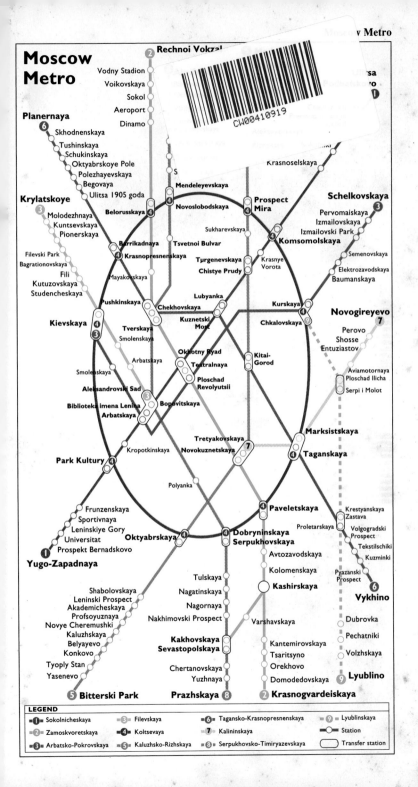

Moscow Metro

Planernaya
Krylatskoye
Kievskaya
Park Kultury
Yugo-Zapadnaya

Rechnoi Vokzal
Vodny Stadion
Voikovskaya
Sokol
Aeroport
Dinamo

CW00410919

v Metro

Skhodnenskaya
Tushinskaya
Schukinskaya
Oktyabrskoye Pole
Polezhayevskaya
Begovaya
Ulitsa 1905 goda

Molodezhnaya
Kuntsevskaya
Pionerskaya

Filevski Park
Bagrationovskaya
Fili
Kutuzovskaya
Studencheskaya

Krasnoselskaya

Mendeleyevskaya
Novoslobodskaya
Belorusskaya

Prospect Mira
Schelkovskaya

Pervomaiskaya
Izmailovskaya
Izmailovski Park
Komsomolskaya

Barrikadnaya
Krasnopresnenskaya
Tsvetnoi Bulvar

Sukharevskaya

Mayakovskaya

Turgenevskaya
Chistye Prudy

Krasnye Vorota

Semenovskaya
Elektrozavodskaya
Baumanskaya

Pushkinskaya
Chekhovskaya
Tverskaya
Smolenskaya

Lubyanka
Kuznetski Most

Kurskaya
Chkalovskaya

Novogireyevo
7

Perovo
Shosse
Entuziastov

Arbatskaya
Smolenskaya

Okhotny Ryad
Teatralnaya
Ploschad Revolyutsii

Kitai-Gorod

Aviamotornaya
Ploschad Ilicha
Serpi i Molot

Aleksandrovski Sad
Biblioteka imena Lenina
Arbatskaya

Borovitskaya

Kropotkinskaya

Tretyakovskaya
Novokuznetskaya

Marksistskaya

Taganskaya

Park Kultury

Polyanka

Frunzenskaya
Sportivnaya
Leninskiye Gory
Universitat
Prospekt Bernadskovo

Oktyabrskaya

Dobryninskaya
Serpukhovskaya

Paveletskaya

Krestyanskaya
Zastava
Proletarskaya
Volgogradski
Prospect
Tekstilshiki
Kuzminki

Avtozavodskaya
Kolomenskaya

Pyazanski
Prospect

Vykhino
6

Shabolovskaya
Leninski Prospect
Akademicheskaya
Profsoyuznaya
Novye Cheremushki
Kaluzhskaya
Belyayevo
Konkovo
Tyoply Stan
Yasenevo

Tulskaya
Nagatinskaya
Nagornaya
Nakhimovski Prospect

Kashirskaya

Varshavskaya

Dubrovka
Pechatniki
Volzhskaya

Lyublino
9

Kakhovskaya
Sevastopolskaya

Chertanovskaya
Yuzhnaya

Kantemirovskaya
Tsaritsyno
Orekhovo
Domodedovskaya

Bitterski Park 5

Prazhskaya 8

Krasnogvardeiskaya 2

LEGEND

1 Sokolnicheskaya	3 Filevskaya	6 Tagansko-Krasnopresnenskaya	9 Lyublinskaya
2 Zamoskvoretskaya	4 Koltsevaya	7 Kalininskaya	Station
3 Arbatsko-Pokrovskaya	5 Kaluzhsko-Rizhskaya	8 Serpukhovsko-Timiryazevskaya	Transfer station

Moscow

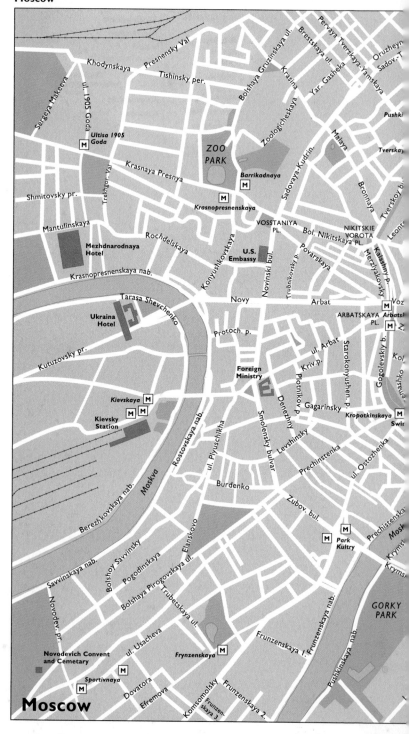

Moscow

Moscow

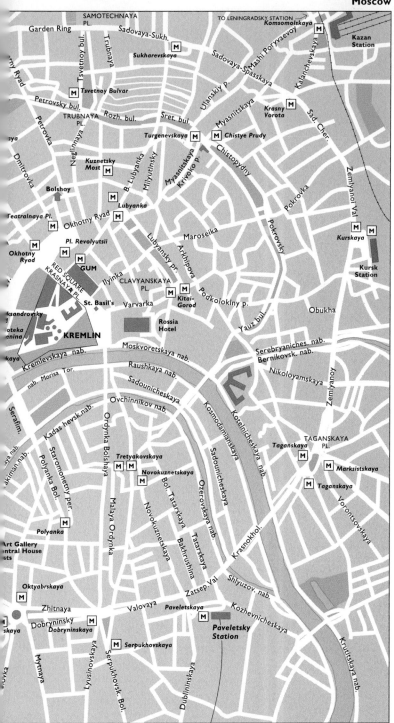

Москвоский Метро

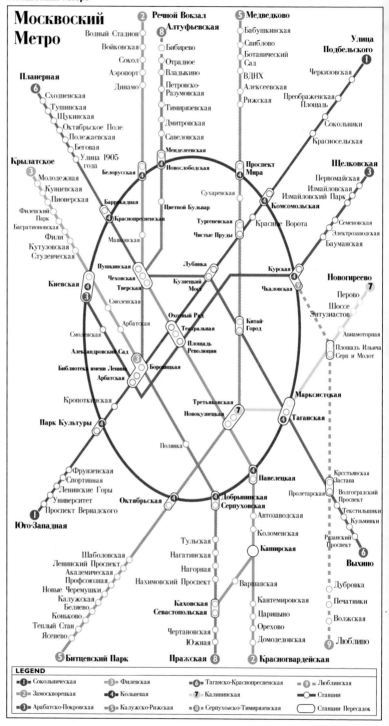

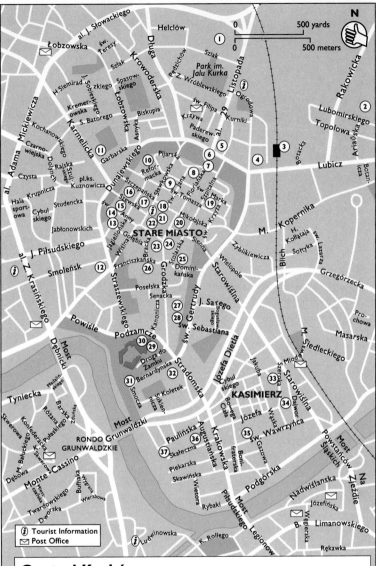

Central Kraków

Akademia Ekonomiczna, **2**
Almatur Office, **24**
Barbican, **6**
Bernardine Church, **32**
Bus Station, **4**
Carmelite Church, **11**
Cartoon Gallery, **9**
City Historical Museum, **17**
Collegium Maius, **14**
Corpus Christi Church, **35**
Czartoryski Art Museum, **8**
Dominican Church, **25**
Dragon Statue, **31**

Filharmonia, **12**
Franciscan Church, **26**
Grunwald Memorial, **5**
Jewish Cemetery, **33**
Jewish Museum, **34**
Kraków Głowny Station, **3**
Monastery of the
    Reformed Franciscans, **10**
Muzeum Historii Fotografii, **23**
Orbis Office, **19**
Pauline Church, **37**
Police Station, **18**
Politechnika Krakowska, **1**

St. Andrew's Church, **28**
St. Anne's Church, **15**
St. Catherine's Church, **36**
St. Florian's Gate, **7**
St. Mary's Church, **20**
St. Peter and Paul Church, **27**
Stary Teatr (Old Theater), **16**
Sukiennice (Cloth Hall), **21**
Town Hall, **22**
University Museum, **13**
Wawel Castle, **29**
Wawel Cathedral, **30**

Prague

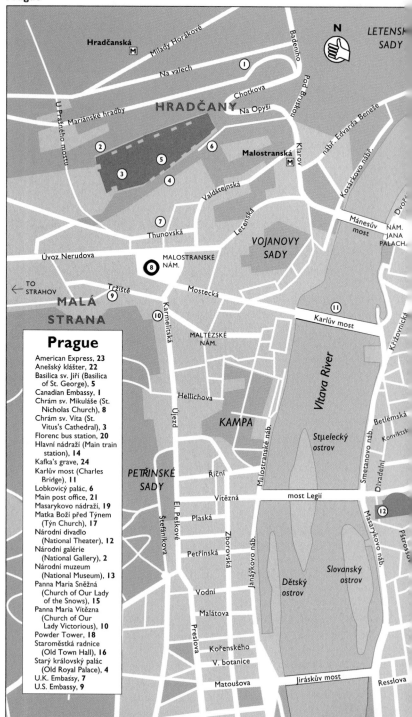

N

LETENSK SADY

Hradčanská Ⓜ

Milady Horákové

Na valech

①

Chotkova

Na Opyši

HRADČANY

Badeniho

Pod Bruskou

U Pražného mostu

Mariánské hradby

②

⑤

⑥

Malostranská Ⓜ

Klárov

③

④

nábř. Edvarda Beneše

Kosárkovo nábř.

Valdštejnská

Letenská

Dvořá

⑦

Thunovská

VOJANOVY SADY

Mánesův most

NÁM. JANA PALACH.

Úvoz Nerudova

MALOSTRANSKÉ NÁM.

⑧

TO STRAHOV →

Tržiště

⑨

Mostecká

⑪

Karlův most

Křižovnická

MALÁ STRANA

Karmelitská

⑩

MALTÉZSKÉ NÁM.

Hellichova

Újezd

KAMPA

Vltava River

Betlémská

Konviktsk

Střelecký ostrov

Smetanovo náb.

Divadelní

PETŘÍNSKÉ SADY

Říční

Malostranské náb.

Prague

American Express, **23**
Anežský klášter, **22**
Basilica sv. Jiří (Basilica of St. George), **5**
Canadian Embassy, **1**
Chrám sv. Mikuláše (St. Nicholas Church), **8**
Chrám sv. Víta (St. Vitus's Cathedral), **3**
Florenc bus station, **20**
Hlavní nádraží (Main train station), **14**
Kafka's grave, **24**
Karlův most (Charles Bridge), **11**
Lobkovicý palác, **6**
Main post office, **21**
Masarykovo nádraží, **19**
Matka Boží před Týnem (Týn Church), **17**
Národní divadlo (National Theater), **12**
Národní galérie (National Gallery), **2**
Národní muzeum (National Museum), **13**
Panna Maria Sněžná (Church of Our Lady of the Snows), **15**
Panna Maria Vítězna (Church of Our Lady Victorious), **10**
Powder Tower, **18**
Staroměstská radnice (Old Town Hall), **16**
Starý královský palác (Old Royal Palace), **4**
U.K. Embassy, **7**
U.S. Embassy, **9**

Vítězná

⑫

Plaská

Zborovská

Petřínská

Janáčkovo náb.

Masarykovo náb.

Pštross

El. Peškové

Štefánikova

Vodní

Dětský ostrov

Slovanský ostrov

Malátova

Preslova

Kořenského

V. botanice

Matoušova

Jiráskův most

Resslova

most Legií

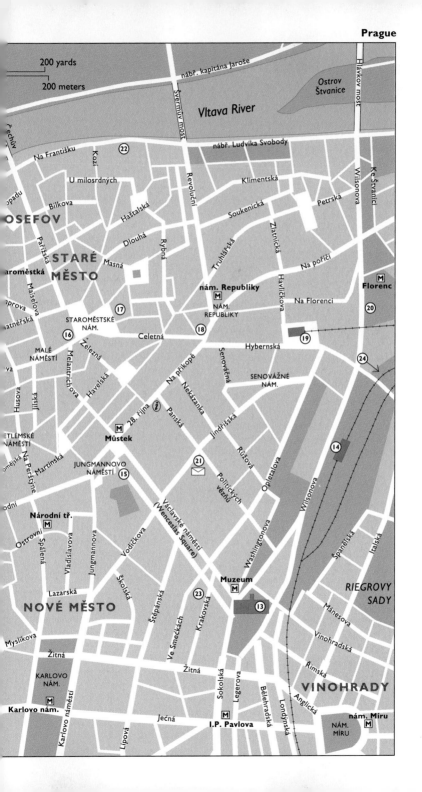

200 yards

200 meters

nábř. kapitána Jaroše

Vltava River

Švermův most

Hlávkův most

Ostrov Štvanice

nábř. Ludvíka Svobody

Na Františku

Kozí

22

r̆ echův

popadu

Na Františku

U milosrdných

Klimentská

Soukenická

Petrská

Wilsonova

Ke Štvanici

Bílkova

Haštalská

Zlatnická

OSEFOV

Pařížská

Dlouhá

Rybná

Truhlářská

Na poříčí

Florenc

M

aroměstská

STARÉ
MĚSTO

Masná

Maiselova

Havlíčkova

NÁM. Republiky

M

iprova

Masná

STAROMĚSTSKÉ
NÁM.

17

Celetná

18

NÁM.
REPUBLIKY

Na Florenci

20

atnéřská

16

Železná

Hybernská

19

MALÉ
NÁMĚSTÍ

Melantrichova

Havelská

Na příkopě

Senovážná

SENOVÁŽNÉ
NÁM.

24

va

Husova

píšíř

Na příkopě

Nekázanka

28. října

ⓘ

Panská

Jindřišská

Růžová

Opletalova

14

ETLÉMSKÉ
NÁMĚSTÍ

omějská

Na Perštýně

Martinská

JUNGMANNOVO
NÁMĚSTÍ

15

Můstek

M

21

✉

Politických
vězňů

Wilsonova

Národní tř.

M

Ostrovní

Spálená

Vladislavova

Jungmannova

Václavské náměstí
(Wenceslas Square)

Vodičkova

Washingtonova

Španělská

Italská

**RIEGROVY
SADY**

Lazarská

Školská

Muzeum

M

Máchova

NOVÉ MĚSTO

Štěpánská

23

13

Vinohradská

Myslíkova

Žitná

Ve Smečkách

Krakovská

Sokolská

Legerova

Bělehradská

Římská

VINOHRADY

KARLOVO
NÁM.

Žitná

Anglická

Karlovo nám.

M

Karlovo náměstí

Lipová

Ječná

I.P. Pavlova

M

Londýnská

NÁM.
MÍRU

nám. Míru

M

Central Budapest

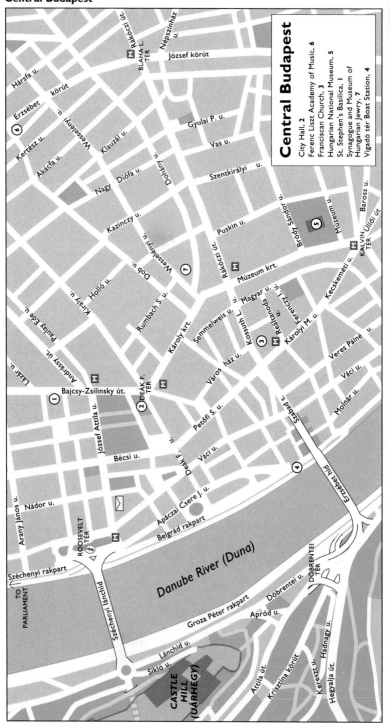

Central Budapest

City Hall, 2
Ferenc Liszt Academy of Music, 6
Franciscan Church, 3
Hungarian National Museum, 5
St. Stephen's Basilica, 1
Synagogue and Museum of
Hungarian Jewry, 7
Vigadó tér Boat Station, 4

Let's Go:
Eastern Europe

"Lighthearted and sophisticated, informative and fun to read. *[Let's Go]* helps the novice traveler navigate like a knowledgeable old hand."

—*Atlanta Journal-Constitution*

"The guides are aimed not only at young budget travelers but at the independent traveler, a sort of streetwise cookbook for traveling alone."

—*The New York Times*

◼ Let's Go writers travel on your budget.

"Retains the spirit of the student-written publication it is: candid, opinionated, resourceful, amusing info for the traveler of limited means but broad curiosity." —*Mademoiselle*

"The writers seem to have experienced every rooster-packed bus and lunar-surfaced mattress about which they write." —*The New York Times*

"All the dirt, dirt cheap." —*People*

◼ Great for independent travelers.

"A world-wise traveling companion—always ready with friendly advice and helpful hints, all sprinkled with a bit of wit." —*The Philadelphia Inquirer*

"Lots of valuable information for any independent traveler."

—*The Chicago Tribune*

◼ Let's Go is completely revised each year.

"Unbeatable: good sight-seeing advice; up-to-date info on restaurants, hotels, and inns; a commitment to money-saving travel; and a wry style that brightens nearly every page." —*The Washington Post*

"Its yearly revision by a new crop of Harvard students makes it as valuable as ever." —*The New York Times*

◼ All the important information you need.

"Enough information to satisfy even the most demanding of budget travelers...*Let's Go* follows the creed that you don't have to toss your life's savings to the wind to travel—unless you want to."

—*The Salt Lake Tribune*

"Value-packed, unbeatable, accurate, and comprehensive."

—*The Los Angeles Times*

Let's Go Publications

Let's Go: Alaska & the Pacific Northwest 1998
Let's Go: Australia 1998 **New title!**
Let's Go: Austria & Switzerland 1998
Let's Go: Britain & Ireland 1998
Let's Go: California 1998
Let's Go: Central America 1998
Let's Go: Eastern Europe 1998
Let's Go: Ecuador & the Galápagos Islands 1998
Let's Go: Europe 1998
Let's Go: France 1998
Let's Go: Germany 1998
Let's Go: Greece & Turkey 1998
Let's Go: India & Nepal 1998
Let's Go: Ireland 1998
Let's Go: Israel & Egypt 1998
Let's Go: Italy 1998
Let's Go: London 1998
Let's Go: Mexico 1998
Let's Go: New York City 1998
Let's Go: New Zealand 1998 **New title!**
Let's Go: Paris 1998
Let's Go: Rome 1998
Let's Go: Southeast Asia 1998
Let's Go: Spain & Portugal 1998
Let's Go: USA 1998
Let's Go: Washington, D.C. 1998

Let's Go Map Guides

Berlin	New Orleans
Boston	New York City
Chicago	Paris
London	Rome
Los Angeles	San Francisco
Madrid	Washington, D.C.

Coming Soon: Amsterdam, Florence

Let's Go Publications

LET'S GO
Eastern Europe
1998

Ruth M. Halikman
Editor

Rachel Eelkema
Associate Editor

Bede M. Sheppard
Associate Editor

Macmillan

HELPING LET'S GO

If you want to share your discoveries, suggestions, or corrections, please drop us a line. We read every piece of correspondence, whether a postcard, a 10-page email, or a coconut. Please note that mail received after May 1998 may be too late for the 1999 book, but will be kept for future editions. **Address mail to:**

Let's Go: Eastern Europe
67 Mount Auburn Street
Cambridge, MA 02138
USA

Visit Let's Go at **http://www.letsgo.com,** or send email to:

fanmail@letsgo.com
Subject: "Let's Go: Eastern Europe"

In addition to the invaluable travel advice our readers share with us, many are kind enough to offer their services as researchers or editors. Unfortunately, our charter enables us to employ only currently enrolled Harvard-Radcliffe students.

Published in Great Britain 1998 by Macmillan, an imprint of Macmillan General Books, 25 Eccleston Place, London SW1W 9NF and Basingstoke.

Maps by David Lindroth copyright © 1998, 1997, 1996, 1995, 1994, 1993, 1992, 1991, 1990, 1989, 1988 by St. Martin's Press, Inc.

Map revisions pp. xvi, xvi, xviii, xix, 45, 53, 54, 61, 69, 77, 84, 95, 123, 125, 132, 139, 154, 165, 177, 197, 205, 227, 234, 242, 243, 247, 279, 289, 300, 307, 323, 331, 341, 350, 357, 364, 369, 373, 382, 383, 399, 423, 439, 462, 471, 473, 513, 536, 563, 573, 575, 581, 587, 598, 599, 601, 623, 636, 643, 654, 672, 679, 688, 700, 701, 703, 715, 721, 725, 737, 746, 753, 780 by Let's Go, Inc.

Published in the United States of America by St. Martin's Press, Inc.

ISBN: 0 333 71176 9

First edition
10 9 8 7 6 5 4 3 2 1

Let's Go: Eastern Europe is written by Let's Go Publications, 67 Mount Auburn Street, Cambridge, MA 02138, USA.

Let's Go® and the thumb logo are trademarks of Let's Go, Inc.
Printed in the USA on recycled paper with biodegradable soy ink.

ADVERTISING DISCLAIMER

Contents

HUNGARY (MAGYARORSZÁG) 234

LATVIA (LATVIJA) 300

LITHUANIA (LIETUVA) 323

F. Y. R. MACEDONIA (МАКЕДОНИЈА) 350

MOLDOVA 364

POLAND (POLSKA) 373

ROMANIA (ROMÂNIA) 462

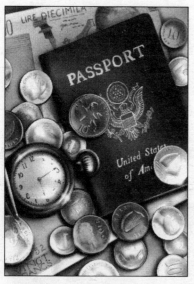

Maps

Color Maps

About Let's Go

Back in 1960, a few students at Harvard University banded together to produce a 20-page pamphlet offering a collection of tips on budget travel in Europe. This modest, mimeographed packet, offered as an extra to passengers on student charter flights to Europe, met with instant popularity. The following year, students traveling to Europe researched the first, full-fledged edition of *Let's Go: Europe,* a pocket-sized book featuring honest, irreverent writing and a decidedly youthful outlook on the world. Throughout the 60s, our guides reflected the times; the 1969 guide to America led off by inviting travelers to "dig the scene" at San Francisco's Haight-Ashbury. During the 70s and 80s, we gradually added regional guides and expanded coverage into the Middle East and Central America. With the addition of our in-depth city guides, handy map guides, and extensive coverage of Asia and Australia, the 90s are also proving to be a time of explosive growth for Let's Go, and there's certainly no end in sight. The first editions of *Let's Go: Australia* and *Let's Go: New Zealand* hit the shelves this year, expanding our coverage to six continents, and research for next year's series has already begun.

We've seen a lot in 38 years. *Let's Go: Europe* is now the world's bestselling international guide, translated into seven languages. And our new guides bring Let's Go's total number of titles, with their spirit of adventure and their reputation for honesty, accuracy, and editorial integrity, to 40. But some things never change: our guides are still researched, written, and produced entirely by students who know first-hand how to see the world on the cheap.

HOW WE DO IT

Each guide is completely revised and thoroughly updated every year by a well-traveled set of over 200 students. Every winter, we recruit over 140 researchers and 60 editors to write the books anew. After several months of training, Researcher-Writers hit the road for seven weeks of exploration, from Anchorage to Adelaide, Estonia to El Salvador, Iceland to Indonesia. Hired for their rare combination of budget travel sense, writing ability, stamina, and courage, these adventurous travelers know that train strikes, stolen luggage, food poisoning, and marriage proposals are all part of a day's work. Back at our offices, editors work from spring to fall, massaging copy written on Himalayan bus rides into witty yet informative prose. A student staff of typesetters, cartographers, publicists, and managers keeps our lively team together. In September, the collected efforts of the summer are delivered to our printer, who turns them into books in record time, so that you have the most up-to-date information available for your vacation. And even as you read this, work on next year's editions is well underway.

WHY WE DO IT

We don't think of budget travel as the last recourse of the destitute; we believe that it's the only way to travel. Living cheaply and simply brings you closer to the people and places you've been saving up to visit. Our books will ease your anxieties and answer your questions about the basics—so you can get off the beaten track and explore. Once you learn the ropes, we encourage you to put *Let's Go* down now and then to strike out on your own. As any seasoned traveler will tell you, the best discoveries are often those you make yourself. When you find something worth sharing, drop us a line. We're Let's Go Publications, 67 Mount Auburn St., Cambridge, MA 02138, USA (email: fanmail@letsgo.com).

HAPPY TRAVELS

Acknowledgments

Team EEUR thanks: Many people helped us assemble this book, a task we certainly could not have accomplished on our own. Special thanks to: everyone who typed and proofed, especially Elena, Nic Rapold, and Leeore (the funniest proofer around); the tourist offices and embassies that supplied letters of introduction; Prof. Susan Suleiman; Mihkel Tarm at *City Paper—The Baltic States*; Mrs. Žagrović; Nicole Jacoby; Asti Pilika; Laurel Holman; Andrew Dudley for finding the answer to every question; Eric Roston for emergency Russian literature aid; and Anne Chisholm for her good cheer and impeccable judgment. **Team EEUR**

Thanks to: Rachel for her miraculous dependability and calm, not to mention ability to rise early; Bede for tireless energy and creativity, as well as the best CDs around; and Kate for her integrity and guidance—if only she weren't moving to Bosnia. Also to the many friends who offered support over the summer, especially Catherine, David, Danny, and Jenny. Finally, to Mom, Gwen, Dad, Sue, and all other family, especially my grandparents, to whom I owe my love for Eastern Europe. **RMH**

To Ruth for stunning competence and compassion, to Bede for dedication and cheer, and to Kate for all the extra work she didn't have to do. Also, to Caroline for still being a good example. Appreciation and respect to the Brothers of Phi Delta Theta, from whom I continue to learn. Love and deepest gratitude (and even that doesn't say enough) to Samantha and Alain Gerhart, Marcella and the Sabatini/Calfon families, Hillary, Hadley, and Sara; to Adam for advice, support, and friendship; to Bernardo for caring; and to my family—Dad, Mom, Anne, Gretchen, Grace. **RE**

Appreciation and respect for Ruth who proves that even Polish can be sexy. Thanks to Rachel for letting me explain about the painter, and to Kate, for amazing me. Thanks to: Andrew, for all the stuff; those who crashed at #7: Adam, ADD, Garfinkle, Joel, JMK, Mike, Pinto, Stoller, and Taya; the Becks, Dudleys, Krebs, and Weiners, for food and board; Amy, Dave, Esti; Claire, Claude, Dave, James and Né for remembering; finally, to Isä ja Äiti, without whom I wouldn't be (literally, even). **BMS**

Editor	Ruth M. Halikman
Associate Editor	Rachel Eelkema
Associate Editor	Bede M. Sheppard
Managing Editor	Kate Galbraith
Publishing Director	John R. Brooks
Production Manager	Melanie Quintana Kansil
Associate Production Manager	David Collins
Cartography Manager	Sara K. Smith
Editorial Manager	Melissa M. Reyen
Editorial Manager	Emily J. Stebbins
Financial Manager	Krzysztof Owerkowicz
Personnel Manager	Andrew E. Nieland
Publicity Manager	Nicholas Corman
Publicity Manager	Kate Galbraith
New Media Manager	Daniel O. Williams
Associate Cartographer	Joseph E. Reagan
Associate Cartographer	Luke Z. Fenchel
Office Coordinators	Emily Bowen, Chuck Kapelke
	Laurie Santos
Director of Advertising Sales	Todd L. Glaskin
Senior Sales Executives	Matthew R. Hillery, Joseph W. Lind
	Peter J. Zakowich, Jr.
President	Amit Tiwari
General Manager	Richard Olken
Assistant General Manager	Anne E. Chisholm

Researcher-Writers

Alexander Atanasov   *Macedonia, Yugoslavia, Bosnia, Dubrovnik*
Sasho would want us to write this as a lawyer would—so read between the lines.
Our native Bulgarian's itinerary took him to email terminals everywhere as he
attempted to cross problematic Balkan borders. Yet on his adventure-filled journey
from Bulgaria to Bosnia and back again, the only injury Sasho suffered was stepping
on a piece of glass. Although Sasho unfortunately couldn't tell us about much of what
he found on his travels, from the little we know, it sounds like he thoroughly enjoyed
himself.

Chris Brooke   *Czech Republic, Slovakia*
Vegetarians can thank Chris's fiancée—perhaps it was for her sake that he found so
many tofu-happy eateries in carnivorous Slovakia and the neighbouring Czech Rep.
Brits may appreciate the authentic English flavour we couldn't quite edit out of his
staggeringly brilliant copy, which ruthlessly punctured the base superstition that so
pervades Prague—and he even found the Hard Rock Cafe. In true stiff-upper-lip style,
Chris didn't even let days of rain in the Tatras prevent him from walking up his share
of hills—or from sending back his acerbic, accurate, and always punctual copy.

Katia Dianina   *Central and Northwest Russia*
Despite Katia's thorough research and evocative descriptions of the mighty Volga,
her real claim to fame at Let's Go is her sexy Russian accent. A second-year grad student in comp lit, she got to use her knowledge of Old Church Slavonic in exploring
the myriad churches and monasteries of northern Russia. On the more modern side
of things, she also discovered all of Peter's coolest *tusovki*. Her words of advice:
always be apologetic when trying to get information out of Russians (they really think
their country makes sense), and don't drink the water in St. Petersburg.

Dan Epstein   *Bulgaria, Moldova, Odesa*
Though Dan's trip got off to a shaky start when he was robbed of his trusty *Let's Go:
EEUR,* he bounced back quickly, thanks to the support of the million friends that
kept giving us letters to pass on to him, the TLC of the myriad Bulgarian friends he
picked up, and a few conference calls to Italy. Trekking his way all the way to the
exotic Moldova, Dan managed to outwit Yugoslav smugglers, transport "antiquities"
across various national borders, and dig up the one and only bagel shop in the Czech
Republic.

Gregory Feifer   *Estonia, Latvia, Lithuania*
Greg bounded through the Baltics, evading bad Estonian food, crazed Latvian drivers,
and the tourist hordes in Vilnius. Though he spoke more regularly with our answer-
ing machines than with us, his copy always arrived well-researched and free of cli-
chés. Greg discovered melting sand dunes, dined on wild boar, and acquainted
himelf with every beer the Baltics have to offer (all in the name of research, of
course).

James Markham   *Southern Russia, Eastern Ukraine, Moscow*
Cute Jamie gives the Army a good name—it was undoubtedly his ROTC training (or
maybe the Power Bars) that sustained him in the face of arrests, constant harassment,
and the countless other inconveniences of travel in Russia and Ukraine. Our first
researcher out of the nest and the first to cross the finish line, Jamie came back with
cool Russian clothes, piles of photos, plenty of stories of all the *babushki* who fell in
love with him, a new appreciation for all the comforts of the U.S. of A., and copy that
made us weep with laughter.

Eugene D. Mazo

Belarus, Kaliningrad, Moscow, Trans-Siberian Railroad, Vilnius

As this book goes to print, Gene is still out there in the depths of Central Asia; we had no idea his itinerary included Ukraine, Mongolia, Kyrgystan, and Beijing. Last year's *Let's Go: Germany* editor and a native Russian, Gene was an obvious choice for the demanding Trans-Siberian itinerary, and his copious copy arrived already in *Let's Go* format. Bribing his way everywhere, Gene nonetheless took a minute to call his mother on her birthday. He informs us that Mongolia, not Vilnius, is the next Prague. Watch out, Oxford—here comes Jumpin' Gene!

Benjamin Paloff

Poland

Ben nearly lost his title as the "Antonio Banderas of budget travel" when he sent his first copybatch by surface-mail. Pub-crawling his way across Poland, Ben scared away the ghosts in Sandomierz, had an epiphany in the Trail of Eagles' Nests, and discovered the truth of the Łódź Principle. His writing was witty, his phone calls were frequent (even after he got back to Michigan), and he sure found a lot of bars serving Guinness. He wishes to thank: the topologists in Kazimierz Dolny, the Scandinavians in Warsaw, and the Manchester Brits in Gdańsk.

Sasha Radin

Kraków, Eastern Slovakia, Eastern Hungary, Western Ukraine

From Hungarian grandmothers to Ukrainian rock stars, Sasha charmed the pants off everyone she met. Whether she was bopping around Kraków or taking on the Hungarian *puszta,* people fell all over themselves to help her find train prices, cheap hotels, and the best spots for pastries. Her list of friends is too numerous to mention each by name: let's just say she'd like to thank all her Eastern European acquaintances. Sasha's experiences prove the truth of the advice she gives in her copy: a little politeness and a smile will get you a long way in Eastern Europe—even in Ukraine.

Anne Toole

Romania

Anne's obvious enthusiasm for Romania has almost—*almost*—ignited in us the desire to see the country for ourselves. After hastily disabusing us of any notion that Bram Stoker ever set foot in Romania, she discovered Carpathian resorts, camped with the hippies on the Black Sea Coast, and even managed to find good things to say about Bucharest, perhaps the most maligned of all Eastern European capitals. It must have been her training in anthropology that gave her such a sensitive eye for the Romanian people—especially all those cute monks!

Bojan Žagrović

Slovenia, Croatia, Western Hungary

Were it not for Bojan, we would never have known just how many nude campgrounds existed in Eastern Europe. Our native Croat definitely provided us with an intimate look at his home country and neighboring Slovenia—as well as the most romantic story in a guide loaded with romance. Bojan's copy inspired so much devotion in us, in fact, that even the threat of bodily harm couldn't prevent us from attempting to retrieve it personally from a certain international express mail service. We're sure that lovestruck Bojan will find poetry even among the neurons he'll study at Stanford.

Brittany Applestein   *Helsinki, Finland*

Alexandra DeLaite   *Istanbul, Turkey*

Aykan Erdemir   *Istanbul, Turkey*

Stuart Shapley   *Berlin, Germnay*

Jasmine Vasavada   *Vienna, Austria*

Let's Go Picks

Of all the beds we slept in, of all the clubs we crashed, of all the views that made us wish we had a 3-D camera with smell-scope and sound, these picks are the sleeps, sights, and attractions that EEUR '98 loved the most. Check 'em out or discover your own; either way, post us some mail—"e" or snail—and tell us what *you* thought.

Spots to Crash Although not astronomically priced, the youth hostel in **Bled, SLN,** shines as "a bright supernova in the backpacker's dark sky" (p. 682). Hotel George, in **Lviv, UKR,** is as lovely as this charming city itself (p. 739). The heavenly *schronisko* in **Kraków, POL,** provides comforts both material and spiritual (p. 395). Although it doesn't need any more plugging, the new Clown and Bard Hostel in **Prague, CZ,** is the hippest new kid on this city's tired accommodations scene (p. 166). But then again, there's nothing like going *au naturel*—and apparently **Croatia's** coast is one of the best places to do it (p. 144, p. 145, and more).

Views for Which to Kill While the sight of the Bucegi mountains from the monastery in **Sinaia, ROM,** is certainly nice, the views of the cute monks are even better (p. 496)! Then again, we'd be hard pressed to make a decision about where the cutest monks in Eastern Europe are—with votes for the Visoki Dečani monastery near **Peć, Yugoslavia** (p. 762) and the Kievo-Pecherska Lavra in **Kiev, UKR,** the jury is still out (p. 709). The view from the tower at **Frombork, POL,** made us wonder why Mikolaj Kopernik (a.k.a. Copernicus) ever took up astronomy—the view across is so lovely, why look up (p. 443)? The Crow's Cliff at **Slovenský Raj, SLK,** best demonstrates why this region is called "Slovak Paradise"(p. 663).

Buffest Bods The revolutionary monks at the Capuchin monastery in **Brno, CZ,** discovered that air-drying works just as well for people as for food—and they've got the bodies to prove it (p. 199)! Kudos to **Szeged, HUN,** for having the most pumped police force in all of Eastern Europe (p. 271), although Novorossijsk, RUS, is a close runner-up. The famed thick-necked youths of **Bulgaria** are not to be missed—or messed with. And when the desire for exhibitionism strikes, Eastern Europe provides countless venues to show off your own stuff: some of the best are the mud baths in **Tuzlata, BUL** (p. 127), and the Gellért spa in **Budapest, HUN** (p. 258).

Best of the Bizarre The Devil Museum in **Kaunas, LIT,** has created a merry little hell populated by nearly 200 devil icons gathered from all around the world (p. 343). If this whets your appetite for diabolical delights, **Hel, POL** (p. 446), isn't too far away. Michael Jackson's new estate in Poland won't be finished for awhile yet, but you can admire the larger-than-life marzipan sculpture of him in **Szentendre, HUN** (p. 260). The Ben & Jerry's shop (yes, the ice cream company) in **Petrozavodsk, RUS,** is reason enough to make the 9hr. trip from St. Petersburg (p. 629). No, indeed, there's nothing bizarre about ice cream...but what are Ben and Jerry doing in Petrozavodsk?! It's a little weird that there's a bust of Frank Zappa in **Vilnius, LIT** (p. 335), but it's even weirder that **Ulan Ude, RUS,** way out in the depths of Asian Siberia, claims the biggest bust of Lenin known to man (p. 571).

Watering Holes Saddle up to the Szalony Koń (Crazy Horse) bar in **Wrocław, POL** (p. 418), where you can take the Chevy for a spin (no drinking and driving though, okay?). While away an afternoon in the shade of the beer gardens in **Rīga, LAT,** and watch your troubles evaporate in the foam (p. 313). Fortify yourself with Bull's Blood wine in **Eger, HUN**—you'll need strength for the Valley of the Beautiful Women (p. 264). If you like your *Cuba Libres* virgin, pick up the cheapest Coke in Eastern Europe at the post office in **Oradea, ROM** (L1000; p. 488).

XVII

Railways of
Eastern Europe

How to Use this Book

Travelers of the world, unite!

The words of a certain manifesto have influenced life in Eastern Europe for much of the 20th century. Though the wisdom found in this fourth edition of *Let's Go: Eastern Europe* comes pretty darn close to the perfect ideology, the book remains only a guide. Follow it, and you will be taken to Europe's wildest—and cheapest—regions, places most travelers couldn't even visit before 1990. Our researchers have braved run-ins with the police, the mafia, and crazed hostel-owners, to find some of the cheapest, freshest spots in Eastern and Central Europe.

Wherever your destination, take time to peruse our **Essentials** *before* heading for the airport. Slashing through the "Red" tape, this section is chock-full of info to demystify the intricacies of passports and visas, to help you find the cheapest flights, and to tell you where traveler's checks will be worth more than a Spanish dictionary in Estonia. We suggest some alternatives to traditional sightseeing, and provide information specifically of interest to women, older travelers, bisexual, gay, and lesbian travelers, minority travelers, and people with disabilities.

The heart of this book lies in its 19 alphabetically arranged country chapters. Each country gets down-and-dirty with an **Essentials** section of its own. Their history, literature, and current event essays in **Life and Times** might just inspire you to read something heftier than this guide on your next train trip. After the fact-filled intro to each country, the capital city comes first, followed by other towns grouped into geographical regions. In each town's **Orientation and Practical Information** section, we give you the low-down on how to get around and where to find valuable services—exchange bureaus, tourist offices, or the train to Ulaan Baatar. The **Accommodations** section spills the beans on the best beds, whether they be in hotels, hostels, private rooms, or tents. **Food** follows, with open-air markets, old-style Socialist cafeterias, and a list of restaurants with the best deals in town. The **Sights** section not only ensures that you don't miss Red Square, but also tells you where to find the rarely seen iconostasis or the bizarre Frank Zappa bust. The **Gateway Cities** section, which includes Berlin, Helsinki, Vienna, and, new this year, Istanbul, lets you expand your horizons.

Want to know what temperatures to expect in Bucharest? Need the phone code for Albania? Got to brush up on your Latvian? Then head to the **Appendix.**

We're thrilled to introduce Yugoslavia to our book this year—we're covering Belgrade for the first time since 1992. Also new this year, we chug even farther down the Trans-Siberian, now as far as Ulan Ude in the heart of Siberia.

Eastern Europe is busy reinventing itself every day. Like all manifestos, even this yellow one doesn't offer answers to everything. Take this guide, choose any of the many unbeaten paths that still run through Eastern and Central Europe, and when you find something new, drop us a line.

A NOTE TO OUR READERS

The information for this book is gathered by *Let's Go*'s researchers from late May through August. Each listing is derived from the assigned researcher's opinion based upon his or her visit at a particular time. The opinions are expressed in a candid and forthright manner. Other travelers might disagree. Those traveling at a different time may have different experiences, since prices, dates, hours, and conditions are always subject to change. You are urged to check beforehand to avoid inconvenience and surprises. Travel always involves a certain degree of risk, especially in low-cost areas. When traveling, especially on a budget, always take particular care to ensure your safety.

ESSENTIALS

PLANNING YOUR TRIP

Sometimes frustratingly bureaucratic, sometimes utterly lawless, travel in Kafkaesque Eastern Europe is never predictable. Start your planning well in advance: begin stalking consulates for visas the moment you decide to go, contact the useful organizations we list, faithfully follow the news, plan out every detail of your itinerary—and be prepared to scrap the whole thing once you arrive. Things change quickly in Eastern Europe: exchange rates, telephone numbers, borders. The most important thing to bring along is flexibility.

What we have called "Eastern Europe" is not a single monolithic bloc but an area containing 19 very different countries. *Let's Go: Eastern Europe* can take you as far east as the middle of Siberia; as far north as Petrozavodsk, Russia; as far south as the Greek border; and west into the very heart of Central Europe. We urge you to unleash your curiosity and to follow your own spirit, whether it leads you to historic cultural centers such as Prague, Budapest, or St. Petersburg; an alpine hike in Slovenia; or beach towns along the Adriatic, Baltic or Black Seas.

■ Useful Information

REGIONAL TOURIST AND TRAVEL AGENCIES

Albania: U.S.: Kutrubes, 328 Tremont, Boston, MA 02116 (tel. (617) 426-5668; fax (617) 426-3196).

Bulgaria: U.K.: Balkan Holidays, Sofia House, 19 Conduit St., London W1R 9TD (tel. (0171) 543 5555; fax 543 5577). **U.S.:** Balkan Holidays, 20 E. 46th St., #1003, New York, NY 10017 (tel. (212) 822-5900; fax 822-5910).

Baltic States (Estonia, Latvia, Lithuania): Canada: Orav Travel, 5650 Yonge Street, North York, Ont. M2M 4G3 (tel. (416) 221-4164; fax 221-6789). **Finland:** Baltic Information Center, Yrjömkatu 21bA, 00100 Helsinki (tel. for Estonia info (358 9) 61 53 74 70; for Latvia and Lithuania 61 53 74 71; fax 61 53 74 02).

Croatia: U.K.: Linen Hall, 162-168 Regent St., London W1R 5TB (tel. (0171) 306 3105; fax 306 3166). **U.S.:** 300 Lanidex Plaza, Parsippany, NJ 07054 (tel. (201) 428-0707; fax 428-3386).

Czech Republic: Canada: P.O. Box 198, Exchange Tower, 2 First Canadian Place, Toronto, Ont. M5X 1A6 (tel. (416) 367-3432; fax 367-3492). **U.K.:** 95 Great Portland St., London W1N 5RA (tel. (0171) 291 9920; fax 436 8300). **U.S.:** 1109-1111 Madison Ave., New York, NY 10028 (tel. (212) 288-0830; fax 288-0971).

Hungary: U.K.: 46 Eaton Pl., London SW1 X8AL (tel. (0171) 823 1032; fax 823 1459). **U.S.:** 150 E. 58th St., 33rd Fl., New York, NY 10155 (tel. (212) 355-0240; fax 207-4103; email huntour@gramercy.ios.com).

Macedonia: U.S.: Ohrid Travel, 294 Parker Ave., Clifton, NJ 07011 (tel. (201) 340-9124; fax 340-9124).

Poland: U.K.: 1st Floor, Remo House, 310-312 Regent St., London W2R 5AJ (tel. (0171) 580 8811; fax 580 8866). **U.S.:** 275 Madison Ave., #1711, New York, NY 10016 (tel. (212) 338-9412; fax 338-9283; http://www.polandtour.org).

Romania: U.K.: 823a Marylebone High St., London W1M 3RD (tel./fax (0171) 224 3692). **U.S.:** 342 Madison Ave., #210, New York, NY 10173 (tel. (212) 697-6971; fax 697-6972).

Russia: Canada: 1801 McGill College Ave., #930, Montréal, Qué. H3A 2N4 (tel. (514) 849-6394; fax 849-6743; http://www.interknowledge.com/Russia). **U.K.:** 219 Marsh Wall, London E14 9PD (tel. (0171) 538 8600; fax 538 5967; http://

www.intours.demon.co.uk). **U.S.:** Intourist, 610 5th Ave., #603, New York, NY 10020 (tel. (212) 757-3884; fax 459-0031).

Slovakia: U.S.: 10 E. 40th St., #3604, New York, NY 10016 (tel. (212) 213-3865; fax 213-4461).

Slovenia: U.K.: 2 Canfield Pl., London NW6 3BT (tel. (0171) 372 3767; fax 372 3763). **U.S.:** 345 E. 12th St., New York, NY 10003 (tel. (212) 358-9686; fax 358-9025; http://sloveniatravel.com).

Ukraine: U.S.: Scope Travel, 1605 Springfield Ave., Mapelwood, NJ 07040 (tel. (201) 378-8998; fax 378-7903).

TRAVEL ORGANIZATIONS

Council on International Educational Exchange (CIEE), 205 E. 42nd St., New York, NY 10017-5706 (888-COUNCIL; fax (212) 822-2699; http://www.ciee.org). Administers work, volunteer, academic, internship, and professional programs around the world. Also offers identity cards (including the ISIC and the GO25) and a range of publications, including the useful magazine *Student Travels* (free).

International Student Travel Confederation, Herengracht 479, 1017 BS Amsterdam, The Netherlands (tel. (31 20) 421 28 00; fax 421 28 10; http://www.istc.org). A non-profit confederation of student travel organizations whose focus is to develop, promote, and facilitate travel among young people. Member organizations include the International Student Surface Travel Association (ISSA), Student Air Travel Association (SATA), IASIS Travel Insurance, the International Association for Educational and Work Exchange Programs (IAEWEP), and the ISIC.

Federation of International Youth Travel Organizations (FIYTO), Bredgade 25H, DK-1260 Copenhagen K, Denmark (tel. (45) 33 33 96 00; fax 33 93 96 76; http://www.fiyto.org). International organization promoting educational, cultural and social travel for young people. Member organizations include language schools, educational travel companies, national tourist boards, accommodation centers, and other suppliers of travel services to youth and students. Sponsors the GO25 Card (http://www.go25.org).

USEFUL PUBLICATIONS

Although *Let's Go* tries to cover all aspects of budget travel, we can't put *everything* in our guides. You might supplement your *Let's Go* library with publications that serve more specific purposes. **Wide World Books and Maps,** 1911 N. 45th St., Seattle, WA 98103 (tel. (206) 634-3453; fax 634-0558; http://www.travelbooksand-maps.com), stocks hard-to-find **maps.** Maps, guidebooks, railpasses, train and ferry schedules, and youth hostel memberships can be purchased from the **Forsyth Travel Library, Inc.,** 1750 E. 131 St., P.O. Box 480800, Kansas City, MO 64148 (tel. (800) 367-7984; fax (816) 942-6969; http://www.forsyth.com). Write for their free catalogue and newsletter. **The College Connection, Inc.,** 1295 Prospect St. Suite B, La Jolla, CA 92037 (tel. (619) 551-9770; fax 551-9987; email eurailnow@aol.com; http://www.eurailpass.com), sells railpasses with student discounts and publishes *The Passport,* a booklet listing hints about traveling and studying abroad (free to *Let's Go* readers; request it by email or fax). Veteran traveler Rick Steves's excellent series, which includes *Europe through the Back Door,* with great advice on the "do"s and "don't"s of budget travel (US$20), is published by **John Muir Publications,** P.O. Box 613, Santa Fe, NM 87504 (tel. (800) 888-7504; fax (505) 988-1680). **Transitions Abroad,** P.O. Box 1300, 18 Hulst Rd., Amherst, MA 01004 (tel. (800) 293-0373; fax 256-0375; http:/ /transabroad.com), is an invaluable magazine that lists publications and resources for overseas study, work, and volunteering (US$25 for 6 issues, one copy US$6.25). They also publish *The Alternative Travel Directory,* a comprehensive guide to living, learning, and working overseas (US$20, postage US$4). The biannual **Specialty Travel Index** (US$6) is an extensive listing of "off the beaten track" and specialty travel opportunities; contact 305 San Anselmo Avenue, #313, San Anselmo, CA 94960 (tel. (415) 459-4900; fax 459-4974; http://www.spectrav.com).

GETTIN' IT ON-LINE ;)

Keeping up-to-date with politics in Eastern Europe is an art. Though events in the former Yugoslavia and USSR are energetically covered by the mainstream press, other areas receive scant attention unless Madonna happens to be filming in town. Luckily, the **Internet** offers a vast amount of information and resources to travelers, from daily news digests to on-line airline, hotel, hostel, or car rental reservations. There are numerous ways to access the **Internet.** Most popular are commercial services, such as **America Online** (tel. (800) 827-6364) and **CompuServe** (tel. (800) 433-0389). Many employers and schools also offer gateways to the Internet, often for free.

The World Wide Web Increasingly the Internet forum of choice, the **World Wide Web (WWW)** provides its users with text, graphics and sound. **Search engines** (services that search for web pages under specific subjects) aid the search process. **Lycos** (http://a2z.lycos.com) and **Infoseek** (http://guide.infoseek.com) are two of the most popular. **Yahoo!** is a more organized search engine; check out its travel links at http://www.yahoo.com/Recreation/Travel. However, it is often better to know a good site and start "surfing" from there.

For general travel info, check out **Let's Go's** own page (http://www.letsgo.com), which features an always-current list of links. The following are some of our favorite sites of departure for budget travel information. **Big World Magazine** (http://www.paonline.com/bigworld) has a web page with a great collection of links to travel pages. **Shoestring Travel** (http://www.stratpub.com) is a budget travel e-zine with feature articles, links, user exchange, and accommodations information. **The Student and Budget Travel Guide** (http://asa.ugl.lib.umich.edu/chdocs/travel/travel-guide.html) is just what it sounds like, as is **Cybercafes of Europe** (http://www.xs4all.nl/~bertb/cybercaf.html). **Foreign Language for Travelers** (http://www.travelang.com) can help you brush up on many Eastern European languages, from Bulgarian to Ukrainian.

For a general overview of Eastern Europe, visit **City.Net** (http://www.city.net/regions/europe/) which provides maps, links, and accommodation and general information, not to mention the weather today in Bucharest. Given the instability in much of Eastern Europe, the daily news reports sent to subscribers to the **RFE/RL newsline** (email listserv@listserv.acsu.buffalo.edu) are invaluable, and it's a good idea to drop in on the U.S. State Department's **Travel Warnings Page** (http://travel.state.gov/travel_warnings.html), preferably right before you leave home.

■ Documents & Formalities

Travel to most of Eastern Europe has become much less bureaucratic than it once was. However, procuring appropriate travel documents, especially from Russia, Belarus, and Ukraine can be time-consuming and expensive. Be sure to file all applications several weeks or months in advance of your planned departure date.

When you travel, always carry two or more forms of identification; a passport combined with a driver's license or birth certificate usually serves as adequate proof of identity and citizenship. Many establishments require several IDs to cash traveler's checks. Never carry all your IDs together. Also carry several passport-size photos that you can attach to the sundry IDs or railpasses you will eventually acquire abroad. If you plan an extended stay, register with the nearest embassy or consulate.

EMBASSIES AND CONSULATES

Albania: U.S. (Embassy): 1511 K St. NW, #1010, Washington, D.C. 20005 (tel. (202) 223-4942; fax 628-7342).

Belarus: U.K. (Embassy): 6 Kensington Court, London, W8 5DL (tel. (0171) 937 3288; fax 361 0005). **U.S. (Embassy):** 1619 New Hampshire Ave. NW, Washington, D.C. 20009 (tel. (202) 986-1604; fax 986-1805).

Bosnia-Herzegovina: Australia (Embassy and Consulate): (tel. (61 6) 257 5798); fax 257 7855) in Canberra. **U.K. (Embassy):** 320 Regent St., London W1R 5AB (tel. (0171) 255 3758; fax 255 3760). **U.S. (Embassy):** 1707 L. St. NW, Washington 20036 (tel. (202) 833-3612; fax 833-2061). **(Consulate):** 866 U.N. Plaza, # 580, New York, NY 10017 (tel. (212) 593-1042; fax 751-9019.

Bulgaria: Australia (Consulate): 1/4 Carlotta Rd., Double Bay, Sydney, NSW 2028 (tel. (02) 93 27 75 81; fax 93 27 80 67). **Canada (Embassy):** 325 Stewart St., Ottawa, Ont. K1N 6K5 (tel. (613) 789-3215; fax 789-3523). **U.K. (Embassy):** 186-188 Queensgate, London SW7 5HL (tel. (0171) 584 9400; fax 584 4948). **U.S. (Embassy):** 1621 22nd St. NW, Washington, D.C. 20008 (tel. (202) 387-7969; fax 234-7973).

Croatia: Australia (Embassy): 14 Jindalee Crescent, O'Malley, Canberra ACT 2606 (tel. (06) 286 69 88; fax 286 35 44). **Canada (Embassy):** 130 Albert St., #1700, Ottawa, Ont. K1 P5 G4 (tel. (613) 230-7351; fax 230-7388). **New Zealand (Consulate):** 131 Lincoln Rd., Henderson, P.O. Box 83200, Edmonton, Auckland (tel. (09) 836 55 81; fax 836 54 81). **South Africa (Embassy):** 1160 Church Street, P.O. Box 11335, 0028 Hatfield, 083 Colbyn Pretoria (tel. (012) 342 12 06; fax 342 18 19). **U.K. (Embassy):** 21 Conway St., London W1P 5HL (tel. (0171) 387 2022; fax 387 0574). **U.S. (Embassy):** 2343 Massachusetts Ave. NW, Washington, D.C. 20008 (tel. (202) 588-5899; fax 588-8936).

Czech Republic: Australia (Embassy): 38 Culgoa Circuit, O'Malley, Canberra, ACT 2606 (tel. (06) 290 13 86; fax 290 00 06). **Canada (Embassy):** 541 Sussex Dr., Ottawa, Ont. K1N 6Z6 (tel. (613) 562-3875; fax 562-3878). **Ireland (Embassy):** 57 Northumberland Rd., Ballsbridge, Dublin 4 (tel. (031) 668 1135; fax 668 1660). **New Zealand (Honorary Consul):** 48 Hair St., Wainuiomata, Wellington (tel. (04) 564 6001; fax 564 9022). **South Africa (Embassy):** 936 Pretorius St., Arcadia, Pretoria 0083, or P.O. Box 3326, Pretoria 0001 (tel. (012) 342 34 77; fax 43 20 33). **U.K. (Embassy):** 26 Kensington Palace Gardens, London W8 4QY (tel. (0171) 243 1115; fax 727 9654). **U.S. (Embassy):** 3900 Spring of Freedom St. NW, Washington, D.C. 20008 (tel. (202) 274-9100; fax 966-8540). **(Consulate):** 10990 Wilshire Blvd., #1100, Los Angeles, CA 90024 (tel. (310) 473-0889; fax 473-9813).

Estonia: Australia (Honorary Consul): 86 Louisa Rd., Birchgrove 2041, NSW (tel. (02) 98 10 74 68; fax 98 18 17 79). **Canada (Honorary Consul):** 958 Broadview Ave., Toronto, Ont. M4K 2R6 (tel. (416) 461-0764; fax 461-0448). **South Africa (Honorary Consul):** 16 Hofmeyr St., Welgemoed 7530 (tel. (021) 913 2579; fax 933 5048). **U.K. (Embassy):** 16 Hyde Park Gate, London SW7 5DG (tel. (0171) 589 3428; fax 589 3430). **U.S. (Embassy):** 2131 Massachusetts Ave. NW, Washington, D.C. 20008 (tel. (202) 588-0101; fax 588-0108).

Hungary: Australia (Consulate): Edgecliff Centre 203-233, #405, Head Rd., Edgecliff, Sydney, NSW 2027 (tel. (02) 93 28 78 59; fax 93 27 18 29). **Canada (Embassy):** 299 Waverley St., Ottawa, Ont. K2P 0Z9 (tel. (613) 230-2717; fax 230-7560). **Ireland (Embassy):** 2 Fitzwilliam Pl., Dublin 2 (tel. (01) 661 2903; fax 661 2880). **South Africa (Embassy):** P.O. Box 27077, Sunnyside 0132, 959 Arcadia St., Arcadia, Pretoria (tel. (012) 43 30 30; fax 43 30 29). **U.K. (Embassy):** 35/B Eaton Pl., London SW1X 8BY (tel. (0171) 235 7191; fax 823 1348). **U.S. (Embassy):** 3910 Shoemaker St. NW, Washington, D.C. 20008 (tel. (202) 362-6730; fax 686-6412). **(Consulate):** 11766 Wilshire Blvd., #410, Los Angeles, CA 90025 (tel. (310) 473-9344; fax 479-0456).

Latvia: Australia (Embassy): P.O. Box 457, Strathfield NSW 2135 (tel. (02) 97 44 59 81; fax 97 47 60 55). **Canada (Embassy):** 112 Kent St., Place de Ville, Tower B, #208, Ottawa, Ont. K1P 5P2 (tel. (613) 238-6014; fax 238-7044). **Ireland (Honorary Consul):** 88-95 Grafton St., Dublin 2, Ireland (tel. (01) 679 56 66; fax 679 52 60). **South Africa (Honorary Consul):** P.O. Box 34, Cyrildene, Johannesburg 2198 (tel. (011) 782 58 12; fax. 888 55 00). **U.K. (Embassy):** 45 Nottingham Pl., London W1M 3FE (tel. (0171) 312 0040; fax 312 0042). **U.S. (Embassy):** 4325 17th St. NW, Washington, D.C. 20011 (tel. (202) 726-8213; fax 726-6785).

Lithuania: Australia (Honorary Consul): 40B Fiddens Wharf Rd., Killara NSW 2071 (tel. (02) 94 98 25 71; fax 94 98 25 71). **Canada (Embassy):** 130 Albert St., #204, Ottawa, Ont. K1P 5G4 (tel. (613) 567-5458; fax 567-5315). **South Africa (Honorary Consul):** P.O. Box 1737, Houghton 20141 (tel. (011) 486 36 60; fax 486 36 50). **U.K. (Embassy):** 84 Gloucester Pl., London W1H 3HN (tel. (0171) 486 6401; fax

486 6403). **U.S. (Embassy):** 2622 16th St. NW, Washington, D.C. 20009 (tel. (202) 234-5860; fax 328-0466).

F.Y.R. of Macedonia: U.K. (Embassy): 10 Harcourt House, 19A Cavendish Sq., London W1M 9AD (tel. (0171) 499 5152; fax 499 2864). **U.S. (Embassy):** 3050 K St. NW, #210, Washington, D.C. 20007 (tel. (202) 337-3063; fax 337-3093).

Moldova: U.S. (Embassy): 2101 S St. NW, Washington, D.C. 20008 (tel. (202) 667-1130; fax 667-1204).

Poland: Australia (Embassy): 7 Turrana St., Yarralumla ACT 2600 Canberra (tel. (06) 273 12 08 or 273 12 11; fax 273 31 81). **Canada: (Embassy):** 443 Daly St., Ottawa, Ont., K1N 6H3 (tel. (613) 789-0468; fax 789-1218). **Ireland (Embassy):** 5 Ailesbury Rd., Dublin 4 (tel. (01) 283 08 55; fax 283 75 62). **New Zealand (Embassy):** 17 Upland Rd., Kelburn, Wellington (tel. (04) 71 24 56; fax 71 24 55). **South Africa (Embassy):** 14 Amos St., Colbyn, Pretoria 0083 (tel. (012) 43 26 21; fax 43 26 08). **U.K. (Embassy):** 47 Portland Place, London W1N 4JH (tel. (0171) 580 4324; fax 323 4018). **(Consulate):** 2 Kinnear Rd., Edinburgh EH3 5PE (tel. (0131) 552 0301; fax 552 1086).**U.S. (Embassy):** 2640 16th St. NW, Washington, D.C. 20009 (tel. (202) 234-3800; fax 328-6271). **(Consulate):** 12400 Wilshire Blvd., #555, Los Angeles, CA 90025 (tel. (310) 442-8500; fax 442-8515).

Romania: Australia (Consulate): 333 Old South Head Rd., Bondi, Sydney (tel. (02) 91 30 57 18; fax 93 65 32 38). **Canada (Embassy):** 655 Rideau St., Ottawa, Ont. K1N 6A3 (tel. (613) 789-5345; fax 789-4365). **South Africa (Embassy):** 117 Charles St., Brooklyn 0011, POB 11295, Pretoria (tel. (012) 466 941; fax 466 947). **U.K. (Embassy):** 4 Palace Green, Kensington, London W8 4QD (tel. (0171) 937 9666; fax 937 8069). **U.S. (Embassy):** 1607 23rd St. NW, Washington, D.C. 20008 (tel. (202) 332-4846; fax 232-4748).

Russia: Australia (Embassy): 78 Canberra Ave., Griffith ACT 2603 Canberra (tel. (06) 295 90 33; fax 295 18 47). **Canada (Embassy):** 285 Charlotte St., Ottawa, Ont. K1N 8L5 (tel. (613) 235-4341; fax 236-6342). **(Consulate)** 52 Range Rd., Ottawa, Ont. K1N 8J5 (tel. (613) 236-6215; fax 238-6158). **Ireland (Embassy):** 186 Orwell Rd., Dublin 14 (tel. (01) 492 3525). **New Zealand (Embassy):** 57 Messines Rd., Karori, Wellington (tel. (04) 476 61 13; fax 476 38 43). **U.K. (Embassy):** 13 Kensington Palace Gardens, London W84 QX (tel. (0171) 229 3628; fax 727 8625). **U.S. (Embassy):** 1706 18th St. NW, Washington, D.C. 20009 (info tel. (202) 232-6020; Consular tel. 939-8907; fax 328-0137). **(Consulate):** 9 East 91st St., New York, NY 10128 (tel. (212) 348-0926; fax 831-9162). **(Consulate):** 2790 Green St., San Francisco, CA 94123 (tel. (415) 202-9800).

Slovakia: Australia (Embassy): 47 Culgoa Circuit, O'Malley, Canberra ACT 2606 (tel. (06) 290 15 16; fax 290 17 55). **Canada (Embassy):** 50 Rideau Terrace, Ottawa, Ont. K1M 2A1 (tel. (613) 749-4442; fax 749-4989). **South Africa (Embassy):** P.O. Box 12736, Hatfield 0028, Pretoria (tel. (012) 342 20 51; fax 342 36 88). **U.K. (Embassy):** 25 Kensington Palace Gardens, London W8T 4QY (tel. (0171) 243 0803; fax 727 5824). **U.S. (Embassy):** 2201 Wisconsin Ave. NW, #250, Washington, D.C. 20007 (tel. (202) 965-5161; fax 965-5166).

Slovenia: Australia (Embassy): P.O. Box 1301, Level 6, 60 Marcus Clarke St., Canberra ACT 2601 (tel. (06) 243 48 30). **Canada (Embassy):** 150 Metcalfe St., #2101, Ottawa, Ont. K2P 1P1 (tel. (613) 565-5781; fax 565-5783). **U.K. (Embassy):** Cavendish Court 11-15, #1, Wigmore St., London W1H 9LA (tel. (0171) 495 7775; fax 495 7776). **U.S. (Embassy):** 1525 New Hampshire Ave. NW, Washington, D.C. 20036 (tel. (202) 667-5363; fax 667-4563).

Ukraine: Australia (Honorary Consul): #3, Ground Floor, 902-912 Mt. Alexander Road, Essendon, Victoria 3040. **Canada (Embassy):** 310 Somerset St. West, Ottawa, Ont., K2P 0J9 (tel. (613) 230-2961; fax 230-2400). **South Africa (Embassy):** 398 Marais Street, Pretoria (tel. (12) 46 19 43; fax 46 19 44). **U.K. (Embassy):** 78 Kensington Park Rd., London W1 12PL (tel. (0171) 727 6312; fax 792 1708). **U.S. (Embassy):** 3350 M St. NW, Washington, D.C. 20007 (tel. (202) 333-0606; fax 333-0817).

Yugoslavia: Australia (Embassy): 11 Nuyts St., Red Hill, Canberra (tel. (06) 295 14 58; 239 61 78). **Canada (Embassy):** 17 Blackburn Ave, Ottawa, Ont., KIN 8A2 (tel. (613) 233-6289; fax 233-7850). **U.K. (Embassy):** 5-7 Lexham Gardens, London W8 5JU (tel. (0171) 370 6105; fax 370 3838). **U.S. (Embassy):** 2410 California St. NW, Washington, D.C. 20008 (tel. (202) 462-6566; fax 462-2508).

PASSPORTS

Citizens of Australia, Canada, Ireland, New Zealand, South Africa, the U.K., and the U.S. all need valid passports to enter any Eastern European country and to re-enter their own country. Some countries do not allow entrance if the holder's passport expires in under six months; returning home with an expired passport is illegal, and may result in a fine. Some countries require children to carry their own passports.

Before you leave, **photocopy** the page of your passport that contains your photograph, passport number, and other identifying information. Carry one photocopy seperate from your passport, and leave another copy at home. These will help prove your citizenship and facilitate the issuing of a new passport if you lose the original document. Consulates also recommend that you carry an expired passport or an official copy of your birth certificate separate from other documents.

If you do **lose** your passport, immediately notify the local police and the nearest embassy or consulate of your home government. To expedite its replacement, you will need to know all information previously documented and show identification and proof of citizenship. A replacement may take weeks to process, and it may be valid only for a limited time. Some consulates can issue new passports within 24 hours if you give them proof of citizenship. Any visas stamped in your old passport will be irretrievably lost. In an emergency, ask for immediate temporary traveling papers that will permit you to reenter your home country.

Your passport is a public document belonging to your nation's government. You may have to surrender it to a foreign government official, but if you don't get it back in a reasonable amount of time, inform the nearest mission of your home country.

Australia: Citizens must apply for a passport in person at a post office, a passport office, or an Australian diplomatic mission overseas. An appointment may be necessary. Passport offices are located in capital cities and Newcastle. A parent may file an application for a child who is under 18 and unmarried. Adult passports, valid for 10 years, cost AUS$126 (for a 32-page passport) or AUS$188 (64-page), and a child's, valid for 5 years, is AUS$63 (32-page) or AUS$94 (64-page). For more info, call toll-free (in Australia) 13 12 32.

Canada: Application forms are available at all passport offices, Canadian missions, many travel agencies, and Northern Stores in northern communities. Citizens may apply in person at any of 28 regional Passport Offices across Canada; ask a travel agent for the nearest location. Canadian citizens residing abroad should contact the nearest Canadian embassy or consulate. Children under 16 may be included on a parent's passport. Passports cost CDN$60, are valid for 5 years, and are not renewable. Processing takes approximately 5 business days for in-person applications, 10 days by mail. For additional info, contact the **Canadian Passport Office,** Department of Foreign Affairs and International Trade, Ottawa, Ontario, K1A 0G3 (tel. (613) 994-3500; http://www.dfait-maeci.gc.ca/passport). Travelers may also call (800) 567-6868 (24hr.); in Toronto (416) 973-3251; in Vancouver (604) 775-6250; in Montréal (514) 283-2152. Refer to the booklet *Bon Voyage, But...,* free at any passport office or by calling InfoCentre at (800) 267-8376, for further help and a list of Canadian embassies and consulates abroad. You may also find entry and background information for various countries by contacting the **Consular Affairs Bureau** in Ottawa (tel. (800) 267-6788 (24hr.) or (613) 944-6788).

Ireland: Citizens may apply for a passport by mail to either the Dept. of Foreign Affairs, Passport Office, Setanta Centre, Molesworth St., Dublin 2 (tel. (01) 671 1633), or the Passport Office, Irish Life Building, 1A South Mall, Cork (tel. (021) 272 525). Obtain an application at a local Garda station or request one from a passport office. The new **Passport Express Service,** available through post offices, allows citizens to get a passport in 2 weeks for an extra IR£3. Passports cost IR£45 and are valid for 10 years. Citizens under 18 or over 65 can request a 3-year passport that costs IR£10.

New Zealand: Application forms for passports are available from travel agents and **Dept. of Internal Affairs Link Centres** in the main cities and towns. Overseas, forms and passport services are provided by New Zealand embassies, high commissions, and consulates. Applications may also be forwarded to the Passport Office, P.O. Box 10526, Wellington, New Zealand. Standard processing time in New Zealand is 10 working days. An adult passport, valid for 10 years, costs NZ$80; a child's passport, valid for 5 years, is NZ$40. An **urgent passport service** is also available for an extra NZ$80. Different fees apply overseas: 9 posts including London, Sydney, and Los Angeles offer both standard and urgent services (adult NZ$130, child NZ$65, plus NZ$130 if urgent). The fee at other posts is adult NZ$260, child NZ$195; passports issued within 3 working days. Children's names can no longer be endorsed on a parent's passport—they must apply for their own.

South Africa: Citizens can apply for a passport at any **Home Affairs Office** or **South African Mission.** Tourist passports, valid for 10 years, cost SAR80. Children under 16 must be issued their own passports, valid for 5 years, which cost SAR60. If a passport is needed in a hurry, an **emergency passport** may be issued for SAR50. An application for a permanent passport must accompany the emergency passport application. Time for the completion of an application is normally 3 months or more from the time of submission. Current passports less than 10 years old may be **renewed** until December 31, 1999; every citizen whose passport's validity does not extend far beyond this date is urged to renew it as soon as possible, to avoid the expected glut of applications as 2000 approaches. Renewal is free, and turn-around time is usually 2 weeks. For further information, contact the nearest Department of Home Affairs Office.

United Kingdom: British citizens, British Dependent Territories citizens, British nationals (overseas), and British overseas citizens may apply for a **full passport,** valid for 10 years (5 years if under 16). Application forms are available at passport offices, main post offices, many travel agents, and branches of Lloyds Bank and Artac World Choice. Apply in person or by mail to one of the passport offices in London, Liverpool, Newport, Peterborough, Glasgow, or Belfast. The fee is UK£18. Children under 16 may be included on a parent's passport. Processing by mail usually takes 4-6 weeks. The London office offers same-day, walk-in rush service; arrive early. The formerly available **British Visitor's Passport** has been abolished; every traveler over 16 now needs a standard passport. For more information, contact the U.K. Passport Agency (tel. (0990) 21 04 10; http://www.open.gov.uk/ukpass).

United States: Citizens may apply for a passport at any federal or state **courthouse** or **post office** authorized to accept passport applications, or at a **U.S. Passport Agency,** located in Boston, Chicago, Honolulu, Houston, Los Angeles, Miami, New Orleans, New York, Philadelphia, San Francisco, Seattle, Stamford, or Washington, D.C. Refer to the "U.S. Government, State Department" section of the telephone directory or the local post office for addresses. Parents must apply in person for children under age 13. You must apply in person if this is your first passport, if you're under age 18, or if your current passport is more than 12 years old or was issued before your 18th birthday. Passports are valid for 10 years (5 years if under 18) and cost US$65 (under 18 US$40). Passports may be **renewed** by mail or in person for US$55. Processing takes 3-4 weeks. **Rush service** is available for a surcharge of US$30 with proof of departure within 10 working days (e.g., an airplane ticket or itinerary), or for travelers leaving in 2-3 weeks who require visas. For more info, contact the U.S. Passport Information's **24-hour recorded message** (tel. (202) 647-0518). U.S. citizens may receive consular information sheets, travel warnings, and public announcements at any passport agency, U.S. embassy, or consulate, or by sending a self-addressed stamped envelope to: Overseas Citizens Services, #4811, Department of State, Washington, D.C. 20520-4818 (tel. (202) 647-5225; fax 647-3000). Additional information (including publications) about documents, formalities, and travel abroad is available on the **Bureau of Consular Affairs** homepage at http://travel.state.gov, or the State Department site at http://www.state.gov.

ENTRANCE REQUIREMENTS AND VISAS

In addition to a passport, many countries in Eastern Europe also require a **visa,** which sometimes must be supported by an **invitation** from a sponsoring individual or organization. A **visa** is an endorsement that a foreign government stamps into a passport which allows the bearer to stay in that country for a specified purpose and period of time. Prices for visas to Eastern Europe vary greatly, depending upon the country as well as the applicant's nationality. We list prices in each country's **Essentials** section. Requirements are always subject to change. For more information, send for *Foreign Entry Requirements* (US$0.50) from the **Consumer Information Center,** Department 363D, Pueblo, CO 81009 (tel. (719) 948-3334; http://www.pueblo.gsa.gov), or contact the **Center for International Business and Travel,** 25 West 43rd St. #1420, New York, NY 10036 (tel. (800) 925-2428 or (212) 575-2811 from NYC), which secures visas for travel to and from all countries for a variable service charge.

When you enter a country, dress neatly and carry **proof of your financial independence,** such as a visa to the next country on your itinerary, an airplane ticket to depart, or enough money to cover the cost of your living expenses. Admission as a visitor does not include the right to work, which is authorized only by a work permit. Entering certain countries to study requires a special visa, and immigration officers may also want to see proof of acceptance from a school and proof that the course of study will take up most of your time in the country, as well as proof that you can support yourself.

Upon entering a country, you must declare certain items from abroad and must pay a duty on the value of those articles that exceed the allowance established by that country's **customs** service. Keeping receipts for purchases made abroad will help establish values when you return. It is wise to make a list, including serial numbers, of any valuables that you carry with you from home; if you register this list with customs before your departure and have an official stamp it, you will avoid import duty charges and ensure an easy passage upon your return. Be especially careful to document items manufactured abroad.

Certain countries in Eastern Europe, including Bulgaria, Croatia, Russia, and Ukraine, require travelers to **register** with the local police or a special office upon arrival. Other countries require travelers to keep a **statistical card** on which they must keep track of where they spend each and every night while in the country. Again, this info is listed in each country's general introduction. Unless you are studying in the country, extending your stay is difficult. You must contact the country's immigration officials or local police well before your time is up, and show proof of financial resources.

Russia, Belarus, and Ukraine will only issue visas to travelers possessing **invitations** from friends, relatives, or a sponsoring organization in the country. Moldova requires invitations for everyone but Americans. If you don't have someone to invite you, several organizations in the West can arrange the appropriate paperwork for a fee. Visas to Russia and Ukraine also require a list of all the cities and towns on the itinerary. Although this rule is inconsistently reinforced, local police and hotel managers can be nasty when the mood strikes them.

CUSTOMS: GOING HOME

Upon returning home, you must declare all articles acquired abroad and pay a **duty** on the value of those articles that exceed the allowance established by your country's customs service. Goods and gifts purchased at **duty-free** shops abroad are not exempt from duty or sales tax at your point of return; you must declare these items as well. "Duty-free" merely means that you do not pay a tax in the country of purchase.

Australia: Citizens may import AUS$400 (under 18 AUS$200) worth of goods duty-free, in addition to 1.125L alcohol and 250 cigarettes or 250g tobacco. You must be over 18 to import alcohol or tobacco. There is no limit to the amount of Australian or foreign cash that may be brought into or taken out of the country, but amounts of AUS$10,000 or more, or the equivalent in foreign currency, must be reported. All foodstuffs and animal products must be declared on arrival. For information, contact the Regional Director, Australian Customs Service, GPO Box 8, Sydney NSW 2001 (tel. (02) 9213 2000; fax 9213 4000).

Canada: Citizens who remain abroad for at least 1 week may bring back up to CDN$500 worth of goods duty-free any time. Citizens or residents who travel for a period between 48 hours and 6 days can bring back up to CDN$200. You are permitted to ship goods except tobacco and alcohol home under the CDN$500 exemption as long as you declare them when you arrive. Goods under the CDN$200 exemption, as well as all alcohol and tobacco, must be in your hand or checked luggage. Citizens of legal age (which varies by province) may import up to 200 cigarettes, 50 cigars or cigarillos, 400g loose tobacco, 400 tobacco sticks, 1.14L wine or alcohol, and 24 355mL cans/bottles of beer; the value of these products is included in the CDN$200 or CDN$500. For more information, write to Canadian Customs, 2265 St. Laurent Blvd., Ottawa, Ont. K1G 4K3 (tel. (613) 993-0534), phone the 24hr. Automated Customs Information Service at (800) 461-9999, or visit Revenue Canada at http://www.revcan.ca.

Ireland: Citizens must declare everything in excess of IR£142 (IR£73 per traveler under 15 years of age) obtained outside the EU or duty- and tax-free in the EU above the following allowances: 200 cigarettes, 100 cigarillos, 50 cigars, or 250g tobacco; 1L liquor or 2L wine; 50g perfume; and 250mL toilet water. Goods obtained duty and tax paid in another EU country up to a value of IR£460 (IR£115 per traveler under 15) will not be subject to additional customs duties. Travelers under 17 may not import tobacco or alcohol. For more info, contact The Revenue Commissioners, Dublin Castle (tel. (01) 679 27 77; fax 671 20 21; http://www.revenue.ie) or The Collector of Customs and Excise, The Custom House, Dublin 1.

New Zealand: Citizens may import up to NZ$700 worth of goods duty-free if they are for personal use or are unsolicited gifts. The concession is 200 cigarettes, or 250g tobacco, or 50 cigars, or a combination of all 3 not to exceed 250g. You may also bring in 4.5L of beer or wine and 1.125L of liquor. Travelers over 17 may import tobacco or alcohol. For more information, contact New Zealand Customs, 50 Anzac Ave., Box 29, Auckland (tel. (09) 377 35 20; fax 309 29 78).

South Africa: Citizens may import duty-free: 400 cigarettes, 50 cigars, 250g tobacco, 2L wine, 1L of spirits, 250mL toilet water, and 50mL perfume, and other consumable items up to a value of SAR500. Goods up to a value of SAR10,000 over and above this duty-free allowance are dutiable at 20%; such goods are also exempted from payment of VAT. Items acquired abroad and sent to the Republic as unaccompanied baggage do not qualify for any allowances. You may not export or import South African bank notes in excess of SAR2000. For more information, consult the free pamphlet *South African Customs Information,* available in airports or from the Commissioner for Customs and Excise, Private Bag X47, Pretoria 0001 (tel. (012) 314 99 11; fax 328 64 78).

United Kingdom: Citizens or visitors arriving in the U.K. from outside the EU must declare goods in excess of the following allowances: 200 cigarettes, 100 cigarillos, 50 cigars, or 250g tobacco; still table wine (2L); strong liqueurs over 22% volume (1L), or fortified or sparkling wine, other liquors (2L); perfume (60 cc/mL); toilet water (250 cc/mL); and UK£136 worth of all other goods including gifts and souvenirs. You must be over 17 to import liquor or tobacco. These allowances also apply to duty-free purchases within the EU, except for the last category (other goods), which has an allowance of UK£71. Goods obtained duty- and tax-paid for personal use (regulated according to set guide levels) within the EU do not require any further customs duty. For more information, contact Her Majesty's Customs and Excise, Custom House, Nettleton Road, Heathrow Airport, Hounslow, Middlesex TW6 2LA (tel. (0181) 910 37 44; fax 910 37 65).

United States: Citizens may import US$400 worth of accompanying goods duty-free and must pay a 10% tax on the next US$1000. You must declare all purchases, so have sales slips ready. The US$400 personal exemption covers goods purchased for personal or household use (this includes gifts) and cannot include more than 100 cigars, 200 cigarettes (1 carton), and 1L of wine or liquor. You must be over 21 to bring liquor into the U.S. If you mail home personal goods of U.S. origin, you can avoid duty charges by marking the package "American goods returned." For more information, consult the brochure *Know Before You Go,* available from the U.S. Customs Service, Box 7407, Washington D.C. 20044 (tel. (202) 927-6724), or visit the Web (http://www.customs.ustreas.gov).

YOUTH, STUDENT, & TEACHER IDENTIFICATION

The **International Student Identity Card (ISIC)** is the most widely accepted form of student identification. Flashing this card can procure you discounts for sights, theaters, museums, accommodations, meals, train, ferry, bus, and airplane transportation, and other services. Present the card wherever you go, and ask about discounts even when none are advertised. It also provides insurance benefits, including US$100 per day of in-hospital sickness for a maximum of 60 days, and US$3000 of accident-related medical reimbursement for each accident (see **Insurance,** p. 19). In addition, cardholders have access to a toll-free 24hr. ISIC helpline whose multilingual staff can provide assistance in medical, legal, and financial emergencies overseas (tel. (800) 626-2427 in the U.S. and Canada; elsewhere call the U.S. collect (713) 267-2525).

Many student travel agencies around the world issue ISICs, including STA Travel in Australia and New Zealand; Travel CUTS in Canada; USIT in Ireland and Northern Ireland; SASTS in South Africa; Campus Travel and STA Travel in the U.K.; Council Travel, Let's Go Travel, and STA Travel in the U.S.; and any of the other organizations under the auspices of the International Student Travel Confederation. When you apply for the card, request a copy of the *International Student Identity Card Handbook,* which lists some of the available discounts by country. You can also write to Council Travel for a copy. The card is valid from September to December of the following year (e.g. September '97-December '98) and costs US$19 or CDN$15. Applicants must be at least 12 years old and degree-seeking students of a secondary or post-secondary school. Because of the proliferation of phony ISICs, many airlines and some other services require other proof of student identity, such as a signed letter from the registrar attesting to your student status and stamped with the school seal, or your school ID card. The US$20 **International Teacher Identity Card (ITIC)** offers the same insurance coverage and similar discounts. For more information consult the organization's web site (http:www.istc.org; email isicinfo@istc.org).

Federation of International Youth Travel Organizations (FIYTO) issues a discount card to travelers who are under 26 but not students. Known as the **GO25 Card,** this one-year card offers many of the same benefits as the ISIC, and most organizations that sell the ISIC also sell the GO25 Card. A brochure that lists discounts is free when you purchase the card. To apply, you will need a passport, valid driver's license or copy of a birth certificate; and a passport-sized photo with your name printed on the back. The fee is US$19, CDN$15, or UK£5. Information is available on the web at http://www.fiyto.org or http://www.go25.org, or by contacting Travel CUTS in Canada, STA Travel in the U.K., Council Travel in the U.S., or FIYTO headquaters in Denmark (see **Budget Travel Agencies,** p. 29 and **Travel Organizations,** p. 2).

DRIVING PERMITS AND CAR INSURANCE

If you plan to drive while abroad, you may need an **International Driving Permit (IDP),** though certain countries allow travelers to drive with a valid American or Canadian license for a limited number of months. Many car rental agencies don't require the permit. Call an automobile association to find out if your destination country requires the IDP. You may want to get one anyway, in case you have an accident or get stranded in a smaller town where police may not read or speak English.

Your IDP, valid for one year, must be issued in your own country before you depart. A valid driver's license from your home country must always accompany the IDP. An application for an IDP usually needs to include one or two photos, a current local license, an additional form of identification, and a fee. Australians can obtain an IDP (AUS$12) by contacting their local **Royal Automobile Club (RAC),** or the **National Royal Motorist Association (NRMA)** if in NSW or the ACT. Canadian license holders can obtain an IDP (CDN$10) through any **Canadian Automobile Association (CAA)** branch office, or by writing to CAA Central Ontario, 60 Commerce Valley Drive East, Thornhill, Ont. L3T 7P9 (tel. (416) 221-4300). Citizens of Ireland should drop into their nearest **Automobile Association (AA)** office, where an IDP can be picked up for IR£4, or phone (01) 283 35 55 for a postal application form.

In New Zealand, contact your local **Automobile Association (AA),** or the main office at 99 Albert Street, PO Box 5, Auckland (tel. (09) 377 46 60; fax 309 45 64), IDPs cost NZ$8 + NZ$2 for return postage. In South Africa, visit your local **Automobile Association of South Africa** office, where IDPs can be picked up for SAR25. For more info phone (011) 466 66 41, or write to P.O. Box 596, 2000 Johannesburg. In the U.K. IDPs are UK£4; you can either visit your local **AA Shop,** or call (01256) 49 39 32 and order a postal application form (allow 2-3 weeks). U.S. license holders can obtain an IDP (US$10) at any **American Automobile Association (AAA)** office or by writing to AAA Florida, Travel Agency Services Department, 1000 AAA Drive (mail stop 28), Heathrow, FL 32746-5080 (tel. (407) 444-4245; fax 444-4247).

Many credit cards cover standard **insurance.** If you rent, lease, or borrow a car, you will need a **green card,** or **International Insurance Certificate,** to prove that you have liability insurance. Obtain it through the car rental agency; most include coverage in their prices. If you lease a car, you can obtain a green card from the dealer. Some travel agents offer the card; it may also be available at border crossings. Verify whether your auto insurance applies abroad; even if it does, you will still need a green card to certify this to foreign officials. If you have a collision abroad, the accident will show up on your domestic records if you report it to your insurance company. Rental agencies may require you to purchase theft insurance in countries that they consider to have a high risk of auto theft.

■ Money

If you stay in hostels and eat occasional meals in restaurants, you may expect to spend approximately US$30 per day plus transportation (more in Slovenia, Croatia, Russia, and the Baltics). Don't sacrifice health or safety for a cheaper tab. Also remember to check the financial pages of a large newspaper for up-to-the-minute exchange rates before embarking on your journey. Certain countries in Eastern Europe are experiencing high levels of inflation and currency depreciation. Many prices are given in **U.S. Dollars** or in **Deutschmarks** (see **Gateway Cities: Berlin,** p. 763, for the exchange rates between DM and US$).

CURRENCY AND EXCHANGE

It is more expensive to buy foreign currency than domestic—i.e., Hungarian forints will cost less in Hungary than in the U.S. However, converting some money before you go will allow you to zip through the airport while others languish in exchange lines. Check commission rates closely, and scan newspapers to get the standard rate of exchange. Bank rates are generally the best, but at times tourist offices or exchange kiosks have better rates; *Let's Go* indicates this in the appropriate sections.

Always save **transaction receipts,** as some countries require you to reconvert unused local currency on your way out. Exchanging some of your old currency before moving on to a new country is good insurance against arriving after hours or in a bankless town. **American Express** offices usually charge no commission, but they often have slightly worse rates than other exchanges. In general, carry a range of denominations since charges may be levied per check cashed. Australian and New Zealand dollars and South African rand are virtually impossible to exchange in much of Eastern Europe. U.S. dollars are generally preferred, though certain establishments only accept Deutschmarks. Western currency is sometimes the preferred payment in Eastern European hotels; find out which hotels and restaurants require hard currency, and don't use Western money when you don't need to—throwing it around to gain preferential treatment is offensive and makes you an instant target for theft.

TRAVELER'S CHECKS

Traveler's checks are the safest way to carry money: if they get lost or stolen, travelers get reimbursed by the checks' issuers. However, many establishments in Eastern Europe do not accept them. In general, you will find it very difficult to exchange traveler's checks outside of capitals and major cities, and in Bosnia and Yugoslavia, you should not count on being able to exchange them at all. Checks should be ordered in advance, especially if large sums are being requested. Keep check receipts and a record of which checks you've cashed in a separate place from the checks themselves. Leave a photocopy of check serial numbers with someone at home in case you lose your copy. Never countersign checks until you're prepared to cash them. Finally, be sure to bring your passport with you any time you plan to use the checks.

American Express: Call (800) 25 19 02 in Australia; in New Zealand (0800) 44 10 68; in the U.K. (0800) 52 13 13; in the U.S. and Canada (800) 221-7282. Elsewhere, call U.S. collect (801) 964-6665 (http://www.aexp.com). American Express Traveler's Cheques are now available in Australian, British, Canadian, German, and other currencies. They are the most widely recognized worldwide and the easiest to replace if lost or stolen. Checks can be purchased for a small fee at American Express Travel Service Offices, banks, and AAA offices (AAA members can buy the checks commission-free). Cardmembers can also purchase checks at American Express Dispensers at Travel Service Offices at airports, or via phone (U.S. and Canada tel. (800) ORDER-TC (673-3782)). AmEx offices cash their checks commission-free (except where prohibited by national governments), although they often offer slightly worse rates than banks. They also sell Cheques for Two which can be signed by either of two people. Request AmEx's *Traveler's Companion,* which lists travel office addresses and stolen check hotlines for each European country.

Citicorp: Call (800) 645-6556 in the U.S. and Canada; in Europe (44) 171 508 70 07; from elsewhere call U.S. collect (813) 623-1709. Sells both Citicorp and Citicorp Visa traveler's checks in U.S., Australian, British, Canadian, and German currencies. Commission is 1-2% on check purchases. Checkholders are automatically enrolled for 45 days in the Travel Assist Program (call U.S. collect (202) 296-8728), which provides travelers with English-speaking doctor, lawyer, and interpreter referrals as well as check refund assistance. Citicorp's World Courier Service guarantees worldwide hand-delivery of replacement traveler's checks.

Thomas Cook MasterCard: Call (800) 223-9920 in the U.S. and Canada; in the U.K. call (0800) 622 101 or collect (1733) 50 29 95 or (1733) 31 89 50; elsewhere call U.S. collect (609) 987-7300. Offers checks in currencies including U.S., Canadian, Australian, British, German, South African, and the ECU. Commission 1-2% for purchases (lower at a Thomas Cook office).

Visa: Call (800) 227-6811 in the U.S.; in the U.K. (0800) 89 54 92; from elsewhere call (44 1733) 31 89 49 and reverse the charges. They will let you know where the nearest office is or help you with lost checks.

CREDIT CARDS AND CASH CARDS

Credit cards can be either invaluable or a frustrating nuisance. For the most part, only expensive, Western-oriented establishments in Eastern Europe take them, but they allow you to withdraw money from some ATMs and get cash advances at many banks. Major credit cards like **MasterCard (MC)** and **Visa** are the most likely to be recognized. Cash advances can be a great bargain, since credit-card companies get the wholesale exchange rate—generally 5% better than the retail rate used by banks and even better than that used by other currency-exchange establishments. **American Express (AmEx)** cards work in some ATMs, as well as at AmEx offices and major airports. All such machines require a **Personal Identification Number (PIN).** Ask your credit card company to assign you one before you leave; without this PIN, *you will be unable to withdraw cash.* Keep in mind that MasterCard and Visa have different names elsewhere ("EuroCard" or "Access" for MasterCard and "Carte Bleue" or "Barclaycard" for Visa). Credit cards are invaluable in an emergency—an unexpected hospital bill or ticket home, or the loss of traveler's checks—which may leave you temporarily without other resources. Credit cards also offer an array of other services, from car insurance to emergency assistance; these depend completely, however, on the issuer. American Express (tel. (800) 843-2273) provides some services that might be of use to travelers, including a 24-hour hotline offering medical and legal assis-

ESSENTIALS

tance in emergencies (from abroad call U.S. collect (310) 214-8228). At AmEx offices abroad, members can pick up mail and find assistance in changing airline, hotel, and car-rental reservations. MasterCard (tel. (800) 999-0454) and Visa (tel. (800) 336-8472) are issued in cooperation with individual banks or other organizations.

ATMs (Automated Teller Machines) are increasing in number in Eastern Europe, but still rare or non-existent in some countries. Banks in larger cities are most likely to be connected to an international money network, usually **CIRRUS** (tel. (800) 4-CIR-RUS (424-7787)) or **PLUS** (tel. (800) 843-7587). Cirrus charges US$3-5 to withdraw money, depending on your bank. ATMs also dispense the money at the same whole-sale rate you get with credit cards, so using a cash card can pay off in the long run. An important note: European ATMs may not have letters on their keypads, so be sure you memorize your PIN by its numbers before you take off (it must be 4 digits).

American Express allows cardholders to cash personal checks at any of its major offices and many of its representatives' offices with no service charge and no interest. There is also an Express Cash service, which tranforms your card into a debit card that makes withdrawals from a bank account instead of a line of credit. To enroll in Express Cash, call (800) CASH NOW (227-4669) or, outside the U.S., collect (904) 565-7875. Unless using this service, avoid cashing checks in foreign currencies: they may take weeks and a US$30 fee to clear.

MONEY FROM HOME

Money can be **wired** abroad through international money transfer services operated by **Western Union** (tel. (800) 325-6000). The money is usually available in the country to which you're sending it within an hour, although this may vary; the fee for this service, however, is often very steep.

In emergencies, U.S. citizens can have money sent via the State Department's **Citizens Emergency Center, American Citizens Services,** Consular Affairs, Public Affairs Staff, Room 4811, U.S. Department of State, Washington, D.C. 20520 (tel. (202) 647-5225, at night and on Sundays and holidays 647-4000; fax 647-3000; http://travel.state.gov). For US$15, the State Department forwards money within hours to the consular office nearest you. This service is only for Americans; citizens of other countries should contact their embassies for information on wiring cash.

■ Safety and Security

Safe travel in Eastern Europe calls for some special effort. Laws can be minimally observed, and con artists abound, in official positions as well as unofficial ones. Should an emergency arise, contact your local embassy; the police in Eastern Europe usually don't speak English, and may not be helpful to foreigners. To avoid unwanted attention, try to blend in as much as possible. If you respect local customs, you are less likely to be heckled. The gawking camera-toter is a more obvious target than the low-profile local look-alike. Walking into a cafe or shop to check your map beats checking it on a street corner. Better yet, look over your map carefully before leaving your hotel room. Muggings are often impromptu; walking with nervous, over-the-shoulder glances can be a tip that you have something valuable to protect. Look like you know where you're going at all times—even when you don't.

Carry all your valuables (including your passport, railpass, traveler's checks, and air-line ticket) in either a **money belt** or **neckpouch** stashed securely *inside* your cloth-ing; this will protect you from skilled thieves who use razors to slash open backpacks and fanny packs. You should keep valuables on your person at all times, including trips to the shower—try hanging the pouch from the showerhead. Making photo-copies of important documents will help you replace them if they are lost or stolen. Carry one copy separate from the documents and leave another copy at home. A sim-ple but effective deterrent is a small padlock, available in luggage stores, to ensure that your pack stays shut (though not unslashed). If you must carry a shoulder bag, make sure that the strap passes over your head and runs diagonally across your torso.

When exploring a new **city,** extra vigilance is wise, but avoid turning precautions into panic. Carry a small whistle to scare off attackers or attract attention. When walking at night, keep to crowded, well-lit places and don't attempt to cross parks, parking lots, or other deserted areas. **Con artists** are on the prowl in many cities. Be aware of classic ploys, sob stories requiring money or a spill on your shoulder to distract you while your bag is snatched. Hustlers often work in groups, and children are among the most effective. A firm "no" should communicate that you are no dupe. Contact the authorities if a hustler acts particularly insistent or aggressive.

Trains are notoriously easy spots for thieving. Professional thieves wait for tourists to fall asleep and then carry off everything they can. If you're traveling in pairs, sleep in alternating shifts. When alone, use good judgment in selecting a train compartment; never stay in an empty one, and try to get a top bunk. Wrap the straps of your luggage securely around you or tie or lock them to the overhead luggage racks. Trains from major Western cities like Vienna and Berlin (e.g., Berlin-Warsaw, Vienna-Budapest) are generally considered to be more dangerous than countryside trains. Travelers on these lines, and on the Moscow-St.Petersburg route, should be especially vigilant; a powerful odorless gas derived from ether has reportedly been used by criminals to drug passengers to prevent their waking during a robbery. Travelers are advised to secure their door with heavy wire while they sleep.

Sleeping in your **automobile** is one of the more dangerous ways to get your rest. If you must, park in a well-lit area as close to a police station or 24-hour service station as possible. **Sleeping outside** is often illegal and exposes you to even more hazards— camping is recommended only in official, supervised campsites. *Let's Go* does not recommend **hitchhiking,** particularly for women; see **Getting There,** p. 29, for more.

A good self-defense course will give you more concrete ways to react to different types of aggression, though it might cost more than your trip. **Impact, Prepare,** and **Model Mugging** can recommend local self-defense courses in the U.S. (tel. (800) 345-KICK; US$50-400). Community colleges often offer cheaper self-defense courses.

For official **United States Department of State** travel advisories, including crime and security, call their 24-hour hotline at (202) 647-5225 or check their website (http://travel.state.gov), which provides travel information and publications. Travel publications such as the pamphlet *A Safe Trip Abroad* may be ordered by writing to Superintendent of Documents, U.S. Government Printing Office, Washington, D.C. 20402, or by calling (202) 512-1800. Official warnings from the **United Kingdom Foreign and Commonwealth Office** are on-line at http://www.fco.gov.uk; or call the office at (0171) 238 45 03. The **Canadian Department of Foreign Affairs and International Trade (DFAIT)** offers advisories and travel warnings (tel. (613) 944-6788 in Ottawa; (800) 267-6788 elsewhere in Canada). This info is also available on the Web at http://www.dfait-maeci.gc.ca.

■ Health

The **Centers for Disease Control and Prevention** in the U.S. have issued two current warnings particular to outbreaks of disease within Eastern Europe. A **diphtheria epidemic,** which began in Russia in 1990, has now spread to the remaining New Independent States of the former Soviet Union. Cases generally arise in urban areas, but incidents are increasingly reported in rural areas. The Advisory Committee on Immunization Practices recommends that travelers to these areas should be up-to-date for diphtheria immunization. The CDC also advises of an outbreak of **poliomyelitis** (polio) in Albania. Those bound for Albania who have received a primary series of polio vaccine should receive a booster dose before leaving. Travelers who are inadequately vaccinated against polio, or whose past vaccination history is uncertain, should contact their physician to discuss polio vaccination options before departure.

Common sense is the simplest prescription for good health while you travel: eat well, drink and sleep enough, and don't overexert yourself. Drinking lots of fluids can help prevent dehydration and constipation, and wearing sturdy shoes and clean socks and using talcum powder can help keep your feet dry. To minimize jet lag, "reset" your body's clock by adopting the schedule of your destination immediately upon arrival. Most travelers adjust to a new time zone after two or three days.

BEFORE YOU GO

Though no amount of planning can guarantee an accident-free trip, preparation can help minimize the likelihood of contracting a disease and maximize the chances of receiving effective health care in the event of an emergency. For minor health problems, bring a compact **first-aid kit,** including bandages, aspirin or other painkiller, antibiotic cream, a thermometer, a Swiss Army knife with tweezers, moleskin, decongestant, motion sickness remedy, medicine for diarrhea or stomach problems, sunscreen, insect repellent, and burn ointment.

In your passport, write the names of any people you wish to have contacted in case of a medical emergency, and also list any allergies or medical conditions. If you wear **glasses** or **contact lenses,** carry an extra prescription, a pair of glasses, and cleaning solution, or arrange to have your doctor or a family member send a replacement pair in an emergency. **Allergy** sufferers should find out if their conditions are likely to be aggravated in the regions they plan to visit, and obtain a full supply of any necessary medication before the trip, since matching a prescription to a foreign equivalent is not always easy, safe, or possible. Carry up-to-date, legible prescriptions or a statement from your doctor, especially if you use insulin, a syringe, or a narcotic. While traveling, be sure to keep all medication in carry-on luggage.

Take a look at your **immunization** records before you go. Some countries require visitors to carry vaccination certificates. Travelers over two years old should be sure that the following vaccines are up to date: measles, mumps, and rubella; diphtheria, tetanus, and pertussis; polio; haemophilus influenza B; and hepatitis B. A booster of tetanus-diphtheria is recommended once every 10 years, and adults traveling to most of the New Independent States of the former Soviet Union, as well as to Albania, should consider an additional dose of **polio vaccine** if they have not had one during their adult years (see the warning, above). **Hepatitis A** vaccine and/or **immune globulin** (IG) is recommended for travelers to Eastern Europe. Remember that no matter how bad the needles are, they're better than the diseases they prevent.

For up-to-date information about which vaccinations are recommended for your destination and region-specific health data, try the **United States Centers for Disease Control and Prevention** hotline, an excellent source of information for travelers (tel. (404) 332-4559; fax 332-4565; http://www.cdc.gov). Or write: Centers for Disease Control and Prevention, Travelers' Health, 1600 Clifton Rd. NE, Atlanta, GA 30333. The CDC publishes the booklet *Health Information for International Travelers* (US$20), an annual global rundown of disease, immunization, and general health advice, including risks in particular countries. This book may be purchased by sending a check or money order to the Superintendent of Documents, U.S. Government Printing Office, P.O. Box 371954, Pittsburgh, PA 15250-7954. Orders can be made by phone (tel. (202) 512-1800) with a credit card. For more general health information, contact the **American Red Cross,** which publishes a *First Aid and Safety Handbook* (US$5), available for purchase by calling or writing to the American Red Cross, 285 Columbus Ave., Boston, MA 02116-5114 (tel. (800) 564-1234).

Those with medical conditions (i.e. diabetes, allergies to antibiotics, epilepsy, heart conditions) may want to obtain a stainless-steel **Medic Alert** I.D. tag (US$35 the first year, and US$15 annually thereafter), which identifies their condition and gives a 24-hour collect-call info number. In the U.S., call Medic Alert at (800) 825-3785, or write to Medic Alert Foundation, 2323 Colorado Ave., Turlock, CA 95382. Diabetics can contact the **American Diabetes Association,** 1660 Duke St., Alexandria, VA 22314 (tel. (800) 232-3472), to receive copies of the article *Travel and Diabetes* and an ID card, which carries messages in 18 languages explaining the carrier's diabetic status.

If you are concerned about being able to access medical support while traveling, contact one of these two services: **Global Emergency Medical Services (GEMS)** has products called *MedPass* that provide 24-hour international medical assistance and support coordinated through registered nurses who have on-line access to your medical information, your primary physician, and a worldwide network of screened, credentialed English-speaking doctors and hospitals. Subscribers also receive a personal medical record that contains vital information in case of emergencies. For more information call (800) 860-1111, fax (770) 475-0058, or write: 2001 Westside Drive, #120, Alpharetta, GA 30201. The **International Association for Medical Assistance to Travelers (IAMAT)** offers a membership ID card, a directory of English-speaking doctors around the world who treat members for a set fee schedule, and detailed charts on immunization requirements, various tropical diseases, climate, and sanitation. Membership is free, though donations are appreciated and used for further research. Contact chapters in **Canada,** 40 Regal Road, Guelph, Ont. N1K 1B5 (tel. (519) 836-0102) or 1287 St. Clair Avenue West, Toronto, Ont. M6E 1B8 (tel. (416) 652-0137; fax (519) 836-3412), the **U.S.,** 417 Center St., Lewiston, NY 14092 (tel. (716) 754-4883; fax (519) 836-3412; email iamat@sentex.net; http://www.sentex.net/íiamat), or **New Zealand,** P.O. Box 5049, Christchurch 5.

ON-THE-ROAD AILMENTS

Common sense goes a long way toward preventing **heat exhaustion:** relax in hot weather, drink lots of non-alcoholic fluids, and lie down inside if you feel awful. Continuous heat stress can eventually lead to **heatstroke,** characterized by rising body temperature, severe headache, and cessation of sweating. Wear a hat, sunglasses, and a lightweight, long-sleeved shirt to avoid heatstroke. Victims must be cooled off with wet towels and taken to a doctor as soon as possible.

Always drink enough liquids to keep your urine clear. Alcoholic beverages, coffee, strong tea, and caffeinated sodas are dehydrating. Be sure to eat enough salty food to prevent electrolyte depletion, which causes severe headaches. If you're prone to **sunburn,** bring sunscreen with you (it's often more expensive and hard to find when traveling), and apply liberally and often to avoid burns and risk of skin cancer. If you do get sunburned, drink more fluids than usual.

Extreme cold is just as dangerous as heat—overexposure to cold brings the risk of **hypothermia.** Warning signs are easy to detect: body temperature drops rapidly, resulting in the failure to produce body heat. You may shiver, have poor coordination, feel exhausted, have slurred speech, hallucinate, or even suffer amnesia. *Do not let hypothermia victims fall asleep*—their body temperature will drop more, and if they lose consciousness they may die. Seek medical help as soon as possible. To avoid hypothermia, keep dry and stay out of the wind. In wet weather, wool and most synthetics will keep you warm, but most other fabric, especially cotton, will make you colder. Dress in layers, and watch for **frostbite** in cold weather and strong winds. Look for skin that has turned white, waxy, and cold; if you find frostbite do not rub the skin. Drink warm beverages, get dry, and slowly warm the area with dry fabric or steady body contact. Take serious cases to a doctor as soon as possible.

Travelers to **high altitudes** must allow a couple of days to adjust to lower oxygen levels before exerting themselves. Be careful about alcohol, especially if you're used to U.S. standards for beer—many foreign brews and liquors pack more punch. At high altitudes, where the air has less oxygen, any alcohol will do you in quickly.

When hiking, camping, or working in forest regions, use mosquito nets, tuck long pants into socks, and wear clothes that cover most of the body. Always use insect repellent; the ingredient to look for is DEET, which is the strongest and most effective repellent. Consider purchasing an insect-killing spray to use in living and sleeping areas. For greater protection, soak or spray your clothes and bednets with permethrin. Natural repellents can also be useful: taking vitamin B-12 pills or garlic regularly can eventually make you smelly to insects, but be sure to supplement your vitamins with repellent. Calamine lotion or topical cortisones may stop insect bites from itching, as can a bath with a half-cup of baking soda or oatmeal. Consider buying your own portable mosquito net. **Ticks**—responsible for Lyme and other diseases— can be particularly dangerous in rural and forested regions all over Europe. Brush off ticks periodically when walking, using a fine-toothed comb on your neck and scalp. Do not try to remove ticks by burning them or coating them with nail polish remover or petroleum jelly. Topical cortisones may help quell the itching.

Tick-borne encephalitis is a viral infection of the central nervous system transmitted by tick bites or ingestion of unpasteurized dairy products. Symptoms range from none to the abrupt onset of headache, fever, and flu-like symptoms to actual swelling of the brain (encephalitis). A vaccine is available in Europe, but the immunization schedule is impractical for most tourists, and the risk of contracting the disease is relatively low, especially if you take precautions against tick bites and avoid unpasteurized dairy products.

Ticks also carry the infamous **Lyme disease,** a bacterial infection marked by a circular bull's-eye rash of two inches or more that appears around the bite. Other symptoms include fever, headache, tiredness, and aches and pains. Antibiotics are effective if administered early. Left untreated, Lyme can cause problems in the joints, the heart, and the nervous system. Again, avoiding tick bites in the first place is the best way to prevent the disease. If you do find a tick attached to your skin, grasp the tick's head with tweezers as close to your skin as possible and apply slow, steady traction in a counter-clockwise direction. However, the ticks that carry Lyme disease are mostly deer ticks, which are about the size of a the head of a pin and cannot be removed. If you are able to remove a tick before it has been attached for more than 24 hours, you greatly reduce your risk of infection. You are at risk for Lyme disease when hiking, camping, or visiting rural areas in Eastern Europe.

For most Eastern European countries there is a risk of **rabies,** a viral infection that affects the central nervous system and is transmitted by warm-blooded animal bites, especially by dogs and foxes. Do not handle any animals. Any animal bite should be promptly cleaned with large amounts of soap and (clean) water and should receive medical attention. Vaccination is recommended for those visiting for more than 30 days, visiting areas where rabies is known to exist, and spelunking.

Food- and water-borne diseases are the number-one cause of illness to travelers in Eastern Europe. Viruses and bacteria can cause diarrhea and a range of other ailments. To ensure that your food is safe, make sure that everything is cooked properly (deep-fried is good, for once), and be positive the water you drink is clean. Don't order meat rare, and eggs should be thoroughly cooked, not served sunny-side up.

Cholera is an intestinal infection caused by a bacterium that lives in contaminated water or food; it causes voluminous diarrhea, dehydration, vomiting, and muscle cramps. While incidents of cholera have been reported in Eastern Europe, the CDC reports that risk of infection for Westerners is low if they follow the usual tourist itineraries and stay in standard accommodations. Otherwise, eat only thoroughly cooked food; peel your own fruit; drink only boiled water, bottled carbonated water, or bottled carbonated soft drinks; and avoid fish and shellfish. A vaccine is only recommended if you have stomach ulcers, use anti-acid therapy, or will be living in unsanitary conditions in areas of high cholera activity. Cholera may be treated by simple fluid and electrolyte-replacement therapy, but treatment must be immediate.

Hepatitis A is a viral infection of the liver that is most frequently transmitted through contaminated water, ice, shellfish, unpeeled fruits, or uncooked vegetables. It can also be transmitted through direct contact with an infected person. Symptoms include fatigue, fever, loss of appetite, nausea, dark urine, jaundice, vomiting, aches and pains, and light stools. Intermediate rates of hepatitis A exist in Eastern Europe. There is no specific treatment and no vaccine, but an injection of Havrix or immune globulin (IG) is highly recommended by the CDC before travel to Eastern Europe.

Parasitic infections result from eating or drinking contaminated food or water, from direct contact with soil or water containing parasites or their larvae, or from insect bites. Symptoms include swollen lymph nodes, rashes or itchy skin, digestive problems such as abdominal pain or diarrhea, eye problems, and anemia. Again, travelers should eat only thoroughly cooked food, drink safe water, wear shoes, and avoid contact with insects, particularly mosquitoes, biting flies, gnats, and midges. **Giardia,** for example, is one serious parasitic disease you can get by drinking untreated water from streams or lakes all over the world. Many backpackers and campers not scrupulous about their water get giardia, and it sometimes stays with them for years. St. Petersburg has particularly dangerous water. Have a doctor prescribe the cure—metronidazole—before you leave. Water purification tablets and boiling water (at least 10min.) will kill giardia before it enters your system.

Typhoid fever is a risk for travelers visiting smaller cities, villages, or rural areas in Eastern Europe. While mostly transmitted through contaminated food and water, it may also be acquired by direct contact with another person. Symptoms include fever, headaches, fatigue, loss of appetite, constipation, and a rash on the abdomen or chest. Antibiotics treat typhoid fever. You can lower the risk of infection by drinking only bottled or boiled drinks and eating only thoroughly cooked food. The CDC recommends vaccinations (70-90% effective) if you will be staying for six weeks or more, or going off the "usual tourist itineraries," that is, hiking, camping, or staying in small cities or rural areas.

On the Run in Eastern Europe

Traveler's diarrhea, the most commonly reported illness for travelers in Eastern Europe, is the dastardly consequence of drinking untreated water. The illness can last from three to seven days, and symptoms include diarrhea, nausea, bloating, and malaise. If the nasties hit you, eat quick-energy, non-sugary foods—like salted crackers—with protein and carbohydrates to keep your strength up. Over-the-counter remedies (such as Immodium) may counteract the problem, but can complicate serious infections. Avoid anti-diarrheals if you suspect you've been exposed to contaminated food or water, which puts you at risk for other diseases. The most dangerous effect of diarrhea is dehydration; one of the simplest and most effective anti-dehydration formulas is a glass of water with ½ tsp. of sugar or honey and a pinch of salt. Down several of these remedies a day, rest, and wait for the illness to run its course. If you develop a fever or your symptoms are severe, consult a doctor. Consult a doctor if children develop traveler's diarrhea, since treatment is different.

Travelers should take precautions to protect themselves against **sexually transmitted diseases (STDs)** by using latex condoms. All condoms are not equal, however; purchase well-known brands and bring them with you. Check the **Essentials** sections for each country to see where buying reliable condoms—a must for preventing any **STD**—is problematic. Even "safe sex" isn't that with some non-Western brands.

Hepatitis B is a viral infection of the liver transmitted by sharing needles, having unprotected sex, or coming into direct contact with an infected person's lesioned skin. If you think you may be sexually active while traveling, if you will be a health worker overseas, or if you will be in rural areas, you are typically advised to get the vaccination for hepatitis B. Ideally, the vaccination series begins six months before travel, but it should be started even if it will not be finished before you leave. Risk is moderate in Eastern Europe.

Human Immunodeficiency Virus (HIV), which causes Acquired Immunodeficiency Syndrome **(AIDS),** is found worldwide. HIV can be transmitted through contact with an infected individual's body fluids or through the transfusion of infected blood. There is no assurance that someone is not infected: HIV tests only show antibodies after a six-month lapse. Some new strands of HIV are not testable. Never have sex without a condom, and never share intravenous needles. The U.S. Center for Disease Control's 24-hour **AIDS Hotline** can refer you to organizations with information on European countries (tel. (800) 342-2437).

Sexually transmitted diseases (STDs) such as gonorrhea, chlamydia, genital warts, syphilis, and herpes are a lot easier to catch than HIV, and can be just as deadly. It's a wise idea actually to *look* at your partner's genitals *before* you have sex. Warning signs include: swelling, sores, bumps, or blisters on sex organs, rectum, or mouth;

burning and pain during urination and bowel movements; itching around sex organs; swelling or redness in the throat; and flu-like symptoms with fever, chills, and aches. If symptoms develop, see a doctor immediately. During sex, condoms may protect you from certain STDs, but oral or even tactile contact can lead to transmission.

BIRTH CONTROL AND ABORTION

Reliable contraceptive devices may be difficult to find while traveling. Women on the Pill should bring enough to allow for possible loss and should bring a prescription, since forms of the Pill vary. If you use a diaphragm, be sure that you have enough contraceptive jelly on hand. Though condoms are increasingly available, you might want to bring your favorite brand with you, as availability and quality vary.

Women overseas seeking information on **abortion** should contact the **National Abortion Federation Hotline** (U.S. tel. (800) 772-9100; Mon.-Fri. 9:30am-12:30pm, 1:30-5:30pm EST; 1775 Massachusetts Ave. NW, Washington, D.C. 20036). The hotline can direct you to organizations which provide information on the availability of and techniques for abortion in other countries. Or contact your embassy to receive a list of obstetrician/gynecologist doctors who perform abortions. For general information on contraception, condoms, and abortion worldwide, contact the **International Planned Parenthood Federation,** European Regional Office, Regent's College Inner Circle, Regent's Park, London NW1 4NS (U.K. tel. (0171) 486 0741; fax 487 7950).

WOMEN'S HEALTH

Women traveling in unsanitary conditions are vulnerable to urinary tract and bladder infections, common and severely uncomfortable bacterial diseases that cause a burning sensation, and painful and sometimes frequent urination. Drink tons of vitamin C-rich juice, plenty of clean water, and urinate frequently, especially right after intercourse. Untreated, these infections can lead to kidney infections, sterility, and even death. If symptoms persist, see a doctor. If you often develop vaginal yeast infections, take along an over-the-counter medicine, as treatments may not be readily available in Eastern Europe. Women may also be more susceptible to vaginal thrush and cystitis, two treatable but uncomfortable illnesses. Tampons and pads can be hard to find when travelling; your preferred brands may not be available, so it may be advisable to take supplies. Some women also use diaphragms or cervical caps for a few hours to temporarily trap menstrual flow, but be aware of the risks of Toxic Shock Syndrome. Refer to the *Handbook for Women Travellers* by Maggie and Gemma Moss (published by Piatkus Books) or to *Our Bodies, Our Selves* (published by the Boston Women's Health Collective) for more info specific to women's health on the road.

■ Insurance

Beware of buying unnecessary travel coverage—your regular policies may extend to many travel-related accidents. **Medical insurance** (especially university policies) often covers costs incurred abroad; get details from your provider. **Canadians** are protected by their home province's health insurance plan for up to 90 days after leaving the country; check with the provincial Ministry of Health or Health Plan Headquarters for details. **Australia** has Reciprocal Health Care Agreements (RHCAs) with certain countries, in which traveling Australians are entitled to many of the services they receive at home. The Commonwealth Department of Human Services and Health can provide more information. **Homeowners' insurance** often covers theft during travel and loss of travel documents (passport, plane ticket, etc.) up to US$500.

ISIC and **ITIC** provide basic insurance benefits, including US$100 per day of in-hospital sickness for a maximum of 60 days, and US$3000 of accident-related medical reimbursement (see **Student Identification,** p. 10). Cardholders have access to a toll-free 24-hour helpline, whose multilingual staff can provide assistance in medical, legal, and financial emergencies (tel. (800) 626-2427 in the U.S. and Canada; elsewhere call the U.S. collect (713) 267-2525). **Council** and **STA** (see **Travel Organiza-**

tions, p. 2) offer a range of plans that can supplement your basic insurance coverage, with options covering medical treatment and hospitalization, accidents, and baggage loss. Most **American Express** cardholders receive automatic car rental (collision and theft, but not liability) insurance and travel accident coverage (US$100,000 in life insurance) on flight purchases made with their card (U.S. tel. (800) 528-4800).

Insurance companies usually require a copy of police reports for thefts, or evidence of having paid medical expenses (doctor's statements, receipts) before they will honor a claim, and they may have time limits on filing for reimbursement. Always carry policy numbers and proof of insurance. Check with each insurance carrier for specific policies. Most of the carriers listed below have 24-hour hotlines.

Globalcare Travel Insurance, 220 Broadway, Lynnfield MA, 01940 (tel. (800) 821-2488; fax (617) 592-7720; http://www.nebc.mv.com/globalcare). Complete medical, legal, emergency, and travel-related services. On-the-spot payments and special student programs, including benefits for trip cancellation and interruption.

Travel Assistance International, by Worldwide Assistance Services, Inc., 1133 15th St. NW, #400, Washington, D.C. 20005-2710 (tel. (800) 821-2828; fax (202) 828-5896). 24hr. hotline. Per-Trip (from US$65) and Frequent Traveler (from US$235) plans include medical, travel, and communication assistance services.

Travel Guard International, 1145 Clark St., Stevens Point, WI 54481 (tel. (800) 826-1300; fax (715) 345-0525; http://www.travel-guard.com). Comprehensive insurance programs from US$40. Programs cover trip cancellation/interruption, medical coverage abroad, emergency assistance, and lost baggage. 24hr. hotline.

Travel Insured International, Inc., 52-S Oakland Ave., P.O. Box 280568, East Hartford, CT 06128-0568 (tel. (800) 243-3174; fax (203) 528-8005). Insurance against accident, baggage loss, sickness, trip cancellation and interruption, travel delay, and default. Covers emergency medical evacuation. Automatic flight insurance.

■ Alternatives to Tourism

STUDY

Foreign study programs have multiplied rapidly in Eastern Europe. Most American undergraduates enroll in programs sponsored by U.S. universities, and many colleges staff offices that provide advice and information on study abroad. Local libraries and bookstores are also helpful sources for current information on study abroad, or check out http://www.studyabroad.com/liteimage.html. Take advantage of academic counselors and put in some hours at their libraries, or request the names of recent program participants and get in touch. Depending on your interests and language skills, you may wish to enroll directly in an Eastern European university. This can be much less expensive and a more intense cultural experience. Contact the nearest consulate for a list of institutions in your country of choice. The largest official programs offer study mostly in Russia and the Czech Republic, but you can find the occasional Latvian university exchange. There are also several international and national fellowships available (i.e. Fulbright, Rotary) to fund adventures abroad.

American Field Service (AFS), 198 Madison Ave., 8th Fl., New York, NY 10016 (students tel. (800) AFS-INFO (237-4636), administration (800) 876-2376; fax (503) 241-1653; email afsinfo@afs.org; http//www.afs.org/usa). AFS offers summer, semester, and year-long homestay international exchange programs for high school students and recent high school graduates. Financial aid available. Exchanges in the Czech Republic, Latvia, Russia, Slovakia, and other countries around the world.

College Semester Abroad, School for International Training, Kipling Rd., P.O. Box 676, Brattleboro, VT 05302 (tel. (800) 336-1616; fax (802) 258-3500). Offers extensive semester-long study abroad programs worldwide. Programs cost US$9300-11,500, including tuition, room and board, and airfare. Scholarships are available and federal financial aid is usually transferable from home college or university. Programs in the Czech Republic and Russia.

Institute of International Education (IIE), 809 United Nations Plaza, New York, NY 10017-3580 (tel. (212) 984-5413; fax 984-5358). For book orders: IIE Books, P.O. Box 371, Annapolis Junction, MD 20701 (tel. (800) 445-0443; fax (301) 206-9789). A nonprofit international and cultural exchange agency with a library of study-abroad resources open to the public Tues.-Thurs. 11am-3:45pm. Publishes *Academic Year Abroad* (US$43 plus US$5 shipping) and *Vacation Study Abroad* (US$37 plus US$5 shipping). Write for a complete list of publications.

Language Immersion Institute, State University of New York at New Paltz, 75 South Manheim Blvd., New Paltz, NY 12561 (tel. (914) 257-3500; fax 257-3569; http://www.eelab.newpaltz.edu/lii). Provides language instruction in Czech, Hungarian, Polish, Russian, Ukrainian, and many other languages. Weekend courses offered at New Paltz and in NYC. 2-week summer courses, overseas learning vacations, and customized corporate instruction. Program fees are about US$295 for a weekend and US$625 for a 2-week course. College credit is available.

Youth For Understanding (YFU), 3501 Newark St. NW, Washington, D.C. 20016 (tel. (800) 833-6243; fax (202) 895-1104; http://www.yfu.org). Places high school students worldwide for year, semester, summer, and sport homestays.

WORK AND VOLUNTEER

The good news is that there's no better way to immerse yourself in a foreign culture than to become part of its economy. The bad news is that in many Eastern European countries it's difficult to find a temporary unskilled job: even the most menial labor may be taking needed employment away from locals. There are opportunities to work in agriculture, as an *au pair,* in summer camps, as an English teacher, or at tourist sites. Be warned: these jobs are rarely glamorous and may not even pay for your plane ticket home.

On the flip side, many foreign companies are infiltrating Eastern Europe and often require office workers who speak English and are familiar with Western business practices. Before leaving, find out which companies in your country have offices in Eastern Europe and get the name of a contact person in the country that interests you. Once abroad, your best bet is to be brazen and contact the local offices of any foreign company that you come across, and to look for ads in local newspapers. If you speak an Eastern European language, translation jobs are easy to find. Another possibility is to try your luck with the local English-language newspaper.

Teaching English has long been the traditional job for foreign visitors to Eastern Europe. These days, so many foreigners are descending on Prague, Budapest, and Warsaw that finding a position is difficult, but not impossible. Teacher of English as a Foreign Language (TEFL) certification is becoming an increasingly necessary credential. Work in rural areas is easier to find. Universities' foreign language departments may have official or unofficial connections to job openings abroad. Post a sign in markets or learning centers stating that you are a native speaker, and scan the classifieds of local newspapers, where residents often advertise for language instruction. Various organizations in the U.S. will place you in a (low-paying) teaching job. Professional English-teaching positions are harder to get: many schools require at least a bachelor's degree and training in teaching English as a foreign language.

Like paid jobs, **volunteer** jobs are not necessarily as readily available in Eastern Europe as in the West; nevertheless, they do exist. You may receive room and board in exchange for labor, and the work can be fascinating. Opportunities include community service, workcamp projects, and office work for international organizations. You can sometimes avoid extra fees by contacting workcamps directly; check with the organization. English-language newspapers and some international aid agencies also love unpaid interns. In the Balkans, you can often simply arrive in an area and find volunteering opportunities on the spot, particularly if you can pay for your own housing. Bosnia and Croatia abound with relief organizations that can always use an extra hand; just bring a resume and a letter of recommendation. Listed below are some sources providing more detailed information:

Council has a Voluntary Services Dept., 205 E. 42nd St., New York, NY 10017 (tel. (888) COUNCIL (268-6245); fax (212) 822-2699; email info@ciee.org; http://www.ciee.org). 2- to 4-week environmental or community services projects offered in Czech Republic, Lithuania, Poland, Russia, Slovakia, Ukraine and many other countries. Participants must be at least 18 years old. Minimum US$295 placement fee; additional fees may also apply for various countries.

InterExchange, 161 Sixth Ave., New York, NY 10013 (tel. (212) 924-0446; fax 924-0575; http://www.interexchange.org). Places *au pairs* for 2- to 18-month jobs in the Czech Republic, Hungary, Latvia, Poland, Russia, and many Western European countries (US$250-450 placement fee). Also offers teaching programs in the Czech Republic, Hungary, and Poland; must have a B.A. and some previous teaching experience (US$400 application fee).

Now Hiring! Jobs in Eastern Europe, by Clarke Canfield. An excellent and comprehensive source of information about all aspects of finding work and accommodations in the Czech Republic, Hungary, Poland, and Slovakia. Can be found in most bookstores (Independent Publishers Group; US$15; U.S. tel. (312) 337-0747).

Peace Corps, 1990 K St. NW, Room 8508, Washington, D.C. 20526 (tel. (800) 424-8580; fax (202) 606-4469; http://www.peacecorps.gov). Opportunities available in developing nations in agriculture, business, education, the environment, and health the world over, including Bulgaria, Estonia, Hungary, Czech Republic, Latvia, Lithuania, Macedonia, Poland, Romania, Russia, Slovakia, Ukraine and Yugoslavia. Volunteers must be U.S. citizens, age 18 and over, and willing to make a 2-year commitment. A bachelor's degree is usually required.

Peterson's Guides, P.O. Box 2123, Princeton, NJ 08543-2123 (tel. (800) 338-3282; fax (609) 243-9150; http://www.petersons.com). Their annual *Study Abroad* (US$30) guide lists programs all over the world and provides information on the study abroad experience in general. Their new *Learning Adventures Around the World* (US$25) annual guide to "learning vacations" lists volunteer, museum-hopping, study, and travel programs. Copies available at bookstores or by calling their toll-free number in the U.S.

Service Civil International Voluntary Service (SCI-VS), 5474 Walnut Level Rd., Crozet, VA 22932 (tel. (804) 823-1826; fax 823-5027; http://wworks_com/~sciivs). Arranges placement in workcamps in Europe (ages 18 and over), including Belarus, Bulgaria, Croatia, Czech Republic, Hungary, Latvia, Lithuania, Poland, Romania, Slovenia, Ukraine and Yugoslavia. Local organizations sponsor groups for physical or social work. Registration fees US$50-250, depending on the camp location.

Volunteers for Peace, 43 Tiffany Rd., Belmont, VT 05730 (tel. (802) 259-2759; fax 259-2922; http://www.vfp.org). Arranges placement in 2-3 week workcamps comprising 10-15 people. Over 1,000 programs in 70 countries. Up-to-date listings provided in the annual *International Workcamp Directory* (US$15). Registration fee US$200. Some work camps are open to 16-and 17-year-olds for US$225. Free newsletter.

WorldTeach, Harvard Institute for International Development, 1 Eliot St., Cambridge, MA 02138-5705 (tel. (617) 495-5527; fax 495-1599; http://www.igc.org/worldteach). Volunteers teach English, math, science, and environmental education to students of all ages in developing countries, including Lithuania and Poland. Room, board, and a small stipend are provided during the period of service, but volunteers must pay a program fee which covers health insurance, airfare, and training. Rolling admission. Bachelor's degree required for most programs.

■ Specific Concerns

WOMEN TRAVELERS

Women exploring on their own face additional safety concerns. Trust your instincts; if you'd feel better somewhere else, move on. Always carry extra money for a phone call, bus, or taxi. Consider staying in hostels that offer single rooms that lock from the inside or in religious organizations that offer rooms for women only; avoid any hostel with "communal" showers. Stick to centrally located accommodations, and avoid late-night treks or metro rides. Hitching is never safe, even for two women traveling together. Choose train compartments occupied by other women or couples, or ask the conductor to put together a women-only compartment.

Women in Eastern Europe almost never go to restaurants alone; women travelers may be significantly harassed if they do, even at midday. Small cafes and cafeterias are much safer options; even hotel restaurants may be dangerous. In crowds, you may be pinched or squeezed by oversexed slimeballs; wearing a wedding band may help prevent such incidents. The look on your face is the key to avoiding unwanted attention. Feigning deafness, sitting motionless, and staring at the ground will do a world of good that no indignant reaction will ever achieve. If need be, turn to an older woman for help in an uncomfortable situation; her stern rebukes will usually be enough to embarrass the most persistent jerks. It's a good idea to observe the way local women dress and to invest in the newest "in" thing, even if you wouldn't dream of wearing it at home. The best way to repulse amorous Eastern European men is to don a *babushka*-style kerchief, tied under the chin.

Don't hesitate to seek out a police officer or a passerby if you are being harassed. Memorize or keep note of the emergency numbers in the countries you visit. Carry a whistle or an airhorn on your keychain, and use it in an emergency. A **Model Mugging** course (see **Safety and Security,** p. 13) will not only prepare you for a potential mugging, but will also raise your level of awareness of your surroundings as well as your confidence. Women also face additional health concerns when traveling (see **Health,** p. 14). All of these warnings and suggestions should not discourage women from traveling alone. Be adventurous in your travels, but avoid unnecessary risks.

Handbook For Women Travellers, by Maggie and Gemma Moss (UK£9). Available from Piatkus Books, 5 Windmill St., London W1P 1HF (tel. (0171) 631 0710).

A Journey of One's Own, by Thalia Zepatos (US$17). Full of good advice, with a useful bibliography. From Eighth Mountain Press, 624 Southeast 29th Ave., Portland, OR 97214 (tel. (503) 233-3936; fax 233-0774; email eightmt@aol.com).

Women Going Places (US$15). A women's travel and resource guide emphasizing women-owned enterprises. Advice geared toward lesbians, but appropriate for all women. From Inland Book Company, 1436 W. Randolph St., Chicago, IL 60607 (tel. (800) 243-0138; fax (800) 334-3892).

A Foxy Old Woman's Guide to Traveling Alone, by Jay Ben-Lesser (Crossing Press, US$11). Info, informal advice, and a resource list on budget solo travel.

OLDER TRAVELERS

Seniors are rarely given discounts in Eastern Europe, but it doesn't hurt to ask. Proof of senior citizen status is required for many of the services and discounts below.

Elderhostel, 75 Federal St., 3rd Fl., Boston, MA 02110 (tel. (617) 426-7788; fax 426-8351; http://www.elderhostel.org). For those 55 or over and their spouses (any age). 1- to 4-week programs at universities on varied subjects in over 70 countries.

National Council of Senior Citizens, 8403 Colesville Rd., Silver Spring, MD 20910-31200 (tel. (301) 578-8800; fax 578-8999). Membership costs US$13 a year, US$33 for 3 years, or US$175 for a lifetime. Offers hotel and auto rental discounts, a senior citizen newspaper, and use of a discount travel agency.

Pilot Books, 127 Sterling Ave., P.O. Box 2102, Greenport, NY 11944 (tel. (800) 797-4568; fax (516) 477-0978; http://www.pilotbooks.com). Publishes a large number of guides including *Doctor's Guide to Protecting Your Health Before, During, and After International Travel* (US$10) and *Senior Citizens' Guide to Budget Travel in Europe* (US$6). Postage US$2. Call or write for a complete list of titles.

Unbelievably Good Deals and Great Adventures That You Absolutely Can't Get Unless You're Over 50, by Joan Heilman (Contemporary Books, US$10). After you finish the title page, check inside for some great tips on senior discounts.

BISEXUAL, GAY, AND LESBIAN TRAVELERS

Attitudes toward bisexual, gay, and lesbian travelers are particular to each country and to the cities within it. Homophobic views persist throughout much of Eastern

Europe, and a degree of caution should be exercised. In Belarus, Bosnia, and Romania, homosexuality remains illegal, and in other countries laws forbidding "scandalous homosexual activity" or public displays of homosexuality can give local authorities an excuse to be troublesome. Even within major cities, gay nightclubs and social centers are often clandestine and frequently change location. Therefore, while we try to list local gay and lesbian bars and clubs, word of mouth is often the best method for finding the latest hotspots. Listed below are contact organizations and publishers which offer materials addressing gay and lesbian concerns.

International Gay and Lesbian Travel Association, P.O. Box 4974, Key West, FL 33041 (tel. (800) 448-8550; fax (305) 296-6633; http://www.rainbow-mall.com/igta). An organization of over 1300 companies serving gay and lesbian travelers worldwide. Call for lists of travel agents, accommodations, and events.

International Lesbian and Gay Association (ILGA), 81 rue Marché-au-Charbon, B-1000 Bruxelles, Belgium (tel./fax (32 2) 502 24 71; email ilga@ilga.org). Provides political information, such as homosexuality laws of individual countries.

Are You Two...Together? A Gay and Lesbian Travel Guide to Europe. Anecdotes and tips for gays and lesbians traveling in Europe. Includes overviews of regional laws relating to gays and lesbians, lists of gay/lesbian organizations, and establishments catering to, friendly to, or indifferent to gays and lesbians (US$18).

Ferrari Guides, P.O. Box 37887, Phoenix, AZ 85069 (tel. (602) 863-2408; fax 439-3952; email ferrari@q-net.com; http://www.q-net.com). Gay and lesbian travel guides: *Ferrari Guides' Gay Travel A to Z* (US$16), *Ferrari Guides' Men's Travel in Your Pocket* (US$16), and *Ferrari Guides' Women's Travel in Your Pocket* (US$14). Available in bookstores or by mail order (postage/handling US$4.50 for 1st item, US$1 for each additional item. Overseas, call or write for shipping cost).

Gay's the Word, 66 Marchmont St., London WC1N 1AB (tel. (0171) 278 7654). The largest gay and lesbian bookshop in the U.K. Mail-order service available. No catalog of listings, but they will provide a list of titles on a given subject.

Giovanni's Room, 345 S. 12th St. Philadelphia, PA 19107 (tel. (215) 923-2960; fax 923-0813; email giolphilp@netaxs.com). International feminist, lesbian, and gay bookstore with many of the books listed here. Call or write for a free catalogue.

Spartacus International Gay Guides (US$33), published by Bruno Gmünder, Postfach 61 01 04, D-10921 Berlin, Germany (tel. (30 61) 50 03 42; fax 591 34). Lists bars, restaurants, hotels, and bookstores around the world catering to gays. Also lists hotlines for gays in various countries and homosexuality laws for each country. Available in bookstores and by mail from Giovanni's Room (see above).

DISABLED TRAVELERS

Eastern Europe tends to be relatively inaccessible to travelers with disabilities. Contact your destination's consulate or tourist office in advance for information. Arrange transportation well in advance to ensure a smooth trip. If you give sufficient notice, some major car rental agencies offer hand-controlled vehicles at select locations. Guide-dog owners should inquire as to the specific quarantine policies of each destination country. At the very least, they will need to provide a certificate of immunization against rabies. The following organizations provide information or publications that might be of assistance:

Graphic Language Press, P.O. Box 270, Cardiff by the Sea, CA 92007 (tel. (760) 944-9594; email niteowl@cts.com). Advice for wheelchair travelers, including accessible accommodations, transportation, and sightseeing for various European cities.

The Guided Tour, Inc., Elkins Park House, 114B, 7900 Old York Rd., Elkins Park, PA 19027-2339 (tel. (800) 783-5841 or (215) 782-1370; fax 635-2637). Organizes travel programs for persons with developmental and physical challenges and those requiring renal dialysis. Call, fax, or write for a free brochure.

Mobility International, USA (MIUSA), P.O. Box 10767, Eugene, OR 97440 (tel. (514) 343-1284 voice and TDD; fax 343-6812; email info@miusa.org; http://miusa.org). Contacts in 30 countries. Information on travel programs, international workcamps, accommodations, access guides, and organized tours for those with physical disabilities. Membership US$30 per year. Sells *A World of Options: A Guide to International Educational Exchange, Community Service, and Travel for Persons with Disabilities* (US$30, nonmembers US$35; organizations US$40).

Moss Rehabilitation Hospital Travel Information Service (tel. (215) 456-9600; TDD 456-9602). A telephone information resource center on international travel accessibility and other travel-related concerns for those with disabilities.

Society for the Advancement of Travel for the Handicapped (SATH), 347 Fifth Ave. #610, New York, NY 10016 (tel. (212) 447-1928; fax 725-8253; email sath-travel@aol.com; http://www.sath.org). Publishes quarterly color travel magazine *OPEN WORLD* (free for members; subscription for nonmembers US$13). Also publishes a wide range of information sheets on disability travel facilitation and accessible destinations. Annual membership US$45, students and seniors US$30.

Twin Peaks Press, P.O. Box 129, Vancouver, WA 98666-0129 (tel. (360) 694-2462; MC or Visa orders (800) 637-2256; fax (360) 696-3210; http://netm.com/mall/info-prod/twinpeak/helen.htm). Publishes *Travel for the Disabled,* which provides travel tips, lists of accessible tourist attractions, and advice on other resources for disabled travelers (US$20); *Directory for Travel Agencies of the Disabled* (US$20); *Wheelchair Vagabond* (US$15); and *Directory of Accessible Van Rentals* (US$10). Postage US$3.50 for first book, US$1.50 for each additional book.

DIETARY CONCERNS

Vegetarian and kosher travelers will have their work cut out for them in Eastern Europe. Most of the national cuisines tend to be meat- and especially pork-heavy. Markets are always a safe bet for fresh vegetables, fruit, cheese, and bread. In Belarus, watch out for veggies and dairy products from near the Chernobyl region—ask the sellers where their food comes from.

Travelers who keep **kosher** should contact synagogues in larger cities for information on kosher restaurants; your own synagogue or college Hillel should have access to lists of Jewish institutions across Eastern Europe. If you are strict in your observance, bring supplies to prepare your own food on the road.

The International Vegetarian Travel Guide (UK£2), last published in 1991. Order back copies from the Vegetarian Society of the UK (VSUK), Parkdale, Dunham Rd., Altringham, Cheshire WA14 4QG (tel. (0161) 928 07 93). VSUK also publishes other titles, including *The European Vegetarian Guide to Hotels and Restaurants.* Call or send a self-addressed, stamped envelope for a catalog.

The Jewish Travel Guide lists synagogues, kosher restaurants, and Jewish institutions in over 80 countries. Available from Ballantine-Mitchell Publishers, Newbury House 890-900, Eastern Ave., Newbury Park, Ilford, Essex, U.K. IG2 7HH (tel. (0181) 599 88 66; fax 599 09 84). Available in the U.S. from Sepher-Hermon Press, 1265 46th St., Brooklyn, NY 11219 (tel. (718) 972-9010; US$15, postage US$2.50).

MINORITY TRAVELERS

The minority which encounters the most hostility in Eastern Europe is Gypsies (*Romany*). Travelers with darker skin of any nationality might be mistaken for Gypsies and face some of the same unpleasant consequences. Other minority travelers, especially those of African or Asian descent, will usually meet with more curiosity than hostility, especially outside of big cities. Travelers of Arab ethnicity may also be treated more suspiciously. Skinheads are on the rise in Eastern Europe, and minority travelers, especially Jews and blacks, should regard them with caution. Anti-Semitism is still a problem in many countries, including Poland and the former Soviet Union; sad to say, it is generally best to be discreet about your religion.

■ Packing

If you want to get away from it all, don't take it all with you.

PACK LIGHT! The more you know, the less you need, so plan your packing according to the type of travel and the high and low temperatures in the area you will be visiting (refer to the **Appendix,** p. 795, for climate charts). The more you have, the more you have to carry and the more you have to lose. Eschew colorful luggage that screams "rich Western tourist" for boring brown or drab gray to keep muggers away. The larger your pack, the more cumbersome it is to store safely. Before you leave, pack your bag, strap it on, and imagine walking uphill on hot asphalt for hours. At the least sign of heaviness, unpack something. A general rule is to pack only what you think you absolutely need, then take half the clothes and twice the money.

LUGGAGE

Backpack: If you plan to cover most of your itinerary by foot, a sturdy backpack is unbeatable. In general, **internal-frame** packs are easier to carry and more efficient for general traveling purposes. If you'll be doing extensive camping or hiking, you may want to consider an **external-frame** pack, which offers added support, distributes weight better, and allows you to strap on a sleeping bag. In either case, get a pack with a strong, padded hip belt to transfer weight from your shoulders to your hips. Always avoid excessively low-end prices—you get what you pay for. Quality packs cost US$150-420.

Suitcase/trunk/other large or heavy luggage: Fine if you plan to live in one or two cities and explore from there, but a bad idea if you're going to be moving around a lot. Features to look for: wheels on suitcases, PVC frame for soft luggage, and the 3 main characteristics of any good piece of luggage: weight, durability, and maneuverability. Remember: you bring it, you carry it.

Duffel bag: If you aren't backpacking, an empty, lightweight duffel bag packed inside your luggage will be useful: once abroad, you can fill your luggage with purchases and keep your dirty clothes in the duffel.

Daypack or courier bag: Essential. Bringing a smaller bag in addition to your pack or suitcase allows you to leave your big bag behind while you go sightseeing. It can also be used as an airplane carry-on to keep essentials with you.

Moneybelt or neck pouch: Guard your money, passport, railpass, and other important articles in one of these, and keep it with you *at all times.* Available at any good camping store. See **Safety and Security,** p. 13, for more information on protecting you and your valuables.

CLOTHING AND FOOTWEAR

Comfortable **shoes** are crucial; any kind of sneakers will do. In hot weather, **sandals** or other light shoes serve well. It might be worth the extra bulk to carry two pairs of shoes: you might not want to go out in the same shoes you've been trekking in all day. For heavy-duty walking, sturdy lace-up **hiking boots** are necessary. Make sure they have good ventilation. A double pair of **socks**—light absorbent cotton inside and thick wool outside—will cushion feet, keep them dry, and help prevent blisters. Putting talcum powder on your feet can prevent sores, and moleskin is great for blisters. Bring a pair of light **flip-flops** for protection against the fungal floors of hostel and hotel showers. **Raingear** is also essential. A waterproof jacket plus a backpack rain cover will take care of you and your pack at a moment's notice.

MISCELLANEOUS

Carry extra toiletries—especially aspirin, razor blades, and tampons—and either buy or bring toilet paper. Eastern European trains are grimier than those in the West and the toilet facilities are unreliable. Trains are not air-conditioned, and on-board soft drinks are overpriced. Bring a sturdy plastic **water-bottle.** Also consider taking the following items: pocketknife, needle and thread, safety pins, electrical tape (for patching tears), umbrella, garbage bags, **contact lens supplies,** a rubber squash ball to stop up the sink, flashlight, cutlery (for grocery-store meals), soap, an alarm clock, a bath towel, bags that seal shut (for damp clothing, soaps, or messy foods), sunglasses, earplugs, sunscreen, and a padlock. It is always a good idea to bring along a **first-aid kit.** Pack extra rolls of **film:** it can be quite expensive in well-touristed areas. And don't forget your travel journal! You might not believe it at the moment, but the day will come when you'll want to remember that 1000th church or castle you visited or that horrifying face rash you picked up in Volgograd.

Across Eastern Europe, **electricity** is 220 volts AC, enough to fry any 110V North American appliance. Visit a hardware store for an adaptor (which changes the shape of the plug) and a converter (which changes the voltage). Do not make the mistake of using only an adaptor, or you'll melt your radio.

GETTING THERE

■ Budget Travel Agencies

Students and people under 26 ("youths") with proper ID qualify for enticing reduced airfares. These are rarely available from airlines or travel agents, but rather from student travel agencies which negotiate special, reduced-rate bulk purchases with the airlines, then resell them to the youth market. Return-date change fees also tend to be low (around US$35 per segment through Council or STA). Most flights are on major airlines, though in peak season some agencies may sell seats on less reliable chartered aircraft. Student travel agencies can also help non-students and people over 26, but probably won't get them the same low fares.

Campus Travel, 52 Grosvenor Gardens, London SW1W 0AG (http://www.campus-travel.co.uk). 46 branches in the U.K. Student and youth fares on plane, train, boat, and bus travel. Discount and ID cards for students and youths, travel insurance for students and those under 35, and maps and guides. Telephone booking service: in Europe call (0171) 730 3402; worldwide call (0171) 730 8111; in Manchester call (0161) 273 1721; in Scotland call (0131) 668 3303.

Council Travel (http://www.ciee.org/travel/index.htm), the travel division of Council. A full-service travel agency specializing in youth and budget travel. Discount airfares on scheduled airlines, railpasses, hosteling cards, low-cost accommodations, guidebooks, budget tours, travel gear, and international student (ISIC), youth (GO25), and teacher (ITIC) identity cards. U.S. offices include: 10904 Lindbrook Dr., **Los Angeles,** CA 90024 (tel. (310) 208-3551); 205 E. 42nd St., **New York,** NY 10017 (tel. (212) 822-2700); 3300 M St. NW, **Washington, D.C.** 20007 (tel. (202) 337-6464). **For U.S. cities not listed,** call 800-2-COUNCIL (226-8624). Also 28A Poland St. (Oxford Circus), **London,** W1V 3DB (tel. (0171) 287 3337), as well as other European capitals.

Council Charter: 205 E. 42nd St., New York, NY 10017 (tel. (212) 661-0311; fax 972-0194). Offers a combination of inexpensive charter and scheduled airfares from a variety of U.S. gateways to most major European destinations. One-way fares and open jaws (fly into one city and out of another) are available.

CTS Travel, 220 Kensington High St., W8 (tel. (0171) 937 33 66 for travel in Europe, 937 33 88 for travel world-wide; fax 937 90 27). Specializes in student/youth travel and discount flights.

Let's Go Travel, Harvard Student Agencies, 17 Holyoke St., Cambridge, MA 02138 (tel. (617) 495-9649; fax 495-7956; email travel@hsa.net; http://hsa.net/travel). Railpasses, HI-AYH memberships, ISICs, ITICs, FIYTO cards, guidebooks (including every *Let's Go*), maps, bargain flights, and a complete line of budget travel gear. All items available by mail; call or write for a catalogue (or see catalogue in center of this publication).

Rail Europe Inc., 226 Westchester Ave., White Plains, NY 10604 (tel. (800) 438-7245; fax 432-1329; http://www.raileurope.com). Sells Eurail products and passes,

national railpasses, and point-to-point tickets. Up-to-date information on all rail travel in Europe.

STA Travel, 6560 Scottsdale Rd. #F100, Scottsdale, AZ 85253 (tel. (800) 777-0112 nationwide; fax (602) 922-0793; http://sta-travel.com). A student and youth travel organization with over 150 offices worldwide offering discount airfares, railpasses, accommodations, tours, insurance, and ISICs. U.S. offices include: 7202 Melrose Ave., **Los Angeles,** CA 90046 (tel. (213) 934-8722); 10 Downing St., Ste. G, **New York,** NY 10003 (tel. (212) 627-3111); 2401 Pennsylvania Ave., **Washington, D.C.** 20037 (tel. (202) 887-0912); In the U.K., 6 Wrights Ln., **London** W8 6TA (tel. (0171) 938 4711). In New Zealand, 10 High St., **Auckland** (tel. (09) 309 97 23). In Australia, 222 Faraday St., **Melbourne** VIC 3050 (tel. (03) 93 49 69 11).

Travel CUTS (Canadian Universities Travel Services Limited), 187 College St., Toronto, Ont. M5T 1P7 (tel. (416) 979-2406; fax 979-8167; email mail@travelcuts). Canada's national student travel bureau, with 40 offices across Canada. Also 295-A Regent St., London W1R 7YA (tel. (0171) 637 3161). Discounted domestic and international airfares open to all; special student fares to all destinations with valid ISIC. Issues ISIC, FIYTO, GO25, and HI hostel cards, as well as railpasses. Offers free *Student Traveller* magazine, as well as information on the Student Work Abroad Program (SWAP).

USIT Youth and Student Travel, 19-21 Aston Quay, O'Connell Bridge, Dublin 2 (tel. (01) 677 8117; fax 679 8833). In the U.S.: New York Student Center, 895 Amsterdam Ave., New York, NY, 10025 (tel. (212) 663-5435; email usitny@aol.com). Offices all over Ireland. Specializes in youth and student travel. Offers low-cost tickets and flexible travel arrangements all over the world. Supplies ISIC and FIYTO-GO25 cards in Ireland only.

Wasteels, 7041 Grand National Drive #207, Orlando, FL 32819 (tel. (407) 351-2537); in **London** (0171) 834 7066; fax 630 7628). A huge chain in Europe, with 200,000 locations. Sells the Wasteels BIJ tickets, which are discounted (25-40% off regular fare) 2nd class international point-to-point train tickets with a number of stopovers (must be under 26 on the first day of travel); sold *only* in Europe.

■ By Plane

Finding a cheap airfare to Eastern Europe in the airline industry's computerized jungle will be easier if you understand the airlines' systems. Call every toll-free number and don't be afraid to ask about discounts; if you don't ask, they won't be volunteered. Have knowledgeable **travel agents** guide you; better yet, find an agent who specializes in the region(s) you'll be traveling to. Remember that travel agents may not want to do the legwork to find the cheapest fares (for which they receive the lowest commissions). Students and people under 26 should *never* pay full price for a ticket. Seniors can also get great deals; many airlines offer senior traveler clubs or airline passes and discounts for their companions as well. Major Sunday newspapers have travel sections that list bargain fares. Outsmart airline reps with the phonebook-sized *Official Airline Guide* (check your local library), a monthly guide listing nearly every scheduled flight in the world (with prices) and toll-free numbers for all airlines that allow you to call in reservations directly. More accessible and incredibly useful is Michael McColl's *The Worldwide Guide to Cheap Airfare* (US$15).

There is also a steadily increasing amount of travel information to be found on the Internet. The *Official Airline Guide* now has a website (http://www.oag.com) which allows access to flight schedules (one-time hook-up fee US$25; user's fee 17-47¢ per min.) The site also provides info on hotels, cruises, and rail and ferry schedules. The **Air Traveler's Handbook** (http://www.cis.ohio-state.edu/hypertext/faq/usenet/travel/air/handbook/top.html) is an excellent source for general information on air travel. **Airlines of the Web** (http://www.itn.net/airlines) provides links to pages and 800 numbers for most of the world's airlines. The newsgroup **rec.travel.air** is a good source of tips on current bargains. And a few airlines have begun holding auctions on their websites, including **Icelandair** (http://www.centrum.is/icelandair) and **Finnair** (http://www.us.finnair.com).

Most airfares peak between mid-June and early September. Weekday (Mon.-Thurs. morning) round-trip flights run about US$40-50 cheaper than on weekends; weekend flights, however, are generally less crowded. Traveling from larger cities or travel hubs will almost always win a more competitive fare than from smaller cities. Return-date flexibility is usually not an option for the budget traveler; traveling with an "open return" ticket can be pricier than fixing a return date and paying to change it. Try to pick up your ticket well in advance of the departure date, confirm the flight within 72 hours of departure, and arrive at the airport at least three hours early.

COMMERCIAL AIRLINES

The commercial airlines' lowest regular offer is the **APEX** (Advance Purchase Excursion Fare); specials advertised in newspapers may be cheaper, but have more restrictions and fewer available seats. APEX fares provide you with confirmed reservations and allow "open-jaw" tickets (landing in and returning from different cities). Generally, reservations must be made seven to 21 days in advance, with seven- to 14-day minimum and up to 90-day maximum stay limits, as well as hefty cancellation and change penalties (fees rise in summer). Book APEX fares early during peak season; by May you will have a hard time getting the departure date you want.

Look into flights to less popular destinations or on smaller carriers. Check out: **Icelandair** (U.S. tel. (800) 223-5500), **Finnair** (U.S. tel. (800) 950-5000; http://www.us.finnair.com), and **Martinair** (U.S. tel. (800) 627-8462). Another option that may save you money is to fly into a main city such as Amsterdam or Paris, and then take the train or bus to your Eastern European destination.

Even if you pay an airline's lowest published fare, you may waste hundreds of dollars. For the adventurous or the bargain-hungry, there are other options, perhaps more inconvenient or time-consuming, but before shopping around it is a good idea to find out the average commercial price in order to measure just how great a "bargain" you are being offered.

EASTERN EUROPEAN AIRLINES

The safety and service of airlines in Eastern Europe varies wildly. Some airlines have completely modernized since 1989 and operate according to Western standards; others have seen their reputations deteriorate. The type and age of the aircraft used often indicate the airline's safety level—aircraft not produced by Boeing, Airbus, McDonnell Douglas, or Fokker sometimes fall below acceptable standards, and aircraft over 20 years old require increased levels of maintenance. Travel agencies and the *Official Airline Guide* (http://www.oag.com) can tell you the type and age of aircraft on a particular route (particularly useful in Eastern Europe, where less reliable equipment is often used for inter-city travel). The **International Airline Passengers Association** (tel. (972) 404-9980) publishes a survey of accident rates on foreign airlines and provides safety information on carriers worldwide. The **Federal Aviation Administration** (http://www.faa.gov) reviews the airline authorities for countries whose airlines enter the U.S. and divides the countries into three categories: stick with carriers in category 1. Check with the **U.S. State Department** (tel. (202) 647-5225; http://travel.state.gov/travel_warnings.html) to check for posted travel advisories which sometimes involve foreign carriers. In 1997, the **British Foreign and Commonwealth Office** advised travelers to Russia to avoid domestic carriers and routes, due to safety concerns. However, Eastern European airlines' low fares can make air travel in the area an option well worth considering. For information on individual national airlines, see the **Getting There** sections of each country.

TICKET CONSOLIDATORS

Ticket consolidators resell unsold tickets on commercial and charter airlines at unpublished fares. Look for their tiny ads in weekend papers (the Sunday *Times* in New York or London is best), and start calling them all. In London, the **Air Travel Advisory Bureau** (tel. (0171) 636 5000) provides a list of consolidators. There are rarely age constraints or stay limitations; tickets are also heavily discounted (30-40%), and may offer extra flexibility or bypass advance purchase requirements, since you aren't tangled in airline bureaucracy. But unlike tickets bought through an airline, you won't be able to use your tickets on another flight if you miss yours, and you will have to go back to the consolidator, rather than the airline, to get a refund.

Be a smart and careful shopper. Contact the local Better Business Bureau to find out how long the company has been in business and its track record. Ask to receive your tickets as quickly as possible so you have time to fix any problems. Get the company's policy in writing: insist on a **receipt** that gives full details about the tickets, refunds, and restrictions, and record the full name of who you talked to and when. It may be worth paying with a credit card (despite the 2-5% fee) so you can stop payment if you never receive your tickets. Ask also about accommodations and car rental discounts; some consolidators have fingers in many pies. Consult Kelly Monaghan's *Consolidators: Air Travel's Bargain Basement* (US$7 plus US$2 shipping), available from the Intrepid Traveler, P.O. Box 438, New York, NY 10034 (email intreptrav@aol.com), a valuable source for more information and lists of consolidators by location and destination. Also useful is Edward Hasbrouck's informative World Wide Wanderer web site (http://www.tmn.com/wwwanderer).

For destinations worldwide, try **Airfare Busters** (tel. (800) 232-8783), **Pennsylvania Travel** (tel. (800) 331-0947), or **Cheap Tickets** (tel. (800) 377-1000). For a fee that depends on the itinerary and number of travelers, **Travel Avenue** (tel. (800) 333-3335; fax (312) 876-1254; http://www.travelavenue.com) will search for the lowest international airfare available and even give you a rebate on fares over US$300.

CHARTER FLIGHTS

The theory behind **charter** flights is that a tour operator contracts with an airline to fly extra loads of passengers to peak-season destinations. Charters are often cheaper than flights on scheduled airlines, especially during peak seasons, and their restrictions on minimum advance-purchase and minimum stay are relatively lenient. However, charters' prices can be beat by fare wars, consolidator tickets, and small airlines, and charters fly less frequently than major airlines, make refunds particularly difficult, and are almost always fully booked. Schedules and itineraries may also change or be cancelled at the last moment (as late as 48 hours before the flight, and without a full refund), and check-in, boarding, and baggage claim are often much slower. As always, pay with a credit card, and consider traveler's insurance against trip interruption. Try **Travac** (tel. (800) 872-8800; fax (212) 714-9063; email mail@travac.com; http://www.travac.com); **Interworld** (tel. (305) 443-4929; fax 443-0351), or **Rebel** (tel. (800) 227-3235; fax (805) 294-0981; email travel@rebeltours.com; http://rebeltours.com). Don't be afraid to call every number to find the best deal.

Eleventh-hour **discount clubs** and **fare brokers** offer members savings on travel, including charter flights and tour packages. Research your options carefully. **Last Minute Travel Club,** 100 Sylvan Rd., Woburn, MA 01801 (tel. (800) 527-8646 or (617) 267-9800), and **Discount Travel International,** New York, NY (tel. (212) 362-3636; fax 362-3236), are among the few that don't charge a membership fee. Others include **Moment's Notice,** New York, NY (tel. (718) 234-6295; fax 234-6450; http://www.moments-notice.com), which offers air tickets, tours, and hotels for a US$25 annual fee; **Travelers Advantage,** Stamford, CT, (tel. (800) 548-1116; http://www.travelersadvantage.com; US$49 annual fee); and **Travel Avenue** (tel. (800) 333-3335; see **Ticket Consolidators,** above). Study your contracts closely; you don't want to end up with an unwanted overnight layover—or worse.

STAND-BY FLIGHTS

Very flexible budget travelers might try **stand-by flights,** for which you buy a promise that you will get to a destination near where you're going within a window of time (usually five days) from a location in a specified region. You call in before your date-range to hear all of your flight options for the next week or so and your probability of boarding. You then decide which flights you want to try to make and present a

voucher at the airport which grants you the right to board a flight on a space-available basis. This procedure repeats for the return trip. When flying standby, be sure to read all the fine print in agreements. It may be difficult to receive refunds, and vouchers may not be honored if the airline fails to receive payment in time. **Air-Tech, Ltd.,** 588 Broadway #204, New York, NY 10012 (tel. (212) 219-7000; fax 219-0066) sells standby tickets for around US$169-239 one way, and also arranges courier flights and regular confirmed-reserved flights at discount rates. With **Airhitch,** 2641 Broadway, 3rd. fl., New York, NY 10025 (tel. (800) 326-2009 or (212) 864-2000; fax 864-5489) and Los Angeles, CA (tel. (310) 726-5000), one-way runs US$175-269. Several European offices handle return registration; the main one is in Paris (tel. (01) 47 00 16 30).

COURIER COMPANIES

Those who travel light should consider flying as a **courier.** The company hiring you will use your checked luggage space for freight; you're only allowed to bring carry-ons. You are responsible for the safe delivery of the baggage claim slips (given to you by a courier company representative) to the representative waiting for you when you arrive—don't screw up or you will be blacklisted as a courier. You will probably never see the cargo you are transporting—the company handles it all—and airport officials know that couriers are not responsible for the baggage checked for them. Restrictions to watch for: you must be over 21 (18 in some cases), have a valid passport, and procure your own visa (if necessary); most flights are round-trip only with short fixed-length stays (usually one week); only single tickets are issued; and most flights are from New York. Round-trip fares to Western Europe from the U.S. range from US$250-400 (off-season) to US$400-550 (summer). For an annual fee of US$45, the **International Association of Air Travel Couriers,** 8 South J St., P.O. Box 1349, Lake Worth, FL 33460 (tel. (561) 582-8320) informs travelers (via computer, fax, and mailings) of courier opportunities worldwide. **Travel Unlimited** is a monthly update of courier options as well as general information on low-budget travel (write P.O. Box 1058A, Allston, MA 02134 for a free sample newsletter; subscription runs US$25 per year). **NOW Voyager,** 74 Varick St. #307, New York, NY 10013 (tel. (212) 431-1616; fax 334-5243; http://www.nowvoyagertravel.com), acts as an agent for courier flights worldwide, offering last-minute deals to such cities as London, Paris, and Frankfurt for as little as US$200 round-trip plus a US$50 registration fee. The company also acts as a consolidator. Other agents to try are **Halbart Express,** 147-05 176th St., Jamaica, NY 11434 (tel. (718) 656-5000; fax 917-0708; offices in Chicago, Los Angeles, and London), and **Discount Travel International** (tel. (212) 362-3636).

You can also go directly through courier companies in New York, or check your bookstore or library for handbooks such as *Air Courier Bargains* (US$15, plus US$2.50 shipping) from the Intrepid Traveler, P.O. Box 438, New York, NY 10034 (email intreptrav@aol.com). *The Courier Air Travel Handbook* (US$10, plus US$3.50 shipping) explains traveling as an air courier and contains names, phone numbers, and contact points of courier companies. It can be ordered from Bookmasters, Inc., P.O. Box 2039, Mansfield, OH 44905 (U.S. tel. (800) 507-2665).

ONCE THERE

■ Travel in the Region

BY PLANE

Flying across Eastern Europe on regularly scheduled flights can devour your budget. **Alitalia** (tel. (800) 223-5730) sells "Europlus": in conjunction with a transatlantic flight on Alitalia, for US$299 you may purchase a package of three flight coupons good for anywhere Alitalia flies within Europe; unlimited additional tickets cost

ESSENTIALS

US$100. **Lufthansa** (tel. (800) 645-3880) offers "Discover Europe" to U.S. residents, a package of three flight coupons which cost US$125-200 each depending on season and destination; up to six additional tickets cost US$105-175 each. Student travel agencies also sell cheap tickets. Consult budget travel agents and local newspapers and magazines. London's **Air Travel Advisory Bureau** (tel. (0171) 636 5000) can point the way to discount flights. In addition, many European airlines offer visitor ticket packages, which give intercontinental passengers discount rates on flights within Europe after arrival. Check with a travel agent for details.

BY TRAIN

Many train stations have different counters for domestic and international tickets, seat reservations, and information; check before lining up. On major routes, reservations are always advisable, and often required, even with a railpass; make them at least a few hours in advance at the train station (US$3-10). In the former Soviet Union, you may need to purchase tickets days in advance.

Railpasses You may find it tough to make your railpass pay for itself in Eastern Europe, where train fares are rising quickly, but still reasonable. Ideally conceived, a railpass allows you to jump on any train in Europe, go wherever you want whenever you want, and change your plans at will. The handbook that comes with your railpass tells you everything you need to know and includes a timetable for major routes, a map, and details on ferry discounts. In practice, it's not so simple. You still must stand in line to pay for seat reservations, supplements, and couchette reservations, as well as to have your pass validated when you first use it. More importantly, railpasses don't always pay off. To figure out whether it's wise to purchase one, consult Rick Steve's *Europe Through the Back Door* newsletter or the **Rail Europe** railpass brochure for prices of point-to-point tickets. Add them up and compare with railpass prices. If you're under 26, the BIJ tickets are probably a cheaper option (see below).

Eurailpass covers only Hungary in Eastern Europe, while the **European East Pass** covers Austria, the Czech Republic, Hungary, Poland, and Slovakia. You'll almost certainly find it easiest to buy a pass before you arrive in Europe. Contact Council Travel, Travel CUTS, or Let's Go Travel (see **Budget Travel Agencies,** p. 29), or other travel agents. **Rail Europe,** 226-300 Westchester Ave., White Plains, NY 10604 (tel. (800) 438-7245; fax (800) 432-1329 in the U.S.; tel. (800) 361-7245; fax (905) 602-4198 in Canada; http://www.raileurope.com) provides extensive information on pass options and also offers a number of passes good in individual Eastern European countries for various durations and prices.

Discount Rail Tickets For travelers under 26, **BIJ** tickets (Billets Internationals de Jeunesse; sold under the names **Wasteels, Eurotrain,** and **Route 26**) are a great alternative to railpasses. Available for international trips within Europe as well as most ferry services, they knock 25-40% off regular second-class fares. Tickets are good for 60 days after purchase and allow a number of stopovers along the normal direct route of the train journey. Issued for a specific international route between two points, they must be used in the direction and order of the designated route without side- or backtracking and must be bought in Europe. They are available from European travel agents, at Wasteels or Eurotrain offices (usually in or near train stations), or occasionally at ticket counters. Contact Wasteels in Victoria Station, adjacent to Platform 2, London SW1V 1JT (tel. (0171) 834 7066; fax 630 7628).

Useful Resources The ultimate reference for planning rail trips is the **Thomas Cook European Timetable** (US$28; US$39 includes a map of Europe highlighting all train and ferry routes; postage US$4.50). This timetable, updated regularly, covers all major and most minor train routes in Europe. In the U.S. and Canada, order it from **Forsyth Travel Library** (see **Useful Publications,** p. 2). In Europe, find it at any **Thomas Cook Money Exchange Center.** Available in most bookstores or from Houghton Mifflin Co., 222 Berkeley St., Boston, MA 02116 (tel. (800) 225-3362; fax (800) 634-7568) is the annual *Eurail Guide to Train Travel in the New Europe* (US$15), giving timetables, instructions, and prices for international train trips, daytrips, and excursions in Europe. The annual railpass special edition of Rick Steves's free *Europe Through the Back Door* travel newsletter and catalogue provides a comprehensive comparative analysis of railpasses with national or regional passes and point-to-point tickets. Contact 120 Fourth Ave. N., P.O. Box 2009, Edmonds, WA 98020 (tel. (425) 771-8303; fax 771-0833; email ricksteves@aol.com; http://www.ricksteves.com). **Hunter Publishing,** P.O. Box 7816, Edison, NJ 08818 (tel. (908) 225-1900; fax 417-0482; email hunterpub@emi.net; http://www.hunterpublishing.com), offers a catalogue of rail atlases and travel guides. Titles include *The Trans-Siberian Rail Guide* (US$18), and *European Rail Atlas: Scandinavia & Eastern Europe* (US$16).

BY BUS

All over Eastern Europe, short-haul buses reach rural areas inaccessible by train. In addition, long-distance bus networks may be more extensive, efficient, and occasionally even more comfortable than train services. In the Balkans, air-conditioned buses run by private companies are a godsend. **Eurolines,** 4 Cardiff Rd., Luton LU1 1PP (tel. (01582) 40 45 11; fax 40 06 94; in London, 52 Grosvenor Gardens, Victoria (tel. (0171) 730 8235), is Europe's largest operator of coach services, offering passes (UK£159-249) for unlimited 30- or 60- day travel between 20 major tourist destinations, including spots in Eastern Europe and Russia.

BY CAR

Cars offer speed, freedom, access to the countryside, and an escape from the town-to-town mentality of trains. Unfortunately, they also insulate you from the *esprit de corps* rail travelers enjoy and subject you to the dangers of road travel in Eastern Europe. Rail Europe and other railpass vendors offer **rail-and-drive** packages for both individual countries and all of Europe. The availability of **rental cars** varies across Eastern Europe, and rates there are the most expensive in Europe. One option is to rent a car in a Western European country and drive it eastward if the rental agreement allows. However, a loss/damage waiver then becomes mandatory. Car-rental agencies in the Balkans often require you to rent a driver along with the car. The former Soviet Union is generally off-limits to cars rented in the West.

You can rent a car from a U.S.-based firm with European offices, such as **Alamo** (tel. (800) 522-9696; http://www.goalamo.com), **Avis** (tel. (800) 331-1084; http://www.avis.com), **Budget** (tel. (800) 472-3325) or **Hertz** (tel. (800) 654-3001; http://www.hertz.com); from a European-based company with local representatives such as **Europcar** (tel. (800) 227-3876; in Canada (800) 227-7368; in France (1) 45 00 08 06); from a tour operator that will arrange a rental for you from a European company at its own rates, such as **Auto Europe** (tel. (800) 223-5555; http://www.autoeurope.com), **Bon Voyage by Car** (tel. (800) 272-3299; in Canada (800) 253-3876), **Europe by Car** (tel. (800) 223-1516; http://www.europebycar.com), or **Kemwel Holiday Autos** (tel. (800) 678-0678; http://www.kemwel.com); or from a local agency. Rates vary considerably by company, season, and pick-up point; expect to pay over US$100 per day, plus tax, for a teensy stick-shift car. Check if prices include tax and collision insurance; some credit card companies cover this automatically. Ask about student and other discounts, and ask your airline about special packages. Sometimes you can get up to a week of free rental. Minimum age restrictions vary by country; often you must be at least 25.

Before setting off, be sure you know the laws of the countries in which you'll be driving. Be careful, road conditions in Eastern Europe are rarely driver- or pedestrian-friendly. The **Association for Safe International Road Travel (ASIRT)** can provide more information about conditions in specific countries. They are located at 5413 West Cedar La., #103C, Bethesda, MD 20814 (tel. (301) 983-5252; fax 983-3663; http://www.horizon-web.com/asirt). ASIRT considers road travel (by car or bus) to be relatively unsafe in Latvia, Bulgaria, and Poland. Unleaded gas is almost nonexistent in Eastern Europe.

Moto-Europa, by Eric Bredesen (US$16; shipping US$3, overseas US$7), available from Seren Publishing, 2935 Saint Anne Dr., Dubuque, IA 52001 (tel. (800) 387-6728; fax (319) 583-7853), is a comprehensive guide to all these moto-options. From itinerary suggestions to a motorists' phrasebook, it provides loads of tips, whatever the mode of transport, and chapters on leasing and buying vehicles. More general info is available from your local **Automobile Association.** For addresses and phone numbers, see **Driving Permits and Car Insurance,** p. 10.

BY BOAT

Sometimes, yes, boats go to Yalta…but not today.
—Ferry ticket clerk in Odesa

Ferries serving Eastern Europe divide into two major groups. **Riverboats** acquaint you with many towns that trains can only wink at. The legendary waterways of Eastern Europe—the Danube, the Volga, the Dnieper—offer a bewitching alternative to land travel. However, the farther east you go, the more often your travel plans may be interrupted by fuel shortages. Most riverboats are palatial and well-equipped; the cheapest fare usually still gives you full use of the boat—including reclining chairs and couchettes that allow you to sleep the trip away in the sun or shade. Schedule information is scarce; inquire in the area of your trip.

Ferries in the **North Sea** and **Baltic Sea** are prized by Scandinavians for their duty-free candy and alcohol shops; they are also universally reliable, and go everywhere. Those content with deck passage rarely need to book ahead. You should check in at least two hours early for a prime spot and allow plenty of time for getting to the port. It's a good idea to bring your own food and avoid the astronomically priced cafeteria cuisine. Fares jump sharply in July and August. Always ask for discounts; ISIC holders can often get student fares, and Eurail passholders get many reductions and free trips (check the brochure that comes with your railpass). You'll occasionally have to pay a small port tax (under US$10). Advance planning and reserved ticket purchases through a travel agency can spare you several tedious days of waiting in dreary ports.

For complete listings of schedules and fares for ferries, steamers, and cruises throughout Europe, find a copy of the quarterly *Official Steamship Guide International* at your travel agent. **Thomas Cook** also lists complete ferry schedules (see **By Train,** p. 36). Links to some major European ferry companies can be found at http://www.youra.com/intnlferries.html. For information on cruises throughout Europe and visa-free cruises to Russia contact **EuroCruises,** 303 W. 13th St., New York, NY 10014 (tel. (800) 688-3876, (212) 691-2099, or (212) 366-4747; email euro-cruises@compuserve.com).

BY BICYCLE

Biking is one of the key elements of the classic budget Eurovoyage. With the proliferation of mountain bikes, you can do some serious natural sightseeing. Be aware that touring involves pedaling both yourself and whatever you store in the panniers (bags that strap to your bike). Prepare by taking some reasonably challenging rides at home, and have your bike tuned up by a reputable shop. Wear visible clothing, drink plenty of water (even if you're not thirsty), and ride on the same side as the traffic. Learn and use the international signals for turns. Know how to fix a modern derailleur-equipped mount and change a tire, and practice. A few simple tools and a good bike manual will be invaluable. For information about touring routes, consult national tourist offices or the numerous books available.

Most airlines will count your bike as your second free piece of luggage (you're usually allowed two pieces of checked baggage and a carry-on). As an extra piece, it'll cost about US$60-110 each way. Bikes must be packed in a cardboard box with the pedals and front wheel detached; airlines sell bike boxes at the airport (US$10), but bring your own tools. Most ferries let you take your bike for free or for a nominal fee. You can always transport your bike on trains; the cost varies from small to substantial.

Riding a bike with a frame pack strapped on it or on your back is about as safe as pedaling blindfolded over a sheet of ice; panniers are essential. The first thing to buy, however, is a suitable **bike helmet.** At about US$25-50, they're a much better buy than head injury or death. U-shaped **Citadel** or **Kryptonite locks** are expensive (starting at US$30), but the companies insure against theft for one to two years.

BY THUMB

> *Let's Go* strongly urges you to seriously consider the risks before you choose to hitch. We do not recommend hitching as a safe means of transportation, and none of the information presented here is intended to do so.

No one should hitch without careful consideration of the risks involved. Not everyone can be an airplane pilot, but almost any bozo can drive a car. Hitching means entrusting your life to a random person who happens to stop beside you on the road. You risk theft, assault, sexual harassment, and unsafe driving. In spite of this, many who live by the thumb see benefits to hitching. Favorable hitching experiences allow hitchers to meet local people and get to places where public transportation is sketchy. If you decide to hitch, consider where you are. Hitching remains common in Eastern Europe, though Westerners are a definite target for theft. In Russia, the Baltics, and some other Eastern European countries, there is no clear difference between hitchhiking and hailing a taxi. The choice, however, remains yours.

BY FOOT

Eastern Europe's grandest scenery can often be seen only on foot. *Let's Go* describes many daytrips for those who want to hoof it, but native inhabitants (Europeans are fervent, almost obsessive hikers), hostel proprietors, and fellow travelers are the best source of tips. There are also numerous books with tales of the Great Outdoors that can give you ideas and practical advice on hiking in Eastern Europe. Check your local wilderness store or bookstore for regional or country-specific guides.

■ Accommodations

If you arrive in a town without a reservation, your first stop should be the local tourist office. These offices often distribute extensive accommodations listings free of charge and will also reserve a room for a small fee (though some favor their friends' establishments). As a rule, expect all prices to rise each January.

ROOMS IN PRIVATE HOMES

Throughout Eastern Europe, it is commonplace for locals with rooms to rent to approach tourists in ports or train stations. This may seem dangerous, but it is an accepted custom and is often a more attractive option than a night in an overpriced 1970s-revival hotel. In small villages in the Balkans, travelers find a roof for the night simply by walking the streets and knocking on doors, or by asking locals for tips. The conditions are sometimes far superior to those at local hotels. However, there is no guarantee of these hawkers' trustworthiness or of the quality of their establishments. Carry your own baggage, ask for identification, check the bathroom facilities, have them write down the offered price, and make sure the place is located conveniently or near a bus or tram stop.

HOSTELS

For tight budgets and beating those lonesome traveling blues, hostels can't be beat. Hostels generally offer dorm-style accommodations, often in large single-sex rooms with bunk beds, although some do offer private rooms for families and couples. They sometimes have kitchens and utensils for your use, bike or moped rentals, storage areas, and laundry facilities. There can be drawbacks: some hostels close during certain daytime "lock-out" hours, have a curfew, impose a maximum stay, or, less frequently, require that you do chores. Hostel quality also varies dramatically. Some require sheets or sleepsacks; make your own by sewing shut two sides of a folded sheet, or buy one at a youth hostel federation. Fees range from US$5 to $25 per night, and hostels associated with one of the large hostel associations have lower rates for members. The **Internet Guide to Hostelling** (http://hostels.com) includes hostels from around the world in addition to oodles of information about hosteling and backpacking worldwide. **Eurotrip** (http://www.eurotrip.com/accommodation/accommodation.html) also has information on budget hostels and several international hostel associations. Reservations for over 300 **Hostelling International (HI)** hostels (see listing below) may be made via the International Booking Network (IBN), a computerized system which allows you to make hostel reservations months in advance for a nominal fee (tel. (202) 783-6161). Depending on your travel plans, it may be worthwhile to join one of these associations.

Hostelling International-American Youth Hostels (HI-AYH), 733 15th St. NW, #840, Washington, D.C. 20005 (tel. (202) 783-6161; fax 783-6171; email hiayhserv@hiayh.org; http://www.hiayh.org). 35 offices in the U.S. 1-year HI memberships: US$25, under 18 US$10, over 54 US$15, family US$35. These can be purchased at many travel agencies (see p. 29) or the national office in D.C. Reservations may be made by letter, phone, fax, or through the IBN.

Australian Youth Hostels Association (AYHA), Level 3, 10 Mallett St., Camperdown NSW 2050 (tel. (02) 95 65 16 99; fax 95 65 13 25; email YHA@zeta.org.au). AUS$44, renewal AUS$27; under 18 AUS$13.

Hostelling International-Canada (HI-C), 400-205 Catherine St., Ottawa, Ont. K2P 1C3 (tel. (613) 237-7884; fax 237-7868). IBN booking centers in Edmonton, Montréal, Ottawa, and Vancouver. 1-year membership CDN$25, under 18 CDN$12; over 18 2-year CDN$35; lifetime CDN$175.

Youth Hostels Association of England and Wales (YHA), Trevelyan House, 8 St. Stephen's Hill, St. Albans, Hertfordshire AL1 2DY (tel. (01727) 85 52 15; fax 84 41 26). Enrollment fees are: UK£9.50; under 18 UK£3.50; UK£19 for both parents with children under 18 enrolled free, UK£9.50 for 1 parent with children under 18 enrolled free; UK£130 for lifetime membership.

An Óige (Irish Youth Hostel Association), 61 Mountjoy St., Dublin 7 (tel. (01) 830 4555; fax 830 5808; email anoige@iol.ie). 1-year membership IR£7.50; under 18 IR£4; family IR£7.50 for each adult with children under 16 free.

Youth Hostels Association of New Zealand (YHANZ), P.O. Box 436, 173 Gloucester St., Christchurch 1 (tel. (03) 379 99 70; fax 365 44 76; email info@yha.org.nz; http://www.yha.org.nz). Annual membership NZ$24.

Youth Hostels Association of Northern Ireland (YHANI), 22 Donegall Rd., Belfast BT12 5JN (tel. (01232) 32 47 33 or 31 54 35; fax 43 96 99). Annual memberships UK£7, under 18 UK£3, family UK£14 for up to 6 children.

Scottish Youth Hostels Association (SYHA), 7 Glebe Crescent, Stirling FK8 2JA (tel. (01786) 891400; fax 891333; email syha@syha.org.uk; http://www.syha.org.uk). Membership UK£6, under 18 UK£2.50.

Hostel Association of South Africa, P.O. Box 4402, Cape Town 8000 (tel. (021) 24 25 11; fax 24 41 19; email hisa@gem.co.za; http://www.gen.com/hisa). Membership SAR45; group SAR120; family SAR90; lifetime SAR250.

HOTELS

In hotels, couples can usually get by fairly well (rooms with a double bed are generally cheaper than those with two twin beds), as can groups of three or four. Always specify that you want the cheapest room available; some managers assume that Westerners expect rooms with phone, fridge, and TV—and that they're willing to pay for the privilege. Inexpensive East European hotels may come as a rude shock to pampered travelers. You'll share a bathroom down the hall; one of your own is a rarity and costs extra when provided. Check to make sure that toilets flush. Hot showers may also cost more, *if* they're available. Some hotels offer "full pension" (all meals) and "half pension" (breakfast and lunch). Unmarried couples will generally have no trouble getting a room together, although couples under age 21 may occasionally encounter resistance.

ALTERNATIVE ACCOMMODATIONS

In university and college towns, **student dormitories** may be open to travelers when school is not in session. Prices are usually comparable to those of youth hostels, and you probably won't have to share a room with strangers or endure stringent curfew and eviction regulations. Also, some **monasteries** and **convents** open their doors for weary backpackers. A letter on stationery from a clergy member at home could facilitate matters. Sleeping in European train stations is a time-honored tradition. Though free and often tolerated by authorities, it's neither comfortable nor safe. Don't spend the night in an urban park unless you place a low value on your life.

■ Camping & the Outdoors

The wilds of Eastern Europe can be experienced at one of the sometimes beautiful and sometimes simply enormous **organized campgrounds** that exist in many of the cities and rural areas. Most are accessible by foot, car, or public transportation. Showers, bathrooms, and a small restaurant or store are common; some sites have more elaborate facilities. Prices are US$1-10 per person, with an additional charge for a tent. Money and time expended in getting to the campsite may eat away at your budget and your patience, but camping will bring you into the vacation subculture of young Eastern Europeans, since it is often the only affordable accommodation for locals. For travelers who opt for the lighter, tent-free backpack, many campgrounds also offer cabins or bungalows for a slightly higher fee.

CAMPING EQUIPMENT

Prospective campers will need to invest a lot of money in good camping equipment and a lot of energy in carrying it on their shoulders. Many of the better **sleeping bags** are rated according to the lowest outdoor temperature at which they will still keep you warm. Sleeping bags are made either of down (warmer and lighter) or synthetic material (cheaper, heavier, more durable, and warmer when wet). **Foam sleeping-bag pads** run from US$15. If you plan on doing a lot of camping, the amount of comfort a pad or mattress provides makes up for its bulk; they also come in handy for sitting on hard train station floors. The best **tents** are free-standing, with their own frames and suspension systems—they set up quickly and require no staking. Low profile dome tents are the best all-around. Good two-person tents start at US$150, four-person tents at US$400. If you intend to do a lot of hiking, you should have a **frame backpack.** Although the costs of all this might seem daunting, you can often find last year's version for half the price. See **Luggage,** p. 28, for hints on backpacks and a continuation of the eternal internal/external frame debate.

Other camping basics include a battery-operated **lantern** (gas is inconvenient and dangerous) and a simple plastic **groundcloth** to protect the tent floor. Don't go anywhere without a **canteen** or water bottle. **Camp stoves** come in all sizes, weights, and fuel types, but none are truly cheap (US$30-120) or light. Consider GAZ-powered stoves, which come with bottled butane/propane that is easy to use and widely available in Europe. The lower-tech camper should bring a small **metal grate** or a grill to take advantage of the campfire. A **first-aid kit, waterproof matches, Swiss army knife, insect repellent,** and a **"space blanket"** (US$5-15) are essential items. For more information about camping concerns, contact the **Automobile Association,** AA Publishing, P.O. Box 194, Rochester, Kent, ME2 4QG, U.K. (tel. (01634) 29 7123; fax 29 80 00). They publish a wide range of maps, atlases, and travel guides, including *Camping and Caravanning: Europe* (UK£8). Also try **The Caravan Club,** East Grinstead House, East Grinstead, West Sussex, RH19 1UA, U.K. (tel. (0342) 32 6944; fax 41 02 58), which produces a detailed English-language guide to campsites in Europe.

WILDERNESS AND SAFETY CONCERNS

The three most important things to remember when hiking or camping: stay warm, stay dry, stay hydrated. The vast majority of life-threatening wilderness problems stem from a failure to follow this advice. On any hike, however brief, you should pack enough equipment to keep you alive should disaster befall. This includes **rain gear,** warm layers of **synthetic materials** or **wool** (*absolutely not* cotton!)—especially **hat** and **mittens, a first-aid kit, high energy food,** and **water.** *There are no exceptions to this list.* Always check weather forecasts and pay attention to the skies when hiking. Let someone know that you are going hiking; tell either a friend, your hostel, a park ranger, the police or a local hiking organization. Do not attempt a hike beyond your ability—you'll be endangering your life.

Use caution when encountering any untamed animal, and cultivate a respect for the environment while remembering that the environment will not always return the favor. Weather patterns can change instantly. A bright blue sky can turn to rain—or even snow—before you can say "hypothermia." If you're on a day hike, and the weather turns nasty, turn back. If on an overnight, start looking immediately for shelter. You should never rely on cotton for warmth. This "death cloth" will be absolutely useless should it get wet. Instead, wear wool or synthetic materials designed for the outdoors. Fleece jackets and Gore-Tex© raingear are excellent choices.

Be sure to wear **hiking boots** appropriate for the terrain you are hiking. Two watchwords sum up the essentials of good footwear: ankle support. Twisted or sprained ankles could keep you from walking for hours or days. Your boots should fit snugly and comfortably over one or two wool socks and a thin liner sock. Be sure that the boots are broken in. A bad blister will ruin your hike. If you feel a "hotspot" coming, cover it with moleskin immediately.

The most important thing to remember while camping is to protect yourself from the environment. This means having a proper tent with rain-fly, warm sleeping bag, and proper clothing. See **Health,** p. 14, for information about outdoor ailments and diseases, as well as basic medical concerns and first aid.

Be concerned about the safety of the environment. Don't unnecessarily trample vegetation by walking off established paths. Because firewood is scarce in popular areas, campers are asked to make fires using only dead branches or brush; using a campstove is a more cautious (and efficient) way to cook. Don't cut vegetation or clear new campsites. Make sure your campsite is at least 150 feet from water supplies or bodies of water. If there are no toilet facilities, bury human waste (but not paper) at least four inches deep and 150 feet or more from any water supply or campsite. Pack your trash in a plastic bag and keep it with you until you reach a trash can.

▓ Keeping in Touch

MAIL

Sending Mail to Eastern Europe Mail can be sent internationally through **Poste Restante** (the international phrase for General Delivery) to most cities or towns; it's well worth using, and more reliable than you might think. Mark the envelope "HOLD" and address it, for example, "Andrew <u>DUDLEY</u>, Poste Restante, City, Country." The last name should be capitalized and underlined. The mail will go to a special desk in the central post office, unless you specify a post office by street address or postal code. For towns in the Czech Republic and Slovakia, you should put a "1" after the city name to ensure mail goes to the central post office. In Hungary, the last name is written first (i.e. <u>DUDLEY</u>, Andrew). As a rule, it is best to use the largest post office in the area; sometimes mail will be sent there regardless of what you write on the envelope. Letters are often opened by criminals in search of valuables or post office employees in search of contraband; *never* send cash. The cheapest letters you can send are aerograms (available at the post office), which provide a limited amount of writing space and fold into envelopes (no enclosures).

When picking up your mail, bring your passport or other ID. If the clerk insists there is nothing for you, ask them to check under your first name. In a few countries you have to pay a minimal fee per item. *Let's Go* lists post offices in the **Practical Information** section for each city and most towns.

American Express offices worldwide will act as a mail service for cardholders if contacted in advance. Under this free **"Client Letter Service,"** they hold mail for 30 days, forward upon request, and accept telegrams. Just like *Poste Restante,* the last name of the person to whom the mail is addressed should be capitalized and under-lined. Some offices offer these services to non-cardholders (especially those who have purchased AmEx Traveler's Cheques), but call ahead to make sure. Check the **Practical Information** sections of the cities you plan to visit for AmEx office locations. A complete list is available from AmEx (U.S. tel. (800) 528-4800) in the booklet *Traveller's Companion* (see p. 11) or on-line at http://www.americanexpress.com.

Sending Mail from Eastern Europe Allow at least one to two weeks for **airmail** from Eastern Europe to reach the U.S. or U.K., and more for Australia, New Zealand, and South Africa. Mail from parts of Eastern Europe can require up to six weeks. From Russia to anywhere has been known to take a year. It is far from guaranteed that the letter will actually reach its final destination, though chances are better in Central Europe and the Baltic States than in the former Soviet Union.

Surface mail is by far the cheapest and slowest way to send mail. It takes one to three months to cross the Atlantic, appropriate for sending large quantities of items you won't need to see for a while. It is vital, therefore, to distinguish your airmail from surface mail by explicitly labeling airmail in the appropriate language or writing *"par avion,"* which is universally understood. You can find how to say airmail in the local language by consulting the **Communication** section of each country's introduction. When ordering books and materials from another country, include one or two **International Reply Coupons (IRC),** available at the post office, with your request. IRCs provide the recipient of your order with postage to cover delivery.

TELEPHONES

The **country code** is listed in *Let's Go* at the beginning of each country's chapter with the exchange rates. In large cities and towns, city **phone codes** are listed at the end of the **Practical Information** sections. For smaller towns, look for the local code at the end of a paragraph within the write-up.

Some countries in Eastern Europe do not have an international dialing code to dial out; you must go through the operator. In some others, you must wait for a tone after the international dialing code. For more information, see each country's **Essentials.**

You can sometimes make **direct international calls** from a pay phone, but you may need to feed money in as you speak. In some countries, pay phones are card-operated; some even accept credit cards. English-speaking operators are often available for assistance. Operators in many Eastern European countries will place **collect (reverse charge) calls** for you, but it's cheaper to find a pay phone and deposit just enough money to be able to say "Call me" and give your number (though some pay phones can't receive calls).

Some companies, seizing this "call-me-back" concept, have created **callback phone services.** Under these plans, you call a specified number, ring once, and hang up. The company's computer calls back and gives you a dial tone. You can then make all the calls as you want, at rates about 20-60% lower than you'd pay using credit cards or pay phones. This option is most economical for loquacious travelers, as services may include a US$10-25 minimum billing per month. For information, call **America Tele-Fone** (U.S. tel. (800) 321-5817), **Globaltel** (tel. (770) 449-1295), **International Telephone** (U.S. tel. (800) 638-5558), and **Telegroup** (U.S. tel. (800) 338-0225).

A **calling card** is another alternative; your local long-distance phone company will have a number for you to dial while traveling (either toll-free or charged as a local call) to connect instantly to an operator in your home country. The calls (plus a small surcharge) are then billed either collect or to a calling card. For information in the U.S., call **AT&T Direct** services at (tel. (888) 288-4685, from abroad (810) 262-6644); **Sprint** (tel. (800) 877-4646, from abroad (913) 624-5335); or **MCI WorldPhone** (tel. (800) 444-4141). In Canada, contact **Canada Direct** (tel. (800) 565-4708); in the U.K., **BT Direct** (tel. (800) 34 51 44); in Ireland, **Ireland Direct** (tel. (800) 25 02 50); in Australia, **Australia Direct** (tel. 13 22 00); in New Zealand, **Telecom New Zealand** (tel. 123); and in South Africa, **Telkom South Africa** (tel. 09 03).

FAXES, EMAIL, AND MORE

Major cities have bureaus (often at the post office) where you can pay to send and receive **faxes.** If you're spending a year abroad and want to keep in touch with friends or colleagues, **electronic mail** ("email") is an attractive option. It takes a minimum of computer knowledge and a little prearranged planning, and it beams messages anywhere for no per-message charges. Befriend college students abroad and ask if you can use their email accounts. If you're not the finagling type, **Traveltales.com** (http://traveltales.com) provides free web-based email for travelers and maintains a list of cybercafes, travel links, and a travelers' chat room. Other free web-based email providers include **Hotmail** (http://www.hotmail.com), **RocketMail** (http://www.rocketmail.com), and **USANET** (http://www.usa.net). Many free email providers are funded by advertising, and some may require subscribers to fill out a questionnaire. Search through http://www.cyberiacafe.net/guide/ccafe.htm, or in the **Practical Information** sections of our major cities to find a list of cybercafes around the world in which you can drink a cup of joe and email him, too.

ALBANIA (SHQIPËRIA)

US$1 = 155 lekë	100 lekë =	US$0.63
CDN$1= 112 lekë	100 lekë =	CDN$0.89
UK£1 = 247 lekë	100 lekë =	UK£0.41
IR£1 = 227 lekë	100 lekë =	IR£0.44
AUS$1 = 113 lekë	100 lekë =	AUS$0.89
NZ$1 = 98 lekë	100 lekë =	NZ$1.08

SAR1 = 33 lekë	100 lekë = SAR3.03
DM1 = 85 lekë	100 lekë = DM1.18
Country Phone Code: 355	International Dialing Prefix: 00

The U.S. State Department has issued a **Travel Warning** advising against unnecessary travel to Albania. Due to the political situation in Albania, *Let's Go* did not send a researcher to the country for this edition. However, information in this chapter has been checked by phone this year. During summer 1997, a state of emergency existed in Albania, including a 10pm-5am curfew. According to a State Department update issued August 14, 1997, the curfew and state of emergency have been lifted, and the government has "reasserted limited control" over the capital. Nonetheless, the situation is still "cause for concern, due to the continuation of bombings and sporadic gunfire...as well as an increase in criminal activity...American citizens should avoid travel outside the capital unless absolutely necessary." American citizens in Albania are urged to register with the U.S. embassy in Tirana. For updates on this travel warning, contact the U.S. State Department (see **Essentials: Safety and Security**, p. 14).

Proud, fierce, and defiant, Albania has played a part in every upsurge of the struggle between East and West. Over the centuries, the nation has had barely a moment's rest between attacks from its neighbors, yet every time it has resisted with a fury that frightened far stronger powers. "Albanians have always had a taste for killing or getting themselves killed. They have killed each other when they haven't had anyone else to fight," snorts a frustrated enemy general in Albanian author Ismail Kadarë's novel *The General of the Dead Army.* Sadly, Albania's recent descent into anarchy poignantly illustrates the general's sentiment.

ALBANIA ESSENTIALS

A visa is not required of citizens of Australia, Canada, Ireland, New Zealand, the U.K., or the U.S. South Africans need a visa (US$15), which is valid for three months. Although not necessary, a letter of invitation, or even a letter explaining the reason for the trip, can facilitate your application. The application process takes two weeks. You may obtain a visa extension at the Ministry of Foreign Affairs in Tirana. Travelers of all nationalities may or may not need to pay an unofficial US$20 "entrance fee" at the door, depending on whether the border guards feel like demanding it. A similarly unofficial "exit fee" of US$10 may be necessary. Welcome to Albania.

GETTING THERE AND GETTING AROUND

The most convenient way to reach Albania is by **plane.** Alitalia and Swissair operate flights from Zurich and Rome, and the Slovenian Adria Air links Tirana with major European cities, including London, and Paris. Albanian Airlines flies to Tirana from Frankfurt. **Ferries** link Durrës with Italian ports. International **buses,** of a higher quality than domestic ones, but still not 100% reliable, run to Athens, Istanbul and Sofia.

Between cities, **buses** are the least offensive choice. Albanian roads cling to steep mountains, while giant, old vehicles compete like road warriors on the narrow paths. There are no traffic lights outside the capital, nor are there road rules. **Trains** are slower and less comfortable, but cheaper. Substantial sections of track were destroyed during the anti-Communist upheaval of 1991, and again during the unrest in 1997. All rails lead to Durrës, and trains run to many other towns within Albania, but no foreign cities. **Car rental** is one way to see the countryside without restricting yourself to train or bus "schedules." A driver often comes with the deal. Find one through an agency in Tirana or Durrës, or simply by approaching a taxi in the street. It's possible to argue the price down to a third of the first quoted price. A good way to get a low price is to ask if anyone knows a friend willing to drive. Renting a car is possible with an international driver's license. Driving in Albania without insurance is not recommended. **Hitchhiking** is legal, and those who do it hold out one hand and wave. Riders are expected to pay. Accidents on Albania's narrow mountain roads are usually head-on collision or cliff dives. In light of this, entrusting a motoring yahoo with one's life may not be such a great idea, and *Let's Go* does not recommend it.

TOURIST SERVICES AND MONEY

Travel agencies are usually open 9am-7pm, with a long afternoon break (typically 1-4pm). Most travel bureaus that sell international bus tickets speak English. **American Express** in Tirana performs all the tasks of a tourist agency.

The monetary unit is the **lek**, the plural of which—lekë—is pronounced the same way. In reaction to the devaluation of the lek during the economic crises of 1997, the **U.S. dollar** is presently the currency of choice; Deutschmarks, however, are not a widely accepted hard-currency alternative. **Traveler's checks** are virtually unknown outside of Tirana. **Moneychangers** offer the highest rates and are especially trustworthy in smaller towns, but be sure you know what the lek looks like. In larger towns, **exchange bureaus** offer good rates and safety. **Credit cards** are slowly coming into use. American Express is commonly accepted in hotels; Visa and MasterCard may be more difficult to use. The lek was devalued by a factor of 10 in 1965, but, surprisingly, many still quote prices in old lekë.

COMMUNICATION AND LANGUAGE

Postal service within Albania is reliable but slow. Airmail in Albanian is *postë ajrore*. The **telephone** is probably faster, although only occasionally capable of international calls. International calls can be made via a local operator, or direct from certain locations. Avoid calling from your hotel, as they may charge upwards of US$10 per minute to the U.S. Most Albanian towns have no direct telephone code. Public telephones can be found at post offices.

Years of **Italian** television account for the popularity of the language in Tirana, although younger Tiranans are liable to speak some **English** too. Older Albanians may speak **Russian**. **Greek** is common in the south. Beware if you are attempting to communicate non-verbally that Albanians nod to mean "no" and shake their heads to indicate "yes." "No" is also indicated by a wagging of the index finger. This can be very confusing when you're trying to ascertain where a bus is headed or whether a hotel is in a particular direction. Reinforce your own responses with *po* (yes) and *jo* (no).

Albanian (called *Shqip* by Albanians) is the only surviving descendant of Illyrian. During centuries of foreign rule, it adopted many words from Latin, Greek, Turkish, Italian, and Slavic languages. Two main dialects can be distinguished: *Geg* (or *Gheg*) in the north and *Tosk* in the south. **Pronunciation** is phonetic. There are seven **vowels:** *i* (ee), *e* (eh), *a* (ah), *o* (oh), *u* (oo), *ë* (e as in "chooses"), and *y* (ü as in German "über"). The final *ë* is silent. **Consonants** are as in English, except for: *ç* (ch as in "chimichanga"), *dh* (th as in "this"), *gj* (j as in "jinx"), *j* (y as in "yen"), *q* (ch as in "cheesy"), *x* (dz as in "adze"), and *xh* (j as in "judge"). See the **Glossary,** p. 797.

HEALTH AND SAFETY

During summer 1997, the U.S. State Department issued a **travel warning** advising against travel to Albania. At press time, the government had regained some control over Tirana, the capital, but large portions of the rest of the country, particularly the south, were considered **extremely dangerous.**

Single **women** travelers may feel uncomfortable, since foreign women are sometimes seen as "easy." Although Albanian men are fairly polite, they are prone to catcalls. Later in the day, there are many more men than women on the streets, and women almost never go into a cafe or restaurant alone. However, even there you will likely encounter surprise, not hostility. Avoid loud cafes; the crowd there has probably had a good deal of *raki* (the local firewater). Going out alone at night is not advised.

Electrical grids cover only a block or two, so even if you have no power, your neighbor might. Power outages are worst in winter. Currently, tap **water** is available only three times a day: 8am, 2pm, and 8pm. Bottled water is a much better bet for drinking and is easily available. Although there are **pharmacies** in many cities, they are not very well-stocked. Foreign brands of shampoo, razors, and tampons are common in Tirana, but less so elsewhere.

ACCOMMODATIONS AND CAMPING

Private hotels are springing up with encouraging frequency. These range from gorgeous and friendly to cramped but still friendly, and the facilities are generally better than those of their state-run counterparts. Many larger hotels may be refurbished in the next few years. Rooms run 1000 to 3000 lekë (US$10-30) per person. As of yet, the only **hostels** in Albania are connected with missionary groups. A few travel agencies in Tirana find **private rooms** for those who inquire. Although hot water, or water at all, is usually not guaranteed, the stay is much more pleasant than in a large hotel. Many people you meet will offer a night in their home for US$5-15. Whether you find your lodging through an agency or through luck, you will probably be given the largest bed in the house, possibly in a room with a few other people, and be fed dinner, coffee, and *raki*. There are no **camping** facilities in Albania. Free camping is legal—but consider the safety risks. You might see tents in the countryside, but they are likely the homes of impoverished Albanians.

FOOD AND DRINK

Albanian **cuisine** revolves around *mish* (meat) and *patate* (potatoes), which usually can be ordered *me garniturë* (with vegetables), probably salted and oiled. The predominance of *djathë* (feta cheese) recalls Greek cuisine. *Kos,* Albanian yogurt, is served at most meals. Also popular are *oriz më tamel,* a sheep's-milk rice pudding, and *byrek,* meat or cheese dumplings. Salads are a popular prelude to a meal and are often accompanied by *raki,* made of fruit juice and drunk in small sips. Poverty and anarchy have shortened the menu for most Albanians. Bread may constitute more than 50% of one's diet. The remaining portion consists mainly of milk products, most notably feta and yellow cheese (*kaçkaval*).

CUSTOMS AND ETIQUETTE

Albanian **hospitality** is influenced by the *Kanun*—the legendary code of the medieval lawgiver Lek Dukagjini, who succeeded Skanderbeg as leader of the Krujë fortress. It will even override revenge, so that a house will shelter and feed a man who has killed one of its members. (The *Kanun* is available in English, with prescriptions on all aspects of life from vendetta etiquette to the ritual of the first haircut.) Assuming things don't get so dramatic, you will be served coffee and *raki* and offered a smoke whenever you enter a home. It is polite to accept it, but no offense will be taken if a cigarette is refused. It is customary to take off your shoes upon crossing the threshold of a house. In the north, it is considered a sign of satisfaction if you wipe your plate with bread at the end of your meal. In restaurants, **tipping** is expected (about 10%).

For women, **dress** is more conservative in Albania than elsewhere in Europe, although shorts and jeans are becoming more common, especially in larger cities. Men rarely wear shorts, even under the hottest sun. Long hair and beards, forbidden under the Communist regime, are increasingly popular, especially among young 'uns. A two-sided kiss is the normal greeting and farewell between women. Men greet each other with several kisses on the cheek and often walk around arm in arm. **Homosexuality** was legalized in Albania in 1995, thanks to international pressures. A harmful by-product of Albanian nationalism is **racial prejudice**, which is directed mainly against gypsies.

LIFE AND TIMES

HISTORY

Archaeological and anthropological studies indicate that Albanians are the direct descendants of the ancient **Illyrian tribes** who inhabited the west part of the Balkans in the 12th and 11th centuries BC. In the 8th century BC, the **Greeks** began founding colonies in the region—most notably, Epidamnus (modern Durrës) and Apollonia (near modern Vlorë). Illyrian tribes began to create alliances, thus forming the basis for future kingdoms. In the late 3rd century BC, the **Roman Empire** defeated Illyria. Throughout this period, the Illyrians managed to maintain their own culture, although Latin came into use and the Illyrian religion was increasingly replaced by Christianity after it was introduced in the 1st century AD.

In 395, the Roman Empire was divided, and the area of modern Albania became part of the **Byzantine Empire.** Illyrian lands were invaded regularly by tribes of Visigoths, Huns, Ostrogots and Slavs until the 6th century, but the southern Illyrian tribes resisted assimilation, and succeeded in preserving their unique tongue. The name Illyria over time became **Albanoi,** then **Arbëri,** and, finally Albania. In the 17th century, Albanians started calling themselves shqiptarë, meaning "sons of eagles," and their country Shqipëri, "the land of the eagle."

The Albanian Church was controlled from Rome until 732 when it began to fall under Constantinople's jurisdiction. Albania experienced its first religious fragmentation in 1054 when the Christian church split between the East and Rome. North Albania reverted to the control of the Pope, and Greek and Latin became the official languages for cultural pursuits. Albanian was recognized by neither church nor state as an official language. The Byzantine Empire proved too weak to protect Albania from successive invasions by Bulgarians, Normans, and Venetians, and in 1347, the country was occupied by the **Serbs.**

Under later **Ottoman** rule, Albania was built on a feudal system of landed estates (*timars*). As the empire declined, the power of the *timar*-holding military lords increased. Some tried to create separate states within the empire, but were overthrown by the sultan. To escape persecution, two-thirds of the population had converted to Islam by the 17th century. Turkey eventually abolished the *timar* system in 1831, and power passed from feudal lords to tribal chieftains.

In response to the oppressive Ottoman rule, the **Albanian League** was founded in 1878 with the goal of unifying all Albanian territories (Kosovo, Shkodër, Monastir, and Janina) and stimulating the growth of Albanian language, literature, and education. By the time the Turks suppressed the League in 1881, and its leaders went into exile, it had become a symbol of national feeling and desire for independence. When the Balkan states declared war on Turkey in October 1912, Albanians issued the **Vlorë Proclamation** of independence to protect Albania from Slavic invaders. After the defeat of Turkey, the **conference of the Great Powers** agreed to recognize independent Albania. Ethnic divisions were ignored, however: Kosovo—still an object of Balkan ethnic strife today—was given to Serbia, and other regions went to Greece.

> **Enver Hoxha formed and then rejected ties with the USSR, Yugoslavia, and China, finally closing Albania's doors to foreigners entirely.**

During **WWI,** Albania's neighbors threatened to partition the country; U.S. President Wilson vetoed this possibility at the **Paris Peace Conference of 1918,** and Albania became independent again. In the early 1920s, Albania experienced internal conflict between conservatives, led by the chieftain **Ahmed Zogu,** and liberals, led by **Bishop Fan Noli.** Noli was elected prime minister in 1924 and began democratization. The process lasted only a few months before Zogu overthrew the government. He crowned himself King Zog I in 1928, but his reign collapsed under Italian occupation in 1939. The ethnically Albanian regions of Kosovo and Çamëria were reunified with the rest of Albania by the Axis powers in 1941, but after the war, the territories were reincorporated back into the neighboring countries and Albania once again fell under the heavy yoke of dictatorship. This time the yoke was the self-aggrandizing Communist **Enver Hoxha,** who had led the wartime resistance. Until his death in 1985, he formed and then rejected ties with Yugoslavia, the Soviet Union, and China, finally closing Albania's doors to foreigners entirely. Travel abroad was severely restricted and religion banned, but Hoxha's portrait was found in every home.

Hoxha's successor, **Ramiz Alia,** faced growing opposition after the fall of Communism throughout Eastern Europe in 1989. Seeking to preserve the regime, Alia granted the right to travel abroad, restored religious freedom, and endorsed the creation of independent political parties. Finally, after numerous concessions to the opposition (largely intellectuals, the working class, and youth), the regime collapsed when it lost the March 1992 elections. Alia was succeeded as president by **Sali Berisha.** In 1996, Berisha's Democratic Party won the Parliamentary election, but the results and procedures of the election were contested by the opposition—mostly notably the former Communists, now renamed the Socialist Party.

LITERATURE

For centuries, politics and power have controlled the tongues in which Albanian authors could express themselves. Albanians have not taken this cultural subservience lying down, however, and have protested with counter-attacks of their own.

Latin dominated the written language until medieval times. The earliest known Albanian work is the 1462 "Baptizing Formula," by **Archbishop Paul Angelus.** During the period of Ottoman occupation, Albania was subject to cultural constraints and isolated from the rest of Europe. During the 16th and 17th centuries, only Roman Catholic missionaries were able to secure permission from the Ottoman rulers to publish books in Albania. Many Albanians, rejecting Ottoman cultural dominance, migrated to Southern Italy, forming a group now known as the **Arbëresh.**

In the 1870s, literary renewal accompanied the political attempt to emerge from under the thumb of the Turks. Arbëresh journalist and poet **Jeronim de Rada** (1814-1903) essentially fathered the movement, compiling arcane fragments of folklore and reconstituting them into poetic epics such as *Skanderbeg* (1873). Unable to express overt nationalism within Albania, expatriates established societies abroad to publish the patriotic works of writers and poets, and smuggle them into Albania. Other participants in this Renaissance, such as the poet **Ndrë Mjeda,** considered new alternatives for the alphabet, and a revised, standard orthography using Roman letters was constructed by the poet **Gjergj Fishta** and adopted by the **Monastir Congress** at Bitola (in modern Macedonia) in 1908-09.

> The change to a consolidated form of Albanian served to eliminate ideas espoused by the Gheg writers.

Following Albania's independence in 1912, novels and dramas recounting the role of Albanian highlanders in the fight for independence were produced by the likes of **Mihal Grameno, Foqion Postoli,** and **Mehdi Frashëri.** Between the World Wars, the translations of **Bishop Fan Noli** were responsible for introducing Albania to the works of Shakespeare and other foreign playwrights.

Under socialism, the Party attempted to formulate a "unified" Albanian language from the Gheg and Tosk variants as part of the **"Albanian Cultural Renaissance"** (1966-69). The product of this concoction was a Tosk-oriented language that actually eliminated numerous words employed in literary Gheg. While Tosk writers, such as the poet **Naim Frashëri** (1846-1900), had already enriched the literary language of their dialect enough to allow such a change, some saw the move as a politically motivated decision by the Communists. The change to a consolidated form of Albanian served to eliminate ideas espoused by Gheg writers, as students attempting to read a northern writer would have been unable to find the necessary vocabulary in any dictionary. The "Cultural Renaissance" in reality occasioned "cultural suppression," and the most independent of the postwar authors were imperiously suppressed. Poet and novelist **Ismaíl Kadarë** did, however, manage to continue his creations, composing numerous fictional works until he went into exile in 1990. These include *Gjenerali i* *ushtërisë së vdekur* (1963; *The General of the Dead Army*), about an Italian army general who enters Albania after the war, and *Doruntine,* set in the medieval period, yet dealing with Communist rule, a conflict between the Eastern and Western churches, Gheg-Tosk divisions, and the longing for the homeland of Albanian writers.

ALBANIA TODAY

In January 1997, shady pyramid savings schemes that had operated for three years—and in which the government is widely believed to have colluded—finally collapsed. Many Albanians who had invested their life savings in the get-rich-quick schemes were enraged, and anti-government riots became widespread. Albania's leadership responded to the protests with force. The deadliest violence erupted in Tirana and in the south. In March, as Parliament re-elected **Sali Berisha** as president (opposition leaders boycotted the vote), a state of emergency was declared and government troops introduced curfews and censorship. Western nations evacuated their citizens, and Albanians desperately attempted to flee the country. With rebels in control of the entire south, Berisha agreed to form an interim government, in preparation for new elections. In April a U.N.-approved multinational force arrived with humanitarian aid. Deadly violence marred June's elections, in which Berisha's Democratic Party lost to Fatos Nano's Socialist Party. Berisha resigned in July, and Parliament elected Socialist Party Secretary-General **Rexhep Meidani** as his replacement. After five months of anarchy, the new government's first concern must be order. Until the various militia groups and gangs are disarmed, investors won't employ the cheap Albanian labor, and tourists will steer clear of Albania's gorgeous landscapes and unspoiled rugged stone cities.

Tirana (Tiranë)

Appearing from nowhere among the Albanian hills, Tirana is one of those places where horses and carts still jostle in traffic with the latest European and Japanese cars. In some ways the entire city looks like a construction zone, with open man-holes, crumbling exteriors, broken glass, and banana peels scattered over the streets. The unprepared little village heroically withstood a series of grandiose Communist designs to become what it is now—a somewhat awkward, but still endearing city. Established as the capital in 1920, when it was only a few huts divided by a cobbled path, Tirana could never be accused of being glamorous, yet it is anything but dull.

ORIENTATION AND PRACTICAL INFORMATION

In general, Albanians are not big on grids, street names, or street numbers. A street may not be marked, and if it is, the name may not correspond to that on the map; building numbers present an equally baffling prospect. To identify with the locals' sense of landmarks, position yourself in **Sheshi Skanderbeg** (Skanderbeg Sq.) facing south. Through the square runs **Bulevardi Dëshmorët e Kombit,** the town's main thoroughfare, which extends towards Tirana University in the south, and the **train station** to the north. The staff of **Albania Travel & Tours,** Rr. Durresit 102 (tel./fax 329 83 or 339 81), books plane and ferry tickets and speaks English (open Mon.-Fri. 8am-7pm, Sat.-Sun. 8:30am-1:30pm). Private **exchange offices** generally offer decent rates. The **U.S. Embassy** is located at Rr. Elbasanit 103 (tel. 328 75 or 335 20; fax 322 22). Walk toward the university on Blvd. Dëshmorët e Kombit, turn left after the Prime Minister's office, right at the TV station, then immediately left. The street ends when it hits Rr. Elbasanit; the yellow embassy is ahead and to the right (open Mon.-Fri 8am-4:30pm, consular section open 1-4:30pm). **American Express,** 65 Rr. Durrësit (tel. 279 08; fax 320 27 or 279 08), provides cash advances and emergency cash, cashes traveler's checks in lekë and US$ for a 1-4% commission (depending on the sum), stocks **maps,** holds mail for members (others are not officially refused), sells ferry tickets, rents cars and drivers, arranges private accommodations, and organizes group and individual tours (open Mon.-Fri. 8:30am-3pm, Sat.-Sun. 8:30am-1pm). **Rinas Airport** is 26km from town. The **train station** lies at the north end of Blvd. Dëshmorët e Kombit. **Albes-Turist** (tel. 421 66) sends **buses** to Istanbul (US$40) and Sofia (US$25). **Travel Agency Memedheu** operates out of a kiosk on the left of Tirana International Hotel and runs buses to Istanbul (2 per week, US$40), Sofia (2 per week, US$25), and Skopje (daily, DM30). There's a **pharmacy** at Blvd. Dëshmorët e Kombit, on the corner opposite Hotel Arberia (tel. 245 42; open daily 8am-9pm). The **post office** is behind the National Bank, a bit to the right (open daily 7am-7pm). A **postal code** is not required for letters to Albania. **Phone code: 42.**

ACCOMMODATIONS AND FOOD

Older hotels' offerings are usually poor value, while more desirable private hotels and rooms are becoming easier to find. Any time you meet an Albanian, it is worth finding out whether he or she knows anyone willing to let a room. Otherwise, **American Express** makes such arrangements in a more organized fashion (private rooms US$10 per person and up). It's worth asking whether a hotel has its own supply of water and water-heating facilities, as, despite promises by the government, tap water is often cold or just plain unavailable.

As part of the inexplicable building boom, restaurants and cafes seem to pop up like mushrooms after the rain. A few bottles of *raki,* some music, and a jolly crowd of Tiranans discussing the world and patting each other on the back make the day go by in a flash. Summer street vendors sell fruits and vegetables; these are usually safe to eat, but be sure to wash and peel them. **Bakeries,** identifiable by *Bukë* signs, are more common on quiet streets off the main thoroughfares. Read the posted prices, hand your money through the window, and your bread will be handed back. **Kiosks,** selling chocolate bars and soft drinks, are like the police force—numerous and strategically placed.

SIGHTS AND ENTERTAINMENT

Communism has not been entirely eradicated from Skanderbeg Sq. Stark architecture stares from blank facades, and a **Socialist mural "Albania"** adorns the front of the **National Historic Museum,** which offers a crash course in Albanian history on three floors. The once-ominous site now serves as a playground with bumper cars and swirly rides. **Skanderbeg's statue** stands near an **18th-century mosque** (don't forget to take off your shoes). Down Blvd. Dëshmorët e Kombit on the left, the **National Art Gallery** exhibits contemporary paintings, some definitive works of Albanian Communist Realism, anonymous Renaissance works, and, of course, several large busts and paintings featuring the omnipresent Skanderbeg. Further along, the immense pyramidal **Cultural Center**—a must in all Eastern Bloc capitals—houses temporary displays arranged by various industrial or political groups. **Tirana University** fills the adjacent area. Behind it, **Parku i Madh** (Big Park) provides a welcome rush of untamed greenery. **Krujë fortress** is an hour away from Tirana.

Beyond the top of the hill, local kids have turned a **lake** into an impromptu beach. Along the "river" and in the park that begins at the corner of Dëshmorë e Kombit and Myslym Shyri is the biggest concentration of **cafes**—enough to accommodate all of Tirana's citizens. The **opera house** holds evening performances. The ticket window is on the left of the facade. **Soccer** games are popular weekend entertainment.

ALBANIA

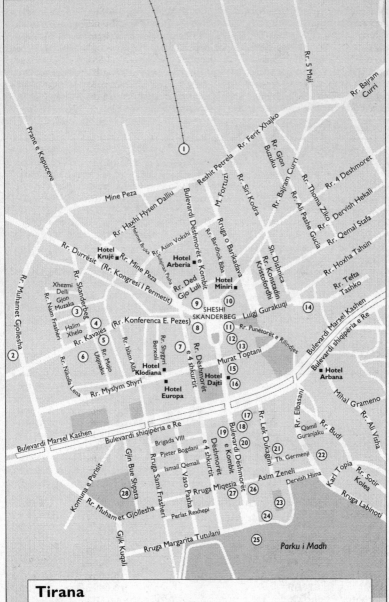

Tirana

Catholic Church, 5	National Bank, 8	Post Office, 7
City Hall, 12	National Theater, 13	Radiotelevision, 21
Cultural Center, 17	Office of the President, 27	Savings Bank, 19
Embassies, 3	Office of the Prime Minister, 20	Stadiumi Dinamo, 28
Embassy USA, 22	Orthodox Church, 6	Stadiumi Q. Stafa, 23
Historical Museum, 9	Opera House, 10	Taxi Station, 14
Ministry of Finance, 18	Palace of Congresses, 26	Tirana University, 24
Ministry of Tourism, 16	Pharmacy, 4	Train Station, 1
Mosque, 11	Police, 2	
National Art Gallery, 15	Polytechnic University, 25	

BELARUS
(БЕЛАРУСЬ)

US$1	= 27,500BR (Belarusian rubles)	10,000BR =	US$0.36
CDN$1	= 20,430BR	10,000BR =	CDN$0.49
UK£1	= 43,170BR	10,000BR =	UK£0.23
IR£1	= 44,800BR	10,000BR =	IR£0.23
AUS$1	= 20,480BR	10,000BR =	AUS$0.49
NZ$1	= 18,220BR	10,000BR =	NZ$0.55
SAR1	= 7600BR	10,000BR =	SAR1.32
DM1	= 18,000BR	10,000BR =	DM0.57
Country Phone Code: 375		**International Dialing Prefix: 810**	

> Inflation is rampant in Belarus, meaning that the Belarusian ruble is likely to lose much of its value. We list many prices in U.S. dollars for comparative purposes.

For as long as anyone can remember, Belarus has always been the backwater of someone else's empire, and today it remains the black sheep of Eastern Europe. The fall of the USSR left Belarus directionless, grasping for a national identity. While other republics were toppling their statues of Lenin, Belarusians polished theirs. Soviet bureaucracy persists needlessly in much of the nation: businesses lack effective management and services, border and travel regulations discourage tourism and unnecessarily restrict natives, and taxes and regulations make living devastatingly difficult. If capitalism is seeping into Belarus, it's acting more like a nest of termites than the Big Bad Wolf. Burdened by low wages, rising prices, crippling inflation, and a nightmare of a legal system, the Belarusian people, known to be the most patient of the Slavs, are finding it hard to hold their breath.

BELARUS ESSENTIALS

To visit Belarus, you must secure an invitation and a visa—an expensive and head-spinning process. If you have an acquaintance in Belarus who can provide you with an official invitation, you may obtain a 90-day single-entry (5-day service US$50, next-day US$100) or multiple-entry (5-day processing US$300; no rush service) visa at an embassy or consulate (see **Embassies and Consulates,** p. 3). Together with the visa application and fee (by personal check or money order), you must submit your passport and one photograph. Those without Belarusian friends may turn to **Russia House** (see **Russia Essentials,** p. 514), which will get you an invitation and visa in five business days (US$145; rush service US$215). **Host Families Association (HOFA)** provides invitations for HOFA guests (see **Russia Essentials,** p. 514). You may also obtain an invitation by planning your trip through a **Belintourist** office. They will provide you with documentation after you have pre-paid all your hotel stays. Transit visas (US$20-30), valid for 48 hours, are issued at a consulate or at the border, but if your train leaves while you're still outside getting your visa, that's your problem. At some Belarusian embassies and consulates, such as those in Daugavpils, Latvia and Kiev, Ukraine, transit visas may be cheaper. At the border, expect to be carefully watched, documented, interrogated, and escorted as scads of soldiers do the old-school evil-empire thing. Don't worry, it's harmless.

GETTING THERE AND GETTING AROUND

You can fly into Minsk from London, Berlin, Frankfurt, Vienna, Warsaw, and Moscow on **Belavia,** Belarus's national airline (if you trust old Aeroflot planes, that is). **LOT** also flies from Warsaw, and **Lufthansa** has daily direct flights from Frankfurt. Leaving Belarus by air can be a nightmare, as customs officials rip through your bags. **Buses** and **trains** connect Brest to Warsaw, Prague, Kiev, and Lviv, and Hrodna to Warsaw, Białystok in Poland, and Vilnius. Brest and Hrodna are massive railway junctions— you'll see more trains headed there than Lenin statues in Minsk. Tickets for same-day **trains** within Belarus can be purchased at the station. Information booths in the stations charge 2000BR per inquiry; it's better to ask a cashier. For **city buses,** buy tickets at a kiosk (or, for a slight surcharge, from the driver) and punch them on board. **Hitchhiking** is popular outside of the large cities, and locals do not consider it dangerous. To catch a car, people point their forefingers to the ground. *Let's Go* does not recommend hitchhiking.

TOURIST SERVICES AND MONEY

Belintourist (Белінтурíст) is the organizational remnant of the once-omnipotent Intourist. It varies from mostly helpful to merely rubble, but is often the only resource available. The staff hands out cool Soviet-era brochures and sometimes offers pricey tours, but seems to cater to businesspeople, locals, or often nobody. **Private travel agencies** are springing up, including the very helpful **Belarusian Society for Friendship and Cultural Relations with Foreign Countries** in Minsk.

Be sure to carry a hefty supply of hard **cash.** U.S. dollars, Deutschmarks, and Russian rubles are the preferred media of exchange; you will have a great deal of trouble changing other currencies, even the British pound. In addition, bills over US$20 may be difficult to exchange—the same is true of bills that are worn, torn, or dated pre-1993. A black currency market still exists, and its kings will easily fool naive foreigners. There are no **ATMs** aside from one or two that have recently popped up in Minsk, and bank clerks leaf through their English dictionaries at the mention of "traveler's checks." Some hotels accept **credit cards,** mostly AmEx, EC, and Visa. Cash advances on Visa and sometimes MC are available (for a 4% commission) at Priorbank (Приорбанк) offices in most cities, and at the occasional hotel lobby.

COMMUNICATION

Avoid the unreliable **mail** system at all costs; there is an off chance that something sent will reach you by *Poste Restante,* but it may be opened and read by the KGB first. Public **telephones** have poor sound quality. **Local calls** require tokens purchased at kiosks (2500BR), or magnetic cards, available at the post office (100,000-200,000BR). **International calls** must be placed at the post office and paid for exorbitantly in advance, in cash. To call the U.S. (35,000BR per min.), Western Europe (11,000-20,000BR per min.), or Australia or New Zealand (up to 40,000BR per min.), write down the number you're calling and say *"Ya ba-tchoo po-ZVAH-neet"* ("I'd like to call...") followed by the name of the country; pay for the call with exact change. You will be told the number of a phone booth, which you then enter to make your call. Blue magnetic **cardphones** in the post office, train station, and some hotels also do the trick; buy cards at the post office (100,000-200,000BR). International access numbers include: **AT&T,** tel. 8 800 101; **BT Direct,** tel. 8 800 44; **MCI,** tel. 8 800 103 from Minsk, Hrodna, Brest, or Vitebsk, or tel. 8 10 80 01 03 from Homel or Mogilev. Wait a few seconds after the first 8 before dialing the rest of the number.

LANGUAGE

Belarusians have been more Russified than any other ethnic minority in the former Soviet Union, to the extent that most Belarusians speak mostly **Russian** and only very rarely Belarusian (see **The Cyrillic Alphabet,** p. 797, and the **Russian Glossary,** p. 811). In Hrodna and Brest, **Polish** is fairly common. Some young people will also speak a little **German** and **English.** Most street and place names have been converted into Belarusian, although locals still use the old Russian versions, which can lead to a bit of confusion. If you can handle substituting the Belarusian "i" for the Russian "и" and other minor spelling changes, you'll be fine. The only major difference is that the Cyrillic letter "г," which is pronounced "g" in Russian, is transliterated as "h" in Belarusian. *Let's Go* lists place names in Belarusian in deference to the official line, but keep in mind that in order to be understood, you may have to replace "h" with "g" (i.e., "Hrodna" is more commonly pronounced "Grodno").

HEALTH AND SAFETY

Emergency Numbers: Fire: tel. 01. **Police:** tel. 02. **Ambulance:** tel. 03.

Belarus was more affected by the 1986 **Chernobyl** accident than any other region. The faulty reactor was situated in Ukraine just 12km south of the Belarusian border, and winds happened to blow north for the first six days after the explosion; hence, nearly 70% of the radioactive material blew into Belarus and sank into the soil of the southeast quarter of the nation. An area of approximately 1200 sq. km just north of Chernobyl has been completely evacuated on account of the extremely high concentrations of strontium-90, plutonium-239/240, and cesium-137. Today, more than 10 years after the Chernobyl tragedy, it is safe to travel through the formerly contaminated areas; experts say that a week's stay there will affect you no more than receiving an X-ray. None of the cities *Let's Go* covers are in affected regions. There's no need to panic, but it is important to be aware of a few safety considerations when choosing food and drink. Avoid inexpensive **dairy products,** which are likely to come from contaminated areas (opt instead for something German or Dutch), and also stay away from **mushrooms** and **berries,** which tend to collect radioactivity. Drink only bottled water; **tap water,** especially in the southeast, may be contaminated.

Belarusian **crime** seems as underdeveloped as the rest of the country, but economic hardship has brought many opportunists. Your embassy is probably a better bet than the police in an emergency—especially because some police have been known to have dealings with the mafia and may not be helpful to foreigners unless bribed. Although streets are usually safe and well-lit, the alcohol problem in Belarus is escalating, and it is generally not a good idea to go out alone after dark. For children under 18 years old unaccompanied by an adult, there is a **mandatory 11pm curfew.** If you are approached by someone asking if you need your bottle once your drink is empty, give it to them—they can collect the deposit, which they'll need more than you do. **Toilet paper** is available in most supermarkets, but is generally absent from public toilets. **Condoms** and **feminine hygiene supplies** from the other side of the former Iron Curtain are beginning to turn up in droves.

ACCOMMODATIONS AND CAMPING

There are no **hostels** in Belarus, apart from *turbazy* ("tour-bases"), which only Stalinist pioneers with Siberian upbringings will be able to bear. Remember to keep all those little receipts from your hotels, because you just might have to show them to the authorities to avoid fines on your way out of the country. **Hotels** have three sets of rates—very cheap for Belarusians, outrageous for foreigners, and in between for citizens of the CIS. The desk clerks will probably ask you where you are from and request your passport, making it easier to get nookie in a nunnery than to pass as a native. Some **private hotels** don't accept foreigners at all for some arcane reason, but those that do are usually much cheaper and friendlier than the Soviet dinosaurs. To find a **private room,** look around for postings at train stations, or ask taxi drivers, who may know of a lead. If you speak some Russian, a good bet would be to approach the *babushki* and give them a sob story about being a poor student with no money; if you play your cards right, you'll get coddled and fed for US$10 or less.

FOOD AND DRINK

Belarusian cuisine consists purely of what farmers can either grow or fatten: potatoes, bread, chicken, and pork. Thanks to Stalinist repatriations, however, many Georgian and Uzbek chefs have made Belarus their home and are sprinkling distant spices on the cholesterol. Brest basks in the glory of having the best restaurant south of Tallinn (see p. 67), while each town's *rynak* (рынак; market) displays a spectrum of veggies and fruits. If you guess at a menu or are a guest in a home, you'll probably receive bread, sausage, and a vegetable. Fried entities like meat-filled, crispy *cheburiki* (чебурики; meat wrapped in pancake; 3000-6000BR) or puffy, divine *panchiki* (панчики) will fill you up for a dollar and hospitalize you for two. The favorite Belarusian drink is a bread-based alcohol, *kvas* (квас), which is sold at any store—just look for the long line. (For more on *kvas,* see **"Just for the Taste,"** p. 694.)

CUSTOMS AND ETIQUETTE

If invited to a Belarusian's house for dinner, bring a bottle of wine for men, or a bouquet of odd-numbered flowers (never even) for women. Nearly all shops and restaurants close an hour for lunch, dinner, and occasionally breakfast. **Discrimination** exists in Belarus, especially against people with dark skin. Also, if you want to fit in, don't smile too much. **Homosexuality** is definitely frowned upon, and a gay man is bound to be beaten if he winks at a local skinhead, but no one will assume you are gay unless you openly announce your sexual preferences.

NATIONAL HOLIDAYS

Belarus celebrates: January 1, New Year's; January 7, Orthodox Christmas; March 8, International Women's Day; March 15, Constitution Day; April 12, Catholic Easter;

April 19, Orthodox Easter; April 28, Radinitsa (9th day after Orthodox Easter); May 1, Labor Day; May 9, Victory Day (1945) and Mother's Day; July 3, Independence Day; November 1, Orthodox New Year; November 2, Dzyady (Remembrance Day); November 7, October Revolution Anniversary; December 25, Catholic Christmas.

LIFE AND TIMES

HISTORY

The land that is now Belarus was among the first to be settled by early **Slavic** tribes during the 8th and 9th centuries. Trading settlements mushroomed along the Dnieper River, which became part of the "river road" stretching all the way from Constantinople to the Baltic Sea. The ties this trade created between what would become Russia, Ukraine, and Belarus foreshadowed future union, particularly since from the 9th century on, Belarusian principalities—including Pinsk, Polatsk, and Minsk, among others—were subject to the first East Slavic state, **Kievan Rus.**

When the **Mongols** overthrew Kiev in 1240, many Belarusian towns were destroyed, and those that survived became dependents of the Mongol empire (the Golden Horde). Over the next 150 years, the **Grand Duchy of Lithuania** gradually swelled to include a large portion of Belarus. After Lithuania united with Poland in 1386, Polish cultural and political influences were added to the melting pot of Belarusian identity. Simultaneously, a distinctly Belarusian language and culture began to develop. The Belarusian aristocracy was mainly Polish-speaking and Roman Catholic, and its feudal system stripped Eastern Orthodox Belarusian peasants of their liberties. The 1596 **Union of Brest-Litovsk** attempted to strike a compromise between the Catholic and Eastern Orthodox Churches, but the "solution" was unsuccessful.

Unhappy with Polish rule, Belarusian peasants, led by Cossacks, staged rebellions from 1648 to 1654. At the same time, Poland and Russia struggled over Belarusian territory. Under the three **Partitions of Poland,** Russia succeeded in taking over Belarus, gaining eastern Belarus after the first partition (1772), central Belarus after the second (1793), and the rest after the third and final partition (1795) that erased Poland from the map. From this period until the formation of the Belarusian Soviet Socialist Republic (SSR) in 1919, Belarus's fate was entirely tied to Russia's. Small timber and glass industries grew up in towns, but many areas—especially the remote Pripet Marshes—remained economically stagnant. The **emancipation of the serfs** in the 1860s gave Belarusian industry a shot in the arm, but the regional economy was still so impoverished that between 1896 and 1915, more than 600,000 people left Belarus—for Siberia.

> The regional economy was so impoverished that between 1896 and 1915, more than 600,000 people left Belarus—for Siberia.

The area witnessed heavy fighting between German and Russian troops during **WWI.** In early 1918, Russia ceded part of Belarus to Germany, only to get it back a few months later at the end of the war. At the same time, Belarus slowly stumbled toward statehood. The **1905 Russian Revolution** triggered peasant revolts in the region, and in 1918—while under German occupation—Belarus declared itself a democratic republic. As soon as Germany left Belarus, however, the Bolsheviks muscled in, while Polish troops marched in from the west. In 1919, Russia and Poland divided the region among themselves, and the Russian portion metamorphosed into the **Belarusian SSR.** Moscow tacked on bits of nearby territory, meanwhile establishing new industries and purging the republic of dissidents and intellectuals.

WWII brought more turmoil to Belarus and shifted the country's borders once again. Soviet troops occupied Poland up to the Bug River, taking back some of the Belarusian land ceded to Poland in 1921. German armies quickly occupied the Belarusian SSR in 1941, despite the brave resistance of a Belarusian garrison at Brest. When a postwar treaty between the USSR and Poland returned western Belarus to the Soviets, they deported the region's Polish population to Poland. Wartime damage was rapidly repaired, and major cities were further industrialized, sapping rural areas of their population. In 1986, the explosion of the nuclear plant in **Chernobyl,** Ukraine spewed radioactive material across the southern part of the republic.

While the nearby Baltic republics struggled fiercely to break away from Moscow in the late 80s, Belarus moved sluggishly. Separatism grew slowly under *glasnost* and *perestroika.* Belarus finally declared **sovereignty** on July 27, 1990, and independence on August 25, 1991, amid political turmoil in Moscow. The fledgling Republic of Belarus joined the **Commonwealth of Independent States**—a weak amalgam of former Soviet Republics—but faced a tough path to capitalism and independence.

LITERATURE

The Belarusian language did not emerge as a literary medium until the 15th and 16th centuries, when chroniclers began writing in a distinctive Belarusian idiom. Polatsk-born **Frantsysk Skaryna,** a writer, translator, printer, and physician, stoked national pride during the 16th century with his Old Church Slavonic translation of the Bible (the first book printed in Eastern Europe), which included original prefaces and post-scripts in Belarusian. By the end of the 16th century, **Andrej Rymsha** and others were creating a new genre of poetry—the **panegyric,** which replaced a formal dedication at the beginnings of books. **Simion Polotsky,** a monk from Polatsk, is known as the founder of Russian syllabic verse, and became court poet in Moscow in 1664.

As Poland gained increasing control over Belarus in the 18th century, and a Polish ruling class began banning and confiscating Belarusian literature, the home literary movement slowed to a halt. A century later, **Dunin-Martsinkievich** reflected the Polish influence with his translation of the Polish epic *Pan Tadeusz.* In 1906, the Belarusian literary journal *Nasha niva (Our Cornfield)* was founded, drawing contributions from nearly 500 villages. With its egalitarian approach, *Nasha* served as a springboard for many Belarusian writers, including **Yanka Kupala** and **Yakub Kolas,** whose interwar work depicts the Belarusian cultural predicament in the face of war and revolution. Although the Belarusian National Republic, created in 1918, had the life-span of a mayfly, the spirit of nationalism continued with an official policy of Belarusification. A slew of literary groups spawned a generation of poets who attacked both the aristocratic past and Communist repression, although by the end of the 1920s, the state had nearly complete control over cultural life. Many writers "disappeared" during Stalin's purges (1936-39), and not until the 50s did a new generation focus on the preservation of Belarusian as a language. In the region under Polish control, literature flowed a bit more freely; one standout is the poet **Natalla Arsenara.**

After the death of Stalin, prose and poetry were able to flourish and diversify. A few big names include **Pimen Pachanka** and **Arkady Kalyashov,** poets; and **Yanka Bryl** and **Ivan Shamyakin,** novelists.

BELARUS TODAY

Of all the former Soviet republics, Belarus had the weakest national identity, was the most Russified, and clamored least for independence. Indeed, President **Alyaksandr Lukashenka** publicly decreed that Belarus was to be "Slavic, Russian, and Orthodox"—in ethnicity, language, and religion, that is—and on April 2, 1996, the country took a step back toward the fold, signing an integration treaty with Russia. The treaty created the "Community of Sovereign Republics," the closest political and economic relationship of any former Soviet states, and calls for a coordinated foreign and military policy; and unification of taxation, transport, and energy legislation. To make matters worse, Lukashenka has become Europe's most ruthless totalitarian ruler, suppressing the media and cracking down on dissenters in secret midnight arrests. As the president gained in power and foreign investment dropped, Lukashenka's paranoia drew international attention. Most recently, **Serge Aleksandrov,** first secretary of the U.S. embassy in Minsk, was

> **Of all the Soviet republics, Belarus had the weakest identity, was the most Russified, and clamored the least for independence.**

expelled from the country two days after the U.S. cut off its $40 million aid to the country because of its poor human rights record; and Belarusian authorities fined the **Soros Foundation** US$3 million, after it had already donated more than US$13 million to Belarusian hospitals, libraries, and schools. Meanwhile, the tragic legacy of **Chernobyl** still haunts Belarus; as much as 30% of the country was contaminated with radioactive cesium, which has triggered a rash of thyroid cancer among children. Minsk marked the 10th anniversary of the 1986 disaster with a **violent demonstration** of 50,000—200 were arrested. And in a country with the most oppressive political climate in Europe, complete with purges in education and the press, the repression only worsens as Lukashenka tightens his grip on the economy, which grew only 2.6% in 1996. **Taxes** on profits are so high (80%) that they discourage private enterprise, and **inflation** ran an estimated 244% in 1995 and 40% in 1996.

Minsk (Мінск)

If you're looking for the supreme Soviet city, skip Moscow and head to Minsk, where the fall of Communism has been only a reluctant shuffle, rather than a wanton gallop to the West. Lenin's statue still stands in pl. Nezalezhnastsi, streets named after Red Army heroes and Soviet leaders still intersect, and statues of Felix Dzerzhinski—the Belarusian founder of the KGB—line avenues bearing his name. Flattened in WWI, the city was redesigned as a showpiece of Soviet style, with wide avenues and stereotypical Stalinist architecture. As the headquarters of the CIS, it's "back in the USSR."

ORIENTATION AND PRACTICAL INFORMATION

Minsk appears to have been built for the super-sized youths of Soviet statues. The main area is contained in the 3km between northeast **pl. Peramohi** (Перамогі) and southwest **pl. Nezalezhnastsi** (Незалежнасці; Independence Square), with **pr. Frantsishka Skaryny** (Францішка Скарыны) running between the two squares. **Pr. Masherava** (Машэрава) runs perpendicular to pr. F. Skaryny. The Svislac River roughly divides the city in two. The **train station** sits behind **Privakzalnaya pl.** (Прывакзальная)—walk up vul. Kirava (Кірава) and take a left on Svyardlova (Свярдлова) to reach pl. Nezalezhnastsi. Get your hands on a copy of the indispensable *Minsk in Your Pocket*, a humorous, frequently updated city guide with maps and restaurant recommendations (US$1). **Jaywalking** is illegal and carries a stiff penalty (75,000BR—more if you don't speak Russian); always use the underpasses to cross major streets.

Tourist Office: Belintourist (Белінтурист), pr. Masherava 19 (tel. 226 98 40), next to Gastsinitsa Yubileynaya. Take the metro to "Nemiga." A remnant of the old Soviet Intourist, but working harder than ever to please. Books rooms (for free), offers visa registration and extensions, sells plane tickets and railpasses, and arranges tours of Minsk. English and German spoken. Open Mon.-Fri. 9am-7pm. **Belarusian Society for Friendship and Cultural Relations with Foreign Countries,** vul. Zakharava 28 (Захарава; tel. 233 15 02). Lives up to its names with the most effusive treatment of any government agency. Open Mon.-Fri. 9am-6pm.

Passport Office: In theory, all foreigners visiting Minsk must **register** their passport with **OVIR** (ОВИР), pr. F. Skaryny 8, room 132 (tel. 220 29 82 or 220 15 05), although some short-term visitors (under 1 week) do not register. Hotels will register you automatically. To extend your visa, you must plead with whomever provided your original visa invitation to apply for the extension with the **Ministry of Foreign Affairs** (tel. 222 26 74 or 232 64 29).

Currency Exchange: Follow the Абмен Валюты (*Abmen Valyuty*) signs, but do not be deceived by the posted hours or services—they're completely random. The exchange office in **Gastsinitsa Yubileynaya** provides US$ advances on MC or Visa (4% commission) and cashes Thomas Cook traveler's checks (open 24hr.), as does **Prior Bank** (Пріор Банк), vul. V. Kharyzhan 3a (Харыжан; tel. 269 09 64), and other locations throughout Minsk. Open Mon.-Fri. 9am-6pm. An **ATM** in **Belvnesheshe-**

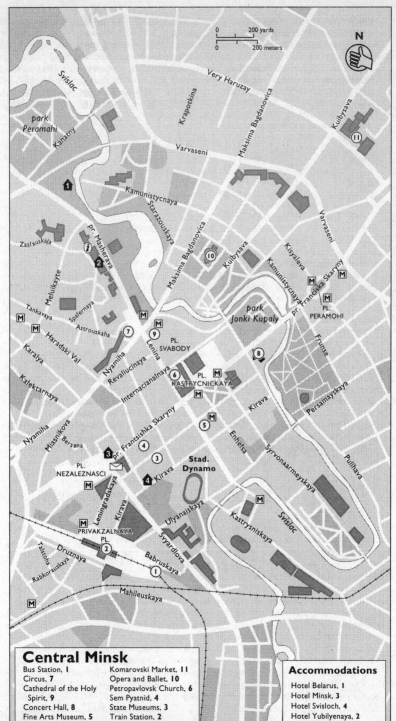

BELARUS

Central Minsk

Bus Station, 1
Circus, 7
Cathedral of the Holy
  Spirit, 9
Concert Hall, 8
Fine Arts Museum, 5

Komarovski Market, 11
Opera and Ballet, 10
Petropavlovsk Church, 6
Sem Pyatnid, 4
State Museums, 3
Train Station, 2

Accommodations

Hotel Belarus, 1
Hotel Minsk, 3
Hotel Svisloch, 4
Hotel Yubilyenaya, 2

conombank, vul. Zaslavskaya 10 (Заславская), north of Gastinitsa Yubileynaya, accepts MC. Open Mon.-Fri. 9am-1pm, 2-4pm.

Embassies: Estonia, vul. Varvasheni 17 (tel. 235 59 65). **Latvia,** vul. Storozhyovskaya 15 (tel. 239 16 12; fax 250 67 84). **Lithuania,** vul. Varvasheni 17 (tel. 234 77 84; fax 276 94 71). **Poland,** vul. Rumyantseva 6 (tel. 239 13 13; fax 276 94 71). **Russia,** vul. Staravilenskaya 48 (Старавіленская; tel. 250 36 65; fax 250 36 64). **U.K.,** vul. Karla Marxa 37 (Карла Маркса; tel. 229 23 03; fax 29 23 06). **Ukraine,** vul. Kirava 17, #306 (tel. 227 27 96; fax 227 28 61). **U.S.,** vul. Staravilenskaya 46 (tel. 234 77 61 or 231 50 00; fax 234 78 53).

Cultural Centers: British Council, vul. Kakarova 21 (tel. 236 79 53; fax. 236 40 47). **Goethe Institut,** vul. Frunze 5 (tel. 236 34 33; fax. 236 73 14). **Israeli Cultural Center,** vul. Uralskaya 3 (tel. 230 18 74; fax 230 81 94).

Flights: The main airport, **Minsk II** (tel. 225 02 31), lies 40km east of the city and can be reached by bus #300 from Avtovakzal Vostochny (1 per hr., 40min., 50,000BR). If you don't speak Russian, a taxi there will cost US$40-60. The Belarusian airline, **Belavia** (tel. 279 13 27), flies to Moscow (2 per day, 1½hr.); **LOT** (tel. 297 37 29) flies daily to Warsaw (1½hr.).

Trains: Tsentralny Vokzal (Центральный вокзал), Privakzalnaya pl. (tel. 220 99 89, info tel. 295 54 10). Same-day local tickets sold on 1st floor; international tickets on 2nd floor. For info on departures and prices, go to window #13 on the 2nd floor, with the Даведка справка (*davedka spravka*) sign. Purchase advance tickets at **Advance Booking Office,** vul. Chkalova 9 (tel. 296 30 67); take trolley bus #2 (open Mon.-Sat. 9am-1pm, 2-6pm). To: Brest (5 per day, 4-5hr., *coupé* 210,000BR); Kiev (1 per day, 14hr., *coupé* 550,000BR); Moscow (10-15 per day, 10-14hr., *coupé* 650,000BR); Rīga (1 per day even dates, 13hr., *coupé* 650,000BR); Vilnius (2 per day, 4½hr., 200,000BR); and Warsaw (6-10 per day, 12hr., US$30).

Buses: There are 2 stations. **Avtovakzal Tsentralny** (Автовакзал Цэнтральный), vul. Babruyskaya 6 (Бабруйская; tel. 227 78 20), just east of the train station. Buses to most points west of Minsk. To Vilnius (3 per day, 4hr., 77,000BR) and Warsaw (1 per day, 11hr., 245,000BR). **Avtovakzal Vostochny** (East Station) is almost 9km from town at vul. Vaneyeva 34 (Ванэева; tel. 248 08 81). Take trolleybus #20 from Kirava, near Avtovakzal Tsentralny, about 9 stops to "Автовакзал восточный." It's the concrete-and-glass monstrosity on the opposite side of the traffic circle. Most connections are within Belarus, though buses also serve Rīga (1 per day, 12hr., 378,000BR). Make sure you know which station your bus arrives at.

Public Transportation: The **Metro,** crowded as hell, has 2 efficient lines that cover downtown Minsk; they cross at Kastrichnichskaya (Кастрычніцкая). Trains run 6am-1am (2000BR). Buses, trolleys, and trams run 5:35am-12:55am (2000BR). Monthly passes 45,000BR. Pick up a pass and **map** at most kiosks around the city.

Taxis: Free-enterprise "competition" in Minsk consists of one company driving Volvos and one with Ladas (tel. 061 or 270 90 11). **State taxis** are supposed to charge 30,000BR every time the meter hits 100; otherwise, fares are negotiable. If you speak Russian, pay no more than 60,000BR for a 10min. ride. If you don't, tell the driver your destination, and bargain the price below 80,000BR before getting in.

English Bookstore: Tsentralny Knizhy Magazin, pr. F. Skaryny 19 (tel. 227 49 18). Paperbacks and foreign dictionaries. Open Mon.-Sat. 10am-3pm and 4-7pm.

What's So Special about 930?

Minsk's authorities cleaned grime, painted old dilapidated buildings, and planted flowers everywhere to celebrate Minsk's 930th birthday on July 3, 1997. The party they threw was surely unforgettable. "But 930?" you ask. "What kind of birthday is that?!" Well, the date has historical significance, for it was on July 3, 1944 that the Red Army "liberated" Minsk from the Nazis, and on that same date in 1991 that Belarus liberated itself from the Soviets on what has come to be known as *Den Nezalezhnastsi* (День Незалежнасці; Independence Day). But that still doesn't answer, why 930? Rumor has it that the date was chosen to boost morale and compete with Moscow, which celebrated its 850th birthday in 1997. And how was this birthday shebang funded? With money extorted from foreign businesses, according to some sources at the U.S. Embassy.

Laundromat: Khimchistka (Химчістка), vul. Dolhobrodskaya 35 (Долгобродская; tel. 38 64 48). Another location at vul. Kubuchkina 64. Open daily 7am-8pm.

24-Hour Pharmacy: At Tsentralny Vokzal (tel. 20 99 89).

Express Mail: FedEx, vul. Asanalieva 9, #31 (tel./fax 275 10 94).

Post Office: pr. F. Skaryny 10 (tel. 227 15 67), opposite Gastsinitsa Minsk. To send or receive packages, enter on vul. Svyardlova (Свярдлова) and go up to the 2nd floor. Open daily 7:30am-11pm. **Postal code:** 220050.

Telephones: Telephones take *zhetony* (жетоны; tokens; 2400BR) and phone cards (50-100,000BR); both can be purchased at kiosks. **Central Telegraph Office,** in the hall to the left immediately upon entering the post office. Calls to the U.S. 35,000BR per min, to Western Europe 11,000-20,000BR per min. All numbers in Minsk are 7 digits and start with a "2," so if you come across a 6-digit number, add an initial "2." But watch out—some pay phones can only handle 6-digit numbers; if you can't get through, drop the 1st "2." Open daily 7:30am-11pm. **Faxes** at booth #6 (tel. 226 02 22; fax 226 05 30). Open Mon.-Fri. 8am-8pm. **Phone code:** 0172.

ACCOMMODATIONS

Youth hostels as such don't exist here, despite a long list of so-called hostels in the phonebook (e.g. the poetic "October Revolution Tractor Plant no. 9 Tool-Makers' Association Hostel of Comrades"). *Minsk in Your Pocket* lists some cheaper hotels. **Private rooms** are another option; taxi drivers may know about them. Remember to ask how far the room is from the city center, and to agree on a price (around US$10) before settling. For slightly more money, former-Soviet hotels that cater to travelers from the CIS will be happy to accommodate you as well.

Gastsinitsa Svisloch (Гасцініца Свіслочь), vul. Kirava 13 (tel. 20 97 83). From the train station, walk up vul. Kirava; the hotel is about a block up on the left. Hot water is turned off for one month every summer; ask in advance. Small, dusty rooms with hardwood floors. Bring your own toilet paper. Singles 370,000BR; doubles 680,000BR, with toilet and bath 860,000BR; quads 1,080,000BR.

Gastsinitsa Minsk (Мінск), pr. F. Skaryny 11 (tel./fax 220 01 32), in the center of town. Renovated rooms with TV, phone, fridge, toilet paper, and showers. Singles US$41; doubles US$60. Breakfast included. AmEx, Diners Club, MC, Visa.

Gastsinitsa Yubileynaya (Юбілейная), pr. Masherava 19 (tel. 226 90 24; fax 226 91 71). Clean, modern, Western-style rooms. Casino downstairs open nightly 4pm-4am. Singles with TV, phone, and shower US$55; doubles US$65. MC, Visa.

Gastsinitsa Druzhba (Дружба), vul. Tolbukhina 3 (tel. 66 24 81). Communal bathrooms and a dark interior, but not even the KGB could beat the price. Take the metro to "Park Chelyuskintsev" (Парк Челюскинцев), northeast of the city center. Doubles 160,000-180,000BR; triples 162,000-200,000BR. Reserve ahead.

Gastsinitsa Belarus (Беларусь), vul. Starazoyskaya 15 (Старазоўская; tel. 239 17 05; fax 239 12 33), on the north side of the river 3km out of town, opposite Gastinitsa Yubileynaya. Rooms on floors 4-5 of this 23-story monster have been "renovated" to higher prices. Private bath, TV, sauna. Singles US$50; doubles US$60. AmEx, Visa. Roll the rest of your cash away at the casino (open nightly 5pm-5am).

FOOD

Restaran Uzbekistan (Ресторан Узбекистан), vul. Y. Kupaly 17 (tel. 227 75 51), at the corner of pr. F. Skaryny. Spicy Uzbek dishes in a tiny co-op restaurant. *Shurpa* (шурпа; soup) goes for 78,000BR; *Plov po uzbeski* (плов по узбески) is rice with lamb (78,200BR). Open daily 8am-11am, noon-4:30pm and 6pm-midnight.

Zio Pepe (Зио Пэпэ), pr. F. Skaryny 25 (tel. 227 02 95), in the center of town. Original location at vul. Rabkorovskaya 17a (Рабкоровская; tel. 210 28 57), behind the train station. Delicious thin-crust pizza pies (80,000-110,000BR). Open 11am-1pm.

Sem Pyatnid (Сем Пятнід), pr. F. Skaryny 19 (tel. 27 69 01). This Polish restaurant is crowded in the evenings, so go for lunch. Start your meal with *solyanka* (солянка), full of raisins, peanuts, and green onions (28,000BR); add *zharkoe s chernochlivom* (жаркое с черночливом), a rich dish of pork with prunes (35,200BR); and finish with coffee (7600BR). Open daily noon-5pm and 7pm-4am.

Restaran Novolune (Рэстаран Новолунэ), vul. Zakharava 31 (Захарава; tel. 36 74 55), 500m east of pl. Peramohi. A cozy semi-underground place just past the British Embassy. The best (and the only) Czech cuisine in town (main courses 50,000-200,000BR). Open daily noon-midnight.

Cafe Berezka (Кафэ Бэрэжка), pr. F. Skaryny 40 (tel. 33 15 89). Beloved by the locals for reasonable prices and its specialty—stuffed fish *Berezka* (40,200BR). Various salads (around 8900BR). Outdoor seating. Open daily 11am-5pm and 6-11:30pm.

SIGHTS

Following its decimation in WWII, Minsk was named one of the 13 "Hero Cities" of the Soviet Union. More than 80% of all the buildings and nearly 60% of the population, including almost all of the 300,000 Jews who lived here, were obliterated between 1941 and 1944. The city was rebuilt in grand Stalinist style, with gargantuan buildings and wide boulevards, and today Minsk is most noteworthy for its utter Sovietness, a state of mind that exudes from the architecture, emanates from the people, and radiates from every street name. In 1997, Minsk cleaned itself up for its **930th birthday,** an unforgettable bash that brought millions of people to the streets.

Start your tour of Minsk at **pl. Nezalezhnastsi,** one block north of the train station. The enormous monoliths that surround the square exemplify Communist-era architecture; the grandiose giant at the far west end of the square was the headquarters of the KGB. From pl. Nezalezhnastsi, stroll northeast along pr. Frantsishka Skaryny, Minsk's main shopping street. A left onto ul. Lenina (Леніна), which eventually turns into pr. Masherava, leads to ul. Nyamiha and the "Nyamiha" Metro stop. On pl. Svobody (Свободы), the square east of the Metro stop, stands the dazzling 17th-century white **Svetadukha Kafedralny Sobor** (Светадуха Кафедральный Собор; Cathedral of the Holy Spirit), vul. Mefodiya 3 (tel. 27 66 09). Built in 1642 as a Bernardine monastery, the building later burned down, only to be rebuilt by the Russian Orthodox Church. Closed by the Soviet regime, it was reopened in 1990 and only restored to its present beauty in 1996. Just west, about 200m down vul. Nyamiha, stands the yellow **Petropavilsky Sobor** (Петропавилский Собор; Cathedral of St. Peter and St. Paul), vul. Rakovskaya 4 (Раковская; tel. 26 74 75), the oldest church still standing in Minsk. Built in 1612, it too was closed by the Soviets, but reopened in 1992.

Minsk's reconstructed **Old Town,** east of vul. Nyamiha on the north bank of the Svislac, is a nice area for a mid-afternoon stroll through souvenir shops and beer gardens. Very few of the buildings in these blocks are authentic, however, as most of the originals were destroyed in WWII. North of the Old Town, a little bridge leads to an eerie structure with four entrances that stands alone on a small island; this is a **monument** dedicated to Belarusians who died fighting for the Soviet army in Afghanistan.

Before WWII, Jews comprised 52% of Minsk's population; today this figure has dwindled to 1%. A **Jewish memorial stone** stands on vul. Zaslavskaya, behind Gastsinitsa Yubileynaya, to commemorate the more than 5000 Jews who were shot and buried on this spot by the Nazis in 1941. Minsk's **synagogue,** vul. Kropotkina 22 (Кропоткина; tel. 34 22 73), can only be viewed from the outside.

Up pr. Masherava, past the Planeta Hotel, the vast flatness is broken by the painfully pointy Soviet **war memorial** spike. Go down the hill at the back of the memorial, and you'll find yourself in a rare area of prewar Minsk, complete with a park and bathing beach (paddle boat rental 25,000BR per hr.).

Minsk's museums all seem to be dedicated to Belarusian history, WWII, railroads, the militia, and not much else—but then again, this is Minsk we're talking about. **Muzey Velikoy Otechestvennoy Voyny** (Музей Великой Отечественной Войны; Museum of the Great Patriotic War), pr. F. Skaryny 25a (tel. 26 15 44), gives a suitably grim, detailed picture of the war in Belarus, which lost 20% of its population (open Tues.-Sun. 10am-6pm; 9000BR; call ahead for a tour in English for 60,000BR). The **National History and Culture Museum,** vul. K. Marxa 12 (К. Маркса; tel. 27 43 22), explores the history of everything Belarusian. Discover arrowheads, 19th-century folk costumes, and whole halls consecrated to the glory of the Belarusian SSR. If you had doubts that Belarus was a country with true culture, this is the place to visit (open Thurs.-Tues. 11am-7pm; 7000BR).

No tour of Soviet Minsk is complete without a visit to the city's parks, the only green you'll find here. Wander up pr. F. Skaryny to reach **Park Gorkoho** (Парк Горкого) on your right and **Yanka Kupala Park** (Янка Купала Парк) on your left, where Minsk residents come to stroll hand-in-hand. Two km northeast of the downtown along pr. F. Skaryny, the **Botanichesky Sad** (Ботанический Сад; Botanical Gardens) will take you away from the grime of the city. Take the metro to "Park Chalyskintskaya" (Парк Чалыскінцкая).

ENTERTAINMENT AND NIGHTLIFE

Minsk's world-renowned **Opera and Ballet Theater,** vul. E. Pashkevich 23 (Пашкевич; tel. 233 17 90), showcases one of the best ballets in the former Soviet Union. Don't miss the chance to see a performance. Tickets (10,000-150,000BR) can be purchased in advance from the **Central Ticket Office,** F. Skaryny 13 (tel. 20 25 70; open Mon.-Sat. 9am-8pm, Sun. 11am-5pm). For acrobatics of a different kind, the **Minsk Circus,** pr. F. Skaryny 32 (tel. 27 22 45; box office tel. 27 78 42), performs twice daily (3 and 7pm; tickets from 10,000BR). The **Belarusian Philharmonic,** pr. F. Skaryny 50 (tel. 33 44 33), organizes chamber and classical music performances daily at 7pm; call for more information. The **Hall of Chamber Music,** pr. F. Skaryny 44 (tel. 33 04 69), boasts organ music (daily at 7pm).

Nightlife in Minsk is developing quicker than the free-market economy, probably because the local mafia, which runs the show, hasn't yet figured out how to extort money from itself. **MiLord,** pr. F. Skaryny 25, boasts a disco and casino that once catered to track-suit-wearing sharks and now attracts screaming kids and those who love them (open daily 9pm-6am; cover 15,000BR; women free Sun.-Thurs.). For a "more sophisticated" crowd, drop by **Art Cafe,** pr. Skaryny 25, right next door. The US$5 cover is a bit steep for Belarusians, but even the broke are sometimes willing to go beyond their means for dancing (open Sun.-Thurs. 6-11pm, Fri.-Sat. 7-11:30pm).

■ Hrodna (Гродна)

On the road between Warsaw and Vilnius, Hrodna is a rarity in Belarus—a city where the towers to God overpower the towers to Stalin. Catholic cathedrals loom over twisting streets of Baroque buildings, their beauty preserved because Hrodna's citizens surrendered quickly during WWII. First mentioned in 1128, Hrodna has a long history of foreign domination by the Poles, Lithuanians, and Russians. Although Soviet planners tried to have their way with the city, today independent Hrodna remains a gem in comparison with what was done to the rest of Belarus. One effect of Soviet occupation you will notice, however, is that everyone calls Hrodna by its Russian name: Grodno. So you can choose: be P.C., or Ruski.

Orientation and Practical Information Hrodna straddles the **Neman River,** north of which lie its downtown and most of the sights. A vast white behemoth rising from a park full of vendors, the **train station,** vul. Budonova (Будонова; tel. 44 85 56), lies 2km northeast of the city center, at the end of vul. Azheshka (Ажэшка). Trains run to Minsk (4 per day, 6-9hr., 75,000BR, *coupé* 100,000BR); Brest (1 per day, 14hr., 76,000BR); Białystok, Poland (2 per day, 3hr., US$6); Druskinikai, Lithuania (Sat.-Sun. 2 per day, 1½hr., 30,000BR); Moscow (daily 3:59pm, 12hr., 470,000BR, *coupé* 750,000BR); Vilnius (daily 5:20am, 4hr., 175,000BR); and Warsaw (1 per day, 5½hr., US$10). Tickets for international trains are sold at windows #13 and 14. **Luggage storage** (*kamery khraneniya;* камеры хранения) is in the station's basement (small bags 8000BR, large bags 13,000BR; open 24hr., except for 7:30-8am, 1-2pm, and 7:30-8pm). **Exchange currency** on the second floor (open 24hr.). The **bus station** (автовокзал; *avtovokzal*), vul. Krasnoarmeyskaya 7a (Красноармейская; tel. 72 37 24), sits 1.5km south of the train station. Bus #15 connects both stations

(2000BR); by foot, cross over the railroad tracks and head south on vul. Krasnoarmey-skaya, and the station will appear on your left (10min.). **Buses** run to: Minsk (10-12 per day, 5½hr., 135,000BR); Brest (2 per day, 7½hr., 135,000BR); Białystok, Poland (5 per day, 3hr., 125,000BR); Druskininkai, Lithuania (2 per day, 1½hr., 19,500BR); Kaliningrad (1 per day, 10hr. 123,000BR); Vilnius (Fri.-Sun. 1 per day, 5hr. 85,000R); and Warsaw (3 per day, 6hr., 185,000BR). Ask someone in the *davetka* (даветка; info office), in the hall to the left, to lock up your bag in the back room (8000BR; open daily 7am-1pm and 2-7pm). The station's **currency exchange** office accepts AmEx traveler's checks (open Mon. and Wed.-Fri. 9am-12:30pm and 1:30-7pm, Sat.-Sun. 8am-2pm). Head west from the train station along vul. Azheshka to reach **vul. Savetskaya** (Савецкая), the main pedestrian thoroughfare. From here, head south to the main square, recently renamed **pl. Stefana Batorya** (Стэфана Баторыя; formerly Sovetskaya pl.). The **tourist office,** vul. Azheshka 49, 2nd floor (tel. 72 17 79), offers assistance in Russian, finds rooms for free, and arranges city tours with prior notice (open Mon.-Fri. 8:30am-5pm, Sat. 8-11am). For advances on your MC or Visa, head to **Prior Bank** (Приор Банк), vul. Savetskaya 10 (tel. 72 17 25; 4% commission). West from the bus station, or due east from pl. Stefana Batorya, is the **post office,** vul. Karla Marxa 29 (Карла Маркса; 8am-8pm, Sat.-Sun. 10am-4pm). Next door, the **telephone office** (tel. 96 75 09) places long-distance calls (open daily 7:30am-10:30pm). **Postal code:** 230025. **Phone code:** 0152.

Accommodations and Food Most hotels in Hrodna aren't used to receiving Westerners. The best deal in town is the reasonably priced and centrally located **Gastsinitsa Neman** (Гасцініца неман), vul. Stefana Batorya 8 (tel. 72 19 36), just south of the main square, which offers simple rooms with TVs (singles 255,000BR; doubles 400,000BR; bring your own toilet paper). Take bus #3 or 14 from the train station. **Gastsinitsa Belarus** (Беларусь), vul. Kalinovskova 1 (Калінoвскога; tel. 44 16 74), has cozy singles (310,000BR) and doubles (525,000BR) with toilet and shower (MC, Visa). Take bus #15 from the train station and get off at "Kinateator Kosmos" (Кінотеатр Космос), the fifth stop. Next door to the hotel, the **Restaurant Belarus** sells *che-buriki* (Чебурики; beef fried in a flaky shell; 8000BR) and other cuisine (open noon-5pm, 6pm-1am). In hot weather, lounge at the outdoor tables of the popular cafe **Magazin Hrodsoup** (Магазин Гродсоуп), at the south end of vul. Savetskaya (coffee 4000BR; open daily 10am-10pm).

Sights and Entertainment Hrodna's quick capture during WWII allowed most of its noteworthy buildings to escape destruction, making it perhaps the most scenic city in Belarus. Start your tour at the awe-inspiring **Farnoy Cathedral** (Фар-ной), pl. Savetskaya 4 (tel. 44 26 77), built by Jesuit missionaries during Polish rule in the 18th century. The dingy light-blue exterior conceals the golden, halo-like chande-liers that bathe the paintings and intricately carved altarpiece with light (open Mon.-Fri. 8am-7pm). Across the square, **ruins** are all that remain of a red-brick Catholic cathedral, razed by the Soviets in the 1950s. Down the street on vul. Karla Marxa stands **Pabrihidsky Sobor** (Пабригидский Собор), in Polish **Najświętsze Serce Jezusa** (Holy Church of Jesus), a former Franciscan monastery turned into a psychiatric hos-pital by the Russian regime and only re-opened to the public in 1990. The beautiful white 16th-century **Barnardinski Kostyol** (Барнардінскі Костёл; Bernardine Church), near the end of vul. Krupskay (Крупскай), was restored in 1996. The main doors lead to a bright interior, where frescoes of Jesus and the angels welcome visitors. The church tour ends with the blue-domed Russian Orthodox **Svetopokrovsky Sobor** (Светопокровский Собор), on vul. Azheshka 23 (tel. 72 29 99), a gem built between 1905 and 1907 in honor of the Russians who died in the 1904-05 war with Japan.

Hrodna's greatest sights are its two castles, reached by heading up vul. Zamkava (Замкава). **Stary Zamak** (Стары Замак; Old Castle), on the right, was built in the 1570s on the ruins of a 15th-century castle used by Lithuanian Grand Duke Vytautas. Climb up to the defensive wall for a gorgeous view of the river below. Inside the cas-tle, a museum devotes 20 rooms to its history (open Mon.-Sat. 9am-6pm, *kassa* closes

5pm; 15,000BR; tours 60,000BR). On the opposite side of the hill, **Novy Zamak** (Новы Замак, New Castle), destroyed in WWII and rebuilt in 1951, houses a worthwhile **History and Archaeology Museum** (tel. 44 40 68), with exhibits devoted to Hrodna's history from its first written mention in 1128 (10,000BR; open Mon.-Sat. 10am-6pm, *kassa* closes 5pm; tours 60,000BR).

■ Brest (Брэст)

Made famous by the 1918 Treaty of Brest-Litovsk, whereby Lenin ceded Poland, the Baltics, Belarus, and most of Ukraine to the Germans to get out of WWI, Brest remained a Polish city between the wars. WWII thrust Brest back into the spotlight, as Krepasts Brest-Litoisk (Brest Fortress) held for over a month against the Germans. Today Brest is a hectic border town that sees legions of traders crossing back and forth, hawking everything from cosmetics to condoms.

Orientation and Practical Information The **Mukhavets** and **Bug** Rivers mark off the south and west boundaries of the city; at their confluence lies **Krepasts Brest-Litoisk** (Brest Fortress). The Bug also demarcates the Polish border. The **train station,** just north of vul. Ardzhanikidze (Арджанікідзэ; info tel. 005), is the main border crossing for Moscow- and Warsaw-bound trains. Trains run to: Minsk (6 per day, 7hr., 80,000BR); Kiev (2 per day, 16½hr., 200,500BR); Moscow (8 per day, 16hr., 400,000BR); Prague (2 per day, 18hr., US$45); and Warsaw (6 per day, US$15). If you're heading to Hrodna, take a bus, as the train route is long and circuitous. **Store luggage** off the main hall (lockers 8000BR; open 24hr.). The **bus station** (tel. 225 51 36) is at the corner of vul. Kuybyshava (Куйбышава) and vul. Mitskevicha (Міцкевіча), near the central market (open daily 6am-11pm). To: Minsk (8-10 per day, 6-7½hr., 155,000BR); Hrodna (2 per day, 7½hr., 134,500BR); and Warsaw (4 per day, 6hr., 185,000BR). From the rail station, cross the overpass to **vul. Lenina** (Леніна) and head left to reach pl. Lenina, the main square; **vul. Pushkinskaya** (Пушкінская) runs off to the left. Farther down is **vul. Gogalya** (Гогаля), the main east-west thoroughfare. **Maps** are available in the kiosk at the train station (21,000BR). **Belintourist** (Белінтурíст), vul. Maskaiskaya 15 (tel. 225 10 71), in Gastsinitsa Intourist, doesn't have many maps or brochures, but the staff speaks English. **Tours** of the fortress in English can be arranged if you call a week in advance (open Mon.-Fri. 8am-6pm). **Five Stars,** vul. Pushkinskaya 10 (tel. 223 86 85), is a private **currency exchange** operation offering possibly the best rates in town (open Mon.-Sat. 9am-9pm, Sun. 9am-7pm). **Prior Bank** (Пріор Банк), vul. Pushkinskaya 16/1 (tel. 223 99 18), gives cash advances on Visa for 4% commission (open Mon.-Fri. 9am-5pm). The **post office,** with **telephones** (open daily 7:30am-9:30pm) inside, is on vul. Pushkinskaya (tel. 226 26 12), at pl. Lenina (open Mon.-Fri. 8:30am-8pm, Sat. 8:30am-5pm, Sun. 8:30am-3pm). All phone numbers in Brest have seven digits and start with "2." If you come across a six-digit number, add a "2" before it. **Postal code:** 224005. **Phone code:** 0162.

Accommodations and Food A budget oasis in the Belarusian accommodations desert, **Gastsinitsa Instituta** (Гасцініца Інстытута), vul. Pushkinskaya 16/1 (tel. 223 93 72), offers basic rooms with sporadic hot water (singles 120,000BR, with shower 170,000BR; doubles 240,000BR, with shower 340,000BR). **Gastsinitsa Vesta** (Веста), vul. Krupskay 16 (Крупская; tel. 223 71 69; fax 223 78 39), is 2km from the train station, in the left back corner of the park-like plaza west of pl. Lenina. The best hotel for the money, the Vesta's marble floors echo with the occasional English conversation, and rooms have fridges and TVs (singles 380,000BR; doubles 660,000BR). **Gastsinitsa Intourist** (Інтурíст), vul. Maskaiskaya 15 (tel. 225 20 83; fax 225 10 70), attracts most of the German and Polish businesspeople swarming around Brest. Rooms have private baths (with hot water!) and TVs (singles 650,000BR; doubles 1,100,000BR).

Diplomats in Minsk drive to Brest on weekends just to dine at the best restaurant between Warsaw and Moscow. **Restaurant India** (Рестаран Індіа), vul. Gogalya 29 (tel. 26 63 25), at vul. K. Marxa, revives your deadened palate with authentic, spicy Indian food. Feast on sumptuous *yakhni sherba* (27,900BR) or creamy *gosht korma* (lamb in sauce; 57,400BR; open daily noon-11pm). There's also a **grocery store** just past the post office (open Mon.-Fri. 7:30am-9pm, Sat. 8am-8pm, Sun. 8am-3pm).

Sights **Krepasts Brest-Litoisk** (Крэпасць Брэст-Літоўск; Brest Fortress) dominates three sq. km of area around the Bug and Mukhavets rivers. Take **bus** #17 down vul. Maskaiskaya or walk 15 minutes to get there. These grassy hills and tree-lined streets used to be the best-equipped fortress in tsarist Russia. After Napoleon's 1812 attack on Russia, several cities in Poland, Lithuania, and Belarus were heavily fortified, with this massive fortress intended to be the central defensive point. From 1838 to 1841, the entire city was moved east to open up the site for the fort. Brick walls 15m thick, moats, rivers, and encasements made this the most formidable battlement in Eastern Europe. In the 1918 **Treaty of Brest-Litovsk,** Lenin ceded Brest to the Germans. The Poles held it between the wars, but another Russian-German agreement, this time the 1939 **Molotrov-Ribbentrop Pact,** brought Brest-Litovsk back into the Russian fold. Embarrassed by the associations of the old name, Stalin dropped the Litovsk, just in time for Hitler's armies to attack on June 22, 1941. While the Germans swept forward to Minsk and beyond, the garrison of Brest stood firm for six weeks. Nearly the entire fortress was reduced to rubble before the Russian Alamo finally surrendered. The defenders' courage earned Brest the honor of being one of the USSR's "Hero Cities." What remains of the always-open fortress has been turned into a sometimes dramatic, sometimes dogmatic testimonial to those heroes. Patriotic Red Army songs and the sounds of gunfire emanate eerily from openings above your head at **Galoiny Iva-khod** (Галоўны ўваход; Principal Entrance), at the end of vul. Maskaiskaya. To the right lies **Uskhodni Fort** (Усходні Форт; Eastern Fort), a football-field-sized complex where tenacious Russians completely cut off from their comrades held their ground for three weeks. To the north lies **Painochnaya Brama** (Паўночная Брама; Northern Gate), the only gate still fully intact. To get a sense of the fortress's former magnitude, remember that the whole place used to look like this. To the right of the main gate, an immense **boulder** towers over the central island of the fortress. Around the base of the soldier-in-the-boulder monolith are **memorials** to the defenders and an eternal flame dedicated to all 13 of the "Hero Cities."

In front of the sculpture are the foundations of **Bely Palats** (Белы Палац; White Palace), where the 1918 treaty was signed. To the right, **Muzey Abarony Brestskay Krepastsi-Geroya** (Музей Абароны Брэсцкай Крэпасці-Героя; Museum of the Defense of the Brest Hero-Fortress), in the reconstructed barracks, recounts the siege during WWII and the perfection of Communism as demonstrated by this heroic defense. A display on the Molotov-Ribbentrop Pact has been added to explain why Soviet soldiers happened to be here when WWII started.

Belavezhskaya Pushcha (Белавежская Пушча), the only virgin forest left in Europe, spreads over 200 acres 40km north of Brest, along the border with Poland. Home to the continent's largest animal—the *zubr* (зубр; East European bison)—this ocean of dark centuries-old coniferous and broad-leaved trees began attracting research scientists as early as the 17th century, and today protects species threatened by extinction elsewhere in Europe, including the European deer, otter, golden eagle, red eagle, black stork, and black grouse. Ask the Brest Belintourist office for info on visiting this eco-labyrinth, or see **Poland: Puszcza Białowieża,** p. 452, for the Polish perspective.

Bosnia-Herzegovina

BOSNIA-HERZEGOVINA

US$1 = 182BHD (dinars, or BAD)	100BHD = US$0.55
CDN$1= 132BHD	100BHD = CDN$0.76
UK£1 = 290BHD	100BHD = UK£0.35
IR£ = 267BHD	100BHD = IR£0.38
AUS$1 = 133BHD	100BHD = AUS$0.75
NZ$1 = 116BHD	100BHD = NZ$0.87
SAR1 = 39BHD	100BHD = SAR2.58
DM1 = 100BHD	100BHD = DM1
HRV KUNA1 = 28BHD	100BHD =KUNA3.52
Country Phone Code: 387	**International Dialing Prefix: 00**

Defying the odds of centuries, the nation of Bosnia-Herzegovina persists, the mountainous centerpiece of the former Yugoslavia. Bosnia's distinction, and its troubles, spring from its self-regard as a mixing ground for Muslims, Croats, and Serbs. In Sarajevo, Bosnia's cosmopolitan capital, that ideal is at least verbally maintained, but in the countryside and smaller towns, ethnic problems continue. Physically, Bosnia is a beautiful country of rolling green hills and valleys. But the past years, as the world knows, have been deadly. The road to Sarajevo passes through endless fields guarded by roofless, abandoned houses. A large part of the population has become refugees, displaced and scattered. The future of Bosnia is uncertain, particularly with the scheduled withdrawal of NATO troops in summer 1999. But the people of Bosnia are resilient, and in this period of post-Dayton peace, the process of rebuilding is underway.

> The U.S. Department of State issued a **Travel Warning** in June 1996 advising against unnecessary travel to Bosnia. The warning cites "landmines and unexploded ordinances throughout the country," as well as "nonexistent civil authority in many regions which are still controlled by Serb militia." Check the State Department Web page at http://travel.state.gov/travel_warnings.html. for updates on this warning. Be aware that the situation in Bosnia will likely have changed dramatically by 1998. If the 30,000-strong peace implementation force (SFOR) pulls out as planned in June 1998, it may be quite unstable.

BOSNIA ESSENTIALS

Citizens of the U.S. and Ireland do not need visas to enter Bosnia; citizens of Australia, New Zealand, the U.K, and South Africa do require visas. Call your nearest Bosnia consulate office (see **Essentials: Embassies and Consulates,** p. 3) for details. Visa applications generally require three or four weeks to process and require you to submit your passport, a visa application, and a small fee (US$15). The Bosnian border, with its congregation of trucks and army vehicles, is somewhat intimidating. However, entrance is a fairly smooth procedure—if the prevailing political climate allows. There are also occasional police checkpoints within Bosnia. Register with your embassy upon arrival, and keep your papers with you at all times.

GETTING THERE AND GETTING AROUND

Commercial **plane** service into Sarajevo is limited and expensive; **Croatia Airlines** (tel. in Zagreb (41) 42 77 52, in Split (21) 362 202) has regular service to Zagreb, and flights also go to Zurich, Ljubljana, and Istanbul (see **Sarajevo: Flights,** p. 76). There are travel agencies in Sarajevo to arrange and change flights, but to buy a ticket, you must pay in cash. **Trains** are barely functional, but **buses** run daily between Sarajevo and Split, Dubrovnik, and Zagreb. They are reliable, but brace yourself for Balkan driving—there is a certain specialty here of passing other cars as narrowly as possible.

STAYING SAFE

> **Emergencies: Police:** tel. 664 211. **Fire:** tel. 93. **Emergency:** tel. 94.

Outside Sarajevo, **do NOT set foot off the pavement** under any circumstances. Even in Sarajevo, use caution—do not venture onto dirt without first watching the locals. Millions of **landmines** and **unexploded ordinances (UXOs)** lace the country. Mine injuries occur daily. Fifteen percent of landmine injuries occur on **road shoulders**—partly because farmers who find unexploded ordinances in their fields occasionally bring them to the sides of the roads for the troops to pick up. If you must take pictures, do so from your car, while the car remains firmly on pavement. If you must go to the bathroom during a road trip, stop at a gas station. **Abandoned houses** are unsafe as well; often they have been laced with booby traps by a retreating army. Absolute caution at all times is essential. The de-mining process is underway, but estimates are that 30 years of intensive, full-time effort would be necessary to declare Bosnia "mine-free"—and even de-mining is not 100% foolproof. See **Sarajevo: Security Information,** p. 76, for details on the Mine Action Center and other safety issues.

TOURIST SERVICES

Few residents of Bosnia are anticipating a tourist influx in the near future. Tourist services are correspondingly limited. Residents of smaller towns may regard foreigners with suspicion, but much depends on the town's political and ethnic affiliation. In Sarajevo and (to some extent) Mostar, travelers are welcomed. Many Bosnians speak **English** or **German,** making the visitor's task easier. In Sarajevo, a fledgling **tourist office** provides guidance to the city. The **U.S. Embassy,** is also a source of useful information. Several independent tourist agencies have sprung up recently, but almost all of them focus on arranging vacations abroad for locals. Despair not: the helpful Bosnian people can often replace the softer functions of a tourist bureau.

MONEY

Bosnia's currency is the **dinar,** which comes in paper only in divisions of 10, 20, 50, 100, 500, and 1000. It is firmly attached to the **Deutschmark** at an exchange rate of 100 dinars per DM1. Transactions take place in either, or both, currencies. There is nothing unusual or suspicious about paying in DM and receiving dinars as change; however, to avoid getting stuck with large amounts of the non-convertible BHD, it is a good practice to ask for DM in return. The Croatian **kuna** was also named an official currency of Bosnia in late summer 1997. Unfavorable exchange rates preclude the kuna's widespread use, but it is the only official currency in the western (Croatian) part of divided Mostar. There are plans for a common Bosnian currency called the **convertible mark,** pegged to the German mark on a one-to-one basis—but that is probably far in the future.

The system of **banks** is quickly improving; within Sarajevo, their number is mushrooming. **ATMs,** however, are non-existent. **Traveler's checks** can be exchanged at some Sarajevo and Mostar banks; Central Banka in Sarajevo has a **wire service.** If your itinerary lies outside of Sarajevo and Mostar, the best advice is BYOD—Bring Your Own Deutschmarks. **Cash** is almost exclusively the method of payment.

Bringing many small Deutschmark bills rather than large ones will save time and hassle; Bosnia's economy operates on a small scale, and even DM10 bills are often not accepted in the marketplace or in cafes. Occasionally, smaller stores will provide sticks of chewing gum or additional produce as a substitute for change.

COMMUNICATIONS

Bosnia's **postal** system, operative since 1996, is slowly gaining more functions. The post offices in Sarajevo and Mostar can accommodate outgoing mail, but it is not wise to rely on mail reaching Bosnia. The only way to receive mail is to befriend a U.S. government employee and borrow their address, as **Poste Restante** is unavailable. Look for the small yellow signs with diagonal lines through them; these mark the post offices. Few towns outside of the capital are equipped with reasonable mail service. Mail to the U.S. usually takes three weeks, somewhat less within Europe. **Postcards** cost DM1 to mail.

Telephone connections have been normalized, and dialing into and out of Bosnia is no longer problematic. To call **AT&T Direct,** dial 008 00 00 10. Calling the U.S. is DM5 per minute, the U.K. roughly DM3.50. **Faxes** can be sent from the post office; the price to the U.S. is DM5 per page, to Australia or the U.K. costs DM3 per page.

LANGUAGE

When in Bosnia, speak **Bosnian.** When in Croatia, Croatian. When in Serbia, Serbian. The distinction is more in name than in substance, but never underestimate its importance. Languages in the former Yugoslavia have been co-opted by the governments as tools of nationalism. If you say you are speaking "Croatian" or "Serbian" in Bosnia, people will immediately correct you. The languages do have certain distinctions. Take, for example, the translation of coffee. *Kava* is the Croatian term, *kafa* the Bosnian. So in the former Yugoslavia, mind your Ps and Qs—and Zs, Ks, Us, and Js. The

BOSNIA

> ## Terminology
>
> Croat, Serb, and Bosnian refer to people with that nation-based, or "ethnic," affil-
> iation. Croatian, Serbian, and Bosnian are terms indicating the country. Thus, to
> say a Bosnian Serb denotes a Serb living in Bosnia (most often in the Republika
> Srpska (RS), the Serb-dominated entity in northeastern Bosnia). Likewise, a Bos-
> nian Croat is a Croat living in Bosnia, and Bosnian Muslims sometimes go by the
> term "Bosniak." Bosnians often refer to their Bosnian Serb enemies as "Četnik,"
> or "Chetnik," a revived WWII ethnic slur. In other words, a Serb is different from
> a Chetnik—do not make this mistake. Another lingual caveat: the Bosnian Army
> is precisely that; it is not the "Muslim army."

standard greeting, "*Šta ima?*" means "What's up?", and the appropriate response is
either "*Nema ništa*" or "*Mane štani,*" both of which mean "Not much." For more
words, see the **Croatian Glossary,** p. 799. **English** and **German** are widely spoken.

FOOD AND DRINK

Sorry, vegetarians, almost every *Bosanski specijalitet* includes meat—beef, lamb, or
to a rarer degree, fish. *Bosanki Lonac* is a stew-like dish that spices up vegetables and
beef with plenty of paprika. Cabbage rolls stuffed with meat and rice are *japrak.*
Slatki is the same but with sugar. *Pite* resembles pie, with the usual meat, cheese,
and potatoes. A shepherd's pie-like concoction, *musaka* features (once again) meat
and potatoes, this time with eggplant. Look for *čevabdžinica* or *aščinica* shops; both
serve Bosnian national dishes and are abundant, particularly in Sarajevo. Vegetarians
with kitchens can subsist on *kruh* (bread), dairy products, and vegetables fresh from
the daily summer **markets.** Or request a sandwich *bez meso* (without meat) from a
lunch stand. Pasta and rice were daily staples of the three-year war; now a bare mention of the words will be met with a grimace. For dessert, baklava and *tufahija*
(apples stuffed with walnuts and topped with whipped cream) are the regional pref-
erence, with *hurmasica* (a glazed cake) a popular third.

It will quickly become apparent that cultural life revolves around a cup—or several—of *kafa.* More daring and uniquely Bosnian selections include varieties of gullet-
stinging *rakija* (brandy). *Loza* is the grape variety, *šlijivovica,* plum.

CUSTOMS AND ETIQUETTE

Tipping is not customary except in more expensive settings—but it is always welcomed. Some places may anticipate that foreigners will tip; the option is yours. Ten
percent is generous; 5% is typical. At restaurants and cafes, the bill is never split.
Instead, one person pays—always the man the first time, and the woman should offer
the second or third time. The man, or the waiter, will also open and pour the
woman's drink. In **Muslim homes,** it is customary to remove one's shoes at the door.
Smoking is practically a national pastime; cigarettes have gone from a wartime black-
market price of DM15 per pack to a reasonable DM1.

Bargaining is possible, particularly in the outdoor clothing markets. Ask a Bosnian
to accompany you; the price will be miraculously lower. **Fashion** was important during the war, when there was little else to focus on, leaving Sarajevo on par with the
rest of Europe. Tourists in grubby T-shirts are easily identified.

Foreigners are welcomed and regarded with great interest in Sarajevo. Even the
taxi driver or the man in the kiosk will ask you friendly questions. America, particularly, is beloved among Sarajevans who amused themselves during the war with
pirated American TV such as the bastion of 90s pop culture, *Beverly Hills 90210.*
And however paradoxically, Sarajevans look to America as an ideal of the diversity
they seek to achieve.

NATIONAL HOLIDAYS

National holidays are: March 1, Independence Day; May 1, Labor Day; April 15, Day of the Army; May 4, Victory Day; and November 25, Day of the Republic.

LIFE AND TIMES

HISTORY

Bosnia originated as a definitive entity in 960, when this small enclave in the center of the Balkan peninsula broke away from the Kingdom of Serbia. Independence proved turbulent: Bosnia was then, as today, the subject of a wrestling match between Serbia and Croatia, and was eventually incorporated into the sphere of the strong medieval Serbian kingdom. From 1386 to 1463, the country came increasingly under the influence of the **Ottoman Empire.** In 1463 Bosnia officially became an Ottoman province, with Sarajevo as its capital. More Bosnians converted to Islam than in neighboring countries, and the mark of Islam remains in the many mosques and examples of Turkish architecture in Sarajevo and Mostar. Yet Bosnia does not wholly reflect Turkish influence: the country's central position means that it has been situated where Christianity and Islam, Roman and Eastern churches, physically converge.

The Ottoman Empire faded in strength through the centuries, its decline facilitated by the increasing power of the Christian empires that surrounded it—Orthodox **Serbia** to the east and Catholic **Croatia** to the north. A series of **peasant revolts** in the late 19th century demonstrated people's increasing restiveness. In 1862, Christian peasants, resentful of higher taxes demanded by their Ottoman overloads, rebelled. Christian powers eventually intervened, but another uprising in Bosnia against the Turks occurred in 1875-6. The situation was uneasily settled when the **Congress of Berlin** in 1878 declared Bosnia an Austrian protectorate.

The nationalistic unrest spreading through Europe in the late 19th century proved infectious. In the Balkans, many intellectuals went to Germany and returned with Bismarckian ideals of achieving nationhood. During the early 20th century, an almost hysterical suspicion of South Slav nationalism developed in the tottering Austria-Hungarian Empire. A desire to dampen South Slav morale (as well as to embarrass the nominal South Slav "protector," Russia) motivated Austria-Hungary's **annexation** of Bosnia-Herzegovina in 1908. Austria-Hungary's antagonism

> Tito strove for equality among the republics—he purged members from all three ethnic groups.

backfired, however, and merely inflamed pan-Slavic sentiments. The notorious anti-Austrian **Black Hand** was one of several terrorist groups that emerged in the new nationalistic context. **Gavrilo Princip,** a member of the Young Bosnians (another Serb nationalist group), assassinated Austrian Archduke Franz Ferdinand in Sarajevo on June 28, 1914. Many consider this to be the act which sparked **WWI,** for it induced Austria-Hungary to declare war on Serbia a month later.

Following WWI, the **Kingdom of Serbs, Croats, and Slovenes** was born, to be renamed **Yugoslavia** in 1929. Power fell to the Serb dynasty Karadjordjević. While the situation was a realization of the long-cherished ideal of South Slav unity, Croats quickly began to chafe under what they perceived as a Serb dictatorship. During **WWII,** Yugoslavia was divided between the German-aligned Croat Ustašas, the Serb Chetniks, and the Communist Partisans, whose stronghold was in mountainous Bosnia, where much of the fighting went on. Concentration camps set up in the region brought the massacre of hundreds of thousands of Serbs; the exact number is a political issue today. Enter Josip Broz, a.k.a. **Tito,** a half-Slovene, half-Croat Partisan during WWII, a Communist Partisan leader during the war, whose break with Stalin in 1948 earned Moscow's disfavor and sanctions. Tito sought to hold Yugoslavia together by decentralizing power, striving for equality among republics; in his great fairness, he purged members from all three ethnic groups. Yugoslavia, under Tito's strong hand, experienced an economic revival. His death in 1980 occasioned the disintegration of the Yugoslav nation. The vacuum was filled in the late 1980s as Serbian Communist **Slobodan Milošević** rose to power, spewing forth nationalistic rhetoric.

The Federal Republic of Yugoslavia began to come apart in 1990. Within a year, two of the country's provinces, **Slovenia** and **Croatia,** had declared independence. Their **secession** was opposed both by the increasingly Serb-dominated federal government and, in the case of Croats, by ethnic Serbs living in the self-declared independent states. In April 1992, events came to a head in Bosnia-Herzegovina, the most ethnically mixed of the former Yugoslav republics. The Bosnian government, unwilling to see the republic remain in a Serb-dominated Yugoslavia, opted for **independence** and was soon recognized by the international community (as were Croatia and Slovenia). The referendum for independence, endorsed by 99% of voters, was largely boycotted by Serbs in Bosnia. Violence broke out as the federal army and Serb militias quickly took control of 70% of Bosnian territory. The capital city, Sarajevo, was placed under a brutal siege that lasted from May 2, 1992 to February 26, 1996. A United Nations force sent to deliver humanitarian assistance **(UNPROFOR)** had little success in stopping the process of ethnic cleansing undertaken principally, though not exclusively, by Serb forces.

READING LIST

A wealth of excellent literature is available on Bosnia and its Balkan neighbors. The long-standing classic is *Black Lamb, Grey Falcon* by Rebecca West, a lively volume of over 1000 pages detailing her impressions during a 1937 journey through Yugoslavia. Facts and opinions are interspersed with spirited (if random) commentary on the male-female dynamic. A more modern, and less physically massive, travel narrative is Brian Hall's *Impossible Country.* Hall, an American, journeyed through Yugoslavia in the summer of 1991, just as the "Impossible Country" began to disintegrate.

For history of the recent war, turn to *The Death of Yugoslavia,* by Laura Silber and Alan Little. Theirs is a scintillating blow-by-blow account of the rise of Slobodan Milošević of Serbia and the tragic events of the war. Misha Glenny's *The Fall of Yugoslavia* covers similar ground; both books were updated in 1997. *Love Thy Neighbor* by Peter Maass, is a more personal, narrative option recounting stories from Maass's days as a *Washington Post* war correspondent.

Bosnian authors too have turned their energies to reflecting upon the war, in poetry, memoirs, and diaries. The simple tale contained in *Zlata's Diary,* by **Zlata Filipović,** a teenager during the seige of Sarajevo, is considered the "Anne Frank" work of the Sarajevo seige. For a more detailed and historical discussion of works by Slavic peoples, turn to **Croatia: Literature** (p. 137) and **Yugoslavia: Literature,** p. 751.

BOSNIA TODAY

Fighting in Bosnia, between Serb, Bosnian, and Croatian forces, continued until October 1995, when a peace agreement was brokered on November 21 at Dayton, Ohio, and signed in Paris later that month. The area under dispute was divided into the Federation of Bosnia-Herzegovina and the Republika Srpska (RS). The destruction caused by the war has been severe in many areas—about two-thirds of Bosnia's population live as displaced refugees, and towns and villages are now largely divided along ethnic lines. The Bosnian national elections of September 14, 1996, gave victory to **Alija Izetbegovič** of the dominant Muslim Party of Democratic Actions (SDA), meaning that he chairs the tripartite presidency which also includes an ethnic Croat, **Kresimir Zubak,** and an ethnic Serb, **Momcilo Krajisnik.**

> About two-thirds of the population of Bosnia live as refugees, and many towns and villages are now divided along ethnic lines.

NATO currently maintains 30,000 Stabilization Force (SFOR) troops in Bosnia, down from the 60,000 that were deployed immediately following the war. Though NATO is scheduled to pull out of Bosnia on June 30, 1998, slow implementation of the Dayton Accords makes it likely that a follow-up force will stay behind. In July 1997, NATO forces killed one Bosnian Serb war crimes suspect and arrested another, an action which raised hopes that NATO would seize "bigger fish" such as **Radovan Karadžic,** the popular wartime leader of the Republika Srpska, and his military henchman, general, **Ratko Mladič.** The tension generated by the arrests precipitated a power struggle in Republika Srpska between the hard-line Karadžic and **Biljana Plavsič,** the President of RS. Travel to RS territory is not advisable.

Sarajevo

Tall, Communist-era buildings tower silently, abandoned, their windows jagged black holes. The city streets, thronged 14 years ago with Olympic fervor, bear the marks of grenades and shrapnel. The arches of the beautiful old library surround a pile of rubble. Sarajevans speak of the prewar beauty of their city; now it possesses a different, strange sort of beauty, as well as a spirit determined to restore what was lost in the four-year siege.

In 1914, Sarajevo struck the alleged spark to WWI, when Serb nationalist Gavrilo Princip shot Austrian Archduke Franz Ferdinand. History buffs can still contemplate Princip's corner, but most other classic tourist features of Sarajevo are largely destroyed or non-functional. It is the city itself that demands to be seen. Internationals crowd Sarajevo, using the peacetime advantage to promote reconstruction efforts. SFOR troops were a common sight in summer 1997, rolling by in armored vehicles or haunting the cafes during off-hours. Sarajevo is stepping slowly toward normalcy—with some tensions, invisible to the tourist, created by the recent influx of refugees from the country. Keep a cautious eye on the political situation, but in the end, you may share with the Sarajevans a total love for this city.

> The following outlying areas of Sarajevo have served as confrontation lines and are thus at particular risk for **mines:** Grbavica, Lukavica, Illidža, and Dobrinja.

ORIENTATION AND PRACTICAL INFORMATION

Sarajevo lies in the heart of Bosnia. Its downtown is easily navigable. **Maršala Titova** (a.k.a. Maršala Tita) is the main street (*ulica*), running east to west through town. At the **eternal flame,** a 1945 marker to the Bosnian state—actually somewhat less than perpetual, due to gas shortages—Maršala Titova branches into **Ferhadija,** a pedestrian-only thoroughfare, and **Mula Mustafe Bašekija,** a street that holds a large market slightly farther down. Most of the cafes, particularly the loudest ones, are arranged along Ferhadija and its intersecting streets. The cobbled streets of **Baščaršija,** the Turkish Quarter, straddle the east end of Ferhadija. Ferhadija and Maršala Titova run roughly parallel to the river **Miljacka,** which borders the downtown area to the south. The road alongside the river is **Obala Kulina Bana;** heading west, it merges with Maršala Titova to become **Zmaja od Bosne** (Dragon of Bosnia), the erstwhile **"Sniper's Alley"** (so-called because its proximity to the front lines made it a constant target of Serb snipers). The yellow **Holiday Inn,** a well-known landmark, lies along Zmaj od Bosne. Farther out of town, the road enters **Novo Sarajevo,** a residential area that shows a heavy Socialist influence. The quarter known as **Skenkerija** lies to the south of the Presidency building (on the west end of Maršala Titova) and extends across the river. The main **market** in town lies beneath the road-bridge between Alipašina and Koševo streets. In the hills above the downtown area, streets become maze-like; it's easy to get lost, but just go downhill, and you'll eventually reach downtown. Streets have acquired new names since the war, but street-signs are clear and up-to-date. Some downtown kiosks and bookstores stock recent city **maps** (DM10).

Embassies and Consulates: Australians should contact their embassy in Vienna at Mattiellistr. 2, 1040 Vienna, Austria (tel. (1) 512 85 80; fax 513 16 56. Open Mon.-Thurs. 9am-1pm, Fri. 9am-1pm. **Canada,** Logavina 7 (tel. 447 900; fax 447 901). Open Mon.-Fri. 8:30am-noon and 1-5pm. Citizens of **New Zealand** should contact their embassy in Rome at Via Zara 28,00 198 Rome, Italy (tel. (6) 440 29 28; fax 440 29 84). Open Mon.-Fri. 8:30am-12:45pm and 1:45-5pm. **U.K.,** Tina Ujevića 8 (tel. 666 129; 444 429; fax 661 131). Open Mon.-Fri. 8:30am-5pm. **U.S.,** Alipašina 43 (tel. 659 969, 659 743, or 445 700; fax 659 722). Open Mon.-Fri. 9am-1pm.

Security Information: Incoming citizens should register immediately with their embassy. At the U.S. embassy, a security briefing is held every few days for government officials—if you ask nicely, you may be included. **Mine Action Center** (tel. 667 610; fax 667 611), in the Tito Barracks on Zmaja od Bosne. Entrance 200m past the Holiday Inn. Provides important pamphlets on the location and nature of landmines (though few are in English). **Mine awareness briefings** are held at schools and local authorities. Call or fax for more information.

Tourist Information: A **tourist bureau,** Zelenih Beretki 22a (tel. 532 281; fax 532 606), is staffed by friendly, chatty old folks who provide hotel information and answer general questions. Open Mon.-Fri. 8am-3pm, Sat. 8am-2pm. The **Consular Department** of the U.S. Embassy (see above) is also a fine source of tourist info.

Travel Agencies: Kompas Tours, Maršala Titova 8 (tel./fax 667 573), past the Presidency building going toward the Holiday Inn. A Slovenian tour agency. Flights from Ljubljana, Zagreb, and other destinations; car rentals; and hotel stays for a visit to the coast (1 week with some meals DM200-300). Open Mon.-Fri. 9am-4pm, Sat. 9am-9pm. **Air Bosna,** 15 Ferhadija (tel. 610 000 or tel./fax 667 954). Flight arrangements on all airlines. Open Mon.-Fri. 9am-5pm, Sat. 9am-2pm.

Currency Exchange: Among the largest of Sarajevo's many banks is **Central Banka,** Zelenih Beretki 54 (tel. 536 688; fax 532 406 or 663 855). Changes AmEx traveler's checks to Bosnian dinars at 1.5% commission. Personal checks up to US$500 cashed immediately; 15-day wait for higher amounts. Money can be **wired** here (2% commission plus DM10). Open Mon.-Sat. 8:30am-7pm; cash counter closes daily at 2pm. Leftover Croatian kuna can be changed at **Gospodarska Banka,** Maršala Titova 56 (tel. 442 959), at a painful rate. Cashes all traveler's checks at 3% commission (maximum amount per day US$300). Will not exchange BHD into foreign currency. Open Mon.-Fri. 9am-4pm, Sat. 9am-1pm.

Flights: To: Istanbul (TOP Air); Ljubljana (Adria Air; US$225-246); and Zagreb (Croatia Airlines; US$215). **Swissair,** Ferhadija 16 (tel. 471 180; tel./fax 471 181) flies to Zurich (DM767). Open Mon.-Fri. 9am-8pm, Sat. 9am-3pm.

Trains: The train station (tel. 617 584) had its first ceremonial run on July 30, 1996. As of summer '97, only two lines were running: one to Konjic (1hr., DM7.10) and another to Zenica (1hr., DM4.80).

Buses: Bus station, Kranjćevića 9 (tel. 670 180 or 445 442), near the old railway station behind the Holiday Inn. Ticket/info window (tel. 213 100) open daily 7am-7pm. **Centrotrans** (tel. 532 874; fax 670 699) services Sarajevo. To: Dubrovnik (7:30am, 8hr., one-way DM40); Frankfurt (Tues., Wed., and Sun., 15hr., DM180); Split (8am, 8hr., DM35); Zagreb (2 per day, 10hr., DM60). DM5 per bag.

Public Transportation: An excellent **tram** network serves downtown; it runs west along Maršala Titova and east along Obala Kulina Bana. Regular service from around 6am to 10pm or midnight, depending on the route (70BHD, buy tickets at a kiosk; they cost DM1 or 100BHD when purchased on the bus). Your ticket will probably not be checked (particularly in view of the disorganized state of the Bosnian government), but hold onto one to show possible inspectors (fine is DM10). **Buses** cover more area but for fewer hours (6:45am-6pm or 9pm). Purchase DM1 tickets on bus. A monthly bus pass is available for under DM10. **Oslobodjenje,** the daily paper (50BHD), lists a complete schedule of trams and buses.

Taxis: Radio Taxi (tel. 970). DM2 initial fare plus DM1 per km (negotiable). Don't call—they charge for getting to you. Make sure the meter's on.

Car Rental: Bosnia Rent-a-Car, Branilaca Sarajeva 19 (tel. 200 182). DM135 per day and up; DM250 deposit required. Open Mon.-Sat. 8am-7pm.

English-Language Press: Available at **Šahinpašic,** Mustafe Bašeskije 1 (tel. 670 676), near the eternal flame on Maršala Titova. Open Mon.-Sat. 9am-8pm, Sun. 10am-

If you're stuck for cash on your travels, don't panic. Western Union can transfer money in minutes. We've 37,000 outlets in over 140 countries. And our record of safety and reliability is second to none. Call Western Union: wherever you are, you're never far from home.

WESTERN UNION | MONEY TRANSFER®

The fastest way to send money worldwide.

Austria 0660 8066 Canada 1 800 235 0000* Czech 2422 9524 France (01) 43 54 46 12 or (01) 45 35 60 60 Germany 0130 7890 or (0180) 522 5822 Greece (01) 927 1010 Ireland 1 800 395 395* Italy 167 22 00 55* or 167 464 464* Netherlands 0800 0566* Poland (022) 636 5688 Russia 095 119 82 50 Spain 900 633 633* or (91) 559 0253 Sweden 020 741 742 Switzerland 0512 22 33 58 UK 0800 833 833* USA 1 800 325 6000*.
*Toll free telephone No.

Get the MCI Card.
The Smart and Easy Card.

The MCI Card with WorldPhone Service is designed specifically to keep you in touch with people that matter the most to you. We make international calling as easy as possible.

The MCI Card with WorldPhone Service....

- Provides access to the US from over 125 countries and places worldwide.
- Country to country calling from over 70 countries
- Gives you customer service 24 hours a day
- Connects you to operators who speak your language
- Provides you with MCI's low rates with no sign-up or monthly fees
- Even if you don't have an MCI Card, you can still reach a WorldPhone Operator and place collect calls to the U.S. Simply dial the access code of the country you are calling from and hold for a WorldPhone operator.

For more information or to apply for a Card call:
1-800-444-1616

Outside the U.S., call MCI collect (reverse charge) at:
1-916-567-5151

Pick Up The Phone.
Pick Up The Miles.

You earn frequent flyer miles when you travel internationally, why not when you call internationally? Callers can earn frequent flyer miles with one of MCI's airline partners:

- American Airlines
- Continental Airlines
- Delta Airlines
- Hawaiian Airlines
- Midwest Express Airlines
- Northwest Airlines
- Southwest Airlines

Please cut out and save this reference guide for convenient U.S. and worldwide calling with the MCI Card with WorldPhone Service.

Your MCI Worldphone Access Numbers

COUNTRY	WORLDPHONE TOLL-FREE ACCESS #
#South Africa (CC)	0800-99-0011
#Spain (CC)	900-99-0014
#Sri Lanka (Outside of Colombo, dial 01 first)	440100
#St. Lucia ✣	1-800-888-8000
#St. Vincent (CC)	1-800-888-8000
#Sweden (CC) ◆	020-795-922
#Switzerland (CC) ◆	0800-89-0800
Syria	0080-13-4567
#Taiwan (CC) ◆	001-999-1-2001
#Thailand ★	1-800-888-8000
#Trinidad & Tobago ✣	00-8001-1177
#Turkey (CC) ◆	1-800-888-8000
#Turks and Caicos ✣	8✱10-013
#Ukraine (CC) ✣	800-111
#United Arab Emirates ◆	0800-89-0222
#United Kingdom (CC) To call using BT ■	0500-89-0222
To call using MERCURY ■	1-800-888-8000
#United States (CC)	000-412
#Uruguay	1-800-888-9000
#U.S. Virgin Islands (CC)	172-1022
#Vatican City (CC)	800-1114-0
#Venezuela (CC) ✣ ◆	1201-1022
Vietnam ●	008-00-102
Yemen	

#	Automation available from most locations.
(CC)	Country-to-country calling available to/from most international locations.
	Limited availability.
✣	Wait for second dial tone.
▶	When calling from public phones, use phones marked LADATEL
■	International communications carrier.
★ ◆	Not available from public pay phones.
	Public phones may require deposit of coin or phone card for dial tone.
●	Local service fee in U.S. currency required to complete call.
▲	Regulation does not permit intra-Japan calls.
✣	Available from most major cities

And, it's simple to call home.

1. Dial the WorldPhone toll-free access number of the country you're calling from (listed inside).

2. Follow the voice instructions in your language of choice or hold for a WorldPhone operator.
   - Enter or give the operator your MCI Card number or call collect.

3. Enter or give the WorldPhone operator your home number.

4. Share your adventures with your family!

MCI

The MCI Card with WorldPhone Service...
The easy way to call when traveling worldwide.

MCI Calling Card
415 555 1234 2244
J.D. SMITH
WorldPhone

For more information or to apply for a Card call:
1-800-444-1616

Outside the U.S., call MCI collect (reverse charge) at:
1-916-567-5151

Please cut out and save this reference guide for convenient U.S. and worldwide calling with the MCI Card with WorldPhone Service.

COUNTRY	WORLDPHONE TOLL-FREE ACCESS #
#American Samoa	633-2MCI (633-2624)
#Antigua (Available from public card phones only)	#2
#Argentina (CC)	0800-5-1002
#Aruba ✦	800-888-8
#Australia (CC) ✦	
To call using OPTUS ■	1-800-551-111
To call using TELSTRA ■	1-800-881-100
#Austria (CC) ✦	022-903-012
#Bahamas	1-800-888-8000
#Bahrain	800-002
#Barbados	1-800-888-8000
#Belarus (CC) From Brest, Vitebsk, Grodno, Minsk	8-800-103
From Gomel and Mogilev regions	8-10-800-103
#Belgium (CC) ✦	0800-10012
#Belize From Hotels	557
From Payphones	815
#Bermuda ❖	1-800-888-8000
#Bolivia ✦	0-800-2222
#Brazil (CC)	000-8012
#British Virgin Islands ❖	1-800-888-8000
#Brunei	800-011
#Bulgaria	00800-0001
#Canada (CC)	1-800-888-8000
#Cayman Islands	1-800-888-8000
#Chile (CC)	
To call using CTC ■	800-207-300
To call using ENTEL ■	800-360-180
#China ❖	108-12
(Available from most major cities)	
For a Mandarin-speaking Operator	108-17
#Colombia (CC)	980-16-0001
Colombia IIIC Access in Spanish	980-16-1000
#Costa Rica ✦	0800-012-2222
#Cote D'Ivoire	1001
#Croatia (CC) ★	0800-22-0112
#Cyprus ✦	080-90000
#Czech Republic (CC) ✦	00-42-000112
#Denmark (CC) ✦	8001-0022
#Dominica	1-800-888-8000
#Dominican Republic (CC) ❖	1-800-888-8000
Dominican Republic IIIC Access in Spanish	1121
#Ecuador (CC) ✦	999-170
#Egypt ✦ (Outside of Cairo, dial 02 first)	355-5770
#El Salvador ✦	800-1767
#Federated States of Micronesia	624

- - - FOLD - - -

COUNTRY	WORLDPHONE TOLL-FREE ACCESS #
#Fiji	004-890-1002
#Finland (CC) ✦	08001-102-80
#France (CC) ✦	0800-99-0019
#French Antilles (CC) ✦ (includes Martinique, Guadeloupe)	0800-99-0019
#French Guiana (CC)	0-800-99-0019
#Gabon	00-005
#Gambia	00112
#Germany (CC)	0130-0012
#Greece (CC) ✦	00-800-1211
#Grenada ✦	1-800-888-8000
#Guam (CC) ✦	950-1022
#Guatemala (CC) ✦	99-99-189
#Guyana	177
#Haiti ✦	193
Haiti IIIC Access in French/Creole	190
#Honduras ❖	122
#Hong Kong (CC)	800-96-1121
#Hungary (CC) ✦	00 ▼800-01411
#Iceland (CC) ✦	800-9001
#India (CC) ✦	000-127
(Available from most major cities)	
#Indonesia (CC) ✦	001-801-11
#Iran ✦ (SPECIAL PHONES ONLY)	172-1022
#Ireland (CC)	1-800-55-1001
#Israel (CC)	177-150-2727
#Italy (CC) ✦	172-1022
#Jamaica ✦	1-800-888-8000
(From Special Hotels only)	873
Jamaica IIIC Access	0039-121▼
#Japan (CC) ✦	
To call using KDD ■	0066-55-121
To call using IDC ■	0044-11-121
To call using ITJ ■	18-800-001
#Jordan	8-800-131-4321
#Kazakhstan (CC) ✦	009-11
#Kenya (CC) ✦	009-12
(Available from most major cities)	
#Korea (CC)	
To call using KT ■	00729-14
To call using DACOM ■	00309-12
Phone Booths* Press red button, 03, then *	
Military Bases	550-2255
#Kuwait	800-MCI (800-624)
#Lebanon ✦	600-MCI (600-624)
#Liechtenstein (CC) ✦	0800-89-0222
#Luxembourg	0800-0112

- - - FOLD - - -

COUNTRY	WORLDPHONE TOLL-FREE ACCESS #
#Macao	0800-131
#Macedonia (CC) ✦	99800-4266
#Malaysia (CC) ✦	800-0012
#Malta	0800-89-0120
#Marshall Islands	1-800-888-8000
#Mexico	
Avantel (CC)	91-800-021-8000
Telmex ▲	95-800-674-7000
Mexico IIIC Access	91-800-021-1000
#Micronesia	624
#Monaco (CC) ✦	800-99-019
#Montserrat	1-800-888-8000
#Morocco	00-211-0012
#Netherlands (CC) ✦	0800-022-9122
#Netherlands Antilles (CC) ❖	001-800-888-8000
#New Zealand (CC)	000-912
#Nicaragua (CC)	166
(Outside of Managua, dial 02 first)	
Nicaragua IIIC Access in Spanish *2 from any public payphone	
#Norway (CC) ✦	800-19912
#Pakistan	00-800-12-001
#Panama	2810-108
#Papua New Guinea (CC)	05-07-19140
#Paraguay ❖	008-112-800
#Peru	0-800-500-10
#Philippines (CC) ✦	
To call using PLDT ■	1026-14
To call using PHILCOM ■	1026-14
Philippines IIIC via PLDT in Tagalog	105-15
Philippines IIIC via PhilCom in Tagalog	1026-12
#Poland (CC) ✦	00-800-111-21-22
#Portugal (CC) ✦	05-017-1-234
#Puerto Rico (CC)	1-800-888-8000
#Qatar ✦	0800-012-77
#Romania (CC) ✦	01-800-1800
#Russia (CC) ✦ ❖	
To call using ROSTELCOM ■	747-3322
(For Russian speaking operator)	747-3320
To call using SOVINTEL ■	960-2222
#Saipan (CC) ✦	950-1022
#San Marino (CC) ✦	172-1022
#Saudi Arabia (CC)	1-800-11
#Singapore	8000-112-112
#Slovak Republic (CC)	00421-00112
#Slovenia	080-8808

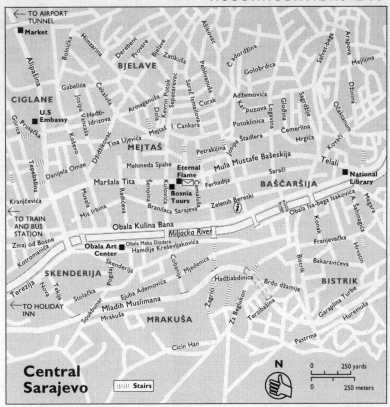

← TO AIRPORT TUNNEL
■ Market

BJELAVE

CIGLANE
U.S ■ Embassy

MEJTAŠ

BAŠČARŠIJA
■ National Library

Eternal Flame
Bosnia Tours

TO TRAIN AND BUS STATION

Obala Kulina Bana
Miljacka River

Obala Art Center

SKENDERIJA

BISTRIK

← TO HOLIDAY INN

MRAKUŠA

Cicin Han

Central Sajevo

:::: Stairs

N

0 — 250 yards
0 — 250 meters

BOSNIA

2pm. *International Herald-Tribune* DM4, *Newsweek* DM5.50. EuroClub (see **Accommodations,** below) has international magazines. The bi-weekly *Time Out,* partly in English, has info on the cultural scene (see **Sights,** p. 79).

Jewish Community Center: La Benevolencija, Hanidije Krevavjakovica 59 (tel. 663 472; fax 663 473; email la_bene@zamir-tz.znt.apc.org), across the river from town, just west of the massive green and yellow building. Cultural and educational organization with about 1000 members. Visitors welcomed and well cared for. As well as religious services, the center arranges housing with host families and organizes tours and volunteer opportunities. Contact in advance. Open Mon.-Sat. 9am-4pm.

Hospital: Koševo, 25 Bolnicka (tel. 666 620 or 444 800), or **City Hospital,** 12 Kranjćevića (tel. 664 724).

Pharmacy: Galas 4, Bulevar M. Selimovića 21 (tel. 640 054). Open 24hr.

DHL: Fra Andela Zvizdovića 1 (tel. 213 900; fax 202 016), very near the Holiday Inn. Open Mon.-Fri. 8am-6pm, Sat. 9am-2pm.

Post Office: "PTT Saobraćaj" Sarajevo, Zmaja od Bosne 100 (tel. 663 617; fax 473 103). No *Poste Restante.* Satellite telephones, faxes. Open Mon.-Sat. 7:30am-8pm. **Postal code:** 71000.

Telephones: At the post office. Calls to U.S. and U.K. DM1.65 per min. To Canada and Australia DM4.18 per min. **Directory information:** tel. 988. **Phone code:** 071.

ACCOMMODATIONS

As the old saying has it, friends are like gold. In Sarajevo, friends *are* gold—plus a few hundred Deutschmarks. Due to the influx of business travelers and a dearth of accommodations, housing is absurdly expensive. Private rooms and *pansions* are the only realistic options (although, as competition regenerates, prices may go down).

The **Jewish Community Center** (see **Practical Information,** above) can arrange housing with a family, given a week's advance notice. **Oglasi,** available for DM1 at newsstands, advertises apartments under the heading *"Iznajmljivanje"*—pronounce this word at your own risk. Typically, the apartment owners will want to rent for a month or more, but wheedle (or get a Bosnian speaker to wheedle for you) and you may be able to negotiate a shorter stay. Try renting a room for one night through an agency and then prolong your stay by negotiating with the landlord independently.

EuroClub, 20 Valtera Perica (tel. 666 240; fax 207 960), in Skenderija. This funky blue- and orange-pillared place can sometimes help with finding cheap housing. Contact them a week in advance. Open Mon.-Sat. 10am-7pm.

Bosnia Tours, Maršala Titova 54 (tel. 202 206; tel./fax 202 207). Private accommodations service. 80 modest but neat, clean rooms with bath in family apartments along Maršala Titova. Sheets provided. 1-2 day stays preferred, as landlord gets paid on a per-traveler basis. Longer stays can be arranged, independently with the landlord, for DM500-700 per month. Call ahead. One bed DM60. Two beds DM100. Open Mon.-Sat. 8am-8pm; those planning to stay Sun. should reserve in advance.

Pansion Mozaik-Train, Haliđa Kajtaza 11 (tel. 200 517; fax 200 522). Rooms are in railroad cars—probably the cheapest and most unique place to sleep in Sarajevo. 1-bed cabin DM30, 2-bed DM40, plus DM3 per person tax. Breakfast included. Water always available. Past the train station, take a left just before the road starts bearing right uphill, then a right (before crossing the tracks). 100m on, past some warehouses, you'll see the *pansion*'s parking lot and tennis court.

Pansion Hondo, Zaima Šarca 23 (tel. 666 564; fax 469 375), above a restaurant in the Bjelave neighborhood. Call for directions or just head uphill (north) from the Cathedral and ask for help. A 25min. hike up, but that's the only direction. 11 spacious rooms with TVs. Some singles with double beds. Large family room with balcony on the top floor. Singles DM80; doubles DM120. Breakfast DM10. Reserve at least 2 days in advance.

UNIS Tours, Ferhadija 16 (tel. 471 181; fax 471 181). Finds private rooms (DM40 per bed in a double, DM50 in a single). Also rents cars. Open Mon.-Sat. 8am-8pm; Sun. 9am-3pm.

FOOD

Though one might not think it given the preponderance of cafes, yes, people in Sarajevo do eat. Scour the Turkish quarter for **Ćevabdžinića** shops; DM3 buys a *ćevapčići* (nicknamed *ćevaps*), small, oblong lamb sausages encased in *somun,* Bosnia's tasty elastic flat bread. The same quick service is found in the numerous **Buregdžinica** shops, where the namesake dish is a meat and potato pie, but vegetarians can usually find *sirnica* (cheese pie) or *zeljanica* (spinach pie). The general poverty among Bosnians means that restaurants are the domain of internationals; in summer 1997, one could rarely eat out without an adjacent table of relaxing SFOR troops, journalists, or businessmen. Usual dining hours are 8-10pm. Two main **markets** bring vegetables to the table during the summer. The larger one, on Alipašina, under the Ciglane bridge, is a five-minute walk from the U.S. Embassy. A more convenient market lies on Mula Mustafe Bašekija a few blocks east from where Maršala Titova splits into Ferhadija and Mula Mustafe Bašekija (open Mon.-Sat. 8am-5pm, Sun. 8am-noon).

Klub Preporod, 30 Branilaca Sarajeva (tel. 205 556), near the National Theater on the street behind Ferhadija. Named after a famed Muslim newspaper. Sit indoors in cavernous armchairs around a low table, or outdoors in the back of the Klub. The music is relatively soft, the food excellent (if a bit greasy) and fairly inexpensive. Classic Bosnian meat and fish main dishes DM7-12. Bread accompanies the meal. Delicious *Lignje* (squid) DM7. No alcohol served—it's dining the Muslim way. Open Mon.-Sat. 8am-10pm.

Ragusa, Ferhadija 10b (tel. 442 541). Expensive, but excellent. A favorite among internationals. More crowded than most places; divine dining on cobbled, love-stirring outdoor patio in back. *Lignje* is swimmingly delicious at DM11, but DM20 is a more standard main-dish price. Open daily 8am-11pm.

Aeroplan, Sarci bb (tel. 535 690), at Ferhadija in the Turkish quarter. A local favorite that now lures the international after-work crowd. Waiters in traditional attire serve excellent food (*lonac*—vegetables and meat in a traditional small pot—DM3). No alcohol. Tomato soup DM2, excellent cheese pie DM3. Main dishes DM8-10. English menu. Open daily 8am-10pm.

Galija, Ćhobanija 20 (tel. 443 350), across the river from the center, 200m up the road. The superior Sarajevo pizza spot for atmosphere and food; frequented by locals. *Quattro Stagione* DM7. Prayers from the nearby mosque can be heard around 8:30pm. Open Mon.-Fri. 9am-11pm, Sun. 2-11pm.

Ćevabdžinica Hodžic, Bravadžiluk 34 (tel. 532 866), near the library in the old quarter. Among the best *ćevap* places for taste and variety, in a pristine white-arched building. All kinds of meat on display, but vegetarians can eat too—try *Raymak,* a melted cheese sandwich on *somun* (DM2). Open daily 8am-10:30pm.

Dom Pisaca, Kranjćevića 24 (tel. 471 158; fax 443 514), directly behind the Holiday Inn on the street parallel to Zmaja od Bosne; look for a glass-fronted building. Sketches of literary luminaries peer down from the walls in the renowned "Writer's Club" of Sarajevo. Two levels of dining: below with glass walls, or above in a peaceful outdoor garden. Rumors of snobbery come perhaps from the prices: steak main dishes DM12-15. Spaghetti *milanese* DM10. Open 24hr.

Bazeni, Bentbasa bb (tel./fax 441 240), on the river a few hundred meters past the burned library heading east out of town. Peaceful and open-air; views of the river and tall rock walls by the road. Eat below on the green mini-golf surface, or above on the wood balcony. Small bands tune up at night. Excellent lamb, steak, and fish. Main dishes DM8-20. Chef's specialty DM40 for two. Open daily 8pm-2am.

SIGHTS

The **eternal flame** (*not* burning in summer '97, due to gas shortages), on Maršala Titova in the center of town, where Ferhadija branches off, actually does not specifically commemorate the recent war. Rather, it is a 1945 marker to all Sarajevans who died in WWII. Evidence of the more recent, four-year siege is not hard to find, however; the souvenir cartoon-style map (DM10) sold at **Šahinpašić** (see **English Language Publications,** p. 76), highlights points of interest. At least half of Sarajevo's buildings sustained varying degrees of damage as a result of the war. The **National Library,** at the east end of town on Obala Kulina Bana, the road running alongside the river, exemplifies the tragedy. Dating from the late 19th century, the building was once regarded as the most beautiful in Sarajevo. It functioned as the City Hall until 1945, when it was declared a library. It is now an open-air structure housing piles of rubble, its pillars still standing as testimony to the lost beauty of the Austro-Hungarian structure. The besieging Serbs, attempting to demoralize the city, targeted civilian institutions early on in the war; the library was an early victim, firebombed on August 25, 1992—exactly 100 years after construction was begun. Most of the books and the archives of old periodicals were burned.

Up in the hills, a **treeline** is sharply evident, demarcating the front lines. The Bosnians trapped in Sarajevo cut down all available wood for winter warmth; the besieging Serbs had no need to do so. In hilly **Bistrik,** the neighborhood on the other side of the river, an old **road** with a beautiful view of the city snakes along, passing an old railway station. **Do NOT, however, leave the pavement at any time.** Though mines are not thought to be in this area, it's good practice.

Back in town, note the four different religious structures—their proximity is representative of Sarajevo itself: a Catholic church, an Orthodox church, a mosque, and a synagogue, all in the downtown area. In summer '97, all but the synagogue had been repaired enough to be open to visitors; the most active is the Catholic **Katedrala Srce Isusovo** (Cathedral of Jesus' Heart), on Ferhadija. Dating from 1889, it was designed by Josipa Vancasa, a prolific Sarajevan architect whose mark appears on numerous other city buildings. The somewhat modern interior of the yellowish-brown Orthodox **Pravoslavna Crkva** (tel. 472 672), on Zmaja od Bosne, might be worth a peek (open Mon.-Sat. for 6pm service and 1hr. before and after, Sun. 8am-7pm).

Fired-Up News

Some days the only newsprint was green, some days lavender, and all days in limited supply. But *Oslobodjenje,* Sarajevo's oldest and best independent newspaper, continued to print daily during the war. The *Oslobodjenje* offices were 50m from the front lines; by June 1992, they were destroyed. The printers, cloistered in a bunker below, were saved. The bunker gained some beds and became *Oslobodjenje*'s lightless wartime offices. Electricity to run the printers was totally cut off, so the paper turned to oil-operated generators. Oil also was in short supply, occasionally provided by the UN Protection Force (UNPROFOR), and occasionally sneaked in via the makeshift airport tunnel that was then the only, albeit high-risk, route to Sarajevo. Generator power lasted about two hours each day, a window during which the newspaper was madly compiled. Editors and reporters spent the rest of the day surviving. Wartime circulation reached about 200, or as many copies as possible, and 4-8 pages was the norm.

Today, *Oslobodjenje*'s circulation within Sarajevo approaches 10,000, and its page count is high in the 20s. Internationally, around 25,000 copies circulate to Slovenia, Austria, Italy, and Germany, where they are available to Bosnian refugees. So at least once, heed the call: *"Oslobodjenje, Oslobodjenje."*

The cobbled **Baščaršija** (known as the Turkish quarter) lies on the east end of town, farther east on Ferhadija. Jewelry and brasswork shops proliferate; sometimes the bronze-makers can be seen at work. If you wish to make a purchase, tell a Bosnian friend what you want, and do a vanishing act—prices double in a funny way around a foreigner. The charming 17th-century **Morića Han,** slightly set off from Ferhadija in Baščaršija, served as an inn for passing merchants for many centuries while Sarajevo was a station between East and West. Diners and *kafa* drinkers now occupy the former horses' stables; the rooms of the former inn are above.

The 1888 **Zemaljski Muzej** (Regional Museum), Zmaja od Bosne 3, across from the Holiday Inn, is among the Balkans' most famous, with botanical gardens and a superb ethnographic collection. On the front lines, the museum was severely damaged during the war. Many exhibits were saved, but the museum remains closed to visitors.

And finally, the act that made Sarajevo famous: on the corner of Obala Kulina Bana and Zelenih Beretki, near a white-railinged bridge about 200m before the library, is a plaque on a building wall commemorating the birthplace, debatably, of **WWI.** It was here that Gavrilo Princip shot Austrian Archduke Franz Ferdinand on June 28, 1914, leading to Austria's declaration of war on Serbia and the subsequent maelstrom of spiraling events that have become world history. During the recent war, the more dramatic plaque which formerly marked the historic spot with Princip's footprints was ripped out of the ground because Princip was a Serb from Belgrade.

Aspirants to culture can consult *Time Out,* a bi-weekly newsprint leaflet tucked inside the Sarajevo papers *Oslobodjenje* and *Slobodna Bosna. Time Out,* partly in English, gives info on the art, festival, and museum scene. Sarajevo has several art galleries. The **Obala Art Center,** Obala Maka Dizdara 3 (tel. 524 127; fax 664 547), in the yellow mosque-type building across the river, showcases rotating month-long exhibitions of contemporary art (open Tues.-Sun. noon-6pm). Most galleries are free.

Upcoming Sights

Many of Sarajevo's traditional tourist sites were damaged during the war; inquire at the U.S. Embassy or at the tourist agency for an update. In Baščaršija, the **Gazi Husref-Gebova Mosque** has towered over Ferhadija since its 1530 construction by the Ottoman Turks. Renovations should be completed by 1998; meanwhile, the mosque is open to visitors daily from 5am-11pm. The **Jewish Museum** (tel. 535 688), on Mula Mustafe Bašekija near the old quarter of town, was built as a synagogue in 1580, when Jews fleeing the Spanish Inquisition arrived in Bosnia. Now it has exhibits tracing the history of Jewish settlement in Bosnia (expected to re-open summer 1998, check with the Jewish Community Center). Renovations of the **airport tunnel** for tourist purposes are being discussed. The tunnel was built during the siege and served as the only wartime route in and out of Sarajevo.

ENTERTAINMENT AND NIGHTLIFE

Sarajevo drips with **cafes,** freer than ever with the abolishment of the 11pm "police hour." In the summer, everyone is outside, relaxing with *kafa*—remember, only the Croatians say *kava* or *pivo* (beer). American pop music-lovers will dig the cafes along **Ferhadija,** the pedestrian street. Equipped with outdoor speakers, the cafes seem to compete for airwaves. The international crowd plugs in at the **Internet Cafe,** Maršala Titova 5 (tel. 205 426), which boasts draft Czech *Budweiser,* the self-proclaimed best beer in town, as well as a fantastic variety of cocktails and shots, and frequent live music. The French cook prepares a different lunch menu every weekday (served 11am-3pm; DM6-8); an American-style brunch is featured Sunday and Monday (cafe open Sun.-Thurs. 10am-1am, Fri.-Sat. until 3am). **Cafe-Club Cocktail,** Kranjčevića 1, lacks the Internet Cafe's elegance, but profits from its proximity. This is also the only place in town where there's **dancing** every night, perhaps because the floor is small enough to look full with a paltry crowd (open 24hr.; most crowded Sun.-Thurs. 11pm-1am, Fri.-Sat. until 3am).

Alternatives to the cafe scene are limited, and generally are more popular during winter when it's too cold to be outdoors. The **S.B.C. Bock** (also known as FIS), 10 Mis-Irbina, occupies a basement room in the sports complex behind the Presidency building. A journalists' wartime hangout, its attraction now is a pool table, occasional live blues at 8pm, and a strange, mixed, but usually sparse crowd. The scene, we hear, is *much* better in winter (open daily 5pm-midnight; in winter 5pm-2am). **Senator,** Štosmajerova bb (tel. 200 443), is just another of the plush cafes lining the alley off the Catholic church downtown—except on Friday and Saturday nights, when this quotidian spot harbors the best **disco** in town (open 8pm until people leave). Smaller (cozy, even), quieter, and not so generic, **Marquee,** Radičeva 2, at the intersection with Obala Kulina Bana along the river, features Hard Rock Cafe-like decor and ceiling fans to dispel the summer heat (open 24hr.—yes, even when it appears closed).

Shoppers will find clothing and tourist items, like the Turkish coffee sets sold in the Turkish quarter, to be rather expensive. It is permissible to bargain, however, and getting a Bosnian to bargain for you can render the prices much more reasonable, particularly at open-air stalls or in the Turkish quarter.

It's lights, camera, action time in mid-September when the fourth annual **Sarajevo Film Festival** starts rolling: the city turns out for eight days of movies, many of them contemporary European productions. Last year's festival recruited the likes of Ingmar Bergman, Susan Sarandon, and Richard Gere for its "Honorary Board." The festival is organized by the Obala Art Center, 10 Obala Kulina Bana (tel. 524 127; fax 664 547). Since 1984 (read: Olympic nostalgia), Sarajevo has held an annual **Winter Festival,** a celebration of culture and art, which carried on even through the siege. For more details, call Sarajevo Winter (tel. 670 676). The bi-weekly *Time Out* (see **Sights,** above) details concerts and upcoming cultural events.

■ Mostar

For 400 years, Mostar beguiled visitors with its 16th-century Turkish bridge, which rose in a slender cobalt arc over the Neretva River. Tragically, in November 1993, the bridge was destroyed by shelling; a swinging metal bridge stands as a replacement. As the main city in Herzeg-Bosna (the mostly Croat-controlled part of Bosnia), Mostar suffered severely from the recent war. Fighting between Muslims and Croats has left the city physically divided, and reminders of war are everywhere, in countless bullet-scarred and windowless buildings. Even still, Mostar's medieval Turkish architecture is serenely beautiful, and the aqua waters of the Neretva River cannot be quenched.

Mostar is divided, with the Neretva River serving as a rough borderline. The Muslims are on the east, and the Croats on the west side (though the Muslims also occupy a thin strip along the west bank of the river). Locals rarely find good reason to cross over into the opposite side. In summer 1997, Mostar was considered reasonably safe. Animosity between Croats and Muslims remains strong, however; sniping erupted in spring of 1997, when Croats fired into a graveyard on the Muslim side, and no one can predict what will happen if the international military force pulls out as scheduled on June 30, 1998.

Orientation and Practical Information The closed **train station** is adjacent to the **bus station** (tel. 56 04 95) in the Muslim part of town, very near the river. **Buses** go to Sarajevo (4 per day, 2½hr., DM10); Zenica (10am, 4hr. DM15); Zagreb (8:45am, 18hr., DM40); Dubrovnik (10am, 3hr., DM27); and Split (10:30am, 4hr., DM16). **Tourist agencies Atlas,** Kardinala Stepinca bb (tel./fax 31 87 71) and **Reise Service** (tel./fax 31 56 66) sit next to each other in the same building as **Hotel Ero;** walk across the bridge opposite the bus station into the Croat part of town, continue about 100m, and Hotel Ero will appear on the left. Both agencies specialize in organizing vacations for locals, but can also answer general questions about the city and provide makeshift, photocopied **maps** (both open Mon.-Fri. 8am-4pm and Sat. 8am-12pm; English spoken). **Traveler's checks** can be exchanged at **Hrvatska banka** (tel./fax 31 21 20), in the same building (1.5% commission for kuna, 2.5% for DM). Visa **cash advances** can also be made (1% commission for DM and commission-free for kuna; open Mon.-Fri. 8am-2pm and Sat. 8am-11:30pm). The Croat **post office,** around the corner from the hotel, has 15kn maps that are fancier but no more detailed than those available in the tourist agencies. Phone cards are also sold (100 impulses for 29kn). *Poste Restante* is at window #12. Be aware that mail sent from Mostar is extremely slow (office open Mon.-Fri. 7am-8pm, Sat. 7am-7pm). **Postal code: 88101. Phone code: 88.** On the Muslim side, a post office can be found at Brace Feica 10 (open daily 8am-8:30pm). **Postal code: 88104. Phone code: 88.**

Accommodations and Food All hotels except Bristol lie on the Croat side. In summer 1997, however, Bristol was closed for reconstruction. **Hotel Ero,** Ante Starcevica bb (tel. 31 71 66; fax 31 43 94), has bright white singles (DM70) and doubles (DM120) with TV and a view of the enchanting rocky hills; prices include breakfast. Comparable prices and quality are offered by **Hotel Mostar,** Kneza Domagoja bb (tel. 31 79 50; fax 31 56 93), on a street west of and almost parallel to Ante Starcevica. Several kilometers from the bus station is the cheaper private hotel **Nikola Coric,** Fra Didaka Buntica 125a (tel. 31 95 60; fax 31 95 59; DM50 per person).

The food on the Croatian side is unexceptional. You can get pizza (25kn) and *kava* (3kn) at **Cafe-Pizzeria Milano,** K. Tomislava (tel. 31 29 08; open Mon.-Fri. 8am-11pm, Sat.-Sun. 8am-midnight). **Lasta,** Kraljice Katarine (tel. 31 34 12; fax 31 71 36), very close to trg H. Velikana, has what's probably the best food in the Croatian part, as well as a befountained courtyard divided by a long bed of flowers. Hunting steak is 37kn, tomato soup 5kn, and *spaghetti frutti di mare* goes for 30kn. Other main dishes run 35-45kn (open daily 7am-midnight).

On the Muslim side, across the makeshift bridge, the restaurants use the steep banks of the river and the rubble of the war to intensify the dining experience. **Babylon,** Tapmana bb, offers delicacies like roasted trout (DM10), brains in bread crumbs (DM10), and grilled calf's liver (DM6; open daily 9am-11pm). Restaurants with magnificent views also huddle along the thin strip that the Muslims control on the west bank of the river.

Sights and Entertainment Mostar's most famous sight is now remembered for its absence—the famous bridge which gave the town its name (*most* means bridge) was destroyed on November 9, 1993, by Croat nationalists eager to eradicate the legacy of the Ottoman Empire. The bridge had been built in the mid-16th century by the Turkish sultan, and almost single-handedly fostered the growth of Mostar. Currently spanning the river in its place is a makeshift, iron rope-and-panel bridge. Most of the sights that survived the war or have been reconstructed are in the **old Turkish quarter;** these include several 14th-century **mosques** and the **Turkish house,** Biscevica 13 (tel. 56 24 46), which is always open to show its now rare visitors "the Orient in the west," depicted in gorgeous photos and paintings and exquisite pottery. The Turkish quarter also holds a wealth of crafts, handmade in the small shops lining the streets. In his workshop at Kujundziluk 4 (tel. 55 00 22), master Ramiz Pandur fashions his world-famous etchings and reliefs. A sight in Mostar that the war was thankfully unable to defile is the beautiful **Neretva river;** in its clear green waters, swimming and rowing are possible.

On Friday, Saturday, and Sunday nights the disco lovers go to **Paladium,** trg Hrvatskih Velikana 1 (tel. 31 58 06), where the disco hops (10pm-4am; 10kn cover). On the Muslim side, the smaller **disco-bar Milano,** Glavna ulica 75a (tel. 55 15 84), has no cover (open daily 7pm-around 3am).

BOSNIA

Bulgaria

N

Monasteries
Camping Sites

0 — 50 miles
0 — 50 kilometers

Bucharest

ROMANIA

Vidin

Dunarea (Danube) R.

Ruse

Belogradchik

Mihajlovgrad

Pleven

Razgrad

Kaspichan 7

Balchik
Kavarna

Varna

YUGO-
SLAVIA

Lovech

Preobrazhensky
Monastery

6

Shumen

Albena
Kranevo

Zlatni Pyasatsi

Sofia

Troyan
Monastery

5

Gabrovo

Veliko Tarnovo

Byala

Kamchiya
Obzor

1 Pernik

STARA PLANINA

Nesebar

Black
Sea

Koprivshtitsa

Valley of
Roses

Shipka

Sliven

Emona
Ravda
Pomorie
Sozopol

Zemen

2 Rila
Monastery

Karlovo

Kazanlak

Burgas

Kyustendil

Sredna Gora

Nova Zagora

Primorsko

Blagoevgrad

Rila Range

Pazardzhik

Plovdiv

Stara
Zagora

Mitsurin

Ahtopol

Razlog

Bansko

Maritsa R.

Bachkovo
Monastery

4

TURKEY

F.Y.R.
MACEDONIA

Sandanski

Rozhen

Melnik

3

RODOPI MTS.

Haskovo

Svilengrad

GREECE

Thessaloniki

Meric R.

Monasteries

Aladzha monastery, 7
Bachkovo monastary, 4
Preobrazhensky
monastery, 6
Rila monastery, 2
Rozhen monastery, 3
Troyan monastery, 5
Zemen monastery, 1

Aegean Sea

BULGARIA

BULGARIA
(БЪЛГАРИЯ)

US$1	= 1810 lv (leva, or BGL)	100 lv=	US$0.06
CDN$1	= 1309 lv	100 lv=	CDN$0.08
UK£1	= 2879 lv	100 lv=	UK£0.04
IR£1	= 2654 lv	100 lv=	IR£0.04
AUS$1	= 1317 lv	100 lv=	AUS$0.08
NZ$1	= 1149 lv	100 lv=	NZ$0.09
SAR1	= 385 lv	100 lv=	SAR0.26
DM1	= 994 lv	100 lv=	DM0.10

Country Phone Code: 359   **International Dialing Prefix: 00**

From the pine-clad slopes of the Rila, Pirin, and Rodopi mountains in the southwest, to the lush Valley of Roses transersing the middle of the country, to the rocky and sandy beaches of the beautiful Black Sea, Bulgaria pleases the eye. Evidence of its 2500-year history appears everywhere: Greco-Thracian ruins on the coast, 9th-century citadels in the eastern mountains, and tiny National Revival villages dotting the land. Today, the Bulgarians love their history but hate their immediate past. The desperate pursuit of the West in a country too poor to hide its flaws provides fascinating insight into Bulgarian history, culture, and nature.

BULGARIA ESSENTIALS

Citizens of the U.S. and the EU may visit Bulgaria visa-free for up to 30 days. Citizens of other countries, or anyone planning to stay more than 30 days, must obtain a visa (single-entry US$53, multiple-entry US$123, transit US$43, double transit US$63) from their local embassy or consulate (see **Essentials: Embassies and Consulates,** p. 4). The application requires a passport, a photograph, a self-addressed stamped envelope, and payment by cash or money order. Single-entry visas take 10 business days to process; five-day rush service costs US$68, and immediate issuance is US$88. For multiple-entry visas, immediate service costs US$153. Visas are valid for three months from the date of issuance and may be extended at any time at a Bureau for Foreigners (located in every major Bulgarian city) before the date of expiration. The visa price includes a US$20 border tax which those who do not need visas are required to pay upon entering the country.

GETTING THERE

For tourist info, contact **Balkan Holidays,** 317 Madison Ave., #508, New York, NY 10017 (tel. (212) 573-5530; fax 573-5538). Bulgarian **trains** run to Budapest, Romania (enter through Ruse), Yugoslavia, Greece, and Turkey. **Balkan Air** flies directly to Sofia from New York and other cities. **Rila** is the main international train ticket company. **Group Travel buses** run to Romania, Greece, and Turkey. There are ferries from coastal cities to Istanbul and other cities on the Black Sea, including Odesa.

GETTING AROUND

In terms of frequency of transportation and accessibility, western Bulgaria is easier to navigate by bus, while trains are better for the north and east. Transportation everywhere is cheap, but not always quick. The **train** system is comprehensive, though slow, crowded, and aged. There are three types of trains: *ekspres* (експрес), *burz* (бърз; fast), and *putnicheski* (пътнически; slow). Avoid the *putnicheski* trains—they stop at anything that looks inhabited. Arrive at the station well in advance, and try to get onto the train itself as soon as possible if you want a seat. Purchase *couchettes* in advance. To buy an **international ticket,** go to the appropriate office, usually in the town center (look for Rila Travel), or go to the international ticket counter in the railway station. **Domestic tickets** are sold at stations. Buying a ticket on the train entails an unregulated surcharge. Stations are poorly marked, often only in Cyrillic. Know when you should reach your destination, bring along a map of the route, or ask a friendly person on the train for help.

Express trains usually have cafes with snacks and alcohol. Be prepared for smoke-filled corridors, unaesthetic bathrooms, breathtaking views, and friendly travelers. First-class seating (*purva klasa*; първа класа) is very similar to second class (втора класа; *vtora klasa*), and probably not worth the extra leva. Some useful words: *vlak* (влак; train); *avtobus* (автобус; bus); *gara* (гара; station); *peron* (перон; platform); *kolovoz* (коловоз; track); *bilet* (билет; ticket); *zaminavashti* (заминаващи; departure); *pristigashti* (пристигащи; arrival); *ne/pushachi* (не/пушачи; non-/smoking); *spalen vagon* (спален вагон; sleeping car).

Rising train ticket prices make **bus** travel an attractive, and often quicker, option—you'll save up to three hours traveling from Sofia to the Black Sea coast. For long distances, **Group Travel** and **Etap** offer modern buses with A/C, bathrooms, and VCRs at around 1½ times the price of trains. Buy a seat in advance from the agency office, or pay when boarding. Buses stop in many towns en route and let passengers off for snacks. Some buses have set departures; others leave only when full. Public buses are a sometimes grueling physical experience—bring water and (in summer) dress for a hot and sweaty trip. Two important departure points are the parking lot next to the Novotel Europa in Sofia, across the street from the train station, and the parking lot next to the train station in Blagoevgrad; both are unregulated clearinghouses of buses to everywhere. Private companies have great package deals on international travel, and many representatives speak English.

Balkan Air domestic fares have swollen enormously (Sofia to Varna or Burgas: US$159 one-way), and there are no youth discounts on domestic flights. Major **car rental** companies such as **Hertz** and **EuroDollar** are in most large cities. The cheapest prices, usually for a Fiat, average US$70-80 per day. Be prepared for speeding, questionable maneuvers, and unfamiliar signs. **Taxis** are everywhere in larger towns. Avoid private taxis; official taxis are all the same make and have the company name and number on the side. Refuse to pay in dollars and insist on a metered ride ("*sus apparata*"). Ask the distance and price per km to do your own calculations. Some Black Sea towns can only be reached by taxi. **Hitchhiking** is risky, but it can yield a heapin' helpin' of Bulgarian *gostelyubivnost* (hospitality) to those who are cautious, polite, gracious, and, above all, patient. *Let's Go* does not recommend hitchhiking.

TOURIST SERVICES AND MONEY

Balkantourist, the former national tourist bureau, still has some offices, though many have been privatized. The agency changes money and books hotel and private rooms. Hotels often maintain tourist offices. **Balkan Holidays,** a spin-off on the Black Sea Coast, is into reservations at expensive hotels, but the staff usually speaks English. It may be difficult to get information unless you're booking a tour or hotel room.

The **lev** (lv; plural leva) is the standard monetary unit. Ten leva coins exist, and bills reach as high as 50,000lv. We list many prices in U.S. dollars due to the ever-changing value of the lev; Bulgaria has fallen prey to some of the worst inflation in history. As of July 1, 1997, the European Currency Board and Bulgarian government pegged the lev to the Deutschmark in an attempt to curb inflation; 1000lv=DM1.

The official rate coincides with rates offered by private banks and **exchange bureaus.** The latter tend to have extended hours (24hr. ones have a "Change Non-Stop" sign in English) and better rates, but may not be able to change anything other than dollars and major European currencies. Old, worn, or ripped foreign bills will not be accepted. A few private exchange bureaus take AmEx **traveler's checks,** and some banks accept major credit cards for **cash advances** (MC is the most widely accepted). Banks have a fixed commission or percentage, while exchange bureaus have a lower (20-30lv) rate for checks than cash. Hotels generally have unfavorable rates. Cash AmEx traveler's checks into dollars or leva at major banks such as **Bulbank, Biohim Bank,** or **Obedinena Bulgarska Banka.** The lack of hard currency has caused many banks to stop cashing traveler's checks in the currency in which they are issued. Credit card cash advances are most often done in leva as well. **Credit cards** are not widely accepted, except in larger hotels and more expensive resorts. Do not be misled by credit card stickers in store windows; many are for show. Never change money with hawkers who approach you offering good rates. Any Bulgarian bill from before 1974 is worthless—check carefully. Your best bet is to carry US$ or DM well-hidden on your body, although **ATMs** are becoming an alternative to carrying cash (most take Cirrus, EC, and MC). Almost everybody will take dollars or DM in Bulgaria, but most official institutions (tourist bureaus, travel agencies, or anywhere you pay in large amounts) may ask for leva, fearing counterfeit hard currency.

COMMUNICATION

Making international **telephone** calls from Bulgaria requires tremendous patience. **AT&T Direct** (tel. 008 00 00 10), **Australia Direct** (1 800 032 329), **British Telecom** (tel. 00 800 99 44), **MCI** (tel. 008 00 00 01), and **Sprint** (tel. 008 00 10 10) provide direct calling card connections. To call collect, dial 01 23 for an international operator or have the phone office or hotel receptionist order the call. The operator won't speak English, the post office may claim they can't make the call, and hotel receptionists are protective of phones. In Sofia or Varna, try the AmEx office. The Bulgarian phrase for collect call is *za tyahna smetka* (за тяхна сметка). You can make international calls at most post offices, but connections are poor outside large cities and often break down during a call. Calls to the U.S. average US$2 per minute, but expect to pay as much as US$4 per minute at hotels. **Betkom** or **Bulfon** direct-dial phones with digital displays are at major hotels and resorts, as well as on the street and at the post office in large cities. They service only Europe and the Middle East, and require a special calling card, usually sold from a kiosk near the phone (5000lv and up). **Faxes** are widely used; send and receive them from post offices. A few hotels have business centers with faxes, typewriters, and phones, all for a steep fee. **Email** can be sent from the Sofia Sheraton or the NDK (National Palace of Culture). Some universities also have access to the Internet—beg or befriend a student or two.

Foreign papers can be found in large hotels; the *International Herald Tribune* and *USA Today* are at the Sheraton and TSUM (Central Department Store) in Sofia. Catch **CNN** in the lobbies of major hotels. The **BBC** and **VOA Europe** (103.5 FM in Sofia) play all day on Bulgarian radio. "С въздушна поща" on letters indicates airmail.

LANGUAGE

Bulgarian is a South Slavic language of the Indo-European family. A few words are borrowed from Turkish and Greek, but by and large Bulgarian is most similar to **Russian,** which is widely understood. **English** is spoken by many young people and in tourist areas. Bulgarian-English phrasebooks are sold at bookstands in Sofia (3000-5000lv). **German** is understood in many big cities and throughout the tourist industry. Street names are in the process of changing; you may need both old and new names. Bulgarian transliteration is much the same as Russian (see p. 797) except that "x" is *h*, "ш" is *sht*, and "ъ" is either *â* or *u* (pronounced like the "u" in b*u*g). *Let's Go* transliterates this letter with a *u*. Some useful words and phrases include: *poshta* (поща; post office); *chastna kvartira* (частна квартира; private room); *govorite-li angliski?* (говорите-ли английски?; do you speak English?); *toaletna* (тоалетна; toilet—Ж for women, М for men); *otvoreno/zatvoreno* (отворено/ затворено; open/closed), and the all-purpose *dobre* (добре; OK—used in almost every sentence). Words frequently used in this book include *Stari Grad* (Стари Град; Old Town); *tsurkva* (църква; church); *hizha* (хижа; hut); and *kushta* (къща; house). See the **Bulgarian Glossary,** p. 798.

HEALTH AND SAFETY

> **Emergency Numbers: Ambulance:** tel. 150. **Fire:** tel. 160. **Police:** tel. 166.

Public **bathrooms** often are simply holes in the ground; pack a small bar of soap and toilet paper, and expect to pay 20-50lv. The sign Аптека (*Apteka*) denotes a **pharmacy.** There is always a "night-duty" pharmacy in larger towns; its address is posted on the doors of the others. *Analgin* is headache medicine; *analgin chinin* is for colds and flu; bandages are *sitoplast;* cotton wool is *pamuk.* **Condoms** (*prezervatif*) can also be purchased in pharmacies—foreign brands are safer. Imported medications are popping up in larger cities. **Contact lens** wearers should bring supplies; in cities, the deceptive Оптика (optician, supposedly) usually just signifies a guy selling sunglasses, but some may have what you need. **Tampons** are not widely available.

While Sofia is as safe as most other European capitals, there is a certain sense of lawlessness. Locals generally don't trust the police, and stories circulate of people being terrorized by the local mafia. Contact your embassy in an emergency. Don't buy bottles of **alcohol** from street vendors, and be careful with homemade liquor—there have been cases of poisoning and contamination. Sofia's **streets** can be deadly; pedestrians do not have the right of way, and Bulgarians park and often drive on sidewalks. Walking in the dark is generally more frightening than dangerous, but still inadvisable, especially if you're alone. **Homosexuality** is coming gradually to Bulgaria, but discretion is a good idea, particularly in the countryside. Bulgarian females' tendency to be physically affectionate makes life easier for lesbians, but gay men may have a tough time outside the Спартакус (Spartakus) dance clubs in Sofia and Varna.

ACCOMMODATIONS AND CAMPING

Upon crossing the border, most people are given a yellow **statistical card** to document where they sleep; without it, you may have difficulty getting a hotel room. If you don't get a card at all (which could be the case if you don't need a visa to enter), don't worry. If you are staying with friends, you'll have to register with the **Bulgarian Registration Office.** See the consular section of your embassy for details.

Private rooms are arranged through Balkantourist or other tourist offices for US$3-11 per night. Be sure to ask for a central location. To brave it alone, look for signs reading частни квартири (private rooms). It is also common for people to offer private accommodations in train and bus stations. In crowded locations, such as the Black Sea resorts in the summer, this may be your only chance to get a room. Be very careful if you're by yourself. *Babushki* (grandmotherly old women) are the safest bet. Bargain if you're up to it. Bulgarian **hotels** are classed on a star system and licensed by the Government Committee on Tourism; rooms in one-star hotels are almost identical to those in two- and three-star hotels, but have no private bathrooms; they average about US$20 for singles and US$30 for doubles. Private hotels in converted homes are often a good option. *Chuzhdentsi* (чужденци; foreigners) are always charged higher prices. The majority of Bulgarian **youth hostels** are in the countryside and are popular with student groups; many give ISIC discounts, and almost all provide bedding. In Sofia, make reservations through **ORBITA,** Hristo Botev 48 (Христо Ботев; tel. (02) 80 01 02; fax 88 58 14); ORBITA may also be able to arrange university housing or sell you discount vouchers. Outside major towns, **campgrounds** provide a chance to meet backpackers. Spartan bungalows await at nearly every site, but are often full. Freelance camping is popular, but you risk a fine (and your safety).

FOOD AND DRINK

Food from **kiosks** is cheap (1000-2000lv); **restaurants** average 4000lv per meal. Kiosks sell *kebabcheta* (кебабчета; small sausage-shaped hamburgers), sandwiches, pizzas, *banitsa sus sirene* (баница със сирене; cheese-filled pastries), and filled rolls. Fruit and vegetables are sold in a *plod-zelenchuk* (плод-зеленчук), *pazar* (пазар; market), and on the street. Find 24-hour snacks at mini-markets. In summer, Bulgaria is blessed with delicious **fruits and vegetables,** especially tomatoes, peaches, cherries, and strawberries. Try *shopska salata* (шопска салата), an addictive mix of tomatoes, peppers, cucumbers, and onions with feta cheese. *Kyopoolu* (кьопоолу) and *imam bayaldu* (имам баялдъ) are eggplant dishes. *Tikvichki s mlyako* (тиквички с мляко) is fried zucchini in milk and garlic sauce. *Gyuvech* (гювеч) is stew with meat, onion, peppers, potatoes, and other veggies. Also try *tarator* (таратор)—a cold soup made with yogurt, cucumber, and garlic, ideally also with walnuts. *Purzheni kartofi* (пържени картофи) are french fries; you'll see "пържени" (fried) with lots of other dishes, too. Bread is *hlyab* (хляб); fruit is *plodove* (плодове).

The Bulgarian menu emphasizes **meat.** Try *kavarma* (каварма)—a meat dish with lots of onions and sometimes an egg on top, or organ-based dishes such as *mozik* (мозик; brain) or *ezik* (език; tongue). *Skara* (скара; grills) are a cheaper option. *Shishche* (шишче) is chunks of pork grilled on a spit and *kyufte* (кюфте) is a small ground meat patty. Bulgarians are known for cheese and yogurt—the bacterium that makes yogurt from milk bears the scientific names *bacilicus bulgaricus*. *Sirene* (сирене) is a feta cheese, and *kashkaval* (кашкавал) is a hard yellow cheese. Baklava and *sladoled* (сладолед; ice cream) are in shops marked сладкарница (*sladkarnitsa*).

Well-stirred *airan* (айран; yogurt with water and ice cubes) and *boza* (боза; similar to beer, but sweet and thicker) are popular drinks and excellent with breakfast. Don't drink unpasteurized milk unless it's been well heated. Bulgaria exports mineral water; locals swear by its healing qualities (good brands are Gorna Banya and

Hissaria). Delicious red and white wines are produced in various regions; the most expensive bottles are US$1-2. Melnik is famous for its red wine, and the area around the old capitals in the northeast makes excellent white wines. Bulgarians begin meals with *rakiya*, a grape brandy. Be careful; it's got a kick. The traditional toast is "*Na zdrave*" (to your health). Good Bulgarian beers are *Astika* and *Zagorka*.

CUSTOMS AND ETIQUETTE

Businesses open at 8 or 9am and take an hour lunch break some time between 11am and 2pm. Banking hours are usually 8:30am-4pm, but some banks close at 2pm. Tourist bureaus, post offices, and shops remain open until 6 or 8pm; in tourist areas and big cities shops may close as late as 10pm, but are often shut Sundays. "Every day" (всеки ден; *vseki den*) usually means Monday through Friday. **Tipping** is not obligatory, but 10% doesn't hurt. A 7-10% service charge will occasionally be added automatically. The word for bill is *smetka* (сметка). Restaurants and *mehani* (taverns) usually charge a small fee to use the restrooms. Bulgarians shake their heads to indicate "yes" and "no" in the opposite directions from Brits and Yanks. It is easier to just hold your head still while saying *da* or *neh*. It is customary to share tables in restaurants and taverns. In churches, it is respectful to buy a candle or two from the souvenir stand out front. Candles are placed high in honor of the living and low in remembrance of the dead.

NATIONAL HOLIDAYS

Bulgaria observes: January 1-2, New Year's; January 7, Orthodox Christmas; March 3, 1878 Liberation Day; April 19, Orthodox Easter; May 1, Labor Day; and May 24, Cyrillic Alphabet Day.

LIFE AND TIMES

HISTORY

Ancient **Thracian** tribes occupied Bulgaria during the Bronze Age from at least 3500BC. Influenced and colonized by the **Greeks** from the 8th century BC, southern and eastern Thrace served as a crossroads for Greek-Persian trade and warfare until the Macedonian conquest of 343-342BC. The death of Lysimachus of Thrace (323-281BC), a general of Alexander the Great, ushered in 200 years of chaos punctuated by Celtic invasions. By the year 46, the Thracian kingdom had fallen to the **Romans,** under whose rule the land that is now Bulgaria was divided between the provinces of Moesia and Thrace, straddling the main land trade route from the west to the Middle East. The crumbling of the Roman empire led to invasion in the 370s, as **Goths, Huns, Avars,** and **Bulgars** successively swept in. Tribes of **Slavic** agriculturalists gradually repopulated the region, but it was the Bulgars who eventually came to dominate. A Turkic group of warlike horsemen living in the steppes to the north of the Black Sea, the Bulgars are first mentioned in sources around 600. Bulgar khan **Asparukh** moved down south of the Danube in the late 6th century, conquering or expelling Slavic tribes in the area and defeating the army of Byzantine emperor Constantine IV. In 681, Byzantium recognized Bulgar control of the region between the Danube and the Balkan Mountains; this is considered the beginning of the Bulgarian state.

A Turkic group of warlike horsemen living in the steppes north of the Black Sea, the Bulgars are first mentioned around 600AD

The 8th century was rough; relations with Byzantium were hostile, and the Bulgarians were usually the losers in the continual small battles waged between the two states. In the 9th century, however, Bulgaria enjoyed peace with Byzantium, and prospered. Saints **Cyril and Methodius** created the first Bulgarian alphabet, *glagolitsa*; their disciple Kliment Ohridski was the author of the **Cyrillic** alphabet.

BULGARIA

Tsar Boris I (852-889) accepted **Orthodox Christianity** in 864, establishing the Bulgarian Church. The adoption of a common religion facilitated the assimilation of the Bulgar conquerors into the more numerous population of subdued Slavs, and an independent church helped ward off the ambitions of the Constantinople Patriarchate and the *Curia Romana*. The powerful **First Bulgarian Empire,** created under Tsar Simeon (893-927), united Southern Slavs under Bulgarian rule and overthrew the Byzantines in the Balkans. Under Simeon's successors, however, Bulgaria was beset by assaults from Magyars, Pechenegs, the Rus, and Byzantines. In 1014, Byzantine emperor **Basil II** won a decisive victory against the Bulgarians; Bulgaria remained subject to Byzantium from 1018 until 1185, when, taking advantage of the attacks of the crusaders and the Seljuq Turks, which weakened the Byzantine empire, the brothers **Ivan** and **Peter Asen** of Turnovo revolted and forced Constantinople to recognize Bulgarian independence. Thus arose the **Second Bulgarian Empire** (1185-1242), which reached its apogee during the reign of **Tsar Ivan Asen II** (1218-41). Under his rule Bulgaria was the leading power in the Balkans, its borders extending from the Black Sea to the Aegean and the Adriatic after the 1204 sack of Constantinople. Wars with the Serbian and Hungarian Kingdoms soon weakened the new nation, however, as did internal upheavals and attacks by the **Mongols** from the north. In the second half of the 14th century, the **Ottoman Turks** invaded the Balkan Peninsula. By 1396, the last semblance of Bulgarian independence was lost, and for the next 500 years, Bulgaria was a nation of oppressed peasants under the "Turkish yoke."

Over time, a **haidouk** (guerrilla or bandit) movement emerged. The *haidouks,* living in the mountains and surviving by robbing the Turks, lacked a strong sense of national consciousness, but kept the spirit of resistance alive. As churches were turned into mosques, monasteries became repositories of Bulgarian culture. Liturgical books were transcribed into Bulgarian, ensuring the continuation of a national language and literature. Meanwhile, Bulgarian towns grew, and an urban bourgeoisie developed trade. In the early 19th century, Bulgaria lagged behind its neighbors Serbia and Greece in the creation of an independence movement, but by the 1870s, the **National Revival** movement had engendered a strong new sense of Bulgarian national consciousness.

The large Bulgarian state envisioned by the Russians after the Russo-Turkish War, with boundaries stretching from the Danube to the Aegean and from the Vardar and Morava valleys to the Black Sea, represented the fulfillment of Bulgaria's territorial ideal, but the idea of such a vast, Russian-influenced state was intolerable to **Austria-**

The National Revival in a Nutshell

Father Paisy of the Hilendar Monastery is the recognized founder of the National Revival movement; his 1762 *Slavo-Bulgarian History* reminded Bulgarians of their past greatness and urged them to take pride in their own language and customs. The National Revival had three main components: the spread of education, the cultural movement against Greek influence, and the national revolution. Bishop Sofrony of Vratsa, Vasil Aprilov, and the monk Neofit Rilski were important educators in the early 19th century; due to their influence, over 2000 free Bulgarian-language schools had been established by the 1870s. The desire for freedom from the religious domination of the Greek patriarch was fulfilled with the Sublime Porte's 1870 establishment of an independent Bulgarian church.

The church became a leading force in Bulgarian life, helping to spread both education and national feeling, while writer/revolutionaries (see **Literature,** below) also inflamed nationalist sentiments. The political revolution began in the 1860s, led by Georgi Rakovski's *haidouk*-inspired legion and by Lyuben Karavelov and Vasil Levski. Hanged in Sofia while spreading the revolutionary message, Levski is considered the greatest hero of the movement. The revolutionaries' April Uprising in 1876, which resulted in the Turkish massacre of 15,000 Bulgarians near Plovdiv, helped lead to the Russo-Turkish War (1877-78), after which Russia imposed the Treaty of San Stefano on Turkey, creating an independent Bulgaria.

Hungary and **Britain.** The 1878 **Berlin Congress** redrew the boundaries, creating a much smaller Bulgaria, autonomous but under the sovereignty of the Ottoman Empire. Simmering Balkan tensions soon erupted in the **First and Second Balkan Wars** in the 1910s. The result was a further loss of territory for Bulgaria, which, frustrated, sided with the Central Powers (Germany, Austria-Hungary, and Turkey) in **WWI.** Troops mutinied, however, leading to an early armistice and further losses of territory. Bulgarian claims on Macedonia led the nation to support Germany in **WWII;** still, Bulgaria protected its Jewish population and resisted German pressure to declare war on the USSR. An anti-German movement emerged in 1942, as Agrarian and Social Democrats, leftist intellectuals, military reserve officers called *Zveno* (Link), and the underground Communist Party joined in the **Fatherland Front,** whose influence grew as Germany's military situation deteriorated. In 1944, faced with the continuing German collapse, Bulgaria attempted to declare neutrality. However, the Soviet Union declared war on Bulgaria on Sept. 5, the Fatherland Front led a successful *coup d'état* four days later, and the new prime minister sought an immediate armistice with the Soviets. 1945-46 elections left Bulgaria a Communist republic.

> The haidouks, bandits who lived in the mountains and survived by robbing the Turks, kept alive the spirit of resistance.

The late 1940s saw the collectivization of agriculture and the beginnings of industrialization. Under Communist leader **Georgi Dimitrov,** good economic and political relations with the USSR allowed Bulgaria to specialize in light manufacturing and serve as the breadbasket of the Eastern Bloc. **Todor Zhivkov** was Bulgaria's prime minister from 1962 until 1989; his dictatorial regime brought stability, restraint, massive industrialization and fanatical alignment with the Soviet Union.

On November 10, 1989, the Bulgarian Communist Party retired Zhivkov, by then unpopular and much-ridiculed, and held elections after changing its name to the **Bulgarian Socialist Party.** Despite initial socialist victories, Bulgaria succeeded in establishing a non-Communist government in November 1991. The country's first open presidential elections, held in January 1992, re-elected sociologist **Zhelyu Zhelev** as president and poet **Blaga Dimitrova** as vice-president. The following year, however, Dimitrova resigned in protest of economic and social policies supported by the government. In recent elections, the **Turks,** who make up approximately 10% of the Bulgarian population, have exercised a disproportionate influence on the country's politics through their party, the Movement for Rights and Freedoms. Meanwhile, Bulgaria's other major ethnic group, the **Gypsies,** remain politically unconsolidated, discriminated against, and on the fringes of mainstream society.

LITERATURE

Old Bulgarian literature developed in the 10th century, Bulgaria's Golden Age. Its beginnings are closely related to Tsar Boris I's adoption of **Christianity** in 864 and subsequent efforts to spread the new religion. The first Slavic literary school, under the patronage of the royal court of Preslav, was established in 893 by the pupils of **Cyril and Methodius,** the inventors of the **Cyrillic** alphabet. Golden Age literature is principally ecclesiastical, with its focus on translating (and thus Slavicizing) Greek liturgical texts and other religious writings, although it also includes uncanonical and didactic fiction, most notably an early 10th-century short story (*Chudo s bulgarina*), probably the earliest Slavic example of this genre and probably by Tsar Simeon himself. During this early medieval period, Bulgarian culture was closely tied to that of Constantinople and the **Byzantine Empire,** but managed to avoid being drowned by it; Bulgarian writings conveyed Byzantine and Greek Orthodox thought and ideas, but with a Slavic structure and lexicon.

However, Constantinople's capture of Bulgaria in the early 11th century completely subjugated the country to Byzantine rule, hindering all literary developments until the 13th century—the **Middle Bulgarian,** or Silver, Age of the Asen and Shishman dynasties. The taste was at first for historical themes, which in the late 14th century gave way to mystical doctrines focusing on the quest for "inner light": this was

BULGARIA

the doctrine of **Theodosius of Turnovo** and his celebrated pupil **Patriarch Evtimii,** leading figures of the Turnovo School, whose attempts to revive Old Church Slavonic literature brought about stylistic cleansing and standardization.

A second lull in forging a nation through literature occurred after Mongols overran Bulgaria in 1242, followed by the Turks in 1352. The hush lasted until 1762, the date on **Paisy of Hilendar's** *Istoria slavyanobulgarska* (*Slavo-Bulgarian History*). The *History* romantically evoked Bulgaria's independent past while appealing to the people's national identity; coupled with the publication of **Bishop Sofrony's** 1806 *Nedelnik* (*Sunday-Book*), the first text in modern Bulgarian, it sparked off the **National Revival** movement (*Vuzrazhdane*). Writers of the National Revival functioned simultaneously as poets, scholars, publicists, and revolutionaries, shaping an image of the renascent state. Modern Bulgarian Realism emerged in the narrative prose and drama of **L. Karavelov** and **V. Drumev,** with their depictions of rural and small-town life. **Hristo Botev** wrote impassioned revolutionary poetry; **Petko Slaveykov's** nationalist verse was influenced by folklore and Greek popular songs; and **G. Rakovski** zealously exploited Bulgaria's illustrious medieval past and surviving folklore to spur the people toward Bulgarian national identity. **Ivan Vazov's** epics, novellas, short stories, and plays earned him the title of "national poet," while his 1894 *Pod igoto* (*Under the Yoke*), vividly describing the Bulgarian struggle against the Turks, gained the status of a "national novel." Vazov's most popular play, *Hushové* (1894), depicted the pre-liberation ordeal of Bulgarian expatriates in Romania. Detailed eyewitness accounts of the Bulgarian uprisings were given by **Z. Stoyanov,** in *Zapiski po bulgarskite vuzstania* (*Notes on the Bulgarian Uprisings;* 1883-85).

The national and social awareness that characterized the 19th-century Romanticism was rejected by the early 20th-century **Misul** (Thought) group. This school glorified the frustrated intellectual, encouraging individual freedom over societal good. One author who incorporated elements of both the Romantic and the post-Romantic ages was **Pencho Slaveykov,** who based his famous *Simfonya na beznadezhnosta* (*Symphony of Hopelessness*), a tale of Bulgaria's centuries-long suffering, on the legend of Prometheus. Unlike those of the Romantics, Slaveykov's works describe personal philosophies of life rather than adopting a moralizing tone.

A "modernist" phase, akin to the Symbolist movement in Western poetry, appeared in the early 20th century, most notably in the poems of *Misul* member **P. Yavorov,** whose lyrics reflect his restless spiritual development and, more than the works of any of his contemporaries, exploit the musical and evocative potentials of the Bulgarian language. Realist writers continued to depict Bulgarian society, some, such as **Anton Strashimirov,** with cynicism; others, such as **Elin Pelin,** with wit and humanity. The effects of the war were vividly described in the work of **Yordan Yovkov,** whose short story *Vecheri v Antimovskia khan* (*Evenings in the Antimovo Inn;* 1928) provides, in classical narrative prose, deep insight into the Bulgarian mind. Meanwhile, **Emilian Stanev** in *Prez zimata* (*During the Winter*) followed the saga of a partridge family in his search for knowledge of human reality, while medieval Bulgaria was portrayed mystically and fantastically in the neo-Romantic works of art historian **Nikolay Raynov.** After the 1944 Communist coup, **Socialist Realism** became the publicly enforced current; against the uniformity, the novels of **D. Dimov** and **D. Talev** stand out, particularly Talev's work on 19th-century Macedonia.

National Revival writers, shaping an image of the state, functioned as poets, publicists, scholars, and revolutionaries.

In recent literary history, several female poets stand out. The promise in the works of **Petya Dubarova** was cut short by her death at age 17, in 1979; her collection *Here I Am, in Perfect Leaf Today* has been recently published in an English translation by Don D. Wilson. Bulgaria's most important 20th-century poet, **Elisaveta Bagryana,** who died in 1991, gained inspiration from technological progress for her love poems, which successfully fused traditional and experimental influences and stylistic devices. Bagryana's heir, the country's first post-Communism vice president **Blaga Dimitrova,** edited a collection of her poetry, the 1993 *Zhivota, koito iskah da bude* *poema: izbrana poezia* (*Life, That Strives to be a Poem: Selected Poems*). Dimitrova has also recently published several works of her own, most notably *Noshten dnevnik* (*Night Diary*), a collection of 70 poems written between 1989 and 1992, and *The Last Rock Eagle,* an English translation of several of her poems.

BULGARIA TODAY

The 90s have been rocky for Bulgaria: financial difficulties resulting from the government's privatization attempts led the political tide back in favor of the ex-Communists, with the **Bulgarian Socialist Party,** supported by the mainly Turkish **Movement for Rights and Freedoms** and the **New Union for Democracy,** a breakaway group from the former majority **Union of Democratic Forces,** ruling the **Narodno Subranie** (National Assembly) with an absolute majority between 1994 and 96. However, a financial crisis in 1996 which led to a sharp devaluation of the lev, massive inflation (over 700%), a serious grain shortage, and substantial unemployment due to layoffs from state-owned enterprises, led to a renewed rejection of the former Communists and espousal of conservatism. **Petar Stojanov** was elected President in the fall of 1996, and in the most recent elections, his party, the Union of Democratic Forces, along with its agrarian and social-democratic supporters, holds a majority in the Narodno Subranie, under Prime Minister **Ivan Kostov.** Bulgaria is one of the poorest countries in Europe, with its situation exacerbated by the continuing inflation. Despite all hardships, the country has remained peaceful, and unrest is not expected.

> Bulgaria is one of Europe's poorest countries, and its situation is exacerbated by continuing inflation.

Sofia (София)

Like the 6th-century church from which it derives its name, Sofia (SO-fee-ya) stands on 1500 years of history. Yet, as the city's motto puts it, "Sofia grows, but never ages." The skyline includes modern Socialist- and capitalist-style high-rises along with spires and minarets; and palaces, museums, and monuments share space with banks, hotels, and the landmark Natsionalen Dvorets Kultura (NDK; Национален Дворец Култура; National Palace of Culture). Amid the fumes of buses, BMWs, and Moskviches dwell more than a million Bulgarians, some wearing business suits and talking on cellular phones, some in rags parading around with dancing bears. The 21st century is coming to Bulgaria's capital in bumps and jerks (and some of the jerks stand on the street offering outrageous currency exchange rip-offs), but Sofia remains a pleasant city, offering coffee and pastries for dimes, and culture and nightlife for quarters.

ORIENTATION AND PRACTICAL INFORMATION

Sofia's 1.2 million inhabitants occupy the center of the Balkan peninsula, 500km southeast of Belgrade. Good **maps** of the city are sold in most hotels and tourist agencies, as well as in the thousands of kiosks and change bureaus. **Bul. Patriarh Evtimii** (бул. Патриарх Евтимий), **bul. Hristo Botev** (Христо Ботев), **bul. Aleksandr Stamboliiski** (Александър Стамболийски), **bul. Knyaz Aleksandr Dondukov** (Княз Александър Дондуков), and **bul. Vasil Levski** (Васил Левски) surround the most important administrative and tourist sites. **Pl. Sveta Nedelya** (пл. Света Неделя), Sofia's center, is marked by the Tsurkva Sv. Nedelya and the enormous Sheraton Hotel and Tsentralen Universalen Magazin (TSUM). **Bul. Knyaginya Maria Luiza** (Княгиня Мария Луиза) connects pl. Sveta Nedelya to the train station. Young people often meet at **Popa,** the irreverent nickname for Patriarch Evtimii's monument, where Patriarh Evtimii meets the intersection of Vasil Levski and **Graf Ignatiev** (Граф Игнатиев). Two good "post-name-change" publications with useful phone numbers, site guides, and maps are the monthly **Sofia City Guide** (free at the airport, hotels, and travel agencies; includes a list of cultural events) and the less frequent **Sofia Guide** (1000lv at Balkan Tour).

> **Tourist Offices: Balkan Tour,** Stamboliiski bul. 27 and 37 (tel. 987 72 33 or 988 52 56; fax 88 07 95 or 83 20 88). From pl. Sveta Nedelya, walk 3 blocks up Stamboli-iski. Agency books rooms in hotels (singles US$27; doubles US$44) and private homes (singles US$18; doubles US$22; students US$15 and US$18), exchanges cur-rency and traveler's checks, and sells current maps. Arranges bus travel to Istanbul, Prague, Budapest, Warsaw, and other cities. Rila Monastery tours with English-speaking guide US$30 per person for groups of 5 or more. Open daily 8am-7pm.
>
> **Budget Travel: ORBITA Travel,** Hristo Botev 48 (tel. 80 15 06 or 80 01 02; fax 988 58 14). From pl. Sveta Nedelya, walk up Stamboliiski and take a left on Hristo Botev. University dorm rooms (US$4, summer only) and hotel rooms (doubles with student or teacher discount, 2-star US$6, 4-star US$10). Issues and renews ISICs and ITICs. Airline and bus discounts. Open Mon.-Fri. 9am-5:30pm.
>
> **American Express: Megatours,** ul. Levski 1 (tel. 981 42 01; fax 981 21 67). Take Tsar Osvoboditel (Цар Освободител) to left of mausoleum. Cashes traveler's checks (commission US$4 for under US$100, 4.5% for over US$100), replaces AmEx cards, and sells plane and bus tickets. Office in Hotel Rila, ul. Kaloyan 6 (Калоян; tel. 980 88 89), Sofia 1000, holds mail. Open Mon.-Fri. 9am-6:30pm, Sat. 9am-noon.
>
> **Embassies and Cultural Centers:** Citizens of **Australia, Canada,** and **New Zealand** should contact the British embassy. **South Africa,** Vasil Aprilov ul. 3 (Васил Априлов; tel. 44 29 16). Open 8:30am-noon. **U.K.,** bul. (*not* ul.) Vasil Levski 38 (tel. 980 12 20 or 980 12 21), 3 blocks northwest of NDK. Open Mon.-Thurs. 8:30am-12:30pm and 1:30-5pm, Fri. 8:30am-1pm. **U.S.,** ul. Suborna 1a (Съборна; tel. 88 48 01 through 05), 3 blocks from pl. Sv. Nedelya behind the Sheraton. Consular sec-tion at Kapitan Andreev 1 (Капитан Андреев; tel. 65 94 59), behind Economic Tehni-kum. Americans are advised to register with the consular section upon arrival in Bulgaria. Open Mon.-Fri. 9am-4:30pm. USIS **American Center,** Vitosha 18 (tel. 980 48 85; fax 980 36 46; http:\\www.usis.bg), has a library stocked with American lit-erature and newspapers. Center open Mon.-Fri. 8:30am-5pm, library open 1-5pm.
>
> **Currency Exchange:** Vitosha, Stamboliiski, and Graf Ignatiev are home to the largest concentration of exchange bureaus. **Bulbank** (Булбанк), pl. Sv. Nedelya 7 (tel. 84 91), across from the Sheraton, changes traveler's checks to leva (US$1 per transac-tion). Open Mon.-Fri. 8:30am-12:30pm and 1-4:30pm. The many branches of **7M** give Visa cash advances at 6% commission. Open Mon.-Fri. 9am-5pm (some branches until 10pm), Sat. 10am-1pm. **ATMs** accepting Cirrus, EuroCard, and MC, are located at Bulbank and at **Purva Investitsionna Banka** (Първа Инвестиционна Банка), Stefan Karadzha 51 (Стефан Караджа), next to the telephone office.
>
> **Flights: Airport Sofia** (tel. 79 32 11, info tel. 72 24 14, international flights tel. 79 32 11 22). Take bus #84 (100lv) to city center. The bus stop is to the left of interna-tional arrivals; ask for *tsentur* (център). Some airlines offer youth fares for travelers under 26. **Balkan Airlines,** pl. Narodno Subranie 12 (tel. 88 06 63, reservations tel. 68 41 48; fax 68 94 18), flies to Moscow, Warsaw, Prague, London, Athens, and Istanbul. Open Mon.-Fri. 8am-7pm, Sat. 8am-2pm. **Lufthansa,** Suborna 9 (tel. 980 41 41; fax 981 29 11). Open Mon.-Fri. 9am-5:30pm. **Air France,** Suborna 2 (tel. 981 78 30). Open Mon.-Fri. 9am-1pm and 2-6pm. **British Airways,** 56 Alabin (Алабин; tel. 981 69 99). Open Mon.-Fri. 9am-5:15pm.
>
> **Trains:** Tsentralna Gara (Централна Гара; Central Train Station) is north of the center on Knyaginya Maria Luiza. Trams #1 and 7 travel to pl. Sv. Nedelya; trams #9 and 12 head down Hristo Botev. Buses #85, 213, 305, and 313 get you to the station from different points in town. Tickets for northern Bulgaria sold on ground floor. To Ruse (7 per day, 6800lv) and Varna (7 per day, 8240lv). Southern Bulgaria and international tickets in the basement. To: Burgas (8 per day, 6800lv); Plovdiv (18 per day, 2920lv); and Blagoevgrad (8 per day, 2450lv). International tickets sold daily 7am-11pm. Info, international and domestic tickets, and reservations also at the all-purpose **ticket office** (Bulgarian tickets tel. 65 84 02; international tel. 65 71 86), down the stairs in front of the main entry of NDK. Daily to: Athens (50,000lv); Budapest (70,000lv); Istanbul (30,000lv); and Thessaloniki (36,000lv). Open Mon.-Fri. 7am-3pm, Sat. 7am-2pm.

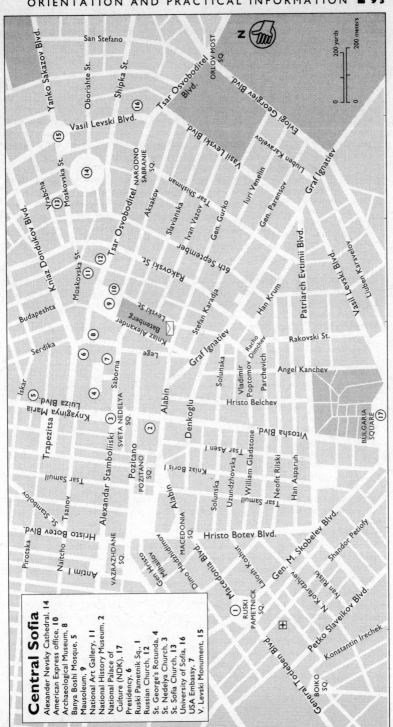

BULGARIA

Central Sofia

Alexander Nevsky Cathedral, 14
American Express office, 10
Archaeological Museum, 8
Banya Boshi Mosque, 5
Mausoleum, 9
National Art Gallery, 11
National History Museum, 2
National Palace of
  Culture (NDK), 17
Presidency, 6
Ruski Pametnik Sq., 1
Russian Church, 12
St. George's Rotunda, 4
St. Nedelya Church, 3
St. Sofia Church, 13
University of Sofia, 16
USA Embassy, 16
V. Levski Monument, 15

Buses: Ovcha Kupel (Овча Купел), along Tsar Boris III bul. (Цар Борис III), reachable by tram #5 or 4. For info and tickets, try the office under the NDK (tel. 65 71 87). Private **international and domestic** buses leave from the parking lot across from the central train station—the quickest and cheapest spot for buses. Get tickets at the Billetni Tsentur (Биллетни Център) kiosks, or check on the buses themselves. Pay in leva, US$, or DM. For more of a walk but much less confusion, try private company **Group Travel,** Ivan Vazov 13 (tel. 981 07 04). From the Sheraton, walk up Knyaz Dondukov bul. and take a left on Rakovski. To Budapest (US$40) and Prague (DM65). **Matpu** (Матпу), ul. Damyan Gruev 23 (Дамян Груев; tel. 52 50 04 or 51 92 01). To: Athens (1 per day except Sat., US$37; students $30); Belgrade (1 per day except Sun., US$21); Istanbul (3 per week, US$20); Skopje (1 per day, US$10); and Tirana (2 per week, US$26). Pay in leva.

Public Transportation: The system of trams, trolley buses, and buses is gleefully cheap (100lv per ride, day pass 400lv, 5-day pass 1500lv). Buy tickets at kiosks or from the driver; punch 'em in the machines between the bus windows. Operating hours officially 4am-1am, but most lines don't run later than 11pm or earlier than 6am. Ticketless riders are fined and mercilessly thrown off the vehicle.

Taxis: Everywhere. A green light in the front window means that the taxi is available. **Softaxi** (tel. 12 84) or **INEX** (tel. 919 19). From the airport, don't pay more than US$10 to reach the center. Fares are 250-350lv per kilometer (and rising with gas prices), with a 10% increase after 10pm, which in most cases is the only time when it's really wise to take a taxi.

Car Rental: Hertz and **Europcar** all over. **Eurodollar,** William Gladstone 38 (Уйлиам Гладстон; tel. 87 57 79), offers Fiats (US$57-98 per day). Open Mon.-Fri. 9am-6pm.

Luggage Storage: Downstairs at the central train station. Look for "гардероб" (*garderob*) signs. 300lv per piece. Open 5:30am-midnight.

Laundromats: None per se, and larger hotels are often unwilling to wash non-guests' dirty underwear. Private room hosts may do it for a minimal charge. A good dry cleaner is **Svezhest** (Свежест), Vasil Kolarov 19 (Васил Коларов). From pl. Sveta Nedelya, walk up Vitosha and make a left on Vasil Kolarov. Pants 1600lv, shirts 2200lv. Open Mon.-Fri. 7am-8pm, Sat. 8am-2pm.

Pharmacies: Purva Chastna Apteka (Първа Частна Аптека), Tsar Asen 43, at the intersection of Neofit Rilski. Well-stocked with condoms and feminine hygiene products. Open *dyenonoshte* (денонощне; 24hr.). **Megapharma,** Vitosha 69 (tel. 980 53 99), across from the NDK. Open daily 8am-11pm.

Medical Assistance: State-owned hospitals offer foreigners emergency aid free of charge. **Pirogov emergency hospital,** Gen. Totleben bul. 21 (Ген. Тотлебен; tel. 515 32 43), across from Hotel Rodina. Open 24hr. Dr. Anton Filchev is an English-speaking **dentist** with modern equipment (tel. 66 29 84). There's a 24hr. dentist at Lyulin Planina 17 (Люлин Планина; tel. 54 58 11); take Buludzha (Булуджа) 3 blocks south from the Ruski Pametnik (Руски Паметник).

Internet Access: ICN (tel. 916 62 213), on the lower floor of **NDK.** 5000lv per hr. Also in the **Business Center** in the basement of the Sheraton, US$6 per hr. Telnet connections may be unreliable, like every other phone connection in Bulgaria.

Express Mail: DHL, Tsar Osvoboditel 8 (Цар Освободител; tel. 987 79 27). Next-day delivery to New York, Washington, D.C., and Western Europe. Accepts AmEx, Diners Club, MC, and Visa. Elsewhere 2-3 business days. Open Mon.-Fri. 9am-5:30pm, Sat. 10am-2pm. **UPS,** Graf Ignatiev 13A (Граф Игнатиев; tel. 80 50 88). Similar services and prices.

Post Office: General Gurko 2 (Гурко). Walk down Suborna behind Sv. Nedelya, turn right on Knyaz Batenberg and left on Gurko. 60lv charge for *Poste Restante.* Open Mon.-Fri. 8am-8pm. Many hotels provide postal services. **Bulpost** express mail service open Mon.-Fri. 8-11:30am and 1-3:30pm. **Postal code:** 1000.

Telephones: On ul. Stefan Karadzhna (Стефан Караджа), near the post office. 1min. to: U.S. and Canada 5500lv; U.K. 2745lv; Australia, South Africa, New Zealand 7320lv. Use 10lv coins for local calls. Bulgarian phone cards also sold here. **Fax** available 8am-9:30pm. Open 24hr. **Phone code:** 02.

ACCOMMODATIONS

Hotels are rarely worth their price—**private rooms** are an ideal alternative. In addition to ORBITA Travel (see **Budget Travel,** p. 94), which arranges hotel discounts for students (US$6-10 per person) and dorm rooms (US$3-4 per person), try **Markela** (Маркела), Knyaginya Maria Luiza 23A (tel. 981 64 21), across from TSUM. They will stamp your statistical card and give you keys and directions (singles with hot showers US$4-6; doubles US$8-10. Open Mon.-Sat. 8:30am-8:30pm). **Camping Vrana** (tel. 78 12 13) is 10km from the center on E-80, and **Cherniya Kos** (tel. 57 11 29) is 11km away on E-79; ask at Balkan Tour for details.

Orbita Hotel, James Baucher bul. 76 (Джеймс Баучер; tel. 639 39), next to Hotel Vitosha. Take tram #9 south past NDK to Anton Ivanov, 3 stops after it emerges from the tunnel. A 2-star behemoth, even larger than Stalin's ego. Clean rooms with private bath, phone, and fridge. Singles US$35, students US$16; doubles US$46, students US$20. Breakfast included with non-discount rates. Rocking disco awaits.

Hotel Baldjieva (Балдиева), Tsar Asen 23 (tel. 87 29 14 or 87 37 84). A private hotel in the city center. Walking from Sv. Nedelya to the NDK, Tsar Asen is on the right, parallel to Vitosha. Clean, small rooms, with direct-dial phones, fridges, mini-bar, and laundry. The complimentary bathrobe makes you forget the bathrooms are shared. Potted plants surround the lounge for peace and photosynthesis. Doubles US$35. Add US$3 for breakfast. Pay in dollars or leva.

Hotel Niky, Neofit Rilski 16 (tel. 51 19 15 or 951 51 04), off Vitosha. Shared toilet, private showers, phone, and satellite TV. The wood panelling smells like it's fresh out of the forest. Billiard room, cafe, and restaurant. Pay in dollars, DM, or leva. Check-out at noon. Single or double US$20 per person, US$18 for students.

Hotel Tsar Asen (Цар Асен), Tsar Asen 68 (tel. 54 78 01 or 70 59 20). Walking toward the NDK on Tsar Asen, cross Patr. Evtimii and continue 40m. Ring the doorbell at the gate and the friendly English-speaking receptionist will let you in. 4 doubles (US$34) that also serve as singles (US$28). Cable TV and private shower.

To avoid the expensive and sometimes unpleasant hotels in central Sofia, stay in the suburb **Dragalevtsi** (Драгалевци), which offers many private, clean, and cheap hotels. Take tram #9 or 12 to the last stop, then pick up bus #64. Get off after 5 stops, in the main square.

Hotel Orhideya (Орхидея), Angel Bukoreshtliev 9 (Ангел Букорешлиев; tel. 67 27 39). As you exit the square on Yabulkova Gradina (Абълкова Градина), take a left on Angel Bukoreshtliev. Comfy, marble-tiled doubles US$20.

Hotel Darling (Дарлинг), Yabulkova Gradina 14 (tel. 67 19 86). It's the unvarnished house next to Hotel Orhideya. Nicely furnished, airy rooms, with a good hillside view of the city. Doubles DM20.

FOOD

From fast food to Bulgarian specialties, inexpensive meals are easy to find in Sofia. Supermarket **Zornitsa** (Зорница), Denkogli 34 (Денкогли), off Vitosha, is particularly well-stocked, with the exception of fresh fruit and vegetables. Open Mon.-Sat. 8am-8pm. 24-hour supermarkets line Vitosha. An **outdoor market** known as the *zhenski pazar* (женски пазар; women's market) extends for several blocks. Take Knyaginya Maria Luiza from pl. Sveta Nedelya, then make a left on Ekzarh Yosif (Екзарх Йосиф); bring your own bag for fresh fruit and vegetables (open daily).

Restaurants

Kushtata (Къщата, House), Verila 4 (Верила; tel. 52 08 30), off Vitosha near the NDK. No thick-necked Bulgarian youths here—swank is the name of the game inside this beautiful old house, where Bulgaria's *nouveau riche* consume *spaghetti mafiosa* (спагети мафиоса; meat, tomato sauce, zucchini, 3440lv) amid delicate paintings and flowers. Main dishes 4000-8000lv, salads 800-3000lv, soups 860-2400lv. English menu. Open daily noon-midnight.

BULGARIA

Borsalino (Борсалино), Chervena Stena 10 (Червена Стена; tel. 963 01 12), behind Hotel Orbita. At night, take a taxi (about 2000lv from central Sofia). Heavy wooden tables, fireplace, cozy outdoor area. Tasty Bulgarian specialties like *sarmi lozov list* (сарми лозов лист; meat-stuffed vine leaves served with Bulgarian sour cream, 1980lv), or *svinsko sus zele* (свинско със зеле; stewed pork with cabbage, 2400lv). *Pulneni guby* (пулнени губи; filled mushrooms) are made from a secret recipe (2490lv). English menu. Open 24hr. Takes US$ and DM.

Eddy's Tex-Mex Diner, Vitosha 4 (tel. 981 01 96). Mosey down the stairs and break through the saloon doors into one of Sofia's hippest eateries. Buffalo wings (2500lv), nachos (2000lv), and fajitas (4000lv) grace the imaginative English menu. Add a cold margarita to feel a bit more south of the border. Live music nightly from 9:30pm. Poduene Blues Band with Vasko Krupkata ("The Patch") appears every Thurs. English menu. *Sofia City Guide* found here. Open daily 12:30pm til the last customer leaves (kitchen closes 12:30am). Takes US$, DM, or leva.

Ramayana, Hristo Belchev 32 (Христо Белчев; tel. 980 43 11), 1 street over from Vitosha between the NDK and the Sheraton. Sofia's first Indian restaurant. Outdoor seating area and A/C to cool you down while you gulp the extra-hot curry. The chefs offer real *samosas,* spicy shrimp, chicken, and lamb dishes, and lots of veggie specials (around 3200lv). Main dishes 5400-7700lv. English menu. Open daily 11am-3pm and 6-11pm.

Chinese Restaurant Chen, Rakovski 86 (tel. 87 34 99), across from the Opera House. Genuine Chinese staff serves genuine Chinese dishes. Main dishes 2150-6000lv, vegetarian 1200-8000lv, seafood 5000-20,000lv. Spring rolls 1650lv. Chinese/English/Bulgarian menu. English spoken. Open daily noon-11:30pm.

Korona (Корона; the Crown), Rakovski 163A (tel. 87 47 08). Go up Rakovski from pl. Slaveikov. When in Bulgaria, eat as the Bulgarians do. Vegetarians may like *grutski sumichki* (stuffed vine leaves, 860lv) or "cheeses on grill Bella" (2500lv). Carnivorous main dishes 3000-5000lv. *Agneshki rultsa* (lamb rolls, 3500lv) are the meat specialty. A/C. English menu and English spoken. Open daily 11am-10:30pm.

Cafes

Markrit (Маркрит), Patriarh Evtimii 61 (tel. 54 92 41). Close to the NDK. A heaven for lovers of sweets. Excellent fresh pastries, fruit cakes, fruit salads, and ice cream. Another branch in Hotel Hemus. Coffee, cake and a soda for 2000-3000lv. Open daily 9am-midnight.

Cafe Luciano (Лучано), Rakovski 137 (tel. 81 36 24), 2 blocks from Hotel Sevastopol. A chain of cafes worth visiting every time you pass one. Low prices and excellent, jet-black caffeine. Coffee and cake for less than US$1. Open daily 9am-midnight.

SIGHTS

The 4th-century **Sv. Georgi** (Св. Георги; St. George's Rotunda), one of Sofia's two most venerable churches, hides behind padlocked doors in the courtyard of the Sheraton Hotel, accompanied by a complex of ruins that used to be a Roman bath system. Sv. Georgi itself is a brick structure with 11th- to 14th-century murals and a long, complicated history. After being converted from a bath to a church in the 5th century, it served as a holy place under Bulgarians, Byzantines, and Turks, then again as a church, later as a museum, and now finally as a historical monument (open 10:30am-1pm and 2:30-5pm). Sofia's other ancient church, the 6th-century **Sv. Sofia** (Св. София), stands on the pl. Aleksandr Nevsky. The city adopted the saint's name in the 14th century. During the 19th century, while the church was used as the city's main mosque, a series of earthquakes repeatedly destroyed the minarets. The Ottoman rulers interpreted the catastrophes as a warning and gave up St. Sofia as their house of prayer. Amazingly, the 5th-century floor mosaic survived intact (south wing open daily 7am-7pm; in summer 1997, the north wing, nave, and transept were all under renovation, including the floor mosaic).

Across the square from St. Sofia looms the gold-domed **Sv. Aleksandr Nevsky** (Св. Александър Невски), erected 1904-1912 in memory of the 200,000 Russians who died in the 1877-78 Russo-Turkish War, and named after the patron saint of the tsar-liberator. During the first few years of frail democracy after 1989, politicians of all creeds used the cathedral steps as a podium to speak to their supporters, who gathered in the square by the thousands. The **crypt** houses a spectacular array of painted icons and religious artifacts from the past 1000 years, undoubtedly the richest collection of its kind in Bulgaria (cathedral open daily 9:30am-7pm; 1500lv; English tour 4500lv; crypt open Wed.-Mon. 10:30am-12:30pm and 2-6:30pm). The **Katedralen Hram Sv. Nedelya** (Катедрален Храм Св. Неделя; Cathedral of St. Nedelya), the focal point of pl. Sveta Nedelya, is a reconstruction from 1925, when a bomb destroyed the 14th-century medieval original in an attempt on the life of Boris III. The tsar escaped, but the cupola buried 190 generals and politicians. The current frescoes were created in 1975 (open daily 7am-6:30pm). In the underpass between pl. Sv. Nedelya and TSUM, the tiny 14th-century **Tsurkva Hram Sv. Petya Samardzhiiska** (Църква Храм Свэ Петя Самарджийска; Church of St. Petya Samardzhiiska) contains some eye-grabbing frescoes. The bones of Vasil Levski, Bulgaria's national hero, are rumored to have been found inside. A museum during Communist times, Sv. Petya is again an operating church (open Mon.-Sat. 8am-6pm, Sun. 8am-3pm).

Along the way to the central train station from pl. Sv. Nedelya, the **Banya Bashi Mosque** (Баня Баши) sits on Maria Luiza. Built in the 16th century and named after the nearby mineral baths, it is again a place of worship (open daily 9am-10pm, even if it looks closed; no shorts; remove shoes at the door). Across the street, behind what used to be the *tsentralny hali* (централни хали; central market), the **Tsentralen Sinagog** (Централен Синагог), Exarh Yosif 16, opened for services in 1909. The building's foundation was built with stones from Sofia's Jewish cemetery; its six towers, six domes, and 12 stars point toward Jerusalem. Down Tsar Osvoboditel from sv. Nedelya, the 1913 Russian **Sv. Nikolai** (Св. Николай), named for the miracle-maker, has five traditional Russian Orthodox-style onion domes. A chandelier reminiscent of Foucault's pendulum hangs below the central dome (open Thurs.-Sun. 9am-10pm).

As you stroll down Tsar Osvoboditel, keep in mind that your boots are soiling the first paved street in Sofia, weighted down on either end by the House of Parliament and the royal palace. The **National Assembly,** built in 1884 and finished with materials from Vienna, provides a backdrop for a dramatic equestrian statue of the tsar *osvoboditel* (liberator) himself, Russian Tsar Aleksandr II, towering astride his charger over the pl. Narodno Subranie (Народно Събрание) with the Declaration of the War of Liberation (the Russo-Turkish War of 1877-78) in his hand.

Continuing up Tsar Osvoboditel, a left on Rakovski leads to the **National Opera House,** Rakovski 59 (main entrance at Vrabcha 1; Врабча), built in 1950 to seat 1270. The box office is to the right of the main entrance (call 87 13 66 for tickets or info; open Mon. 9am-5:30pm, Tues.-Fri. 8:30am-7:30pm, Sat. 9am-7pm; tickets 300-10,000lv). Rakovski is Bulgaria's Broadway, with half a dozen theaters in a half-mile stretch. The Neoclassical **Ivan Vazov National Theatre,** Levski 5, was built in 1907, destroyed by fire in 1923, and restored in 1927. Although the theater takes a break during the summer, you can catch any number of shows there the rest of the year (see **Entertainment,** p. 100, for details).

The **University of Sofia,** Tsar Osvoboditel 15, on the corner of Vasil Levski, was designed by the French architect Breancon and built between 1920-31. The sculptures at the main entrance represent Evolgi and Hristo Georgiev, who funded the University's construction. Students hang around as late as the end of July, when candidates for admission visit the "wall of tears"—the spot where acceptance results are posted after a series of rigorous exams. Nearby, on Vasil Levski, is the **Narodna Biblioteka Sv Sv. Kiril i Metodii** (Народна Библиотека св. св. Кирил и Методий; National Library Sts. Cyril and Methodius), Bulgaria's largest depository of knowledge. The **Suyuz na Bulgarskite Hudozhnitsi** (Съюз на Българските Художници; Bulgarian Artists' Union) has a four-floor gallery on Shipka (Шипка; tel. 433 51, ext. 214), behind the University. Bi-weekly literary exhibits grace the marble halls (open Mon.-Sat. 10am-6pm; free). See the posters by the entrance for schedules.

The **Natsionalen Dvorets Kultura** (Национален Дворец Култура; National Palace of Culture) is located at the end of Vitosha. Opened in 1981 to celebrate the 13th centennial of Bulgaria's creation, the NDK contains restaurants, theaters, and movie halls, including the best cinema in the country, which shows mostly subtitled American movies. Buy tickets (2000lv) from the ticket office (билletни център) to the left of the main entrance. Also ask here about tickets for plays, operas, shows, or exhibitions.

The labels in the **Natsionalen Istoricheski Muzey** (Национален Исторически Музей; National Museum of History), Vitosha 2 (tel. 88 41 60), off pl. Sv. Nedelya, are in Bulgarian only, but a guided tour in English is available. The exposition goes all the way back to 200,000BC; from Thracian treasures to medieval war glory, it has it all (open May-Sept. Mon.-Fri. 9:30am-6:30pm, Oct.-April Mon.-Fri. 9:30am-4:30pm; box office closes 3:45pm; 5000lv, students 2500lv; English, French, German, Italian, Russian tours 7500lv). The **Arheologicheski Muzey** (Археологически), Suborna 2, houses items from the Thracian, Greek, Roman, and Turkish settlements. Don't miss the amazing coins, weapons, and statues from up to 2000 years ago (open Tues.-Sun. 10am-6pm; donation requested). Traditional Bulgaria is preserved at the **Natsionalen Etnograficheski Muzey** (Национален Етнографически; tel. 87 41 91), in the Royal Palace building. Founded immediately after the 1878 liberation, the museum contains a vast collection of items from the past 400 years (open Wed.-Sun. 10:30am-5pm; 3000lv, students 1500lv). The **Natsionalna Hudozhestvena Galeriya** (Национална Художествена Галерия; Museum of Fine Arts) is also located in the Royal Palace. Its pride is a permanent exhibit of Bulgarian Old Masters (open Tues.-Sun. 10:30am-6pm; 1500lv, students 750lv).

There are two **artists' markets** in Sofia. In front of **Nevsky Cathedral,** you can find antiques, Soviet paraphernalia, and handmade crafts. Diagonally to the other side of the square, the market continues with lots of Bulgarian *babushki* offering handmade lace and embroidery. In the second park, in the underpass between the Sheraton and TSUM, artists of varying talent display their works in a sea of kitsch.

A great escape from the metropolis is the invigorating **Vitosha Planina** (Витоша Планина; Vitosha mountain). On a clear day, the panorama extends to the southern Rila mountains. There are several chalets, lodges and campsites. In winter, Vitosha becomes a popular **skiing area.** It can be reached by **bus** from Hladilnika (Хладилника; last stop of trams #9 and 12; take bus dir. "Vitosha"). Bus #66 takes you to **Hizha Aleko** (Хижа Алеко; Aleko Hut) in the middle of the skiing area (45min.). A **gondola** also goes there from the suburb of Simeonovo (Симеоново). To get to the lift, take bus #122 from Hladilnika (30min. to Aleko). For information on booking winter rooms with either of the hotels on the mountain, **Moreni** (Морени) or **Prostor** (Простор), call the Balkan Tour office at Vitosha 1 in Sofia (tel. 433 31). Vitosha is also home to **monasteries** and **churches,** including the 14th-century **Dragalevtsi Monastery** and the 10th-century **Boyans Church.**

ENTERTAINMENT

Nightlife in the center of Bulgarian civilization gets wilder every year. Outdoor cafes and bars share **Vitosha bul.** with musicians and dancing bears. **Frankie's Jazz Club/ Piano Bar,** Kurnigradska 15 (Кърниградска), right off Vitosha across from the American Center, invites some of Bulgaria's best jazz musicians (cover 500lv; no music in summer; open 10am-2am). Smartly dressed Sofians fill up the cafes around the **park** outside the NDK to scam and be scammed. When out on the town, though, remember that the thick-necked mafia runs the show; mind your own business, and don't pick fights. A crowd of regulars congregates religiously from 10pm until 4am at **Yalta** (Ялта; tel. 981 01 43), one of Sofia's most venerable discos, on the corner of Tsar Osvoboditel and Vasil Levski (1000lv cover). **Spartakus** (Спартакус), under the Grand Hotel Sofia by the pl. Narodno Subranie, serves both gay and straight clientele, although it's exceedingly exclusive—unless you know someone with a membership card, you may be out of luck. The club **Biblioteka** (Библиотека), which is actually *in* the Sts. Cyril and Methodius Library (enter from the Oborishte (Оборище) side), packs in 1500-2000 people on big nights (Wed.-Sat.). With a 500lv cover and live music, it's jumping until 5am.

The **opera** and **theater** seasons run from September to June. Good seats at the opera can be found for less than US$1 (tel. 87 70 11; box office open daily 9:30am-

7pm; no performances Mon.). You can get tickets for the **Ivan Vazov National Theater** at Rakovski 98 (tel. 07 23 03), or ask at the NDK ticket center. Cinemas often show subtitled Hollywood films—try Vitosha 62 and pl. Vasil Levski 1.

SOUTHERN MOUNTAINS

■ Rila Monastery

Holy Ivan of Rila built **Rilski Manastir** (Рилски Манастир) in the 10th century to serve as a refuge from the lascivious outer world. The monastery sheltered the arts of icon painting and manuscript copying during the Byzantine and Ottoman occupations, and remained an oasis of Bulgarian history and culture during the nation's hardest hours (well, more like five centuries). The quickest way to get to Rila town is to take a bus from Sofia's **Novotel Europa** to Blagoevgrad (8-10 per day, 2hr., 1200lv), then from Blagoevgrad to Rila town (6 per day, 1½hr., 600lv), and then catch the bus up to the monastery (2 per day, 1hr., 500lv). Try to get the earliest connections you can, because the last bus to the monastery leaves at 3:15pm. **Balkantourist** and **Group Travel** arrange guided **tours** in English to the monastery (US$30 per person). Bring a sweater—Rila is always chilly. **Exchange money,** but not traveler's checks, in Rila town at **Hebros Bank** (Хеброс Банк; open Mon.-Fri. 8am-noon and 1-3:45pm).

Inquire in room 170—or with any monk—about staying in a heated **monastery cell** (US$15 per person) with toilet and cold mountain water (tel. 22 08; reception open 9am-noon and 2-4pm; after 6pm in room 74; lockout midnight). The three-star **Hotel Rilets** (Рилец; tel. 21 06), a 15-minute walk from the monastery (follow the signs), rents fairly clean singles for US$24, doubles for US$36, and accepts Visa, MC, EuroCard, and Diners Club. **Restaurant Rila** (tel. 22 90), outside the monastery, sells phone cards and serves up a beautiful view and delicious *balkanska pasturva* (балканска пастърва; trout; 4000lv). The few vegetarian options revolve around eggs (1200-3000lv; open daily 7:30am-11:30pm). The **monastery bakery** tops the list of breakfast options; try the delicious *mekitsi* (мекици; fried dough with sugar; 150lv), bread (600lv per loaf), and the thick, sweet traditional Bulgarian drink *Boza* (Боза; 250lv per bottle; bakery open daily 7am-6:30pm).

The monastery's vibrant **murals** were created by National Revival artists of the Samokov and Bansko schools of painting, most notably the brothers Dimitar and Zahari Zograf. Not only are these two famous for their other work at the Troyan and Bachkovo monasteries, but their surname actually means "one who paints murals." The 1200 **frescoes** on the central **chapel** and surrounding walls form an outdoor art gallery. Inside you can find the grave of Bulgaria's last tsar, Boris III (no cameras, no shorts). The monastery also houses a **museum** displaying religious objects, coins, weapons, jewelry, and embroidery. The exhibit includes a carved wooden cross that took 12 years to finish and left its master, the monk Rafail, without his eyesight (open daily 6am-dusk; services 6:30am or 4:30pm; 1500lv, English tours 4000lv per person).

You can find maps and suggested **hiking** routes (2-9hr.) outside the monastery, or look in the alcove labeled **Manastirski Padarutsi** (Манастирски Падаръци) for a map in Cyrillic with all the *pateki* (патеки; paths; 1500lv). Hiking trails in Bulgaria are marked by colored lines on white background painted on rocks, trees, or anything that doesn't look like it'll walk away. Infrequent signs with directions and time remaining pop up along the way. Try to see the beautiful **Sedemte Ezera** (Седемте Езера; Seventh Lake) or climb a peak near **Malyovitsa** (Мальовица). Breathtaking views, dozens of mountain lakes, and welcoming *hizhi* (huts) await. Follow the yellow markings to **Hizha Sedemte Ezera** (Хижа Седемте Езера; 6½-hr. trek). Blue leads to **Hizha Malyovitsa** (Мальовица; 7hr.). Red leads to the highest hut in the Balkans: **Ivan Vazov** (Иван Вазов; 6hr.). Expect to pay around US$2 for a spot (not necessarily a bed) to sleep. Be prepared—weather in high mountains changes quickly, and the terrain can be pretty rough, so good hiking boots are a must.

BULGARIA

▨ Blagoevgrad (Благоевград)

The epitome of Stalinist urban planning in Bulgaria, much of Blagoevgrad (blah-GOY-ehv-grahd) came into being in the 1950s, making for big, open pedestrian squares and orderly streets. While Blagoevgrad is not nearly a cultural center like Plovdiv or Sofia, it is *the* transportation hub of the southwest, and the student element from the American University of Bulgaria gives the city a young and lively downtown, as well as making it the most English-friendly city in Bulgaria.

Orientation and Practical Information Blagoevgrad's **bus** and **train** stations are located right next to each other, along the southwest side of **Sv. Dimitur Solunski** (Св. Димитър Солунски). **Trains** head to Sofia (8 per day, 2hr., 2450lv) and Sandanski (8 per day, 1½hr., 1800lv). **Buses** depart from the *avtogara* (автогара) to: Sofia (every hr., 2hr., 1500lv); Sandanski (5 per day, 2hr., 1000lv); Melnik (1 per day, 3hr., 1500lv); Rila (6 per day, 1½hr., 500lv); and Bansko (7 per day, 3hr., 2100lv). To get to the center of town from the stations, take any bus up the thoroughfare **Sv. Sv. Kiril i Metodii** (Св. Св. Кирил и Методий) from the bus stop across the street from the train station. Three or four stops later is the **American University of Bulgaria (AUB),** a huge building that used to be the Communist Party regional headquarters. The befountained **pl. Makedoncheto** (Пл. Македончето) sits behind the university. Heading toward downtown, you'll find the **pl. Makedonia** (Македония), **pl. Bulgaria** (България), and the pedestrian commercial street **Todor Aleksandrov** (Тодор Александров), which runs parallel to the **Bistritsa** river (Бистрица) back toward Sv. Dimitur Solunski. State-run **Balkan Tour,** Sv. Sv. Kiril i Metodii 1 (tel. 232 18 or 230 31), in Hotel Alen Mak, sells **maps** (200lv) and other brochures and sets up private rooms (doubles US$10; open Mon.-Fri. 8am-5:30pm). The myriad change bureaus deal with cash only, but **Bulgarska Banka** (Българска Банка), 2 Trakia (Тракия; tel. 220 26), changes traveler's checks into leva (1% commission) or US$ (1.5% commission; open 8am-5pm). An **ATM** next to the main entrance of the AUB takes Cirrus, MC, and Eurocard. A healthy selection of English-language reading material can be found at the **AUB bookstore** (tel. 254 21, ext. 228), inside the AUB (open 8am-5pm). A **pharmacy** is at 8 Mizia (Мизия; open daily 8am-10pm). The **post office** is across from the big onion dome in pl. Makedoncheto (tel. 231 31; open 7am-10pm). **Postal code:** 2700. **Telephones** are inside the post office (4880lv per min. to the U.S., 2684lv per min. to the U.K.; open 24hr.). **Phone code:** 073121.

Accommodations and Food **Alphatour**, at Krali Marko 4 (Крали Марко; tel. 235 98), arranges private rooms for 8000lv per person (open Mon.-Fri. 8am-6pm, Sat. 9am-2pm). Balkan Tour (see above) offers slightly steeper private rooms and vouchers for the elusive Hotel Bor ($4 discount with voucher). Otherwise, check out **Dom Narodni Armi** (Дом Народни Арми), Ivan Vazov 7 (Иван Вазов; tel. 223 87), in the Voennen Klub (Военнен Клуб) just north of the pl. Makedonia. The best bet in town—clean beds in comfortable, if concrete, doubles with sinks cost 9000lv per person, and the shared bathroom on the third floor even has a working toilet. Another option is the **Hotel Bor** (Хотел Бор; tel. 224 91), on a hill across the river in the Loven Dom Park (Ловен Дом Парк). Take a taxi or hike—take the steps to the right of the Istoricheski Muzey and bear left until you get to a big dish-like fountain. Then go right up the steps until you come to a path of white flagstones next to a stream. Follow the path to the right (downstream) until you come to a red flagstone path on your left; this one leads to the hotel. Clean doubles with bath run 20,000lv per person (DM20, US$12, breakfast included; US$8 with Balkan Tour voucher).

The cheapest and freshest food can be found at the **Kooperativen Pazar** (Кооперативен Пазар), an outdoor market open Wednesday (the busiest day) through Sunday, dawn till late afternoon, on the opposite side of the river. Cross the bridge at Petko D. Petkov (Петко Д. Петков) or Krali Marko. The legion of restaurants and cafes on **Todor Aleksandrov** and the squares provide standard Bulgarian fare (soups, salads, omelettes, meat dishes) at standard prices (1000-4000lv). Away from the main drag, one option is the **Cafe Foto Stefcho** (Кафе Фото Стефчо) at Doctor Hristo Tatarchev 30 (Доктор Христо Татарчев; tel. 67 14), on a vine-covered patio in the park in the center of town. Fish is 1000-2200lv, Bulgarian beer 450-600lv. To get there, follow Doctor Hristo Tatarchev from the intersection of Todor Aleksandrov and Batumi (Батуми; cafe open 8:30am-1am).

Sights and Entertainment The **Loven Dom Park** on the hillside across the river offers quiet, peaceful, and potentially romantic walks away from the capitalist din below. The **Istoricheski Muzey** (Исторически Музей; Historical Museum; tel. 290 20) provides interesting exhibits of early Bulgarian art and crafts (open Tues.-Sat. 9:30am-4:30pm; 100lv). Okay, there's not that much to do during the day, but Blagoevgrad shines at night. Students come crawling out to the many cafes and bars on the squares, like **Rock House** on the south side of pl. Bulgaria. The discos **Galactica** (Галактика), in the basement of the building between the AUB and the Drama Theater, and **Tsentral** (Централ), on pl. Makedoncheto by the First Private Bank (Първа Часна Банка), start to fill up after 9pm on Monday, Wednesday, and Saturday (100lv; women free at Tsentral). For something more intellectual, try the **Dramaticheski Teatr Nikola Vaptsarov** (Драматически Театр Никола Вапцаров; tel. 234 75), next to the AUB (nightly performances Sept.-June; 500lv, students 300lv).

■ Bansko (Банско)

At the base of the Pirin mountains, Bansko (BAHN-sko) is a gateway to 180 lakes and more than 100 steep peaks scattered across a sea of forget-me-nots and alpine poppies. The highest peak, Vihren, reaches 2914m. The mountain range around Bansko offers summer hiking and winter skiing, while wonderfully preserved stone houses, taverns, and hotels line the narrow, cobbled streets of the town itself.

Orientation and Practical Information Take a bus from Sofia's Ovcha Kupel station (4 per day, 3½hr., 2800lv), Blagoevgrad (8 per day, 1½hr., 1200lv), or Plovdiv (1 per day Mon., Wed., Fri., 3hr., 3100lv). From Bansko's **bus station,** Patriarh Evtimii (Патриарх Евтимий), cross the street, walk straight to Todor Aleksandrov (Тодор Александров), and take a right toward **pl. Demokratsia** (пл. Демокрация), the town center. Make a left on **Tsar Simeon** (Цар Симеон) to get to **Hotel Pirin** (Пирин), which sells a useful **map** (200lv). Nearby is **Tourist and Change Bureau Bansko** (tel. 24 86) which also sells maps (600-1500lv) and **exchanges cash only**—no traveler's checks (open daily 9am-8pm). **Pirin Pharm** (Пирин Фарм), 57 Tsar Simeon, at the northwest corner of pl. Demokratsia, has a sufficient supply of basic medicine (tel. 23 43; open daily 7:30am-8pm). The **post office,** 69 Tsar Simeon, is across from Hotel Pirin (see above; open Mon.-Fri. 7:30am-4:30pm). **Telephones** in the post office are open daily 7am-10pm (2684lv per min. to the U.K.; no service to the U.S.). **Postal code:** 2770. **Phone code:** 07443.

Accommodations and Food **Private rooms** can be arranged informally with locals for US$2-5 a head, or through the **Piri Tourist Agency** (Пири), pl. Demokratsia 2 (tel. 25 76; fax 51 98), which books private rooms for US$2 per night (US$3 in winter) or hotel space for US$4 (US$5 in winter). Book in advance for winter (open Mon.-Sat. 10am-8pm, Sun. 11am-2pm). An exemplary private hotel is **Mir** (Мир), Neofit Rilski 28 (Неофит Рилски; tel. 25 00 or 21 60), with spotless bathrooms, 24-hour hot water, and firm beds (singles, doubles, and triples with breakfast US$12 per person, US$15 in winter). **Edelweis** (Еделвайс; tel. 22 71), on pl. Vuzrazhdane (Възраждане), offers bedding and sinks with rooms, but the shared showers long for Lysol. Doubles, triples, and quads cost US$5. For a cheaper but amenity-free sleep, **hizhi** (huts) dotting the mountains shelter hikers for around US$2 per night.

With a **mehana** (механа; tavern) hiding in almost every house or courtyard, Bansko is a dining heaven—at least for carnivores. **Sireshtova Kushta** (Сирешова Къща; tel. 46 68), Yane Sandanski 12 (Яне Сандански), occupies the oldest preserved house in town, which dates from the 17th century. The wooden menu offers main courses for 2000-3500lv and beer for 480-600lv. Vegetarians will appreciate the *ovcharska salata* (овчарска салата; shepherd's salad; 2400lv), a mix of cucumbers, tomatoes, onions, baked peppers, mushrooms, parsley, cheese, and a boiled egg. On weekends you can hear old Bansko folk songs, live (open daily 8am-past midnight). **Dudo Pene** (Дъдо Пене), Aleksandr Buinov 1 (Александър Буйнов; tel. 50 71), can sate the healthiest appetite around its heavy wooden tables. A specialty is *shish po haidushki* (шиш по хайдушки; shish kebab with garnish; 3300lv); salads (650-2000lv) and wines (5000lv) are also popular. Veggie options hover around 1500lv. Live folk music after 7:30pm (open daily 10am-whenever).

Sights and Hiking Although the increase in tourism in the past 10 years is pushing the town towards modernity, the 20th century has not destroyed Bansko's established way of life. Traditional habits are still alive and stomping—around 7pm, the streets fill with cattle and sheep strolling back from the pastures. Pleasant, well-kept museums and century-old houses make Bansko a living homage to the National Revival. The **Kushta-Muzey Nikola Vaptsarov** (Къша-музей Никола Ванцаров; Nikola Vaptsarov House-Museum; tel. 30 38), on the corner of pl. Demokratsia and Vaptsarov, recalls the life and works of the 20th-century poet who gave his life in the struggle against the Bulgarian brand of Fascism in the 1940s. The newer, connected **Dom Poezi i Iskustvo** (Дом Поези и Искуство; House of Poetry and Art) shows images of the National Revival movement and of the liberation struggles of southern Bulgaria at the outset of the century. (Taped tours available in English, French, German, and Russian; open Tues.-Sun. 8am-noon and 2-6pm; 500lv, taped tours 500lv.) **Velianova Kushta** (Велианова Къща; Velianov House; tel. 41 81), a twist and a turn down Velian Ognev (Велиан Огнев) from pl. Vuzrazhdane, is named after the painter from Debur (formerly in Bulgaria, now in Macedonia) responsible for the interior decoration of Bansko's Sveta Troitsa church. A typical Revival house, its thick walls once protected the inhabitants from *kurdzhali* brigands. (Open Mon.-Fri. 9am-noon and 2-5pm; 500lv; taped tours in English, French, German, and Russian 500lv.) **Kushta-Muzey Neofit Rilski** (Къша-Музей Неофит Рилски; tel. 25 40), at the corner of Pirin and Rilski, was the house of one of the initiators of the National Revival movement. A man of letters, a collector of folk songs and sayings, and one of the founders of the Rila school of church singing, Neofit Rilski also once taught the muralist Zahari Zograf (open Tues.-Sun. 9am-noon and 2-5pm; 500lv; taped tours in English, French, German, and Russian 500lv). Subdued church music accompanies the stroll through the **ekspozitsiya na ikoni** (експозиция на икони; icon exhibit), a dozen paces down Yane Sandanski from pl. Vuzrazhdane (open Tues.-Sat. 9am-noon and 2-5pm; taped tours in English, French, German, and Russian 500lv). Pl. Vuzrazhdane's 1835 **Tsurkva Sveta Troitsa** (Църква Света Троица; Holy Trinity), on the corner of Neofit Rilski, was once surrounded by a wall, and served as a shelter during many attacks on the city. Most wealthy houses in town were connected to the churchyard by a network of tunnels, which older people may even remember playing in as kids. The church itself is Bulgaria's second largest (open daily 7:30am-noon and 1-6pm).

For hikers and skiers, Bansko offers Pirin trails, four ski lifts, and a rope-tow. **Hiking routes** are marked with different-colored signs. From the town, look for signs for Pirin National Park (Народен Парк Пирин) and follow that road southwest out of town and up. Hike (6hr.) or drive up the paved road to **hizha Vihren** (хижа Бихрен; Vihren hut) past **hizha Bunderitsa** (Бъндерица) and **baikushevata mura** (байкушевата мура), a fir tree that's as old as the Bulgarian state (1300 years). Vihren hut is the jumping-off point for a number of *pateki* (патеки; mountain paths). A good trail map is available at Hotel Alpin in Bansko (see below), although the paths are well-marked. One *pateka* will lead you up Vihren peak (2914m) to **hizha Yavora** (Яворов; Javor's hut; 1740m). Be careful—not everyone can handle the beauty and excitement of the **koncheto** (кончето; horse) trail, a narrow path flanked by a precipice on either side. Buses await in **Razlog** (Разлог) in the valley below. Another hike from *hizha* Vihren takes you around **Todorin** peak (Тодорин) to **Hizha Demyanitsa** (Демяница) in about six hours.

Hizha Bezbog (Безбог), which is becoming increasingly popular as a ski resort, is another eight hours away. A **lift** connects it to **Hizha Gotse Delchev** (Гоце Делчев), which is two hours by foot from the village of **Dobrinishte** (Добринище). Buses to Bansko or Razlog can be caught there. Expect to pay around US$2 for a place to sleep (not necessarily a bed) in mountain huts, and bring your own food. **Hotel Alpin** (Алпин), Neofit Rilski 6, **rents skis** (US$25-30); walk down Pirin past pl. Vuzrazhdane and make a left on Neofit Rilski.

■ Melnik (Мелник)

Deep in a sandstone gorge, tiny Melnik (MEL-nik) quietly produces delicious wine in exquisitely preserved National Revival houses. Although its population has been waning during this century, neither the town's beauty nor its ability to welcome its guests has diminished. The 1754 **Kordopulova Kushta** (Кордопулова Къща), the biggest National Revival house in Bulgaria, it also contains the largest wine cellar in Melnik— the caves inside the sandstone hill took a full 12 years to carve and can store up to 300 tons of wine. To get there, take the main road's right fork, look for the biggest house on the hillside to your left, and walk up the stone path (open dawn to dusk; free). Mitko Manolev's **Izba za Degustatsiya na Vino** (Изба за Дегустация на Вино; wine-tasting cellar; tel. 234) is a 200-year-old establishment that offers naturally air-conditioned caverns and some of the best Melnik wine (glass 300-400lv, bottle 1200-2000lv). A brochure in English and German (800lv) could come in handy if you want to try at-home viticulture (open daily 8am-9pm). Turn left at the fork and climb up the hill on the right, through the ruins of the 10th-century **Bolyarska Kushta** (Болярска Къща), or simply continue on the path leading to the Kordupoulova Kushta. A 15-minute walk up the path behind the sv. Nikola church leads to a plateau from which all of Melnik and the surrounding hills can be seen. Take a right to reach the ruins of the **Despot Slav Krepost** (Деспот Слав Крепост), a fortress built by Aleksii Slav in the early Middle Ages to protect and serve as a refuge for the townspeople. Two rings of walls surround a central **church** whose altar still remains. Be careful not to get lost on the way up, though—some of what appear to be paths are only seasonal water courses! The 13th-century **Rozhenski Manastir** (Роженски Манастир; Rozhen Monastery) presents beautiful 16th-century murals, 17th-century stained glass, an icon collection, and carved lecterns. Seven km from Melnik, the monastery can be reached by **bus** (1 per day, leaves around noon, 700lv), but the bus doesn't return to town, allowing (or necessitating) a nice afternoon hike. Or hike *to* the monastery: from the bottom of Melnik's single street, take a right and follow the main road. Another hike will take you to the **Tsurkva Sveta Zona** (Света Зона)—ask about the miraculous icon of Bogoroditsa Iverska.

Buses arrive here via Sandanski (Sofia-Sandanski 1 per day, 2½hr., 2400lv; Sandanski-Melnik 4 per day, 40min., 600lv) or Blagoevgrad (1 per day, 1hr., 800lv). Melnik's main street, running along a dry river bed, is also its only street. There are no tourist bureaus in town, but **maps** are sold at hotels and restaurants (1000lv). **Private rooms** cost around 2000-4000lv and can be arranged with almost anyone you meet in town. **Hotel-Vinarna MNO** (МНО; tel. 249), whose sign proclaims simply "Hotel, Restaurant, Winery" (Хотел, Ресторант, Винарна), is on the left, 50m past the post office. Its 30 beds are divided among large doubles and triples with private showers (15,000lv or US$10 per person). On your way, you'll pass by **Uzunova Kushta** (Узунова Къща; tel. 270), with pleasant rooms and home-cooked breakfast included (doubles with bath US$15 per person, quads US$13 per person). When it comes to culinary delights, Melnik's offerings belie its size. **Mehana Loznitsite** (Механа Лозиците; tel. 283) is on the right side of the river bed, just over the second bridge into town. *Svinska purzhola s gubi* (свинска пържола с губи; pork chop with mushrooms and sauce; 3000lv) can be savored under the grapevines of this National Revival house, complemented with *chorba* (чорба; soup, 500-600lv) and local wine (450lv glass, 2200lv bottle; open noon-midnight). The **Mencheva Kushta** (Менчева Къща) serves up a delicious *poveche po chorbadzhiiski* (повече по чорбаджийски), a hearty dish with beef, potato, two cheeses, mushrooms, and an egg (2400lv), as well as a host of salads and vegetarian dishes (450-2000lv), local beers and wines (400-2500lv), and other meat dishes (1800-3800lv). It also has three homey double rooms (shared bath; 5000lv per person) and can provide you with a good map (1000lv). It's found on the right fork of the town street. The **mini-market** (мини маркет) near the beginning of the main street presents a do-it-yourself option with a variety of sandwich materials and drinks (open 6am-10pm). Up the main street is a **pharmacy** (Аптека) with all the basics (tel. 388; open Mon.-Fri. 8am-12pm and 2-7pm). Two doors down is the **post office** with **telephones** (open Mon.-Fri. 7:30am-noon and 1-7pm; 4880lv per min. to the U.S., 6344lv per min. to the U.K.). **Postal code:** 2820. **Phone code:** 0997437.

■ Plovdiv (Пловдив)

Bulgaria's second city, Plovdiv (PLOV-deev), is a microcosmic kaleidoscope of Bulgarian history and culture. Pass by the neighborhoods of Soviet-style apartment blocks and head for the medievally convoluted **Stari Grad** (Стари Град; Old Town), where the upper stories of National Revival houses protrude over the cobblestones below, windows stare into alleys at impossible angles, and churches and mosques hide in secluded corners. Founded around 600 BC as Philipopolis (named for Philip of Macedon, father of Alexander the Great), Plovdiv quickly achieved prominence as a center of trade and culture—a distinction that has survived from antiquity to today. Its two annual trade fairs are the focus of the Bulgarian business world, and the city now rivals Sofia as a tourist and cultural center.

ORIENTATION AND PRACTICAL INFORMATION

Plovdiv is a veritable mess of streets, but the downtown area's south border is relatively defined by the east-west thoroughfare **Hristo Botev** (Христо Ботев). Perpendicular to Hristo Botev, heading to the **Maritsa River** (Марица), are **bul. Tsar Boris III Obedinitel** (бул. Цар Борис III Обединител; Conqueror) and **bul. Ruski** (Руски). The **train station** is located at the corner of Hristo Botev and Ruski. In the middle of town, Tsar Boris III Obedinitel runs tangent to the east side of **pl. Tsentralen** (пл. Централен; Central Square), which is dominated by its huge **poshta** (поща; post office). From the northwest corner of pl. Tsentralen, **Knyaz Aleksandr** (Княз Александър), the main commercial street, runs north to **pl. Dzhumaya** (Джумая), where **bul. Suborna** (Съборна) rises east over the hill into the **Stari Grad**. North of the Maritsa, **bul. Bulgaria** (България) parallels the river. To get to pl. Tsentralen from the train station, take bus #2, 20, or 26 (buy 150lv tickets on the bus). Or walk: cross Hristo Botev via the underground pass, and take **Ivan Vazov** (Иван Вазов) to the square. While many street names have changed, most maps now have all the current names, and streets are generally known by their new names. The only exception is **Mitropolit Paisii** (Митрополит Паисий), which often goes by its old name—**Haine** (Хайне).

Tourist Office: Puldin Tours (Пълдин), bul. Bulgaria 106 (tel. 55 38 48), has a map in English, but with Communist-era street names. (Street vendors sell good Cyrillic maps for around 3000lv.) Some English and German spoken. Arranges tours, changes money, and provides info. Private rooms also arranged (see **Accommodations**, p. 107). From train station, ride trolley #102 or 2 (150lv) nine stops to bul. Bulgaria and backtrack a block. By foot, cross the river via Tsar Boris III Obedinitel, pass Hotel Maritsa, and look for Puldin on the corner with bul. Bulgaria. Open Mon.-Fri. 9am-5:30pm (until 9pm during fairs).

Currency Exchange: Exchange bureaus await on Knyaz Aleksandr, and almost everywhere else too. **Bulbank** (Булбанк), 5 Patriarh Evtimii (Патриарх Евтимий) (tel. 26 02 70) cashes traveler's checks at US$1 per transaction. Open Mon.-Thurs. 9am-3pm, Fri. 9am-1pm. **ATM:** In the post office on pl. Tsentralen. Theoretically accepts Visa and Plus cards—when it works.

Trains: Most trains from Sofia to Istanbul or Burgas stop in Plovdiv. To Sofia (approx. every hr., 2½hr., 1820lv). Good local train connections. Only **Rila**, bul. Hristo

Botev 31a (tel. 44 61 20), sells international tickets. Open Mon.-Fri. 8am-7pm, Sat. 8am-4pm. **Luggage storage** is also available (approx. 1000lv).

Buses: Three separate stations serve the areas indicated by their names. **Yug** (Юг; South; tel. 22 69 37), east of the train station, on the north side of Hristo Botev, sends buses south, as well as to Sofia (every hr., 1hr., 2000lv). **Rodopi** (Родопи; tel. 20 24 60), south through a maze of pedestrian underpasses under the trains, and then past a labyrinth of kiosks and food stands, serves the Rodopi mountains. **Sever** (Север; North; tel. 55 37 05), north of bul. Bulgaria on Dimitur Stambolov (Димитър Стамболов) near its intersection with Pobeda (Победа—which Ruski becomes when it crosses the river), sends buses north—take bus #2 from pl. Tsentralen. **Traffic Express** (Трафик Експрес), bul. Hristo Botev 45 (tel. 26 57 87; fax 26 51 51), at the Yug station, sells tickets for the Black Sea Coast. **Matpu** (Матпу; tel. 22 26 33; tel./fax 22 24 42), in the underpass below Tsar Boris III Obedinitel next to Hotel Trimondium (Тримондиум), deals with all Balkan connections: direct to Istanbul (US$20), Athens (US$43, under 26 US$35), and Thessaloniki (US$28/22). The buses to Greece on Wed. and Fri. have connections with ferries to Italy. Open daily 8am-7pm. **Agency Suzana** (Сузана; tel./fax 55 91 74) also runs direct buses to Istanbul. Open Mon.-Fri. 9am-9pm.

24-Hour Pharmacy: Pharmacy #47 "The Tunnel" (Аптека 47 Тунела), Tsar Boris III Obedinitel 64 (tel. 27 07 93), on the opposite side of the automobile tunnel from pl. Tsentralen. **Fleming** (Флеминг), Knyaz Aleksandr 22 (tel. 26 00 57). Open daily 8:30am-8pm. Both well-stocked with Western **condoms** and **feminine products.**

Express Mail: DHL, bul. Svoboda 9 (Свобода; tel. 44 21 11 or 44 19 90).

Post Office: pl. Tsentralen. *Poste Restante* in the room to the left of the western entrance. Open Mon.-Sat. 7am-7pm, Sun. 7-11am. **Postal code:** 4000.

Telephones: In post office. Direct international calling (to the U.S. 5490lv per min., U.K. 2745lv per min.). Open daily 6:30am-11pm. Send or receive **faxes** (fax 493 00 44) for 1831lv per page. Fax open daily 6:30am-9pm. **Phone code:** 032.

ACCOMMODATIONS

Prices can rise 500% during trade fairs, which are generally during the first two weeks of May and September. At these times, **private rooms** may be your only hope. **Puldin Tours** (see above) arranges singles (US$13), doubles (US$16), and 1-bedroom apartments (US$20). **Prima Vista Agency** (Прима Виста), Ivan Vazov 74 (tel. 27 27 78; fax 27 20 54), open daily 10am-6pm, also finds private lodgings. **Bureau Esperanza** (Буро Есперанса), Ivan Vazov 14 (tel. 26 06 53, info in English 22 50 51), specializes in rooms downtown (12,400lv per person; open daily 10am-7pm).

Hostel Turisticheski Dom (Туристически Дом), P.R. Slaveykov 5 (П.Р. Славейков; tel. 23 32 11), in Stari Grad. From Knyaz Aleksandr, take Patriarh Evtimii into Stari Grad, passing under Tsar Boris III Obedinitel, and take a left on Slaveykov at pl. Vuzrazhdane (Възраждане). Clean 1- or 2-bed old-style dorm rooms with sinks in a spacious National Revival building listed among Plovdiv's monuments. Shared bathrooms. Cafe/restaurant. Lockout midnight. 18,000lv per room.

Hotel Feniks (Феникс), Kapitan Raicho 79 (Капитан Райчо; tel. 22 47 29). From pl. Tsentralen, cross Tsar Boris III Obedinitel to Kapitan Raicho. Reception on 3rd floor of the first entry off Kapitan Raicho. TV and laundry. Unintentionally antique but still functional furniture. Shared bathrooms. Singles US$15; doubles US$30.

Trakia Camping (Тракия Къмпинг; tel. 55 13 60), on the E-80 highway to Sofia. Take the #23 bus from the train station (leaves every hr.). Orange mini-van taxis drop you off 100m away (200lv); buses #4 and 44 stop ½km away. Bungalows have 2 rooms, each with shower. Every June, Bulgaria's Hell's Angels hold their annual "festival" here, and the place looks it. Open year-round.

FOOD

Plovdiv can offer a generous culinary program for less than US$5. On the way to the Hostel Turisticheski Dom on Patriarh Evtimii, the **Ponedelnik Pazar** (Понеделник Пазар; outdoor market) in pl. Vuzrazhdane sells fresh fruit and veggies for about

1000-2000lv per kilo. Kiosks in all parts of the city sell snacks and drinks for no more than 2000lv; in most restaurants and cafes, a meal runs 4000-5000lv.

Kambanata (Камбаната), Suborna 2B (tel. 26 06 65), a short way up Suborna from pl. Dzhumaya. Vegetarians will be surprised at its large selection of traditional veggie dishes—*kyopoolu* (eggplant), *pecheni chushki* (baked peppers), *tikvichki* (zucchini with milk sauce)—for under US$0.50. Main courses hover at US$1-2. The chef's specialty, "Kambanata," is a concoction of filet of pork or veal, cream, mushrooms, smoked cheese, and spaghetti (US$2). English menu. A/C. Open daily 10:30am-midnight.

Union Club (Юнын Клуб), Mitropolit Paisii 5 (formerly Haine; tel. 27 05 51). Take Suborna from pl. Dzhumaya, then turn right up the steep alley before the church and head up the steps (yes, this is still the street) through a forbidding wooden gate to the lovely outdoor garden. Frequented by local *intelligentsia*. English menu of 230 items contains stewed vegetable dishes and veggie-stuffed pancakes, too. Open daily 9am-late.

Alafrangite (Алафрангите), Kiril Nektariev 17 (Кирил Нектариев; tel. 26 95 95), in an Old Town National Revival house. From behind the Dzhumaya mosque, follow Suborna and take the third right. The chef cooks up a mean *vreteno* (вретено;spindle), a pork or veal filet with cheese and mushrooms (7800lv). Classic Bulgarian dishes run 2500-7500lv. English menu. Open daily 11:30am-midnight.

Cocktail Restaurant Maniika (Манийка), P.R. Slaveykov 4, serves up a number of organ-based dishes (for the Leopold Bloom in you) and other main courses for around US$1. Happenin' National Revival courtyard. Open daily 11am-midnight.

SIGHTS

With more than 150 houses designated as cultural monuments, Plovdiv's Stari Grad is a giant historical museum. Its narrow cobblestone alleys are irresistible. Stari Grad's location on three hills (the **Trimontium**), makes the tiny streets steep as they wind up and down between tightly packed rows of houses. The area's most ancient treasure is the Roman marble **Antichen Teatr** (Античен Театр; amphitheater), dating from the 2nd century. Take a right off Knyaz Aleksandr to Stanislav Dospevski (Станислав Доспевски) and walk ahead to the theater. Today, the amphitheater hosts the **Festival of the Arts** in summer and early fall (contact Puldin Tours for details; see p. 106) and opera singers cross their voices in noble competition during the annual **Opera Festival** in June. In the middle of pl. Dzhumaya lies **Philipopolis Stadium.** Contemplation of its ancient stones becomes almost impossible at night, when parading Plovdiv youths steal the show and fill up the nearby cafes. The building that gave its name to pl. Dzhumaya is the **Dzhumaya Dzhamiya** (джамия; mosque) whose colorful minaret peers around the other buildings.

At the end of Suborna, the **Etnografski Muzey** (Етнографски Музей; Museum of Ethnography; tel. 22 56 56) displays ancient Bulgarian crafts, including an interesting exhibition on the production of precious rose oil (open Tues.-Sun. 9-11am and 1-5pm). Colorful **Baroque houses** can be found down the hill, through the Roman gate. For more Bulgarian history, try the **National Revival and National Liberation Museum**, Tsanko Lavrenov 1 (Цанко Лавренов; tel. 22 59 23). Make a right at the end of Suborna and go through the Turkish gate (open Tues.-Sun. 9-11am and 1-5pm). Ancient history is also preserved in the **Archaeological Museum** at pl. Suedinenie (Съединение), but unfortunately the museum itself is not holding up as well as its artifacts—when last visited, it was being renovated. To check if it's open again, walk down Raiko Daskalov (Райко Даскалов) from pl. Dzhumaya and take a left on 6 Septemvri (6 Септември). Its pride is one heavy collection of golden vessels from the 4th century BC. **Durzhavna Hudozhestvena Galeria** (Държавна Художествена Галерия; State Gallery of Art; tel. 22 42 12) has a permanent collection of Bulgarian masters at Suborna 14a and holds bi-weekly temporary exhibits of contemporary graphics, sculptures, and watercolors at its other location on Knyaz Aleksandr 15 (open Tues.-Sun. 9-11am and 1-5pm).

BULGARIA

For an out-of-museum experience, wander down little Strumna (Стръмна) alley and watch the few remaining Plovdiv artisans pound and polish in workshops, just as their ancestors did. The **park** in the west side of town, beyond the train tracks and near the stadium, provides a welcome break from the steep cobblestone streets and the antiquity of touristed areas. There you will find the Plovdiv **zoo**, outdoor **swimming pools,** and the biggest man-made **rowing canal** in Bulgaria. On a cool evening, head to the fountainside cafe in **Tsentralni Park** (Централни Парк), near pl. Tsentralen, where multicolored strobes illuminate the spring. As a last resort, one of the many **movie theaters** on Knyaz Aleksandr is bound to be showing a film in English. .

■ Near Plovdiv: Bachkovo Monastery

Twenty-eight km south of Plovdiv lies Bulgaria's second-largest monastery, the 11th-century **Bachkovski Manastir** (Бачковски Манастир) built by Georgian brothers Grigorii and Abazii Bakuriani. Mostly destroyed by the Turks in the early 14th century, it was rebuilt a century later. Always an oasis of Bulgarian culture, history, and literature, this holy site maintained and even strengthened its spirit during five centuries of Ottoman rule. The monastery's treasure is the miracle-working **ikona Sveta Bogoroditsa** (икона Сбета Богородица; icon of the Virgin Mary and Child), which is said to heal the sick (open daily 7am-dark). The **Hram Sveti Nikola** (Храм Свети Никола; Chapel of Saint Nikola) is blessed with the work of **Zahari Zograf** (1840) and cursed with the work of some modern fans who have etched their marks next to his on the outside murals. To get to Bachkovo, take a **train** from Plovdiv to Asenovgrad (every 30min., 25min., 600lv); once there, catch a bus to the monastery (10min., 250lv). **Buses** to Smolyan from Plovdiv's Rodopi bus station also get you there (40min., 700lv). Inquire about spartan **accommodations** at the administrative office on the monastery's second floor; ask for Brother German (tel. (03327) 277). Ten- to 20-person dorms share bathrooms (2000lv per bed; cold water only). Brother German says you wouldn't like it, though, and encourages Western travelers to stay at the **campground** (къмпинг) at the base of the hill, where 20 slightly grungy bungalows with functional plumbing house 2 people each for 2000lv per night. The monks also allow visitors to pitch **tents** on the monastery lawn for free. Around Christmas and Easter, the monastery is booked solid, so call ahead. Every August 15th, believers flock to Bachkovo to celebrate the holiday of the Virgin Mary. Everyone crashes in the courtyard (free) "for good health" after the **kurban** (курбан; feast).

Continuing along the road above the monastery, escaping the swarming hordes, there are other small shrines and paths that make for great day-hiking, with picnic areas and some of the most gorgeous mountain vistas in Bulgaria. Below, several gift shops, cafes, and food stands flank the road leading to the monks' haven. The **Vodapada** (Водапада; waterfall) restaurant (tel. from Plovdiv (9) 93 23 89), named for the stream that cascades down into a pool next to its *gradina* (градина; patio), sits at the bottom of the road. Here you can feast on *balkanska pasturva* (балканска пастърва; trout; 4500lv) and great wine—try *magareshko mlyako* (магарешко мляко; donkey's milk; 7500lv per bottle).

VALLEY OF ROSES (РОЗОВА ДОЛИНА)

■ Koprivshtitsa (Копривщица)

Koprivshtitsa's (KOP-riv-SHTEET-sa) revolutionary roots are well concealed among its innocent-looking, sleepy little wood and stone houses. Todor Kableshkov's 1876 "letter of blood," which announced an uprising against Ottoman rule, started its tour of the country here. Quelled in the most violent manner, the uprising nevertheless succeeded in turning Europe's eye toward the small nation; the Russo-Turkish war of 1877-78 ensued and brought Bulgaria freedom after five centuries under Turkish

BULGARIA

domination. Every five years, the tranquility of this otherwise peaceful city is shaken by the thousands who come to enjoy the **Koprivshtitsa International Folklore Festival.** Book rooms early (the next one takes place in August 2000).

Orientation and Practical Information Trains from Sofia (10 per day, 1½-2hr., 500lv) stop at the Koprivshtitsa train station (the stop after Anton or, on a *burz* (бърз; fast) train, the one after Pirdop), 10km from town. Other trains arrive from Plovdiv via Karlovo (change trains at Karlovo; total time 3½hr.; 1520lv). A bus awaits to take you into town (10min.; 300lv). Get off at the Koprivshtitsa **bus station** (a dark wooden building), which posts the bus and train schedules but is usually vacant, so questions are out of the question. To reach the **main square,** backtrack a bit along the river that bisects the town. The few streets have no names. **Banka Biohim** (Биохим; tel. 21 86), across the river and next to the school, **exchanges money** (open Mon.-Fri. 8:15am-3pm). The alley to the right of the monument on the main square leads to a private **pharmacy** (open daily 9am-noon and 3-6pm). The **post office** sits behind the bus station, on the town's other square (open Mon.-Fri. 7:30am-noon and 1-3pm; **telephones** open Mon.-Fri. 7:30am-6pm; Sat.-Sun. 8am-4pm; closed daily noon-1pm). **Postal code:** 2017. **Phone code:** 07184.

Accommodations and Food Hotel Byaloto Konche (Бялото Конче; tel. 22 50), up the steep street from the main square, has five doubles in a classic Koprivshtitsa house (US$8 per person; breakfast included). Go to the *mehana* to ask for a room. **Hotel Dalmatinets** (Далматинец; tel. 29 04), Georgi Benkovski 62 (Георги Бенковски), near the end of town upstream from Banka Biohim, has five doubles with private showers and 24-hour hot water (US$10, with breakfast US$12). Arrange **private rooms** through the English-speaking owner of the Mlechkov (Млечков) souvenir shop (tel. 21 64) in the square advertising *chastni kvartiri* (частни квартири; US$5 per person; shop open daily 10am-6pm). Seize the opportunity to buy all kinds of **tourist maps** of Bulgaria—the owner is a geographer by education. In the main square, Tsonka Tormanova deals in private rooms (4000lv) out of her **Kvatirno Byuro "Alis 15"** (Квартирно Бюро Алис; tel. 25 16; open daily 9am-noon and 1-6pm).

Byaloto Konche has a separate tavern with home-cooking and a cozy atmosphere, offering splendid *sirene po trakiiski* (сирене по тракийски, 2500lv; open 8am until last person leaves). **Pod Starata Krusha** (Под Старата Круша; tel. 21 63), at the bus station, is undisturbed by traffic in the evenings—only birds, frogs, or an occasional dog may accompany your meal. The specialty, *pileshka purzhola s drobcheta* (пилешка пържола с дробчета; chicken steak with liver; 3000lv) goes well with a salad (400-900lv) and wine (2500-6000lv per bottle). The **food market** by the stream, past the buses and post office, is well-stocked with fresh produce; vendors hang out from early morning to mid-afternoon. A **bakery** lies nearby (delicious bread 500lv).

Sights Old houses are Koprivshtitsa's main attraction—masterpieces of three distinct stages of National Revival architecture remain wonderfully preserved and open to tourists. The houses in which the first settlers lived are low plank structures. The second type are sturdy, half-timbered, early 19th-century homes with open porches, high stone walls, and sparse ornamentation. The third, most common, type feature enclosed verandas and delicate woodwork reflecting the mercantile prosperity of the mid-19th century. Many homes of the 1876 Uprising leaders have become museums, and all are easy to find with a map (50lv at administration office or Oslakovma Kushta). The 1845 **Kushtata-muzey Todor Kableshkov** (Къщата-музей Тодор Каблешков; Todor Kableshkov Museum-House) is one of the third stage's grandest achievements, dressed with an impressive facade, ingeniously carved ceilings, and the hero's personal possessions—all soaked in revolutionary spirit (tel. 21 54; open Tues.-Sun. 8am-noon, 1:30-5:30pm). The 1831 **Kushtata-muzey Georgi Benkovski** (Георги Бенковски; tel. 28 11), near the statue of Benkovski, immortalizes the life and deeds of the leader of the "Flying Troop" of horsemen, more a symbolic than effective battle force in the April Uprising. Look for Benkovski's unusual rifle (closed

Tues.). The **Kushtata-muzey Dimcho Debelyanov** (Димчо Дебелянов; tel. 20 77) is the birthplace of one of Bulgaria's best lyric poets. Debelyanov died in the First World War; a sculpture of his mother vainly awaiting his return sits in the yard (closed Mon.). The houses of two merchants—**Oslekov** and **Lyutov**—are examples of the most prosperous Revival houses. Besides ornate ceiling work, the **Lyutovata kushta** (Лютовата къща) has original exhibits of non-woven carpets (closed Tues.). The **Oslekovata kushta** (Ослековата къща), supported by three columns of imported Lebanese cedar, has some stunning murals and wood carvings (closed Mon.). The 1817 **Uspenie Bogorodichno** (Успение Богородично; Assumption Church) was built in 11 days, according to legend, but looks much better. Inside you can find some masterpiece icons by **Zahari Zograf.** (Museums open Tues.-Sun. or Wed.-Mon. 8am-noon and 1:30-5:30pm. A 1500lv ticket valid for all museums may be purchased at any one of the houses or at a *kupchinitsa* (купчийница) booth nearby. English and French tours (2400lv) are possible; ask at the museum administration office in the main square or try the office in the Oslekovata Kushta, across the street from the Byaloto Konche.)

More Precious Than Gold

More expensive by weight than gold, "attar of roses" (rose oil) drips from the fertile valleys of Bulgaria, producing more than 70% of the world's supply. A single gram requires 2000 petals snatched before sunrise, and from late May through early June, workers pick furiously to supply enough rose juice for the world to keep feeling fresh. Apart from perfume and rose water, Bulgarian rose petals are used in medicine, jam, tea, vodka, sweet liquor, and syrup. Picking season ends with the annual rose festival (Прозник на Розата; *Proznik na Rozata*), held in Karlovo and Kazanluk during the first weekend of June.

■ Kazanluk (Казанлък)

Kazanluk (KAHZ-ahn-luk) has always been the center of Bulgaria's rose-growing world. Rather undistinguished throughout the year, the town acquires a sweet scent during the **Rose Festival** (the first week of June), which perfumes the performances of traditional song-and-dance troupes, comedians, and soccer stars.

Orientation and Practical Information Take a **train** from Sofia (5 per day, 3hr., 1960lv); Burgas (3 per day, 3hr., 1960lv); Karlovo (11 per day, 1½ hr., 800lv); or a **bus** from Plovdiv's Sever station (2 per day). **Store luggage** at the train station (opens only 10min. within arrival or departure of trains; 300lv). 100m west of the train station, bul. Rozova Dolina (Розова Долина) leads to the main **pl. Sevtopolis** (Севтополис). The main street runs west as the tongue-twisting 23rd Pehoten Shipchenski Polk (23ти Пехотен Шипченски Полк), and continues east as Knyaz Aleksandr Batenberg (Княз Александър Батенберг). **Banka Biohim** (Банка Биохим), Rozova Dolina 4 (tel. 239 81), **changes** all major currencies (open 7am-6pm). **Bookstore Tezi** (Тези), 23rd Pehoten Shipchenski 16 (tel. 490 58), stocks useful English **maps** of town (1000lv; open Mon.-Fri. 9:30am-7pm, Sat. 10am-2pm). The **post office** is on the other side of 23rd Pehoten Shipchenski (open Mon.-Fri. 7:30am-6:30pm, Sat. 8am-1pm; **telephones** open 7am-10pm; **faxes** (256 05) open 7:30am-8pm). **Postal code:** 6100. **Phone code:** 0431.

Accommodations and Food Accommodation options are limited. Be sure to make reservations for the Rose Festival. **Hotel Voennen Klub** (Военнен Клуб), Rozova Dolina 8 (tel. 221 64), 30m down the street from pl. Sevtopolis toward the train station, offers lived-in tiled rooms with private showers and hot water (10,000lv per person). The **Hotel Vesta** (Веста; tel. 477 40), Chavdar Voivoda 3 (Чавдар Войвода), behind the monolithic cultural center, offers much newer rooms for much higher prices. The private showers have 24-hour hot water (singles US$43; doubles US$48).

Campground Krunsko Hanche (Крънско Ханче), 3km away, is open year-round. Take a bus to Gabrovo, or city bus #6, and ask the driver to stop at the campground. Part of the new Tourist Complex Moshi (Туристически Комплекс Моши; tel. 242 39 or 270 91), the campground has two refurbished bungalows (US$5 per person; tents US$4 per person). For budget dining, search out **Starata Kushta** (Старата Къща), Dr. Baev 2 (Др. Баев; tel. 212 31). From pl. Sevtopolis, take the second left onto Gen. M. Skobelev, then the first right onto Gen. Gurko. Dr. Baev is the first right. Try the *shishche* (шишче; Bulgarian shish kebob; 800lv) or *kavarma* (2040lv; restaurant open 24hr.). **Supermarket** Hali (Хали) can be found at Ivan Vazov 3 (Иван Вазов; tel. 244 07), just off Rozova Dolina by pl. Sevtopolis (open Mon.-Fri. 7am-7:30pm, Sat. 7am-1:30pm). An **open market**, Kooperativna Pazar (Кооперативна Пазар) is on ul. L. Hilendarski (Л. Хилендарски)—follow Otets Paisii (Отец Пайсий) from pl. Sevtapolis until it crosses a main thoroughfare and disjointedly picks up again as L. Hilendarski.

Sights Kazanluk's **Trakiiska Grobnitsa** (Тракийска Гробница; Thracian Tomb) resides in the city park, a 10-minute walk from pl. Sevtopolis. Climb the stairs to the top of the hill. The original resting place of the tomb, which is now sealed, dates from the turn of the 3rd century BC. The interior has been re-created 20m away. The early-Hellenistic frescoes in the corridor and dome chamber are original; those in the replica are from the more recent Socialist period (tel. 247 50; open daily 8:30am-noon and 1:30-6pm; closed Nov.-Feb.; US$1, students US$0.50).

As you walk back down the stairs out of the park, take a left on General Radetski (Генерал Радецки) and the first right onto the cobblestone Knyaz Mirski (Княз Мир-ски), which leads into the heart of **Koulata** (Кулата), the oldest part of Kazanluk, which preserves the architecture and traditions of the National Revival. In the enclosed courtyard, the **Etnografski Kompleks Koulata** (Етнографски Комплекс Кулата; tel. 217 33) displays two buildings—a village house and a city dwelling from the Revival years—and is probably the only museum in the world to treat you to a shot of genuine rose brandy and jam. In its wonderfully sculpted garden courtyard, a primitive distillery shows how rose oil and liquor are made the old-school way (complex open daily 8:30am-noon and 1:30-6pm; US$2, students US$1). The **Hudozhestvena Galeriya i Istoricheski Muzey Iskra** (Художествена Галерия и Исторически Музей Искра; Art Gallery and Historical Museum Iskra; tel. 263 22), Kiril i Metodii 9, features an exhibit on ancient history, Thracian culture, and the rose in the life of Kazanluk. The gallery also contains a rich permanent collection of Bulgarian masters and some icons. To find it, follow Iskra (Искра) straight from the north end of pl. Sevtopolis (open daily 9am-noon and 1-5pm; US$1). For those who still hunger for info on the oil-giving rose, 30 minutes away from pl. Sevtopolis sits the **Muzey na Rozata** (Музей на Розата; Rose Museum; tel. 260 55 or 263 22). From the square, head down Gen. Skobelev, go right at the fork and continue on bul. Osvobozhdenie (Освобождение) towards Gabrovo. If you're lucky, you may catch the irregular buses #5 or 6 across from Hotel Kazanluk (4 stops; 100lv). Located next to the **Scientific Research Institute of the Rose, Essential Oil-Yielding, and Medicinal Plants,** the museum displays, with the help of tools and photos, the technology used over the centuries to produce rose oil. The institute's experimental **gardens** are home to over 250 varieties of roses. The souvenir shop sells English brochures and some indispensable rose products—liquor (2000lv), jam (2000lv), and precious rose oil (naturally derived US$4, chemical version 1000lv. Museum open March 15-Oct. 15 8:30am-5pm; US$1, students US$0.50). For another kind of entertainment, head to **Dramaticheski Teatr Yambol** (Драматически Театр Ямбол), where you can catch the weekly show for 300-1500lv (Sept.-June).

■ Near Kazanluk

ETURA (ЕТЪРА)

Etura's (EH-tu-rah) charming **Ethnographic Complex** makes it a worthwhile stop en route from Kazanluk (8 buses per day, 40min.) to Veliko Turnovo, or vice versa (7 buses per day). This **outdoor museum** consists of a couple of dozen National Revival-style buildings, workshops, and mills. Climb through tiny doors and up narrow staircases into workshops that look as if time had stopped 100 years ago, featuring artisans making woodcarvings, metalwork, silver jewelry, icons, musical instruments, and ceramic pottery just as they've done for centuries. Visit the candy store for sweet and sticky sesame and honey bars (300lv), or the bakery for fresh breads and pastries. (Complex open daily May-Sept. 8am-6pm, off-season 8am-4pm; 3900lv, students 2300lv; multilingual tours US$3.)

Buses to Etura actually stop in **Gabrovo. Store luggage** at the station for 300lv. If you can find **bus** #7 or 8 from the center of Gabrovo, take it east, away from the station, and go direct. Otherwise, take **trolley** #32 or bus #1 to the end-stop, "Bolshevik" (15min., 150lv), then bus #7 or 8 and ask to be dropped off at Etura (5min., 15lv). All buses stop by **Hotel/Restaurant Etura** (tel. 424 19 or 420 26), which offers comfy but expensive rooms with private bath (singles US$46; doubles US$57). Downstairs is a small *mehana* (open 8am-midnight). The steps leading there also head up to the Ethnographic Complex; cross the bridge to find the ticket kiosk.

SHIPKA PASS (ШИПКЧЕНСКИ ПРОХОД)

At the Rose Valley's north edge looms the legendary **Shipkchenski Prohod** (Shipka Pass; ship-CHEN-skee pra-HOHD), site of the bloody and pivotal battle that lasted an entire winter and ultimately liberated Bulgaria from the Turks in 1878. The village at the base lies overshadowed and struggling—this time with the new cutthroat economy. Ten minutes up a little road from the main village square sits the memorial **St. Nicholas**, built in honor of the Russian soldiers who lost their lives here (open daily 8:30am-5:30pm; 2500lv, students 1500lv). Shipka Pass is 20km up the paved road to Gabrovo; a hike starts at the memorial church (about 2km). Locals don't recommend it, warning of "*volki, medvedi, partizani!*" (wolves, bears, guerrilla fighters!), but it's usually safe enough, although it's very steep and could be better marked. For non-hikers, **buses** running from Kazanluk to Gabrovo pass through (2 per day, 750lv). Views of the Valley of Roses are exquisite from the top of the **Pametnik na Svobodata** (Паметник на Свободата; Monument to Liberty), which has crowned the famous battle site since August 26, 1934 in memory of the Russian and Bulgarian dead. Many of the writing fragments inside the monument come from Ivan Vazov's legendary poem "Shipka" (see **Literature,** p. 91), which most Bulgarian students learn by heart (monument open daily 8:30am-5pm; 2500lv, students 1500lv).

From Kazanluk, take **city bus #6,** departing from the train station or across from Hotel Kazanluk, in the direction away from the post office (every 30min., 15min., 300lv). Buses also arrive from Gabrovo, dropping their loads off in Shipka town in front of the now-defunct Hotel Shipka. You **cannot exchange currency** here. You also **cannot sleep**—the only hotel is up in the pass. If you're really stuck, though, try the manager of **Snack Bar Asprovalta** (Снек Бар Аспровалта; tel. 21 05), on the square; he has a back room with a mattress. The **post office** is to the right on Hristo Patrev (Христо Патрев), the cobbled street above the square (open Mon.-Fri. 8am-noon and 1-4pm). **Postal code:** 6150. **Phone code:** 94324.

A **grocery** hides under the remains of old Hotel Shipka (open 7am-7pm). **Restaurant Pronto** (Пронто; open daily 7am-midnight), across the square, conjures up a meal with some kind of *chorba* (чорба; soup), grills, *shopska salata*, and a tall, cool one for less than US$3. Up in the pass, the other **Hotel Shipka** (tel. 247 50) has singles and doubles with shared bath (10,000lv per person), and three-person apartments with private bath (US$10).

NORTHERN BULGARIA

■ Pleven (Плевен)

With 150 memorials to the Battle of Pleven, this town is a living monument to the Russo-Turkish War of 1877-78. But not to worry—Pleven offers its history in a fresh, relaxing atmosphere of parks, flowerbeds, and possibly the most beautiful (but definitely the most functional) fountains in Bulgaria. The per capita volume of cafes gives staggering proof of Pleven's number of young people.

Orientation and Practical Information Take a **bus** (1 per day, 4hr., 2400lv) or **train** (17 per day, 3hr., 1840lv) from Sofia; bus (1 per day, 3hr., 1600lv) or train (6 per day, 3½hr., 1220lv) from Ruse; train from the Gorna Oryahovitsa international station, the big rail hub just outside Veliko Turnovo (17 per day, 1½hr., 1100lv); or train from Plovdiv (1 per day, 5½hr., 2860lv). **Store luggage** at the train station (left of main entrance; closed 8:15-8:45am and pm; 300lv). The focal points of Pleven are its Siamese twin squares—**pl. Svobodata** (Свободата) and **pl. Vuzrazhdane** (Възраждане)—connected by rows of trees and fountains, and by a short stretch of the pedestrian **Vasil Levski** (Васил Левски), which then continues toward the train station. From the train station, walk down **Danail Popov** (Данаил Попов), which turns into **Osvobozhdenie** (Освобождение) and eventually hits pl. Svobodata. Or, take **Asen Halachev** (Асен Халачев) to the right of the train station and turn left on Vasil Levski, Pleven's commercial and culinary artery. Hunt down a **map** (600lv) from the booksellers on Vasil Levski. **Orbita,** Dr. Zamenhof 3 (Др. Заменхоф; tel. 265 27; tel./ fax 332 88), specializes in youth tourism and tourist info. The staff gives away English brochures, issues ISICs, and arranges dorm rooms in July and August (US$3 per person; office open Mon.-Fri. 9am-5pm). The **Obedinena Bulgarska Banka** (Обединена Българска Банка), Vasil Levski 1 (tel. 80 12 56), charges US$3 to change traveler's checks (open Mon.-Fri. 8am-4pm). There's also an **ATM** (Cirrus, EuroCard, and MC).The **post office** is in pl. Svobodata (open daily 7am-7pm). **Postal code:** 5800. The **phone office** sits across the hall (open daily 7am-10pm). **Phone code:** 064.

Accommodations and Food Private rooms can be found, although not that easily. Two-star **Rostov na Don** (Ростов на Дон), Osvobozhdenie 2 (tel. 80 18 92), on the left as you enter pl. Svobodata from the train station, has acceptable singles (US$17) and doubles (US$28) with clean bathrooms, and apartments with bed, couch, TV and tub (US$34; MC, Visa, and EuroCard accepted). **Hotel Pleven,** pl. Republika 2 (Република; tel. 301 81, 363 20, or 363 22), is near the bus and train stations (singles US$27; doubles US$44; Diners Club, MC, and Visa accepted).

The well-hidden **Mehana Stari Oreh** (Механа Стари Орех; Old Walnut Tavern), Vasil Levski 17, serves memorable meals. Grab a seat in the garden and indulge in the specialty, the "Stari Oreh" pork filet stuffed with mushrooms, cheese, and sausage (3450lv; open daily 11:30am-midnight). The famous **Peshterata** (Пещерата; tel. 225 72) is 3km from town in **Kailuka Park.** Built in a sandstone cave, the loud restaurant has outdoor tables and plenty of space. *Kavarma* with omelette costs 2600lv. Take trolley #3 or 7 from San Stefano (100lv), behind the post office, heading away from the main square. From the end, follow the main street along the green park for 20 minutes (open daily 10am-late).

Sights The granddaddy of Pleven's sights, the **Panorama** (Панорама; tel. 373 06), a museum with huge murals, including a 360° panorama, depicts the third Russo-Turkish Battle of Pleven and the liberation of Bulgaria. Hire a guide, or it'll just be a bunch of beautiful pictures (open Tues.-Sat. 9am–5:30pm5000lv, English guide 5000lv, bother them about a student discount, and you might get in for 200lv). From the center, take bus #1, 9, or 12 (ask for the Panorama), then hike up. Down the path from the main entrance is the old battlefield, now **Park Skobelev** (Парк Скобелев). Some wild greenery, guns, and an ossuary make for a spooky walk.

In the center of the first park-graced space left of Vasil Levski lies the small **Muzey Osvobozhdenieto na Pleven** (Музей Освобождението на Плевен; Museum of the Liberation of Pleven). A small house that was the nicest in Pleven 120 years ago, this was the quarters of Russian Tsar Aleksandr II, the Osvoboditel himself (open Tues.-Sat. 9am-noon and 1-6pm). Next door, outside the park, stairs lead down to the 1834 **Sv. Nikolai** (Св. Николай; tel. 372 08), built two meters underground in compliance with a requirement that no church be higher than the local mosques. Holes in the walls and ceiling hold more than 600 clay pots, said to enhance the acoustics (open daily 8:30am-6:30pm, services at 8am and 5pm). Midway between the two main squares on the right (coming from the train station), the former **Turkish Bathhouse,** Doyran 75 (Дойран; tel. 383 42) is now an art gallery with a fascinating melange of Bulgarian and international classical and modern painting and statuary, formerly the private collection of Svetlin Rusev (open Sun.-Thurs. 11am-8pm; free).

At the end of pl. Svobodata is the **Kostnitsa** (Костница; mausoleum; tel. 300 33), built from 1902 to 1904. The outside resembles a Baroque chapel; inside are Socialist Realist murals, ancient icons, and a vault holding the remains of many Russian and Romanian soldiers. Call ahead to arrange a tour in English (mausoleum open Tues.-Sat. 9am-noon and 1-6pm; free; English tours 1000lv). The huge **Istoricheski Muzey** (Исторически Музей; Historical Museum), Sv. Zaimov 3 (Св. Заимов; tel. 235 69), is minutes from the center. Go through the park at the end of pl. Vuzrazhdane or walk down Vardar (Вардар) and take a left on Zaimov. Two floors take you through archaeology, ethnography, and National Revival exhibits, ending with the Russo-Turkish war and early 20th-century history (open Tues.-Sat. 8am-noon and 12:30-5:30pm; 5000lv; Bulgarian-only signs make the 5000lv English guide a must—call in advance). Across the street is the **Hudozhestvena Galeriya "Iliya Beshkov"** (Художествена Галерия "Илия Бешков"; Iliya Beshkov Art Gallery), bul. Skobelev 1 (tel. 300 30), named after a famous Bulgarian caricaturist. Temporary exhibits have seen the likes of Rembrandt and Picasso (open Tues.-Sat. 9am-5pm; free admission and German tour). During the day, rent rowboats at the small pond in **Kailuka Park,** south of the city. The park, with two lakes surrounded by restaurants, fountains, and flowers, provides a beautiful (and cool) setting for a stroll on a hot summer evening.

▓ **Veliko Turnovo** (Велико Търново)

Perched on steep hills above the twisting Yantra River, Veliko Turnovo (veh-LEEK-uh TUR-nuh-vuh) has been watching over Bulgaria for 5000 years. The town has given the country revolutionaries, kings, and, following the overthrow of the Turks, the first Bulgarian constitution. The spirit of historical significance still lives here in Bulgaria's biggest treasure trove of ruins, but gives way to a relaxed atmosphere: stroll past ice cream stands and sip cheap wine while looking out over the river.

ORIENTATION AND PRACTICAL INFORMATION

Veliko Turnovo is situated around a loop in the river. The town is on the outside bank, with the center, **pl. Maika Bulgaria** (Майка България), at the top of the loop. From the bus station, off toward the west, take bus #7 or 10 five stops to the center, where **Nezavisimost** (Независимост) extends around the loop, turning into **Stefan Stambolov** (Стефан Стамболов) and subsequently **Nikola Pikolo** (Никола Пиколо) as it stretches toward the **Tsarevets Krepost** (Царевец Крепост). A *knizharnitsa* (Книжарница; bookstore) right across from the gate has good **maps** (500lv). Coming out of the train station, which is located inside the loop of the river, take a left to walk up the loop and then cross the bridge, which leads to **Aleksandr Stamboliiski** (Александър Стамболийски). Turn right onto the big **Hristo Botev** (Христо Ботев) to reach the center (15min.). Alternatively, take almost any of the infrequent buses from the train station (150lv; ask *"za tsentur?"*—"to the center?").

Currency Exchange: Biohim Bank (Биохим), Rafael Mihailov 2 (Рафаел Михайлов). Changes traveler's checks into US$ or leva (US$2.20 commission per check), but ask the tellers, not the security guard! From pl. Maika Bulgaria, walk east on Neza-visimost, and it's the first left. Open Mon.-Fri. 8:30am-noon and 1-4pm.

Trains: To: Burgas (5 per day, 2480lv); Sofia (8 per day, 2480lv); Varna (5 per day, 2480lv); Gabrovo (7 per day, 700lv; change in Tsareva Livada); Ruse (6 per day, 1280lv); and Pleven (11 per day, 1440lv). Trains north all have connections through nearby Gorna Oryahovitsa (Горна Оряховица), 7km northeast of town. To go direct out of Gorna, take bus #10 east from pl. Maika Bulgaria (500lv).

Buses: Nikola Gabrovski. Five stops from the center by bus #7 or 10. To Stara Zagora (1 per day, 2hr., 2100lv). **Group Travel** (tel. 282 92) in the Hotel Etur building. To Sofia (4 per day, 3hr., 3800lv) and Varna (2 per day, 3hr., 3800lv). Open Mon.-Fri. 9am-6:30pm, Sat.-Sun. 10am-noon and 3:30-6pm.

Luggage Storage: At the train station (300lv per day).

Pharmacy: ul. Vasil Levski 23 (Васил Левски). Open daily 8am-8pm.

Post Office: pl. Maika Bulgaria. Open Mon.-Fri. 7am-noon and 12:30-6:30pm, Sat. 8am-noon and 2-5:30pm. *Poste Restante* down the stairs to the next building, 30m left of main entrance. **Postal code:** 5000.

Telephones: At the post office. Open daily 7am-10pm. **Faxes** (fax 298 77) can be sent and received here. Fax open daily 7am-7pm. **Phone code:** 062.

ACCOMMODATIONS

While the daredevil traveler may find a deal by scouring the streets for a private room (as little as 5000lv, if you can pull it off), the more circumspect traveler should not have any problems finding a room either.

Hotel Orbita (Хотел Орбита), Hristo Botev 15 (tel. 220 41), on the way to Hotel Etur (see below). Backpacker-oriented triples and quads on the 4th floor share a func-tional bathroom with squatter toilets. 24hr. hot water. 10,000lv per person.

Hotel Trapezitsa (HI; Хотел Трапезица), Stefan Stambolov 79 (tel. 220 61). An excel-lent youth hostel. From the post office, walk straight, and follow the street right. Fresh, new rooms with private bathrooms. Apartments for 2 with fridge US$10 per person. Doubles 12,000lv, non-members 18,000lv. Lockout midnight.

Hotel Comfort, Panayot Tipografov 5 (Панайот Типографов; formerly Yanaki Donchev (Янаки Дончев); tel. 287 28). From Stambolov, walk left on Rakovski, and turn left at the small square. Well-hidden in a private house. Clean rooms, beautiful bathrooms, and amazing views. US$15 per person. The luxury top floor apartment sleeps 4 and its balcony affords a great view of the evening light shows (US$48).

FOOD

A large **outdoor market** sells fresh fruit and veggies daily from dawn to dusk at the corner of Bulgaria and Nikola Gabrovski. Multiple **taverns** capitalize on the balconies of old houses overlooking the river. **Mehana Medovina** (Механа Медовина), Ivan Panov 5 (Иван Панов; tel. 201 90), off Stambolov to the right of Hotel Trapezitsa, serves great veal "medalion" with mushrooms (5100lv). Other main courses run 2500-5000lv, wine 2500-6000lv (open daily 11am-2:30pm and 4pm-1am). **Starata Mehana** (Старата Механа), on Stambolov, five minutes from Hotel Trapezitsa, is small and friendly with animal skin decor (*kavarma* 2600lv, soups 800-1800lv; open 10am-midnight). **Sladkarnitsa Lotos** (Сладкарница Лотос), the "Snack Bar" next to Hotel Trapezitsa, offers oodles of cake: try the chocolate *garash* (гараш; 470lv). On the ter-race, both the view and the cappuccino are cheap (220lv; open daily 6am-11pm).

SIGHTS AND ENTERTAINMENT

The ruins of the **Tsarevets** (Царевец), a fortress that once housed the royal palace and a cathedral, stretch across an overgrown hilltop surveying the city. Nikola Pikolo leads to the gates (open daily in summer 8am-7pm, off-season 8am-5pm; 2500lv, stu-dents 1500lv). From the heights near **Baldwinova kula** (Балдуинова кула; Baldwin's tower), you'll be standing where the imprisoned Latin emperor Baldwin of Flanders spent his last days after an unsuccessful attempt to conquer Bulgaria in 1205. Climb up the hill to **Tsurkva Buzneseniegospodne** (Бъзнесениегосподне; Church of the Ascension), restored in 1981 on the 1300th anniversary of the Bulgarian state.

Near the fortress off ul. Ivan Vazov, the **Muzey Vtoroto Bulgarsko Tsarstvo** (Музей Второто Българско Царство; Museum of the Second Bulgarian Kingdom) traces the region's history from the Stone Age to the Middle Ages with Thracian pottery, a collection of medieval crafts from Turnovo, and copies of religious frescoes (open Tues.-Sun. 8am-noon and 1-6pm; 2500lv, students 1500lv). Next door, in the **Muzey na Vuzrazhdaneto** (на Възраждането; National Revival), the English signs on some exhibits help even foreigners understand the depth of the movement (open Wed.-Mon. 8am-noon and 1-6pm; 2500lv, students 1500lv; group tours 3500lv).

On summer evenings there is often a **sound and light show** above Tsarevets Hill: different-colored lasers play out Bulgaria's history in symbols. Check at **Interhotel Veliko Turnovo** off Stamboliiski for dates, although they may not know if the show will go on until 8pm. The Interhotel's indoor **swimming pool** is also open to visitors (2000lv per hr. after 1:30pm). The building identifiable by the big БАР ПОЛТАВА sign in the main square houses a **disco** (200lv, dead except on weekends) and a **movie theater** (500lv; Thurs.-Fri. only).

■ Near Veliko Turnovo

ARBANASI (АРБАНАСИ)

Four kilometers east of Veliko Turnovo, 15th-century **Arbanasi** (ar-bahn-AH-see) is packed with beautiful hill-top mansions turned museums. The restored white houses hide indoor murals dripping with color and intricately-carved wooden ceilings and furnishings. Todor Zhivkov, Bulgaria's long-time Communist leader, had a residence here, and the town is now a luxury resort. From the *pazar* (пазар; market) in Veliko Turnovo, **minivans** will take you there for around 2000lv, taxis for even more. **Bus #16**, on its way to Gorna Oryahovitsa, will drop you off where the road splits off for Arbanasi (500lv), but the best way to get there may be on foot. Follow Nikola Pikolo out of town and when you start to see some houses on the hillside, take the unmarked paved road that splits off to the right for another kilometer or so. It loops past **Sveti Nikola monastery** (Свети Никола) and Zhivkov's old hangout—now the Arbanasi Palace Hotel—to land in the middle of Arbanasi, a town too small for street names. Take a sharp left to find the sights. One ticket (3000lv, students 1500lv) lets you into **Hadzhi Ilievata kushta** (Хаджи Илиевата Къша; Hadzhi Iliya house; open Wed.-Thurs. 9am-noon and 1-6pm), **Tsurkva Rozhdestvo Hristovo** (Рождество Христово; Church of the Nativity; open daily 9am-noon and 1-6pm), **Constantsalievata Kushta** (Константалиевата Къша; open daily 9am-noon and 1-6pm), and **Tsurkva Arhangeli Gavrail i Mihail** (Архангели Гавраил и Михаил; Archangels Gabriel and Michael; open Wed.-Thurs. 9am-noon and 1-6pm). Ask at the kiosk or Constantsa-lievata Kushta for an English guide (4500lv per group).

To spend the night, go to **Restaurant Galeria** (tel. 305 54) and ask the owner to recommend one of Arbanasi's 13 **private hotels.** He knows them all, together with prices (US$5-8) and location. The restaurant also has excellent food—they will cook (almost) anything you want. Baked lamb is worth the 4500lv (open Mon. 6pm-11pm, Tues.-Sun. 10am-11pm). There are several other **taverns** lining the main drag (all with fresh trout); don't miss the **bazaar**—a bargain-hunter's dream come true, with vendors selling icons, wood carvings, handmade lace, and various antiques.

TRYAVNA (ТРЯВНА)

Fiercely independent during the centuries of Ottoman occupation, Tryavna (tr-YAHV-nah) was an important center of the National Revival movement. Works of the 17th-century Tryavna School of Woodworking and Icon Painting remain as a reminder of the settlement's greatest years. The 12th-century **Tsurkvata Sv. Arhangel Mihail** (Църквата Св. Архангел Михаил; Church of the Archangel Michael), Angel

BULGARIA

Kunchev 9 (Ангел Кънчев), is across the street and a little way down from the post office. The church's treasure is the **Tsarskiyat Krutst** (Царският Кръст; Tsar's Crucifix), a wooden relic with 12 scenes from the Gospels carved on it—ask the *pop* (priest) to unlock it and show it to you (open daily 7am-noon and 3-6pm). The **Muzey Shkolo** (Музей Школо; Old School) stands at #7 pl. Kapitan Dyado Nikola (Капитан Дядо Никола), the only preserved National Revival square in Bulgaria. The museum displays timepieces, art, and "graphicatures" (open daily April-Sept. 9am-6pm; off-season 8am-noon and 1-5pm; 1600lv; French tours 2000lv).

Cross the little arched bridge by the clocktower and turn left to find **Daskalova Kushta** (Даскалова Къща; Daskalov's House), Slaveykov 27a (Славейков). A wood-carving museum (including portraits of famous historical figures) occupies the first floor. The second exhibits the carved ceilings of competing masters (open daily April-Sept. 9am-6pm; off-season daily 8am-noon and 1-5pm; 1000lv). To find the **Muzey Trevnenska Ikonopisna** (Музей Тревненска Иконописна; Museum of the Tryavna School of Icon Painting), backtrack 30m on Slaveykov, take a left toward the hill, and cross the train tracks. Take a left on Breza (Бреза), and, after the buildings end, head up the stairs on the right. Over 160 icons tell the story of the oldest icon-painting school in Bulgaria. Don't miss the exhibits of a *zograf*'s (зограф; painter) instrumentarium and the stages in an icon's creation. Taped tours in *Bulglish* (open daily in summer 8am-4pm; 1000lv; English city guide-map 500lv).

To get to Tryavna, take a **bus** from Gabrovo (1 per hour, 45min., 500lv) or a **train** from Veliko Turnovo (8 per day, 45min., 700lv). Cross the little square in front of the bus/train station and turn right down Angel Kunchev. Religiously follow its fickle turns; it's 10 minutes to the center, which is marked by a big library on the right and Hotel Tryavna on the left. To get to **Chastna Zemedelska i Investitsionna Banka** (Частна Земеделска и Инвестиционна Банка), continue along Angel Kunchev and turn right at the T-intersection. The bank changes **cash only** (open Mon.-Fri. 9am-12:30am and 1-4:45pm). Ahead is the **post office** (open Mon.-Fri. 8am-noon and 1-5pm). **Postal code:** 5350. **Phone code:** 677.

Accommodations are hard to come by. **Hotel/Restaurant Tryavna,** in the town center, has small, basic, clean rooms with bathrooms and phones (tel. 25 98; singles US$20; doubles US$18 per person; triples US$16 per person; apartments US$50). Hot water runs 6-9am and 6-9pm. The restaurant is open daily 11am-2pm and 6:30pm-midnight. Locals praise **Restaurant Pri Maistora** (При Майстора; tel. 32 40). The chef's specialty is a dish of veal and pork with cheese in the shape of a pyramid (3400lv; open daily 11am-midnight). Take Chuchura (Чучура) from the old square, go straight through the intersection, and turn right on Kaleto.

■ Ruse (Русе)

Voyagers have drifted down the Danube for centuries, bringing music, art, and architecture. Clever Ruse (ROO-seh) made the most of all the attention. This city still lives and dies with the river and its ships; recently, the war in Yugoslavia cut important links with Central Europe and affected Ruse's all-important shipping livelihood. Most of its museums are closed because the new private owners have no money for maintenance and renovation. Nonetheless, Ruse's center remains one of the most beautiful in Bulgaria, reminiscent of its better-known Danubian brothers and sisters.

ORIENTATION AND PRACTICAL INFORMATION

Despite its size, Ruse is very easy to navigate. The **train** and **bus stations,** far from the center, are connected to the main **pl. Svoboda** (Свобода) by **Borisova** (Борисова). The main street is **ul. Aleksandrovska** (Александровска), which cuts through the main square. The statue in the main square looks toward the Danube, which runs parallel to Aleksandrovska, a five-minute walk away. A few blocks east of the square, intersecting Aleksandrovska and running south toward the stations, is the main motor (and bus) drag, **Tsar Osvoboditel** (Цар Освободител).

Tourist Office: Dunav Tours (Дунав Турс), pl. Han Kubrat 5 (Хан Кубрат; tel. 22 30 88 or 22 52 50). From pl. Svoboda, take ul. Aleksandrovska in the direction indicated by the statue's left hand. Arranges private rooms (singles US$9; doubles US$13) and provides maps and brochures.

Budget Travel: Orbita, General Skobelev 21 (Ген. Скобелев; tel. 22 47 81; fax 23 42 03), near the intersection with Borisova. Sells ISICs and sets up dorm rooms year-round for US$4-5 per person. Open Mon.-Fri. 9am-5pm.

Currency Exchange: Bulbank, pl. Sv. Troitsa (Св. Троица; tel. 231 32 31, 32, or 33), in an old yellow house on a small square connected to the southeast corner of pl. Svoboda. Changes traveler's checks (US$1 commission per transaction). Open 9am-4pm. An **ATM** is near the western end of ul. Aleksandrovska (Cirrus, EuroCard, MC).

Trains: To: Bucharest (3 per day, 6hr., 4250lv); Sofia (4 per day, 7hr., 3740lv); Varna (2 per day, 4hr., 2120lv); Plovdiv (1 per day, 5hr., 3200lv); and Burgas (1 per day, 5hr., 3200lv). **Rila,** Knyazheska 33 (tel. 22 39 20), sells international train tickets. Open Mon.-Fri. 8am-noon and 1-5pm.

Buses: To Varna (2 per day, 3½hr., 2400lv) and Pleven (1 per day, 2hr., 2400lv). **Group Travel,** pl. Svoboda (tel. 23 20 08), at Dunav Hotel, sends buses to Sofia (3 per day, 5hr., 4700lv). Open Mon.-Fri. 8am-noon and 1-6pm. Buy tickets from the hotel desk Sat.-Sun. 7:30am-noon and 1-4:30pm.

Public Transportation: Buy 180lv tickets on board for the **buses** and **trolleys.**

Taxis: tel. 189. 250lv per km.

Pharmacy: Apteka Nikolovi, ul. Aleksandrovska 89 (tel. 27 03 86). Open daily 8am-8pm. **Night pharmacy,** ul. Aleksandrovska 97 (tel. 23 70 51). Open Mon.-Fri. 9pm-7am, Sat.-Sun. 10pm-8am. Small entry to left of the daytime door.

Post Office: Sredets 1 (Средец), on the left side of Svoboda (facing the river). Open Mon.-Fri. 7:30am-9pm., Sat. 7:30am-6pm. **Postal code:** 7000.

Telephones: At the post office. Open daily 7am-10pm. **Faxes** (fax 23 36 00) can be sent and received 7am-8pm. **Phone code:** 082.

ACCOMMODATIONS AND CAMPING

Private rooms or **student dorm rooms** are the best option; go to Dunav Tours or Orbita (see above). Small hotels are few, and the former state ones, like the museums, have fallen into ruin while they're being privatized.

Hostel Prista (Хижа Приста; tel. 23 41 67), in Prista Park, 8km west of the city center by the Danube. Buses #6 and 16 run here from the center with unpredictable frequency (10min., 180lv). Get off at the stop after the campground, backtrack about 30m, follow the side road to the restaurant, and take a right. Then take the first left. A taxi from the stations costs 1500-2000lv. Bare rooms with big beds. The renovations underway during summer '97 may help out the private baths. Lockout 11:30pm. US$5-7 per person.

Hotel Petrov (Петров; tel./fax 22 24 01), in the same park as Hotel Prista. Take bus #6 or 16 to the "Camping" stop, but continue past the campground, take a right at the service station, and follow the road all the way to the end (30min. hike). Small, private hotel with a restaurant and great views. English spoken. Laundry, ironing board, even complimentary slippers. Restaurant open daily 8am-midnight. Doubles with bath US$40.

Campground Ribarska Koliba (Рибарска Колиба; tel. 22 40 68). This, too, is in Prista Park. Follow directions for Hotel Petrov, above. Spartan but clean bungalows and trailers at US$4 per bed (get one in the shade—the others may cook you alive). Tents US$2 per person. Outdoor bathrooms and mosquitoes included (avoid the campground during the nightly bug bomb). Restaurant down the road (see below).

FOOD

Food in Ruse centers around **ul. Aleksandrovska,** with the **Hali** (Хали) supermarket right at the intersection with Tsar Osvoboditel (open Mon.-Sat. 8am-8pm, Sun. 8am-2pm). **Leventa** (Левента; tel. 282 90), a few kilometers south of the train station underneath the tallest TV tower in the Balkans (take bus #17), serves main courses (2500-4600lv), salads (800-1500lv), omelettes, and cheese vegetarian dishes (1200-

2800lv). Located in what was once a Turkish fort guarding the Danube, the restaurant has a room dedicated to each nation the river runs through. The house gypsy orchestra plays nightly if there's a crowd (open daily 11:30am-midnight). Try **Bara Panorama** (Бара Панорама) on the top of the TV tower for delicious chocolate *torta garash* (860lv): Cappuccino is a mere 370lv—but don't forget the 80lv for the elevator ride. Ask to borrow the binoculars—you can see the whole Danube Valley from above (open daily 4-11:30pm; reservations suggested). **Restaurant Ribarska Koliba** (tel. 22 43 57), 15 minutes down the road from the eponymous campground (take a right at the auto shop), is a Ruse institution known for *ribena chorba* (рибена чорба; fish soup, 1800lv). Fish delicacies average 3400-9000lv, salads 500-1600lv (open 10am until the last customer leaves).

SIGHTS AND ENTERTAINMENT

Ruse centers around **pl. Svoboda,** which is marked by beautiful and colorful Baroque, Renaissance, and Art Deco architecture. This peaceful square is full of places to sit and rest in the coolness of fountains and trees. On the right side lies another square, **pl. Sv. Troitsa** (Св. Троица), on which stand the **Opera House** (tel. 23 43 03; box office open Mon.-Fri. 9am-1pm and 3-6pm) and **Sveta Troitsa** (Holy Trinity Church), erected in 1632 during the Ottoman occupation (open Sat.-Sun. 6am-8:30pm). **Sveti Pavel** (Свети Павел; St. Paul's), one of the few Catholic churches in Bulgaria, is found on a small street off Knyazheska. In the evening, locals head to the popular **Mladezhki Park** (Младежки Парк) on the east side of the city to stroll or swim in its **outdoor pool** (500lv). At night, try one of the **movie theaters** on ul. Aleksandrovska or the **discos** in the Riga and Dunav Hotels. Buy **theater** tickets through the Kontsertno Byuro (Концертно Бюро) on pl. Svobody (tel. 22 53 64; tickets US$12; season runs Sept.-June 30). And don't forget the annual **March Music Days,** Bulgaria's symphonic music festival (March 12-31; see the Kontsertno Byuro for info). Close by is **Basarbovo Manastir** (Басарбово Манастир); take bus #8 from Iv. Dimitrov. Ask at Dunav Tours for more information.

■ Shoumen (Шумен)

Relaxing and pleasant, Shoumen is notable mainly for its proximity to Bulgaria's treasured archaeological sites at Preslav, Pliska, and Madara. Monolithic historical monuments, a busy main street, and some well-preserved specimens of early 20th-century architecture keep a traveler's tired eyes busy.

Orientation and Practical Information Shoumen can be reached by **train** from Ruse (1 per day, 3hr., 1600lv); Sofia (5 per day, 6hr., 3420lv); Varna (12 per day, 1½hr., 1160lv); or anywhere else via the rail hub of Gorna Oryahovitsa, just outside Veliko Turnovo. **Group Travel** (tel. 627 13) has a kiosk outside the train station that sends **buses** to: Sofia (3 per day, 6hr., 4800lv); Veliko Turnovo (3 per day, 2½hr., 2600lv); and Varna (2 per day, 1hr., 2300lv). **Store luggage** at the train station (300lv; open 24hr.). Buses #4, 6, 8, 9, and 10 (150lv; buy ticket on the bus) run to the central pl. Oborishte (Оборище). Get off at "Hotel Shoumen." To get to the main **bul. Slavyanski** (Славянски), a two-level walkway with cafes, trees, and benches between levels, take Hristo Botev from pl. Oborishte. Or walk from the station—go up the steps to the park that lies behind the row of food stands between the bus and train stations, and walk through the park to the traffic circle, pl. Bulgaria (България), which marks the beginning of Slavyanski. The **tourist office,** pl. Oborishte 6a (tel. 553 13), arranges **private rooms** at US$8 per person and provides maps (old street names, but useful for still-accurate bus routes) and brochures (open Mon.-Fri. 8:30am-5pm, Sat. 8:30am-4pm). **Biohim Bank,** just up Slavyanski from the traffic circle in pl. Bulgaria, next to Kino Herson (Кино Херсон), changes traveler's checks for a small commission (open Mon.-Fri. 9am-5pm). The **post office** is at the top of bul. Slavyanski, right by

Hotel Madara (open Mon.-Fri. 7:30am-noon and 1-6pm; **telephones** open daily 7am-9:30pm). **Postal code:** 9700. **Phone code:** 054.

Accommodations and Food Other than **private rooms** (US$5-8), options for lodging are slim. Try **Hotel Orbita** (tel. 523 98) in Kyoshkovete Park (Кьошковете Парк), at the western end of town near the Shoumen brewery. Take bus #6 from the train and bus stations to its last stop. You're in the right place if everything smells like beer. Enter the park, and walk down the alley. Clean, recently renovated rooms boast showers, shaded terraces, and firm mattresses, and don't reek of beer (15,000lv per person, 4-person suite US$50). Three-star **Hotel Madara** (tel. 575 98), at the beginning of bul. Slavyanski, has rooms with a view, TV, fridge, bath, and occasional cockroach (singles US$31; doubles US$38; breakfast included).

Bul. Slavyanski is lined with places to eat and relax. **Popsheytanova Kushta** (Попшейтанова Кьща), pl. Oborishte (tel. 574 02), has an outdoor garden overgrown with ivy. A touristy folk tavern, it offers live music nightly, and prepares exotic salads and *starata kushta* (старата кьща), a filet with cheese, mushrooms, and tomatoes (4920lv; open 10am-late; music after 7pm; English menu). For a real treat, drop by the **Shoumen Brewery** restaurant across from Hotel Orbita, home of the famous Shoumen beer. Rattan chairs and a grand piano welcome guests to try *Shoumensko pivo*.

Sights and Entertainment The 1744 **Tombul Dzhamiya** (Томбул Джамия; Tombul Mosque; tel. 568 23), the second-largest mosque in the Balkans, is a few hundred meters west of Hotel Shoumen. It features a beautiful stone courtyard with a fountain in which believers wash before Friday services (open daily 9:15am-4:15pm; 800lv, students 650lv). The history of Shoumen, named for Bulgarian King Simeon (864-927), dates back to the early 10th century, but its monuments are from still earlier. Two buses per day (150lv) run by the mosque to **Shoumenska Krepost** (Шуменска Крепост; Shoumen Fortress). By foot, take the asphalt road by the last stop of bus #6 (30min.). Built by Thracians in the 5th century BC, the fortress was later used by Romans and Byzantines (open daily 8am-5pm; US$1, students US$0.50; English, German, Russian tours US$3). A map outside the main gate depicts suggested **hiking** routes (1½-3hr.) in the area. One of them (1½hr.) leads to the tall hilltop structure overlooking Shoumen, the **Pametnik Sozdatel Bulgarski Durzhava** (Паметник Създател Български Държава; Monument to the Founders of the Bulgarian State; tel. 625 98), erected in 1981. Exactly 1300 steps, reflecting the 13 centuries of Bulgaria's existence, get you there from the middle of bul. Slavyanski—the tiring hike is rewarded with a view and beautiful mosaics representing scenes from medieval Bulgarian history (open daily 8:30am-4:30pm; 100lv). Dance the night away under the stars in open-air disco **Lucky**, next to the station (open daily 10pm-3am). Or choose the refined **Terminator 2** disco at Hotel Shoumen (open daily 9am-5am). If you're in the mood for something more relaxing, chill out with a *Shoumensko* and all of Shoumen's youth in one of the numerous cafes along bul. Slavyanski.

■ Near Shoumen

PLISKA (ПЛИСКА) AND VELIKI PRESLAV (ВЕЛИКИ ПРЕСЛАВ)

Pliska (PLEE-ska; 681-893) and Veliki Preslav (Veh-LEEK-ee PRES-lav; 893-972), first and second capitals of Bulgaria, remain mute witnesses to the nation's history, from its birth to its greatest might. They share similar maps: a walled "inner city" circled by a lightly defended "outer city." They also share the tragic neglect of a country too poor to take care of its treasures.

Pliska lies 23km northeast of Shoumen and is accessible by **bus** (4 per day, 30min., 630lv). A huge archaeological **excavation** has unearthed parts of palaces and fortifications 3km from the village. No public transportation goes there—many walk or hitch. Unmarked remains of round fortress towers and the somewhat rebuilt **king's palace**

struggle to stay above the top of upstart grasses and bushes. To get there from the bus stop, cross the big white tiled area behind the cafe, then head left on Han Krum (Хан Крум) and settle in for the long haul.

Preslav, 18km south of Shoumen, can be visited in a daytrip from Shoumen by **bus** (7 per day, 30min., 400lv). Walk up from the hotel to find the *pazar* (food market). From there, a walk uphill leads to the **Veliki Preslav Archaeological Reserve** and its complex of medieval ruins. The graffiti-embellished English map is the only one available. Enter the park, walk straight, past the statue and bearing right at the next intersection to the cafe, then take a left onto a paved path (30min. from center) to **Arheologicheski Muzey** (Археологически Музей; Archaeological Museum; tel. 32 43; open April-Sept. 8am-6pm, winter 9am-4pm). The museum has exhibitions of ancient artwork and craftsmanship, as well as a 15-minute English film on the town. Ask for an English guide (1500lv, students 750lv). Walk down the road from the museum through a stone gate to find the ruins. Make sure to see the **Golden Temple** ruins (built in 908) and its well-preserved floor mosaic. The king's palace is marked by a column, and parts of the **fortress wall** of the inner city remain.

MADARA (МАДАРА)

Madara (mah-DAH-rah), 16km east of Shoumen, is home to the famous **Madara Horseman** (Мадарски Конниц) stone relief. On a vertical cliff 25m above ground, the lifesize relief features a horse with rider, lion, and dog—an ensemble so legendary it graces the backs of all leva coins and the labels of *Shoumen* beer. The artist is unknown, but the work was created in the 8th century and supposedly symbolizes the victories of Bulgarian ruler Han Tervel over the broken Byzantine empire. A path leads methodically through prehistoric Stone and Copper Age caves (3500BC). The largest one became the **Trakicheski Svetilishte** (Тракически Светилище; Temple of Three Thracian Nymphs; 4th-1st centuries BC) and now houses the annual festival **Madaraski Musikalni Dni** (Мадарски Музикални Дни; Madara Music Days) every June. More than 150 cells are carved into the rock, the one-time home of ascetic monks and heretics—proof of Madara's importance as a perennial cult center. On top of the plateau sit the remains of the 4th-century **Madara Fortress,** which once worked with the Shoumen Fortress to guard the way to Pliska and Preslav. Nearly 400 exhausting steps get you to the top (open daily in summer 8:30am-7pm; winter 8:30am-4:30pm; 1500lv, students 750lv). To get to Madara, take a **bus** (2 per day, 20min., 500lv) or a **train**—any *putnicheski* (slow train) to Varna will do (9 per day, 3 stops away, 20min., 400lv). From the train station, follow the crowd toward the village center, then turn left across the railroad tracks, with the Univermag (Универмаг) on your left, to reach the main road to Madara (go left and up; 30min.).

BLACK SEA COAST

The Black Sea beaches represent a sentimental journey through the sweet stuff of every Bulgarian's life: bare-bottomed childhood vacations, summer jobs flipping *kebabche,* first loves, second loves, and... The many campgrounds and international youth centers have long been popular with young party-bound backpackers; for years, the coast was the only place Bulgarians could come in contact with "the West." Go north for rocky cliffs and small villages; go south for popular resorts and beautiful beaches. Unlike elsewhere in Bulgaria, English is not uncommon on the Black Sea Coast. Many Russian and German tourists hang out here as well, especially at the resort towns Slunche Bryag (Слънче Бряг; Sunny Beach) and Zlatni Pyasutsi (Златни Пясъци; Golden Sands), built specifically to suck up tourist rubles, marks, and dollars.

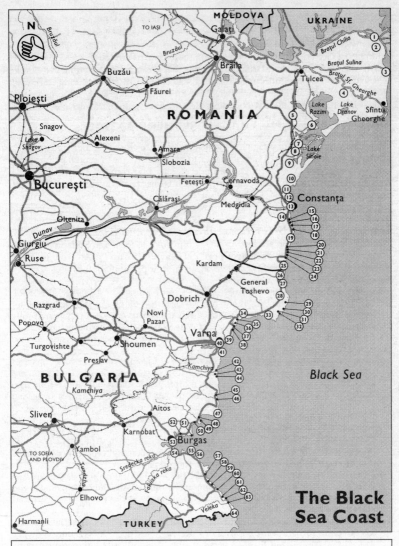

The Black Sea Coast

COASTAL TOWNS			
1 Periprava	17 Eforie Sud 🏊🏕	33 Bulgarevo	49 Nesebur 🏊🏕
2 C.A. Rosetti	18 Vasile Roaită	34 Tuzlata 🏊🏕	50 Ravda
3 Sulina 🏊	19 Costineşti	35 Balchik 🏕	51 Pomorie 🏕
4 Dunevăţo de Jos 🏕	20 Neptun 🏊	36 Albena 🏊🏕	52 Saratovo
5 Babadag 🏕	21 Jupiter 🏊🏕	37 Kranevo 🏕	53 Burgas 🏊
6 Jurilovca	22 Venus 🏊🏕	38 Zlatni Pyasutsi 🏊🏕	54 Kraimorie 🏕
7 Sinoie	23 Saturn 🏊	39 Sveti Konstantin 🏊🏕	55 Chernomorets 🏕
8 Istria	24 Mangalia	40 Varna 🏊	56 Sozopol 🏊🏕
9 Săcele	25 Vama Veche 🏊	41 Galata 🏕	57 Primorsko 🏊🏕
10 Corbu	26 Durankulak	42 Kamchiya 🏊🏕	58 Kiten 🏕
11 Mamaia-Sat 🏕	27 Krapets 🏕	43 Novo Oryahovo 🏕	59 Lozenets 🏕
12 Mamaia Băi 🏊	28 Shabla 🏕	44 Shkorpilovtsi 🏕	60 Tsarevo 🏕
13 Constanţa 🏊	29 Tyulenovo	45 Byala 🏕	61 Varvara
14 Cumpăna	30 Kamen Bryag	46 Obzor 🏊🏕	62 Ahtopol 🏕
15 Agigea 🏊	31 Sveti Nikola	47 Emona 🏕	63 Sinemorets 🏕
16 Eforie Nord 🏊	32 Rusalka 🏊	48 Slunchev Bryag 🏕	64 Rezovo 🏕

🏊 Towns with beach   🏕 Towns with campsite nearby

■ **Varna** (Варна)

Varna was crawling with sunburned Greek sailors as early as 600BC, when it was a young port city known as Odessos. By the time Romans arrived in the 2nd century, Varna was busy trading and doing the things that cosmopolitan cultural centers do. These days, Bulgaria's third-largest city and sea capital harbors an alluring Stari Grad, Roman ruins, and an ideal beach backdrop for rollerblading. Long experience as a tourist hub has taught the city countless ways to squeeze out a traveler's last cent.

ORIENTATION AND PRACTICAL INFORMATION

Although Varna is a sprawling city, the major sights are close together, and the Latin script on street signs makes the city easier to navigate. To get to central **pl. Nezavisimost** (Независимост), go through the underpass to **Tsar Simeon I** (Цар Симеон I). Varna's main pedestrian artery, **bul. Knyaz Boris I** (Княз Борис I), starts at pl. Nezavisimost. Both **Slivnitsa** (Сливница) and **Tsar Osvoboditel** (Цар Освободител) connect bul. Knyaz Boris I with a multi-name parallel street that shows up as **Osmi Primorski Polk** (Осми Приморски Полк), **Maria Luiza** (Мария Луиза) by the cathedral, and **Hristo Botev** (Христо Ботев). **Preslav** (Преслав), near Maria Luiza, continues past pl. Nezavisimost to the **train station,** forking at one point to form **San Stefano** (Сан Стефано), which leads to the **passenger port** and **beach.** Walk up Preslav from pl. Nezavisimost to the **Sv. Bogoroditsa cathedral,** a major stopping point for buses.

Tourist Offices: Varnenski Bryag (Варненски Бряг), Musala 3 (Мусала; tel. 22 55 24; fax 25 30 83), between Preslav and bul. Knyaz Boris I off pl. Nezavisimost. Staff dispenses transportation info and arranges **private rooms** (US$10-14). Open in June daily 8am-7pm, July-Aug. 7am-8pm, Sept.-May 8am-5pm. Another branch (tel. 22 22 06) is at pl. Slaveykov 6, across from the train station—the sign reads only "Частни Квартири." Same hours as other office.

Currency Exchange: United Bulgarian Bank, 77 Osmi Primorski Polk. Changes traveler's checks to leva or dollars (1% and 1.5% commission, respectively) and has an **ATM** outside (Cirrus, EC, MC). Open Mon.-Fri. 8:30am-noon and 1-4pm. The bank also operates an ATM next to the Festivalen Complex (Фестивален Комплекс) at the bottom of Slivnitsa. **PExchange bureaus** litter the city, but rates are much worse in summer and on weekends.

American Express: Megatours, Slivnitsa 33 (tel. 22 00 47 or 22 00 58), in the Hotel Cherno More. Holds mail, sells traveler's checks, and cashes them (3% fee). Buy checks with your AmEx card, then receive cash for them right there. **Free maps** of downtown. Open Mon.-Fri. 9am-6:30pm, Sat. 9am-noon.

Flights: From the airport (tel. 442 13), take bus #409 to the cathedral. **Balkan Airlines** (tel. 22 26 04), in the Varna Community House of Art, the tall building at the intersection of Slivnitsa and Maria Luiza. To: Sofia (US$159); Burgas (US$159); and Odesa (US$234).

Trains: Near the commercial port by the shore. To: Sofia (7 per day, 7hr., 3900lv; 2200lv extra for *couchette*); Plovdiv (3 per day, 5½-7hr., 3000lv); Burgas (1 per day, 3hr., 1700lv); and Ruse (2 per day, 4hr., 1900lv). **Rila** international trains bureau, ul. Preslav 13 (tel. 22 62 73 or 22 62 88), sells tickets to Budapest, Athens, and Istanbul. Open Mon.-Fri. 8am-6:30pm, Sat. 8am-3pm.

Buses: ul. Vladislav Varnenchik (Владислав Варненчик). Take city bus #22 or 41 from either the train station or the north side of the cathedral. Buses are the best way to and from Burgas (8 per day, 3hr., 3500lv). **Group Travel,** bul. Knyaz Boris I 6 (tel. 25 67 34 or 23 04 87), hidden under a SONY sign. Sends buses to: Sofia (2 per day, 6½hr., 4700lv); Warsaw (Tues. 6pm, 40hr., DM100); and Odesa (Wed. noon, 24hr., US$36). Open Mon.-Fri. 10am-3pm, Sat.-Sun. 10am-1pm. Buy tickets in advance.

Ferries: At the passenger port (Морска Гара; tel. 22 23 26). Ferries sail between coast resorts and are a pleasant alternative to hot, crowded buses. Cashier open 1hr. before departure. **Information kiosk** open Mon.-Fri. 7:30am-6:30pm. Daily **ferries** (hydro-buses) depart from Varna at 8:30am for Sveti Constantin (40min., 3000lv); Golden Sands (1½hr., 3750lv); and Balchik (2½hr., 6400lv). A **cargo ferry** sells pas-

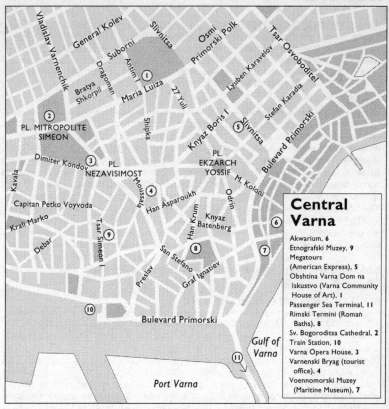

Central Varna

Akwarium, 6
Etnografski Muzey, 9
Megatours
(American Express), 5
Obshtina Varna Dom na
Iskustvo (Varna Community
House of Art), 1
Passenger Sea Terminal, 11
Rimski Termini (Roman
Baths), 8
Sv. Bogoroditsa Cathedral, 2
Train Station, 10
Varna Opera House, 3
Varnenski Bryag (tourist
office), 4
Voennomorski Muzey
(Maritime Museum), 7

BULGARIA

sengers tickets from Beloslav, 30km from Varna, to Ilichovsk, Ukraine, a short bus ride from Odesa. Call 60 20 12 or 60 34 38 for info.

Public Transportation: City **buses** cost 160lv (pay on bus). Look for the resort name on the front of the bus or **minivan** at the cathedral. Take bus #22 or 41 from the train station to the cathedral.

Car Rental: Europcar, at AmEx (see above). Unlimited mileage US$65 and up; otherwise US$24 plus US$0.24 per km and up. 22% VAT not included.

Luggage Storage: At the train station. 300lv. Open daily 6-11:30am and noon-10pm.

Pharmacy: bul. Knyaz Boris I 29 (tel. 22 22 87). Open Mon.-Fri. 7:30am-8pm, Sat.-Sun. 10am-5pm. Also at Debur 2 (Дебър; tel. 22 12 77), off Preslav. Open 24hr.

Post Office: bul. Suborni (Съборни), across the street from the cathedral. Open Mon.-Fri. 7am-9pm, Sat. 7:30am-9pm, Sun. 8am-noon. **Postal code:** 9000.

Telephones: At the post office. Open daily 7am-10:30pm. **Faxes** (fax 24 40 30) open Mon.-Fri. 7am-8:30pm, Sat. 8am-1pm. **Phone code:** 52.

ACCOMMODATIONS

There may be more **private room bureaus** in Varna than private rooms. Reserve ahead in July and August. It is generally easier to find rooms in Varna or Burgas than at the resorts. Location determines the price. In addition to **Varnenski Bryag's** two offices (see above), **Isak** (Исак; tel. 60 23 18), at the train station, finds rooms for US$5-7 per person (open daily 5am-10pm).

Hotel Musala (Мусала), Musala 3 (tel. 22 39 25), next to Varnenski Bryag. Mediocre but affordable, in a cool old building with a beautiful (and long) staircase inside. Spartan, clean rooms and tiled bathrooms. Singles with sink US$14; doubles US$20; triples US$24.

Hotel Orel (Орел), bul. Primorski 131 (Приморски; tel. 22 42 30; fax 25 92 95), along the seaside gardens. Cool doubles and triples with shared bath. US$20 per person. The beach is 50m away. 24hr. cafe to indulge cravings for *Astika* beer.

Hotel Orbita (Орбита), Tsar Osvoboditel 25 (tel. 22 51 62). Nice rooms have satellite TV, fridge, phone, radio, and private shower. Singles US$30; doubles US$40; 10% ISIC discount. Regular rooms (shared bath, no TV) are US$15/US$20, respectively.

FOOD

Pedestrian **bul. Knyaz Boris I** and **Slivnitsa** swarm with cafes, kiosks, and vendors selling everything from foot-long hot dogs to corn on the cob and cotton candy, as well as locally produced *Albena* champagne (US$1 per bottle). The many restaurants along the beach have great seafood and are full of young people. A block up Preslav from pl. Garov, **"Happy" English Pub** bursts with youth—staff and clientele—and serves all your favorite Bulgarian dishes at moderate prices. The specialty is pork filet stuffed with ham and mushrooms (4150lv; English menu; open daily 8am-midnight). The bright **Restaurant Musala** (Мусала; tel. 60 19 28), pl. Nezavisimost, stirs up goulash (5700lv) and Asian specials like sweet and sour chicken (8000lv), as well as imaginative cocktails like Zombies (1868lv) and fantastic desserts—try the *crème caramel* (700lv; open daily 8:30am-11:30pm, music from 8pm). **Baba Tonka** (Баба Тонка), a tiny sweets booth on Tsar Simeon, cooks up delicious *palachinki*—thin pancakes filled with apple jam (150lv). Various pastries (150-400lv) make a great breakfast (open daily 6am-8pm).

SIGHTS AND ENTERTAINMENT

The beautiful, sandy, family-dominated **beaches** can be reached through the seaside gardens. The **Akvarium** (Аквариум) features a stuffed monarch seal and some lively fish (open Mon. noon-7pm, Tues.-Sun. 9am-7pm; 1000lv, children 800lv). The **Dolphinarium** (tel. 82 60 69), in the north part of the park, has 30-minute shows at 11am, 2pm, and 3:30pm (open Tues.-Sun.; 740lv, ages 2-10 370lv; ticket office open Tues.-Sun. 10am-4pm). Take bus #8, 9, or 14 or walk through the seaside gardens. On the way, you'll pass by the **zoo** (open 8:30am-8pm; 500lv). Hidden among the fountains and trees is a vine-covered **open-air theater,** home of international ballet competitions and festivals (May-Oct.). Buy tickets at the gate or at the ticket office near Hotel Cherno More (Хотел Черно Море).

The well-preserved **Rimski Termi** (Римски Терми; Roman Baths) stand on San Stefano (open Tues.-Sun. 10am-5pm; 1000lv) in the city's old quarter—**Grutska Mahala** (Грыцка Махала). Bulgaria's second-largest cathedral, **Sv. Bogoroditsa,** is in the city center across from the post office between Maria Luiza and Suborni. It was built in 1882-86 in honor of the Russian soldiers who fought for the liberation of Bulgaria.

The big red **Opera House** (tel. 22 33 88, reservations tel. 22 30 89) on the main square, has a reduced summer schedule: inquire at the ticket office. Performances (1000lv) start at 7:30pm. At ul. L. Karavelov 1 (Лэ Каравелов), up Maria Luiza at its intersection with Slivnitsa, the **Obshtina Varna Dom na Iskustvo** (Община Варна Дом на Искуство; Varna Community House of Art), hosts chamber music concerts; get a schedule at the tourist bureau. **Nightlife** centers around bul. Slivnitsa and bul. Knyaz Boris I. The **Festivalen Complex,** with a cinema and disco, is a popular hangout for younger crowds. The music festival **Varnensko Lyato** (Варненско Лято) takes place for about six weeks, starting in mid-June. Hotel Orbita's **disco** is popular with students (open nightly 11pm-sunrise). In summer, a good number of discos and bars open by the beach. Try **Spider** (tel. 25 00 22), close to the port—dance the night away under glowing arachnids (gets better after midnight; 500lv). **Spartakus** (Спартакус), a self-advertised "private mixed club welcoming all sexual orientations," is in the Opera House.

Every summer, Varna chills out during its **International Jazz Festival** (last weekend in July); for the cynical, the **"Love is Folly" film festival** takes place in the festival complex (last week of Aug.-1st week of Sept.). For cultural info, try the Festivalen

Complex or the **International Advertisement office** (tel. 23 72 84), two floors below the entrance on Slivnitsa.

■ North of Varna

BALCHIK (БАЛЧИК)

An underrated jewel among the northern seaside resorts, **Balchik** (BAHL-chik), dotted with orange-roofed white houses carved into rocky cliffs, captivates with simple and spontaneous beauty. This sleepy fishing village is a perfect base for a northern Black Sea Coast vacation—it has most of the conveniences of a resort without the high prices and crowds. Right before you reach the beachside, pl. Ribarski (Рибарски; fisherman) is a lively **outdoor market,** and a vegetarian heaven. The **public beach** is small but clean, with showers, changing rooms, bar, volleyball, umbrellas, and *vodna koleva* rental (paddleboats; 3000lv per hour). A smaller, less-crowded beach lies 0.5km in the other direction along the beach. Above the slightly rocky shoreline lies Romanian Queen Marie's **summer palace,** where you can sit in her marble throne and tour the **rose garden** and the **largest cactus collection in the Balkans** (open daily 8am-8pm; entry to both 4000lv, students 500lv). At night, relax at a beachside cafe or dance at **Cariba disco,** right on the beach (10pm until sunrise; free).

Buses run from Varna (6 per day, 1hr., 1350lv), but intermittent **minivans** across the street from the bus station make the trip faster and charge the same price (they leave when full). From Balchik's bus station, walk downhill on Cherno More (Черно Море) to the main square, pl. Nezavisimost, and then continue following it to pl. Ribarski. Ul. Primorska (Приморска) runs along the shore. At ul. Primorska 1, just right of pl. Ribarski, sits **Balkan Tourist Dionisopolis** (tel. 28 62), which finds private rooms (US$7) and sells **maps** (800lv; open 9am-9pm). The **post office** is in pl. Nezavisimost (open Mon.-Sat. 8am-7pm; **telephones** and **fax** open daily 7am-9pm; fax 31 00). **Postal code:** 9600. **Phone code:** 0579.

Hotel Esperanza (Хотел Есперанса), Cherno More 16 (tel. 51 48), is small, but has spacious rooms (US$8 per person). A satellite TV plays in the common room, and a kitchen is available. Dozens of nameless food joints advertise their menus on chalkboards along the beach (3000lv assures a healthy meal). From the beach, work up an appetite by climbing the vegetation-covered stairs to **Emona** (Емона), Emona 14. A sign leads the way to delicious fish and chicken dishes and an unrivaled view of the harbor from the ship-like building (full meal less than US$4; open daily 5pm-midnight). For an epidermal treat, visit the mud baths of **Tuzlata,** 7km to the north. Three **buses** per day leave from the Balchik bus station (15min., 400lv; **taxi** from pl. Ribarski about 2500lv; ask for the sanatoria). Although the spa has seen better days, you can still have yourself a great *grazni banya* (грязни баня). Go in the right side for women, the left for men; get naked; take a preparatory dip in the water; then rub mud all over yourself and sit in the sun while it dries. It's good for skin problems, rheumatism, or just for fun (open 8am-4pm; 200lv).

ALADZHA MANASTIR (АЛАДЖА МАНАСТИР)

Known as the *skalen* (rock) monastery, **Aladzha Manastir** (tel. 35 54 60), 14km from Varna, was carved out of the side of a mountain during the 13th and 14th centuries. No written records about the monastery exist, and its Christian name remains a mystery ("*aladzha*" is Turkish for "patterned"). The monastery's two levels were carved directly into the 40m limestone cliff; the chapel on the second level preserves a likeness of Madonna with child and other frescoes. An **art gallery,** to the left as you enter the premises of the monastery, exhibits medieval mural paintings. An excellent guidebook in English is available at the ticket office (3000lv). The **catacombs,** a group of three-level caves that once served as the homes of hermits, sit 800m northeast. (Monastery open June-Oct. daily 9am-6pm; Nov.-May Tues.-Sun. 10am-5pm; 1560lv, students 800lv.)

Take **bus** #29 from the Varna cathedral to the foot of a hill, minutes from the monastery (only 2 per day, early morning and evening, 30min., 160lv). If you miss it, take

#53 and get off at the fork marked "Golden Sands—Aladzha monastery." Going left and up, it's a 15-minute hike (provided landslides do not render the road impassable). On the way down, have a snack at the small **cafe**, or dine at **Lovna Sreshta** (Ловна Среща; tel. 35 51 90) for thrice the price. *Gligan pemen* (глиган пемен; wild boar; 8500lv) and various fish (4500-6800lv) top the menu, and mind-boggling outdoor folk shows feature "*Nestinari*" dancers—people prancing barefoot on hot coals (open daily 11am-midnight; show 9:30-10:30pm, call ahead to see if the show will go on).

■ Burgas (Бургас)

Used mainly as a transport link to the villages and beaches of the south coast, Burgas (BOOR-gahs) is decidedly underrated by tourists. The consummate Bulgarian beach town, Burgas is filled with people strolling just about everywhere, but especially through the city's lively center and its seaside gardens.

ORIENTATION AND PRACTICAL INFORMATION

The Burgas **bus** and **train stations** are near the port at **Garov pl.** (Гаров). **Aleksan-drovska** (Александровска), the main pedestrian drag, begins across the street. The first of many tourist offices is one block east. Up Aleksandrovska and to the right, pedestrian **Aleko Bogoridi** (Алеко Богориди) leads to **Demokratsia** (Демокрация), beyond which are the seaside gardens and beach. **Ferdinandova** (Фердинандова) lies on the other side of Aleksandrovska.

Tourist Office: Primorets Tourist, pl. Garov (tel. 427 27), a block east of Aleksan-drovska under the sign Частни Квартири. The first of Burgas' dozens of such offices offers private rooms at the going rate (US$4). Open 8am-8pm.

Currency Exchange: Bulbank, right across the street from the huge Hotel Bulgaria on Aleksandrovska. Cashes traveler's checks at US$1 per transaction and has an ATM inside (Cirrus, EC, MC). Open Mon.-Fri. 8:30am-11:30am and 1-3:30pm. Some private bureaus take AmEx traveler's checks. **Obedinena Bulgarska Banka** (Обе-динена Българска Банка) also has an **ATM** (Cirrus, EC, MC) on the left side of Ale-ksandrovska as you approach pl. Svoboda from the train station.

Trains: To: Ruse (1 per day, 6hr., 3200lv); Sofia via Plovdiv or Karlovo (8 per day, 7hr., 4100lv; 2 express per day, 6hr., 4000lv); Varna (2 per day, 4½hr., 1960lv); and Plovdiv (6 per day, 4hr., 2660lv).

Buses: Station **Yug** (Юг), by the train station, serves the Black Sea coast and any-where else you please, including Varna (8 per day, 3hr., 3500lv). In the lobby of Hotel Bulgaria, tickets are sold for the **Group** and **Maksitur** bus lines to Sofia, Odesa, and more. Open daily 8:30am-noon and 1-5:30pm. There's also a **minibus** stand for the resorts at the opposite end of the train station from the bus station.

Pharmacy: Bogoridi, near the corner of Aleksandrovska. Open Mon.-Fri. 9am-9pm, Sat.-Sun. 9am-7pm.

Luggage Storage: Near the bus and train stations. Look for the big "Гардероб" sign. 300lv per day. Open daily 6am-10pm.

Post Office: ul. Hristo Botev (Христо Ботев), parallel to Aleksandrovska. Milin Kamuk (Милин Камък), across Aleksandrovska from Hotel Bulgaria, leads right to it. Open Mon.-Fri. 7am-8pm, Sat. 8am-6pm. **Postal code:** 8000.

Telephones: At the new post office, on the corner of San Stefano (Сан Стефано) and bul. Osvobozhdenie 70 (Освобождение). From the bus/train station, ride 4 stops on bus #211. Open 7am-10:30pm. **Phone code:** 056.

ACCOMMODATIONS AND FOOD

Private rooms in Burgas are plentiful, affordable (about US$4), and often convenient. Secure them at **Primorets Tourist** (see above) or other accommodations bureaus. **Hotel Park** (tel. 329 51 or 297 32), in the farthest northern reaches of the seaside gar-dens (take bus #4 from the center or a taxi—it's about 5km from the station), offers clean rooms with balcony, shower, and phone (doubles 60,000lv, single travelers in doubles 45,000lv; restaurant on premises). **Camping Kraymorie** (Къмпинг Крайморие; tel. 240 25), 10km from Burgas by hourly bus #17, rents out motel rooms by wide, clean beaches and tennis courts (doubles US$20; bungalows US$12).

Ul. Bogoridi and **Aleksandrovska** are full of restaurants, cafes, hamburger joints, and ice cream stands. If you choose to feast near the waves, walk up the alley along the beach and look around. Many places—from homely kiosks to refashioned ships—serve fish and seafood, especially at the north end of the seaside gardens, opposite the train station. **Art Restaurant** (Арт Ресторан; tel. 422 39), on Bogoridi in the courtyard of the "CDC" building, cools you off with the shade of a huge fig tree and a mini fountain to get you ready for some healthy fish portions (1875-6000lv). A great place for dessert—try a Bulgarian interpretation of the banana split (1200lv) or some *palachinki* (pancakes) with fruit, cream, and chocolate (1130lv; 5% service charge; English menu; open daily 5pm-midnight). Even farther down Bogoridi, on the right just before the seaside gardens, the loud **Restaurant Odesa** (Одеса) serves national specialties (3600-8600lv), salads (850-1400lv), and *mish-mash* (a local vegetarian concoction of peppers, eggs, and cheese; 850lv), on a terrace overlooking the stream of people at night. Live music gets especially lively on weekends.

SIGHTS AND ENTERTAINMENT

The center of Burgas—Aleksandrovska and Bogoridi—is colorful, friendly, unimposing, and filled with happy foreigners and young Bulgarians. The walkway along the beach affords a pleasant stroll, and the sand strip is nowhere near as overrun as in Varna, although it is problematic ecologically. The **Archaeological Museum,** Bogorodi 21 (tel. 452 41), houses the oldest marble statue found in Bulgaria (5th century BC; open in summer Mon.-Sat. 9am-5pm, off-season Mon.-Fri. 9am-5pm; US$1, students US$0.50; free English guidebook). At night, try the open-air **Dance Club Strena,** right by Taverna Neptune, a few hundred meters north of Hotel Primorets in the Seaside Gardens. Also fun is the **Neptune Nightclub,** right next door.

■ Near Burgas

NESEBUR (НЕСЕБЪР)

Nesebur (neh-SEH-bur), a museum town atop the peninsula at the south end of Sunny Beach, is a sweet alternative to generic coastal tourist ghettos, though it gets crowded in high season. Medieval churches and Thracian, Byzantine, and Roman ruins dot the town, sometimes referred to as the jewel of Bulgaria's Black Sea coast. A walk through Nesebur's **Stari Grad** is a genuine walk through time. On the north shore, stone **fortress walls** from the 3rd century still survive. The Byzantine **gate** and **port** date back to the 5th century, and the 6th-century church **Starata Mitropoliya** (Старата Митрополия; Old Metropolitan) stands roofless in Nesebur's center. The temple of **Ioan Krustitel** (Йоан Кръстител; John the Baptist), now an art gallery, has been around since the 10th century (free). The 11th-century **Tsurkvata Sveti Stefan** (Църквата Свети Стефан; St. Stephen's) is plastered in 16th-century frescoes (open 8:30am-7pm; 1200lv, students 500lv). The church **Hristos Pantokrator** (Христос Пантократор; Christ the Almighty) in the main square dates from the 13th century, and in summer doubles as an art gallery (open daily 9am-11pm; free). On Mitropolitska, the **Tsurkvata Sveti Spas** (Свети Спас; Church of St. Spas; 1609) offers a written tour in English about its 17th-century frescoes. The gravestone of a Byzantine princess is found inside (open 9:30am-5pm; 800lv, children 400lv). The **Arheologicheski Muzey** (Археологически Музей; Archaeological Museum; tel. 60 18), to the right of the town gate, exhibits a fascinating collection of ceramics, coins, icons, and naval implements (open May-Oct. daily 9am-6pm, Nov.-April Mon.-Fri. 9am-6pm; 1500lv, students 250lv; English tours 2000lv per group). **Artists** sell their wares along the alleys and in front of churches and ruins.

Get to Nesebur by **bus** from Burgas (every 40min., 40min., 1250lv). Buses stop at the Old Nesebur port and gate leading to town. The main **Mesembria** goes right, while **Mitropolitska** goes left at the central square fork. The town is small but intricate, so stop by **Tourist Bureau Menabria** (Менабрия; tel. 60 91), and get a **map;** the office is on Mesembria, on the left side from the beginning of town. The staff arranges **accommodations** (US$8 per person; open 9am-8:30pm). **Bank Biohim,** Mesembria 19 (tel. 29 32), cashes traveler's checks at 4% commission (open Mon.-Fri. 8:45am-12:30pm and 1:30-4pm). **Private exchange offices** accept traveler's checks with better rates. The **post office** is in the main square (open daily 7am-5pm; **phones** open daily 7am-10pm). **Postal code:** 8231. **Phone code:** 0554.

In high season, it may be difficult to find a room for less than a three-night stay. It is cheaper and easier to sleep across the isthmus on the mainland. **Mesembria Hotel,** Ribarska 2 (Рибарска; tel. 32 55), near the post office, may be a possibility (50,000lv per person). **Hotel Panorama** (Панорама; tel. 32 83) has clean doubles with bathrooms and terraces (US$12 per person). To reach the hotel, follow the left street at the fork coming out of Stari Grad, turn right at the next fork, and walk uphill for five minutes. People on the street can be approached for private rooms (US$3-5), but it is wise to be choosy about where and with whom you stay.

Along the harbor, munch on fresh fish with fries and *shopska* salad at street **kiosks** (US$3). Or order steaming-hot seafood and add fresh veggies from the **farmers' market. Kapitanska Sreshta** (Капитанска Среща; Captain's Table; tel. 34 29), on Chayka (Чайка), serves up superbly prepared treasures of the sea at reasonable rates. Groove to the nightly live music from 6 to 11pm (open daily 8am-midnight).

SOZOPOL (СОЗОПОЛ)

Sozopol (soh-ZO-pohl), 34km south of Burgas, is Bulgaria's oldest Black Sea town, settled in 610BC. It was once the resort of choice for Bulgaria's artistic community, and still caters to a more creative set than its Black Sea neighbors. The town is quieter and less expensive than Nesebur or Golden Sands, and works to fill the needs of visitors who don't travel in tour buses. Century-old houses line the cobbled streets of its **Stari Grad,** which sits on a rocky peninsula. The **bus station** is in the middle of an isthmus straddling a park connecting the old part of town to the new (hourly **buses** from Burgas 6am-8pm, 45min., 960lv). At the end of the park, turn left on Republikanska (Републиканска) toward Novi Grad. Tourist bureau **Lotos** operates at the bus station (tel./fax 282) and in the Novi Grad main square, Ropotamo 1 (Ропотамо; tel. 429). The staff arranges private rooms (US$7 per person) and organizes trips (open daily 8am-5pm). **Biohim Bank,** Republikanska 5 (tel. 423), in Novi Grad, changes traveler's checks (open 9am-noon and 1-4pm). The **post office** is in Stari Grad, a block past the bus station on the main street, **Apolonia** (open Mon.-Fri. 7am-9:30pm; Sat.-Sun. 7-11am and 2-8pm; **phones** daily 7am-9:30pm; send or receive **faxes** at fax 306 daily 7:30am-8pm). **Postal code:** 8130. **Phone code:** 5514.

Private rooms abound and can be arranged at Lotos (see above) or with locals (US$3-5 per person). The cheapest hotel in town is the **Voennensko Club** (Военненско Клуб; tel. 283), at the intersection of Republikanska and Ropotomo (US$5 for a bed in a double or quad, US$6 with private bath and shower). **Hotel Radik** (Радик), Republikanska 4 (tel. 17 06), offers doubles, communal baths, and a panoramic view (US$10 per person). Camping at **Zlatna Ribka** (Златна Рибка) is five minutes away by bus, 10 by boat. **Camping Kavatsite** (Каваците; 3km away; tel. 354), **Chernomorets** (Черноморец; 10km away) and **Gradina** (Градина; halfway between the two) can be reached by bus (all are on the Burgas-Sozopol bus route). Contact **Lotos** (see above).

Apolonia is the site of an ongoing craft fair and home to many **kiosks** offering fresh fried fish and calamari. For a delicious meal, walk to restaurant **Vyaturna Melnitsa** (Вятърна Мелница), Morski Skali 27a (Морски Скали; tel. 844), the street running along the tip of the peninsula; look for the little windmill. The specialty, *gyuvech,* is a meat-and-potato dish served over a burning flame in exquisite clay pots (3500lv; main dishes 2300-12,400lv; open daily 8am-midnight). For a little pre-dinner adventure, take a **boat cruise** (1hr., US$10 for groups of up to 8 or 10) from the seaport around Sozopol and have a peek at the two adjacent islands, St. Peter and St. Ivan. The best time to go is around sunset. One of the most popular night spots is the misleadingly named **Country Club,** right on the beach. Look out for rave nights (open daily 10pm-sunrise; free). During the first 10 days of September, Sozopol hosts the **Arts Festival Apolonia**—artists, actors, and their friends move here for a while.

PRIMORSKO (ПРИМОРСКО)

Young Bulgarians know Primorsko (pree-MOR-sko) as site of the **Mezhdugarodni Mladezhki Tsentur** (Международни Младежки Център; ММЦ; International Youth Center), where the best *komsomoltsy* and pioneers were once sent to strengthen international comradeship. Today, Zhivkov would blush at this rocking, inexpensive resort piled with scantily-clad foreign youths. At the manicured **beach,** equipped with dunes and some of the cleanest Black Sea water, you can rent a *vodna koleva* (paddleboat; 200lv per hr.). In the oak forest, play **tennis** (US$6 per hr., equipment US$2), volleyball, basketball, or handball (fields US$5 per hr.). The complex also has a **medical center,** open-air **theater,** and **cinema.** The **tourist office** (tel. 21 01), in Hotel Druzhba (Хотел Дружба), has maps and books hotel rooms (doubles US$20) and bungalows (US$4-10 per person). People in town may also approach with **private room** offers (300lv per person). To reach the ММЦ, walk back past the post office, heading out of town, then take a left at the big intersection. Cross the bridge over Dyavolska Reka (Дяволска Река; Devil's River) and keep going for another 20 minutes to reach the entrance to the center (45min. walk; a cab shouldn't cost more than 2000lv). Once inside the center, walk about 300m on the main street, then hang a left by the tiny post office to get to the **information office** (tel. 21 01), which has maps and books hotel rooms (US$13-15 per person in July and Aug.; otherwise US$10-12) and bungalows (similar rates). If all are full, they'll try to arrange a private room (US$5; open daily 8am-5pm).

Take a southbound coastal **bus** to Primorsko from Burgas (every hr., 1½hr., 1550lv) to the main street, **Cherno More** (Черно Море). **Exchange cash** at a kiosk near the bus station (open daily 8am-8:30pm), or traveler's checks at **Bulbank,** Cherno More 9 (open Mon.-Fri. 9:30-11:45am and 1-3pm). The **post office** and phones are a little ways back, toward the beginning of town (open Mon.-Fri. 7:30am-noon and 1:30-5pm; phones open daily 6:30am-9:30pm). **Postal code:** 8290. **Phone code:** 5561.

AHTOPOL (АХТОПОЛ)

Only 25km from the Turkish border, **Ahtopol** (ah-TOE-pohl) is a humble town of 1400 inhabitants. Man-made attractions are few, but hidden rocky bays with crystal clear water and the highest seawater temperature of all of Bulgaria's resorts more than make up the difference. The public **beach** competes with several small bays (try the one at the lighthouse). To get to the public beach, take Levski from the bus station to the end, then follow the paved path past the "жп район пловдив" sign.

Get to Ahtopol by **bus** from Burgas (2 per day, 2½hr., 2500lv). The bus station is on the main drag, **Trakiya** (Тракия). All points of interest are within a 15-minute walking radius. **Tourist office CREDO-OK** is at the bus station (tel. 340). A helpful staff provides free **maps, private rooms** (US$4 per person), and sells **bus tickets** to Sofia (1 per day, 7½hr., US$5) and Istanbul (1 per week, US$60). An **exchange bureau** waits on the way to the post office (open daily 9am-1pm and 4-7pm). The **post office** is at the end of Trakiya by the harbor (open Mon.-Fri. 8am-12:30pm and 2:30-6:30pm, Sat. 9am-noon; **phones** open Mon. 8am-noon and 2:30-10pm, Tues.-Fri. 7:30am-10pm, Sat. 8am-noon and 4-10pm). **Postal code:** 8280. **Phone code:** 995563.

Private rooms are the accommodations of choice (US$3-4), but a few private hotels also exist. Try **Valdi** (Валди; tel. 320), Cherno More 22a (Черно Море). Take a left on Veleka (Велека) from Trakiya, then a right on Cherno More—Valdi is on the right (clean doubles with shower 25,000lv). The small town leads a surprisingly active culinary life, busiest along **Kraymorska** (Крайморска)—left and right off Trakiya at the quay. On the other side of Trakiya, **Restaurant Sirius** (Сириус; tel. 372), on Kraymorska, offers cheap grills (700-1000lv) and fish (750-3000lv; open daily 11am-midnight). Left and up the street is **Chetirimata Kapitana** (Четиримата Капитана), Kraymorska 29 (tel. 366). Draped in fishing nets, it offers imaginatively named and prepared dishes (2200-4800lv; open daily 11am-3pm and 6pm-midnight). A couple of **discos** operate by the beach until sunrise.

Croatia

CROATIA (HRVATSKA)

US$1	= 6.4kn (kuna)	1kn =	US$0.16
CDN$1	= 4.63kn	1kn =	CDN$0.22
UK£1	= 10.19kn	1kn =	UK£0.10
IR£1	= 9.39kn	1kn =	IR£0.11
AUS$1	= 4.66kn	1kn =	AUS$0.22
NZ$1	= 4.06kn	1kn =	NZ$0.25
SAR1	= 1.36kn	1kn =	SAR0.73
DM1	= 3.52kn	1kn =	DM0.28

Country Phone Code: 385　　　　　**International Dialing Prefix: 00**

Sprawled along the spectacular Dalmatian coast, Croatia came away from the 1991 breakup of Yugoslavia with some of the finest resort towns in Europe. The war dampened tourism, but peacetime is luring European visitors back in droves to sail the blue Adriatic Sea, sip coffee in Zagreb's cafes, and explore the historic walled cities of Dubrovnik and Split. Even as Croatia savors its long-sought independence, unrest between ethnic Serbs and Croats casts a pall on the interior regions of the Krajina and

Slavonia, and a police presence remains visible throughout the country. Set politics aside, however, and follow the Romans, Venetians, and Slavs across the Adriatic to this exotic corner of Europe.

CROATIA ESSENTIALS

Citizens of Australia, Ireland, New Zealand, the U.K, and the U.S. do not need visas to enter Croatia. South African citizens require visas; send a visa application, two pass-port-sized photos, and a $29 check or money order to the nearest embassy and con-sulate (for your nearest Croatian representative, see **Essentials: Embassies and Consulates,** p. 3). Citizens of any country staying more than 90 days should fill out a routine extension of stay form at a local police station.

GETTING THERE AND GETTING AROUND

By plane, train, or bus, Zagreb is Croatia's main entry point. **Croatia Airlines** flies there from many cities, including Chicago, Frankfurt, London, New York, Paris, and Toronto, and continues to Dubrovnik and Split. **Trains** travel to Zagreb from Budap-est, Ljubljana, and Vienna, continuing to many additional destinations throughout Croatia. On the schedules posted around the stations, *odlazak* means departures, *dolazak* arrivals.

Though slow, stuffy, and often crowded, **buses** are sometimes more convenient than trains, and occasionally the only option. From Zagreb, they run to Dubrovnik, Rijeka, Split, and most islands. To reach Istria, travel from Koper (Slovenia) or Rijeka to Poreč or Pula. Tickets are sold on the bus, as well as at the station. In theory, lug-gage (including backpacks) must be stowed—and paid for—separately. Consider being brash and bringing it on—everyone else does, but it might be tight if the bus gets crowded. Renting a **car** is possible in larger cities, but downtown parking can be expensive, and those traveling through the Krajina region and other conflict areas should stay on paved roads to avoid possible off-road land mines. Contact the **Croat-ian Automobile Association** (HAK; tel. (1) 455 4333) for further info.

Ferry service is run by **Jadrolinija.** Boats sail the Rijeka-Split-Dubrovnik route, stop-ping at islands along the way. Ferries also float from Split to Ancona, Italy, and from Dubrovnik to Bari, Italy. Although even slower than buses, they're much more com-fortable. The basic fare provides only a place on the deck. Cheap beds sell out fast, so purchase in advance for overnight international trips. Sometimes the agency will only offer a basic ticket; in that case, *run* to get a bed. Additional local ferries and more expensive **hydrofoils** are run by private companies.

TOURIST SERVICES

Most major cities and sites have a public tourist office (*turist biro*), which provides information and maps, but usually doesn't arrange accommodations. Some private agencies also crop up, like the two conglomerates **Kompas** and **Atlas,** that exchange money and find private rooms. Tourist offices are usually open weekdays 8am-6pm and Saturdays 9am-2pm; on the crowded coast, they may take a midday break and then stay open until 10pm, even on Sundays.

MONEY AND COMMUNICATION

Most banks, tourist offices, hotels, and transportation stations offer **currency exchange,** but **traveler's checks** are accepted by only a smattering of banks; even American Express offices in small cities refuse them. Croatia's monetary unit, the **kuna** (kn)—divided into 100 **lipa**—is theoretically convertible, but impossible to exchange abroad, except in Hungary and Slovenia. **ATMs** are still rare, but their num-bers are on the rise. Most banks give **MC** or **Visa** (or both) **cash advances,** but only pricey stores, restaurants, and hotels accept plastic.

CROATIA

Mail from the U.S. arrives in 10-14 days; if addressed to *Poste Restante,* it will be held for 90 days at the main (not always the most central) post office. *Avionskim putem* is Croatian for airmail. **Post offices** usually have public **telephones** available to the public; pay after you talk. Dial 993 85 42 88 for **AT&T Direct,** 99 38 00 44 for **British Telecom Direct,** or 99-385-0112 for **MCI World Phone.** Technically, this operator assistance is free, but some phones demand a **telekarta** card, and calls to the United States are expensive (about 20kn per min.). Local calls require a *telekarta* (phone card), available at newspaper stands and the post office.

LANGUAGE

The Croats speak a language of the southern Slavic family, and write in Latin characters. Words are pronounced exactly as they are written; "*č*" and "*ć*" are both pronounced "ch" (only a Croat can tell them apart), "*š*" is "sh", and "*ž*" is a "zh" sound. The letter "*r*" is rolled, except when there's no vowel, then it makes an "er" sound as in "Brrrr!" The letter "*j*" is equivalent to "y," so *jučer* (yesterday) is pronounced "yuchur." In Zagreb and tourist offices, many know **English,** but the most popular languages on the coast are **German** and **Italian.** Almost everyone involved in the tourist industry speaks the former, as do many private room renters. Street designations on maps often differ from those on signs by "*-va*" or "*-a*" because of grammatical declensions. For a little Croatian vocabulary help, see the **Glossary,** p. 799; also see **Bosnia: Language,** p. 71, for the differences between Croatian, Bosnian, and Serbian.

HEALTH AND SAFETY

> **Emergency Numbers: Police:** tel. 92. **Fire:** tel. 93. **Ambulance:** tel. 94.

The **climate** is mild and continental around Zagreb and Mediterranean along the coast. Although Croatia is currently at peace, travel to the Slavonia and Krajina regions is still dangerous due to **unexploded mines.** Travel to the coast and islands is considered safe, but check in advance to make sure that all is calm in Bosnia, just a few miles inland. The **police** require foreigners to **register** with them upon first arriving in Croatia. Hotels, campsites, and accommodations agencies should do this for you, but those staying with friends or in private rooms must do it themselves. Failure to register has led to exclusion and fines. Police may check foreigners anywhere. **Crime,** especially violent crime, is quite low.

Croatians are generally friendly toward foreigners. Traveling for **women** is usually safe, though having a companion may help ward off an unreasonably large number of pick-up lines. Croatians are just beginning to accept the presence of **homosexuals** in their own society; discretion is still wise. There is no age limit for alcohol consumption, and you are also welcome to drink in public.

ACCOMMODATIONS AND CAMPING

Most **hotels** are expensive, with a 20-50% tourist surcharge that can often be avoided by asking to pay in kuna. Prices for pleasant *Sobe* (rooms to let; also indicated by *Zimmer*) are increasing. Sharing a double room with someone is significantly cheaper than trying to find a single. Agencies generally charge 30-50% more if you stay less than three nights. Bargain them down to a price 20% less than tourist offices charge, and check the room before paying. Organized **campgrounds,** open April or May through September or October, speckle the country and are usually packed. All accommodations are subject to a **tourist tax** of 5-10kn (another reason the police require foreigners to register). Arriving on a weekend may cause lodging problems.

FOOD AND DRINK

After years of wartime drought, restaurants are eagerly expecting guests. *Puricas mlincima* (turkey with pasta) is the regional dish in the Zagreb area. The spicy Slavonian *kulen* sausage, which is available everywhere, is considered one of the world's best sausages. Along the coast, try *lignje* (squid) or *pršut* (smoked Dalmatian ham). Culinary nymphomaniacs should know that the oysters from the Ston Bay have received a number of awards at international competitions. If your budget does not allow for such treats, *slave srdele* (salted sardines) are a tasty substitute, if less of an aphrodisiac. Even though the vegetarian culture is still underdeveloped in Croatia, there are a number of excellent meatless dishes. *Cyrašak varivo* (green bean stew), *tikvice va le šo* (steamed zucchini in olive oil), and *grah salata* (beans and onion-salad) are some of the favorites. The eclectic nature of Croatian culture is best witnessed in the diversity of desserts. If you always ask for a regional specialty, you will never eat the same dessert twice. *Zagorski štrukli* (cooked dough with cheese) in Zagreb and *fritule* (thin baked pastry) in Dalmatia are some of the all-time favorites.

Croatia offers several excellent brands of wine: the price is usually the best indicator of quality. Mix red wine with tapwater to get popular *bevanda*, and white wine with carbonated water to get *gamišt*. *Karlovačko* and *Ožiysko pivo* are the two most popular brands of beer.

CUSTOMS AND ETIQUETTE

Tipping is not expected, but you may round off to the nearest whole figure. **Clothing** is unpretentious in northern Croatia, but style becomes increasingly important as one moves farther south. Likewise, the rhythm of life changes; on the southern islands, it is common to see people eating dinner at 10pm. The style of communication in the south is friendlier and more direct. Many stores don't close until 8pm, with shorter Sunday stints, but in warmer areas they may take a break from noon to 6pm, re-opening for several hours in the evening. Generally, only restaurants are open between Saturday at noon and Monday at 8am.

NATIONAL HOLIDAYS

Croatia observes: January 1, New Year's; January 7, Orthodox Christmas; April 13, Catholic and Orthodox Easter Monday; May 1, Labor Day; May 30, Statehood Day; June 22, Croatian National Uprising Day; August 15, Assumption Day; November 1, All Saints' Day; December 25-26, Christmas.

LIFE AND TIMES

HISTORY

The ancestors of Croatia's present inhabitants settled the Adriatic's shores in the 6th and 7th centuries. They were **Slavs** who followed a largely unknown native religion until **Catholicism** arrived slowly over the next two centuries. The Croats successfully resisted Charlemagne's attempts to gain control of their area, and King Tomislav (910-28) earned his country papal recognition, consolidating Croatian independence. King Zvonimir expelled the Byzantines and was crowned by Pope Gregory in 1076, decisively strengthening Croatia's orientation toward Catholic Europe.

The Slavs who settled the Adriatic shores in the 6th century were followers of a native religion that is today unknown.

In 1102, the Kingdom of Croatia-Slavonia entered as a junior partner into a dynastic **union with Hungary,** in which it preserved some independence in the form of *sabors* (noble assemblies) and *bans* (viceroys). This partnership would tie Croatia's history to that of Hungary for the next 800 years. Instability prevailed after 1241, when **Mongol** invaders swept through Eastern Europe, crushing the Hungarians at the Sajo River. Local rulers became more powerful at the expense of the Hungarian king of Hungary-Croatia until the kingdom's recovery in the late 14th to early 15th centuries. During this period, other Balkan kingdoms—Serbia, Bulgaria, Albania, Moldova, Greek Constantinople, and Wallachia—fell to the Ottomans. After the Ottoman victory over Hungary at

CROATIA

Mohács in 1526, Croatia became an embattled, divided border region. Over the centuries, Ottomans and Hungarians tugged at the territory, but Croats did not raise a unified protest until the 19th century. After Hungarian was declared the official language and minority rights were curbed in the 1830s and 1840s, an **independence movement** began to emerge. When Hungary revolted against Austria in 1848, the Croats sided with the latter and convened a diet in Zagreb demanding self-government. **Josip Jelačić,** chief of the Zagreb diet, ordered Croatia to break with Hungary, proclaimed loyalty to the Austrian Emperor Franz Josef, and led an army toward Budapest. Though defeated by the Hungarians at Pákozd in 1848, the struggle continued into 1849; Croat participation on the Habsburg side helped defeat the Magyars. Following a devastating defeat by Prussia in 1866, however, Austria was forced to grant a constitution and more independence to Hungary.

With this compromise of 1867, the empire became known as the **Austro-Hungarian Dual Monarchy,** though the Habsburgs retained the upper hand. Croatia-Slavonia, including Zagreb and Rijeka, became part of the **Hungarian kingdom,** while most of the coast, including Istra, Zadar, and Dubrovnik, was incorporated into the Austrian half of the kingdom. Initially, the Hungarian government adopted a liberal attitude, but between 1875 and 1890, Tisza's Liberal Party campaigned to Magyarize Hungary, re-instituting Hungarian as the only official language.

During **WWI,** Croatian troops fought on the side of the Germans along with the rest of Austria-Hungary, but after November 1914, political exiles proposed the idea of political unity between the Serb, Croat, and Slovene nations as a way to further independence. On October 29, 1918, after the collapse of the Central Powers, Croatia broke with Hungary and the Dual Monarchy. Austria-Hungary sued the Allies for peace on November 3, and on December 1 the **Kingdom of the Serbs, Croats, and Slovenes** (the original name for **Yugoslavia**) declared its independence, with two rival governments: the National Council in Zagreb and the Serb royal government in Belgrade. Croats and Slovenes demanded a federal state, but the Serbian monarch, King Alexander, failed to work for reconciliation, and proclaimed a dictatorship in 1929. In 1934, he was assassinated by Croat nationalists during a visit to Marseille.

In 1939, Croatia finally achieved **autonomous** administration and government. Neutral at the outbreak of **WWII,** Yugoslavia nearly joined the Axis for protection, but British-assisted Greek triumphs over Italy provoked a pro-Allied coup in Belgrade in 1941. Hitler diverted forces into Yugoslavia, and German bombers reduced Belgrade to rubble with the help of Hungary and Bulgaria. Italy annexed Split and parts of Slovenia, while Croatia and Serbia were occupied. WWII saw savage fighting between Serbs and Croats. The puppet state created by Croat **Ustaše** fascists under Ante Pavelić collaborated with the Germans and worked to exterminate the Serbian population. Nonetheless, the majority of the Croatian population either joined or indirectly supported the anti-fascist Partisan forces led by Communists and **Josip Broz Tito,** a half-Croat, half-Slovene. Partisan resistance in Yugoslavia was fierce, and eventually led to the liberation of Yugoslavia.

Yugoslav Croatia recovered Istra, Rijeka, the Adriatic islands, and Zadar from Italy after the war and became part of the Socialist Republic of Yugoslavia. In 1945, **Tito** placed all industry and natural resources under state control. Under his unchallenged rule Yugoslavia broke with Stalin in 1948 and decentralized the administration. Ethnic rivalries were suppressed, and Yugoslavia became a relatively tolerant, prosperous Communist country. In 1971, the Croatian Communists asked for greater autonomy within Yugoslavia, and Tito, under pressure from the army, dismissed and replaced the entire leadership with more obedient Communists. Tito ruled until his death in 1980. Yugoslavia, with its volatile ethnic mix, proved highly susceptible to quick disintegration and descent into violence after Communism's wholesale defeat and collapse in Europe. In April 1990, the nationalist **Franjo Tudjman** was elected president of Croatia and the people of Croatia, simultaneous with the neighboring Slovenes, declared **independence** on

Under the rule of Josip Broz Tito, ethnic rivalries were suppressed, and Yugoslavia became a prosperous and relatively tolerant country.

CROATIA

June 25, 1991. Autonomy was declared in April; and tensions began to rise with the significant Serbian minority, which disliked the idea of Croatian independence. The Serbs, who controlled the Yugoslav National Army, expelled hundreds of thousands of Croatians from Eastern Slavonia. Shelling was directed at Dubrovnik and, to a lesser extent, Split, during 1991. On January 15, 1992, Croatia was recognized as an independent country by the EC and an UNPROFOR presence kept any further fighting at bay. In early May of 1995, Croatia, frustrated with the continued lack of control of over one-half of its territory, began an operation in Western Slavonia, and in August, decisively seized the Serb-controlled **Krajina,** expelling over 150,000 Serbs. Since a late-1995 agreement with the Serbs, there has been relative peace in Croatia, but tension has not altogether dissipated.

LITERATURE

The first Croatian texts date from the 9th century, and for the next 600 years, offerings in Croatian consisted almost entirely of translations of Europe's greatest literary hits. Renaissance influences from the West made their way to the Dalmatian coast in the 1500s when the first Croatian poets, such as **Marko Marulić,** finally moved from devotional to secular writing. The 16th-century dramatist **Marin Držić** and the 17th-century poet **Ivan Gundulić** raided Italy for models (of the literary type), combining them with influences from the oral traditions back home. After Dubrovnik's devastating 1667 earthquake, the focus of Croatian literature shifted north.

> Ugresic's personal novels took on political overtones during the recent war, when she publicly opposed the president.

The largely German-speaking middle class and the constant fear of attack from the Ottoman Empire left little room for Renaissance and Reformation ideas. The Counter-Reformation brought the Franciscans and the Jesuits, who expanded education and established Zagreb as a cultural center. The most important 18th-century Croatian authors were two Franciscans, **Filip Grabovac** and **Kačić-Miošić,** and the Slavonian **Matej Reljković.** The political domination of Croatia by Germany and Hungary threatened to become a linguistic domination in the following century—**Ljunedit Gaj** led the movement to reform and codify the vernacular as the standard literary language. With the work of the poet **Ivan Mažuranić,** the revival of Croatian literature was established at last. **August Šenoa,** Croatia's most important 19th-century literary figure, played a key part in the formation of a literary public and in completing the work that Gaj had begun. Mirroring European trends of the later 1800s, prose dominated, especially that of **Ujeneslav Novak** and **Ante Kovačić.**

Poetry returned in multiple incarnations in the 20th century, the first stimulated by Croatian Modernist **Anton-Gustan Matoš** and then by interwar avant-garde writers **Anton Branko Šimić** and **Tin Ujević.** Croatian prose also sparkled in the 20th century, inspired in the 30s by the novels of **Miroslav Krleža,** and again in the 70s, as young prose writers dubbed the Borgesites wove fantastic themes into short stories and novels. Among the Borgesites was **Pavao Pavlilic,** a popular author of numerous mystery and crime novels set in Zagreb. Another Borgesite is the controversial **Dubravka Ugresić.** Her personal, reflective novels took on political overtones during the recent war, when she publicly opposed Croatian President Tudjman. Now she lives abroad, and her works, which discuss nostalgia and revision of history, are instant best-sellers in Croatia, much to the chagrin of the state media apparatus. Another novelist and contemporary feminist, **Slavenka Drakulić;** is more popular abroad than at home. Her works in English include *Balkan Express: Fragments from the Other Side of War* and *Cafe Europa*.

CROATIA TODAY

As Croatia copes with the problems of a burdened economy, the euphoria of independence has faded. Tensions between Serbs and Croats remain high in the former Serb-held areas of the Krajina and Western Slavonia, and return of refugees amounts to a trickle. Serb-held **Eastern Slavonia,** an area administered by NATO, is scheduled to be turned over to the Croatian government in January 1998, in fulfillment of a long-delayed stipulation of the Dayton Peace Agreement.

Croatian politics are dominated by the Croatian Democratic Party (HDZ), which won elections in April 1997. Franjo Tudjman remains the president; however, he is thought to be dying of cancer, despite Yeltsin-like attempts to conceal his condition.

International preassure is mounting on Croatia to institute reforms and loosen its state-controlled media; Croatia's aspirations to join the EU gives the international community some leverage. With the war-related problems and exorbitant taxes, the cost of living remains high. Prices in Croatia are close to those in Italy—still not as high as in northern Europe, but higher than in most of Central Europe.

Zagreb

After bearing much of the weight of the war, Zagreb is embracing its new role as a modern Central European capital. Developed as the third most important city in the powerful Austro-Hungarian empire, Zagreb remained a "younger sister" to the bigger and more popular Vienna and Budapest. But beware the charm of the 900-year-old little sister: this mid-sized city has a magic of its own, from the towering arches of St. Stephen's Cathedral to the Austro-Hungarian architecture of many of the downtown buildings. A lively street scene completes the atmosphere, with the Dolac market cheerfully overflowing with peasants hawking their vegetables and fish. Come nightfall, to see or be seen is the object of the fashionable young crowds which thrive on the lively cafes and beer halls. Home to many international festivals and world-renowned museums, Zagreb is also a city of culture, tradition and history.

ORIENTATION AND PRACTICAL INFORMATION

Zagreb is 30km from the Slovene border; Austria and Hungary are about 100km away. **Trains** arrive here from many European capitals, via Ljubljana or Budapest. To reach the main square, **Trg bana Josipa Jelačića,** from the train station, walk north along the parks, then along **Praška.** Uphill are the cathedral and cobblestone streets of the old **Gornji Grad** (Upper Town); nearby is the main shopping street, **Ilica.**

Tourist Office: Tourist Information Center (TIC), Trg J. Jelačića 11 (tel. 481 40 54; fax 481 40 56), in the southeast corner of the square. Helpful staff distributes tons of **maps** and pamphlets *gratis,* organizes trips, and sells souvenirs and books on Zagreb and Croatia. Study the huge map outside. Open Mon.-Fri. 8am-8pm, Sat.-Sun. 9am-6pm. Another TIC office offering similar services is located at Trg N.Š. Zrinjskog 14 (tel. 455 28 67; fax 455 28 69).

Embassies: Australia, Mihanovićeva 1 (tel./fax 457 74 33). Open Mon.-Fri. 10am-2pm. **Canada,** Mihanovićeva 1 (tel. 457 79 05; fax 457 79 13). **U.K.,** Vlaška 121 (tel. 455 55 00; fax 455 51 65). Open Mon.-Fri. 9am-12pm. **U.S.,** Hebrangova 2 (tel. 455 55 00, Citizen Services ext. 276; fax 455 25 01). Open Mon.-Fri. 8am-4:45pm. An **American Cultural Center,** Zrinjevac 13, is around the corner. Open Mon.-Wed. and Fri. 9am-4pm, Thurs. 9am-6:30pm.

Currency Exchange: Zagrebačka Banka has several branches throughout the city; the convenience outweighs the slight gains made by those who find a better *mjenjačnica* (private exchange office). Traveler's checks cashed (1.5% commission). Open Mon.-Fri. 7:30am-7pm, Sat. 7:30am-noon. At the railway station, Zagrebacke Banka-Mjenjačnica "Croatiaexpressa," Trg krakja Tomislava 12, is open 24hr. Several **Zagrebačka Banka** locations have Cirrus/MC/EC-linked **ATMs.**

American Express: Atlas, Zrinjevac 17, 41000 (tel. 42 76 23). Mail held and cards replaced. May start taking traveler's checks in '98. Open Mon.-Fri. 8am-7pm, Sat. 8am-noon.

Flights: Croatia Airlines, Teslina 5 (tel. 42 77 52; fax 42 79 35). Flies to most major airports around the globe. Also inquire here to book flights on other airlines. Buses

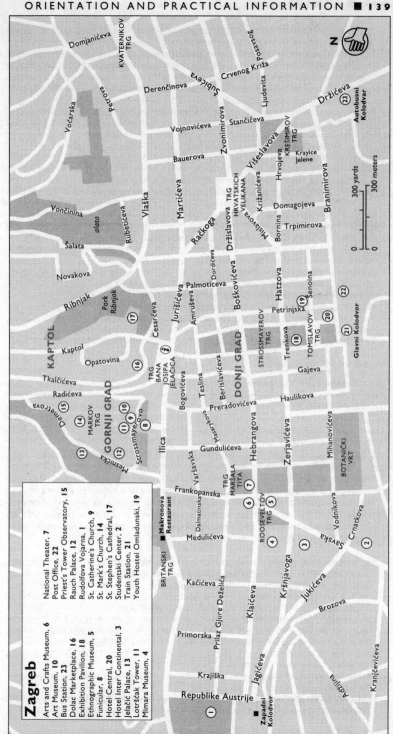

CROATIA

Zagreb

Arts and Crafts Museum, 6
Art Museum, 10
Bus Station, 23
Dolac Marketplace, 16
Exhibition Pavilion, 18
Ethnographic Museum, 5
Funicular, 8
Hotel Central, 20
Hotel Inter Continental, 3
Jelačić Palace, 13
Lotrščak Tower, 11
Mimara Museum, 4

National Theater, 7
Post Office, 22
Priest's Tower Observatory, 15
Rauch Palace, 12
Rudolfova Vojarna, 1
St. Catherine's Church, 9
St. Mark's Church, 14
St. Stephen's Cathedral, 17
Studentski Center, 2
Train Station, 21
Youth Hostel Omladunski, 19

depart from the bus station to the **airport** (tel. 456 21 82; buses Mon.-Sat. every 30min. 3am-8pm; Sun. schedule differs a bit).

Trains: Trains provide fast, efficient service to coastal Croatia as well as to countries to the north and west. All passenger trains arrive and depart from **Glavni Kolodvor** (main station), Trg kralja Tomislava 12 (tel. 27 23 42). To: Budapest (4 per day, 7hr., 165kn); Ljubljana (5 per day, 2½hr., 41kn); Venice (1 per day, 8hr., 152kn); and Vienna (2 per day, 6½hr., 262kn).

Buses: Croatia's bus system is better developed than its rails. The **bus station** (tel. 060 31 33 33) is just south of the railway tracks on Držićeva Cesta. Information and tickets are on the 2nd floor. Prices are often quoted in DM and converted on the spot. To: Frankfurt (7 per week, DM142); Ljubljana (6 per day, 3hr., 55kn); Sarajevo (2 per day, 9hr., DM60); and Vienna (8hr., 173kn).

Public Transportation: The city itself is ruled by trams. Buy tram tickets at any newsstand (3.70kn); punch 'em in the boxes near the tram doors.

Taxis: Rates are expensive but usually fair. Larger companies like **Radio Taxi** (tel. 68 25 05 or 68 25 58) are the most reliable. Average fare: 15kn plus 5kn per km.

Luggage Storage: At the train station. 9kn per piece per day.

Laundromat: No self-service laundromats exist yet; one of the most reliable **dry cleaners** in town is at the **Hotel Intercontinental,** Kršnjavoga 1 (tel. 455 34 11, ext. 17 49), around the back. Priced per item, 50% more for fewer than 3 items or for 24hr. service. Shirts 9kn. Open Mon.-Fri. 8am-4pm.

Photocopies: Photocopy offices abound; look for *fotokopiranje* signs. **Super Copia,** Petrinjska 32a (tel. 430 619). 0.30kn per page. Open daily 8am-6pm.

24-Hour Pharmacy: Centralna Ljekarna, Trg J. Jelačića 3 (tel. 27 63 05).

Medical Assistance: Đordićeva 26 (tel. 44 44 44 or 94).

Post Office: Branimirova 4 (tel. 271 593) and Jurišiceva 13 (tel. 4811-092), a block east of Trg J. Jelačića. Open Mon.-Sat. 7am-8pm. **Postal code:** 10000.

Telephones: Located outside the post office, or use the ones inside and pay afterward. Phone cards for public phones are available at all newsstands and post offices. **Phone code:** 01.

ACCOMMODATIONS

To stay in Zagreb, you'll have to open that wallet (or moneybelt) and pay, pay, pay. Hotel prices are on par with much of Eastern Europe, but with so few young vacationers, there has been little to no demand for true budget accommodations. For help with **private rooms,** contact **Staza,** Heinzelova 3 (tel. 21 30 82), near Kvaternikov trg. From the train station, take tram #4 to Dubrava (rooms about 150kn per person, plus a 30% fee for stays fewer than three nights; open Mon.-Fri. 9am-4pm). **Di-Prom,** Trnsko 25a (tel. 655 02 33), offers singles (170kn) or doubles (110kn), with the same multi-day deal (open Mon.-Fri. 9am-3:30pm). From the train take tram #2 or 3 to "Autobusni kolodvor." Change for tram #7 to "Velesapim"; get off one stop after Velesajam and walk toward the bridge across the Sava river. The TIC (see **Tourist Offices,** p. 138) doesn't make reservations, but may be willing to call hotels and private agencies to see where there is a room.

Student Hotel Cvjetno, Odranska 8 (tel. 611 84 44). Converted dorms. Hall bathroom and toilets. Doubles 296kn; no singles, but they might pair you up with someone else for half the price. From the train station, take tram #4; direction "Savski most"; get off at "Vjesnik." Continue walking in the same direction as the tram; Odranska is the first street on your left. Open July 15-Oct. 1.

Omladinski Turistički Centar (HI), Petrinjska 77 (tel. 42 64 61; fax 42 76 27). From the train station, facing King Tormislav's statue, walk right on Branimirova. Petrinjska will be on your left 1 block down the road. Clean but slightly worn-out rooms with tiny bathrooms. Singles 132kn, with shower 190kn; doubles 255kn, with shower 310kn; dorm beds 70kn.

Hotel Stjepan Radić, Jarunska 2 (tel. 33 42 55). From the train station, take tram #4, going to "Savski most"; change for #14, 17, or 5 at "Vjesnik" and get off at "Studentski dom." Relatively cheap student housing relatively far from the center. Hall bathrooms. Singles 70kn; doubles 130kn. Open July 15-Aug. 30.

Hotel Central, Branimirova 3 (tel. 42 57 77; fax 42 05 47). Rooms facing the train station are a bit noisy, but it's central. Tiny rooms (with shower and cable TV) are newly furnished and extra-clean. Singles 308-358kn. Doubles 446-566kn. Breakfast included. AmEx, Diners Club, Visa.

FOOD

The specialties of the Zagreb area are *purica z mlinci* (turkey with homemade dough) and *vinski gulaš* (pork and potato stew cooked in wine). Historians still argue about whether *Zagorski štrukli* (a dessert made from dough and cottage cheese) is what has made so many want to conquer Zagreb throughout history. Along with bars and cafes, **slastićarne** (pastry shops), famous for their exquisite ice cream, play an important part in the Zagreb experience. Across the street from the railway station, an escalator leads to a huge **underground mall,** replete with inexpensive cafes, bakeries, sandwich shops, and pizzerias. Behind Trg J. Jelačića is a daily **market** (open Mon.-Sat. 6am-2pm, Sun. 7am-noon). For a complete list of the best restaurants and pubs, pick up a free copy of *Zagreb-Gastro* at the tourist office.

Gostionica Tempo, Petriyska ulice 33a (tel. 43 16 66). Dark wood and deer horns adorn this huge cellar-restaurant specializing in meat prepared *à la* Croatia. Affordable daily *menüs* that include dishes like *grah s mesom* (beans with meat, 25kn) and *viuski gulaš* (wine stew, 22kn) will make every budget eater happy.

Makronova, Jlica 72/1 (tel. 42 63 52). One of the few vegetarian oases in Zagreb. Meatless à la carte options plus excellent daily *menüs* (40kn). Make a reservation. Open Mon.-Fri. noon-6pm, Sat. noon-2:30pm.

Mimice, Jurišićeva 15. An old budget seafood restaurant with a soul: nostalgic Zagreans come here for their daily fix of *sardeliće* (fried sardines; 9kn) or *skuše* (mackerel; 14kn). Open Mon.-Fri. 7am-10pm, Sat. 7am-6pm.

Bistro-Pizzeria "Delfino," Dežmanvo prolaz 2 (tel. 42 65 04). One of many excellent pizza places in the center of Zagreb. Pizzas 25-30kn. If you don't like your Italian food shaped round, there's *gnocchi*, lasagne, and spaghetti. Open 8am-11pm.

Centar, Jurišićeva 24. If you eat 2 ice creams every day, it will take you about 2 months to go through all of the flavors available at Centar. Not to mention cakes, or even shakes…you may as well stay in Zagreb for good. Pastries and baklava 6kn. Open daily 9am-11pm.

SIGHTS

Tours of Zagreb leave from the TIC office, Zrinjevac 14, every Wednesday at 10am (minibus 75kn, on foot 45kn). If you want to be your own guide, strolls through old Zagreb generally begin and end around the huge horse statue and beautiful facades of **Trg bana Josipa Jelačića.** Visible from many parts of the city, **Zagrebačka katedrala** (Zagreb cathedral), lies just around the corner. Neo-Gothic structures blend seamlessly with the remains of the 13th-century building. Tours (Mon.-Sat. 10am-5pm, Sun. and holy days 1-5pm) point out most of the interesting features of the structure, including an altar attributed to Dürer. This elegant building, however, is still much more a place of worship than a tourist attraction.

Today, the former clerical city of **Kapitol** and the craftsmen's province of **Gradec**—the twin seeds that grew into modern-day Zagreb—comprise the area called **Gornji Grad** (Upper Town). The medieval core remains the same, including such structures as the **Kamenita Vrata** (Stone Gate), on Radićeva, and **Crkva sv. Marka** (Church of St. Mark), with its Gothic entrance and the charming painted roof. Despite the other small churches on the hill, Zagreb's visitors tend to head straight for **Kula Lotrščak** (Lotrščak tower), Strossmayerovo šetalište 9, and its splendid **panorama** of the city (open Tues.-Fri. 10am-6pm, Sat.-Sun. 10am-1pm; 7kn). The romantic **Strossmayerovo šetalište** (Strossmayer's promenade) edges the west half of the hill. Follow it to its end to return to the heart of the city, or, from the east side of the promenade, take the stairs or the funicular. All routes from Gornji Grad end on **Ilica,** the main shopping district. South of here is **Donji Grad** (Lower City).

Zagreb takes pride in its many well-stocked museums which, newly redecorated, await visitors after a few years of wartime hiatus. A complete list of all the museums can be found in the free *Zagreb: Events and Performances,* published monthly and available at TIC (see **Practical Information,** p. 138). It also lists numerous galleries, as well as plays, festivals, concerts, and sporting events.

Muzej Mimara (Mimara Museum), Rooseveltiv trg 4 (tel. 44 80 55). Da Vincis, Michelangelos, and Monets, together with a collection of glass and Chinese art. Open Mon. 2-5pm, Tues.-Fri. 10am-5pm, Sat.-Sun. 10am-1pm. 20kn, students 15kn.

Muzej za umjetnost i obrt (Arts and Crafts Museum), Trg Maršala Tita 10 (tel. 455 41 22). Paintings, clocks and watches, furniture, glass and ceramics from Gothic to Art Deco. Judaic collection is one of the biggest and most renowned in the world. Frequent special exhibits. Open Tues.-Fri. 10am-6pm, Sat.-Sun. 10am-1pm. 20kn.

Etnografski muzej, Mažuranićev trg 14 (tel. 455 85 44). The most amazing section of this fine museum features traditional folk robes from all parts of Croatia. Open Tues.-Thurs. 9am-1pm and 5-7pm, Fri.-Sun. 9am-1pm. 10kn, students 5kn.

Strossmayerova galerija starih majstora HAZU (Strossmayer Gallery of Old Masters), Trg Nikole Šubića Zrinjskog 11 (tel. 43 34 44). Permanent collection of European paintings from the 14th to 19th centuries, exhibited in the Croatian Academy of Arts and Sciences building. Open Tues. 10am and 5-7pm, Wed.-Sun. 10am-1pm.

Galerija primitivne umjetnosti (Gallery of Naïve Art), Cirilometodska 3 (tel. 42 36 69). Permanent collection of naïve art, a Croatian art form consisting of rustic and peasant motifs. Open Tues.-Fri. 10am-6pm, Sat.-Sun. 10am-1pm.

Muzej grada Zagreba (City Museum), Opatička 20 (tel. 27 46 42). Unless you meet a history major at the University of Zagreb, this place is the best bet if you want to learn something about Zagreb's past. Open Tues.-Fri. 10am-6pm, Sat.-Sun. 10am-1pm. 10kn.

ENTERTAINMENT

Hrvatsko Navodno Kazalište (Croatian National Theater), Trg Maršala Tita 15 (tel. 447 644), is the place to be for those who prefer more refined entertainment. Ballet, opera, and drama are equally represented under the roof of one of the most beautiful Baroque buildings in the city. In mid-June, Zagreb hosts the annual **World Festival of Animated Film** in Vatroslav Lisinski Concert Hall on Trg S. Radića 4. Films range from the best of Disney to high-tech Japanese *anime.* Folklore fetishists flock to Zagreb toward the end of July for the **International Folklore Festival,** a premier gathering of European folk dancers and singing groups. July and August see open-air concerts and theatrical performances during the **Zagreb Summer Festival;** some of the best concerts take place in the Museum Gallery Atrium, Jezuitski trg 4 (tel. 27 89 57). **Zagreb Fest,** in November, balances the offerings with a festival of pop. **Eurokaz,** a yearly festival of progressive European theater, takes place at the end of June all around Zagreb. Puppet-lovers shouldn't miss the huge **International Puppet Festival,** at the beginning of September, which celebrated its 30th anniversary in 1997.

The numerous sidewalk **cafes** along **Tkalčiceva ulica,** in Gornji Grad, beckon a young, mixed crowd. Those who care to imbibe are in luck: bars are a civic institution, busy from morning till night. Many **discos** are empty during the week, but fill with revelers. For a complete listing of all discos and nightclubs in Zagreb, consult the free *Zagreb: Events and Performances* available at TIC.

Hard Rock Caffé, Gajeva 10. Reputedly a branch of the famous chain regardless of the second "f." Replete with records, memorabilia, and a pink Cadillac. T-shirts 219kn. Open daily 9am-midnight.

BP Club, Teslina 7 (42 55 20), in the same hallway as Hard Rock Caffé. The venue for jazz in Zagreb. Open daily 10am-2am. Cover varies.

Pivnica Medvedgrad, Savska cesta 56. Long wooden tables and dim lights attract crowds of both students and businessmen. Brews its own beer; try *Crna kraljica,* a dark beer masterpiece. Open daily 10am-midnight.

The Best, Horvačanski zavoj bb (tel 30 16 01). Chic youth, famous athletes, and movie stars come here for their weekly dose of techno and dance music. Open Fri.-Sat. 9:30pm-5am, Sun. 5-11pm. Cover varies; occasional concerts.

Big Ben, Bogovićeva 7 (tel. 42 57 06). A good disco near the center of town. Open Fri.-Sat. 10pm-4am.

Sokol Club, Trg Maršala Tita 6 (tel. 41 00 12). Live Latin music on Wed. nights. Open Wed.-Sun. 10pm-4am. Cover 30kn.

Gjuro II, Medveščak 58 (tel. 26 67 00). Currently the hippest hangout of Zagreb's college youth. Smooth enough to attract the med-school students, but also crazy enough to please the aspiring artists. Open Wed.-Sun. 9pm-2am. Cover 25kn.

■ Near Zagreb: Hrvatsko Zagorje

Nested on the hilltops surrounding Zagreb, the cool and mysterious **castles** of **Hrvatsko Zagorje** wait to be conquered—this time with Canons instead of cannons. The following three are the most popular; for a more comprehensive listing consult the free *Zagreb and Surroundings,* available at TIC. **Medvedgrad,** a royal fortress that has guarded Mount Medvednica since the 13th century, can be seen from almost any point in Zagreb. You'll hardly get a better view of the city than from this stone beauty, which has become the symbol of Croatia's struggle for independence. From Trg bana J. Jelačića, take tram #14 to Mihaljevac; change to #15 to Gračani. From Gračani, follow a well-marked path up the hill to Medvedgrad (approx. 1½hr.). **Veliki Tabor** (tel. (049) 34 30 52), yellow and bulky, is as awesome as castles get (open 10am-5pm; 20kn, students 10kn). Built in the 15th century, this Romantic/Gothic structure is home not only to several permanent art and archaeological collections, but also one **ghost.** Every year in June, a colorful fencing tournament takes place in the castle. **Grešna Gorica,** a nearby restaurant serving exclusively national special-ties, should not be missed (*štrukli* 12kn, *srnei gulaš*—deer goulash—22kn). From the Zagreb bus station, take a bus for Desinić (8 per day, 1¼hr., 27kn). **Trakošcan** (tel. 042 79 62 81) is probably the most beautiful castle in Croatia. Newly renovated and complete with original furniture, this romantic 14th-century pearl belongs to the realm of fairy tales (open daily 9am-6pm; 20kn, students 10kn). Guided tours in English are available; make a reservation. From the Zagreb bus station take a **bus** to Varardin (12 per day, 80min., 29kn), and then change to a local bus to Trakošćan.

ISTRIA

While it lacks the prominence of islands farther south, this peninsula's Roman cities, crystalline waters, and proximity to the landlocked north draw a huge tourist crowd.

▨ Poreč

Though a municipality since before Caesar's time, Poreč (PO-retch) has never been as lively as it is today. Along the polished stone pavement, the buildings glisten, the ice-cream vendors juggle their wares, and live bands play on every corner. Somewhere, the Roman gods must be smiling.

Orientation and Practical Information Buses link Poreč with the rest of Croatia, Slovenia, and Italy. Five minutes south of the town center, the **bus station,** Rade Končara 1 (tel. 321 53), sends buses to Zagreb (6 per day, 5hr., 74-105kn); Pula (11 per day, 45min., 22kn); Ljubljana (1 per day, 4½hr., 83kn); and Trieste (2 per day). **Store luggage** at the station (open Mon.-Sat. 6am-8pm; 5kn per piece). **Tur-istički Informatisni Centar,** Zagrebačka 11 (tel. 45 14 58; fax 45 16 65), provides free **maps,** pamphlets, and advice: while they can't organize accommodations, they'll tell you where to try (open in summer daily 8am-10pm; off-season 9am-4pm). To reach the main **trg Slobode** (Freedom Square), walk toward the water and head right on

Bože Milanovića. **Exchange currency** at **Zagrebačka Banka,** on Maršala Tita by the harbor (open Mon.-Sat. 8:30am-7pm). A Cirrus/EC/MC **ATM** and automatic bill changer wait outside. A **pharmacy** (*apoteka*) is at trg Slobode 12 (open Mon.-Sat. 7:30am-10pm, Sun. 8am-noon and 5-8pm). The **post office,** equipped with phone booths, sits in trg Slobode 14 (tel. 43 18 08; open Mon.-Sat. 7am-9pm, Sun. 9am-noon). **Postal code: 52440. Phone code: 052.**

Accommodations and Food Poreč has several accommodations options, most with a DM2 daily **tourist tax.** Although prices are quoted in Deutschmarks, they can be paid in the kuna or dollar equivalent. Off-season travelers should note that many institutions refuse visitors from November to March. For **private rooms,** try **Passage,** Zagrebačka 17 (tel. 43 17 81; fax 43 17 38), near the tourist office (singles DM12-27; doubles DM40-67; apartments DM40; open daily 8:30am-9:30pm). If these rooms are full, there are agencies on every corner—shopping around is worthwhile. Encouraged by the ever-increasing demand, owners often refuse to rent rooms to those staying less than three nights. Paying extra for a day or two that you won't be there may still be better than staying at a hotel (the cheapest, "Neptun" and "Poreč," are roughly DM40 per person per night). Large **Laternacamp** (tel. 44 34 88; fax 44 30 93), often dubbed "Little Europe," is far to the east, with good facilities (sites DM13 per night, DM6 per person; open April-Oct.). Nudist camp and apartment-village **Solaris** (tel. 44 34 00), next to Laterna, is a paradise for those who think Adam and Eve should never have bothered with fig leaves. Ten **buses** per day go from Poreč bus station to Laterna.

For fine Italian food on a quiet side street, try **Barilla,** Eufraziana 26 (tel. 45 27 42). Pasta specialties and plentiful vegetarian selections (25-40kn) make up for less-than-generous portions (open daily noon-1am). **Grill Sarajevo,** M. Vlačića, off Dekumana, offers Bosnian and Croatian specialties like *pljekavica* (30kn) and Sarajevo-style steak (40kn). Soup and beer both cost 10kn (open daily 11am-10pm). Self-service restaurant **Peškera,** N. Tesla off Dekumana, is an obligatory hangout for budget travelers. A decent lunch, including salad and soup, costs about 30kn (open daily 9am-10pm).

Sights Stari Grad's main street is the historic **Dekumana,** lined with shops, cafes, and restaurants. From trg Slobode, walk past—or even climb up—the 15th-century Gothic **Peterokutna kula** (Pentagon Tower), a relic of Poreč's Venetian days. The awe-inspiring remains of the Roman **Veliki hram i Neptunov hram** (Great Temple and Temple of Neptune), from the first century, await at the end of Dekumana. At Narodni trg, south of Dekumana, rises **Okruglakula** (Round Tower), another creatively named 15th-century edifice. From its terrace, one can view Poreč and the big, bad, blue Adriatic. The **Eufrazijeva bazilika** (Euphrasius Basilica), one block north of Dekumana, is the city's most important monument. Composed of 6th-century foundations, late Gothic choir stalls, and a Renaissance belltower, the basilica contains a millennium and a half of art history—don't worry, there's no quiz at the end. The Jerry-Garcia-art-appreciation award goes to the phantasmagorical Byzantine mosaics adorning the interior. The Byzantine version of perspective reveals a refreshing, simple, highly symbolic style—or maybe just the need for some better glasses.

Most stores close down at midday in observance of the ancient Croatian tradition of the fun-in-the-sun summer afternoon. The best **beaches** are south of the Marina, around **Zelena Laguna** (Green Lagoon) and **Plava Laguna** (Blue Lagoon). While you won't spot Brooke Shields or Christopher Atkins re-living their 80s movie, there are even more scantily clad bods at the beaches marked "Naturists." To escape the crowds, find the rocky areas where the tide has cut small coves into the base of a hill, each with room for two or three people—depending on how those people use the space. A **ferry** leaves beside the Hotel Rivera for the less exciting, but quieter, beaches of the island of **Sveti Nikola** (Saint Nicholas; round-trip 10kn). Any area of the coast that has a name also has a hotel complex and **disco** (generally open nightly 10pm-4am). If a walk down the beach sounds too strenuous, join the crowd at **Capitol,** Vladimira Nazora 9, smack in Stari Grad (cover 10kn; dress casual). **Club No. 1,**

Marafor 9, has a higher bar-to-dance floor ratio (open nightly 9pm-4am). If you're no John Travolta, stores and boutiques abound in Stari Grad; most are open as late as midnight. **Pubs** are crowded and open late. At the popular bar **Casablanca,** Eufrez-ijeva 4, Sam plays it again until 2am. **Bar Ulixes,** Dekumana 2, hides from tourists in a narrow alley off of Dekumana, with a cool cellar and outdoor garden making it a rock-ing all-weather choice.

▒ Rovinj

Located in one of the most prosperous tourist areas in Croatia, Rovinj (ro-VEEN) is a charmingly eclectic city. The serenity of the sun-washed buildings and narrow stone streets of the medieval quarter is balanced by the joyful clutter of yachts in the mod-ern marina across the bay. The Italian connection is clearly felt here, and the entire town seems bilingual, with "Rovingo" in evidence as often as "Rovinj." *Capice?*

Orientation and Practical Information With no train station, Rovinj depends on **buses** (tel. 81 14 53) to get to Poreč (6 per day, 1hr., 16kn) and Pula (21 per day, 1hr., 15kn). There are no platforms, so watch carefully. To reach Stari Grad, proceed up the busy pedestrian street. **Taxi** drivers wait in front of the bus station, or call 81 11 00. **KEI Istra** (tel. 81 11 55; fax 81 50 46), on Nello Quarantotto across from the bus station toward the sea, will serve you a tall, cool glass of that favorite summer cocktail: "info 'n' pamphlets" (open daily 9am-8pm). **Exchange currency** at **Istarska Banka,** by the water north of KEI Istra, which has decent rates but sometimes inept service (open Mon.-Fri. 7:30am-8pm, Sat. 7:30am-noon). Use the **post office** (tel. 81 14 66) next to the bus station on M. Benussi-Cio, or the numerous **telephones** outside (open Mon.-Sat. 7am-9pm, Sun. 8am-noon). **Postal code:** 52210. **Phone code:** 052.

Accommodations and Food With its well-developed tourist industry, Rovinj has much to offer in terms of accommodations. A DM2 tourist tax and 30% surcharge for one- to three-day stays is standard; peak season high prices last from mid-July to mid-August. KEI Istra (see above) arranges private rooms (DM14-22 per person, dou-ble apartments from DM53). The other 17 tourist agencies in Rovinj use the same price list, so whichever you choose, you won't lose. Rovinj is one of the oldest Euro-pean resorts for nudists. The, er, well-equipped Naturist Holiday Village **Monsena** (tel. 81 30 44; fax 81 33 54), just 3km outside of Rovinj, has apartments, athletic facil-ities, and more (singles 56kn; doubles 57kn per person; half-board). If you prefer camping with your clothes on, visit **Camping Polari** (tel. 81 34 41; fax 81 13 95), east of town with cold water, a supermarket, and nearby bars (DM9.5 per campsite, DM5 per person; off-season 10% less; closed Nov.-March). Take the hourly bus to Polari.

Seafood is a frequent culinary theme—the Adriatic's calamari (squid) is highly esteemed, but pasta comes cheaper. For a **grocery store,** look next to the bus station (open Mon.-Sat. 6am-9pm, Sun. 7am-11am). **Gostionica Cisterna,** in the heart of the medieval quarter on trg Matteotti, has many main dish options (calamari 35kn, schnit-zel 30kn, salads 10kn; open daily 9am-11pm). At one of Rovinj's most celebrated fish restaurants, **Amfora Riblji Restaurant,** Rismondo 23 (tel. 81 55 25), the cheapest *menü* includes spaghetti, soup, and crepes (75kn; open daily 11am-midnight).

Sights and Entertainment Half the fun of Rovinj lies in exploring the **medi-eval quarter,** inland on the jutting peninsula. Most of the narrow alleys and hilly cob-blestone streets eventually lead to **Crkva sv. Eufemije** (St. Euphemia's Church), with a Baroque Venetian tower that dominates the town (open 10am-noon and 5-7:30pm). The church's sheer size and its Italian exterior are impressive, though most come to see the 6th-century Byzantine sarcophagus, containing the remains of St. Euphemia, the 3rd-century patron of Rovinj. At age 15, Euphemia refused to deny her Christian faith and was put to the lions, who killed her, but chose not to eat her. One misty morning 500 years later, according to legend, the sarcophagus containing her remains floated into the harbor of Rovinj; it now lies behind the right-hand altar. You can also climb the **bell tower,** 50 years older than the rest of the church, for a quick cure for Stairmaster withdrawal (5kn). The **Museum of National Heritage,** trg Maršala Tita 11, contains the work of local masters from 1100BC to the present (open Tues.-Sat. 9am-noon and 7-10pm, Sun. 7-10pm; 5kn). Every second Sunday in August, the traditional open-air art festival **Grisia** takes place in the street of the same name. Those who prefer works signed by Mother Nature should hop aboard one of the boats anchored in the harbor for a trip around the 22 islands in the area (90kn).

For the nicest **beaches** in the area, walk past the marina following the path along the shore and weigh anchor wherever you feel like it. Or, right after the marina, cut through the park **Zlatni rt** (Golden Cape) to reach a staircase-shaped, natural beach highly recommended by natives (30min. walk, well worth it). You can also take a ferry from the main quay to **Katarina** (10kn) or **Crveni otok** (Red Island, 15kn).

At night, Rovinj is not nearly as boisterous as nearby Poreč or Pula. Check for shows at **Gandusio Theater,** Valdibora 17 (tel. 81 15 88), or visit a **cafe** after dark. There seem to be enough tourists to keep **Discoteca Monte Mulini,** in the eponymous hotel, hopping (open nightly 10pm-5am).

■ Pula

At Istria's south tip, 3000-year-old Pula was founded by sailors who had failed in their quest to defeat the Argonauts and retrieve the Golden Fleece. Legend claims that since the unlucky seafarers couldn't bear the shame of returning home empty-handed, they built Pula instead. However fantastic the myth, Pula is home to a fascinating array of Roman ruins. Handsome tree-lined avenues from the Habsburg days and narrow winding streets in the medieval quarter combine with Pula's ancient heritage and modern energy to make an eminently worthwhile destination.

Orientation and Practical Information From the **train station** (tel. 54 17 33), exit and turn right, on **Vladimira Gortana;** continue until it turns into **Istarska,** near the amphitheater. When it becomes **Giardini,** the circular **Stari Grad** will be on your right. The **bus station** is downtown between Istarska and Balote Mate. **Luggage storage** here is cheaper and more accessible than at the train station (open daily 5-11pm; 5kn). **Buses** run to Zagreb (12 per day, 5-6hr., 74-103kn) and Rijeka (20 per day, 2½hr., 41kn). **Trains** to Zagreb (4 per day, 7hr., 78kn) and Rijeka (4 per day, 2½hr., 39kn) are slow and expensive. Brave the sometimes cantakerous train or bus officials, to confirm the posted times, which aren't always correct. For a **taxi,** call 232 28, or try the stand at Giardini and Balote Mate. The helpful staff at the **Tourist Information Center,** Istarska 13 (tel. 335 57; fax 418 55), provides free **maps** and cultural programs (open July-Aug. daily 8am-1pm and 2-8pm, Sept.-June Mon.-Fri. 8am-1pm). **Istarska Banka,** Istarska 12, and throughout the city, **exchanges cash** and has an outdoor Cirrus **ATM** (open Mon.-Fri. 7:30am-7:30pm). A **pharmacy, Ljekama Centar,** sits at Giardini 15 (tel. 225 44; open Mon.-Fri. 7:30am-8pm, Sat. 7:30am-2pm). Find the **post office** and **telephones** at Istarska 5 (open Mon.-Fri. 7am-8pm, Sat. 7am-4pm). **Postal code:** 52100. **Phone code:** 052.

Accommodations and Food A plethora of travel agencies, many on Giardini, helps tourists find overpriced hotels, somewhat expensive apartments, and reasonably priced private rooms. **Arenaturist,** Giardini 4 (tel. 343 55; fax 21 22 77), may seem a bit brusque, but their rooms are in the toniest locations (singles 81kn for the first night, 2-3 nights 70kn per night, 4 nights or more 56kn per night; daily tourist tax 7kn; registration fee 6kn; doubles 50% more). South of Pula, youth hostel **Ferijalni Savez Valsaline (HI),** Zaljev Valsaline 4 (tel. 345 95), with decent rooms and its own beach area, often fills to capacity, so call ahead. Take bus #2 or 4 towards Verudela, then exit at Vila Idola (75kn per night with HI card; breakfast included). **Stoja Camping** (tel. 241 44), lies on the tip of Pula's western peninsula. From Giardini, take bus #1 towards Stoja to the end (DM6 per person, DM3 per tent or car, plus DM2 daily tourist tax and DM1.20 registration fee).

Well-stocked **grocery stores** abound in Pula (generally open Mon.-Sat. 6am-8pm and Sun. 8am-noon). **Pizzeria Orfej,** Gorana Kovačića 8, in the medieval quarter, offers small pizzas (20-25kn; open Mon.-Sat. 7am-11pm). **Restaurant Delfin,** trg sv. Tome 1 (tel. 222 89), off Gorana Kovačića, across from the 4th-century cathedral (visible from the terrace), provides cheap but excellent seafood in a pleasant setting (seafood risotto 23kn, calamari 32kn; open daily 11am-10:30pm). **Bistro Barbara,** Kandlerova 5, a block from Orfej, has grill and seafood treats on the obligatory terrace or in rustic interior setting (calamari 30kn, grilled sardines 15kn).

Sights and Entertainment Visitors to Pula are understandably enchanted with the Roman ruins. The number-one must-see sight is the **amfiteatar,** a wonder of ancient Roman architecture built in the first century, now used again for concerts (open for visits daily 8am-9pm; 14kn, students 7kn). From the bus station, walk south along Istarska, then Giardini—a tree-lined boulevard recalling the era of Habsburg influence. At the southern tip stands the 29BC **Slavoluk obitelji Sergi** (Arch of the Sergians). Through the gates, stroll along narrow, shop-crammed **I Maja ul.,** a little street that comes alive in the evening. **Forum,** at the end of 1 Maja ul., holds the columned Augustov hram (Temple of Augustus). As well-preserved as Elizabeth Taylor, it was originally constructed 2BC-14AD. Smile back at the worn faces on the Roman statuary inside (open daily 9am-9pm; 4kn). Pass through the **Dvojna vrata** (Twin Gate), just north of the bus station, and climb the hill to the **Arheološki Muzej Istre** (Archaeological Museum of Istria), Mate Balote 3 (tel. 334 88). The museum offers an overview of Pula's history from prehistoric to medieval times, with an emphasis on Roman stone artifacts—following the old Latin truism, "Rocks rock" (open May-Sept. Mon.-Sat. 9am-8pm, Sun. 9am-3pm; Oct.-April Mon.-Fri. 9am-2pm). Looking from Stari Grad to the shipyards, you wouldn't guess that Pula had **beaches** at all. Purchase a bus ticket from the kiosk Giardini (8kn; punch on one side going one way and on the other going back) to hop a bus to where the real sand castles stand. All the southbound buses pass a beach or two; just follow the crowds holding towels and buckets.

Pula is a city of **cafes,** though during the evenings most also serve as pubs. Several first-rate ones inhabit Forum, at the end of 1 Maja ul.; if they appear dormant during the day, return after 8pm. **Bistro Sirena** and **Cafe Carius** are always buzzing with espresso-energized conversation (open daily until midnight). Of those in Narodni trg, **Caffé Milan** is smack in the middle. Enjoy an espresso (3kn) or a pint of *pivo* (beer; 10kn; open daily until 11pm). Spend nights in one of Pula's nine discotheques. The natives particularly praise the pyramid-shaped **Piramida** and techno/rave heaven **Fort Bourguignon,** both on Zlatne Stijene (cover 15kn; take bus #3 to Zlatne Stijene).

▓ Rab

Guarding a harbor on the south coast of the eponymous island, the fortified medieval town of Rab masterfully blends its 2000-year history into modern tourism-oriented schemes. Its white stone streets have watched fashions change from simple Roman togas to intricate Byzantine dresses, and from monks' robes to Speedos. The British King Edward VIII challenged the idea of fashion altogether by staying at one of Rab's nudist resorts more than 60 years ago. A stroll along the city's **Gornja ul** (Upper St.) takes you from the remains of **Crkva sv. Jvana** (St. John's Church), an outstanding Roman *bazilika,* to **Crkva sv. Justine** (St. Justine's Church), which houses a museum dedicated to Christian art (open Mon.-Sat. 9-11am and 7:30-9:30pm; 5kn). Climbing the church's belltower at sunset is as addictive as Dalmatian wine (tower open Mon.-Sat. 7:30-10pm; 5kn). The 12th-century **Katedrala Djevice Marije** (Virgin Mary Cathedral) and nearby 14th-century **Samostan sv. Antuna** (St. Anthony Monastery), farther down Gornja ul, complete the tour of this history-laden quarter.

There are sand **beaches** on the island, but to get to places with names like "Sahara," you'll have to board a bus to Lopar, on the island's northwest corner (every 2hr.; 14kn). However, Rab's real assets are its tiny, craggy beaches, perfectly isolated from tourist hordes. These can best be reached by **taxi-boats** waiting in the harbor.

CROATIA

Turistička Zejednica-Informationi Centar, at Mali Palit, right next to the bus station, has info and pamphlets, but does not arrange accommodations (tel. 77 11 11; open 8am-10pm). The **bus station** stands next to the tourist office (open Mon.-Sat. 5:30am-7:30pm, Sun. 11am-6pm). Buses run to Zagreb (2 per day, 6hr., 99kn) and Rijeka (2 per day, 3hr., 74kn). The friendly, English-speaking staff can also help you with ferry schedules (ferry departs Mon. 4:15am for Rijeka; Fri. 9:25pm for Split/ Dubrovnik). **Hitchhikers** report success getting off a Split-bound bus at Jablanac, catching a ride to the ferry (9kn per person), and staying on until Rab. To **exchange currency,** stop by **Riječka Banka,** trg Municipium Arba (tel. 72 40 99; open Mon.-Sat. 8am-noon and 5-9pm). **Numero Uno,** J. de Marisa 22 (tel./fax 72 46 88), facing the harbor as you enter Stari Grad, offers singles or doubles (50-80kn per person; open daily 8am-10pm). **Camping III Padova** (tel. 72 43 55; fax 72 45 39), 1km east of the bus station, is close to town without being co-dependent (14kn per tent, 18kn per person). The **supermarket** is at the beginning of the peninsula (open daily 7am-10pm). Try the Hunter's cutlet (35kn) at **Gostiona Labirint,** one block from Stjepana Radića (open daily 11am-2pm and 6-11pm). **Buffet Harpun,** Donja ul. 15, will hook you with affordable prices and a homey atmosphere. It serves Adriatic calamari (30kn) and spaghetti (25kn; open Mon.-Sat. 10am-2am). **Phone code:** 052.

DALMATIAN COAST

Crystal-blue waters once lured Romans and Venetian traders to this region, and today they bring flocks of tourists to bask on the beach and gaze at the awesome Roman structures. The term "Dalmatian Coast" generally designates the south-central stretch of the Adriatic coastline, and is Croatia's main tourist draw. Contrary to popular belief, the Dalmatian Coast cities of Split and Dubrovnik were hardly damaged during the war; the old stone walls of Dubrovnik's fortress sustained such slight damage from shelling in 1991 that you would almost never know a war had touched the city.

■ Split

There are very few places in the world where the love of people for their hometown is more clearly felt than in Split; the residents of Dalmatia's largest city are energetic, stylish, and happy to enjoy the long-awaited peace near the blue Adriatic waters. With the Stari Grad (Old Town) literally founded on the Roman Emperor Diocletian's early 4th-century palace, Split is an architectural jewel wedged between the high mountain range and a palm-lined waterfront.

ORIENTATION AND PRACTICAL INFORMATION

The **train** and **bus stations** lie across from the ferry terminal on **Obala kneza Domagoja.** Leaving the stations, follow Obala kneza Domagoja to the waterside mouthful **Obala hrvatskog narodnog preporoda,** which runs roughly east to west. To the north lies **Stari Grad,** inside the walls of **Dioklecijanova palača** (Diocletian's Palace).

Tourist Office: Obala hrvatskog narodnog preporoda 12 (tel./fax 34 21 42). English-speaking staff knows it all. **Maps,** pamphlets, and currency exchange. Open Mon.-Fri. 7:30am-8pm, Sat. 8am-1pm.

Budget Travel: Croatia Express, Obala kneza Domagoja 9 (tel. 34 26 45; fax 36 24 08). Youth discounts for international bus, train, and plane fares. Also sells B.I.J. Wasteels tickets. Open daily 7am-9pm.

Currency Exchange: Splitska Banka, Obala hrvatskog narodnog preporoda 10. Good rates and takes Visa and traveler's checks (2% commission). Open Mon.-Fri. 7am-1pm and 2-8pm, Sat. 8-11:30am. Next door, a Cirrus/MC **ATM** sits in front of the **Zagrebačka Banka,** which also exchanges money and traveler's checks (1.5% commission).

American Express: Atlas Travel Agency, Trg Preporoda 7, 58000 (tel. 430 55). Open May-Sept. Mon.-Sat. 8am-8pm, Sun. 9am-noon; Oct.-April Mon.-Fri. 8am-2pm and 3pm -7pm.

Trains: (tel. 35 53 88). Trains running north out of Split offer fewer choices but cheaper prices than buses. To Zagreb (3 per day, 9hr., 106kn).

Buses: Domestic and international (*medunarodni promet*) tickets are sold at the outside ticket counters (tel. 34 50 47). To: Zagreb (30 per day, 6½-9hr., 60-99kn); Dubrovnik (6 per day, 4½hr., 70kn); and Sarajevo (3 per day, 8-9hr., 130kn).

Ferries: (tel. 35 55 57). **Jadrolinija,** south of the stations, sells tickets to Italy and domestic cities. To Dubrovnik (3 per week, 8-12hr., 67kn) and Ancona, Italy (daily, 9hr., one-way 228kn).

Public Transportation: Tickets for **buses** are good for 2 trips; buy them from the driver (8kn) and punch them on board. Most buses run every 30min.

Taxis: Call 477 77. Average fare 14kn, plus 7kn per km.

Luggage Storage: At the **bus station** (7kn per day). Open daily 6am-9pm. Or at the **train station**—follow *garderoba* signs (8kn per day). Open daily 5:30am-10pm.

Pharmacy: The private pharmacies take turns staying open 24hr. Try **Ljekarna,** Istarska 2, north of the market. Open Mon.-Fri. 7am-8pm, Sat. 7am-1pm.

Police: Trg hrvatske bratske zajednice 9 (tel. 30 72 81).

Hospital: Clinical Hospital Center (tel. 51 50 55), Spinčićeval at Firule, southeast of Stari Grad.

Post Office: ul. Kralja Tomislava 9, north of Stari Grad. Go straight in the main doors to send mail, through the left-hand doors for **telephones, fax,** and **telegrams,** and through the doors on the right for *Poste Restante*. Open Mon.-Fri. 7am-9pm, Sat. 7am-2pm. **Postal code:** 21000. **Phone code:** 021.

ACCOMMODATIONS AND FOOD

The tourist office (see above) finds **private rooms** (singles 50-89kn; doubles 70-140kn; tourist tax 7kn per night). Old ladies at the bus station offer rooms that are held to a somewhat lower standard, but may have cheaper and more negotiable prices. **Prenoćište Slavija,** Buvinova 2 (tel. 470 53), in Stari Grad east of Trg braće Radića, has seen better days, but is sparkling clean (singles 160kn, with bath 200kn; doubles 200kn, with bath 240kn; breakfast included; tourist tax 7kn). There are several medium-sized **camps** in and around Split: inquire at the tourist office.

Emperor Diocletian: Hey, subject! My men and I have just survived a horrible storm. We are wet and hungry, so tell us quickly what your village has to offer! Fisherman Duje: My master, if you like fish and good wine, welcome. Heavenly **Dionis,** at Marmontova 3 (on the west border of Stari grad) will take care of your crew with large, hearty *menüs* (25kn). There's an excellent rustic atmosphere, and live music at night (open daily 7am-11pm). **Restaurant Sarajevo,** Domaldova 6 (tel. 474 54), is the oldest restaurant in Stari Grad for a few reasons; class, candlelight, and delicious grills. The royal fish-*menü,* including soup and dessert, is well worth the money (80kn; open daily 10am-midnight). **Hotel Central,** Narodni trg 1, provides worthy dining at any hour, but before 11:30am the brunch prices are an absolute steal; try *bakalar* (codfish stew; 15kn; open daily 9am-midnight). Finally, **Delta,** Trumbićeva Obala 12, offers sandwiches with piles of toppings, pizza, and alluring pastry (sandwiches 10kn; open daily 7am-1am). If you want to wash out the seawater from your mouth, just ask for a *bevanda,* red wine mixed with water. Emperor Diocletian: Cool! I think I'll build a palace here.

SIGHTS

Split's **Stari Grad** (Old Town), the eastern half of which inhabits the one-time fortress and summer residence of the late-3rd century Roman Emperor Diocletian, is a living, thriving museum of classical and medieval architecture. The best entrance is easily overlooked—it sits just past the line of taxis on the south side of the city. This small **portal** (open daily 9am-10pm) leads into the **cellars** of the city. At the entrance, turn either direction to wander around this labyrinth. The dark stone passages originally created a flat floor for the emperor's apartments; the 1700 years of trash stored here

CROATIA

has metamorphosed into an archaeologist's paradise. Some of these archaeological finds are displayed in hallways to the left of the entrance, which also hold a complex of dripping domes. The airier right side is used as a space for **modern art** displays (tickets to either side 6kn, students 3kn).

Straight through the cellars and up the stairs is the open-air **peristyle,** a colonnaded square used for outdoor operas and ballets. Up a few stairs and behind you is the open-domed **vestibule,** which becomes the backstage during the **Summer Festival.** Explore it freely during the day. The **cathedral** on the west end of the peristyle, is one of architecture's great ironies—it was originally the mausoleum of Diocletian, an emperor known to history primarily for his violent persecution of Christians. This ancient genealogy makes it the world's oldest Catholic cathedral. Its small, circular interior with intricately wrought stonework leaves almost no room for the faithful or the tourists who come to gawk at the magnificent inner door and altar. The adjoining **Zvonik Sv. Duje** (belltower of St. Domnius), begun in the 13th century, took 300 years to complete. Conquering this 60m beast will make an instant honorary *Splića-nin* out of you (cathedral and tower open daily 7am-noon and 4-7pm; entrance to tower 5kn). Walk north from the peristyle along ul. Dioklecijana, then right on ul. Papalićeva to the **Muzej grada Splita** (City Museum), Papalićeva 1 (tel. 34 12 40). The collection inspires less than the rich medieval palace housing it (open Tues.-Wed. and Fri.-Sun. 9am-1pm, Thurs. 9am-5pm; 10kn, students 5kn).

Several gates exit from Stari Grad, so choose your own adventure. Exiting by the east **Srebrua Vrata** (Silver Gate) leads to the main **market.** Outside the north **Zlatna Vrata** (Golden Gate) thunders a huge statue of **Grgur Ninski** (Gregorius of Nin), the 10th-century Slavic champion of commoners' rights. In Ivan Meštrović's rendering, he looks like a grandiose wizard. Alternatively, exit the palace's walls through the western **Željezna Vrata** (Iron Gate). You'll still be in Stari Grad on Narodni trg. The 15th-century Venetian former **town hall** sits on the north side. It houses the **Etnograf-ski muzej** (Ethnographic Museum; under renovation in summer 1997). Though this side of town lacks the otherwise omnipresent excavations, medieval architecture still dominates. Browsing through the many boutiques, it's hard not to run into a centuries-old church or an equally old residential section.

Headless statues meander in a beautiful garden north of Stari Grad—visitors are welcome to join them. Or dig up the **Arheološki muzej** (Archaeological Museum), Zrinsko Frankopanska ul. 25 (tel. 34 45 74; open Tues.-Sun. 9am-1pm; 10kn). The nearby **Umjetnička galerija** (Gallery of Fine Arts), Lovretska ul. 11 (tel. 34 12 50), was closed in 1997 for renovation and relocation. The gallery will open in 1998 in its new home at Kralja Tomislava 15. Similarly, the **Meštrović Gallery,** Šetaliste Ivana Meštroćia 46 (tel. 358 71 90), is scheduled to open in 1998 after renovation.

The rocky cliffs, green hills, and sandy beaches on the west end of the peninsula now make up **City Park Marjan,** and serve as reminders of why Diocletian once vacationed here. Romantics, or those who just love the smell of evergreens and prefer to simply *see* the sea, will appreciate this area. Paths are indicated on the tourist map; you can find your own, but watch for signs indicating that a trail leads to private lands—the dogs do bite.

ENTERTAINMENT

Beaches flank Split, but since the nearby water is dirty, the best ones require a bus ride (#60) outside the city. At night, Stari Grad transforms into a teeming, vibrant mass of people spilling in and out of the local bars. In fact, Split's nightlife far surpasses that of its posher island rivals. From mid-July to mid-August, Split hosts its annual **Summer Festival.** Every night, the city's best *artistes* join international guests in presenting ballets, operas, plays, and classical concerts among the town's churches and ruins. At other times of the year, visit the **Hrvatsko Narodno Kazalište** (Croatian National Theater), Trg Gaje Bulata 1 (tel. 58 59 99), to see and hear the same indoors (box office open daily 9am-noon and 6:30-8:30pm). Pick through the monthly Croatian *Splitska Scena,* free at the tourist office, for more listings.

Discoteque Night Cafe, Osječka 66, at the Koteks center. From Kralja Zvonimiva, turn left on Slobode and follow it to the mall-like Koteks center. Don't let the name fool you: on weekends the guests in this high-tech, techno, and dance disco are counted in thousands. No cover. Open 9pm-3am.

Obojena sujetlost (The Colored Light), at Uvala Zvončac. Walk along Šetalište Ivana Meštroviča to Meštrovič Gallery, then go down to the beach. This beach pub hosts popular and less popular Croatian and international rock 'n' roll, blues, or "we-play-it-all" bands on its beachfront, open-air stage. Something goes on every night: have a beer and let the colored lights shine on you. No cover. Open 7am-4am.

Jazz planet, Grgura Ninskoga 3. Hidden on a tiny back street in Stari Grad, the stone interior is so mellow it draws more people than the sunny outdoor tables. Occasionally live music. Open daily 7am-midnight.

"Song," Mihovila Širina 1. If you don't want your new Armani suit to go unnoticed, have a beer at this chic Stari Grad bar. Drinks cost the same as in other bars in Split, but here you'll mingle with the especially beautiful and elegant. Open 8am-1am.

■ Near Split: Hvar

After having visited 250 islands around the globe, an American journalist included Hvar among the ten most beautiful islands in the world. Hvar is more of a phantasmagorical palette than an island—the fields of lavender challenge the blue of the sea, the yellow facades dance with the ivory white cobblestone. The Venetian-style town, gleaming enticingly against the water, is as enchanting as the entire island. The **main square** sits northeast of the docks. Various museum-going thirsts can be quenched at the central **Gallery Arsenal** (open daily 8am-noon) or at the **Last Supper Collection** of art in the **Franciscan monastery,** with the famous oil *Last Supper* by Matteo Ignoli (open daily 9am-noon and 6-7pm). The monastery also hosts the outdoor performances of the **Hvar Summer Festival.** Indoor performances take place in Europe's **oldest municipal theater,** above the Arsenal, dating from 1612. The towers at the Franciscan and the **Domincan monastery** farther north are off limits, but you can climb the **cathedral tower** (open daily 9am-noon and 5-7pm; 10kn).

A more enjoyable way to see the city from above is to climb the path to the 1551 **Venetian fortress.** To reward your efforts, it houses a **museum of underwater archaeology** (open daily 9am-3pm; 10kn). On the lower, western hill stands a pseudo-fortress whose outdoor patio plays soft dance hits in the early evening, disguising the fact that after midnight it morphs into a **disco** so loud and fast that it draws hordes of youth off the mainland (open nightly 10pm-5am; free). Some of the Adriatic's clearest and bluest water surrounds Hvar, but the gravel **beaches** don't measure up. Abandon them for the island's stone outcroppings; or, better yet, head to the small nearby **Pakleni otoci** (Hellish islands): Jevolim, Stipanska, and Parmižana. Boats in the harbor run a taxi service between them (round-trip 10kn).

The only easy way to get to Hvar is the **Jadrolinija Ferry** from Split (3 per day, 2hr., 23kn). Another option is to board the Jadvolinja Ferry that visits the island four days per week on its trip from Split to Dubrovnik and back (Tues., Wed., Fri., and Sun., 2hr., 50kn). Three daily **buses** run from the station east of Hvar's main square to Stari Grad (10kn), where you can catch a local ferry back to Split. Walking north from the ferry landing will bring you to the **tourist office Pelegrin** (tel. 74 22 50; open Mon.-Sat. 9am-noon and 6-9pm, Sun. 6-8pm), which rents **rooms** (singles 70kn; doubles 120kn). The nearby **Mengola** (tel. 74 20 99) offers more expensive rooms with private bathrooms (singles 88kn; doubles 132kn). Either *might* help you bypass the 30% per night additional fee for shorter stays, but it's probably easier to follow the women at the ferry terminal offering rooms for comparable prices. **Hotel Bodul** (tel. 74 17 44) isn't exactly a steal, but it's the cheapest hotel in town (singles 171kn; doubles 272kn). Hvar's seafood restaurants, though among Dalmatia's best, are pricey. Try **Jerolim,** on the west side of the harbor, which serves up spaghetti (20kn) and squid (35kn; open daily 10am-11pm). The well-stocked **Razvitka market** is on the north side of the main square (open Mon.-Sat. 6am-9:30pm, Sun. 7am-noon). Everything else you'll need is on the waterfront. North of the ferry, **Splitska Banka** gives Visa

CROATIA

cash advances and **exchanges money** (open Mon.-Fri. 7am-1pm and 2-8pm, Sat. 8:30-noon). Farther on, the **Atlas** office will give you kunas on your **AmEx** card and cash traveler's checks (open Mon.-Sat. 8:30am-12:30pm and 6-8pm, Sun. 6:30-8:30pm). **Phone code:** 021.

■ Dubrovnik

Picturesquely sandwiched between the Dinaric Alps and the calm Adriatic, the walled city of Dubrovnik appears in every piece of Croatian tourist literature. Less idyllic images of the city were broadcast around the world as Dubrovnik suffered attacks during the war in 1991-92. Those expecting to see still-smoking ruins will be disappointed—the damage is hardly noticeable, and this city, possessed with Croatia's vibrant cafe culture, brims with energy and pride.

Orientation and Practical Information The **bus station,** Put Republike 38 (tel. 230 88; fax 237 25; open 4:30am-9pm) lies about 2km north of Stari Grad. **Buses** travel to: Split (15 per day, 5hr., 46-71kn depending on the company); Zagreb (8 per day, 11hr., 135kn); Mostar (2 per day, 3hr., 53-78kn); and Sarajevo (7:30am, 7hr., 153kn). The **ferry landing,** Obala S. Radića 40 (tel. 41 10 00; fax 41 81 11), is a few hundred meters farther north (open Mon.-Fri. 8am-8pm, Sat. 8am-2pm, Sun. 8-9:30am, 12:30-2:30pm, and 7-8pm). **Ferries** make their way to Rijeka (20hr., 145kn) and Split (8hr., 70kn). You can base yourself in this area, or catch a bus (any but #7) to the Stari Grad gates from the stop on Starčevića across the parking lot (dir. "Pile"; tickets cost 5kn on board and 4kn from kiosks). Or, walk up **ul. Ante Starčevića** from the bus station (20min.). For a **taxi,** check outside the city gates next to the bus station, or call 243 43 (15kn to start; 7kn per km). Many of the tourist facilities are scattered on Lapad peninsula, to the west, but all the attractions wait within the city gates. The **tourist office** (tel. 263 54; fax 263 55) is just through the main gates on the right side of the main street, after the fountain (open Mon.-Sat. 8am-9pm, Sun. 9am-1pm). Exiting from the gates to the left, you'll find **Atlas tourist agency,** Starčevića 17 (tel. 44 27 27; fax 44 27 20), which answers pertinent questions, gives out prolific guides to Dubrovnik, and runs city tours (75kn; open Mon.-Sat. 8am-7:30pm). **Gulliver,** Obala S. Radića 31 (tel. 41 10 88; fax 41 20 88), is a travel and **rental car** agency very close to the ferry landing. You can also rent a scooter (40kn per hour, 154kn per day; includes insurance and tax). The agency also cashes traveler's checks, commission-free (open Mon.-Sat. 7am-8pm, Sun. 8am-noon). Farther down the main street from the tourist office, on the left, you'll see a branch of **Dubrovačka banka** (fax 41 19 67; open Mon.-Fri. 7:30am-1pm and 2-8pm, Sat. 7:30am-1pm). The main office (tel. 41 29 67; fax 41 10 35) is next to the bus station; it gives cash advances in kuna and from Visa cards only (open Mon.-Fri. 8am-4pm). **Zagrebačka banka,** Republike 5 (tel. 43 18 93; fax 43 18 90), just opposite Dubrovačka banka's main office, accepts MasterCard for cash advances (no commission) and has an **ATM** in front of its entrance. Money is given in kuna only, and 1.5% commission is taken to exchange either cash or traveler's checks (open Mon.-Fri. 8:30am-3pm, Sat. 9am-noon). The **post office,** Ante Starčevića 2, is up the street from the main gate. **Telephones** and *Poste Restante* (3kn) are found here (open Mon.-Fri. 7am-8pm, Sat. 7am-7pm, Sun. 8am-2pm). **Postal code:** 20 000. **Phone code:** 020.

Accommodations and Food Having once housed the special police, the **HI youth hostel,** Bana J. Jelačića 15/17 (tel. 232 41; fax 41 25 92), is ultra-clean, friendly, and always happy to host guests. Up a quiet alley, but still within reach of some happening bars, each of its 82 beds is a steal at 60kn (sheets provided; breakfast 7kn extra). From the bus station, walk up ul. Ante Starčevića about 10 minutes, turn right at the traffic light, and then turn right again after 30m. Continuing, pass a short chain of small bars and watch for a sign on the left. A narrow, concrete stair-street will lead you up to the hostel's terrace (reception open daily 7am-2pm). If you happen to arrive when nobody is at the reception desk, use the public phone on the wall inside to call the director's number, posted there. For **private rooms,** women will meet you at the transportation terminals (singles 80kn; doubles 130kn). The longer your stay, the more open they are to bargaining; the recent shortage of tourists also makes it easy to get a good price. **Globtour,** Zeljarica 5/II (tel. 289 92; fax 263 22) offers high-quality private rooms, bath and breakfast included (singles DM30; doubles DM50; open Mon.-Sat. 8am-8pm). Globtour also has an office and exchange bureau in Stari Grad, about 20m from the gates. Not its fanciest, but definitely Dubrovnik's least expensive hotel sits right across from the ferry terminal. **Hotel Petka,** Obala S. Radića 38 (tel. 41 80 08; fax 41 80 58), charges 175kn for a single and 300kn for a double (breakfast included; 20% less for stays over 3 days). **Hotel Zagreb,** Šestalište Kralja Zvonimira 57 (tel. 43 10 11; fax 235 81), also includes breakfast in its price (singles 168kn; doubles 292kn). **Camping Solitude** (tel. 44 81 66), on the Loped peninsula, was still closed in '97 after being hit in the 1991 attack, but may reopen by '98.

If you are outside Stari Grad, look around your neighborhood; you'll probably find some cheap eats, even if they're not as stylish as their more central counterparts. **Raguse 2,** Zamanjina 2 (tel. 224 35; fax 347 27), cooks up spaghetti (30kn), octopus salad (30kn), and *mussels bouzzara* (30kn; English-speaking staff; open daily 8am-11pm). **Domino,** Od Domina 6 (tel. 43 28 32), has first-class local caviar served on ice with onions, butter, and toast. The only catch is that it costs 65kn. If you like frog's legs or snails *a la française* (55kn), this is your place (open daily 11am-midnight). A cheaper and less secluded place is **Restaurant Jadran** (tel. 235 47), probably the only place in town offering a vegetarian option—a platter of beautifully arranged carrots, peas, potatoes, eggplant, mushrooms, and spinach-like greens (30kn). Live instrumental music plays under the massive stone archways (open daily 9am-11pm).

Sights and Entertainment Dubrovnik's **Stari Grad** resembles no other on the Croatian coast. The most impressive legacy of this former naval city-state is the awesome **gradske zidine** (city walls). Stretching up to 25m, they were mostly complete by the 14th century, but didn't receive finishing touches until the 17th. Climbing to the top of the walls yields a glorious view of the old city, right up against the sparkling blue Adriatic. Once atop the walls, take an hour to stroll the unforgettable 2km all the way around (walls open daily 9am-7:30pm; 10kn, children 5kn). Entering Stari Grad on its main street, the **Franjevački samostan** (Franciscan Monastery) will be on the left, the **Dominikanski samostan** (Dominican Monastery) at the other end. For all you mortar-and-pestle fans, the Franciscan one holds Europe's third-oldest working pharmacy (exhibition open daily 9am-5pm; 5kn). Its Dominican partner in penance has an especially rich collection of Renaissance paintings, art, and books (open daily 9am-6pm; 5kn). Nearby, the street opens into a large square, with **Crkva sv. Vlaha** (St. Blaise's Church) sitting on the same side as the **katedrala.** Between the two is the town's best museum, the 1441 **Knežev dvor** (Rector's Palace; tel. 264 69), which, holds old furniture, paintings, old coins, and collections of weaponry, all dating from the 16th and 17th centuries (open Mon.-Sat. 9am-1pm and 4-7pm, Sun. 9am-1pm; 10kn, guidebooks 4kn). Less pious visitors lie out on the **rocks** east of Stari Grad. The steep descents into the sea make for great diving, but you may instead want to take the ferry from the harbor to **otok Lokrum** (Lokrum island). The view of Dubrovnik on the return trip is well worth the price (round-trip 15kn). For Dionysian **disco** deca*dance,* follow the noise in Stari Grad to the **Arsenal** (open nightly 11pm-5am; cover 10kn). **Sun City** is livelier and showier. The grown-up youth of Dubrovnik flock here at night and stay until sunrise (open Fri.-Sat. 10pm-5am; cover 30kn with live music, 10-15kn without).

CROATIA

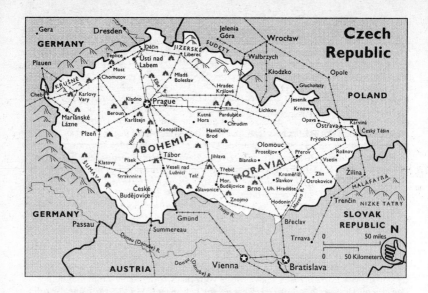

CZECH REPUBLIC
(ČESKÁ REPUBLIKA)

US$1	= 34.20kč (koruny)	10kč =	US$0.29
CDN$1	= 24.73kč	10kč =	CDN$0.40
UK£1	= 54.41kč	10kč =	UK£0.18
IR£1	= 50.14kč	10kč =	IR£0.20
AUS$1	= 24.88kč	10kč =	AUS$0.40
NZ$1	= 21.70kč	10kč =	NZ$0.46
SAR1	= 7.28kč	10kč =	SAR1.37
DM1	= 18.78kč	10kč =	DM0.53
Country Phone Code: 420		**International Dialing Prefix: 00**	

On New Year's Day, 1993, after more than 75 years of relatively calm coexistence, the Czech and Slovak Republics bloodlessly split. The notion of self-determination is relatively new to the Czech people. From the Holy Roman Empire up to the Nazis and the Soviets, foreigners have driven their internal affairs; even the 1968 Prague Spring was frozen by the iron rumble of Soviet tanks. Today, the Czech Republic is facing a more benevolent invasion, led by enamored tourists sweeping in to savor the magnificent capital, historic towns, and the world's best beer.

CZECH REPUBLIC ESSENTIALS

U.S. citizens may visit the Czech Republic visa-free for up to 30 days, U.K. or Canadian citizens for up to 180 days, and Irish citizens for up to 90 days. Australians, New Zealanders, and South Africans need visas, valid for 30 days. Visas may be obtained at three border crossings: Rozvadov, Dolní Dvořiště, or Hatí, or at an embassy or consulate. See **Essentials: Embassies and Consulates,** p. 4. Processing takes three days by mail, one day in person. With the application, you must submit: your passport; two photographs (for a double-entry visa send two applications and four photos; for multiple-entry, two photos); a self-addressed, stamped envelope (certified or overnight mail); and a cashier's check or money order for the amount of the fee. Single-entry and transit visas cost US$22 (US$60 at the border), double-entry US$36, and 90-day multiple-entry visas US$50 (180-day US$90). South Africans willing to settle for a 30-day, single-entry visa can get it gratis. You may apply for an extension (up to 6 months) at the local Passport and Visa Authorities.

GETTING THERE AND GETTING AROUND

Eastrail is accepted in the Czech Republic, but **Eurail** is valid only with a special supplement. Although cheap, trains are slow, rarely direct, and in the middle of any ride the conductor might announce that the stretch from X to Z has to be done by bus—a head-spinning affair. The fastest trains are *expresný*. *Rychlík* trains cost as much as *expresný,* while the few *spešný* (semi-fast) trains cost less; avoid *osobný* (slow) trains. **ČSD,** the national transportation company, publishes the monster *Jízdní řád* (train schedule; 74kč), helpful if only for the two-page English explanation in front. *Odjezd* (departures) are printed in train stations on yellow posters, *příjezd* (arrivals) on white. If heading to **Austria** or **Hungary,** it's cheaper to buy a Czech ticket to the border; once inside the country, buy a separate ticket to your destination. When coming from **Poland,** it's cheapest to walk across the border at Cieszyn/Český Těšin (see p. 460). Seat reservations (*místenka*, 6kč) are recommended on almost all express and international trains and for all first-class seating; snag them at the counter labeled with a boxed "R." A slip of paper with the destination, time, date, and a matching "R" expedites the transaction. IC and EC trains require an additional supplement, which can double the ticket price.

Buses can be significantly faster and only slightly more expensive than trains. **ČSAD** runs national and international bus lines. From **Prague,** buses run a few times per week to Munich, Milan, and other international hubs; buses depart from **Brno** to many destinations in Austria. Consult the timetables posted at stations or buy your own bus schedule (25kč) from kiosks.

Because of the inherent risks, *Let's Go* does not recommend **hitchhiking** as a safe means of transportation. However, hitchhikers report that it still remains a popular option in the Czech Republic, especially during morning commuting hours (6-8am).

TOURIST SERVICES

Čedok, the official state tourist company and a relic of centralized Communist bureaucracy, has been transformed into a travel agency. **CKM,** its junior affiliate, remains helpful to the student and budget traveler, serving as a clearinghouse for youth hostel beds and issuing ISICs and HI cards. The quality and trustworthiness of private tourist agencies varies; use your instincts. **Municipal tourist offices** in major cities provide heaps of printed matter on sights and cultural events, as well as lists of hostels and hotels. City maps (*plán města*) are available for 30-60kč. Bookstores sell a fine hiking map of the country, *Soubor Turistických Map,* with an English key.

MONEY

The Czech unit of currency is the **korun,** plural *koruny* (kč). The black exchange market no longer exists in the Czech Republic, while banks bear seemingly endless streams of **ATMs. Traveler's checks** can be exchanged in every town, if only because **Komerční banka** operates wherever a human being earns cash; its many branches accept all sorts of checks. Banks generally work weekdays from 9am to 5pm and close for the weekend.

COMMUNICATION

The Czech Republic's **postal system** has been converted to capitalist efficiency; letters generally reach the U.S. in less than 10 days. When sending a package by air mail, stress that you want it to go on a *plane* ("*leteckou poštou*" in Czech, but "*par avion*" works if you say it without a Southern drawl). The postmaster might seem surprised that anyone wants to spend so much money on mail, but even registered mail is inexpensive compared to prices in western Europe.

To make calls within the country, a phone card (150kč for 50 impulses) is a must and a godsend. It can be used in new gray and green phones. The old blue ones demand coins—but rarely return them—and generally drive you up the wall. Local calls cost 2kč regardless of length. Making calls abroad through an operator does not require a card—just dial the toll-free number of an international long-distance system (avoiding the hefty charges of the Czech telephone bureaucracy). Calls run 31kč per minute to the U.K.; 63kč per minute to the U.S., Canada, or Australia; and 94kč per minute to New Zealand. To reach **AT&T Direct,** dial 00 42 00 01 01; **MCI WorldPhone,** tel. 00 42 00 01 12; **Canada Direct,** tel. 00 42 00 01 51; **British Telecom Direct,** tel. 00 42 00 44 01.

LANGUAGE

Russian *was* every student's mandatory second language. These days, **English** will earn you more friends. A few **German** phrases go further, especially in the western spas, but might gain you some enemies. English-Czech dictionaries are indispensable; before you leave home, pick up a phrasebook. A handy phrase is "*Zaplatíme*" (ZAH-plah-tee-meh—We're ready to pay). If you've learned Czech abroad and arrive in Prague ready to romp, beware the Prague cockney—or just allow for some imaginative "mispronunciations." See the **Czech Glossary,** p. 800.

> ### The World's Most Difficult Sound
>
> Not quite a Spanish "r" and simply not the Polish "rz" (pronounced like the second "g" in "garage"), Czech's own linguistic blue note, the letter "ř," lies excruciatingly in between. Although many of Prague's ex-pats would sacrifice a month of Saturdays at Jo's Bar to utter the elusive sound just once, few manage more than a strangely trilled whistle. Most foreigners resign themselves to using the "ž" (akin to the Polish "rz") in its place, but what we consider a subtle difference often confuses Czechs. For all those linguistic daredevils in the audience, here's a sure-fire method of tackling the randy Mr. Ř: roll your tongue and quickly follow with a "ž", repeat. Oh, yeah—and start when you're two.

HEALTH AND SAFETY

> **Emergency Numbers: Fire:** tel. 150. **Ambulance:** tel. 155. **Police:** tel. 158.

The greatest risk of ill-feeling comes from food—it can be cheap and stodgy. **Pharmacies** *(lékárna)* and supermarkets together carry a sufficient variety of hygiene and health products. Check a town's Yellow Pages for 24-hour pharmacies. **Crime** has increased dramatically since 1989; beware purse-snatchers and pickpockets prowling among the crowds in Prague's main squares, on the way to the Castle, and on trams. Lost wallets and purses sometimes appear at embassies with only the cash missing. In an **emergency,** notify your consulate—police may not be well-versed in English. There is less danger of crime in smaller towns. Reach the toll-free **AIDS** emergency number (Mon.-Fri. 1-6pm) at tel. 060 64 44 44.

ACCOMMODATIONS AND CAMPING

Converted **university dorms** are the cheapest option in July and August; comfy two- to four-bed rooms go for 200-400kč per person. CKM's **Junior Hotels** (year-round hostels that give discounts to both ISIC and HI cardholders) are comfortable but often full. Private hostels have usurped CKM's monopoly, but do not necessarily surpass its reliability. Showers and bedding are usually part and parcel, and sometimes breakfast too, especially outside of Prague.

Across the country, **private homes** have become a legal and feasible option. In Prague, hawkers offer expensive rooms (US$16-30, but don't agree to more than US$20) that often include breakfast. Scan train stations for *Zimmer* signs. Quality varies, so do not pay in advance. Make sure anything you accept is easily accessible by public transport, including at night (much transport stops running at midnight); be prepared for a lengthy commute to the town center. Outside of Prague, **local tourist offices** and **Čedok** handle private room booking, although private agencies are burgeoning around train and bus stations. If you're sticking to **hotels,** reserve ahead from June to September in Prague and Brno, even if pre-payment is required. In smaller towns, it's easier to find a bed on the spot.

Inexpensive **campgrounds** are available throughout the country, ranging from 60 to 100kč per person (most sites are open only mid-May to September). The book *Ubytování ČSR,* in decodable Czech, comprehensively lists the hotels, inns, hostels, huts, and campgrounds in Bohemia and Moravia.

FOOD AND DRINK

Anyone in the mood for true Czech cuisine should start learning to pronounce *knedlíky* (KNED-lee-kee). These thick pasty loaves of dough, feebly known in English as dumplings, serve as staples of Czech meals, soaking up *zelí* (sauerkraut) juice and the unbelievably schmaltzy sauces that smother almost every local dish. The Czech national meal is *vepřové* (roast pork), *knedlíky,* and *zelí,* but *guláš* (stew) runs a close second. Subsidies on meat and dairy products have managed to strip most meals of fruits and vegetables; the main food groups seem to be *hovězí* (beef), *sekaná pečeně* (meatloaf), and *klobása* (sausage). Meat can be *pečené* (roasted), *vařené* (boiled), or *mleté* (ground). *Kuře* (chicken) is eaten less often than in North America. *Ryby* (fish) include *kapr* (carp) and *pstruh* (trout). If you are in a hurry, grab a pair of *párky* (frankfurters) or some *sýr* (cheese) at a *bufet, samoobsluha,* or *občerstveni,* all variations on a diner. Vegetarian restaurants serve *šopský salat* (mixed salad with feta cheese) and other *bez masa* (meatless) specialties. *Káva* (coffee) is almost always served Turkish-style, with a layer of grounds at the bottom. *Kobliby* (doughnuts), *jablkový závin* (apple strudel), and *palačinky* (pancakes) are favorite sweets, but possibly the most beloved is *koláč*—a tart filled with either poppy-seed jam or sweet cheese. If you love ice cream, master the consonants of *zmrzlina.*

Produced chiefly in Moravia, Czech wines are worth a try. *Rulandské,* from Znojmo in South Moravia, is good, but the quality of *Müller-Thurgau* varies. Any *Welschriesling* is drinkable. Wine is typically drunk at a *vinárna* (wine bar). Wine bars also serve a variety of hard spirits, including *slivovice* (plum brandy) and *becherovka* (herbal bitter), the country's favorite drink next to *Plzeňský Prazdroj* (*Pilsner Urquell*)—internationally famed as the world's best beer.

CUSTOMS AND ETIQUETTE

Everyone in the country addresses all of their friends, family, and foes with "*ty vole*" (you ox). This does *not* mean, however, that you should do here as oxen do: screw all the cows and crap on public lawns. Although by no means uptight, the Czechs do have certain rules of etiquette, most of which relate to dinner-table behavior. When beer is served, wait until all raise the common "*na zdraví*" toast, then drink. Similarly, before biting into a sauce-drowned *knedlík,* wish everyone "*dobrou chut,*" and when wished that by others, answer "*děkuji.*" At the end of the meal, the Czechs don't **tip** waitrons, but round upward to the nearest whole and tell the waitron how much they're paying. So learn your numbers.

NATIONAL HOLIDAYS

Czechs celebrate: January 1, New Year's Day; April 12, Easter; May 1, Labor Day; May 8, Liberation Day; July 5, Cyril and Methodius Day; July 6, Jan Hus Day; October 28, Republic Day (1918); December 24-26, Christmas.

CZECH REPUBLIC

LIFE AND TIMES

HISTORY

A fertile plain protected by a ring of mountains, the area now known as the Czech Republic has always been a great place to start a culture. The earliest evidence of humans in the area date back 600,000 years ago, and **Paleolithic** tribes hunted mammoths here a mere 25,000 years ago, and just 19,000 years later, **Neolithic** farmers in Bohemia made a big splash in the European fashion scene; their Linear pottery decorations dominating Central European art for 2000 years. The area became populated by **Celtic** and **Germanic** tribes, bringing improved trade, a warrior aristocracy, a fetish for cremation, and by 450BC, an urban civilization. By the 6th century, **Western Slavs** had arrived: Moravians in the southwest, and Czechs in the west.

At the end of the 9th century, the **Přemysl Dynasty** united the Czechs and quickly created a strong autonomous state. The legendary **Sv. Václav** (c.903-935; known as Good King Wenceslas, though he was never a king), later patron saint of Bohemia and Christmas-carol cameo, was one of the dynasty's earliest rulers. Following defeat to the German King Otto I, the area became incorporated into the Holy Roman Empire. In 1140, the region became a hereditary kingdom under **Vladislav II,** and reached a peak under Přemysl Otakar II (1253-1278), who conquered Austria and Slovenia. Otakar II grew too big for his boots, however, and he hoped to claim the imperial crown. The job, however, went to Rudolf Habsburg, someone Otakar considered less qualified than himself, leading a dissatisfied Otakar into conflict and defeat by the founder of the Habsburg dynasty.

Holy Roman Emperor Karel (Charles) IV (1346-1378) made Bohemia the center of Imperial power, and Prague experienced its **Golden Age.** Charles established Prague as an Archbishopric, founded the first university in Central Europe, and constructed hundreds of buildings, including the Charles Bridge. Charles's son Václav "the Lazy" was clearly not as productive. During Václav's reign, the Rector at Prague University, **Jan Hus** (1369-1415) spoke out against the corruption of the Catholic hierarchy and was burned to death as a heretic. The thus created Hussite movement led to the **first Defenestration of Prague,** in which Hussite protestors threw the royalist mayor and several of his councillors out of the window of the Council House in Prague. The **second Defenestration of Prague** launched the set of religious and dynastic conflicts known as the **Thirty Years' War** (1618-1648), during which Bohemian losses led to forced Catholic conversion, coerced German emigration, and the utter destruction of Bohemia, resulting in the deaths of over one-third of its inhabitants. The Czech Protestants suffered an early and very harsh blow in the **Battle of Bílá hora** (White Mountain), fought outside Prague on November 8, 1620: after the battle, 27 Protestant nobles were executed in Prague's Staroměstské nám., and five-sixths of the Czech nobility went into exile, their property given to loyal Catholic families. While the Counter-Reformation inspired the building of magnificent churches, the absorption of Czech territory into the **Austrian Empire** turned into the three centuries of oppressive rule that directly inspired Franz Kafka's nightmare world.

> **Charles founded the first university in Central Europe and built the Charles Bridge. His son Vaclav "the Lazy" was less productive.**

As the spirit of national invention swept Europe from west to east, Bohemia became the home of Czech nationalism, and Josef Dobrovský and Josef Jungmann revived and standardized the Czech language. During the **1848 revolutions,** Czech nationalism was crushed by imperial conservatism. Unquenched nationalism congealed into extremist groups in the late 19th century, including Pan-Slavs, Young Czechs, and Pan-Germans. While **WWI** did nothing to increase harmony among the nationalities of the Hapsburg Empire, it did help unite the Czechs and Slovaks, and in the post-war confusion, **Edvard Beneš** and **Tomáš Masaryk** convinced the victorious Allies to legitimize a new state which united Bohemia, Moravia, and Slovakia into

CZECH REPUBLIC

Czechoslovakia. Uniquely in Eastern Europe, Czechoslovakia remained a parliamentary democracy between the wars, only to be torn apart as Hitler exploited the Allies' **appeasement** policy in the infamous 1938 **Munich Agreement,** whereby Czech territory was handed over to Germany. The following year, Hitler brutally annexed Bohemia and Moravia as a protectorate and turned Slovakia into an independent fascist state. Most of Czechoslovakia's Jews were murdered by the Nazis during the five-year occupation. In 1945, Soviet and American troops met in Czechoslovakia. The Communists, under **Klement Gottwald,** won 38% of the vote in the 1946 elections, and following the collapse of the Popular Front coalition in 1948, they seized power. In 1968, Communist Party Secretary **Alexander Dubček** sought to implement "socialism with a human face," dramatically reforming the country's economy and easing political oppression during the **Prague Spring.** Not pleased with the new developments, the Warsaw Pact states suppressed Dubček's counter-revolution. **Gustáv Husák** introduced an even more repressive system that lasted 21 years. After the demise of the Communists in Hungary and Poland and

> Czechoslovakia remained a democracy between the wars, only to be torn apart as Adolf Hitler exploited the Allies' appeasement policy.

the fall of the Berlin Wall, the **Velvet Revolution** rippled into Czechoslovakia. Despite crackdowns, Czechs increasingly demonstrated and went on strike in Prague and other cities in November, and within a month, the Communist government had resigned; **Václav Havel** became president soon afterwards. A combination of three years of debate, the winning of a plurality in the 1992 elections by nationalist parties in the Slovak areas, and a perception by many Czechs that the Slovaks were resistant to rapid economic liberalization, lead to the separation of the two nations on **January 1, 1993.** Although Havel temporarily stepped down in protest at the divorce with Slovakia, Czechs today have much respect for their playwright-president and generally are embracing the economic transition process.

LITERATURE

In the Czech Republic, literature and life are inextricably intertwined. From former foreign minister **T.G. Masaryk** to current president **Václav Havel,** writers have retained an immense influence over the political process, posing a real threat to the terrors of totalitarianism and Communism. This is not because they have proposed alternative programs. Instead, as Havel himself describes in *The Power of the Powerless,* authors expose ideology and propaganda for what they are merely by describing life in all its intricacies.

The themes of justice and technology pervade Czech literature, tempered by characteristic humor. From the Defenestration of Prague to the mysterious demise of T.G. Masaryk (see **"High Windows,"** p. 173), the Czech government has almost always meant corruption. Obliged to face this fact in their daily life, Czech writers mused on paper about what was fair, and came to their own conclusions. Authors also expressed ambivalence about the Czech Republic's rapid industrialization—the result of its location at the border between East and West. Science fiction prose and dramas served to satirize and debunk the grandiose ideas of the Party line.

Music also reappears frequently in Czech literature. Twentieth century novelist **Josef Škvorecký** writes in his foreword to *Bassaxofon* (The Bass Saxophone), "jazz was a sharp thorn in the sides of the power-hungry men, from Hitler to Brezhnev, who ruled in my native land." A popular and spontaneous form of emotional expression, jazz threatened the powers that be—just as in the American movie *Swing Kids.* Havel himself began the human rights organization "Charter 77" when a rock group was put on trial under the Soviet system, and **Milan Kundera,** among others, writes of music in *Kniha smíchu a zapomnění* (The Book of Laughter and Forgetting).

Swing Kids is not the sole American movie that resembles a work of Czech literature. Indeed, more icons of foreign culture have been co-opted from Czech literature than you might think. The renowned South American poet Pablo Neruda adopted his pseudonym in emulation of the Czech poet **Jan Neruda,** while the replicants of the

80s film *Blade Runner* distinctly resemble the robots in **Karel Čapek's** *Rossum's Universal Robots* (Čapek invented the word "robot"!)

In terms of early literary development, two works stand out: the **Unitas Fratrum scholars'** translation of the bible, dubbed the *Kralice Bible* (1579-93), which set a standard for the Czech language, and **Jan Ámos Komenský's** *Labyrint sveta a ráj srdce* (Labyrinth of the World and Paradise of the Heart;1631), composed after the author had been sent into exile by the Habsburgs. While the indigenous tradition was stifled during the period of Habsburg oppression, other Czech literary production occurred elsewhere, yet it was not until the 19th century that a literary renaissance took place.

Fueled by scholarly endeavors to revitalize the language, **Karel Hynek Mácha** created his lyric epic *Máj* (May; 1836). Considered one of the masterpieces of Czech poetry, these verses recounted the age-old tale of seasonal death and rebirth. The simple theme finds perfect expression in Mácha's consummate artistic work. The respect that it commanded throughout Czech literary circles prompted a later 19th century circle of writers christened themselves the "Máj group," despite their rather different aims. Besides novelist Karolina Světlá and poet Vitězslav Hálek, poet and story-teller **Jan Neruda** was the principal player in "The Máj Group."

In the 1870s, **Jaroslav Vrychlický** and his companions clustered around the periodical *Lumir* tried to steer Czech culture toward that of the rest of Europe. **Svatopluk Čech,** representative of the rival publication *Ruch* (Stir) disagreed, claiming that Czech writing should deal with subjects of national importance. Political leader **T. G. Masaryk** followed in this vein with his newspaper articles and other compositions. German oppression supplied an incessant theme for **Petr Bezruč,** and **Otakar Březina** retained a lyrical style verging on the mystical.

> Although he never explicitly discussed politics, Franz Kafka alluded to the evils of the state in all his novels.

The next generation of authors included **Franz Kafka, Karel Čapek, František Langer, Jaroslav Hašek,** and **Vladislav Vončura.** Although he never explicitly discussed politics, Kafka alluded to the evils of the state in all his novels.

Today, the novels of **Milan Kundera** and **Josef Skvorecký** and the dramas of **Václav Havel** remain part of the Czech Republic's daily life, and continue to serve as introductions for readers new to the Czech tradition. The streets that Czech writers have so affectionately depicted, in Prague and other cities around the country, now bear their names.

CZECH REPUBLIC TODAY

The Czech Republic is enjoying its status as the ex-Communist pet of Western investors and politicians. Foreign money is pouring in faster than the Czechs can build new dumpling factories or breweries, although some national economists voice doubts about the soundness of the transformation's fundaments. The coalition government, led by the Civic Democratic Party leader Václav Klaus, has ruled the economy with an iron hand since democratization. Although the 1996 elections changed parliament's spectrum, turning the Klaus-led coalition into a minority government relying on the support of the Social Democrats, the political, social, and economic process will continue to evolve in the same, capitalistic direction. Meanwhile, President Václav Havel keeps careful watch, despite lung-cancer surgery and the death of his wife. He is eligible to run for another five-year term in the Presidential elections to be held early 1998.

In July 1997, the Czech Republic was offered NATO membership, and is expected to be formally admitted in time for NATO's 50th anniversary in 1999. Also in July 1997, floods—the worst natural disaster to hit Central Europe in centuries—caused billions of dollars worth of damage. The financial burden of recovery has forced the Czechs to turn to their EU neighbors for aid, adding fuel to critics who say that expanding EU membership would only be a burden to present members. Nonetheless, accession negotiations are scheduled to open in early 1998.

Prague (Praha)

I see a city whose glory will touch the stars; it shall be called Praha.
—Princess Libuše

From its mythological inception to the present, benefactors have placed Prague on the cusp of the divine. Envisioning a royal seat worthy of his rank, King of Bohemia and Holy Roman Emperor Karel IV refashioned Prague into a city of soaring cathedrals and lavish palaces. Mazes of shady alleys, along with legends of demons and occult forces, lent the "city of dreams" a dark side and provided frightening fodder for Franz Kafka's 20th-century tales of paranoia. Be it benevolent or evil, a dreamy spell hangs over Prague, where the clocks run backwards or not at all.

In recent years, this spell has begun to break. After the Iron Curtain fell, hordes of Euro-trotting foreigners flooded the Czech Republic's venerable capital seeking history and cheap beer. In August, most of central Prague's citizens leave for the country, and the foreigner to resident ratio soars above nine to one. Masses pack some streets so tightly that crowd-surfing could become a summer pastime. Although today's tourists chase daytime ghosts away, at night Rabbi Loew's *golem* still runs amok, and a phantom baby can be heard crying under Charles Bridge. A growing number of international expats has chosen to savor the city before the magic is gone. Some believe it already is, but those willing to explore for themselves might find a bit of stardust left in the cobblestone cracks.

ORIENTATION AND PRACTICAL INFORMATION

Straddling a bend in the Vltava, Prague is a gigantic mess of suburbs and curvy streets. Study a map. **Staré Město** (Old Town) lies along the southeast riverbank. Across the Vltava sits **Hradčany** castle, with **Malá Strana** (Lesser Side) at its south base. Southeast of Staré Město spreads **Nové Město** (New Town), and farther east across **Wilsonova** lie the **Žižkov** and **Vinohrady** districts. **Holešovice** in the north has an international train terminal. **Smíchov,** the southwest end, is the student-dorm suburb. All train and bus terminals are on or near the **metro** system. *Tabak* stands and bookstores vend indexed *plán města* (maps). The English-language weekly *The Prague Post* provides numerous tips for visitors, as well as the usual news.

> The reform of Prague's phone system continues, with businesses sometimes getting just three weeks' notice that their numbers will change, driving them to drink, despair, and lose revenue. The eight-digit numbers are least likely to be obsolete by the time you read this—but, then again, nothing is sacred.

Useful Organizations

Tourist Offices: The "i"s of Prague signify the multitude of tourist agencies that book rooms and tours and sell maps, bus tickets, postcards and guidebooks. Be a bit wary: with money on their minds, these firms didn't pop up just to aid tourists.
Pražská Informační Služba (Prague Info Service), Staroměstské radnice (in the old town hall; tel. 24 48 25 62, English tel. 54 44 44). Burbles information in English and sells **maps** (40kč) and **tickets** to shows. Open Mon.-Fri. 9am-7pm, Sat.-Sun. 9am-6pm. Other offices at Na příkopě 20 (open Mon.-Fri. 9am-7pm, Sat.-Sun. 9am-5pm), Hlavní nádraží (open Mon.-Fri. 9am-7pm, Sat. 9am-3pm), and in the tower on the Malá Strana side of the Karlův most (same hours as Na příkopě 20).
Čedok, Na příkopě 18 (tel. 24 19 71 11). A formidable institutional memory stemming from 40 years of socialist monopoly on tourist information, but not yet fully user-friendly. Fairly comprehensive range of travel and tourist services. Open Mon.-Fri. 8:30am-6pm, Sat. 9am-1pm.
Budget Travel: CKM, Jindřišská 28 (tel. 24 23 02 18; fax 26 86 23; email ckm-prg@mbox.vol.cz). Sells budget air tickets for students and those under 26, and the discount cards you need to qualify for them (ISIC and GO25 150kč; Euro26 200kč).

Also books accommodations in Prague (from 300kč). Open Mon.-Thurs. 9:30am-1pm and 1:30-5pm, Fri. 9:30am-1pm and 1:30-4pm. The office at Žitná 12 (tel. 24 91 57 67) sells bus and train tickets. Open Mon.-Fri. 10am-6pm. But this office doesn't do HI stuff—to buy a card or book HI hostels anywhere in the world, go to **KMC,** Karoliny Světlé 30 (tel. 24 23 06 33). Open Mon.-Thurs. 9am-noon and 2:30-5pm, Fri. 9am-noon and 2:30-3:30pm.

Passport Office: Foreigner police headquarters at Olšanská 2 (tel. 683 17 39). Metro A: Flora. Walk down Jičinská, and turn right onto Olšanská. Or take tram #9. To get a visa extension, get a 90kč stamp just inside the door, line up in front of doors 2-12, and wait up to 2hr. Little English spoken. Open Mon.-Tues. and Thurs. 7:30-11:45am and 12:30-2:30pm, Wed. 7:30-11:30am and 12:30-5pm, Fri. 7:30am-noon.

Embassies: Canada, Mickiewiczova 6 (tel. 24 31 11 08). Metro A: Hradčanská. Open Mon.-Fri. 8am-noon and 2-4pm. **Hungary,** Badeniho 1 (tel. 36 50 41). Metro A: Hradčanská. Open Mon.-Wed. and Fri. 9am-noon. **Ireland,** Tržiště 13 (tel. 53 09 02). Metro A: Malostranská. Open Mon.-Fri. 9:30am-12:30pm and 2:30-4:30pm. **Poland (Consulate),** Václavské nám. 49 (tel. 24 22 87 22). Open Mon.-Fri. 7am-noon. **Russia,** Pod Kaštany 1 (tel. 38 19 45). Metro A: Hradčanská. Open Mon, Wed, and Fri 9am-1pm. **Slovakia,** Pod Hradbani 1 (tel. 32 05 21). Metro A: Dejvická. Open Mon.-Fri. 8:30am-noon. **South Africa,** Ruská 65 (tel. 67 31 11 14). Metro A: Flora. Open Mon.-Fri. 9am-noon. **U.K.,** Thunovská 14 (tel. 57 32 03 55). Metro A: Malostranská. Open Mon.-Fri. 9am-noon. Travelers from **Australia** and **New Zealand** are lucky enough to have their own honorary consuls (tels. 24 31 00 71 and 25 41 98, respectively) but should contact the British embassy in an emergency. **U.S.,** Tržiště 15 (tel. 57 32 06 63, emergency after hours tel. 53 12 00). Metro A: Malostranská. From Malostranské nám., head down Karmelitská and take a right onto Tržiště. Open Mon.-Fri. 8am-1pm and 2-4:30pm.

Currency Exchange: The best rates are for AmEx and Thomas Cook's traveler's checks when cashed commission-free at the appropriate office. Exchange counters are everywhere—hotel lobbies, tourist information agencies, and littering the streets—with wildly varying rates. **Chequepoints** are mushrooming around the center of town, and may be the only places open when you need to change cash, but they can cream off a 10% commission. **Komerční Banka,** main branch Na příkopě 33 (tel. 24 02 11 11; fax 24 24 30 20). Buys notes and checks for 2% commission. Open Mon.-Fri. 8am-5pm.

ATMs: All over the place. The one at **Krone supermarket,** Václavské nám. 21, is hooked up to Cirrus, EuroCard, Eurocheque, MC, Plus, and Visa.

American Express: Václavské nám. 56 (tel. 24 21 99 92; fax 22 21 11 31). Metro A or C: Muzeum. The **ATM** outside takes AmEx cards. Address mail to "Peter Sarris, American Express, Client Letter Service, Václavské nám. 56, 113 26 Praha 1, Czech Republic." MC and Visa cash advances (not just to AmEx cardholders) at 3% commission. Exchange office open daily 9am-7pm; travel office open May-Sept. Mon.-Fri. 9am-6pm, Sat. 9am-2pm; Oct.-April Mon.-Fri. 9am-5pm, Sat. 9am-noon. Another exchange office near the Karlův most at Mostecká 12. Open daily 9:30am-7:30pm.

Thomas Cook: Národní tř. 28 (tel. 21 10 52 76; fax 24 23 60 77). Cashes Cook's checks commission-free. MC cash advances. Open Mon.-Sat. 9am-7pm, Sun. 10am-6pm. Also at Staroměstké nám. 5/934 (tel. 24 81 71 73). Open daily 9am-7pm.

Post Office: Jindřišská 14. Metro A or B: Můstek (tel. 24 22 88 56, info tel. 24 22 85 88). Open daily 24hr. (some windows have shorter hours). Stamps sold at window 16; letters and small parcels go to #12-14. Window 9 is for information; #17 is *Poste Restante*. Address mail to "Rebecca KORZEC, POSTE RESTANTE, Jindřišská 14, 110 00 Praha 1, Czech Republic." Window open Mon.-Fri. until 8pm. Airmail to and from the U.S. takes about 10 days. To send a package of more than 2kg abroad, go to the **Celní stanice** (customs office), Plzeňská 139. Take tram #4, 7, or 9 from Metro B: Anděl to "Klamovka" and go up the road. Open Mon.-Tues. and Thurs.-Fri. 7am-3pm, Wed. 7am-6pm.

Telephones: Everywhere, especially at the post office. Cardphones are becoming increasingly common. Phonecards sell for 3kč per unit at kiosks, post offices, and some exchange places: don't let kiosks rip you off. **Phone code:** 02.

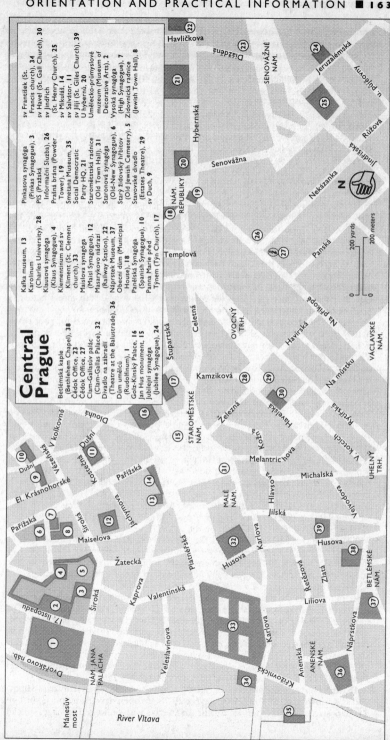

Central Prague

Betlémská kaple
(Bethlehem Chapel), 38
Čedok Office, 23
Čedok Office, 27
Clam-Gallasův palác
(Clam-Gallas Palace), 32
Divadlo na zábradlí
(Theatre at the Balustrade), 36
Dům umělců
(Rudolfinum), 1
Golz-Kinsky Palace, 16
Jan Hus monument, 15
Jubilejní synagóga
(Jubilee Synagogue), 24

Kafka museum, 13
Karolinum
(Charles University), 28
Klausová synagóga
(Klaus Synagogue), 4
Klementinum and sv
Kliment (St. Clement
church), 33
Maislova synagóga
(Maisl Synagogue), 12
Masarykovo nádraží
(Railway Station), 22
Národní Muzeum, 37
Obecní dům (Municipal
House), 18
Panělská synagóga
(Spanish Synagogue), 10
Panna Marie před
Týnem (Týn Church), 17

Pinkasova synagóga
(Pinkas Synagogue), 3
PIS (Pražská
Informační Služba), 26
Prašná brána (Powder
Tower), 19
Smetana Museum, 35
Social Democratic
Party HQ, 21
Staroměstská radnice
(Old Town Hall), 31
Staronová synagóga
(Old-New Synagogue), 6
Starý židovský hřbitov
(Old Jewish Cemetery), 5
Stavovské divadlo
(Estates Theatre), 29
sv Duch, 9

sv František (St.
Francis church), 34
sv Havel (St. Gall Church), 30
sv Jindřich
(St. Henry Church), 25
sv Mikuláš, 14
sv Salvator, 11
sv Jiljí (St. Giles Church), 39
U hybernů, 20
Umělecko-průmyslové
muzeum (Museum of
Decorative Arts), 2
Vysoká synagóga
(High Synagogue), 7
Židovnická radnice
(Jewish Town Hall), 8

Transportation

Flights: Ruzyně Airport (tel. 20 11 11 11), 20km northwest of the city. Take bus #119 from Dejvická. **Airport bus** (tel. 20 11 42 96) collects travelers at nám. Republiky (90kč) and Dejvická (60kč). Taxis to the airport can be extremely expensive. Many major carriers, including **Air France,** Václavské nám 10 (tel. 24 22 71 64), **British Airways,** Ovocný trh 8 (tel. 22 11 44 44), **ČSA** (tel. 20 10 43 10), **Delta,** Národní tř. 32 (tel. 24 23 36 38), **KLM,** Václavské nám. 37 (tel. 24 22 86 78), **Lufthansa,** Pařížská 28 (tel. 24 81 10 07), and **Swissair,** Pařížská 11 (tel. 24 81 21 11).

Trains: info tel. 24 22 42 00, international fare info tel. 24 61 52 49. Prague has 4 terminals—make sure you go the right one. **Praha Hlavní Nádraží** (tel. 24 61 72 50; Metro C: Hlavní Nádraží) is the biggest, but most international services run out of **Holešovice** (tel. 24 61 72 65; Metro C: Nádraží Holešovice). To: Berlin (5 per day, 5hr., 1342kč; Wasteels 1128kč); Budapest (6 per day, 8hr., 1018kč; Wasteels 741kč); Vienna (4 per day, 5hr., 709kč; Wasteels 453kč); Warsaw (3 per day, 10hr., 722kč; Wasteels 449kč); and Bratislava (9 per day, 5hr., 231kč). Domestic trains go from **Masarykovo** (tel. 24 61 72 60; Metro B: nám. Republiky) on the corner of Hybernská and Havličkova, or from **Smíchov** (tel. 24 61 72 55; Metro B: Smíchovské Nádraží), opposite Vyšehrad. **B.I.J. Wasteels:** Office at Hlavní Nádraží (tel. 24 61 74 54; fax 24 22 18 72) sells cheap international tickets to those under 26 and books couchettes (open Mon.-Fri. 8:45am-5:45pm, daily in summer). Wasteels tickets also available from the **Czech Railways Travel Agency** at Holešovice (tel. 80 08 05; fax 80 69 48). Open Mon.-Fri. 8am-5pm, Sat. 9am-3pm.

Buses: ČSAD has several *autobusové nádraží.* The biggest is **Florenc,** Křižíkova 4 (tel. 24 21 49 90; info 24 21 10 60; Metro B or C: Florenc). Staff rarely manages English, but the timetables aren't too horrible: the ones inside have explanations of the symbols posted in English. Start by looking up bus stop numbers for your destination. Info office open Mon.-Fri. 6am–9pm, Sat. 6am-6pm, Sun. 8am-8pm. Get tickets in advance—they sometimes sell out. To: Berlin (1 per day, 6hr., 750kč); Vienna (6 per week, 8½hr., 330kč); and Sofia (1 per day, 26hr., 1200kč). Students might get 10% discount. The **Tourbus** office upstairs (tel. 24 21 02 21) sells tickets for Eurolines and the airport buses (open Mon.-Fri. 8am-8pm, Sat.-Sun. 9am-8pm).

Ferries: PPS, Rašínovo Nábřeží (tel. 29 38 03; fax 24 91 38 62) to Vyšehrad and the zoo. Metro B: Karlovo nám. Exit into Palackého nám.; PPS is between Jiráskův and Palackého bridges. Various river trips 9:30am-8pm daily; 2hr. Vltava cruise 200kč.

Public Transportation: The **metro, tram,** and **bus** services are pretty good, and share the same ticket system. Buy tickets from newsstands, machines in stations, or **DP** (*Dopravní Podnik;* transport authority) kiosks. Punch tickets upon first use. Basic 6kč ticket good for one short ride; more useful 10kč ticket valid 1hr. (90min. 8pm-5am and all day Sat., Sun, and holidays), allowing you to switch from bus to tram to metro and back again. Large bags 5kč each, as are bikes and prams without babies in them (*with* babies free, so don't forget the baby). To remind you to punch your ticket, plainclothes DP inspectors roam Prague issuing 200kč spot fines. Make sure you see their official badge and get a receipt. The metro's 3 lines run daily 5am-midnight: A is green on the maps, B is yellow, C is red. **Night trams** #51-58 and **buses** run all night after the last metro; look for the dark blue signs at bus stops. DP also sells **tourist passes** valid for the entire network (24hr. 50kč, 3 days 130kč, 1 week 190kč). **DP offices** by the Jungmannovo nám. exit of Můstek station (tel. 24 22 51 35; open daily 7am-9pm) or by the Palackého nám. exit of Karlovo nám. station (tel. 29 46 82; open Mon.-Fri. 7am-6pm).

Taxis: Taxi drivers are notorious rip-off artists. Before getting into the cab, check that the meter is set to zero, and ask the driver to start it by saying *"Zapněte taximetr."* For longer trips, agree on a price before you set off. Always ask for a receipt (*"Prosím, dejte mi paragon"*) with distance traveled, price paid, and driver's signature on it. If the driver doesn't write the receipt, you aren't obligated to pay. Taxi drivers can set their own price per km, but must state what it is, often with a sign on the door. 15-20kč per km is reasonable, along with a 20-30kč flat charge for getting in. **Taxi Praha** (tel. 24 91 66 66) and **AAA** (tel. 24 32 24 32) run 24hr.

Car Rental: Hertz, at the airport (tel. 312 07 17; fax 36 59 98; open daily 8am-10pm) and at Karlovo nám. 28 (tel. 29 01 22; fax 29 78 36; open daily 8am-8pm). Must be 21. Cars start at 2314kč per day for the first 4 days with unlimited mileage; special

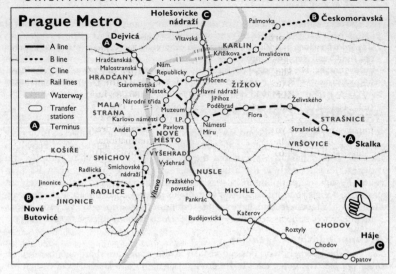

Prague Metro

— A line
•••• B line
---- C line
++++ Rail lines
░░░░ Waterway
◯ Transfer stations
Ⓐ Terminus

weekend rental rates. **Czechocar,** 5. května 65 (tel. 61 22 20 79; fax 61 17 24 32). Škodas for 1600kč per day plus insurance. Travel agents can provide full details.

Hitchhiking: Hitchhiking in and around Prague has become increasingly dangerous; luckily, cheap and extensive train and bus service renders it an unnecessary risk. Those hitching east take tram #1, 9, or 16 to the last stop. To points south, they take Metro C to "Pražskeho povstání" and walk left 100m, crossing nám. Hrdinů to 5. květná (highway D1). To Munich, hitchers take tram #4 or 9 to the intersection of Plzeňská at Kukulova/Bucharova, then hitch south. Those going north take a tram or bus to "Kobyliské nám.," then bus #175 up Horňátecká. *Let's Go* does not recommend hitchhiking as a safe form of getting around.

Other Practical Information

Luggage Storage: Lockers in all train and bus stations take 2 5kč coins. If these are full, or if you need to store your suitcase, backpack, or Maltese falcon for longer than 24hr., use the left luggage offices in the basement of **Hlavní nádraží** (15kč per day for up to 15kg; 25kč per day over 15kg; open 24hr.) and halfway up the stairs at **Florenc** (10kč per day up to 15kg; 20kč per day 15-30kg; open daily 5am-11pm).

English Bookstores: The Globe Bookstore, Janovského 14 (tel. 66 71 26 10). Metro C: Vltavská. From the Metro, walk under the overpass on the right, then turn right onto Janovského. New and used books and periodicals, together with a big noticeboard and coffeehouse. A legendary (pick-up) center of Anglophone Prague. Open daily 10am-midnight. **Big Ben Bookshop,** Malá Štupartská 5 (tel. 231 80 21; fax 231 98 48; email bigben@terminal.cz). Metro A: nám. Republiky. Open Mon.-Fri. 9am-6pm, Sat.-Sun. 10am-5pm. **U Knihomola International Bookshop,** Mánesova 79 (tel. 627 77 70; fax 627 77 69; email zazie@terminal.cz). Metro A: Jiřího z Poděbrad. Open Mon.-Thurs. 10am-11pm, Fri.-Sat. 10am-midnight, Sun. 11am-8pm.

Laundromat: Laundry Kings, Dejvická 16 (tel. 312 37 43), 1 block from Metro A: Hradčanská. Cross the tram *and* railroad tracks, then turn left onto Dejvická. Wash 60kč; dry 15kč per 8min. Soap 10-20kč. Use the spinner to save on drying. Full-service 30kč more and takes up to 2 days. Beer 11kč. Filled with soiled and thirsty travelers who watch CNN while they wait. Bulletin board for apartment seekers, English teachers, and those trying to locate friends. Open Mon.-Fri. 6am-10pm, Sat.-Sun. 8am-10pm. **Laundryland,** Londýnská 71 (tel. 25 11 24; delivery tel. 06 03 41 10 05). Wash 43kč; dry 10kč for 8min. Soap 10-20kč. Full-service 30kč more. In some private flats, laundry service can be informally arranged.

Pharmacies: Pharmacies are plentiful in Prague and offer a variety of foreign products at foreign prices. You may need to ask for *kontracepční prostředky* (contraceptives), *náplast* (bandages), or *dámské vložky* (tampons). **24hr. pharmacies** at Koněvova 210 (tel. 644 18 95) and Štefánikova 6 (tel. 24 51 11 12).

Gay Information: SOHO, the Association of Organizations of Homosexual Citizens in the Czech Republic. Info tel. 24 22 03 27.

Emergencies: Na Homolce (hospital for foreigners), Roentgenova 2 (tel. 52 92 21 46, after hours 57 21 11 11). Open Mon.-Fri. 8am-4pm. **American Medical Center** (tel. 80 77 56); **Canadian Medical Centre** (tel. 316 55 19).

ACCOMMODATIONS AND CAMPING

While hotel prices rise beyond your wildest dreams, the hostel market is glutted; prices have stabilized around 200-300kč per night. The smaller hostels provide a friendly, communal atmosphere, but they're often full. The Strahov complex and other student dorms bear the brunt of the summer's backpacking crowds. Year-round hostels are popping up in some of the most convenient and inconvenient places, so weigh your options. A few bare-bones hotels are still cheap, and a growing number of Prague residents have begun renting rooms. Although everyone knows someone who's done it, sleeping on Prague's streets is too dangerous to consider.

Accommodations Agencies

Many of the hawkers who besiege visitors at the train station are agents hired by other people. The going rates hover around US$15-30 (500-1000kč), depending primarily on proximity to the city center. Haggling is possible. Arrangements made in this way are generally safe, but if you're wary of bargaining on the street, try a private agency. Staying outside the center is fine if you're near public transport, so ask where the tram, bus, or metro stop is. Don't pay until you know what you're getting—if in doubt, ask for details in writing. You can often pay in US$ or DM.

Konvex 91, Ve Smečkách 29 (tel. 96 22 44 44; fax 22 21 15 02). Specializes in apartment rental, around 440-590kč per person per night near the TV tower or 590-720kč in Staré Město. Hostels from 340kč per night. English and French spoken.

Ave., Hlavní Nádraží (tel. 24 22 32 26; fax 24 23 07 83), left from the main hall of the train station. The burgeoning firm offers hundreds of rooms (shared and private) starting at 440kč per person and books hostels from 170kč. Open daily 6am-10pm.

Hello Travel Ltd., Senovážné nám. 3, between Na příkopě and Hlavní Nádraží (tel. 24 21 26 47). Arranges every sort of housing imaginable. Singles in pensions from US$23 (low season) or US$35 (high); doubles US$38/56; hostels US$10-13. Payment in kč, DM, or by credit card (AmEx, Diners, MC, Visa). Open daily 10am-9pm.

Hostels

In the Strahov neighborhood, west of the river next to the Olympic stadium, an enormous cluster of dorms frees up for travelers in July and August. These rooms may be the best bet for those who arrive in the middle of the night without having a reservation. Many prefer the smaller hostels, where there's a fighting chance the staff will remember your name. Since a lot of places don't take reservations, it's best to phone the night before you arrive, or at 10am when they know who's checking out, to snap up a bed. The staff generally speaks good English. Curfews and sleeping sheets are distant memories.

The Clown and Bard, Bořivojova 102 (tel. 27 24 36). Metro A: Jiřího z Poděbrad. Walk down Slavíkova and take a right onto Ježkova; continue until the intersection with Bořivojova. Prague's newest hostel provides beds in the roomy attic dorm for 200kč, private rooms for 250-350kč per person, or apartments from 300kč per person, all in a converted 19th-century Žižkov building. Wildly popular in summer '97, owing much to the cellar bar, where guests line their stomachs with toasties before the traditional consumption of beer and Leonard Cohen (open 8am-1am).

Slavoj Wesico (a.k.a. **Hostel Boathouse**), V náklích 1a (tel. 402 10 76). From Holešovice station or Metro A: Staroměstská, take tram #17 south to "Černý Kůň." Descend by the balustrade on the river side and walk all the way to the Vltava; be sure to look for it during the daytime. Friendly and energetic staff offers meals (big cooked breakfasts 50kč, dinners 70kč) and laundry service (80kč per load) while keeping the place strikingly clean. Beds in 3- to 5-bed dorms perched above a working boathouse 250kč (300kč for just one night). 50kč key deposit. Call ahead.

V podzámčí, V podzámčí 27 (tel. 472 27 59). From Metro C: Budějovická, take bus #192 to the third stop—ask the driver to stop at "Nad Rybníky." Eva, the Czech in charge, is a delight to talk to. Kitchen, satellite TV, laundry service (100kč), and 2 cats. 2- to 4-person dorms with beds and loft mattresses 240kč per person.

Libra-Q, Senovážné nám. 21 (tel. 24 23 17 54; fax 24 22 15 79). Metro B: nám. Republiky or C: Hlavní Nádraži. Scores high on location—just above the *Elle* and *Bohemian Model* offices. Oh, and also right by the edge of Staré Město. Triples and quads 300kč per person; 8-bed dorms 280kč per person.

Domov Mládeže, Dykova 20 (tel. 25 06 88; fax 25 14 29). From Metro A: nám. Jiřího z Poděbrad, follow Nitranská and turn left on Dykova. Possibly the most enjoyable hostel trek ever. 60 beds in the tree-lined Vinohrady district. So peaceful you might forget you're in Prague. Clean but not sterile 2- to 7-person dorms 300kč per person (lone double 630kč). Breakfast included.

ESTEC Hostel, Vaníčkova 5, blok 5 (tel. 57 21 04 10; fax 57 21 52 63). Take bus #217 or 143 from Metro A: Dejvická to "Koleje Strahov." A mega-Strahov operation with hundreds of beds. Try for a double in the refurbished basement of blok 5; otherwise, mostly ordinary student doubles (280kč per person), with some singles (400kč), triples (250kč per person), and crowded basement dorms (180kč). Comfy bedding. Check-out 9:30am, check-in 2pm. 24hr. reception. Bar open 8pm-4am. Breakfast 50kč. Exchange office (3% commission). AmEx, Eurocard, MC, Visa.

Traveller's Hostels: Now with 8 city-center hostels, these summertime big-dorm specialists make you feel comfortable with large murals of TV newsreaders. Brand new outfits at **Dlouhá 33** (tel. 231 13 18), in Staré Město—it's the same building as the Roxy club, so let's hope it's got good soundproofing (doubles 450kč per person; triples 390kč per person; 6-bed dorms 250kč); and at **Neklanova 32** (tel. 24 91 55 32), Metro C: Vyšehrad; head down Slavojova and it's on the left. No-bunks dorm 270kč. The one at **Husova 3** (tel. 24 21 53 26) is still the classiest, with dorm beds for 400kč per person. Smack dab in Staré Město. Take Metro A to Národní třída, turn right onto Spálená (which turns into Na Perštýně after Národní), and then Husova. **Střelecký ostrov** (tel. 24 91 01 88), on the island off most Legii (Metro B: Národní třída). 300kč. **Mikulandská 5** (tel. 24 91 07 39). Metro B: Národní třída. 270kč. **Křížovnická 7** (tel. 232 09 87). Metro A: Staroměstská. 230kč. **Růžova 5** (tel. 26 01 11). Metro C: Hlavní nádraží. 220kč. **U lanové drahy 3** (tel. 53 31 60). Tram #6, 9, 12 to "Újezd" and up the stairs. 200kč.

Welcome Hostel, Zikova 13 (tel. 24 32 02 02; fax 24 32 34 89). Metro A: Dejvická; from the escalators, follow Šolinova to Zikova. A free beer welcomes weary travelers. Singles 350kč; bed in a double 240kč. Check-out 9:30am, check-in 2:30pm. They also run a Strahov dorm, Vaničková 5, blok 3 (tel. 52 71 90; same directions as for ESTEC, above). Singles 300kč; doubles 440kč.

Hotel Junior, Žitná 12 (tel. 29 29 84; fax 24 22 39 11), right next to CKM. Metro B: Karlovo nám. Decor on the cutting edge of 1970s revival. The hotel is expensive and block-booked months in advance, but they also run a **hostel:** dorm beds 500kč, 400kč with ISIC/HI card (400/300kč Nov.-Dec.). Big buffet breakfast included.

Hotels and Pensions

With so many tourists infiltrating Prague, hotels are upgrading both service and appearance, and budget hotels are now scarce. Beware that hotels may try to bill you for a more expensive room than the one you in which you stayed. Arm yourself with pen, paper, and receipts. The good and cheap ones require reservations up to a month in advance. Call, then confirm by fax.

Hotel Standart, Přístavní 2 (tel. 87 52 58 or 66 71 04 71; fax 80 67 52). From Metro C: Vltavská, take tram #1,3,14, or 25 to "Dělnická." Continue along the street, then make a left onto Přístavní. Very quiet neighborhood that gets very dark at night. Spotless hall showers and WC. Singles 595kč; doubles 750kč; triples 995kč; quads 1090kč. All rooms 350kč per person for HI members. Breakfast included.

Pension Unitas, Bartolomějská 9 (tel. 232 77 00; fax 232 77 09), in Staré Město. Metro B: Národní. An old monastery where Beethoven once performed, then a

Communist jail where Václav Havel was incarcerated. Havel's basement room (P6) is now a quad outfitted with bunk beds, small windows, and heavy iron doors (1900kč). Singles 1000kč; doubles 1200kč; triples 1650kč. The Convent of the Gray Sisters still owns the place, so no smoking or drinking in the rooms.

Hotel Unitour, Senovážné nám. 21 (tel. 24 10 25 36; fax 24 22 15 79). The budget hotel arm of Libra-Q (above) has clean singles (750kč, with shower 890kč); doubles (810kč/1250kč); triples (1200kč/1480kč); and quads (1400kč).

B&B U Oty (Ota's House), Radlická 188 (tel./fax 57 21 53 23; http:// www.bbuoty. netforce.cz). 400m from Metro B: Radlická, up the slope. Ota is an affable Anglophone. Kitchen facilities and free laundry services available after 3 nights. Singles 450kč; doubles 700kč; triples 900kč; quads 1200kč. 100kč per person additional if staying only 1 night. Free parking, provided you won't use the car while in Prague.

Pension U Medvídků, Na Perštýně 7 (tel. 24 21 19 16; fax 24 22 09 30). Metro B: Národní. Very central. Upstairs from a popular pub, the renovated rooms somehow escape the noise. Price varies during the year but is usually 500kč per person off-season and 650kč June-Sept., breakfast included. 3 doubles and 5 triples; single travelers pay 50% extra for a room of their own.

Hotel Kafka, Cimburkova 24 (tel. 27 31 01; fax 24 22 57 69), in Žižkov near the TV tower. Brand-new hotel amid 19th-century buildings, near restaurants and *pivnice*. In July: singles 1150kč; doubles 1600kč; triples 1950kč; quads 2300kč; all with WC. In August, add 200-300kč. Off-season, subtract 550-800kč. Breakfast 90kč.

Pension Sunshine, Drahobejlova 17 (tel./fax 82 31 88). Metro B: Českomoravská. The Welcome Hostel's foray into the budget hotel business, away from the center but near the metro. Singles 500kč; doubles, triples and quads with bath 380kč per person. Breakfast included.

Purple House, Krásova 25 (tel. 27 14 90; fax 271 84 71). Metro A: Jiřího z Poděbrad, then along Slavíkova, right onto Kubelíkova, and left down Krásova. More pink than purple. Two apartments with baths go for US$40-50, depending on number of guests (up to 4) and length of stay. Dorm beds US$10. One double with shower US$25.

Camping

Campsites have taken over not only the outskirts, but also the centrally located islands on the Vltava. Their bungalows must be reserved in advance, but tent space is generally available. Should one campsite be all booked up, chances are another lies across the fence. Tourist offices sell a guide to sites near the city (15kč).

Císařská Louka, on a peninsula on the Vltava. Metro B: Smíchovské nádraží, then almost any tram to "Lihovar." Walk toward the river and onto the shaded path. Alternatively, take the ferry service from Smíchovské nádraží. **Caravan Park** (tel. 54 09 25; fax 54 33 05) sits near the ferry, and **Caravan Camping** (tel. 54 56 82) is near the tram. Both charge 95kč per person, 90-140kč per tent. Caravan Park has 2-bed bungalows for 480kč and 4-bed ones for 720kč. Caravan Camping has singles for 365kč, doubles for 630kč, and triples for 945kč.

Sokol Troja, Trojská 171 (tel./fax 688 11 77). Prague's largest campground, north of the center in the Troja district. From Metro C: Nádraží Holešovice, take bus #112 to "Kazanka," the fourth stop, then walk 100m. 70-150kč per tent, 90kč per person. Dorm, bungalow, and flat accommodation at 155kč, 165kč, and 135kč per person respectively. If full, at least 4 nearly identical places are on the same road.

Na Vlachovce, Zenklova 217 (tel./fax 688 02 14). Take bus #175 or 102 from Nádraží Holešovice toward Okrouhlická, get off, and continue in the same direction. If you've ever felt like crawling into a barrel of *Budvar*, this bungalow city provides romantic 2-person barrels at 200kč per bed. If you miss the beer, the pub in front pours it for 15kč. Great view of Prague. Reserve a week ahead. The pension attached has doubles with bath for 900kč, breakfast included.

FOOD

The basic rule—there are exceptions—is that the nearer you are to the tourist throngs on Staroměstské nám., Karlův most, and Václavské nám., the more you'll pay. Check your bill carefully—you'll pay for anything the waiter brings, including ketchup and bread, and restaurants have been known to massage bills higher than they ought. In Czech lunch spots, *hotová jídla* (prepared meals) are cheapest: away from the center you can have pork, cabbage, dumplings, and a pint of beer for 50kč. Outlying metro stops become impromptu marketplaces in the summer; look for the daily vegetable market at the intersection of Havelská and Melantrichova in Staré Město. A number of vegetarian eateries are opening up, but in many Czech restaurants veggie options are still limited to fried cheese dishes and cabbage.

Supermarkets

Go to the basement level for food halls in Czech department stores or supermarkets.

Krone department store (tel. 24 23 04 77), on Václavské nám. at the intersection with Jindřišská. Metro A or B: Můstek. Open Mon.-Fri. 8am-7pm, Sat. 8am-6pm, Sun. 10am-6pm.

Kotva department store (tel. 24 21 54 62), corner of Revoluční and nám. Republiky. Metro B: nám. Republiky. Consistently well-stocked. Food halls open Mon. 7am-7pm, Tues.-Fri. 7am-8pm, Sat. 8am-6pm.

Tesco's, Národní 26 (tel. 24 22 79 71). Right next to Metro B: Národní tř. Open Mon.-Fri. 7am-8pm, Sat. 8am-6pm, Sun. 9am-6pm.

Staré Město

Lotos, Platnéřská 13 (tel. 232 23 90). Metro A: Staroměstská. Vegetarian restaurant which deserves applause for its veggie Czech food (soy cubes with dumplings 52kč) and for liberal use of the leek (leek soup 15kč; lentil salad with leek, carrot, and raisins 39kč). Wheat-yeast *Pilsner* 22kč for 0.5L; 7-herb tea 19kč. Open daily 11am-10pm.

Klub Architektů, Betlémské nám. 169 (tel. 24 40 12 14). Walk through the gates and descend to the right. A 12th-century cellar thrust into the 20th century with sleek table settings and copper pulley lamps. Plenty of veggie options (60-70kč); meat dishes around 100kč. Chinese cabbage soup 20kč. Open daily 11am-midnight.

U Medvídků, Na Perštýně 7 (tel. 24 22 09 30), outskirts of Staré Město. Metro B: Národní tř. There's a *restaurace* and a *pivnice*, but the latter is cheaper and more fun. Pretty good Czech food at very good prices has been consumed here since 1466, including "Bear's Foot toast" (35kč) and beef sirloin with cranberries (71kč). Open Mon.-Sat. 11:30am-11pm, Sun. 11:30am-10pm.

Shalom, Maiselova 18 (tel. 24 81 09 29; fax 24 81 09 12). Metro A: Staroměstská. Fine kosher lunches in the old Jewish Quarter. Set menu each day 120-350kč. Buy tickets beforehand from T.A. Mantena, the travel agent across the road (tel. 232 10 49; open Sun.-Thurs. 9am-6:30pm). Order tickets well in advance for holidays. Restaurant open daily 11:30am-2pm.

Country Life, Melantrichova 15 (tel. 24 21 33 66). Metro A and B: Můstek. The Prague link in an international chain, this might be the best veggie takeout place in town. Filled rolls around 30kč, veggie *guláš* 21kč, and a range of juices. Prices 25% lower after 5pm. Open Mon.-Thurs. 10am-6pm, Fri. 10am-2:30pm, Sun. noon-6pm. Attached health food shop open Mon.-Thurs. 8:30am-6pm, Fri. 8:30am-2:30pm.

Nové Město (New Town)

Velryba (The Whale), Opatovická 24 (tel. 24 91 23 91). Metro B: Národní tř. Relaxed with a bit of chic, this cafe-restaurant stores a gallery in the back. Mixed crowd of locals, American expats, business types, and tourists enjoys inexpensive Czech dishes (60-90kč) and drinks coffee, beer, and Twining's tea. Can you see the whale on the sea-green wall? Open daily 11am-2am.

Restaurace U Pravdů, Žitná 15 (tel. 29 95 92). Metro B: Karlovo nám. A deservedly popular Czech lunch spot, where spillover from the high-ceilinged wood-and-white-plaster dining room gets to sit in the shady beer garden. Fish dishes 61-76kč, soya "meat" 37kč, pork 77kč, potato *knedlíky* 15kč. Big glass of *Staropramen* beer 16kč, *Radegast* 19kč. Open Mon.-Fri. 10am-11pm, Sat.-Sun. 11am-11pm.

Černý Pivovar, Karlovo nám. 15 (tel. 294 45 23). Metro B: Karlovo nám. Under reconstruction in '97, but should be worth a visit in '98 *if* they've kept the heroic socialist murals. The Czech usuals—pork (60kč) and salads (25kč). Non-socialist AmEx and thoroughly bourgeois MC accepted. Open daily 11am-10pm.

CZECH REPUBLIC

Jáma (The Hollow), V Jámě 7 (tel. 90 00 04 13). Metro A and C: Muzeum. Hidden off Vodičkova. Attracts a diverse but largely non-Czech crowd. Weekend brunches (89-119kč) all come with very civilized free coffee refills. Other options include a "super veggie burro" (124kč) and burgers (99-116kč). Open daily 11am-1am.

Góvinda, Soukenická 27. Metro B: nám. Republiky. Rama and Krishna gaze upon diners and their delicious vegetarian stews. A plate with the works for 50kč. Menu changes daily so you won't get bored. Lectures on the *Bhagavadgitá* every Wed. at 6:30pm. Open Mon.-Sat. 11am-5pm.

Pizzeria Kmotra, V jirchářích 12 (tel. 24 91 58 09). Metro B: Národní tř. Downstairs pizza joint with pleasant ground-floor cafe. Queue for your table and then enjoy hot cabbage salad (30kč), mugs of *Gambrinus* (17kč per 0.3L), and big pizzas (56-83kč) with huge peppers on them. Open daily 11am-1am.

U Rozvařlů, Na poříčí (tel. 24 21 93 57). Metro B: nám. Republiky. The last of a Communist breed evolving to survive. The glass and steel remain—but shine has replaced the grit. Nowadays you can sit down with *guláš* (34kč) and Coke or beer (12kč). This is still as close as it comes to the red old days, so pay your respects. Open Mon.-Fri. 8am-7:30pm, Sat. 8am-7pm, Sun. 10am-5pm.

Malá Strana (Lesser Side)

Bar bar, Všehrdova 17 (tel. 53 29 41). Metro A: Malostranská. Left off Karmelitská walking down from Malostranské nám. A jungle jungle of salads salads with meat meat, fish fish, cheese cheese or just veggies veggies (54-89kč). The other choice is, surprisingly, not fried pork with french fries, but pancakes pancakes—sweet sweet (18-48kč) or savory savory (49-92kč). The stuttering eatery has a good vibe, good music, and 40 varieties of good whiskey (from 41kč). *Velkopopovický kozel* on tap (15kč per 0.5L). Open Mon.-Fri. 11am-midnight, Sat.-Sun. noon-midnight.

Bohemia Bagel, Újezd 16 (tel. 53 10 02). Metro A: Malostranská, or tram #22 to "Újezd." Following fast on the heels of Budapest's New York Bagels, Bohemia Bagel provides a 2nd place in Eastern Europe for bagelophiles to get their fixes. All the usual flavors, plus some surprising ones. Bagel with cream cheese 35kč, 5 plain ones for 60kč. Open Mon.-Fri. 7am-2am, Sat.-Sun. 9am-2am.

Malostranská Hospoda, Karmelitská 25 (tel. 53 20 76), just by Malostranské nám. Metro A: Malostranská. Chairs spill out onto the square from the pub's vaulted interior. The usual long table in the corner surrounded by beer and *becherovka* fans is made up of women. Good *guláš* (58kč), Batman! Draft *Staropramen* 13kč per 0.5L. English menu. Open Mon.-Sat. 10am-midnight, Sun. 11am-midnight.

U Švejků, Újezd 22 (tel. 52 56 29; fax 29 14 76). Metro A: Malostranská. Aggressively touristy with a nightly violinist, but prices are low and portions large, though there's practically nothing for vegetarians. But the place does have a picture of Emperor Franz Josef on the wall—fans of Hašek's novel may wonder about its condition…Good soldiers should partake of beef in cream sauce (79kč), dumplings (10kč), or garlic soup (19kč). Open daily 11am-midnight.

Cafes

When Prague journalists are bored, they churn out yet another "Whatever happened to cafe life?" feature. Ignore their pessimism, and try some of the places listed below.

U malého Glena, Karmelitská 23 (tel. 535 81 15 or 90 00 39 67), just south off Malostranské nám. Metro A: Malostranská. The "light entrée" menu has veggie plates (70kč) and *croque-m'sieur* (80kč). Baked potatoes go for 90-130kč, and the delicious stuffed pita breads are 70-95kč. Czechs and foreigners hang around here; some descend to the Maker's Mark basement bar for nightly jazz or blues at 9pm (cover 50-70kč). Open daily 7:30am-2am.

U zeleného čaje, Nerudova 19 (tel. 53 26 83), up from Malostranské nám. Metro A: Malostranská. Part of the admirable effort to get Czechs drinking tea, this small cafe serves 4 salads (15kč per 100g) and a huge variety of teas (15-40kč), all lovingly and multi-lingually described in the extensive tea menu. Open daily 10:30am-7:30pm.

Kavárna Medúza, Belgická 17. Antique shop masquerading as a cafe. Fluffed-up Victorian seats and lots of coffee (17-27kč), with 18 versions of the alcohol-added variety (37-62kč). Open Mon.-Fri. 11am-1am.

Blatouch, Vězenská 4 (tel. 232 86 43). Metro A: Staroměstská. Women-run cafe in Staré Město. Ever-so-slightly artsy feel, but stops well short of insufferable. Cocktails are 50-70kč, a bowl of olives to chew on 32kč, and a pleasantly large *Bernard* beer 24kč. Open daily 11am-midnight.

Cafe-Bar Bílý Orel (White Eagle), Minská 10, in Malostranské nám. Metro A: Malostranská. The stylish interior—an improbable mix of UFO-like globules, odd curves, and fish—makes up for the higher prices (asparagus in bechamel sauce 129kč). 0.3L Pilsner 35kč, coffees from 30kč, and lots of spirits. Open daily 8:30am-1:30am.

U Knihomola, Mánesova 79 (tel. 627 77 68). Metro A: Jiřího z Poděbrad. An extended living room with comfy couches and coffee-table literature. Smooth jazz lulls coffee-sippers to nirvana. Coffee 20kč; carrot cake 75kč. Open Mon.-Thurs. 10am-11pm, Fri.-Sat. 10am-midnight, Sun. 11am-8pm.

The Globe Coffeehouse, Janovského 14 (tel. 66 71 26 10). Metro C: Vltavská. Tasty, bitter black coffee (20kč per cup; no free refills), a slightly pricey weekend brunch menu (omelette 120kč), and lots of English-speaking voices in pleasant literary surroundings. Open daily 10am-midnight.

U červeného páva, Kamzíková 6 (tel. 24 23 31 68). Metro A: Staroměstská. Wander down Celetná from the square and look for the sign. The Red Peacock is proof that not everything around Staroměstské nám. is over-touristed ghastliness. Quiet cafe-bar for gays and straights. Espresso 28kč, *Staropramen* 22kč.

SIGHTS

Central Prague is structured by three streets that form a leaning "T." The long stem of the T is the boulevard **Václavské nám.** (Wenceslas Sq.). The **Národní Muzeum** sits at the bottom of the T. Busy and pedestrian, **Na příkopě** forms the right arm, leading to **nám. Republiky.** On the left, **28. října** becomes **Národní** after a block, leading to the **Národní Divadlo** on the river. A maze of small streets leads to **Staroměstské nám.,** two blocks above the T. There are two prominent **St. Nicholas churches**—in Malá Strana near the castle and in Staroměstské nám.—and two **Powder Towers**—one in the castle and another in nám. Republiky. Strollers will find that Prague has plenty of green space along Malá Strana's **Petřínské Sady.** Miles of pathways traverse the Kinsky, Strahov, Lobkowic, Schönborn, and Seminář **gardens,** but most are badly eroded. Many try the promenade on the banks of the Vltava south of **most Legií** along Nové Město's **Masarykoro nábřeží.** Gorgeous greenery lies southeast of Staré Město in **Vinohrady.** This quarter's hills also offer great views of the town.

Václavské Náměstí (Wenceslas Square)

> I've taken my grandchildren to the top of Wenceslas Square where St. Wenceslas looks over the entire square. I tell them to imagine all the things St. Wenceslas might have seen sitting there on his horse: the trading markets hundreds of years ago, Hitler's troops, the Soviet tanks, and our Velvet Revolution in 1989. I can still imagine these things; it's the boulevard where much of our history, good and bad, has passed.
> —Bedřich Šimáček, tram #22 driver, quoted in *The Prague Post*

Not so much a square as a broad boulevard, **Václavské nám.** owes its name and fame to the equestrian statue of the Czech ruler and saint **Václav** (Wenceslas), in front of the National Museum. Václav has presided over a century of turmoil and triumph, witnessing no fewer than five revolutions from his pedestal. The perfectionist sculptor Myslbek completed Václav after 25 years of deliberation: as others gasped at its 1912 unveiling, poor Myslbek just mumbled, "It could have been bigger." The statue is big enough for most and has stood for nearly a century as a symbol of Czech national identity. The new Czechoslovak state was proclaimed here in 1918, and in 1969, Jan Palach set himself on fire in protest against the 1968 Soviet invasion.

Václavské nam. sweeps down from the Národní Muzeum past department stores, stately parks, posh hotels, fast food joints, and trashy casinos. The view of the museum from Můstek's base is hypnotic at full moon, but keep your wits about you:

despite frequent police sweeps, the square has become one of the seediest areas in Prague. Behind the museum, the monstrous six-lane **Wilsonova** runs across the Vltava and all the way to Holešovice. Originally named Vitězného února (Victorious February) in honor of the 1948 Soviet-backed Communist seizure of power, the street was re-christened in 1989 after U.S. President Woodrow Wilson, who helped forge the interwar Czechoslovak state. The **Radio Prague Building,** behind the National Museum, was the scene of a tense battle during Prague Spring between Soviet tanks and Prague citizens trying to protect the radio studios by human barricade. The station managed to transmit impartial reports for the first 14 hours of the invasion. North of the Václav statue, the Art Nouveau style, expressed in everything from lampposts to windowsills, dominates the square. The premier example is the 1903 **Hotel Evropa.** Since its construction, the hotel and its cafe have been a socialite center.

From the north end of Václavské nám., take a quick detour to Jungmannovo nám. and **Panna Maria Sněžná** (Church of Our Lady of the Snows). Founded by King Charles IV in 1347, this edifice was intended to be the largest church in Prague. The Gothic walls are, indeed, higher than those of any other house of worship, but the rest of the structure is still unfinished—there was only enough cash to complete the choir. It feels tiny, despite the Baroque altar and magnificently vaulted ceiling. Enter **Františkánská zahrada** through the arch at the intersection of Jungmannova and Národní. No one knows how the Franciscans who tend the rose gardens have managed to maintain such a bastion of serenity in Prague's commercial district, perhaps because most friars are too busy talking to the birds to answer questions (open daily in summer 7am-10pm, winter 8am-7pm). Under the arcades halfway down Národní stands a **memorial** honoring the hundreds of Prague's citizens beaten on November 17, 1989. A march, organized by Communists to commemorate the 50th anniversary of the Nazi execution of nine Czech students, was savagely attacked by the police— sparking further massive protests against the police and the regime itself. Václav Havel's Civic Forum movement was based at the **Lanterna magika (Magic Lantern)** theater, Národní 4, during the tense days now known as the Velvet Revolution.

Staroměstské Náměstí (Old Town Square)

A labyrinth of narrow roads and Old World alleys lead to **Staroměstské nám.,** Staré Město's thriving heart. **Jan Hus,** the Czech Republic's most famous martyred theologian, sweeps across the scene in bronze. In summer, masses of travelers sit at the base of his robes, drinking, smoking, slinging woo, and performing a hundred other deeds upon which Jan can only frown. No less than eight magnificent towers surround the square. The expansive cobblestone plaza leaves room for everyone, even the ranks of horse carriages (500kč for 20min.) and blacksmiths selling twisted metal for the price of a Trabant. The building with a bit blown off is the **Staroměstská radnice** (Old Town Hall), partially demolished by the Nazis in the final week of WWII. Prague's *radnice* has long been a witness to violence—**crosses** on the ground mark the spot where 27 Protestant leaders were executed on June 21, 1621 for staging a rebellion against the Catholic Habsburgs. The tourist office inside offers tours of the town hall's interior (open in summer daily 9am-5pm; 30kč, students 20kč). The **Old Senate,** with a magnificent coffered ceiling, boasts a Baroque stove with a figure of Justice and a sculpture of Christ. The inscription reads, "Judge justly—sons of Man." Crowds gather on the hour to watch the wonderful **astronomical clock** *(orloj)* chime with its procession of apostles, a skeleton, and a thwarted Turk. They say that the clockmaker's eyes were put out so he couldn't design another—but they say that about the man who built St. Basil's in Moscow, too.

Across from the *radnice,* the spires of **Matka Boží před Týnem** (Týn Church) rise above a huddled mass of medieval homes. The famous astronomer **Tycho Brahe** is buried inside; he overindulged at one of Emperor Rudolf's lavish dinner parties. To the left of the church, the austere **Dům U kamenného zvonu** (House at Stone Bell) shows the Gothic core that lurks beneath many of Prague's Baroque façades. The flowery **Goltz-Kinský palác** on the left is the finest of Prague's Rococo buildings. **Sv. Mikuláš** (Church of St. Nicholas) sits just across Staroměstské nám. (open Tues.-Sun.

High Windows

At decisive moments in European history, unlucky men fall from Prague's window ledges. The Hussite wars began after Catholic councillors were thrown to the mob from the New Town Hall on Karlovo nám., July 30, 1419. The Thirty Years' War devastated Europe, starting when Habsburg officials were tossed from the windows of Prague Castle's Bohemian Chancellery into a heap of steaming manure, May 23, 1618. These first and second defenestrations echo down the ages, but two more falls this century continue this somewhat macabre tradition. Fifty years ago, March 10, 1948, liberal foreign minister Jan Masaryk fell to his death from the top floor of his ministry just two weeks after the Communist takeover, and murder was always suspected but never proved. And then on February 3, 1997, Bohumil Hrabal, popular author of *I Served the King of England* and *Closely-Observed Trains*, fell from the fifth floor of his hospital window and died in his pajamas aged 82. Nothing unusual here—except that two of his books describe people choosing to fall—out of fifth-floor windows.

10am-5pm). Kilian Ignaz Dienzenhofer built the church in only three years; Dienzenhofer and his dad then built the **Sv. Mikuláš** in Malá Strana, right by the castle. Between Maiselova and Sv. Mikuláš, a plaque marks **Franz Kafka's** former home.

At Malá Štupartská, behind Matka Boží před Týnem, a thief's arm has been dangling from the entrance of **Kostel sv. Jakuba** (St. Jacob's Cathedral) for 500 years. Legend holds that a thief tried to pilfer one of the gems from the **Virgin Mary of Suffering** statue, whereupon the figure came to life, seized the thief's arm at the elbow, and wrenched it off. The monks took pity on the repentant, profusely bleeding soul and invited him to join their order. He accepted and remained pious; the arm hangs as a reminder to the faithful.

Nám. Jana Palacha, next to the Staroměstská metro, used to be called "Red Army Square" in honor of the Russians who liberated Prague in 1945. During popular unrest in 1969 and then again in November 1989, students renamed the square in honor of the late **Jan Palach,** who studied at the philosophy faculty of Charles University here on the square. In 1990, the name change was officially approved. A copy of Palach's death mask is mounted on the faculty building wall.

Josefov (Jewish Quarter)

Prague's historic Jewish neighborhood, Josefov, is located north of Staroměstské nám., along Maiselova and several side streets. Its cultural wealth lies in five well-preserved synagogues. In 1179, the Pope decreed that all good Christians should avoid contact with Jews; a year later, Prague's citizens complied with a 12-foot wall. For the next 500 years, the city's Jews were exiled to this cramped ghetto in northwest Prague. The gates were opened in 1784, and the walls came down in 1848, when the Jews were granted civil rights. The closed city bred exotic legends, many focusing on **Rabbi Loew ben Bezalel** (1512-1609), whose legendary *golem*—a creature made from mud that supposedly came to life—predates Frankenstein's monster by 200 years. The century following 1848 was not a happy one for Prague's Jews. The open quarter rapidly became a disease-racked slum, and many old buildings were demolished as the area was modernized. Finally, the Jewish people themselves were annihilated as the Nazis deported them to Terezín and then to death camps.

Hitler's perverse decision to create a "museum of an extinct race" resulted in the preservation of the old cemetery and five of the synagogues. Today the ghetto walls have been replaced by a steep admission fee to see the synagogues and museum (all sights open daily 9am-5:30pm; 450kč, students 330kč). At the 90-degree bend in U Starého hřbitova, **Starý židovský hřbitov** (Old Jewish Cemetery) remains the quarter's most popular attraction. Between the 14th and 18th centuries, 12 layers of 20,000 graves were laid. The 700-year-old **Staronová synagóga** (Old-New Synagogue) is Europe's oldest operating synagogue. En route to Staronová synagóga, **Klausová synagóga** displays rotating exhibitions of paintings and Judaica.

Next to the Staronová synagóga is the 16th-century **Vysoká synagóga** (High Synagogue). The neighboring **Židovská radnice** (Jewish Town Hall) was once the administrative control center of Josefstadt, as Jews referred to Josefov in the early 19th century. The Hebrew clock in the pink Rococo exterior of the town hall runs counterclockwise. Walk down Maiselova and turn right on Široka until you reach the **Pinkasova synagóga.** After a period of Communist neglect, the synagogue's walls once again list the names of victims of Nazi persecution. Turning right onto Maiselova again, the ornate **Maiselova synagóga** is now used to exhibit treasures from the extensive collections of the Jewish Museum—back in the hands of the city's Jewish community only since 1994.

Karlův most (Charles Bridge)

Head out of Staroměstské nám. on Jilská, and go right onto Karlova. Wandering left down Liliová leads to Bethlémské nám., where the **Betlémská kaple** (Bethlehem Chapel) stands. The present building dates from the 1950s—it's a fine reconstruction of the medieval chapel made famous by Jan Hus, the great Czech religious reformer (open daily 9am-6pm; 30kč, students 20kč). Turning back onto Karlova and left toward the river leads to **Karlův most,** which throngs with tourists and people trying to sell them things. Five years ago it was Red Army gear and dodgy black market currency deals; now it's boring watercolors and other souvenir knicknacks. King Karel (Charles) IV built this 520m bridge to replace one that washed away in 1342. The foundation stone was laid at 5:31am on July 9, 1357, the most significant astrological point for Leo—the mascot of Bohemia and now the name of a Czech porn magazine in the post-communist society. Legend has it that the builder made a pact with the devil in order to complete the massive bridge. Satan was allotted the first soul to cross the completed bridge, but the builder's wife and newborn baby unwittingly traversed the finished structure first. The devil could not take the baby's pure soul, so he cast a spell over the bridge instead. In the evening, some claim to hear the faint cry of a ghostly infant—or is it the whining of prepubescent hostel youth?

When darkness falls, the street musicians emerge—but the penalty for requesting "Wish You Were Here" is being tied up in a goatskin and lowered into the Vltava. This happened to Sv. Jan Nepomucký, although for a different reason: at the center of the bridge, the eighth statue from the right is a depiction of hapless Jan being tossed over the side of the Charles for faithfully guarding his queen's confidences from a suspicious King Václav IV. Torture by hot irons and other devices failed to loosen Jan's lips, so the King ordered that he be drowned. A halo of five gold stars supposedly appeared as Jan plunged into the icy water. The right-hand rail, from which Jan was supposedly ejected, is now marked with a cross and five stars between the fifth and sixth statues. If you like Prague, place one finger on each star and make a wish: not only is it guaranteed to come true, but any wish made on this spot will at some point in the future whisk the wisher back to Prague.

Climb the Gothic **defense tower** on the Malá Strana side of the bridge for a superb view of the city (open daily 10am-5:30pm; 30kč, students 20kč) or on the Staré Město side (same hours, same prices, different view). The stairs on the left side of the bridge (as you face the castle district) lead to **Hroznová,** where a mural honors John Lennon and the 1960s peace movement. Once interesting when the authorities kept trying to suppress it, the mural is now crumbly and the graffiti staggeringly unimaginative.

Malá Strana (Lesser Side)

The seedy hangout of criminals and counter-revolutionaries for nearly a century, the cobblestone streets of Malá Strana have, in the strange sway of Prague fashion, become the most prized real estate on either side of the Vltava. Yuppies now dream of a flat with a view of Sv. Mikuláš. Affluent foreigners sip beers in the haunts where Jaroslav Hašek and his bumbling soldier Švejk once guzzled suds (see **Food,** p. 170). The current trend seems to fit the plans of the original designer, King Otokar II, who in the 13th century dreamed of creating a powerful economic quarter. This was not to occur until the 15th century, when Austrian nobility erected grand churches and palaces. As nationalism mounted, however, the quarter became known as a rat's den of surly sailors, dealers, and drunken brawls. The 1989 revolution brought a new appreciation for the district's architecture, and careful restorations have made it one of the most enjoyable sections of Prague to visit. From Karlův most, continue straight up Mostecká and turn right into **Malostranské nám.** Dominating the square is the magnificent Baroque **Chrám sv. Mikuláše** (Church of St. Nicholas; tel. 53 69 83) with its remarkable high dome. Expensive and boring classical music concerts take place nightly. (Church open daily 9am-4pm; 25kč, students 15kč. Concert tickets an absurd 350kč, students 250kč.) Nearby on Karmelitská rises the more modest **Panna Maria Vítězna** (Church of Our Lady Victorious). The famous polished-wax statue of the **Infant Jesus of Prague,** which is said to bestow miracles on the faithful, resides within. The figurine has an elaborate wardrobe of more than 380 outfits; every sunrise, he's swaddled anew by the nuns of a nearby convent. The statue first arrived in town in the arms of a 16th-century Spanish noblewoman who married into the Bohemian royalty; mysteriously, the plague bypassed Prague shortly thereafter. In 1628, the Barefooted Carmelite nunnery gained custody of the Infant and allowed pilgrims to pray to the statue; the public has been infatuated with it ever since (open daily summer 7am-9pm, winter 8am-8pm; English mass Sun. at 12:15pm).

Designed by father-son team Kristof and Kilian Ignaz Dienzenhofer, the duo responsible for the Břevnov Monastery's undulating facade (see **Outer Prague,** p. 176), **sv. Tomáš** stands at Letenská off Malostranské nám., toward the Vltava. Rubens facsimiles await within, adjacent to the saintly reliquaries adorning the side altars. A simple wooden gate just down the street at Letenská 10 opens onto **Valdštejnská zahrada** (Wallenstein Garden), one of Prague's best-kept secrets. This tranquil 17th-century Baroque garden is enclosed by old buildings that glow golden on sunny afternoons. General Albert Wallenstein, owner of the palace of the same name and hero of Schiller's grim play, held his parties here among Vredeman de Vries's classical bronze statues—when the works were plundered by Swedish troops in the waning hours of the Thirty Years' War, Wallenstein replaced the original casts with facsimiles. **Frescoes** inside the arcaded loggia depict episodes from Virgil's *Aeneid* (open May-Sept. daily 9am-7pm). A 10-meter wall keeps the city out. Across the street from the Malostranská metro station, a plaque hidden in a lawn constitutes the **Charousková Memorial,** the sole monument to those slain in 1968. It commemorates **Marie Charousková,** a graduate student who was machine-gunned by a Soviet soldier for refusing to remove a black ribbon protesting the invasion.

Pražský Hrad (Prague Castle)

Founded 1000 years ago, Pražský Hrad has always been the seat of the Bohemian government and the center of its politics. For centuries, conflicts between medieval dynasties, Czechs and Germans, or Protestants and Catholics have played out within—sometimes plummeting down beside—its walls. This century, liberal presidents, Nazi despots, and Communist apparatchiks have all held court here. The final ideological struggle saw the socialists replaced by playwright Václav Havel, who has been known to ride his tricycle along the castle's corridors. Give the castle a full day—just don't make it Monday.

From Metro A: Malostranská, climb up the **Staré Zámecké Schody** (Old Castle Steps), and peer over the battlements on the left for a fine cityscape before passing between the two armed sentries into the castle. Museums loom almost immediately—on the right is the **Muzeum Hraček** (Museum of Toys; tel. 24 37 22 94; open daily 9:30am-5:30pm; 40kč, children and students 15kč). Left, the **Lobkovický Palác** contains a replica of Bohemia's coronation jewels and a history of the Czech lands (open Tues.-Sun. 9am-5pm; 40kč, students 20kč). Halfway up Jiřská, the tiny **Zlatá ulička** (Golden Lane) heads off to the right. Once alchemists worked here; later Kafka lived at #22; and today there is a small forest of cramped souvenir shops for tourists to squeeze in and out of. When Jiřská opens into a courtyard, to the right stand the **convent** and **basilika sv. Jiří.** The convent is home to the **National Gallery of Bohemian Art,** from the Gothic to the Baroque. In the medieval galleries, Master Theodorik's ecclesiastical portraits, the relief from Matka Boží před Týnem, and the so-called Kapucínský cycle of Christ and the apostles stand out; upstairs, the paintings by Michael Leopold Willmann (1630-1706) deserve scrutiny (open Tues.-Sun. 10am-6pm; 50kč, students and seniors 15kč; free first Fri. of each month). The basilica next door was built in 921. The tomb in the right-hand corner is St. Ludmila's, with skeleton on full display. A mason who snitched the thighbone supposedly activated a vicious curse that killed three before the mason's son restored the bone to the grave. The ticket you buy to enter the basilica (100kč, students 50kč) is also good for the cathedral, Old Royal Palace, and Powder Tower, so hold onto it (sights all open daily 9am-5pm; ticket valid for three days).

Across the courtyard stands Pražský Hrad's centerpiece, the colossal **Chrám sv. Víta** (St. Vitus's Cathedral), which may look Gothic but in fact was only finished in 1929—600 years after it was begun. To the right of the high altar stands the **tomb of sv. Jan Nepomucký,** 3m of solid, glistening silver, weighing two tons. Look for an angel holding a silvered tongue—Jan was allegedly tied in a goatskin and chucked into the Vltava for refusing to reveal the details of Queen Sophia's confession to her husband, King Václav IV. His tongue was somehow recovered and eventually silvered. The story was officially declared false in 1961, but the tongue is still on display.

Emperor Karel IV has his own bridge, university, and fortress (at **Karlštejn**)—but his tomb is in the **Royal Crypt** below the church, along with a handful of other Czech kings and all four of Karel's wives, tactfully buried in the same grave to his left. Back up the stairs in the main church, the walls of **Svatováclavská kaple** (St. Wenceslas's Chapel) are lined with precious stones and a painting cycle depicting the legend of this saint, although you won't find him looking out on the feast of Stephen anywhere. In an adjoining but inaccessible room, the real crown jewels of the kings of Bohemia are stored. More superstition claims that people who try them on inappropriately meet sticky ends—and the last to do so was Hitler's *Reichs-Protektor* Reinhard Heydrich, later assassinated by the Czech resistance. Finally—if you have mountain goat thighs—try the 287 steps of the **Cathedral Tower,** which lead to a good view of the entire city.

The **Starý královský palác** (Old Royal Palace), past the Last Judgment mosaic across the courtyard, houses the lengthy expanse of the **Vladislav Hall,** where jousting competitions once took place; upstairs is the **Chancellery of Bohemia,** the site of the second Defenestration of Prague. On May 23, 1618, angry Protestants flung two Habsburg officials (and their secretary) through the windows and into a steaming dungheap which broke their fall, signalling the start of the quite extraordinarily bloody Thirty Years' War in Europe.

There are two ways out of the Hrad. Crossing **Prašný most** (Powder Bridge), you'll see the entrance to the serene **Královská zahrada** (Royal Garden), sculpted in 1534 to include the glorious and newly renovated Renaissance palace **Belvedér.** Devastated by Swedes and Saxons during the Thirty Years' War, today the garden houses an **Orangery** and a **Fig Garden** (open Tues.-Sun. 10am-5:45pm). If you exit the castle though the main gate instead, you'll pass the **Šternberský palác** (tel. 20 51 46 34), home of the National Gallery's European art collection, whose gems include an 1815 Goya portrait; three Rubens paintings, one a fine *Visitation;* and Leonard Bramer's *Raising of Lazarus,* next to Willem Droost's *Annunciation,* formerly attributed to Rembrandt on the not unreasonable grounds that it bore his authentic signature. The genuine Rembrandt is in the next room, the *Scholar in His Study* from 1634 (hours same as basilica, above). Continuing straight for 300m after leaving the Hrad's main gate gets you to the **Loreta,** Prague's own Baroque replica of the Virgin Mary's house. Odd as it is, it's still not as strange as the grim array of cherubs that parade outside (open Tues.-Sun. 9am-12:15pm and 1-4:30pm; 45kč, students 25kč).

Outer Prague

The largest gardens in Prague, **Petřínské sady,** provide some of the most spectacular views of the city. A cable car runs to the top (6kč; look for *lanová dráha* signs), leaving from just above the intersection of Vítézná and Újezd. It stops once to deposit visitors at **Nebozízek,** Prague's most scenically endowed cafe (open daily 11am-6pm and 7-11pm). A bag of goodies stands at the summit: a small Eiffel tower; the city's observatory (info tel. 57 32 05 40); a **church of St. Lawrence;** and the ever-so-wacky laby-

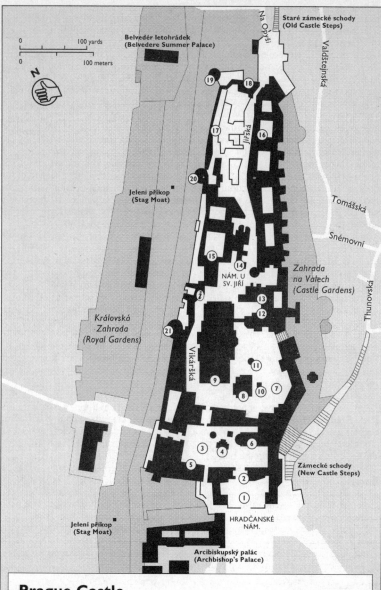

CZECH REPUBLIC

0   100 yards

0   100 meters

N

Staré zámecké schody
(Old Castle Steps)

Belvedér letohrádek
(Belvedere Summer Palace)

Na Opyši

Valdštejnská

Jeleni příkop
(Stag Moat)

Tomášská

Snémovní

Zahrada
na Valech
(Castle Gardens)

Thunovská

Královská
Zahrada
(Royal Gardens)

NÁM. U
SV. JIŘÍ

Jiřská

Vikářská

Zámecké schody
(New Castle Steps)

Jeleni příkop
(Stag Moat)

HRADČANSKÉ
NÁM.

Arcibiskupský palác
(Archbishop's Palace)

Prague Castle

Bazilika Sv. Jiří (Basilica
of St. George), 14

Bílá věž (White
Tower), 20

Cerná věž (Black
Tower), 18

Chrám Sv. Víta (St.
Vitus's Cathedral), 9

Daliborka (Daliborka
Tower), 19

I. nádvorí
(First Courtyard), 1

II. nádvorí
(Second Courtyard), 3

III. nádvorí
(Third Courtyard), 7

Jizdárna (Riding School;
Art Gallery), 13

Kaple Sv. Kríže s
klenotnicí (Chapel of
the Holy Rood), 6

Kohlova kašna (Kohl's
Fountain), 4

Lobkovický palác
(Lobkovic Palace), 16

Matyášova brána
(Matthias Gate), 2

Monolit (Monolith), 10

National Gallery of
Bohemian Art, 15

Prasná věž (Powder
Tower), 21

Socha Sv. Jiří (Statue of
St. George), 11

Španělský sál (Spanish
Hall; Castle Picture
Gallery), 5

Staré probošství
(Old Provost's
House), 8

Starý královský palac
(Old Royal Palace), 12

Zlatá ulička (Golden
Lane), 17

rinth of mirrors at **Bludiště** (open daily 10am-7pm; 20kč, students and children 10kč). Just east of the park is Strahov Stadium, the world's largest, covering the space of 10 soccer fields.

Take tram #22 west of the castle to "Břevnovský klášter" to reach **Břevnov Monastery,** Bohemia's oldest Benedictine order. The monastery was founded in 993 by King Boleslav II and St. Adalbert, each independently guided by a divine dream to create a monastery atop a bubbling stream. **Kostel sv. Markéty** (St. Margaret's Church), a Benedictine chapel, waits inside the complex. Beneath the altar rests the tomb of St. Vintíř, who, even in Bohemia, vowed to forego all forms of meat. On one particular diplomatic excursion, St. Vintíř met and dined with a German king, who was a fanatical hunter; the main course was an enormous pheasant slain that morning by the monarch's own hand. The saint prayed for delivery from the myriad *faux pas* possibilities, whereupon the main course sprang to life and flew out the window. The green belltower and red tile roof of the monastery building are all that remain of the original Romanesque construction; the complex was redesigned in high Baroque by the Dienzenhofer father and son team. During the Soviet occupation, the monastery was allegedly used to store truckloads of secret police files. Guided tours set off around the grounds (Sat. 9am; Sat.-Sun. 10:30am, 1, 2:30, and 4pm; 30kč).

Bus #112 winds from Metro C: Nádraží Holešovice to **Troja,** the site of French architect J. B. Mathey's masterful **château.** The pleasure palace, overlooking the Vltava from north of the U-shaped bend, includes a terraced garden, an oval staircase, and a collection of 19th-century Czech paintings (open Tues.-Sun. 9am-5pm). The tourist office carries schedules of **free concerts** in the château's great hall.

The former haunt of Prague's 19th-century romantics, **Vyšehrad** is clothed in nationalistic myths and the legends of a once-powerful Czech empire. It is here that Princess Libuše prophesied the founding of Prague and embarked on her search for the first king of Bohemia. The 20th century has passed the castle by, and Vyšehrad's elevated pathways now escape the shotgun tourists of Staré Město. Quiet walkways lead between crumbling stone walls to a magnificent **church,** a black Romanesque rotunda, and one of the Czech Republic's most celebrated sites—**Vyšehrad Cemetery** (home to the remains of Dvořák and Božena Němcová of the 500kč bill). Even the Metro C: Vyšehrad subway stop has a movie-sweep vista of Prague (open 24hr.).

For a magnificent view of Staré Město and the castle from the east, stroll up forested **Pohled z Vítkova** (Vítkov Hill), topped by the world's largest equestrian monument. One-eyed Hussite leader Jan Žižka scans the terrain for Crusaders, whom he stomped out on this spot in 1420. From Metro B: Křižíkova, walk down Thámova, through the tunnel, and up the hill.

Although less a pilgrimage destination than the Old Jewish Cemetery, the **New Jewish Cemetery,** far to the southeast, is one of Central Europe's largest burial grounds. Kafka is interred here; obtain a map and, if you're male, a mandatory head covering from the attendant before you start hunting for the tombstone. The main entrance is at Metro A: Želivského (open Sun.-Thurs. 9am-5pm, Fri. 9am-1pm).

Prague's ancient wine-growing district, **Vinohrady** is short on history but wins the gold for greenest. Nature has overrun the streets with plane trees and vines, but the crumbling mansions never put up a fuss, and enjoy the shade of a luscious canopy. Tranquil terrace bars sprout up throughout the quarter.

Museums

Národní muzeum (National), Václavské nám. 68 (tel. 49 71 11). Metro A or C: Muzeum. Soviet soldiers mistook this landmark for a government building and fired on it; traces of the damage are still visible. This fact is more interesting than the collection inside. Open daily May-Sept. 10am-6pm, Oct.-April 9am-5pm. Closed first Tues. each month. 40kč, students 15kč. Free first Mon. each month.

Národní galérie: It's spread around nine different locations—the **Šternberský palác** and **Klášter sv. Jiří** are described above in the "Pražský Hrad" section. The other major gallery is the **Klášter sv. Anežky** (St. Agnes's Cloister), where the 19th-century Czech art collection is displayed. Metro A: Staroměstská. These 3 are all open Tues.-Sun. 10am-6pm. 50kč, students 15kč. A booklet describing the other venues is available at the cashier.

Bertramka Mozart muzeum, Mozartova 169 (tel. 54 38 93). Metro B: Anděl. Take a left on Plzeňská, and look for a green sign pointing up the slope on the left. Mozart, a guest at Villa Bertramka, dashed off the overture to *Don Giovanni* here the day before it opened in 1787. Open daily 9:30am-6pm. 50kč, students 30kč. Concerts are held Wed.-Fri. in summer: call for ticket info. The gardens are free, restful, and near the Malá Strana cemetery.

Muzeum hlavního města Prahy (Municipal), Na poříčí 52 (tel. 24 81 67 72). Metro B or C: Florenc. Holds the original calendar board from the town hall's astronomical clock and a 1:480 scale model of old Prague, precise to the last window pane of more than 2000 houses and all of Prague's great monuments. See what your hostel looked like in 1834. Leave a 100kč deposit at the desk to borrow an English guidebook to walk you through the fine historical galleries. Open Tues.-Sun. 9am-6pm. 20kč, students 5kč. Other exhibits from the collection reside in the **Dům U kamenného zvonu,** Staroměstské nám., left of Matka Boží před Týnem. Open Tues.-Sun. 10am-6pm. 75kč, students 35kč.

Památník národního písemnictví (National Literature), Strahovské nádvoři 1 (tel. 81 67 72). Walk from the castle's main gate and bear left. The star attraction here is the **Strahov library,** with its magnificent **Theological and Philosophical Halls.** The frescoed, vaulted ceilings of the two Baroque reading rooms were intended to spur enlightened monks to the loftiest peaks of erudition. Great pagan thinkers of antiquity oversee their progress from the ceiling in the Philosophical Hall. Open Tues.-Sun. 9am-5pm. 15kč, students 5kč.

Rudolfinum, Alšova nábř. 12 (tel. 24 89 32 05; fax 231 92 93). Metro A: Staroměstská. The Czech Philharmonic shares a building with one of Prague's oldest galleries. Rotating art exhibits in an immense Art Nouveau interior. The columned cafe at the end seems too elegant to be self-serve. Open Tues.-Sun. 10am-6pm. 40kč, students 20kč.

Uměleckoprůmyslové muzeum (Decorative Arts), 17. listopadu 2 (tel. 24 81 12 41), across the street from Rudolfinum. Metro A: Staroměstská. Fun furniture exhibit with detailed English handouts so you know what's what. Some glass, too. And a good view of the Old Jewish Cemetery, from the windows by the WC. Open Tues.-Sun. 10am-6pm. 40kč, students 10kč.

ENTERTAINMENT

For a list of current concerts and performances, consult *The Prague Post, Threshold,* or *Domĕsta-Downtown* (the latter two are free and distributed at many cafes and restaurants). Most shows begin at 7pm; unsold tickets are sometimes available 30 minutes before showtime. Most of Prague's theaters shut down in July and return in August only to provide tourists with re-running attractions. The selection is more varied off-season: the peak happens around mid-May to early June, when the **Prague Spring Festival** draws musicians from around the world. Tickets (300-2000kč) may sell out as early as a year in advance; try **Bohemia Ticket International,** Salvátorská 6, next to Čedok (tel. 24 22 78 32; fax 24 81 03 68; open Mon.-Fri. 9am-6pm, Sat. 9am-4pm, Sun. 10am-3pm). Prague is particularly fine for the budget opera buff: **Národní divadlo, Stavovské divadlo,** and **Státní opera** all churn out the stuff, and while performances rarely scintillate, the staggeringly low prices do. One worthwhile film club is the **Kino** cafe-bar, Karlovo nám. 19 (entry on Odborů; tel. 24 91 57 65), which shows Czech films with English subtitles (50-60kč).

Národní divadlo (National Theater), Národní třída 2/4 (info tel. 24 91 34 37). The "Golden Shrine" features drama, opera, and ballet. Tickets 100-1000kč. Box office open Mon.-Fri. 10am-6pm, Sat.-Sun. 10am-12:30pm and 3-6pm, and 30min. before performances.

Stavovské divadlo (Estates Theater), Ovocný trh 1(info tel. 24 21 50 01). Metro A or B: Můstek. Recently renovated, this is where *Don Giovanni* premiered all those years ago. Mostly classic theater now, some opera and ballet, with earphones for simultaneous translation. Use the Národní divadlo box office, above, or turn up 30min. before the show and try your luck.

Státní opera (State Opera), Wilsonova 4, between the Metro A or C Muzeum stop and Hlavní Nádraží (tel. 26 53 53). Though not as famous as the Národní or Stavovské divadlo, the opera retains an impressive program. Tickets 50-600kč. Box office open Mon.-Fri. 10am-5:30pm, Sat.-Sun. 10am-noon and 1-5:30pm.

Lanterna magika (The Magic Lantern), Národní 4 (tel. 24 21 26 91). Once revolutionary and internationally influential as the headquarters of the Velvet Revolution, the Lanterna magika now serves up touristy "multimedia" spectaculars that don't really come off. Box office open Mon.-Fri. 10am-8pm, Sat.-Sun. 3-8pm.

Říše Loutek (Marionette Theater), Žatecká 1 (tel. 232 34 29), in Staré Město. Metro A: Staroměstská. Puppetry is taken seriously in the Czech Republic, and isn't just for kids. The touristy-but-great-fun version of *Don Giovanni* will almost certainly still be running. Tickets 490kč, students 390kč. Box office open 10am-8pm.

NIGHTLIFE

As everywhere else in Europe, club owners in Prague know the best way to rake in the cash is to pump out Abba all night to the traveling hordes. Or you can retreat to the Karlův most to sing along with Eurotrash or—better—aspiring Britpop guitarists. The most authentic way to enjoy Prague at night is through an alcoholic fog; the clubs and live venues below should satisfy the need for a *pivo* and an injection of *takzvaná populární takzvaná hudba*—so-called popular so-called music.

Beerhalls and Pubs

U Vystřeleného Oka, U božích bojovníků 3 (tel. 49 24 47 57), off Husitská. From Metro A: Flora or Metro C: Hlavní Nádraží, take tram #26 to "Lipanská." Walk 1 block east of Seifertova, turn right on Chlumova through Prokopovo nám., turn left on Husitská, and then right on the tiny long-named street. All-Czech, all-student. A bright hangout for dark-clad, dark-souled folks, some of whom prefer to sit around the tables outside. *Radegast* 10kč. Open Mon.-Sat. 3:30pm-1am.

Taz Pub, U Obecního Domu 3 (tel. 21 10 11 13). Metro B: nám. Republiky, on the street running along the right side of the county house. A somewhat young, mostly Czech crowd comes here to drink, listen to loud music, and smoke pot (legal in the Czech Republic, although dealing is not). Imported beers (30-40kč). Open Mon.-Fri. noon-2am, Sat.-Sun. 2pm-2am.

Cafe Gulu Gulu, Betlémské nám. 8 (tel. 90 01 25 81). A hangout for the Czech university crowd and summer backpackers. Fun-loving, from the graffiti to the frequent impromptu musical jams. By 11pm, people are hanging out of windowsills to get a place to sit. *Eggenberg* 25kč. Open daily 10am-1am.

Újezd, Újezd 18 (tel. 53 83 62). Metro A: Malostranská. The business card features a bespectacled smoker, but neither the basement beer cave nor the upstairs cafeclub shows a trace of pretense. A mid-20s crowd laughs the night away even on Mon. DJ or live music (acid jazz) 3 times a week. Open nightly 6pm-3am.

Molly Malone's, U obecního dvora 4. Metro A: Malostranská. Irish prove they're the best fun at the cozy bar and washing room. The drying drawers are just for show. A draft of *Staropramen* is 30kč, and Guinness is cheaper than in Ireland at 65kč per pint. Open Sun.-Thurs. noon-midnight, Fri.-Sat. noon-1:45am.

Cafe Marquis de Sade, a.k.a. **Cafe Babylon,** Templová 8 (tel. 232 34 06), between nám. Republiky and Staroměstské nám. Metro B: nám. Republiky. Enough breathing space, even if no seating space. The band strikes up old pops when in full ensemble, but mellows out to jazz when only a couple of members show up. The "de Sade" of the cafe appears only on the walls—the burgundy/orange color looks more like coagulated blood than paint. Beer 25kč. Open daily until 1am or later.

U Fleků, Křemencova 11 (tel. 24 91 51 18). Founded in 1491, the oldest surviving brewhouse in Prague is a work of art. The beer garden boasts graffitied walls, looming shade-trees, and a gazebo where bands play nightly. The 39kč per 0.4L of home-brewed beer ensures no one gets drunk. Open daily 9am-11pm.

U Sv. Tomáše, Letenská 12 (tel. 57 32 01 01). Metro A: Malostranská. The mighty dungeons echo with boisterous beer songs and slobbering toasts. The homemade brew is 30kč, as are the other six beers on tap. Live brass band starts nightly around 7pm. Open daily 11:30am-midnight.

Sport Bar Praha, Ve Smečkách 30 (tel. 24 19 63 66). Nonstop ESPN spouting from 3 wide-screen TVs. The schedule of what the baseball-capped masses will be watching is posted. Beer 32kč. Open Sun.-Thurs. 10am-2am, Fri.-Sat. till 4am.

Jo's Bar, Malostranské nám. 7 (tel. 53 12 51), Metro A: Malostranská. If you can't bear the idea that the people at the next table might not speak English, all-American Jo's Bar may be for you. Other guides say this is where the *Let's Go*-toting summer crowds come. We like to think they're more adventurous than that. *Staropramen* 25kč. Long Island iced tea 95kč. Cuban cigars 90-490kč.

Clubs and Discos

Roxy, Dlouhá 33 (tel. 231 63 31). The Roxy's not afraid to experiment with a variety of music, which means the inspired and the less inspired happily rub shoulders. The venue, a beat-up old theater, is a lot of fun; the moody crowd looks perfectly at home. Open nightly from 8pm.

Agharta, Krakovská 5 (tel. 24 21 29 14), just down Krakovská from Václavské nám. The "Jazz Centrum" also operates a CD shop. Nightly live jazz ensembles, starting at 9pm. 80kč cover, and beer an expensive 40kč, but the music is great and the vibration moderately groovy. Open nightly 7pm-1am.

Radost FX, Bělehradská 120 (tel. 25 69 98). Metro C: I.P. Pavlova. Tourists do come here, but it's still the place where Czechs want to be seen. Prague's slickest outfit tries to take music seriously. *Staropramen* 35kč. Cover from 50kč. The vegetarian cafe upstairs serves chili until 5am (95kč). Open 8pm-dawn.

Klub X, Na příkopě 15 (tel. 24 21 60 73). Metro A and B: Můstek. Lots of noise in this amiably shabby basement club. Men dance in sneakers, women in chunky black shoes—or maybe they're practicing for the Stairmaster? 26kč for 0.5L beer. Open Mon.-Thurs. 9pm-6am, Fri.-Sat. 9pm-noon, Sun. 9pm-6am.

Rock Cafe, Národní 20 (tel. 24 91 44 16). Anything but grunge. The bands that play here are the best that pass through Prague. Look for the Communist mural in hot pink, and the punk dominatrix threatening with a whip: "The wages of sin are death." On live-musicless nights, dominatrix wannabes rule the dance floor. Cover 50kč. Open Mon.-Fri. 10pm-3am, Sat.-Sun. 8pm-3am.

Palác Akropolis, Kubelíkova 27 (tel. 697 64 11). Metro A: Jiřího z Poděbrad, then down Slavíkova and right onto Kubelíkova. Live bands several times a week; doors open at 7:30pm. Top Czech act Psi Vojaci are occasional visitors.

The Maker's Mark, Karmelitská 23 (tel. 535 81 15), below "U malého Glena" (see **Cafes,** p. 170). This small bar hosts bouncy jazz or white blues from Stan the Man nightly at 9pm. Beer 25kč. Cover 50-70kč. Open daily 8pm-2am.

Lávka, Novotného lávka 1 (tel. 24 21 47 97). Tourists from around the world make Prague memories under Karlův most. Otherwise devoid of character. The fluorescent disco downstairs pops eyeballs. Cover from 50kč. Open nightly 10pm-5am.

Hard Rock Cafe—Praha, Nepravda 69 (tel. 495 94 12), next to the Turkish baths. Metro D: Zabloudil jsi. Kafka once made "the Rock" his home, but now it's just full of bewildered tourists trying to buy a t-shirt. Guinness is 5kč; local *levné pivo* goes for the same price. Open daily 6am-6am.

THE FAGUE AND THE DRAGUE OF PRAGUE

If Prague had a desert, *Priscilla II* could be shot here. The scene is developing fast and in many directions: transvestite shows, stripteases, discos, bars, cafes, restaurants, and hotels aimed at gay and lesbian travelers can be found easily, although not by asking the random *babushka* selling cherries. At any of the places listed below, you can pick up a copy of the monthly *Amigo* (15kč), the most comprehensive guide to gay life in the Czech Republic and Slovakia, or *SOHO* (40kč), a glossier piece of work with less in English. Almost all gay life happens behind closed doors, but don't be afraid to ring the bell.

U Střelce, Karoliny Světlé 12 (tel. 24 23 82 78), under the archway on the right. Gay club that pulls a diverse crowd for its Fri. and Sat. night cabarets, when magnificent female impersonators take the stage, occasionally sitting on unwary audience members. Beer 25kč. Cover 80kč. Open nightly 6pm-4am.

Penzion David, Holubova 5 (tel./fax 54 98 20). Take tram #14 (catch it by the main post office) to its end at Laurová, take a left off the main street and then a right on Holubova. Some of the best food in town on a quiet terrace surrounded by plants. Meat dishes mostly 90-125kč, fine veggie plates 45-70kč, beer 13kč, and kangaroo medallions (!) 130kč. Lunch menu a dirt-cheap 45kč. Open Mon.-Fri. 11am-11pm, Sat.-Sun. noon-midnight.

A Club, Milíčova 25, off Seifertova, "Lipanská" stop on tram #26 from Metro A: Flora or Metro C: Hlavní Nádraží. A nightspot for lesbians, although men come here too. The cafe is all class, with wire sculptures, soft light, and some comfy couches near the bar. Disco in the back starts jamming at 10pm nightly, but don't come before midnight if you want a crowd. Beer 30kč. Open nightly 6pm-6am.

L-Club, Lublaňská 48 (tel. 90 00 11 89). Metro C: I.P. Pavlova. Great fun for both the guys and the dolls with a dancing floor, bar, and cafe. Neon purple lights to make the white shirts glow. Mostly gay men. Open nightly 8pm-4am. Cover 50kč.

Rainbow Club, Kamzíkova 6 (tel. 24 23 31 68). Metro A: Staroměstská. Below "U červeného páva" (see **Food,** p. 171), the Rainbow Club is a good, somewhat quiet central spot for gays to meet, drink, and chat. Open daily noon-1am.

Tom's Bar, Pernerova 4 (tel. 232 11 70). Metro B: Křižíkova. Backtrack from the metro, take a right on Křižíkova, a left at the square, and a right onto Pernerova. It's on your left (10min.). An all-around spot with a cafe, bar, disco, darkroom, and videoroom. The music is bearable, but in the disco-bar area downstairs it's hard to see anything but eyes and teeth, since the only lights are black. Men only. Open Tues.-Thurs. 9pm-2am, Fri.-Sat. 9pm-4am.

■ Near Prague

TEREZÍN (THERESIENSTADT)

The fortress town of Theresienstadt was built in the 1780s on Habsburg Emperor Josef II's orders to safeguard the northern frontier with the German states. In 1940, Hitler's Gestapo set up a huge prison in the Small Fortress, and in 1941 the town itself became a concentration camp for Jews—by 1942, the entire prewar civilian population had been evacuated. 140,000 Jews were deported to the ghetto, first from the "Bohemia-Moravia Protectorate," later from all over the Reich. Around 35,000 died there of starvation or disease, or at the hands of brutal guards; 85,000 others were transported to death camps in the east, primarily Auschwitz. Twice, Terezín was beautified in order to receive delegations from the Red Cross, who were wholly deceived about the true purpose of the place. More than 30,000 prisoners were held in the fortress itself, and many Czech resistance fighters and Communists were shot there. After the Red Army liberated Terezín, the Czechoslovak regime used the camp to hold Sudeten Germans awaiting deportation: the Czech and German governments recently exchanged apologies for the "ethnic cleansing" both countries attempted during this ghastly time. Terezín's population never recovered its prewar levels—the last census recorded fewer than 2000 inhabitants.

The **bus** from Prague-Florenc (every 1-2hr., 1hr., 43kč) stops by the central square, where the tourist office sells a map for 40kč (open until 6pm). The **Ghetto Museum,** Komenského (tel. (0416) 78 25 77) displays lots of contemporary documents, helpfully setting Terezín in the wider Nazi context—all explanatory text is provided in English. The museum also shows various films and displays harrowing children's art from the ghetto alongside some staggeringly good adult work. (Open daily 9am-6pm. 80kč, students 60kč; including Small Fortress 100kč, students 60kč. Guided tour in English 220kč.) South of the town, the **cemetery** and **crematorium** have been well-preserved. Men should cover their heads as a mark of respect (crematorium open March-Nov. Sun.-Fri. 10am-5pm).

East of the town, the **Small Fortress** is the other major sight. Much of the fortress is left bare for visitors to explore freely; permanent exhibitions chart the town's development from 1780-1939, and—in the **museum**—the story of the fortress during World War II (open daily 9am-5:45pm).

KUTNÁ HORA

An hour and a half east of Prague, the former mining town of **Kutná Hora** (Silver Hill) has a history as morbid as the bone church that made the city famous. Founded when lucky miners hit a vein, the city boomed with 100,000 gold diggers until the plague hit, when men who had rushed there like flies began dropping like them. A 13th-century abbot sprinkled soil from Golgotha on the cemetery, which made the rich and superstitious keen to be buried there. Neighbors started to complain by about the 15th century, so the Cistercian order that ran the meadow of death built a chapel and started cramming in bodies. In a fit of whimsy, the monk in charge began designing flowers with pelvi and crania. He never finished, but the artist František Rint completed the project in 1870 with flying butt-bones, femur crosses, and a grotesque chandelier made from every bone in the human body. Some lucky corpse even got to spell out the artist's name, and there's an amazing rendering of the Schwarzenberg family crest (open April-Sept. daily 8am-noon and 1-6pm, Oct. 9am-noon and 1-5pm, Nov.-March 9am-noon and 1-4pm; 20kč, students 10kč). The *kostnice* (tel. 611 43) is 2km from the bus station: walk, or take a local bus to "Sedlec Tabák" and follow the signs. It's near the train station.

The 13th-century silver boom and subsequent bust in the 16th century left snapshots of a thriving medieval town replete with burghers' houses, cobblestone alleys, church spires, and a vaulted cathedral on a hill southwest of town. From Palackého nám., follow 28. října to Havlíčkovo nám. Originally a storehouse for Kutná Hora's stash, the imposing **Vlašský Dvůr** (Italian Court; tel. 28 73) got its name after Václav IV made a home out of it and invited the finest Italian architects to refurbish the palace with more than just silver. It also served a stint as the royal mint. The tour leads through only a few rooms, but each one deserves a look. The **audience hall** witnessed the election of Vladislav II as King of Bohemia, and a life-size mural depicts the tense event. The **Chapel of St. Václav and Vladislav** has been draped with painted flowers and smirking saints since a 20th-century couple renovated the sanctuary in Art Nouveau (open daily 9am-6pm; tours every 15min.; 20kč, students 10kč; infrequent English tours 50kč, students 25kč). Behind the museum, a terrace looks upon the sweeping valley, and trails lead down to the garden **Letní scéna** below. Coming back around the Italian Court, go past the ancient **St. James Church** and follow Barborská, which becomes lined with statues and ends at the beautiful Gothic **St. Barbara's Cathedral** (open Tues.-Sun. 9am-5pm; 20kč, students 10kč).

Infocentrum, Palackého nám. 5 (tel. 23 78), a trip along Lorecká, then Vocelova, then Vladislavova from the bus station, sells maps (15kč or 40kč), books beds for 165kč and up, and gives info on the concerts in Vlašský Dvůr and the cathedral (open Mon.-Fri. 9am-7pm, Sat.-Sun. 9am-6pm). **Buses** arrive from Prague's Florenc station (6 per day, 1 per day Sat.-Sun., 1½hr., 44kč) and station #2 at Metro A: Želivského (9 per day, 2 per day Sat.-Sun., 1hr. 40min., 44kč). If you miss the last bus back, try catching one to Kolín, which has a bigger train station. **Phone code:** 0327.

KARLŠTEJN AND KONOPIŠTĚ

The Bohemian hills around Prague contain 14 castles, some built as early as the 13th century. A train ride southwest from Hlavní Nádraží or Praha-Smíchov (45min., 12kč) brings you to **Karlštejn** (tel. (0311) 68 46 17), a walled and turreted fortress built by Karel IV to house his crown jewels and holy relics. The **Chapel of the Holy Cross** is decorated with more than 2000 inlaid precious stones and 128 apocalyptic paintings by medieval artist Master Theodorik. (Open Tues.-Sun. 9am-5pm. English guide 150kč; cheaper for students, with Czech guides, or with no guide at all.) Ask at tourist information in Prague if they've finished restoring the chapel before setting out.

Animal-rights activists might wish to avoid mighty **Konopiště,** south of Prague in **Benešov** (buses from Prague-Florenc leave at least every hr. 6am-6pm, 1½hr., 22kč), a Renaissance palace with a luxurious interior from the days when Archduke Franz Ferdinand bagged game here, displaying more than 300,000 taxidermized animals. The Renaissance facade hides a castle-like Gothic body. The **Weapons Hall** contains a fine collection of 16th- to 18th-century arms (tel. (0301) 213 66; open Tues.-Sun. 9am-5pm; with English guide 100kč, students 60kč; in Czech 50kč, students 30kč.)

WEST BOHEMIA

Bursting at the seams with curative springs, West Bohemia is the Czech mecca for those in search of a good bath. Over the centuries, emperors and intellectuals have soaked in the waters of Karlovy Vary and Mariánské Lázně, but nowadays the spa-goers consist mainly of German tourists in search of cheap sulphurous draughts. Expelled from the Sudetenland in 1945, the Germans are now returning *en masse,* taking advantage of the Deutschmark's awesome purchasing power. It's not all spa life, however: Plzeň is something of a grimy industrial town, but known as the home of the world-famous *Pilsner* beer.

■ Karlovy Vary

On a routine deer hunt, Holy Roman Emperor and King of Bohemia Karel IV stumbled upon a fountain spewing hot water high into the air. So impressive was the sight that he built a personal lodge on the spot. Over the next 600 years, the spa—then known as Karlsbad—developed into one of the "salons" of Europe, visited by such diverse personalities as Johann Sebastian Bach, Peter the Great, and Sigmund Freud. It was during this period that present-day Karlovy Vary (KAR-lo-vih VA-rih) was built, largely by two tongue-twisting Viennese architects—Ferdinand Fellner and Hermann Helmer. The spa's therapeutic springs continue to be its premier tourist attraction, but perhaps the most beneficial of the waters comes in a bottle: *Becherovka,* the secret alcoholic synthesis of various herbs and just the right amount of sugar.

Orientation and Practical Information Trains run from the main **Horní nádraží** to Prague via Chomutov (5 per day, 4hr., 80 or 100kč). To get to town, take bus #11 or 13 (6kč per person or backpack—buy tickets at the kiosk), departing across the street from the station, to the last stop. Or, it's an easy 10-minute walk downhill from the bus stop: bear left, and a right at the bridge leads straight to the post office at the start of **Masaryka,** the city's administrative street. Intercity buses are much quicker than the train; they zoom from **Dolní nádraží,** on Západní, to Plzeň (10 per day, 1½hr., 60kč) and Prague (16 per day, 2½hr., 84kč). The **ČSAD office** is nearby, just before Západní runs into nám. Republiky (open Mon.-Fri. 6am-6pm, Sat. 7:30am-12:30pm). To get to the center from Dolní nádraží, turn left on Západní, continue past the Becher building, and bear right onto Masaryka, which runs parallel to the other main thoroughfare, **Bechera.** **City-Info** (tel./fax 233 51), in a little white booth on Masaryka across from the post office, sells brochures and maps, books rooms from 330kč, and may have information on nightlife. *Promenáda* is a monthly paper, partly in English, listing concerts, films, and hotels, with a handy map of the town in the middle (11-25kč; available at every kiosk). The **American Express** desk in the travel agency at Vřídelní 51 (tel. 322 18 15) cashes traveler's checks with no commission (and not just AmEx checks either; open Mon.-Fri. 9am-5pm, Sat.-Sun. 9am-noon). Nearby, outside **Komerčni Banka,** Tržiště 11 (tel. 322 22 05), there's a 24-hour Cirrus/MC/Visa **ATM.** Summon a **taxi** at tel. 322 30 30. There is a **pharmacy** at Bechera 3 (tel. 248 20; open Mon.-Fri. 7:30am-6pm, Sat. 8am-noon). The **post office** is at Masaryka 1 (tel. 322 49 30; open Mon.-Fri. 7:30am-7pm, Sat. 8am-1pm, Sun. 8am-noon). **Postal code:** 360 01. Coin- and card-operated **telephones** stand at the junction of Masaryska and Bechera. **Phone code:** 017.

Many establishments are adding an initial "32" to their telephone numbers.

Accommodations Budget accommodations in Karlovy Vary are becoming scarce. **Autotourist,** nám. Dr. Horákové 18 (tel. 322 28 33), will book you a double in a private house for 900kč (open Mon.-Fri. 9am-5pm, Sat. 9am-noon; off-season closed noon-1pm). **City-Info** (see above) also books rooms, as does **A-Z Travel,** Krymská 9 (tel./fax 322 84 37; open Mon.-Fri. 9:30am-5pm). **Pension Kosmos,** Zahradní 39 (tel.

322 31 68), is bang in the center of town on the banks of the Teplá just down from the post office. The pension offers amply sized, simply furnished singles (400kč, with bath 700kč) and doubles (660kč, with bath 1200kč). The area around **Hotel Adria,** Západní 1 (tel. 322 37 65), can get hairy at night, but it's near the main nightclub strip and opposite the buses. The old hotel offers clean singles (752kč), doubles (1168kč), and triples (1680kč), and while the crude picture of a bare-breasted woman in the lobby doesn't inspire much confidence, at least all rooms have bathrooms and breakfast is included. **Pension Romania,** Zahradní 49 (tel. 228 22) has comfy singles, doubles, and triples with bathroom and TV for 820kč per person, breakfast included.

Food A **supermarket** is located at Horova 1 in the large building with the Městská Tržnice sign overlooking the local bus station (accepts Visa and MC; open Mon.-Fri. 6am-7pm, Thurs. until 8pm, Sat. 7am-1pm). The food in Karlovy Vary's eateries is generally either expensive or tasteless—or the waitrons are rude. An exception is **Vegetarian restaurant,** Pavlova 25 (tel. 322 90 21), in the back of the building (follow the signs), which combines (mostly) veggie cooking with the traditional dark Czech interior suitable for serious beer drinking. Fruit kebab is 45kč, veggie goulash and dumplings 35kč, and beer starts at 12kč (open daily 11am-9pm). **Pizzeria Heluan,** Tržiště 41 (tel. 257 57), above the Plague Column, cooks up some odd pizzas and a few normal ones. Most arrive at the table for 38kč, but the "seafruit pizza," with oysters and shrimp, goes for 65kč. Those who like their stomachs bathed in sugar goo should order the fruit pizza (37kč; open daily 10am-9pm). **E&T,** a more expensive eatery with better service and faithful regulars, sits at Zeyera 3 (tel. 322 60 22), between Bechera and Masaryka. A leafy terrace and gleaming interior take in a mixed homo-hetero crowd feeding on various meat dishes (80-130kč) and salads (30kč) and drinking beer (20kč; open daily 10am-11pm).

Sights and Entertainment Between Masaryka and the Teplá, **Smetanovy sady** (gardens) are noted for their spa house and plants arranged to spell the date. Masaryka and nábř. Osvobození fuse into **Zahradní,** which connects to **Dvořákovy sady.** These gardens are named after the Czech composer, a frequent visitor who premiered his "New World" symphony here. Along the south rim of the Dvořákovy sady lies the Victorian **Kolonáda,** where you can sip the curative waters of Karlovy Vary's 12th spring, **Sadový Pramen.** The pedestrian **Mlýnské nábř.** meanders alongside the Teplá under the cool protection of shady trees. Pop into Lázně (Bath) 3 (tel. 322 56 41; fax 322 34 73) to get an underwater massage (DM22, US$15, or—if they condescend to take Czech money—a much cheaper 110kč).

Pramen Svobody (Freedom Spring) is next, and more drinkable than most. Bring your own drinking vessel, or buy little souvenir porcelain cups from the kiosks (40-200kč). The good news for the budget traveler is that the spring waters are free to drink, although you may be able to manage only a few sips of the extremely metallic stuff—it's much stronger than any so-called mineral water you'll get in a restaurant. Next door, the imposing **Mlýnská (Mill) kolonáda** shelters six different springs. Farther along the spa area, the former **tržiště** (market) appears with the delicate white **Tržní kolonáda,** where two more springs bubble to the surface. Look out for some mediocre Latin hexameters celebrating the springs (there's a Czech translation on the left to help you) and also for the **Zawojski House,** now the Živnostenská Banka, a gorgeous cream-and-gold Art Nouveau building from the turn of the century. Crossing the Teplá to the steps of the baroque **Kostel sv. Maří Magdalená** gets you a good view of the other side of the Zawojski House, and takes you past the **Vřídlo** spring (*Sprudel* to the Germans), which shoots 30 liters of water into the air each second at 72° (and that's not Fahrenheit!).

Follow Stará Louka until signs point you to the **funicular** up to the **Diana Rozhledna** (tower; 555m) for a magnificent panoramic view. (Funicular runs daily 9am-7pm, every 15min.; 20kč, round-trip 30kč. Tower open until 6:30pm; 150 steps; 5kč.) Stará Louka comes to a grand end at **Grandhotel Pupp.** Founded in 1774 by Johann Georg Pupp, the Grandhotel was the largest hotel in 19th-century Bohemia. The intricate facade you see today is the work of the Viennese Helmer-Fellner duo.

The interior features luxurious suites, a concert hall, and multiple ballrooms. The woods on the hillside above Stará Louka have sloping, well-maintained paths lightly punctuated with lookout spots and monuments to famous spa visitors. Descend back to the town along Petra Velikého to see a statue of **Karl Marx**—hardly unusual in the former Eastern bloc, except that this one marks not his revolutionary contribution to socialist theory, but rather his visits to the spa and to one Dr. Fleckles in 1874-76.

Promenáda (see **Orientation and Practical Information,** p. 184) lists a gratifying number of concerts around town, including opera in the summer. Karlovy Vary's **International Film Festival** (http://www.tlp.cz/internet/iffkarlovy_vary), showcasing independent film from all parts of the globe (with a particular emphasis on Eastern Europe), runs July 3 through 11 in 1998. To speed up the sipping and strolling routine, a handful of nightclubs are dotted around. Ask around for the latest tips—one joint with staying power is **Propaganda,** Jaltská 5 (tel. 222 92), off Bechera, which attracts a young and local crowd (open Mon.-Sat. 5pm-2am, Sun. 5pm-1am).

■ Mariánské Lázně

In 1779 Dr. Nehr discovered more than 100 curative springs here, and Marienbad—today's Mariánské Lázně (MA-ree-AHN-skay LAHZ-nyeh)—sprouted up atop peat bogs within 50 years. Heads of the world's political, cultural, and sexual life have all mingled here to gather up new energy and ideas. Young backpackers who have plenty of the above in store might leave this town off their itineraries, but the spa provides splendid strolling grounds for families and anyone else tired of raving youths.

Orientation and Practical Information Mariánské Lázně is linked by **train** to Karlovy Vary (8 per day, 1¾hr., 24kč), Plzeň (11 per day, 1hr., 32kč), and Prague (7 per day, 3hr., 80kč). **Buses** go to Plzeň (7 per day, 1½hr.) and to Prague (5 per day, 3hr.). The **train station** (tel. 62 53 21) and the string of 10 **bus stops** (tel. 33 11) next door lie a laborious 2km from the spa's compact center. **Trolley #5** connects the town and its train station (throw 5kč in the box on the trolley), but for the powerful and the poor: head straight out of the station, take a right, and turn left on the main **Hlavní třída,** which runs past the tiny steel and glass tourist booth and then leads to luxurious "hotel row." The staff of **City Service,** Hlavní tř. 626 (tel. 62 38 16; fax 62 42 18), books rooms starting at an impressive 150kč and continuing up to an equally impressive 5100kč, and sells maps and brochures (open Mon.-Fri. 8am-12:30pm and 1-5pm, Sat. 10am-2pm). The good samaritans at **Komerční Banka,** Hlavní tř. 132 (tel 62 60 11), take only a 2% commission on currency exchange, but be ready for lines (open Mon.-Fri. 8am-5pm). The bank also has a Cirrus/Visa/MC/AmEx **ATM.** There is a **pharmacy** at Lidická 311 (tel. 62 25 26); find it by going down Hlavní tř. and turning right onto Dykova—you can't miss the green and white Lékárna Rea sign (open Mon.-Fri. 8am-6pm, Sat. 8am-noon). For **taxis,** call 27 08. The **post office** is at Poštovní 17 (tel. 36 07; open Mon.-Fri. 8am-6pm, Sat. 7am-2pm, Sun. 8am-noon). **Postal code:** 353 01. **Telephones** are outside. If a phone number doesn't work, add 62 to the beginning and try again—change is underway, but going slowly. **Phone code:** 0165.

Accommodations Private rooms and cheap hotels bubble up everywhere. **City Service** (see above) books cheap **private rooms.** The only way to escape the sneaky 15kč "spa" tax is to sleep in the woods. **Hotel Evropa,** Třebízského 101 (tel. 62 20 63; fax 62 54 08), is set in the ranks of "hotel row" without the rank prices. Climb Hlavní tř. to its end and take a left. The orange-patterned wallpaper and orangey-brown carpets in some rooms aren't great, but the prices are: singles 400kč, with shower or bath and WC 600kč; doubles 600kč, with extras 950kč; triples 800kč, with the goods 1200kč. Halfway up the hill, **Hotel Suvorov,** Ruská tř. 76 (call the associated Hotel Kossuth at tel. 62 28 61 or fax at 62 28 62), enjoys panoramic views of the spa. Climb Hlavní tř. and take a left only after Ruská appears a second time, following it through a 90° turn left. Rooms boast plush rugs and sofa beds (singles 450kč, with bath 510kč; doubles 600kč, with bath 790kč; breakfast 70kč). **Juniorhotel Krakonoš (HI)** (tel. 62 26 24; fax 62 23 83) lurks in the wooded hills to the east of the town.

From the town center take bus #12 to "Krakonoš" (infrequent, 5kč), or walk along Dusíkova until you reach the cable car. If it's operating (unlikely), get it; if not, take the path to its right—after a bit you'll meet the road again and signs will lead you to the hotel (30min.). A vast mansion-with-turrets-turned-hostel, Krakonoš has one- to four-bed rooms (335kč per person, breakfast included, or 235kč with an HI card). **Motel Start** (tel. 62 20 62), Plzeňská, offers three-person rooms in dormitory-style "comfort" at 150kč per head. Take a right off Hlavní almost as soon as you enter it from the train/bus stations (before the Dyleň supermarket) and another right onto the busy Plzeňská. The steel motel sits on the left; go past the smoky slot-machine-filled lobby to get to the reception. Every two rooms share a bathroom.

Food Mariánské Lázně is famous for a distinctive sweet treat known as *oplatky:* wafers layered with vanilla, chocolate, or almond filling (25-40kč per box). Also try the popular beer *Chodovar,* brewed in a nearby village. A butcher, a baker, and an orange-juice maker sell groceries and a few prepared dishes at **Trio,** Hlavní tř. 30 (open Mon.-Fri. 7am-6pm, Sat. 8am-7pm, Sun. 8am-6pm). Plunk a handful of Swedes down in Bohemia—possibly the first in the region since the Thirty Years' War—and what do they do? Yup—they cook pizzas at **Tre Kronor,** Lidická 154/9 (tel 44 49), near Hlavní's intersection with Dykova (look for the sign). This blue-and-yellow joint swims with pizzas (40-99kč), some Swedish specialities, and bottled beer (16-20kč; open daily 11am-11pm). Not so budget, but worth a look, is the **Classic** restaurant, Hlavní tř. 131/50 (tel. 28 07), unusual for offering vegetarian main courses (56-63kč) and for the angelfish swimming in the airy dining room. (Soups 15kč, fish 138kč, meat 108-158kč, a glass of fruity Moravian wine 19kč. Accepts MC/Visa/AmEx.)

Sights Everyone seems to be on a prescription to stroll. Elderly ladies, stodgy old men, young tots, and their sunny parents all move like snails along Hlavní tř. sipping from porcelain and munching on *oplatky.* Grab some wafers, put on some shades, and get ready to meander. At the town's highest point, stately **Goethovo nám.** recreates the aura of Marienbad's heyday with well-kept gardens, lawns, and 19th-century lampposts. In the center, a stone Goethe touches his chin and gazes at strollers; the famed author spent less pensive time in **spa-house #11** (tel. 27 40), tasting the waters with lascivious Ulrike. The building is now a museum housing exhibits on minerals, spa visitors, and the 1945 liberation at the hands of Patton's 97th infantry division (20kč, students 15kč; open Tues.-Sun. 9am-4pm).

Across the gardens of Goethovo nám., **Kostel Nanebevzeté Panny Marie** (Assumption church) stands under a large neo-Byzantine dome. Coming out at the front, the huge *kaisergelb* buildings on your left form the complex that houses the New Baths and the Casino. On the right, people sample the waters of **Karolina pramen** (spring) under a snow-white colonnade. The second fountain is the so-called **zpívající fontána** (singing fountain). Once the water made musical noises as it hit steel spheres; now it just squirts funny patterns. Reconstructed in 1975-81, the nearby **Novobarokní kolonáda** (colonnade) resembles a mix of neo-Baroque and 60s tie-dye. The painter must have been tripping or living in a fish bowl with cherubs. Springs come in hot and cold. To rinse your mouth out afterwards, use a tap marked "*trinkwasser*" or "*pitná voda*" (taps open daily 6am-noon and 4-6pm).

The **Anglikáský kostelík** (Anglican church), Ruská 98 (tel. 62 21 96), has recently been renovated: this is where King Edward VII came during his spa visits in 1903-9 (open Tues.-Sun. 9am-4pm; 15kč, students 10kč). The **Ruský pravoslavný kostel sv. Vladimíra** (Russian Orthodox church) houses prize-winning icons. (Open May-Oct. Mon.-Fri. 8:30am-noon and 1-4:30pm, Sat.-Sun. 8:30am-4:30pm; Nov.-April daily 9:30-11:30am and 2-4pm. 10kč, students 5kč. Mass Sun. 9:15am.)

▓ Plzeň

Tell a Czech that you're going to Plzeň (Pl-ZEN-yeh), and they might say "to je škoda." The unfortunate pun on "Škoda," which means "pity," alludes to the notorious arms factory turned notorious auto plant that helped place Plzeň on the list of Bohemia's most polluted cities. For the visitor, however, Plzeň offers an intriguing Gothic and Renaissance old town center, a thriving youth culture rooted in the local University of West Bohemia, and, of course, its hometown brew, the world-famous *Pilsner Urquell*. If the highbrow is your game, hit Prague; come here for hard-jamming rock, flowing pints, and a pinch of soot.

ORIENTATION AND PRACTICAL INFORMATION

Náměstí Republiky, the central square, lies amid a rectangular grid of narrow streets. A few blocks west and parallel to the square's east side runs **Sady Pětatřicátníků,** which becomes **Klatovská** farther south. At the name-change point, the busy street meets the perpendicular **Americká,** which runs east to the train station. From the **train station,** hang a right onto **Sirková,** dive into the underpass and emerge where the sign points to "Americká." Turn off down **Jungmannova,** which runs north to the square, morphing into **Smetany** before reaching it. From the bus station, follow any street east toward the spires. You'll fall in love with **tram #2,** which runs from the train station to the square to the bus station to the youth hostel, and beyond.

Tourist Offices: MIS (Městské informační středisko), nám. Republiky 41 (tel. 723 65 35; fax 722 44 73). Helpful staff sells maps (40kč) and books rooms from 300kč up. Good English spoken. Open Mon.-Fri. 10am-4:30pm, Sat. 9am-1pm. The town hall publishes a very helpful listings brochure, *Plzeň Open Town,* for 33kč.

Budget Travel: CKM, Dominikánská 1 (tel. 723 63 93; fax 723 69 09), off the central square's northwest corner. Books private rooms (300kč and up) and sells ISICs and HI cards. Open Mon.-Fri. 9am-6pm.

Currency Exchange: Komerční Banka, Zbrojnická 4 (tel. 721 42 11), off nám. Republiky's southeast corner. 2% commission (min. 50kč) on traveler's checks. Open Mon.-Fri. 8am-5pm. A **cash exchange machine** outside of **Československá Obchodní Banka,** Americká 60, changes major currencies into koruny. Open 24hr. **ATMs** (Visa/Cirrus/MC) at Československá Obchodní Banka and Komerční Banka.

Trains: Americká (info tel. 22 20 79). To Prague (13 per day, 1hr. 40min., 48kč). International tickets and info on the 2nd floor.

Buses: Husova 58 (tel. 22 37 04). Many cheap Eurolines buses pass through en route to Prague from France, Switzerland, or Germany. To Prague (more than 1 per hr., 2hr., 54kč) and a heap of West Bohemian spas.

Public Transportation: Tram #2 serves the "practicalities route"; tram #4 gets the "fun route." The other means of transport are not nearly as exciting. 6kč per tram ride; backpacks (and dogs) are 3kč extra. Get tickets from *Tabaks* and punch them on board. Catch #4 opposite the Synagogue. When the trams stop running at night, identically numbered **buses** take over.

Taxis: Big stands at the train station and Palackého 2.

Luggage Storage: At the train station. 5kč, with English instructions. 24hr.

AIDS Hotline: tel. 27 36 60. 24hr.

Post Office: Solní 20 (tel. 22 45 60). Open Mon.-Fri. 6am-8:30pm, Sat. 7:30am-2pm, Sun. 7:30am-noon. **Postal code:** 301 00.

Telephones: A row of mostly card phones can be found on Sedláčkova, around the corner from the post office. **Phone code:** 019.

ACCOMMODATIONS

MIS or CKM will book rooms for you, with pension prices starting at 300kč per person. Or try these:

SOU (HI), Vejprnická 58, pavilion #8 (tel. 28 20 12). Take tram #2 to "Internáty," walk back 50m, and head left into the fenced compound. A former Škoda workers' hostel that still houses some long-term residents. Each pair of doubles or triples shares a bathroom. Institutional atmosphere, but cheap at 189kč per person.

Penzion v Solní ulice, Solní 8 (tel. 723 66 52), mere yards from nám. Republiky's northwest corner. Three delightful rooms (with bath) in a newly renovated 16th-century house. Call ahead to book; the landlady speaks English. Reception open daily 9am-6pm. Singles 510kč; doubles 850kč. Extra bed 170kč. Good breakfast 90kč. Prices 20% higher in July and Aug.

Morrison Hotel, Thámova 9 (tel. 27 09 52; fax 27 54 80), off Klatovská. Take tram #4 to "Chodské nám." Clean rooms with dark wood beds, alabaster walls, shower/bath, and WC. Restaurant in the same building. Singles 750kč; doubles 1100kč; triples 1500kč. Accepts MC and Visa.

FOOD

No one should eat a meal in Plzeň without including a pint of either *Prazdroj* or its dark equivalent, *Purkmistr*. If you can't decide between the two, they combine in *Řezané* (Czech-style black-and-tans). The restaurants listed below also serve as entertainment spots. There are plenty of places to buy groceries, including a large **Tesco's** just outside the train station.

U Dominika, Dominikánská 3 (tel. 22 32 26), off the square's northwest corner. A crowd of students comes here mostly to chat over coffee (13-20kč) or beer (15kč). Offers the usual selection of ready-mades, ranging from pork to pork to pork, at 50-70kč per dish; also pizzas (pork optional) 42-65kč. Open Mon.-Sat. 11am-midnight, Sun. 7pm-midnight. The beer garden next door is popular even on rainy days. Open nightly 6pm-1am.

U bílého lva, Pražská 15 (tel. 722 69 98), entrance on Perlova. The "White Lion" boasts an open-air *orangerie* for beer-drinking in the company of plant life, and a low-ceilinged restaurant with a stuffed duck on the wall in which to eat pork surrounded by groups of happy Czechs. Bulgarian salad 35kč, goulash with dumplings 57kč, *palačinky* (pancakes) 34kč, 0.5L beer 15kč. Open daily 10am-11pm.

Na spilce, U Prazedroje 7 (tel. 706 27 54; fax 706 27 03). If Na spilce had been around in 1945 when armies marched through Plzeň, it probably could have fed the whole lot. This gigantic dining hall under Prazdroj Brewery now accommodates Plzeň's every guest with quality food and fast service. As a result, it's very touristy. Soups 17-20kč, salads 20-40kč, apple strudel 25kč, and house brew 17kč per 0.5L. English menu. AmEx/Visa/MC. Open Mon.-Thurs. and Sat. 11am-10pm, Fri. 11am-11pm, Sun. 11am-9pm.

U Salzmannů, Pražská 8 (tel. 723 58 55). Plzeň's oldest beerhall (founded 1637), although the recent refurbishment makes it feel more like a brand-new theme pub than an authentic antique. Good beer for 17.50kč, but the food isn't up to much; goulash 59kč. Open Mon.-Sat. 11am-11pm., Sun. 11am-10pm.

SIGHTS

Empire dwellings loom over the marketplace, but none out-tower the belfry of **Kostel sv. Bartoloměje.** For a vertiginous view of the town and the Škoda factory, tourists can pay 18kč (students 12kč) to climb 60 of the 103m to the observation deck, where they can read sad stories about why the town no longer has an outsized bell called Bartholomew (Bárta to its friends). Bárta was cracked, removed, smelted in a fire, shot at, and cracked once more before being melted down to make bullets during WWII. Now no one has the heart or the money to forge another. Inside, a rich collection of Gothic statues and altars bows to the stunning 14th-century polychrome **Plzeňska Madona,** recalling Bohemia's glory days under Charles IV. The **Morový sloup** (Plague Column) in the square seems to be working: residents may suffer from industrial diseases and liver complaints, but the plague hasn't been here for a while. Also in the square, Plzeň's golden-clock-topped Renaissance **radnice** connects on the inside to the 1607 **Císařský dům** (Kaiser House).

From the northeast part of nám. Republiky, Pražská leads to **Masné krámy** (tel. 722 39 48), the former slaughterhouse, at #16. It features changing art exhibitions and hosts concerts (open Mon.-Fri. 10am-6pm, Sat. 10am-1pm, Sun. 9am-5pm; 15kč, students 8kč). Across the street, the **Vodárenská věž** (water tower), Pražská 19, stored the crystal-clear water needed for fine beer. The well's dried up, so the **Trigon Gallery** (tel. 22 54 71) doesn't have to worry about water damage to its cool independent art (open Mon.-Thurs. 10am-6pm, Fri. 10am-5pm, Sat. 10am-1pm; free except for the upstairs exhibit, which is 10kč, students 5kč). The Vodárenská věž and **Plzeňské podzemí** (underground; tel. 722 52 14) can be visited on a tour that starts inside Perlová 4 near the tower and leads through the cellars, which were used for the storage and the covert mass consumption of beer (open Tues.-Sun. 9am-4:20pm; 30kč).

Perlova ends at Veleslavínova, where the **Pivovarské muzeum** (brewery), Veleslavínova 6 (tel. 723 55 74), exhibits beer paraphernalia from medieval taps to a collection o' coasters. The original malt-house room displays the top-secret Pilsner process (no cameras). The last room, labeled "miscellaneous," is probably the most fun, with gigantic steins, wacky pub signs, and a statue of Shakespeare's most famous drunk, Sir John Falstaff (open daily 10am-6pm; 40kč, students 12kč).

Return down Veleslavínova to Rooseveltova, which becomes Františkánská on the other side of the square. The gate of the **Františkánský kostel a klášter** leads into a quiet cloister garden, with statues in despairing Gothic poses. The church also houses a fine Baroque main altar and the renowned **Black Madonna of Hájek,** an 18th-century sculpture. Further along are the **Kopeckého sady** (gardens). People stroll and relax here in the shade of the trees as brass bands perform polkas, waltzes, and folk tunes. Moving west along the promenade, Kopeckého sady becomes Smetanovy sady; at its intersection with Klatovská stands the Neo-Renaissance **Divadlo J. K. Tyla** (J. K. Tyl Theater). North of the theater along Sady pětatřicátníků lies the 1892 **synagogue,** an impressive monument to Plzeň's once-large Jewish community.

In 1840, over 30 independent brewers plied their trade in the beer cellars of Plzeň. Some of the suds were good, but some were awful, so the burgher brewers formed a union with the goal of creating the best beer in the world. Many would agree that the **Měšťanský Pivovar Plzeňský Prazdroj** (Pilsner Urquell Burghers' Brewery; tel. 706 28 88) succeeded with its legendary *Pilsner Urquell*. The entrance to the complex lies 300m east of the Staré Město, where Pražská becomes U Prazdroje. A huge neo-Renaissance gate welcomes visitors to this pastel palace of the brewing arts. Guided tours run once each weekday at 12:30pm. After the stimulating "kaleidoscope" film (with Czech, English, and German subtitles) about Prazdroj's past and present, the group divides into Czech, German, English, and French subgroups. The English one collects few people, so you'll be able to bombard the knowledgeable guide with questions (70kč; the tour lasts 75min.).

ENTERTAINMENT

For early-evening highbrow entertainment, **Divadlo J.K. Tyla** (tel. 22 25 94) offers **plays** and good **opera** cheap. The schedule is posted outside. Get tickets an hour before the performance (shows usually start at 7pm) in the theater or in advance at the Předprodej office, Sedláčkova 2 (tel. 722 75 48), a block southwest of the main square (open Mon.-Fri. 10am-5pm; best seats 60kč). To get to the theater, take tram #4 to "U synagogy," or walk along Přešovská from nám. Republiky's southeast corner and turn left along the main road (Sady pětatřicátníků, which becomes Klatovská).

Bars and Clubs

Thanks to West Bohemia University students, Plzeň booms with bars and late-night clubs. The young English-speaking summer staff at the tourist office eagerly gives suggestions. Some clubs have resorted to placing "members only" signs on the doors, but bouncers rarely ask for cards. Things get hoppin' around 9:30pm on weekends.

Bílej Mědved, Prokopova 30 (tel. 22 24 45), off Americká. The "White Bear" is where the long- and short-haired herds congregate at weekends, drinking *Budvar* (19kč per 0.5L) at the bar or in the beer garden at the back, listening to droning rock at high volume, and periodically breaking out into bouts of slam-dancing. Open Mon.-Thurs. 6pm-3am, Fri.-Sat. 6pm-4am, Sun. 8pm-2am.

Subway, Sady 5. května 21 (tel. 22 28 96). Descend left down the first flight of stairs off the overpass at the end of Rooseveltova (off nám. Republiky's northeast corner). This popular underground cellar bar, which plans to refurbish itself for summer '98, packs lots of people into a fairly small space and plays Anglo rock oldies at high volume. Dance if you can find space. Open Wed.-Fri. 10pm-2am.

Kapsa, nám. Míru 140, next to the tram #4 stop. Attracts a slightly older crowd with fewer body parts pierced (they must be graduate students) who chat, smoke and drink prize-winning *Herold* beer (14.50kč per 0.5L) in the basement bar or, in warmer weather, on the terrace. Open Mon.-Fri. 11am-2am, Sat.-Sun. 5pm-2am.

Moravská Vinárna, Bezručova 4 (tel. 723 79 72). Wine from wooden barrels in a generously sized glass for 19kč, or 94kč for a bottle of *Müller Thurgau* to drink in a good-natured, mixed-age crowd of locals and visitors. Open Mon.-Sat. 10am-10pm, Sun. 11am-9pm.

American Center Plzeň, Dominikánská 9 (tel. 723 77 22), provides a spot for homesick Americans to watch CNN, read old copies of the *Herald Tribune,* and drink American beer in the downstairs cafe. Open Mon.-Fri. 8am-11pm.

SOUTH BOHEMIA

Rustic and accessible, South Bohemia is a scenic ensemble of scattered villages, unspoiled brooks, and castle ruins. Low hills and plentiful attractions have made the region a favorite of Czech bicyclists, who ply the countryside watching for wildlife, visiting castles, and paying homage to the famous *Budvar* beer.

■ České Budějovice

No amount of beer will help you correctly pronounce České Budějovice (CHESS-kay BOOD-yeh-oh-vee-tsay). Pint-guzzlers worldwide can be thankful the town was known as Budweis in the 19th century, when it inspired the name of the popular but pale American Budweiser. But tourists come to Budějovice for more than just *Budvar* (which shares little in common with its American cousin). Mill streams, the Malše, and the Vltava wrap around the city center, which is a fascinating amalgam of Gothic, Renaisssance, and Baroque houses scattered along winding medieval alleys and impeccably straight 18th-century streets. České Budějovice is also a great launchpad for trips to South Bohemia's castles and natural wonders.

Orientation and Practical Information Staré Město centers around nám. Přemysla Otakara II. Cheap rooms, generally found outside Staré Město's walls, are reachable by **buses** and **trolley-buses** (6kč tickets sold at kiosks; punch them on board). The **train station** is 10 minutes on foot from the main square. From the station, take the pedestrian **Lannova tř.,** which becomes **Kanonická** after the moat, and finally pours out into the gigantic nám. Otakara II. **Turistické Informační Centrum,** nám. Otakara II 2 (tel./fax 594 80), has helpful English-speaking staff who book private rooms (from 350kč near the center, cheaper farther out) for a 10kč commission (open Mon.-Fri. 9am-5pm, Sat.-Sun. 9am-noon). **Komerční Banka,** Krajinská 15 (tel. 774 11 47), off nám. Otakara II, cashes traveler's checks for a 2% commission (min. 50kč). An **ATM** waits outside; more 24-hour Cirrus/MC ATMs can be found along Lannova and opposite the train station. **Trains,** Nádražní 12 (tel. 82 34 34), ply the rails to Brno (4 per day, 4½hr., 100kč); Plzeň (10 per day, 2hr., 56kč); and Prague (11 per day, 2½hr., 72kč). **Buses** (tel. 558 04) congregate across the street from the train station, spewing smoke to Brno (8 per day, 4hr., 123kč); Plzeň (3 per day, 3hr., 85kč); and Prague (20 per day, 2½hr., 95kč). **Taxis** are summoned by phoning 731 25 38. A few places **rent bikes** for 100kč per day—ask the tourist office or a hostel manager where to go. A **pharmacy** heals on the main square at #26 (tel. 530 63; open Mon.-Fri. 7am-6pm, Sat. 8am-noon). The **post office,** Senovážné nám. 1 (tel. 773 41 22), sits south of Lannova as it enters Staré Město (open Mon.-Fri. 6am-7pm, Sat. 7am-noon). **Postal code:** 37001. **Phone code:** 038.

Accommodations The University of South Bohemia **dorms** (tel. 777 44 00) on Studenstská open to tourists in July and August (doubles 280kč). Inexpensive year-round **pensions** flourish near the center. By far the friendliest place to stay, however, is the hostel-like **Penzion U Výstaviště,** U Výstaviště 17 (tel. 724 01 48), where pale-blue stairs lead to a corridor lined with stenciled clouds and homemade cartoons. Take bus #1, 13, 14, or 17 from the bus station five stops to "U parku," and continue 150m along the street that branches off to the right at the bus stop. If you phone from the station, the English-speaking staff may offer a free lift. The common room contains a kitchen and a list of all the cheap restaurants in town. Call ahead (250kč for the first night, 200kč thereafter). If you have to catch the 5am train to Brno, the **Hotel Grand,** Nádražni 27 (tel. 565 03; fax 565 62), is right opposite the station (singles from 700kč; doubles 900kč; triples 1100kč; quads 1800kč; all with some kind of washing facilities).

Food Despite the town's many restaurants, it's difficult to find anything but meat, dumplings, and *Budvar* at meal time. One grocery is **Večerka**, Placého 10 (entrance on Hroznova; open Mon.-Fri. 7am-8pm, Sat. 7am-1pm, Sun. 8am-8pm). **U paní Emy,** Široká 25 (tel. 731 28 46), near the main square, does fine Czech cooking. Aid your digestion of Tábor steak (95kč), large salads (60kč), or veggie dishes (50-70kč) with a tall *Budvar* (19kč per 0.5L). A buzzing local crowd throngs **Restaurace Na Dvorku**, Kněžsná 11, where main dishes—the Czech usuals—are a bargain (29-79kč; open Mon.-Fri. 9:30am-10pm, Sat.-Sun. 10am-10pm).

Sights and Entertainment Surrounded by Renaissance and Baroque buildings, cobbled **nám. Otakara II** is the largest square in the Czech Republic. In the center, **Samsonova kašna** (Samson's fountain; 1726) doesn't flow with the local brew of the same name—maybe that's why the faces spewing water look a little anguished. The *náměstí's* impressive 1555 **radnice** stands a full story above the other buildings on the square. Jazzed up in 1730, it sports a fine set of gargoyles. Near the square's northeast corner, **Černá věž** (Black Tower; tel. 635 25 08) stands over the town. To taste all 72m and see all the bells costs nothing, but to get to the 360° balcony after the climb costs 6kč. Beware: the treacherous stairs are difficult even for the sober (open July-Aug. Tues.-Sun. 10am-7pm; Sept.-Nov. 9am-5pm, March-June 10am-6pm). The tower once served as a belfry for the neighboring 13th-century **Chrám sv. Mikuláše** (Church of St. Nicholas), which became a cathedral when the town gained a bishop in the 18th century. The creamy interior's altar is from 1791; the Way of the Cross cycle around the sides is from the 1920s (tel. 731 12 63; open 7am-6pm daily). The city's most famous attraction, the **Budweiser Brewery,** Karoliny Světlé 4 (tel. 770 51 11; fax 731 11 35), can be reached by bus #2, 4, or 5 from the center. Tours of the factory are available for groups of six or more. In theory these ought to be booked weeks in advance from the tourist office; in practice travelers turning up early, either alone or in small groups, often manage to get inside.

You can drink *Budvar* almost anywhere in town, but the former medieval meat market, **Masné krámy,** Krajinská 13 (tel. 379 57), now a 280-seat restaurant and bar, is worth a look, even if you decide it's a glossy tourist trap (0.5L beer 18kč; open daily 10am-10pm). In summer, lakes around the town host open-air disco concerts (ask hipsters at the tourist office). Later in the evening, a younger, livelier crowd (some leather, a bit of facial hair) drinks at the **Fidel Castro Bar** on the corner of Nova and Otakarová, where *Samson*—the *other* local brew—runs 10kč for 0.5L (open daily 6pm-5am). Quieter types can settle for a nice cup of tea at **Dobrá Čajovna,** Hroznova 16, where regulars take off their shoes to drink sweet herbal brews (11kč and up) and talk desperately quietly in deference to the thrum of the sitar (open Mon.-Sat. 1-10pm, Sun. 3-10pm).

■ Near České Budějovice: Hluboká nad Vltavou

Hluboká is an ordinary town blessed with an extraordinary castle. This Disneyland of towers owes its success to Eleonora Schwarzenberg, who renovated the original Renaissance-Baroque castle into a Windsor-style fairytale stronghold in the mid-19th century. The castle has 141 rooms in all, and the 45-minute tour takes in a dozen or so, starting with some seriously mahoganized interiors and ending with the library of

This Bud's for EU

Many Yankees, having tasted the malty goodness of a *Budvar* brew, return home to find that the beer from Budweis is conspicuously unavailable. The fact that *Budvar* is the Czech Republic's largest exported beer, beating out even *Pilsner Urquell* in 1995, makes its absence from American store shelves even stranger. About the only way to sip an authentic *Budvar* on a porch in New York is to sneak a few bottles in your pack and pray they don't shatter in transit.

So where's the *Budvar*? The answer lies in a tale of trademarks and town names. České Budějovice (Budweis in German) had been brewing its own style of lager for centuries when the Anheuser-Busch brewery in St. Louis, Missouri came out with its Budweiser-style beer in 1876. Not until the 1890s, however, did the Budějovice Pivovar (Brewery) begin producing a beer labeled "Budweiser." International trademark conflicts ensued, and in 1911 the companies signed a non-competition agreement: Budějovice Pivovar got markets in Europe, and Anheuser-Busch took North America. But the story continues...A few years ago, Anheuser-Busch tried to end the confusion by buying a controlling interest in the makers of *Budvar*, but the Czech government refused. Coincidentally, Anheuser-Busch didn't order its usual one-third of the Czech hop crop the following year. Anheuser-Busch is now suing for trademark infringement in Finland, while Budějovice Pivovar is petitioning the EU to make the moniker "Budweiser" an exclusive as "Champagne," meaning that any brand sold in the EU under that name would have to come from the Budweiser region. As long as the battle continues, there is little chance that a *Budvar* in America will be anything but an illegal alien, so fill up while you can (and take a few for the road).

rare books. En route, there are more Schwarzenberg portraits than you could care to shake a stick at, as well as tapestries, paintings (including Raphael and da Vinci copies), and absurdly ornate wooden furniture. Irritatingly as ever, guided tours are compulsory, and English tours only happen when groups (usually bus tours) book them in advance. If there is one, though, others are "free" to tag along (120kč). Czech tours (55kč, 30kč students) are frequent and much cheaper. (Castle open April, Sept.-Oct. Tues.-Sun. 9am-noon and 12:30-4:30pm; May-June Tues.-Sun. 9am-noon and 12:30-5pm; July-Aug. daily, same hours.)

Buses run from České Budějovice to "Hluboká pod kostelem" (25 min., 11kč) frequently, although there are many fewer on weekends—look for buses with "Týn nad Vltavou" as their final destination. The most pleasant way of daytripping here is by bike. You can also walk it from České Budějovice (2hr.). From the bus stop, hike up the hill on any of the converging paths. **Štekl**—the greeting "lobby"—was superbly renovated in 1996—the real castle is a little further up the path.

■ Český Krumlov

Winding medieval streets, scenic promenades, aging stone courtyards, and the looming presence of Bohemia's second-largest castle might have earned Český Krumlov its coveted UNESCO-protected status, but that's only half the story. The town's wonderful location on the banks of the Vltava in the gentle South Bohemian countryside makes it truly ideal for relaxation. Herds of 10-speeds wait outside cafes as their riders tank up for the road, while canoers and kayakers maneuver through the "Venice of Bohemia's" windy waterways. The town's hostel log-books heave with variations on the same "I-only-meant-to-stay-here-one-night-and-ended-up-staying-forty" theme.

Orientation and Practical Information Located 16km southwest of České Budějovice, the town is best reached by frequent **buses** (Mon.-Fri. 10 per day, fewer on weekends; 35min., 18kč). If you get off at the small **"Špičak"** stop on the northern outskirts of town, it's an easy march downhill to the medieval center and the tourist office. From "Špičak," pass through **Budějovice gate** and follow **Latrán** past the castle and over the Vltava. The street becomes Radniční as it enters Staré

CZECH REPUBLIC

Město and leads into the main **nám. Svornosti.** The **tourist office,** nám. Svornosti 1 (tel. 71 11 83), is in the town hall building and books pensions (starting at 550kč) or private rooms, which can be a bit cheaper. They also sell local maps for planning cycling trips (39-59kč; open Mon.-Sat. 9am-6pm, Sun. 10am-6pm). **Moravia Bank,** Soukenická 34, (tel. 71 13 77) cashes traveler's checks at 1% commission (min. 20kč; open Mon.-Fri. 9am-5pm, Sat. 9am-noon). The **train station,** Nádražni 31 (tel. 32 75), is a 2km uphill hike from the center, and connections to České Budějovice take nearly twice as long as buses, but they're also cheaper, and on weekends they run more frequently (8 per day, 1hr., 14kč). The **main bus terminal,** Kaplická 439 (tel. 34 15), lies to the southeast. **Vltava Travel,** at Kájovská 62 (tel./fax 71 19 78), rents boats (July-Aug. from 250kč, off-season 150kč) and mountain bikes (300kč per day, with a vast 3000kč deposit!) and will transport you and your stuff to the start of various trips (open daily 8am-6pm). The main **post office,** Latrán 193 (tel. 71 19 98), has 24-hour card-operated **telephones** outside (open Mon.-Fri. 7am-5:30pm, Sat. 7-11am). **Postal code:** 381 01. **Phone code:** 0337.

Accommodations Every street has a story, and every house a room to rent. Just look for the *Zimmer frei* or *ubytování* signs hanging outside. Pension and hotel accommodation is quite expensive nowadays, but the town does have three fine hostels. The **Moldau Hilton** sits at Parkan 116 (no tel.). Take Radniční from nám. Svornosti, turn right on Parkan, and pray for the "Goddamit! We have space!" sign to be hanging on the door. With 12 beds stuffed in between the roof beams in the attic, the Moldau Hilton prides itself on being the best place in Český Krumlov to watch electrical storms over the castle at night; it may also be the only place that charges Czechs (300kč per person) more than foreigners (200kč). New baths and toilets will be in place for 1998, but the hostel will be shut mid-January to mid-May as the extraordinary (and Anglophone) Czech owner flies south for the winter. At **U vodníka,** Po vodě 55 (tel. 71 19 35), beds are 180kč in the two quads, or 500kč for the solitary double. The friendly native-English-speaking staff will also do your laundry (75kč per kilo), rent you a mountain bike (150kč per day), lend you books from their fine library, arrange boat rentals, and log you into cyberspace for (100kč per hour; contact them in the final frontier at vodnik@ck.bohem-net.cz). Get off at the main bus station, bear left toward the town spires, then hang a right into town and follow the signs. Spillover can be put up at the **Krumlov House** just up the road at Rooseweltova 68 (same management, same telephone). Finally, the 17-bed **Ryba** (fish) **Hostel,** Rybářska 5 (tel. 71 18 01), overlooking the Vltava just across from the town center, offers the same prices (180kč dorms, 500kč double) as well as the benign and welcoming management of Jessica from New Jersey. From the central square, set out from the right-hand corner across from the tourist office, drift left onto Kájovská, head over the bridge and straight down Rybářská. You'll see it from the bridge.

Food and Entertainment On weekdays or Saturday mornings, ask your hostel manager where the nearest grocery is. There's a **SPAR** at Linecká 49 (open Mon.-Fri. 7am-6:30pm, Sat. 7am-6pm, Sun. 9am-6pm). Hunt out great Czech cooking at **Na louži,** Kájovská 66 (tel. 71 12 80), where tables of satisfied customers spill out into the cobbled street. Pork, dumplings, and cabbage go for 54kč, fried cheese dishes are 59-65kč, skewered meat—the house specialty—is 120kč, and it all goes down with half a liter of beer for 13kč (open daily 10am-10pm). The **Cikanská jízba** (Gypsy bar), Dlouhá 31 (tel. 55 85), fills up with English-speaking expats and tourist-friendly locals. Good *gulaš* goes for 65kč, and *Eggenberg* pours for 16kč per 0.5L (open Mon.-Thurs. 4-11pm, Fri.-Sun. 4pm-1am). To get there, follow Radniční out of the main square and turn left down Dlouhá. **U Matesa,** Rybářska 24, a bit farther along the waterfront from the Ryba Hostel, is a fine spot for drinking into the night. A half-liter of dark *Bernard* beer goes for 12kč and light *Kozel* for 14kč; you'll get better food elsewhere, though (open Mon.-Thurs. noon-1am, Fri. noon-2am, Sat. 2pm-2am, Sun.2pm-midnight). Finally, ask your hostel manager how to find the summer-only midnight spot, **Myší díra** (Mousehole, a.k.a. The Boat Bar), which makes the river a little more interesting by supplying booze to rafters, canoers, and kayakers who stop at the Vltava hut each time they drift by (completely idiosyncratic opening hours).

Sights Perversely, pollution may have been Český Krumlov's biggest boon. In the early 20th century, an upstream paper mill began to putrefy the river, and most citizens moved to the town's outskirts. Under such benign neglect, the medieval inner city escaped "development." Originally a 13th-century fortress, the **castle** fell into the hands of wealthy families who had nothing better to do than fill it with fancy stuff. The length of stone courtyards is open to the public for free. Two separate tours cover the castle—the first visits the older wing, taking in the **Chapel of St. George,** passing through the Baroque Schwarzenberg chambers, and finally emerging in the **ballroom,** which is adorned with frescoes of masques. The second tour explores the older, Renaissance-style rooms before moving into the 19th-century areas of the castle and ending with the splendid Baroque **theater.** Czech tours are only 45kč, but to understand anything more than "Blah, blah, Schwarzenberg, blah," take the English tour (50min.; 100kč, students 50kč; open April and Oct. 9am-noon and 1-3pm; May, June and Sept. 9am-noon and 1-4pm, July-Aug. 9am-noon and 1-5pm). You can also visit the castle **tower** (25kč, students 15kč) and ascend 147 steps for a fine view of the town (open April-Oct. daily 9am-6pm); wander through the **galleries of the crypt** where local artists' sculptures and ceramics are evocatively displayed (open May-Oct. 10am-5pm; 25kč, students 15kč); or stroll in the castle **gardens,** which house a riding school and a summer palace (open May-Sept. 8am-7pm; April and Oct. 8am-5pm).

The Austrian painter Egon Schiele (1890-1918) found Český Krumlov so enchanting that he decided to set up shop here in 1911. Sadly, the citizens ran him out after he started painting burghers' daughters in the nude. Decades later, the citizens realized how silly they'd been and founded the **Egon Schiele International Cultural Center,** Široká 70-72 (tel. 42 32; fax 28 20), which contains hours of browsing material. Schiele's works, including his infamous nudes, share wall space with paintings by other 20th-century Central European artists. Admission is steep (120kč, students 80kč), but very well worth it (open daily 10am-6pm). The **city museum,** Horní 152 (tel. 71 16 74), covers Krumlov's history with bizarre folk instruments, bone sculptures, and log barges that once plied the river (open May-Sept. daily 10am-12:30pm and 1-5pm; 30kč, students 5kč).

■ Near Český Krumlov

Local firms and hostels rent out mountain bikes (see p. 194) for the express purpose of getting you out into the South Bohemian countryside. And if you can't, won't, or don't want to pay to be transported to the start of a day excursion trail, here are a couple of routes that can be done from Český Krumlov itself. The first is a 70km loop along the banks of the Vltava, the second a much shorter, somewhat up-and-down trip to a couple of interesting local sites. Check the weather before you go, get a good map, and take food and plenty to drink!

ALONG THE VLTAVA

Follow the road signs to **Rožmberk** (24km), which boasts the first real sight along the way. The route leads through the towns **Vetřní** and **Záton.** The former hosts a paper mill largely responsible for the polluted condition of the river, while the latter is so small it would be unnoticeable except for a lovely church perched atop a hill some 200m to the left of the road. Carry on along the banks of the river, with strains of Smetana continually playing in your brain, until you see a pale fortress tower up on the left. Rožmberk is just around the next bend. You can stop here and pop up to see the **castle** (tel. 74 98 38; fax 74 98 13), the mighty seat of the mighty Rožmberks (Rosenbergs), but you need to pay for a guided tour to get in. (Tours leave June-Aug. Tues.-Sun. at 9am and 4:15pm; May and Sept. Tues.-Fri. at 9am and 3:15pm; and April and Oct. Sat., Sun. and holidays at 9am and 3:15pm. 30kč, students 20kč.)

If you don't like to climb, head back to Český Krumlov (48km round-trip). Otherwise, press on 9km to **Vyšší Brod.** The town's claim to fame is a cloister, the charm if which resides in its utter non-spectacularity. The simple white church, with some surrounding buildings, almost blends into the other part of Vyšší Brod's "urban" complex. The plaster is crumbling faster than in Český Crumble-off, and no one seems to care. Few foreigners visit, making Brod a top-notch place for a cheap Czech lunch.

Lipno lies another 9km upstream, and on this strip the "up" makes itself particularly evident. **Frymburk** sits along the lake shore 8km west. With a waterside church, it smacks of Swiss quaintness and is a better spot for a break than Lipno. From Frymburk, a road leads back to Český Krumlov, mostly downhill for 22km, to close the 70km loop. If you can't make it this far, you have to retreat the way you came: there's no alternate route.

ROUTE NORTH: REMNANTS OF A GLORIOUS PAST

Unlike the road up that curves around the Vltava, this route heads through hillside meadows. From Český Krumlov, head toward České Budějovice and take a left off the highway toward Srnín. Be careful crossing railway tracks without a crossing guard—fortunately, approaching trains tend to whistle a lot. Whiz through Srnín and follow the signs to **Zlatá Koruna.** The long descent ends at the gate of the 1263 monastery. Over the course of its tumultuous history, the local order of monks was almost abolished several times, managed to introduce potatoes to the region, and was stripped of its property rights by beerlord Eggenberg before finally being sent into the lay world in 1785. Since then, the building has been a pencil factory and an underestimated tourist attraction (tel. 74 31 26). The tour (20kč per person, min. 5 people; available in English) leads through the massive complex's courts, halls, library (the second largest in the country), and the obligatory convent, chapel, and church (open May-Sept. Tues.-Sun. 8am-noon and 1-5pm; April and Oct. 9am-noon and 1-4pm; last tour 1hr. before closing). From here, walk your bike back up the hill, and at the T-junction go straight on towards Kremže (left leads back the way you came).

After entering **Třísov,** take the second right (by the village notice-board) and cross the railway line just below the tiny station. Continue down this sometimes bumpy path, and you'll reach a few houses, the river bank, and, as the path bends to the left, a metal bridge. Leave your bike here, and make a short trek over the bridge and to the left. Be sure not to cross the second metal bridge you come to; trot up the steps to the right instead to get to the 1349 ruins of the castle **Dívčí Kamen.** Find some shade for lunch or brood on the mysteries of the violent past (there's not a lot else to do here) before rejoining your bicycle. Once you've climbed back out of Třísov, it's downhill (almost) all the way home.

MORAVIA

Wine-making Moravia makes up the easternmost third of the Czech Republic. The home of the country's finest folk-singing tradition and two of its leading universities, it's also the birthplace of a number of Central European notables: Tomáš G. Masaryk, founder and first president of Czechoslovakia; composer Leoš Janáček; and psychologist Sigmund Freud. Gustav Mahler was born in Bohemia, but grew up in the Moravian town of Jihlava (Iglau) before heading off to Vienna. Brno and Olomouc are the towns worth visiting—ignore industrial Ostrava—but South Moravia also harbors the remarkable caves of the Moravský Kras, and the architectural pearl Telč.

■ Brno

The Czech Republic's second city, Brno (bruh-NO) industrialized early and still attracts keen business interest in its frequent trade fairs, as well as the attention of motorcycling fans fixated on the annual Grand Prix. That's just one side of the city, however: the tourist is more likely to enjoy a fine collection of Gothic and Baroque churches, a thriving local arts scene, and the lively atmosphere created by and for the students at Masarykova Univerzita.

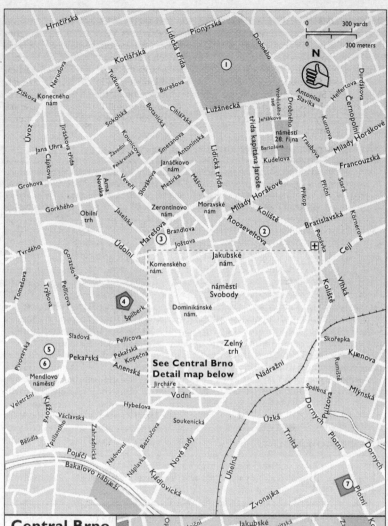

CZECH REPUBLIC

Central Brno

Augustinian Monastery, 5
Bus Station, 7
Capucin Church, 15
Cathedral of St. Peter and Paul, 14
Čedok, 16
Church of St. James, 9
CKM, 8
Janáček Theater, 2
Lužánky Gardens, 1
Mahen Theater, 10
Mendelianum, 6
Moravian Museum, 13
New Town Hall, 11
Old Town Hall, 12
Red Church, 3
Špilberk Castle, 4
Train Station, 17

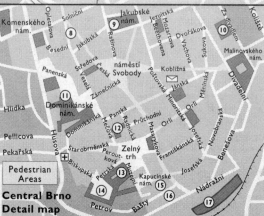

Pedestrian Areas

Central Brno Detail map

ORIENTATION AND PRACTICAL INFORMATION

Brno's compact center makes almost everything, except clubs and accommodations, accessible by foot. To reach the center from the train station, cross the three tram lines and the packed **Nádražní** onto **Masarykova.** Continuing on Masarykova leads to the city's main square, **nám. Svobody.** To get to the tourist office, turn left before the square at **Zelný trh.** The tourist office is on **Radnická,** in the old town hall.

Tourist Office: Kulturní a Informační Centrum Města Brna, Radnická 8 (tel./fax. 42 21 10 90). The multilingual staff books hotels and rooms and sells guidebooks and city maps (29kč) from a treasure trove of literature on Brno and the region. Open Mon.-Fri. 8am-6pm, Sat.-Sun. 9am-5pm.

Currency Exchange: Komerční Banka, Kobližná 3 (tel. 42 12 71 11; fax 42 21 64 76). Provides Visa cash advances and cashes most traveler's checks at 2% commission (min. 50kč). AmEx/Cirrus/MC/Visa **ATM** in front entrance. Open 24hr. **Taxatour,** at the train station, cashes many forms of dough, and charges a hefty 5% as they do. **American Express,** Starobrněnska 20 (tel. 42 21 80 13). Traveler's checks exchanged commission-free. Open Mon.-Fri. 9am-noon and 1:30pm-5pm.

Trains: (tel. 42 21 48 03). To: Bratislava (9 per day, 2hr., 83kč); Budapest (2 per day, 4½hr., 851kč); České Budějovice (3 per day, 4½hr., 100kč); Prague (12 per day, 3hr., 110kč); and Vienna (1 per day, 2hr., 400kč). The international booking office handles *Wasteels* tickets. Open 24hr.

Buses: Zvonařka (tel. 43 21 77 33), behind the train station. Descend into the large area under the train station and follow the ČSAD signs. To Prague (lots per day, 3hr., 105kč) and Vienna (2 per day, 2½hr., 225kč).

Public Transpotation: Adult fare for **trams, trolleys, and buses** is 5kč, or 8kč for a ticket that lets you change lines. Luggage 4kč extra. 24hr. passes 40kč. Buy tickets at a *tabák* or kiosk. Ticket checks happen, and are accompanied by 200kč fines. Half the tram routes run all night; the rest run 5am until 8pm, 10:30pm, or 11pm.

Taxis: Radiotaxi, tel. 42 21 88 88. Loads on streets after dark.

Luggage storage: At the train station. 10kč per bag per day.

Pharmacy: Kobližná 7 (tel. 42 21 02 22). Open Mon.-Fri. 7am-7pm, Sat. 8am-1pm.

Post Office: Poštovská 3-5 (tel. 42 32 11 01). Open Mon.-Fri. 7am-9pm, Sat. 7am-1pm. **Postal code:** 602 00.

Telephones: Common at the station and in the squares. Card phones are a funny green color. **Phone code:** 05.

ACCOMMODATIONS

Brno's hotel scene is strongly geared towards business visitors, so it was no surprise when one of the genuine budget hotels was replaced by the "Moulin Rouge erotic night club disco"—a fairly gloomy sign of the times. The hostel listed below is good, and the pension is dead central; otherwise, the tourist office or Taxatour can arrange private rooms in the center or a 10-minute tram ride away.

Interservis (HI), Lomená 38 (tel. 45 23 31 65; fax 33 11 65). Take tram #9 or 12 from the train station to the end at "Komárov." Continue along Hněvkovského, and turn left onto the unmarked Pompova (the penultimate turn before the bridge). The hostel will appear on the right. Outgoing staff brightens up this high-class hostel with smiles and daily scrubbing. Lone double 575kč; 5-bed flatlets 265kč per person, 300kč with breakfast; with ISIC or HI card 220/260kč. MC/Visa accepted.

Bulharský Klub, Skrytá 1(tel. 42 21 10 63). One hall of double rooms with a shared shower and toilet. Little amenities like fluffy bath rug and patterned tiles. Bar, too. Doubles and triples 300kč per person. Reception open 9am-noon and 5-10pm.

FOOD

Street-side pizza joints far outnumber traditional *párek* peddlers. A fruit and vegetable **market** thrives on Zelný trh (Mon.-Sat. 9am-6pm). A **Tesco's** waits right behind the train station (open Mon.-Fri. 7am-8pm, Sat. 7am-6pm, Sun. 8am-5pm).

Livingstone, Starobrněnska 1 (tel. 42 27 51 56), on the corner of Zelný trh. The cut-out giraffe on the wall presides over a young Czech crowd. Fine light *kuřeci prsa* (chicken breasts; 45kč) go well with salad (25kč) and *krokety* potatoes (15kč). The beer is *Krušovice* (0.5L 16.50kč). Open Mon.-Fri. noon-1am, Sat.-Sun. 6pm-1am.

Sputnik, Česka 1, just off Svobody nám. (tel. 42 21 06 75). Self-serve cafe with plenty of grilled chicken. Quarter bird with fries 40kč; *gulaš* with *knedlíky* 32kč. *Jarošovské* beer only 7kč per 0.5L. Open Mon.-Fri. 8am-6pm.

Stopkova Plzeňska Pivnice, Česká 5. Founded in 1554, this beerhall serves traditional *svíčková* (roast pork; 49kč). Order something else, though, if you don't like whipped cream with your meat. *Pilsner* 14kč. Open daily 10am-11pm.

SIGHTS

Veterans of Kutná Hora and fans of the Capuchin fathers' place in Rome will love the **Hrobka Kapucínského kláštera** (Capuchin Monastery Crypt; tel. 42 21 23 32) just to the left of Masarykova as you come up from the station. The monks there developed a revolutionary embalming technique involving extensive ventilation, preserving 100-plus 18th-century monks and assorted worthies. The results are now on display, along with fine slogans about human mortality that both impress and humble (open Tues.-Sat. 9am-noon and 2-4:30pm, Sun. 11-11:45am and 2-4:30pm; 20kč, students 10kč). On the left when entering **Zelný trh** (Cabbage Market), the Dietrichsteinský Palác houses **Moravské Zemské Muzeum** (Moravian Museum; tel. 42 32 12 05) in its never-ending halls. The historical galleries are good, and the museum boasts 180 wooden mushrooms (open Tues.-Sat. 9am-5pm; 12kč, students 6kč).

At Radnická 8, the tower of the **Stará radnice** (Old Town Hall) looms even larger over the vegetable market after a 1905 extension. The *radnice's* strangely crooked Gothic portal purportedly got bent after the carver who created it spent his whole commission on too much good Moravian wine. Legend has it that the dismayed stone face inside is the petrified head of a burgher who met his doom behind the town-hall wall after siding with the Hussites in 1424. The most famous of the tales involves the stuffed "dragon" hanging on one wall. Sometime in the Middle Ages, the reptile was ravaging the town; to stop him, a valiant knight stuffed quick-lime into an ox carcass and offered the venomous confection to the dragon. After devouring the bait, the dragon quenched his thirst in a nearby river; the lime began to slake, and the poor fire-breather's belly exploded—thus the seam that marks his stomach today. The dragon is actually an Amazonian crocodile offered to the town by Archduke Matyáš to garner favor among the burghers (*radnice* open daily 9am-5pm). Towering above Zelný trh on Petrov Hill is the **Katedrála sv. Petra a Pavla** (Cathedral of St. Peter and St. Paul). Although destroyed in the Swedish siege during the Thirty Years' War, the replacement church was neo-Gothicized 100 years ago. You may hear the bells strike noon at eleven o'clock. Don't panic, Moravia isn't in a new time zone: allegedly Brno was saved from the Swedish siege one day in 1645, when the besieging general gave his army until noon to capture the town, or else he would withdraw. The townsfolk found out about this, rang the bells early, and the Swedes slunk away. The bells have been striking like this ever since (cathedral open Mon.-Sat. 8:15am-6pm; Sun. 7am-6pm). The unexciting crypt museum is around the back (open Mon.-Sat. 10am-5pm, Sun. 11:45am-5pm; 10kč, students 7kč).

Biskupská curves from the cathedral down to Šilingrovo nám. and across into Dominikanská, which flows into Dominikanská nám. The **Kostel sv. Michala** (St. Michael's Church) is worth a glance—enter through the side door—as is the **Nová radnice** (New Town Hall). The short street in front of this building leads to nám. Svobody, Brno's largest square. Its partially gold **Morový sloup** (Plague Column) has successfully warded off infections for the last 300 years, but recently McDonald's has broken through. North of nám. Svobody along Rašínova, the great **Kostel sv. Jakuba** (Church of St. James) points its strangely thin tower ("the toothpick") into the skyline. Built for Brno's medieval Flemish and German communities, the church has undergone more than 10 renovations. The French Huguenot Raduit de Souches, who helped save Brno from the Swedish armies in 1645, rests inside in a great stone monument. Follow Jezuitská east to reach Rooseveltova and an exercise in comparative architecture study. Two minutes to the right sits the grand **Mahenovo divadlo** (Mahen Theater), built by Viennese duo Helmer and Fellner in the late 19th century; two minutes to the left takes you past the 1960s **Janáčkovo divadlo** (Janáček Theater), home of the Brno opera.

From the corner with Jezuitská, Rooseveltova runs northwest to a set of traffic lights. Turning left here, toward the center, leads to the **Kostel Zvěstování Panny Marie a sv. Tomáše** (Church of the Annunciation and of St. Thomas). Built in 1350 as an Augustinian monastery, the church shelters the remains of its founder—the brother of Charles IV, yes, he of the bridge—right in front of the main altar. Down Joštova, the **Červený kostel** (Red Church) is an 1860s medieval pastiche erected by Heinrich Ferstel, who also built Vienna's neo-Gothic Votivkirche. It commemorates the 17th-century Protestant pedagogue Jan Ámos Komeský (Comenius) who revolutionized the philosophy of education, earning him the (declined) offer of the presidency of the fledgling Harvard College.

Head down Husova and up the hill on the right to reach **Hrad Špilberk** (tel. 42 21 41 45), the mighty Habsburg fortress-turned-prison where Hungarian, Italian, Polish and Czech patriots and revolutionaries were incarcerated in somewhat grim conditions. The journey through the prison corridors is more intriguing than the rather weak collection of torture-related exhibits. (Open daily June-Sept. 9am-6pm, Oct.-March 9am-5pm; 20kč, 10kč students. English leaflet available, or pay 200kč for an English-speaking guide.)

From Šilingrovo nám., a walk along Pekařská leads to the heart of Old Brno, **Mendlovo nám.** The high Gothic **Basilika Nanebevzetí Panny Marie** (Basilica of the Assumption of the Virgin Mary) houses the 13th-century *Black Madonna*, the Czech Republic's oldest wood icon, which purportedly held off the Swedes in 1645 (church open daily 5pm-7:15pm, Sun. also 7am-12:15pm). The Augustinian monastery next door was the home of **Johann Gregor Mendel,** who laid out the fundamental laws of modern genetics. It took the scientific world 50 years to appreciate his work, but as his words now accurately predict in stone, *"Má doba přijde!"* ("My time will come!") The **Mendelianum,** Mendlovo nám. 1a, documents Mendel's life and works, explaining his remarkable experiments with peas and bees. The Lysenkoist Communists took down his statue—it's now back in the courtyard (open daily July-Aug. 9am-6pm, Sept.-June 8am-5pm; 8kč, students 4kč; 5kč for English pamphlet).

A lengthy walk on Milady Horákové and a left on Černopolní leads to **Tugendhat Vila,** one of the finest examples of Functionalist architecture. It was built by Mies van der Rohe for the Tugendhats before they were chased out by the Nazis; now it's part of the municipal museum (open Wed.-Sun. 10am-6pm; 80kč, students 40kč).

A left on Schodová leads to **Lužánky Park,** the largest in Brno (open daily 8am-dusk). The 200-year-old trees once belonged to the Jesuits but now please the public, providing paths and shade just to let visitors walk off dumpling-heavy lunches. From the park's southwestern corner, Smetanova will take you past the **Janáčkovo Muzeum,** Smetanova 14 (tel. 41 21 28 11), which celebrates the extraordinary Moravian composer Janáček (open Mon.-Fri. 8am-noon and 1pm-4pm).

ENTERTAINMENT

The *Stará radnice* hosts frequent recitals and concerts—to get tickets for these and other events, go to the tourist office's **ticket agency,** Běhounská 16 (open Mon.-Fri. 9am-5pm). Get **theater and opera** tickets at the office at Dvořákova 11. Rock and pop events and films are advertised on posters all over town. Surprisingly, it's easier to find a *pivnice* than a wine pub in the heart of wine-producing Moravia, but a *vinárna* does occasionally appear (bottles 80-100kč).

Pivnice Minipivovar Pegas, Jakubská 4 (tel. 42 21 01 04; fax 42 21 12 32). This 1992-founded microbrewery has a loyal following. Light and dark brews ferment behind the bar. Pints 17kč. Moravian food also served. Open daily 9am-midnight.

Mersey, Minská tř. 14 (tel. 41 24 06 23), a 30min. walk north along Veveří, which becomes Minská. Or ride tram #3 or 11 from "Česká" to "Tábor." Hosts visiting bands and DJs, sometimes from "overseas." Mostly rock, some techno and jungle. Walk through the dancers to get to the bar (beer a cheap 12kč). Open from 2pm daily; music starts around 9pm.

H46, Hybešova 46 (tel. 43 23 49 45), a 10min. walk west from the train station, or a couple of stops on tram #1 or 2. If the door is locked, ring the bell. Inside, a mostly gay, partly lesbian, others-welcome bar pours beer (18kč). Open nightly 6pm-4am.

Club Philadelphia, Milady Horakové 1a (tel. 57 77 30). Smaller and lighter than H46, this gay-and-lesbian-only space gets packed and smoky by the bar. Open nightly 4pm-12:30am.

■ Near Brno

MORAVSKÝ KRAS

The traveler may spend a few hours in sleazy buffets waiting for bus connections to get to Moravský Kras (mo-RAHV-skee krahs), but no matter how much time is spent en route to and from Brno, it's still a good trip. Inside the forested hills, a network of caves around Skalní Mlýn has been opened up for visitors. The most popular is **Punkevní,** where the tour groups pass magnificent stalactites, stalagmites, *and* stalagmites—many with their own silly names (like *rokoko panenko,* "rococo doll")—to emerge at **Propast Macocha,** "Stepmother's Abyss." Legend has it that a wicked stepmother from a nearby town threw her stepson into the gaping hole. When villagers found the boy suspended from a branch by his trousers, they saved him and threw the woman in instead. Over the last 20 years, 50 people have committed suicide by jumping off the abyss's 140m ledge. During the summer, cavetrekkers are then rowed back along the underground Punkva river in a wobbly boat. Buy tickets for the tour at Skalní Mlýn's bus stop or in the entrance booth. Bring a sweater; it gets chilly even in midsummer. (Exact hours vary from month to month; in summer a first tour at 8:20am and last at 3:50pm is typical. Ask at the tourist office in Brno, or call Skalní Mlýn at (0506) 553 79. 25kč, students 10kč.)

Just around the corner from Skalní Mlýn, the equally fine but much less visited **Kateřinská jeskyně** (Catherine Cave, named for a shepherdess who went inside looking for a stray and never re-emerged) is also worth a look. Huge halls with stunning rock formations, asthma-curing properties and perfect acoustics (proved by blasts of Verdi) await (30min. tour; open 8:20am-4pm in summer; 25kč, students 10kč).

To get there before the caves are overrun with tour groups and possibly sold out for the day, go early. Catching a **train** around 6:30am to Blansko (7 per day, 30min., 10kč) will get you to the caves before 9am, whether you **hike** the 8km from Blansko to Skalní Mlýn along a well-marked trail (follow the green blazes) or take the **bus** (5 per day, 15 min., 6kč) from the bus station just up the road from the trains. At Skalní Mlýn there's a ticket and information office ((0506) 553 79) and a silly tourist mock-train shuttle to the cave entrance (round-trip 30kč, students 20kč), or it's another 1.5km walk along the yellow-marked route. The BVV travel agency in Brno, Starobrněnská 20 (tel. 42 21 77 45), organizes afternoon tours (520kč per person) for those who don't want to get up early.

TELČ

The Italian aura of Telč (TELCH) stems from a trip **Zachariáš of Hradec,** the town's ruler, took to Genoa in 1546. He was so enamored of the new Renaissance style that he brought back a battalion of Italian artists and craftsmen to fix up his humble Moravian castle. The town's thriving burghers asked the craftsmen to spruce up their houses too, and a heated battle-of-the-Joneses soon transformed the center into an Italian export, ultimately putting it on UNESCO's list of world heritage monuments.

Castle tours are Telč's most popular attraction. There are two options—*trasa* A (1hr.) and *trasa* B (45min.)—buy your ticket, wait in the courtyard, and when there are enough people and a guide is ready, a tour will begin. *Trasa* A takes you through the Renaissance hallways past tapestries, through the old **chapel,** and under extravagant ceilings; *Trasa* B leads through the rooms decorated in later styles. Any of the guidebooks on sale around town (30kč and up) provide useful commentary (open May-Aug. Tues.-Sun. 9am-noon and 1-5pm; April and Sept.-Oct. Tues.-Sun. 9am-noon and 1-4pm; 45kč per tour, students 25kč; foreign-language guide 90kč per group; the final tour leaves 45min. prior to closing). In the arcaded courtyard, a **museum** displays examples of Telč's folklore (same hours as castle; 14kč, students 7kč; pick up an English leaflet). The **gallery** off the walled garden is a memorial to artist **Jan Zrzavý** (1890-1977), who trained as a neo-Impressionist, dabbled in Czech Cubism, and produced some striking religious paintings (open May-Aug. Tues.-Sun. 9am-5pm; Sept. and April Tues.-Fri. 9am-noon and 1-4pm, Sat. 9am-1pm; 10kč, students 5kč).

Buses run between Brno and České Budějovice (7 per day, 2hr., 59kč to either). The **tourist office,** nám. Zachariáše z Hradce 1 (tel. (066) 96 21 45), in **Městský Úřad,** books hotels and private rooms (200-400kč). They also have info on the town's **cultural festival,** which takes place during the first two weeks of August (open Mon.-Fri. 7am-5pm, Sat.-Sun. 9am-5pm). The **bus station** lies five minutes from nám. Zachariáše z Hradce. Follow Staňkova and turn left on Masarykova, which leads to the square. **Pod kaštany,** Štěpnická 409 (tel. (066) 721 30 42) has clean, shower-equipped singles (400kč) and doubles (660kč) and accepts MC. Call ahead, or risk being directed by the friendly staff to another hotel or *penzion*. To get there, cross the bridge at the far corner of the main square by the castle, and bear right.

■ Olomouc

The historic capital of North Moravia, Olomouc (OH-lo-mots) won't stir up any new emotions in the visitor's heart, but it will bring to mind the best aspects of the Czech Republic. The masterfully rebuilt town center offers yet another network of promenades amid flaunts and friezes—perhaps even better than elsewhere. Foreign visitors are by far outnumbered by local students, and the young scholars of Comenius and Hus do their best to infuse the eerily quiet, traffic-free squares with life. If you come soon, the 99%-pure-nearly-free-of-guided-tours taste of Olomouc might still fill the air.

ORIENTATION AND PRACTICAL INFORMATION

All trams from the **train station** head downtown (4 stops, 6kč per ticket). The **bus station** lies one stop beyond the trains in the other direction on tram #4 or 5. Take the tram to the gigantic copper **Prior** department store and follow 28. října 50m to **Horní nám.,** the town's main square.

Tourist Office: Horní nám. (tel. 551 33 85; fax 522 08 43; email tourist@risc.upol. cz), in the *radnice*. Tons of info on Olomouc and the surrounding region. Books hotels, hostels and private rooms (from 230kč per person). In summer, student housing fliers are posted at the desk. The staff also offers 10kč trips to the top of the town hall tower (daily at 11am, 12:30pm, 3pm and 5pm). Open daily 9am-7pm.

Budget Travel: CKM, Denisova 4 (tel. 522 21 48; fax 522 39 39). Books rooms and sells train tickets and ISICs. Open Mon.-Fri. 9am-5pm.

Currency Exchange: Komerční Banka, Svobody 14 (tel. 550 91 11). Charges 2% to cash most traveler's checks and handles MC cash advances. Open Mon.-Fri. 8am-5pm. Its annex, Denisova 47 (tel. 550 91 69), does the same during the same hours. Komerční Banka's 24hr. **ATMs** suck'n'spit your AmEx, Cirrus, MC, and Visa plastics where Riegrová 1 meets the town square and at the Prior bus stop.

Trains: Jeremenkovo 60 (info. 476 21 75). To Brno (12 per day, 1½hr., 40kč) and Prague (12 per day after 7am, 3½hr., 110kč).

Buses: Sladkovského 37 (tel. 332 91). To Brno (1 per hr. 5:30am-8pm, 1½hr., 61kč) and Prague (2 per day, 175-200kč).

Public Transportation: The city's **trams** and **buses** all require 6kč tickets, sold at kiosks marked with a big yellow arrow. All trams run between the train station and the central Prior department store before branching off.

Taxis: Call **Ekotaxi** at 522 06 66, or wave one down on the street.

Luggage storage: At the train station. 10kč per piece per day; 24hr. lockers 5kč.

Pharmacy: Lots; try the corner of Ostružnicka and Horní nám. Open Mon.-Fri. 8am-6pm, Sat. 8am-noon.

Post Office: nám. Republiky 2 (tel. 522 40 83). Open Mon.-Fri. 7am-7pm, Sat. 8am-noon. **Postal code:** 771 00.

Telephones: Outside the post office, and many other places. **Phone code:** 068.

ACCOMMODATIONS

Cheap beds (100kč) appear in summer when **dorms** open to tourists; it's possible to snag them by mid-June. A few dorms have vacancies year-round. Olomouc levies a 15kč tax on all rooms.

Hostel Envelopa, 17. listopadu 54 (tel. 522 38 41). From the train station, take any inbound tram 2 stops to "Žižkovo nám." and head down the road to the left of Masaryk's statue. It's the huge building to the left. Student dorm, refurbished somewhat in 1997. Beds in doubles 220kč with communal washing facilities, or 276kč if they're shared with just one other room. ISICs knock the prices down to 122kč/171kč. 1 person alone in a double pays 183kč. Summer only.

Pension na Hradbách, Hrnčířská 14 (tel. 523 32 43). From Horní nám., head down Školní, go straight along Purkrabská, and turn right onto Hrnčířská. Small, friendly pension in the quiet old streets of the town center. Not much space, so call ahead. Singles 500kč; doubles a good value at 600kč.

Palavecký Stadión, Legionářská 11 (tel. 41 31 81; fax 541 32 56), at the swimming stadium. Take any tram from the train station to nám. Národních hrdinů. Backtrack through the bus park, head left under the airplane, and go around the pool buildings. The hostel is part of the pool complex—airy in the morning, but with a chlorinated tang by the afternoon. Doubles 380kč; triples 420kč. Swimming 30kč.

FOOD

There's a **24-hour grocery** at Komenského 3 and nearby, at Žižkovo nám., a cheap Czech diner, **Bufet "Na růžku"** (open Mon.-Thurs. 7am-6pm, Fri. 7am-5pm).

U červeného volka, Dolní nám. 39 (tel. 522 60 69). Tofu pioneers in Olomouc, with four delicious soy dishes (44kč) and fine veggie starters and salads. The unreconstructed Czech diner can wash down porky plates (48-71kč) with *Velkopopovický kozel* beer (13 kč). Open daily 10am-10pm. MC, Visa.

Cafe Caesar, Horní nám. (tel. 522 92 87), in the *radnice*. A million conversations rumble and echo in the gothic vaults as patrons munch their way through impressively garlicky pizzas (31 varieties, mostly 49-109kč). Plates of pasta are cheap (13kč), but you pay extra for sauce (37-59kč). Chase it with beer (*Drak* 25kč) or more Italianate cappuccino (19kč). Caesar was, so they say, the legendary founder of Olomouc. Open Mon.-Sat. 9am-1am, Sun. 11am-midnight. AmEx, MC, Visa.

Restaurace U Huberta, 1. máje 7 (tel. 522 40 17). The only non-traditional thing here is the sign in the dining room requesting patrons not to smoke from noon to 3pm. Better-than-average Czech cuisine, with daily *hotová jídla* (prepared meals; 34-46kč) and veggie fried cheese options (28-54kč). Open Mon.-Sat. 10am-10pm.

SIGHTS

The imposing spires of **Chrám sv. Václava** (St. Wenceslas Cathedral) are probably the only way to find tiny Václavské nám., tucked away in the northeast corner of Staré Město. The high-vaulted church interior is in impeccable condition, having been reworked virtually every century since the fire of 1265. The crypt exhibits Christian paraphernalia, including the gold-encased skull of Olomouc's protectress St. Pauline. Nothing here is outstanding, but the collection does give the viewer a feel for Moravian Catholicism (open Mon.-Thurs. and Sat. 9am-5pm, Fri. 1pm-5pm, Sun. 11am-5pm; donations requested). The **Přemyslovský Palác** (Přemysl palace) next door is a Gothic cloister with fine 15th-century frescoes, unique Romanesque window designs, and the 13th-century **Kaple sv. Jana Křtitele** (Chapel of John the Baptist). Descend Dómská and climb up Wurmova to reach Biskupské nám. On the east side is the Renaissance **Arcibiskupský palác,** a 17th-century palace and the place where Franz Josef ascended the Habsburg throne during the revolutionary turbulence of 1848.

Follow Mariánská to nám. Republiky, where **Vlastivědné muzeum** (Museum of National History and Arts), nám. Republiky 5 (tel. 522 27 41), presents the history of *homo olomouciensis* from mammoth to noble, as well as the pre-Communist history of the *radnice*'s astrological clock. The temporary exhibits are the museum's highlights (open Tues.-Sun. 10am-5pm; permanent exhibit 10kč, students 5kč; entire museum 30kč, students 15kč). From the museum, take a left on Univerzitní after the pretty (but closed) church, past the Jesuit **Kaple Božího Těla** (open Tues.-Sun. 9am-5pm; 10kč, students 5kč) and up to the **Kaple sv. Jana Sarkandra** (Jan Sarkander Chapel), which commemorates the Catholic priest tortured to death by Protestants in 1620 after he refused to divulge a confessor's secret. There's an exhibit on the "threefold torture" he suffered inside—if no regular hours are posted and you *really* want to see it, ask a priest at the nearby **Kostel sv. Michala** (St. Michael's Church—a good example of the Baroque style at its most confident) to let you in.

A right on Mahlerova leads to the bustling **Horní nám.** The massive 1378 **radnice** and its spired clock tower dominate the center, while fountains gush on both sides. A wonderful astronomical clock is set in the *radnice*'s north side. Apparatchiks in 1954 contributed to the building of Socialism when they replaced the mechanical saints with mechanical steelworkers, who strike the hour with their hammers. **Sloup Nejsvětější Trojice** (Trinity Column) soars over 35m in black-and-gold glory. North along 28. října, next to the massive copper cube of the Prior department store, the blocky Gothic **Kostel sv. Morice** might well have been the minimalist eyesore of its day, but the rich interior is all decoration. Most of the sculptures date from 1399 to 1540. One of Europe's largest Baroque organs bellows on Sundays in the church's resonant hall, and is the star of the international organ festival each September. South of Horní nám., stately homes line Dolní nám. The oldest building is the 1580 **Hauenschildův palác,** at the corner of Lafayettova, but the square's centerpiece is the **Morový sloup** (Plague Column), which gathers eight saints around a Madonna and child.

ENTERTAINMENT

Start the evening's drinking at the Student Center's **Kavárna Terasa,** Křížovského 14, sitting out on the terrace. A pint of *Gambrinus* (11kč) smoothly accompanies the fall of evening on the forested gardens below. Inside, students squeeze onto silvery-gray sofas, and the conversation and the beer flow freely (open Mon.-Thurs. 10am-midnight, Fri. 10am-2am, Sat. 2pm-2am). Moving back towards the center, **Depo No. 8,** nám. Republiky 1 (tel. 522 12 73) offers Czech food (with some tofu) and *Staropramen* (18kč) in three underground rooms with metallic decor and comfy seats (open Mon.-Thurs. 10am-4am, Fri.-Sat. 10am-6am, Sun. 4pm-1am). For a change of scene, try **Vitriol,** Univerzitní 6, where Chinese lampshades, Indian music, maps of old Moravia, and wooden pub tables mingle with dozens of teas (from 20kč), several coffees (from 10kč), *Lobkowicz* beer (12kč), and a gritty vibe that prevents too much of a drift toward naff New Age spaciness (open Mon.-Thurs. 5pm-midnight, Fri.-Sun. 5pm-1am).

ESTONIA (EESTI)

US$1	= 14.55EEK (Estonian Kroons)	10EEK =	US$0.69
CDN$1	= 10.52EEK	10EEK =	CDN$0.95
UK£1	= 23.15EEK	10EEK =	UK£0.43
IR£1	= 21.34EK	10EEK =	IR£0.47
AUS$1	= 10.59EEK	10EEK =	AUS$0.95
NZ$1	= 9.24EEK	10EEK =	NZ$1.08
SAR1	= 3.10EEK	10EEK =	SAR3.23
DM1	= 7.99EEK	10EEK =	DM1.25

Country Phone Code: 372   **International Dialing Prefix: 800**

Volvos, cellular phones, designer shops, and an ever more stylish young public seem to attest that Estonia is benefitting from its transition to democracy and capitalism. Material trappings, however, mask declining living standards in the face of growing inflation. Historically and culturally identifying with its Nordic neighbors, Estonia is redefining its identity and forgetting its Soviet past, to the chagrin of the 35% of the population who are ethnically Russian. Having overcome successive centuries of domination by the Danes, Swedes, and Russians, the Estonians' serene, patient pragmatism has matured into a dynamic and, some would say, Scandinavian attitude.

ESTONIA ESSENTIALS

Citizens of Australia, Canada, Ireland, New Zealand, the United Kingdom, and the United States do not need a visa to visit Estonia for up to 90 days. South Africans can obtain a visa at the border for 400EEK. It is cheaper for South Africans to apply for a visa at the closest Estonian consulate before departure, although this requires a notarized invitation. When arranged before departure, 30-day, single-entry visas are US$10, and multiple-entry visas $50. To obtain a visa extension, contact the visa department of the Estonian Ministry of Foreign Affairs in Tallinn (tel. 631 74 40).

GETTING THERE AND GETTING AROUND

Several **ferry lines** connect to Tallinn's harbor (general info tel. 631 85 50 or 43 12 50). **Tallink** (tel. 640 98 00) is a popular line, with three boats per day between Helsinki and Tallinn (3½hr., 375-430EEK, students 175EEK). **Tallinn Line Express** (tel. 60 14 55) runs two hydrofoils, making six round-trips per day (1½-2hr.; late spring to late fall only, Mon.-Fri., 360-400EEK). **Estline** (tel. 631 36 36) sails the *Regina Baltica* between Stockholm and Tallinn (1 every other day, 13hr., deck space 500EEK, students 380EEK, cabin space 126EEK). **Silja Line** (tel. 631 83 31) sails two beautiful boats per day between Tallinn and Helsinki (3½hr., 140 Finnish Marks and up). For contact details of ferry companies across the Baltic in Helsinki, see **Gateway Cities,** p. 774. In Estonia, reservations for all ferry lines can be made through **Baltic Tours,** in Tallinn (tel. 631 35 55 or 43 06 63).

Buses and trains radiate to all points from Tallinn and Tartu. Three **train** lines cross the Estonian border; one heads from Tallinn through Tartu to Moscow, another goes to Rīga and on to Warsaw, and the third goes through Narva to St. Petersburg. The **Baltic Express** is the only train from Poland that skips Belarus, linking Tallinn to Warsaw via Kaunas, Rīga, and Tartu (1 per day; 20hr.; 660EEK, private compartment 1049EEK). Major towns such as Pärnu and Haapsalu are all connected to Tallinn, but trains can be scarce. Diesel trains, as opposed to local electric trains, are express. Estonian rail tickets are the most expensive in the former Soviet Union. **Buses** thoroughly link all towns, often more cheaply and efficiently than the trains. It's even possible to ride buses direct from the mainland to towns on the islands (via ferry) for less than the price of the ferry ride alone. During the school year (Sept. 1-June 25), students receive half-price bus tickets. On the islands, where buses have up to 12-hour gaps between trips, bike and car rentals can be relatively inexpensive and an excellent way of exploring the remote areas. Those who **hitchhike** stretch out an open hand. *Let's Go* does not recommend hitchhiking as a safe form of transportation.

Estonian Air (tel. 640 11 60 or 44 63 82) flies between Tallinn and Helsinki (4 per day; round-trip US$142, under 25 US$86). **Finnair** (tel. 611 09 50) also connects Tallinn to Helsinki (4 per day; one-way US$142, under 25 US$43), and **SAS** (tel. 631 22 40) goes to Stockholm (1 per day, US$338).

TOURIST SERVICES

Unlike most of the former Soviet Union, Estonia is grasping the importance of tourist services; most small towns now offer city maps, while larger towns and cities may have well-equipped tourist offices with literature and staff who can help you find hotels, restaurants, and whatever else you need. Info booths marked with a green (or sometimes blue) "i" sell maps and give away brochures; staff can generally answer questions in English. The main tourist offices arrange tours and make reservations.

MONEY

The unit of currency is the **kroon** (EEK), divided into 100 **senti,** which is tied to the Deutschmark. Most banks (*pank*) cash **traveler's checks.** Increasingly more restaurants and shops take credit cards, mostly **Visa** and **MasterCard.** Hotel Viru in Tallinn, as well as many other banks across the country, provides Visa cash advances. **ATMs** take only local bank cards.

COMMUNICATIONS

A letter abroad costs 6.70EEK. To use a pay telephone, you must insert a digital card, obtainable at any bank or newspaper kiosk. Cards come in denominations of 30, 50, and 100EEK. If you dial a cell phone number, you get to foot the bill, at around 6EEK per minute. **AT&T Direct** is available in Estonia by dialing 80 08 00 10 01 from any phone. **International long-distance** calls from Estonia can be made at post offices. Calls to the Baltic states and Russia cost 8.50EEK per minute (10.50EEK with a card). Phoning the U.S. runs a steep 30EEK per minute from Tallinn and 36EEK from other cities (40.80EEK with a card). International calls can be ordered through the operator in the post office; it should take about 10 minutes for the call to go through.

In an attempt to update and modernize their phone system, the Estonians have come up with a system that proves that the universe, despite everything, tends toward disorder. There are three phone systems in Tallinn: a crude medieval system, a new digital system, and a cellular system. Each system has its own area code. For the **old system,** phone numbers have 6 digits, and the area code is 22. For the **new system,** in which phone numbers have 7 numbers, the first of which is a 6 (often mistakenly placed in parentheses), the area code is 2. The increasing popularity of the cellular system is evident in the upscale city center, where every other person has a cell phone in hand. For **cellular phones,** the area code is 25. The digital system and the old system can call each other without the area code within a given city. Calling from a cell phone, however, means always having to dial using an area code. To call Tallinn from outside Estonia on the old system, dial 37 22 and then the number; on the digital system, dial 372. To call a cell phone anywhere in Estonia, dial 37 25. To call from **Russia** with love, the old Soviet codes still apply: dial 014 instead of 372, then the appropriate area code.

To call out of Estonia on the old system dial 8, wait for the second, more mellow, tone, then dial 00, the country code, and the rest of the number. From digital phones, dial 800 without waiting for a tone. From a cell phone, just dial 00 and the number. To call Eesti Telefon's **information** number dial 07. If you get lost in the chaos of the Estonian phone system, or need any information, call the English-speaking **Ekspress Hotline** (tel. 631 32 22 in Tallinn, elsewhere, dial 8, then 11 88).

English-language **books** and **newspapers** are relatively easy to find in Estonia, especially in Tallinn. The English-language weekly *The Baltic Times* (5EEK), has an excellent entertainment listing for all three Baltic countries, as well as detailed news and features about the Batlic region. The English-language weekly *Baltic Independent* is a good source for info on the latest in Tallinn and Tartu, or keep an eye out for *City Paper—The Baltic States,* at hotels, kiosks, and tourist info points (US$1.50).

LANGUAGE

Estonians speak the best **English** in the Baltic states; most young people know at least a few phrases. Many also know **Finnish** or **Swedish,** but **German** is more common among the older set. **Russian** was learned in schools, but Estonians in secluded areas are likely to have forgotten much of it since few, if any, Russians live there. Moreover, Estonians are usually averse to using Russian. Always try English first, making it clear you're not Russian, and then switch to Russian if necessary. Estonian is a Finno-Ugric language, with 14 cases and all sorts of letters. One popular Estonian rock group calls itself Jää-äär, translated as "on the edge of the ice." You won't master Estonian in a day, but basic words help: *bussijaam* (BUSS-ee-yahm; bus station); *raudteejaam* (ROWD-tee-yahm; train station); *avatud* (AH-vah-tuht; open); *suletud* (SUH-leh-tuht; closed). Also see the Estonian Glossary, p. 802.

HEALTH AND SAFETY

In Tallinn: Fire: tel. 001. **Police:** tel. 002. **Ambulance:** 003.
Elsewhere: Fire: tel. 01. **Police:** tel. 02. **Ambulance:** tel. 03.

Public **toilets** (*tasuline*), marked by "N" or a triangle pointing up for women and "M" or a triangle pointing down for men, usually cost 3EEK and include a very limited supply of toilet paper. Try not to drink any unboiled tap water; bottled water is always a safer choice. While the **crime** rate is low, women should avoid going to bars and clubs alone or walking alone at night, even during white nights. For English-speaking help in an emergency, contact your embassy.

ACCOMMODATIONS AND CAMPING

Each **tourist office** will have listings and prices of accommodations in its town and can often arrange a place for visitors. Even some of the upscale hotels have hall toilets and showers. Many hotels provide **laundry** services for an extra charge. Some hostels are part of larger hotels, so be sure to ask for the cheaper hostel rooms. Between the range of expensive western hotels, US$100-per-night ex-Intourist abodes, and the cheap, drab hotels with no hot water, a few companies have set up youth hostels and started to arrange stays at private homes. Tallinn's **Baltic Family Hotel,** Mere pst. 6 (tel./fax 44 11 87), **Bed and Breakfast,** Sadama pst. 11 (tel./fax 60 20 91), and **CDS Reisid** (Baltic Bed and Breakfast), Raekoja plats 17 (tel. 44 52 62; fax 31 36 66), offer rooms in homes throughout the Baltic countries. BFH charges US$9-15 per person; CDS is computer-efficient but charges US$25.

FOOD AND DRINK

It's hard to define Estonian food; go to any local restaurant and you'll see the same assortment of drab sausages, lifeless schnitzel, greasy bouillon, and cold fried potatoes that plague all of the former USSR. If there is a difference in Estonia, it is that there is more fish on the menu. Trout is especially popular, and often the ham-laden *soljanka* you knew as meat stew in Rīga and Moscow will undergo a seaward-change here into a deliciously thick whitefish soup. Beer is the national drink in Estonia for good reason—not only is it inexpensive, it's also delicious and high-quality. The national brand *Saku* is excellent, as is the darker *Saku Tume*. Local brews, like the *Saaremaa* beer available in Kuressaare, can be volatile. Some restaurants and cafes take an hour break during the late afternoon. If dining late, try to get in before 10pm.

CUSTOMS AND ETIQUETTE

Businesses take hour-long **breaks** at noon, 1, or 2pm, and most are closed on Sundays. No one **tips** in Estonia, although a service charge can be included in the bill at some restaurants. Most Estonian doorkeepers are friendly to Westerners, although you'll occasionally meet a hard-headed Stalinist. Try smiling and speaking English, German, or French. **Women** traveling alone are a rarity, so expect some questions. Also, women in Estonia never go to bars or clubs alone, and in some towns, women dining alone might get some stares, especially if they order beer—and especially if it's anything but *Saku* original. **Homosexuality** is legal in Estonia, but public displays are not socially accepted, even in bigger cities. Much late-night entertainment in cities and resort towns caters to *mafiosi* and the like, and on weekend nights most clubs throw expensive erotic shows involving naked women on neon floors.

NATIONAL HOLIDAYS

Estonians observe: February 24, Independence Day (1918); May 1, May Day; June 23, Victory Day (Battle of Võnnu, 1919); June 24, Jaanipäev (St. John's Day); and November 16, Rebirth Day (1988).

LIFE AND TIMES

HISTORY

Estonia's new-found freedom shines against a history of foreign domination and repression. Archaeological evidence dates the first settlement to the middle of the 8th millennium BC. Five thousand years later, **Finno-Ugric** tribes arrived, mixing with the previous settlers and forming farming villages around 1500-1300BC. **Viking** invasions, beginning in the 8th century AD, shook up the rural peace. **King Canute** of Denmark launched attacks in the 1000s, and after 200 years of diligent pillaging, **Denmark** conquered Northern Estonia in 1219. The Germans, Swedes and Russians also tried, at times successfully, to get a piece of the Estonian pie. By 1227 all of Estonia had been conquered, and small feudal states divided the land between the **Livonian Order** (crusading German knights), the Danes, and the **Bishops of Tartu and Saare-Lääne.**

During the 15th century, Estonia clashed with Lithuania, Novgorod and Pihkava, eventually leading to conflict with Moscow. In 1558, **Prince Ivan IV** of Moscow conquered the tiny feudal states. In an effort to force Ivan out, the defeated states searched for foreign assistance: the Bishop of Saare-Lääne sold his land to Denmark (1559), and northern Estonia capitulated to Sweden, as did southern Estonia to Polish rule (1561). By 1583, Russia had lost control of Estonia, and in 1625, as a product of the Swedish-Polish wars, most of Estonia fell into Sweden's hands.

The **Swedish interlude** (1629-1710) was a relative respite for the Estonians, as it curbed the worse abuses of the feudal system. During this era, Estonian-language schools and Tartu University were established. Amidst the crossfire of the Northern War, in which Russia's **Peter the Great** and Sweden's **King Charles XII** duked it out in northern and central Europe, Estonia again changed hands. Following Peter's victory, the 1721 **Peace of Nystad** awarded him the Baltics. Russian rule reversed the reduction of the nobility's power that had begun under the Swedes, and serfs lost all rights until 1819, when **serfdom was abolished,** 45 years earlier than in Mother Russia herself. Benefiting from a wave of reforms, Estonian peasants owned two-fifths of all privately owned land by the end of the 19th century. Following the coronation of **Tsar Alexander III,** Russia clamped down, prompting an Estonian nationalistic backlash led by **Konstantin Päts,** editor of the radical newspaper *Teataja.*

> As the Red Army slowly pushed the Nazis out, tens of thousands of Estonians died at sea trying to escape their homeland.

The **1905 Russian Revolution** sparked rebellions in Estonia that were met by harsh reprisals. At the outbreak of **WWI,** Estonians were in a difficult position; many were drafted into the Russian Army, while the Estonian-German population sided with Prussia. The **Russian Revolution of 1917** intensified the Estonian struggle for independence. After occupation by Germany, Estonia declared **independence** in 1918 but was subsequently taken by the Red Army. Only with British and Finnish help did Estonians recapture their land and declare their right to **self-rule.** From 1919-33, a coalition government ruled. The decentralized government was unable to cope with economic depression and unemployment in the early 1930s, forcing President Päts to proclaim a state of emergency and rule as a benevolent dictator from 1934-36 before resuming democratic elections. In 1940, as previously agreed in the secret protocol of the **German-Soviet Nonaggression Pact,** Estonia was occupied by the Russians, who formed the **Estonian Soviet Socialist Republic.** Päts and other Estonian leaders, as well as a significant portion of the Estonian population, were arrested, deported, or killed. A year later, however, **Hitler** reneged on the Nonaggression Pact, and Germany invaded and occupied the country 1941-44. As the Red Army slowly pushed the Nazis out in mid-1944, tens of thousands of Estonians fled to Germany or Sweden; thousands more died at sea trying to escape their war-ravaged homeland.

The Singing Revolution

Over the past century, Estonia has done more with music than just sing away its blues. The Russian-dominated nation made its musical debut in 1869, as 10,000 patriots joined voices to praise Estonia at the country's first song festival. Over the decades, as Russia tightened its grip, the sing-a-thons became focal points of protest for independence, increasing national pride and adding momentum to the ever-feisty Estonian freedom movement. Under Stalin, singing patriotic hymns became a sure-fire pass to a Siberian wonderland, yet the sing-alongs continued underground. By 1988, Estonians couldn't keep the music in any longer, and at a raucous political rally, 10,000 voices raised a tune that had been outlawed for 40 years. That summer, rebellious hymns resounded throughout the country, as marches and rallies united the disgruntled Estonians, frightened the Soviet government and ultimately, in 1991, gained Estonia its freedom.

ESTONIA

The 50s saw extreme repression and Russification under **Soviet rule;** deportations and immigration reduced the percentage of ethnic Estonians in the population from 90% in 1939 to 60% in 1990. Internal purges removed the few native Estonians holding seats in the Republic's Communist party. *Glasnost* and *perestroika* eventually permitted breathing room for an Estonian political renaissance. In 1988, a **Popular Front** emerged in opposition to the Communist government, pushing a resolution on independence through the Estonian legislature. Agitators for independence won a legislative majority in the 1990 elections; following the foiled Moscow coup of 1991, Estonia became truly independent.

LITERATURE

The first written work in Estonian, a rough translation of the Lutheran catechism, appeared in 1535. **Anton Thor Helle's** 1739 translation of the Bible helped create a common Estonian language primarily out of the northern dialect and heralded the **Estophile period** (1750-1840), which increased the volume of Estonian literature, especially lyric poetry rooted in national folktales and Finnish epics. Folklore provided the basis for **Friedrich Reinhold Kreutzwald's** *Kalevipoeg* (1857-61). The epic's eponymous hero slays castle-loads of Teutons. Chained to the gates of Hell, he is prophesied to return, his own release bringing new life to the nation. This tale became the rallying point of Estonian national rebirth in the Romantic period, of which **Lydia Koidula's** poetry and drama, imbued with protest, marked the peak.

Deepening class barriers in the 1800s shifted the intelligentsia's attention away from national problems to social ones. Still, the entrance of Realism into Estonian literature was painful. **Eduard Vilde's** novels attacking the relationship between feudal landowner and serf drew moral criticism. In the 1905 Revolution, Vilde helped popularize Socialist ideas. At the same time, the pro-revolutionary Neo-Romantic **Noor-Eesti** (Young Estonia) movement appeared. Its writers focused primarily on literary form, although **Gustav Suits's** stylistic experiments produced poems which called on youth to fight for liberty and truth. Suits's later work, however, reflected the poet's disillusionment, a pessimism justified by the outbreak of WWI.

> Chained to the gates of Hell, the hero of the epic "Kalevipoeg" is prophesied to return, bringing new life to the nation.

The interwar years saw the development of tragic poetry haunted by visions of human suffering and war. Realism-starved poets protested against newly independent Estonia's bourgeois rule. **Anton Tammsaare's** prose evolved with the changing literary styles. A turn-of-the-century naturalist, he joined the Noor-Eesti group only to surprise the public again with realist novels in the 20s. Tammsaare's *Tõde ja õigus* (*Truth and Justice,* 1926-33), a search for the meaning of life, canonized him in Estonia's literary hagiography. The resurgence of Realism did not dampen the Estonian literati's interest in mysticism. **Maria Under's** earthy love sonnets and **Heiti Talvik's** doomsday predictions gained popularity in the 1930s. The latter seemed to foresee WWII and the enlargement of the USSR; both hindered the growth of Estonia's literary tradition. After 1940, many novelists went into exile and used symbolic and erotic writing to confront their new life and contemporary society. Later emigrés penned ironic and self-critical verses. **Socialist Realism** at home sent many to temporary exile in Siberia. **Jaan Kross** managed to get away with criticizing Soviet reality in *The Tsar's Madman* (1978). **Aimée Beekman** avoided head-on conflict with the authorities, shedding light on modern women's dilemmas in *The Possibility of Choice* (1978).

ESTONIA TODAY

Estonia is within reach of Scandinavian standards of living, but prices stay low. Thousands, however, are out of work. A recovery plan, instigated by former Prime Minister **Tiit Vähi,** continues to work under current Prime Minister **Mart Siimann** of the Coalition Party and Rural Union. Estonia stands as one of the first of the Eastern European countries in line for **EU membership.**

Estonia's main foreign policy problem is **Russia.** Moscow promised to honor Estonian borders in the 1920 **Treaty of Tartu,** but annexed 5% of Estonia's territory after invading in 1940, and unilaterally demarcated the borders. Estonia still refuses to accept the loss of these regions. Closer to home, nearly 35% of Estonia's residents are Russian immigrants or children of immigrants. In July 1996, Soviet passports—which most Russians in Estonia possess and use—expired, leaving Russian citizens without passports and forcing them either to opt for Estonian citizenship or to live as illegal residents. The first option is complicated by a difficult language test that all would-be Estonians must pass. The test has been waived for some returning ethnic Estonians, leading Russians to protest that Estonians are trying to disenfranchise the Slavs and squeeze them out of the country. The government has responded slowly, allowing Russians to live in Estonia without passports, though "foreigner" status brings difficulties with travel or even registering a car.

Tallinn

With medieval Germanic spires climbing skyward, vendors pouring *Saku* in Raekoja plats, and cobbled streets winding through wonders of history and architecture, Tallinn's cityscape is now complemented by hip cosmopolitan shops, bars, restaurants, and a very fashionably dressed young crowd. The most renowned town of the German Hanseatic league in the 14th and 15th centuries, Tallinn is beginning to boom again. Nonetheless, the city center's prosperity cannot hide Tallinn's drab outskirts, which remain as squalid as if frozen in Soviet rule. But even farther out in suburbia, expensive new houses are reinventing Tallinn's glory days.

ORIENTATION AND PRACTICAL INFORMATION

Tallinn's **Vanalinn** (Old Town) is an egg-shaped maze ringed by four main streets—**Põhja puiestee, Mere pst., Pärnu maantee,** and **Toom pst. Narva mnt.** runs east from the junction of Mere pst. and Pärnu mnt. to the looming **Hotel Viru,** Tallinn's central landmark. Vanalinn peaks at the fortress-rock **Toompea,** where 13th-century streets are level with the church steeples of **All-linn** (Lower Town). To reach Vanalinn from the **ferry terminal,** walk 15 minutes along Sadama to Põhja pst., then go south on Pikk between the stone towers. From the train station, cross **Toom pst.** and go straight through the park along **Nunne;** the stairway up **Patkuli trepp** on the right leads directly to Toompea. In Vanalinn, **Pikk tee** (Long Street), the main artery, runs from the seaward gates of All-linn to Toompea via **Pikk Jalg** tower. **Raekoja plats** (Town Hall Square) is the scenic center of All-linn.

> **Tourist Office:** The **Tourist Information Center** at Raekoja plats 10, across the square from the town hall, sells and gives out brochures and a useful **map** of the city showing major landmarks. Another **Tourist Information Center,** Sadama 25 (tel. 631 83 21), at the harbor (terminal A), offers info on small hotels.
> **Tours: CDS Travel,** Raekoja plats 17 (tel. 44 52 62; fax 631 36 66; email cds@zen.estpak.ee). Gives English walking tours of the city (May 15-Sept. 15 daily at 2pm, 1½hr., 50EEK). Office open Mon.-Fri. 10am-6pm, Sat.-Sun. 10am-4pm. **REISI Ekspert,** Rooskirautsi 17 (tel. 44 52 76), also gives tours daily at 10am (180EEK). Buy tickets at Hotel Viru. The shop on Hotel Viru's second floor has free copies of *Tallinn This Week.*
> **Embassies: Canada,** Toomkooli 13 (tel. 44 90 56, emergencies tel. 630 40 50). Open Mon.-Fri. 9am-4:30pm. **Latvia,** Tõnismägi 10 (tel. 631 13 66; fax 68 16 68). Open Mon.-Fri. 10am-noon. **Russia,** Lai 18 (tel. 60 31 66; visa section fax 646 62 54). Open Mon.-Fri. 9:30am-12:30pm. **U.K.,** Kentmanni 20 (tel. 631 33 53; fax 631 33 54). Open Tues.-Thurs. 10am-noon. **U.S.,** Kentmanni 20 (tel. 631 20 21; fax 631 20 25). Open Mon.-Fri. 8:30am-5:30pm.

ESTONIA

Currency Exchange: Five *valuutavahetus* (currency exchange windows) line the inside of the central post office, offering some of the best rates in Tallinn. **ATM** and Visa **cash advances** at Hotel Viru, Viru väljak.

American Express: Suur-Karja 15, EE-090 (tel. 631 33 13; fax 631 36 56). Sells and cashes traveler's checks, books hotels and tours, sells airline, ferry, and rail tickets, and arranges visas to the other Baltics, Russia, and the rest of the CIS. Members can receive mail and get cash advances. Open Mon.-Fri. 9am-6pm, Sat. 9am-3pm.

Flights: Bus #2 runs every 20min. from the **airport,** Lennujaama 2 (tel. 21 10 92; fax 638 87 33), to near Hotel Viru.**Estonian Air,** Vabaduse sq. 10 (tel. 44 63 82); 4 per day to Helsinki, US$142. Open Mon.-Fri. 9am-5:30pm. **Finnair,** Liivalaia 14 (tel. 631 14 55); 4 per day to Helsinki, US$142. **SAS,** Roosikrantsi 17 (tel. 631 22 40); 7 per day to Helsinki, round-trip US$248.

Trains: Toom pst. 35 (tel. 45 68 51). Trams #1 and 2 travel between station and Hotel Viru. Trains are modern, announcements are in English, and there are no shoving crowds. To St. Petersburg (1 per day, 10hr., 195EEK, *coupé* 393EEK). Buy same-day international tickets at window #8, or buy them in advance at window #8 upstairs. Domestic tickets (same-day only) at windows #15-18 in the older building on the other side of the tracks. The *Baltic Express* goes to Warsaw via Rīga and Kaunas, with a change at Šeštokai, Lithuania (1 per day; Warsaw: 21hr., 660EEK, *coupé* 1049EEK; Rīga: 7hr. 303EEK, *coupé* 501EEK). Buy tickets at window #7.

Buses: Lastekodu 46 (tel. 42 25 49), just south of Tartu mnt., 1.5km southeast of Vanalinn. Tram #2 or 4 and bus #22 connect to the city center. Windows #1-9 sell domestic tickets. The *As sebe* window deals with international links. To Rīga (8 per day, 7hr., 114EEK) and St. Petersburg (2 per day, 9hr., 150EEK).

Ferries: At the end of Sadama, 15min. from center. Terminal A sends ferries to Finland, terminal B to Sweden. Bus #92c goes from the ferry to the center of town. Bus #90 runs from the ferry to the train station. **Estline,** Sadama 29 (tel. 631 36 36), sails to Stockholm (every other day; 15hr.; deck 500EEK, students 380EEK). **Tallink,** Sadama 4 (tel. 44 24 40). To Helsinki (3 per day; 1½hr., 375-430EEK). **Viking,** Sadama 25 (tel. 631 86 23). To Helsinki (6 per day, 1½hr., 350-600EEK).

Public Transportation: Buses, trams, and **trolley-buses** cover the entire metropolitan area; each category has separate stops marked with symbols. All run 6am-midnight. Tram #2 connects the bus and train stations. Kiosks sell tickets (4EEK), or you can buy them from the driver (exact change only on the tram and trolley). If you're in Tallinn for a while, buy a 10-day transit card (*kümne päeva kaart;* 50EEK) at a kiosk, which is good for unlimited rides on all public transportation.

Taxis: Find a *Takso* stand, or call 60 30 44, 639 59 59, 31 27 00, or 43 03 30. "Volga" model taxis have low rates. Cabs with meters may charge up to 5.50EEK per km; around Hotel Viru they might overcharge you.

Car Rental: Europcar, Magdaleena 3 (tel. 650 25 59, airport office tel. 638 80 31), is less expensive than others: 11,000EEK per day for a Toyota Corolla with unlimited mileage. Make reservations two days in advance (open daily 9am-5pm). When **parking,** buy tickets from the black boxes on street corners, and place ticket in a visible place inside the windshield.

Luggage Storage: Lockers downstairs in the train station (6EEK—one 3EEK token to open it and another to retrieve your stuff). Open 5am-12:30am. Lockers at the bus station 2-9EEK per day. Open daily 5am-noon and 12:30-11:40pm.

Bookstores: Homeros, Vene 20 (tel. 631 10 59), just off Raekoja plats. A wide variety of books and magazines in English. Open Mon.-Fri. 10am-7pm, Sat.-Sun. 11am-5pm. Buy reference materials, city guidebooks, and Baltic travel books at **Kupar,** Harju 1 (tel. 44 83 09) southeast of Raekoja plats. Open Mon.-Fri. 10am-6pm, Sat. 11am-4pm.

Laundry: Washcenter, Maakri 23 (tel. 646 65 81). Wash your own clothes (55EEK per load), or have them done for you (for considerably more).

Pharmacy: RAE Apteek, Pikk 47 (tel. 44 44 08). A broad selection of Scandinavian medical supplies. Open Mon. 11am-6pm, Tues.-Fri. 9am-8pm, Sat.-Sun. 9am-3pm.

Express Mail: EMS, Toom pst. 33a (tel. 631 39 81). A 10-page document to the U.S. costs 400EEK; to the U.K. 300EEK; to Australia 550EEK.

Internet Access: Internet room at main library, Tõuismäqi pst. 2 (tel. 45 25 27); register first. Open Mon.-Tues., and Fri. noon-6pm, Wed.-Thurs. noon-4pm.

Tallinn

Alexander Nevski
Cathedral, 9
City Concert Hall, 2
City Museum, 4
Dome Church, 7
"Estonia" Theater and Concert Hall, 12
Ferry Terminal, 1
Information Ctr., 14
Intercity Bus Station, 18
Kadriorg Palace, 15

Maritime Museum, 3
Museum of Peter the Great, 16
Post and Telephone Office, 13
Puppet Theater, 5
Song Festival Grounds, 17
Toompea Castle, 8
Tower Museum
"Kiek in de KoK", 10
Town Hall and Museum, 11
Train Station, 6

500 yards
500 meters

Pirita tee
Kurtistku
Lasnamäe
Kadrioru park
Mäekalda
Oktobri tee
A. Weizenberg
Lasnamäe
Tartu mnt.
Pallasti
Pae
Vesi värava
J. Vilmsi
J. Poska
Gonsiori
K. Türnpu
Tartu mnt.
Lastekodu
Juhkentali
Herne
Karu
Narva mnt.
Pronksi
F. R. Kreutzwaldi
Estonia pst.
Lembitu
Liivalaia
Sakala
Veerenni
Filtri tee
Ahtri
Mere pst.
Sadama
Põhja pst.
Suur-Patarei
Soo
Vana-Kalamaja
Rannamäe
Põhja pst.
Telliskivi
Kopli
Rohu
Tehnika
Toompuiestee
Nunne
Pikk
Lai
RAEKOJA PLATS
Harju
Rüütli
Vabaduse väljak
Toompea
Falgi tee
Toompuiestee
Luise
Koidu
Endla
Liha
Suur Ameerika
Kaarli pst.
Lilleküla

ESTONIA

Post Office: Narva mnt. 1, 2nd floor, across from Hotel Viru. Open Mon.-Fri. 8am-8pm, Sat. 9am-5pm. **Postal code:** EE-0001.
Telephones: For all phone services and inquiries, go to window #45 at the post office. **Fax** services (fax 631 30 88). A 1-page fax to the U.S. costs 50EEK. **Phone code:** See **Estonia Essentials: Communication,** p. 206, for help with dialing. The short version: 22 or 2 for new digital lines; 25 for cellular phones.

ACCOMMODATIONS

Inquire at the information desk in the bus station about beds there (communal bathrooms; 100EEK). No reservations accepted. **Karol Travel Agency,** Lembitu 4/7 (tel. 45 49 00; fax 31 39 18), sets tourists up in hostels for as low as 100EEK (40EEK reservation fee). In summer, make reservations one day ahead (open Mon.-Fri. 9am-6pm). **Baltic Family Hotel Service,** Mere pst. 6 (tel./fax 44 11 87), near Hotel Viru, off the street through the alleyway, arranges private rooms with access to bathrooms and kitchen. Call a couple of days ahead, though rooms can sometimes be arranged at the last minute (singles start at 220EEK; central doubles 360EEK; open daily 10am-6pm).

The Barn, Väike-Karja 1 (tel. 44 34 65), in Vanalinn. A find for budget travelers, with unbeatable location and cleanliness. Newly renovated. Doubles 495EEK, shared baths. 38-person dorms 150EEK per person. 10EEK extra for sheets, blankets, and towels. HI Members get a 10% discount. Kitchen and laundry services. Call ahead: this place is extremely popular.

Kuramaa 15 Hostel, Vikerlase 15 (tel. 632 77 81; fax 632 77 15). This hostel's major flaw is that you may never find it. Take bus #67 from across the street from Hotel Viru to the last stop (7-10min.). Go up the stairs and straight into the first courtyard of the building complex. "Hostel" is barely visible in a window toward the right that also reads *"Juksuur."* The office is on the first floor (on the left) of the entryway to the right. Huge rooms with use of a full kitchen. Each apartment has 2-3 rooms, each with 2 beds (many queen size). Shared bathroom within apartment. 140EEK per person, 130EEK with an HI card. Reception open Mon.-Sat. 9am-9pm, but call ahead and someone will wait for you.

Hotel Dorell, Karu 39 (tel. 626 12 00), 5min. from Vanalinn. Clean, but still smacks of Soviet times. Rooms have televisions and telephones. Small singles 350EEK, large singles 400EEK; doubles 460EEK. Breakfast included. Cash only.

Hotel Scard, Liivalaia 2 (tel. 44 61 43), left off Pärnu mnt. Institutional, standard-issue rooms, but clean. The toilets smell a little; worth it for the central location. No English spoken. 100EEK per person. Open July-Aug. only.

FOOD

Although cheaper than in western Europe, restaurants in Vanalinn are becoming increasingly expensive as the kroon sinks and more tourists make their way to Tallinn. The city has many well-stocked **supermarkets,** where you can see Americans weep with joy at the chance to buy Hawaiian Punch and Pop-tarts. The most centrally located is **Kaubahall,** Aia 7, near the Viru Gates (open Mon.-Sat. 9am-8:30pm, Sun. 9am-8pm). The smaller **Kauplus Tallinn,** Narva mnt. 2 (tel. 64 01 10), stays open later and has lower prices (open daily 9am-10pm). Both take Visa and MC. Fast food places, including McDonald's (Big Mac meal 36EEK), are opening everywhere.

Eeslitall, Dunkri 4 (Donkey Stable; tel. 31 37 55). Tallinn's best place for Balto-Russian cuisine; there's been a restaurant in these halls since the 1300s. Eat outside or in a rustic interior with painted beams. Great place for vegetarians; salad buffet (25EEK), vegetable salad (26EEK), and baked potato with mushrooms (42EEK). Good for meat-eaters, too; herring with sour cream and potatoes (26EEK) and steak (67-132EEK). Thronged with tourists in summer, so call ahead for dinner. Open Sun-Thurs. 11am-11pm, Fri.-Sat. 11am-1am. Visa, MC.

Rüütli Baar, Kohtu 2, in the portico across from the Toomkirik. Local and cheap. The Germanic menu includes schnitzel (25EEK) and steak (25EEK), both of which happen to be an Eastern European hamburger. With a glass of *Saku* for only 13EEK, this is a budget traveler's dream. Open noon-6pm Mon-Fri.

Merevarikus, Rahukohtus, on Patkuli Vaateplats (lookout). This cafe/restaurant has amazing views from outdoor and indoor tables. Pork, chicken, mutton, and shrimp main courses 70-90EEK. MC, Visa.

Sanjay's, Rataskaevu 5 (tel. 44 02 54), on the 2nd floor of a Sovietesque 4-restaurant complex, next to the nonstop strip-tease lasso bar. Delicious Chinese spring rolls 30EEK. Service is impeccable, and prices are competitive. Rice dishes 16-59EEK, lamb dishes 69-72EEK, *Saku* 25EEK. Open noon-11pm. Visa, MC.

Teater Restoran, Lai 31 (tel. 631 45 18). With jazzy blues in the background, this affordable basement restaurant is romantic and just plain cool. Choose which medieval cave to dine in, or try outdoors. Spicy creole food with an Estonian touch: seafood gumbo (76EEK), Creole pork chops (79EEK), and salads (from 18EEK). Throw in a glass of *Saku* (25EEK). Open daily 11am-1am. Visa, MC.

SIGHTS

Vanalinn (Old Town)

Get acquainted with Vanalinn by starting at Hotel Viru, walking down Narva mnt., then continuing along Viru through the 15th-century **Viru City Gate.** Along Uus, which runs north just inside the walls, a large **sweater market** sets up in summer; in winter, it moves into the flower stalls that line Viru. Further up Viru lies **Raekoja plats** (Town Hall Square), where handicrafts are sold on summer evenings and folk songs and dances are performed on a small outdoor stage. **Vana Toomas** (Old Thomas), a 16th-century cast-iron figurine of the Tallinn's legendary defender, guards the **raekoda** (town hall), built 1371-1404. Thomas has done a good job so far; this is the oldest surviving town hall in Europe. Behind the *raekoda,* the medieval town jail, **Raemuuseum,** Raekoja 4/6 (tel. 44 99 03), now displays early Estonian photography and contemporary Estonian sculpture (open Tues. and Thurs. 11am-5:30pm and Wed. 2-5:30pm; 7EEK, students and seniors 3EEK). On the north side of the square, Saia kang (Bread alley) twists onto Pühavaimu, where the 14th-century **Pühavaimu kirik** (Church of the Holy Ghost) sports a 15th-century bell tower and an intricate 17th-century wooden clock (open Mon.-Sat. 10am-5pm).

For a view of the medieval city's north towers and bastion, head up Vene from Viru, take a right on Olevimägi, and head up Uus. Along the way are roomfuls of 19th-century knick-knacks at **Linnamuuseum** (City Museum), Vene 17 (tel. 44 65 53; open Wed.-Fri. 10:30am-5:30pm, Sat.-Sun. 10:30am-4:30pm; 7EEK, students 3EEK). Founded by Dominicans in 1246, **Dominiiklaste Klooster,** Vene 16 (tel. 44 46 06), across the street and through a courtyard, contains a Gothic limestone courtyard, two Catholic churches, a windmill, stone carvings, and a granary. The monastery's **Katariina kirik** (Church of St. Catherine) borders the cloister (open daily 10am-6pm; 7EEK). In the large squat tower known as **Paks Margareeta** (Fat Margaret), the **Meremuuseum** (Maritime Museum), Pikk 70 (tel. 60 18 03), houses changing exhibits on Tallinn's history as a busy port (open Wed.-Sun. 10am-6pm; 7EEK, students 3EEK, seniors 3EEK).

Going back down Pikk, **Oleviste kirik** (St. Olav's Church), the tallest church in town, rises to the right. The murals inside the adjoining chapel illustrate the architect's death; he fell from the tower (open Sun. 9am-noon and 5-8pm, Mon. 5-9pm, Thurs. 5-8pm). Go to the end of Pikk and hang a left on Rataskaevu to see **Niguliste kirik** (St. Nicholas's Church, tel. 44 41 40), frequent site of organ concerts, and its mighty spire. Inside is a fragment of Bernt Notke's medieval masterpiece, *Danse Macabre* (open Wed. 2-9pm, Thurs.-Sun. 11am-6pm). At the base of the hill, WWII ruins lie undisturbed as a reminder of Russian bombing that gutted much of south Tallinn in 1944. Farther south along Rüütli, the **Kiek in de Kök tower** (Peek in the Kitchen; 1475CE), Komandandi 2 (tel. 44 66 86), once offered voyeuristic views into the homes of 16th-century Tallinnites. The tower is still pockmarked with embedded cannonballs; its **museum** keeps six floors of art and historical exhibits (open Tues.-Fri. 10:30am-5:30pm, Sat.-Sun. 11am-4:30pm; 7EEK, students and seniors 3EEK).

Straight ahead, the cafe **Neitsitorni** (Virgin Tower), Lühike jalg 9a (tel. 44 08 96), features *hõõgvin* (hot mulled wine, 12EEK; open daily 10am-11pm; balcony closed in winter, but tower open 11am-10pm).

Toompea

Following Lühike jalg uphill onto Toompea from Niguliste kirik leads to Lossi plats, a square dominated by **Aleksandr Nevsky katedral,** begun under Tsar Alexander III and finished a few years before the Bolshevik Revolution. A marble marker from 1910 recalls Peter the Great's 1710 victory over Sweden. The exterior renovations are not complete, but the rich interior is worth a look (open daily 8am-7pm). The **Toompea Castle,** present seat of the Estonian *riigikogu* (parliament), stands here, but the door is barred to prying eyes. Directly behind, a fluttering Estonian flag tops **Pikk Hermann** (Tall Hermann), Tallinn's tallest tower. The **Eesti Kunstimuuseum** (Art Museum), Kiriku plats 1 (tel. 44 14 78), across from Toomkirik higher up on Toompea, displays Estonian art from the 19th century to the 1940s, including a compelling exhibition of Art Nouveau/avant-garde book printing from independent Estonia (open Wed.-Mon. 11am-5:30pm; 10EEK, students and seniors 3EEK). There are three excellent viewpoints from Toompea, all framed by artists selling watercolor versions of the views—the best is at Kohtu's north end, on Toompea's west side.

Rocca-al-mare

In **Rocca-al-mare,** a peninsula 12km west of Tallinn, the **Vabaõhumuuseumi** (Estonian Open-Air Museum), Vabaõhumuuseumi 12 (tel. 656 02 30; fax 656 02 27), collects 18th- to 20th-century wooden mills and farmsteads. Visitors crawl into log cabins, see crocheted and macramé decorations, climb rickety stairs, and hide in horse stables, while intricately dressed actors sing and dance. Weaving machines, wooden clocks, and sheep abound. There are 68 buildings on 84 hectares, including a well, a mill, and **Sutlepa kabel** (chapel), where a choir sings in Estonian and Swedish during holidays. Estonian folk dance troupes perform regularly (open May-Oct. daily 10am-8pm, some buildings close at 6pm; 25EEK, students 10EEK). From Tallinn's train station, take bus #21 (regular 4EEK ticket; ½hr.).

ENTERTAINMENT

To start planning, check *Tallinn This Week* for performance wheres and whens (free at the tourist info center, Raekoja plats). **Pühavaimu kirik** holds performances by students from the Estonian Music Academy and Tallinn Music School. **Niguliste kirik** is famous for its organ concerts and choirs. **Toomkirik** (the Dome of St. Mary's) also holds organ concerts. Listings for these churches are posted outside Rae Museum. During the **Organ Festival** (August 1-10 in 1997), Niguliste kirik, Nõmme-Rahu, and Dome churches host recitals. Tickets are sold in Niguliste kirik (daily from July 1, 2-8pm), or at the door one hour before concerts.

Tallinn loves music festivals. **Old Town Days** are June 6-10, when open-air concerts take place throughout Vanalinn, and a stage on Raekoja plats is erected for fashion shows, singing, and skit performances. Mid-June brings *Kantripäeväd* (Country Music Days). In June or July, Tallinn shifts musical gears, hosting **Rock Summer,** which draws students and bands from around the world for a week-long music fest. In 1997, over 60 of the world's hottest bands performed on 3 stages (600EEK for the whole event, 150EEK for 1 day; for info contact Makarov Music Management, tel. 23 84 03). Come October, it's time for a **jazz festival,** as Tallinn stages *Jazzkaar.*

Estonian Kontserdisaal, Estonia pst. 4. Classical music almost every night, with festivals dedicated to composers and singers. Prices depend upon performers, usually around 40EEK. Ticket office (tel. 44 31 98; fax 44 53 17) open daily 1-7pm.

Vaualinnastudio, Sakala 23 (tel. 44 84 08). A popular comedy theatre. Call for prices.

Eesti Draamateater, Pärnu mnt. 5 (tel. 44 33 78). The biggest dramas in town. Ticket office open Aug.-June Tues.-Sun. 1-7pm.

Estonia Teater, Estonia pst. 4 (tel. 44 90 40). Opera, ballet, musicals, and chamber music. Ticket office open daily noon-7pm, closed in July.

Tallinna Linnateater, Lai 23 (tel. 44 85 79). Drama and comedies in a medieval merchant's mansion (tickets 30-90EEK). Ticket office open Mon.-Fri. 10am-7pm, Sat.-Sun. noon-6pm.

NIGHTLIFE

Bars have sprouted on almost every street of Vanalinn; most bars have a loyal clientele, though all but the most popular are generally empty by 11pm, as the local scene moves to the nightclubs. While some are dominated by young mafioso, expats and tourists are also quickly creating a niche for themselves.

Von Krahli Teater/Baar, Rataskaevu 10, (tel. 631 39 27), on the west edge of lower Vanalinn. The avant-garde theater showcases Baltic and other European talent, from Lithuanian jazz to experimental dance to cutting-edge blends of Gregorian chant and techno. Attached split-level eclectic bar with *Saku* (20EEK) and a dance floor is popular with the local artsy crowd. Tickets for bands in the bar are 35EEK. The theater has shows most nights 7-9pm (tickets 35-40EEK). Open Mon.-Thurs. 7am-2am, Fri.-Sat. 7am-4am.

Nimeta Baar (The Pub with No Name), Suur-Karja 4 (tel. 44 66 66), across from The Barn. If you couldn't figure it out from the men in kilts, it's Scottish-owned. Draws a large, boisterous crowd on many nights, some of which end in shot-drinking competitions. Open Sun.-Thurs. 11am-3am, Fri.-Sat. 11am-4am. Visa/MC).

Hell Hunt (The Gentle Wolf), Pikk 39 (tel. 60 25 61). A rocking Irish pub with Guinness and Kilkenny on tap. Back room serves cottage pie (49EEK) and Irish coffee (45EEK). In summer, a beer garden across the street dispenses suds as long as it's light. Live music some nights, including "local" Irish bands. Open Sun.-Mon. 11am-1am, Tues.-Thurs. 11am-2am, Fri.-Sat. 11am-3am).

George Browne's Irish Pub, Harju 6 (tel. 631 05 16), 300m south of Raekoja plats on the north edge of Vabaduse väljak. Ground-level pub has live music in the evenings, 11 types of beer, a pool table, and good snacks. Excellent fries cure the drinking munchies (20EEK). Open daily 11am-2am. Live music Fri.-Sat. after 9pm.

■ Near Tallinn: Lahemaa National Park

Founded in 1971, Lahemaa Rahvuspark (Bay Area) was the Soviet Union's first, and is now Estonia's only, national park. Nature trails lead over rolling hills and tranquil fields to jagged coasts and forest bogs. Gargantuan boulders, the legacy of glaciers, punctuate the land. The park preserves more than just an ecological zone; the Soviet authorities that planned the park intended to protect the region's rural heritage.

Orientation and Practical Information Small villages pepper the plains. Some villages connect by bus; others require a bike or walk to reach. Luckily, most lie within two hours walking distance of each other. **Buses** from Tallinn travel to Viitna (12 per day, 1hr., 19EEK). There, check the schedule of buses to Palmse mõis (Palmse plantation). Buses run from Viitna to Käsmu (Mon., Wed., Fri., and Sun. at 12:40pm, 10EEK), so biking, and hiking are the only way to get there if you don't want to wait. Hitchers also report success. In Palmse mõis, the English-speaking **Palmse information center** (tel. (32) 341 96; fax 456 59) has info on Lahemaa Rahvuspark (open daily April-Aug. 9am-7pm, Sept. 9am-6pm, Oct.-March 9am-2pm).

Accommodations and Food There are many hotels, hostels and home lodgings in Lahemaa. The Palmse information center offers advice, and can sometimes arrange for private-room owners to pick you up by car. The bed and breakfast in Altia (tel. 825 252 355) has a sauna (100EEK per hr.) and **rents bicycles** (70 EEK per day; rooms 200EEK). At Viitna, past the bus stop, take the first right under the wooden arch, and the **camping office** in the trees can set you up with tent space or narrow-bedded singles (100EEK) and doubles (150EEK) in log cabins with clean new hall toilets and showers. For the best lodging, head for Kämsu. The seaside **Merekalda Pansion,** Neema tee 2 (tel. (232) 99 451), offers rooms (220EEK per person) and a beautiful sauna (200EEK per hour). The hostess also has three beds in a room above the garage for poor students (150EEK per person, including breakfast). Rent a water bike (50EEK per hour), a yacht (150EEK per hour), or a **bike** (100EEK per hour) here. Make reservations a week early. Cheaper lodgings in Käsmu await at **Lainela Puhke-baas** (tel. (232) 991 33), at the end of Neema tee. Once a Soviet pioneer camp, the hotel/campground has basketball, tennis and volleyball courts. They offer rooms (singles 80EEK, 100EEK with shower; 20% discount after 5 days) and use of a kitchen. The **restaurant** behind the hotel serves breakfast (omelette 25EEK) and lunch (open daily 1pm-5pm, bar open noon-midnight). The **Park Hotell Restaurant** (tel. (237) 341 67), on the Sagadi mõis manor grounds, prepares fresh salads (15EEK), *soljanka* (20EEK), and chicken Kiev (45EEK; open daily noon-10pm).

Sights Wolves and bears make tracks through the park in winter, while in summer it's elk, storks and lynx. Lahemaa is also home to 838 plant species, of which 34 are rare. To see how Estonia's German aristocracy lived, go to **Palmse mõis,** a plantation-turned-**museum** (tel. 341 91; fax 324 45 75; email teet@lklm.envir.ee). From 1674, members of the von Pahlen family resided among the manor's slightly ostentatious gazebos and swan ponds, before the government reclaimed all private land in 1923. Peter Ludwig von Pahlen was involved in the 1801 assassination of Russian Tsar Paul I, and Alexander von Pahlen initiated the building of the Tallinn-St.Petersburg railroad (1879). The main house is being restored; eclectic furniture carted in from around Estonia includes examples of Russian late-Classical and Empire styles, huge ornate stores and a horrendous-sounding 19th-century music box from St. Petersburg (open April-Aug. Wed.-Mon. 10am-7pm; 25EEK, students 13EEK).

In **Käsmu,** at the end of Neemetee and through the dirt path in the woods, the **stone hill** sometimes grants wishes to those who give the mound a nice new rock. Ice Age glaciers brought boulders all the way from Finland, and here they remain, reaching 8m above the sand. To the east, **Altja,** an old fishing village turned Soviet military border lookout. The small island out at sea still holds a Russian border patrol station. The century-old fishing huts in the town are part of a **museum** (open 24hr.).

Sagadi lies 5km south of Altja. The **Museum of Forestry,** the first white building on the left through the gates, features exhibits on the park's plant and tree life, its historical uses, and the frightening effects that humans have had on the ecosystem (open Tues.-Fri. 11am-4pm, Sat.-Sun. 11am-6pm; 10EEK; students 3EEK). The restored **Sagadi mõis** (manor) holds, in addition to original artifacts from the household, a collection of Estonian folk costumes. The Baroque building is more modest than some of the other Lahemaa estates, and the grounds look more "natural" in their less well-kept state. Climb the spiral staircase to the attic, half of which displays the manor's old furniture; the other half offers a look at the fauna the master of the house brought back with after his hunts (open Tues.-Sun. 11am-6pm; 15EEK, students 5EEK).

■ Tartu

First mentioned in the annals of history in 1030, when the Kievan Prince Yaroslav the Wise defeated the native population and set up a fortress, Tartu—Estonia's second largest city—is the oldest city in the Baltics. Since that inauspicious date, 55 separate fires have turned Tartu to ashes, destroying any remnants of its medieval past; so Tartu's classical architecture dates mostly from after 1775. Founded in 1632, Tartu University long served as one of the Russian Empire's premier universities and was a focal point for the development of Estonian nationalism. Westernized Tartu now buzzes with the energy of 10,000 collegians, though the city's small size and expansive parks give it a relaxed atmosphere.

ORIENTATION AND PRACTICAL INFORMATION

The **bus** and **train stations** border the center of town. The main artery, **Riia mnt.,** runs into the center from the southwest, and ends by the bus station. Perpendicular to it is **Turu pst.,** which turns into **Vabaduse pst.** and runs from the bus station along the **Emajõgi River** toward the northeast. **Raekoja plats** (Town Hall Square), the city's geographical and social center, stretches west from the **Emajõgi** river toward the old castle hills. **Rüütli** heads north from the square; its end at Lai marks the boundary of the historic center. Behind the town hall, **Lossi** meanders uphill between the two peaks of **Toomemägi** (Cathedral Hill) and intersects **Vallikraavi,** a crooked, cobblestone road that follows the path of the old moat circling the hills and joins **Kuperjanovi,** which leads southwest to the train station.

Tourist Office: Tartu Infobüroo Turistinfo, Raekoja plats 14. Provides info and organizes travel, transportation, and tours (Tues., Thurs., and Sat. 3pm, 1½hr., 90EEK). **Maps** 12EEK. Open Mon.-Fri. 10am-6pm, Sat. 10am-3pm. Travel agency open Mon. 10am-6pm, Tues.-Fri. 10am-5pm.

Currency Exchange: At the train station (tel. 39 22 87). Open daily 8am-10pm. Countless banks in town, including **Eesti Forekspauk,** Ülikooli 6a (tel. 39 05 10), which gives EC, MC, and Visa cash advances, and cashes AmEx traveler's checks. Open Mon.-Fri. 9am-4:30pm. **ATMs** at Rahvapauk, Raekoja plats 14, accept MC and Visa. Open Mon.-Fri. 9am-5pm.

American Express: Kompanii 2, 3rd floor, EE-2400. While they don't cash traveler's checks, they do issue them, and offer cash advances. Open Mon.-Fri. 9am-5:30pm.

Trains: Vaksali 6 (tel. 29 22 20), at intersection of Kuperjanovi, 1.5km from city center. Info booth open daily 7am-noon and 1-7pm. To: Tallinn (5 per day, 3hr., 67-85EEK); Moscow (1 per day, 18hr., 162EEK, *coupé* 363EEK); Rīga (1 per day, 5hr., 95EEK, *coupé* 220.50EEK); Kaunas (1 per day, 9hr., 202.50EEK, *coupé* 391EEK).

Buses: Turu 2 (tel. 47 53 55), on the corner of Riia, 300m southeast of Raekoja plats along Vabaduse. The information booth is open daily 8am-1pm and 2-8pm. To: Tallinn (40 per day, 2-5hr., 60-70EEK); Narva (3 per day, 3-4hr., 64EEK); Pärnu (10 per day, 4hr., 66-68EEK); Rīga (1 per day, 4½hr., 110EEK).

Public Transportation: Buses cost 4EEK. **Bus #5** and **6** go from the train station around to Raekoja plats, the central square, and the bus station. **Bus #4** travels down Võru. Buses #3, 6, 7, 11, and 21 travel down Riia.

Taxis: Outside the bus and train stations (4EEK per 1km within the city, 5EEK outside). A cross-town ride between the stations runs around 15EEK.

Luggage Storage: Lockers in train station. Buy tokens in the room in the main lobby marked "*Vaksali Korraldaja*" (6EEK—one 3EEK token to open it and one to retrieve your stuff). Open 24hr. In the bus station, there is luggage storage on the left side of the main hall. 3EEK per bag. Open Mon.-Fri. 8am-7pm, Sat. 8am-noon.

Pharmacy: Raekoja Apteek (tel. 43 35 28), on the north side of the town hall. Open Mon.-Fri. 8am-9pm, Sat. 10am-5pm. EC, MC, Visa.

Internet Access: Arvutuskeskus (University Computing Center), Liivi 2, south of where Lossi meets Vallikraavi west of Toomemägi. Ask a student or staff member if you can use a computer for free. They'd prefer if you flashed some student ID.

Post Office: Vanemuise 7 (tel. 44 06 21). Telephones, faxes, express mail. Open Mon.-Fri. 9am-7pm, Sat. 9am-3pm, Sun. 10am-3pm. **Postal code:** EE-2400.

Telephones: Lai 29 (tel. 43 16 61; fax 43 39 93), at the corner of Rüütli, north of the post office. Cardphones and **fax** machine. Open Mon.-Fri. 8am-6pm, Sat.-Sun. 9am-4pm. Almost all street phones take digital **phonecards,** obtainable at the telephone office, main post office, or any kiosk in units of 30, 50, or 100EEK. **Phone code:** 07.

ACCOMMODATIONS

Tartu's few budget options consist of standard Soviet hotel fare. The tourist office can help find cheap accommodations if those below are full.

Tartu Võõrastemaja (Hotel Tartu), Soola 3 (tel. 43 20 91), in the center of town behind the bus station in an aging yellow building. Bare rooms with newly tiled communal showers. Sauna (100EEK per hour). Private toilet with hot water. Comfortable renovated singles 370EEK; doubles 640EEK. Breakfast included. MC, Visa.

Külalistemaja Tähtvere, Laulupeo pst. 19 (tel. 42 17 08), in a quiet green spot northwest of the historic center, in front of the looming beer factory pictured on bottles of *Tartu* beer. This 16-bed hotel has singles (150EEK); doubles (250EEK); and a 4-person suite with fireplace and fridge (600EEK). Decent private baths.

Hotel Salimo, Kopli 1 (tel. 47 08 88), 3km southeast of the train station off Võru. Take bus #4 from the beginning of Riia opposite the Kaubamaja to "Karete." Backtrack and take the first left on Sepa, then the second left on Võru; Kopli is the first right. The office is on the 2nd floor. Generic rooms with bare-bones furnishings and dingy white paint. Singles 75EEK; doubles 150EEK. Two rooms share a bath.

FOOD

It's strange that in a university town there aren't more cheap, downscale restaurants. **McDonald's** has opened on Turu near the bus station. The **Kousum,** Riia 2 (tel. 47 62 31), sells staples (open Mon.-Fri. 9am-9pm, Sat. 9am-8pm, Sun. 10am-8pm; MC, Visa). The newly redone **turg** (market) is on the corner of Va baduse and Vanemuise, opposite the bus station (open Tues.-Fri. 7am-6pm, Sat. 7am-4pm, Sun. 7am-3pm).

Pinguin, Vabaduse pst. 2a (tel. 43 46 01), at the base of Raekoja plats. Ice cream 4EEK, pastries 2-3EEK, schnitzel with fries 11EEK, pizza 11EEK, sandwiches 3.50EEK. Open Mon.-Fri. 7:30am-10pm, Sat.-Sun. 10am-10pm.

Püssirohukelder, Lossi 28 (tel. 43 42 31). This cavernous 18th-century gunpowder cellar in the side of Toomemägi now houses a cellar bar and restaurant that turns a great room into kitsch. An older, staid crowd comes here. French salad (canned peas et al in a bowl) 14EEK, flamed pepper steak (popular with the Finns here) 70EEK, beef fillet in wine sauce 65EEK. 0.5L *Saku Originaal* 20EEK. Open Sun.-Thurs. noon-1am, Fri.-Sat. noon-2am. Cover after 8pm 10EEK, 20EEK if there's a show. The variety/erotic show goes up every Wed., Fri., and Sat. at 10:15pm. Visa.

Rüütli Kelder, Rüütli 1 (tel. 43 37 52). This basement restaurant right off Raekoja plats has typical Estonian meals. Summer salad (mixed vegetables) 21EEK, cheese omelette 21EEK, pork with sauerkraut 43EEK. 0.5L *Tartu Alexander* beer 12EEK. Open Mon.-Thurs. 11am-midnight, Fri.-Sat. 11am-2am, Sun. noon-midnight.

SIGHTS

Strolling through the historic center (and stopping occasionally for a glass of *Saku*) is one of the best ways to experience the charm of Tartu like a local student, and see all the sights—in double. **Raekoja plats** (Town Hall Square), the center of Tartu, dates from 1775. The pink and white **raekoda** (1782-89) at the top of the square was constructed in the Dutch town hall style. Most buildings rest on wooden pylons, and some are sinking slowly into the marshy ground. Raekoja plats 18, once the house of **Barclay de Tolly** (an exiled Scottish mercenary who became famous in the war against Napoleon) slumps at one of the craziest angles you'll ever see (it's not just the beer). At the far end of the square next to the bridge across the Eurajõgi stands a photograph of the 1784 Kivisild stone bridge, blown up by the Red Army retreating from the Nazis in 1941.

Ülikooli runs behind the town hall. To the north, it passes the main building of **Tartu Ülikool** (Tartu University), built in 1809 with six imposing Corinthian columns. The university was founded to teach government officials and Protestant clergy, and was modeled on the Swedish Uppsala University. A statue of Gustavas II Adolphus, unveiled in 1992 by Swedish King Carl XVI Gustaf, stands at the back of the building. The Great Northern War closed the school's doors in 1700, but when Tsar Alexander I reopened it in 1802, the institution became a source of government officials for the Russian empire and a model the Russians respected and copied. Inside the main building is the **Museum of Classical Art,** a small collection of Roman and Greek plaster copies with a temporary exhibition of original antiquities (tel. 43 53 84; open Mon.-Fri. 11am-4:30pm; 6EEK, students 2EEK). The attic keeps a collection of students' detention-time doodles (7EEK, students 4EEK). The only Russian university with the right to have fraternities, the school has used its privilege well. The **Estonian National Awakening** began here with the founding of **Eesti Üliõpilaste Selts** (Estonian Student Association) in 1870. The nationalists who constituted the fraternity became so central to Estonia's struggle for independence that when the country won its freedom in 1919, the frat's colors (blue, black, and white) became those of the national flag.

Farther up Ülikooli (which becomes Jaani), **Jaani-kirik** (St. John's Church), Lutsu 16-24 (tel./fax 43 38 60), completed in 1323, was unique in Gothic architecture with thousands of terra-cotta saints, martyrs, and other figures. The Russian recapture of Tartu in 1944 nearly destroyed the church, and only a few hundred figures remain in the scarcely standing edifice. Restoration began in the 80s, but is still not completed. Across the street, the **Museum of the 19th-Century Tartu Citizen,** Jaani 16 (tel. 44 19 34), displays furnishings and objects relevant to its name (open Wed.-Sun. 11am-6pm; 4EEK, students 2EEK). Farther up, at Lai 40, is the **Botaanikaaed** (Botanical Garden; open May-Sept.).

To reach **Toomemägi** (Cathedral Hill), which dominates Tartu from behind the *raekoda,* climb up any number of roads or stairs. At the bottom of the hill by Lossi is a statue of Nikolai Pirogov, a pioneer in the field of anaesthesia in the 19th century who graduated from the university. On the west hump, the majestic 15th-century **Toomkirik** (Cathedral of St. Peter and Paul) served stints as a granary (1600s) and university library (1800s). Today, it houses the **Tartu University Museum** (tel. 43 53 35), an in-depth series of displays, including scientific instruments and a social history of the university (open Wed.-Sun. 11am-5pm; 7EEK, students 3EEK; English guide available). Near the church and two Swedish 17th-century cannons, **Musumägi** (Kissing Hill), once part of a prison tower, is now a make-out spot and the site of an ancient pagan **sacrificial stone.** It stands in front of a small stage used for evening drama performances and an arch of rocks thought to have been part of a fortification. These days, students burn their notes here after exams. A **statue of Karl Ernst von Baer** (the embryologist who adorns the 2EEK note) tops this hill.

Two bridges lead to the east hump of Toomemägi—the pink wooden **Inglisild** (Angel's Bridge), built in the 1830s, and the concrete **Kuradisild** (Devil's Bridge), from 1913. An annual competition between the university **choirs** takes place on these bridges: men on the Devil's Bridge, women on the Angel's Bridge. On this part of Toomemägi, the 19th-century **observatory** (tel. 43 49 32) houses what was once the largest telescope lens in the world. On the northwest side of the hill at Oru 2 stands Tartu's **City Museum** (tel. 42 20 22). Aside from the usual Stone Age spearheads, 19th-century furniture, and various trinkets, a table is displayed here on which the Peace Treaty of Tartu was signed between Russia and the nascent Estonian Republic on February 2, 1920, ending the Estonian War of Independence (open Wed.-Sun. 11am-6pm; closed on the last day of every month; 3EEK, students 2EEK). The **Tartu Kivisilla Art Gallery,** Raekoja plats 18 (tel. 44 10 80), has interesting 19th- and 20th-century works, including those of Johann Köler and Ants Laikmaa, who founded the first studio in Tartu (open Wed.-Sun. 11am-6pm; 5EEK, students 2EEK; Fri. free). The **Estonian National Museum,** J. Kuperjanov 9 (tel. 42 13 11), gathers scads of ethnographic material, including textiles, folk costumes, and furniture, and discusses the 19th-century National Awakening, begun in Tartu (open Wed.-Sun. 11am-6pm; 5EEK, students 3EEK; temporary exhibit 8EEK, students 5EEK).

ENTERTAINMENT

Tartu comes alive in the evenings with revelers roaming and biking around **Raekoja plats** and stopping at the town's growing number of bars. Bulletin boards inside the entrance of the main university building (Ülikooli 20) have fliers advertising local happenings. Various events around town include the August "Rock Box" rock festival showcasing Estonian bands (tel. 42 21 08 for info), and folk-instrument festivals, also in August, that take to the town's streets. The **Dionysia** arts festival is held in May, and includes processions, drama and dance performances, film screenings, and visual art exhibitions all over Tartu. The first Estonian-language theater, **Vanemnine Theater,** Vanemuise 6 (tel. 43 40 59), was founded in 1870. Performances include operas and classical concerts (ticket office open Mon., Wed., and Fri. 1-6pm; closed in summer).

Zavood, Lai 30 (tel. 43 26 89). A smoky basement den with billiard tables. Popular with students. Enter from the right side of the building through a narrow alley. *Saku* 20EEK. Open daily 8pm-4am.

Krooks, Jakobi 34, just at the bottom of Toomemägi. Usually packs the house in the evenings. *Saku* 20EEK. Open daily noon-4am.

Atlantis, Narva mut 2 (tel. 44 15 09). This behemoth of a disco/restaurant/casino/pool hall is the most happening place in town. Neon lights illumine DJ Cool D, who spins most nights for the hip youngsters. Go-go dancers Fri. Cover 14EEK. Disco open Sun.-Thurs. 10pm-4am, Fri.-Sat. 10pm-5am. MC, Visa.

■ Viljandi

At first glance, the town of Viljandi (VEEL-yan-dee) appears as dead as the knights who founded the castle here, but the decorated wooden houses, peaceful lake, castle ruins, and surrounding forests, make Viljandi a worthwhile daytrip. The medieval **Jaani kirik** (St. John's Church) stands in the central castle park. The ruins of a 1466 Franciscan monastery destroyed in the 1560s are visible in the basement. A dirt path leads left to the **Ordulinnuse varemed** (Ruins of the Order's Castle), founded by the Knights of the Sword in the 13th century. Possibly the largest fortress in the Baltics, its stone walls were begun in 1224. The ruins afford the best view of Viljandi järv (the lake) and forests. Children climb around as if the ruins were a jungle gym; wear suitable shoes if you want to play too. The 1879 red and white **Rippsild** (suspension footbridge) leading to town was sent to Viljandi in 1931 by a German count to stop his daughter from racing her horses over it. The town hall peers past a statue of Estonian artist Johann Köler onto **Laidoneri plats,** the former marketplace. A hut at the nearby **beach** rents paddle **boats.** Or swim—the lake's clean. At the **Viljandi Muuseum,** Laidoneri plats 10 (tel. 333 16), find stuffed animals, Stone Age implements, and objects from Viljandi's more recent past (open in the summer Wed.-Sun. 11am-6pm, off-season 10am-5pm; 6EEK, students 3EEK).

The main street, **Tallinna,** runs from beyond the bus station to the castle ruins. From the **bus station,** Ilmarise 1 (tel. 336 80), buses run to: Tallinn (12 per day, 3-4hr., 50-56EEK); Pärnu (9 per day, 2hr., 32-34EEK); and Tartu (14 per day, 2hr., 23-28EEK; station open Mon.-Fri. 8am-1:30pm and 3:30-6pm, Sat. 8am-1:30pm). At the bottom of Tallinna, **Vaksali** runs west toward the **train station.** At the **tourist office,** Tallinna 4 (tel. 337 55), buy a **map** (23EEK; open Mon.-Fri. 10am-5pm, Sat. 10am-2pm). **Exchange currency** at any bank, including **Tallinna Pank,** Tartu 11 (tel. 344 25), which offers Visa cash advances (open Mon.-Fri. 9am-4pm, Sat. 9am-3pm). Both the **post** and **telephone offices** are at Tallinna 11 (open Mon.-Sat. 8am-6:30pm; 24hr. phones). **Postal code:** EE2900. **Phone code:** 43.

The only place to stay in the center of town, **Hotell Viljandi,** Tartu 11 (tel. 338 52), is badly in need of refurbishment (singles 50EEK, double 100EEK; with grim private baths: singles 175EEK, doubles 350EEK; hot water schedule; cash only). The significantly nicer **Hotell Männimäe,** Riia 38 (tel. 366 85), is housed in a Brezhnev-era concrete structure, a 15-minute walk on Vaksali and south on Riia (doubles 240EEK-440EEK depending on facilities; breakfast 40EEK; cash only). At **Restoran Iva,** Tasuja 3 (tel. 344 93), carrot salads (6EEK). Bland mushroom soup (15EEK), and greasy pork cutlet with soggy boiled potatoes (59EEK) round out the menu (open daily 8am-9pm). The **Tasuja Kohvik,** Vadabuse plats 2, has veal schnitzel (28EEK; open Mon.-Fri. 9am-9pm, Sat.-Sun. 11am-9pm). There are numerous **grocery stores,** including one on Keskväljak (open Mon.-Fri. 9am-8pm, Sat.-Sun. 9am-5pm).

■ Pärnu

Seawater, sand...and mud. Pärnu (PAR-noo), established as a resort in the early 19th century, tends to be a little cold for swimming and half-empty outside of July and August. Nevertheless, new stores and restaurants line Rüütli pst, the main street. Grand old summer residences, traditional Germanic-Baltic stone and wooden structures, and 1920s and 30s Functionalist and Modernist architecture evoke the atmosphere of a bygone era. The mud baths, famed throughout the Russian Empire, continue to soothe the skin and spirits of visitors.

Orientation and Practical Information At the **tourist office,** Mungu 2 (tel. 406 39; fax 456 33), one of the least helpful in Estonia, pick up **maps** and info (open Mon.-Fri. 9am-6pm, Sat. 9am-4pm, Sun. 10am-3pm). You can **exchange currency** at Hotel Pärnu (open 24hr.), but rates are better at the post office or any bank. Find a Visa **ATM,** change traveler's checks, and obtain cash advances at **Eesti Ühis Pank** (tel. 408 80), next to the tourist office (bank open Mon.-Fri. 9am-6pm, Sat. 9am-2pm). The **train station** (tel. 407 33) is located east of the city center, by the corner of Riia and Raja (take bus #40 from the central post office to "Raeküla Rdtj."). **Trains** travel to Tallinn (4 per day, 3½hr., 30EEK). **Buses,** however, are the best way to reach Pärnu; the station, Ringi 3 (tel. 415 54), lies in the town center, a block down on the right from the bus parking lot (open Mon.-Fri. 8am-6pm, Sat. 8am-4pm). Buses go to: Tallinn (32 per day, 2-3 hr., 50EEK); Haapsalu (2 per day, 3hr., 42EEK); Kuressaare (2-3 per day, some heading to Virtsu, 3hr., 70EEK); Tartu (8 per day, 5hr., 60-68EEK); and Rīga (5 per day, 4hr., 76EEK). For a **taxi,** call 412 40 (6EEK per km). **Rattasõit,** Ria 95 (tel. 440 32), rents **bikes** (50EEK per day). **Store luggage** at the bus station, through the "*Pakihoid*" door opposite the ticket office (large bag 6EEK; open Mon.-Fri. 8am-7pm, Sat.-Sun. 8am-5pm). The **post office,** Akadeemia 7 (tel. 409 69), is at the west end of Rüütli, less than 1km from the bus station (open Mon.-Fri. 8am-6pm and Sat.-Sun. 9am-3pm). The **telephone office** is around the corner to the right, on Rüütli (tel. 409 69; open daily 7am-10pm). **Postal code:** EE-3600. **Phone code:** 244.

Accommodations The small **Hotell Seedri,** Seedri 4 (tel. 433 50), near the beach, offers hall showers and rather grim toilets, but rooms have a fridge and sink (single bed in double room 140EEK; doubles 170EEK; triples 215EEK; quads 345EEK; reservations recommended). **Hotell Kajakas,** Seedri 2 (tel. 430 98), provides a sauna (80EEK per hour), but has older, Soviet-style rooms and hall toilets and showers (singles 160EEK; doubles 220EEK). Though located in an unattractive area, **Hotell Yacht Club,** Lootsi 6 (tel. 314 20), boasts fairly new furnishings and bathrooms in every room. Some rooms have views of the port (singles 230EEK; doubles 350EEK; sauna 100EEK per hr.; breakfast 30EEK; bike rental 100EEK per day). **Villa Marleen,** Seedri 15 (tel. 458 49), a small, attractive, completely refurbished building, offers comfortable furniture, telephone, and satellite TV, and is spotless. Some rooms have private baths (singles 250EEK; doubles 350EEK; breakfast included).

Food Trahter Postipoiss, Vee 12 (tel. 402 04), is a great courtyard cafe and restaurant in a building that housed a butcher in the 19th century. Estonian chicken salad (chicken, pasta, and veggies; 23EEK) and cheese schnitzel (59EEK) are among the offerings. All main dishes come with greens and potatoes (open Mon.-Sat. 11am-midnight, Sun. 11am-10pm). **Restoran Jahtklubi Körts,** Lootsi 6, under the hotel, serves large portions of chicken schnitzel with fries (58EEK), and ham and cheese omelette (20EEK) in a semi-ship-like atmosphere (open 11am-midnight). A popular spot for an inexpensive meal is **Georg,** on the corner of Rüütli and Hommiku, a buffet-style restaurant offering *plov* (chicken and rice; 16.50EEK), salads (5.50EEK), and schnitzel with fries (23EEK; open Mon.-Fri. 7:30am-7:30pm, Sat.-Sun. 9am-7:30pm). A **turg** (market) is at the intersection of Sepa and Karja (open Tues.-Sun. 7am-1pm).

Sights and Entertainment Facing Hotell Pärnu at Rüütli 53, the **Pärnu Rajoonide Vaheline Koduloomuuseum** (Pärnu City Museum; tel. 434 64) displays local artifacts like Stone Age tools, 13th- to 20th-century weapons, traditional clothing, and taxidermic animals (open Mon.-Sat. 11am-5pm; 4EEK, students 2EEK). The **Lydia Koidula Museum,** Jannseni 37 (tel. 416 63), across Pärnu river, commemorates the 19th-century poet who led a revival in Estonian verse and drama (see **Literature,** p. 210; open Wed.-Sun. 10am-4pm; 3EEK, students 1EEK). South from Rüütli on Nikolai stands the 1747 Baroque rust-red **Eliisabeti kirik,** named after the Russian tsarina. Farther west, at the corner of Uus and Vee a block north of Rüütli, the Russian Orthodox **Ekatariina kirik** is a multi-spired, silver-and-green edifice built in the 1760s under the order of Catherine the Great. Rüütli ends at an **open-air theater** where

ESTONIA

The Dirtiest Bath This Side of the Baltics

Mud has never looked or felt better than at Pärnu's Neo-Classical **Mud Bath Establishment,** Ranna pst. 1 (tel. 424 61). Since 1838, when the mud baths and health resort were founded, the privilege of rolling around in gooey mud has not been limited to pigs and small children. Workers at the mud bath and many health professionals insist that Pärnu's sea mud has a curative effect on disorders of the bones, joints, and peripheral nervous system. There's even a special ward for patients with myocardial infarction and cardiovascular diseases. After a brief consultation, patients can choose between General Mud, Local Mud, and Electric Mud. And, for those tough-to-reach areas, there's the ever-so-popular mud tampon. No day at the mud bath is complete without a massage (200EEK), a "curative" bath or shower, and a cup of restorative herb tea—no mud added. (Mud treatment, massage, and shower costs around 380EEK, but varies with procedure length; open daily 8am-3pm.) Or stay at the establishment's hotel and get full board and 2-3 "procedures" for 450EEK.

---

music and drama performances are given in summer (starting July). The formidable **Tallinna värav** (Tallinn Gate), the only gate that led into the city under the Swedes, is the only surviving Baltic town wall gate from the 17th century. The office at Rüütli 1a is a celebrated example, built in 1933, of Pärnu's Functionalist architecture.

The broad, tree-lined street stretching south from Tallinna värav leads to a long pedestrian zone just behind the white-sand **beach.** There's a whirly slide open in summer (daily 11am-7pm; 5EEK per swoosh). Be careful at the bottom—the pool is only one meter deep. A small **amusement park,** Jalaka 5 (tel. 421 01), with a ferris wheel (3EEK), lies just off the boardwalk (open in summer daily 11am-7pm). The beaches and water are clean, if a bit cold before July. **Nude bathers** wander up the beach to the right, well past Rannasalong.

To play **tennis,** go to Ratta Sport, Ringi 14a (weekdays before 6pm 60EEK, weekends and nights 80EEK; racquets free; open daily 10am-10pm). **Tallinna Baar** (tel. 450 73), a small, dark, stone tavern, sits atop the gate (*Saku* 18EEK; open daily noon-11pm). The disco **La Pera Vida,** Mere 22 (tel. 473 964), is housed in a wooden 1930s dance hall. It plays the usual pop and techno, but sometimes has theme nights (cover 25EEK, open daily 10pm-5am). **Diskoklub "Hamilton,"** Rüütli 1, near the outdoor theater, hosts disc-spinners from all over Estonia (cover 25EEK, higher when bands play; open daily 9pm-5am). An **outdoor cafe/beer garden**, Lootsi 6 (tel. 419 48), bustles next to the yacht club (open daily 11am until whenever they decide to close). At **Väike Klaus** (Little Saint), Supeluse 3 (tel. 421 30), foreigners and locals down glasses of *Saku* (16EEK), *Heineken,* or *Grolsch* inside or outside (open Mon.-Thurs. 11am-midnight; Fri.-Sun. 11am-2am). There's a **cinema** at Mere 22, in the same building as La Pera Vida; films are usually in English with Russian and Estonian subtitles (25EEK). Around **Jaanipäev** (Midsummer Night), Pärnu hosts the **FiESTa International Jazz Festival,** a week of jazz, blues, and world music during which around 40 groups perform. **Baltoscandal,** an extravaganza of Baltic and Scandinavian drama, is put on at the same time, and features about 20 avant-garde theater groups.

■ Haapsalu

In the first half of the 13th century, Haapsalu (HOP-sa-loo) became the seat of the Saare-Lääne (Ösel-Wiele) bishopric, encompassing most of western Estonia. The town was almost destroyed during the Russo-Livonian War (1558-1583), then taken over by the Swedes in 1581, and by the Russians in 1710. In the 19th century, it was famed for its curative mud baths. In the 20th century, the Soviets built an airbase there. Today, populated by 14,000 people, the sleepy town is known for its sailing, and as a quickly-westernizing tourist attraction.

Orientation and Practical Information The bus drops its passengers off on Tallinna mnt. To get to the **tourist information office,** Posti 39 (tel. 332 48), walk up Tallinna (in the direction the bus drives) and turn right on Posti. The helpful English-speaking staff sells **maps** (15-25EEK), and hands out brochures like the free *Two Weeks in Haapsalu* with info on events in town. A **travel agency,** Haapsalu Travel Services, is located at Karja 7 (tel. 450 37; fax 443 35). **Exchange money** at most banks, including **EUP,** Karja 27 (tel. 447 56; open Mon.-Fri. 8am-6pm, Sat. 8am-2pm). Hotels may also change money (some 24hr.). **Trains** no longer run to Haapsalu, though Tsar Nicholas II came here so often he had a massive covered platform built to make sure none of his party would get wet while disembarking. Curiously, the station, Randtee 2 (tel. 576 64), is being renovated and sells bus tickets. **Buses** run from here to: Tallinn (4 per day, 2hr., 16-30EEK); Kärdla (3 per day, 3hr., pay 40EEK on the bus); and Pärnu (daily, 3 on Mon. and Wed., 2-3hr., 40EEK; ticket office open daily 5-8:30am and 9:30am-7pm). For information on the Kärdla bus, call 965 02. From **Rohuküla,** 9km west of Haapsalu, **ferries** (tel. 336 66; port tel. 316 30) leave to Heltermaa on Hiiumaa (12 per day, 1½hr., 25EEK). Bus #1 runs to Rohuküla from stop #1 at the Haapsalu station (almost hourly, 25min., 4EEK). It is cheaper to take a bus from Haapsalu to Kärdla (Hiiumaa) or Sviby (Vormsi) than to ride the ferry and grab a bus once you arrive on the islands. For a **taxi,** call 333 30 (4EEK per 1km). **Police:** tel. 441 48. The **post office** is at Posti 1 (tel. 445 55; open Mon.-Fri. 7:30am-6pm, Sat. 8am-4pm), and the **telephone office,** Tamme 21a (tel. 352 57), is nearby (open daily 7am-10pm). **Postal code:** EE-3170. **Phone code:** 247.

Accommodations and Food The **Hotell Laine** (Hotel Wave), Sadama 9/11 (tel. 441 91), welcomes visitors on the shores of Väike-viik. A sanatorium in a previous life, the hotel still offers massages (75EEK for 25min.). Follow Posti north until it ends near the castle, go two blocks west on Ehte, then two blocks north on Sadama; the entrance is at the rear of building. Ask for a view of the swan-filled sea (singles 275EEK; doubles 420EEK; includes bath, balcony, and breakfast). The **Tamme Guest House,** Tamme 10a (tel. 575 50), has clean singles (150EEK). The **Yacht Club,** Holmi 5a (tel. 455 82) is near the Hotell Laine (singles 140EEK; doubles 280EEK; showers 10EEK; breakfast 35EEK).

Rootsituru Kohvik, Karja 3 (tel. 450 58), a pink building in the castle's shadow on the corner of Ehte, serves unassuming food. Its fried bass (65EEK) is reminiscent of fish and chips. Salads come smothered in sour cream (10EEK; open 10am-10pm). The new **Restoran Central,** Karja 21 (tel. 446 73), is bathed in shades of green. Locals hang out in the bar downstairs or go to the dining room upstairs to eat pepper beef with fries (65EEK) or fried trout with cream and spinach (89EEK). The place gets crowded on weekends (open Mon.-Fri. noon-midnight, Sat.-Sun. noon-2am). The **turg,** or **market,** is one block from the train station on the corner of Jürlöö and Jaama (open April to mid.-Oct. 7am-3pm, mid.-Oct. to March 9am-2pm). There are several good **supermarkets,** including **Rema 1000,** Linula 3 (open 9am-9pm; Visa, MC).

Sights and Entertainment From Lossiplats, the square just east of the north end of Kavja, one enters **Lossi Park** (open 7am-11pm). Here stands the limestone **Piiskopilinnus** (Bishop's Castle), where the Bishop of Saare-Lääne lived until moving to Saaremaa in 1358. The castle is mostly a set of picturesque ruins surrounding the tower and Episcopal chapel. Adjoining the chapel is the newly renovated museum with chamber guns and cannons from the 15th and 16th centuries, plaques outlining Haapsalu's history, and period costumes (open daily 10am-6pm; 10EEK, students 5EEK). From here, enter the whitewashed inside of the chapel. Classical concerts and choir performances are held here some evenings (consult *Two Weeks in Haapsalu*). Outside, 10EEK (students 5EEK) lets you climb the treacherous, winding steps to the top of the tower. The chapel was thrice destroyed and abandoned, most recently by a storm in 1726, after which it was left unrepaired until 1887 (open Mon.-Fri. 11am-4pm, Sat. 9am-3pm; 3EEK donations requested for concerts). On August's full moon, Haapsalu's **White Lady,** the ghost of a woman walled up in the cathedral for crossing

ESTONIA

its threshold in the 1280s (a time when only men were allowed inside), makes an apparitional appearance in one of the cathedral windows. The event is celebrated by a week-long **festival**. The **Aafrikarand** (Africa Beach) promenade, northeast of the castle at the end of Rüütli, runs 2km to the yacht club. **Kaluri**, farther east, makes for beautiful walks amid weathered Baltic wooden houses, marsh grasses, and ducks.

One of the few places to hang out at night is the **Cafe Rondo**, Posti 7. It has a cafe upstairs and a dark bar downstairs. On weekends, local bands play in the courtyard until 2am (cafe open Mon.-Thurs. 7:30am-7pm, Sat.-Sun. 9am-7pm; bar open Sun.-Thurs. noon-11pm, Fri.-Sat. noon-2am). **Africa Discotheque,** Tallinna mnt. 1 (tel. 452 91), at the south end of Posti, is as good as any club in the Baltics. The disco boasts tuxedoed staff and *nouveau-riche* customers (open Wed. 9pm-3am, Thurs. and Sun. 9pm-4am, Fri.-Sat. 9pm-5am; cover Fri.-Sat. 70EEK, cheaper other nights).

ESTONIAN ISLANDS

Estonia precociously expands its territory far out to sea, speckling the Baltic with over 1500 islands. Worried about providing an easy escape route to the West, the Soviets restricted foreigners and Estonians alike from visiting the islands; even boat ownership was banned, stifling the traditional fishing industry. Today's traveler will discover, however, that 50 years of isolation had the unintended side effect of preserving much of the islands' and Estonia's old way of life.

■ Saaremaa

The largest and most frequented of the islands, Saaremaa (SA-reh-ma) boasts windmills, churches, manors, springs, and a medieval fortress in the main town, Kuressaare. The island is reckoned to be more Estonian than Estonia itself; much of the population lives in traditional farmhouses huddled around a palace abandoned in the 16th century.

KURESSAARE

A major resort before Soviet occupation, Kuressaare (KOO-re-sa-re), on Saaremaa's south coast, is now making a comeback. Bars, restaurants, and hotels are multiplying, and young Estonians from the mainland increasingly visit in greater numbers to party and hit the beaches, particularly during the peak of white nights (around June 21).

Orientation and Practical Information Between the **Linnus-Kindlus** (Episcopal Castle) and the **bus station,** is only a 15-minute walk. **Buses,** Pihtla tee 2 (info tel. 573 80, reservations tel. 562 20), at the corner of Tallinna, go to: Tallinn (9 per day, 4hr., 96EEK); Muhu (11 per day, 1½hr., 24EEK); Orissaare (8 per day, 1hr., 20EEK); Pangu (3 per day, 2hr., 11.50EEK); and Pärnu (2 per day, 3hr., 70EEK). To get to the mainland, it's easier and cheaper to take a direct bus (which gets first priority on the ferries). A new **ferry** route allows you to island-hop between north Saaremaa's Triigi port and south Hiiumaa's Orjaku port (3 per day, 45min., 45EEK; buses don't run from Orjaku to Hiiumaa's main town, Kärdla). **Raekoja plats** is the narrow town square; the **tourist office,** Tallinna 2 (tel. 551 20), inside the *raekoda* (town hall), sells **maps** (20EEK) and answers questions in English on food, lodging, and events (open Mon.-Fri. 9am-5pm, Sat. 10am-5pm). Baltic Tours, a **travel agency** at Tallinna 1 (tel. 334 80; fax 334 81), on Raekoja plats, helps with ferry info, English-language tours, and hotels (open Mon.-Fri. 9am-6pm, Sat. 10am-3pm). **Exchange currency,** cash traveler's checks, and get Visa/MC advances at **Hansapank,** Kohtu 1 (tel. 559 55; open Mon.-Fri. 8am-6pm, Sat. 8am-2pm). You can also exchange currency at various **supermarkets** in town, such as Saaremaa Kanbamaja, behind the town hall (open Mon.-Fri. 9am-7pm, Sat. 9am-5pm, Sun. 10am-5pm). **Taxis** (tel. 533 33) run from behind the town hall, the bus station, and Smuuli pst. (4-5EEK per km).

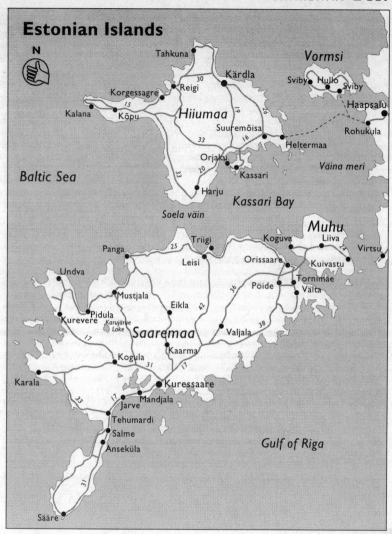

Estonian Islands

N

Tahkuna

Kärdla

Vormsi

Svíby · Hullo · Sviby

·Haapsalu

Korgessagre · Reigi

30

Kalana · Kõpu

15

Hiiumaa

61

26

Suuremõisa

Rohukula

33

16

Heltermaa

Baltic Sea

Orjaku

20

Väina meri

33

Kassari

· Harju

Kassari Bay

Soela väin

Muhu

Triigi

Koguva

Liiva

Panga

25

Virtsu

Leisi

Orissaare

24

Undva

Kuivastu

Tornimäe

36

Põide

Välta

Mustjala

Eikla

42

Kurevere · Pidula

Karujärve Lake

Saaremaa

17

Valjala

38

Kogula

Kaarma

31

17

Karala

· Kuressaare

33

17 · Mandjala

Gulf of Riga

Jarve

· Tehumardi

· Salme

· Anseküla

31

Sääre

Rent **bikes** at Elektrum, Tallinna 16 (tel. 590 42; 180EEK a day; open Mon.-Fri. 9am-6pm, Sat. 9am-4pm). Priit Rent, Aia 54a-1 (tel. 397 33; cell phone 250 879 19), rents **cars** (Opel Rekords 300EEK per day; unlimited mileage). The **post office,** Torni 1 (tel. 543 45), on the corner of Komandandi, a block north of Tallinna, offers **photo-copying** (open Mon.-Fri. 8am-6pm, Sat.-Sun. 8:30am-3pm) and **telephones** (daily 8am-9pm). As the island upgrades its telephone system, numbers are constantly changing. **Postal code:** EE-3300. **Phone code:** 0245; for faxes dial 5 instead.

Accommodations and Food New pensions and small B&Bs are opening all the time; check with the tourist office. Hotel management students run **Mardi Öömaja,** Vallimaa 5a (tel. 332 85; fax 332 80), the cheapest hotel/hostel in town, with clean, institutional-style rooms. The hostel has older rooms and narrow beds, but the common bathrooms have recently been redone (100EEK per bed; hotel singles 240EEK; doubles 380EEK; breakfast 50EEK). The family-run **Suve Hotell,** Suve 6

ESTONIA

(tel. 54 851), provides tolerable rooms with clean toilets and showers (200EEK per person; breakfast included). **Hotell Pärna,** Pärna 3 (tel. 57 521), has recently refurbished rooms and offers the use of a kitchen (doubles 400EEK, with bath 550EEK; sauna 150EEK per hour; breakfast included). **Mändjela Puhkeküla** (tel. 751 93), Kuressaare Vald, lies 11km outside Kuressaare at the "Kämping" stop on the Kuressaare-Järve bus. One of many campsites across the island, this place is hidden on a clean beach among secluded pine woods (4-bed dorms 160EEK per person; breakfast included; tent sites 50EEK per person; open May 30-Sept. 1).

New bars, restaurants, and cafes are constantly opening, and prices are rising as the town grows more cosmopolitan. **Vanalinna,** Kanba 8 (tel. 553 09), is one of the best eateries in Kuressaare, offering salted trout in sour cream (65EEK), wild boar (120EEK), and *Saku* (20EEK; open daily noon-midnight; Visa). **Kodulinna Local,** Tallinna 11 (tel. 541 78), in a basement off Raekoja plats, is a restaurant/bar popular with locals, who come here to eat pork and peppers (53EEK) and drink the local *Saaremaa* beer (17EEK) late into the night (open noon-6am; kitchen closes 2am; 15EEK cover after 9pm). Like the hotel of which it is part, **Kass Restaurant,** Vallimaa 5a (tel. 332 95), is run by Kuressaare Trade School students. The house specialty is perch (53EEK; open daily 7:30-10am and noon-midnight; Visa, MC). A hip coffeehouse, **Hausa Kohvik,** Tallinna 9 (tel. 543 21), on Raekoja plats, has walls adorned with works by Estonian artists (open Mon.-Sat. 9:45am-7pm, Sun. 9:45am-3pm).

Sights and Entertainment

Seventeenth-century buildings surround **Raekoja plats** (Town Hall Square); most notable is the 1670 Nordic Baroque **raekoja,** a squarish building built by the Swedish landowner Marcus Gabriel de la Gardie which still serves as a the town hall. Past the square's south end, a **statue** of an Estonian soldier commemorates the 1918-20 struggle for independence. Down Lossi, **Nikolai kirik** (St. Nicholas's Church) was built in 1790 for newly arrived Russian troops.

Farther south, through a sleepy park and across a moat, lies **Linnus-kindlus** (Episcopal Castle), the town's main attraction. Built in 1260 shortly after the Teutonic Order subdued the islanders, it was reconstructed 1336-80 as the island home of the Bishop of Saare-Lääne; he liked it so much that in 1358 he declared it the bishopric's administrative center. The castle changed hands a number of times; in 1559 the bishop sold it to the Danes, and it later became a Swedish, and then a Russian, stronghold. The tsar finally retired the venerable late-Gothic fortress from military use in 1899; it now houses one of the more interesting museums in the Baltics, the **Saaremaa Regional Museum** (tel. 563 07). An eclectic collection from all periods of the island's history is on display, including intricately carved coats-of-arms, national costumes, carriages, antiques, military and maritime objects, and photographs and short biographies of Saaremaa intellectuals and politicians. The innumerable twisting and turning passages, stairwells, towers, and halls are enough to keep visitors busy all day; pick up a much-needed map (10EEK) at the entrance (castle and museum open daily 11am-7pm, last entry 6pm; 20EEK, students 10EEK). On the top floor of the defense tower, Tornikohvik, a **cafe,** has a view of the sea and castle (beer 20EEK; open daily 11am-5:30pm). On the west side of the park, the tiny **Citizen's Museum,** Pärgi 5 (tel. 563 07), displays turn-of-the-century furniture in a middle-class house typical of the time (open Wed.-Sun. 11am-6pm; 4EEK, students 2EEK). The house belonged to the parents of Victor Kingissepp, a Communist revolutionary shot by the first Estonian national government in 1922. Kuressaare's name was changed in the 1940s to Kingissepp by the Soviets; the town only regained its former name in 1990.

At night, the mellow crowd is at **Lonkav Konn,** Kauba 6 (tel. 534 49), an Irish bar in the inimitable Eastern European style. Eat *seljanka* (14EEK) and beef stroganoff (45EEK) or drink *Saku* (14EEK) and Guinness (28EEK; open daily 10am-2am). Revelers head to **Disko Skala,** in the old cinema on Tallinna, north of Raekoja plats, next to a casino. Drink prices are steep (50EEK for a double gin and tonic). The crowd under the neon lights is noticeably less *mafioso* (open Fri.-Sat. 10pm-4am, during white nights open daily; 20-35EEK cover). A cultural events calendar is available at the tourist office; listings include Estonian art exhibits around town, classical and pop concerts in the castle yard, and festivals held during white night.

WEST SAAREMAA

Saaremaa's most interesting sights lie in the west. One of the island's more beautiful churches is in **Käärma.** You can bicycle the 20km here by taking Tallinna mnt. north out of Kuressaare and turning left at the sign to Upa, then following signs to Käärma. **Käärma Kirik** is a 13th-century structure under renovation. Attached is a serene straw-roofed parsonage. Across the road is the site of the **Käärma stronghold.** To see the **Saaremaa dolomite mines,** take the road to Saia; the mines will be on the left several kilometers out of Käärma. Doesn't sound fascinating? Then you should know that dolomite is one of Saaremaa's few export materials, and stone from here was used for Kuressaare's castle and the Palace of Congresses in Moscow's Kremlin.

To get to unspoiled **Karujärve Lake,** continue on the same road, which becomes unpaved, about 15km to Karla. At the main intersection in Karla, take a right on a paved road. After 5km you'll see the Karujärve **campground,** Karla vald (tel. 726 81) on the left. The campground has small A-frame 2-person cabins with thin mattresses (180EEK), or you can simply get a bed (50EEK without sheets). The showers have hot water (open May 15-Sept. 15). Swimming is possible at the small, sandy beach. A couple of kilometers farther, opposite the "Karujärve 11" bus stop, is a dirt road on the right that leads to an abandoned Soviet **military base.** If you follow the main road, past barracks and shooting ranges, you will arrive at a row of massive missile hangars.

If the cliffs to the south are unsatisfying, try the 60m drop at **Panga,** on the north coast of Saaremaa (depicted on the back of the 100EEK note). **Buses** to Panga leave Kuressaare infrequently (3 per day, 2hr., 6EEK), so be careful not to get stuck. At the cliffs, you can climb halfway up the lighthouse, which is nothing more than a ladder surrounded by steel scaffolding. Be careful: the steps are steep and the wind blustery. A stand at Panga sells sausages (3 for 12EEK) and beer (13EEK; open daily 10am-8pm). From Panga's cliffs it's a 12km cycle south to **Mustjala;** bear right on the unpaved road to Võhma and follow the coast. In Mustjala stands **Anna Kirik** (Anna's Church), built in 1864 on the site of a medieval burial ground. For an excellent **view** of the surrounding forest, sea, and fields, climb the steeple to the bells. Hungry travelers should walk a few meters down the road, following the signs to **Käsitöösahver,** where they rustle up sandwiches (5EEK) and salads (15EEK; open daily 11am-7pm).

Continuing down the road until Silla and turning right on the unpaved road to **Pidula** leads to the natural **Odalätsi Springs,** which are said to bring eternal youth to young ladies who splash its water on their faces. Apparently the local matrons haven't tried it. **Pidula Manor** is a bit farther south on the unpaved road. Built in the 18th century, the modest building, once a school, is now in an advanced state of decay. Farther along the road, turn right down the hill to **Kihelkonna,** where the 14th-century **Kihelkonna Kirik** holds choral concerts almost every day in the summer. Only 2km down the paved road from Kihelkonna is the **Mihkli Farm Museum** in Viki (open daily 10am-6pm; 10EEK, students 5EEK). In **Angla,** not far from the Triigi port (6km) in the north, crawl around inside five preserved **windmills** (5EEK).

SOUTHWEST SAAREMAA

One of the best ways to explore this area is to rent a bike. The first stop on the route south should be the quiet beaches of **Mändjala** and **Järve,** 8-12km west of Kuressaare. The beaches are sandy, but punctuated by marsh grasses and sometimes strewn with algae. To reach the popular Mändjala, take the first left after the "Mändjala 1" bus stop. For the beach in **Järve,** turn left after the "Ranna" bus stop. More beaches dot the road south. At **Tehumardi,** a giant concrete sword with four faces chiseled into it marks the location of a 1944 battle. Across from it are rows of memorials for the dead soldiers. Farther on, the town of **Salme,** 17km out of Kuressaare, makes a good lunch stop. The restaurant **Ago & Co.** (tel. 715 34), on the main road, serves fried trout (58EEK), and salad (15EEK; open Mon.-Sat. noon-midnight, Sun. noon-6pm).

ESTONIA

About 2km out of Salme, a sign points right along an unpaved road to **Lide,** cutting over to the west side of **Sõrve poolsaar** (the peninsula), where the slightly choppier waters of the open Baltic meet rockier beaches. At **Kaugatuma,** the locals make too much of the "cliffs," but there is a good lookout from the lighthouse and you can sunbathe alongside grazing cows on the fossil-strewn, pebbly beaches. Five kilometers farther down the road, the ruins of the WWII **Lõpe-Kaimiri kaitseliini rajatised** (defense line) are visible. Staying on the major gravel road, which now cuts inland, 12km of travel will bring you to the (real) cliffs at **Ohessaare.** At **Sõrve säär,** the very tip of Sõrve poolsaar, clear weather opens up a view of Latvia, 25km south across the Baltic. The **lighthouse** is open to visitors (5EEK, students 2EEK). On the trip back, the road going through **Mõntu** (the opposite direction from Jämaja) passes through the **national park** (look out for foxes and deer). Warning: the ride, especially on the one-speed bikes rented in Kuressaare, may leave you with a sore rump; bring cushioning and plenty of mosquito repellent. If you're tired, take a bus home; ask the driver to put the bike in the luggage area.

EAST SAAREMAA

From Kuressaare, you can take a bus toward Orissaare, get off in **Käo,** bike 5km north to the turn to Tornimäe, and take that right to reach **Pöide.** Take the first left, onto a sandy path, and bike to the end of the road to get to **Pöidekirik.** Built as a Catholic church in the 13th century, it later became Lutheran, Russian Orthodox, and then Lutheran again. The Teutonic Knights used the edifice as a fortress against the locals. The outlines of the old church can still be seen (its small bottom windows remain). Southwest of **Orissaare** in the small town of **Valjala** is **Valjala Kirik** (1230), the oldest stone church in Estonia, built with buttresses to serve as a stronghold when needed.

Several kilometers south along the main road to Kuressaare lies **Kõljala.** Turn right at the sign to reach **Kõljala Manor,** a pink Classical building in better shape than most of the island's old manors. Slightly farther up the road in **Kaali** lies a **meteorite crater.** You can climb down steps to reach the bottom, where a pond has formed.

■ Muhu

From Orissaare, continue east, then north through coastal scenery along the main road to Kuivastu for 10km, and over the causeway to Muhu Island. Here, take a sharp left turn to get to **Koguva.** At the end of the road (7km), the Koguva **open-air museum** consists of an old-fashioned farm, complete with a well and houses made from hay (open summer daily 10am-7pm; 18EEK, students 10EEK). People actually live in some of the museum's houses. Pedaling back past the turn to Orissaare leads to **Linnuse,** where, on the left, you can crawl inside a **windmill.** The windmill was built in 1980 on the site of an 1881 mill (open daily 10am-6pm; 4EEK, students 2EEK).

■ Hiiumaa

By restricting access to Hiiumaa (HEE-you-ma) for 50 years, the Soviets unwittingly preserved many of the island's rare plant and animal species, as well as its unhurried way of life. Native residents tell stories of spirits, giants, trolls, and devils who inhabited Hiiumaa before them. Visitors find unadorned churches, history-laden light-houses, and sites where legends were born. A woody wilderness unblemished by human habitation, Hiiumaa is not for the partier: come here for peace and respite.

KÄRDLA

Swedish settlers named this sleepy spot Kärr-dal, which means lovely valley. Although not awarded town status until 1938, when it became Hiiumaa's capital, settlement began here in 1830 to support a large textile works. While the residents total only 4300, this number almost triples in summer.

Orientation and Practical information The main square (okay, geometrically speaking, triangle) is **Keskväljak,** near which are most of the town's shops. From the **bus** station, Sadama 13, north of Keskväljak (tel. 965 02), catch buses to: Tallinn (3 per day, 4hr., 80EEK); Haapsalu (2-3 per day, 3hr., 30-40EEK); and Kassari (1 per day Tues.-Sun., 50min., 15EEK; station open Mon.-Fri. 7am-7pm, Sat. 9:30-11am, 2:30-3:30pm). **Ferries** to Hiiumaa arrive at Heltermaa and Orjaku (see **Elsewhere on Hiiumaa,** p. 232); a bus shuttles to Heltermaa's port from the Kärdla bus station (4 per day, 45min., 14EEK). It's theoretically possible to take local buses to any point of the island with a house on it, since a mailbox is equivalent to a bus stop, but buses run to remote areas only once per day at most. Even between Kärdla and Käina, there can be six-hour gaps in service. The island's English-speaking **tourist office,** Kõrgessare mnt. 1 (tel./fax 330 33; http://www.hiiumaa.ee), can be found by heading south from Keskväljak on Võidu; Kõrgessare mnt. is the first on the right. They provide info on accommodations, and sell **maps** (25EEK) and *The Lighthouse Tour* (20EEK), a guidebook to sights on Hiiumaa (open in summer Mon.-Fri. 9am-6pm, Sat.-Sun. 10am-2pm; off-season Mon.-Fri. 10am-4pm). A **travel agency,** Tiit Reisrd, stands at Keskväljak 9 (tel. 320 54). At Tallinna Pank, Keskväljakul 7 (tel. 320 40), you can **exchange money** and get Visa cash advances (open Mon.-Fri. 9am-5pm, Sat. 10am-3pm). All **taxis** (tel. 316 95) are based in Keskväljak; the catch is that you have to pay for both directions of the driver's journey (5EEK per km). Rent a **bike** with more gears than anyone knows what to do with (50EEK per day), or even a **car,** from Dagotrans, Sõnajala 11 (tel. 918 46), on the left in the little house at the gate that says not to enter on the left side of the street (open 24hr.). The island's main **post office** is at Posti 13, about 200m north of the bus station, opposite the church (open Mon.-Fri. 9am-4:30pm, Sat. 9am-1pm). To make **telephone** calls, head to Leigri väljak 9 (tel. 315 37; 24hr.). **Postal code:** EE-3200. **Phone code:** 0246.

Accommodations and Food Hiiumaa's hotels have cheaper rates than anywhere else in Estonia. There's no need to be limited to staying in Kärdla, however; to check out other accommodations available on the rest of the island, see **Elsewhere on Hiiumaa,** p. 232. A white building near the corner of Vabaduse and Valli is the institutional, but meticulously clean **Võõrastemaja Kärdla,** Vabaduse 13 (tel. 965 77). Its sauna is open daily 11am-7pm (Fri. women-only). There are only 24 places; consider calling ahead (singles 135-220EEK; doubles 220-240EEK; quads 250-340EEK). Adjoining a tennis club, **Hotell Sõnajala,** Leigri väljak 3 (tel. 312 20; fax 320 36), has clean and comfortable rooms, as well as a kitchen, and a common room with satellite TV. The staff speaks German and Russian. Walk south on Rookopli from Keskväljak, turn right on Kõrgessaare mnt. (the major intersection with a big stone head on the corner), and left on Sõnajala; the hotel is in the complex on the right in 20 minutes (singles 150EEK; modern shared bathrooms).

The grub on Hiiumaa is mediocre at best. Expect canned peas with every dish, and vegetarians will only find salads smothered in sour cream. The largest grocery shop on Hiiumaa is **Tiigi Pood,** Tiigi 5 (tel. 990 88), which stocks western and Estonian foods and accepts Visa and MC (open daily 9am-10pm). Some of the best eats can be found outside of Kärdla (see **Elsewhere on Hiiumaa,** p. 232). The pink wooden building at the corner with Posti, **Priiankru,** Sadama 4 (tel. 962 95; fax 963 05), serves perch fillet (35EEK), thick *seljanka* (18EEK), or *puljong pirukaja* (broth with meat pie, 10EEK; open daily 8am-midnight). By the water at the end of Lubjaahju, **Rannapargu** (tel. 912 87), with a balcony to watch the people venturing into the waves, is perfect for a drink by the sea (open 10am-midnight).

Sights The **Pühalepa Kirik,** Pikk 26 (tel. 911 20), contains the graves of the Baltic-German Count Ungeru-Stenberg's family. The Count, who came to the island in 1781, the year Catherine the Great deported all of Hiiumaa's Swedes, wanted to acquire the entire island, but his shipping and salvage business was cut short when he killed one of his ship captains in a dispute. The Count built Reigi Kirik (on the highway between Kärdla and Kõrgessaare) in 1802 in memory of his son Gustav, who committed suicide after accruing gambling debts. The **Tahkuna Lighthouse** is northwest of Kärdla. Built in Paris in 1874, the lighthouse was consistently ineffective in warning ships about the coast's shallow waters. Perhaps locals purposefully made sure the lighthouse never worked, since their economy perked up when salvaging ships' loot and rescuing passengers. For a spectacular view, climb to the top of the lighthouse, which is usually left unlocked. The Tahkuna lighthouse was shipped to Hiiumaa along with another, shorter lighthouse (now standing on Hiiumaa's western tip); it is believed the two were placed in their present locations by mistake, since the taller Tahkuna Lighthouse should have been the first to be seen by ships coming from the west. Near the Tahkuna Lighthouse stands a **memorial** to the Russian soldiers who were to fight a battle here during WWII but were surprised and taken as prisoners. Gun emplacement and bunkers still stand in the area; bunkers are open, but it's advisable not to enter without a flashlight.

ELSEWHERE ON HIIUMAA

The interior of Hiiumaa is made up largely of old farms. Roads (mostly paved) ring the island; and a good one cuts 20km across the island to link Kärdla with **Käina,** Hiiumaa's second-largest town (pop. 200), 16km away on the south coast. From Rohuküla, just south of Haapsalu on the mainland, **ferries** make the crossing to **Heltermaa** on the east tip of the island (in summer Sun.-Fri. 8-12 per day; Sat. 6 per day; 90min.; 25EEK, students 10EEK; off-season 2 per day, up to 36hr. in icy conditions, 19EEK, students 9EEK). For **schedules,** call the ports (tel. 316 30 in Heltermaa, tel. 911 38 in Rohuküla). Buses shuttle from Heltermaa's port to Kärdla's bus station (4 per day, 45min., 14EEK). Another ferry operates between the tiny southern Hiiumaa port at **Orjaku** and the **Saaremaa** town of Triigi (10am and 6pm, 45EEK), but note that there's no bus from Orjaku to Kärdla.

More than two-thirds of all the plant species in Estonia exist only on Hiiumaa. Due to the variety of plants and waterfowl, much of the island now belongs to the **West-Estonian Islands Biosphere Reserve. Hiking** and **camping** are permitted and encouraged, but be sure to pick up info at the tourist office about regions off-limits. Motor vehicles are not allowed on the seashore and certain other areas. Because of dry conditions, **campfires are prohibited.** Lighthouses dot the island, most notably the **Kõpu Lighthouse,** a pyramid-shaped tower on Hiiumaa's west peninsula, constructed in the early 1500s by the Hanseatic League. The stairwell was an afterthought, hacked out of solid rock to provide access to the top. The view from the top (100m) is a panorama of the Baltic Sea, including all of Hiiumaa and, on a sunny day, the island of Saaremaa to the south (5EEK, but no one collects tickets, and the workers at the food stand/ticket booth forget to sell them). Farther west of Kõpu is an abandoned Soviet **radar facility** at the tip of the island, at what used to be the Soviet Union's northwesternmost point.

Not far northeast of Käina, **Suuremõisa Palace,** a beautiful example of northern Baroque architecture, stands in disrepair. The palace was built by the Swede Jakob de la Gardie, who purchased the entire island from the Swedes in 1624. The estate languished under Russian rule, but the current building was rebuilt by Margarethe Stenbock, a relative of de la Gardie's, in 1775. The palace is now a school, and its rooms have been converted into rather depressing classrooms (5EEK, students 2EEK).

Crossed Paths

Legend claims that long ago at **Ristimägi** (Hill of Crosses), two wedding parties once met and, neither wanting to cede the hill to the other, fought. The groom from one party and the bride from the other were killed in the scuffle. The remaining bride and groom decided to get married and, in memory of their dead loved ones, planted the first cross on this hill. Another legend has it that Ristimägi commemorates the last church service held there by Swedes, who were forced to leave the island in 1781. Today, tradition holds that in remembrance of either tale, anyone who passes the spot must plant a cross constructed out of objects occurring naturally in the area (such as grass, sticks, leaves, or rocks).

A kilometer northeast of the palace stand the **Põhilise leppe kivid** (Contract Stones), Hiiumaa's Stonehenge. The large rocks were placed by human hands, but their purpose is a mystery. Some islanders insist that a 6th-century Swedish king and his gold rest in peace under the stones. Others argue that sailors carried a large stone to the site before a voyage as a show of faith in God, hoping He would grant them safe passage (hence the term "contract stones"). Still other "experts" believe the stones served a purpose for worshippers of an ancient Hiiumaa religion.

One kilometer from Käina's center, **Lõokese Hotell,** Lõokes 14 (tel. 92 10 70), provides a welcome change from the institutional rooms of other hostels. The hostel, attached to a hotel, offers spacious rooms with modern furnishings and bathrooms (singles 200EEK; doubles 280EEK, with sink 320EEK; quads 480EEK; sauna 100EEK).

The island's **best restaurant** hides in the hamlet of **Kõrgessaare** (also called **Viskoosa**), 17km west of Kärdla. The large granite-block building that **Viinaköök** (Vodka Kitchen; tel. 933 37) inhabits was first a 19th-century silk factory and later a vodka distillery. They specialize in genuine Hiiumaa wild boar, though it's not always available, as well as vegetable salad (12EEK), roast salmon (60EEK; probably the best-tasting dish on Hiiumaa), pork fried with cheese (55EEK) and *Saku* (14EEK; open Tues.-Sat. 11am-3am, Sun.-Mon. 11am-10pm). **Lõokese Restoran,** Lõokes 14 (tel. 372 46), in Käina, serves cream of mushroom soup (15EEK), roast cod fillet (55EEK), and *Saku* 14EEK. If you're beginning to tire of *Saku,* **Humala Baar,** a tiny wooden pub on the main road just south of Partsi in eastern Hiiumaa, offers its own homemade brew (open daily noon-10pm).

■ Kassari

The tiny island of Kassari (ka-SA-ree), south of Hiiumaa, is home to even thicker woods and wilder sights. Perhaps the most beautiful of the island's natural sights is **Sääretirp,** a one- to three-meter wide peninsula extending over 3km out into the sea, lined with wild strawberries and juniper bushes. Legend holds that this is the remains of a bridge built by the giant Leiger between Hiiumaa and Saaremaa so that his brother Suur Tõll could come for a visit. West of Sääretirp, near the broken-down windmill, visit the **Hiiumaa Koduloomuuseum** (tel. 971 21) to see Hiiumaa's last gray wolf and exhibits on the island's history and wildlife. The museum is a one-story orange-roofed barn-house (open Mon.-Fri. 10am-5:30pm; 5EEK, students 2EEK). On the northeastern tip of the island is **Kassari Kirik,** a small white church on the sea with a hay roof. Check out the moss-covered **Devil's Stone,** near **Suure-Maise Kirik.** According to legend, the Devil, intending to throw the stone at someone, accidentally threw it here.

Campground Puulaid (tel. 921 26), only a few kilometers from Orjaku/Sadama port (ask the bus driver to let you off at Puulaid), could compete with some of the nicer budget hotels in Estonia, with spacious shared rooms, modern toilets, a huge high-tech sauna and shower, use of a full kitchen, and a splendid view of the sea (100EEK per person; breakfast 40EEK, supper 60EEK).

ESTONIA

HUNGARY (MAGYARORSZÁG)

US$1	= 198 forints (Ft, or HUF)	**100Ft =**	**US$0.51**
CDN$1	= 143Ft	**100Ft =**	**CDN$0.70**
UK£1	= 314Ft	**100Ft =**	**UK£0.32**
IR£1	= 290Ft	**100Ft =**	**IR£0.35**
AUS$1	= 144Ft	**100Ft =**	**AUS$0.70**
NZ$1	= 125Ft	**100Ft =**	**NZ$0.80**
SAR1	= 42Ft	**100Ft =**	**SAR2.38**
DM1	= 109Ft	**100Ft =**	**DM0.92**
Country Phone Code: 36		**International Dialing Prefix: 00**	

Forty-five years of isolation and relative powerlessness under Soviet rule were a mere blip in Hungary's 1100-year history, and traces of Socialism are corroding with each iron-free day. Budapest is the focal point of the country, though the capital by no means has a monopoly on cultural attractions, and no provincial center is more than a three-hour train ride away through corn and sunflower fields. Try not to forsake the beauty of the countryside for a whirlwind tour of the capital—you'll have seen the heart of Hungary, but missed its soul entirely.

HUNGARY ESSENTIALS

Citizens of Canada, Ireland and the U.S., can travel to Hungary visa-free with a valid passport for 90 days; South African citizens for 30 days; U.K. citizens for 6 months. Australians and New Zealanders must obtain 90-day tourist visas from a Hungarian embassy or consulate, as no border-control posts issue visas. (See **Embassies and Consulates**, p. 4.) For green card holders, visa prices are: single-entry US$40, double-entry US$75, multiple-entry US$180, and 48-hour transit visa US$38. Non-U.S. residents pay US$65, US$100, US$200, and US$50, respectively. Obtaining a visa takes one day and requires proof of means of transportation (such as a plane ticket), as well as a valid passport, three photographs (5 for double visas), payment by cash or money order, and a self-addressed, stamped (certified mail) envelope. You will also receive an entry-exit form that you must keep in your passport. Visa extensions are not awarded frequently; apply at police stations in Hungary.

GETTING THERE AND GETTING AROUND

Hungary's national airline, **Malév**, has daily direct flights from New York to Budapest. Most **rail** lines swerve through the capital. Use **buses** to travel among the outer provincial centers. Hungarian **trains** (*vonat*) are reliable and inexpensive, although theft is particularly high on the Vienna-Budapest line. **Eurail** and **EastRail** are valid in Hungary. Travelers under 26 are eligible for a 33% discount on some **domestic** train fares; inquire ahead and be persistent. An **ISIC** commands discounts at IBUSZ, Express, and station ticket counters. Book international tickets in advance. The student discount on **international** trains is roughly 30%, but sometimes you need to be persistent. Try flashing your ISIC and repeat "student," or the Hungarian, "*diák*" (DEE-ahk).

Személyvonat trains are excruciatingly slow; *gyorsvonat* (listed on schedules in red) cost the same and move at least twice as fast. Large provincial towns are accessible by the blue *expressz* rail lines. Air-conditioned *InterCity* trains are fastest. A seat reservation is required on trains labeled "R." Some basic vocabulary will help you navigate the rail system: *érkezés* (arrival), *indulás* (departure), *vágány* (track), and *állomás* or *pályaudvar* (station, abbreviated *pu.*); see the **Glossary**, p. 803, for more. The platform (*peron*) for arrivals and departures is rarely indicated until the train approaches the station—and then the announcement will be in Hungarian.

The cheap but crowded **bus** system links many towns that have rail connections only to Budapest. The **Erzsébet tér** bus station in Budapest posts schedules and fares. *InterCity* bus tickets are purchased on the bus (get there early if you want a seat). In larger cities, tickets for **public transportation** must be bought in advance from a newsstand and punched on board; they can't be bought from the driver, and there's a fine if you're caught ticketless. In smaller cities, you generally pay when you board (usually 60Ft). The Danube **hydrofoil** floats to Vienna via Bratislava (one-way 11,000Ft; round-trip 16,000Ft; 50% discount for Eurail pass holders).

Either IBUSZ or Tourinform can provide a brochure about **cycling** in Hungary that includes maps, suggested tours, sights, accommodations, bike rental locations, repair shops, and recommended border-crossing points. Write to: **Hungarian Tourist Board,** 1065 Budapest, Bajcsy-Zsilinszky út 31, or **Hungarian Cycling Federation,** 1146 Budapest, Szabó J. u. 3, for more information. Some rail stations rent bicycles.

TOURIST SERVICES

Knowledgeable and friendly **Tourinform** has branches in every county and is probably the most useful tourist service in Hungary. The staff usually does not arrange accommodations, but will be glad to direct you to other agencies. **IBUSZ** offices throughout the country make room arrangements, change money, sell train tickets, and charter tours, although they are generally better at helping with travel plans than at providing information about the actual town. Snare the pamphlet *Tourist Information: Hungary* and the monthly entertainment guides *Programme in Hungary* and *Budapest Panorama* (all free and in English). **Express,** the former national student travel bureau, handles hostels and changes money. The staff generally speaks German, and sometimes English. Regional agencies are most helpful in the outlying areas. **Tourist bureaus** are usually open Monday to Saturday 8am-8pm in summer (some until noon on Sunday); off-season, hours shrink to Monday to Friday 10am-4pm.

MONEY

The national currency is the **forint,** divided into 100 **fillérs,** which are quickly disappearing from circulation. Since inflation in Hungary is unpredictable, change money only as you need it. Make sure to keep some U.S. dollars or Deutschmarks to purchase visas, international train tickets, and (less often) private accommodations. New Zealand and Australian dollars, as well as South African rand and Irish pounds, are not exchangeable. **American Express** offices in Budapest and IBUSZ offices around the country convert **traveler's checks** to cash at about 6% commission. Generally, it is wise to cash traveler's checks at **OTP Bank** and **Postabank** offices. Cash advances on credit cards are available at most OTP branches, but with the already abundant and ever-increasing number of **ATMs,** many banks no longer give cash advances. Machines that automatically change foreign cash into forints are popping up all over and tend to have excellent rates. They may take a little while though, so don't get impatient and walk away without your money. Major **credit cards** are accepted at expensive hotels and many shops and restaurants. At exchange offices with extended hours, the rates are generally poor. The maximum permissible commission for cash-to-cash exchange is 1%. Allow 30 minutes to exchange money. IBUSZ may offer a marginally lower rate. Black market exchanges are common, but illegal.

COMMUNICATION

The Hungarian **mail** system is reliable (airmail—*légiposta*—to the U.S. takes 5-10 days). Note that if you're mailing to a Hungarian citizen, the family name precedes the given name, as in "Krebs, Justin."

Almost all phone numbers in the countryside have six digits and begin with a "3." For intercity calls, wait for the tone and dial slowly; "06" goes before the phone code. **International calls** require red phones or new, digital-display blue ones, found at large post offices, on the street, and in Metro stations. Though the blue phones are more handsome than their red brethren, they tend to cut you off after three to nine minutes. Phones suck money so fast you'll need a companion to feed them. The public phones throughout the country increasingly require **phone cards** (*telefonkártya*), available at kiosks, train stations, and post offices in denominations of 750Ft and 1500Ft. You don't save money either way, but the cards are convenient and seriously collectable. Direct calls can also be made from Budapest's phone office. To call **collect,** dial 09 for the international operator. To reach international carriers, put in a 10Ft and a 20Ft coin (which you get back), dial 00, wait for the second tone, then dial the appropriate number: **AT&T Direct,** tel. 80 00 11 11; **Australia Direct,** tel. 80 00 61 11; **British Telecom Direct,** tel. 80 04 40 11; **Canada Direct,** tel. 80 00 12 11; **Ireland Direct,** tel. 80 00 35 31; **New Zealand Direct,** tel. 80 00 64 11; **MCI World-Phone,** tel. 80 00 14 11; **Mercury Call UK,** tel. 80 00 44 12; **Sprint,** tel. 80 00 18 77.

English **press** is available in many Budapest kiosks and large hotels, but rarely in other cities. The weekly *Budapest Sun* (280Ft) is oriented mostly toward news and hard business information, but its *Style* section will help navigate through the cultural life of Budapest. English-language radio and TV programming is found in *Budapest Week*, which also has excellent listings, survival tips, and articles about life in Hungary (published Thurs.; 145Ft, free at AmEx offices and larger hotels). Also published weekly, the Magyar flyer *Pestiest* lists movies, concerts, and performances in Budapest; pick up a free copy in restaurants, theaters, and clubs. Used bookstores (*antikvárium*) often have English, German, and French books at fire-sale prices.

Three **radio** stations have Anglophone programming: Danubius, Juventus, and Radio Bridge. The frequencies vary from region to region, but in the Budapest area they are 103.3, 89.5, and 102.1FM respectively.

LANGUAGE

Hungarian belongs to the Finno-Ugric family of languages, which includes Finnish and Estonian; but Hungarian and Finnish—probably the two most similar—are only as closely related as German and Italian. After Hungarian and **German, English** is the country's distant third language. "*Hello*" is often used as an informal greeting or farewell. "*Szia!*" (sounds like "see ya!") is another greeting—you'll often hear friends cry: "Hallo, see ya!" See the **Hungarian Glossary,** p. 803, for more.

A few starters for pronunciation: "*c*" is pronounced "ts" as in "cats"; "*cs*" is "ch" as in "chimichanga"; "*gy*" is "dy" as in "*adieu*"; "*ly*" is "y" as in "yam"; "*s*" is "sh" as in "shovel"; "*sz*" is "s" as in "Seattle"; "*zs*" is "zh" as in "pleasure"; and "*a*" is "a" as in "*a*lways." The first syllable always gets the emphasis.

HEALTH AND SAFETY

> **Emergency Numbers: Ambulance:** tel. 104. **Fire:** tel. 105. **Police:** tel. 107.

Tap water is usually clean and drinkable (except in the town of Tokaj, where it bears an uncanny resemblance to the neighboring Tisza River). **Bottled water** is available at every food store. Public **bathrooms** vary tremendously in cleanliness: pack soap and a towel, and don't forget 20Ft. Gentlemen should look for *Férfi*, and ladies for *Női* signs. Should you get sick, contact your embassy for a list of English-speaking doctors. **Pharmacies** (*gyógyszertar*) are usually well-stocked, and in bigger towns there is always a 24-hour pharmacy. Violent **crime** in Hungary is low. However, in larger cities, especially Budapest, foreign tourists are a frequent target of petty thieves and pickpockets. Be extremely careful and don't carry large amounts of money.

ACCOMMODATIONS AND CAMPING

Many travelers stay in **private homes** booked through a tourist agency. Singles are scarce—it's worth finding a roommate, as solo travelers must often pay for a double room. Agencies may try to foist off their most expensive rooms on you; be persistent. Outside Budapest, the best and cheapest office will specialize in the region (i.e. Eger-Tourist in Eger). These agencies will often call ahead to make reservations at your next stop. After staying a few nights, you can frequently make further arrangements directly with the owner, thus saving the 20-30% commission the agencies charge.

Some towns have cheap **hotels,** but most of these are rapidly disappearing. As the hotel system develops and room prices rise, **hosteling** becomes more attractive, although it is difficult to find hostels that are open year-round outside of Budapest. Hostels are usually large enough to accommodate peak-season crowds, and **HI cards** are becoming increasingly useful. Sheets are rarely required. Many hostels can be booked at Express, the student travel agency, or sometimes at the regional tourist office. From late June through August, university **dorms** metamorphose into hostels. Locations change annually; inquire at Express. Many dorms require a minimum 12-hour reservation—always call ahead.

More than 300 **campgrounds** are sprinkled throughout Hungary. If you rent a **bungalow** you must pay for unfilled spaces. Most sites stay open May through September. Tourist offices offer the annual booklet *Camping Hungary* for free. For more info and maps, contact **Tourinform** in Budapest (see **Budapest,** p. 241).

FOOD AND DRINK

Paprika, Hungary's chief agricultural export, colors most dishes red, and the food is more flavorful and varied than in much of Eastern Europe. In Hungarian restaurants (*vendéglő* or *étterem*), begin with *gulyásleves,* a delicious and hearty beef soup seasoned with paprika. Alternatively, try *gyümölesleves,* a cold soup made from cherries, pears, or other fruit, usually topped with whipped cream. *Borjúpaprikás* is a veal dish with paprika, often accompanied by small potato-dumpling pasta. Vegetarians can find the tasty *rántott sajt* (fried cheese) and *gombapörkölt* (mushroom stew) on most menus.

In a *cukrászda,* you can satisfy the relentless desire of your sweet tooth for dangerously few forints. Pastries in Hungary are cheap and usually delicious. *Túrós rétes* is a chewy pastry pocket filled with sweetened cottage cheese. *Somlói galuska* is a fantastically rich sponge cake of chocolate, nuts, and cream, all soaked in rum. After the Austrians stole the recipe for *rétes,* they called it "strudel" and claimed it as their own, but this delicious concoction is as Hungarian as Zsa Zsa Gabor. *Kávé* means espresso, served in thimble-sized cups and so strong your veins will be popping before you finish your first sip.

Hungary produces a diverse array of fine wines (see **A Mini-Guide to Hungarian Wine**, p. 268). Unjustly less famous, Hungarian *sör* (beer) ranges from the first-rate to the merely acceptable. *Dreher Bak* is a rich, dark brew; good light beers include *Dreher Pils*, *Szalon Sör*, and licensed versions of *Steffl*, *Gold Fassl*, *Gösser*, and *Amstel*. Hungary also produces different types of *pálinka*, a liquor that resembles brandy. Among the best tasting are *barackpálinka* (similar to apricot schnapps) and *szilvapálinka* (plum brandy). *Unicum*, advertised as the national drink of Hungary, is a very fine herbal liqueur that Habsburg kings used to cure digestive ailments.

CUSTOMS AND ETIQUETTE

Business hours in Hungary are Monday to Friday 9am-5pm (7am-7pm for food stores). Banks close around 3pm on Friday, but hours are lengthening. **Museums** are usually open Tuesday to Sunday 10am-6pm, with occasional free days on Tuesday. ISIC holders often get in free or pay half-price.

Rounding up the bill as a **tip** for all services—especially in restaurants, but also for everyone from taxi-drivers to hairdressers—is standard for a job well done. Remember in restaurants to give it as you pay—it's rude to leave it on the table. Waiters often don't expect foreigners to tip, so they may start to walk away while you're still fumbling for your money. The bathroom attendant gets 20Ft.

The frequency and extent of public displays of affection, among young and old, may be startling, or at least distracting. Every bus has an obligatory couple exchanging lesser bodily fluids. Taste in **clothing**, especially for men, is casual and unpretentious, but try not to laugh when you see men over 50 sweeping the streets in Speedos. Modesty is not a strong point of women's fashions, though women in smaller towns dress more conservatively.

Hungarians love exercise—if they're watching others do it. They are serious about cigarettes, however. Dogs are family members, far bigger than the European average—no poodles here, thank you—and are spoiled rotten. **Homosexuality,** though legal, is still not fully accepted in Hungarian society; discretion is wise.

NATIONAL HOLIDAYS

Hungarians observe: January 1, New Year's Day; April 10, Good Friday; April 12, Catholic Easter; May 1, Labor Day; August 20, St. Stephen's Day; October 23, Republic Day (1956); December 25-26, Christmas.

LIFE AND TIMES

HISTORY

After a long series of tenants dating back to the Late Stone Age—hunters, gatherers, Neolithic farmers, and Scythians—Celtic tribes settled Hungary in the 3rd century BC, building a fort on what would later be Budapest's Citadel. The city was founded by the **Romans,** who conquered Hungary in 10AD. Roman peace lasted until the 3rd century, when waves of Vandals, Huns, Avars, and Franks trampled the remains of the Romano-Celtic civilization in Hungary.

Magyars, mounted warrior tribes from Central Asia, arrived in 896. Led by **Prince Árpád**, it took them only a few years to establish control over the Mid-Danube Basin. Árpád's descendant, Stephen I, was crowned King of Hungary with papal benediction on Christmas Day 1000, accepting the authority of the pope and decreeing the conversion of his subjects.

The Árpád dynasty ruled Hungary for another 300 years. In 1222, the **Arany Bulla** (Golden Bull) officially recorded the rights of the various Hungarian classes. These rights were promptly revoked by the **Mongols** when they invaded in 1241. The

Árpáds revived briefly, then died out in 1301, to be replaced by a variety of families from across Europe. One of these imported rulers, János Hunyadi, defeated the encroaching Turks in 1456 at Nandorfehérvár near modern Belgrade. His son, Mátyás Hunyadi, known as **Matthias Corvinus** (1458-1490), ruled as king over Hungary's Renaissance, restoring prosperity and the administration of the country and acquiring territory (Bohemia and Lower Austria). In the century following Corvinus's death, Hungary witnessed civil war, peasant rebellion (1514), civil rights setbacks, and Turkish invasion.

After destroying the Hungarian army at Mohács in 1526, the Turks occupied Hungary for almost 150 years. Divided between Habsburgs, Turks, and Turkish allies, the land fell to plague and persecution. More damage came with "liberation." The **Habsburgs** took hold in the early 17th century, ushering in another era of foreign domination. A new **war of independence** began in 1848, led spiritually by the young poet Sándor Petőfi and politically by Lajos Kossuth. The war resulted in the establishment of the **first Hungarian republic.** Kossuth's state held out for one year, but in the summer of 1849, Habsburg Emperor Franz Josef I retook Budapest with support from Tsar Nicholas I of Russia.

Despite a period of repression, Hungary was granted its own government in 1867, in league with the Austrian crown; the Austro-Hungarian Empire came to be known as the **Dual Monarchy.** While the late 19th century witnessed economic development hitherto unseen, Hungary adopted a language policy that favored Magyars over other linguistic groups. In response, national movements emerged among Romanians, Serbs, Croats, Swabians, and Slovaks.These divisions erupted during **WWI,** which resulted in the permanent destruction of

> During the "events of 1956," Imre Nagy declared a neutral government in the capital, but Soviet tanks crushed the revolt.

the empire and the loss of two-thirds of Hungary's territory. During WWI, many of these minority groups remained loyal to Hungary, and the post-war Trianon Treaty awarded political independence only to some at the expense of others. The **Bourgeois Democratic Revolution** that overthrew the monarchy in 1918 was followed by the 133-day-long Communist Hungarian Republic of Councils under the leadership of **Béla Kun.** Counter-revolutionary forces took control, brutally repressing those involved with the Communist administration, as the fascist dictatorship of Admiral Miklós Horthy de Nagybanya settled in for 24 years of control (1920-44). The depressed interwar years were followed by a tentative alliance with Hitler in **WWII,** then by the year-long Nazi occupation and the almost total destruction of Budapest during the two-month Soviet siege of 1945. Two-thirds of Hungary's Jews, whose numbers had approached one million before the war, were murdered in WWII. Survivors fled the country.

Hungary became a **People's Republic** in 1949. Communist Hungary was ruled by **Mátyás Rákosi** and the Hungarian Workers Party (later the Magyar Szocialista Munkáspárt), under which it became strongly tied to the USSR both economically and politically. Rákosi went out with the **"events of 1956,"** a violent uprising in Budapest during which **Imre Nagy** declared a neutral, non-Warsaw Pact government in the capital. Soviet troops rolled in to crush the revolt; Nagy was executed and thousands died in the fighting.

Over the next two decades, under Nagy's replacement, **Janos Kádár,** borders were partially opened and the national standard of living improved, until inflation and a lack of economic growth halted the process in the 1980s. Democratic reformers in the Communist Party pushed aside Kádár in 1988, pressing for a market economy and increased political freedom. In autumn 1989, the Hungarian people broke away from the Soviet orbit in a bloodless revolution. The 1990 elections transferred power to the center-right **Hungarian Democratic Forum,** led by Prime Minister **József Antall** and President **Arpád Göncz,** a former Soviet political prisoner. Slow progress, however, led the renamed-and-revamped Socialists to be trusted with power again, in 1994. Change continues at a dizzying pace, but Hungarians have adapted admirably since the last Soviet troops departed in June 1991. In 1996, Hungary celebrated its 1100th anniversary.

HUNGARY

LITERATURE

A Finno-Ugric tongue, distantly related to Finnish and Estonian, **Magyar** is a stranger in a strange linguistic land. The feeling of isolation created by such a unique and impenetrable language has defined the literary, social, and political history of its speakers. Since the Reformation, Magyar writers have dealt with the problems of Hungarian identity and establishing an independent role in the European system.

There is little record of literary Magyar before the 11th century; the earliest extant written example is a deed from 1055 founding a Benedictine Abbey, which contains a number of Hungarian proper nouns (now kept at Pannonhalma Abbey; see p. 296). Not until Christian missionaries came to the region did the Hungarian language emerge from under the dominant Latin culture—Latin actually remained the language of state until 1844. The history of Hungarian literature has also been affected by the problems of censorship; the Ottoman occupation censored Hungarian writers for over 150 years. As the Turks receded in the early 18th century, novels in French and German entered the country in translation. During the Enlightenment, members if the Hungarian nobility like **Count Miklós Bethlen** wrote memoirs in the style of Voltaire and Rousseau. As evidenced by the street names of post-Communist Hungary, the writers leading up to the revolution of 1848 played an important role in Hungary's history, as well as literature. **Ferenc Kazincsy** (1759-1831) organized language reform, elevating the status of Hungarian. Romantics like **Mihály Vörösmarty** (1800-1855), as well as the Populist anti-Romantic **Sándor Petőfi** (1823-1849), provided the nationalistic rhetoric required for revolutions. This period bound together changing literary ideals with the quest for social reform and political independence. Outside of a few poets, such as **Arany** (1817-1882), the 19th century produced fewer great works until the initiation of a new literary era with the founding of the Nyugat (West) literary journal in 1908. **Endre Ady, Mihály Babits,** and **Dezso Kosztolány** embraced Symbolism and psychoanalysis in their poetry, expanding the creative field for Hungarian Expressionist writing. Unconnected with Nyugat, the avant-garde poet **Lajos Kassák** concerned himself with Hungarian working-class life.

László Németh was one of the most influential authors to emerge from the new Populist movements of the interwar period in Hungary. He crafted plays that used a stark Realism to depict the battle of the individual against the world. After WWII, Communism again silenced the Magyar writers who worked in the **Socialist Realist** style until a new generation appeared that was able to more freely develop individualistic styles. **György Konrád** (1933-) writes both novels such as *Latogato* (The Case Worker; 1969) and important political treatises like *Antipolika* (Antipolitics; 1984), both of which were crucial in defining the dissident movements all over Central Europe. Less concerned with social issues and more interested with the post-modern quest to redefine the meaning of use of words themselves, **Péter Esterházy** and his innovative books, such as *Kis Magyar Pornografia* (A Little Hungarian Pornography; 1984) and *An Introduction to Literature* (1986), founded a new movement in Magyar literature and brought it again to the world cultural scene. Since the end of Communism, political motivations have had to be redefined, and the search is on for a new source of energy for this generation of Hungarian writers.

> The unique Magyar tongue fosters a sense of isolation that has come to define the literary, social, and political history of the Hungarians.

HUNGARY TODAY

Although still aglow with political triumphs, Hungarians are experiencing an economic hangover. High prices for daily necessities, widespread unemployment, and yawning inequities in income harshly remind Hungarians of the competitive side of liberty. However, along with Poland, the Czech Republic, and Slovakia, Hungary is one of the prosperous **Visegrád Four,** named after an economic pact signed in the town of Visegrád in 1991. Realizing that there are no quick solutions, most Hungarians are resigning themselves to a painful transition. In an attempt to curb the rapidly increasing deficit, and to bring the economy into line with guide-lines set by international creditors and the EU, Prime Minister **Gyula Horn** has overseen large cuts in the fat public sector in the face of strikes and protests. The Ministry of Finance predicts 17-19% inflation for 1997, which, although high, is down from the 24% rate of 1996, and the economy in general is stable enough that the EU will begin accession negotiations in early 1998. Against the protests of former Warsaw Pact ally Russia, Hungary was offered NATO membership in July 1997.

Aside from economic woes, the most visible vestiges of the old regime are now benevolent: efficient public transportation, clean parks and streets, and a low incidence of violent crime. Led by Gyula Horn, the former Communists, renamed the Hungarian Socialist Party, returned to power in the 1994 election with promises of easier reforms, rather than a return to the past. Horn's present popularity and authority will be put to the test by the general elections in May 1998.

Budapest

A cosmopolitan European capital and the stronghold of Magyar nationalism, Budapest still has spirit after its years in a Communist coma. Endowed with an architectural majesty befitting the Habsburg Empire's number-two city, the Hungarian capital is huge but graceful, multifaceted but not contradictory. WWII punished the city, but the Hungarians rebuilt it from rubble with the same pride that fomented the ill-fated 1956 Uprising, weathered the Soviet invasion, and overcame decades of subservience. Today, the city maintains its charm and a vibrant spirit—neon lights and legions of tourists have added a new twist to the Budapest rhapsody, but below it all the main theme is still expertly played by genuine, unspoiled Magyar strings.

ORIENTATION AND PRACTICAL INFORMATION

Budapest straddles the **Duna** (Danube), 250km downstream from Vienna; regular trains and boats connect the two capitals. Previously two cities, **Buda** and **Pest,** separated by the Duna, Budapest has retained a distinctive character on each side of the river. Buda inspires artists with its hilltop citadel, trees, and cobblestone Castle District. On the east side, **Pest,** the commercial heart of the modern city, buzzes. Here you'll find shopping, banks, Parliament, the Opera House, and theaters.

Three central bridges lace Budapest together. **Széchenyi lánchíd** connects Roosevelt tér to the base of the cable car, which scurries up **Várhegy** (Castle Hill). To the south, the slender white **Erzsébet híd** extends from near **Petőfi tér** and **Március 15 tér** up to the monument of St. Gellért at the base of **Gellért-hegy** (Gellért Hill). Farther along the Duna, the green **Szabadság híd** links **Fővám tér** to the south end of Gellért-hegy, topped by **Szabadság Szobor** (Liberation Monument). **Moszkva tér,** just down the north slope of Várhegy, is Budapest's bus and tram transportation hub. One Metro stop away in the direction of Örs vezér tere, **Batthyány tér** lies on the west bank, opposite **Országház** (Parliament); this is the starting point of the **HÉV commuter railway,** which leads north through Óbuda and into Szentendre. Budapest's three **Metro** lines (M1, M2 and M3) converge at **Deák tér,** beside the main international bus terminal at **Erzsébet tér.** Deák tér lies at the core of Pest's loose arrangement of concentric-ring boulevards and spoke-like avenues. Two blocks west toward the river lies **Vörösmarty tér.** As you face the statue of Mihály Vörösmarty, the main pedestrian shopping zone, **Váci u.,** is to the right.

If you feel like you're walking in circles, remember that streets arbitrarily change names from one block to the next, and many street names in Budapest occur more than once; always check the district as well as the kind of street: **út** is a major thoroughfare, **utca** (u.) is a street, **körút** (krt.) is a circular artery, and **tér** means square. Addresses in Budapest begin with a Roman numeral that represents one of the city's 23 **districts.** Central Buda is I; downtown Pest is V. The middle two digits of the

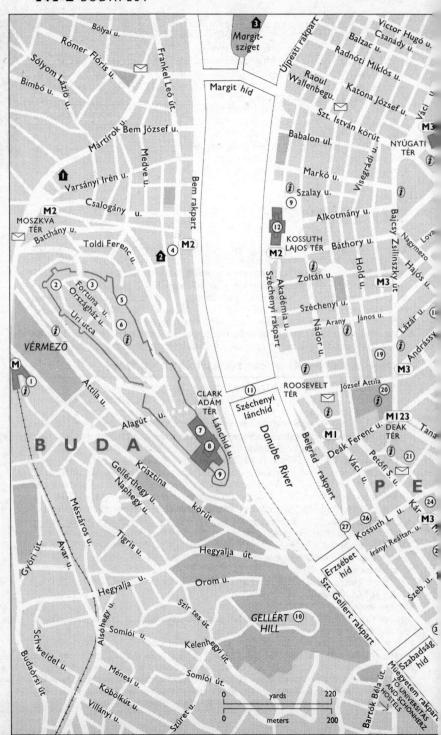

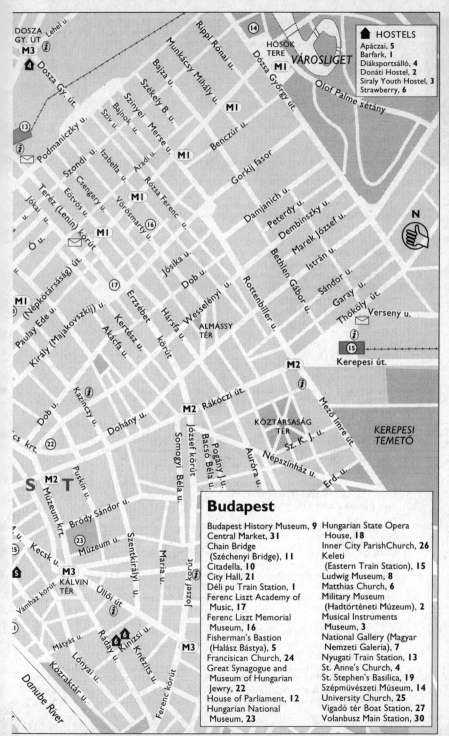

HOSTELS

Apáczai, 5
Barfark, 1
Diáksportsálló, 4
Donáti Hostel, 2
Siraly Youth Hostel, 3
Strawberry, 6

Budapest

Budapest History Museum, 9
Central Market, 31
Chain Bridge
  (Széchenyi Bridge), 11
Citadella, 10
City Hall, 21
Déli pu Train Station, 1
Ferenc Liszt Academy of
  Music, 17
Ferenc Liszt Memorial
  Museum, 16
Fisherman's Bastion
  (Halász Bástya), 5
Franciscan Church, 24
Great Synagogue and
  Museum of Hungarian
  Jewry, 22
House of Parliament, 12
Hungarian National
  Museum, 23

Hungarian State Opera
  House, 18
Inner City ParishChurch, 26
Keleti
  (Eastern Train Station), 15
Ludwig Museum, 8
Matthias Church, 6
Military Museum
  (Hadtörténeti Múzeum), 2
Musical Instruments
  Museum, 3
National Gallery (Magyar
  Nemzeti Galeria), 7
Nyugati Train Station, 13
St. Anne's Church, 4
St. Stephen's Basilica, 19
Szépmüvészeti Múseum, 14
University Church, 25
Vigadó tér Boat Station, 27
Volanbusz Main Station, 30

postal code also correspond to the district number. Because many streets have shed their Communist labels, an up-to-date **map** is essential. The **American Express** and **Tourinform** offices have good free tourist maps, or pick up *Belváros Idegenforgalmi Térképe* at any Metro stop (150Ft).

Useful Organizations

Tourist Offices: Tourinform, V, Sütő u. 2 (tel. 117 98 00; fax 117 95 78), off Deák tér just behind McDonald's. M1, 2, or 3: Deák tér. This busy, multilingual tourist office provides information about everything from sightseeing tours to opera performances, but doesn't arrange accommodations. Make room in your pack for all the free brochures. Open Mon.-Fri. 9am-7pm, Sat.-Sun. 9am-4pm. Sightseeing, accommodation bookings, and travel services are available at almost every private travel agency, including IBUSZ and Budapest Tourist (offices in train stations and tourist centers). **IBUSZ** central office, V, Apácsai Csere J. u. 1 (tel. 118 57 76; fax 117 90 00), a block west of Vörösmarty tér. Books airline tickets, sightseeing packages (3200Ft per 3hr. tour; 12 languages), accommodations, and provides cash advances on Diner's Club and Visa. Open 24hr. At all tourist offices you can purchase the **Budapest Kártya** (Budapest Card), which truly, as the ad says, "puts the whole city in your pocket." For 2900Ft, you get 3 days of public transportation, entrance to all museums, and discounts at a number of shops and restaurants.

Tourist Police: KEO, V, Városligeti Fasor 46/48 (tel. 112 15 37), 2 blocks southeast of Andrássy út. M3: Nyugati Pu. Visa extensions. Open Tues. 8:30am-noon and 2-6pm, Wed. 8:30am-1pm, Thurs. 10am-6pm, Fri. 8:30am-12:30pm.

Budget Travel: Express, V, Szbadság tér 16 (tel. 131 77 77). Some reduced international air and rail fares for the under-26 crowd (train ticket reductions also available at train stations). Pick up an ISIC (700Ft). Open Mon. and Wed.-Thurs. 8am-4:30pm, Tues. 8am-6pm, Fri. 8am-2:30pm. Bring your own photos for the ISIC; there is a photo booth (4 for 500Ft) at the top of the escalators at the Moskva tér and other major subway stops. Amazing discounts for those under 26 as well as standby tickets (purchase 2 days before flight) available at the office of **Malév** airlines, V, Dorottya u. 2 (tel. 266 56 16; fax 266 27 84) on Vörösmarty tér. Open Mon.-Fri. 7:30am-5pm.

Embassies and Consulates: Australia, XII, Kriályhágó tér 8/9 (tel.201 88 99). Open Mon.-Fri. 9am-noon. Take M2 to Déli pu. and then bus #21 to Királyhágó tér. **Canada,** XII, Zugligeti út 51-53 (tel. 275 12 00). Take bus #158 from Moszkva tér to the last stop. **U.K.,** V, Harmincad u. 6 (tel. 266 28 88), just off the northeast corner of Vörösmarty tér. M1: Vörösmarty tér. Open Mon.-Fri. 9:30am-noon and 2:30-4pm. **U.S.,** V, Szabadság tér 12 (tel. 267 44 00). M2: Kossuth Lajos, then walk two blocks down Akademia and take a left on Zoltán. Open Mon. and Wed. 8:30-11am, Tues. and Thurs.-Fri. 8:30-10:30am.

Currency Exchange: The bureaus open late often have less favorable rates. Most exchange offices turn traveler's checks into hard currency for a commission. **General Banking and Trust Co. Ltd.,** Váci u. 19/21 (tel. 118 96 88; fax 118 82 30). Some of the best rates in town. Open Mon.-Fri. 9am-4:30pm. **IBUSZ,** V, Petőfi tér 3, just north of Erzsébet híd. Cash advances on Visa. Cirrus **ATM.** Open 24hr. **GWK Tours** (tel. 322 90 11), in the Keleti Station. Excellent rates. Very convenient for rail travelers. Open daily 6am-9pm. **Magyar Külkereskedelmi Bank,** V, Szent István tér 11. M: Deák tér. Two blocks north of the Metro, at the basilica's entrance. Perhaps the most comprehensive exchange place in town; with very good rates. Open Mon.-Thurs. 8am-2pm and Fri. 8am-1pm. Outdoor Cirrus/EC/MC/Visa **ATMs.** This chain of banks is among the few to give MC and Visa cash advances (forints only; go inside the bank if you don't have a PIN code) and cash traveler's checks in US$ (2% commission). **ATMs** are all over town. At the Tourinform office, ask for the free OTP/Postabank brochure listing the locations of more than 100 Cirrus/MC/Visa ATMs. Citibank and American Express also have ATMs.

American Express: V, Deák Ferenc u. 10 (tel. 266 86 80; fax 267 20 28). M1: Vörösmarty tér, next to Hotel Kempinski. Sells traveler's checks for hard cash, moneygrams, or cardholders' personal checks. Cashes US$ traveler's checks (6% commission). Cash advances only in forints. Free **maps.** Pick up the free *Budapest Week* here. Holds mail; address as follows: "Claudia WEBBER, American Express,

Hungary Kft., Deák Ferenc u. 10, H-1052 Budapest, Hungary." Free pickup for AmEx cardholders; 555Ft otherwise. AmEx **ATM.** Office open July-Sept. Mon.-Fri. 9am-6:30pm, Sat. 9am-2pm; Oct.-June Mon.-Fri. 9am-5:30pm, Sat. 9am-1pm.

Luggage storage: At the train station, Keleti pu. in yellow lockers across from the international cashier (80Ft). Also at the Volánbusz main bus station, V, Erzsébet tér (80Ft). Open Mon.-Thurs. 6am-7pm, Fri. 6am-9pm, Sat.-Sun. 6am-6pm.

Post Office: V, Városház u. 18 (tel. 118 48 11). Pick up *Poste Restante* here. Open Mon.-Fri. 8am-8pm, Sat. 8am-3pm. 24hr. branches at Nyugati station, VI, Teréz krt. 105-107, and Keleti station, VIII, Baross tér 11c. **Postal code:** 1052.

Telephones: V, Petőfi Sándor u. 17. English-speaking staff. Fax service. Open Mon.-Fri. 8am-8pm, Sat.-Sun. 8am-2pm. At other times, try the post office. Many of the public phones in Budapest now use **phone cards,** available at newsstands, post offices, and metro stations. 50-unit card 750Ft, 120-unit card 1750Ft. Use **card phones** for **international calls.** They will automatically cut you off after 10-20min., but it's more time than the coin phones will give you (**local operator** tel. 01, **international operator** 09). **Phone code:** 1.

Transportation

Flights: Ferihegy Airport (tel. 267 43 33, info 157 71 55, reservations 157 91 23, telephone check-in 157 75 91). Terminal 1 is for foreign airlines and Malév flights to New York and Vienna. Terminal 2 is for all other Malév flights, Lufthansa, and Air France. **Volánbusz** takes 30min. to get to terminal 1 and 40min. to terminal 2 from Erzsébet tér (every half hour between 5:30am and 9pm, 300Ft). The **airport shuttle bus** (tel. 296 85 55) will pick you up anywhere in the city at any time of day or night, or take you anywhere in the city from the airport (1000Ft); call for pick-up a few hours in advance. The cheapest way to the airport is to take the M3 to Köbanya-Kispest and then follow the signs to the Ferihegy bus; it's well-marked with lots of pictures of airplanes (40min. to terminal 1, 50min. to terminal 2).

Trains: Domestic info tel. 322 78 60, international info tel. 142 91 50. *Pályaudvar,* often abbreviated "pu," means train station. Those under 26 are eligible for a 33% discount on international tickets; show your ISIC and tell the clerk *"diák"* (student). English may not be understood, so write your destination on a piece of paper and show that to the clerk. The three main stations—**Keleti pu.** (113 68 35), **Nyugati pu.** (149 01 15), and **Déli pu.** (175 62 93)—are also Metro stops. The railway stations are favorite spots for thieves and pickpockets, so be careful. Most international trains arrive at Keleti pu., but trains to and from a given location do not necessarily stop at the same station; trains from Prague may stop at Nyugati pu. or Keleti pu. Nyugati pu. serves east Hungary; Déli pu. serves west Hungary. Each station has schedules for the others. To: Belgrade (4 per day, 6½hr., 6350Ft); Berlin (5 per day, 12½hr., 16,200Ft); Bucharest (3 per day, 12hr., 15,800Ft); Prague (8 per day, 7½hr., 8230Ft); Vienna (5 per day, 3½hr., 5100Ft); and Warsaw (2 per day, 10hr., 8430Ft). The daily **Orient Express** travels between Berlin and Bucharest.

Train Ticket Agencies: International Ticket Office, Keleti pu. Open daily 7am-6pm. **IBUSZ** (see p. 244). Generous discounts on international rail tickets. Several days' advance purchase may be necessary for international destinations. **MÁV Hungarian Railways,** VI, Andrássy út 35 (tel. 322 82 75; fax 322 84 05), and at all train stations. International and domestic tickets. About 25% discounts for those under 26; be insistent and whip out all your student/youth IDs. Open Mon.-Fri. 9am-6pm. **Wagons-lits,** V, Dorottya u. 3 (tel. 266 30 40), across from Malév just northeast of Vörösmarty tér. 25-50% discounts for seniors and youth. Open Mon.-Fri. 9am-12:45pm and 1:30-5pm.

Buses: Info tel. 117 29 66. **Volánbusz main station,** V, Erzsébet tér (tel. 117 25 62; international ticket office tel. 118 21 22; fax 266 54 19). M1, 2, 3: Deák tér. International cashier upstairs (open Mon.-Fri. 6am-7pm, Sat.-Sun. 6:30am-4pm). Most domestic buses to East Hungary and buses to most the Czech Republic, Poland, Romania, Slovakia, Turkey and Ukraine depart from **Népstadion,** Hungária körút 48/52 (tel. 252 18 96). M2: Népstadion. Domestic buses are usually cheaper than trains, but may take longer. Buses to the Danube Bend leave from **Árpád híd** station. To: Berlin (4 per week, 14½hr., 13,800Ft); Bratislava (1 per day, 3½hr., 1450Ft); Prague (4 per week, 8½hr., 3100Ft); Vienna (1 per day, 3hr., 3150Ft).

Public Transportation: Built in 1896, the Budapest **Metro** was the first in continental Europe and has been consistently rapid and punctual ever since. The subway, **buses,** and **trams** are inexpensive and convenient. The Metro has 3 lines: yellow (M1), red (M2), and blue (M3). An "M" indicates a stop, but you will not always find the sign on the street; it's better to look for stairs leading down. All lines converge at the **Deák tér** station. Public transportation stops about 11:30pm; don't be surprised to find the subway gates locked 15min. earlier. Buses whose numbers are marked with an "E" run along major routes 24hr. Bus #78E runs along the same route as M2. The subway, buses, and trams all use the same yellow **tickets,** (60Ft) sold in Metro stations, *Trafík* shops, and by some sidewalk vendors. Tickets are valid through Óbuda on the HÉV; to go beyond that, you'll have to buy one on the train. Punch tickets in the orange boxes at the gate of the Metro or on buses and trams. 10-trip tickets (*tíz jegy;* 540Ft) and 20-trip tickets (1000Ft), as well as passes, are available (1-day 500Ft, 3-day 1000Ft, 1-week 1300Ft, 2-week 1640Ft, 1-month 2460Ft). Tickets are checked mostly on the Metro and at the beginning of the month; 800Ft fine if you're caught without a ticket, or 2000Ft if you can't cough up the cash on the spot. If you change Metro lines or buses, you must use a new ticket. The **HÉV commuter rail** runs between Batthyány tér in Buda and Szentendre, 40min. north on the Danube Bend. Trains leave about every 15min. At every metro station you can buy an extremely useful *Budapest közlekedési hálózata* (Network Map of Budapest Transport Ltd.; 220Ft); all you ever wanted to know about public transportation in Budapest.

Hydrofoils: MAHART International Boat Station, VI, Belgrád rakpart (tel. 118 15 86; fax 118 77 40), on the Duna near Erzsébet híd. Info and ticketing. Open Mon.-Fri. 8am-4pm. Or try **IBUSZ,** VII, Dob u. (tel. 322 16 56, fax 322 72 64). M2: Astoria. Open Mon.-Fri. 8am-4pm. Arrive at the docks 1hr. before departure for customs and passport control. Eurailpass holders receive a 50% discount. To Vienna (April 8-May 19 and Sept.4-Oct. 29 daily 9am; May 20-Sept. 3 daily 8am and 4pm; 6hr. via Bratislava; one-way 12,100Ft, students 9000Ft; round-trip 20,500Ft, students 13,000Ft; bicycles 1600Ft). All charges payable in Ft, US$, or with AmEx and Visa.

Car Rental: Most rental agencies charge over US$100 per day for their cheapest cars. If you must rent, try **Budget,** I, Krisztina krt. 41/43 (tel.156 63 33; fax 155 04 82), in Hotel Mercure Buda; Ferihegy Airport terminal 1 (tel. 157 81 97), or terminal 2 (tel. 157 84 81). Open Mon.-Sat. 8am-8pm, Sun. 8am-6pm. The cheapest unlimited mileage option is the Opel Corsa (13,500Ft per day; minimum age 21). A more economical option is to travel with **Super Kenguru KFT,** VIII, Kőfaragó u. 15 (tel. 138 20 19). M2: Astoria. This **carpool** service charges 6.40Ft per km for both domestic and international trips. If you're driving somewhere and would like to take passengers, notify Kenguru 3-4 days in advance. If you want to go somewhere, they'll need to know 4-5 days in advance. Open Mon.-Fri. 8am-6pm, Sat.-Sun. 10am-2pm.

Taxis: Főtaxi, tel. 222 22 22. **Budataxi,** tel. 233 33 33. 100Ft base plus 80Ft per km. Probably the most reliable. Taxis are more expensive at night.

Other Practical Information

English Bookstore: Bestsellers KFT, V, Október 6 u. 11 (tel./fax 112 12 95), near the intersection with Arany János u. M: Deák tér or M1: Vörösmarty tér. Small but eclectic. Literature, pop novels, current magazines, and local travel guides. Also carries **The Phone Book,** an English language "yellow pages," invaluable for people planning to spend an extended period of time in the city (US$4). Open Mon.-Fri. 9am-6:30pm, Sat. 10am-6pm. Nearby, **CEU Academic Bookshop,** V, Nador u. 9 (tel. 327 30 96), has a more erudite selection; particularly strong on Eastern Europe. Open Mon.-Fri. 9am-6pm, Sat. 2pm-5pm.

Photocopies: Photocopying offices abound. Try the friendly photoshop V, Petőfi Sándor u. 11 (tel. 118 54 84), near the main post office. Copies 10Ft per page.

Laundromats: Irisz Szalon, VII, Rákóczi út. 8b. M2: Astoria. Wash: 5kg, 350Ft per 40min. Dry: 120Ft per 15min. Pay the cashier before you start. Open Mon.-Fri. 7am-7pm, Sat. 7am-1pm. Many hostels let you use their washing machines for a fee.

24-Hour Pharmacies: I, Széna tér 1 (tel. 202 18 16). VI, Teréz krt. 41 (tel. 111 44 39). IX, Boráros tér 3 (tel. 117 07 43). IX, Üllői út. 121 (tel. 133 89 47). At night, call the number on the door, or ring the bell to summon the sleepy manager; you will

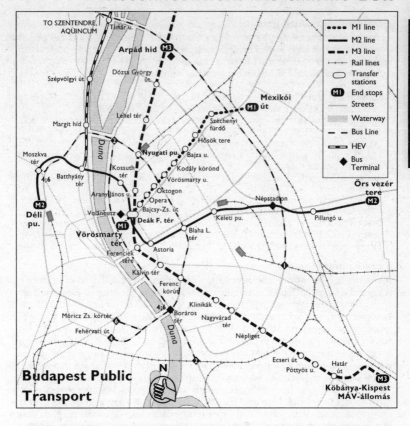

Budapest Public Transport

be charged a slight fee for the service. State-owned pharmacies are the only source for all medicines, including aspirin; little is displayed and everything is dispensed from behind the counter. To find a pharmacy look for the tan-and-white motif with *Gyógyszertár, Apotheke,* or *Pharmacie* in black letters in the window.

Gay Hotline: Try **Cruise Victory Co.,** II, Váci. itca 9 (tel./fax 267 38 05), for a free brochure with gay listings and a gay map of Budapest. Open Mon.-Fri. 9am-6pm. (Also see **Gay Budapest,** p. 259).

AIDS Hotline: Tel. 166 92 83. Mon., Wed., and Thurs. 1pm-5pm; Tues. and Fri. noon-8pm.

Medical Assistance: Személyi Orvosi Szolgálat, VIII, Kerepesi út 15 (tel. 204 55 00, 204 55 01). English spoken. Open 24hr. Emergency medical care is free for foreigners. The U.S. embassy has a list of English-speaking doctors. The ubiquitous emergency medical assistance number is 104.

ACCOMMODATIONS AND CAMPING

Travelers arriving in Keleti station enter a feeding frenzy as hostel solicitors and proprietors huckstering their rooms elbow their way to tourists. Don't be drawn in by promises of free drinks or special discounts; the hostel-hawkers get paid by the customer and have been known to stretch the truth. The easiest options are **hostels, private rooms,** or family-run **guesthouses.** Get your bearings before you go with anyone. Always make sure that the room is easily accessible by public transportation, preferably by Metro. Ask to be shown on a map where the lodging is located. Though the runners are generally legit, see the room before you hand over any cash. And remember: price is not always the best indicator of quality.

Accommodations Agencies

Accommodation services are overrunning Budapest. Rates (1200-5000Ft per person) depend on the location and bathroom quality. Haggle stubbornly. Arrive around 8am, and you may get a single for 1400Ft or a double for 1800Ft. Travelers who stay for more than four nights can obtain a somewhat better rate.

Pension Centrum, XII, Szarvas Gábor út 24 (tel. 201 93 86 or 176 00 57). Makes reservations in private rooms (commission free). Open daily 10am-7pm.

IBUSZ, at all train stations and tourist centers. 24hr. accommodation office, V, Apáczai Csere J. u. 1 (tel. 118 39 25; fax 117 90 99). An established service. Private rooms 1800-3600Ft per person. Swarms of people outside IBUSZ offices push "bargains"; quality varies, but they're legal. Old women asking "*Privatzimmer?*" are vending private rooms.

Budapest Tourist, V, Roosevelt tér 5 (tel. 117 35 55; fax 118 16 58), near Hotel Forum, 10min. from Deák tér on the Pest end of Széchenyi lánchíd. A well-established enterprise offering 2000-2800Ft singles and 4800Ft doubles. Open Mon.-Thurs. 9am-5pm, Fri. 9am-3pm. Same hours at branches through the city.

Duna Tours, Bajcsy-Zsilinszky út 17 (tel. 131 45 33; fax 111 68 27), next to Cooptourist. Doubles from 2400Ft. The English-speaking staff swears that their rooms are located only in districts V and VI. Open Mon.-Fri. 9:30am-noon and 12:30-5pm.

Year-Round Hostels

If you're eager to meet young people, hostels are the place to be. Most hostel-type accommodations, including university dorms, are under the aegis of **Express.** There is an office in the 5th district, Semmelweis u. 4 (tel. 117 66 34 or 117 86 00); leave Deák tér on Tanács krt., head right on Gerlóczy u., then take the first left. Or try the branch at Szabadság tér 16 (tel. 131 77 77), between M3: Arany János and M2: Kossuth tér. Hostels advertise in the train stations and on billboards and flyers. Before accepting lodging, make sure you're not being brought to one of the new private hostels that cram hordes of tourists into tiny rooms. Within two minutes of arriving at Keleti pu., you're bound to be familiar with Traveller's Youth Hostels/Youth Way, Universum, and Strawberry—three companies that run youth hostels all over the city. Most rooms have bunk beds and linoleum floors that, despite avid cleaning, never quite look clean. Many provide in-room refrigerators and TV rooms on each floor. Some offer laundry machines. Prices at the company-run hostels are rising quickly in response to demand. The Travellers' Youth Hostels's Diáksportszálló is famous for its party scene. Universum hostels are usually quieter. One caveat with these large companies—they may quote a price at the train station only to claim later that all such rooms are taken.

Backpack Guesthouse, XI, Takács Menyhért u. 33 (tel. 185 50 89), a 20min. commute from central Pest. From Keleti pu. or the city center, take bus #1, 7, or 7A heading toward Buda and disembark at "Tétenyi u.," immediately after the rail bridge, 5 stops past the river. From the bus stop, head back under the bridge, turn left, and follow the street parallel to the train tracks for 3 blocks. Look for the most colorful house on the block. Carpeted rooms, clean bathrooms, and humor in every niche. Young, friendly, and very helpful staff. 5- and 8-bed dorms 1000-1100Ft per person; showers, private locker, and use of kitchen, TV, and VCR included. Rotating day program; try spelunking, horseback riding, rock climbing, or waterskiing, all in the Budapest area (1800Ft). The bulletin board lists special trips, programs, and information. Free tennis.

Nicholas's Budget Hostel, XI, Takács Menyhért u. 12 (tel. 185 48 70). Follow the directions to the Backpack Guesthouse, then continue a half block down the road. Not as corporate as the competition, but more spacious and clean, and just as friendly. TV, garden, kitchen, lockers and laundry (5kg 1600Ft). 12-bed dorm 1000Ft per person. Doubles 3200Ft. Bedding 500Ft. Reservations accepted.

Diáksportszálló, XIII, Dózsa György út 152 (tel. 140 85 85 or 129 86 44). Entrance on Angyalföldi, 50m from M3: Dózsa György. Huge and hugely social (dubbed "party hostel"), but not the best choice if safety, cleanliness, and quiet are major concerns. It seems to have remained the same under new "Travellers' Youth Hostels" management, but they claim improvements are in the works. Check-out 9am. Singles 2000Ft; doubles 3800-4000Ft, with shower 4200Ft. Triples and quads 1650Ft per person. 8- to 12- person dorms 1200Ft per person. 10% discount with HI card. Bar open and occupied 24hr.

Best Hostel, VI, Podmaniczky u. 27 I/13 (tel. 332 49 34; fax 269 29 26). Ring bell #27. Run by a very young management team working hard to justify the name. Newly refurbished, with spotless bathrooms and a well-equipped kitchen, centrally located and actually affordable. Dorm 1000Ft per person. Doubles 3000Ft; quads 3900Ft; dorms 1000Ft per person. HI members get 10% discount.

Summer Hostels

Almost all of the **Technical University** (Műegyetem) dorms become youth hostels in July and August; these are conveniently located in district XI, around Móricz Zsigmond Körtér. From M3: Kálvin Ter, ride tram #47 or 49 across the river to "M. Zsigmond." For more information, call the **International Student Center** (tel. 166 77 58 or 166 50 11, ext. 1469). In summer, the center also has an office in Schönherz. For bookings, try the **Express Office** (see Year-Round Hostels, above).

Strawberry Youth Hostels, IX, Ráday u. 43/45 (tel. 218 47 66), and Kinizsi u. 2/6 (tel. 217 30 33). M3: Kálvin tér. Two converted university dorms within a block of each other in Pest, on a smaller street running south out of Kálvin tér. Spacious rooms without bunk beds. All rooms have refrigerators, sinks and drying racks. Disco on premises. Use the old washing machines for free, or the new ones for 160Ft. Check-out 10am. Doubles 4080Ft; triples and quads 1920Ft per person. 10% off with HI card.

Bakfark Hostel, I, Bakfark u. 1/3 (tel. 201 54 19). M2: Moszkva tér. From the Metro, stroll along Margit krt. and take the first side street after Széna tér.; the street is not marked, but the hostel is. 78 beds in quads and 6-bed dorms (1900Ft). Some of the coolest hostel rooms in town, with lofts instead of bunks. Check-out 9am. Sheets, locker, and storage space included. No shower curtains. 10% off with HI card. Reservations recommended. Laundry 300Ft per load.

Apáczai, V, Papnövelde u. 4/6 (tel. 267 03 11; fax 275 70 46), 3 blocks south of M3: Ferenciek tér. Probably the most central summer hostel, with the usual amount of linoleum. Doubles 3600Ft. Quads and sixes 1600Ft per person. Spacious dorms 1100Ft per person. HI members get 10% off.

Baross, XI, Bartók Béla út 17 (tel. 186 83 65; fax 275 70 46), 2 blocks from Géllert tér. Lived-in college dorms—Madonna pin-ups and all. From simple singles to quads with sink and refrigerator in the room. Hall bathrooms. Check-out 9am. Doubles 1990Ft; triples and quads 1700Ft. 10% discount with HI card. New washer (140Ft; washing powder 50Ft). Open late June-Aug.

Hostel Rózsa, XI, Bercsényi u. 28/30 (tel. 463 42 50), 3 stops after the river on tram #4 on the side street next to Kaiser's supermarket. 65 doubles with big desks, wood floors, fridge, and sink. Better-than-average hall bathrooms. 2300Ft per person. Newly refurbished. Laundry 160Ft (wash only). Free transportation from bus or train stations. 10% off with HI card. Free Hungarian lessons on request.

Martos, XI, Stoczek u. 5/7 (tel. 463 37 76; tel./fax 463 36 51; email reception@hotel.martos.bme.hu), near the Technical University. Independent, student-run summer hostel with the cheapest rooms in town. Free use of washers and dryers, phones on each floor for incoming calls, and communal kitchens. Internet access available. Hall bathrooms. No curfew. Check-out 9am. Singles 1800Ft; doubles 2400Ft. Plush 6-person apartment 9000Ft.

Universitas, XI, Irinyi József u. 9/11 (tel. 463 38 25 or 463 38 26). First stop after crossing the river on tram #4 or 6. Large square dorm with 500 beds. In-room fridges. Communal bathrooms. No curfew. Check-out 9am. Doubles 4320Ft. Wash 200Ft. Satellite TV; and a very active nightlife in the disco and bar on weekends. HI members 10% off. Fine cafeteria with affordable *menüs* (540Ft including beer).

Guest Houses

Guest houses and rooms for rent in private homes include a personal touch for about the same price as an anonymous hostel bed (do not confuse these with pensions, or *panzió,* which are larger and rarely charge less than 4000Ft per person). Owners usually pick travelers up at the train stations or the airport, and often provide services such as sightseeing tours or breakfast and laundry for a small extra fee. Most allow guests to use their kitchens, and are on hand to provide general advice or help in emergencies. Visitors receive the keys to their rooms and the house, and have free reign to come and go. Although proprietors spend much of their time looking for clients in Keleti station, they carry cellular telephones so they can always be reached for reservations. In stations, bypass the pushier hostel representatives and look for a more subdued group of people hanging around in the background.

Caterina, V, Andrássy út 47, III. 48 (tel. 291 95 38, cellular 06 20 34 63 98). At "Oktogon" (M1 or tram #4 or 6). The home of "Big" Caterina Birta and her daughter "Little" Caterina is in a century-old building on the grand Andrássy boulevard only a few min. from downtown Pest. Stay in a double, a small loft with two beds, or a large airy room for 8-10 people. Two guest bathrooms. Neither Caterina is fluent in English, but they compensate with enthusiasm. All beds 1000Ft per person. Laundry 500Ft per 4kg load.

"Townhouser's" International Guesthouse, XVI, Attila u. 123 (cellular tel. 06 30 44 23 31; fax 342 07 95). M2: Örs Vezér tere, then five stops on bus #31 to Diófa u. A quiet residential area 30min. from downtown in east Pest. Home of Béla and Rózsa Tanhauser, whose kind dog Sasha protects the family of guinea pigs living in the garden. The house has 5 large guest rooms, with 2 or 3 beds each, and 2 guest bathrooms. Béla speaks German, English, and some Korean, Japanese, and Spanish. Kitchen available and the cleanest bathrooms you'll find for the price. Béla transports guests to and from the train station. 1200Ft per person.

Weisses Haus, III, Erdőalja u. 11 (cellular tel. 06 20 34 36 31). Take bus #137 from Flórián tér to "Iskola." On a hillside in residential Óbuda, about 20min. from the city center. Panoramic view of northern Pest across the Danube. The 4 doubles and a triple are carefully decorated. 2 guest bathrooms. 4000Ft per room. Breakfast included. German and some English spoken.

Ms. Vali Németh, VIII, Osztály u. 20/24 A11 (tel. 113 88 46, cellular 06 30 47 53 48). 400m east of M2: Népstadion. Convenient for travelers arriving or leaving from Népstadion bus station. The first floor of a 4-story apartment complex in central Pest. Grocery stores and a cheap restaurant with an English menu are nearby. 2 doubles and one triple. One guest bathroom. 1500Ft per person.

Mrs. Ena Bottka, V, Garibaldi u. 5, (tel. 302 34 56; cellular 06-30-518-763; email bottkavi@ursus.bke.hu), 5th fl. a block south of M2: Kossuth tér. Live the Bohemian life in the tiny rooms overlooking gabled rooftops and Parliament building. Small kitchen. Doubles 2900Ft. Also apartments. Call in the morning or evening to reserve. Mrs. Bottka speaks fluent French and *poco italiano* and *español*, while her son speaks flawless English and very good German.

Hotels

Budapest's few inexpensive hotels are frequently clogged with groups; call ahead. Proprietors often speak English. All hotels should be registered with Tourinform.

Hotel Góliát, XIII, Kerekes út 12-20 (tel. 270 14 55; fax 149 49 85). M1: Arpad hid. Take the tram away from the river and get off before the overpass. Walk down Reitler Ferere ut. until you see the 10-story yellow building on the left. Clean, spacious rooms are a step up from hostels at the same prices. Singles 2000Ft; doubles 2500Ft. Bathrooms are still down the hall.

Hotel Citadella, Citadella Sétány (tel. 166 57 94; fax 186 05 05), atop Gellért Hill. Take tram #47 or 49 3 stops into Buda to "Móricz Zsigmond Körtér," then catch bus #27 to "Citadella." Perfect location, built right in the Citadel. Spacious, with hardwood floors. Doubles, triples, and quads US$40-58. Usually packed, so write or fax to reserve. Safe deposit at reception 100Ft per day.

Hotel Flandria, XIII, Szegedi út 27 (tel. 270 31 81; fax 120 88 53). M2: Lehel, then either the #12 or 14 tram one street past Karoly Körut. Then a 5min. walk down Szegedi út. Acceptable rooms and an inexpensive restaurant downstairs. Singles 4100Ft; doubles 5400Ft; quads 7400Ft.

Camping

The pamphlet *Camping Hungary,* available at tourist offices, describes Budapest's campgrounds.

Római Camping, III, Szentendrei út 189 (tel. 168 62 60; fax 250 04 26). M2: Batthyány tér, then take the HÉV commuter rail to "Római fürdő," and walk 100m towards the river. 2500-person capacity with tip-top security, a grocery, and tons of restaurants around. Disco, swimming pool, and huge park on the site; Roman ruins nearby. Communal showers. 700Ft per tent, students 600Ft. Bungalows 1800-6000Ft. Open mid-April to mid-Oct.

Hárs-hegyi, II, Hárs-hegyi út 5/7 (tel./fax 200 88 03). 7 stops on bus #22 from "Moszkva tér" to "Dénes u." Exchange for cash and traveler's checks. A good, cheap restaurant on the grounds. Credit cards accepted. 600Ft per tent, students 550Ft.

Riviera Camping, III, Királyok u. 257/259 (tel. 160 82 18). Take the HÉV commuter rail from "Batthyány tér" to "Romai fürdő," then bus #34 10min. until you see the campground. 500Ft per tent. Bungalows 2300Ft. There's an affordable, popular restaurant. Open year-round.

FOOD

Even the most expensive restaurants in Budapest may fall within your budget, though the food at family eateries is often cheaper and tastier. A 10% tip has come to be expected in many restaurants; another 10% is added if your meal is accompanied with live music. Cafeterias lurk under *Önkiszolgáló Étterem* signs (meat main courses 300-400Ft, vegetarian 180Ft). The listings below are just a nibble of what Budapest has to offer. Seek out the *kifőzés* or *vendéglő* in your neighborhood for a taste of Hungarian life. For the times when you want an infusion of grease or need to see a familiar menu late at night, the world's largest branch of Burger King is located on the Oktogon, and McDonald's and Pizza Hut are everywhere. Travelers may also rely on markets and raisin-sized 24-hour stores labeled *Non-Stop* for staples. The king of them all is the **Central Market,** V Kőzraktár tér u. 1 (M3: Kelvin tér). Marvel at the enormous display of fruit, vegetables, bread, cheese, meat, and just about any other kind of food you can imagine. Come for the aesthetic experience, stay for the best eating bargain around (open Mon. 6am-4pm, Tues.-Fri. 6am-6pm, Sat. 6am-2pm). Take a gander at the produce market, IX, Vámház krt. 1/3, at Fővám tér (Mon. 6am-3pm); the **ABC Food Hall,** I, Batthyány tér 5/7 (open Sun. 7am-1pm); or the **Non-Stops** at V, Október 6. u. 5, and V, Régi Posta u., off Váci u. past McDonald's.

Pest

Vegetárium, V, Cukor u. 3 (tel. 267 03 22). A block and half from M3: Ferenciek tere. Walk up Ferenciek tere (formerly Károlyi M. u.) to Irány u. on the right; a quick left puts you on Cukor u. A great place to detox after a week of meat. Elaborate and imaginative vegetarian and macrobiotic dishes (520-900Ft), as well as tempura (560Ft). Although they prepare a few ultra-healthy dishes that would meet with even Californian approval, the food still tends to be far from low-fat. Classical guitar in the evening from 7-10pm. Smoke-free environment. Menu in English. Open daily noon-10pm. 15% student discount with ISIC. 10% service charge.

Picasso Point Kávéhaz, VI, Hajós u. 31 (tel. 169 55 44). Make a right onto Hajos u. 2 blocks north of M3: Arany János. A Bohemian hang-out for students, intellectuals and foreigners. The English/Hungarian menu is an eclectic mix of traditional Hungarian and everything else, including chili (220Ft), onion soup (120Ft), and crepes (200Ft). Dance club downstairs; when live bands play there may be a cover charge (200Ft). Open daily from noon to some vaguely defined point after 4am.

Alföldi Kisvendéglő, V, Kecskeméti u. 4 tel. 267 02 24). M3: Kálvin tér, 50m past the Best Western. Traditional Hungarian cuisine—even the booths are paprika-red. The spicy, sumptuous homemade bread rolls (60Ft) are reason enough to come. Main courses 400-800Ft. Open daily 11am-midnight.

New York Bagels (The Sequel), VI, Bajcsy-Zsilinszky út 21. (tel. 111 84 41). M3: Arany János u. Hungary's largest bagel shop, with 9 more branches throughout the country. Assorted bagels baked hourly, freshly made spreads, sandwiches, salads, and Budapest's only chocolate chip cookies. Daily special bagel sandwiches (300Ft) or design your own. Owned by a former *Let's Go* Researcher-Writer and gleeful Wall Street escapee. Open daily 7am-10pm.

Marquis de Salade, VI, Hajós u. 43 (tel. 153 49 31), corner of Bajcsy-Zsilinszky út 2 blocks north of M3: Arany János. A self-service mix of salads, Middle Eastern, and Bengali food (all, unfortunately *sans* Spanish fly) in a cozy storefront the size of a large closet. The Azeri owner speaks English and posts notes about her regulars on the walls. Most dishes 500-700Ft. Open daily noon-midnight.

Sancho, VII, Dohány u. 20 (tel. 267 06 77). Walk up Károly krt. from M2: Astoria. American-Mexican pub and restaurant serving tacos, burritos, chimichangas, and their like (from 400Ft). Popular local bands perform evenings. At "tequila time" (11pm), the waiter puts on a sombrero and carries around a tray of half-priced shots. English menu. Open Tues.-Thurs. and Sun. 6pm-2am, Fri.-Sat. 6pm-4am.

Apostolok, V, Kígyó u. 4/6 (tel. 267 02 90; fax 118 36 58). Visible from M3: Ferenciek tere, on a pedestrian street toward the bridge. Eclectic, swinging combination of Gothic ambience and superb food in an old beer hall. Most main courses 500-1000Ft. Open daily noon-midnight.

Fészek Müvész Klub Étterem, VII, Kertész u. 36 (tel. 322 60 43), corner of Dob u. 2 blocks southwest of Erzsébet krt. M1: Oktogon, or tram #4 or 6 to "Király u." Once the dining hall of a Golden Age private club for performing artists. Excellent Hungarian food and very low prices; the 5-page single-spaced menu ranges from beef and fowl to venison and wild boar. Main courses 490-1370Ft, but 150Ft cover. In summer, walk through to the leafy courtyard. Open daily noon-1am.

Bagolyvár, XIV, Allatkerti krt. 2 (tel. 351 63 95; fax 342 29 17). M1: Hősök tere. Directly behind the Museum of Fine Arts—a perfect and elegant place to deconstruct the chromatic schema presented on your supper plate. Exceptional, yet remarkably affordable, Hungarian cuisine, with a menu that changes daily. Main courses 1300-3000Ft. Open daily noon-11pm. The Gundel Restaurant next door is Budapest's most famous—and most expensive.

Paprika, V, Varosáz u. 10. Cafeteria food from 260Ft, but come here for the bakery. Tasty snacks 50-80Ft. Open Mon.-Fri. 11am-4pm, Sat. 11am-3pm.

Fatâl Restaurant, V, Váci itca 67 (tel. 266 26 07). Currently one of the most popular restaurants in Budapest. Large, hearty Hungarian meals, carefully garnished and extremely delicious, served in pleasant, rustic surroundings. Main courses 450-1000Ft. If dim lights, colored glass windows and red bricks are meant to stimulate the appetite, it sure works. Open daily 11am-11pm.

Buda

Söröző a Szent Jupáthoz, II, Dékán u. 3 (tel. 212 29 29). 50m from M2: Moszkva tér; entrance on Retek u. Venture down the modest stairway, then right back up into an open-air hall. Enormous portions and friendly staff. "Soup for Just Married Man" 240Ft. Main courses 400-1100Ft. Open 24hr.

Remiz, II, Budakeszi út 8 (tel. 275 13 96). Take bus #158 from "Moszkva tér" to "Szépilona" (about 10min.) and continue past three stores beyond the stop. Traditional and tasty Hungarian cuisine in a cosmopolitan setting. Frequented by Hungarian tennis-racket-wielding yuppies. Prices are average (main courses 720-1400Ft), but it's just fancy enough for special occasions. Outdoor seating in warm weather; live music; English menu. Open daily 9am-1am. Call for reservations.

Marxim, II, Kis Rókus u. 23 (tel. 212 41 83). M2: Moszkva tér. With your back to the Lego-like castle, walk 200m along Margit krt. and turn left down the very industrial road. KGB pizza and Lenin salad are just a few of the revolutionary dishes served in structurally constrained, barbed-wire-laden booths. Food prepared by the staff according to their abilities, consumed by the patrons according to their needs. Join the locals in thumbing their noses at the erstwhile oppressive vanguard. English menu. Salads 120-200Ft. Pizza 300-700Ft. Open Mon.-Thurs. noon-1am, Fri.-Sat. noon-2am, Sun. 6pm-1am.

Marcello's, XI, Bartók Béla út 40 (tel. 166 62 31), just before Móricz Zsigmond Körtér, on the river side. One of the few pizzerias in Budapest to use tomato sauce rather than ketchup. Classy to boot. Pizzas 360-500Ft. Small salad 220Ft, large 380Ft. Reservations suggested. Open Mon.-Sat. noon-10pm.

Cafes

A cafe in Budapest is more a living museum of a bygone era than a place to indulge in scrumptious desserts and coffee. These amazing establishments were once the pretentious haunts of Budapest's literary, intellectual, and cultural elite. A leisurely repose at a Budapest cafe is a must for every visitor; best of all, the absurdly ornate pastries are inexpensive, even in the most genteel establishments.

Cafe New York, VII, Erzsébet krt. 9/11 (tel. 322 38 49). M2: Blaha Lujza tér. One of the most beautiful cafes in Budapest, and the staff knows it. Velvet, gold, and marble, but still as affordable as it was for turn-of-the-century *artistes*. Cappuccino 200Ft. Ice cream and coffee delights 300-500Ft. Filling Hungarian main courses (920Ft) served downstairs noon-10pm. Open daily 9am-midnight.

Művész Kávéház, VI, Andrássy út 29 (tel. 267 06 89), diagonally across from the National Opera House. M1: Opera. This acclaimed cafe draws pre- and post-Opera crowds with Golden Age wood paneling and gilded ceilings. Considered one of the Budapest's most elegant. Fabulous *Művész torta* 140Ft. Open daily 10am-midnight.

Ruszwurm, I, Szentháromság u. 7 (tel. 175 52 84), just off the square on Várhegy. Confecting since 1826 and strewn with period furniture. Stop by to relax after the majesty of Mátyás Cathedral down the street. You won't be hurried. Ice cream 35Ft per scoop. Cakes 80-200Ft. Open daily 10am-7pm.

Litia Literatura & Tea, I, Hess András tér 4 (tel. 175 69 87), in the Fortuna Passage. Choose from an immense selection of teas in this airy gardenhouse cafe in a quiet courtyard. For the full literary experience, pick up some reading material in the adjoining artsy bookstore. Coffee 100Ft. Open daily 10am-6pm.

Cafe Pierrot, I, Fortuna u. 14 (tel. 175 69 71). Antique clown dolls hang from the curvaceous walls. Espresso 120Ft. Fantastic crepes (*palacsinta*) 350Ft. Open daily 11am-1am. Live piano music daily from 8:30pm.

Cafe Mozart, VII Erzsébet krt. 36. (tel. 352 06 64). M2 to Blaha Lujza Tér. Newly opened cafe serves 75 different coffee drinks (120Ft-310Ft) and almost as many ice cream creations. Shiny, glitzy environment goes well with the heavenly Mozart music, but where did the waitresses get those funky period uniforms? Still, some of the best drinks in town. Open Sun.-Fri. 11am-6pm, Sat. 12am-6pm.

SIGHTS

In 1896, as part of Hungary's 1000th birthday bash, Budapest received several architectural marvels. Among the works commissioned by the Habsburgs were **Országház** (Parliament), **Hősök tere** (Heroes' Square), **Szbadság híd** (Szbadság Bridge), **Szent István Bazilika** (St. Stephen's Basilica), **Vajdahunyad vár** (Vajdahunyad Castle), and continental Europe's first metro station. The domes of **Országház** and **Szent István Bazilika** are both 96m high—vertical references to the historic date. Slightly grayer for wear, these monuments still attest to the wealth of the Austro-Hungarian Empire at the height of its power.

Várhegy (Castle Hill)

The **Castle District** towers above the Duna, atop the surprisingly named **Várhegy** (Castle Hill). The castle was built in 1242, but was leveled in consecutive sieges by Mongols and Ottoman Turks. Habsburg forces razed the rebuilt castle while ousting the Turks after a 145-year occupation. A reconstruction was completed just in time to be destroyed by the Germans in 1945. Determined Hungarians pasted the castle together once more, only to face the new Soviet menace—bullet holes in the palace facade recall the 1956 Uprising. In the postwar period, sorely needed resources were channeled into the immediate reconstruction of the castle. During this rebuilding, extensive excavations revealed artifacts from the earliest castle on this site, which are now housed in **Budapesti Történeti** (Budapest History Museum) in **Budavári palota** (Royal Palace). The castle walls, just to the left of the cable car peak station, envelop numerous other collections, and statues lurk everywhere (for a full descriptions of Várhegy's many **museums,** see p. 256). Find one of the many paths up, or cross **Széchenyi lánchíd** and ride the *sikló* (cable car) to the top of the hill (150Ft; open daily 7:30am-10pm, closed 2nd and 4th Mon. of the month). The upper lift station sits just inside the castle walls.

From the castle, stroll down Színház u. and Tárnok u. to reach **Szentháromság ter** (Trinity Square), site of the Disneyesque **Halászbástya** (Fisherman's Bastion). This arcaded stone wall supports a squat, fairy-tale tower, but you'll have to pay for the magnificent view across the Duna (50Ft). Behind the tower stands the delicate, Gothic **Mátyás templom** (Matthias Church), which, with its multicolored tiled roof, is one of the most-photographed buildings in Budapest. It served as a mosque for 145 years following an overnight conversion on September 2, 1541, when the Turks seized Buda. These days, high mass is celebrated Sundays at 10am with orchestra and choir (come early for a seat). On summer Fridays at 8pm, organ concerts reverberate in the resplendent interior. The holy edifice also conceals a **crypt** and a **treasury;** descend the stairway to the right of the altar. Besides the treasury's ecclesiastic relics, don't miss Queen Elizabeth's stunning marble bust, next to the entrance to **Szent István Kápelna** (St. Stephen's Chapel). The marble was hewn from the Italian Carrara mine, where Michelangelo shopped for rock (treasury open daily 9am-5:30pm; 100Ft). A second side chapel contains the **tomb of King Béla III** and his wife, Anna Chatillon; this was the only sepulcher of the Árpád dynasty spared from Ottoman looting. Outside the church is the grand **equestrian monument** of King Stephen, with his trademark double cross (open daily 7am-7pm).

Next door, the brash **Budapest Hilton** incorporates the remains of Várhegy's oldest church, a 13th-century abbey. Intricate door-knockers and balconies adorn the hill's other historic buildings; ramble through **Úri u.** (Gentlemen's Street), with its Baroque townhouses, or **Táncsics Mihály u.,** in the old Jewish sector. You can enjoy a tremendous view of Buda from Várhegy's west walls. By **Becsi kapu** (Vienna Gate), at the District's north tip, frequent minibuses run to Moszkva tér, though the walk down Várfok u. takes only five minutes.

Várhegy doesn't just offer sights above ground; some awesome ones lurk below, too. **Barlangrendszer Budavárában** (the cavern system of Buda Castle), formed by thermal springs and rich in stone formations, was created when Budapest's only residents were unicellular. Enter at the corner of Dárda u. and Orszagház u. (open April-Oct. 10am-6pm, Nov.-March 10am-4pm; 200Ft, students 100Ft).

Elsewhere in Buda

Szabadság Szobor (Liberation Monument) watches over the city and crowns **Gellért-hegy** (Gellért Hill). The 30m bronze woman presiding over the city was created to honor Soviet soldiers who died while "libertating" Hungary, though the Communist star has since been removed. Hike up to the monument and the adjoining **Citadella**—built as a symbol of Habsburg power after the 1848 revolution—from Hotel Gellért or from beneath the St. Gellért statue on the other side. Bus #27 also drives up. The view from the top is especially spectacular at night, when the Duna and its bridges shimmer in black and gold. Overlooking Erzsébet híd near the base of Gellért Hill is the **statue of St. Gellért,** accompanied by colonnaded backdrop and glistening waterfall. The Pope sent Bishop Gellért to the coronation of King Stephen, the first Christian Hungarian monarch, to assist in the conversion of the Magyars. Those unconvinced by his message hurled the good bishop to his death from atop the hill that now bears his name.

Fresh forest air awaits in the suburban Buda Hills, far into the second and twelfth districts. Catch bus #22 from "Moszkva tér," north of Várhegy, and ride up to the "Budakesci." There you'll find the **Vadaskert** (Game Park), where boar roam while deer and antelope play—here, people speak optimistically, and the skies are supposedly cloudless. The **Pál-völgyi Caves** gape east of Vadaskert. Even first-time spelunkers can enjoy the 15m-high caverns, remarkable stalactite formations, and such attractions as the **Cave of the Stone Bat** and the 25m-deep **Radium Chamber.** Be sure to wear your polar fleece, even in the summer—it's quite cool inside. Take the #86 bus from Batthyany tér to "Kolosyi tér." Then take bus #65 to the caves (open Wed.-Sun. 10am-4pm; 160Ft, students 80Ft)

HUNGARY

Between the caves and the castle, **Margit híd** leads over the Duna to **Margitsziget** (Margaret Island). Off-limits to private cars, the island offers capacious thermal baths, luxurious garden pathways, and numerous shaded terraces. Here you can **rent bikes,** run along the river, or prance around the tennis courts. A little **zoo** adds scent to the island's east part, while open-air clubs on the west half jockey for audiences in the evenings. According to legend, the *sziget* is named after King Béla IV's daughter; he vowed to rear young Margit as a nun if the nation survived the Mongol invasion of 1241. The Mongols left Hungary decimated, but not destroyed, and Margaret was confined to the island convent. Take bus #26 from "Szt. István krt." to the island.

Like a Troubled Bridge Over Water

The citizens of Budapest are justly proud of the bridges that bind Buda to Pest. The four great lions that have guarded **Széchenyi lánchíd** (Chain Bridge) since 1849 make this bridge one of the most recognizeable in the city. These exotic beasts were created by the master János Marschalkó in a naturalistic style, with the tongues resting far back in their gaping mouths. The anatomical correctness of their new city mascots did not impress the citizens of Budapest, and distraught by public ridicule over this apparently missing feature in his creations, Marschalkó jumped from the bridge to his death. *Let's Go* does not recommend sculpting lions without visible tongues.

Pest

Cross the Duna to reach Pest, the capital's animated commercial and administrative center. The old **Belváros** (Inner City), rooted in the pedestrian zone of Váci u. and Vörösmarty tér, is a tourist haven. Filled with souvenir shops, Pest's riverbank sports a string of luxury hotels leading up to the magnificent neo-Gothic **Országház** (Parliament) in Kossuth tér (arrange 1500Ft tours at IBUSZ or Budapest Tourist).

Sz. István Bazilika (St. Stephen's Basilica), two blocks north of Deák tér, is by far the city's largest church, with room for 8500 worshippers under its massive dome. A very Christ-like depiction of St. Stephen adorns the high altar. Climb 302 spiraling steps to the Panorama tower, central Pest's highest building, for a 360° view (tower open April-Oct. daily 10am-6:30pm; 200Ft, students 100Ft). St. Stephen's holy **right hand,** one of Hungary's most revered religious relics, is displayed in the **Basilica museum.** (Basilica open Mon.-Sat. 9am-5pm, Sun. 1-5pm; 120Ft, students 60Ft. Museum open April-Sept. Mon.-Sat. 9am-4:30pm, Sun. 1-4:30pm; Oct.-March Mon.-Sat. 10am-4pm, Sun. 1-4pm.)

Another grand religious destination is the **Zsinagóga,** at the corner of Dohány u. and Wesselényi u., the largest active synagogue in Europe and the second largest in the world. The Moorish-style building was designed to hold almost 3000 worshippers (open to visitors Mon.-Sat. 10am-2:30pm, Sun. 10am-1:30pm; 400Ft, students 200Ft). The building has been under renovation since 1988, and much of the artwork is likely to be blocked from view. The **Jewish Museum** here juxtaposes magnificent relics and artwork from Hungary's rich Jewish past with haunting Holocaust photos and documents (open April-Oct. Mon.-Fri. 10am-3pm, Sun. 10am-1pm; closed Nov.-March). In the back garden behind the museum, an enormous metal tree stands as a **Holocaust Memorial** over mass graves dug 1944-45. Inscribed on each leaf of the dramatic sculpture is the name of a victim. The harmonies of organ and mixed choir float through the entire structure during Friday evening services (6-7pm).

Andrássy út, Hungary's grandest boulevard, extends from the northeast corner of Erzsébet tér in downtown Pest and arrives some 2km later in **Hősök tere** (Heroes' Square). A stroll down Andrássy út from Hősök tere toward the inner city best evokes Budapest's Golden Age, somewhat tarnished by Soviet occupation. The most vivid reminder of this period is **Magyar Állami Operaház** (Hungarian National Opera House), Andrássy út 22 (M1: Opera). Laden with sculptures and paintings in the ornate Empire style of the 1880s, the building is even larger than it appears to be from the street; the gilded auditorium seats 1289 people. If you can't actually see an opera, make sure to take a tour (English tours daily 3 and 4pm; 400Ft, students 200Ft).

Andrássy út's most majestic stretch lies at the end, between Hősök tere and Oktogon. Hősök tere is dominated by **Millenniumi emlékmű** (Millennium Monument), which showcases the nation's most prominent leaders and national heroes from 896 to 1896, when the structure was erected for the 1000th anniversary. The seven fearsome horsemen led by Prince Árpád represent the seven Magyar tribes who settled the Carpathian Basin. Overhead is the Archangel Gabriel, who, according to legend, offered Stephen the crown of Hungary in a dream. It was King (later Saint) Stephen, the colonnade's first figure, who made Hungary a Christian state with his coronation on New Year's Eve, 1000.

Behind the monument, **Városliget** (City Park) contains a permanent circus, an amusement park, a zoo, a castle, and the impressive **Széchenyi Baths** (see **Bathouses,** p. 258). Originally constructed out of canvas and wood, **Vajdahunyad Vár** (Vajdahunyad Castle) was redone with more durable materials in response to popular outcry. Created for the Millenary Exhibition of 1896, the facade, intended to chronicle 1000 years of architecture, is a stone collage of Romanesque, Gothic, Renaissance, and Baroque styles. Outside the castle, broods the hooded statue of **Anonymous,** the secretive scribe to whom we owe much of our knowledge of medieval Hungary. Rent a **rowboat** (June to mid-Sept. daily 9am-8pm) or **ice skates** (Nov.-March daily 9am-1pm and 4-8pm; 80Ft) by the lake next to the castle.

The ruins of the north Budapest garrison town, **Aquincum,** Szentendrei út 139 (tel. 168 82 41), crumble in the outer regions of the third district. From M2: Batthyány tér, take the HÉV to "Aquincum;" the site is about 100m south of the HÉV stop. These are the most impressive vestiges of the 400-year Roman occupation. The settlement's significance increased steadily over that time, eventually attaining the status of *colonia* and becoming the capital of Pannonia Inferior; Marcus Aurelius and Constantine were just two of the emperors to bless the town with a visit. The **museum** on the grounds contains a model of the ancient city, as well as musical instruments and other household items (open daily March-Oct. 10am-6pm, Nov.-Feb. 10am-4pm; 100Ft, students 50Ft). The remains of the **Roman Military Baths** are visible to the south of the Roman encampment, beside the overpass at Flórián tér near the "Árpád híd" HÉV station. From the stop, just follow the main road away from the river.

Museums

Though at times they may seem haphazardly thrown together, Budapest's museums are beautiful and, happily, extremely affordable. If you're in the mood to try to discover that up-and-coming new artist, head to the galleries on both sides of the river; search for them in the *Budapest Panorama* and drop in on a few.

Buda Castle, I, Szent György tér 2 (tel. 175 75 33). Leveled by Soviet and Nazi combat, the reconstructed palace now houses an assortment of fine museums.

Wing A contains **Kortárs Művészeti Múzeum** (Museum of Contemporary Art) and **Ludwig Museum,** a collection of international modern art that includes the works of Zsigmond Kÿrolyi, Károly Keliman, Roy Lichtenstein, Robert Rauschenberg, and Andy Warhol. Frequent special exhibitions; get the exhibit calendars at a tourist office. Open Tues.-Sun. 10am-6pm. 100Ft, students 50Ft, Tues. free.

Wings B-D hold **Magyar Nemzeti Galéria** (Hungarian National Gallery), a vast hoard containing the best in Hungarian painting and sculpture, spanning a millennium. Its treasures include a collection of Mihály Munkácsy, a founder of Hungarian Realism; Pál Mersei, a Hungarian Impressionist; and Károly Markó, a classical landscape painter. Open Tues.-Sun. 10am-6pm. 150Ft, students 40Ft; one ticket is valid for all 3 wings. English tour 200Ft.

Wing E houses **Budapesti Történéti Múzeum** (Budapest History Museum), a chronicle of the development of Óbuda, Buda, and Pest. Open Tues.-Sun. Jan.-Feb. 10am-4pm; March-Oct. 10am-6pm; Nov.-Dec. 10am-5pm. 100Ft, students 50Ft, Wed. free.

Szépművészeti Múzeum (Museum of Fine Arts), XIV, Dózsa György út 41 (tel. 343 67 55). M1: Hősök tere. Simply spectacular. One of Europe's finest collections of artwork, from Duccio and Goya to Rembrandt and Bruegel, with a particular emphasis on Italian art. Highlights include an entire room devoted to El Greco and a display of Renaissance works. All your favorite Impressionists, too. Open Tues.-Sun. 10am-5:30pm. 200Ft, students 100Ft. Tours for up to 5 people 1500Ft. English guidebooks for individual sections (around 100Ft).

Hadvtöténeti Múzeum (Museum of Military History), I, Tóth Árpád Sétány 40 (tel. 156 95 86), in the northwest corner of Várhegy just west of Kapisztrán tér. An intimidating collection of ancient and modern weapons, from the most functional to the most ornate. Some swords seem too splendid to sully with petty disembowelments. The upper floor presents the military history of WWII and a day-by-day account of the 1956 Uprising; don't miss the severed fist from the massive Stalin statue toppled in the Uprising. Open Tues.-Sun. 10am-6pm. 250Ft, students 80Ft, ISIC-holders free. English guide 600Ft.

Néprajzi múzeum (Museum of Ethnography), V, Kossuth tér 12 (tel. 312 48 78), opposite the Parliament in the erstwhile home of the Supreme Court. Outstanding exhibit of folk culture, from the late 18th century to WWI. Covers the whole cycle of peasant life and customs, from childhood to marriage to death (and taxes). Open Tues.-Sun. March-Nov. 10am-6pm, Dec.-Feb. 10am-4pm. 200Ft, students 60Ft.

Magyar Nemzeti Múzeum (Hungarian National Museum), VIII, Múzeum krt. 14/16 (tel. 138 21 22). Chronicles Hungarian settlements and holds the Hungarian Crown Jewels, supposedly the crown and scepter used in the coronation of King Stephen in 1000 AD. Don't miss Mihály Munkácsy's enormous canvas *Golgotha;* in the room at the top of the stairs. Open Tues.-Sun. 10am-6pm, cashier closes 5:30pm. 200Ft, students 90Ft. English tour 200Ft. English guidebook 840Ft.

Vasarely Museum, III, Szentlélek tér 6 (tel. 250 15 40). Take HÉV from M2: Batthyány tér to "Árpád híd." Filled with Viktor Vasarely's arresting Op-A rt. Yes, it's modern and it's abstract. Open Tues.-Sun. 10am-6pm. 50Ft, students 20Ft.

Iparművészeti Múzeum (Museum of Applied Arts), IX. Üllői út 33-37 (tel. 217 52 22). Fine permanent exhibition on "Arts and Crafts," and temporary exhibitions on the history of styles. Open Tues.-Sun. 10am-6pm. 80Ft, students 20Ft.

ENTERTAINMENT

Performances

Budapest hosts a healthy number of cultural events year-round. The English-language monthlies *Programme in Hungary, Budapest Panorama,* and *Pestiest* contain listings of all concerts, operas, and theater performances in the city. They're all free at tourist offices. The "Style" section of the weekly English-language *Budapest Sun* is another good source for entertainment schedules.

The **Central Theater Booking Office,** VI, Andrássy út 18 (tel. 312 00 07), next to the Opera House (open Mon.-Fri. 10am-6pm, Sat. 10am-5pm), and the branch at Moszkva tér 3 (tel. 212 56 78; open Mon.-Fri. 10am-6pm) both sell tickets without commission to almost every performance in the city. An extravaganza at the gilded, Neo-Renaissance **Magyar Állami Operaház** (State Opera House), VI, Andrássy út 22 (tel. 332 81 97; M1: Opera), one of Europe's leading performance centers, can be witnessed for US$4-5. The box office (tel. 153 01 70), on the left side of the building, discounts tickets for operas and occasional ballets a half-hour before showtime (open Tues.-Sat. 11am-1:45pm and 2:30-7pm, Sun. 10am-1pm and 4-7pm). The world-renowned **Philharmonic Orchestra** gives concerts almost every evening from September to June. The ticket office, Vörösmarty tér 1 (tel. 117 62 22), is on the west side of the square; look for the Jegyroda sign. (Open Mon.-Fri. 10am-6pm, Sat.-Sun. 10am-2pm; tickets 1000-1500Ft; less on day of performance.)

In late summer, the Philharmonic and the Opera take a break, but the tide of culture never ebbs: **summer theaters** are ready to pick up the slack. In July, classical music and opera are performed nightly at 8:30pm in the **Hilton Hotel Courtyard,** I, Hess András tér 1/3 (tel. 214 30 00), next to Mátyás templom on Várhegy; buy tickets at reception (300-800Ft; small discount if bought just before performance). **Mátyás templom,** Szentháromság tér, holds organ, orchestral, and choral recitals most Wednesdays and Fridays at 8pm (Wed. 600Ft, Fri. 500Ft, occasionally free). **Mar-**

gitsziget Theater, XIII, on Margitsziget, (tel. 111 24 96), features opera and Hungarian-music concerts on its open-air stage. Take tram #4 or 6 to "Margitsziget." Try **Zichy Mansion Courtyard,** III, Fő tér 1, for orchestral concerts. **Pesti Vigadó** (Pest Concert Hall), V, Vigadó tér 2 (tel. 118 99 03; fax 175 62 22), on the Duna bank near Vörösmarty tér, hosts operettas almost every other night (cashier open Mon.-Sat. 10am-6pm; tickets 3200Ft). Folk-dancers stomp across the stage at the **Buda Park Theater,** XI, Kosztolányi Dezső tér (tel. 117 62 22); brochures and concert tickets flood the ticket office at Vörösmarty tér 1 (open Mon.-Fri. 11am-6pm; tickets 70-250Ft). For a psychedelic evening, try the laser shows at the **Planetarium** (tel. 134 11 61), M3: Népliget. The multimedia sorcery even brings the Beatles to life on occasion (Mon., Fri. 8 and 9:30pm; Tues. 6:30 and 9:30pm; Wed.-Thurs. and Sat. 6:30, 8, and 9:30pm). The **Budapest Spring Festival,** in late March, is an excellent chance to see the best in Hungarian art and music.

Hungary has an outstanding cinematic tradition; most notable among its directors are Miklós Jancsó and István Szabó. **Cinemas** screening the latest Hungarian and foreign films abound in Budapest. The English-language *Budapest Sun* and *Budapest Week* list a surprising number of reasonably current movies in English; check the kiosks around town. If *szinkronizált* or *magyarul beszélő* appears next to the title, the movie has been dubbed into Hungarian. Tickets are 350-450Ft.

If you still miss international pop culture, many of the world's biggest shows come to Budapest, and prices are reasonable; check the **Music Mix 33 Ticket Service,** V, Vaci u. 33 (tel. 266 70 70; open Mon.-Fri. 10am-6pm, Sat. 10am-1pm). Touring companies *à la* Andrew Lloyd Webber also stop by—watch for *Cats* on roller skates. Tickets can be bought at the **Madách Theater** box office, VII, Madách tér 6 (tel. 322 20 15; open Mon.-Sat. 2:30-8pm). **Óbudai sziget** (Óbudai island) hosts the week-long **Sziget Festival** in the middle of August, perhaps Europe's biggest **open-air rock festival.** For info call 372 06 50 (daily tickets 1000Ft, week-long ticket 5000Ft).

Bathhouses

To soak away weeks of city grime, crowded trains, and yammering camera-clickers, sink into a **thermal bath,** an essential Budapest experience. The post-bath massages vary from a quick three-minute slap to a royal half-hour indulgence. Some baths are meeting spots, though not exclusively, for Budapest's gay community.

Gellért, XI, Kelenhegyi út 4-6 (tel. 166 61 66). Take bus #7 or tram #47 or 49 to Hotel Gellért, at the base of Gellért-hegy. Venerable indoor thermal baths, segregated by sex, where you may soak nude if you like. The only spa with signs in English. An indoor pool surrounded by statues and enormous plants; rooftop sundeck; and wave pool for the young or young at heart. Besides all this, there is a huge range of inexpensive *à la carte* options, from mudpacks to pedicures. Thermal bath 400Ft, with pool privileges 1200Ft. 15min. massage 250Ft. Open May-Sept. Mon.-Fri. 6am-6pm, Sat.-Sun. 6am-4pm; Oct.-April Mon.-Fri. 6am-6pm, Sat.-Sun. 6am-2pm. Pools open daily until 7pm except weekends Oct.-April, when they close at 5pm.

Király, I, Fő u. 84 (tel. 202 36 88). M2: Batthány tér. Bathe in the splendor of Turkish cupolas and domes. Steam bath 300Ft. Thermal bath 200Ft. Massage 300Ft per 15min. Men only Mon., Wed., and Fri. 6:30am-6pm. Women only Tues. and Thurs. 6:30am-6pm and Sat. 6:30am-noon.

Széchenyi Fürdő, XIV, Állatkerti u. 11-14 (tel. 321 03 10), in Városliget, 7min. north of M1: Hősök tere. These public thermal baths (300Ft) command a devoted following among the city's venerable gentry, while the large **outdoor swimming pool** delights their grandchildren. Bring your swimsuit. Massage 600Ft per 30min. Open Mon.-Fri. 6am-7pm, Sat. 6am-1pm. July-Aug., the baths are men-only on Mon., Wed., and Fri.; women-only Tues., Thurs., and Sat.

Rudas, Döbrentei tér 9 (tel. 175 83 73), right on the river under a dome built by Turks 400 years ago. Take the #7 bus to the first stop in Buda. The centuries haven't altered the dome, the bathing chamber, or the "men only" rule. Swimming pool open to women, too (300Ft); bath (1½hr.; 350Ft). Open Mon.-Fri. 6am-6pm; Sat.-Sun. 6am-1pm.

Király Fürdő, II, Fő u. 84 (tel. 201 43 92). Open exclusively to men on Mon., Wed., and Fri., and popular among Budapest's gay community.

Palatinus Strandfürdo, (tel. 112 30 69) on Margit island, is another gay hangout.

HUNGARY

NIGHTLIFE

After a few drinks, you'll forget you ever left home. Global village alternateens wearing the usual labels and grinding to an electronic beat make the club scene in Budapest familiar to anyone who has ever partied in America or Britain. A virtually unenforced drinking age and cheap drinks may be the only cause for culture shock. As clubs become more and more technically endowed, cover prices are rising—a night of techno may cost the same as a night at the opera, although both are cheap by Western standards. Despite tons of tourists and overcrowded nightclubs, the streets of Budapest are surprisingly empty at night, echoing pre-capitalist times.

Bars

Old Man's Pub, VII, Akácfa u. 13 (tel. 322 76 45). M2: Blaha Lujza tér. Live blues and jazz under the newspapered ceilings. Classy and upscale environment. Kitchen serves pizza, spaghetti, salads, and delicious cold fruit soup (240Ft). Occasional free samples of beer. Nightly blues and folk concerts. Open Mon.-Sat. 3pm-dawn.

Fat Mo's Speakeasy, V, Nyári Pal Utca 11 (tel. 267 31 99). M3: Kalvin tér. Pricey food, but hip bands and reasonably priced beer (quart of Guinness 310Ft) go well with the Prohibition-era decor. Open Mon.-Sun. 12pm-2am.

Morrison's Music Pub, VI, Révay u. 25 (tel. 269 40 60), just to the left of the opera house. M1: Opera. Half pub, half dance club (beer 240Ft). A young, international crowd. May be the one place in Europe where Jim's not buried. Functional English red telephone booth inside. June-Aug. cover 400Ft. Open daily 8:30pm-4am.

The Long Jazz Club, VII, Dohány u. 22-24 (tel. 322 00 06). A new jazz club in town: orange painted walls, David Lynchean atmosphere, smoke, live jazz, and young jazz-loving crowd. Beer 200Ft. Open daily 6pm-2am.

Discos

Bahnhof, (tel. 302 85 99) north side of Nugati train station. M3: Nyugati pu. One of the most popular dance clubs, and with good reason; no technical wizardry, but two superb dance floors (rock and disco). Well ventilated. Guaranteed NO TECHNO. Cover 300Ft. Open Mon.-Sat. 6pm-4am.

Made-Inn Music Club, VI, Andrássy út 112. (tel. 111 34 37), M1: Bajza u. Crowds come for the frequent live bands in this cavernous disco/funk club. Cover 300-500Ft. Open Wed.-Sun. 8pm-5am.

Véndiák (Former Student), V, Egyetem tér 5 (tel. 267 02 26). M2: Kálvin tér. Walk up Kecskeméti u. Late-night bar with a lively dance floor. Popular with students during school year. Picks up after midnight. Open Mon. 9pm-2am, Tues.-Sat. 9pm-5am.

E-Play Cyberclub, VI, Terezkrt 55 (tel. 302 28 49), by the McDonald's in Nyugati pu. M3: Nyugati pu. More fog and more lights per person than any other dance club. Two floors of techno, but little difference between them. Cover 600Ft.

Franklin Trocadero Cafe, V, Szent István körút 15 (tel. 111 4691). Spacious dance hall quickly fills up with Latin salsa dancers. Live music; dance lessons on Tues. Open daily 9pm-5am. Cover 300Ft.

GAY BUDAPEST

For decades, gay life in Budapest was completely underground; it is only now starting to make itself visible. The city still has its share of skinheads, so it is safer to be discreet. If there are problems of any sort, call the gay hotline (tel. 166 92 83), open during somewhat irregular afternoon hours. **Cruise Victory Co.,** II, Váci u. 9 (tel/fax 267 38 05), can provide a gay guide and map with listings and addresses of organizations and popular gay locations (open Mon.-Fri. 9am-6pm). Below are several locations that are either gay-friendly or have primarily gay clientele. For gay **bathhouses,** see p. 258.

Capella Cafe, V, Belgrád rkp. 23, (tel. 118 62 31). An amicable bar just south of Erzsebet bridge. Different themes for each day of the week, from transvestite shows to cabarets. At times the candlelit, psychedelic walls transform into a disco.

Angel Bar, VII, Rákóczi út 51 (tel. 113 12 73). M2: Blaha Lujza tér. Regulars complain of an increasingly mixed crowd. Popular disco Thurs.-Sun. Open daily 1pm-sunrise.

No Limit Gay Bar, V, Vitkovics Mihaly 11-13 (tel. 267 03 26). Advertised as Budapest's highest standard gay bar, No Limit offers various theme nights in a dimly-lit, exclusive surrounding. Open daily 10am-5am.

THE DANUBE BEND

North of Budapest, the Danube sweeps south in a dramatic arc called the *Dunakanyar* (Danube Bend) as it flows east from Vienna along the Slovak border. This lush and relaxed region is deservedly one of the great tourist attractions in Hungary. Ruins of first-century Roman settlements cover the countryside, and medieval palaces and fortresses overlook the river in Esztergom and Visegrád. An artist colony thrives today amid the museums and churches of Szentendre. All this is within two hours of Budapest by bus, but the longer ferry ride is well worth the time for the relaxing, refreshing, and re-energizing rest it provides the weary traveler.

■ Szentendre

Szentendre (sen-TEN-dreh) is by far the most tourist-thronged of the Danube Bend towns, but its proximity to Budapest, narrow cobblestone streets, and wealth of art galleries and museums keep the visitors coming. On Szentendre's **Templomdomb** (Church Hill), above Fő tér, sits the 13th-century Roman Catholic church. Facing it, the **Czóbel Museum** houses works by Béla Czóbel, Hungary's foremost Impressionist painter (open March 15-Oct. 31 Tues.-Sun. 10am-4pm, off-season Fri.-Sun. 10am-4pm; 90Ft, students 50Ft). To the north across Alkotmány u., the Baroque **Szerb Ortodox Templom** (Serbian Orthodox Church) displays Serbian religious art (open Wed.-Sun. 10am-4pm; 60Ft). Szentendre's most impressive museum, **Kovács Margit Múzeum,** Vastagh György u. 1, exhibits brilliant ceramic sculptures and tiles by the 20th-century Hungarian artist Margit Kovács (open March 15-Oct. 31 Tues.-Sun. 10am-6pm, Nov. 1-March 14 Tues.-Sun. 10am-4pm; 250Ft, students 150Ft). **Szabó Marcipán Múzeum,** Dumtsa Jenő u. 7 (tel. 31 14 84), puts the structural properties of this sticky sweet to the test; if the marzipan Parliament doesn't tempt you, the larger-than-life statue of Michael Jackson will. You can't beat it—it's a real almond-flavored thriller. Pick up a pastry from the shop (60-130Ft; open daily 10am-6pm; 100Ft, students and seniors 50Ft). In June 1996, Szentendre hosted the first **Danube Carnival,** a celebration of folk art dance groups from along the Danube; it's now an annual event, along with hordes of other summer music, dance, theater, and craft festivals.

The HÉV commuter rail, train, and bus station is 10 minutes south of town; to get to Fő tér, go through the underpass, and head up Kossuth u. **HÉV** travels to Budapest's Batthyány tér (every 20min., 45min., 168Ft). **Buses** run from Budapest's Árpád bridge station (every 10-40min., 30min.-1hr., 126Ft), many continuing to Visegrád (45min.) and Esztergom (1½hr.). **MAHART boats** leave from a pier 10-15 minutes north of the city—just walk along the river past town until you see the sign—for Budapest (3 per day; 420Ft, students 295Ft); Visegrád (2 per day; 420Ft, students 295Ft); and Esztergom (2 per day; 460Ft, students 395Ft; May 17-Aug. 31 only). The helpful staff of **Tourinform,** Dumsta Jenő u. 22 (tel. 31 79 65 or 31 79 66), provides maps (50Ft) and brochures (open Mon.-Fri. 10am-4pm, Sat.-Sun. 10am-2pm). **OTP Bank,** Dumsta Jenő u. 6 (tel. 31 02 11), compensates for its slowness with great **currency exchange** rates and a 24-hour **ATM** (bank open Mon. 8am-5pm, Tues.-Thurs. 8am-3pm, Fri. 8am-12:30pm). **IBUSZ,** Bogdányi u. 4 (tel. 31 03 33), has rates that are almost as good, and finds private doubles (2000-3000Ft) with no commission (open Mon.-Fri. 9am-4pm, June 15-Sept. 30 also Sat.-Sun. 10am-2pm). **Ilona Panzió,** Rákóczi Ferenc u. 11 (tel. 31 35 99), near the center of town, rents decent doubles with private baths (3500Ft; 2500Ft for one person, breakfast included). **Pap-szigeti Camping** (tel. 31 06 97), 1km north of the center on Pap-sziget Island, has motel rooms with three beds (2500Ft for 2 people and 1000Ft for 1 person), bungalows (triples 3000Ft), and tent sites (600Ft per person). The constant flow of tourists has made restaurants, especially in town, expensive by Hungarian standards—budget travelers should return to Budapest or continue to Visegrád for dinner. **Grocery stores** wait near the rail station for those requiring immediate gratification. **Phone code:** 26.

■ Visegrád

During medieval times, rural Visegrád (VEE-sheh-grad) served as the royal capital of Hungary. King Béla built a palace in this serene setting in 1259 to host elaborate feasts with the monarchs of Bohemia and Poland. The partially reconstructed **Királyi Palota** (Royal Palace; tel. 39 80 26; fax 39 82 52), at the foot of the hills above the west end of Fő u., has begun to resemble truly ancient ruins, with bleached stone and open-air mazes of rooms looking out over the river (open April-Oct. Tues.-Sun. 9am-5pm; 100Ft, students 50Ft). During the second weekend of July, the town hosts the **International Palace Games** on the palace grounds, complete with royal parades, knight tournaments, living chess, concerts, and medieval crafts (tel. (01) 166 17 80 for more info). Named for a king imprisoned here in the 11th century, the hexagonal **Alsóvár Salamon Torony** (Solomon's Tower), at the end of Salamontorony u., now keeps watch over the palace complex. The **King Matthias Museum** inside displays artifacts and stone carvings found in the ruins of the palace when it was re-discovered in 1934 (open May-Sept. daily 9am-5pm; 100Ft, students 50Ft). High above the Danube, the 13th-century **citadel** was built above a Roman outpost and commands a dramatic view of the river and surrounding hills (open April-Nov. daily 8:30am-6pm; 50Ft, students 30Ft). Catch a **minibus** (tel. 39 73 72 for service; 900Ft) to the fortress's remains, or make the demanding 30-minute walk up Kalvaria, a ridge of the Pilis Forest, lined with stations of the cross (iconographic elements depicting the death of Christ). Residents have built a **wax museum** inside devoted to medieval torture, and an exhibit on local life (open daily 9am-6pm; 200Ft, students 100Ft). If you really get carried away by the 13th-century scenery, go ahead and test your archery skills in front of the castle (40Ft per arrow).

Visegrád Tours, Rév u. 15 (tel. 39 81 60; open daily April-Oct. 9am-6pm; Nov.-March 10am-4pm), between the pier and Nagy Lajos u., provides pamphlets and **maps,** and finds **private rooms** (doubles DM12-15). **Buses** to Budapest's Árpád Híd metro station (1 per hr., 1½hr., 356Ft) and Esztergom (45min., 145Ft) pass through. **MAHART boats** run to Budapest (3 per day, 2½-3hr., 440Ft), Esztergom (2 per day, 2hr., 420Ft), and Szentendre (2 per day, 1¼hr., 400Ft). **Phone code:** 26.

To try your luck without an accommodation agency, look for *Zimmer Frei* signs along Fő u. **Elte Guest House,** Fő u. 117 (tel. 39 81 65), offers rooms with fridge, bath, and balcony (1600Ft per person). **Hotel Salamon,** Salamontorony u. 1 (tel. 263 82 78), has simple but adequate singles, doubles, and triples (1100Ft per person). **Diófa Restaurant,** Fő u. 48 (tel. 34 18 52), serves Swedish and Hungarian dishes (300-1200Ft). The friendly owner's parents were Swedish and Hungarian—that's why. **Gulás Csárda,** Nagy Lajos u. near Fő u., delivers tasty Hungarian fare in a room strung with paprika (500Ft and up; open daily 11:30am-10pm). **Vegyesbolt supermarket,** at the crossing of Rév and Fő u., sells apple juice (120Ft) and other necessities (open Mon.-Fri. 6am-6pm, Sat. 6am-2pm, Sun. 6am-noon).

■ Esztergom

A fantastic hilltop cathedral has shaped the 1000-year-old religious history of Esztergom (ESH-ter-gom) and it is chiefly responsible for the town's nickname: the Hungarian Rome. A basilica was originally built here in 1010, but the present Neoclassical behemoth—Hungary's biggest church—was consecrated in 1856. On a smaller scale, the red marble **Bakócz Chapel** on the south side of the cathedral is a masterwork of Renaissance Tuscan stone-carving. Climb to the 71.5m-high **cupola** for a view of Slovakia and the mighty Danube bend (50Ft), or descend into the solemn **crypt** to honor the remains of Hungary's archbishops (open daily 9am-5pm). The **Kincstáv** (Cathedral Treasury), on the north side of the main altar, is Hungary's most extensive ecclesiastical collection of works of gold, textiles, and historical and legal relics, going back a millennium. The jewel-studded cross labelled #78 in the case facing the entrance to the main collection is the **Koronázási Eskükereszt** (Coronation Cross), on which Hungary's rulers pledged their oaths from the 13th century until 1916 (open daily 9am-4:30pm; 130Ft, students 65Ft). Beside the cathedral stands the restored 12th-century **Esztergom Palace** (tel. 31 59 86; open Tues.-Sun. summer 9am-4:30pm; winter 10am-3:30pm; 60Ft, students 10Ft, free with ISIC). To survey the kingdom, ascend to the roof (10Ft). At the foot of the hill, **Keresztény Múzeum** (Christian Museum), Berenyi Zsigmond u. 2 (tel. 31 38 80), houses an exceptional collection of Renaissance religious artwork (open Tues.-Sun. 10am-6pm; 100Ft, students 50Ft).

The **train station** sits at the south edge of town. Get to central Rákóczi tér by walking up Baross Gábor út, making a right onto Kiss János Altábornagy út, and bearing straight as it becomes Kossuth Lajos u. **Gran Tours,** Széchenyi tér 25 (tel./fax 41 37 56), at the edge of Rákóczi tér, provides **maps** and finds **private accommodations** (singles 1400Ft; doubles 2500Ft; open Mon.-Fri. 8am-4pm, in summer also Sat. 8am-noon). **OTP,** on Rákóczi tér, has the best exchange rates in town. **Trains** connect Esztergom to Budapest (11 per day, 1½hr., 278Ft). Catch **buses** a few blocks south of Rákóczi tér (take Simor János u. straight up) to: Budapest (every 30min., 1½hr., 292Ft); Szentendre (1 per hr., 1hr., 214Ft); and Visegrád (5 per day, 30min., 156Ft). **MAHART boats** (tel. 31 35 31) depart from the pier at the end of Gőzhajó u., on Primas Sziget island, stopping three times per day at Visegrád (1½hr., 420Ft) and Szentendre (3½hr., 880Ft) on the way to Budapest (5hr., 1218Ft). Twice a day on weekends, a **hydrofoil** leaves from the same pier to Budapest (1hr.) and Visegrad (40min.). **Phone code:** 33.

One of several centrally located pensions, **Platán Panzió,** Kis-Duna Sétány 11 (tel. 31 13 55), between Rákóczi tér and Primas Sziget, rents digestible singles (1120Ft) and doubles (2464Ft) with shared toilets and bath. **Gran Camping,** Nagy-Duna Sétány (tel. 31 13 27), in the middle of Primas Sziget, within walking distance of the sights, was closed in 1997 because of a flood: check out if you still need an anchor to tent there. **Vadászkert Vendeglő,** (tel. 31 70 19) Széchenyi tér, lets you relax on the terrace overlooking Esztergom's most attractive square. The restaurants do *sertés* (schnitzel) in many ways (500Ft and up; open daily 11am-9pm). **Szalma Csárda** (tel. 31 10 52), in the middle of Primas Sziget near the pier at the end of Gőzhajó u., serves the catch of the day straight from the Danube (400Ft; open daily noon-midnight).

NORTHERN HUNGARY

Hungary's northern upland is comprised of a series of six low mountain ranges running northeast from the Danube Bend along the Slovak border. The towns of the north are known for their skill at satisfying two of life's vital needs: recreation and alcohol. The Bükk and Aggtelek National Parks beckon hikers and explorers with their scenic trails and cave systems, while the dry volcanic soil of the hillsides yields the grapes for the justifiably famous white *Tokaj* and red *Egri Bikavér* wines.

■ Eger

In 1552, Captain Dobó István and his tiny army, holed up in Eger (EGG-air) Castle, held off the invading Ottomans for an entire month. They credited their fortitude to the potent *Egri Bikavér* (Bull's Blood) wine they quaffed before battle. Today, Dobó's name and likeness appear throughout the city, and the sweet red *Bikavér* flows copiously and cheaply in Eger's tiny wine cellars. As if the wine wasn't enough to produce a warm, fuzzy glow, the 17th and 18th centuries brought a wealth of Baroque architecture, which has characterized the town ever since.

Orientation and Practical Information The **train station** (tel. 31 42 64), on Vasút u., sends trains to: Budapest's Keleti station (5 direct per day, 2hr., 800Ft); Füzesabony (11 per day, 20min., 84Ft), which connects to Budapest and Miskolc (1½hr., 380Ft); and Szilvásvárad (6 per day, 70min., 140Ft). Budapest trains split in Hatvan (a third of the way), so make sure you're in the right car. From the **train station** to the center, take bus #10, 11, 12, or 14 to the bus terminal or walk: head straight from the train station for a minute, then take a right onto **Deák u.,** a right and a quick left onto Széchenyi u. (at the cathedral), and a final right on **Ersek u.** (20min.). **Buses** head to: Budapest (15-22 per day, 2hr., 820Ft); Szilvásvárad (every 30min.-1hr., 45min., 190Ft); Aggtelek (1 per day, morning departure, afternoon return, 3hr., 690Ft); and Debrecen (3-6 per day, 3 hr., 820Ft). The **bus station** (tel. 41 05 52) lies five minutes uphill and west of central Dobó tér. To get to the center, head right on the main street in front of the station, then turn right on the first street. Follow the stairs down and turn right at the "T" on **Széchenyi u.** A left down a side street will take you to Dobó tér. The upbeat, English-speaking **Tourinform,** Dobó tér 2 (tel./fax 32 18 07), stocks brochures, English newspapers, good **maps** (60Ft), and accommodations info, and will research anything it doesn't already know (open in summer Mon.-Fri. 9am-6pm, Sat.-Sun. 9am-2pm; off-season Mon.-Fri. 9am-6pm and Sat.-Sun. 10am-1pm). **OTP,** Széchenyi u. 2 (tel. 31 08 66), gives advances on AmEx, EC, MC, and Visa, and charges no commission on most traveler's checks. A **24-hour ATM** outside takes Cirrus, EC, MC, and Visa (open Mon.-Tues. and Thurs. 7:45am-3:15pm, Wed. 7:45am-5pm, Fri. 7:45am-12:45pm). **Bank Posta,** Fellner u. 1 (tel. 31 35 40; fax 31 19 44), just south of Dobó tér, cashes traveler's checks, gives Visa cash advances, and has a Cirrus/EC/MC/Plus/Visa **24-hour ATM** (open Mon.-Thurs. 8am-4pm, Fri. 8am-3pm). The **post office** (tel. 31 32 32), **telephones** included, is at Széchenyi u. 22 (open Mon.-Fri. 8am-8pm, Sat. 8am-2pm). **Postal code:** 3300. **Phone code:** 36.

Accommodations The best and friendliest accommodations are in **private rooms;** look for *Zimmer Frei* signs outside the city center. There may be several on Almagyar u. and Mekcsey u. near the castle. **Eger Tourist,** Bajcsy-Zsilinszky u. 9 (tel. 41 17 24; fax 41 17 68), arranges private rooms in the center (around 1400Ft per person; open June-Sept. Mon.-Fri. 10am-6pm, Sat. 9am-noon; Oct.-May Mon.-Fri. 8:30am-5pm). The agency also operates a very basic **Tourist Motel,** Mekcsey u. 2. An interesting hue of aqua "mixes" with pink and red in the corridors, but the rooms are calmer and clean (doubles 2400Ft, with bath 3200Ft; triples 3000Ft, with bath 3900Ft; quads 3200Ft, with bath 4400Ft). **Eszterházi Károly Kollégiuma,** Leányka u. 2/6 (tel. 41 23 99), is a short ways up the hill beyond the castle, but not well-marked; it's the first big block-like building on the left (800Ft per person in triples and quads; open July to early Sept.; call ahead). **Autós Caravan Camping,** Rákóczi u. 79 (reserve through Eger Tourist), is 20 minutes north of the center on bus #5, 10, 11, or 12 (open April 15-Oct. 15; 250Ft per tent, 320Ft per person).

Food Grocery stores or fast food and pizza places are the quickest and cheapest way to eat. **HBH Bajor Söház,** Bajcsy-Zsilinsky u. 19 (tel. 31 63 12), in the southwest corner of Dobó tér, is a Bavarian beer house serving Hungarian specialties. Main dishes (450-1000Ft) include "Beer Drinkers Passion" (pork with cold brains baked in beer batter, rice, and chips; 499Ft; open May-Oct. daily 10am-10pm, Nov.-April Mon.-Sat. 10am-10pm). In the Valley of the Beautiful Women, the vine-draped courtyard of **Kulacs Csárda Borozó** (tel./fax 31 13 75) keeps the crowds coming for the roasted fish with fries (370Ft) and Parisian pork with peas and rice (540Ft; open Tues.-Sun. noon-10pm). **Gyros Étterem,** Széchenyi u. 10 (tel. 31 01 35), serves gyros (585Ft), souvlaki (555Ft), and small but tasty Greek salads (299Ft). For caffeine and sugar, **Sarvari,** Kossuth u. 1, past the Lyceum (tel. 41 32 98), serves up pastries (40-65Ft) and espresso that javaholics will love (open Mon.-Fri. 6:30am-6pm, Sat.-Sun. 9am-6pm).

Sights and Entertainment Eger can be explored in a morning, but you can spend an entire afternoon and evening in the wine cellars of **Szépasszonyvölgy (Valley of the Beautiful Women).** Land on the volcanic hillside was sold cheaply after World War II, and now holds some 25 open wine cellars, as well as hundreds more used for storage. Most open cellars consist of little more than 20m of tunnels and a few tables and benches, but each has its own personality: some are subdued and gentle, while rowdy Hungarians and Gypsies hold candlelit sing-alongs in others. Although locals also pride themselves on white wines, Eger is Hungary's red wine capital; the most popular libations are the dry *Bikavér* (Bull's Blood) and the sweeter *Medok*. Little glasses for tasting are free; 100mL shots run 30-50Ft. The valley is designed for people coming to buy (300Ft per 1L; less if you bring your own container), but many spend hours in the friendly, smoky cellars, or outside chatting around the picnic tables in the small park. Visitors force small coins into the spongy fungus on the cellar walls—legend has it that if your coin sticks, you'll return. Most cellars are open from around 10am and begin to close around 6 or 7pm, or whenever their owners have had enough. Some stay open as late as 10pm, but the best time to go is late afternoon. A South African woman at cellar #2 will give you a thorough and entertaining introduction to the area's wines if you descend into her cavern (usually open 3pm-late). Otherwise, you'll most likely be confronted with broken German. For the best *Medok* around, go to cellar #16 (you might be let in the back). Get to the Valley by walking west from the 1956 monument on Deák u. down Telekessy u., which with a quick jog to the left becomes Király u. and then Szépasszonyvölgy u. About 15 to 20 minutes from Deák, the valley appears; walk past the buses and stands to the wine cellars. The wise (and kind) thing to do here is to enjoy all the samples you want, and then buy a bottle of a variety you particularly like—that way the cellars can continue to give free tastings.

The yellow **Bazilica** on Eszterházy tér is Hungary's second-biggest church; it was built in 1837 by big-thinker Joseph Hild, who also designed the country's largest in Esztergom. Distinguishing the real marble from the painted illusions is a challenge—albeit not a particularly tough one. Half-hour **organ concerts** are held here from May to mid-October (Mon.-Sat. 11:30am, Sun. 12:45pm; 200Ft, under 18 60Ft). Opposite the cathedral is the Rococo **Lyceum.** The fresco in the library on the first floor depicts an ant's-eye view of the Council of Trent, which spawned the edicts of the Counter-Reformation (a slim lightning bolt at one end is blasting a pile of heretical books). Upstairs, a small **astronomical museum** houses 18th-century telescopes and instruments of the building's old observatory. A marble-line depression in the floor represents the meridian; when the sun strikes the line through a tiny aperture in the south wall, it is astronomical noon. There is also an observation deck with great views of the city and surrounding hills. Two floors up, a periscope projects a live picture of the surrounding town onto a table in a periously stifling room (open Tues.-Fri. 9:30am-1pm, Sat.-Sun. 9:30am-noon; 200Ft, students 100Ft).

On the south side of Dobó tér stands the Baroque pink **Minorita Templom** (Minorite Church), built in 1773. It overlooks a statue of Captain Dobó and two co-defenders, including a possessed female poised to hurl a rock upon an unfortunate Turk. Hungarians revere the medieval **Vár** (castle; tel. 31 27 44). It was here that Dobó István and his 2000 men repelled the unified Ottoman army, halting their advance for another 44 years. The castle's innards include subterranean barracks, catacombs, a crypt, and, of course, a wine cellar (open daily 8am-7:30pm; 50Ft, students 20Ft). One ticket buys admission to the three museums in the castle: a **picture gallery** showing Hungarian paintings from as early as the 15th century, the **Dobó István Vármúzeum,** which displays excavated artifacts, armor, and an impressive array of sharp, spiky, and pointy weapons, and the **dungeon exhibition,** a collection of torture equipment that inspires sadists and masochists alike (museums open Tues.-Sun. 9am-5pm; underground passages on Mon.; 200Ft, students 100Ft; English tours 2000Ft). The 400-year-old wine cellars are also open to the public for wine tasting (open Tues.-Sun. 10am-5pm).

Just north of Dobó tér, capture another Kodak moment from the 40m **Minaret,** the Ottomans' northernmost phallic symbol (open daily 10am-6pm, closed in winter; 30Ft). The steep spiral staircase is not much wider than the average 20th-century person. The 18th-century **Szerb Ortodox Templom** (Serbian Orthodox Church), Vitkovics u. at the town center's north end, parallel to Széchenyi u., displays magnificent murals and an equally magnificent altar (open daily 10am-4pm; free).

Eger celebrates its heritage during the **Baroque Festival,** held throughout August. Nightly performances of operas, operettas, and medieval and Renaissance court music are held in the Franciscan Church's yard, the basilica, and Dobó tér. Buy tickets (300Ft) at the place of performance. An international folk-dance festival, **Eger Vintage Days,** is held daily in the end of June. Ask at Tourinform (see **Practical Information,** p. 263) for schedules.

■ Near Eger: Aggtelek and Jósvafő

The **Baradla caves** are a 25km-long system of tunnels that wind between Hungary and Slovakia. Each chamber is a forest of dripping stalactites, stalagmites, and fantastically shaped stone formations. Entrances (permitted only with a tour) in Hungary are at **Aggtelek** (AWG-tel-eck) and **Jósvafő** (YOSH-va-fuer). A variety of tours are available (tel./fax (48) 35 00 06), including hour-long tours at Aggtelek (300Ft, students 150Ft; daily at 10am, 1pm, 3pm, and 5pm or whenever more than 10 people are waiting; tours in Hungarian, but there are English pamphlets) and at Jósvafő (300Ft, students 150Ft; tours daily at noon, 5pm, and sometimes also 10am and 2pm). At Aggtelek, a large chamber with perfect acoustics has been converted into an auditorium, and spelunkers pause here for a 1970s-esque light-and-sound show. Another hall contains the cemetery of the **Halstatt man,** where 13 people are buried in a sitting position. The tunnels along the tour are all well-lit, but the guide turns the lights off as you pass to discourage stragglers. The caves' temperature is 10°C year-round, so bring a jacket.

The one daily **bus** leaves Eger at 8:40am, whizzes through Szilvásvárad at 9:20am, and arrives in Aggtelek at 11:20am (400Ft) in front of Cseppkő Hotel, 200m uphill from the cave entrance. The bus back to Eger leaves at 3pm; the one to Miskolc is at 5:30pm. **Baradla Camping,** at the mouth of the cave (tel./fax (48) 34 30 73), has 4- to 9-bed dorms (April 16-Oct. 15 420Ft; Oct. 16-April 15 490Ft; sheets 80Ft), as well as bungalows and campsites (4-person bungalow 1800Ft; tent 500Ft per person; 100Ft tax, students exempt). The rooms in the dorms are acceptable, but don't count on hot water. Up the hill, at the two-star **Cseppkő Hotel** (tel./fax (48) 34 30 75), the rooms all come with shower, TV, radio, and breakfast (singles 4000Ft; doubles 5000Ft; triples 6500Ft; quads 9000Ft). The hotel also has **currency exchange** with not-so-great rates (Visa and MC accepted).

Ten minutes by bus (68Ft) past Aggtelek lies **Jósvafő,** a town of red roofs and roosters. From the first bus stop in town, walk back out of town by the main road and bear right at the sign to the cave. In 15 minutes, you will reach the Jósvafő entrance to the Baradla caves. For overnight spelunkers, one of the only options here is **Tengerszem Szálló,** Tengerszem oldal 2 (tel. (48) 35 00 06; singles 1400Ft, 2100Ft with shower; doubles 2100Ft/2800Ft; extra beds 560Ft; 80Ft tax). **Tengerszem Étterem** has English menus and the standard Hungarian main dishes (320-750Ft). Buses run between Aggtelek and Jósvafő every two to three hours.

■ Szilvásvárad

Beloved for its carriages, Lipizzaner horses, and surrounding national parks, Szilvásvárad (SEAL-vash-vah-rod) trots along at its own dignified clip, oblivious to the huge concrete factories 5km to the southwest. Recreational opportunities abound, from leisurely strolls in the Szalajka Valley to hikes in the fauna-filled Bükk mountains.

Orientation and Practical Information Trains run to Eger (8 per day, 70min., 140Ft); **buses** go to Eger (every ½-1hr., 45min., 190Ft) and Aggletek (9:20am,

1¾hr., 324Ft). The town's one big street, **Egri út,** extends northeast from the Szilvás-várad-Szalajkavölgy train station (the first one in Szilvásvárad when coming from Eger) and bends north at the info cottage. **Szalajka u.** extends south from the turn and leads to the national park. Farther north, Egri út turns into **Miskolci út.** There is no bus station; after passing the looming concrete factories of Bükkszentmárton, Szil-vásvárad is the next town. Don't get off at the first bus stop in town, unless you want to investigate the *Zimmer Frei* signs. The second stop is just north of the info cot-tage, where **Tourinform** sells maps of the national park (late June-Sept.). Laid-back, friendly, and eager to speak English, the staff can help find accommodations, but doesn't make reservations. **Maps** are also available from Dohány-Ajándék, a stand by the entrance to the park. A **currency exchange** and a few phones reside in the **post office,** Egri út 10 (tel. 35 51 01; open Mon.-Fri. 8am-8pm, Sat. 8am-2pm, Sun. 8am-noon). **Hegy Camping,** Egri út 36a (tel. 35 52 07), changes money 24hr. from May to October, but for only moderately good rates. **Postal code:** 3348. **Phone code:** 36.

Accommodations and Food Private rooms usually start at 600Ft per person without breakfast, but expect to pay a little more if you'd like water or heat. **Lipicai Hotel Szállására,** Egri út 12 (tel./fax 35 51 00), is one of the town's nicest budget options. It's a trifle gray, but clean, and you can get a black-and-white TV on request. Students are exempt from room tax (doubles 1500Ft weekdays, 2000Ft weekends; triples 4500Ft/ 6000Ft; quads 6000Ft/8000Ft; tax 100Ft). The rooms of the regal, hill-top **Kastély Hotel Szilvás,** Park u. 6 (tel. 35 52 11; fax 35 53 24), 15 minutes east of the main drag, are not as elegant as the building, but they are Szilvásvárad's cleanest, have showers, include breakfast, and are cloistered by trees and formal gardens (sin-gles 3465 Ft; doubles 4300Ft, with TV, refrigerator, and bath 5200Ft). **Hegy Camping** (see **Practical Information,** above) offers great views of the valley from the grassy and groomed campground (tents 280Ft, more than 2 people 380Ft; 360Ft per person; students 288Ft). Bungalows have shower and toilet (doubles 2200Ft; triples 3000Ft; quads 3600Ft; tax 100Ft per person; open May-Oct.).

   Csobogó, Szalajka u. 1 (tel. (30) 41 52 49), on the road to the national park, lies among all sorts of *büfé* and little restaurants. In addition to traditional meals made for tourists seeking Hungarian culture, it offers random dishes from around the world, including vegetarian meals (250Ft). Check out Carpathian *borzaska* (450Ft) or *Ban-daguzda tlates pecsenijeje* (pork cutlet, bacon, herbs, garlic, and tomato; 450Ft; open daily 11am-8pm; summer and Oct.-April open Sat.-Sun. until midnight). **Szala-jka Inn,** Egri út 2 (tel. 35 52 57), immerses the visitor in folk decor and cuisine. Try the Bükk-style wild boar with mushrooms (810Ft) or forester's goulash soup (370Ft). Live Gypsy music plays on weekends (open daily 7am-midnight).

Sights and Entertainment Horse shows kick into action on weekends in the arena across from Tourinform on Szalajka u. (300Ft per person). Or get into the thick of things by learning how to drive a carriage, brandish a whip, or ride a steed—all with the 400-year-old race of Lipizzaner horses for which Hungary is famous. Many farms offer horse-riding, especially in July and August. **Péter Kovács,** Egri út 62 (tel. 35 53 43), rents horses (1500Ft per hr.) and two- and four-horse carriages (2000Ft and 3500Ft respectively). Equestrians should also gallop to the **Lipicai Múzeum** (Horse Museum), Park u. 8 (tel. 35 51 55), full of riding paraphernalia from the region's horsey history (open Tues.-Sun. 9am-5pm; 150Ft). In early September, the three-day **Lipicai Festival** (info tel. 35 51 55) ushers carriage drivers from all over the world for a grand international competition of horses and reins.

   Leafy walks through the **Bükk mountains** and the **Szalajka valley** are beautiful, but not always particularly relaxing. The most popular destination—and we do mean popular—is the **Fátyol waterfall,** the rocks of which look like steps designed for giants. It only takes 45 minutes to walk here, or 15 minutes by the little open-air choo-choo train. Catch the train at the entrance to the park just to the right of the stop sign (100Ft, students 50Ft). This is not the place for solitude, but steeper hikes up the mountain attract fewer people. To cover more distance and enjoy bouncing over potholes, **rent a bike** at Szalajka u. 28 (tel. (60) 35 26 95), just past the stop sign at the entrance to the park. You can't miss it, thanks to the racks of fluorescent green mountain bikes lining the patio. The shop also arranges trips to the local plateaus for groups of 10 or more for the cost of a day's rental (300Ft per hr., 1200Ft per day; open in summer daily 9am-dusk; off-season in good weather only). A 30-minute hike beyond the waterfalls leads to the **Istálósk cave**, which once sheltered a bear cult during the Stone Age. Talk about perfect acoustics—*La Traviata* sounds as good in here as in a tile bathroom. Follow the road (with the brook always to the right), and then scramble up the switchbacks. On the path to the waterfall, two museums are of moderate interest. The **Erdészeti Muzeum** displays logging techniques and other elements of life in the forest (open Nov.-April 15 daily 9am-2:30pm; April 16-April 30 Tues.-Sun. 8:30am-4pm; May 1-Sept. 30 Tues.-Sun. 8:30am-4:30pm; Oct. Tues.-Sun. 8:30am-3pm; 60Ft, students 40Ft). The **Open Air Erdei Museum** exhibits huts similar to those once used by the region's woodsmen (open daily 9am-3pm; free).

The **Orbán-ház Museum,** Miskolci út 5, has a collection of all the archaeological treasures of the area. Fossils! (Open May-Oct. Thurs.-Sun. 9am-5pm; 60Ft, students 20Ft.) Just up the hill in front stands the white, rotund, and perfectly Classical **Keréktemplom**—a 19th-century reform temple, the interior of which appears even more austere than most Protestant creations. Great views of the fields and valleys roll out from this vantage point.

■ Tokaj

Locals say that King Louis XIV called Tokaj (toke-EYE) wine "the wine of kings and the king of wines." Tokaj itself is just one of the 28 small towns and villages that take advantage of the volcanic yellow soil and sunny climate at the foot of the Kopasz Mountains to produce unique whites, but it lends its name to the entire class of wine.

Orientation and Practical Information Trains, Baross G. u. 18 (tel. 35 20 20), puff to Miskolc (13 per day, 1hr., 266Ft) and Nyíregyháza (9 per day, 30min., 166Ft), which links to Debrecen (2hr., 440Ft). The only **bus** service is to local towns. The train station sits 15 minutes southwest of town; with your back to the station, walk left along the railroad embankment until you reach an underpass, then turn left on Bajcsy-Zsilinszky u. At the Hotel Tokaj fork, stay on the left road. Tokaj's center can be crossed on foot in about 15 minutes. The main **Bajcsy-Zsilinszky u.** becomes **Rákóczi u.** and, beyond the center at Kossuth tér, **Bethlen Gábor u.** Some pensions' brochures include primitive street **maps**—these may be the only ones you'll find. **Tokaj Tours,** Serház u. 1 (tel./fax 35 22 59), at Rákóczi u., arranges private and hotel rooms (no fee), organizes tours of the region and wine-tastings, and can set you up with a horse, canoe, or rafting tour (open Mon.-Sat. 9am-4pm). **Exchange currency** and traveler's checks or get MC and Visa cash advances at **OTP,** Rákóczi u. 35 (tel. 35 25 21; open Mon.-Thurs. 8am-3:30pm, Fri. 8am-2:30pm). There's a 24-hour **ATM** outside the bank. The **post office** is at Rákóczi u. 24 (tel. 35 24 17; open Mon.-Fri. 8am-5pm, Sat. 8am-noon). **Telephones** are sprinkled throughout the center; they're also in the post office. **Postal code:** 3910. **Phone code:** 47.

Accommodations and Food See what Tokaj Tours has to offer, but *Zimmer Frei* and *Szoba Kiadó* signs abound—your best bet is to walk along Rákóczi u. and venture down random streets to choose one you like (singles generally 1200Ft-1400Ft; doubles 2750Ft). Don't be afraid to bargain, but beware: your host may well take you into a small wine cellar and talk you into sampling—and buying—her homemade vintage. **Grof Széchenyi István Students Hostel,** Bajcsy-Zsilinszki u. 15-17 (tel. 35 23 55), between the train station and the center, is the best deal around, with fresh, recently renovated doubles (3800Ft with bath) and sparse but clean quads (3000Ft; open July-Aug. only). **Makk-Marci Panzió-Pizzéria,** Liget Köz 1 (tel. 35 23 36; fax 35 30 88), facing Rákóczi u., provides relaxing, bright rooms with bath (singles 2464Ft; doubles 3584Ft; triples 4816Ft; quads 6048Ft; breakfast included; EC,

MC, Visa). The cafe's offerings include pizza (215-935Ft) and spaghetti (175-225Ft). Reserve ahead. The concrete and plexiglass-bubbled **Hotel Tokaj,** Rákóczi u. 5 (tel. 35 23 44; fax 35 27 59), has comfortable singles (3425Ft) and doubles (4050Ft) that include breakfast and baths; some even overlook the Tisza River (EC, MC, Visa). If you think you're tougher than the mosquitoes that control the banks of the Tisza (and you might want to think again), proceed across the river (only 5min. from center). The best bet is **Camping Tisza,** on the right as you cross the river (tents 470Ft per person, with vehicles 600Ft; Rover will run you an extra 50Ft). Two- or four-person tiny bungalows are also available (450Ft per person). To the left, the extraordinarily friendly **Tisza Vízisport Centrum,** Horgász u. 3 (tel. 35 26 45), with an English-speaking proprietor, is expected to shed its drab Communist cover soon. Both students and athletes frequent this modest establishment. Reservations are recommended during the second half of July (4- to 12-person dorms 450Ft per person; sheets 150Ft; open May 1-Oct. 15 only).

Gödör, in the Tisza Vízisport complex, cooks up heavy meat dishes and some veggie ones (the usual cheese, mushrooms, and potatoes). The menu is in French and German (meals 200-400Ft; open Mon.-Fri. 9am-11pm, Sat.-Sun. 7am-11pm). The informal **Bacchus Etterem,** centrally located at Kossuth tér 17 (tel. 35 20 54), cooks up standard Hungarian foods (goulash 330Ft) and pizza (250-300Ft)—it also serves breakfast (180-250Ft; open 8am-10pm). Supermarket **Árunáz,** right in Kossuth tér, is another cheap option (open Mon.-Fri. 6am-7pm, Sat. 6am-1pm, and Sun. 7-11am).

Sights and Entertainment Signs reading *Bor Pince* herald **private wine cellars.** The owners of these cellars are generally pleased to let visitors sample their wares (50mL 90-300Ft, depending on the cellar)—walk on in, or ring the bell if the cellar looks shut. The big flashy cellars on the main road are more touristy—explore the side streets for higher-quality wines. Serious **tasting** takes place at the best-respected and largest of the lot: **Rákóczi Pince,** Kossuth tér 15 (tel. 35 20 09; fax 35 21 41), now a French-Hungarian joint venture. This 1.5km-long system of 24 tunnels was dug from volcanic rock in 1502. In 1526, János Szapohjai was elected king of Hungary in the elegant and surprisingly large hall; the tunnel served as the imperial wine cellar for two centuries, until the end of WWI. The tunnel walls are coated with 500 years' worth of the dripping, spongy fungus—it turns from cotton-ball white to sooty black with age—that keeps the cellar at a constant 10°C and 80% humidity. A jacket is a good idea down here, even in summer. **Wine-tastings** and **group tours** of the cellar, which has a 25,560L barrel, are usually held on the hour, but can be pre-empted by tour groups. **Individual tours** can also be arranged. (English-speaking guides available July-Aug. 200Ft for the 15-20min. tour, 300Ft for the tour and a glass of wine, and 700Ft for 6 glasses. Open daily 10am-7pm; AmEx, MC, Visa.) Another winery-museum hybrid, the **Borpince Múzeum,** Bem u. 2 (tel. 35 24 16), in the 16th-century cellar of a former king, is run by the Várhelyi family. (English spoken; exhibit free; taste 5 wines for 250Ft. Open until 10pm.)

A Mini-Guide to Hungarian Wine

Wine connoisseurs have been aware of the merits of Hungarian wines for years, and budget travelers have long appreciated the low prices. The exotic names on the labels, however, might intimidate those used to *Chardonnay.* The main local products are *Furmint,* a basic dry or sweet white wine, and *Hárslevelú,* a slightly more complex white. *Szamorodni* is an aperitif that ages in barrels for a year and a half. *Aszú* is *Furmint* sweetened with "noble rot" grapes (which ripen and dry out more quickly than others in the same bunch) and aged for three years. Getting a little more technical, sweetness is measured in three, four, five or six *puttony*—units of *Aszú* grapes added (six is the sweetest). It's said that 1972, 1988, and 1993 were especially good *Aszú* years. *Fordítás,* a dessert wine aged for three years, is made from the byproduct of *Aszú.* Experts sample wines in order from driest to sweetest, and do not *ever* swallow. The idea of wasting good wine offends our budget ethic, though, so go ahead. Drink up!

The **Tokaji Múzeum,** Bethlen Gábor u. 7 (tel. 35 26 36), exhibits the tools and equipment used in wine production, as well as the glass bottles and porcelain decanters in which wine has been stored and served for the least 300 years. Unfortunately, the lack of signs in English detracts from the museum's comprehensibility (open Tues.-Sun. 9am-5pm; 100Ft, students 50Ft). **Tokaji Galléria,** Bethlen Gábor u. 15, in an old red-and-cream Greek Orthodox Church, puts on free exhibitions by local artists that include funky paintings and sculptures (open June-Oct. Tues.-Sun. 10am-4pm). The century-old **Zsinagoga,** Serház u. 55, guarded by a family of beautiful storks (look up!) one block behind the gallery by way of József Attila u., survived WWII by doing duty as German barracks. It is newly yellow outside, but awaits renovations inside (closed to the public).

Outdoor opportunities are multiplying as fast as cellar fungi. **Vízisport Centrum** rents bikes (400Ft per day; reserve ahead) and canoes (1000Ft per day, 500Ft for ½-day); will drive you to the beginning of the Tisza for a long canoe trip (100Ft per km); and arranges horseback-riding (600Ft per hr., 1000Ft with trainer). **Camping Tisza** rents canoes (4-seater 1000Ft per day) and kayaks (500Ft per day).

With all the wine around, bars and discos aren't that common here. In summer, a **boat disco** floats on the river near Bajcsy-Zsilinszki u. The fun starts at 10pm (open June-Aug. only). **Veres Szekér Söröző,** Rákóczi u. 30-32, quickly fills with students and other young people in the evenings (0.5L beer 80-130Ft, 100mL wine 30-180Ft; pool 50Ft per game; open daily 5pm-2am).

NAGYALFÖLD (THE GREAT PLAIN)

Romanticized in tales of cowboys and mirages rising from its flat soil, Nagyalföld is an enormous grassland stretching southeast of Budapest over nearly one-half of Hungary's territory. Also called the *puszta,* meaning "plains" or "ravaged land," Nagyalföld was once a forest before the Turks chopped down the trees. Much of the plain is either pasture or farmlands, but a train ride through endless fields of sunflowers leads to the beautiful towns of Debrecen, Kecskemét, and Szeged.

▓ Debrecen

Protected by the Phoenix, Debrecen (de-bre-TSEN)—one of the few cities in the world with neither natural waterways nor defensive physical features—has burned down between 30 and 40 times, thanks to its scorching summers. It began as Nagyalföld's bread basket, and later became a wealthy business center; it's still known as the unofficial capital of eastern Hungary. Once the "Calvinist Rome," a Protestant center during the Reformation, Debrecen is still home to a large number of Protestants. Modern and 19th-century buildings alternate along Debrecen's broad streets, which draw a mix of cultures, thanks to the town's position near the Romanian border.

Orientation and Practical Information Trains (tel. 32 67 77) ply the rails to: Budapest (13 per day, 3hr., 1168Ft; *InterCity* 5 per day, 2½hr., 1418Ft); Kecskemét (1 per day, 3½hr., 1000Ft); Miskolc (5 per day, 2½-3hr., 700Ft); Eger (through Füzesabony, 3 per day, 3hr., 600Ft); Oradea, Romania (destination "Tîrgu Mureş"; 1 per day, 3½hr. or more depending on border crossing, 1034Ft); and Szeged (through Cegléd, 7 per day, 3½hr., 1336Ft). **Store luggage** at the train station (100-200Ft depending on size; open 24hr.) or in lockers (150Ft for 24hr.). From the **bus station** (tel. 41 39 99), at the intersection of Nyugari ú. and Széchenyi ú., buses run to: Tokaj (2 per day, 2hr., 478Ft); Szeged (2 per day, 4-5½hr., 1260Ft); Kecskemét (2 per day, 5½hr., 1260Ft); Miskolc (30 per day, 2hr., 530Ft); and Oradea (1 per day, 3½hr., 400-700Ft). The town center lies at **Kálvin tér** and **Kossuth tér.** Running south, broad Piac u. ends at Petőfi tér and the train station, about a 15-minute walk from the center. Piac u. becomes Péterfia u. at Kálvin tér and runs 3km north to **Nagyerdei Park**

and **Kossuth Lajos Tudományegyetem** (KLTE; Kossuth Lajos Technical University). Tram #1 (the one and only) runs from Petőfi tér through Kálvin tér into the park. Ticket checks are frequent and menacing (fine 2500Ft)—get tickets from the kiosk by the train station (50Ft) or pay the driver (60Ft). The tram is the best route to the town center from the train station; tourist offices are on the triangular Kossuth tér. The **bus station** lies 10 to 15 minutes southwest of the center. From the center, walk down Piac u. and turn right on Széchenyi u. The station is on the corner of Széchenyi u. and Nyugati u. At **Tourinform,** Piac u. 20 (tel. 41 22 50; fax 31 41 39), English-speaking agents give away or sell city **maps** and provide info on concerts (open June-Aug. daily 8am-8pm; Sept.-May Mon.-Fri. 8:30am-4:30pm). **OTP,** Hatvan u. 2/4 (tel. 41 95 44), has fairly good rates, gives Cirrus, EC, and MC cash advances, accepts most traveler's checks, and has a 24-hour **ATM** (bank open Mon.-Fri. 8am-3pm). For a taxi, dial 44 44 44 or 44 45 55. **Alternativ Könyvesbolt,** right in the center at Hatvan u. 11a (tel. 31 01 37), sells **English-language books** (open Mon.-Fri. 9am-6pm and Sat. 9am-1pm). The **medical emergency** room (tel. 41 43 33) is just south of the bus station at the intersection of Erzsébet u. and Szoboszlój u. **Internet access** is available at the aptly named **Internet Club,** Timár u. 15, on a small out-of-the-way street between the train station and the youth hostel (tel. 34 96 62 or 45 87 99; email hermes@weste1900.net). Email, internet, and WWW access are all available (30min. 180Ft, students 150Ft); up to 5 pages per day of printing are free (open daily 9am-9pm) The **post office,** Hatvan u. 5/9 (tel. 41 23 74), lies west of Kálvin tér (open Mon.-Fri. 7am-8pm, Sat. 8am-2pm, Sun. 8am-noon). **Postal code:** 4001. **Phone code:** 52.

Accommodations **Hajdútourist,** Kálvin tér 2 (tel. 41 55 88; fax 31 96 16), arranges central private singles (1000Ft) and doubles (1700Ft; open June-Aug. Mon.-Fri. 8am-5pm, Sat. 8am-12:30pm, Sept.-May Mon.-Fri. 8am-4:30pm); **IBUSZ** does the same (800-1500Ft per person). In July and August, many dorms rent out rooms (500-700Ft per person)—ask at Tourinform. Twenty minutes from the center and about 10 minutes from the train station, the youth hostel **West Tourist,** Wesselényi u. 4 (tel. 42 08 91; fax 41 32 66), offers adequate doubles (1800Ft, with bath 2900Ft), triples (2700Ft), and quads (3600Ft). In July and August, call ahead (100Ft tax and 10% discount for HI members on all rooms). Close to the train station, right off Piac u., lies the sea-green **Hotel Fönix,** Barna u. 17 (tel. 41 33 55; fax 41 30 54). Rooms are spotless, if occasionally stuffy (singles 1300Ft; doubles 2400Ft, 4000Ft with shower; spare beds 500-800Ft extra; tax 130Ft; EC, MC, Visa). Treat yourself to a bath (150Ft). **Hotel Stop,** Batthyány u. 18 (tel. 42 03 01), parallel to Piac u., occupies a pleasant courtyard near the center, but the rooms are a little dingy (doubles with shower 2500Ft). Hidden in Nagyerdei Park is **Termál Camping,** Nagyerdei körút 102 (tel./fax 41 24 56), accessible from the train station by tram #1 or bus #10 or 14. Get off once you're in the park—you should see Hotel Termál on the left—and backtrack past the crossroads. The campground is about five minutes down the road on left. (Quads 1600Ft; with shower 4100Ft. Tents 780Ft per person; caravans 930Ft per person. 100Ft tax per person. Reserve rooms 1 month in advance. Open May 1-Oct. 15.)

Food In the brick cellar of **Csokonai Söröző,** Kossuth u. 21 (tel. 41 08 02), waiters accustomed to foreigners enthusiastically greet their customers and then allow them to try their luck with a roll of the dice for a free meal. The city's best menu includes English translations and photographs of the main dishes (320-795Ft). Everything from snails (395Ft) to wild hog goulash (595Ft); stuffed turkey breast with rice, corn, and peas is for the less adventurous (535Ft). Veggie options are also available (lentil soup with cabbage 320Ft; open Mon.-Sat. noon-11pm, Sun. 4pm-11pm). **Régi Posta Étterem,** Széchenyi u. 6 (tel. 41 72 92), named for an old stagecoach stop, has fried food and attentive waiters (main dishes 340-490Ft; open daily 11am-10pm). The **University Dining Halls** offer lunch (300-500Ft) during the school year. Look for the building marked "Menza" behind the main university building on Egyetem tér (open daily noon-4pm; cheap leftovers until approximately 6pm 200-250Ft).

Sights and Entertainment Hungary's largest Protestant church, the 1863 twin-spired **Nagytemplom** (Great Church; tel. 32 70 17), looms over Kossuth tér's north end. The T-shaped interior can hold 3000 people, and the huge organ threatening to crush the pulpit serves as the only major adornment. A great view extends from the bell tower, though the narrow, rickety stairs and low ceilings might make the claustrophobic a bit nervous (open Mon.-Fri. 9am-noon and 2-4pm, Sat. 9am-noon, Sun. 11am-4pm; 30Ft, students 15Ft). The **Református Kollégium,** Kálvin tér 16 (tel. 41 47 44), in back of the church, was established in 1538 as a center for Protestant education. The present building has housed the government of Hungary twice—in 1849 when Lajos Kossuth headed the Parliament in the Oratory, and again in 1944. Today, it houses Calvinist schools, as well as a collection of religious art and an exhibit on the history of Protestantism in Debrecen. The 650,000-volume **library,** Hungary's second-oldest, displays 16th-century Bibles (open Tues.-Sat. 9am-5pm, Sun. 9am-1pm; 60Ft, students 30Ft; Hungarian and German explanations).

Two blocks west in Déri tér stands the **Déri Museum** (tel. 41 75 77), with a collection that ranges from local history to Japanese lacquerware. Check out the exhibit on folkcraft since the 16th century and the marvelous collection of gold- and silver-work. Upstairs are three awe-inspiring murals by Mihály Munkácsy of Christ's trial and crucifixion. The artist painted himself into *Ecce Homo* as the old man in the crowd, next to the arch (open Tues.-Sun. 10am-6pm; 180Ft, students 90Ft).

Debrecen is famous for its young population, and you'll find them all in **Nagyerdei Park,** which provides thermal baths as well as bike lanes, paddle boats, bars, tattoo salons, and an overabundance of single men sitting around in tank tops. **Programs in Debrecen** is a series of summer events, ranging from equestrian competitions in the first weekend of July to musical performances to air shows, and culminating in the huge **Flower Carnival** parade on August 20. Every year, the **Jazz Days** festival features well-known musicians and bands (dates variable). See Tourinform for the two *fêtes'* schedules and tickets (usually 300-700Ft). Every odd year, the **International Military Band Festival** blows its horn in the last week of June. Every even year, the **Béla Bartók Choir Festival** attracts great choirs from around the world in the first week of July. Master the unmasterable—the Debrecen summer school at KLTE offers cheap and popular **Hungarian language programs** for more than 500 students from around the world. Contact Debreceni Nyári Egyetem, Egyetem tér 1, M-4010 Debrecen (tel./fax 32 91 17 or tel. 31 66 66, ext. 3003). Then practice your new skills with the young, lively crowd in smoky **El Tornado,** Pallagi u. 2 (tel. 34 05 90), in Nagyerdei Park. This spirited pub even cranks out some country music every once in a while (0.5L *Borsodi* 110Ft; open daily May-Sept. 4pm-4am, Oct.-April 6pm-4am). In addition to the Internet Club (see **Practical Information,** p. 270), the cafe **Csokonai Kávénáz,** Kossuth u. 21 (tel. 41 29 58), also offers Internet and email services (280Ft per 30min., 500Ft per hr.). The less crowded **Yes Jazz Bár,** Kálvin tér 4 (tel. 41 85 22), is usually filled with low conversations rumbling under the live jazz and blues (Guinness 180Ft; cover 100-300Ft; open daily 2pm-2am).

■ Szeged

The easygoing charm of the Great Plain's cultural capital belies the status of Szeged (SEH-gedd) as the nation's only planned city; after an 1879 flood practically wiped out the town, streets were laid out in straight lines and orderly curves punctuated by large stately squares. Row after row of colorful neo-Renaissance and Art Nouveau buildings now complement each other in shape and style. Equally colorful legends hold that Attila the Hun was buried here, where the Tisza and Maros Rivers unite.

ORIENTATION AND PRACTICAL INFORMATION

Szeged is split in two by the **Tisza river.** The downtown area sits on the west bank. **Újszeged** (New Szeged), on the east bank, is mostly parks and residences. A curved *körút* (boulevard) connects the streets that radiate from the center. The inner road,

Tisza krt., is a half-circle, with **Klauzál tér** in the middle, next to **Széchenyi tér,** which starts upriver and circles around to downriver. The outer road—named at different segments for the European cities that helped rebuild Szeged after the flood—is a nearly complete circle that crosses the river from the downtown's northeast section. Most travel bureaus are on or near Klauzál tér. **Tram #1** connects the **train station** in the south with Klauzál tér (5 or 6 stops away) and continues northeast to the **bus station.** Tickets (50Ft) can be purchased at the train station from people standing at the exit and at the bus station kiosks, or on the tram (75Ft). The tram stop is just north of the bus station on **Kossuth sugárút.** It's a 10- to 15-minute walk from the bus station to the center; the trains are about 20 minutes in the opposite direction.

Tourist Offices: Szeged Tourist, Klauzál tér 7 (tel. 32 18 00; fax 31 29 28). Maps, summer bus and boat tours in July and Aug. (bus 450Ft, under 18 300Ft), and international bus tickets with 10% student discount. Open Mon.-Fri. 9am-5pm and Sat. 9am-1pm; off-season closed Sat.

Currency Exchange: OTP, Klauzál tér 5. Cashes traveler's checks without commission and gives EC/MC/Visa cash advances. Open Mon. 7:45am-4:30pm, Tues.-Thurs. 7:45am-2pm, Fri. 7:45-11:30am. **Budapest Bank Ltd.,** next door at Klauzál tér 4 (tel. 48 55 85), offers **Western Union** services. Open Mon. and Wed. 8:30am-5pm and Tues. and Thurs.-Fri. 8:30am-1pm. **K&H Bank,** Károly u. 2, by Széchenyi tér, has a **24hr. ATM** (Cirrus/EC/MC/Plus/Visa) and the best exchange rates.

Trains: 1 block east of Boldogasszony sugárút, the main drag leading into town (tel. 42 18 21). To: Arad, Romania (3 per day, change in Békés Csaba, 5-7hr., 2600-2730Ft); Belgrade (2 per day, 6hr., 4009Ft); Budapest (*InterCity* 14 per day, 2½hr., 1000Ft); Debrecen (7 per day, change in Cegléd; 3-4hr.; 1336Ft); Kecskemét (dir. "Budapest," 12 per day, 1hr., 440Ft, *InterCity* 576Ft); and Pécs (1 per day, 1724Ft). International cashier on 2nd floor. Open daily 6am-5:45pm.

Buses: Mars tér (tel. 42 14 78), 10min. west of Londoni krt. along Merey u. or Kossuth u. To: Budapest (7 per day, 3½hr., 1200Ft); Debrecen (2 per day, 5¼hr., 1500Ft); Kecskemét (13 per day, 1¾hr., 630Ft); Pécs (6 per day, 4½hr., 1260Ft); Győr (2 per day, 6hr., 1890Ft); and Eger (2 per day, 5hr., 1580Ft).

Taxis: tel. 470 470, 490 490, 480 480, or 488 488.

Luggage storage: At the train station. 60Ft until 4pm, then 120Ft. Open 4am-11pm.

English Bookstores: Kőnyvesbolt, Kárász u. 16 (tel. 31 23 28). Open Mon.-Fri. 10am-6pm, Sat. 9am-1pm. **Délhir I Bolt,** Dugonics tér (tel. 31 21 18). International magazines and newspapers. Open Mon.-Sat. 5am-8pm, Sun. 5am-7pm.

Pharmacy: Kígyó Richter Referenciapatika, Klauzál tér 3 (tel. 11 11 31). One of many. Open daily 7am-8pm.

Medical Assistance: The center at Kossuth Lagos sgt. 15 (tel. 47 43 74) provides medical care. In an **emergency,** dial 04.

Post Office: Széchenyi tér 1 (tel. 47 62 76), at Híd u. Open Mon.-Fri. 8am-8pm, Sat. 8am-2pm, Sun. 8am-noon. **Postal code:** 6720.

Telephones: Both inside and outside of the post office. **Phone code:** 62.

ACCOMMODATIONS AND CAMPING

Szeged Tourist (see above) finds the best deals on rooms (singles 900-1800Ft; doubles 2400Ft). University dorms are generally cheapest, especially for solo travelers, but are only open in July and August.

Fortuna Panzió, Pécskai u. 8 (tel./fax 43 15 85). A serene neighborhood setting, across the bridge. Worth the walk and search. Go across Belvárosihid bridge and take a left onto Szent-Györgyi Albert u. After passing a huge hotel complex on the left, turn left onto Pécskai u. Air-conditioned, spacious rooms and sparkling bathrooms. Doubles with bath 4500Ft. EC, MC, Visa.

Napfény, Dorozsmai u. 4 (tel. 42 18 00; fax 46 75 79), west of downtown. Hotel and campground. Take tram #1 to the last stop, go up the overpass behind you, then take a left. After about a 10min. walk on this major road, you'll see Napfény on the left. Rooms in motel-like bungalows are reasonably priced (doubles 1900Ft; campsites 200Ft per tent and 300Ft per person). Open year-round.

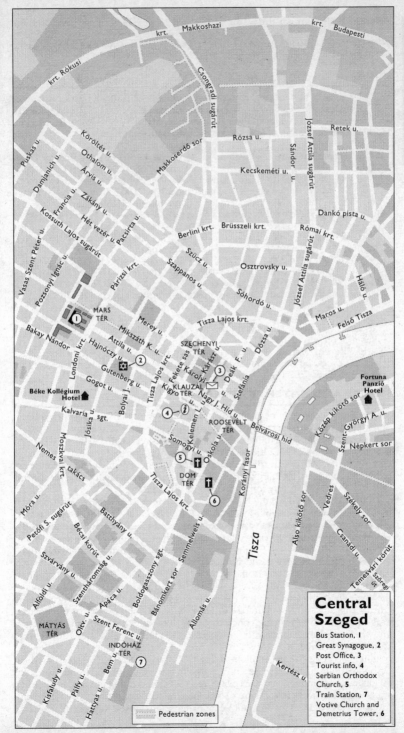

Central Szeged

Bus Station, **1**
Great Synagogue, **2**
Post Office, **3**
Tourist info, **4**
Serbian Orthodox
Church, **5**
Train Station, **7**
Votive Church and
Demetrius Tower, **6**

Pedestrian zones

Apáthy Kollégium, Apáthy u. (tel. 45 40 00; fax 45 57 29) Centrally located dorm. Singles 1800Ft, doubles 2400Ft, and triples 3000Ft. Open July-Aug. The nearby **Béke Kollégium,** Béke u. 11/13 (tel. 31 14 88), was closed for renovation during summer 1997, but should reopen in 1998.

FOOD

Szeged is known both for university culture and food—it is the home of the famous Pick salami, the source of sweet paprika, and the best place for *halászlé*, a spicy fish soup. For late-night cravings and weekend supplies, there is a **non-stop ABC market,** Mars tér, near the corner of Londoni krt. and Mikszáth Kálmán u.

Aranykorona Étterem, Déak Ferenc u. 29 (tel. 32 17 50), at the corner of Victor Hugo u. Mouth-watering Hungarian dishes are the cheapest of their kind around (red wine and fish with tomato sauce 370Ft). Veggie dishes don't depart much from the standard fried cheese and mushroom type (180-350Ft). No fish on Mon. Open Mon.-Thurs. 11am-11pm, Fri.-Sat. 11am-2am, Sun. 11am-10pm.

Roosevelt téri Halászcsárda (Sótartá Étterem), Roosevelt tér 14 (tel. 42 43 33 or 42 41 11), on the square's southeast side next to the river. The place to sample the spicy fish soup for which Szeged is famous. Try any of the "*hallé*" (fish soup) dishes—they're only spicy if you add the green paprika served on the side (550-900Ft). Catch of "the day" (literally) and other hefty meals (350-1500Ft). English, Croatian, and German menu. Open daily 11am-11pm or until last guest leaves.

Bounty Pub (tel. 32 65 00), on Roosevelt tér across from the Móra Ferenc Múzeum. Seafaring atmosphere feels more like a ship than a restaurant. Specializes in "Lava Rock grilling," in which gravy is steamed in with the meat (grilled pork chops, chili, and bean stew 580Ft). Bar offers more than 70 types of whiskey (150-1700Ft), as well as the usual wine and beer. Restaurant open noon-midnight; bar open until around 3am in summer, off-season 1-2am.

Bárka Élterem, Kálmán Lajos u. 4 (tel. 31 59 14). Smoky interior and cheap prices attract everyone from students to old men discussing politics. Dishes include *halaszle* (fish; 570Ft) and spaghetti (430-470Ft). Open 8am-midnight.

SIGHTS AND ENTERTAINMENT

Szeged's downtown can be easily seen in an afternoon. Park-like **Széchenyi tér,** a block north of Klauzál tér, is near the geographical center of the city. The yellow **Városháza** (town hall) on the square's west edge was re-shingled with red and green majolica ceramic tiles after the 1879 deluge destroyed most of the city. The bridge connecting the *Városháza* to the drab building next door (which once held the tax office) was built for Habsburg Emperor Ferenc József's inspection of the reconstruction, to prevent His Majesty from having to go up and down.

To the east by the river, the huge Neoclassical **Móra Ferenc Múzeum,** Roosevelt tér 1/3 (tel. 47 03 70), exhibits folk art from the 18th century to the present. Keep an eye out for the waffle irons that look like giant salad tongs. The museum details the life of the long-vanished Avars, who occupied the Carpathian basin from the 6th through the 9th centuries. Exhibits include precise explanations in English (open Tues.-Sun. 10am-5pm; 80Ft, students 20Ft).

Oskola u. leads south to Dóm tér, where the red-brick **Fogadalmi Templom** (Votive Church) pierces the skyline with its twin 91m towers. Built by survivors of the great flood, the structure has too many tiny steeples and arches to be graceful. One of Hungary's largest churches, it houses a 10,000-pipe organ that often exerts itself in afternoon or evening concerts (open Mon.-Sat. 9am-6pm, Sun. 12:30-6pm; known for closing haphazardly). Alongside the church stands the 12th-century **Dömötör Torony** (Demetrius Tower), Szeged's oldest monument. Smaller and brighter than Fogadalmi Templom is the 1778 **Palánki Szerb Templom** (Serbian Orthodox Church), Somogyi Béla u. 3, across the street. Inside, the iconostasis holds 60 gilt-framed paintings, and the ceiling fresco of God creating the Earth swims in a sea of stars (open whenever there's someone around to collect the 50Ft admission). Just southwest of Dóm tér on Aradi Vértanuk tér stands **Hősök Kapuja** (Hero's Gate), an arch erected in 1936 in honor of Horthy's White Guards, who brutally cleansed the nation of "Reds."

At the corner of Hajnóczi u. and Jósika u. lies the 1903 **Zsinagoga,** Jósika u. 8. The temple's Moorish altar and gardens, Romanesque columns, Gothic domes, and Baroque facades combine to make this the most beautiful synagogue in Hungary. The cupola, decorated with designs symbolizing Infinity and Faith, seems to grow deeper the longer you look up into it. The walls of the vestibule are lined with the names of the 3100 members of the congregation killed in concentration camps. English-speaking guides explain every detail of the building (open May-Sept. Sun.-Fri. 9am-noon and 1-6pm; 100Ft, students 50Ft). Next door, **Régi Zsinagoga** (Old Synagogue), now a theater, is disintegrating at the same speed that renovation progresses.

Frolic on the Tisza River on the summer-only disco boat **Szőke Tisza,** just off Roosevelt tér (*Kaiser* beer 150Ft; no cover; open daily until 4am). Discoers move on to **Sing-Sing** in Mars tér once the weather gets colder. During the school year, join *Szegedi* students in their very own heavy metal joint at **Jate Klub,** in the Toldi u. entrance to the central university building on Dugonies tér, for a little taste of America (Rolling Rock 120Ft). Party nights are Thursday, Friday, and Saturday (200-300Ft cover), and the doors don't close until 4am. The recently-opened **Grand Cafe,** an artsy little joint on the third floor of Deák Ferenc u. 18 (tel. 31 35 78), is the place to relax with friends or meet young Hungarians (beer 120Ft). At the **HBH Bajor Serfőzde (Beer House),** Deák Ferenc u. 4 (tel. 31 39 34), in the heart of the city, you can see how beer is made and promptly forget what you've learned (130-192Ft per glass; open Mon.-Sat. 11:30am-midnight, Sun. 11:30am-11pm).

The **Szegedi Szabadtéri Játékok** (Open-Air Theater Festival), mid-July to mid-August, is Hungary's largest outdoor theater festival. International troupes perform folk dances, operas, and musicals in an amphitheater with Fogadalmi Templom as a backdrop. Tickets (400-1500Ft) are sold at Deák u. 28/30 (tel. 47 14 66; fax 47 13 22) and at Tourinform.

■ Kecskemét

Nestled amid vineyards, fruit trees, and the *puszta* (plains), Kecskemét (CATCH-keh-MATE) lures tourists with museums and its famous *barack pálinka* (apricot brandy). On the old road between Istanbul and Hamburg, Kecskemét developed as the crossing point of traders' routes, and was mentioned as early as 1368 as a market town. The architecture captivates at every turn, with everything from Hungarian Art Nouveau to colorful mosaic tile. The road between Szeged and Budapest passes near the *puszta,* the sandy lands of which surround Kecskemét.

ORIENTATION AND PRACTICAL INFORMATION

The town centers around a loosely connected string of squares. The town hall rises on **Kossuth tér,** which leads east into **Szabadság tér** and **Kálvin tér. Katona tér** is immediately south of the town hall, and **Jokai tér** and **Széchenyi tér** are two blocks north. The **train station** lies 10 to 15 minutes east of town along the main boulevard, **Rákóczi út.** The **bus station** is around the corner from the train station. **Local buses** head into town from the train station. **Volán bus** will leave you next to the local bus station immediately north of Kossuth tér. Tickets are available from the driver (63Ft).

Tourist Offices: Tourinform, Kossuth tér 1 (tel./fax 48 10 65), in the town hall's right-hand corner. Tons of free brochures organized by language. Basic maps free, detailed ones will cost you. Lots of info on opportunities in the *puszta;* get it here, because obtaining it in English on the plains is harder than making a horse drink. Open Mon.-Fri. 8am-6pm, Sat.-Sun. 9am-1pm; off-season Mon.-Fri. 8am-5pm, Sat. 9am-1pm. **Cooptourist,** Kettemplom kőz 9 (tel. 48 14 72), on the little pedestrian street between Szabadság tér and Kossuth tér. Good rates on private rooms (see **Accommodations,** below). **IBUSZ,** Kossuth tér 3 (tel. 48 69 55; tel./fax 48 05 57), next to Hotel Aranyhomok. Private rooms, visas, and discount international bus, train, and plane tickets. Open Mon.-Fri. 8am-5:30pm, Sat. 9am-noon.

Currency Exchange: Numerous banks in the city center offer services and rates similar to those at **Budapest Bank,** at the intersection of Nagykőrősi u. and Wesselenyi u. Forints for traveler's checks, and a **24hr. ATM** (Cirrus, EC, MC, and Visa). Open Mon. and Thurs. 8am-1pm and 3-5pm, Tues.-Wed. 8am-1pm, Fri. 8am-11:30am.

Trains: Kodály Zoltán tér, at the end of Rákóczi út (tel. 32 24 60). To: Budapest (13 per day, 1¼hr., 600Ft); Szeged (17 per day, 1hr., 376Ft); and Pécs (via Kiskunfélegyháza, 5hr., 988Ft).

Buses: Kodály Zoltán tér (tel. 32 17 77). To: Balatonfüred (1 per day, 5hr., 1260Ft); Budapest (26 per day, 1½hr., 560Ft); Debrecen (2 per day, 5hr., 1260Ft); Eger (3 per day, 2½hr., 1010Ft); Pécs (3 per day, 5hr., 1260Ft); and Szeged (13 per day, 1¾hr., 568Ft).

Public Transportation: Volán buses (50Ft from kiosks, 63Ft from driver). Timetables are posted at most stops—service winds down around 10pm. The main local bus terminal is just north of Kossuth tér.

Car Rental: Hunguest Travel Bureau, Lestártér 2. Open June 15-Aug. 31 Mon.-Fri. 9am-5pm, Sat. 9am-noon; off-season Mon.-Fri. 9am-5pm.

Taxis: 24hr. from stands around the city, or call 48 48 48.

Luggage storage: At the train station. 100Ft per day. Open daily 7am-7pm.

Pharmacy: Mátyás Király Gyógyszertár, Szabadság tér 1 (tel. 48 07 39). Open Mon.-Fri. 7:30am-8pm, Sat. 8am-5pm.

Medical Assistance: tel. 104. Two facilities alternate 24hr. duty: Nyíri út 38 (tel. 48 17 81), northwest of town, and Izsáki u. 5 (tel. 48 43 84), southwest of town.

Post Office: Kálvin tér 10-12 (tel. 48 65 86; fax 48 10 34). Open Mon.-Fri. 8am-8pm, Sat. 8am-2pm, Sun. 8am-noon. **Postal code:** 6000.

Telephones: Both inside and outside the post office. **Phone code:** 76.

ACCOMMODATIONS AND CAMPING

Summer offers all sorts of cheap accommodations in dormitories. Winter travelers have considerably fewer options; the best deals are in private rooms or pensions. Most tourist agencies (see p. 275) locate private rooms. **Cooptourist** rents singles and doubles (2000Ft for two people), with a 30% additional fee on the first day for stays of less than 3 days. **IBUSZ** also has rooms (1200-1500Ft per person).

Hotel Pálma, Hornyik János u. 4 (tel. 32 10 45 or 32 30 94), as close to the heart of the city as possible. Despite the name, it's the Reformed College's dormitory. Rooms are newly redone and super-clean. Bunk beds, showers, toilets, and telephones. Watch out for heat and mosquitoes on the top floor. Doubles 3500Ft; triples 4000Ft; quads 4800Ft; 4- to 8-bed dorms (with lockers) 2000Ft per person.

Tanitóképzo Kollégiuma, Piaristák tér 4 (tel. 48 69 77 or 48 73 48), 2min. from Kossuth tér. Beds in spacious doubles, triples, and quads 1000Ft per person. Washing machine 150Ft. Theoretically only open July-Aug., but try off-season, too.

Caissa Panzió, Gyenes tér 18 (tel./fax 48 16 85), on the 5th floor of a townhouse cloistered behind trees 5-10min. north of Kossuth tér. Head north from the northwestern corner of Jókai tér. Rooms are small, but clean and modern. Singles 2200-2700Ft, with bath and TV 3400Ft; doubles 2700-3200Ft, with bath and TV 4200Ft; triples 4800Ft; quints 4800Ft. Breakfast 390Ft. Curfew 10pm. German and some English spoken. Call ahead.

Autós Camping, Sport u. 3 (tel. 32 93 98). About 15min. southwest of town by Volán bus #1 or 11. Tent sites 350Ft. 400Ft per person, 100Ft tax. Electricity and parking 400Ft each. 4-bed bungalows 4000Ft. Open mid-April to mid-Oct.

FOOD

Numerous restaurants serve standard Hungarian food—lots of onions, flavorful sauces on meat (goose, pork, beef), and the inevitable dish of paprika. The apricot brandy tastes great, but will put hair on your chest.

Öregház Vendéglő, Hosszú u. 27 (tel. 49 69 73), next to Széchenyi krt, a 10-15min. walk from the center. Meat 'n' potatoes Hungarian-style, in a spacious, airy neighborhood restaurant. Main dishes include goulash (260Ft) and "chicken breast à la

Santiago" (390Ft). Open Sun.-Thurs. 11am-10pm, Fri.-Sat. 11am-midnight. 20% discount Sat.-Sun.

Göröd Udvär Étterem, Hornyik J. 1 (tel. 49 25 13). Enjoy Greek food in the courtyard or at small tables indoors. *Szuvlaky* 650Ft; veggie dishes 510Ft; pizza 420Ft. Open daily 11am-11pm.

Borozó, Rákóczi út 3 (tel. 32 22 40). Head here for a quick swig of the local wines (100mL 200Ft) and *barack pálinka* (50mL 95Ft). Open Mon.-Thurs. 6:30am-7pm, Fri. 6:30am-6pm, Sat. 6:30am-noon.

SIGHTS AND ENTERTAINMENT

The salmon-colored **town hall,** Kossuth tér 1 (tel. 48 36 83), built in 1897 during the height of the Hungarian Art Nouveau movement, is Kossuth tér's most impressive building (tours by appointment daily 7:30am-6pm; call 48 36 83 and ask for Földi Margit; 50Ft, in English 300Ft). The 1806 **Roman Catholic Big Church** brandishes its Neoclassical features on Széchenyi tér (open Tues.-Fri. 9am-noon and 3-6pm), and you can brave its rickety wooden floors and wobbly stairs to reach a superb view at the top of the tower (open June-Aug. daily 10am-8pm; 200Ft). If you're not going to the *puszta,* visit the **Magyar Népi Iparművészet Múzeuma** (Museum of Hungarian Folk Art), Serfőző u. 19/a (tel. 32 72 03). In addition to clothes, furniture, and ceramics, the museum displays a sadistic collection of horse whips and painted Easter eggs. Don't worry; the eggs won't hurt you (open in summer Wed.-Sun. 10am-6pm; off-season 9am-5pm; 80Ft, students 50Ft). The **Szórakatémusz Játékszín és Múzeum** (Toy Museum), Gáspár u. 11 (tel. 48 14 69), rotates exhibitions and a permanent collection of old miniature castles, soldiers, and dolls (open Tues.-Sun. 10am-6pm; 50Ft, students 30Ft, Thurs. free). At the same address, the **Naív Muvészek Múzeuma** (Museum of Amateur Artists), Gáspár u. 11 (tel. 32 47 67), displays the sculptures and paintings of amateur artists from the area in a white 18th-century manor (open Tues.-Sun. 10am-6pm; 100Ft, students 50Ft, Thurs. free).

The Art Nouveau **Kecskeméti Galéria,** Rákóczi út 1 (tel. 48 07 76), displays the works of *Kecskeméti* artists (open Tues.-Sun. 10am-5pm; 100Ft, students 60Ft, Thurs. free). Inside the cupola-topped **synagogue** (now the Technika Háza), Rákóczi út 2 (tel. 48 76 11), sit 15 full-size copies of Michelangelo sculptures, including the head of *David* and a *Pietà* (open Mon.-Fri. 9am-6pm; 40Ft, students 20Ft). The **Katona József Színhaz** (Theater), Katona tér 5 (tel. 48 32 83), not only puts on excellent drama, but is also located in a magnificent 1896 building (off-season operettas 400-500Ft). For raucous disco fun, here's to you, **Club Robinson,** Akadémia krt. 2 (tel. 48 58 44; open 7pm-3am). For a more laid-back evening, try **Kilele Music Cafe,** Jokai 34 (tel. 32 67 74). Beer runs 160Ft for 0.5L, and there's sometimes live rock or jazz (100-150Ft cover; open Mon.-Fri. noon-2am, Sat. 6pm-4am, Sun. 6pm-1am).

Kecskemét has produced such greats as composer Zoltán Kodály (1882-1967) and author József Katona (1791-1830), and continues its artistic tradition each March with the **Kecskemét Spring Festival,** featuring music, theater, literature, and visual art. In late August and early September, witness the "Hírös" ("famous") **Food Festival.**

■ Near Kecskemét: Bugac

Bugac (boo-GATS)—where cowboys roam the *puszta* and rustle up goulash under the stars—brushes up against the Kiskunság National Park. Sand lizards and vipers share the park with gray cattle, twisted-horned sheep, and the Mangalica pig. Bugac is very large—start with a visit to **Bugac Tours,** Szabadság tér 5/A, Kecskemét (tel. 48 25 00; fax 48 16 43; email: bugac@mail.datanet.hu; http//www.datanet.hu/~bugac), to find out how to make the most of your day. The most popular destination for those with fast-shutter cameras is the 40-minute **horse show.** Since the cowboys were constantly on the move due to raids, they taught their horses all kinds of tricks, such as lying down with their masters to hide. When the Hungarian half-breeds perform now, it's all for show: tricks include sitting at the dinner table and shaking hands with their masters. The performance culminates with the breathtaking "Koch five-in-hand," in which a horseman drives a band of five horses at a staggering speed while he stands with one foot on the rumps of the two back horses. (Shows take place May 1-Sept. 15 at 1 and 3 pm and in April and Oct. with enough people. Tickets 1400Ft, students 700Ft, including park admission and a carriage ride; without carriage ride 700Ft, students 350Ft. 30min. trek from bus stop to horse show.)

The national park offers some lovely hikes and bike rides in the hilly juniper forest. **Táltos Panzió** (tel. 37 26 33; fax 37 25 80), next to Bugaci Csárda in Bugac-Felső, or Bugac Tours in Kecskemét are the best places to arrange horseback riding (1200-1500Ft per hour), carriage rides (800Ft per hour), bike rentals, and wintertime sledding (must be arranged in advance). At the intersection of Beton út and Főld út, a summer souvenir shop offers **tourist information** and directions. The **national park ticket office,** about 1km past the souvenir shop and right before Bugac-Puszta, offers a lot of info, but the staff's English ability depends on who is working that day.

Bugac Puszta, where you'll find the horse shows, is about 6km north of Bugac and not directly accessible by public transportation—prepare to walk! The **narrow-gauge train** (tel. 32 24 60) leaves from Kecskemét's little train station (not the main station), on Halasi u. Head down Batthyány u. from the center and cross the overpass (about 20min. walk). The train (1hr.) stops at four places in the Bugac area. The first—**Bugac-Puszta**—is *not* where the horse shows are. The next—**Bugac** town—is best if you're looking for a private room. **Bugac-Felső** is closest to the riding school and Bugaci Csárda (see below), about halfway between the town of Bugac and where the horse shows take place. This is the most central stop. Continue along the tracks until a sand path crosses the tracks, turn right, and follow the path for 10 minutes. If your only destination is the *puszta,* get off at **Móricgát-Tanyak** and walk west across the fields toward the white houses in the distance. For a good daytrip, take the 8:25am train, which meanders through the countryside to Bugac (250Ft, students 125Ft; buy tickets on the train). Return to Kecskemét either by the 6:35pm train or bus from Bugac. The Kecskemét tourist office also arranges daytrips (see p. 275).

To spend the night, head for the **private rooms** in Bugac proper (about 1500Ft per person). Several *csárdas* in town serve the specialties of the *puszta,* with dancing and Gypsy music to boot. Live the high life at the elaborate **Bugaci Csárda** (tel. 37 25 22), which sated—nearly—even the appetites of the horse-mad British royal family (hence the pictures). The house specialties are the ham-filled pancakes (400Ft), deep-pot goulash (300Ft), and for dessert, *palacsinta* (pancakes with apricot marmalade, 250Ft; open daily 8am-10pm).

TRANSDANUBIA

Transdanubia, the southwest half of Hungary, is known for rolling hills and expansive sunflower fields. Originally Pannonia, a Roman province, Transdanubia later witnessed the 1566 bloody Battle of Szigetvár that ended the Ottoman's push for Vienna. The Austro-Hungarian Empire rewarded the region with Baroque and Rococo architecture. Towns like Tata, Székesfehérvár, and Fertőd—home of the "Hungarian Versailles"—cause your Budapest-dominated perception of Hungary to fade away.

■ Pécs

Take 2000 years of history, add raucous collegians, and you have the recipe for Pécs (PAY-ts). On the street, students and locals sit, sip, and stroll, while towering monuments recall the city's more turbulent years under Roman, Ottoman, Habsburg, and Nazi rule. Tourists have long appreciated the town's dynamic combo, and each year foreigners flock to admire ancient history over a cup of java.

ORIENTATION AND PRACTICAL INFORMATION

Pécs rests on the knees of the Mecsek mountain range; conveniently, north and south correspond to up and down the hillside. Tourists bustle through the historic **inner**

HUNGARY

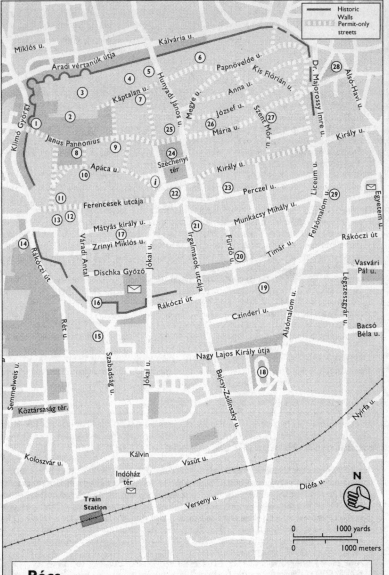

Pécs

Amerigo Tot Museum, **4**
Barbakán (Barbican), **1**
Belvárosi templom (Church of inner town), **24**
Bóbita Bánszínház, **27**
Bus Station, **18**
Csontváry Museum, **9**
Ferences templom (Franciscan Church), **13**
IBUSZ, **22**
Irgalmasok temploma (Church of the Brothers of Mercy), **21**
Jakováli Haszán Museum, **14**
Janus Pannonius Museum, **6**

Kis Galéria (Small Gallery), **11**
Liszt Ferenc Zeneművészeti Foisbola (Francis Liszt Academy of Music), **17**
Mecseki Bányászati Múzeum (Mining Museum of Mecsek), **26**
Memi pasa fürdője--romok (Memi Pasha's baths--ruins), **12**
Modern Magyar Képtár Kortás Gyüjtemény (Picture Gallery of Hungarian Modern Art), **15**
Nemzeti színház, **23**
Néprajzi Museum, **16**
Ókeresztény mausóleum (Old-Christian Mausoleum), **8**

Püspöki palota (Bishop's Palace), **2**
Régészeti Múzeum (Archeological Museum), **25**
Római sírkápolna (Roman Mausoleum), **10**
Synagogue, **20**
Székesegyház (Cathedral), **3**
Szt. Ágoston-templom (St. Austin's Church), **28**
Termeszettudományi Múzeum (Museum of Natural Science), **19**
Várostörténeti Múzeum (Museum of the History of Pécs), **29**
Vasarely Museum, **7**
Zsolnay Museum, **5**

city, a rectangle bounded by the remnants of the city wall. The middle of the inner city is **Széchenyi tér,** where **Jokai u., Király u., Hunyadi Janos u., Ferencesek u.,** and **Janus Pannonius u.** converge, and where most tourist offices are located. The inner city is small enough for pack-toters to visit on foot; it takes less than 20 minutes to cross from north to south (more to get back uphill).

Tourist Office: Tourinform, Széchenyi tér 9 (tel. 21 33 15; fax 21 26 32). Info on local entertainment and travel. Xeroxed maps (free), tourist **maps** (250Ft), and a building-by-building guide to Pécs's history (60Ft). English spoken. Open daily June-Aug. 9am-2pm; Sept.-May 8am-4pm.

Budget Travel: Mecsek Tours, Széchenyi tér 1 (tel. 21 33 00; fax 21 20 44). This travel agency specializes in trips out of Pécs, sells telephone cards and bus tickets, changes money, and arranges tours and private rooms. English spoken. Open June-Aug. Mon.-Fri. 9am-5pm, Sat. 9am-1pm; Sept.-May Mon.-Sat. 8am-3:30pm.

Currency Exchange: IBUSZ bank, at Széchenyi tér's south, end cashes most traveler's checks with no commission. Open Mon. 8:15am-5pm, Tues.-Thurs. 8:15am-4pm, Fri. 8:15am-3pm, Sat. 9am-noon. 24hr. **ATM** takes Cirrus, EC, MC, and Visa.

Trains: (tel. 31 24 43). Just beyond the bottom of the city's historic district, 10min. by bus #30 or 34 from the center of town. Several regular trains chug daily from Budapest-Déli station (3hr., 1112Ft). *InterCity* trains (tel. 21 27 34) speed to Budapest (2 per day, 2½hr., 1112Ft plus 250Ft reservation). 4 trains per day leave for various towns around Lake Balaton. Purchase tickets at the **MÁV travel office** in the station or at Rákóczi út 39c.

Buses: (tel. 41 52 15). Walking distance from the center, at the intersection of Nagy Lajos Király út. and Alsómalom u. To Budapest (8 per day, 3hr., 980Ft) and Szigetvár (8-14 per day, 40min., 204Ft).

Public Transportation: City bus tickets cost 60Ft.

Bookstores: International English Center, Mária u. 9 (tel. 31 20 10). New and used books, and English newspapers. Open Mon.-Fri. 10am-6pm. The Center runs a cafe/library that stocks *Newsweek* and *National Geographic.* Open July-Aug. Mon.-Fri. 10am-6pm; Sept.-June Mon.-Fri. 10am-8pm, Sat. 9am-1pm.

Post Office: Jókai Mór u. 10 (tel. 21 44 22). Open Mon.-Fri. 8am-8pm, Sat. 8am-2pm, Sun. 8am-noon. **Postal code:** 7621. **Phone code:** 72.

ACCOMMODATIONS AND CAMPING

Private rooms can be arranged at the inner city's tourist offices. For stays of less than three nights, a 30% fee is added to the first night's price. **Mecsek Tours** (see above) seeks out singles (1100Ft) and doubles (1800Ft).

Janus Pannonius University Dormitory has several campuses around Pécs; rooms are available July-Aug.; call ahead Sept.-June to see if there is space. **Universitas u. 2** (tel./fax 32 44 73). Take bus #21 from main bus terminal to the wooded "48-es tér." Worn but pleasant wood-paneled rooms for up to 3 people (700Ft per person). Laundry facilities. **Szántó Kovács u. 1** (tel./fax 25 12 03). Less central. Take bus #21 from the main bus terminal to "Nendtvich Andor u." The university is across the main road and to the left. Lower floors stay cooler. Laundry facilities. Neat triples (700Ft per person) with floor bathrooms.

Szent Mór Kollégium, 48-es tér 4 (tel. 31 11 99). Take bus #21 to "48-es tér." Doubles (700Ft) in a gorgeous old building. Bathrooms in hall are cleaned daily. Sign up for laundry. Kitchen, meaning a stove and a sink.

Hotel-Camping Mandulás, Angyán János u. 2 (tel. 31 59 81). Take bus #34 from the train station directly to the hills above the city, where tent sites (DM12 for 2 people), 3-bed bungalows (DM35), and doubles with breakfast in a 1-star hotel (DM45) are located at the entrance to hiking trails in the Mecsek Hills. Discounts in low season. Open mid-April to mid-Oct. Call ahead for same-day reservations. For advance reservations, call Mescek Tours (see above).

FOOD

Countless restaurants, cafes, and bars line Pécs's touristy streets —especially Király u., Apáca u., and Ferencesek u.—offering varied menus and crowd-watching opportunities. **Konzum,** Kossuth tér, is an all-purpose grocery (open Mon.-Fri. 6:30am-8pm, Sat. 6:30am-2pm).

Liceum Söröző (tel. 32 72 84), in a cellar off Király u. 35 opposite the Liceum church and through a courtyard. Low prices and a choice selection of beers make this a favorite with the student community. *Gold Fassl* 160Ft. Main courses from 330Ft. English menu. Open Mon.-Thurs. 11am-10pm, Fri.-Sat. 11am-11pm.

Caflisch Cukrászda Café, Király u. 32. Possibly the best and trendiest cafe in town. Sit inside to savor Hungarian sweets, or enjoy the sun with a cold drink and watch Pécs go by. Pastries from 60Ft. Open Sun.-Thurs. 8am-10pm, Fri.-Sat. 8am-11pm.

DÓM Vendéglő Restaurant, Király u. 3 (tel. 21 00 88), through the courtyard, last door on your right. The interior is an impressive two-level wooden reproduction of a church, complete with stained-glass windows. Many roasted meat dishes. German menu. English spoken. Main courses 420-840Ft. Open daily 11am-11pm.

Kolping, Szent István tér 9 (tel. 32 47 12), just north of Ferencesek u. Good *borda* (cutlet) and a rainbow of colorful veggies, with a heavy emphasis on German food. Main courses 420-840Ft. 0.5L *Gösser* beer 280Ft. Open daily 11am-10pm.

SIGHTS

The ornate buildings surrounding Széchenyi tér center around the **Ghasi Khasim Pase Belvarosi Templom** (Ghasi Khasim Pasha Inner City Parish Church), a converted and exorcised 16th-century Turkish mosque built on the site of an earlier Christian church—a fusion of Christian and Turkish history emblematic of Pécs. Cursive Arabic excerpts from the Koran remain as decorative wall designs in the church's interior, and a former absolution basin, where the Turks washed their feet before entering the mosque, has now been turned into a baptismal font. A Rococo alien in the square, **Patika Múzeum** (Pharmacy Museum), Apáca u. 1 (tel. 31 57 02), testifies to the belief that leeches and blood-letting were good and sound techniques to cure anything from stubbornness to political incorrectness (open Mon.-Fri. 7:30am-4:30pm). Stroll along Ferencesek u. to the **Ferences Templori és Kolostor** (Franciscan Church), whose serene exterior hides joyful, exuberant Baroque furnishings. **Jakováli Hasszán Pasa Dzsámija,** Rákóczi u. 2, is a functioning 16th-century mosque (no shorts; open Sun.-Wed. 10am-1pm and 2-6pm; 60Ft, students 30Ft).

North of the Franciscan Church, numerous trees shield Szent István tér from the hot afternoon sun. On the square's east side, 4th-century **Roman ruins** have been slowly decaying since Jupiter and Venus went out of business. Underneath lies the largest known burial site in Hungary (open Tues.-Sun. 10am-6pm). Rising above a **mausoleum,** across an open square, the **Bazilika** (cathedral) stands proudly as Pécs's centerpiece. Masons have been piling on additions to the 4th-century foundation since the first bricks were laid (open Mon.-Sat. 9am-1pm and 2-5pm, Sun. 1-5pm; 200Ft, students 100Ft). To the west, the **Barbakán** is a popular walking spot and a vestige of the great double-walled defense of the 15th century.

East of the inner-town, **Várostörténeti Múzeum** (History Museum), Felsőmalom u. 9 (tel. 31 01 65), chronicles Pécs's subordination under the Ottomans, Habsburgs, Nazis, and Communists. Pécs was above dreary labor productivity races, and programmed its conveyor belts to turn out elegance—porcelain, musical instruments, and champagne (open Tues.-Sun. 10am-4pm; 100Ft, students 50Ft, off-season students free). **Zsolnay Múzeum,** Káptalan u. 2, exhibits the finest examples of the world-famous Zsolnay porcelain produced in Pécs since the mid-19th century (open Tues.-Sun. 10am-6pm; 160Ft, students 80Ft). The neighboring **Vasarely Múzeum,** Kaptalan u. 3, houses the works of one of the most important Hungarian 20th-century artists, Pécs-born Viktor Vasarely, the father of the Op-Art movement (open Tues.-Sun. 10am-6pm; 160Ft, students 80Ft). South of Széchenyi tér, a 19th-century **synagogue** stands on Kossuth tér (open Sun.-Fri. 9am-5pm; 60Ft, students 40Ft). The

Jewish population in Pécs hovers at 300; 88% of the prewar population was killed during the Holocaust.

ENTERTAINMENT

Nightlife in Pécs settles in the crowded, cheerful bars and restaurants near Széchenyi tér, especially on the first two blocks of Király u. For pierced body parts and loud music, the local alternative scene is the best outside of Budapest.

Rózsakert Sörkert/Rosengarten Biergarten, Janus Pannonius u., east of the cathedral. The place to go for a sobering breeze and live Hungarian gypsy music in a German-inspired outdoor setting. 0.5L *Gold Fassl* 180Ft. Open daily 11am-11pm.

Kioszk Eszpresszo, opposite Janus Pannonius u. 1. A cafe/beer garden popular with lesbians, gay men, and heteros alike (open daily 11am-11:45pm).

Blues Pub, Apáca u. 2. On weekends, this pub attracts slightly more mature Pécs youths who've learned to converse, carouse, and consume one cigarette after another. After a few *Stella Artois* (160Ft), you might begin to feel dizzy in this 5-level Surrealist structure. Open daily 11am-1am.

Hard Rák Cafe, Ipar u. 7 (tel. 22 71 44), at the corner of Bajcsy-Zsilinszky u. Plays rock, alternative, and hard-core. The grotto inside comes complete with cave paintings. Don't get run over by the bands arriving in VW buses. Open Mon.-Sat. 7pm-past 4am. Cover 240Ft when live bands play.

■ Near Pécs

SZIGETVÁR CASTLE

In 1566, 50,000 Turks besieged the Croatian viceroy Nikola Šubić Zrinski (Miklós Zrínyi in Hungarian) and his 2500 soldiers in **Szigetvár Castle.** After a month-long struggle, with their drinking water exhausted and the inner fortification in flames, Zrínski's army launched a desperate attack against their aggressors. They were wiped out, but managed to kill a quarter of the Turkish force in the process. This event terminated the Ottoman Empire's expansion to the west. The castle ruins are remnants of a structure built well after the battle and consist mostly of red brick walls with a pleasant park inside. The **Zrínyi Miklós Museum** chronicles the siege (open Tues.-Sun. May-Sept. 9am-6pm; April-Oct. 9am-4pm; 80Ft, students 40Ft).

Buses from Pécs, 33km west (8-14 per day, 204Ft), stop at the town's south end. Walk north 15 minutes to the castle. The English-speaking reception at **Hotel Oroszlán,** Zrínyi tér 2 (tel. 31 01 16; fax 31 29 17), on the way, rents bath-outfitted doubles (3800Ft). **Mecsek Tours** (tel. 31 01 16) in the hotel distributes **maps** (132Ft; open Mon.-Fri. 7:30am-4pm). **Phone code:** 73.

■ Székesfehérvár

With its old narrow streets, 18th-century pastel buildings, and Baroque steeples, one would hardly guess that Székesfehérvár (SAY-kesh-FEH-hair-var) once served as Hungary's first capital. The one-time basilica, built in the early 11th century, hosted all state events until the Turks occupied and ruined the town in 1543. Much of the architecture from the following century remains intact, and ongoing exploration continues to unearth artifacts from earlier periods. A concrete embrace of highrises has given new life to one of Hungary's friendliest and most unpretentious towns.

Orientation and Practical Information Pedestrian **Fő u.** bisects the inner old town. Central **Városház tér** and nearby **Koronázó tér** branch off Fő u. to the west and east, respectively. Székesfehérvár is a major transportation link for Transdanubia. **Trains** ply the rails to: Budapest (30 per day, 1hr., 302Ft); Siófok (18 per day, 1hr., 216Ft); and Veszprém (12 per day, 1hr., 200Ft). **Buses** pass by wide fields of corn on their way to: Budapest (12 per day, 1½hr., 380Ft), Siófok (6 per day,

1hr., 248Ft), and Veszprém (21 per day, 1hr., 248Ft). Trains generally run slightly more frequently than buses, but the bus terminal is more centrally located. From the **bus station,** Piac tér (tel. 31 10 57), just west of Fő u., both **Liszt Ferenc u.** and **Megyeháza u.** travel to Városház tér. From the **train station,** Béke tér (tel. 31 22 93), walk along **Prohászka Ottokár út** until it becomes **Várkőr út.** The old town will be just to your left. The cheerful staff at **Tourinform,** Városház tér 1 (tel./fax 31 28 18), speaks English, gives out free brochures, and sells **maps** (280Ft and up; open Mon.-Fri. 9am-noon and 1-4:30pm). **OTP Bank,** at the corner of Fő u. and Várkapu u., is equipped with a Cirrus/EC/MC/Visa **ATM** (open Mon.-Thurs. 8am-3:30pm, Fri. 8am-1pm). A 24-hour **currency changer** sits at Kossuth u. 14. The **post office** is at Kossuth Lajos u. 16 (tel. 31 22 68; open Mon.-Fri. 8am-8pm, Sat. 8am-2pm, Sun. 8am-noon). **Postal code:** 8000. **Phone code:** 22.

Accommodations and Food The folks at **Albatours,** Kossuth Lajos u. 14a (tel. 31 24 94; fax 32 70 82), offer four-person apartments (1800Ft; open Mon.-Fri. 9am-5pm). The staff at **Tourinform** (see above) know everyone in town who has rooms, and will be glad to direct you. **Rév Szálló,** József Attila u. 42 (tel. 31 44 41; fax 32 70 61), at the corner of Bodai út, equips its doubles with TVs (2200Ft), but strips triples down to the bare minimum (1800Ft); all rooms have shared baths. Call ahead—they are often full. The summer dorms of **József Attila Kollégium,** Széchenyi István u. 13 (tel. 31 31 55), cost 1000Ft per bed. Space might be available even before school lets out in late June. The dorms are cleaner than average, but still have no shower curtains. **Campground Székesfehérvári Kemping,** Bregyó-köz 1 (tel. 31 34 33), runs a well-equipped, pleasant campground and three-person bungalows (650FT per person; 315Ft per tent and 250Ft per person). Athletic facilities abound nearby.

Skip the abundant pizza places in favor of the inexpensive, untouristed restaurants serving national cuisine. The local favorite, **Ősfehérvár Étterem,** Koronázó tér 2 (tel. 31 40 56), has German, French, and Russian menus, and a Hungarian list of daily specials. Outdoor tables are right over the basilica's excavation work (main courses 290-800Ft; open daily 11am-10pm). There's live gypsy music every day except Sunday. Come to **Arany Csengő Vendéglő,** Megyeház u. 10, for *galuska* (dumplings; 120Ft) and tasty *káposztasaláta* (coleslaw; 60Ft). Simple, good eatin', and not a tourist in sight (open Mon.-Sat. 5pm-8pm). The **McDonald's** across from the bus station is open 24 hours. **Kaiser's** supermarket, Kyegl Györg u., just northeast of the Romkert (Garden of Ruins), has everything you'll need (open Mon.-Fri. 8am-7pm, Sat. 8am-1pm).

Sights and Entertainment Start your walking tour of Székesferhérvár in **Városház tér,** the old town's center. The **fountain** in the middle represents the royal orb, which, along with the crown and scepter, served as one of the three symbols of the Hungarian king's authority. The lime-green Baroque **városház** (town hall), was built in 1698 and enlarged in 1936-37. Directly to the east, on Koronázó tér, spreads the **Romkert** (Garden of Ruins). This courtyard contains the remains of Hungary's first **basilica;** St. Stephen, the country's first Christian king, built the basilica between 1016-38, when Székesfehérvár was the Hungarian capital. Here, 37 kings were crowned and 17 buried. Unfortunately, all that's left is some riveting rubble. When the Turks took the city in 1543, they used the basilica as a gunpowder storehouse; in 1601, an accidental explosion blew the building to smithereens. The excavation that has turned most of Koronázó tér into a sand pit is currently unearthing parts of the basilica that fared slightly better. Scattered throughout the garden and displayed near the walls are fragments of stonework and sculpture. Archaeologists now generally concur that the sarcophagus on the right as you enter once contained the remains of St. Stephen himself (open April-Oct. Tues.-Sun. 9am-5pm; 50Ft, students free).

Koronázó tér's long, yellow **Püspöki Palota** (Bishop's Palace), built from 1790-1801, soon after the city became a bishopric, was constructed largely of stones from the old basilica. It is still the bishop's residence, but tourists can occasionally wheedle a glimpse of the 40,000-volume library. The twin-spired building to the south of the square on Arany János u. is **Szent István templom** (St. Stephen's Cathedral), not to be confused with the church of St. János of Nepomuk, which is also yellow and also has two towers, but is smaller and north of Varosház tér on Fő u. St. Stephen's was built between 1759 and 1778 on the site of the tomb of Stephen's dad, Grand Duke Géza, the founder of Székesfehérvár. Unless mass is in session, visitors must view the airy hall with its Baroque frescoes from the glass doors in the vestibule. The white paving stones on the street in front outline the foundations of the 10th-century church thought to have contained Géza's tomb. Don't miss the original, bent crucifix adorning the northern facade of the church. The white 1470 **Szent Anna-Kápolna** (St. Anna's Chapel), on the north side, was a mosque during the Turkish occupation. On the cathedral's east side is **Hősök tere,** dedicated to WWI heroes.

A courtyard off Jókai u. holds a wrought iron sign that says **Törökudvar** (Turkish Yard). From the street, it resembles a small vacant lot gone to weed, but it's the site of a 16th-century Turkish bath now under excavation. Stonework and brick arches are becoming visible as work progresses. The **Szent István Király Múzeum** (King St. Stephen Museum) fills several buildings in town with Hungary's second-largest collection, after the National Museum in Budapest. The main building's **Állandó Régeszeti Kiállítása** (Permanent Exhibition of Archeology), Fő u. 6 (tel. 31 55 83), spans the history of Fejér county from the first settlement to the 1600s, including a particularly large collection of Roman artifacts. There is even a small exhibition on the Turkish bath on Jókai u. (English explanations; open Tues.-Fri. 10am-4pm, Sat.-Sun. 1-5pm; 80Ft, students 40Ft). **Rotating art exhibitions** are shown in the branch of the museum at Országzászló tér 3 (tel. 31 17 34; open Tues.-Sun. 10am-4pm; 100Ft, students 50Ft).

Budenz-ház Ybl Gyűjtemény (Budenz House: Ybl Collection), Arany János u. 12 (tel. 31 30 27), shelters the collection of the Ybl family, including their 18th- to 20th-century Hungarian art and furniture. The house itself, named after the linguist József Budenz, who lived here from 1858 to 1860, was built in 1781, but its foundations date from the Middle Ages (open Tues.-Sun. 10am-2pm; 100Ft, students 50Ft). Jesuits built **Fekete Sas Patikamúzeum** (Black Eagle Pharmacy Museum), Fő u. 5 (tel. 31 17 34), in 1758 and it remained a functioning pharmacy until 1971. All the original woodwork is still intact (open Tues.-Sun. 10am-6pm; donations encouraged).

One man's expression of artistic whimsy, the ferro-concrete-and-brick **Bory-vár** (Bory Castle), at Bory tér on the city's northeast edge, could be the playground for the ultimate game of hide-and-seek. Over 40 summers, architect and sculptor Jenő Bory (1879-1959) built it by hand as a memorial to his wife. The towers, gardens, crooked paths, winding staircases, incongruous statuary of historical figures, and stone chambers crowded with works of art were all meant for exploring. It is nearly deserted on weekdays. Take bus #26a from the terminal at Piac tér or #32 from the train station to the intersection of Kassai u. and Vágújhelyi u. (next to the white storefront with turquoise trim; tickets cost 60Ft on the bus, 40Ft at the terminal). Then walk north on Vagújhelyi u. to Bory tér (open Mon.-Fri. 9am-5pm, Sat.-Sun. 10am-noon and 3-5pm; 100Ft, students 50Ft). North of town, a chain of exceptionally well-kept parks and lakes offers ample opportunity for relaxation. At the far end is a **sports park** with facilities for volleyball and tennis (350Ft per hour).

Late-night carousers can grab a cold draft *Dreher* (0.5L 150Ft) at **Dreher Maximka Söröző,** Ady Endre u. 4 (open Sun.-Thurs. 10am-midnight, Fri.-Sat. 10am-4am). **Vörösmarty Theater,** Fő u., and the **open-air theater,** Pelikán u., put on music and theater performances nearly every night. Get tickets (300Ft and up) and schedules at the box office at Fő u. 3 (tel. 31 45 91; open Mon.-Fri. 9am-6pm).

■ Szombathely

Big Szombathely (SOM-ba-tay) likes to act small, as if it were still Claudia Savaria, a first-century Roman colony. Seat of Vas county and a major crossroads between Transdanubia and Austria, the city fills on weekends, with clusters of people promenading among 2000-year-old ruins and Baroque facades. Szombathely's unparalleled selection of cafes, pubs, and restaurants refuel tired strollers readying for yet another crawl through the town's architectural treasures.

ORIENTATION AND PRACTICAL INFORMATION

The inner city of Szombathely can be crossed on foot in 20 minutes. The town focuses on several squares, the largest of which is **Fő tér.** The main tourist offices are located around **Mártírok tere,** a few blocks north. The **train station** lies northeast of the inner city; to reach Mártírok tere, take **Széll Kálmán u.** straight down. The **bus station** is in the northwest part of the inner city; find Mártírok tere by following **Petőfi Sándor u.** east and **Király u.** south.

Tourist Office: For German information and maps, your best bet is Tourinform-licensed **Savaria Tourist,** Mártírok tere 1 (tel. 31 22 64). Open Mon.-Fri. 8am-5:30pm, Sat. 8am-noon. If you speak German, buy a slightly outdated, but still valuable *Reise-Führer: Komitet Vas* describing all the sights in the entire Vas region.
Currency Exchange: OTP Bank, Király u. 10, across the street from the tourist office. Open Mon.-Thurs. 8am-3pm, Fri. 8am-1pm. Around the corner at Széll Kálmán u. 1, stands a Cirrus/MC **ATM.**
Trains: (tel. 31 20 50). To: Budapest (7 per day, 3½hr., 1168Ft); Győr (2 per day, 3hr., 600Ft); Keszthely (2 per day, 3½hr., 700Ft); Sopron (7 per day, 2hr., 326Ft); and Veszprém (12 per day, 2½hr., 700Ft).
Buses: (tel. 31 20 54). To: Budapest (3 per day, 3½hr., 1214Ft); Győr (7 per day, 2hr., 704Ft); Keszthely (3 per day, 3hr., 500Ft); Sopron (7 per day, 2hr., 690Ft); and Veszprém (3 per day, 2hr., 1010Ft).
Post Office: Kossuth Lajos u. 18 (tel. 31 15 84). Open Mon.-Fri. 8am-8pm, Sat. 8am-2pm, Sun. 8am-noon. **Postal code:** 9700.
Telephones: Inside and outside of the post office. **Phone code:** 094.

ACCOMMODATIONS AND CAMPING

There aren't many private rooms to rent in Szombathely, and they're difficult to discover on your own. **Savaria Tourist** offers centrally located doubles (1700-2000Ft) in the homes of people who could be your grandparents. **IBUSZ,** Fő tér 44 (tel. 31 41 41), also offers doubles (2000Ft; open Mon.-Fri. 8am-5:30pm, Sat. 9am-noon).

Orlay Hostel, Nagy Kar u. 1/3 (tel. 31 23 75), next to the bus station. 8-bed dorms (500Ft per person). More spacious than most, but still no shower curtains. Check-out 8am. Open in summer daily, off-season weekends.
405 Kollégium, Ady tér 2 (tel. 31 21 98), next to bus station. Clean college dorm. 4-bed dorms (500Ft per person). Open in summer daily, off-season weekends.
Hotel Liget, Szent István Park 15 (tel. 31 41 68). From the bus station, the #7 bus stops outside. Sparkling doubles with private baths, TVs, and breakfast (5850Ft).
Péterfy Kollégium, just west of the inner city at Magyar László u. 2 (tel. 31 26 53), near the bus station. 2- and 7-bed rooms (450Ft per person). Open in summer daily, July-Aug. weekends.
Camping: Tópart Camping, Kondics u. 4 (tel. 31 47 66). 4-person bungalows 3000Ft (6000Ft with bath); 5-person bungalows for 2800Ft. To camp, it's 300Ft per tent and 300Ft per person. Open May 1-Sept. 30.

FOOD

Szombathely offers a wide selection of top-notch restaurants and supermarkets. The **Julius Meinl** supermarket, Fő tér 16, isn't the best stocked, but will gladly accept MC and Visa (open Mon.-Fri. 7am-8pm, Sat. 7am-2pm).

Gődőr Étterem, Hollán Ernő 10. Exquisite Hungarian specialties for more-than-reasonable prices. Low ceilings, subtle lighting, and a classy staff make this Szombathely's top choice for a dinner date. The delicious *bakonyi sertésborda* (bakony schnitzel) is worth every forint at 440Ft. Main courses 400-560Ft, wine 60Ft per glass. Open Mon.-Thurs. 11am-11pm, Fri.-Sat. 11am-midnight, Sun. 11am-3pm.

HUNGARY

Gyöngyös Étterem, Széll Kálmán u. 8 (tel. 31 26 65). Reliable and popular. Main dishes run 350-550Ft, but there's also a cheaper daily set menu. Specialties include *pörkölt* (stew) and *sertésszelet* (schnitzel). Open Tues.-Sun. 10am-10pm.

Király Bisztró, Király u. 3. Cheap Hungarian sausages, sandwiches, and pastries for around 150Ft. Pizza 235Ft. Open Mon.-Fri. 6am-6pm, Sat. 6am-1pm.

Korzó étterem, Mártírok tere 5. Slightly classier and slightly less Magyar than others, this fine restaurant offers excellent meat specialties such as *marhagulyás* (beef stew; 480Ft) and *borjú pecsenye* (steak; 550Ft). Open daily 10am-11pm.

SIGHTS AND ENTERTAINMENT

The **Katedrál** at Templom tér, built in 1797 as a cross between Baroque and Neoclassical styles, is adorned with frescoes and gilt ornaments. An Allied bombing raid in 1945 all but flattened the building, and so far the efforts at reconstruction have been slow; hence the bare ceilings and lack of pews. Directly behind the cathedral stretches the north side of the **Romkert** (Garden of Ruins), the center of the city's original first-century Roman colony. The ruins from several different periods have been excavated, and visitors can walk among town walls, roads, a bathhouse, parts of a palace, official buildings, and floor mosaics. An English-speaking guide may be around to explain everything in copious detail (open April-Oct. Tues.-Sun. 10am-6pm; Nov.-March 10am-4pm; 100Ft, students 50Ft).

The **Smidt Múzeum** (Smidt Museum), Hollán Ernő u. 2, is the result of Dr. Lajos Smidt's obsession with collecting just about everything he could lay his hands on. Like a garage sale gone berserk, each case is packed with weapons, watches, coins, clothing, tableware, Roman artifacts, and ancient maps. The museum vividly conveys 19th-century Szombathely life, and an antique beer mug's inscription *"Bier ist Gift!"* (Beer is Poison!) warns of premature death from cirrhosis—what's the population of Germany these days? (Open Tues.-Sun. 10am-5pm; 80Ft, students 40Ft.)

Iseum, Rákóczi Ferenc u. 2, is the reconstructed remains of the Temple of Isis built by Roman legionnaires in the 2nd century, but it looks more like the wreck of an urban municipal building; all the missing parts were rebuilt using concrete, and the edifice stands in a weed-strewn lot bordered by an office block. The shed-like structure at the north side houses an exhibit about the temple (open Tues.-Sun. 9am-4pm). Across the street at Rákóczi Ferenc u. 3, shoot up the two spires of the former **synagogue,** a late 19th-century Moorish-revival structure. The unchanged facade hides an interior that has been remodeled into a concert hall. A **memorial** outside remembers the 4228 Jews deported to Auschwitz from that spot during the Holocaust.

The **Savaria Múzeum,** Kisfaludy Sándor u. 9 (tel. 31 25 54), unearths the roots of Vas county, including natural history exhibits and Roman and medieval artifacts (open Tues.-Fri. 10am-5pm, Sat.-Sun. 10am-4pm; 100Ft, students 40Ft).

West of the inner city spreads the **Múzeum falu** (Village Museum), Árpád u. 30, a re-created village consisting of 150- to 200-year-old farmhouses transplanted from throughout the region. The rooms of each home are authentically decorated; the "owner's" clothes are even laid out. All maintenance is done using traditional techniques, although knowledge of them is rapidly dwindling; a century ago, a thatched roof could last 60 years, but nowadays no one can figure out how to make them secure for more than 20. The English-speaking guide can explain everything, but is usually off on Saturdays. A visit here is worth the 25-minute walk from Fő tér (open May-early Nov. Tues.-Sun. 10am-5pm; 80Ft, students 40Ft).

On the west side of town, a series of **parks** provides opportunities for relaxation. Perhaps with Budapest in mind, Szombathely set a large, abstract **monument** dedicated to the 1945 liberation on the highest hill they could find. Farther north, a lake, complete with island, offers a more romantic atmosphere. Swimming is only allowed, however, in the huge **pool,** across the street at Jazsai M. u. 2 (open Mon.-Fri. 9am-8pm; 100Ft). Near the summer solstice, these parks host the season's festivities.

On weekends and evenings, **Fő tér** is the site of concerts, other performances, or primo people-watching. For something even sweeter, get tasty pastries, like *krémes* (cream-pie; 120Ft), at **Rózsa Cukrászda,** Éhen Gyula tér 2, (open Mon.-Fri. 10am-

8pm, Sat.-Sun. 9am-7pm). **Gődőr Söröző,** Hollán Ernő 10, is a popular pub housed in the cellar of the bishop's 19th-century brewery (0.5L *Amstel* draft 140Ft; open Mon.-Sat. 11am-midnight). **Zipfer Söröző,** Aréna u. 1 (tel. 31 17 89), serves fine meals (250-680Ft) and even finer lagers in the wood-and-plaster surroundings of the former Franciscan monastery's cellars (open Mon.-Sat. 11am-11pm).

■ Near Szombathely: Kőszeg

Kőszeg (KEW-seg), on the Austrian border, is almost venerated by the natives, who treasure this tiny fortification for its picturesque medieval cityscape, its history, and especially its 15th-century **Szent Jakab Templom** (St. Jacob's Church)—one of Hungary's best-known Gothic edifices. Between **Város Kapu** (City Gate) and its counterpart, **Bécsi Kapu** (Vienna Gate), medieval burghers' dwellings line Rájnis and Schneller u. The biggest, if not the most impressive, sight in town is the **Jurisich vár** (Jurisich Castle), Rájnis u. 9. First built in the 13th century, it was rebuilt in the 18th century after a fire. In the summer, the inner yard of the castle serves as an open-air theater (castle museum open Tues.-Sun. 10am-6pm; 100Ft, students 50Ft). **Trains** reach Kőszeg from Szombathely (1 per hr., 30min., 70Ft); **buses** come less often from Szombathely (6 per day, 45min., 114Ft) and Sopron (3 per day, 1½hr., 190Ft). The Szombathely bus from Sopron stops first at the train station and then closer to the center. Step off, and turn right on Kossuth Lajos u.; one block up is **Várkör** (Castle Ring), one of the main streets. From the train station, cross the little bridge and bear right up Rákóczi u. about 1km into the center. **Savaria Tourist,** Várkör 69 (tel. 36 02 38), offers doubles in **private homes** (2000Ft; German spoken; open Mon.-Fri. 8am-4pm, Sat. 8am-noon). The upscale yet affordable **Bécsikapu Söröző,** Rájnis 3 (tel. 36 02 97), prepares pork according to recipes that hark from Kiev and Tokaj (400-1000Ft; open daily 11am-10pm). Decipher the Magyar menu and enjoy local delicacies or plentiful beer with the locals at **Kiskakas Vendéglő** (open daily 9am-9pm). Opposite is the **Julius Meinl supermarket** on Rákóczi u. 25 (open Mon. 6am-6pm, Tues.-Fri. 6am-6:30pm, Sat. 6am-2pm). **Phone code:** 94.

LAKE BALATON

Aspiring to be the glam Baywatch beach-land of Central Europe, shallow Lake Balaton has become one of the most coveted vacation spots in the area. Villas first sprouted along its shores during the Roman Empire, and when a railroad linked the lake to its surroundings in the 1860s, the area mushroomed into a favored summer playground. Today, the region's rich scenery and comparatively low prices draw mobs of German, Austrian, and Hungarian vacationers. Once school lets out, the lakeside becomes raucous and crowded with young people, but at other times you will meet mostly retirees and kids.

> Storms roll in over Lake Balaton in less than 15 minutes, raising dangerous whitecaps on the otherwise placid lake. Amber lights on top of tall hotels and the Meteorological Research Center at Siófok's harbor give **weather warnings;** 30 revolutions per minute means stay within 500m of shore; 60 revolutions per minute means swimmers must be within 100m and boats must be tied on shore.

■ Siófok

Siófok (SHEE-oh-fok) is not only the largest town on Lake Balaton, but is also its main tourist center. The fact that more tourist offices per square kilometer congregate here than in any other Hungarian city says something about the numbers of surf- and bargain-starved German-speaking tourists who descend on Siófok each year. May to September, Siófok is abuzz by day at its beach, and by night at its discos. In cooler months, tourists vanish and the town all but closes down.

Orientation and Practical Information Siófok runs east-west along Bala-ton's south shore. **Trains** run to Budapest (7 per day, 3hr., 540Ft) and Pécs (6 per day, 3½hr., 902Ft). A **gyorsjárat** (fast bus) leaves for Budapest (4 per day, 2½hr., 718Ft), and another goes to Pécs (3 per day, 3hr., 796Ft). The quickest way to the north side of the lake is by the hourly **MAHART ferry** that docks next to the verdant **Jókai Park,** 10 minutes from the train station (Balatonfüred, 50min.; Tihany, 80min.; 350Ft to either port). The **train** and **bus stations** are adjacent to each other in roughly the center of town. The main **Fő u.** is just south of the train station. A **canal** connect-ing the lake to the Danube bisects the town. The **Arany-part** (Gold Coast) on the east side is the home of the older, larger hotels, while the **Ezüst-part** (Silver Coast) on the west has the newer, less expensive ones. **Tourinform,** Fő u. 41 (tel. 31 53 55; fax 31 01 17), in the base of the wooden water tower, has English-speakers on staff and car-ries **maps** (open July-Aug. Mon.-Sat. 8am-8pm, Sun. 8am-1pm; Sept.-June Mon.-Fri. 9am-4pm). **IBUSZ,** Fő u. 174, 2nd floor (tel. 31 14 81), is a bit closer to the bus and train stations (open June-Aug. Mon.-Sat. 8am-6pm, Sun. 9am-1pm; Sept.-May Mon.-Fri. 8am-4pm). To **exchange currency,** visit **Postabank,** Fő u. (tel. 17 41 76). An **ATM** and a **bill changer** lurk outside (open Mon.-Sun. 9:30am-noon and 12:30-7pm). There is a **pharmacy** at Fő u. 202 (tel. 31 00 41; open Mon.-Fri. 9am-3:30pm). The **police** sta-tion is at Sió u. 14 (tel. 31 07 00). **Telephones** stand outside the **post office,** at Fő u. 186 (tel. 31 02 10; open Mon.-Fri. 8am-6pm, Sat. 8am-1pm). **Postal code:** 8600. **Phone code:** 84.

Accommodations and Food A myriad of agencies offer **private accommo-dations.** If you prefer to search on your own, **Erkel Ferenc u.,** to the west of the canal, and **Szent László u.,** to the east, are residential streets close to the water with rows of *Panzió* and *Zimmer Frei* signs. **Tourinform** (see above) charges no commis-sion and will mediate in the negotiation of rates. Doubles in the center of town aver-age 2200Ft in July and August; prices drop slightly off-season. **IBUSZ** (see above) offers doubles for 2000Ft in July and August. There is a 30% surcharge for staying fewer than four nights. **Tuja Panzió,** Szent László u. 74 (tel. 31 49 96), provides well-equipped singles and doubles with satellite TV, shower, and fridge (2600Ft per per-son; less off-season). **Hunguest Hotel Azúr,** Vitorlás u. 11 (tel. 31 20 33), off Erkel Ferenc u., offers bright doubles with bathrooms (2000Ft). **Aranypart Camping,** Szent László u. 183-185 (tel. 35 28 01), 5km east of the town center, opens April to September (500Ft per person plus 1000Ft tax).

Csárdás, Fő u. 105 (tel. 31 06 42), serves up traditional Hungarian dishes and live native music. Main courses hover around 600-900Ft (open daily 11am-11pm). The central **Kálmán Imre,** Kálmán Imre sétány 1, near Fő u. and Mártirok u., prepares spiced turkey breasts (780Ft) and chicken paprika (580Ft); its taps run with *Steffl* beer (0.5L 280Ft; open daily 10am-10pm). The less-expensive **Kristály Étterem,** Petőfi sétány 1, dishes out schnitzel with *lecsó* (pepper and tomato; 460Ft) and *Gösser* beer (240Ft). There is a massive fruit and vegetable **market** south of Fő u. just west of the canal. Look for the **Vásárcsarnok** building (open Mon.-Fri. 7am-6pm, Sat. 7am-1pm, Sun. 7am-noon). Next door to the market, gourmands can find the choic-est crumpets at the **Julius Meinl grocery** (open Mon.-Fri. 6:30am-8pm, Sat.-Sun. 6:30am-1pm).

Sights and Entertainment Most attractions in Siófok pale in comparison with the **Strand,** which is not a beach but a series of park-like lawns that run to the extremely un-sandy concrete shoreline. There are public and private sections, with some private spots charging at least 80Ft per person, depending on the location and whim of the owner. The most centrally located section is the town park, but swim-ming isn't allowed. The largest private part lies right to the east (open Mon.-Fri. 8am-7pm; 150Ft). Most sections rent water bikes and sailboards. **Nightclubs** of varying degrees of seediness line the lakefront, while amphibious lounge lizards frolic to ABBA and the Bee Gees on the funky **Disco Boat** (500Ft; leaves the harbor July 9-Aug. 21 nightly 9:30pm). Another boat, with a live pop music band, offers a 1½-hour

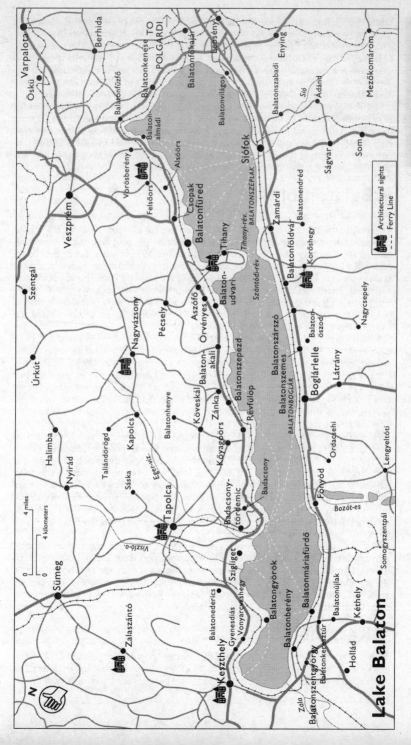

Lake Balaton

Architectural sights
Ferry Line

N

4 miles
4 kilometers

cruise (500Ft; July-Aug. 21 nightly 7 and 9pm). If you're out of Dramamine, dance the night away at **Flört Disco,** Sió u. 4 (open nightly 9pm-5am). **Kajman Pub Disco,** Fő u. 212, swears it doesn't play techno (open nightly 10pm-4am; cover 200Ft). For a taste of home—if you're German—the **Sörbár,** Kálmán Imre étany, west of the pedestrian overpass, is a pleasantly shaded beer garden with *Zipfer* and *Weiselburger* on tap (open daily till midnight). Since many of Siófok's night clubs feature nude or semi-nude dancers; inquire beforehand if you're not into that kind of entertainment.

Siófok is also the hometown of composer Imre Kálmán. In his honor, an **operetta** is performed nightly in the Kultúrcentrum, Fő tér 2, near the water tower. During high season, the town hosts the annual, four-day **International Folk Dance Festival.** For info on schedules and tickets, visit the **Kálmán Imre Múzeum,** Kálmán Imre sét-any, next to the train station (open daily 9am-5pm; 100Ft). The church at Fő u. 57 has biweekly evening organ concerts (400Ft, students 300Ft).

◼ Balatonföldvár

Celtics, and then Romans, settled the area of Balatonföldvár (BA-la-ton-FEWLD-var) long before the Magyars had even bought a copy of *Let's Invade: Eastern Europe.* In the mid-17th century, the village of Földvar became the property of the powerful, aristocratic Széchenyi family, and at the end of the 19th century Count Széchenyi converted it into one of the most beautiful tourist towns on Balaton. Voted "the most flowery town in Hungary" in 1995, and winning the "Europe Prize" for its cleanliness and floral ornament in 1994, the town of Balatonföldvár truly enthralls with its parks and promenades. If you are a flower lover, a walk through the **central park** around Bajcsy Zsilinszky u. may take you long time. The 1200m long promenade along the lake borders a fine **Strand,** Balaton-style.

Trains connect Balatonföldvár to Budapest (8 per day, 3¼hr., 700Ft) and Pécs (4 per day, 3¼hr., 900Ft). From the train station, walk west until you hit the main tourist artery, Széchenyi út. **Buses** zoom to Budapest (4 per day, 2¾hr., 720Ft) and Siófok (22 per day, 30min., 90Ft) from the bus stop on the main Budapesti út. From the bus stop, walk down Széchenyi út toward the lake to reach the **Siotour office,** Széchenyi út 9-11 (tel. 34 00 99). It offers free **maps** and pamphlets and help with accommoda-tion (private doubles 1800Ft per person). The **post office** sits on the corner of Bajor Gizi and Hősök útja. **Phone code:** 84.

Hotel Park, Szécheny u. 1 (tel. 34 01 18; fax 34 04 53), has cozy, newly refurbished doubles (2000Ft per person; including breakfast). **Magyar Tenger Camping,** Kemp-ing u. 6 (tel. 34 02 40), is clean, well-equipped, and close to the beach, although it is also very close to the train tracks (700Ft for tent, 500Ft per person per day). Széche-nyi u. abounds with restaurants and pubs—take your pick. For excellent Hungarian-style pizzas (420-800Ft), try **Mini-Italia pizzeria,** Szechenyi u. 5. **Vitamin,** Camping út. 6/b (tel. 34 06 82), reels in splendid Hungarian fish specialities (from 300Ft). A well-equipped **Julius Meinl** grocery store awaits on Budapesti út. near the bus stop (open Mon.-Sat. 7am-8pm, Sun. 7am-midnight).

The 80s and 90s beats of popular **Keringő Disco,** on Széchenyi u. near the post office, attract crowds of Germans and Austrians (open daily 10pm-morning; 300Ft cover). **Disco-ship M.S. Gulács** departs from the main quay for two hours of wild "boat-rocking" (Tues.-Wed. and Fri.-Sun. 9am; 600Ft, children 360Ft). The second weekend in June witnesses the colorful **Földvárer Festival;** with folk music, amateur sport competitions, and arts and crafts flea market.

◼ Keszthely

With its 18th-century architecture and large student population, Keszthely (KESS-tay) graces the lake's west tip. The town's claim to fame is the elegant and decadent Fes-tetics Kastély (Festetics Palace), but its parks and beaches are also worth exploring.

Orientation and Practical Information In summer, **ferries** run to and from Keszthely, and **boats** take passengers to Badacsony on the north shore (1 per day, 2hr., 340Ft) and Balatonboglár on the south shore (1 per day, 2½hr., 450Ft). **Express trains** run between Keszthely and Budapest (5 per day, 3hr., 920Ft). **Slow trains** make the trip to Szombathely (2 per day, 2hr., 648Ft). **Buses** beat trains for local travel: Balatonfüred (8 per day, 2hr., 384Ft); Pécs (5 per day, 3hr., 560Ft); and Veszprém (16 per day, 2hr., 402Ft). Some buses leave from the terminal, while others use stops in the town center at either Fő tér or Georgikan u. Each departure is marked with an "F" or a "G" to indicate which stop it uses. The **train station** and **bus terminal** are adjacent to each other, about 250m from the water. The main **Kossuth Lajos u.** runs north-south, with the **Festetics Kastély** (Festetics Palace) at its head. After **Fő tér,** it becomes a pedestrian street. To reach Kossuth Lajos u. from the train station, walk straight up **Mártirok u.** Turn right to get to Fő tér. **Tourinform,** Kossuth Lajos u. 28 (tel./fax 31 41 44), sits just north of Fő tér (open Mon.-Fri. 9am-5pm, Sat.-Sun. 9am-1pm). **IBUSZ** (tel. 31 29 51) occupies Kossuth Lajos u. 27 (open June-Aug. Mon.-Sat. 8am-6pm, Sun. 9am-1pm; Sept.-May Mon.-Thurs. 8am-4pm, Fri. 8am-3pm). **OTP Bank,** at the corner of Kossuth Lajos u. and Helikon u., **exchanges currency** (open Mon.-Thurs. 8am-3pm, Fri. 8am-1pm) and offers a Cirrus/MC/Visa **ATM.** An agency **rents bikes** at Kossuth Lajos u. 54 (900Ft per day). The **post office,** Kossuth Lajos u. 48 (tel. 31 42 32), lies two blocks south of Fő tér (open Mon.-Fri. 8am-8pm, Sat. 8am-noon). **Postal code:** 8369. **Phone code:** 83.

Accommodations and Food Tourinform (see above) finds four-person apartments (7000Ft). **IBUSZ** (see above) offers private doubles (2500Ft). **Zalatour,** Kossuth Lajos u. 1 (tel. 31 43 01), also has doubles (2200Ft; open Mon.-Sat. 8am-9pm, Sun. 8am-noon). If you'd rather strike out on your own, homes with *Zimmer Frei* signs are most common near the Strand, especially on Erzsébet Királyné u. **Mr. Athla Lukic's** cozy *panzió,* Jókai Mór u. 16 (tel. 31 12 32), has attractive doubles (6000Ft). **Vajda J. Középiskola Kollégiuma,** Gagarin u. 4 (tel. 31 13 61), can provide a dorm bed (1200Ft; open late June-Aug.); reserve at least two days ahead. **Castrum Camping,** Móra Ferenc u. 48 (tel. 31 21 20), has four-person bungalows (4000Ft) and tent sites (400Ft per tent, 400Ft per person; open May-Sept.).

The restaurants centered around Fő tér are obscenely overpriced, but there are more remote, and reasonably priced, eateries farther from the center. **Béke Vendéglő** (tel. 31 24 47), on the corner of Kossuth Lajos u. and Balaton u., offers generous quantities of tasty food in a shaded courtyard (main courses 520-900Ft). Drafts of good *Zipfer* run 200Ft (open Mon.-Thurs. 11am-10pm, Fri.-Sat. 11am-11pm). **Gösser Restaurant,** Erzsébet Királyné u. 23, north of the Strand, creates culinary delights out of the rich fish stocks of Lake Balaton, including carp and trout (400-900Ft; open Mon.-Sat. 11am-10pm). **Donatello,** Balaton u. 1b, brings Italian cuisine to Hungary with a plethora of pastas (320-800Ft) and pizzas (340-720Ft; open daily noon-11pm).

Sights Keszthely's pride is the **Helikon Kastélymúzeum,** in the **Festetics Kastély** (Festetics Palace). Built by one of the most powerful Austro-Hungarian families, the storybook palace does Baroque architecture proud. Of the 360 rooms, tourists may visit only the central wing. The palace includes the 90,000-volume Helikon Library, an arms collection that spans a thousand years, and rooms full of artwork and period furniture. **Concerts** are often held in the mirrored ballroom during summer. Check your bag at the door and pad through the collection wearing tie-on shoe covers (open Tues.-Sun. 9am-6pm; 560Ft, students 230Ft; English or German tour 2000Ft). The surrounding **English park** provides a vast and well-kept strolling ground. To find the palace, follow Kossuth Lajos u. north until it becomes Kastély u. You can't miss it—it's the only one on the block.

Keszthely is very much alive during the day at the **Strand,** which covers much of the coast on the side of the train tracks opposite the town. With rocks instead of sand and swamp instead of waves, it's a wonder that it's still such a major people magnet (120Ft). **Balatoni Múzeum,** Múzeum út. 2 (tel. 31 23 51), on the corner of Mártirok u., displays Balaton's indigenous wildlife and ethnographic history (open Tues.-Sun. 10am-5pm; 80Ft, students 50Ft). **Georgikon Majormuzeum** (Georgikon Farm Museum), Bercsényi u. 67 (tel. 31 15 63), presents an amusing deification of György Festetics, who founded Europe's oldest agricultural university here in 1797. Exhibits detail the history of European agriculture (open April-Oct. Tues.-Sat. 10am-5pm, Sun. 10am-6pm; 60Ft, students 30Ft). Don't miss the **church** on Fő tér; its pastel green tower, built in 1896, hides the fact that the main part of the structure, dating from 1386, remains one of the most important standing works of Gothic architecture in Hungary. There are no Baroque frescoes here, but some beautiful stained glass, and 14th-century wall paintings in the sanctuary.

Six kilometers northwest, **Hévíz** is home to Europe's largest **hot-water lake,** covered in gigantic lilies. The water is a calm-inducing 26-33°C (77-91°F). The huge lake covers 4.5 hectares, but the spring filling the lake pumps so fast that the water is entirely replaced every 28 hours. A large **bathhouse,** Dr. Schüller Vilmos sétány 1 (tel. 34 04 55) extends right to the center of the lake (open daily 8:30am-5pm; 349Ft for 3 hr.). Buses from Keszthely's Fő ter visit this gigantic hot tub hourly.

■ Tihany

With its lush vegetation, luxurious homes, and extensive panoramas, the Tihany (TEE-hain) peninsula is the pearl of Balaton. Although every bit as touristy as the rest of the lake, Tihany has somehow managed to escape rampant commercialization. The main attraction is the magnificent **Bencés Apátság** (Benedictine Abbey), with its Baroque altars, pulpit, and organ (open daily 9am-6pm; 120Ft, students 60Ft). In the same complex, the **I. András kriptája** (András I crypt) from 1055 contains the remains of one of Hungary's earliest kings. Next door, an 18th-century monastery has been reincarnated as the **Tihany Museum,** with psychedelic dreamscapes, colorized etchings, and Roman inscriptions displayed in a cool, subterranean lapidarium (open March-Oct. Tues.-Sun. 10am-6pm; 60Ft). Follow the *strand* signs along the Promenade behind the church to get to the beach (open daily 7am-7pm; 100Ft). Clearly Tihany's strangest sight, the **garage-gallery** of painter, artist, writer, and professor Gergely Koós-Hutás, Fürdőtelep 43, lies only a five-minute climb from the wharf, and includes massive canvases of didactic Lenins. Better yet, **hike** across the Peninsula (check out the map by the church first). It only takes an hour or two along the dirt roads and paths that pass through hills, forests, farms, and marshes. Best of all, you may never see another person except the occasional worker pruning his vineyard.

Buses frequently pass by the beaches at both Tihany and the more popular Tihanyi-rév. In summer, the **ferry** to Tihany departs from Balatonfüred's pier (every 20min., 20min., 180Ft). **Balatontourist,** Kossuth Lajos u. 12 (tel. 44 85 19), a block from the bus stop, can arrange a room in the village (2800-3800Ft; open Mon.-Sat. 8:30am-6:30pm, Sun. 8:30am-1pm). It's expensive, but not as pricey as the lakefront rooms five minutes away. For some nourishment, the outdoor terrace of **Rege Coffeehouse,** Kossuth u. 22 (tel. 31 82 80), next to the church, sells drinks, ice cream, and what may be the best pastries along Lake Balaton.

THE ŐRSÉG

In the far west corner of Hungary, low-flying storks guard the bucolic region known as the Őrség. During the Cold War, authorities discouraged visitors and Hungarian citizens alike from entering the Őrség, as it was too close to the capitalist Austrian and Titoist Yugoslav borders. Thus, a region that had always been a little behind the times—electricity didn't arrive until 1950—became even more distanced from the step of the modern world. Tourists now arrive more frequently to catch this slice of timelessness, and the locals of the Őrség hardly mind; here, hospitality is a way of life.

■ Őriszentpeter

Rolling hills, cool forests, and beautiful countryscapes combine to make the Őrség a biker's and hiker's paradise. The centrally located Őriszentpeter (Ö-ree-sent-PEH-ter) makes an excellent starting point. Foremost of the tiny Őrség villages, the town still regulates its busiest intersection with yield signs. The bridgeless street running north-west-southeast will take you to a sign for **camping** up a short driveway to the left. The reception is **Savaria Tourist,** Városszer 57 (tel. 42 80 46); the same friendly folks run the **Fogadó,** the local inn, and can arrange **private rooms.** (Some German spoken. Camping 200Ft per tent, 400Ft per person; a room inside with a shared shower is 2000Ft. Open whenever someone's around.) You may be able to pick up a **map** of the Őrség area at Savaria Tourist, real or hand-drawn. Try finding a map in larger towns before you arrive. They also **rent bikes** (400Ft per day). To reach another **campground** (tel. 92 37 14 67), turn right from the station, then left on Petőfi u. until you see a trail off to the right at #131 to **Borostyán lake** (tent 300Ft, 400Ft per person; 2-person bungalows 1600F; **rent bikes** 500Ft per day). **Zalalövő** is the village closest to the lake.

The decent **Centrum Etterem,** at the main intersection, dishes out main courses (400Ft). **ABC Market** (open Mon.-Fri. 7am-noon and 1-5pm, Sat. 7am-noon) and a few **bars** cluster around the main intersection 110m downhill from the **bus station;** no trains run here. The quickest way to get here is to take the **train** to **Körmend** (10 per day from Szombathely, 45min., 102Ft), and then turn left and walk parallel to the tracks until you reach the bus station (13 per day to Őriszentpeter, 30min., 136Ft). Less frequent **buses** also arrive here from the nearby towns of Zalalövő and Svent-gotthard (both on the rail line), as well as Sopron and Szombathely. **Postal code:** 9941. **Phone code:** 94.

Hiking, Biking, and Sights Hiking offers choice choices in the Őrség. The entrance to the trail network is just past Őriszentpeter's Savaria Tourist, up the stairs to your left—climb every mountain, ford every stream, follow…Wait! This is Hungary, not Austria. (For *The Sound of Music,* see *Let's Go: Austria and Switzerland*).

The old saw about "the journey, not the destination" becomes clear in this scenic area. Select roads at random to feel the whole rhythm of life. **Museums** freckle the Őrség, and more medieval **churches** stand here than anywhere in Hungary. Visitors shouldn't be shy about knocking on nearby doors and asking for keys; this is also true for the local **artisans' studios** (marked *Fazekasház* in the case of potters).

You might wish to "randomly" select one of the following routes. Leaving Őriszent-peter to the west, after 6km you will pass through the village of **Szalafő.** Before you reach the town, a sign to your left will point to a 13th-century **church.** Continue past the town and over the bridge, veer left, and at the top of the hill you'll find a model 19th-century **farm community.** Wander around the silent houses, and peek in the windows (the museum is theoretically open March-Nov. daily 10am-6pm; 60Ft, students 30Ft). Farther past Szalafő lies **Fetete-to,** a huge peat bog home to a number of rare, insectivorous plants (open May-Oct. 7am-sunset, Oct.-May 7am-4pm). About 12km south of Őriszentpeter, the villagers in **Magyarszombatfa** stoke backyard kilns in which to fire plates, bowls, and jugs (so sturdy you can cook *gulas* in them). Or, approaching Őriszentpeter from the north, be sure to catch **Batthyány Castle** in Kör-mend (open Tues.-Sun. 10am-6pm) and the 1256 **Romanesque church** in Ják.

■ Győr

Although closely associated with the Rába truck factory, Győr (dyur) maintains a cer-tain charm. Some of Hungary's finest 17th- and 18th-century buildings crowd the inner city, and an occasional horse-drawn cart still plods through rush-hour traffic at the lazy pace of the Danube tributaries that nourish the town.

Orientation and Practical Information The train station lies south of the inner city; the underpass that links the rail platforms leads to the **bus station.** **Trains** chug to: Budapest (11 per day, 2½hr., 700Ft); Veszprém (7 per day, 2hr., 380Ft); and Vienna (6 per day, 2hr., 3618Ft). **Buses** head to Budapest (every hr., 2½hr., 670Ft) and Veszprém (every hr., 2hr., 504Ft). Packed with free **maps,** brochures, and friendly smiles, a **Tourinform kiosk** awaits at Árpád ú. 32 (tel. 31 17 71), one block north of the train station (open Mon.-Sat. 8am-8pm, Sun. 9am-1pm). A few blocks north, **IBUSZ,** Kazinczy u. 3 (tel. 31 17 00), is bigger, but less Győr-oriented (open Mon.-Tues. and Thurs. 8am-3:30pm, Wed. and Fri. 8am-3pm). **OTP Bank,** at the corner of Czuczor Gergely u. and Árpád u., has good **exchange** rates, but to cash traveler's checks, you'll have to go to a post office (open Mon.-Fri. 7:45am-3pm, Sat. 7:45am-1:30pm). The **ATM** at **Magyar Külkereskedelmi Bank,** Bajcsy-Zsilinsky út 19, links to Plus and Cirrus. The **post office** is at Bajcsy-Zsilinszky út 46 (tel. 31 43 24; open Mon.-Fri. 8am-8pm). Cash traveler's checks at the *Postabank* desk (no commission). **Postal code:** 9001. **Phone code:** 96.

Accommodations and Food In July and August, accommodations in downtown Győr overflow, and rooms can be hard to find without reservations. **Tourinform** (see above) makes various **private rooms** available (singles start at 1800Ft; doubles 2200Ft). **IBUSZ** (see above) only has doubles (2000Ft and up). If you stay for less than four nights with either agency, expect to pay a 30% surcharge. The English-speaking staff of **Hotel Szárnyaskerék,** Révai Miklós u. 5 (tel. 31 46 29), right outside the train station, rents clean doubles (2750Ft, with private bath 4200Ft). Just north of the Mosoni-Duna River, **2sz. Fiú Kollégium** (Boys' Dormitory No. 2), Damjanich u. 58 (tel. 31 10 08), offers 3-4 bed dorms (600Ft per bed; open daily mid-July through Aug.; off-season weekends). **Széchenyi Istvan Főiskola Kollégiuma,** entrance K4, Hédevári út 3 (tel. 42 97 22), north of the river, has dorm-room triples (600Ft per bed, students 550Ft; open mid-July through Aug.). Let the large mosquitoes smashed on the walls be a warning to close the windows at night. **Kiskút liget Camping,** Kiskút liget (tel. 31 89 86), has a year-round motel, as well as camping and bungalows open April 1-October 15 (motel triples 3300Ft, quads 4000Ft, 6-bed dorms 5000Ft; 4-person bungalows 2800Ft; campsites 400Ft per tent, 400Ft per person).

The enthusiastic teenage waitstaff at **Sárkányluk** (Dragon's Hole), Arany János u. 27 (tel. 31 71 16), runs a popular bistro that fill quickly (main courses 320-900Ft; open Mon.-Sat. 11am-9pm, Sun. 11am-3pm). **Napoleon Pince,** Munkácsy Mihály u. 6 (tel. 32 03 14), just south of the Petőfi Bridge, is a French restaurant with an English menu, slightly more upscale than the run-of-the-mill *étterem* (main courses 480-1000Ft; open daily noon-midnight). The bar/restaurant **Paradiso,** Kazinczy u. 20, offers huge, tasty *menűs* (500Ft). At night, the ground floor transforms into a smooth bar (open daily 9am-1am). A good **Julius Meinl** grocery store sits at the corner of Baross Gábor and Árpád (open Mon.-Fri. 6am-8pm, Sat. 6am-1pm).

Sights and Entertainment The **city hall** is the most magnificent building in Győr; it stands a few steps from the train station. Most sights, however, lie within a rough triangle between Bécsi Kapu tér, Káptalandomb, and Széchenyi tér. Bécsi Kapu tér is the site of the yellow 18th-century **Karmelita-templom** (Carmelite church) and the remains of a **medieval castle** built to defend the town from the Turks. A small branch of **Xantus János Múzeum** (János Xantus Museum), built into the castle at Bécsi Kapu tér 5, contains a lapidarium with Roman stone carvings and monuments (open Tues.-Sun. 10am-6pm; 50Ft, students 30Ft). To the east of the square at Kiraly u. 4, the house where **Napoleon Bonaparte** spent his only night in Hungary now contains an art gallery and music school called **Napóleon Ház.**

At the top of **Káptalandomb** (Chapter Hill), the **Székesegyház** (Episcopal Cathedral) has suffered constant additions since 1030. Its exterior is now an incoherent hybrid of Romanesque, Gothic, and Neoclassical styles. The Baroque splendor inside deserves more attention, with dozens of golden cherubim flying around magnificent frescoes. A priest fleeing **Oliver Cromwell's** regime in the 1650s brought the miraculous **Weeping Madonna of Győr** all the way from Ireland. On St. Patrick's Day 1697, the painting is rumored to have spontaneously wept blood and tears for three hours in compassion for persecuted Irish Catholics. The **Herm of King St. Ladislas,** a masterwork of Gothic goldsmithery in the Hédeváry chapel on the cathedral's south side, is a wide-eyed bust of one of Hungary's first saint-kings. **Egyházmegyei Kincstáv** (Ecclesiastical Treasury) on the hill, presents an extensive assortment of ornate gold and silver religious accessories dating back to the 14th century, but the real eye-catcher is an impressive collection of 15th- and 16th-century illuminated texts. The exhibits are marked in English (open Tues.-Sun. 10am-5pm; 100Ft, students 50Ft). The way to Széchenyi tér leads through Gutenberg tér past the religious monument **Frigylada szobov** (Ark of the Covenant), built by the king in 1731, with funds levied on his mercenaries in order to keep them impoverished and in line.

Patkó Imre Gyűjtemény (Imre Patkó Collection), in **Vastuskós ház** (Iron Log House; named for the stump into which traveling 17th-century craftsmen drove nails when they spent the night), Széchenyi tér 4, contains two floors of fine works by modern Hungarian artists, and a smaller room devoted to foreign masters such as Picasso and Chagall. The loft holds a collection of Asian and African works that Patkó amassed in his travels (open Tues.-Sun. 10am-6pm; 50Ft, students 20Ft). The entrance is from the narrow street between #3 and #5. **Kovács Margit Gyűjtemény** (Margit Kovács Museum), Rózsa Ferenc u. 1, one block north of the square, displays the artist's distinctive ceramic sculptures and tiles (open Tues.-Sun. April-Oct. 10am-6pm, Nov.-March 10am-5pm; 100Ft, students 50Ft). Some will love it, some will call it kitsch, but all must agree that there is something extremely smile-inducing about Kovács's queens and soldiers.

The Iron Rooster Crows Again

Unmarked against a corridor wall in the **János Xanthus Museum** leans an inconspicuous iron rooster weathervane with a half-moon at its base. When Turks invaded and occupied Győr, they erected it on the town's highest tower, and bragged that they would hold the town until the cock crowed and the half-moon changed phase. The Hungarians took the boast seriously, and crowed like cocks under a full moon as they began the siege that eventually retook the city.

In summer, do as the locals do—spend less time in the musty museums, and more time splashing in the water and enjoying the sun. Across the river from the center of town, **thermal springs** serve as the basis for a large water park (Czirákytér and Tőltésszev u. 24), complete with swimming, saunas, massages, and water slides (open Mon.-Fri. 6am-8pm, Sat.-Sun. 7am-6pm; 160Ft, students 130Ft). Work on your tan with a good portion of the city. Fishing, rowing, and swimming in the river are all popular, but if the murky water doesn't appeal, check out the several shady, though poorly kept, **parks** south of the train station. Head straight down u. Zrínyi or Tihanyi Árpád út. The best park is one block east of the city hall. A peaceful resting spot of another kind is the **temető** (cemetery) at the southern edge of town; the most interesting memorials lie just inside the gates (open daily 7am-8pm). The white church at the west side of the cemetery deserves a peek; head out through the modern, **sliding stained-glass doors** and back to town. The **market** on the river transmogrifies into a **bazaar** on Wednesday, Friday, and Saturday mornings.

Wine drinkers crowd the mellow **Troféa Borozó,** Bajcsy-Zsilinszky 16 (open daily 6am-10pm), and beer-bellies gurgle in unison at the **Komédiás Biergarten,** in the courtyard at Czuczor Gergely u. 30 (*Amstel* 160Ft; open daily until midnight).

Győr frolics away June and July with **Győri Nyár,** a festival of daily concerts, drama, and ballet. Buy tickets at the box office on Baross Gábor út or at the performance venue. Schedules are found at Tourinform and IBUSZ.

■ Near Győr: Archabbey of Pannonhalma

Eighteen kilometers southeast of Győr, the hilltop **Pannonhalmi Főapátság** (Arch-abbey of Pannonhalma; tel. (96) 37 01 91) has seen 10 centuries of destruction and rebuilding since it was established by the Benedictine order in 996. It now boasts a 13th-century Romanesque and Gothic basilica, a library of 360,000 volumes, a small art gallery, and one of the finest boys' schools in Hungary. The Benedictine abbey at Tihany was established by a 1055 royal charter—the oldest document bearing Hungarian words—that is also kept here (see **Literature**, p. 240). If you walk back and forth in front of the painting *The Body of Christ* in the gallery, the body seems to rotate so that the feet always point toward the viewer. There is also a **Gregorian chant mass** every Sunday at 10am for the chic and religious. Frequent classical music concerts take place in the acoustic halls of the abbey: inquire at Pax Tourist (tel. 57 01 92). To see the abbey, join an hourly tour group at the Pax Tourist office at the entrance. English-speaking guides are usually available for the mandatory one-hour tour; otherwise, follow along with an excellent English brochure (abbey open daily 8:30am-4pm; 400Ft, students 150Ft). Pannonhalma is an easy daytrip from Győr by **bus** (7 per day, 45min., 158Ft; ask for Pannonhalma vár), but bring a snack—there's nothing to eat or drink here.

■ Tata

The quiet vacation town of Tata stretches around lakes, canals, and a 14th-century castle, providing a restful training ground for the Hungarian Olympic team. If you'd rather go for the beach than the gold, this popular place for sunbathing, boating, and fishing retains the charm of an isolated medieval town. The still waters of the north tip of the lake reflect **Öregvár**, the old castle. Inside the castle is Tata's main tourist attraction, **Kuny Domokos Múzeum,** which holds two millennia of the area's history. Breeze through the two lower floors and head for the third, which hides the work of 18th-century master craftsmen in wood, metal, and porcelain (open Tues.-Sun. 10am-6pm; 120Ft, students 70Ft). The Baroque-style **Eszterházy mansion,** built in 1765 and now used as a hospital, sits between Kastély tér and Hősök tere. Nearby, a converted synagogue at Hősök tere houses **Görög-Római Szobormásolatok Múzeum** (Greek-Roman Statuary Museum), a collection of copies of ancient statues and friezes that once lined the paths of Angol Park (open Tues.-Sun. 10am-6pm; 60Ft, students 30Ft). **Angol Park,** around Cseke-tó, was Hungary's first English-style park, and has managed to maintain its elegance *sans* statuary.

You probably won't see the town name on the **train station,** but get off at the dilapidated yellow building. From the station, walk south on Bacsó Béla u. and make a right on Somogyi Béla u, which ends at Országgyűlés tér. Trains pass through on their way to Budapest (18 per day, 1½-2hr., 524Ft), but you can avoid the mile-long hike into town by taking the **bus** from Budapest (4 per day, 1½hr., 494Ft). Most of the sights and stores lie along the northwestern shore of **Öreg-tó** (Old Lake). **Komturist,** Ady Endre 9 (tel. 38 18 05), on the main drag, sells **maps** (120Ft; open Mon.-Fri. 8:30am-4pm). If the well-stocked **Supermarket Spar** (open Mon.-Fri. 8am-7pm, Sat. 8am-4pm, Sun. 8am-noon) is closed, try the little bakery/food store at Egység u. 18 (open daily 6am-10pm). The **post office** is at Kossuth tér (open Mon.-Fri. 8am-6:30pm, Sat. 8am-noon). **Postal code:** 2890. **Phone code:** 34.

Komtourist (see above) can provide four-person lakefront houses (5600Ft), but more affordable rooms lie along the main street. **Patak Motel,** Fényes fasor 2890 Pf. 62 (tel. 38 28 53), offers clean and pleasant doubles (2200Ft) and quads (4000Ft). The **Hattyú Panzio,** Ady Endre u. 56, supplies tidy, well-furnished singles (2200Ft) and doubles (2900Ft) with private shower and toilet. *Bad-Camping* signs point from the bus station to **Fényes-Fürdő** (tel./fax 38 15 91). Don't worry, it's just a funny attempt to combine German with English: the camp is clean and well-equipped with 4 swimming pools, tennis courts, and laundromat (4-person bungalow 4000Ft; tents 900Ft per person; open May 1-Sept. 30). Follow the signs from the bus station

(2.5km) or take a bus (every 30min.). Locals recommend the fish at **Halaszcsárda** (main courses 360-600Ft; English menu), halfway down the eastern shore, one of many lakefront restaurants.

On weekend nights, the lake comes alive. Live bands play outside on the southern tip; at the north end, the DJ pumps up dance mixes at **Lovas Disco,** just off Tanoda tér; follow the lights in the sky (open Fri.-Sat. 10pm-2am; cover 400Ft). Local youth party late at **Zsigmond Vigadó** (tel. 24 77 46), a hip bar located in the underground caverns on the castle grounds (beer 160Ft per pint; open Mon.-Wed. noon-midnight, Fri.-Sat. 11am-2am, Sun. 10am-10pm).

▓ Sopron

With its soaring spires and winding cobblestone streets, the medieval quarter of Sopron (SHO-pron) feels decidedly German. Yet, as any local will remind you, Sopron is considered "Hungary's most loyal town." In 1920, the Swabians of Ödenburg (as Sopron was then called) voted to remain part of Hungary instead of joining their linguistic brethren in Austria. This fidelity notwithstanding, Sopron is deluged daily by Austrians drawn by low prices for medical care and sausage—especially sausage.

Orientation and Practical Information Belváros (inner town), the historic center, is a 1km-long horseshoe, bounded by **Ógabona tér** and **Várkerület.** At the north end, **Fő tér** is the center of town. The **bus station** is two blocks to the northwest, on Lackner Kristóf, and the **train station** is a 10-minute walk south on Mátyás Király út. **Ciklámen Tourist,** Ógabona tér 8 (tel. 31 20 40), offers free **maps** and advice, but only in German and Hungarian (open Mon.-Fri. 8am-4:30pm, Sat. 8am-1pm). To **exchange currency,** skip the smaller agencies in favor of **Budapest Bank,** Színház u. 5 (open Mon.-Fri. 8am-1pm). **ATMs** outside are linked to Cirrus and Plus. A 24-hour machine that changes many currencies into forints stands at **K&H Bank,** Ogabona tér 9. **Trains** dash to Budapest (7 per day, 3-4hr., 1140Ft), Győr (7 per day, 1hr., 440Ft), and Vienna (16 per day, 1hr., 2578Ft). **Buses** buzz to Budapest (5 per day, 4hr., 1200Ft), Győr (about 1 per hr., 2hr., 568Ft), and elsewhere. The **post office,** Széchenyi tér 7/10 (tel. 31 31 00), lies at the south edge of Belváros (open Mon.-Fri. 8am-8pm, Sat. 8am-noon). **Postal code:** 9400. **Phone code:** 99.

Accommodations and Food Ciklámen Tourist (see above) finds **private rooms** (singles 1600Ft; doubles 2000Ft). **Locomotiv Turist,** Új u. 1, near Fő tér, arranges singles (1400Ft) and doubles (1900-3200Ft; open Mon.-Sat. 9am-5pm). **Talizmán Panzió,** Táncsics u. 15 (tel. 31 16 20), has small but impressively well-kept doubles with TV and shower, but shared toilet (2350Ft). **Középiskolai Fiú Kollégium,** Erzsébet u. 9 (tel. 31 12 60), in the city center, and its sister dorm, **Középiskolai Leány Kollégium,** Ferency János u. 60 (tel. 31 43 66), just west of the center, offer four-bed dorms (560Ft per person; June 20-Aug. 20, off-season weekends). Call in advance to reserve. **Lővér Campground** (tel. 31 17 15), at the south end of town on Köszegi u., has fun four-person bungalows (4100Ft), threesome ones (3300Ft), and huts for conservative couples (2100Ft), as well as campsites (300Ft per tent, 500Ft per person; open April 15-Oct. 15).

Várkerület Restaurant, Várkerület 83 (tel. 31 92 86), near Széchenyi tér, serves up tasty *sertés pörkölt* (stews), homemade dumplings, and veggie main courses (440-800Ft), as well as 0.5L *Zipfer* and *Steffl* (300Ft). There's live piano music in the beer garden (English menu; open daily 10am-midnight). **Pince Csárda,** Széchenyi tér 4 (tel. 34 92 76), upholds its good reputation with a tremendous array of chicken, venison, and veal dishes (450-900Ft; open Mon.-Thurs. 10am-11pm, Fri.-Sat. 10am-midnight). At Széchenyi tér 12, the **John Bull English Pub** (tel. 31 68 39) is a first-class emergency unit for all nostalgic Brits. Fantastic *bázinyulcomb caprima rtássl* (haunch of rabbit with Capri dressing; 690Ft), and vegetarian meals like *trappista sajt rántva* (porsault cheese in bread crumbs; 490Ft); pint of Guinness (378Ft; open daily

10am-2am). **Julius Meinl grocery,** Várkerület 100-102, is one of the town's best-stocked shops (open Mon.-Fri. 6:30am-8pm, Sat. 6:30am-3pm).

Sights and Entertainment Tűztorony (Fire Tower), on Fő tér's north side, consists of a 17th-century spire atop a 16th-century tower on a 12th-century base straddling a Roman gate. Its clock is the source of the chimes heard throughout town. Visitors squeeze up a narrow spiral staircase to the balcony for a view of Sopron's steeples and surrounding hills (open Tues.-Sun. 10am-6pm; 100Ft, students 50Ft). Across the square stands **Bencés Templom** (Benedictine Church), built in the 13th century with funds from a happy herder whose goats found a cache of gold. Two queens and one king were crowned in this church: not bad for a place that has goats frolicking on the heraldic design above the main entrance. The small **kolostor** (monastery) next door also dates from the 13th century. Visitors can enter its Chapter Hall, a room of textbook Gothic architecture enriched by 10 sculptures of human sins and taped Gregorian muzak (church and hall open daily 10am-noon and 2-5pm). The crab stands for fickleness, just in case you were wondering.

The Gothic **Fabricius House,** Fő tér 6, is divided into three separate exhibits. The first and second floors hold a rather dry historical/archaeological collection. On the third floor are re-creations of domestic life in 17th- and 18th-century Sopron. Tour guides demand to know your native language as you enter each room, and thrust upon you a photocopied guide in your confessed *Sprache* describing each article of the gorgeous antique furnishings. Inside the vaulted cellar—originally a Gothic chapel, and now the coolest place in town on a hot day—the **Római Kőtár** (Roman Lapidarium) exhibits stonework and monuments dating to Sopron's start as the colony Scarbantia. The 2nd century trio of Jupiter, Juno, and Minerva that adorn the hall once sat in the forum (open Tues.-Sun. 10am-6pm; each exhibit 60Ft, students 30Ft; buy tickets from the cashier as you enter the house).

Just to the right, the **Storno-ház** (Storno House), Fő tér 8, may be the most interesting of the town's 13 museums. The Stornos were 19th-century Swiss-Italian restorers of monuments and cathedrals; their taste in restoration is often unimpressive, but their home and personal collections of furniture and artwork spanning from the Renaissance to the 19th century are exquisite. The cashier hands you your ticket and sends you up to the first floor, where there is a dry and poorly marked historical exhibit. Don't worry, that isn't the collection; the number on your ticket is the time your 40-minute guided tour on the second floor starts. The guide says almost nothing—instead, she carries around a tape recorder with narration in Hungarian or German and points out each item as it's mentioned, like a flight attendant giving pre-flight safety instructions. English speakers get a photocopied fact sheet (open Tues.-Sun. 10am-6pm; 100Ft, students 50Ft).

Angyal Patika Muzeúm (Angel Pharmacy Museum), Fő tér 2, traces the history of the profession from the 15th to 20th centuries (open Tues.-Sun. 9:30am-2pm; 20Ft). Down Új u., once known as Zsidó u. (Jewish street), stand two rare 14th-century synagogues that evoke the life of the local medieval Jewish community, expelled in 1526. **Középkori Ó-Zsinagóga** (Old Synagogue), at #22, first built around 1300, has been reconstructed to show the separate rooms for each gender, the stone Torah niche, the wooden pulpit, and the deep well used as a ritual bath (in a small building in the courtyard; open Wed.-Mon. 9am-5pm; 80Ft, students 40Ft). At #11, **Új-Zsinagóga** (New Synagogue), is new only because it was built 50 years later. After centuries of ignominy, it is now being restored. For a list of other museums, ask at Ciklámen Tourist (see **Practical Information** above).

For a brief but thorough tour of old Sopron, take a short walk down Templóm u. to **Evangélikus Templom** (Evangelical Church) with its late Baroque interior, especially the organ. Return to Fő tér via Szent György u. and peek inside **Szent György Templom** (St. George's Cathedral) to be amazed by the exquisite blend of Gothic and Baroque ornamentation concealed by the church's plain exterior.

Just north of the inner town at Bécsi út. 5, **Pékmúzeum** (Bakery Museum) illustrates the history of professional baking from the 15th to 20th centuries in the restored home and shop of a successful 19th-century baker (open Wed., Fri., Sun. 10am-2pm and Tues., Thurs., and Sat. 2-6pm; 50Ft, students 20Ft). Five minutes south of the inner town at the corner of Deák tér and Csatkai Endre u., **Liszt Ferenc Múzeum** (Franz Liszt Museum) houses a collection of folk crafts and has no apparent connection to the composer (open Tues.-Sun. 10am-6pm; 100Ft, students 50Ft).

The two biggest **discos** in Sopron are the next-door neighbors **The Rockline** and **The Dancing Bar,** at Selmeci u. and Lacknev Kristóf u., one block north of the bus station. Lively and unpretentious, these places brim with Sopron youth, especially on Wednesday and Thursday, when there is no cover (open daily 10pm-4am; Fri.-Tues. cover 200Ft). During the **Sopron Festival Weeks** (June-July), the town hosts opera, ballet, and concerts, some set in the **Fertőrákos Quarry** caverns 10km away, reached by hourly buses from the bus terminal (quarry 20Ft for students; concerts 500-600Ft). Buy tickets for all events from the **Festival Bureau,** on Széchenyi tér across from the post office (open Mon.-Fri. 9am-5pm, Sat. 9am-noon). **Kolostor,** Kolostor u. 9, south of Fő tér, has *Szalon* from the royal Pécs brewery on tap (0.5L 100Ft; open daily until 10pm). A 17th-century cellar house, **Cézár Pince,** Hátsókapu 2 (tel. 31 13 37), quenches its guests' thirst with *Soproni Kékfrankos* (open daily 10am-9pm).

■ Near Sopron: Fertőd

In tiny **Fertőd** (FER-tewd), 27km east of Sopron, stands the magnificent Baroque **Eszterházy Palace,** Bartók Béla u. 2 (tel. (99) 37 04 71), nicknamed the "Hungarian Versailles." Miklós Eszterházy, known as **Miklós the Sumptuous** before he squandered his family's vast fortune, ordered the palace built in 1766 to hold his multi-day orgiastic feasts. Visit the inside of the mansion, now a museum, to see what time has done to the magnificent art (open April 16-Dec. 15 Tues.-Sun. 9am-5pm, Dec. 16-April 15 Tues.-Sun. 9am-4pm; 500Ft, students 100Ft). **Josef Haydn** composed and conducted here, and **concerts** still resound within. Tours in Hungarian only; non-Hungarian-speaking visitors can get a short written guide in their language of choice. **Buses** leave every hour for Fertőd from platform 11 in Sopron's station on Lackner Kristóf (45min., 190Ft). Buses continue on to Győr (5 per day, 2hr., 440Ft). Fertőd has dorms and a few rooms, but groups often fill them. Book with Ciklámen Tourist in Sopron.

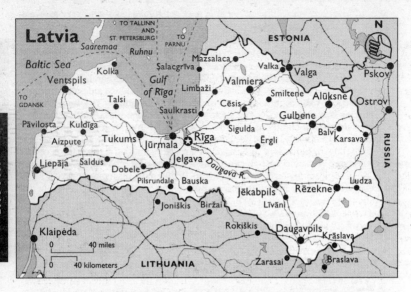

LATVIA (LATVIJA)

US$1	= 0.59Ls (lats)	1Ls =	US$1.71
CDN$1	= 0.42Ls	1Ls =	CDN$2.36
UK£1	= 0.93Ls	1Ls =	UK£1.07
IR£1	= 0.86Ls	1Ls =	IR£1.16
AUS$1	= 0.43Ls	1Ls =	AUS$2.34
NZ$1	= 0.37Ls	1Ls =	NZ$2.69
SAR1	= 0.13Ls	1Ls =	SAR8.01
DM1	= 0.32Ls	1Ls =	DM3.11
Country Phone Code: 371		**International Dialing Prefix: 00**	

Except for 20 years of independence that ended with the 1939 Molotov-Ribbentrop Pact, Latvia has been ruled by Germans, Swedes, and Russians from the 13th century until 1991. The country (pop. 2.6 million) is now rebuilding after almost 50 years of Soviet occupation, but remains less affluent and developed than Estonia, its Baltic neighbor to the north. Attitudes toward the Russians who still live in the country are softening: Latvians speak Russian well and are willing to use it more often than Estonians. But evidence of national pride abounds, from patriotically renamed streets virtually bleeding with crimson-and-white flags, to a reemergence of native holidays predating even the Christian invasions. Rīga, Latvia's only large city, is a westernizing capital where many corporations have established their Baltic headquarters. The rest of the country is mostly a provincial expanse of deep green hills dominated by tall birches and pines, dairy pastures, and quiet settlements.

LATVIA ESSENTIALS

Irish, U.K., and U.S. citizens can visit Latvia visa-free for up to 90 days. Citizens of Australia, Canada, New Zealand, and South Africa require 90-day visas, obtainable at a Latvian consular office (see **Essentials: Embassies and Consulates,** p. 4) or at Rīga's airport. Single-entry visas cost US$15; multiple-entry cost US$30; 24-hour rush processing costs US$60 (single-entry) or US$90 (multiple-entry). Multiple-entry visas are issued only if an official invitation from a Latvian government agency or an officially registered organization is submitted with the visa application. Allow 10 days for standard processing. With the application, send your passport, one photograph, and payment by check or money order. For extensions, apply to the Department of Immigration and Citizenship and Immigration (see **Rīga:** Passport Office, p. 306).

GETTING THERE AND GETTING AROUND

Flights to Latvia use the overworked Rīga Airport, the only runway of which was short enough to cause safety concern when U.S. President Clinton visited in 1994. **Air Baltic, Czech Airlines, Finnair, Lufthansa,** and others make the hop to Rīga from their hubs. However, consider taking **trains,** which link Latvia to Berlin, Moscow, St. Petersburg, Tallinn, and Vilnius. Trains are cheap and efficient, but stations aren't well-marked, so get a map. The **suburban rail** system, centered in Rīga, qualifies almost the entire country as a suburb. Diesel trains, often express, stop only at towns marked on the board in Rīga by a white dot.

Latvia's efficient long-distance **bus** network reaches Prague, Tallinn, Vilnius, and Warsaw. Buses, usually adorned with the driver's bizarre collection of Christian icons, stuffed animals, are quicker than trains for travel within Latvia, but they stop in places so isolated you'll wonder where all those waiting to get on came from. Beware the standing-room-only long-distance jaunt. **Hitchhiking** is common, and is considered more dangerous for drivers than passengers; hitchers may be expected to pay. *Let's Go* does not recommend hitching as a safe means of transport. **Ferries** run to Rīga from Stockholm, Sweden and Kiel, Germany—but from Stockholm, a train via Tallinn is cheaper, and from Kiel, buses run via Klaipéda.

TOURIST SERVICES

Look for the big green **i** marking some tourist-info offices across the land; offices, with one or two exceptions, vary in usefulness from being possibly helpful to acting incredulous at the thought of actually dispensing any information. The same goes for their more subtly adorned "i"-deprived brethren. Most provide services for a fee and resent doing anything for free. In Rīga's forest of tourism, the **Tourist Club of Latvia** stands out for quantity of info, and **Latvijas Universitātes Tūristu Klubs** plans nifty outdoor (and other) adventures, with prices geared to students rather than international businesspeople (see **Rīga:** Tourist Offices, p. 306).

MONEY

The Latvian currency unit is the **Lats** (100 santīmi=1 Lats; abbreviated Ls). There are a few **ATMs** in Rīga linked to Cirrus, MasterCard, and Visa. In most towns, there are usually some nicer restaurants, banks, and hotels accepting **Visa** and **MasterCard. Traveler's checks** are harder to use; both AmEx and Thomas Cook can be converted in some Rīga banks, but Thomas Cook is a safer bet outside the capital.

COMMUNICATION

Buy **phone cards** for the newly digitalized telephones at the local post office, kiosks, stores, and anywhere else you see a phone-card sticker (lowest denomination 2Ls). If you see a dot written within a phone number, wait for a tone before dialing the rest of the digits. Within Rīga's commuting range and in some Baltic coastal spots, **digital telephones** are common; otherwise, trek to the post office to make **international calls.** The **AT&T Direct** number in Latvia is 700 70 07; it's not a free call, but it's your best option for an English-speaking operator. The gradual switch to digital phones has made making a connection something like cracking a safe—sometimes you must dial a 2 before a number, sometimes a 7. Trial and error is nothing to be ashamed of. From an analog phone, an 8 followed by an old Soviet phone code zaps you across the fallen empire; from a digital phone, dial 007 before the country code. To call outside the CIS from an analog phone, you have to phone the operator: dial 8, wait for the tone, then dial 15 or 194; it may take up to three hours to connect your call. From a digital phone, it's simple and direct: dial 00, then the country code. If you tire of Russian-roulette dialing, check a phone office or *Rīga in Your Pocket* for the latest in digit disasters. Asking for *gaisa pastu* at the post office will get you airmail.

LANGUAGE

A blend of German, Russian, Estonian, and Swedish influences, **Latvian** (see **Glossary,** p. 804) is, with Lithuanian, a member of the Baltic language group. Life, however, proceeds bilingually. Nearly 65% of the people in Rīga are Russians who speak little (if any) Latvian, while the populations of some cities are over 95% Latvian. A language law requires that signs, menus, and other public writing be in Latvian; this can seem obnoxious when, after struggling to order from a Latvian menu, you discover that your waiter speaks only **Russian.** Many young Latvians study **English,** but the older set know some **German.** Most Latvians speak Russian well, though some prefer not to, even though animosity toward Russians is waning from the heady days of the early 90s. In smaller towns, Russian may bring hostility, which can be softened by attempting it apologetically or as a last resort. *Alus* (beer) is a crucial word in any language. Key places are the *autoosta* (bus station), *stacija* (train station), *lidosta* (airport), *viesnīca* (hotel), and *pasts* (post office).

HEALTH AND SAFETY

Emergency Numbers: Fire, tel. 01. **Police,** tel. 02. **Ambulance,** tel. 03.

Bathrooms are marked with an upward-pointing triangle for women, downward for men. There are rumors that Rīga **tap water** is drinkable, but boil all water for 10 minutes to be safe. Many Latvian **drivers** seem aggressive enough to win the Indy 500, though they'd all be disqualified for slamming on the pedal before the light turns green. Be very cautious around roadways. If you're **attacked** or feel threatened, speak Russian instead of English, if possible; locals may not notice your accent. "*Ej prom*" (ey prawm) means "go away"; "*Lasies*" (lahsioos prawm) says it more offensively, and "*Lasies lapās*" (lahsioos lahpahs; "go to the leaves"), poetic though it may be, is even ruder. Your **consulate** is often a better bet for English-speaking help than the police.

ACCOMMODATIONS AND CAMPING

The **Tourist Club of Latvia** lists budget lodgings, makes travel arrangements, and books accommodations (see **Rīga:** Tourist Offices, p. 306). In Rīga, **Patricia** provides English info and arranges homestays (average 8.50Ls per night without breakfast) and apartment rentals (see **Rīga:** Accommodations, p. 309). Many towns have only one **hotel** (if any) in the budget range; expect to pay 3-12Ls per night, with price variations reflecting a monopoly, not higher quality.

FOOD AND DRINK

Heavy and filling, Latvian food tries to fatten you up for winter. Many restaurants, however, are serving more Western dishes. National specialties, tasty on the whole, include smoked *sprats* (once the fame of Rīga), the holiday dish *zirņi* (gray peas with onions and smoked fat), *maizes zupa* (bread soup usually made from cornbread, and full of currants, cream, and other goodies), and the warming *Rīgas (Melnais) balzams* (a black liquor great with ice cream, Coke, or coffee). Dark rye bread is a staple, and homemade bread and pastries are deliciously worth asking for. Try *speķa rauši,* a warm pastry; *biezpienmaize,* bread with sweet curds; or the dark-colored *kaņepju sviests,* hemp butter, which is good but too dilute for medicinal purposes. Latvian beer, primarily from the Aldaris brewery, is pretty good and should cost 0.55Ls for 0.4L, 0.65Ls for 0.5L; *Porteris* is best. If imported beers aren't 1.50Ls or less, you're paying for the atmosphere.

CUSTOMS AND ETIQUETTE

Tipping is increasingly common; it will probably be expected in any restaurant accustomed to foreign patrons. As elsewhere in the region, expect to be bought a drink if you talk with someone a while—repay the favor in kind. **Shops** sometimes close for an hour or two between noon and 3pm, and restaurants may take a break between 5 and 7pm. **Homosexuality,** though legal, may not be tolerated.

LIFE AND TIMES

HISTORY

Ancient Latvia was inhabited by the **Balts,** an Indo-European people who arrived in the area of the eastern Baltic Sea in the 3rd millennium BC. Isolated by the sea, forest, and swamps, the westernmost Balts, ancestors of today's Latvians and Lithuanians, were able to protect their pagan culture until the Middle Ages, while the other Balts were absorbed completely into more powerful civilizations, such as that of the Slavs. During the 8th, 9th, and 10th centuries, the Balts in Latvia suffered from the expansionist pressure of the Scandinavian **Vikings** from the northwest and the **Slavs** from the east, before being subjected to the more lasting dominance of German-speaking warriors. The **Order of the Brothers of the Sword,** founded in 1202 and known as the **Order of Teutonic Knights of Livonia** after 1237, conquered and Christianized most of Latvia, forcing its residents into the position of serfs within the **Livonian Confederation** system of estates ruled by the Knights. However, while the Germans ruled the Latvians, they proved insufficiently strong to Germanize them; Rīga remained a free city, and the Latvian Balts were not subsumed within the Teutonic culture.

The unstable Confederation of Livonia fell apart at the end of the 16th century, when **Russian Tsar Ivan IV,** "the Terrible," invaded, beginning the 25-year **Livonian War** (1558-83), during which the Knights' territory was divided up by the **Polish-Lithuanian state** and **Sweden.** Livonia was broken up into three duchies: Courland, Estland, and Livonia, the third of which, with its capital, Rīga, was ruled briefly by Lithuania before being ceded to Sweden under the **1629 Truce of Altmark.** Swedish control of Latvia lasted only a century, but the Latvians prospered under it; the Swedes introduced compulsory elementary education, opened a secondary school and a university in their Livonian territory, and in general sought to improve the lot of the peasant serfs. Although Sweden successfully defended these eastern Baltic lands concurrently against **Poland** (Polish-Swedish War, 1654-60) and **Russia** (Russo-Swedish War, 1654-61), the Russians refused to give up, and at the conclusion of the **Great Northern War** (1700-21), Sweden was forced to cede the Livonian territories to the greedy Slavic tsars under the **Treaty of Nystad.** By the end of the 18th century, the whole of Latvia was under Russian control.

> The incorporation of Latvia into the Soviet Union was never officially recognized by the United States and other Western countries.

During the period of Russian rule, the German land-owning ruling class was able to maintain and even further expand its power and influence in Latvia, and the serfs' servile status increased. The peasants gained some freedom after the **Napoleonic Wars,** but the issue of land ownership remained contentious, and unrest spread. When serfs were liberated throughout the Russian empire in 1861, Latvian peasants finally won the right to buy the lands their forefathers had farmed for centuries. Calls for independence were increasingly heard, particularly after the 1905 revolution in Russia.

Reacting to the Bolshevik coup of November 1917, the **Latvian People's Council** proclaimed independence on November 18, 1918. The new autonomous government in Rīga—a distant dream—was led by Kārlis Ulmanis. Over the next few years, Latvia was overrun by battling armies. Latvians, Germans, White Russians, British, French, Estonians, Lithuanians, and the Red Army all fought for supremacy. When fighting ended in 1920, the Latvians were in control. **Democratic coalitions** ruled the country, with Ulmanis serving four terms as prime minister. Proposed constitutional reforms created an uproar, however, and the Nazi movement spread in the minority German population. In 1934, Ulmanis established a dictatorship. During **WWII**, the country was incorporated into the USSR, and deportations began. Germany invaded in 1941, but by 1945 the Red Army had driven the Nazis out.

Latvia was one of the wealthiest and most industrialized regions of the Soviet Union. But under **Soviet rule,** it was torn by radical economic restructuring, extreme political repression, and a thorough **Russification** of its national culture. Immigrants from the rest of the USSR poured into the country, rarely bothering to learn the local language or identify with the indigenous population; most local Party leaders were Russian immigrants. Within four decades, ethnic Latvians accounted for only half the population, as compared to three quarters before the war.

Never reconciled to their incorporation into the Soviet Union, which in fact was never officially recognized by the U.S. and other Western countries, the Latvians were more than ready to take advantage of Gorbachev's willingness to reform the Soviet system. Under **glasnost** and **perestroika,** Latvians protested *en masse* in 1987 over environmental protection and created the Popular Front of Latvia in 1988 to oppose the Soviet establishment. The Soviets were trounced in the 1990 elections. On May 4, 1990, the new legislature declared Latvia **independent,** but Soviet intervention sparked violent clashes in Rīga in 1991. Finally, following the foiled Moscow coup in August, the Latvian legislature reasserted its independence, and the nation's sovereignty was recognized by most of the world in early September, 1991.

LITERATURE

The legacy of the ancient Balts is powerful in Latvian literature. The **daina,** a folk song reflecting the pagan Balts' reverence of nature and strong sense of ethics, was not erased from Latvians' memory during their centuries under the influence of varied foreign cultures. Although the first written literature came in late, fostered by German clergymen, it still shows clear evidence of the influence of folklore. The 17th-century poet **C. Fuereccerus,** who introduced new metrical conventions and rhymes, made use of the *daina*'s stylistic elements, and **G. Mancelius,** who founded Latvian prose, fought against the influence of the pagan folk songs.

The mid-19th century brought the National Awakening to Latvia, spurring a wealth of writings as the country asserted its literary independence. The modern Latvian lyric began with **Juris Alunans's** 1856 book of verse *Dziesminas* (*Little Songs*), and the *daina*'s spirit is reflected in the lyrics of **Auseklis (M. Krogzems)** and in **Lāčplēsis** (*Bearslayer*), **Andrējs Pumpurs's** 1888 national epic. A patriotic role-model and symbol of the National Awakening, Lāčplēsis kills a bear and conquers the German Black Knight—only to fall into the Daugava River. Legend foretold that he would return to free Latvia. Some say *Lāčplēsis*'s 20th-century reappearance in the form of **Māra Zālite's** rock opera indeed effected Latvia's independence.

> A patriotic role-model, the epic's hero kills a bear and conquers the German Black Knight—only to fall into the Daugava River.

Realism became very important in the last years of the 19th century, as did social protest literature. The first major Latvian novel, the 1879 *Mērnieku laiki* (*The Times of the Land-Surveyors*), by **Reinis and Matiss Kaudzītes,** was a realistic portrayal of Latvian peasant life. **Jānis Rainis** used imagery from folk poetry to depict contemporary problems, and his wife, **Aspazija,** fought for women's rights. With the 1905 Revolution, another shift in the literary current occurred, as Latvians tried to break away from both imperialistic Russian and local German influence. Lyricism began to predominate, and the ethics of the *daina* were again incarnated in the verse and fairy tales of the poet **Karlis Skalbe.**

More new literary forms diversified Latvia's literature after the country achieved independence in 1918. **Jānis Akurāters'** romantic lyrics exhibit Nietzschean themes such as individual heroism, while **Edvarts Virza** returned to Classicism, glorifying rural life and traditional (read: sexist) familial life. Others, like **Kārlis Zariņš,** grappled with the effects of WWI. The folktale re-entered the scene as a context for analyzing modern Latvia; the ballad was used by **Aleksandrs Čaks** to caricature urban and sub-urban life, although his most outstanding work was *Muzibas skartie* (*Marked by Eternity*), a haunting ballad cycle about the Latvian riflemen of WWI. Many Latvian writers turned to psychological detail in the early 20th century: **Mirdza Bendrupe's** Freudian prose explored human psychology, **Eriks Adamsons** depicted modern neuroses, and **Anslavs Eglitis** reveled in focusing on one human quality and intensifying it to absurdity. Finally, **Aleksandrs Upītis's** work, portraying class struggle and proletarian heroes, grew out of seeds sown by French and Russian naturalists.

After WWII, Upītis became a leading writer, thanks to the political correctness of his texts. Socialist Realism failed to drown other trends, however. **Jānis Medenis,** exiled to a labor camp in Siberia, longed for a free Latvia in his poetry; **Imants Ziedonis** also managed to foster independent Latvian literature despite the authorities' tight censorship, as did **Vizma Belsevica** and **Ojars Vacietis,** poets who gave expression to their individual inner worlds of experience, constrained by external pressures.

LATVIA TODAY

Latvia's transition to capitalism has been rocky. Industrial production has plummeted, and the standard of living continues to fall. Latvia still depends on Russia to provide it with fuel and to serve as a major market for its washing machines, refrigerators, motor scooters, radios, and solid organic fertilizer spreaders. Fiscal austerity, instigated by a Latvian government tightening its belt, has been relatively successful at reducing inflation. Lax regulation has made Latvia a little Switzerland for the ex-Communist countries, and banking has begun to boom. Internal politics has been turbulent. Parties as diverse as the **Latvian Farmers' Union** (LZS), the **National Conciliation Bloc** (NIB; made up of three leftist parties and a right extremist party), and the rightist **National Bloc** (NB) all gaining and losing the upper hand in the **Saeima** (Parliament). The country has also experienced a quick succession of Prime Ministers, although President **Guntis Ulmanis,** of a party comprising the **LZS** and the **Latvian Christian-Democratic Union** in alliance with the **Latgalian Democratic Party,** did manage to secure himself another term in June '96. The current Prime Minister, **Guntar Krasts,** comes from the nationalist **For Fatherland and Freedom** party. Not all Latvians may vote; suffrage is limited to those who have been citizens since 1940 and their descendants. About 34% of all residents, mainly Slavs, are disenfranchised. Relations with Russia, tense due to this discrimination against the Russian minority in Latvia, as well as to the Latvians' desire that all Russian troops be withdrawn, have improved due to new legislation and agreements. Russia still stands in the way of the NATO membership that Latvia desires, however, and EU membership seems distant.

NATIONAL HOLIDAYS

Latvia observes: March/April, Catholic Easter Monday; May 1, Labor Day; 2nd Sunday of May, Mother's Day; June 23, Līgo (Midsummer Festival); June 24, Jāni (St. John's Day); July 6, Mindaugas Day; September 14-16, Ascension Day pilgrimage; November 1, All Saint's Day; November 2, All Soul's Day; November 11, Lāčplēsis day (Veterans' day); November 18, National Day (1918); December 25-26, Ziemsvētki (Christmas).

A Midsummer Night's Eve

Everybody's favorite *Jogānu rituālus* (pagan-esque ritual), Līgo, inflames Latvia on June 23rd—Midsummer. Bonfires consume the hills as young lovers, sent to the woods to find the legendary fern flower that blossoms only on Midsummer's Eve, consume each other—passionately. Men don oak-leaf crowns to assert their fertility, and women wear flower wreaths; *dainas* (folk songs) fill the air, and the whole country stays up all night chasing *Jānu* cheese with rivers of beer and merriment. The whole celebration, bigger than Christmas, New Year's, and even Baryshnikov's birthday, results in a national hangover so severe that many establishments remain closed for the day after Līgo.

Rīga

Founded in 1201 by the Teutonic Order of the Knights of the Sword as a base for conquering Livonian and Latvian tribes, Rīga soon became the seat of a bishopric that fought the knights for control of the city. Later ruled by Poles, Swedes, and then Russians, Rīga grew to be the most prosperous city in the Baltics. Rīga's famed Art Nouveau architecture reveals German influences, while the population and atmosphere reflect the inescapable legacy of the Soviet era. Tensions between disenfranchised Russians, *nouveau riche* businesspeople with cellular phones, and returning Latvians who fled in the 40s after Stalin's takeover make Rīga a hotbed of post-Soviet politics. But the city's eclectic attractions cast a spell on all its residents, and visitors.

ORIENTATION AND PRACTICAL INFORMATION

Rīga's city center consists of an expanding series of concentric half-circles along the banks of the **Daugava river,** engulfing **Vecrīga** (Old Rīga), which is bordered by **Kr. Valdemāra iela** to the north and **Marijas iela** to the south. **Pīlsētas kanāls** (the old city moat), surrounded by a park, marks the first circle—about a 15-minute walk across. Beyond the canal, a ring of parks and boulevards laid out in the 19th century make up the second circle; **Elizabetes iela,** 1km from the river, bounds this newer region. Beyond sprawls the noisy, dirty metropolis. Vecrīga has two sections, divided by **Kaļķu iela** (which becomes **Brīvības bulvāris** in the newer part of the city, and **Brīvības iela** out past Elizabetes iela). The **train** and **bus stations** are located on the southeast edge of the city center. With the trains behind you, take a left onto the busy Marijas iela; once you pass the canal's terminus, you are in Vecrīga.

A city **map** (1Ls), widely available, is a must; you'll get lost in Vecrīga's wandering streets anyway, but it's a great city in which to get lost. *Rīga in Your Pocket* can be very useful, with up-to-date info on most things a traveler needs (0.50Ls); the free *Rīga This Week* is also helpful, though not as good. The informative *City Paper—The Baltic States,* can be picked up at hotels, kiosks, and tourist info points (US$1.50).

Tourist Offices: The best bet for Baltics' omniscience is the **Tourist Club of Latvia** (Latvijas Tūristu Klubs), Skārņu iela 22 (tel. 722 17 31; fax 722 76 80), behind Sv. Pētera baznīca (St. Peter's Church). Can help with a Russian visa (US$15 for 10-day processing, US$60 for 24hr.). English-speaking staff gives out brochures and sells the entire *In Your Pocket* line. Guided tours in English of Vecrīga 17.40Ls (2hr; price includes up to 30 people). Open daily 24hr. **Balta Tourist Agency,** Elizabetes iela 63 (tel. 728 63 49; fax 724 30 99), gives out maps, brochures, and flight timetables. Open Mon.-Fri. 9am-6pm, Sat. 10am-2pm.

Tours: Latvijas Universitātes Tūristu Klubs, Raiņa bulv. 19, room 127 (tel. 722 52 98; fax 782 01 13; email mountain@com.latnet.lv), arranges hiking and canoeing trips (17Ls for 2 days; includes transport, guide, accommodations, and any museum admissions. Open Mon.-Fri. 9am-6pm.

Passport Office: Visa extensions are difficult to get; start by contacting the **Dept. of Immigration and Citizenship,** Raina iela 5 (tel. 721 91 81).

Embassies: Belarus, Elizabetes iela 2 (tel. 732 25 50; fax 73 22 89). Open Mon.-Fri. 10am-2pm and 3-5pm. **Canada,** Doma laukums 4, 3rd fl. (tel. 722 63 15; emergency tel. 755 11 81). Open Mon.-Fri. 10am-1pm. **Russia,** Antonijas iela 2 (tel. 22 06 93), entrance on Kalpaka bulv. Open Mon.-Fri. 10am-1pm. **Ukraine,** Kalpaka bulv. 3 (tel. 33 29 56). Open Mon.-Fri. 10am-1pm. **U.S.,** Raiņa bulv. 7 (tel. 721 00 05). Open Mon.-Fri. 9am-noon and 2-5pm. **U.K.,** Alunāna iela 5 (tel. 733 81 26). Open Mon.-Fri. 9:30am-noon.

Currency Exchange: At any of the innumerable *Valutos Maiņa* kiosks or shops in the city. **Unibanka,** Kaļķu iela 13 (tel. 722 83 51), has generous hours (Mon.-Fri. 9am-9pm, Sat. 9am-6pm), gives MC and Visa cash advances (4% commission), and cashes AmEx and Thomas Cook **traveler's checks** (3% commission). Cirrus/MC/Visa **ATMs** are popping up all over, including at the telephone office (see below).

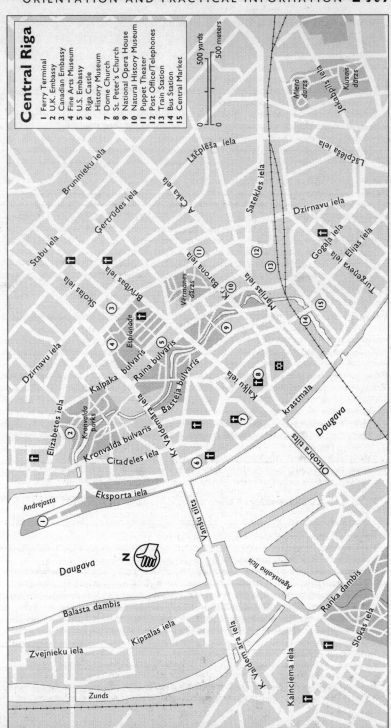

Central Riga

1 Ferry Terminal
2 U.K. Embassy
3 Canadian Embassy
4 Fine Arts Museum
5 U.S. Embassy
6 Riga Castle
7 History Museum
8 Dome Church
9 St. Peter's Church
10 National Opera House
11 Natural History Museum
12 Puppet Theater
13 Post Office/Telephones
14 Train Station
15 Bus Station
16 Central Market

LATVIA

American Express: Latvia Tours, Kaļķu iela 8 (tel. 721 36 52; fax 732 00 20), the Latvian AmEx representative, doesn't cash traveler's checks, but will hold mail. Open Mon.-Fri. 9am-6pm, Sat. 10am-2pm.

Flights: Lidosta Rīga (Rīga Airport; info tel. 20 70 09), 8km southwest of Vecrīga. Take bus #22 from Gogol iela. **Air Baltic** (tel. 207 24 01) flies once daily to Tallinn (US$127), and twice daily to Frankfurt (US$524) and London (US$246). **Lufthansa** (tel. 728 59 01; fax 782 81 99) and **Finnair** (tel. 720 70 10; fax 720 77 55) fly to most major western European cities.

Trains: Stacijas laukums (tel. 007, but don't ask for Mr. Bond), east of Vecrīga and north of the canal. It's really 2 stations, with **long-distance trains** located in the larger building to the left. Departures (*atiešanas*) listed on the board to the right as you enter. To: Berlin (1 per day, 31hr., *coupé* 46.28Ls; on the Baltic Express via Hrodna, Belarus, so get your transit visa); Moscow (2 per day, 17hr., *coupé* 23.53Ls); St. Petersburg (1 per day, 15hr., *coupé* 19.69Ls); Tallinn (1-2 per day, 8½hr., *coupé* 13.98Ls); Vilnius (2 per day, 8hr., *coupé* 10.52Ls); Warsaw (1 per day, 22hr., *coupé* 18.64Ls; also on the Baltic Express). **Suburban trains,** running as far as the Estonian border at Valka (the Latvian section of the Estonian town Valga; on the Lugaži line), leave from the smaller building. The Lugaži line includes Cēsis and Sigulda. Buy same-day tickets in the respective halls, and advance ones in the **booking office** off the right side of the suburban hall. Open Mon.-Sat. 8am-7pm, Sun. 8am-6pm. **Non-CIS tickets** must be purchased at the three windows at Turgeneva iela 14. Open Mon.-Sat. 8am-1pm and 2-7pm, Sun. 8am-1pm and 2-6pm.

Buses: The station (tel. 721 36 11) is 200m south of the train station along Prāgas iela, across the canal from the central market (open daily 5am-midnight). To: Kaunas (2 per day, 7hr., 5-6Ls); Minsk (2 per day, 10hr., 6.20-6.90Ls); Tallinn (8 per day, 6hr., 5-6Ls); and Vilnius (6 per day, 6hr., 6Ls). Buses to Prague (1 per day, 30hr., 38Ls) and Warsaw (1 per day, 14hr., 14.50Ls) can only be booked with the private **Eurolines** company; offices at the bus station to the right of the ticket windows (tel. 721 11 58). Open Mon.-Fri. 9am-6pm, Sat. 9am-7:30pm.

Ferries: Transline Balt Tour, Eksporta iela 1a (tel. 232 99 03; fax 783 00 40), 1km north of Rīga Pils (Castle) at the passenger port. A ship sails from Rīga to Stockholm Mon., Wed., and Fri. at 6pm, arriving at 10am the next day. Deck space 10Ls; 25Ls for a spot in a 4-place cabin with hall showers and toilets. From Stockholm to Rīga: boats leave Tues. and Thurs. 5pm and arrive 11am the next day; a Sat. ferry leaves at 3pm and docks in Rīga at 9am.

Public Transportation: Buses, trams, and **trolleybuses** take 0.14Ls tickets (buy at kiosks, post offices, and on board); punch tickets on board. Transportation runs 5:30am-12:30am.

Taxis: State taxis (tel. 070) are outnumbered by private ones with a green light in the windshield. Haggle over price (0.70Ls per km in town, 0.40Ls in the suburbs).

Car Rental: Europcar Interrent Basteja bulvāris 10 (tel. 722 26 37; fax 782 03 60), rents Opels (US$89; damage liability insurance US$15). Open daily 9am-11pm.

Luggage Storage: In the bus station, on guarded racks (0.50Ls per bag). Open daily 5:30am-noon and 12:30-11pm. At the train station, lockers (0.30Ls) are in the tunnel under the long-distance tracks. Open daily 5am-1am.

Bookstore: Aperto Libro, Kr. Baronas iela 31 (tel. 728 38 10). Comes with attached cafe, **Osiris,** where you can sip cappuccino while you peruse your new *Moby-Dick*. Breakfast combos around 2Ls; free English newspapers; and everywhere Anglophones. Bookstore and cafe open Mon.-Fri. 8am-1am, Sat.-Sun. 10am-1am. For Victorian novels and new pulp fiction, try **Rastāmlietas Grāmatas Bērniem,** Elizabetes iela 85 (tel. 728 66 36), through a courtyard and on the right. English books on the second floor. Open Mon.-Fri. 10am-7pm, Sat. 10am-5pm.

Laundromat: Miele, Elizabetes iela 85a (tel. 271 76 96), in the courtyard opposite the bookstore. Groaning machines take almost 2hr. to wash a load, so plan ahead. Wash 1.89Ls; dry 0.63Ls. Add 1.57Ls a load to have your laundry washed and dried for you; takes 24hr. Open 24hr. Visa, MC.

Pharmacy: Grindex, Audēju 20 (tel. 721 33 40). Open Mon. and Sat. 9am-5pm, Tues.-Fri. 8am-8pm. Visa, MC.

Gay and Lesbian Center: Latvian Association for Sexual Equality, Puškina 1a (tel./fax 722 70 50; http://dspace.dial.pipex.com/town/parade/gf96).

Express Mail: DHL, Brīvības 55 (tel. 701 32 93; fax 701 32 98). 10 pages to the U.S. in 1-2 days 23Ls, to the U.K. 21Ls, to Australia 25Ls. Open Mon.-Fri. 9am-6pm, Sat. 10am-2pm.

Internet Access: Latnet, Raiņa 29 (tel. 721 12 41; http://www.latnet.lv). Open an account for 47.20Ls per month. 1.60Ls per hr. Open Mon.-Thurs. 9am-6pm, Fri. 9am-5pm. There are two **internet cafes** in Rīga: **Bilteks,** Jēkaba 20 (tel. 732 2208), 2Ls per hour, open daily 10am-9pm; and **Internet Cafe Audalūzijas Suns,** Elizabetes iela 83/85 (tel. 724 28 26), 1.50Ls per hr. Open daily noon-10pm.

Post Office: Stacijas laukums 1 (tel. 721 32 57), near railway station. 0.30Ls for a letter abroad; 0.25Ls for a postcard. Express mail (11.67Ls for 250g to the U.S. in 2-5 days, 11.37Ls to the U.K., 10.90Ls to Australia) and *Poste Restante* at window #1. Open Mon.-Fri. 8am-8pm, Sat. 8am-4pm, Sun. 10am-4pm. **Postal code:** LV-1050.

Telephones and Telegraph Office: (tel. 733 12 22) Brīvības bulv. 21. Open daily 8am-10pm. Smaller office at main post office by the train station. Open 24hr. With 24hr. booths and a Cirrus/MC **ATM. Phone code:** 2 for analog numbers, 8 for digital lines, and 9 for cellular phones.

ACCOMMODATIONS

Rīga's prices for decent rooms are generally the highest in the Baltics. However, there are a number of very cheap, if grim, places to stay in town. The English- and German-speaking staff of **Patricia,** Elizabetes iela 22-26, 3rd floor (tel. 28 48 68; fax 28 66 50), 2 blocks from the train, arranges US$15 homestays in Vecrīga (doubles US$30; breakfast an extra US$5; open Mon.-Fri. 9am-7pm, Sun. 9am-1pm).

Arena, Palasta iela 5 (tel. 722 85 83). Located in the heart of the Vecrīga, this is the cheapest place, but by no means the worst, in town. Open April-Oct.; the rest of the year circus performers live here. Some rooms have sinks. Hall shower and communal kitchen for true budgeters. 3Ls per person. Cash only.

Saulite, Merķela iela 12 (tel. 22 45 46), directly across from the train station. Green spiral staircase branches off to clean halls, rooms, and communal showers and toilets. Singles 5.40Ls, with private bath 12-18.20Ls. Doubles 7.80-15Ls, with private bath 15-20Ls. EC, MC.

Studentu Kopmītne (Student Dormitories), Basteja bulvārīs 10 (tel. 721 62 21), above the Europcar Interrent office, on the edge of Vecrīga. Run by the University of Latvia to accommodate guest lecturers and others. Rooms truly spotless and well-maintained. Clean, mostly new communal bathrooms. 2-3Ls per person; with private bath and refrigerator, 5-6Ls per person). Call ahead; this place is popular!

Viktorija, Čaka iela 55 (tel. 27 23 05), 8 blocks from the trains on Marijas iela (which becomes Čaka iela), or 2 stops on trolleybus #11 or 18. The price of the rooms can be seen in the new lobby and the trappings of the renovated section, rather than in the dingy rooms themselves. Grim common toilets. Singles 10Ls; with private bath, TV, breakfast, and fridge 22Ls; doubles 14Ls; with amenities 34Ls. MC, Visa.

Aurora, Marijas iela 5 (tel. 722 44 79), across from the train station. Rooms are old and the toilets, most of which don't have seats, smell. Hall bathrooms. All rooms have sinks with hot water. Singles 3.50-3.70Ls; doubles 5.80-6.20Ls. Cash only.

Hotel Baltija, Raiņa bulv. 33 (tel. 722 74 61), on the corner of Marijas near the train station. The rooms are large, but decorated in the Soviet style. The toilets may be the worst-smelling around; no toilet seats in sight. Rooms have sinks with hot water. Singles 4.70Ls; doubles 7.20Ls, with bath 12.40Ls.

FOOD

Bleary-eyed women tend an insomniac's daydream: 24-hour food and liquor stores. Pricey **Interpegro,** Elizabetes 18 (tel. 287 190), is just one example, selling mostly packaged foods, but also fruits and vegetables (open Mon.-Sat. 10am-10pm, Sun. 10am-7pm). **Universālveikals Centrs,** Audēju iela 16, has food on the first floor of its three-story complex (open Mon.-Fri. 8am-8pm, Sat. 8am-6pm, Sun. 10am-4pm). In five immense zeppelin hangars behind the bus station, **Centrālais Tirgus** (Central Market), one of the largest in Europe, has by far the best selection at the cheapest prices. You can buy anything you want here, but shop around and haggle, as vendors' prices vary quite a bit (open Mon.-Sat. 8am-5pm, Sun. 8am-3pm). **McDonald's** is at Basteja bul. 18.

Lido Bistro-Piceria, Elizabetes 65 (tel. 722 13 18). One of the most popular fast-food type places in Rīga. Decent spaghetti (1.40Ls), shish kebab and rice (1.95Ls), salad (0.50Ls). Open daily 8am-11pm.

Rozamunde, Mazā Smilšu 8 (tel. 722 77 98), 1 block off Filharmonija laukums. An upscale pub run by the Rīga Jazz Company. Try beef tenderloin stuffed with champignons and cheese (3.80Ls), or lamb curry supposedly inspired by Rīga's Englishman's Club in the 1930s (3.95Ls). Open daily 11am-11pm. Musicians play nightly 8-10pm in a candlelit room with white linen tablecloths. Visa, MC, EC.

Fredis Cafe, Audēju iela 5 (tel. 21 37 31). Decent tunes, smoky air, and tiny floodlights flirting with each other, as do the carefully dressed patrons—when they take a break from acting cool. Tiny subs 0.90-1.30Ls. Overcooked spaghetti with mushrooms 2.20Ls. Omelette with mushrooms (heaped with mayonnaise and spaghetti) is 1.90Ls. 0.5L *Aldaris* 0.65Ls. Open daily 9am-midnight.

Arve Restaurant, Aldaru iela 12 (tel. 722 06 49), next to the Swedish Arch. A relatively fancy place in a basement with tables on the narrow street outside. Good bread. Passable *fettucine alfredo* with chicken filet (2.60Ls); vegetarian menu includes tomato, eggplant, and feta cheese (3.15Ls). Open daily noon-11pm.

LuLu Pizza, Ģertrūdes iela 27. Thin-crust pizza is light on the cheese and hearty on the tomato paste, but it's the best in town. Hip new interior with stools that can be made for children. Large pizzas enough for 3 moderately hungry people (2.99-3.99Ls); or slices (0.69-0.95Ls). *Aldaris* 0.85Ls. Open daily 8am-midnight. Visa, MC.

Manhattan Pizza, Čaku iela 52 (tel. 731 24 69). Thin-crust slices (0.30-0.52Ls) to feed the late-night munchies. Open 24hr.

Hotel Latvija Express Bar, Elizabetes iela 55 (tel. 722 22 11), at the corner of Brīvības bul. past the Freedom Monument in the ugly, skyscraping landmark. Renowned breakfast joint serves small portions of pancakes with jam (0.96Ls), and has 23 varieties of omelettes (0.81-3.04Ls). Big windows overlook the park outside in front of the Orthodox Cathedral. Open daily 7am-11pm. Cash only.

Pulvertornis, Vaņu iela 1 (tel. 21 68 80). Cafeteria-style dining in a renovated room of mostly silent people inhaling their food. Cheap and surprisingly good. Beef stroganoff (0.78Ls), rice (0.25Ls), salad (0.36Ls), *Aldaris* beer (0.35Ls). Open Mon.-Fri. 8am-8pm, Sat.-Sun. 9am-6pm.

SIGHTS

Most of Rīga's well-known sights lie in Vecrīga (Old Rīga), but to get a real feel for the city, also explore the newer parts of town. One good route is to turn left on Elizabetes iela from Marijas iela and walk the length of the street. In Vecrīga, at the end of Audēju iela, **Sv. Pētera baznīca** (St. Peter's Church) towers above the city with a dark spire visible throughout the city. First built in 1209, the church now standing dates from 1408. Its tower burned down during WWII and was rebuilt with an elevator in the 70s. From the top of the 103m spire (the platform is 72m), the entire city and the Baltic Sea are visible. Inside exhibits cover the fire that destroyed the original tower (open Tues.-Sun. 10am-7pm; church 0.30Ls; tower 1Ls, students 0.70Ls). Just behind at Skārņu iela 10/20 stands the 1208 **Juras kirik** (St. George's Church; tel. 22 22 35), the oldest stone edifice in Rīga. Constructed for the German Knights of the Sword, the church was secularized in the 1500s and divided into three warehouses by German merchants. Again altered, it now houses the magnificent **Dekoratīvās mākslas muzejs** (Museum of Decorative and Applied Arts), showcasing Latvian ceramics, bookmaking, and tapestries (open Tues.-Sun. 11am-5pm; museum 0.50Ls, students 0.20Ls; exhibitions 0.40Ls, students 0.20Ls).

Farther right on Skārņu iela at the intersection with Jāņa iela stands **Sv. Jāņa baznīca** (St. John's Church), a small 13th-century Dominican, then Lutheran, chapel embellished until the 1830s in a medley of architectural styles, from Gothic to Baroque to Neoclassical. After the Reformation, it served for a time as the city's armory (open Tues.-Sun. 10am-1pm; info tel. 722 40 28). Through a tiny alleyway at the left, **Jāņa sēta** (St. John's Courtyard) is the oldest populated site in Rīga, where the first city castle stood. Part of the old city wall is preserved here. Nearby, the **Latvijas fotogrāfijas muzejs** (Latvian Photography Museum) is on a small side street, Mārstalu 8 (tel. 722 72 31), exhibiting Latvian photography through the years as well as new exhibits (open Wed.-Thurs. 1-7pm, Fri.-Sat. 11am-5pm, Sun. 11am-3pm; 0.50Ls, students 0.20Ls; exhibition 0.40Ls, students 0.20Ls). Three granite soldiers guard the square at Kaļķu iela's base, **Latviešu strēlnieku laukums.** Dedicated during Soviet times to the crack team of Latvian soldiers who served as Lenin's bodyguards after the revolution, the statues meant enough to the nation that they were some of the few Soviet monuments not torn down. Behind them rise the ominous black walls of **Okupācijas muzejs-fonds** (Occupation Museum Fund), Strēlnieku laukums 1 (tel. 21 27 15), one of Rīga's finest museums. Top-notch exhibits labeled in Latvian, English, German, and Russian take two hours to read through. The initial Soviet occupation is depicted so vividly you can almost hear the Red Army marching. A model *gulag* helps explain why the Germans were welcomed as liberators. Don't miss the shot of Latvian girls draping Hitler's soldiers with flowers as the invaders smile in disbelief (open Tues.-Fri. and Sun. 11am-5pm; free).

North of Okupācijas muzejs-fonds along Kaļķu iela, **Filharmonija laukums** is bordered on the northwest by two ancient German guild houses and the felines of the yellow **Cat House.** Down Zirgu iela, between the two guild houses, the cobblestone expanse of **Doma laukums,** Vecrīga's central square, remains timelessly serene despite several vast new outdoor bars that serve tourists and Rīga's *nouveau riche.* Rīga's centerpiece, **Doma baznīca** (Dome Cathedral), begun in 1226, stands on one side of the square (tel. 721 34 98). Inside, an immense pipe organ is one of Europe's largest and reputedly finest (open Tues.-Fri. 1-5pm, Sat. 10am-2pm; 0.50Ls, students 0.20Ls; concerts Wed. and Fri. at 7pm). Behind the *Doma,* Palasta iela 4, the **Rīgas vēstures un kuģniecības muzejs** (History and Navigation Museum; tel. 721 13 58) describes Rīga's complex Germano-Russo-Swedish-Latvian history, houses exhibits on the Latvian naval tradition, and has a veritable shrine to dancer Marta Lberinga (open Wed.-Sun. 11am-5pm; 1Ls, students 0.40Ls).

Rīga pils (Rīga Castle), Pils laukums 2 (tel. 32 30 11), at the street's end, houses three modest museums: the **Latvijas vēstures muzejs** (Latvian History; open Wed.-Sun. 11am-5pm; 0.40Ls), and the **Raiņa literatūras un mākslas vēstures muzejs** (Literature; open Mon.-Sat. 11am-5pm; 0.40Ls) and the **Ārzemju mākslas muzejs** (Foreign Art), which has two exhibitions (0.20Ls each); its displays, dating from the 16th to 19th centuries, include Indian, Japanese, and Chinese art (open Tues.-Sun. 11am-4:30pm). The little-visited trio are labeled in Latvian only.

At Jēkaba iela 11, Latvia's **Saeima** (Parliament; tel. 32 51 35; fax (8) 83 03 33), was barricaded with trucks, barbed wire, sandbags, and nationalism during the 1991 struggle for independence. Call or visit the office, Maztrokšnu iela 2, a day in advance to arrange a free tour. The small street across Jēkaba iela from the Parliament, **Trokšņu iela** (Noisy Street), deserves its name from its location just inside the city walls, where soldiers were always rowdy. A block down this passage is the **Zviedru vārti** (Swedish Gate), built into the city walls in 1698 when Sweden ruled Latvia. Through it, Torņa iela leads to **Pulvertornis** (Powder Tower), one of Rīga's oldest landmarks and the only city tower still standing. Nine cannonballs are still lodged in its 14th-century walls; it's not clear why they're on the side facing *into* the city. Inside, the **Latvijas kara muzejs** (Latvian Museum of War), Smilšu iela 20 (tel. 722 81 47), shows Latvian resistance to Soviet rule; Latvians hated Communism so much that 200,000 enlisted in the German army during WWII (appeals to German heritage were apparently also a factor), and guerrilla bands continued fighting until the mid-50s. Several floors display weapons through the centuries (including the cockpit of a MIG-15), uniforms, and descriptions of conflicts in tones that vary from proud joy to horror (open Tues.-Sun. 10am-6pm; 0.40Ls, students 0.20Ls).

In the park-ring near Pulvertornis, ruins of the old walls remain on **Bastejkalns.** Across and around the city canal, an old defensive moat, five red stone slabs stand as memorials to the dead of January 20, 1991, when Soviet special forces stormed the Interior Ministry on Raiņa bulv. The dead included a schoolboy and two cameramen recording the events. At the north end of the park, on Kr. Valdemāra iela, lies the **National Theater,** where Latvia first declared its independence on November 18, 1918 (open Mon.-Fri. 10am-7pm, Sat.-Sun. 11am-6pm). In the park, Kaļķu iela widens to become Brīvības bulv., where the beloved **Brīvības Piemineklis** (Freedom Monument), nicknamed "Milda," was dedicated in 1935, while Latvia was an independent republic. The Soviets left this standing, yet Intourist used to craftily explain that the mighty figure represented Mother Russia supporting the three Baltic States (it actually shows Liberty raising up the three regions of Latvia—Vidzeme, Latgale, and Kurzeme). The inscription reads "Fatherland and Freedom." Across the **Esplanāde** near Elizabetes iela, the **Valsts mākslas muzejs** (Art Museum), Kr. Valdemāra iela 10 (tel. 32 50 21), has work by Latvian and Russian artists until 1945 (open Wed.-Mon. 11am-5pm; museum 0.50Ls; exhibition 0.40Ls). At Brīvības 23, the Russian **Pareiztcīgo Katedrāle** (Orthodox Cathedral), opposite Hotel Latvija, is part construction site, part functioning church. The cathedral was built in 1884, and was turned into an observatory by the Soviets. Latvians still call it "the planetarium."

Several other sights outside the city center are worth seeing. On Zaķusalas island in the middle of the Daugava River, the viewing platform and cafe of the **TV Tower** (tel. 20 09 43) loom 98m over the city, offering stunning panoramas of Vicrīga. To get there, take trolleybus #19 from behind the train station. To the north, **Mežaparks,** a 6km square woodland area at the end of tram line #11, houses the **city zoo,** pr. Meža 1 (tel. 51 80 35; open daily 10am-7pm; 0.80Ls). On the south end of this expanse, the three main cemeteries of Rīga assumed considerable symbolic significance in the struggle for Latvian nationhood. **Brāļu Kapi** (Brothers' Cemetery) is dedicated to soldiers who fell during the World Wars and the 1918-20 struggle for independence. The poet Jānis Rainis rests in the smaller **Rainis Kapi,** along with other Latvian nationalists, literary figures, and important Communist stooges of the last 50 years. **Meža Kapi** (Forest Cemetery) is a peaceful area filled with stones designed to represent the personalities of the men and women they commemorate. All three can be reached by taking tram #11 to "Braļu Kapi," 11 stops from the starting point at the train station. The much-touted **Rīgas Motormuzejs** (Motor Museum), Eizenšteina 6 (tel. 53 77 30), has a wacky collection of cars and related objects old and new, including Stalin's seven-ton armored *Chaika* limousine and Brezhnev's crashed Rolls Royce Silver Shadow, complete with wax figures of the former dictators. To get there, take bus #21 from Pareiztcīgo Katedrāle on Brīvības to the suburbs, and get out at the Šmerļa iela stop in the Mežciems region (open Tues.-Sun. 10am-6pm; 0.40 Ls, students 0.20Ls). The **Etnogrāfiskais Brīvdabas Muzejs** (Open-Air Ethnographic Museum; tel. 99 41 06), on the shores of the Juglas Ezers (Lake), has collected nearly a hundred 18th- and 19th-century buildings from all regions of Latvia, including churches, complete farmsteads, and a windmill. On the first weekend of June, the annual crafts fair here draws hundreds of artists. To reach the museum, take tram #6 to the end of the line, walk across the bridge, and turn right onto Brīvdabas iela (open daily May-Oct. 10am-5pm).

ENTERTAINMENT AND NIGHTLIFE

Birthplace of Mikhail Baryshnikov, Rīga is home to the **Latvian National Opera** and the **Rīga Ballet.** Theaters are closed during the summer; the rest of the year, purchase tickets at Teātra 10/12 (tel. 722 57 47; open daily 11am-3pm and 4-6pm). The **Russian Drama Theater** is in Vecrīga at Kaļķu 16 (tel. 722 46 60; tickets 0.35-2.00Ls). At the Doma Baznīca, **ērģeļmūzikas koncerts** (organ concerts) employ the third-largest organ in existence. Buy tickets at Doma laukums 1, opposite the main entrance at *koncertzāles kase* (tel. 721 34 98; open daily noon-3pm and 4-7pm). The **Latvian Symphony Orchestra** has frequent concerts in the Large and Small Guilds off Filharmonija laukums, while ensembles and artists from abroad perform in **Vāgnera zāle,** Vāgnera iela (open daily noon-3pm and 4-7pm). The ticket office, which sells tickets for nearly all concerts in Rīga, is on the first floor of the Large Guild, Amatu iela 6 (tel. 22 36 18).

Rīga doesn't sleep at night. Almost every day of the week in summer, into the wee hours, young and old wander or stumble loudly through the streets of Vecrīga and the surrounding area. People drop into countless bars, but mostly gravitate toward the vast beer gardens of Doma laukums and the smaller ones at Filharmonija laukums.

Pulkuedim Neviens Neraksta, Peldu 26/28 (tel. 721 38 86). At night, trendy youth pile over the backlit steel bridge, and a few even dance to the "alternative" (mainstream American rock) sounds. By day, it's a restaurant with an exotic menu. Salad and a brie sandwich (1.55Ls), fish soup (0.76Ls), 0.5L *Aldaris* (0.90Ls). Open Sun.-Thurs. noon-3am, Fri.-Sat. noon-5am. After 9pm, 1Ls cover.

Paddy Whelan's, Grēcineku iela 4. Rīga's first Irish pub. Fast-flowing beer sates a noisy, friendly crowd of local students, backpackers, and the occasional businessman. Pint of Guinness (and other Irish brews) 1.20Ls. *Aldaris* 0.55Ls. Open nightly 5pm-midnight; food served until 8pm. MC, Visa.

Ala (Cave), Audēju iela 11 (tel. 722 89 43). Go through a glass door, and walk through the building to the steep steps on the left. Subscribing to the "ant colony" school of bar design, tunnels and stairways connect little rooms filled with pool tables, bars, slot machines, and young cave-dwellers just hanging out. *Aldaris* 0.50Ls. Open Mon.-Fri. 10am-11pm, Sat. 11am-11pm, Sun. noon-11pm.

M (Maksims) Bars, Čaku iela 45 (tel. 27 54 41). Cozy black interior has wood paneling, low leather booths, and a slightly higher grade of techno. *Shashliks* 1.95Ls. Chicken fillet with mushrooms, red peppers, and cheese, a popular dish, is 2Ls. Sandwiches 0.35Ls. *Aldaris* only 0.36Ls. Open 24hr. Cash only.

Clubs

Rīga's *diskotekas* are growing in number. Things get crowded on weekends, but keep in mind that Friday night is bigger and badder than Saturday, and that the most popular places change quickly. Rīga has two **gay** nightclubs: **Purrs,** Matisa 60/62 (open Tues.-Sun. 9pm-6am; cover 0.50-1.50Ls); and **808,** Kalniņa 8 (open Wed.-Thurs. and Sun. 6pm-midnight, Fri.-Sat. 6pm-6am).

Groks Stacija, Kaļķu iela 22, near the Freedom Monument. The disco downstairs is meant to evoke a metro stop, complete with fluorescent graffiti. The bar upstairs has a small loft with several tables—during the day, it functions as a bistro. Salad 0.20Ls. *Aldaris* 0.65Ls. Open daily noon-6am. 3Ls cover Fri.-Sat. after 10pm.

Olé, Audeju 1 (tel. 722 32 06), in Vecrīga. The painted walls, mainstream music, and central location draw a crowd on weekends to gyrate under colored lights on the second floor. Billiards in basement. Open Tues.-Sat. 10:30pm-5am. Cover 2-3Ls.

Underground, Slokas 1 (tel. 722 19 26). Perhaps the most popular club in Rīga, across the river from Vecrīga. Open Tues.-Sun. 9pm-6am. Cover 1Ls.

Zero Zone, Kandaras 27 (tel. 45 80 62). This disco is the largest in town, with several bars and billiards tables. The crowd ranges from teenagers whose looks could kill to aging tourists. Open Thurs.-Sun. 10pm-6am. Cover 3Ls.

■ Near Rīga

The beaches of **Jūrmala** (see p. 314) or the forests and valleys of the **Gauja National Park** (see p. 320) are the most popular daytrips from Rīga. Sun-lovers who don't care for crowds should head to **Saulkrasti,** an hour north on the suburban trains (0.35Ls), with wider, sparser beaches that get direct sun far into the evening.

DĀRZIŅI

Electric trains travel frequently from Rīga to **Dārziņi** (*not* "Salaspils" on the Krustpils line; 14 per day, 20min., 0.18Ls), the site of the **Salaspils Memorial,** where the Kurtenhof concentration camp was located during WWII. Blue and yellow signs point the way (20min.). At the entrance to the memorial dedicated to 100,000 victims, the overhead inscription reads, "Behind this gate the earth moans." A huge concrete museum-memorial and a field of immense statues depicting the suffering and courage of the camp's victims watch over barracks sites layered in flowers.

PILSRUNDĀLE

The magnificent **Rundāles pils** (Rundāles Palace) is perhaps the most interesting and imposing piece of architecture in the Latvian countryside. It was designed for **Ernst Johann von Bühren** (**Bīrons** in Latvian) by **Bartolomeo Rastrelli,** the Italian master who also planned St. Petersburg's Winter Palace. How such a structure came to be built when Kurzeme (German Courland, the west and south parts of present-day Latvia) wasn't even a part of the Russian empire, but a semi-independent duchy under Polish and Russian influence, tells something of the Baltic Germans' role in the empire. Bīrons was chief advisor and lover of a Russian empress, Anna, who was married to the German **Frederick, Duke of Courland.** Reflecting his power-hungry status, Bīrons decided to build the palace, and Anna duly sent Rastrelli to Courland in 1736. In 1737 Frederick died, and Anna gave the dukedom to Bīrons, who decided to have an even larger palace built in Jelgava. Work on Rundāle slowed and then stopped completely when Anna died in 1740, and the new power structure under Empress Elizabeth found Bīrons more palatable in Siberian exile. In 1763, however, **Catherine the Great** ascended the throne, and Bīrons was allowed to return. Over the next four years, the interior wall decorations of the Baroque Pilsrundāle were completed by **Johann Michael Graff** in Rococo style. Bīrons held onto the palace until 1795, when Russia annexed Kurzeme, and he was forced to flee again.

Used variously by the Soviets as a grain storehouse, hospital, and primary school, the palace was in a dismal state when restoration began. Basketball hoops had been screwed into the walls of the parquet-floored dining room, which was used as a gym until the school moved and restoration work began in 1979. With most of the palace's 138 rooms to refurbish, work will continue for many years, but the restored section includes the most opulent rooms. Up the grand staircase, now redone, is the **Zelta Zāle** (Gold Room), the marble and gold-leaf **throne room,** with dramatic murals and soldiers' graffiti from as long ago as 1812. The **Baltā Zāle** (White Room) was the ballroom; plasterwork cherubim depict the four seasons and the four elements (palace open summer Wed.- Sun. 10am-6pm, off-season 10am-5pm; 1Ls, students 0.70Ls). It'll cost you more, but the exhibit of art recovered from churches brutalized by the Soviets is worth it (2Ls, students 1.40Ls). An English guidebook (0.15Ls) is available, as are info-packed tours (1½-2hr., 8-10Ls; call (239) 621 97 in advance to arrange). The kitchen's immense fireplaces heated the ballroom year-round and cooked an estimated 1200 eggs and one steer every day; refurbished, it now houses a **cafe.** The palace hosts **concerts** on Museum Day (May 18), Independence Day (Nov. 18), and Christmas. Around the third week in July there is an **Early Music Festival** (2Ls for a day of tunes; call the director's office at (239) 622 74 for details).

To get there, you'll have to go through **Bauska,** connected to Rīga by **bus** (22 per day, 1¾hr., 0.40Ls). Then take the bus to Jelgava; ask the driver to drop you off at Pilsrundāle (8-10 per day, 25min., 0.20Ls). From that bus stop, go left at the big Pilsrundāle sign, and walk 1.3km. The palace is around a hedge to the left. Half the daily buses go all the way to the hedge.

■ Jūrmala

Since the late 19th century, Rīgans have spent their summers on this narrow spit of sand 20km from the capital between the Gulf of Rīga and the Lielupe River. In 1959, 14 towns were conglomerated into the city-resort Jūrmala (YOUR-ma-la). A handful of towns dot the coast; from Rīga, beachless Priedaine is the first train stop in Jūrmala; the tracks then pass over the Lielupe river and quickly run through Lielupe, Bulduri, Dzintari, Majori, Dubulti, Jaundubulti, Pumpuri, Melluži, Asari, Vaivari, and Sloka before heading back inland to Kudra and Ķemeri. The **commuter rail** runs one train every 30 minutes in both directions from 5am to 11:30pm. **Public buses** (15 santīmi) string together Jūrmala's towns, each connecting two to four towns.

On the side facing the Gulf, the sand dunes of **Lielupe,** the first town with beach access (from Rīga: 30min., 0.23Ls), are the most dramatic in Latvia, but the towns between **Bulduri** and **Dubulti** are more popular for sunning and swimming. Gulf water is polluted, and swimming is prohibited. Nevertheless, hordes of young and old wade out into the shallow waters to splash around on hot days.

Majori (from Rīga: 35min., 0.32Ls), Jūrmala's center, sees trainloads of people filing to the beach or wandering up and down **Jomas iela,** Majori's pedestrian street, which is lined with cafes, restaurants, and shops. To the left, streets head for the beach; to the right, it's back to the parallel road and train tracks running the length of Jūrmala. The **Jānis Rainis Memorial Museum,** Pliekšāna iela 5/7 (tel. 76 42 95), displays the poet's works, books, and photos in the villa where he died in 1929 (open Wed.-Sun. 10am-4:30pm; 0.50Ls, students 0.20Ls). The **tourist office,** Jomas iela 42 (tel. 642 76), has **maps** (1Ls), a wealth of brochures, and a helpful director who speaks perfect English (open Mon.-Fri. 9am-5pm). The office also books hotel **accommodations** in Jūrmala. **Exchange money** at **Baltijas Tranzitu Banka,** Jomas iela 59 (tel. 613 11; open Mon.-Fri. 9:30am-4pm). The **post office** is on the same side of the street at Jomas iela 2. The **telephone office,** Lienes iela 18 (tel. 643 75), is parallel to the train tracks (open 24hr.). **Postal code:** LV-2015. **Phone code:** 27.

The cheapest place to stay is surprisingly nice: **Sanatoriaja Marienbāde,** Meijerovica Prospekt 43 (tel. 625 18; fax 614 64). It has clean rooms on the beach with private baths (7Ls per person). You can lounge on the beach here or go swimming in the sanatorium's sea-water pool (1Ls). To get there, walk west from Rīga, from the station along Jomas street until it turns into Meijerovica; look for a sign for the sanatorium and a stone arch on the right, and go through the arch.

Majori has a number of **grocery shops,** including one of the biggest, **Majori,** Jomas 65/67 (tel. 610 50). You can also exchange money here (open daily 8am-10pm). **Orients,** Jomas iela 33 (tel. 620 82), is the Big Kahuna of local eateries; the food is as good as you'll find in Latvia. Try Uzbek *plov,* a rice dish (1.60Ls), or tasty beef shish kebab (3.20Ls; open daily 10am-midnight; EC, MC, Visa). At Jomas iela 66/3, **Barbara** (tel. 622 01) smacks a big, bland omelette on your plate (0.79-0.85Ls). Enter on Janna iela (open daily 11am-midnight). One of Majori's many **bars** is **Jomas 77,** at, interestingly, Jomas 77 (tel. 648 25), serving food (hamburgers 1.35Ls) and *Aldaris* beer (0.45Ls; open daily 8am-11pm). The **Vikings** discotheque, Kondordijas 13 (tel. 76 45 57), a red brick building off Jomas iela, hosts DJs and occasional theme shows (open Wed.-Sun. 9pm-6am. Cover 1-2Ls).

At the end of Jūrmala, **Ķemeri** was once the prime health resort of the Russian empire. Therapeutic mud baths, sulphur water, and other cures have operated here since the mid-18th century. The impressive white **Sanatorium** (tel. 76 53 88), built in 1936 vaguely in the style of an Art Deco ocean liner, is an aging palace (singles 5.7Ls; doubles 10Ls). The interior has a restored library complete with period furniture and tapestries. The #6 bus to "Sanitorija Latvia" brings you close; take the paved road next to the bus stop, following the street lights to the original, grand entrance.

■ Kuldīga

Legend has it that Kuldīgas Rumba (the town's waterfall on the Venta River) formed after a rooster's call scared the devil out of the Devil, making him drop a sack of rocks into the river. Once the seat of the Duchy of Courland, Kuldīga (kool-DEE-ga) was battered in the Great Northern War, never to regain its importance. Its typical Baltic architecture, relatively unscathed by Soviet rule, as well as its views of the Venta, make it one of the prettiest stops in Kurzeme, the west region of Latvia.

Orientation and Practical Information About 150km west of Rīga, Kuldīga's town center can be traversed in just 10 minutes. The main street, **Liepājas iela,** is a 15-minute walk from the bus station. **Diku iela** and **Pils iela** hug the castle park across a tributary of the Venta. Only buses come to Kuldīga, arriving at the small **bus station,** Stacijas iela 2 (tel. 220 61; open daily 4:30am-9pm), from Rīga (10 per day, 3hr., 1.90Ls). To get to the center, turn right out of the station and walk to the big, brown-black barn. Take a left on Jelgavas iela, and follow it until it turns into Muce-nieku iela, then take a right on Putnu iela to reach Liepājas iela. The **tourist information office,** Pilsētas lankums 5 (tel. 222 59), off Liepājas iela, sells **maps** (0.50Ls). The office also books one-hour English-speaking tours of the town (5Ls). You can also rent inflatable **boats** here to float around in the Venta (3Ls per day; office open Mon.-Fri. 9am-5pm, Sat. 9am-2pm). **Store luggage** at the bus station (0.10Ls; open daily 6am-6pm). **Exchange money** at **Zemes Banka,** Liepājas iela 15 (tel. 236 89), which accepts AmEx traveler's checks and gives EC and MC cash advances (open Mon.-Fri. 10am-4pm). The **post office** is at Liepājas iela 34 (open Mon.-Fri. 8am-6pm, Sat. 8am-4pm). **Postal code:** LV-3300. The **telephone office** is upstairs from the post office (open daily 7am-10pm). **Phone code:** 033.

Accommodations and Food The Soviet edifice of **Viesnīca Kuršu,** Pilsētas laukums 6 (tel. 224 30), is the most prominent object in the wide square. Clean singles, with private baths but cold water, cost 6Ls (doubles 9Ls). If you like your water hot, it's 11Ls (14Ls for doubles). The new **Jāņa Nams Hotel,** Liepājas iela 36 (tel. 234 56), offers charming doubles with beautiful private baths (20Ls).

Jāņa Nams Hotel has a **cafe** in front with a trendy half-brick interior that serves decent but modestly proportioned dishes, including salad (0.40Ls), pork chops (1.55Ls), and *Aldaris* beer (0.60Ls). One of the cheapest eats in town is crowded **Staburadze Kafejnica,** Liepājas iela 8 (tel. 235 99), closer to the river. Pork *carbonade* (fried in egg) with greasy fries is 1.36Ls (open Mon.-Sat. 7:30am-7pm, Sun. 10am-6pm). For frogs' legs (2.46Ls), go to the popular **Namiņš Restaurant,** Kalna iela 25a (tel. 226 97) near the red-brick bridge over the Venta. You can dine outside on less amphibious options, including pork with mushrooms (1.51Ls), omelettes with cheese (0.83Ls), and salad (0.47Ls; open Mon.-Tues., Thurs.-Fri. 11am-midnight, Sat.-Sun. 11am-1am; Visa, MC, EC). The **Rumba Cafe,** on Pils iela at the top of the castle park, has great views of the *rumba* (waterfall). *Aldaris* is 0.45Ls (open 11am until the last customer leaves). One of Kuldīga's many **grocery shops** is **Gamma,** Liepājas iela 28 (tel. 223 05; open Mon.-Fri. 8am-10pm, Sat. 8am-5pm, Sun. 9am-3pm).

Sights The most famous church in Kuldīga, **Sv. Katrīnas baznīca** (St. Katrina's), is a large white building on Baznīcas iela (services Sun. 10am-noon). Built in 1655, but reconstructed during the 19th and 20th centuries, the Soviets used it as a museum. An 1807 **water mill** stands down the hill. The **oldest house** (built in 1670) ages still further on the same street at #7. The ornate orange-and-brown building at the end of the street is the 1860 **town hall,** Rātslaukums 1, now a library. An **older town hall,** a black wooden building built in the 17th century, is located to the left at Rātslaukums 5. The **Kuldīgas Novada Pētīšanas Muzejs** (Regional Museum), Pils iela 5 (tel. 223 64), features Stone Age implements, weather vanes, and photographs of nude women. The museum also has interesting pictures of the Livonian Order castle before its destruction (open Tues.-Sun. 11am-5pm; 0.20Ls, students 0.15Ls; tours 8Ls, call a couple of days in advance). Outside, a single-vaulted room of the castle, the top covered by earth and glass, forms part of a **sculpture garden.** The **Lutheran Church of St. Anne,** Dzirnavu iela 12, is a brick giant with green-coned tops (open daily 10am-5pm). The stained glass near the pipe organ shows an absurd Sovietesque scene of bounty and family virtue. On Raiņa iela just off Liepājas iela, the Catholic **Sv. Trisvienības baznīca** (Holy Trinity Church; 1640) has a Rococo interior. Farther up Liepājas, away from the river as you head right on Smilšu iela, stands a red-brick **Russian Orthodox Church.** In the third week of July, Kuldīga hosts a **summer festival** with drama performances in various places around town and night classical concerts.

■ Daugavpils

Founded in 1275 by Germans on the banks of the Daugava, what was then Dünaburg languished unnoticed until Ivan the Terrible swept through in 1577 during the Livonian War. For the next 50 years, Poles, Lithuanians, Russians, Germans, and Swedes fought over the city, with the Poles in the end assuming control over what they called Dvinsk. Heavy fighting during WWI reduced the population by 80%. After WWII, the Soviets repopulated almost 90% of Daugavpils (DOW-gav-pils); even now, the industrial town is little more than 10% Latvian. Ironically considered "Latvia's Second City," it betrays its size only by the westernized shops and chemically refined air (which, incidentally, makes for beautiful sunsets). Otherwise, the pedestrian streets and quiet buildings are in harmony with the emerald peace of the countryside.

Orientation and Practical Information Daugavpils is a walkable city carved in half by two hills and railroad tracks. From the train station, the pedestrian **Rīgas iela** leads to the commercial area, **Centrs.** North of the station, tram tracks follow **18. Novembra iela** through **Jaunbūve,** the residential area. A detailed **map** (0.60Ls) is easy to find at any kiosk. The **tourist office,** Viesnīca Latvija (tel. 297 73), #14 on the 1st floor, while not the most helpful, can be pressed for info on sights, accommodation, and transport to and from town. If #14 is locked, try #15 (open Mon.-Fri. 9am-1pm and 2-6pm). There's a 24-hour **currency exchange** booth in the train station, but banks in town offer better rates. At **Zemes Banka,** Rīgas 22 (tel. 288 65), you can cash AmEx **traveler's checks** and get MC and EC cash advances (open Mon.-Fri. 9am-5pm). There is a Cirrus/EC/MC **ATM** outside **Saules Banka,** Rīgas 38. The **train station** (info tel. 005), east of the commercial section at the end of Rīgas iela (open daily 9am-6pm). Trains zoom to: Rīga (5 per day, 3-6hr., 2.18-4.50Ls); St. Petersburg (5 per day, 11-12hr., 6.43-10.84Ls); and Vilnius (7 per day, 4hr., 2.30-5Ls). **Store luggage** downstairs (0.50Ls). Catch **buses** from the station, Viestura iela 26 (tel. 230 00, info tel. 004; open daily 5am-10pm; cashiers 4:45am-7:20pm) to: Aglona (3 per day, 1½hr., 0.84Ls); Vilnius (1 per day, 3hr., 1.60Ls); and Warsaw (Mon., 16hr., 10Ls). Around town, **trams** (0.08Ls) and **buses** (0.09Ls) run daily 6am-1am. Tram #1 goes from the train station past the market and Viesnīca Latvija to Jaunbūve; #3 goes to the same destination from the fortress. Buy tickets on board. With the state taxi service (tel. 254 50), a ride in town (up to 7km) costs 1.50-2Ls. The **post office,** Cietokšņa iela 28 (tel. 223 55), lies one block east and three blocks south of Viesnīca Latvija (open Mon.-Fri. 8am-1pm and 2-7pm, Sat.-Sun. 8am-4pm). It also houses the **telephone office,** Cietokšņa iela 24 (open daily 8am-11pm). **Postal code:** LV-5401. **Phone code:** 254 (from Europe, drop the 2).

Accommodations and Food Even with only two hotels, there's an overabundance of rooms in Daugavpils, except during the mid-August religious festival in nearby Aglona. From the train station, walk 500m on Rīgas iela to get to the Soviet monstrosity **Viesnīca Latvija,** Ģimnāzijas iela 46 (tel. 290 03), on the right. The Soviet rooms come in three almost indistinguishable classes, all with private bath (singles 8.40Ls; doubles 15.40Ls; third class doubles 8Ls; triples 7.50Ls; breakfast included; MC, Visa). Find a good deal at the cheapest place in town, **Viesnīca Celtnieks,** Jelgavas 7 (tel. 325 10), deep in the residential section. Take tram #1 up 18. Novembra iela to "Jelgavas," then make a right onto Jeglavas, and another right on Strādnieku iela. It's the yellow brick sports complex on your left; the hotel, on the fourth floor, sports small, clean doubles (4Ls; with private bath 6Ls). The hall bathrooms are old but clean, and there's a sauna (3-5Ls per hour).

If the restaurant selection leave you unimpressed, there are other options. The **tirgus** (market) on Parādes iela, just behind Viesnīca Latvija, has outdoor produce stalls and indoor meat and fish sections (open daily 7am-4pm). There is a **grocery store, Dinaburga Ceutrs,** at Rīgas iela 22 (tel. 296 11; open daily 7am-midnight). **Mārtiņš,** Muzeja iela 2 (tel. 233 28), a left off Rīgas on Imantas iela then left on Muzeja, is easily the best restaurant in town, attentively serving mushroom salad (0.67Ls), Mexican carbonade (1.46Ls), and chicken filet (1Ls; open daily noon-midnight). Bands sometimes play from 8pm to closing (cover Tues.-Thurs. 0.50Ls, Fri.-Sun. 0.80Ls). The centrally located **Kafejnīca "Vecais Draugs,"** Vienības iela 22 (tel. 221 58), plays loud music and serves tolerable tomato and cucumber salads (0.22Ls) and pork chops with fries and cucumbers (1.30Ls). *Aldaris* is on tap (0.5L 0.38Ls; open daily 9am-11pm). There's nothing American about **Little Johnny's American Pizza** (Jānītis), Rīgas 55, not even the pie (1Ls; open daily 9am-8pm).

Sights and Entertainment The **four churches** district, in the eastern half of Daugavpils, is the city's tourist highlight. To get there, take tram #3 to "Lokomotīve," just past the bridge over the railway tracks. The huge **Borisa-Gleba katedrāle,** Tartac iela 2 (tel. 535 44), is pure fantasy in rich purple, cobalt, and white, topped by starry blue onion domes with gold trim (mass Sun. 8am and 5pm). Inside, dark, classical icons clutter every available surface; a local belief held that every member of the congregation had to have a different patron saint. A block up on 18. Novembra iela, workers slowly refill the burnt-out shell of the **Luterāņu baznīca** after a 1987 fire gutted the church. Just a block farther east, at Andreja Pumpura iela 11a, is the more austere **Jaunavas Marijas katoļu baznīca,** still serving Daugavpils's Polish 13% minority (open daily 9:30am-noon). **Vecticībnieku baznīca** (Church of the Old Believers), on the corner of Pushkin and Tartac iela, reveals a more haphazard construction, its interior cluttered with aged icons surrounding rows of benches. It is home to a perennially persecuted Russian sect that fled to Latvia during Peter the Great's reign. Inside, women must cover their heads and are not permitted behind the wall of icons; everyone must always face the front. Contrary to Russian Orthodox tradition, worshippers cross with three fingers (Sun. service 8am). Abandoned by its spired comrades, **Sv. Pētera baznīca** (tel. 205 84) languishes near Viesnīca Latvija. Modeled in the 1840s after St. Peter's in Rome, it shadows spontaneous Hare Krishna concerts (open Mon.-Thurs. 8:30am-8pm, Fri.-Sun. 9:30-11am and 7-8pm).

The immense **Cietoksnis** (Fortress) was abandoned by the Soviet Air Force in 1992. The Teutonic Order built a stockade on this site as early as 1288, that was later replaced by a larger fort that Ivan the Terrible built in 1577. The current ring of bricks and earthen mounds, at tram #3's north terminus through the railroad trestle, only dates back to the early 19th century; the Nazis used the base as **Stalag-340** during WWII. The immense network of military buildings has been totally stripped, though the families that remained behind in Latvia still live in the other half of the complex. A lone guard keeps nosy visitors out of the central courtyards. The **Regional History and Cultural Museum,** Rīgas iela 8 (tel. 227 09), surrounded by vigilant lions, contains one of the only two extant polyphones, which resembles a midget piano without keys and plays minstrel-like music when wound. The museum houses paintings, a tapestry, a statue, a carriage, and a bottle collection (open Tues.-Sat. 11am-6pm; 0.30Ls, students 0.15Ls).

People don't come to Daugavpils for the nightlife. There are a couple of bars in town, but the biggest draw is the **Nakts Club's disco,** Vienības iela 22 (tel. 262 00), part of a complex that includes a casino. Enter on Rīgas iela and go down a set of stairs to get to the dance floor, surrounded by tables where the under-20 crowd gossip (*Aldaris* 0.52Ls; open Wed.-Sun. noon-5pm and 7pm-5am; cover Wed.-Thurs. and Sun. 0.50Ls, Fri.-Sat. 1Ls). In the same building, the **House of Culture** (tel. 262 68) hosts occasional concerts, ballets, and jazz sets (0.30-1.50Ls). A **student theater,** also in the same building, performs September to May (*kase* open Wed.-Sun. noon-6pm).

About 45km northeast of Daugavpils, the town of Aglona is the site of the annual **Ascension Day pilgrimage** on August 15. Thousands of Catholics walk from all over Latvia to their most revered shrine, many carrying elaborately carved wooden crosses, to celebrate at the 1699 cathedral. Buses run to Aglona (3 per day, 1½hr., 0.84Ls). Don't get caught here overnight; there's not a rentable room in the village.

▦ Sigulda

The attractions of Sigulda (si-GOOL-da), 50km east of Rīga, consist of the ruins of several medieval castles, legendary caves, and other goodies connected by a string of nature trails in a picturesque stretch of the Gauga Valley. Part of the Gauga National Park, Sigulda's bobsled run, funicular, bungee jumping, and hot-air ballooning make it a popular daytrip from the capital.

Orientation and Practical Information From the **bus** and **train stations**, walk up **Raiņa iela** to get to the town center. Continue as it transforms into **Gaujas iela,** then bear right on **Turaidas iela. Bus** #12 takes you to Hotel Senleja (0.15Ls), which provides a variety of valuable services if you're persistent; buy **maps** here (0.50Ls). Next door, **Makara Turisma Birojs,** Peldu iela 1 (tel. 737 24; fax 720 06), **rents bikes** (5Ls per day), canoes (8Ls per day), and boats (6Ls per day). The staff also organizes raft, ski, and bike adventures and even supplies ski instruction (Dec. 1-April 1). **Trains** run from Rīga on the Rīga-Lugaži commuter rail line (18 per day, 1hr., 0.53Ls). **Buses** from Rīga (8-10 per day, 1½hr., 0.36Ls) proceed to the *autoosta* (open daily 6am-10pm). **Exchange money** or get EC/MC/Visa cash advances across the street from the train station at **Rīgas Komerc Banka,** Raiņa iela 1 (tel. 016 90; open Mon.-Fri. 9am-5:30pm, Sat. 9-11am). For a **taxi,** call 718 99. The **post office**, Pils iela 2 (open Mon.-Fri. 8am-noon and 1-5pm, Sat. 8am-2pm), contains the **telephone office** (open daily 7am-9pm). **Postal code:** LV-2150. **Phone code:** 29.

Accommodations and Food Gūtman's cave isn't for rent, but rooms are across the way at **Hotel Senleja,** Turaidas iela 4 (tel. 721 62; fax 790 16 11; doubles with aging but clean common baths 9Ls; MC, Visa). To rough it out cold and toiletless, rent a double occupancy **cottage** near the river (4Ls). The best and cheapest place to eat is the **Kafejuīca/Bistro,** Raiņa iela 1, next to the bank. This cafeteria-style eatery has salads, pork chops, chicken shish kebabs, and rice, all sold by weight (decent-sized meals about 1.5Ls; *Aldaris* beer 0.35Ls; open Mon.-Fri. 7am-10pm, Sat.-Sun. 7am-midnight; MC, Visa). **Siksparnīs Restaurant** serves salads (0.65Ls), shish kebabs (2.25Ls), and *Aldaris* (0.80Ls; open daily 11am-midnight). There is a **grocery store** in the new complex next to the Kafejuīca (open Mon.-Sat. 8am-11pm, Sun. 8am-9pm; MC, Visa).

Sights Perched on a ridge to the right of Gauja iela, on the near side of the gorge, is the **Siguldas dome,** the new "castle" where the Russian **Prince Kropotkin** once lived. Behind, the immense ruins of **Siguldas pilsdrupas** (Sigulda Castle) hint at their former magnificence. Constructed by the German Order of Knights of the Sword from 1207 to 1226, the fortress was destroyed in the Great Northern War. At the end of the paved path opposite the 1225 **Siguldas baznīca** (Sigulda's Church), the **cable car** hangs out (2 per hour, 5min., 0.50Ls). To the right of the terminal, stones still trickle

---

Every Little Thing She Does Is Magic

As a little girl, Maija was brought to Turaida Castle after she was found wandering among the wounded of a 1601 battle. As she grew older, she became a famous beauty for whom suitors would travel from far away. But her heart belonged to Victors, the gardener at the opposing Sigulda Castle. The two would secretly meet at Gūtmaņa ala, a cave located between the castles, until a Polish officer, pretending to be Victors, lured Maija there one day. Maija offered the officer her scarf in return for her freedom, saying it was magical. To test her claim, the officer, believing the scarf would protect Maija, struck her with his sword and killed her. As the gardener said his final farewells, he sought to shade her rest and make his grief immortal by planting a pair of linden trees. Near **Daiņa kalns** (Hill of Songs), two linden trees still bask in the scent of daisies and roses at the **grave of Maija,** "the Rose of Turaida."

from the small remnant of the 1273 **Krimuldas pilsdrupas,** the bulk of it having fallen in the 1601 Polish-Swedish war. Down the slope and about 500m to the left along Turaidas iela, the chiseled maw of **Gūtmaņa ala** (Gūtman's Cave), inscribed with coats of arms and phrases by generations of Latvians and other visitors since the 16th century, continues to erode.

The partially wooden building farther up Turaidas and up the hill to the right is the 1750 **Turaidas baznīca** (Turaida church), now home to a small archaeological museum (tel. 95 16 20; open daily 9:30am-6pm). The **sculpture park** covering the surrounding hills is dedicated to **Krišjānis Barons,** a 19th-century scholar who preserved 20,000 Latvian folksongs. Farther out rise the towers and walls of **Turaidas pils** (Turaidas Castle), begun in 1214 by the Knights of the Sword. Restored earlier in this century, the skyscraping red tower is home to the **Siguldas novadpētniecības muzeja** (History Museum), Turaidas iela 10 (tel. 97 14 02). The tower contains impressive displays on the history of the Liv people, from their immigration to Latvia in the 3rd century to their near-elimination in the 12th-century crusades, complete with English descriptions and *faux* ancient music. Ascend the steep staircase for nauseatingly elevated views of the region and a chance to pretend you're watching a horde of enemy knights through an arrow slit in the 3m-thick wall (open daily 10am-6pm; 0.80Ls; includes museum, tower, and adjacent buildings.)

Sports and Entertainment Hiking options here are numerous. An excellent 2km walk follows the Gauja River to the steep **Piķenes Slopes,** where two caves, the deep **Velna ala** (Devil's Cave) and **Mazā velnala** (Devil's Little Cave), merit mention. The nearby spring is purportedly a **Fount of Wisdom** in which ambitious mothers bathe their babes. Another good hike goes from Siguldas pilsdrupas down to the Gauja, then heads upstream to cross **Vējupite creek.** Upstream another 100m, stairs rise to **Paradīzes kalns** (Paradise Hill), where 19th-century Latvian painter Jānis Rozentāls made the valley view famous. The **Gauja National Park Center,** Baznicas iela 3 (tel. 713 45), has guided English tours (minimum 10Ls per guide, not including cable car and museum prices). Call two days in advance to arrange tours. Visit the center in any case to see the stuffed wild boars in the office (open daily 9am-5pm). For safety info, see **Essentials: Wilderness and Safety,** p. 42.

Visible from the commuter rail, the Olympic-size **bobsled and luge run** plummets from Sveices iela 13 (tel. 739 44; fax 790 16 67). From October to March, you can take the plunge (1Ls; open Sat.-Sun. 10am-8pm). From the bridge, a thin rope supports a tiny red **cable car.** This is the local **bungee jumping** thread; call 762 51 for reservations. Those itching to go one-on-one with gravity climb the wooden stairs, sign a release, and jump away (12Ls; open Sat.-Sun. 6-10pm).

Vade Mecum, Pusas iela 12 (tel. 61 16 14; fax (8) 86 02 06), offers **hot-air balloon** rides (0.50Ls). The **International Ballooning Festival** floats out of town in the third week of May. Next to the Turaidas Museum, Turaidas 10, **horses** are available for hire, with or without a trainer (tel. 745 84; 5Ls per hour; open Tues.-Sun. 10am-6:30pm). Play **minigolf** at Parka iela (tel. 238 08; 0.50Ls before 2pm, 1Ls after) or **tennis** across the street (1Ls per hour before 2pm, 3Ls after; open daily 11am-9pm).

■ Cēsis

The master of the Livonian Order (the German knights who controlled Latvia and Estonia during the 13th-16th centuries) once made his headquarters here, but since a brief stint as a popular 1930s resort, Cēsis (TSEH-siss) has declined in glory. The quiet and deteriorated state of many of its buildings now adds to its sad beauty. The center of Gauja National Park, it's a great base for hikes along the Gauja River.

Orientation and Practical Information Raunas iela runs to the town center from the bus station, then empties into the main square, **Vienības laukums.** **Rigas iela** and **Valnu iela,** heading downhill at the square's south end, meet at **Līvu laukums,** the original 13th-century heart of the city. **Lenču iela,** which runs away from Vienības laukums, travels to **Cēsu pils** (Cēsis Castle). From Rīga, Cēsis is easily reached via suburban **trains** (10 per day, 1½-2hr., 0.93Ls), and **buses** (17 per day, 2hr., 1.10Ls); for convenience, purchase your return ticket in Rīga. The **bus station** is at one with the **train station** (tel. 227 62; open daily 8am-2pm and 3-7pm); ask the cashier to **store luggage.** A **map** (1L) is available at Cēsis Hotel, Vienības laukums 1 (tel. 223 92). The **tourist office,** in a small yellow building at Uzvaras Bulvaris 8 (tel. 222 46), functions best as a travel agency. To get information, be persistent and insist on doing things yourself, as they encourage you to book every excursion through them, as in Soviet days (open Mon.-Fri. 10am-5pm, Sat. 10am-3pm). There is a **market** on Uzvaras Bulvaris between Vienības laukums and the tourist office. The **tourist service** at the hotel offers excursions for large groups, but the friendly staff will point out local places of interest for individuals. Call a few days in advance (open daily 9am-5pm). **Public transportation** consists of two buses (0.15Ls). Bus #9 runs west to the Gauja river; catch it on Vienības laukums from the stop on the woodier side. Bus #11 runs east from the bus station along Poruka iela and down Lapsu iela (Mon.-Sat.). **Exchange currency** at **Unibanka** (tel. 228 03), on Raunas iela, which accepts MC, Thomas Cook, and Visa traveler's checks and gives Visa and MC cash advances (open Mon.-Fri. 9am-5pm, Sat.-Sun. 9am-2pm). The **post** and **telephone offices,** Raunas iela 14-15, sit at the corner of Vienības laukums. The post office (tel. 227 88) is housed in a new red brick building (open Mon.-Fri. 8am-7pm, Sat. 8am-6pm), and the telephone office (tel. 078) is in the old post office, a yellow building across the street (open daily 7am-10pm). You can send a **fax** (tel. 241 09) abroad for 1.85Ls. **Postal code:** LV-4100. **Phone code:** 0241.

Accommodations and Food

The only hotel in the center is the **Cēsis Hotel,** Vienības Lakums 1 (tel. 223 92), run by a Danish company. The rooms are very pleasant, with new furniture and baths, even if they are already slightly deteriorating (singles 12Ls-22Ls; doubles 15-30Ls). **Putniųkrogs,** Saules iela 23 (tel. 202 90), offers modest singles (4-5.50Ls) and doubles (6-8Ls). To hike here, take Valmiera iela away from Vienības laukums, make a hard right onto J. Poruka iela, and another right onto the dirt Puku iela, which leads to the hotel; there's no bus. **Kafejnīca Raunis** (tel. 238 30), where Rauna iela meets the square, presents plentiful if somewhat bland main courses: veal schnitzel (1.60Ls) or chicken filet with cheese (1.65Ls), accompanied by local *Cēsu* beer (0.58Ls; open daily 8am-10pm). **Cēsis Hotel restaurant,** Vienības laukums 1 (tel. 223 92), offers an English menu with more elaborate and tasty meals at higher prices (trout with almonds 3.90Ls, popular avocado soup 0.90Ls). Vegetarians can ask for specially prepared meals (open daily noon-midnight).

Sights and Entertainment

Cēsis was taken by the **Livonian Order** in 1209. During the battle, the **Latvian flag** was inadvertently designed: the Latvian leader died on a white sheet, staining it a deep crimson on two sides while leaving the middle section white. Begun the same year, the **castle** the Germans built to rule the region was a mighty fortress with walls 4m thick by its completion in the 1280s. By the late 16th century, the Order's power had lapsed, but when Russia's **Ivan the Terrible** laid siege to its fortress in 1577, the men preferred to fill the cellars with gunpowder and blow themselves up rather than surrender. Later it was partially reconstructed, but when Russians invaded again in 1703 under **Peter the Great,** the castle was bombarded and left in its present ruined state. To see the castle's insides, you must join a guided tour, complete with inane theatricals (tel. 226 15; 2.50Ls, students 1.50Ls; open Tues.-Sun. 10am-5pm). Constructed by a 19th-century baron, the surrounding **park** is mossy, shaded, and peaceful. A pool reflects families feeding ducks as a stone fisherman struggles with a water-spouting fish. Ask a museum attendant to point out the town's **Lenin statue,** now resting under a giant wood crate resembling a coffin. **Cēsis vēstures muzejs** (Cēsis History Museum), Pils iela 9 (tel. 226 15), fills the two castles with artfully arranged regional ephemera, coins, and jewelry (open Tues.-Sun. 10am-5pm; 0.50Ls).

Virtually next door, **Cēsu alus darītava** (Cēsis Beer Brewery), Lenču iela 9/11 (tel. 222 45), the oldest in Latvia, has produced fine beverages since the 1870s. The shop parts with its wares for 0.23-0.26Ls a bottle (open Mon.-Fri. 8am-7pm, Sat. 8am-5pm, Sun. 8am-1pm). Arrange tours in advance with the director (tel. 235 29). To access the older section of town, take Torņa iela from the parking lot by the castle. The Gothic **Jāņa baznīca** (St. John's; 1280-87) on Baznīcas laukums rises above narrow cobbled streets (open Mon.-Fri. 8-10am and 5-8pm; services Sun. 11am). The Gauja river flows on the east side of town, and a number of good **hiking** trails lead along the many cliffs lining the river. Bus #9 in front of the hotel on Vienības laukums takes you the 3km along Gaujas iela to the base of the trails. The best cliffs are to the south.

To find nightline options, exit the bus or train station and cross the road to the large **bulletin board** on the right. Along with hand-written signs, like "I cure virtually all diseases: adults and kids in same way," there are **ballroom dance, disco,** and **movie** posters. Every late July to early August, Cēsis throws a massive **Beer Festival.**

Buses run daily from Cēsis to Lake Āraiši (7-9 per day, 15min., 0.15Ls). From the bus stop, follow the sign on the right to the **old mill.** Up 400m and left off the main road lie a reconstructed 9th- and 10th-century wooden **island-fortress** and a ruined Livonian Order **castle** on the next peninsula. Some believe the Swedes keep maps of a secret underground road connecting this fortress and the one in Cēsis, and that they will guard the secret until they find a way to spirit its gold across the Baltic.

LITHUANIA (LIETUVA)

US$1 = 4.00Lt (Litai)		1Lt = US$0.25
CDN$1 = 2.89Lt		1Lt = CDN$0.35
UK£1 = 6.36Lt		1Lt = UK£0.16
IR£1 = 5.86Lt		1Lt = IR£0.17
AUS$1 = 2.91Lt		1Lt = AUS$0.35
NZ$1 = 2.54Lt		1Lt = NZ$0.39
SAR1 = 0.85Lt		1Lt = SAR1.18
DM1 = 2.20Lt		1Lt = DM0.46

Country Phone Code: 370

International Dialing Prefix: 810

Lithuania once moshed through Central Europe—spitting in the face of proselytizing Christians, ruling over modern-day Ukraine, Belarus, and Poland, and generally using brutal tactics on its neighbors. Ruined castles and fortifications stand as mute reminders of the glory days, while ancient Vilnius welcomes visitors with green parks, relaxed cafes, and an unassuming skyline. Fun in the sun and the Baltics' best beaches await where the mighty Baltic Sea washes up at Palanga and on the Kuršių Nerija

(Curonian Spit). Lithuania also occupies a bizarre niche in the annals of modern culture; its Olympic basketball team was sponsored by the Grateful Dead, and busts of the likes of Frank Zappa now fill the void left by Lenin's fall from grace.

LITHUANIA ESSENTIALS

Citizens of the U.K., U.S., Australia, and Canada can visit Lithuania visa-free for up to 90 days. Citizens of New Zealand or South Africa who have visas from Estonia or Latvia do not need a visa for Lithuania; otherwise regular 90-day visas are required. Got it? No border posts issue visas. Send one photograph, your passport, application fee (by check or money order), and a stamped, self-addressed envelope to the nearest embassy or consulate (see **Essentials: Embassies and Consulates,** p. 4). Single-entry visas cost US$20; multiple-entry visas US$40; transit visas are US$10. Regular service takes two weeks; rush service costs US$20 for 24-hour service or US$15 for 48-hour service. For visa extensions, contact the Migration Dept. at Šaltoniškų 19, Vilnius (tel. (222) 72 58 53 or 72 39 97).

GETTING THERE AND GETTING AROUND

Vilnius, Kaunas, and Klaipėda are easily reached by **train** or **bus** from Belarus, Estonia, Latvia, Poland, and Russia. Most trains from Poland to Vilnius go through Belarus, requiring a transit visa (US$30). The daily *Baltic Express* departs Warsaw at 2:30pm, passes through Kaunas at 11:55pm (74Lt), and arrives in Tallinn the next day at 1:10pm. There is also one overnight train between Warsaw and Šeštokai, Lithuania; it arrives at 6:30am, two hours before a Šeštokai-Kaunas-Vilnius train departs. These two trains, as well as buses from Poland to Lithuania, do not go through Belarus. Land travel often involves lengthy waits at customs, especially at the Polish border. **Planes** land in Vilnius from Berlin (18hr., 832Lt), Moscow (480Lt), Stockholm (1056Lt), and Warsaw (480Lt). **Ferries** connect Klaipėda with German cities Kiel (34hr., 350Lt) and Muhkran (18hr., 140DM).

Trains around Lithuania are slow, noisy, and often crowded. Two major rail lines cross Lithuania: one runs north-south from Latvia through Šiauliai and Kaunas to Poland, and the other runs east-west from Belarus through Vilnius and Kaunas to Kaliningrad, or on a branch line from Vilnius through Šiauliai to Klaipėda. Slightly more expensive and faster **buses** radiate from all the cities of Lithuania.

TOURIST SERVICES AND MONEY

Litinterp, a network of tourist services, arranges private accommodations, rents cars, and stocks loads of city information. Some cities have tourist information offices that vary in helpfulness. The big three Lithuanian metropoles publish detailed guidebooks on their scenes: *Vilnius in Your Pocket,* thoroughly updated every two months and available at newsstands (4Lt), is a best-seller, as are its younger siblings *Kaunas in Your Pocket* and *Klaipėda in Your Pocket.*

The unit of **currency** is the Litas (1Lt=100 centų), plural Litai. Since March 1994, it has been pegged to the U.S. dollar at US$1 = 4.00Lt. **Traveler's checks** can be cashed at most banks (usually for a 2-3% fee). Cash advances on **Visa** cards can usually be obtained with a minimum of hassle in certain banks. **Vilniaus Bankas,** with outlets in major cities, accepts all major credit cards and traveler's checks and charges little commission. Some cities have 24-hour Visa **ATMs.**

COMMUNICATION

Local **phones** in Lithuania cost 20 centų. Long-distance calls can be made from some of the old gray public phones using gold *žetonai* (tokens; 0.24Lt) sold at post offices. It is easiest to use the new Norwegian **card phones;** cards are sold at phone offices in denominations of 3.54Lt, 7.08Lt, and 28.32Lt. Rates for international calls are: Estonia and Latvia 1.65Lt per minute; Europe 3.54Lt; U.S. 10.50Lt. You can book international calls through the operator at the central phone office (pay when finished), but you'll have to wait 20 to 45 minutes for the call to go through. Only some countries can be dialed directly. Dial 8, wait for the second tone, dial 10, then dial the country code and number. Calls to cities within the former Soviet Union can be placed by dialing 8, then the old Soviet phone code after hearing the second tone. For countries to which direct dialing is not available, dial 8, wait for the second tone, and dial 194 or 195 (English-speaking operators available). To reach the **AT&T Direct operator,** dial (8) 196; for **Sprint Express,** dial (8) 197.

Letters abroad cost 1.20Lt, postcards 0.90Lt. Airmail packages weighing up to 250 grams cost 4.80Lt in addition to a 1Lt registration fee. **EMS** international mail takes 3-5 days. Ask for *oro paštu* if you want airmail.

English-language books are cheap, but not plentiful. The English-language *Lithuanian Weekly* covers Lithuanian events in fair depth (2Lt), but is increasingly hard to find and not available at all outside Vilnius. The Tallinn-based *Baltic Independent* and Rīga's *Baltic Observer* are both available in Vilnius, Kaunas, and Klaipėda, and the ever-informative *City Paper—The Baltic States* can be picked up at hotels, kiosks, and tourist info points (US$1.50). In Vilnius, pick up **Voice of America Radio** 24 hours at 105.6 FM.

LANGUAGE

Lithuanian is the most archaic surviving Indo-European tongue, and one of the only two surviving languages in the Baltic branch (Latvian is the other). All "r"s are trilled. Nearly all Lithuanians speak **Russian,** but attempts to use it might be better received after assays in **English** or **German** first. You may need the words *atidarytas* (ah-tee-DAR-ee-tass; open), *uždarytas* (oozh-DAR-ee-tass; closed), *viešbutis* (vee-esh-BOO-tees; hotel), and *turgus* (tuhr-GUHSS; market). For more, see **Glossary,** p. 805.

HEALTH AND SAFETY

> **Emergency Numbers: Fire:** tel. 01. **Police:** tel. 02. **Ambulance:** tel. 03.

A triangle pointing downward indicates men's **bathrooms;** an upward-facing triangle indicates women's bathrooms. Many restrooms are nothing but a hole in the ground. Well-stocked **pharmacies** are everywhere. Anything German with a picture of a man clutching his cranium is likely to be a reliable pain killer. Tylenol and ibuprofen dot the shelves. Drink bottled mineral water, or boil tap water first if you must drink it.

ACCOMMODATIONS

Lithuania has eight **Youth Hostels (LJNN/HI).** HI membership is nominally required, but an LJNN guest card (US$3 at any of the hostels) will suffice. The head office is in Vilnius (see **Vilnius: Practical Information,** p. 329). Their *Hostel Guide* is a handy booklet with info on bike and car rentals, advance booking, and maps showing how to reach various hostels.

FOOD AND DRINK

Lithuanian **cuisine** is heavy, filling, and sometimes very greasy. Restaurants serve various types of *blynai* (pancakes) with *misa* (meat) or *varške* (cheese). *Cepelinai* are heavy, potato-dough missiles stuffed with meat, cheese, and mushrooms, most prominent in west Lithuania. *Šaltibarščiai* is a beet and cucumber soup, not unlike cold borscht, prevalent in the east half of the country. *Karbonadas* is fried breaded pork fillet. Lithuanian **beer** varies in quality. Most restaurants and shops stock *Kalnapilis,* which is passable. *Baltijos,* brewed in Klaipėda, has several good varieties.

CUSTOMS AND ETIQUETTE

Reserve informal **greetings** for those with whom you've bonded. A *"laba diena"* (good day) whenever you enter a shop ensures good feelings, and you can never say *"prašau"* too many times (both "please" and "you're welcome"). Handshakes are reserved for men; women nod or get their hands kissed. **Homosexuality** is legal, but not always tolerated. For info on gay life, contact the Lithuanian Gay League (tel./fax (22) 65 16 38), Vladimiras or Eduardas at P.O. Box 2862, Vilnius 2000, Lithuania.

NATIONAL HOLIDAYS

Lithuania observes: January 1, New Year's; February 16, Independence Day (1918); March 4, St. Kazimieras's Day; April 12-13, Easter Sunday and Monday; 1st Sunday in May, Mother's Day; June 23, Rasos (Midsummer Night); June 24, Joninės (St. John's Day); July 6, Mindaugas Day; November 1, All Saints' Day; November 2, All Souls' Day; December 25-26, Kalédos (Christmas).

LIFE AND TIMES

HISTORY

In the 3rd millennium BC, an Indo-European people settled in what is now Lithuania. Called **Aestii** by the Roman historian Tacitus, these ancients were the only Baltic group to succeed in creating their own political state. At one point, Lithuanians ruled over parts of modern-day Ukraine, Belarus, Poland, and Russia. While Teutonic armies conquered other Baltic peoples, the Lithuanians, shielded by thick forests and natural moats of swampy marshland, held off the invaders. In the mid-13th century, the Teutonic menace prompted various tribes to unite under a single leader, **Mindaugas.** Pope Innocent IV crowned Mindaugus king in 1253, two years after he accepted Christianity. His coronation incorporated the Lithuanian state into the western political hierarchy. After Mindaugas's assassination 10 years later, however, Lithuania reverted to paganism.

The Lithuanian empire, encompassing modern Lithuania, Belarus, and northwestern Ukraine, was consolidated under the 14th-century ruler **Gediminas** (1315-42). After his death, successors **Algirdas** and **Kestutis** divided the kingdom in two. Algirdas extended the his realm eastward toward Moscow, laying siege on, but not conquering the Russian capital in 1370. After Algirdas died, the internal power struggles between his son **Jogaila** and Jogaila's relatives Kestutis and **Vytautas,** coupled with the increasing external threat posed by the **Teutonic Order** busily conquering and subduing Lithuania's neighbors on all sides, forced the nation to seek out a powerful ally. The choice was between Moscow, entailing acceptance of Orthodoxy, or Poland and the acceptance of Roman Catholicism. In 1385, Jogaila married the 12-year-old Polish queen **Jadwiga,** ascended the Polish throne as **Wladislaw II Jagiełło,** and made peace with his cousin Vytautas. Under Vytautas (1392-1430), Lithuania conquered vast tracts of territory, and Lithuanian culture, language, and religion were affected by Poland much more than by isolated Russia under the Mongol Yoke. The empire reached its zenith in the mid-15th century, stretching from the Baltic to the Black Sea to within 100 miles of Moscow.

Lithuania's union with Poland was strengthened and politicized by the meeting of a joint parliament in Lublin on July 1, 1569, which made the Lithuanian-Polish state officially a **Commonwealth of Two Peoples** (a.k.a. **Union of Lublin**). The political alliance began a period of prosperity and cultural development; Lithuania successfully defended itself against Muscovite incursions for the next two centuries. In the mid-17th century, however, peasant unrest among Ukrainian Cossacks, coupled with endemic war with Sweden over Livonia, began to weaken the Polish-Lithuanian Commonwealth. After Vilnius's first sacking by the Russians in 1655, the **Great Northern War** (1700-21) definitively felled the Lithuanian empire. The three **partitions of Poland** carried out by Russia, Austria, and Prussia in 1772, 1793, and 1795, erased the Commonwealth from the European political map; Russia controlled all of Lithuania by 1815.

Successive uprisings against Russian rule during the 19th century only resulted in further repression and intensified Russification. The tsars closed the 250-year-old University of Vilnius, abolished the Lithuanian legal code, and banned use of the Lithuanian language in public places. But the **1905 Russian Revolution** thawed the freeze on Lithuanian liberties, prompting demands for independence.

WWI ignited a new power struggle. German armies entered Lithuania in 1915, 500 years after their last defeat. The 1918 **Treaty of Brest-Litovsk** ceded the Baltic area to Germany, which attempted to organize puppet states in the region. The Germans recognized the "independence" of the Kingdom of Lithuania on March 23, 1918, but occupied the region until the end of the year. No sooner had Germany departed than the **Soviets** moved in. Lithuania managed to expel the Red Army in 1919 and finally concluded a peace treaty with the Soviets in 1920; their successes inaugurated a brief period of independence, during which time they joined the League of Nations. But a fragile parliamentary democracy floundered before collapsing in a 1926 *coup d'état*. Dictator **Antanas Smetona** banned all opposition parties. Meanwhile, Poland had taken Vilnius from the Red Army in 1919 and refused to give it back. Over the next few years, the Poles and the Soviets battled for the city, while the **Nazis** gazed covetously upon the Lithuanian city of Klaipėda. In 1939, they seized the valuable port.

The facade of autonomy crumbled in 1939, when Moscow forced Lithuania to admit Soviet troops; in return, Lithuania got back Vilnius and about one-third of the territory that Poland had seized in 1920. An ostensibly unanimous parliamentary vote absorbed Lithuania into the vast Soviet Union. **Sovietization** entailed a dismanteling and restructuring of Lithuania's government, economy, culture, and society. On the night of June 13-14, 1941, the Soviets began pulling Lithuanians from their homes; deportations to Arctic or desert regions of the USSR eventually displaced 35,000 Lithuanians. In three years of German occupation, the Lithuanian Jewish community was virtually wiped out; total war and occupation deaths in Lithuania have been estimated at 250,000.

The Red Army expelled the Nazis in 1944 and initiated more **Russification** and repression. But the iron fist of Soviet rule did not go unopposed; Lithuanian guerrilla fighters, at times 40,000 strong, badgered the Soviets into the early 50s. Moscow's grip had relaxed by the early 60s, when **Antanas Sniečkus** slowly transformed the republic's government into a nativized political machine. Unlike Latvia and Estonia, Lithuania resisted an influx of Russian immigrants; ethnic Lithuanians still compose 80% of the population.

> The iron fist of Soviet rule was not unopposed, as guerrilla fighters badgered the Soviets into the early 1950s.

The orthodox backlash of the 70s and early 80s failed to quell Lithuanian nationalism; the republic generated more *samizdat* (dissident underground publications) per capita than any other in the Soviet Union. *Glasnost* and *perestroika* spawned a Lithuanian mass reform movement, imaginatively dubbed **Sajúdis** (Movement). On March 11, 1990, Lithuania shocked the world by declaring its **independence** from the Soviet Union. Moscow immediately began reprisals, starting with ineffectual measures to diconnect the region from oil and gas resources. In January 1991, Moscow launched an assault on Vilnius's radio and TV center, leaving 14 people dead. Only in the wake of the failed Soviet putsch of August 1991 did Lithuania achieve a measure of independence. Despite internal divisions, all Lithuanians rejoiced on August 31, 1993, when the last Russian soldiers left Lithuanian soil.

LITERATURE

Early Lithuanian literature was primarily religious in subject matter. The first known book printed in Lithuanian was **M. Mazvydas's** catechism (1547). The **New Testament** was published in 1701, and the entire Scriptures in 1727. Notable outside of religious literature is the first Lithuanian dictionary, the 1629 *Dictionarium trium linguarum,* by **K. Sirvydas,** as well as the German-influenced hexametric poem *Metai (The Four Seasons)*, written in 1818 by **Kristijonas Donelaitis.**

LITHUANIA

The early 19th century saw a new literary movement focusing on **Romantic** themes and the early Lithuanian history. In the wake of the French Revolution, Western influences triggered a renaissance in Lithuanian literature. From 1864, many writers violated the ban on publishing Lithuanian works in Latin letters (as opposed to Cyrillic), seeking to overthrow Russia's political control and Poland's cultural hegemony. The first modern Lithuanian periodical was founded in 1883 by **Jonas Basanavicius;** its name, *Ausra (Dawn)*, became that by which the literature of the ensuing generation was known. One of the poems of **Vincas Kudirka,** a well-known writer of short stories, became the national anthem of independent Lithuania. Known for both dramatic and lyric poetry, "the poet-prophet of the Lithuanian renaissance" was **Jonas Mačiulis,** whose 1895 *Pavasario balsai (Voices of Spring)* inaugurated modern Lithuanian poetry. After independence in 1918, nationalistic trends intensified, with writers concentrating on developing national culture and a greater degree of literary sophistication. Novelist and dramatist **Vincas Kreve-Mickevicius** was regarded by some as Lithuania's greatest writer, while **Jurgis Baltrusaitis** was a distinguished lyrical poet. Ex-priest **Vincas Mykolaitis-Putinas,** known for his novel *Altorių šešėly (In the Altars' Shadow),* pioneered the modern Lithuanian romance. However, Soviet rule following WWII again gagged and shackled Lithuanian writers. New expressive modes were attempted in the philosophical poetry of **Alfonsas Nyka-Niliunas,** the idylls of **J. Mekas,** and the novels of **Marius Katiliskis.** Talented writers **Sigitas Geda** and **Judita Vaičiūnaitė** took on that ever-present Eastern European phenomenon **Socialist Realism,** challenging it with poetry and drama, a mix of realism and mythological ambience, and urban romanticism.

LITHUANIA TODAY

Despite an early start—Lithuania began dismantling the Soviet economic system even before achieving independence from Moscow—Lithuania's economic reforms have run aground. Approximately 80% of the population is considered poor. Disenchantment with government institutions grows, due as much to corruption as the decline in GNP. An associate member of the **EU** since 1995, Lithuania transacts the same amount of business with the EU as with Russia, but remains heavily dependent on its former ruler for fuel. Russia exploits the situation, demanding the right to transport military equipment over Lithuanian soil to Kaliningrad, its dislocated province. A compromise was worked out between the two nations in 1995, but Russia continues to stand firmly opposed to the **NATO** membership Lithuania desires. **Algirdas Brazauskas** of the **Lithuanian Democratic Labor Party** (the former Communists) continues in the five-year Presidential term to which he was elected in 1993. In the **Seimas** (Parliament), current Prime Minister **Gediminas Vagnorius,** of a party comprising the **Homeland Union** (formed in 1993 out of the remains of the dispirited Sąjūdis organization) and the **Conservatives,** heads a coalition of center parties. They hope this return to the center will help the nation attain the economic and political stability required for admittance to NATO and the EU.

> **Lithuania's dismantling of the Soviet economic system began even before the nation achieved independence from Moscow.**

Vilnius

Once a minor city within the vast Soviet empire, Vilnius was able to escape mass Sovietization, retaining its majestic, Baroque beauty. Thrust into the international spotlight during Lithuania's 1991 revolution for independence, Vilnius is poised once again to show the rest of the world what it's all about. In the 19th century, Wilno, as it was called, was the world center of Jewish scholarship. The "Jerusalem of Europe" was home to the Jewish Enlightenment and many influential Hasidic thinkers, including the great Rabbi Gaon. Today, the city's Old Town is home to Catholic and Russian Orthodox churches and even a synagogue, and visitors will hear Lithuanian, Polish, Russian, Belarusian—and, increasingly, English—spoken on the streets. With foreign investment pouring in and new shops and restaurants opening up daily, Vilnius stands on the brink of becoming the next Prague. See it for yourself, before everyone else gets in on the secret.

ORIENTATION AND PRACTICAL INFORMATION

From the **train** or **bus stations**, directly across from each other, walk east on **Geležinkelio g.** (to your left as you face the train station), and turn left at its end. This is the beginning of **Aušros Vartų g.**, which leads north from the south gates of **Senamiestis** (the Old Town), changing its name first to **Didžioji g.**, then **Pilies g.** At the north end, **Arkikatedros aikštė** (Cathedral Sq.) and the **Castle Hill** loom over the banks of the river **Neris. Gedimino pr.**, the commercial artery, leads west from the square in front of the cathedral's doors. Pick up a copy of *Vilnius in Your Pocket* upon arrival. This semi-monthly gem, available at any self-respecting kiosk or hotel (4Lt), includes everything you could ever want to know about the city.

Tourist Offices: The recently-opened **Tourist Information Centre,** Gedimino pr. 14 (tel. 61 68 67; fax 22 61 18), finds rooms for free, sells tickets for concerts and special events, arranges guided tours of Vilnius and other parts of Lithuania (60-80 Lt), rents cars, hands out free brochures, and sells the ever-wonderful *Vilnius in Your Pocket.* English, German, and Russian spoken. Open Mon.-Fri. 9am-6pm, Sat. 10am-3pm. **Lithuanian Youth Hostels Head Office,** Filaretų g. 17 (tel./fax 26 26 60; email lyh@jnakv.vno.soros.lt), at the Filaretai Hostel (see below). Student travel packages, ISICs, and worldwide hostel reservations. Open daily 8am-6pm.

Budget Travel: Lithuanian Student and Youth Travel, V. Basanavičiaus g. 30, #13 (tel. 22 13 73). Best deals in town for travelers 26 and under. Sells ISICs and GO25 cards, Eurail passes, and student tickets for buses, trains, and airplanes. Open Mon.-Fri. 9am-6pm, Sat. 10am-2pm.

Passport Office: Imigracijos Taryba, Verkių 3, #3, (tel. 75 64 53), 2km north of Senamiestis. Extends visas for 61Lt, for those who demonstrate proof of need to stay in Lithuania. Open Mon.-Fri. 9am-4:30pm.

Embassies: Belarus, P. Klimo g. 8 (tel./fax 26 34 43). Visa services at Muitinės g. 41 (tel. 63 06 26). Open Mon.-Tues. and Thurs.-Fri. 10am-4:30pm. **Canada,** Gedimino pr. 64 (tel. 22 08 98; fax 22 08 84). Open Mon.-Fri. 10am-1pm. **Russia,** Latvių g. 53/54 (tel. 72 17 63; fax 72 38 77; visa info tel. 72 38 93; fax 72 33 75). Open Mon.-Tues. and Thurs.-Fri. 10am-1pm. **Ukraine,** Turniškių g. 22 (tel./fax 76 36 26). Visa services on Kalvarijų 159, 2nd floor (tel. 77 84 13). Open Mon.-Tues. and Thurs.-Fri. 10am-1pm. **U.K.,** Antakalnio g. 2 (tel. 22 20 70; fax 72 75 79). Open Mon.-Fri. 9:30am-12:30pm. **U.S.,** Akmenų g. 6 (tel. 22 30 31; fax 670 60 84). Open Mon.-Thurs. 9-11:30am.

Currency Exchange: Vilniaus Bankas, Gedimino pr. 12 (tel. 61 07 23; fax 22 62 88). Cash advances with no commission from your Diners Club, MC, or Visa. Also cashes AmEx and Thomas Cook traveler's checks. Open Mon.-Thurs. 9am-1:30pm and 2:30-4:30pm, Fri. 9am-4pm. **Bankas Snoras,** A. Vivulskio g. 7 (tel. 65 29 76 or 26 27 71; email root@impar.aiva.lt). Cashes Visa and Thomas Cook checks and gives cash advances on Visa (2% commission) at 35 circular blue-and-white kiosks throughout the city. Open daily 8am-8pm. A Visa **ATM** lurks at **Vilniaus Bankas.** Another one hides out at the airport.

Flights: The **aerouostas** (airport; flight info tel. 63 55 60), Rodūnės Kelias 2, lies 5km south of town. Take bus #1 from the train station, or bus #2 from the "Sparta" stop of trolley bus #16 on Kauno g. (15-20min.). **LOT** (tel. 26 08 19; fax 63 27 72) flies to Warsaw (4 per week, 25min.); **SAS** (tel. 23 60 00; fax 23 31 39) to Copenhagen (daily, 1¾hr.). **Estonian Air** (tel. 26 15 59; fax 26 03 95): to Tallinn (daily, 1½hr.). **Lithuanian Airlines** (tel. 75 25 88; fax 72 48 52): to Berlin (daily, 2hr.); Kiev (3 per week, 1½hr.); London (5 per week, 3hr.); and Moscow (3 per week, 1½hr.).

Trains: Geležinkelio g. 16 (tel. 63 00 86 or 63 00 88). Tickets for **local** trains sold in a separate building, to the left on the main (pink) building. Tickets for international trains can be purchased in the brand-new yellow addition to the left of the main station; windows #1 and 2 are specifically for trains to western Europe. Tickets for non-Lithuania-originating trains can be bought no earlier than 3hr. before departure. **Reservation Bureau** (tel. 62 39 27), in the station hall to the right (open daily 6am-midnight). To: Berlin via Belarus (transit visa a must—1 per day, 19½hr., 309Lt); Kaliningrad, Russia (3 per day, 7hr., 40Lt, *coupé* 65Lt); Minsk (3 per day, 5hr., 32Lt, *coupé* 52Lt); Moscow via Belarus (get that transit visa! 3 per day, 17hr., 80Lt, *coupé* 128Lt); Rīga (1 per day, 7½hr., 41Lt, *coupé* 67Lt); St. Petersburg (2 per day, 18hr., 64Lt, *coupé* 108Lt); Warsaw via Belarus (transit visa required—2 per day, 12hr., 60Lt, *coupé* 115Lt); Kaunas (5 per day, 2hr., 7.30Lt); Klaipėda (3 per day, 5hr., 39Lt); and Trakai (8 per day, 40min.-1hr., 2Lt).

Buses: Autobusų Stotis, Sodų g. 22 (info tel. 26 24 82, reservations tel. 26 29 77 or 63 52 77), opposite the train station. **Priemiestinė Salė**, to the left as you enter, is for buses to local destinations; **Tarpmiestinė Salė** covers long-distance buses and has an info booth open daily 7am-8pm. Windows #13-15 serve destinations outside of the former Soviet Union. To: Kaliningrad (1-3 per day, 8hr., 34-40Lt); Minsk (8 per day, 4hr., 19Lt); Rīga (5 per day, 5-6hr., 25-40Lt); Tallinn (2 per day, 10hr., 81Lt); Warsaw (4 per day, 10hr., 60-65 Lt); Kaunas (21 per day, 1½-2hr., 8-10.40Lt); Klaipėda (9 per day, 4-6 hr., 25-35Lt); and Trakai (30-45 min., 2.30-3.60Lt).

Public Transportation: Buses and **trolleys** don't run in Senamiestis but link Vilnius's train and bus stations, its suburbs, and Senamiestis's edges (daily 6am-midnight). Buy tickets at any kiosk (0.60Lt; 0.75Lt from the driver; punch on board).

Taxis: State Taxis (tel. 22 88 88). 1Lt to start, plus 1Lt per km (double after 10pm). **Private taxis** show a green light in the windshield; debate the fare before you go.

Car Rental: Hertz, Ukmergės g. 2 (tel. 72 69 40; fax 72 69 70). Best rates around. Start negotiations at around US$28 per day for a Ford Fiesta.

Luggage Storage: At the **bus station.** Open daily 7am-10pm. 1.50Lt per bag. Or in the tunnels underneath the **train station.** Open 24hr. 1.50Lt per small bag, 2.50Lt for large bags and backpacks; 2Lt each additional day.

International Bookstore: Penki Kontinentai (Five Continents), K. Stulginskio g. 5 (tel. 22 14 81; fax 22 61 15), off Gedimino pr. Open Mon.-Fri. 10am-7pm.

Late-Night Pharmacies: Gedimino Vaistinė, Gedimino pr. 27 (tel. 61 01 35 or 62 49 30). Open Mon.-Fri. 24hr., Sat. 9am-8pm.

Photocopies: Xerox, Gedimino pr. 4 (tel. 22 70 57), in the Academic Theater Building. 0.30Lt per page. Open Mon.-Fri. 9am-6pm. Also at the post office (see below).

Cultural Centers: America Center (USIA), Pranciškonų g. 3-6 (tel. 22 04 81; fax 22 04 45). **Jewish Cultural Centre**, Šaltinių g. 12 (tel. 62 58 36).

Gay Information Line: tel. 63 30 31. Info about organizations, events, and accommodations for gay men. **Lithuanian Gay and Lesbian Homepage** (http://cs.ektaco.ee/~forter) lists gay and lesbian establishments in Lithuania.

Laundromat: Slayana, Latvių g. 31 (tel. 75 31 12), in Žvėrynas, 5min. west of Senamiestis across the Neris river. Take tram #7 from the train station or tram #3 or 7 from Senamiestis. Do-it-yourself wash and dry 10Lt, full service 18Lt. Detergent 3Lt. Open Mon.-Fri. 8am-8pm.

Medical Services: Baltic-American Medical & Surgical Clinic, Antakalnio g. 124 (tel. 74 20 20), at Vilnius University Hospital. Open Mon.-Fri. 9am-5pm.

Police: 02. **Ambulance:** 03.

Internet Access: Send free email from the offices of the **Soros Foundation,** Šv. Jono g. 3/5 (tel. 22 38 06; call 22 37 to reserve a terminal). Open Mon.-Fri. noon-8pm.

Express Mail: DHL, Dariaus ir Girėno 40 (tel. 26 77 22; fax 26 77 44). Open Mon.-Fri. 9am-6pm, Sat. 9am-2pm. **FedEx,** Geležinio Vilko 12, #52 (tel./fax 61 46 54). Open Mon.-Fri. 9am-5pm.

Post Office: Centrinis Paštas, Gedimino pr. 7 (tel. 61 67 59), west of Arkikatedros aikštė. Letter to the U.S. 1.20Lt. *Poste Restante* on the right side at the window that says "*iki pareikalavimo.*" 0.30Lt to pick up mail. Open Mon.-Fri. 8am-8pm, Sat. 10am-5pm. **Postal code:** LT-2001.

Telephones: In the main post office (info. tel. 62 55 11). Norwegian phones take phone cards (3.54Lt and up) and allow direct dialing abroad (to the U.S. 10.51Lt per min., Eastern Europe 3.57Lt per minute, western Europe 5.80Lt per minute). Open Mon.-Fri. 8am-8pm, Sat. 10am-5pm. **Phone code:** 02.

LITHUANIA

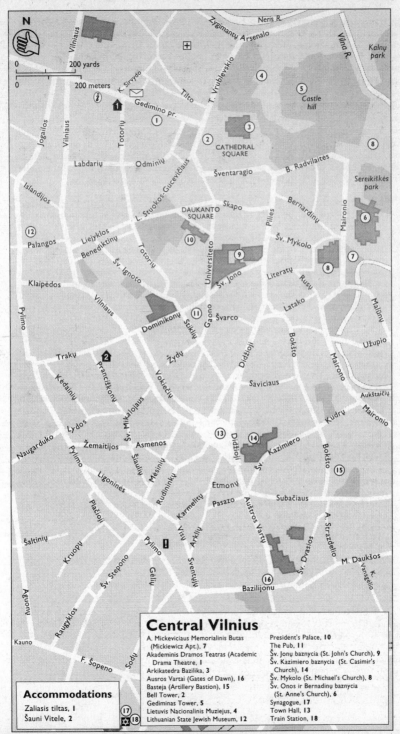

Central Vilnius

A. Mickeviciaus Memorialinis Butas
  (Mickiewicz Apt.), **7**
Akademinis Dramos Teatras (Academic
  Drama Theatre), **1**
Arkikatedra Bazilika, **3**
Ausros Vartai (Gates of Dawn), **16**
Basteja (Artillery Bastion), **15**
Bell Tower, **2**
Gediminas Tower, **5**
Lietuvis Nacionalinis Muziejus, **4**
Lithuanian State Jewish Museum, **12**

President's Palace, **10**
The Pub, **11**
Šv. Jonu baznycia (St. John's Church), **9**
Šv. Kazimiero baznycia (St. Casimir's
  Church), **14**
Šv. Mykolo (St. Michael's Church), **8**
Šv. Onos ir Bernadinų baznycia
  (St. Anne's Church), **6**
Synagogue, **17**
Town Hall, **13**
Train Station, **18**

Accommodations

Zaliasis tiltas, **1**
Šauni Vitele, **2**

LITHUANIA

ACCOMMODATIONS

New accommodations are being built in Vilnius almost daily, although surprisingly few of them cater specifically to budget travelers. The wonderful **Filaretai Youth Hostel**, in a peaceful neighborhood a short walk from Senamiestis, is probably the best bet. Other options include **Litinterp**, Bernardinų 7, #2 (tel. 22 38 50; fax 22 35 59; email litinterp@post.omnitel.net), which arranges homestays with English-speakers and private apartments in Senamiestis (reservations preferred; singles 60-100Lt; doubles 100-140Lt). They can also set you up with an apartment with a kitchen and bath, starting at 160Lt per night (open Mon.-Fri. 9am-6pm, Sat. 9am-4pm). If you arrive late and find yourself in a pinch, head to the overnight office in the main train station, Geležinkelio g. 16 (tel. 69 24 72), to the left of the ticket information office; they'll rent out **a couchette in a non-working stationary train** for the unbeatable price of 15Lt per night (check-in after 8pm; mandatory 8am checkout).

Filaretai Youth Hostel (HI), Filaretų g. 17 (tel. 69 66 27; fax 22 01 49; email filareta@vno.osf.lt), in the quiet Užupis neighborhood, just east of Senamiestis. With your back to the train station, head east on Geležinkelio g. and turn left at its end. Pass through the gates and head down Aušros vartų g., which becomes Didžioji g. Make a right on the tiny Savičiaus g., and at its end turn left onto Išganytojo g., which turns into Užupio g. after you cross the river. Heading uphill, take the left fork off Užupio onto Krivių g., and then a right off Krivių onto Filaretų g.; the hostel is 200m up on the right (30min.). Or take bus #34, which leaves from the right of the station (across the street from McDonald's) to the 7th stop (10min.). Clean kitchen; satellite TV in the common room; hostel reservations in Russia and the Baltics; visa invitations for St. Petersburg (20Lt); oodles of information about Vilnius; and, at no extra charge, staff member Arturas will pull an all-nighter to bring you up-to-date on the latest Lithuanian jokes. Curfew midnight. Reception open 7am-midnight. Cozy, comfortable 2- to 8-bed rooms 24Lt for the first night, 20Lt each additional night; doubles 64Lt for the first night, 56Lt thereafter.

Žaliasis tiltas (The Green Bridge), conveniently located in the center of downtown at two different locations around the corner form each other. The one at **Gedimino pr. 12** (tel. 61 54 50; fax 22 17 16) boasts spacious, sumptuous rooms with high ceilings. Singles with shower and TV 90Lt; doubles with bath and TV 130Lt. The one at **Vilniaus g. 2, #15** (tel. 61 54 60, info and reservations tel./fax 22 17 16), near the Neris, is slightly less expensive. Small but clean singles with shower and toilet 60Lt; doubles 120Lt. Breakfast included. AmEx, Diners Club, MC, and Visa.

Šauni Vietelė, Pranciškonų g. 316 (tel/fax 22 41 10), in a former monastery. Excellent location in the western part of Senamiestis. Extremely comfortable, tastefully decorated rooms with dark wood paneling and TVs. Receive faxes for free at the reception desk. Singles 100Lt; doubles 200Lt. Reserve in advance.

Vilnius Pedagogical University Dormitory, A. Vivulskio g. 36 (tel. 23 07 04; fax 26 22 91). Converted suites with spartan but colorful rooms and creaky floors. Take trolleybus #7, 15, or 16 from the station and switch to trolleybus #10, 13, or 17. Toilets shared between 2 rooms. Singles 28Lt, students 23Lt; doubles 54Lt, students 46Lt.

Rytų Camping, in Rukainai, 25km down the road to Minsk (tel./fax 65 11 95). Satellite TV and electricity hook-ups. 3-5Lt per tent.

FOOD

The four French joint-venture **Iki** supermarkets in Vilnius are stocked with foreign foods. The most convenient one lies at Žirmūnu g. 68 (tel. 77 29 62), 1.5km north across the Neris. Take trolleybus #9, 12, 13, or 17 from Senamiestis (open Mon.-Sat. 9am-9pm, Sun. 9am-8pm). Trendy yet inexpensive restaurants are popping up everywhere, and although there's certainly no stopping the city's nightlife from hitting the stratosphere, Vilnius is also beginning to show signs of a profound cafe culture.

Restaurants

A full meal can be as cheap as US$4-6. Unfortunately, the quality-price correlation seems to be getting increasingly strong. A simple rule to save money: the more English words on the menu, the fancier the establishment and the more you'll pay. Visit a place with a translated menu and take notes before hitting a less touristy joint.

Ritos Slėptuvė (Rita's Hideaway), A. Goštauto g. 8 (tel. 62 61 17), west of Senamiestis along the Neris. *The* place to go. Funky decor and "no sweat-suits allowed"—a subtle ban on the local mafia. Chicago-style 12" pizza (16-25Lt), great chili (8Lt), heaping plates of fresh pasta (5-10Lt), and bottomless cups of coffee (3Lt). Come nighttime, Rita transforms the restaurant into a **bar.** The barmen recently won the "best barmen in Lithuania" competition—we kid you not. Live music and disco start pumping on Fri. and Sat. nights. Open Sun.-Thurs. 7:30am-2am, Fri.-Sat. 7:30am-4am.

Ritos Smuklė (Rita's Tavern), Žirmūnų g. 68 (tel.77 07 86), next to the Iki supermarket. Rita's newest creation is this traditional Lithuanian restaurant where folk music and 19th-century costumes abound. And the food is great! Take trolley bus #12, 13, or 17. Try the homemade *kvass* (gyros; 1.90Lt), *šaltibarščial* (cold beet soup; 3.70Lt), and *vēderai su grietine* (potato links with sour cream; 9.90Lt). Live folk music Fri. and Sat. 8-10pm. Open daily 11am-2am.

Prie Parlamento, Gedimino pr. 46 (tel. 62 16 06). An extremely popular joint, and with damn good reason. Lasagna "reputedly the best in Lithuania" (11Lt). Hefty servings of your favorite East European dishes: Hungarian goulash 10Lt. *Trijų pupų salotos* (three-bean salad) 7Lt. Open Mon.-Fri. 8am-midnight, Sat.-Sun. 10am-2pm.

Stikliai Aludė (Beer Bar), Gaono g. 7 (tel. 22 21 09). Less pricey, equally good, and a warm atmosphere to boot. Main dishes 16-40Lt. Excellent local brew, too: *Biržai Grafas* 4.50Lt, *Kalnapilis Ekstra* 8.50Lt. Open daily noon-midnight.

Cafes and Coffeehouses

A "European" cafe culture is steadily starting to develop, and soon this Prague-like city will be inundated with its own coffeehouses. Beer used to be the only way to go in Vilnius, but with the new times, even this truism is slowly changing.

Cafe Afrika, Pilies g. 28 (tel. 61 71 90), smack in the center of it all. Look for the yellow-and-blue zebra. Soup, salad, and gourmet cup of coffee in this mellow yellow establishment for less than 11Lt. Open daily 10am-11pm.

Užupio Kavinė, Užupio g. 2 (tel. 22 21 38), halfway between Senamiestis and the youth hostel. Beautiful setting on a porch overhanging the banks of the river. *Bifstrogenas* 12.50Lt. Pint of *Dvaro* beer 3-5Lt. Open 11am-11pm.

Cafe Filharmonija, Aušros vartų g. 5 (tel. 22 13 83). Of the sidewalk cafes near Aušros Vartai, this is the pick of the litter, marked by a golden *"Kavine"* sign over the door and a relaxed crowd outside. Truly amazing fries 3.70Lt, main dishes 7-12Lt. The ice cream desserts are incredible (5-7Lt). Open daily 10am-11pm.

Kavinė Romeda, Totorių g. 15 (tel. 62 48 25), at the corner of Odminių, a block south of Gedimino pr. Dark and homey, with an old Italian feel. A brick-walled cafe in one half, a bar in the other. The coffee's so strong, it's hard to pour (1.90Lt). Tiny, rich cakes 2.40-5Lt. Open Mon.-Sat. 10am-8pm.

SIGHTS

With the largest Old Town in Eastern Europe, Vilnius has no shortage of architectural wonders or historic spots. The moment you reach the end of Geležinkelio g. and turn left, **Aušros Vartai** (the Gates of Dawn) welcome you in. Built during the 16th century, the gates are the only surviving portal of the old city walls. Take a map, or just enjoy getting lost in the winding, cobblestone alleyways and crooked streets.

Senamiestis (Old Town)

Through the gates, enter the first door on the right to ascend to the 17th-century **Aušros Vartų Koplyčia** (Chapel of the Gates of Dawn), built around an icon said either to have been captured in Ukraine by Grand Duke Vytautas or to be a portrait of a 16th-century princess. The shrine is usually packed with candles and locals praying…and selling holy paraphernalia. Going back down to the street and entering the doorway at the building's end, will lead you to **Šv. Teresės bažnyčia** (St. Theresa's church). An outpouring of Baroque sculptures celebrate beneath multicolored arches, a frescoed ceiling, and stained glass. A few steps farther down, a gateway leads to the shockingly bright 17th-century **Šv. Dvasios bažnyčia** (Church of the Holy Ghost; tel 62 95 95), seat of Lithuania's Russian Orthodox Archbishop. A functioning monastery, the church is the final resting place of Saints Antonius, Ivan, and Eustachius, martyred in 1371. The usually red-clad bodies, preserved in a glass case under the altar, are dressed in white for Christmas and black for Lent. Beyond the gates, Aušros Vartų g. turns into Didžioji g., leading to the crown-topped **Šv. Kazimiero bažnyčia** (St. Casimir's church), Didžioji g. 34 (tel. 22 17 15). Named after the country's patron saint, this is Vilnius's oldest Baroque church, built by the Jesuits in 1604 to ape the Roman Il Gesù church. Its history, however, is oh-so-very Lithuanian. In 1832, the church gained a Russian Orthodox dome; during World War I, the Germans made it Lutheran; and with their return in World War II, they tore down the dome. After "liberating" Vilnius, the Soviets turned the temple into a museum of atheism, but it's been back in the Catholic fold since 1989. The church's vast salmon-colored interior encases an altar of gold and marble (open Mon.-Sat. 4-6:30pm, Sun. 8am-2pm).

Didžioji g. broadens into **Rotušės aikštė,** an ancient marketplace dominated by the columns of the 18th-century **town hall,** now home to the **Lietuvos Dailės Muziejus** (State Art Museum), Didžioji g. 4 (tel 62 80 30), with a collection rich in late 19th- and 20th-century Lithuanian paintings. The building is now undergoing restoration, but its art is at Didžioji g. 4—the **Vilniaus Paveikslu Gallerija Lietuvos Dailė** (tel. 22 42 58), in a former palace (open Tues.-Sun. noon-6pm; 2Lt, students 1Lt; Sept.-May Wed. free). As Didžioji g. continues north, it passes **Šv. Mikalojaus bažnyčia** (St. Nicholas' Church), Šv. Mikalojaus g. 4 (tel 62 30 69). Lithuania's oldest church, Šv. Mikalojaus was built in 1320 for the city's Hanseatic merchants. Shortly after the church, Didžioji g. widens into a triangular square and merges with the pedestrian **Pilies g.,** lined with peddlers of amber, silver, and leather. At the corner of Pilies g. and Šv. Jono g. stands the main entrance to **Vilniaus Universitetas.** Founded in 1579, the Jesuit university was a major player in the Counter-Reformation. On the east side of the main university courtyard, the 1387 **Šv. Jonų bažnyčia** (St. John's Church), Šv. Jono g. 12 (tel. 61 17 95), served as a museum of science under the Soviets. Go through the arches opposite St. John's to the remarkable 17th-century **Astronomical Observatory,** with zodiac signs on its facade's frieze, once rivaled in importance only by Greenwich and the Sorbonne. The university **library,** Universiteto g., was once among Europe's largest; with more than 5 million volumes, it's still a contender. Students with ID may use the collection.

Continue north on Pilies g. (or Universiteto g.) and you'll come out onto **Arkikatedros aikštė** (Cathedral Square), depicted on the 50Lt note. A church has stood here since 1387, when Grand Duke Jogaila converted his country to Catholicism in order to win the Polish throne. The present 18th-century **Arkikatedra Bazilika** (tel. 61 11 27) resembles a Greek temple—perhaps a reminder that this was also the site of the principal temple to Perkunas, the Lithuanian god of thunder. The contorted figures on the south wall depict Lithuanian grand dukes in religious fervor, with suitably ecstatic poses. Inside, peek into the early Baroque **Šv. Kazimiero koplyčia** (Chapel of St. Casimir), a marble-cake work which houses a royal mausoleum (open Mon.-Sat. 7am-1pm and 2:30-8pm, Sun. 7am-2pm). Back out in the square, the octagonal 1522 **clock tower,** atop one of the lower fortress towers, is one of the city's best meeting points. Behind the cathedral, walk up the long path of the Castle Hill to **Gedimino pilis** (tower) for a great view of Vilnius's spires—and you know what they say about the size of a city's spires…

After you descend the hill, meander through the park to the south until you reach Mairionio g., which leads south to Vilnius's Gothic treasure, **Šv. Onos ir Bernardinų bažnyčia** (St. Anne's Church and Bernardine Monastery), Maironio g. 8 (tel 61 12 36). St. Anne's is a red-brick confection built at the height of the Gothic style, so beautiful that Napoleon is said to have exclaimed that he wanted to carry it back to France. Tough luck for him. The Bernardine monastery in back, part of the city walls in 1520, partly houses the Art Academy and Design School of the University of Vilnius. Across the street, the Renaissance **Šv. Mykolo** (St. Michael's), Šv. Mykolo g. 9 (tel. 61 64 09), was built in 1625 to house a family mausoleum (open Mon. and Wed.-Sun. 11am-5:30 pm). The **A. Mickevičiaus Memorialinis Butas** (Adam Mickiewicz Memorial Apartment), Bernardinų g. 11 (tel. 62 01 48), sits on the road back toward Pilies g. The famous Lithuanian-Polish poet lived here in 1822 (open Tues.-Sun. 11am-7pm; free).

Go south on Mairionio g. from Šv. Mykolo's to the very un-Russian **Russian Orthodox Church of the Holy Mother of God,** a 19th-century restoration of a 16th-century church originally built into the city walls. **Šventosios Dvasios Bažnyčia,** Dominikonų g. 8 (tel. 62 95 95), a gold-and-marble Baroque masterpiece last rebuilt in 1770, was the first Gothic church in Vilnius (open daily 7am-10am and 5-7pm). Continue on Maironio g., and follow the steps up to Bokšto g. for a view of **Užupio** (literally, "across the river"), the oldest area of Vilnius outside the medieval city walls. A poorer neighborhood, today Užupio is increasingly being settled by writers and artists. Cannons, armor, and rusty swords fill the **Bastėja** (Artillery Bastion), Bokšto g. 20/18 (tel. 61 21 49), a restored section of the 17th-century fortifications that once surrounded Vilnius and were built as a defense against the Russians and Swedes (open Wed.-Sun. 11am-6pm). One of the few remains of the city wall extends south, leading the way back to Aušros Vartai. Interrupt a cruise of Gedimino pr. to head south on Jogailos, later Pylimo. Off Pylimo between Kalinausko 1 and 3, a shimmering steel pedestal shoots skyward, topped by a **bust of Frank Zappa** erected in 1995—the most random monument in Eastern Europe. Lenin's gone, but Zappa's in the house.

The Old Jewish Quarter

Once a center of Jewish life on a par with Warsaw and New York, Vilnius had a Jewish population of 100,000 (in a city of 230,000) at the outbreak of World War II. Nazi persecution left only 6000 survivors by the time the Red Army retook the city in 1944. Only one of prewar Vilnius's 96 **synagogues** remains, at Pylimo g. 39 (tel. 61 25 33), 500m west of Aušros Vartai. The Nazis used it to store medical supplies; it's now undergoing its first exhaustive restoration. Despite 50 years of Soviet repression that stalled any immediate post-WWII rebirth, services are also being revived, and are now held regularly on Saturday mornings. Plaques commemorating the community have started to appear, especially around the Stikliai restaurants. Some street names also recall the past: Žydų g. (Jewish St.) runs south of Stiklių g. from the restaurants. The **Lithuanian State Jewish Museum,** housed in two buildings at Pylimo g. 4 (tel 61 79 17), offers a variety of exhibits that testify to the vitality of Yiddish culture in Lithuania and pay homage to the victims of the Holocaust. An **exhibition on Jewish life** houses rotating exhibits and a permanent display of items salvaged from the destroyed synagogues, while the **Teisuoliu Gallerija** (Gallery of the Righteous) memorializes the Lithuanians who saved Jews by hiding them in their homes during the war. The third exhibit, entitled **"Righteous of the World,"** showcases Jewish resistance to Nazi forces, documenting how the city's Jewish community put on full-scale theater performances during the height of the war, even as the Nazis were approaching. The museum also arranges guided tours of Jewish Vilnius in English, Yiddish, Russian, and Lithuanian (info tel. 62 45 90 or 74 24 88; museum open Mon.-Thurs. 9am-5pm, Fri. 9am-4pm; donations requested). The **Green House,** Pamėnkalnio g. 12 (tel. 62 07 30; fax 22 70 83), chronicles the destruction of Vilnius's Jewish community through slides and photographs, including meticulous SS records of daily executions, and documents where 90% of Lithuania's 240,000 Jews were exterminated during the war. Ben-Zvi (1884-1963) and Š.Z. Šazaras (1889-1974), Israel's second and third presidents, respectively, were both originally from Vilnius; their pictures now hang in the museum as testimony to the vigor and intellect of the city's Jewish community (open Mon.-Thurs. 9am-5pm, Fri. 9am-4pm; donations requested)

LITHUANIA

Soviet Vilnius

The tour guides in the **Genocido Aukų Muziejus** (Museum of Genocide Victims) Gedimino pr. 40 (tel. 62 24 49; enter around the corner at Aukų g. 4), in the **old KGB prison,** were once prisoners of its cells. The stately building was originally constructed in 1899 by the Russian tsar to serve as a court, but it was captured by the Nazis during World War II and turned into Gestapo headquarters. The officers of the *Abwehr,* a branch of the SS that was devoted to exterminating the Jews, held court downstairs. When the Soviets came to town, the building became Vilnius's KGB headquarters. The prison is still rife with torture and execution chambers; notice the mounds of documents only partially destroyed by the KGB before they left in 1991 and the dark, damp rooms in which prisoners were tortured and beaten, and then left to stand (not sit!) in solitude for as long as a week (open Tues.-Sun. 10am-4pm; tours in Lithuanian and Russian). Ask for the English guidebook (should be available by summer 1998). Behind the Gedimino pilis (tower), the **Lietuvis Nacionalinis Muziejus** (Lithuanian National Museum), Arsenalo g. 1 (tel 62 94 26), recently underwent some serious *remontas* and now boasts a new red roof. Founded in 1855, the museum chronicles the history of the Lithuanian people from before anyone could remember to 1940. Don't miss the exhibit on the life and times of the 1918-40 independent Lithuanian republic (open Wed.-Sun. 11am-6pm; 4Lt, students 2Lt). The **Nacionalinė Galerija** (National Gallery), Studentų g. 8 (tel. 72 51 67), across the Neris off the riverside Upės g., offers exhibits on the January 1991 crackdown in Vilnius and the deportations to Siberia of the 1940s and 50s—stumps studded with Soviet medals and piles of USSR passports (open Tues.-Sun. noon-6pm; history museum 4Lt, students 2Lt; art section 2Lt, students 1Lt). The **parliament** sits at the west end of Gedimino pr., just before the Neris. In January 1991, the world watched as Lithuanians raised barricades to protect their parliament from the Soviet army. President Landsbergis later said that all of the deputies expected to become martyrs on the night of January 13, but the main attack came instead at the 326m **TV tower,** where 14 unarmed civilians were killed as the Red Army forced the station off the air. Crosses and memorials surround the spot today; the streets in the immediate neighborhood have been renamed in honor of the 14 martyrs. The tower, visible from the city center, is reachable by trolleybus #11 going west from "Skalvija" on Žaliasis bridge's south end toward "Pašilaičai" (14 stops). Ascend the tower for a breathtaking view of the surrounding countryside (12Lt). Upstairs, a revolving restaurant with orange fake-leather 70s seats awaits your tourist dollars (open daily 10am-9pm).

East Vilnius

Above Senamiestis's east side rises the **Trijų Kryžių kalnas** (Hill of Three Crosses), visible from everywhere in Vilnius. White crosses were originally erected here in the 18th century to commemorate seven Franciscan friars crucified on the hill during the 13th century by pagan tribes. During Lithuania's first period of independence, a white stone memorial of three crosses appeared on the hilltop. Torn down by the Soviets in the 50s, the present monument is a 1989 copy; legend dictates that exactly two of the crosses can be seen from anywhere in the city, while a third remains hidden. Check it out for yourself. A final must-see is the 1688 **Šv. Apaštalv Petro ir Povilo bažnyčia** (Sts. Peter and Paul Church), Antakalnio g. 1, a 10-minute walk from the cathedral. Or take trolley bus #2, 3, or 4 from Senamiestis or trolleybus #12 or 13 from "Skalvija" at the foot of the Žaliasis bridge three stops east to "Meno mokykla." Carved figures levitate on the ceiling. The church's humble founder is buried next to the door; his tombstone reads *Hic jacet peccator* (Here lies a sinner).

ENTERTAINMENT

Vilnius's breakneck economic development has opened up the gates for a fast and furious arts scene. Concerts and plays are staged nightly at a rate unrivaled in the Baltics. For a list of performances, check *Vilnius in Your Pocket* or the Lithuanian morning paper *Lietuvos Rytas*. Consult the tourist office at Gedimino pr. 14 (tel. 61 68 67; fax 22 61 18) for info on how to obtain tickets. In summer, music and dance festivals and pop music concerts (the Gypsy Kings played in 1997) come to town, including the annual **Worst Bands Festival,** which features Lithuanian alternative bands. *Vilnius in Your Pocket* has up-to-date listings. Finally, there are an increasing number of art galleries opening their doors to display the works of Lithuania's budding young artists. Wander around Senamiestis, and it won't be long before you find something of value. The **Akademijos Galerija** (Academy of Art Gallery), Pilies g. 44 (tel. 61 20 94), specializes in ceramics and the graphic arts. If it's movies you're after, see them undubbed at **Lietuva Cinema,** Pylimo g. 17 (tel. 62 34 22) and **The Vilnius,** Gedimino pr. 5a (tel. 61 26 76). **Kino Centras Skalvija,** Goštauto g. 2 (tel. 61 05 05), shows the best foreign films in Vilnius.

National Philharmonic Orchestra, Aušros Vartų 5 (info tel. 62 71 65), just north of the Senamiestis gates. Internationally renowned. Tickets 8-24Lt; box office open 10am-2pm and 3-7pm; performances begin at 7pm. Also organizes the annual **Vilniaus Festivalis** (late May to late June), a month of nonstop concerts.

Operos ir Baleto Teatras (Opera and Ballet Theater), Vienuolio 1 (info tel. 62 06 36; tickets tel. 620 27). Performances begin at 7pm.

Muzikos Akademija (Academy of Music), Gedimino pr. 42 (tel. 61 01 44). Choirs and soloists show off their talents on the piano and violin.

Akademinis Dramos Teatras (Academic Drama Theater), Gedimino pr. 4 (tel. 62 97 71). Plays by Lithuanian, Russian, and Polish dramaturgs. Box office open Tues.-Sun. 1-7pm.

Rusų Dramos Theatras (Russian Drama Theater), Arklių g. 5 (tel. 62 86 78). Similar to Akademinis Dramos Teatras, but smaller. Box office open Tues.-Sun. 10am-4pm.

NIGHTLIFE

As if the old Baroque churches weren't entertainment enough, new discos, bars, and clubs are springing up daily to entertain the new influx of foreigners and Vilnius's younger crowd, who have better things to do with their weekends than go to church. Check out posters in Senamiestis or Prie Parlamento's bulletin board, and remember: don't do anything we wouldn't do. Lithuanian hipsters Eduardas and Vladimiras organize a **gay disco** every Saturday night at a different venue. Call them (tel. 63 30 31) for more information (usually midnight-6am; cover 15Lt)

Pubs and Bars

The Pub (Prie Universiteto), Dominikonų g. 9 (tel. 61 83 93; email teranova@ pub.osf.lt), in the heart of Senamiestis. Traditional English pub with heavy wooden interior and a cozy dungeon dating back to the 19th century. Immensely popular with local students. Pint of *Pilsner Urquell* 10Lt. Open daily 11am-2am.

NATO's, Pasažo 2/3 (tel. 61 77 84). Wash down such items as the "Red Army" and "Remains of a Partisan"—smoked, boiled pig's ears—with *EKU Pils* (8Lt). Set in a grey-and-black command post draped in missiles, guns, camouflage, and steel. Open daily noon-3am. Visa and MC accepted for your war debts.

Savas Lampas (Your Corner), Vokiečių g. 4 (tel 22 32 03). A laid-back place for the more mature set, who come here to hear 60s, 70s, and 80s tunes. Local Lithuanian bands play live on Fri. and Sat. nights, when dancers hit the disco floor. Great mix of jazz, blues, and rock. Open daily midnight-3am.

Clubs

Indigo Klubas, Trakų g. 312 (tel. 62 10 45) on the 2nd floor of the Tavola restaurant. The fanciest disco in town, right out of London. Live DJ, excellent mix of music, and a very sophisticated crowd. Don't come if you don't like to dance, because it doesn't get much better than this. Cover 10-15Lt. Wed. is ladies' night, Sun. is jazz. Open Sun.-Thurs. 8pm-3am, Fri.-Sat. 8pm-5am.

Naktinis Vilkas (Night Wolf), Lukiškių g. 3 (tel. 22 47 51). Popular student disco, full of Lenin memorabilia and Communist kitsch. No bourgeoisie allowed, or the ghost of Brezhnev will haunt you in the bathroom! Reputed to have the best singles scene in town, but don't take our word for it; go check out the crazy Bolshevik revolution for yourself. Cover 5Lt. Open daily 5pm-5am.

Ministerija, Gedimino pr. 46 (tel. 62 16 06), in the basement of Prie Parlamento. Ever-popular club under an ever-popular restaurant. Small cozy floor and a "no techno" rule. Open Mon.-Thurs. 5pm-2am, Fri.-Sat. 5pm-4am. Cover 5Lt.

■ Trakai

Trakai's magnificent lakes and fairy-tale castle have inspired legends since the 14th century, when Grand Duke Gediminas built Trakai Castle, which served as the capital of the Grand Duchy of Lithuania in the 14th and 15th centuries. One hundred years later, the duke's grandson Grand Duke Vytautas, returning from a miliary campaign in Crimea, brought back a few hundred families of Karaites, a Turkic-speaking Jewish sect whose members adhere only to the first five books of the Old Testament, to serve as his royal guard. Today, 200 Karaites, as well as Lithuanians, Russians, and Poles, live peacefully in Trakai, while tourists flock to this idyll of lakes and islands to catch a glimpse of the most impressive castle in Lithuania.

Orientation and Practical Information Located 28km from Vilnius, Trakai spreads itself out on a long peninsula surrounded by three lakes. The **bus station,** Vytauto g. 90 (tel. 513 33), sits at the southern end of town, where it receives buses from Vilnius (26 per day, 45min., 2.30-2.60Lt) and Kaunas (2 per day, 2½hr., 11Lt). Buy your tickets on the bus. The last bus for Vilnius departs nightly at 10:07pm, but it has been known to leave early, so beware (station open daily 5am-11:30pm). The **train station,** on Vilnias g., lies 500m south of the bus station, though the bus is faster and more convenient (8 trains daily to Vilnius, 1hr., 2Lt). Trakai's main drag, Vytauto g., runs north from the bus station, eventually veering left to become Karaimų g., which leads directly to the foot-ramp of the castle. The **Trakai Tourism Information Bureau,** Vytauto g. 69 (tel./fax 519 34), in the town's cultural center, provides info about Trakai and its surroundings and also books **rooms** for free (open Mon.-Fri. 9am-5pm, Sat. 10am-3pm). There's a **post office** at Vytauto g. 22 (tel. 525 84) from which you can make **phone calls** (open Mon.-Fri. 8am-6:30pm, Sat. 8:30am-3pm). **Postal code:** LT-4050. **Phone code:** 238.

Accommodations and Food Though most tourists come to Trakai only as a daytrip from Vilnius, there is reason to spend a night here, if only for the serenity of the surrounding woods and lakes. The best option for budget travelers is **Hotel Galvė,** Karaimų g 41 (tel. 513 45), which is conveniently situated in front of the ramp to the castle. The hotel can house up to 24 people in its old but clean rooms, and the management happily organizes tours of Trakai, Vilnius, Kaunas, and Druskininkai in English, Russian, or German (reception open 24hr; singles 25Lt; doubles 50Lt; triples 75Lt). **Svečiu Namal,** Vytauto g. 55 (tel. 510 78), just up the street from the tourist office, rents out apartments with tiny kitchens (singles 120Lt; doubles 100Lt). Four km north of Trakai on the other side of Lake Galvė, **Kempingas Slėnje,** in Totoriskiu village (tel. 513 87; fax 514 74), provides camping spots right on the edge of the lake with a magnificent view of the castle (tents 4-7Lt). They also rent doubles (65Lt), triples (65Lt), and a quad (70Lt), as well as boats, waterbikes, and yachts, and arrange hot-air balloon flights over the castle (400Lt per hr.)

The national food of the Karaites, *kibinai,* can be tasted at **Kibininė,** Karaimų 65 (tel. 521 65), a small restaurant in a wooden house. The Karaites brought *kibinai* with them to Lithuania in the 14th century, and they have apparently been serving it ever since. In addition to *kibinai* (6Lt), also try *troškinyš* (stew), another Karaite staple (7Lt; restaurant open daily 11am-8pm). **Židinys,** Vytauto g. 91 (tel. 531 98), offers German, Polish, and Karaite delicacies (main dishes 5-7Lt), along with beer to wash them down (4Lt; open daily 11am-midnight).

Sights and Entertainment The town's pride and joy is the picture-perfect **Trakai Castle,** which sits in all its splendor on three islands in the middle of Lake Galvė, and is accessible only by a footbridge that connects it to the mainland at

Karaimų g. Construction on the castle was begun by Grand Duke Vytautas in 1406, to replace the ruins of the **first castle,** which had been built on the main Trakai peninsula half a century earlier by his grandfather, only to be captured twice and later besieged by German knights. Trakai Castle went through a lengthy process of restoration from 1952 to 1980; the result is a perfect red-brick monolith that presides majestically over some of the most beautiful lakes and woods in Lithuania. A combined admission ticket allows entrance into both the castle's 30m brick **watchtower** and the City and Castle History Museum. Climb the watchtower's tight, circular staircases to the third floor to catch a magnificent view of the medieval courtyard below. The various rooms in the tower chronicle the history of Lithuania after it came under the rule of tsarist Russia in 1795, as well as the history of the independent Lithuanian republic that existed from 1918 until 40. Downstairs in the dungeon, displays showcase Polish, Russian, Swedish, and Lithuanian coins from the 14th to 17th centuries found in the Trakai region, as well as Lithuanian currency in use during the rule of Zygmonta the Old and Zygmonta Augustas. Across from the tower, the **City and Castle History Museum** (tel. 512 86) features Lithuanian period furniture from the 18th-20th centuries, the clock collection of Bronius Kasperavicus, handmade marble postal stampers, and an immense and interesting collection of tobacco and opium pipes of all shapes, colors, and sizes. To reach the castle, visitors must defend themselves from a flurry of kiosks and souvenir stands, almost as pesky as the crossbow arrows of centuries ago. Give yourself plenty of time to wander around the island, which affords amazing views of the surrounding countryside. (Open daily 10am-7pm. Admission 5Lt, students 2.50Lt; cameras 2.50Lt. Tours in Lithuanian or Russian 30Lt, in English or German 50Lt; students 15Lt and 25Lt, respectively.)

The **Karaites,** who comprise Lithuania's smallest ethnic minority, celebrated the 600th anniversary of their existence in Lithuania in 1997. Grand Duke Vytautas brought back some 300 Karaite families from Crimea after his 1397 campaign there to serve as his royal guard, and they have remained in Trakai ever since. Today, the 200 or so remaining Trakai Karaites make their homes in the wooden cottage-lined residential district along Karaimų g. They place a heavy emphasis on education and work ethic, and most speak fluent Lithuanian, Polish, and Russian. Their square, green-roofed, 18th-century prayer-house, the **Kinesė,** stands quietly at Karaimų g. 30, where it is guarded by a black metal gate; come during services on Saturday mornings if you want a peek at the stained-glass windows inside.

The best way to navigate Trakai is not by foot but by **boat.** Boat owners usually can be found along the lakeshore off Vytauto g.; just befriend one of them, and don't forget to bargain—the going rate is usually 5-7Lt per hour. You can also rent boats to explore the islands from the tourist office (6Lt per hour), or board a yacht from in front of the castle for a guided tour (20-50Lt per hour; try to bargain).

■ Kaunas

Burnt to the ground 13 times, Lithuania's second-largest city has been repeatedly reincarnated as the country's true heart and soul. Indeed, Kaunas (KOW-nas) served as the nations's provisional capital during the Lithuanian independence of 1918-40, when Vilnius was in the hands of Poland. It is now a serene city whose quiet streets and unhurried pace have been little changed by the growing number of bars, restaurants, and shops.

ORIENTATION AND PRACTICAL INFORMATION

At the confluence of the **Nemuna** and **Neris** rivers, Kaunas is a peninsula pointing west, with **Senamiestis** (Old Town) at the western tip, the bus and train stations at the southeast point, and the hilly suburbs of **Žaliakalnis** in the north. **Naujamiestis** (New Town) fills the middle, bisected by the 2km pedestrian **Laisvės al.** At the fork with **Šv. Gertrūdos g.,** Laisvės al. gains new life as it connects with **Vilniaus g.** at the beginning of Senamiestis to lead directly to **Rotušės aikštė. Bus #7** heads west from the stations on **Kęstučio g.**, cuts between Senamiestis and Naujamiestis by going north on **Birštono Gimnazijos g.**, then heads east along the avenue formed by three connected streets: **Šv. Gertrudos g., F. Ožeškienės g.,** and **K. Donelaičio g.** Its route is never more than one block from Laisvės al. Your jeans will bulge in new and exciting ways with *Kaunas in Your Pocket,* a guidebook with maps, restaurant listings, and a public transportation grid (4Lt).

Tourist Offices: Kaunas does not have a tourist office—don't be deceived by the "i" in front of **Delta/Tourist Information,** Laisvės al. 88 (tel. 20 49 11). Nevertheless, this travel agency sells **maps** (8Lt) and gives info on accommodations and sights. Open Mon.-Fri. 9am-6pm, Sat. 10am-2pm. **Litinterp,** Kumelių 15, #4 (tel./fax 22 87 18), in Senamiestis, finds private rooms. Open Mon.-Fri. 9am-6pm, Sat. 9am-4pm.

Currency Exchange: Look for *Valiutos Keitykla* signs on Laisvės al. and Vilniaus g. **Lietuvos Akcinis Inovacinis Bankas,** Laisvės al. 84, gives cash advances and exchanges traveler's checks. Open Mon.-Fri. 10am-5pm, Sat. 9am-7pm.

Trains: Čiurlionio g. 16 (tel. 29 22 60), 1.5km southeast of Naujamiestis, at the end of Vytauto pr. To: Rīga (1 per day, 6hr., 25Lt, *coupé* 55.50Lt); Kaliningrad (2 per day, 15hr., 16.90Lt, *coupé* 52.60Lt); Tallinn (*Baltic Express* 1 per day, 12hr., 36Lt, *coupé* 68Lt); Vilnius (18 per day, 1½-2hr., 7.30-8.70Lt); and Warsaw (*Baltic Express* 1 per day, 9½hr., 74Lt). **Advance Booking Office,** Šv. Gertrūdos 7 (tel. 29 24 08). Open Mon.-Sat. 9am-2pm and 3-7pm. Trolleybuses #3, 5, or 7 take you three stops from the train station to "Gedimino," a block south of Laisvės's end.

Buses: Vytauto pr. 24/26 (reservations tel. 29 24 55; international reservations tel. 29 24 46; info tel. 22 19 42 or 22 19 55). To: Klaipeda (9 per day, 4hr., 24Lt); Palanga (9 per day, 4hr., 26Lt); and Vilnius (1-2 per hr. 4am-9pm, 2hr., 9.40Lt).

Hydrofoils: Raudondvario pl. 107 (tel. 26 13 48), in the trans-Neris town of Vilijampolė. Take trolleybus #7 from the train and bus stations, or #10 or 11 from the stop at the west end of Laisvės al.; get off at "Kedainių," the 3rd stop across the river. In summer, *Raketa* hydrofoils splash to Nida via Nemunas (1 per day, 4hr., 49Lt).

Public Transportation: Tickets for buses and trolleybuses are available from kiosks (0.60Lt) or the driver (0.75Lt). The best way to get around the city, however, is by the **maršrutinis taksis** vans that speed along bus routes in large numbers. To stop one, stick out an arm, then tell the driver where you want to get off (1Lt).

Taxis: State Taxi Company (tel. 23 66 66). 1Lt per km. **Private Taxi** (tel. 23 98 80).

Luggage Storage: In a tunnel under the train station. 1Lt per bag. Open 24hr., except 8-8:30am, 2:15-3pm, and 8-8:30pm. At the bus station, store luggage outside and to the left of the main building. 1Lt per bag. Open daily 7am-9pm.

Pharmacy: Aesculaturas, Gedimino 36 (tel. 20 48 02). Open Mon.-Fri. 9am-7pm, Sat.-Sun. 9am-3pm.

Internet Access: Soros Foundation (Open Society Fund), Laisvės al. 53, 2nd floor (tel. 20 10 81; fax 20 62 24). Free. Open Mon.-Fri. 10am-1pm and 2-6pm.

Post Office: Laisvės al. 102 (tel. 22 62 20). *Poste Restante* at Window #11. Beware: letters waiting for you over 5 days cost 1.50Lt per day for "storage." Open Mon.-Fri. 8am-7pm, Sat. 8am-5pm. **Postal Code:** LT-3000.

Telephone Office: In the hall to the left as you enter the post office; cardphones in the main lobby (tel. 20 33 15). Open daily 8am-10pm, desk open 9am-9pm. **Phone Code:** 027.

ACCOMMODATIONS

Litinterp (see **Practical Information**) arranges B&Bs (singles 60Lt; doubles 100Lt).

Svečių Namai, Prancūzu g. 59 (tel. 74 89 72; fax 22 41 85). This youth hostel in a converted apartment building is the best deal in town. All rooms have kitchens and baths that are clean, if not in the best condition. Cross the tracks behind the train station and turn left at the end of the bridge to Prancūzų g., which wanders uphill through a local neighborhood toward the guesthouse. A bit far. Doubles 124Lt; triples 111Lt; breakfast included. With HI card: singles 40Lt; beds in doubles or triples 24Lt; but no breakfast.

VILIJAMPOLĖ

SENAMIESTIS

Kaunas

Advance Booking Office, 17
Bookstore, 15
Bus Station, 2
Castle, 22
Christ's Resurrection Church, 14
Devil Museum of Kaunas
(A. Zmuidzinavičiaus Museum), 13
Eternal Flame, 10
Freedom Monument, 9
Kaunas Technological University, 8
M. Zilinskis Art Gallery, 5
M.K. Čiurlionis Museum, 12
Museum of Folk Instruments, 18
Perkūnas House, 23
Post Office, 16
Postal Museum, 20
Santakos Parkas, 21
St. Michael the Archangel Church, 4
Town Hall, 19
Train Station, 1
Vienybės aikštė (Unity Square), 6
Vytautas Church, 24
The Vytautas Great War
Museum, 11
Vytautas Magnus University, 7

LITHUANIA

Maisto g.

Marvalės

Nemunas

Neris

Brastos g.

Jurbarko g.

Santakos g.

Rotušės aikštė

Karaliaus dvaro

Jonavos g.

Saukliu

Antakalnio g.

H. ir O. Minkovskiu g.

NEMUNO
SALOS
PARK

ZENTRUM

Karaliaus

Vandens

Muziejaus

Daugirdo

Aleksoto

V. Kuzmos

Kumeliu g.

M. Daukšos

L. Zamenhofo

A. Mapu g.

Palangos

Jablonskio g.

Birštono g.

Druskininku g.

Smalininku g.

Šilutės

Trinito g.

I. Kanto g.

J. Gruodžio

P. Puskos

St. Gertrūdos

Vilniaus

Gimnazijos g.

Benediktinu g.

Levu takas

Jonavos g.

Paminklu g.

Turzenu

Višniu g.

Liskiavos g.

Zūko g.

Skčrio g.

Raseiniu g.

Valančiaus g.

Obuoliu

Kupiškio

Zūko g.

Šatrijos

Savanoriu pr.

A. Mackevičiaus g.

Telšiu g.

Serbentu g.

Avečiu g.

Všokliu

Pakrantes
takas

P. Kalpoko g.

Mindaugo pr.

Kestučio g.

Laisvės alėja

E. Ožeškienes g.

L. Sapiegos g.

Vasario
16g.

Maironio g.

Vienybes
aikštė

V. Putvinskio g.

Aeronomiljos g.

Astros
takas

Žemaičiu g.

Vaisiu g.

Spaustuvininku

A. Mickevičiaus g.

Griunvaldo g.

Miško g.

Gedimino g.

K. Donelaičio g.

Nepriklausomybės
aikštė

Lietuviu g.

Aukštaičiu g.

P. Višinsko g.

Aušros g.

Kaunakiemio g.

Karo
ligonines g.

Vytauto pr.

Šiauliu g.

Bažnyčios g.

Vytauto pr.

Traku g.

K. Bugos g.

AŽUOLYNAS
PARK

Parodos g.

Radastu g.

K. Petrausko g.

Aukštaičiu g.

Vaičaičio g.

V. Kudirkos g.

Minties ratas

J. Mazeikos g.

Vydūno aleja

Radailienu pl.

Prančišku

M.K. Čiurlionio g.

Vaizganto g.

Perkuno aleja

Sporto g.

AŽUOLYNAS PARK

Geliu ratas

J. Krasevskio g.

HOSTELS

a Baltijos Hotel
b Hotel Lietuva II

HOSTEL

Hotel Baltijos, Vytauto pr. 71 (tel. 28 32 02). Basic accommodations a few blocks from the end of Laisvės al. A prime candidate for renovation. Singles 70Lt; doubles 104Lt, with bath 158Lt. Make sure you get a door handle that works.

Hotel Neris, Douelaičio 27 (tel. 20 42 24). A former Intourist hotel trying to go upscale. Singles 150Lt; doubles 200Lt; partially-renovated doubles 180Lt; breakfast included. All rooms have private baths with Western fixtures. EC, MC, Visa.

FOOD

An open-air **market** operates across from the train station, behind Vytauto 12 (open Mon.-Fri. 8:30am-6pm, Sat. 8:30am-3pm). **Parduotuvé SKALSA,** Laisvės al. 103 (tel. 20 29 66), is a large **grocery** (open Mon.-Fri. 8am-8pm, Sat. 8am-6pm, Sun. 8am-2pm).

Liepaité, Donelaičio 66. One of the most comfortable places to wait for your order, this place has tables flanked by low sofas. The food is decent and service is impeccable. Among the offerings are veal with salmon in olive oil (25Lt) and chicken filet with dried apricots (22Lt). Open Sun.-Thurs. noon-midnight, Fri.-Sat. noon-3am.

Pieno Baras, on Laisvės al. at S. Daukanto. The name of this cafe means "milk bar," and they're serious. They whip up whipped milk (1.56Lt), whipped cream with chocolate sauce (1.40Lt), and *blyneliai* (3Lt). Open Mon.-Fri. 9am-7pm, Sat. 10am-6pm. Ultraviolence not included.

Astra, Laisvės al. 76 (tel. 22 14 04). Chic outdoor restaurant. Salad 9Lt, herring with spiced vegetables and walnuts 8Lt, chicken with stewed vegetables 19Lt, "sleeping" banana fried in dough with ice cream and cognac 9Lt. Divine cappuccino 2Lt. Breakfast specials 9-11am; 10% lunch discount 4-6pm. Open Mon.-Thurs. 8:30am-midnight, Fri.-Sat. 8:30am-1am, Sun. 11am-midnight.

SIGHTS

Where Laisvės al. ends, Senamiestis (Old Town) begins; follow Vilniaus g. through an underpass, and you'll be inside the medieval city walls. Two blocks later, a left on Zamenhofo g. leads to the absorbing **Museum of Folk Instruments,** Kurpių g. 12, a collection of hand-carved fiddles, accordions, and strange Lithuanian sound-makers—a dried, inflated sheep's bladder on a string, for one (open Wed.-Sun. 11am-6pm; donation requested). Three blocks farther along Vilniaus g., **Kauno Arkikatedra Bažnyčia** (Kaunas cathedral), one of Lithuania's largest churches, is thought to have been first built during the 1408-13 Christianization of Low Lithuania on the orders of Vytautas the Great. Its vast interior, dating from 1800, is cut in sharp Gothic/Renaissance lines. On the south wall, the **tomb of Maironis** holds the priest from Kaunas whose poetry played a central role in Lithuania's 19th-century National Awakening. West of the cathedral, the **town hall,** a confused stylistic concoction constructed in stages from 1542 to 1771, crowns **Rotušés aikštė,** the central square. Up Karaliaus dvaro, off the north end of the square, the Neris and Nemunas rivers meet at **Santakos Parkas.** The remains of the 13th-century **Kauno pilis** (castle) stands here. Facing it is the late-Baroque **St. Francis Church and Jesuit Monastery** (1666), used by the Russians as an Orthodox Church and by the Soviets as a school.

Follow Aleksoto g. toward the river from the southeast corner of Rotušés aikštė to get to the 15th-century **Perkūnas namas** (Perkūnas House), a late-Gothic edifice built for Hanseatic merchants on the site of a temple to Perkūnas, god of thunder. At the end of the street is the Gothic **Vytauto bažnyčia** (Vytautas Church), also built in the early 1400s. A **funicular** (0.15Lt) leads up the hill to an unrivaled panorama of Kaunas. In the southwest corner of Rotušés aikštė stands a **statue of Marionis.** His hand hides his dog collar, a ploy that duped the Soviets into letting the city erect a statue of a priest. Near the statue at Rotušes 13 is **Marionin Lietuvin Literatūros Muziejus** (Marionis Lithuanian Literature Museum; tel. 20 68 42), in the 18th-century Baroque house where Marionis once lived. The poet's apartment is on display, as well as exhibits dealing with the history of Lithuanian literature (open Wed.-Sun. 10am-6pm, closed last day of each month; 2Lt, students 1Lt).

Away from Rotušes at the east end of Laisvės stands the massive **St. Michael the Archangel Church.** Built in the 1890s for the Russian garrison that came to man the nine forts placed around Kaunas in a period of intense Russification, the sumptuous neo-Byzantine exterior is a feast for the eyes, although the recently redone interior is strangely unattractive (open Mon.-Fri. 8am-5pm, Sat.-Sun. 9am-4pm; services Mon.-Fri. noon, Sat. 10am, Sun. 10am and noon). In the south shadow of the church is the **Mykolo Žilinsko Dailės Galerija** (tel. 22 28 53), with rotating exhibitions of modernist art and a collection of mummies, porcelain, and 19th-century paintings; works by Cézanne, Renoir, and Manet await on the upper levels. Notice the well-endowed statue of a "man" out in front—as if you could miss it (open Tues.-Sun. noon-6pm; 3Lt, students 1.50Lt).

Two blocks down Laisvės al. and right on Daukanto g. lies **Vienybės aikštė** (Unity Sq.), depicted on the back of the 20Lt note. On the south side, **Vytauto Didžiojo universitetas** and the older **Kauno technologijos universitetas** draw in a student population of more than 16,000. Across the street, in an outdoor shrine to Lithuanian statehood, busts of famous Lithuanians flank a corridor leading from the **Laisves paminklas** (Freedom Monument) to an eternal flame commemorating those who died to win freedom in 1918-20. During Soviet occupation these symbols of nationhood disappeared, only to emerge from their hiding place in St. Michael's in 1989.

Several museums surround the plaza. **Vytauto Didžiojo Karo Muziejus** (Vytautas the Great War Museum), Donelaičio g. 64 (tel. 22 27 56), behind two soccer-playing lions, houses all sorts of weapons and the aircraft in which two Lithuanian-Americans, Darius and Girėnas, tried to fly from New York to Kaunas non-stop in 1933 (they crashed in Germany—check out the 10Lt bill; open Wed.-Sun. 11am-5:15pm; 2Lt, students 1Lt). One street north, **M. K. Čiurlionis Museum,** Putvinskio 55 (tel. 22 14 17), displays pastels by the revered artist and composer who sought to combine music and image to depict ideas in their pre-verbal state. High-quality 20th-century Lithuanian works fill the other halls (open Tues.-Sun. noon-6pm, closed last Tues. of every month; 3Lt, students 1.50Lt). Across the street, the hellish **Velnių muziejus** (Devil Museum), Putvinskio g. 64 (tel. 27 48 02), more properly known by its less infernal moniker—the A. Žmuidzinavičiaus kūrinių ir rinkinių (A. Žmuidzinavičiaus Art Collection)—keeps a collection of nearly 2000 devils, most of them Lithuanian folk carvings. Other diabolical creations come from Africa, Siberia, the Urals, and South America. Don't miss Devil Hitler and Devil Stalin chasing each other across bone-covered Lithuania (open Tues.-Sun. noon-6pm, closed last Tues. of every month; 4Lt, students 2Lt). On a high hill behind the museum, **Christ's Resurrection Church,** a famous modernist creation, waits to be finished. Started in 1932, construction ceased in 1940 on account of Stalin's meddling paws. The garish **statue of Vytautas the Great,** "creator of Lithuanian power," on Laisvės al., depicts Russian, Pole, Tatar, and German crusaders bowing in defeat.

The **Pažaislis Monastery and Church,** a vibrant Baroque ensemble with rich frescoes, sits on the Nemunas's right bank 10km east of central Kaunas. It was built in the 17th century and designed by three Florentine masters. Used as a KGB-run "psychiatric hospital" and then as a tourist resort, the monastery was returned to the Catholic Church in 1990 (open Mon.-Sat. 10am-5pm, Sun. 10am-6pm). Take trolleybus #5 or 9 from the train station to the end of the line; then walk 1km down the road. The church is just past a small beach. Classical concerts are held here, as is the much-touted **Pažalis Music Festival** during the summer between June and September.

Across the Neris from the castle lies the town of **Vilijampolė,** which gained infamy during WWII as the Jewish Ghetto of Kaunas, vividly immortalized in Avraham Tory's *Kovno Ghetto Diary.* The **IX Fortas** (Ninth Fort), Žemaičių pl. 73 (tel. 23 75 74), a few kilometers north of the ghetto, was one of the nine forts constructed in the 1880s around Kaunas as the first line of defense against the German Empire. During WWII, it was used as a Soviet deportation center and killing ground until it became a Nazi concentration camp, and was later used by the KGB. The museum focuses on Nazi atrocities, but also includes newer exhibits on the mass deportations of Lithuanians in the 1940s and 50s, and the guerrilla resistance that continued until 1952. Part of the museum is housed in the damp, cold prison cells of the fort, where 30,000 Jews were murdered and inscriptions remain carved in the walls of the "dying cell." Each part of the museum is 2Lt (students 1Lt), and a tunnel connecting the prison with soldiers' barracks can be explored with a guide for 10Lt. Local buses #23, 25, and 45 stop a kilometer away on Žemaičin pl. It's better to take any one of the inter-city buses that stop at "IX Fortas" from the bus station (2-5 per hr., 2am-9pm).

ENTERTAINMENT

Locals are proud of the city's theaters. Theater festivals occur at least two or three times a year; at other times, **Akademinis Dramos Teatras,** Muzikims 11 (tel. 22 31 85), picks up the slack, with everything from classical to modern plays. **Mažasis Teatras** (Small Theater), Daukšos 34 (tel. 22 60 90), covers alternative performances. **Muzikinis Teatras** (The Musical Theater), Laisvės al. 91 (tel. 20 09 33), performs operettas. **Kauno Filharmonija,** Sapiegos g. 5 (tel. 20 04 48), is well-known for its classical concerts. Some of Kaunas's outdoor bars offer live music in the evenings.

Kaunas has a number of folk and music festivals, including the **Kaunas Jazz Festival** (held from April 17-20 in 1997). Any excuse to revive traditional songs, dance, and dress is reason enough in Kaunas; when **Mindaugas's Day** comes around on July 6th, stand back and check out the jigs. For information on dates and prices, look for posters on Laisvės alėja or check the *Kaunas in Your Pocket.*

Skliautai, Rotušės aikštė 26 (tel. 20 68 43). Located in a courtyard, this is a great place to mellow out and watch felines slink around the square. They'd love some herring with onions (3.50Lt). 0.50L *Kalnapilis* (5.50Lt). Open daily 11am-midnight. EC, MC.

Elfu šėlsmas, Laisves 85 (tel. 20 59 56). You might have trouble realizing this is the hippest place in town. Exposed-brick walls surround a packed bar and bands playing countryish blues to dancing revelers every night. 0.5L *Kalnapilis* (6Lt). Open daily 11am-4am. EC, MC.

Trestas, Mickevičiaus 8a (tel. 29 43 96). A young crowd comes to this disco to shake it on the dance floor and ogle one another. Bars downstairs and up, dancing upstairs. *Kalnapilis* 3Lt. Cover 6Lt. Open daily 9pm-2am.

■ Near Kaunas: Šiauliai

On a sunny morning in 1236, German Knights of the Sword, returning after a campaign to Christianize Lithuania, were ambushed and massacred. The town that grew up on the site took its name from the shining *saulė* (sun) of that bloody day, and to commemorate the bloodshed, people began a tradition of placing crosses on **Kryžių Kalnas** (Hill of Crosses), 10km northwest of the city. After the Lithuanian uprisings of 1831 and 1863, the collection grew as Lithuanians brought crosses to remember the dead and the deported. Under the Soviets, more crosses appeared for those killed or exiled to Siberia. During Soviet occupation, the hill became a mound of anti-Russian sentiment, and despite three bouts with a bulldozer, the memorial survived as Lithuanians stealthily replaced the fallen crosses. Independence has brought a new eruption of crosses, as emigrated Lithuanians and relatives of the exiled have returned to place monuments of their own. The stunning number of crosses of all breeds and sizes creates an eerily moving sight as they sway and rattle in the blowing wind. In the industrial town, at the corner of Aušros al. and Tilžės g., the hilltop Renaissance-Baroque **Šv. Petro ir Povilo bažnyčia** (Church of St. Peter and Paul) looms over the city, thrusting its 17th-century steeple, the tallest in Lithuania, 70m skyward (4 daily services on weekends).

Šiauliai (SEE-ow-oo-lee-eye) is best seen as a daytrip from Kaunas; **trains** make the connection (5 per day, 2hr., 6Lt). From the train station, walk left on Dubijos g., right on Višinskio and left on Stoties to the bus station, Tilžės 109. **Buses** run north to Joniškis, Meškuičiai, Rīga, or Tallinn (15 per day); ask the driver to stop at Kryžių Kalnas—it's not a regular stop. Be sure not to take a bus to Kryžkalnis; it's 30km south of

Šiauliai! From the bus stop, a marked road leads down for about 2km. To get back, take any bus that passes the opposite side of the road from where you arrived.

▓ Druskininkai

"You hear the murmur of the pines, so solemn, as if they were trying to tell you something," avant-garde artist, composer, and mystic **Mikolojus Konstantinas Čiurlionis** wrote in 1905. Čiurlionis was born and spent many of his days in Druskininkai, although, to the locals' regret, he died and was buried in Poland. The tiny town (pop. 20,000), situated less than 10km from the Belarusian border, is home to some 40 sanitoria, and boasts several supposedly curative mineral springs. Poles used to flock to Druskininkai to put mud on their faces and bathe in its natural spring waters; after WWII, the town became a favorite vacation resort among Russians. These days, the Russians are gone, but the Poles are returning in droves, forcing the town's residents to sharpen their trilingualism. Spend a few hours among the town's still-whispering pines and you'll understand why Čiurlionis held Druskininkai so dear to his heart. The artist's unique works are kept alive at **M. K. Čiurlionis Memorialinis Muziejus,** Čiurlionio g. 41 (tel. 511 31), which tells the artist's story in four buildings, one of which is the house in which he worked. The museum has mostly prints and focuses on the artist's life and times; for the originals, go to the M.K.C. Museum in Kaunas (see p. 343). Čiurlionis's evocative, mythical images are accompanied by recorded compositions—he intended the visual and audio components to be understood as one integrated art form (open Tues.-Sun. noon-6pm, closed last Tues. of the month; 1Lt, students 0.50Lt; color guidebook with English translations and excerpts from his letters 7Lt). **Piano concerts** on Sunday evenings in summer feature Čiurlionis's own compositions, as well as those of such lesser-known figures as Bach, Debussy, and Ludwig B. (5pm, 1hr., 5Lt). The 5m **statue** of Čiurlionis at the end of Kurdirkas g., not far from the Nemunas River, depicts the artist in a weary and bizarre state, with his hands crossed and what look like handle bars sprouting from his hips—a condition probably caused by attempting to explain his paintings to everyone.

Buses head from the station at Gardino g. 1 (tel. 513 33) to: Vilnius (4 per day, 2½hr., 12-14Lt); Kaunas (6 per day, 3hr., 12-14Lt); Augustów, Poland (1 per day, 3½hr., 20Lt); Hrodna, Belarus (1-2 per day, 1¾hr., 4Lt); and Warsaw (1 per day, 7-7½hr., 48Lt). The **train station,** Gardino g. 3 (tel. 543 43), 400m south of the bus station, sends trains to Vilnius via Parieče, Belarus (you may need a visa; check with the station manager before boarding; 5 per day, 4hr., 10Lt) and Hrodna (2 per day Sat.-Sun., 1½hr., 5.40Lt). Get to Hrodna on weekdays by boarding either the 1:20 or 6:35pm train headed for Vilnius and switching for a Hrodna-bound train in Parieče (1½hr., 5.40Lt.). To get to town, make a left after exiting either station and walk down Gardiono g., which soon becomes V. Kudirkos g., and leads directly to Čiurlionio g., the main artery (5min.). For info on **renting bikes** and booking accommodations, contact the **Druskininkai Tourist Information Agency,** Laisvės al. 18 (tel. 517 77; fax 553 76), at the corner of Vilniaus g., down the street from the Russian Orthodox onion domes (open Mon.-Fri. 9am-6pm). Find your friendly **post office** at the intersection of Čirulionio g. and Kudirkos g. (open Mon.-Sat. 8:30am-2pm and 3-7pm). Long-distance calls can be placed from the **telephone office** next door (open daily 7am-11pm). **Postal code:** LT-4690. **Phone code:** 233.

Druskininkai Hotel, Kudirkos g. 43 (tel. 525 66; fax 522 66), corner of Taikos g., offers comfort and tree-brushing balconies, directly across the street from the picture-perfect Roman Catholic church, which dots the town's postcards. The spartan yet clean rooms are as cheap as they come in Druskininkai (singles with toilet and shower 40Lt; doubles 46Lt, without bath 30Lt; triples 45Lt). Even if you're not hungry, stop by the **Baltoji Astra,** Vilniaus g. 10 (tel. 533 32), to ogle a purple-curtained, white-marble techno-temple to the triumph of ambition and funding over architectural taste (salads 4Lt, main courses 10Lt; open daily noon-midnight).

LITHUANIA

■ Klaipėda

Every time a German tourist calls Klaipėda "Memel," residents recall that for nearly 700 years Klaipėda (klai-PAY-da) was anything but Lithuanian. The city belonged to Prussia from the 16th century until WWI, then was occupied by the French until Lithuania invaded and claimed it in 1923, only to see it annexed by Hitler in 1939. Razed during WWII, Klaipėda was heavily rebuilt under the Soviets, but a number of older streets remain intact. Despite being Lithuania's third largest city, the pace never gets too busy to forget about the peace and quiet by the river or the beaches across the Kuršių marios (Curonian Lagoon).

ORIENTATION AND PRACTICAL INFORMATION

The **Danė River** divides the city into south **Senamiestis** (Old Town) and north **Naujamiestis** (New Town), while the Kuršių marios cuts off **Smiltynė**, Klaipėda's Kuršių Nerija (Curonian Spit) quarter. All of mainland Klaipėda lies close to the **bus** and **train** stations, which are separated by a parking lot. Follow **S. Nėries g.** away from the train to its end, then take a right on **S. Daukanto g.** to reach the heart of the city. **H. Manto g.,** the main north-south artery, changes its name to Tiltų g., then Taikos g., as it crosses the river into Senamiestis. **Liepų g.** (Naujoji sodo at its western end) is the main east-west street in Naujamiestis. Most kiosks sell the useful *Klaipėda in Your Pocket,* an annually updated English guide, complete with **maps** and information on Palanga and the Kuršių Nerija (4Lt).

Tourist Office: Litinterp, S. Šimkaus g. 21/8 (tel. 21 98 62; fax 21 69 62). Arranges private rooms in Klaipėda, Palanga, and on the Kuršių Nerija (singles 60Lt; doubles 100Lt); **rents bikes** (20Lt per day, US$100 deposit); sells **maps** and guidebooks; and answers any questions. Open Mon.-Fri. 9am-6pm, Sat. 10am-4pm.

Currency Exchange: In kiosks surrounding the train station and the bus station, or in one of the many banks. If those 1Lt ferry rides start to add up, refuel at **Vilniaus Bankas,** Daržų g.13 (tel. 39 01 21), which changes AmEx or Thomas Cook traveler's checks (0.5% commission). Open Mon.-Thurs. 9am-1:30pm and 2:30-4:30pm, Fri. 9am-1:30pm and 2:30-4pm. There is a Visa **ATM** in the post office (see below).

Trains: Priestočio g. 7 (tel. 21 46 14, reservations tel. 29 63 56). To Vilnius (3 per day, 5hr., 27Lt) and Kaunas (1 per day, 7½hr., 27Lt).

Buses: Butkų Juzės 9 (tel. 21 48 63, reservations tel. 21 14 34). To: Vilnius (14 per day, 7½hr., 29-30Lt); Kaunas (20 per day, 4hr., 20Lt); Nida (4 per day, 2hr., 7.40Lt); Ventspils (1 per day, 4hr., 18.50Lt); Kaliningrad via Sovietsk (2 per day, 4hr., 22Lt); and Kaliningrad via the Kuršių Nerija (first take the ferry to Smiltynė; 2 per day, 4hr., 22Lt).

Ferries: The **Smiltynė** ferry landing, Žueju 8 (tel. 21 22 24), surprisingly sends ferries to Smiltynė (1-2 per hr. 6am-1.30am, 10min., round-trip 1Lt; cashier open 5:45am-11:30pm). **International ferries** leave from the big boys' port at Perkėlos 10. To: Mukhran, Germany (odd dates at 3pm, 18hr., DM140) and Kiel, Germany (Mon.-Thurs. and Sat. at midnight, Sun. at 7pm; 34hr.; 350Lt). Call **Taurvita** travel agency, Taikos pr. 42 (tel. 21 78 00; open Mon.-Fri. 9am-6pm), for info and tickets.

Public Transportation: City buses (0.50Lt per ride) and the wonderfully convenient **maršrutinis taksis** (route taxis) careen all over town. The latter pick up and deposit passengers anywhere along the way, with flexible fares. Stick out an arm to hail one (1Lt between 6am and 11pm; 2Lt all other times). They serve Kuršių Nerija, going to Juodkrantė (5Lt), but rarely to Nida.

Taxis: State company (tel. 000). Private company (tel. 007; no license to kill). 1.50Lt per km is the standard fare.

Luggage Storage: Lockers at far end of the train station (0.50Lt for a small locker) or racks at the back of the bus station (1.50Lt per bag). Both open 5:30am-11:30pm.

Post Office: Liepų g. 16 (tel. 21 53 78), in an eccentric 1890 neo-Gothic brick building. Open Mon.-Fri. 8:30am-6pm, Sat. 10am-4pm. **Postal code:** LT-5800.

Telephones: Central Telephone Office, Liepų g. 1 (tel. 25 54 46). Pay the attendant or use magnetic blue card phones. Open daily 8am-11pm. **Phone code:** 026.

ACCOMMODATIONS

Litinterp (see Practical Information) arranges homestays with local families (singles 60Lt; doubles 100Lt; MC, Visa).

Hotel Viktorija, S. Šimkaus g. 2 (tel. 21 36 70), on the corner with Vytauto g. The best location in town for the best price. Old rooms are clean, as are the hall showers and toilets. Singles 45Lt; doubles 70Lt; private baths 120Lt.

Vétrunge, Taikos g. 28 (tel. 25 48 01), in a typical Soviet residential block. The rooms are equally Soviet but clean; communal toilets and showers could be cleaner. Singles 75Lt; doubles 90Lt; rooms with private baths 150Lt. Cash only.

Hotel "Jura," Malūnininkų 3 (tel. 39 98 57), in the northwest part of town. The lobby and second floor of this hotel have been renovated; new rooms come with Western furniture, phones, and private baths. Singles 140Lt; doubles 220Lt. Unrenovated singles 80Lt; doubles 100Lt. Visa, MC.

FOOD

Klaipėda's **grocery stores** include **Deimena,** H. Mauto g. 30 (open daily 8am-2pm and 3-7pm). The **central market** is on Turgas aikštė (open daily 8am-6pm).

Skandalas, Kanto 44 (tel. 21 28 85). If you're looking for a reprieve from *carbonadas* and borscht, this is the place to come. Very tasty grilled steaks cut thick with a choice of side dishes are 20Lt before 6pm, 28Lt after. Greek salad 6Lt (8Lt after 6pm). 0.5L *Kalnapilis* 7Lt. The restaurant is also a popular nightspot. Live jazz amid knick-knacks such as the tail of a MIG fighter. Open daily noon-3am. Visa, MC.

Lūja, H. Mauto 20 (tel. 25 94 45). This somewhat formal restaurant has tables outside with fake straw umbrellas. House dishes are quite popular: pancakes with mushrooms (10.30Lt), steak (18.10Lt), salmon (26.10Lt). Open daily noon-midnight.

Restoranas Luiza, Puodžių 4 (tel. 21 98 82), opposite the gargantuan Hotel Klaipėda. Squid stuffed with rice and vegetables (22Lt), stewed veal (15.40Lt). You can sit outside at the restaurant's pleasant bar. *Baltijos* (4.50Lt). Open daily noon-midnight.

SIGHTS

Mainland Klaipėda

The leafy park, **Mažvydo Skulptūrų Parkas,** between Liepų g. and Daukanto g., once served as the town's central burial ground and was turned into a **sculpture garden** by the Soviets. From Egyptian sundials to Chinese candle clocks and a modern quartz watch-pen, every conceivable ticking contraption finds a place at **Laikrodžių Muziejus** (Clock Museum), Liepų g. 12 (tel. 21 35 31), in Naujamiestis, next to the main post office (open Tues.-Sun. 9am-5:30pm; 2Lt). The **old post office** is one of the few interesting buildings in town not ruined in WWII. The **Paveikslų** (Picture Gallery), Liepų 33 (tel. 21 33 19), has some 19th-century portraits and plaster copies of Greek and Roman sculpture, but mostly 20th-century work of Lithuanian artists. Downstairs is a collection of sculptures (open Tues.-Sun. noon-6pm; 2Lt, students 1Lt).

Klaipėdos Dramos Teatras (Klaipėda Theater), Teatro aikštė, on the other side of Mauto g., dominates the Senamiestis (Old Town) center. Built in 1857, the theater is famous as one of Wagner's favorite haunts, and infamous as the site where Hitler personally proclaimed the reincorporation of the town into the German Reich in 1939 (open Tues.-Sun. 11am-2pm and 4:30-7pm; tel. 21 25 89 for tickets). In front, the **Simon Dach Fountain** spouts water over the symbol of Klaipėda, a statue of Ännchen von Tharau. The Memel-born Dach wrote a song for the wedding of young Anna, expressing his love for her. The original statue disappeared in WWII; some say it was taken by the Nazis, who didn't want her back facing Hitler during his speech. The copy standing today was erected by German expatriates in 1989. The fat lady sings at **Klaipedos Muzikinis Teatras,** Danés g. 19 (tel. 21 62 60), which houses operas and other musical events (ticket office open Tues.-Sun. 11am-2pm and 4-7pm). The **Mažosios Lietuvos Istorijos muziejus** (History Museum of Lithuania

Minor), Didžioji vandens g. (tel. 21 06 00), collects clothing, maps, rusty swords, coins and buttons from the Iron Age to the present (open Wed.-Sun. 11am-7pm; 1Lt). The museum's backyard conceals a **Lenin statue** which, before 1991, graced the square next to Hotel Klaipėda. The square also includes several examples of exposed-timber *Fachwerk* buildings for which pre-war Klaipėda was well-known. **Aukštoji g.** is one of the best preserved areas of old Klaipėda. Craftsmen's quarters from the 18th and 19th centuries have been restored for use as shops, cafes, and boutiques. The **castle ruins** are worth a glance as you board for Smiltynė.

Smiltynė

The **Jūrų muziejus ir Akvariumas** (Maritime Museum and Aquarium), Tomo g. 10 (tel. 39 11 33), is housed in an 1860s fortress that protected the entrance to Klaipėda. The outer perimeter, buried deep in underground tunnels, displays the port's naval history. Sea lions now frolic in the inner moat; you can buy fish to toss to them (0.50Lt). Inside, Antarctic penguins press their noses to the glass, confident they know which side of the glass holds the exhibit. Above the still-swishing specimens, the museum's second floor cringes in fear of the bad-ass Crab of Kamchatka and other stuffed seafood (open June-Aug. Tues.-Sun. 11am-7pm; May and Sept. Wed.-Sun. 11am-7pm; Oct.-April Sat. and Sun. 11am-6pm; 4Lt, students 2Lt). Sea lions kiss trainers and spectators in the **sea lion show** in an adjacent pool-theater (1pm, 3pm, and 5pm; 2Lt; photo of a sea lion kissing you 15Lt). Next door, the **Dolphinarium** stages shows at noon, 2 and 4pm (10Lt, students 5Lt). Both aquatic attractions are located in **Kopgalis,** at the head of the Spit, 1.5km from the food-stall-lined ferry landing. Geography buffs will quickly realize that this is also where the Kuršių marios (Curonian Lagoon) meets the Baltic Sea. To the east, several museums and displays line the road to a pier. The **Kuršių nerijos gamtos muziejus ekspozicija** (Nature Museum; tel. 39 11 79), near Landing 1, exhibits the region's natural and human history, including dioramas showing the locations of villages buried by the shifting dunes (open daily 11am-6pm; free). In the **Žvejybos Laivai-veteranai** (Garden of Veteran Fishing Boats), four forlorn ships on concrete pillars sit 20m from the water. The **Ethnografinė Pajūrio Žvejo Sodyba** (Ethnographic Coastal Fishermen's Village) is a reconstruction of a 17th-century settlement (open daily 24hr.; free). Forest paths lead west about 500m to the **beaches.** By walking north before crossing over you can get a patch of sand to yourself. Signs mark gender-restricted areas for **nude bathing**—*moterų* is women, *vyrų* men. On blustery days, sunbathers retreat to the dunes to avoid wind chill and a good sandblasting.

ENTERTAINMENT

The bars of Senamiestis are the staple here, but a number of discos have opened in the past few years to accommodate Klaipėda's growing nightlife.

Meridianas (tel. 21 68 51), Daučs Krautinė (river bank). This old 3-mast schooner moored permanently east of Tiltų is a popular bar. Open daily 3pm-5am.

Baras Senamiestis, Bažnyčių 4 (tel. 25 18 44). Dark, velvety hunting lodge in Senamiestis. Art gallery upstairs. *Baltija* 5Lt. Open noon-midnight.

Nova, Janonino 27 (tel. 31 11 62). A neon palace of a disco, Nova is the most popular place in town. Open Tues.-Sun. 10pm-5am. Cover: 10-20Lt.

▪ Nida

If you're watching the sunrise from a high white dune as the crisp smell of smoked fish rises with sounds of a waking fishing village, you must be in Nida. Encircled by more unruffled sea than any one town has a right to have, this resort village is located in the middle of the Kuršių Nerija (Curonian Spit), 3km north of the border with Kaliningrad.

Orientation and Practical Information From the hydrofoil port, **Taikos g.** runs west inland. Nida's other main street, **Naglių g.**, runs perpendicular to the north, and becomes Pamario g. The **Tourist Information Center,** Taikos g. 4 (tel. 52 34 59), opposite the bus and ferry stations, sells **maps** (3Lt), arranges homestays, and has good accommodation and transport information about Nida and the rest of the Kuršių Nerija (Curonian Spit; open daily in summer 10am-8pm; winter 9am-1pm and 2-6pm). **Exchange money** at **Lietuvos Taupomasis Bankas,** Taikos g. 5 (tel. 522 46), which also cashes AmEx and Thomas Cook traveler's checks, and gives MC, Visa, and Western Union cash advances. The **bus station,** Naglių 2 (tel. 523 34), is just north of Taikos. Buses run to Vilnius (2 per day, 4hr., 35Lt) and Klaipėda (4 per day, 2hr., 7Lt). The *kassa* is open daily noon-4pm, but you can also buy tickets on the bus. A **hydrofoil,** at Naglų 16, runs to Kaunas (Tues.-Sun. 1 per day, 4hr., 49Lt; *kassa* open daily 12:30-3:30pm and 6-9pm). The **post office,** Taikos g. 13, lies up the road (open May-Sept. 10am-6:30pm; Oct.-April 10am-3pm). The adjacent **telephone office** (tel. 520 07) has cardphones (open daily May.-Sept. 7am-midnight; Oct.-April 8am-9pm). **Postal code:** 5870. **Phone code:** 0259.

Accommodations and Food The **tourist office** (see above) arranges bed-and-breakfasts (20-40Lt per person). **Urbo Kalnas,** Taikos g. 32 (tel. 524 28), sprawls over a pine-covered hill above town with big, balconied rooms furnishing clean hot showers (DM37 per person; breakfast included). **Laumė,** Pamario 24 (tel. 523 35), has clean rooms with small beds in a main house by the water (40-50Lt per person, depending upon how long you stay; be sure to haggle), as well as shoddier rooms in another building with slightly smellier common baths and kitchens (20Lt). **Litinterp** (tel. (26) 21 69 62) in Klaipėda hikes its prices for Nida **private rooms** (singles 70Lt; doubles 115Lt).

The local specialty is *rūkyta žuvis* (smoked fish), which is best eaten with beer; selection varies from nondescript "fish" to eel and perch. **Seklyčia,** Lotmiško 1 (tel. 529 45), is considered to be the best restaurant in town. Outdoor tables offer a wonderful view of the dunes while you eat tomato salad (4Lt), *shashlik* (13Lt), and *blyni* (pancakes; 6Lt). Half a liter of *Baltijos* is 4Lt (open daily 9am-3am). **Ešerinė,** Naglių 2 (tel. 527 57), in a wacky thatched-roofed collection of glass-wall huts, is bona fide Hawaiian simulacrum; just the sort of thing you'd expect in a small Baltic village. Dine on cucumber salad (2.40Lt), or pork chops (16.50Lt), and don't forget the *Baltijos Ekstra* (5Lt). Nida's largest **grocery shop** is **Gilija,** Naglių 29 (tel. 523 19; open Mon.-Fri. 9am-9pm, Sat.-Sun. 9am-7pm).

Sights The **Drifting Dunes of Parnidis** rise south of town. Walk along the beach or through forest paths to reach steps leading to surreal mountains and plains of white sand, suspended 60m above the sea and blowing gracefully into it. From a giant sundial at the top are the best views of the lagoon and, across pine forests, the Baltic Sea to the west. Farther south, the nature preserve is technically off-limits, but the footsteps of many incorrigible tourists cross the line. The dunes here are even more spectacular, visibly in motion, and falling off at an incredible angle to the water below.

All of the **wooden houses** clustered along Lotmiškio g. are classified as historic monuments; another two whole villages of them are buried somewhere under the sand. From the center of town, walk north on Pamario or along the promenade along the water and bear right onto Skruzdynės g. to reach the renovated **Tomo Mano Namelis** (Thomas Mann House) at #17 (tel. 522 60; open Tues.-Sun. 11am-6pm; 1Lt). Mann built the cottage in 1930 and wrote *Joseph and His Brother* here, but had to give up the summer house when Hitler invaded. There is now a room of photos of Mann, and the **Tomo Mano Kultūros Centre** puts on classical concerts here during the summer. The **Fishermen's Museum,** Naglių 4 (tel. 423 72), displays objects and furnishings of a typical fisherman of old and has several aging boats by the water (open June-Sept. Mon.-Fri. 11am-7pm, Sat.-Sun. 11am-6pm; Oct.-May Tues.-Fri. 11am-5pm; 1Lt).

Macedonia

Djakovica · Uroshevac

YUGOSLAVIA

Prizren

Kumanovo

Skopje

Tetovo

Gostivar

Sveti Nikole

Kochani

Titov Veles

Shtip

Berovo

Peshkopi

Kichevo

Kavadarci

Zerqan

Krushevo · Prilep

Strumica

Struga

Ohrid

Lake Ohrid

Bitola

Gevgelija

Pogradec

Lake Prespa

ALBANIA

Árnissa · Edessa

Florina

GREECE

Kriva Palanka

BULGARIA

Vardar R.

| ♣ **Mosques** |
| Mustafa Pasa, **1** |
| Yeni and Isak |
| Dzhamiya, **2** |

♣ **Monasteries**	
St. Nikita, **1**	Markov, **7**
Matejcha, **2**	Pschaca, **8**
Staro	Osogovo, **9**
Nagorichane, **3**	Lesnovo, **10**
St. Pantelejmon, **4**	St. Bogorodista,
Matka, **5**	**11**
Andrija, **6**	St. Naum, **12**

0 —— 20 miles
0 —— 20 kilometers

MACEDONIA

FORMER YUGOSLAV REPUBLIC OF MACEDONIA (МАКЕДОНИЈА)

US$1	= 45dn (denars)	10dn =	US$0.22
CDN$1	= 33dn	10dn =	CDN$0.30
UK£1	= 70dn	10dn =	UK£0.14
IR£1	= 72dn	10dn =	IR£0.14
AUS$1	= 34dn	10dn =	AUS$0.30
NZ$1	= 30dn	10dn =	NZ$0.34
SAR1	= 12dn	10dn =	SAR 0.81
DM1	= 26.13dn	10dn =	DM0.38

Country Phone Code: 389   **International Dialing Prefix: 99**

Free but frail Macedonia, its economy damaged by years of UN- and Greek-enforced trade embargoes, continues to struggle financially, although its greater problem now may be the ever-escalating unrest between the country's different ethnic groups. Current problems notwithstanding, Macedonia did manage to stay entirely out of the latest war in the Balkans, and its historical and geographical treasures remain intact and accessible—particularly the spectacular mountain basin that is home to Lake Ohrid.

> For the sake of brevity, *Let's Go* uses the name "Macedonia" throughout this chapter to refer to the Former Yugoslav Republic of Macedonia. *Let's Go* does not endorse any perceived claims of the former Yugoslav Republic to the Greek territory of the same name. Yes, we are toadies to Balkan irrationality.

MACEDONIA ESSENTIALS

Irish and U.K. citizens need only a valid passport to enter Macedonia. Citizens of Australia, Canada, and the U.S. can procure visas at any border crossing at no cost. New Zealanders and South Africans must submit their passports to a Macedonian embassy or consulate (US$14 for 90-day single-entry). Allow 10 days for processing.

GETTING THERE AND GETTING AROUND

You can reach Macedonia by air, bus, or train. The airlines **Adria** (Slovenian), **CRO** (Croatian), **Balkan** (Bulgarian), and **PALAIR** (Macedonian) fly to the capital, Skopje. Many people prefer to travel over land from Sofia, Bulgaria, or Thessaloniki, Greece, to gain access to a broader range of international flights and avoid the smog that causes frequent closures of the Skopje airport. The **train** system is not extensive, and train tickets are usually more expensive than bus tickets. Luckily, buses run reliably and frequently to most destinations. A private **bus** company in Skopje, located near the old train station, is challenging the former monopoly of state-run **Proleter,** which still runs international lines. Buses connect Istanbul, Sofia, Tirana, Belgrade, and other cities to various towns in Macedonia. Be warned: border crossings can take a long time, as there are often traffic backups for miles. Helpful words include *bilet* (билет; ticket), *voz* (воз; train), *zheleznitsa* (железница; railway), *avtobus* (автобус; bus), *stanitsa* (станица; station), *povraten bilet* (повратен билет; return ticket), *liniya* (линија; track), *peron* (перон; platform), *informatsiya* (информација; information), *trugvanye* (тругвање; departures), and *pristignuvanye* (пристигнување; arrivals). **Hitchhiking** in Macedonia—which *Let's Go* does not recommend—is becoming increasingly dangerous, especially for foreigners.

As the country de-Communizes, street names change but old street signs remain. When asking for directions, use both the new and the old names; locals may be unaware of the change. Get a copy of a new map in English as soon as you arrive.

TOURIST SERVICES AND MONEY

Many **tourist bureaus,** mostly private, abound in the main cities. They often give out maps, rent **private rooms,** and sell train and airline tickets. Look for the **"i"** signs. **Shops** are generally open Monday to Friday 8am to 8pm; weekend hours vary. Some **banks,** especially in tourist areas, are open daily. Expect an hour break anytime between noon and 2pm at most offices and shops. In high season, many towns operate at a more frenetic pace, and services stay open later.

The monetary unit is the **denar,** which comes in notes of 10, 20, 50, 100, 500, 1000, and the extremely rare 5000 denars, and in coins of one, two, and five denars. Exchange rates vary little from bank to bank. Hotels have worse rates, and changing money on the street is illegal. Most hard currency prices in Macedonia are given in **Deutschmarks (DM),** although most banks will readily accept U.S. dollars and British pounds and cash **AmEx** traveler's checks. Few places accept **credit cards,** and some major hotels accept only cash. Skopje has some **ATMs** accepting MC and Cirrus.

MACEDONIA

COMMUNICATION

Place international collect calls via Macedonia's **AT&T Direct** operator (tel. (99) 800 42 88). To get an international line, dial 99. Calls to the U.S. average US$2 per minute. At the post office, service is generally efficient, but employees, even in the capital, will probably have no idea that calling card or collect calls can be made from Macedonia. Firmly insist that there is no charge. To make local calls from public phones, you must buy a microchip **phone card** (75dn or 150dn) at a post office. Some kiosks also sell them, or lend their own phones at a small charge.

Faxes can be sent at most phone centers for prices comparable to phone calls. **Photocopy** centers abound; look for the sign Фотокопир. Prices range from 2 to 10 dinars per copy. Large hotels televise **CNN** in their lobbies, kiosks sell *Newsweek* and *Time,* some radio stations occasionally switch to **Voice of America** and **BBC** broadcasts, and local TV features subtitled American movies.

LANGUAGE

Macedonian and **Bulgarian** are mutually intelligible. **Russian** is widely understood, as is **Serbian,** but it would be wise to ask before using either. **English** is quickly becoming the second language of choice in Macedonia, and many young people in urban areas are fluent. Macedonian-English phrasebooks (разговорник; *razgovornik*) are sold at bookstores and kiosks for 210dn. The **head movements** for "yes" and "no" are reversed from in the U.S., although younger Macedonians may do it the familiar way; confirm everything with words. For more information, see **The Cyrillic Alphabet,** p. 797, and the **Macedonian Glossary,** p. 806.

HEALTH AND SAFETY

> **Emergency Numbers: Police:** tel. 92. **Ambulance:** tel. 94. **Fire:** tel. 93.

Recent political events in Albania have made it inadvisable to enter Albania; even traveling near the border may be dangerous, due to bandits as much as to soldiers and police patrols. Crossing into Serbia should not be a problem.

Pack a small bar of soap and some toilet paper for the **public bathrooms.** Basic **medicines** are widely available in Macedonian **pharmacies** (аптека; *apteka*). *Analgin Cafetin* is aspirin, and *Arbid* is cold medicine. Bandages are *Flexogal.* **Condoms** are sold in kiosks and sometimes in pharmacies (10dn); **feminine hygiene products** should be widely available. If you are seriously ill, the Faculty of Medicine at the University in Skopje is the best bet. You will be asked to pre-pay for treatment.

ACCOMMODATIONS AND CAMPING

A hotel or hostel will take your passport at check-in: all businesses offering accommodations are required by law to **register** passports with the police. You'll get the passport back at the end of your stay; try to get it back earlier if you are expecting *Poste Restante* or plan to cash traveler's checks. If you are crashing with friends, they officially must do this as well, although this law is often ignored.

In areas other than Lake Ohrid and Lake Prespa, **private rooms** are expensive (750dn) and difficult to find. Check with the nearest tourist office. In the resorts, you'll be met at the bus and train stations by room-renting locals. Prices improve with haggling. **Hotels** are exorbitantly expensive (2000-3000dn per person in summer). Service is better and prices more reasonable at new private establishments (600-800dn per person). **Youth hostels** are usually outside urban centers; make reservations for most Macedonian hostels at the Skopje hostel. Many **campgrounds** are in a state of disarray; call before heading out. Free-lance **camping** is popular, but you risk a fine and it's not safe. Camping in reserve areas is prohibited.

FOOD AND DRINK

Food is not cheap in Macedonia. Kiosks sell grilled meats (скара; *skara*), especially small hamburgers (плескавица; *pleskavitsa;* 40dn), and *burek* (бурек; delicious, warm filo-dough pastry stuffed with veggies, feta cheese, or meat; 30-35dn). Fruits and vegetables can be bought at an outdoor market, or *pazar* (пазар). The standard *shopska* salad consists of cucumber, tomato, onion, and feta cheese. *Letnitsa*, a type of trout found only in Lake Ohrid, is expensive. *Eyeyar* and *rindzur* are tomato-based pasta dishes. *Chorba* (чорба; a thick type of soup) is a popular mid-morning snack. Wash it all down with delicious Macedonian *vino* (вино; wine) or *rakiya,* a grape or plum brandy. The water is safe to drink, and there are fountains in touristed areas.

CUSTOMS AND ETIQUETTE

Tipping is not customary, but it is appreciated. When restaurants are crowded, share a table with the locals and practice your Macedonian. **Homosexuality** is illegal in Macedonia, and there is a general lack of tolerance towards lesbians and gay men. Life here will be easier if you do not express views or preferences openly.

NATIONAL HOLIDAYS

Macedonians celebrate: January 1-2, New Year's; January 7, Orthodox Christmas; January 13, Old New Year; March/April, Orthodox Easter Monday and Tuesday; May 1-2, Labor Days; September 8, Republic Day; October 11, Partisan Day.

LIFE AND TIMES

HISTORY

Archaeological evidence shows a flourishing civilization in Macedonia between 7000 and 3500BC, which was followed by the immigration into the Balkan Peninsula of semi-nomadic Indo-European tribes, and then, in the first millennium BC, a mixed population of Dacians, Thracians, Illyrians, and Celts. The flourishing Greek culture to the south only seeped into the fringes of the area, then known as **Paeonia.** King **Philip II** of Macedonia (Macedonia being then situated just to the south of the modern Republic of Macedonia) joined Paeonia with his kingdom in 358BC, incorporating it into the Empire that, under his son **Alexander the Great,** would stretch from Albania to the Indus. While none of the empires before that of the Romans succeeded in holding power over the area for long, their rather ephemeral existence is nonetheless extremely politically important today, as both Greece and Albania base their claims to be indigenous inhabitants of the region upon the achievements of the Macedonian and Illyrian states during this pre-Roman period.

Macedonia's diverse Greek and Slavic heritage helped lay the foundation for contemporary conflict in the region.

Following the death of Alexander the Great, Macedonia fell to General Cassander, whose kingdom was lost to invading Celts and the acquisitive **Antigonid** family after his death. Macedonia, including eastern Paeonia, was then ruled by the Antigonids from 279 to 168BC. Alliances with Carthage and Egypt led to losses to Rome in the First and Second **Macedonian Wars,** while the Third Macedonian War (171-168BC) found Paeonia split from its southern neighbors. It remained an independent territory for some years before being incorporated into the larger **Roman** province of Moesia in the year 29. Under Roman rule, Paeonia enjoyed more than five centuries of grazing cattle and quiet *pax,* while the Romans built the foundations of cities that exist today, notably Heraclea Lyncestis (present-day Bitola) and Skupi (present-day Skopje).

Change came in the third century with the arrival of rampaging Goths, Huns, Bulgars, and Avars. The Visigoths tore through the Balkans on their way to Italy and Spain, opening up Paeonia to settlement by **Balkan Slavs,** who arrived steadily over the next 300 years. These Slavs, the ancestors of Macedonia's modern inhabitants, were soon re-incorporated into the Byzantine Empire under a system of tenuous military alliances that lasted well into the 13th century. The **Byzantines** and **Bulgarians** periodically warred over the territory from the 7th to 14th centuries, both empires treating the people as spoils and inserting their own nobles as feudal overlords. Serbian control, which began in 1331, ended with the 1389 **Battle of Kosovo,** and over the next 70 years the territory was completely absorbed into the **Ottoman Empire.**

It is this **diverse heritage** of Greek and Slavic origins that has laid the foundation for contemporary conflict in Macedonia. The Christian government and culture brought by the Greek-speaking Byzantines competed with the traditions of the Slavs. The situation was complicated by the work of the 9th-century missionaries **Cyril** and **Methodius,** whose Cyrillic alphabet (an adaptation of Greek characters to a Slavonic dialect spoken in southern Macedonia) became an important cultural feature uniting the Slavs, while at the same time it enabled the wide-spread transmission into the vernacular of a Christianity very tied to Greek Constantinople. In addition, various Slavic groups (notably the Bulgars and the Serbs) claim Macedonia on historical grounds: the **Bulgars** were a dominant Balkan power under Simeon I (893-927) and later in 976-1014 under Samuel, and Bulgarian is linguistically similar to Macedonian. The **Serb** claims rest on the basis of their predominance in the area under the Serbian Nemanjić dynasty in the 14th century. Least disputed is the influence of the **Ottoman Turks,** who controlled Macedonia from the end of the 14th century until 1913.

> Macedonia was the least successful of the Yugoslav republics economically, though its loyalty remained unwavering.

In the 19th century, the Balkan Slavs began agitating for independence. At the same time, the Great Powers (Austria-Hungary, Britain, France, Prussia, and Russia) became interested in the territories of the faltering Ottoman Empire, and the last quarter of the century saw tremendous jockeying for position and influence among them, as they prepared to pounce on the imminently available lands. One Macedonian reaction to these varied pressures was the 1893 creation of the **International Macedonian Revolutionary Organization (IMRO),** whose slogan was "Macedonia for the Macedonians." Twelve years later, every power in the Balkans fought over Macedonia in the **First Balkan War.** The Ottomans were quickly defeated, but the victors could not agree on how to divide the spoils. Bulgarian troops turned on their Serbian and Greek allies, causing the **Second Balkan War.** The Bulgarians were defeated and most of what would eventually become the Republic of Macedonia fell to Serbia. The **post-WWI** settlement confirmed this partitioning. In the years leading up to WWII, different Macedonias were artificially created (Vardar Macedonia, colonized by Serbia, and Aegean Macedonia, colonized by Greeks) and various countries fought for influence. During **WWII,** Macedonia was again partitioned, this time in 1941 between the Axis powers. Most of Macedonia was occupied by Bulgaria, though parts were combined with Albania and placed under Italian control.

When Macedonia was incorporated into **Yugoslavia,** each Balkan state was given republic status in the federation. Yugoslavia soon broke with the Soviet Union in favor of the non-Warsaw-Pact-Communism of leader **Josip Broz Tito.** Under Tito, Macedonian language, literature, and culture were revived. In 1958, the archbishopric of Ohrid was restored, signifying a break with the Serbian Church. Macedonia was the least successful of the Yugoslav republics economically, though its loyalty to the federation remained unwavering even through debates over republican autonomy and the suppression of liberal Marxism in Macedonia. Eventually, however, popular support for sovereignty could not be denied, and on December 19, 1991, Macedonia declared its **independence** from Yugoslavia.

LITERATURE

Tracing the roots of Macedonian Slav literature is as problematic as giving the fledgling country a politically acceptable name. Occupied by foreign powers for so long, the indigenous population (a portion of which occupies regions of modern-day Bulgaria) had little chance to bring its language to a literary level—Macedonian was not even officially recognized as a literary language until 1946, when Macedonia was established as a constituent republic of Communist Yugoslavia.

The earliest Macedonian literature, unsurprisingly, was Orthodox Christian, produced during Byzantine times. With the Ottoman Empire's rule (from the 14th century until 1913, when Serbian rule supplanted that of the Turks), little was written in Macedonian, and nothing of note, with the exception of the works of **Kosta Misirkov.** A pioneer in the movement to found a national language and literature, Misirkov published the 1903 *Za Makedonskite raboti (In Favor of Macedonian Literary Works)* and, two years later, established the literary periodical *Vardar.* After WWI, nationalist literary efforts were continued by the poet **Kosta Racin,** who promoted the use of Macedonian in the literary journals of the 1930s. Political tensions between the ruling Serbs, who considered Macedonian merely a dialect of Serbo-Croatian, and nationalist writers who attempted to assert its distinctiveness, induced some writers, such as **Kole Nedelkovski,** to work and publish abroad.

After WWII, when Yugoslavia was established and Macedonian was granted official status as a language, new freedom to write and publish in their own language inspired a wealth of postwar literature. Prewar playwrights such as **V. Iljoski** continued to shine, and the stage enjoyed an influx of new blood in **Kole Casule** and **Tome Arsovski.** Noteworthy postwar poets include **Aco Sopov, Slavko Janevski, Gane Todorovski,** and **Blaze Koneski.** The first works focused on the war and patriotic concerns, but soon diversified into themes ranging from the dream-lands of **Zivko Chingo** to the recent *Sok od prostrata (Prostate Gland Juice)* by **Yovan Pavlovski.**

Post-Yugoslavia literary development was stunted by various economic and political problems. With the 1995 lifting of the Greek trade embargo, however, a wonderful wealth of works poured forth. **Ante Popovski's** collection *Prividenija (Providence)*, which intertwines history and theosophy, won the Braca Miladinović Award at the Struga poetry festival as the best book of poetry, while **Sande Stojcevski's** *A Gate in the Cloud,* featuring over 50 of the poet's best lyrics, was published in an elegant English translation by David Bowen et al. Another winner of acclaim is *Skok so stap (Pole Vault)*, by **Dragi Mihajlovski**—a collection of short stories that provide insight into the nature of reality through their union of the grotesque and fantastic. The short stories of **Petre Andreevski,** collected in *Site lica na smrtta (All the Faces of Death)*, combine folk wisdom with modernity, and are read as metaphors for Macedonian life today. Also tapping into Macedonia's history for inspiration (or perhaps stability), there is **Slobodan Mickovic's** *Aleksandr i smrtta (Alexander and Death)*, a novel written in the form of notes sent by Alexander the Great's armorer to Aristotle, and covering the last two years of the life of the legendary Macedonian ruler.

MACEDONIA TODAY

There are half a million more sheep in Macedonia than there are people. If only the people got along as well as the sheep! Ethnic tensions are high in this nation, with its mix of Slavic Macedonians, Albanians, Serbs, Bulgars, and Turks. Mosques mingle with Orthodox churches, and nationalist propaganda is prevalent, the result of 50 years of brainwashing by Serbian leaders. President **Kiro Gligorov,** reelected in October 1994, continues to lead the country after surviving an assassination attempt by car bomb in October 1995, while Prime Minister **Branko Crvenkovski** heads

Macedonia, once weakened by UN embargoes and Greek trade blockades, is now making a comeback.

a coalition government made up of the **Social Democratic Alliance of Macedonia** (SDSM), the **Liberals,** the **Socialist Party,** and the Albanian **Democratic Prosperity Party.** Once weakened by UN-enforced embargoes from the north and Greek trade blockades from the south, Macedonia is now making a comeback. The U.S. is pumping aid into the strategically located nation, and the end of the war to the north is allowing trade routes to re-open. Most importantly, in October 1995, Greece, which originally contended that the new nation's name, currency, flag, and constitution all implied pretensions to the Greek province of the same name, lifted its embargoes. In turn, Macedonia may replace its current compromise prefix "Former Yugoslav Republic of" with a Greek-pleasing "New" or "North."

Skopje (Скопје)

The rolling hills, tilled fields, and orange-roofed suburbs that surround Skopje lend the city an air of serenity—an impression quickly corrected upon the first choking attempt to breathe the smog-filled air in the bustling national capital. Fortunately for those who prefer all things old, despite the disastrous earthquake that destroyed 90% of the city's structures in 1963, fate spared the town's mighty Old Bazaar, and old-school minarets still rise above the city's green parks.

ORIENTATION AND PRACTICAL INFORMATION

Despite being a city of half a million, Skopje has managed to consolidate most points of interest along a small stretch of the **Vardar River.** Several bridges, most notably the stone pedestrian **Kamen most** (Камен мост), connect the old and new sections of the city. The **trgovski tsentar** (трговски центар; central shopping center) is on the river next to **Ploshtad Makedoniya** (Плоштад Македонији; Macedonia Square). **Maps** of Skopje are difficult to find; the ones given out by tourist offices are generally copied onto brochures, and, lacking keys and street names, are about as helpful to the tourist as a compass is to an astronaut. However, there is a detailed map in pl. Macedonia and another posted right by the bus station. While some **street signs** are in Latin script, most are printed in Cyrillic. To add to the confusion, city leaders have changed "red" names to democratic ones, though the signs have not been changed.

Tourist Office: Tourist Association of Skopje (Туристички Сојуз на Скопје), Dame Gruev, blok III, p.f. 399 (Даме Груев; tel. 11 84 98; open Mon.-Fri. 7am-3pm). Runs information and tourist bureaus around town. Look for the **"i"** signs. One of the **tourist agencies** (Туристичка Агенциа; tel. 11 68 54; fax 61 34 47), is around the corner from the bus station across from the low-lying domes of the Turkish Baths, in the building of shopping center "Most" (Мост). Cheery English speakers provide brochures. Books hotel rooms for 800dn including breakfast, private rooms for DM20-30. Polyglot guides US$80-120. Up to 30% discounts on air tickets for travelers under 25. Open Mon.-Sat. 8am-8pm, Sun. 9am-2pm.

Embassies and Cultural Centers: U.K., Velyko Vlahovic 26, 4th floor (Велько Влахо-вик; tel. 11 67 72; fax 11 70 05 or 11 75 55). Open Mon.-Thurs. 8am-1pm and 2-4:30pm, Fri. 8am-1pm. Citizens of **Australia, Canada,** and **New Zealand** should contact the U.K. office. **U.S.,** Bulevar Ilinden (Булевар Илинден; tel. 11 61 80; fax 11 71 03). Open Mon.-Fri. 8am-4:30pm. Also houses the **U.S. Information Resource Center** (tel. 11 66 23; fax 11 84 31), a library that provides English newspapers, books, and **email.** Open Mon.-Fri. 11am-4pm.

Currency Exchange: Stopanska Banka, Tushinska (Тушинска; tel. 11 53 22; fax 11 45 03), across from the bus station. Exchanges money and cashes traveler's checks. Open Mon.-Fri. 7am-7pm, Sat. 7am-1pm. **Komertsiyalna Banka** (Комерцијална Банка) operates 3 Cirrus/MC **ATMs** around town; the most convenient is in the City Shopping Center.

Flights: Skopje Airport (tel. 11 28 75), 23km from downtown, is near the hamlet Petrovech. A taxi there is 800-1000dn. Macedonian **PALAIR** (tel. 23 82 38), at the shopping center.

Trains: Bulevar Kuzman Yosifovski (Кузман Јосифовски; info tel. 23 42 55). International (меѓународна; *megyunarodna*) and domestic tickets sold downstairs. To: Belgrade (5 per day, 12hr., 995dn); Budapest (2 per day, 24hr., 3620dn); Sofia (1 direct per day, 18hr., 913dn); and Thessaloniki (2 per day, 5hr., 575dn).

Buses: At the entrance to the Old Town (info tel. 23 62 54). From the train station, walk 3 blocks to the river, keeping the mountains on your left, then cross the 3rd

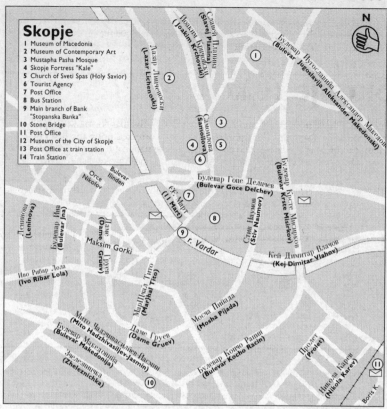

Skopje
1 Museum of Macedonia
2 Museum of Contemporary Art
3 Mustapha Pasha Mosque
4 Skopje Fortress "Kale"
5 Church of Sveti Spas (Holy Savior)
6 Tourist Agency
7 Post Office
8 Bus Station
9 Main branch of Bank
  "Stopanska Banka"
10 Stone Bridge
11 Post Office
12 Museum of the City of Skopje
13 Post Office at train station
14 Train Station

bridge. **Tourist Agency Proleter** (Пролетер; tel. 23 75 32), at the bus station, also
runs buses to Sofia (4 per day, 7hr., 440dn). The international terminal (Македонија
сообракај; *Makedoniya soobrakay*), Mito Hajivasilev 1 (Мито Хаџивасилев; tel. 11
17 20 or 11 63 45), left of the old train station. Open Mon.-Sat. 7am-9pm, Sun. 7am-
4pm. To: Sofia (3 per day, 7hr., DM15); Tirana (8-12hr., DM30; leaves from Tetevo
only; buses to Tetevo from Skopje every 15-30min.); and Istanbul (4 per day, 12hr.,
DM50). All buses require a 30dn reservation fee.

Public Transportation: Buy public **bus tickets** from kiosks (20dn) or from the driver
(30dn); stamp on board. Private buses run the same routes (10dn, pay on bus).

Taxis: Radiotaxi Vodno (tel. 91 91) or **Radiotaxi Jambo** (tel. 91 81). Taxis crawl the
streets with lost-people antennae. 5dn to get in, 15dn per km.

Luggage Storage: Garderoba (Гардероба), at the domestic bus station. 40dn. Open
daily 5am-10pm (often closes by 9:15pm).

24-Hour Pharmacy: Gradska Apteka (Градска Аптека; tel. 23 76 17). The second
pharmacy in the main shopping mall hasn't closed in the last 20 years.

Medical Assistance: Contact a hotel receptionist. Skopje's best hospital is **Medical
Faculty Hospital,** Vodnanska (Воднанска; tel. 11 42 44). **Emergencies:** tel. 94.

Internet Access: At the **U.S. Information Resource Center** (see **Embassies and
Cultural Centers,** above).

Post Office: Cross Kamen bridge from the bus station, take a right along the Vardar,
and follow the yellow "ПТТ"signs. *Poste Restante.* Open daily 8am-8pm. Telephones open 24hr. **Postal code:** 91101. In the train station: passport and 2dn
needed to pick up *Poste Restante* at window #20. Open Mon.-Sat. 7am-7:30pm,
Sun. 8am-2:30pm. **Postal code:** 91000.

Telephones: Next to the post office in the train station. Open Mon.-Sat. 7am-8pm.
The post office along the Vardar has 24hr. phone and fax service. **Phonecards** for

75dn (100 impulses) and 150dn (200 impulses) can also be bought at the post office and used throughout the country (even for international calls). **Kiosk** owners often let people use their phones for a few dinars. **Phone code:** 91.

ACCOMMODATIONS

Accommodations are scarce and overpriced. Most hotels are still state-run and charge 3000-5000dn per person. Some private pensions are popping up, but the best bet may be private rooms booked through the tourist office (700dn; breakfast included). Although haggling will not help in state-run hotels, it often gets a cheaper room in private ones.

Youth Hostel Skopje (HI), Prolet 25 (Пролет; tel. 11 48 49; fax 23 50 29). From the train station, walk toward the river along Kuzman Yosifovski and take the 2nd left onto Prolet to the 3-story building with psychedelic murals. English-speaking reception provides info on nightlife. Doubles with shower and 3-bed apartments with shower and TV 830dn per person; nonmembers 1050dn. Doubles, triples, or quads with hallway showers and stand-up toilet 540dn per person; non-members 610dn. Breakfast at adjacent 24hr. restaurant included.

Student Dorm Gotse Delchev (Гоце Делчев; tel. 36 33 06), Ivo Ribar Lola bb (Иво Рибар Лола). 4km from the center. Bus #5 from the train station; dorm is the four 15-story concrete towers on the right. Spartan rooms DM10. Open July-Aug.

Hotel Laki (Хотел Лаки), Leninova 79 (Ленинова; tel. 23 55 97), in the southwest. Bus #5 goes nearby; get off after you pass Studentski Dom Kuzman on the right coming from the train station. Laki is in a 3-story house at the intersection of Ivo Ribar Lola and Leninova. One of Skopje's 1st private hotels. Private showers. From DM25 per person. Reception open daily 7am-midnight.

FOOD

You'll find Skopje's best dishes toasting over coals in the streets of **Stara Charshiya** (Стара Чаршија; Old Bazaar). *Chorba* (чорба; a thick soup of some kind or another), is a popular dish, as are the more substantial *shish kebabs*, grilled peppers, and the local *tavche gravche* (тавче гравче; greasy beans topped with *shish kebab* bits), which tempt strollers with spicy aromas. Kiosks specialize in inexpensive and generous hot sandwiches (40-50dn). Stara Charshiya's north end hosts a huge vegetable market, and the adjacent **Bitpazar** (Битпазар; flea market) has everything else. Groceries stay open all week, although generally no later than 9pm. Finding vegetarian food in Skopje's eateries is somewhat like searching for intelligent life in the universe—it's not impossible that you'll find something, but don't hold your breath while you look.

Gostilnitsa Tourist (Гостилница Турист; tel. 22 90 04), in Stara Charshiya's fountain square. Feast on a boiled head of lamb (eyeballs and brain included; 100dn) or a lamb's kidney, heart, and liver (300dn). Also serves more mundane salads (50dn) and grills (*kebabs* or burgers; 50dn). Open daily 7am-11pm or midnight.

Pivnitsa An (Пивница Ан; tel. 22 18 17), down the steps and through the wooden gates in Stara Charshiya's fountain square. In the courtyard of a restored old house. Enjoy filet mignon (Филе Миньон; 330dn), less substantial grills (120-160dn), or a Balkan specialty, stuffed grape leaves (сарма от винова лоза; 130dn). Baklava and other desserts (60-100dn). English menu, nice staff. Open 24hr.

Dal Metu Fu (Дал Мету Фу), pl. Makedoniya (tel. 11 24 82). Imaginative pizzas, like the Indiana (tomato, cheese, chicken, and curry sauce; 169dn) or the Chiucculiata (cheese, tuna, salted fish, olives, olive oil, and fried egg; 169dn), pasta (148-169dn), and 25 kinds of chicken, beef, and pork dishes (290-390dn) served in a huge, bright joint. Open Mon.-Sat. 9am-midnight, Sun. noon-midnight.

Restaurant Simplon (Симплон; tel. 23 32 53), in a restored railroad car behind and to the left of the old train station. The *shkembe chorba* (60dn), made of the lining of a lamb's stomach, is a love-or-hate affair with lots of garlic. Meat dishes (140-210dn); salads (30-70dn). Open Mon.-Sat. 8am-midnight, Sun. 3pm-midnight.

SIGHTS AND ENTERTAINMENT

Most of Skopje's historical sights are an easy walk from the bus station. The domes of the 15th-century **Daut-Pashin Amam** (Даут-Пашин Амам; Turkish Baths; tel. 23 39 04), now an art gallery with a different exhibition every month, are visible from the bus station. Perfect acoustics make the baths a desirable venue for concerts from the Festival Skopsko Leto (Скопско Лето; Skopje Summer; gallery open Mon.-Sat. 8am-7pm, Sun. 9am-1pm; 30dn, students with ID free; call for concert schedule). The baths serve as a gateway to **Stara Charshiya's** enchanting streets. Largely Albanian and Muslim, the Old Bazaar stands in stark contrast to the modern side of town. Bear left up to Samoilova (Самоилова) until you reach a small square with a fountain; just across the square is **Sveti Spas** (Свети Спас; Sveti Spas Church; tel. 23 38 12). Frescoes of God and a few angels hover over marble floors and a masterful walnut iconostasis that took seven years to carve. Much of the interior is below ground level; Christian temples were once prohibited from being higher than mosques. In the courtyard, a sarcophagus holds revolutionary Gotse Delchev, who died in 1903 (open Mon.-Fri. 7am-7pm, Sat.-Sun. 7:30am-3pm; 50dn).

Farther up Samoilova, **Mustafa Pashina Jamiya** (Мустафа Пашина Џамија; Mustafa Pasha Mosque) marks its 504th year in this world, a miraculous survivor of the 1963 quake. Every Friday at 1:20pm, hundreds gather to listen to the preaching of the Hodzha (graduate of a theological university). The mosque's key-holder will let you in anytime he's around, usually between 10am and 6pm. The mosque with the insanely tall minaret belonged to Mustafa Pasha's brother, **Jaja Pasha,** who decided to match the height of Mustafa's temple despite the inferior valley site. Nearby, the elegant **Kurshumli Han** (Куршумли Хан; Turkish Inn) recalls five centuries of Ottoman occupation. Located in Stara Charshiya's former ironmongers' district, the inn served a 19th-century stint as a prison before finally becoming part of **Muzey na Makedoniya** (Музеј на Македонија). The museum's main building (tel. 11 60 44) gleams across a large courtyard. Its three permanent exhibits—archaeological, ethnographic, and historical—each present a nationalistic picture of the Macedonian past. An English or Russian tour is included in the ticket price (open Tues.-Fri. 8am-4pm, Sat. 9am-3pm, Sun. 9am-1pm; 50dn, students 20dn). Farther up Samoilova, **Muzey na Sovremenata Umetnost** (Музеј на Современата Уметност; Museum of Modern Art; tel. 11 77 35) occupies the highest point in central Skopje; its spacious halls host works of both national and foreign artists (open Tues.-Sat. 10am-5pm, Sun. 9am-1pm).

Walking back to the Vardar's banks, you'll see that the crumbling **Kale** (Кале; Turkish Fortress) has turned into weedy pastures. On sunny afternoons, the base is covered with Yugos and the picnickers they transported to the vista. Backtrack to the 6th-century **Kamen Most** (Камен Мост; Stone Bridge), one of the few structures to survive the 1963 earthquake. Monopolized by cheap T-shirt and fake-Marlboro peddlers, the aging thoroughfare leads to Skopje's New Town plaza. Since Macedonia's break with Yugoslavia, pl. Marshal Tito sports the name pl. Macedonia. To tune into the psychology of local artists, take a left at the square and visit **Galeriya DLUM** (Галерија ДЛУМ), kej 13 Noemvri bb (кеј 13 Ноември; tel./fax 21 15 33), in the riverside part of the central mall. Every 15 days, the Macedonian Association of Professional Artists presents a new exhibition (open Mon.-Sat. 9am-2pm and 4-8pm; free).

To bar- and disco-hop until the wee hours, party-hungry Skopjans gather at bars in the central mall, some of which often offer live jazz music. Try **Stadivarius Club** on the second floor—scope out the strollers from the breezy terrace. You can follow other disco-zombies to disco club **Playa Vista** at the outdoor swimming complex on the Stara Charshiya side of the river (more or less opposite the stadium). The music is usually loud enough to guide you from miles away (cover 50dn; open daily 9pm-whenever). **Club MNT** (МНТ Клуб) is underneath the City Cultural Center. Geared toward a slightly older crowd, it opens only Friday and Saturday nights (cover 100dn; under 16 8:30-11pm, over 16 12:30am-4am).

MACEDONIA

■ Near Skopje: Matka Canyon

On the Treska River, 15km southwest of Skopje, lies **Matka Canyon.** Several old churches and monasteries are found in the vicinity, of which the closest to the canyon and most impressive is the tiny **Sveta Bogoroditsa.** Built in the 14th century by a woman out of stone, sand, and egg-whites, it survived seven earthquakes and stands amazingly well-preserved today (open daily 7am-7pm). Farther up, just beyond the hydropower station and to the right, you'll find the mouth of the canyon. The spiky, narrow trail, seemingly dug out of the tall rocks, snakes along the steep banks of the Treska; it's a challenging, but beautiful, hike. **Bus #60** goes straight up to Sveti Bogoroditsa via the village of Saraj.

LAKE OHRID

■ Ohrid (Охрид)

Ohrid town is the lake's premier summer resort. A profusion of cafes fan out from the main square by the shore, giving way to small shops on narrow streets up the sloping Old Town. Like so many Balkan towns, Ohrid changed hands frequently; it was Roman, Slavic, Ottoman, and even, in the late 10th and early 11th centuries, the Bulgarian capital. Only the legacy of Yugoslav Socialism, with its penchant for concrete, is largely missing, thanks to UNESCO's designation of Ohrid as a protected town.

Orientation and Practical Information To get to the center from the bus station, make a right onto Partizanska (Партизанска). The collection of orange-roofed, white houses on the hill is the Old Town. At the foot of the hill, **Sveti Kliment Ohridski** (Климент Охридски) serves as Ohrid's pedestrian main street. The **tourist office AD Galeb-Bilyana** (АД Галеб-Билјана), Partizanska 3 (tel. 224 94; fax 241 14), one of many tourist bureaus in the center, finds **private rooms** (400-450dn per person; apartments from 1350dn) and sells new **maps** and brochures. Tour **guides** run 2000dn per day (open daily 7am-9pm; off season Mon.-Sat. 7am-8pm). **Buses** go to Skopje (10 per day, 3½-5hr., 235-270dn). The quickest route (3½hr., 235dn) is via Kichevo; the longer west route winds through the mountains (5hr., 285dn). **Exchange money** and cash AmEx **traveler's checks** at **Ohridska Banka** (Охридска Банка), on the corner of Makedonski Prosvetiteli (Македонски Просветители) and Turistichka bul. (Туристичка; tel. 314 00; open daily 7am-9pm; off-season Mon.-Fri. 8am-5pm, Sat. 8am-1pm). Store **luggage** at the bus station (50dn). The **post office,** on Makedonski Prosvetiteli, also runs an **exchange** (open Mon.-Sat. 7am-8pm). **Telephones** and **faxes** (fax 322 15) are in the post office (open Mon.-Sat. 7am-9pm). **Postal code:** 96000. **Phone code:** 096.

Accommodations and Camping The rates for **private rooms** are good (270-400dn), but lower-end prices usually don't include the 80dn **registration fee.** Find out the location of the room and exactly what the price includes, then bargain. Or shun the madness by going to the **tourist bureau** (rooms 400-450dn). **Lyupcho Mileski,** Dame Gruev 37 (Даме Груев; tel. 322 17), offers a double and two triples with a common shower/bath (US$10/DM15 per person). Similar accommodations and prices are offered by **Trajan Nikodinoski,** Lazo Trpski 14 (Лазо Трпски; tel. 229 01). The town's two **youth hostels** sit together 2.5km from the center. **Hostel Magnus** (Магнус; tel. 216 71; fax 342 14) offers two-, three-, or four-bed rooms with clean bathrooms (800dn with breakfast, 850dn with all meals). A private beach, soccer area, and nightly live music amuse homebodies. **Hostel Mladost** (Младост; tel. 216 26) rents four-person caravans and two- to five-bed rooms (bed DM7; bed and breakfast DM9; full room and board DM17). Take any bus headed for Struga (Струга; every 15min., 35dn) and ask the driver to stop at "Mladost," or walk up Gotse Delchev (Гоце Делчев) and go left at the drugstore "Shkor" (Драгстор "Шкор").

Food A mini-market sells all you need on Sveti Kliment Ohridski (open daily 7am-11pm). The **gradsko pazarishte** (Градско Пазариште; town market) vends fruits and vegetables daily between Gotse Delchev and Turistichka. **Letnitsa** (Летница; tel. 224 96), on the left side of Sveti Kliment Ohridski as you walk toward the lake, occupies a huge building and three terraces (open daily 7am-1am, off-season 7am-11pm), serving the famous Ohrid fish (300dn), soups (50dn), and meat dishes (from 160dn). **Pizzeria Don Giovani,** in the Letnitso complex on a second-floor balcony, offers different kinds of pizzas, including the unusual *Quatro Stagione*—tomato, cheese, calamari, crab, octopus, and other shellfish (195dn; open daily 10am-2pm).

Sights and Entertainment **Sveta Sofia** (Света Софија), Ohrid's oldest church, was built in the 9th century on the foundations of an even earlier church. The 11th-century frescoes, which are in surprisingly good shape, depict scenes from both the Old and New Testaments. During the Ottoman Empire's domination of the town, the church served as a mosque. To get there, take Tsar Samoil at the Lake Ohrid end of Sveti Kliment Ohridski and choose the left branch at the fork (open daily 9am-7pm; 100dn, students 50dn). Performances of the **Festival Ohridsko Leto** (July 12-Aug. 20) and the **Balkan Folklore Festival** (July 5-10) are held with the church as a backdrop. Up the hill from Sveta Sofia, go up Ilindenska, then take a right toward the church of **Sveti Kliment** (Свети Климент), formerly dedicated to the Virgin Mary. Frescoes depict to the holy teachers of the Christian faith, the Virgin, and the life of Christ (open daily 9am-1pm and 6-8pm; 100dn, students 50dn). Across from the church sits the **Icon Gallery,** with works spanning seven centuries, including depictions of stoic saints enduring torture (open Tues.-Sun. 9-10:30am, 11am-2pm, and 5-8pm; 100dn, students 50dn). The 13th-century **Sveti Yovan** (Свети Јован) perches on the lip of a cliff overlooking the lake. Take the steps behind Sveta Sofia (to the left as you exit) to Kocho Ratsin (Кочо Рацин), then follow the cliff path to the church. The sun sets in technicolor over the lizard-covered rocks.

Several **souvenir shops** flank the main street, and many artists with card tables display handmade jewelry crafted with the famed Ohridski Biser (Охридски Бисер; Ohrid Pearl). The **flea market,** part of the larger town market, offers cheap flip-flops good for Lake Ohrid's often-rocky bottom. Ohrid's best beaches can be found on the lake's eastern side, starting at Hotel Park (Хотел Парк), 5km from town. They get even better farther away, around Lagadin (Лагадин), where the wealthy and powerful erect their villas. **Water-taxis** wait on the shores of the town center to transport sun-bathers to better beaches. It'll cost 40dn if you're willing to wait for the boat to fill up. Otherwise, hiring the whole boat runs 300dn to the first beach, 400dn to the second, and 500dn to the third (round-trip). You can also rent **bikes** on the left side of Gotse Delchev, near the entrance to the town market (300dn per day), or you can dance until dawn at the **Disco Club** at Hotel Park. And if you still want to listen to disco music but feel pooped out, try **Cafe B-52** in the Amam Shopping Center on Kliment Ohridski, where people get sloshed and watch passersby from the second-floor window (open daily 9am-2am; off-season 9am-midnight).

The exquisite 10th-century monastery of **Sveti Naum** (Свети Наум) stands 28km to the south. Buses connect Ohrid to Sveti Naum (6 per day, 45min., 65dn).

■ Struga (Струга)

Fifteen kilometers northwest of Ohrid town (buses every 15min., 30min., 35dn), Struga is a poor man's Ohrid. Although it may lack some of the charm of its more famous neighbor, it still fills with tourists in July and August. In late August, poets from around the world come to compete for Struga's golden wreath at the **Strushki Vecheri na Poeziyata** (Струшки вечери на поезијата; Struga Poetry Evenings). Past honorees include W. H. Auden and Allen Ginsberg. The festival commemorates Struga's favorite son—Constantin Miladinovil, founder of Macedonian lyric poetry and author of *Bulgarian Songs*. He lived with his brother Dimitar in the **House of the Miladinov Brothers** on Brachya Miladinovi (Браќа Миладинови). As you go up Marshal Tito, take the first right after Hotel Beograd and follow signs to the house-museum (open daily 8am-3pm; free). **Nikola Nezlobinsky Muzey** (Никола Незлобин-ски Музеј; Museum of Natural Sciences), Boro Kalajdzieski (Боро Калайдзески; tel. 718 55), displays many past and present species of Struga's fragile ecological community. For once, preserved specimens of otherwise warring animals and insects "live" together at peace. A two-headed calf and a one-meter *letnitsa* (16.5kg, the largest ever caught) top a marvelous show of insects, birds, reptiles, and mammals (open daily 7am-7pm; 50dn). If you're in town in early August, you may be able to catch the **National Costume Festival,** a display of traditional Macedonian dress.

To get to the beginning of Struga's main street, Marshal Tito (Маршал Тито), get off the bus and walk to one of the bridges over the Tsrni Drim (Црни Дрим) River—Marshal Tito starts on the second bridge from the lake. **Struga Tours** (tel. 751 46; fax 726 57), on Marshal Tito, offers free brochures and **maps** and arranges **private accommodations** (about 300dn per person; open daily 8am-8pm; off-season 8am-2pm). **Hotel Beograd** (tel. 715 22; fax 751 25), on Marshal Tito, rents singles (DM40) and doubles with balcony and TV (DM60). **Campsite As** is located 11km from Struga on the way to Ohrid (tel. 719 05; DM30 for a caravan). **Exchange currency**—cash or traveler's checks (commission-free!)—at **Stopanska Banka,** across the street from Struga Tours (tel. 718 00; open Mon.-Fri. 7am-3pm, Sat. 7am-2pm; branches throughout town may stay open as late as 7-8pm in high season). Try a meat or cheese *burek* (pastry; 30-35dn) at any of the half-dozen joints inside the shopping complex opposite Hotel Beograd, or relax with a coffee (25dn) or whiskey (100dn) on one of the comfy rattan chairs at **Adagio** (Адаџо; opposite Struga Tours; open daily 8am-2am). The **post office** is situated just over the bridge past Hotel Beograd on the left of ul. J.N.A. (Ј.Н.А.; open Mon.-Sat. 7am-8pm). **Telephones** are at the post office (open Mon.-Sat. 7am-9pm, Sun. 9am-noon and 6-8pm); *Poste Restante* is at the telephone cashier's window. **Postal code:** 96330. **Phone code:** 096.

■ Near Struga: Sveta Bogoroditsa (Света Богородица)

Five kilometers from the center of town, near the village of Kalishta (Калишта), the churches of **Sveta Bogoroditsa** (Света Богородица) and **Sveta Atanasie** (Света Ата-насие) are set into cliffs on the shores of Ohrid. To reach them, take the bus to Radozhda (Радожда; 5 per day, 15dn), get off at Kalishta, and follow the signs for Hotel Biser—the Sveta Bogoroditsa complex is just beyond the hotel. The old Sveta Bogoroditsa consists of three caverns and a little chapel carved into a rock overhanging the lake. During the 14th century, three Christian monks slept and fasted through their last days there. The Ottoman oppressors discovered that the ascetic trio was preaching the forbidden faith and walled them inside their temple (open 6-10am and 5-9pm; 50dn; dress appropriately). Tiny Sveta Atanasie makes similar use of a cliff 100-200m farther up. A lakeside trail, which sometimes briefly disappears into the water, runs to the church from Sveta Bogoroditsa's courtyard. An overgrown path leads to the steps. What time has failed to do to the outside frescoes has successfully been accomplished by vandals. Luckily, the door leading inside is locked. Ask the caretaker of Sv. Bogoroditsa for the key.

CENTRAL MACEDONIA

■ Bitola (Битола)

Ringed by gray-brown apartment buildings and dotted with shiny glass-fronted banks, Bitola hides its heritage well. Macedonia's second city, founded by Philip of Macedon (father of Alexander the Great) in the 4th century BC, can no longer rely solely on its once-strategic location for prosperity, and now depends singularly on **Heraclea Lyncestis,** the ruins of an ancient settlement about 2km from the city center, to attract tourists. To get there, walk to the end of the park, which starts right where Marshal Tito ends, and bear left. Take the first right, after which signs on the right lead the way. You will walk by an abandoned zoo and an overgrown cemetery. At the turn of the millennium, Heraclea was an Episcopal seat; two basilicas and the Episcopal palace have survived, and their floor mosaics are completely intact. The amphitheater is being partially rebuilt with locally quarried stone to accommodate the **Herakleyski Becheri** (Хераклејски Бечери; Heraclean Nights), a cultural event held every July and August. Call the cultural center for more information (tel. 317 36 or 472 23; ruins open dawn to dusk). Many of Heraclea's precious finds sit in the **Zavod Muzey Galeriya** (Завод Музеј Галерија; Zavod Museum and Gallery; tel. 353 87), at the border of the park where Marshal Tito ends—opposite a bizarre white sculpture masquerading as a fountain (open Mon.-Fri. 7am-3pm; 50dn). In the town center, the mosque **Yeni i Isak Jamiya** (Јени и Исак Џамија), is now a gallery of modern art (open Tues.-Sun. 9am-noon and 6-9pm; free). If you take a right along the river (Први Мај; Prvi May) between the two mosques, you will eventually end up at the **Stara Charshiya** (Стара Чаршија; Old Bazaar), with cobbled streets offering the atmosphere the tourist would hope to find in an Old Bazaar, as well as plentiful shops and cafes.

Trains chug to Skopje (5 per day, 2hr., 200dn), and **buses** run to Skopje (every 1½hr., 3½hr., 250dn) and Ohrid (every 1½hr., 1¾hr., 125dn). The **train** and **bus stations** are located across from each other, 10 minutes from the town center. To get to the center, follow the main road opposite the train station until you reach the city park, then take a right on **Ivo Ribar-Lola** (Иво Рибар-Лола), which runs all the way up to the street **Marshal Tito** (Маршал Тито), now a pedestrian zone, lined with **exchange bureaus. Putnik Tours,** Marshal Tito 77 (tel./fax 352 11; open Mon.-Fri. 8am-7pm, Sat. 8am-noon), may have **maps** of the city, but the **Tourist Association** (Туристички Сојуз), Kliment Ohridski 25 (Климент Охридски; tel. 213 96) is probably a safer bet. It's hidden in an apartment block on a street parallel to Marshal Tito on the right side of Hotel Epinal as you stand facing it (open Mon.-Fri. 8am-3pm). **Creditna Banka Bitola,** in the futuristic building at the intersection of Marshal Tito and Radoslavljevik (Радослављевик), accepts traveler's checks (open Mon.-Fri. 7am-8pm, Sat. 7am-1pm). To get to the **post office** (open Mon.-Sat. 7am-7pm), take a right onto Ruzvelt (Рузвелт) from Marshal Tito immediately after the self-service restaurant (restaurant open Mon.-Sat. 7am-9pm). Make international **phone** calls or send **faxes** (fax 333 61) here (open daily 7am-8pm). **Postal code:** 97000. **Phone code:** 097.

A dearth of accommodations is reason enough to make Bitola a daytrip. **Dona Tours,** Gyuro Gyakovich 47 (Ѓуро Ѓаковик; tel./fax 426 34; open daily 9am-7pm), offers **private rooms** (DM15 per night). The only open hotel, **Epinal** (tel. 247 77; fax 247 78), rents unimpressive singles (910dn or DM35) and doubles (1200dn or DM60; breakfast included). Bitola also offers few epicurean options. In a former marketplace, between the mosques in the city center, **Restaurant Kai Kuburot** (Кај Кубурот; tel. 246 55), serves *bistrichka zhelka,* a pork filet stuffed with cheese and veggies (300dn). Quell the mouth-igniting paprikas with Macedonian wine (100dn per bottle; open daily 7am-midnight).

The Secretive Christianity of the Balkans

After spelunking through your 10th church in the caves of far reaching Macedonia, you might wonder, "What were these crazy Christians thinking?" The answer lies not in monkish asceticism, but rather in five centuries of Ottoman domination. The regime imprisoned or tortured Christian teachers and decreed that all churches remain physically, as well as symbolically, lower than mosques. Most churches from the Ottoman era still operate in cellars. To avoid persecution, congregations moved to secret grottos in the outskirts, but, as the three monks of Struga's Sveta Bogoroditsa found out, the empire had ears everywhere. Still, the hermit churches throughout the Macedonian countryside escaped the humiliation bestowed on their larger city "cousins" like Sveta Sofia in Ohrid, which had to wear a minaret until 1912.

MACEDONIA

MOLDOVA

Moldova, like the emblem on its flag, is a strange bird. Occupying the area known as Bessarabia, but a long-time part of Moldavia (one of the three historical provinces of Romania), this region languished in the Soviet Union for 45 years. Seventy percent of Moldova's land and people live on the west bank of the Nistru River, while a high concentration of Russians and Ukrainians hold out on the other side of the river they call the Dniestr. Teetering on the brink of a post-Soviet abyss, Moldova clings to the edge of Europe, a silent battleground of the Slavic and Romanian cultures, with language, signs, history and memory all providing fodder for the fray.

MOLDOVA ESSENTIALS

Citizens of Australia, Canada, Ireland, New Zealand, South Africa, and the U.K. need visas and invitations to enter Moldova; citizens of the U.S. need visas, but not invitations. For U.S. citizens, single-entry visas (valid 1 month) cost US$30, multiple-entry visas run US$50-80 (depending upon length of stay), and transit visas are US$15 for single-entry, US$30 for double-entry. For other nationals, single-entry visas are US$40 (valid 1 month), US$70 (2 months), or US$100 (3 months); transit visas cost US$40, US$50 for double-transit. Regular service takes five to seven days; two-day rush service costs an additional US$20. Together with a visa application, you must submit your passport, photograph, and fee by money order or cashier's check to your nearest Moldovan representative (see **Essentials: Embassies and Consulates,** p. 5.) U.S. citizens can also get visas at the airport in Chişinău. Invitations can be obtained from acquaintances in Moldova, or from Moldovatur after booking a hotel in Chişinău. For a visa extension, visit the Ministry of Foreign Affairs, Consular Section, in Chişinău.

GETTING THERE AND GETTING AROUND

Trains connect Chişinău to Bucharest, Iaşi, Kiev, Moscow, Odesa, Sofia, and many other former Soviet cities (generally via Kiev). The Iaşi-Chişinău trip takes about six hours, of which only two are spent in motion; border controls and wheel-changing (Moldovan rail tracks are of a larger gauge than Romanian ones) take up the rest. If you haven't seen bogies changed before, it's cool. Border guards will probably open your luggage. Internally, trains from Chişinau go to Bălţsi, Tirasopol, and Ungleni, but a railroad network built when Moldova and Ukraine were one country crisscrosses what is now an international border, so **buses** are generally the best way to get around Moldova. Buses arrive in Chişinău from every direction inside Moldova and internationally from Bucharest, Odesa, and even Istanbul (via Romania, not Bulgaria). Beware the bus schedules posted at the station—they're often wrong. Ask the driver or the ticket salespeople instead. The efficiency of a bus driver's work is measured in number of heads per ride, so buses are always packed to bejezus.

TOURIST SERVICES AND MONEY

Moldovatur is the only show in town, and that town is Chişinău. For better or worse, its president is Moldova's Minister of Tourism (not that that keeps him very busy). The Hotel Naţional office provides tours, hotel reservations, visa support, and some of the country's only English. It's not budget- or backpacker-oriented, but provides useful and friendly advice, and sells a map of Chişinău and a booklet about the city (in French only, until lei grease the wheels of an English press).

The monetary unit, the **leu** (plural lei), is worth 100 bani (often called by their diminutive form, bănuti). Unlike the currencies of many nearby countries, the Moldovan leu did not experience serious inflation in 1995-96, and prices remained stable as of summer 1997. Do not confuse the Moldovan leu with the Romanian currency of the same name. Black market sharks are common, but take care: it's better to have receipts for all currency exchanged to tame nasty customs officials, who make you declare all the money you're carrying when you enter the country. **Bringing cash is necessary,** since few places take traveler's checks or give cash advances.

U.S. dollars and Deutschmarks are the things to bring, while Russian rubles, Ukrainian hryvny, and Romanian lei are also occasionally possible to exchange.

COMMUNICATION

AT&T Direct and similar **phone** services are not yet available, but international service in the post office in Chişinău, though predictably expensive (to the U.S. 10 lei per min.), is dependable to as far away as Thailand. For local calls, buy pay phone tokens or a Moldtelecom card for modern cardphones popping up all over Chişinău (12 lei and up). These cards can dial direct internationally, too—watch as your credits plunge like a post-Soviet economy. **Mail** is even slower than the average Eastern European mail; ask for *avion* if you want airmail, but tell your friends back home not to worry if they don't hear from you for some time. For expensive emergencies, **DHL** has landed in both Chişinău and Tiraşopol.

LANGUAGE

As the official language of Moldova, **Romanian** was renamed **"Moldovan"** during the Soviet era for political reasons. Moldovan is essentially Romanian written in the Cyrillic alphabet, although the languages do have some semantic differences. In 1989, the script was changed back to the Latin alphabet, sparking a debate about whether the language should still be called Moldovan. Almost everybody speaks both **Russian** (see the **Russian Glossary,** p. 811, and **The Cyrillic Alphabet,** p. 797) and **Romanian** (see the **Romanian Glossary,** p. 809, and **Romania Essentials: Language,** p. 465). For the first year after the fall of the USSR, it was unusual to hear Russian spoken on the streets of Chişinău. Most ethnic Russians, aware that the times were changing, tried either to leave or to switch to Romanian, which they had avoided for decades. Nowadays, however, Russian is back and stronger than ever. In Chişinău and most of the urban centers, it dominates in all the tourist-oriented services and commercial life in the capital, though you can scrape by with Romanian. Almost nobody speaks **English,** but with perseverance, you should get your message across. Most signs are bilingual (Moldovan-Russian) although it is noteworthy that those on many public institutions are not. In the countryside, Russian drops like a rock, and you may feel a bit like Koko the gorilla trying to get your message across if you don't speak Romanian.

HEALTH AND SAFETY

Emergency numbers: Fire: 901; **Police:** 902; **Ambulance:** 903.

Few travelers make it as far as Moldova. Consequently, most Moldovans treat foreigners with a bit of suspicion. Women traveling alone are likely to feel uncomfortable. Even in Chişinău, streets are poorly lit and empty after 7 or 8pm.

CUSTOMS AND ETIQUETTE

Since Moldova as a nation is only about eight years old, it lacks its own way of life. The countryside reflects the traditions of its Romanian peasantry, while more Russified urban dwellers carry on the customs of their Slavic forebears. One typical Moldovan attitude that seems to have grown out of living in such delicate balance is a level of **courtesy** unsurpassed in Eastern Europe. Moldovans are very helpful to travelers, especially those who impress with a few phrases in Russian or Romanian.

On **homosexuality,** though, Moldova sticks to the old Soviet party line—it is practically unknown here, and as ignorance promotes fear and mistrust, discretion is highly advisable. The same is true for travelers of Jewish descent. Despite its location smack in the middle of the historic Pale of Settlement (the regions to which the Jews were restricted), Moldova retains a strong portion of Soviet-era anti-Semitism. While this may never present a problem, travelers may need a thick skin if discussing politics or history and the Jewish people.

MOLDOVA

LIFE AND TIMES

HISTORY

Present-day Moldova occupies the region known as **Bessarabia,** sandwiched between the Nistru and Prut rivers. During the first millennium BC, it was part of Scythia. Later, the Romans acquired it in a combo with Dacia (present-day Romania). Kievan Rus (10th and 12th centuries), Galician princes (early 13th century), and the Tatars (1241-1300s) all took turns at the "reign." Soon afterwards, Bessarabia was annexed by its western neighbors, **Moldavia** and **Walachia,** and then the whole province was captured by the Turks. In the 15th century, **Ştefan cel Mare** expanded Moldavia's frontiers, pushing back Poles to the north and Turks to the south, and defeating Vlad the Impaler (a.k.a. Dracula), ruler of Walachia. But the Turks got their revenge, extracting tribute from Stefan's son, **Bogdan the One-Eyed.** For the next three centuries, greedy neighbors tore Moldavia apart. Between 1711 and 1812, **Russia** occupied Moldavia five times. Finally, in 1812, under the **Treaty of Bucharest,** the declining Ottoman Empire handed the region over to Russia.

Bessarabia's new rulers attempted to Russify the region's civil and religious institutions, but this had little effect on the largely illiterate peasants, who remained culturally aligned with **Romania.** Bessarabia prospered during this period, however, with its agricultural produce finding a market in the Russian empire. The birth of Romania as an autonomous kingdom (1881) fueled smoldering nationalist sentiment in Bessarabia, but resentment did not erupt in a full-fledged nationalist movement until the **Russian Revolution** of 1905.

The Central Powers tried to use Bessarabia as a lure to get Romania on their side during WWI, but in the end Romania decided to ally with Russia. In **December 1917,** Bessarabia renounced Russia and declared itself an **autonomous republic.** The Bolsheviks reacted by invading the region, but Romanian forces drove them out. Alarmed by the German-sponsored government in nearby Ukraine, the new Moldavian state united with Romania the following year, and the official union of Bessarabia and Romania was recognized at the **Paris Peace Conference** in 1920. The Soviets, however, never accepted Romania's right to the province; in 1924, Moscow set up another tiny "Moldavian" state on Ukrainian territory, across the Nistru River from the "real" one. Meanwhile, Moldavia languished under Romanian control; its exports and had been geared toward Russia, not Romania, and the economy stagnated.

In 1939, the **Soviets invaded** once again, attempting to unite central Bessarabia with part of Bukovina and the miniscule Communist Moldavia in Ukraine. The Red Army expropriated Moldavian lands and expelled the German population to Western Poland. During **WWII,** Romania occupied Bessarabia as Germany's ally, killing or deporting many Bessarabian Jews and resettling the region with Romanian peasants. By 1944, the Soviets had retaken the region, and Moscow reintegrated the war-torn area into the Soviet empire as the **Moldavian Soviet Socialist Republic.** Under Communist rule, the Moldavian S.S.R. was radically collectivized and industrialized. Any kind of autonomous culture or society was stamped out, and the republic was thoroughly Russified, through the mass deportation of Romanian-speaking Moldavians to remote areas of the USSR and the resettlement of the area with ethnic Russians. The ethnic stratification of the Moldavian S.S.R. was intensified when **Russian** became the exclusive language of education and administration, with Romanian only sporadically studied as a foreign language. The weakening of the Soviet Union in the late 1980s allowed open public debate to resume in the country. On August 27, 1991, amid political chaos in Moscow, the Republic of Moldova declared **independence.**

> Under Communist rule, Moldova was thoroughly Russified, and Romanian-speakers were deported to remote areas of the USSR.

MOLDOVA

LITERATURE

Moldovan literature, like much of Moldovan history, is inextricably linked with that of Romania (see **Romania: Literature,** p. 468). After the country was subsumed by the USSR, literature in Moldova suffered the same fate as elsewhere in the Soviet bloc: heavy state control, including stylistic and ideological censorship. One of the most notable writers to surface during this period was **Andrei Lupan** (1912-), who managed to inject a bit of life into Socialist Realist themes. One of the only Moldovan authors translated into English is **Ion Druta** (1928-), whose 1963 novel *Balade de câmpie* (*Ballads of the Steppes*) explores the psyche of the region's rural population. Although both Lupan and Druta wrote in Moldovan, much of their work has been published only in Russian translation by the Soviet-controlled presses in Chişinău.

MOLDOVA TODAY

When the Soviet Union disintegrated, a powerful nationalistic movement in Moldova gathered 600,000 people at a meeting in Chişinău. They forced the Communist leaders to reject the Cyrillic alphabet in favor of the Latin one (thus virtually negating the difference between the Moldovan and Romanian languages) and to select the same national flag and hymn as Romania. These pro-Romanian tendencies alarmed the country's Russian minority (about 30% of the population), who feared reunification with Romania. Russian ultra-nationalists in the **Transdniester** area, on the east bank of the Dniester river, declared independence from Chişinău in September 1990. Hundreds were killed during violent clashes in this area in 1992; the conflict was eventually quashed by Russian forces led by **General Aleksandr Lebed,** which jump-started his political career. In 1994, the **Agrarian Democratic Party** won a parliamentary majority, defeating pro-Romanian and pro-Russian groups. Moldovans voted to maintain autonomy in March 1994, and in April the parliament approved limited membership in the Commonwealth of Independent States (CIS). A constitution, ratified July 28, 1994, granted substantial independence to the Transdniester region, but tensions continued. On May 8, 1997, Moldovan President **Petru Lucinski** (elected in December 1996) and Transdniestr leader **Igor Smirnov** signed an agreement reaffirming a united Moldovan state, and Moscow withdrew its 6000-troop peacekeeping presence. The conflict in this region seems to have abated, and the tanks and border controls of the past should remain a memory. Moldova's economy has also settled down; after inflation reached an incredible 800% in 1993, it has steadily decreased, and in the first six months of 1997 amounted to only 8%.

> **Russian nationalists in the Transdniester area declared independence during 1990; hundreds were killed in clashes in the region.**

Chişinău (Кишинёв)

The capital of Moldova, Chişinău (KEE-shee-nao; Russian kee-shee-NYOF) looks like a Soviet provincial city. It is built on a rectangular grid, with its sparseness punctuated by concrete monsters on a Stalinist scale—yet glimpses of its pre-Soviet past are visible in the pillared mansions along the main street. The area's strange weather, including a tendency for the sun to shine while rain is falling, curiously reflects the residents' attitude. In a country racked by political instability and geographically cut off from Western influences and trade, Chişinău stumbles slowly but doggedly toward modernity. The Adidas and Reebok stores look much better than the decrepit state-run establishments, and the rollicking market place, a huge consumer free-for-all, attracts a great deal of traffic and entrepreneurial ventures—from *morshrutne* taxis to knockoffs of Western fast-food restaurants. Unlike other post-Soviet cities clinging to the past, Chişinău is groping, albeit blindly, toward the future.

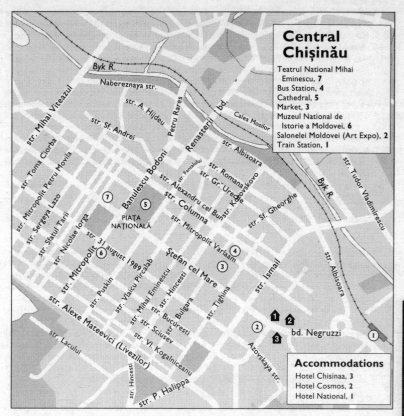

Central
Chișinău

Teatrul National Mihai
  Eminescu, 7
Bus Station, 4
Cathedral, 5
Market, 3
Muzeul National de
  Istorie a Moldovei, 6
Salonelei Moldovei (Art Expo), 2
Train Station, 1

Accommodations
Hotel Chisinaa, 3
Hotel Cosmos, 2
Hotel National, 1

ORIENTATION AND PRACTICAL INFORMATION

To get to the city center from the train station, located in the southeast corner of the city, walk through the park in front. On the left is the **trolley station** (near the vendors). Turn right, walk up to Hotel Cosmos, then turn left on **bd. Negruzzi;** after about 300m, it veers right and becomes **bd. Ștefan cel Mare.** This seemingly endless boulevard spans the city from southeast to northwest; most sights are clustered around it. Most of the trolleys from the train station, including #8, travel along it.

Tourist Office: Moldovatur, bd. Ștefan cel Mare 4 (tel. 26 61 06 or 26 62 47), on the 2nd floor of Hotel Național. Arranges hotel reservations and tours, provides great **maps** (5 lei) and booklets (6 lei), and speaks English. Open Mon.-Fri. 9am-5pm.

Embassies: U.S., str. Alexe Mateevici 103 (tel. 23 37 72; fax 23 30 44). Take trolley #7, 9, 10, or 24 to the university. Open Mon.-Fri. 9am-6pm; citizens' services Wed. 2-4pm. Citizens of other countries should contact their embassies in Romania.

Currency Exchange: One of the few businesses booming in Chișinău. All accept DM and US$. Romanian lei work at bad rates, as do Ukrainian hryvny and Russian rubles. **Bancosind Bank,** at the corner of bd. Ștefan cel Mare and str. Pușkin, cashes AmEx, MC, and Thomas Cook traveler's checks and gives Diners Club and Visa cash advances. Open Mon.-Fri. 8am-7pm, Sat. 8am-4pm.

Western Union: Window #24 in **Banca de Economie al Moldovei,** str. Pușkin 33. Coming from the train station on Ștefan cel Mare, take a right onto Pușkin. Visa cash advances also available. Open Mon.-Fri. 8:30am-3pm, Sat. 9am-3pm.

MOLDOVA

Flights: The **airport** (tel. 52 54 12) is 12km from downtown; take bus #65 from the corner of Izmail and Stef. **Air Moldova,** bd. Negruzzi 3 (tel. 26 40 09), near Hotel Naţional, flies to Athens, Frankfurt, Istanbul, and Moscow. English spoken.

Trains: Info tel. 25 27 35. Somewhat anarchic. You can buy international tickets at the 2nd floor booth, but they're expensive (e.g. Chişinău-Iaşi one-way 25 lei); buying a round-trip ticket in Romania saves about 50%. However, you will have to specify in advance which train you'll be taking back. To: Bălţi (1 per day, 7 lei); Bucharest (1 per day, 55 lei); Kiev (1 per day, 14hr., 60 lei, first-class 90 lei); Minsk (1 per day, 90 lei, first-class 130 lei); Moscow (1 per day, 31hr., 110 lei, *couchette* 180 lei); Odesa (2 per day, 20 lei); and Tiraspol (1 per day, 5 lei). Buy domestic tickets at the booth between the main buildings that has train times posted on it.

Buses: Str. Mitropolit Varlaam 58 (tel. 21 20 84), a block to the right off the main street; take a left after the market. Beware the occasionally erroneous bus times posted in the lobby! Open daily 7am-7pm. The buses are old enough to be declared historical monuments. Crowded transports leave for: Bălţi (every 30min., 14 lei); Tiraspol (every hr., 9 lei); Bucharest (1 per day, 50 lei); Iaşi (5 per day, 17 lei); and Odesa (1 per day, 20 lei). **Kavasoglu lines** (tel. 54 98 22) and **Ozgüleu lines** (tel. 26 34 48) each run 2-7 buses to Istanbul from the train station (24hr., 130 lei).

Express Mail: DHL, 42 Vlaicu Pirkălub (tel. 23 22 46 or 23 22 44). Open Mon.-Fri. 9am-6pm, Sat. 9am-1pm.

Public Transportation: Extensive but slow **trolley** system; buy tickets (50 bani) at kiosks in the stations, and stamp them on board. Scores of **marshrutki**—converted minivans—follow the same routes and are a very quick alternative (1 leu).

Taxis: State-run. Theoretically, 2 lei per km in the city, but, at least with foreigners, drivers set the price in the beginning. If you're slick with Russian or Romanian, bargaining can work wonders.

Post Office: Bd. Ştefan cel Mare 134, right across from city hall and the Mihai Eminescu Theater. Open Mon.-Sat. 8am-7pm, Sun. 8am-6pm. **Postal code:** 277012.

Telephones: Corner of str. Tighina and bd. Ştefan cel Mare, 2 blocks from Hotel Naţional. Phones open 24hr., except for occasional coffee breaks. Phone cards sold. International service to the left as you enter. To call internationally from these phones, dial 810 and the number; after the call is answered, dial 3. **Faxes** (fax 54 91 55) sent and received. Open daily for faxes 8:30am-10pm. **Phone code:** 02.

ACCOMMODATIONS

Coopertiva Adresa, bd. Negruzzi 1 (tel. 26 64 14), across from Hotel Cosmos, rents **private rooms** (16 lei per person; open Mon.-Fri. 9am-9pm, Sat.-Sun. 9am-6pm). Approaching Cosmos from the train station, Adresa is in the first alley on your left as you pass the traffic circle and enter bd. Negruzzi. Look for a small orange, blue, and white sign. Hotels are also affordable. All hotels have a hot-water schedule, so ask for it before you strip down for that long-awaited bath. Most, particularly the fancy-sounding ones, take Visa and have someone on hand who speaks a form of English.

Hotel Meridian, str. Tighina (tel. 26 06 20). As budget as it gets. Noisy but good spot near the market. "Luxury" rooms have TV, fridge, and bath, while normal rooms have the bare necessities. If paying the luxury fee, be sure to get the luxury room. Singles 30 lei, luxury 50 lei; doubles 50 lei, luxury 100 lei.

Hotel Chişinău, bd. Negruzzi 7 (tel. 26 63 41). The lobby resembles a tiny, well-kept train station, with square marble columns and a dark-wood motif. The dim hallways are actually pink. Modest rooms with TV, phone, and bath. Restaurant, exchange office, and room service. Singles 75 lei; doubles 124 lei; triples 182 lei.

Hotel Cosmos, bd. Negruzzi 2 (tel. 26 44 57; fax 26 43 00). Parquet floors, dark checkerboard bedspreads, golden wallpaper, a massage parlor, and a restaurant and bar (restaurant open daily 7:30am-midnight; bar until 4am) complete the ambience. English and French spoken. Doubles 160 lei. Breakfast included.

Hotel Naţional, bd. Ştefan cel Mare 4 (tel. 26 60 83). A former Intourist facility. Bright flowery rooms typical of well-endowed Soviet hotels, with slightly dingy bathrooms. Barber shop, bar, and restaurant (open daily 8am-11:30pm). English spoken. Singles 130 lei; doubles 180 lei.

FOOD

Finding good, cheap dining in Chişinău is a problem, but simply finding food is relatively easy. Try the **marketplace** (open in summer Tues.-Sun. 6:30am-5pm, winter 7am-4pm), off the main street on str. Tighina. You can find vendors selling fresh veggies, fruit, pastries, and *buterbrod* (бутерброт; open-faced sandwiches with meat and veggies for 1-2 lei). Also look for **Nimentarii** or Гастрономи (food stores).

Butoiaş (Little Barrel), Calea Ieşilor 71 (tel. 62 13 68), at the north end of town. Take trolley #11 to the last stop and look for the big barrel on the left. The restaurant inside has atmosphere but not much food. The choices: soup, pork, chicken, veggie side dishes, and various sandwiches (4-12 lei). All meals include bread and mineral water *Răcoarea Codrilor* (Coolness of the Woods), synthetically produced at a Chişinău experimental plant. Watch out, Evian. Open daily 11am-midnight.

Belluno, bd. Ştefan cel Mare 124 (tel. 26 03 42). Perhaps the best and most elegant eating establishment in town, serving so-called Moldo-Italian cuisine. *The* place to go if you want to impress your date. See his or her eyes widen when you pull out your credit card to pay for the 16-lei steak that tops the menu. Meals can easily reach 40-50 lei here. English menu. Open late.

Magic, bd. 31 Aug. 1989 78 (tel. 23 25 80), across from the History Museum. Plastic red arches and summer "Sprite"-emblazoned canopies give it the aura of a fast-food temple. And, indeed, it serves sandwiches: with caviar (4.60 lei), boiled tongue (2.50 lei), and mushroom-stuffed chicken legs (10 lei). Open 10am-11pm.

SIGHTS AND ENTERTAINMENT

To tour most of Chişinău's monuments, just walk up bd. Ştefan cel Mare. In front of Hotel Cosmos, the first statue represents **Kotovski**—Robin Hood for Soviet *apparatchiki,* a bandit for Romanians. In the 1920s, he attacked Romania in flash raids from across the Nistru River. Not as dramatic as Lenin's accomplishments, but then, Kotovski's statue is still up. Follow the boulevard as it bears left and take a left at Hotel Naţional (at the half-nude pillar statue pointing toward the Academy of Science) to view the sky-blue towers of **Cioflii Church** (finished in 1876), perhaps once the most beautiful in Chişinău. Look past the exterior's need for restoration to admire the icons inside, each framed by a different coverpiece-and-column combo (open daily 6am-7pm). Across the street, on the corner of bd. Ştefan cel Mare, is **Salonelei Moldovei** (Art Expo; open Tues.-Fri. 10am-6pm, Sat.-Sun. 11am-4pm), where 2m silver statues representing the classical arts—painting, writing, sculpture—stand outside the wall.

All along the main boulevard, Stalinist blocks and Neoclassical buildings compete for attention. A few blocks up on the left are the Corinthian columns and beige facade of the **Teatrul Naţional Mihai Eminescu** (tel. 25 02 55; ticket office open 10am-1pm and 3-6pm). Close by, two gentle lions guard the **Organ Hall;** check the board for concert schedules (usually at 6:30pm). A flag crowns the small tower above the charming facade of the nearby **City Hall.** A few hundred meters down Vlaicu Pirkălab on the left is the 1887 church **Pantelimona;** its fascinating architecture and beautiful stained-glass windows were defiled in Communist times when it was transformed into a temple of consumerism (a department store). Farther up bd. Ştefan cel Mare, at the intersection with str. Puşkin, is **Piaţa Naţională,** the main square, with an 1846 triumphal arch. Behind it lie a **park** and the temple-like **cathedral,** resembling a Stalin-sized neo-Greek R2-D2. On the square's upper left corner stands the statue of the legendary **Ştefan cel Mare** (Stephen the Great). The statue, created in 1928, was moved around during WWII to avoid the Bolsheviks, but finally fell the hands of the Soviet—who modified its inscription—in 1945. In 1972, it was set up in the park, but the 1990 national revival brought it back to its original resting spot. The park also contains an alley with statues from the classics of Romanian literature.

The **Muzeul Naţional de Istorie a Moldovei,** str. 31 August 1989 121a (tel. 22 66 14), sits near Piaţa Naţională. Take a left on str. Puşkin, then a right (open Tues.-Sun. 10am-5pm, closed last Fri. of the month; museum 50 bani, students 20 bani; treasury 1 leu, students 50 bani). In front of the museum, the statue of a she-wolf feeding the two founders of Rome, Romulus and Remus, stands as a reminder of south Bessarabia's Latin roots. About five blocks left of the main street up str. Puşkin is the central **park,** complete with a lake. On the way you'll pass by the **university;** many of the students who hang out at the cafes around here would welcome the chance to practice their English with you. The department store **Lumea Copiilor** (Children's World), bd. Ştefan cel Mare 136, five blocks up from Hotel Naţional on the corner of Piaţa Naţională, is a living museum of revolutionary Communism (open Mon.-Sat. 8am-8pm, Sun. 9am-4pm). For souvenirs, head for the **Galerie Brancuşi,** in Salonelei Moldovei, which also has cool temporary exhibitions.

■ Near Chişinău

CĂPRIANA

Nestled in the hills 20km northwest of Chişinău, Căpriana (kep-ree-AH-na) centers around Moldova's most celebrated 14th-century monastery. Reasonably accessible as a daytrip from Chişinău, the village and monastery provide a gentle glimpse of the countryside. From the bus stop, walk to the left of the only modern-looking building in sight to gaze upon the spires of the **old and new monastery churches.** The peach-and-light-blue main church has a bright interior filled with paintings in need of restoration. In the monastery's far corner, the gutted old church offers a glimpse of its former beauty, with silver towers melting into one high dome. Clad in scaffolding, this house of worship is now home to many sparrows. Good picnic spots hide in the hills. Like every other town in Moldova, getting to Căpriana involves a fantastically cheap and overcrowded **bus** (daily at 11:30am, Fri.-Sun. also 7:45am; 40min.; 5 lei). Since the only return buses leave the village at 9am and 1pm, you might broaden your transportation choices to include the 7km hike to the Străşeni **train** station. The ever-present (though never scheduled) **Marshrutki** (taxis) that come through every couple of hours could save your feet (2.50 lei). Some hitch a ride into town (3-5 lei expected).

VADUL LUI VODĂ

About 12km northeast of Chişinău, the relaxing riverside resort Vadul lui Vodă hosts hordes of Russian-speaking Moldovans in summer. Although water sports are not popular here (the Transdniestr Republic looming on the opposite bank is a somewhat effective discouragement), you can burn off a few calories with tennis, soccer, and other pastimes. The beach attracts a large Chişinău crowd eager to quench its thirst at the kiosks in this wooded retreat, but watch out for the hideous public toilets, which belong in the Outhouse Hall of Shame. **Bus** #31 runs here directly from the market in Chişinău, as do *marshrutki* (taxis). Ride the bus to the very end (*plaja*), where you'll see globs of people in skimpy Speedos frolicking on the banks of the Nistru. From the bus parking lot, take a right and walk until the first bend in the road to get to a **free campground.** Staying on the path as it crosses the big paved road leads to an alley of *Bazide Odibni* (vacation complexes), where many state-run firms once established rest areas for their employees. Some of these lodgings, such as **Păduricea Verde** (Зелёный Бор, *Zelyony Bor*; tel. 38 20 36), 300m on right, welcome tourists into their log-cabin houses (3-bed cabins 25 lei per person, with meals 45 lei). The snack bar offers reasonably priced food (open daily 9am-noon and 3-11pm). A sauna (50 lei per hr.), furnishings (including fridge and TV), and working toilets make this shady little spot a great little deal.

POLAND (POLSKA)

US$1 = 3.50zł (złoty, or PLN)	1zł = US$0.29
CDN$1 = 2.53zł	1zł = CDN$0.40
UK£1 = 5.57zł	1zł = UK£0.18
IR£1 = 5.14zł	1zł = IR£0.20
AUS$1 = 2.55zł	1zł = AUS$0.39
NZ$1 = 2.22zł	1zł = NZ$0.45
SAR1 = 0.75zł	1zł = SAR1.34
DM1 = 1.92zł	1zł = DM0.52

Country Phone Code: 48　　　　　　　**International Dialing Prefix: 00**

For many Westerners, it's rather odd to think that between 1795 and 1918, Poland simply did not exist on any map of Europe. And after only two decades of freedom, it was soon carved up by Hitler and Stalin. Now, after centuries of partition and occupation, Poland has finally been given a little room to breathe. Westernization and capitalism have run rampant in this country, which has always considered itself more a part of the West than the East. This is not to say that Poland is losing its natural flavor. Rather, political and economic freedoms have helped this rich culture to occupy its own skin once again, even if it's now wearing a pair of Levi's.

POLAND ESSENTIALS

Citizens of the U.S. and Ireland do not require a visa for visits up to 90 days; citizens of the U.K. can stay visa-free up to six months. Make sure your passport is stamped when you enter the country. Australians, Canadians, New Zealanders, and South Africans all need visas. Single-entry visas (valid for 90 days) cost US$40 (children and students under 26 pay US$30); double-entry visas cost US$55 (students US$42); 48-hour transit visas cost US$20 (students US$15). A visa application requires a valid passport, two photographs, and payment by money order, certified check, or cash. Regular service takes four days; rush service (24hr.) costs US$35 extra. See **Essentials: Embassies and Consulates**, p. 5, for a list of Polish embassies. To extend your stay, apply at the local *voivodship* (province) office (*urząd wojewódzki*).

GETTING THERE

LOT, British Airways, and Delta **fly** into Warsaw and from London, New York, Chicago, and Toronto (among other cities). **Trains** and **buses** connect to all neighboring countries, but **Eurail** is not valid in Poland. Almatur offers ISIC holders 25% off international fares for the Polish portion of the trip and sells **Interrail** passes. **Wasteels** tickets and **Eurotrain** passes, sold at Almatur, Orbis offices, and major train stations, get those under 26 40% off international train travel fares. Thefts have been known to occur on international overnight trains; **do not fall asleep.** Ferries run from Sweden and Denmark to Świnoujście, Gdańsk, and Gdynia.

GETTING AROUND

PKP trains scurry to most towns at bargain prices. Train stations have boards that list towns alphabetically, and posters listing trains chronologically. *Odjazdy* (departures) are in yellow; *przyjazdy* (arrivals) are in white. **InterCity** and *Ekspresowy* (express) trains are listed in red with an "IC" or "Ex" in front of the train number. *Pośpieszny* (direct; also in red) are almost as fast. *Osobowy* (in black) are the slowest but are 35% cheaper than *pośpieszny*. All **InterCity, ekspresowy,** and some *pośpieszny* trains require seat reservations; if you see a boxed R on the schedule, ask the clerk for a *miejscówka* (myay-SOOV-ka; reservation). Buy your ticket aboard the train for a surcharge; when doing so, find the *konduktor* before he or she finds you, or risk a fine. Most people purchase *normalny* tickets, while students and seniors buy *ulgowy* (half-price) tickets. Beware: foreign travelers are not eligible for discounts on domestic buses and trains—ISICs will get you nowhere. You risk a hefty fine by traveling with an *ulgowy* ticket without official Polish identification. On Sundays, all tickets cost 20% less. Train tickets are valid only on the day for which they're issued. Lines can be extremely long and move at a snail's pace; make sure you plan for enough time so you don't miss your train. Better yet, buy your ticket in advance at the station or an Orbis office. When traveling by bus or train, be aware that stations are not announced and are sometimes poorly marked. If you are getting off before the final destination, pay attention and ask someone if necessary.

   PKS buses are cheapest and fastest for short trips. Like trains, there are *pośpieszny* (direct; marked in red) and *osobowy* (slow; in black). Purchase advance tickets at the bus station, and expect long lines. Many tickets can only be bought from the driver, however. In the countryside, PKS **markers** (like yellow Mercedes-Benz symbols) indicate bus stops, but drivers will often halt wherever you flag them down. Traveling by bus with a backpack can be a problem (or at least uncomfortable) if the bus is full. Under-bus storage is rarely used, and the overhead bins are so ridiculously small that they can barely accommodate coats.

   Though legal, **hitching** is increasingly dangerous for foreigners. Hand-waving is the accepted sign. *Książeczka autostopu* (*The Hitchhike Book*), sold by PTTK, includes an insurance policy, an ID card, and vouchers that qualify drivers for compensation. *Let's Go* does not recommend hitchhiking as a safe means of transportation.

TOURIST SERVICES

Orbis, the Polish state travel bureau, sells international bus, train, plane, and ferry tickets, as well as domestic train tickets. **Almatur,** the Polish student travel organization, sells ISICs and helps find university dorm rooms in summer. Both provide maps and brochures, as do the **PTTK** and **IT** bureaus in every town. Since 1989, **private tourist agencies** have mushroomed all over Poland; their prices are competitive, but watch out for scams.

MONEY

The Polish **złoty**—plural *złote*—is fully convertible. For cash, private **kantor** offices, except for those at the airport and train stations, offer better exchange rates than banks. **Bank PKO S.A.** accepts **traveler's checks** and gives MC and Visa **cash advances** all over Poland. **ATMs** (Polish *Bankomat*) are flourishing, but still scarce in the east and in small towns. **Wielkopolski Bank Kredytowy (WBK)** is affiliated with Plus and Visa, while Bank PKO S.A. accepts Cirrus and EC/MC.

In January 1995, the National Bank cut four zeroes off all prices, and introduced new bank notes and coins. The old currency has been invalid since January 1, 1997. Learn the difference between the old and the new (posters at the airport and train stations depict the currencies), and never accept old currency. When changing money, it is helpful to ask for smaller bank notes (10zł or 20zł), since businesses and hostels may not be able to give change for the larger notes (50zł or higher). As there are nine types of coins, a change purse can prove extremely helpful.

COMMUNICATION

Mail is becoming increasingly efficient, though there are still incidents of theft. Airmail (*lotniczą*) usually takes seven to 10 days to reach the U.S. For *Poste Restante,* put a "1" after the city name to ensure that it goes to the main post office. When picking up *Poste Restante,* you will usually have to pay a small fee (0.70zł).

Two types of **pay phones** are available. The older ones use *żetony* (tokens; "A" for local calls, "C" for intercity calls). Newer phones use **phone cards,** which come in several denominations. These phones have card slots and instructions in English. Both tokens and phone cards are available at any post office as well as some kiosks. Card phones are becoming increasingly available throughout the country and are no longer constrained to the post office. Long-distance access numbers include: **AT&T Direct,** tel. 01 04 80 01 11 (from outside Warsaw, dial 0 and wait for a tone first); **MCI WorldPhone,** tel. 01 04 80 02 22 or 00 800 111 21 22; **Sprint Express,** tel. 01 04 80 01 15; **Canada Direct,** tel. 01 04 80 01 18; **British Telecom Direct,** tel. 044 00 99 48. To make a **collect call,** write the name of the city or country and the number plus "*Rozmowa 'R'*" on a slip of paper, hand it to a post office clerk, and be patient.

LANGUAGE

Polish varies little across the country, apart from the region of Kaszuby, the distinctive, Germanized dialect of which is classified by some as a separate language, and Karpaty, where the highlanders' accent seems to have been affected by the rivers of goat's milk they drink. In western Poland and Mazury, **German** is the most commonly known foreign language, though students will probably know **English.** Elsewhere, try English and German before **Russian,** which many Poles understand but show an open aversion to speaking. Most Poles can understand **Czech** or **Slovak** if they're spoken slowly. Students may also know **French.**

The fully phonetic spelling is complicated by some letters not in the Latin alphabet: "*ł*" sounds like a "w"; "*ą*" is a nasal "o"; "*ę*" is a nasal "eh"; a dash above a consonant softens it; "*ó*" and "*u*" are both equivalent to an "oo"; "*ż*" and "*rz*" are both like the "s" in "pleasure"; "*w*" sounds like "v." The language also has a few consonantal clusters, which are easier to spit out than they seem: "*sz*" is "sh," "*cz*" is "ch," and "*ch*" and "*h*" are equivalent, and sound like the English "h." See the **Polish Glossary,** p. 807.

HEALTH AND SAFETY

> **Emergency Numbers: Police:** tel. 997. **Fire:** tel. 998. **Ambulance:** tel. 999.
> **AIDS:** tel. 958.

Public restrooms are marked with a triangle for men and a circle for women. They range from pristine to nasty and can cost up to 0.70zł, even if they're gross. Soap, towels, and toilet paper cost extra. **Pharmacies** are well-stocked. Hi-tech medical clinics are opening up around the country. **Tap water** is theoretically drinkable, but to avoid the high chemical and metal content, it is very advisable to drink **bottled mineral water,** which is available carbonated (*gazowana*) or not (*nie gazowana*).

Criminals feed off naive, rich western tourists; carry a bare minimum of cash. As unemployment grows, con artists multiply. Always be on your guard at big train stations. Also be on the lookout for pickpockets, especially when boarding or riding crowded public buses and trams.

ACCOMMODATIONS AND CAMPING

Grandmotherly **private room** owners smother travelers at the train station or outside the tourist office. Private rooms are usually safe, clean, and convenient, but can be far from city centers. Expect to pay about US$10 per person.

PTSM is the national hostel organization. The average **HI youth hostel** (*schronisko młodzieżowe*) is quite nice, though throughout the country they run the range from basic to divine. They're everywhere and average US$3 per night (less for "juniors" under 18 or 26, more for non-members). **Hot water** is standard. **University dorms** transform into spartan but cheap tourist housing in July and August; these are an especially good option in Kraków. The Warsaw office of **Almatur** can arrange stays in all major cities. **PTTK** runs a number of hotels called **Dom Turysty,** which have multi-bed rooms (US$2-5) as well as budget singles and doubles. Many towns have a **Biuro Zakwaterowań,** which arranges stays in private homes. Rooms come in three categories based on location and availability of hot water (1 is the best).

Campsites average US$2 per person; with a car, US$4. **Bungalows** are often available; a bed costs about US$5. *Polska Mapa Campingów* lists all campsites. Almatur runs a number of sites in summer; ask for a list at one of their offices.

FOOD AND DRINK

Monks, merchants, invaders, and dynastic unions have all flavored Polish cuisine—a blend of hearty dishes drawing from the French, Italian, and Jewish traditions. While Polish food is often loaded with cholesterol, it is less starchy than that of the Czech Republic and less fiery than that of Hungary or Bulgaria.

A Polish meal always starts with **soup.** From a typical menu, you will often be able to choose between *barszcz* (beet broth), *chłodnik* (a cold beet soup with buttermilk and hard-boiled eggs), *kapuśniak* (cabbage soup), *krupnik* (barley soup), and *żurek* (barley-flour soup loaded with eggs and sausage). Filling **main courses** include *gołąbki* (cabbage rolls stuffed with meat and rice), *kotlet schabowy* (pork cutlet), *naleśniki* (cream-topped crepes filled with cottage cheese or jam), and *pierogi* (dumplings with various fillings—meat, potato, cheese, blueberry…).

Poland bathes in **beer,** vodka, and spiced liquor. *Żywiec* is the favorite strong (12%) brew; *EB* is its excellent, gentler brother. *EB* also makes *EB Czerwone,* a darker, heavier, very-much-stronger variety. Other beers available throughout the country include *Okocim* and *Piast. Wódka* ranges from wheat to potato. *Wyborowa, Żytnia,* and *Polonez* usually decorate private bars. "Kosher" vodka is rumored to be top-notch, although what makes it kosher remains a mystery. The herbal *Żubrówka* vodka comes with a blade of grass from the region where the bison roam. It is sometimes served as a mixed drink with apple juice (*z sokem jabłkowym*). *Miód* and *krupnik*—two kinds of mead—are beloved by the gentry, and many grandmas make *nalewka na porzeczce* (black currant vodka).

CUSTOMS AND ETIQUETTE

Business hours tend to be Monday to Friday 8am to 6pm and Saturday 9am to 2pm. Saturday hours are especially variable, as all shops in Poland distinguish between "working" (*pracująca*) Saturdays, when they work longer hours, and "free" (*wolna*) ones, when hours are shorter. Unfortunately, each store decides for itself which Saturdays are which, so there's no way of preparing a master shopping plan for any given weekend. Very few stores or businesses are open on Sunday. **Museum hours** are generally Tuesday to Sunday 10am to 4pm. Museums are ordinarily closed on the day after a holiday. In restaurants, a 10-15% **tip** is expected, and usually given when paying the bill. When arriving as a **guest,** bring your host (only if it's a she) an odd number of flowers. You'll then be offered more than you can possibly eat; wolf it all or face eternal damnation. When addressing a man, use the formal "*Pan*"; with a woman, use "*Pani.*" Most Poles eat meals at home; when they eat out, it's usually in the cafeteria-style *bary* and *bary mleczne*. It is not uncommon for **restaurants** to be mostly empty, especially in the evening. **Homosexuality** is legal and a frequent topic of media debate. Warsaw's **Lambda** offers info in English for both gays and lesbians.

NATIONAL HOLIDAYS

Poland celebrates: January 1, New Year's; January 6, Epiphany; March 6, Ash Wednesday; April 9-13, Holy Week and Catholic Easter; May 1, Labor Day; May 3, Constitution Day; May 21, Ascension Day; June 13, Corpus Christi; August 15, Assumption Day; November 1, All Saints' Day; November 11, Independence Day (1918); December 25-26, Christmas.

LIFE AND TIMES

HISTORY

The region around the Wisła River was first settled around 2000BC by Slavic tribes, which branched into several groups: East, West, and South. Between 800 and 960AD, some of the West Slavic tribes united to form small states. When Prince **Mieszko I,** of the Piast dynasty, converted to Catholicism in 966, he united the tribes in the region now known as Wielkopolska. Under Mieszko's son, **Bolesław Chrobry** (the Brave), Poland fought Bohemia, the German Empire, and Kievan Rus with success.

Though the **Mongols** succeeded in reaching the gates of Kraków and defeating a combined Polish-German army at Legnica in 1241, Poland escaped the Mongol yoke. The 14th century, particularly under **King Kazimierz Wielki** (the Great), was a time of prosperity and unprecedented religious and political tolerance; at this time Poland became a refuge for Jews expelled from Western Europe. Kazimierz rebuilt the country's defenses, made strategic peace pacts, and expanded Poland's territories. Scholars codified Polish law in 1347, and a university was founded at **Kraków,** the cultural center and capital of Poland, in 1364.

The Piast dynasty ruled Poland until 1368, when **Jagiełło,** grand duke of Lithuania, married Piast Crown Princess Jadwiga, establishing the Jagiellon dynasty and **uniting Poland and Lithuania.** But after the death of Kazimierz in 1370, Poland experienced increasing international difficulties, particularly with the **Teutonic Knights,** who turned on Poland, taking East Prussia and cutting off Polish access to the Baltic. Poland and Lithuania resoundingly defeated the Teutonic Knights at the **Battle of Grunwald** in 1410. This established the Polish-Lithuanian Union as one of the greatest powers in Europe, and opened up the Baltic to the newly unified region.

After the capital of Poland was moved to Warsaw, the Wazas got their wazoos whipped in bloody wars against Swedish invaders.

The Renaissance reached Poland under the rule of **King Zygmunt I Stary** (the Old). Under the reign of his son, **Zygmunt II August, Copernicus** created a new planetary theory, and the poet **Kochanowski** produced his unparalleled *Treny* (Laments) in

Kraków. In 1572, the nobles in the **Sejm** (Parliament) decided to establish an elected kingship, which gave them the power to survey royal policy, the right to approve taxes, declarations of war, and treaties, and the right to resist the king's decisions. Elections became a major event, and too often an excuse for the highest ranking members of the *szlachta* to indulge in political intrigue and feuds.

In the early 17th century, one of the elected kings, **Zygmunt III Waza,** of a Swedish line, moved the capital to Warsaw. Soon after, the Wazas got their wazoos whipped during the bloody wars against Swedish invaders. **Jan III Sobieski** crushed the Turks and lifted the siege of Vienna in 1683, which further exhausted Poland and left it vulnerable to Prussia and Russia. The three **Partitions of Poland,** in 1772, 1793, and 1795, divided the kingdom among Russia, Prussia, and Austria, wiping Poland off the map for the next 123 years. While the 19th century was for much of Europe an age of empire, expansion, improvement, and progress, for Poland it was an ordeal. Russia suppressed the development of modern institutions in the 1820s, and bloody rebellions in 1831 and 1863 were crushed.

Poland did not regain its **independence** until 1918, when, under American President Woodrow Wilson's principle of self-determination, the Allies returned Poznań and West Prussia, as well as access to the port of Gdańsk, to the newly independent

In 1978, Karol Wojtyla— a.k.a. John Paul II—became the first Polish Pope; his visit to Poland in 1979 helped birth Solidarity.

country. From the 1920s until 1935, Poland was governed by the autocratic **Marshal Józef Piłsudski,** with only formal preservation of parliamentary authority. Once Germany signed the Nazi-Soviet Non-Aggression Pact on August 23, 1939, Poland's defensive treaties with France and non-aggression pact with Germany were rendered worthless. The country fought courageously for a month against the raging Nazi war machine despite a simultaneous Soviet attack from the east. In 1939, Germany occupied the western two-thirds of the country, while the Soviet Union got the rest. With Hitler's invasion of the USSR in 1941, all of Poland fell under Nazi rule. Wartime Poland was the site of massive destruction and unspeakable atrocities. More than six million of its inhabitants died, including three million Polish Jews. Liberated by the Soviet Union, which obstructed the return of the Polish government and installed Communist proxies after the war, Poland spent 45 years bound to Russia in the Soviet Bloc. Strikes broke out in 1956, 1968, and 1970; all were promptly and violently quashed by the militia.

In 1978, **Karol Wojtyła** became the first Polish Pope, taking the name John Paul II. His visit to Poland during the following year helped to unite the still-devout Catholic Poles and was an impetus for the birth of **Solidarność** (Solidarity), the first independent workers' union in Eastern Europe, in 1980. Led by the charismatic **Lech Wałęsa,** an electrician at the Gdańsk shipyards, Solidarnosc was to be one of the most important factors in bringing down Communism. The union's actions resulted in the declaration of **martial law** in 1981 by **General Wojciech Jaruzelski,** then head of the Polish government, allegedly as a means of protecting the Polish nation from a Soviet invasion. Wałęsa was jailed and released only after Solidarity was officially disbanded and outlawed by the government in 1982. The organization continued its fight underground, however.

The first of the 1989 Eastern European shakedowns unfolded in Poland. Solidarity members swept into all but one of the contested seats in the June elections, and **Tadeusz Mazowiecki** was sworn in as Eastern Europe's first non-Communist premier in 40 years. In 1990, the government opted to swallow the bitter dose of capitalism in one gulp, eliminating subsidies, freezing wages, and devaluing the currency in order to attract foreign investment. This threw the already antiquated economy into recession and produced the first unemployment in 45 years. The availability of consumer goods didn't compensate for the rise in prices and unemployment, a fact which led to the victory of the left in the elections of 1993. Wałęsa's popularity slowly declined as he made his own difficult transition from trade union president to President. Steadily rising crime, a fractured and fragile coalition government, and painful reform process also didn't help. Despite some serious setbacks, however, Poland has continued to inch towards economic prosperity and political stability.

POLAND

LITERATURE

The oldest work written in Polish, the religious hymn *Bogurodzica,* dates back to the 14th century. The first author to write consistently in the language was the 16th century's **Mikołaj Rej.** His contemporary **Jan Kochanowski** challenged classical poetic rules in his *Treny* (*Laments*), a cycle of poems about the death of his young daughter.

Another convention-breaker was **Jan Chryzostom Pasek,** whose diaries, written in Baroque Poland's favorite literary style, recount the stormy life of his pet otter. An even greater passion sparked **King Jan III Sobieski's** unabashedly erotic letters written to his French wife, Marysieńka, who languished alone (as far as we can tell) during her hubby's unending military campaigns against the Turks. Diaries, letters, and all other forms of literary expression thrived during the 18th-century Enlightenment under King Stanisław II August Poniatowski's patronage. The tireless, politically involved scribes even managed to compose a constitution.

Ignacy Krasicki's *Historia na dwie księgi podzielona* (*History Divided into Two Parts*) introduced the novel to Poland in 1779, while international tensions and the partitions resulted in many political pamphlets and treatises. Poland's loss of statehood in 1795, followed by the failed 1831 uprising, ushered in Romanticism, which glorified the country, assigning it messianic significance. The works of the three *wieszcze* (national bards)—**Adam Mickiewicz, Juliusz Słowacki,** and **Zygmunt Krasiński**—depict Poland as a noble, suffering martyr and mother. Their poems are often set in the mystical scenery of Polish and Lithuanian folktales.

Like the Enlightenment, Romanticism also ended with a failed uprising in 1863. Disillusioned with the mood of the first half of the century, younger 19th-century authors ushered in **Positivism.** Characterized by naturalistic and historical novels, the new current advocated simple work and integration into one's community as the central goals of each individual. **Eliza Orzeszkowa** voiced such ideas in *Nad Niemnem* (On the Banks of the Niemen), a novel about a pauperized noble's interaction with peasants. A rather different novel, Nobel Prize winner **Henryk Sienkiewicz's** *Quo Vadis?*—a tale of early Christianity amid Roman decadence under Nero—pleads that a wholesome society rests on each person's individual morality.

The daily grind provided inspiration only until the turn of the century. The early 20th-century **Młoda Polska** (Young Poland) movement, which lacked the previous generation's brand of energy, was laden with pessimism and apathy. In his mystery-filled *Wesele* (The Wedding), playwright **Stanisław Wyspiański** built suspense with the promised appearance of a miracle-bearing spirit. In place of a Polish messiah, the end introduces straw men, symbols of weak national leaders. Pessimism, as exemplified by the Surrealist drama of **Witos,** prevailed even after independence in 1918. Unlike Wyspiański, who settled for worrying about Poland's problems, Witos feared for the future of all people. His indignation at the soullessness of mechanized society can be seen in his sex-crazed, psychopathic characters.

The outbreak of WWII proved the relevance of Witos's catastrophic vision. Wartime tragedies inspired numerous writers; outstanding among them is **Tadeusz Borowski,** whose short story *Proszę panstwa do gazu* (*Ladies and Gentlemen, This Way to the Gas*) depicts the horrors of Auschwitz in a brutally realistic light. Reverberations of the war can be heard throughout the works of the most recent generation of Polish poets, including Nobel Prize Winner **Czesław Miłosz, Zbigniew Herbert,** and **Tadeusz Różewicz,** all of whom

> In 1996, poet Wislawa Szymborska became the second Polish writer to win the Nobel Prize in recent years.

struggled to deal with postwar nihilism. At the same time, **Witold Gombrowicz** exaggerated the absurdity of the world in prose works such as *Trans-Atlantyk* (*Trans-Atlantic*) and *Kosmos* (*Cosmos*). In 1996, **Wisława Szymborska** became the second Polish writer to win the Nobel Prize in recent years. Her gently written verse on topics ranging from death to Atlantis deals poignantly and often humorously with the universal trials and joys of life.

POLAND TODAY

In Poland's tightly contested November 1995 election, Lech Wałęsa—former leader of the Solidarity movement and one of the most internationally recognized figures in Central European politics—was replaced by Aleksander Kwaśniewski. As the head of the ex-communist Democratic Left Alliance, Kwaśniewski, who modeled his campaign on U.S. President Bill Clinton's, was elected on a platform of further reform in Poland and strengthening relations with the west, including eventual Polish membership in NATO and the EU. Kwaśniewski's election came as a shock to Polish liberals, many of whom were mistrustful of the role the former Communist had played during the 70s and 80s. Westward-looking Poland has also developed Western-style problems; protests occurred during 1996 against the rise in crime, the first demonstrations since the new government took control. Anti-Semitism is another problem that has not improved since the fall of Communism. Still, Poland's invitation to join NATO in July 1997 indicated that at least as far as the Western powers are concerned, Kwaś niewski has kept his promises.

Warsaw (Warszawa)

Warsaw's motto, *contemnire procellas* (to defy the storms), has been put to the test often during the city's long history. According to legend, Warsaw was created when the lucky fisherman Wars netted a mermaid (Polish *syrena*, now the city's emblem) who begged him to release her, pledging to protect the new city that he and his wife Sawa would establish on the spot where the fantastic catch had been made. Warsaw has needed all the protection it can get; invaders from the north, east, and west have all taken a shot at this bastion of Polish pride. WWII saw two-thirds of the population killed and 83% of the city destroyed, but even that devastation was used as an opportunity to rebuild and revitalize. Once again the world's largest Polish city (a title long held by Chicago), Warsaw is quickly throwing off its Communist legacy to emerge as an important international business center. Tourists come to take in the museums, listen to the concerts, and feast in the restaurants of the city that rebuilt itself from rubble. The university infuses Warsaw with young blood, which keeps the energy high and the nightlife lively. The *syrena* appears to have kept her promise.

ORIENTATION AND PRACTICAL INFORMATION

Poland's principal air and rail hub, Warsaw sprawls in east-central Poland, 150km from the Belarusian border and bisected by the **Wisła River.** The busy downtown area, known as **Śródmieście,** is on the west riverbank. The main train station, **Warszawa Centralna,** is located near the center at the corner of **aleje Jerozolimskie** and **ul. Emilii Plater.** A short walk from here along Al. Jerozolimskie leads to the large intersection with **ul. Marszałkowska,** one of the city's two main north-south avenues. This busy intersection serves as a major stop for most bus and tram lines. Al. Jerozolimskie continues east to the other main north-south avenue, **Trakt Królewski,** which intersects Al. Jerozolimskie at **rondo Charles de Gaulle.** A left on Trakt Królewski runs north up **ul. Nowy Świat,** which becomes **ul. Krakowskie Przedmieście,** and leads directly to **Stare Miasto** (Old Town). A right at rondo Charles de Gaulle puts you on **Al. Ujazdowskie,** which, by way of embassy row, reaches the Łazienki Palace. When you purchase a **map** (try WCIT, see below), buy one that covers the whole city, including the public transportation lines.

Useful Organizations

Tourist Offices: Warszawskie Centrum Informacji Turystycznej (WCIT), pl. Zamkowy 1B (tel. 635 18 81; fax 831 04 64), at the entrance to Stare Miasto. Friendly, busy staff runs an info line and provides maps, guidebooks, hotel and restaurant listings, currency exchange, and hotel reservations. English-language publications on sale include the indispensable *Warsaw Insider* (4zł), jam-packed with useful information, listings, and hilariously written reviews. *The Warsaw Voice* (4zł) is much less useful, but occasionally contains interesting articles. Open Mon.-Fri. 9am-6pm, Sat. 10am-6pm, Sun. 11am-6pm. For info on cultural events, call tel. 629 84 89 (available Mon.-Fri. 10am-9pm, Sat.-Sun. 10am-6pm). **Orbis,** ul. Bracka 16 (tel. 827 45 16 or 827 76 03), entrance on Al. Jerozolimskie near ul. Nowy Świat. Train, ferry, and bus tickets. Open Mon.-Fri. 8am-7pm, Sat. 9am-2pm.

Budget Travel: Almatur, ul. Kopernika 23 (tel. 826 35 12 or 826 26 39; fax 826 35 07), off ul. Nowy Świat. Sells ISICs, international bus and ferry tickets, and plane tickets at student discounts. Often has vouchers for hotels in major Polish cities. Open Mon.-Fri. 9am-6pm, Sat. 10am-2pm. **Room 3,** ul. Krakowskie Przedmieście 24 (tel. 826 99 80; fax 826 47 57), is the train ticket department. Go through the main university entrance to the 1st building on the right. **Interrail** and **Eurotrain** tickets. Open Mon.-Fri. 10am-5:30pm. **PTTK,** Podwale 23 (tel. 635 27 25), in Stare Miasto. Info on budget hotels across Poland, and hitchhiker's guides (6zł). Open Mon.-Fri. 9am-3pm.

Embassies: Clustered around Al. Ujazdowskie. **Australia,** ul. Estońska 3/5 (tel. 617 60 81). Open Mon.-Thurs. 8:30am-1pm and 2-5pm. **Belarus,** ul. Ateńska 67 (tel. 617 39 54). **Canada,** ul. Matejki 1/5 (tel. 629 80 51). Open Mon.-Fri. 9am-1pm and 2-4pm. **Russia,** ul. Belwederska 49, bldg. C (tel. 621 34 53). Open Wed. and Fri. 8am-1pm. **Ukraine,** Al. Ujazdowskie 13 (tel. 629 32 01). **U.K.,** Al. Róż 1 (tel. 628 10 01). Open Mon.-Fri. 9am-noon and 2-4pm. **U.S.,** Al. Ujazdowskie 29/31 (tel. 628 30 41). Open Mon.-Fri. 8:30am-5pm.

Currency Exchange: At hotels, banks, tourist offices, and private *kantors* (which have the best rates) throughout the city. **24hr. exchange** at Warszawa Centralna (tel. 255 050), and the international airport departures area (tel. 469 624 or 469 694). For **traveler's checks** and **cash advances,** head to one of the branches of the **Bank PKO S.A. (Pekao):** pl. Bankowy 2 (tel. 637 10 61), in the blue skyscraper; ul. Mazowiecka 14 (tel. 661 25 59); or ul. Grójecka 1/3 (tel. 658 82 17), in Hotel Sobieski. AmEx and Visa traveler's checks cashed into dollars or złoty for 1% commission; MC, Visa cash advances. All branches open Mon.-Fri. 8am-6pm. Most **Bank PKO S.A.** branches have Cirrus/MC **ATMs. 24hr. ATMs** are located at ul. Mazowiecka 14 and Hotel Sobieski, ul. Grójecka 1/3. There is also a 24hr. AmEx ATM at American Express and at airport.

American Express: ul. Krakowskie Przedmieście 11 (tel. 635 20 02; fax 635 75 56). Holds cardholders' mail and provides members with emergency cash advances. Exchange cash and American Express traveler's checks commission free. For *Poste Restante,* address mail: <u>TROMLEY</u>, Gwen, Box #159, PL 00-950, Warszawa 1, c/o American Express. Open Mon.-Fri. 9am-6pm. Services are also available at the **Marriott Hotel** cash desk. Open Mon.-Fri. 8am-8pm, Sat.-Sun. 10am-6pm.

Western Union: ul. Krakowskie Przedmieście 55 (tel. 635 88 93), in Prosper Bank S.A. Open Mon.-Fri. 8am-6pm.

Internet Access: Cyberia Internet Cafe, ul. Krakowskie Przedmieście 4/6 (tel. 627 14 47; email cafe@cyberia.com.pl; http://www.cyberia.com.pl). Telnet and Netscape 9zł per hr. Open daily 9am-midnight.

Express Mail: DHL, Al. Jerozolimskie 11/19 (tel. 622 12 12; fax 627 23 13). Open Mon.-Fri. 8am-6pm, Sat. 8am-2pm. **Federal Express,** ul. Obornicka 19A, in Hotel Marriott (tel. 642 00 24). Open Mon.-Fri. 8am-6pm, Sat. 8am-2pm.

Post Office: ul. Świętokrzyska 31/33 (tel. 826 60 01). The computer at the entrance doles out tickets; take a number and wait your turn. For stamps and letters, push "D." For packages, push "F." For *Poste Restante*, push "C"; pick it up at window #12 or 13. Letters abroad cost 1.10zł (20g), plus 0.10zł per additional 10g (to Europe); 0.30zł per 10g (to North America); or 0.40zł per 10g (to Oceania). **Fax** bureau (fax 300 021). To the U.S. 15zł per page. Open 24hr. **Postal code:** 00-001.

Telephones: At the post office (see above). Tokens and **phone cards** available. Open 24hr. **Phone code:** 022. **Directory assistance:** 913.

Transportation

Flights: Port Lotniczy Warszawa-Okęcie, ul. Żwirki i Wigury (tel. 650 30 00), commonly referred to as Terminal 1. Take bus #175 to the center (after 11pm, bus #611). Buy bus tickets at the Ruch kiosk in the departure hall or at the *kantor* out-

POLAND

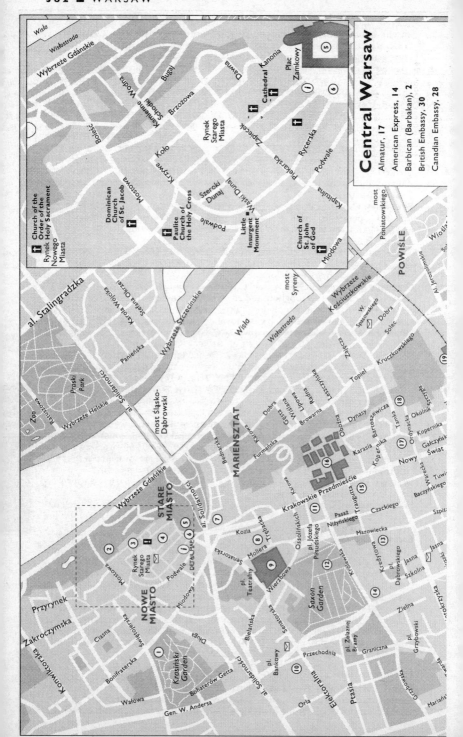

Central Warsaw

Almatur, 17
American Express, 14
Barbican (Barbakan), 2
British Embassy, 30
Canadian Embassy, 28

Caricature Museum, 8
Central Railway Station, 24
Chopin Monument, 33
Chopin Museum, 18
Church of the Holy Cross
(św. Krzyża), 15
Ethnographic Museum, 13
John Paul II Collection, 10
Łazienki Palace, 34
Krasiński Palace, 1
LOT Polish Airlines, 25
Medical Academy, 31
National Museum, 20
Orbis, 14
Orbis, 21
Palace of Culture and Science, 22
Parliament (Sejm), 29
Politechnical University, 32
Powiśle Railway Station, 19
Royal Castle, 5
St. Anne's Church, 7
St. John's Cathedral, 4
Statue of King Zygmunt III, 6
Śródmieście Railway Station, 23
The Grand Theater and Opera
House, 9
Tomb of the Unknown Soldier, 12
US Embassy, 27
Warsaw Historical Museum, 3
Warsaw Operetta, 26
Warsaw University, 16

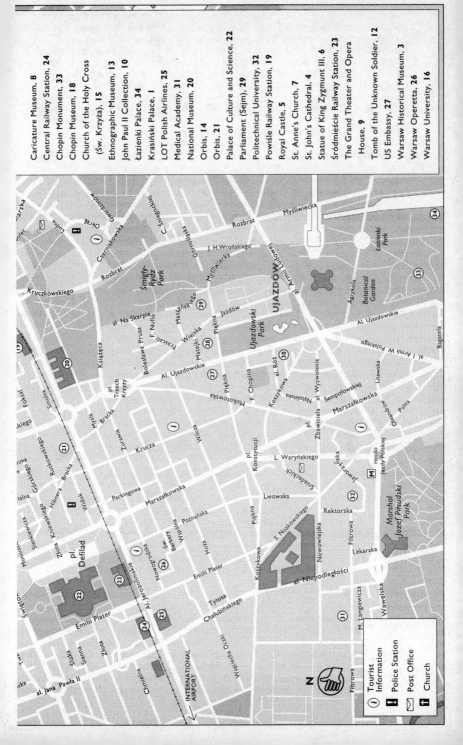

side (1.40zł plus 1.40zł for a large suitcase or backpack). **Airport-City Bus** (5.60zł, students 2zł; luggage free) is a faster way to the center and back (daily 5:30am-11pm; weekdays 3 per hr.; weekends 2 per hr.). Buy tickets from the driver.

Airline Offices: LOT, Al. Jerozolimskie 65/79 (tel. 952 or 953), in Hotel Marriott. **British Airways,** ul. Krucza 49 (tel. 628 94 31), off Al. Jerozolimskie. Open Mon.-Fri. 9am-5pm. **Delta,** ul. Królewska 11 (tel. 827 84 61). Each carrier has at least 1 flight per day to London, and LOT flies directly to New York (6 per week).

> **Warning:** Theft is rising on international overnight trains (to and from Berlin and Prague) as well as in train stations. Travelers should protect their safety and property, and should under no circumstances sleep on night trains.

Trains: Warszawa Centralna, Al. Jerozolimskie 54 (tel. 255 000). Lines can be quite long, and most employees speak only Polish, so write down where and when you want to go, and ask them to write down which *peron* number to head for ("*Który peron?*" means "Which platform?"). To: Berlin (6 per day, 7-8hr., 97zł); Budapest (2 per day, 10hr., 170zł); Kiev (2 per day, 22-24hr., 88zł); Minsk (5 per day, 12hr., 50zł); Moscow (4 per day, 27-30hr., 160zł); Prague (3 per day, 12-14hr., 94zł); and almost every corner of Poland, including Poznań, Gdańsk, and Kraków (several connections per day, all 3-4hr., 13-16zł). **Train information:** tel. 620 45 12 (international); tel. 620 03 61 (domestic).

Buses: PKS Warszawa Zachodnia, Al. Jerozolimskie 144 (tel. 236 494 or 236 495), shares a building, address, and bus stop with the Warszawa Zachodnia train station, and sends buses north and west of the city. Buses from **PKS Warszawa Stadion,** on the other side of the river, head to the east and south. Both stations are easily reached by taking the commuter train from the Warszawa Śródmiescie station (next to Warszawa Centralna; 1.60zł). Check with the International Bus Information window for ever-changing westbound schedules (open Mon.-Fri. 8am-4pm). The private company **Polski Express,** Al. Jana Pawła II (tel. 630 29 67), offers faster and more comfortable bus service from Warsaw to Gdańsk (2 per day, 6hr.), Kraków (3 per day, 6hr.), Lublin (6 per day, 4hr.), and Szczecin (1 per day, 9½hr.).

Public Transportation: Bus and **tram** lines are marked on some maps. Day trams and buses (including express lines) cost 1.40zł, night buses 3zł. Large baggage 1.40zł per piece. Buy tickets at just about any kiosk, or from the driver at night. Punch the ticket (on the end marked by the arrow and *tu kasować*) in the machines on board or face a 70zł fine, plus another 28zł for your unpaid-for pack. Bus #175 is the king of them all, going all the way from the airport to Stare Miasto by way of the central train station, the center of town, and ul. Nowy Świat. Warsaw's **Metro** is still in its early stages; its one line connects the southern border of town with the center. Tickes 1.40zł, available in Metro stations.

Taxis: Call 919 or 96 22. Avoid cabs in front of hotels and at the airport, the train station, and the ul. Marszałkowska-Al. Jerozolimskie rotary; you'll be overcharged. Fares usually start at 3.60zł plus 1.20zł per km; 1.60zł per km is the legal maximum. Rates are 50% more from 10pm to 6am, plus whatever the driver thinks he earned. Cabs with a mermaid on the side are state-run and usually a safer bet.

Car Rental: Avis, at the Marriott Hotel (tel./fax 630 73 16).

Hitchhiking: Hitchers pick up *Książeczka autostopu* (*The Hitchhiker's Book*), at the PTTK office (see above). Locals are hitchhiking less in Warsaw, though it is still quite common in the countryside.

Other Practical Information

Luggage Storage: At the main train station, below the main hall. Lockers come in 3 sizes: "A" (5zł per day), "B" (7zł per day), and "C" (12zł per day). Open 24hr.

English Bookstore: American Bookstore, ul. Krakowskie Przedmieście 45 (tel. 826 01 61). A fine selection of fiction, reference books, and periodicals. Open Mon.-Sat. 11am-7pm, Sun. 11am-4pm; in winter Mon.-Sat. 10am-6pm, Sun. 11am-4pm.

International Press: Empik, across from the Pałac Kultury on the ground floor of the Junior department store. Open Mon.-Sat. 9am-10pm, Sun. 11am-5pm. Also in the lobby of the Marriott Hotel.

Laundromat: ul. Karmelicka 17 (tel. 317 317). Take bus #180 north from ul. Marszałkowska toward Żoliborz, and get off at ul. Anielewicza. Bring your own detergent. Call ahead to make a reservation. Some English spoken. Wash and dry 13zł. Open Mon.-Fri. 9am-5pm, Sat. 9am-1pm.

24-Hour Pharmacy: Apteka Grabowski (tel. 256 984), at the central train station.

Crisis Lines: 24hr. AIDS hotline: tel. 628 03 36. Open Mon.-Fri. 10am-10pm. **Drugs:** tel. 96 33, 622 50 01, or 628 03 36. Open Mon.-Fri. 9am-5pm. **Women's:** tel. 635 47 91. Open Mon.-Fri. 4-8pm. **Mental Health:** tel. 295 813. **STDs:** 629 79 77.

Gay and Lesbian Hotline: tel. 628 52 22. The Lambda Center Information Line runs 2 weekly phone sessions: Wed. 6-9pm for women, Fri. 3-9pm for men. Both in English or Polish. They'll tell you what's up and where.

Medical Assistance: Medical Info Line, ul. Smolna 34/22 (tel. 827 89 62). Directs you to private doctors and dentists. Some English spoken. Open Mon.-Fri 8am-8pm, Sat. 8am-3pm. **24hr. service** and **ambulance,** ul. Hoża 56 (tel. 999 or 628 24 24). **24hr. dental service,** ul. Ludna 10 (tel. 635 01 02 or 625 01 05). **Marriott Hotel Medical Center,** Al. Jerozolimskie 6/7 (tel. 630 51 15).

ACCOMMODATIONS AND CAMPING

Prices rise and rooms become scarce in July and August. The hostels are the first to go, so call ahead. Differences in hotel prices often do not reflect a difference in quality; some hotels just aim for the business traveler and charge more. For help finding **private rooms,** check with **Syrena,** ul. Krucza 17 (tel. 628 75 40), off Al. Jerozolimskie; the staff speaks English (open Mon.-Sat. 9am-7pm, Sun. 9am-5pm; singles start at 45zł; doubles at 65zł). **WCIT** (see **Useful Organizations: Tourist Offices,** p. 380) maintains a list of all accommodations in the city and can help with reservations.

Hostels

Schronisko Młodzieżowe (HI), ul. Smolna 30, top floor (tel. 827 89 52), across from Muzeum Narodowe. A short walk from the train station, or take any tram headed east 3 stops to "Nowy Świat." The price and location can't be beat, but the staff is not the friendliest bunch of English-speakers in Poland. Rules are enforced to the letter, in both languages: 11pm curfew, and 10am-4pm lockout. Kitchen and baggage room, but only 2 showers. If you don't mind skipping nightlife, this popular hostel is a good option. 12zł; nonmembers 15zł; sheets 2.50zł. 3-day max. stay.

Schronisko Młodzieżowe (HI), ul. Karolkowa 53a (tel. 632 88 29). Take tram #22 or 24 west from Al. Jerozolimskie or the train station, and get off at "Okopowa." Turn left on Al. Solidarności, then right onto ul. Karolkowa. The hostel is hard to miss— it's the white building in the sea of gray blocks. Inside, it's well-maintained and not as mobbed as the main one. Doubles and triples include TV and fridge. Kitchen and storage facilities. Great showers. Curfew 11pm. Lockout 10am-5pm. Doubles 50zł; triples 72zł. 4- to 7-bed dorms 16zł, non-members 18zł. Sheets 3.50zł.

Schronisko Młodzieżowe, ul. Międzyparkowa 4/6 (tel. 311 766), close to the river between two parks. Take tram #2, 6, or 18 northbound from ul. Marszałkowska to "K.K.S. Polonia." The hostel is across the street as you continue down the road. Definitely the least formal of the hostels in town, located in a tiny building in an old sports complex. The rooms go with the exterior (a bit rugged), but they do the job. Curfew 11pm. Lockout 10am-5pm. Beds 14.50zł. Sheets 3zł. Open April 15-Oct. 15.

Hotels

Hotel Metalowiec, ul. Długa 29 (tel. 831 40 20; fax 635 31 38), 3 blocks away from Stare Miasto near the "Arsenał" stop. One of the most affordable hotels in the city, and a great location to boot. Spacious, comfortable rooms and clean communal bathrooms. Singles 30zł; doubles 55zł; quads 81zł. Add 10zł for private bath.

Hotel Belfer, Wybrzeże Kościuszkowskie 31/33 (tel. 625 05 71; fax 625 26 00). Same directions as for Hotel Aldona. Overlooks a park, river, highway, and electric plant. Singles 64zł, with bath 94zł; doubles 84zł, with bath 126zł.

Hotel Aldona, Wybrzeże Kościuszkowskie (tel. 628 58 53). From the train station, take any tram east to Most Poniatowskiego, then go north (with the river on your right) along Wisłostrada, which becomes Wybrzeże Kościuszkowskie. On a ship

POLAND

floating in the Wisła. A great budget option, unless the thought of sleeping on a boat makes the land-lubber in ya' queasy. 4 communal bathrooms. Singles 40zł; doubles (bunk beds) 50zł.

Hotel Garnizonowy, ul. Mazowiecka 10 (tel. 682 20 69). Hidden away a little more than a block from ul. Krakowskie Przedmieście off ul. Świętokrzyska, this is one of the most affordable hotels in the downtown area. Feels a bit like barracks, but the rooms are nice for the price. Singles 70zł; doubles 100zł; triples 120zł.

Camping

Camping Gromada, ul. Żwirki i Wigury 32 (tel. 254 391). Take bus #175 (dir. "Port Lotniczy") to "Akademia Medyczna." Cheerful signs point to a crowded campsite. 9zł per person, 4-8zł per tent space. Bungalows 16zł per person. Open April-Sept.

Camping "123," ul. Bitwy Warszawskiej 1920r. 15/17 (tel. 233 748), down the road from the rotary by the main bus station. Take bus #127 to "Zachodnia" and cross the street. Closer to downtown, shadier, and less cramped than Gromada, it's also near a popular swimming pool. 8.56zł per person. Small tent space 6zł, large 8zł. Open year-round.

FOOD

For quick and cheap eats, there are numerous **food stands** along ul. Marszałkowska. You can blow your budget on roast duck or grilled salmon at any of the restaurants bunched around **Rynek Starego Miasta,** but proletarian **cafeterias** are infinitely cheaper and more colorful. There is a **24-hour grocery** at the central train station, as well as **Delikatesy,** ul. Nowy Świat 53. Both are oases for late-night club crawlers and jet-lagged snackers. Many restaurants in Warsaw sell fish, poultry, and meat by weight. Ask in advance how much the average weight is to avoid a nasty surprise when the check arrives.

Bar Uniwersytecki, ul. Krakowskie Przedmieście 16/18, next to the university under a yellow awning. As Polish as it gets. Rice with apples 1.20zł. Soups 1.30zł. Pork chops 3.50zł. English menu. Open Mon.-Fri. 7am-8pm, Sat.-Sun. 9am-5pm.

Bar Pod Barbakanem, ul. Mostowa 27/29 (tel. 831 47 37), entrance on ul. Freta. A popular cafeteria-style eatery between Stare and Nowe Miasto. A full meal runs only 6zł. English menu. Open Mon.-Fri. 8am-6pm, Sat.-Sun. 9am-5pm.

Bar Familijny, ul. Nowy Świat 39. More traditional (fat) Polish (plentiful) food for the lighter-than-air wallet, in a great location. Open Mon.-Fri. 7am-8pm, Sat.-Sun. 9am-5pm.

Zapiecek, ul. Piwna 34/36 (tel. 831 56 93), at the corner of ul. Piwna and ul. Zapiecek in Stare Miasto. Candle-lit, German-style, but Polish cuisine rules the menu. Veal 10zł. Outdoor dining. Open daily 11am-11pm.

Restauracja Boruta, ul. Freta 38 (tel. 831 61 97), on Rynek Nowego Miasta. Dine outside or inside. Roasted duck 7zł. Vegetarian menu. Open daily 11am until the last guest leaves.

Pod Herbami, ul. Piwna 21/23 (tel. 831 64 47). Looks like a medieval tavern, tastes like a Polish restaurant. Main dishes hover around 10-15zł, while grilled salmon and other specialties run 20-30zł. Open Sun.-Thurs. 11am-11pm, Fri.-Sat. 11am-1am.

Pod Samsonem, ul. Freta 3/5 (tel. 831 17 88). Cheap eats on the way from Stare Miasto to Nowe, opposite Maria Skłodowska-Curie's museum. The Polish-Jewish cuisine is supposed to make you big and strong like Samson. You won't know unless you try it. *Cymes* salad 3zł. Open daily 10am-10pm.

Restauracja Ekologiczna "Nove Miasto," Rynek Nowego Miasta 13/15 (tel. 831 43 79). Warsaw's first natural food restaurant. Organically grown vegetarian main dishes 15-40zł. Whole grain desserts, healthy soups, a variety of crepes, and a whole theater of salads, including *Bacchus' Triumph, King Lear,* and *L'Après-midi d'un Faun.* Encores of Polish beer and German wine. Outdoor seating available. Live music nightly. Open daily 10am-midnight.

Restauracja-Kawiarnia "Chmielna" (tel. 827 14 84). At the corner of ul. Chmielna and ul. Zgoda. Real bargains include seasonal salad (2.70zł), penne with mushroom sauce (4zł), and pizza (3zł). Outdoor dining on a lively, pedestrianized street. Open Mon.-Sat. 11am-10pm.

Cafes

Kawiarnia Bazyliszek, Rynek Starego Miasta 3/9 (tel. 831 18 41 or 831 32 35). A relaxing outdoor cafe amid the restored splendor of Stare Miasto and all the tourists who are here to see it. Tortes 3.50zł. Coffee 2.50zł. Open daily noon-midnight.

Gwiazdeczka, ul. Piwna 40/42 (tel. 319 463), in Stare Miasto. The menu is full of innocent snacks and coffees (3-6zł), but beer and cocktails are ever-tempting alternatives (large *Żywiec* 4.50zł). Open daily 9am-10pm.

Cyberia Internet Cafe, ul. Krakowskie Przedmieście 4/6 (tel. 627 14 47; http://www.cyberia.com.pl). A little too Euro-chic for some tastes, but the coffee (5zł), which the helpful, multilingual staff might make you buy to go with your time on the 'Net (see **Internet Access,** p. 381), is quite good. Open daily 9am-midnight.

SIGHTS

Razed beyond recognition during WWII, Warsaw was rebuilt from the rubble by defiant survivors. Thanks to the wonders of Communist upkeep, most of the buildings look much older than their 50 years. The city requires time to explore, as sights are spread out, and some are quite distant from the center.

Stare Miasto (Old Town) and Nowe Miasto (New Town)

Warsaw's postwar reconstruction shows its finest face in the narrow, cobbled streets and colorful facades of **Stare Miasto** (Old Town), at the very end of ul. Krakowskie Przedmieście. At the right side of the entrance to Stare Miasto stands the impressive **Zamek Królewski** (Royal Castle). In the Middle Ages, it served as the residence of the Dukes of Mazovia, and in the late 16th century it replaced Kraków's Wawel as the official royal residence. Burned down in September 1939 and plundered by the Nazis, the castle became a symbolic martyr in the fight for Polish independence. Many Varsovians risked their lives hiding its priceless works in the hope that one day they could be returned. After Poland gained independence in 1945, the castle's plans and some of the treasures were retrieved, and for 30 years, thousands of Poles, Polish expats, and dignitaries worldwide sent contributions in hopes of restoring this symbol of national pride. Work began in 1971 and was completed a few years later. The kingly abode is an impressive example of restoration; visitors will marvel that anything like this was built in the '70s. **Kolumna Zygmunta III Wazy** stands proudly above the square in front of the castle. Constructed in 1644 in honor of the king who transferred the capital from Kraków to Warsaw, it stood here for 300 years before it was destroyed in WWII. The king's crusading figure, now rebuilt, has watched over plac Zamkowy for centuries; his vigil continues with a view of the rollerbladers below.

Leaving the column behind and turning left past the castle onto ul. Świętojańska leads to **Katedra św. Jana** (Cathedral of St. John), Warsaw's oldest church. Almost completely destroyed during the 1944 Warsaw Uprising, it was rebuilt after the war in Vistulan Gothic style. The 1339 case against the Order of Teutonic Knights, who had broken a pact made with Duke of Mazovia Konrad Mazowiecki, is hidden within the walls. The cathedral and its crypts are open to the public; the crypts shelter the graves of the dukes of Mazovia and of famous Poles such as Nobel Prize winner Henryk Sienkiewicz, author of *Quo Vadis,* and Gabriel Narutowicz, first president of independent Poland. One side altar contains the tomb of Cardinal Stefan Wyszyński (open to visitors daily dawn-dusk, except during services).

Ul. Świętojańska takes you straight to the pristinely restored Renaissance and Baroque houses of **Rynek Starego Miasta** (Old Town Square). A stone plaque at the entrance memorializes its reconstruction, which was finished in 1953-54, and recalls the square's prewar history. On the *rynek*'s southeast side at #3/9, **Dom "Pod Bazyliszkiem"** immortalizes the Stare Miasto basilisk (a legendary reptile with a fatal breath and glance), whose stare brought instant death to those unfortunate enough to cross his path. Although most houses around the *rynek* were razed during the Warsaw Uprising, a few managed to survive WWII, including the house at **#31,** which dates back to the 14th century. The *rynek* oozes with cafes, kitschy art, and tourists; for a mere 5-10zł, an ever-ready artist will enter your image into the annals of art history.

POLAND

In the northeast corner of the *rynek* starts ul. Krzywe Koło (Crooked Wheel), which leads to the **Barbakan**, a rare example of 16th-century Polish fortifications and a popular spot for locals and tourists to sit and rest their feet to the accompaniment of street performers. The **Little Insurgent Monument** honors the heroism of the youngest soldiers of the Warsaw Uprising. Around the *Barbakan* are the reconstructed remains of the walls that used to surround the entire Stare Miasto; they are decorated by a statue of the **Warszawska Syrenka** (Mermaid), the symbol of the city.

The Barbakan opens onto ul. Freta, the edge of Nowe Miasto. Despite its name, this is the city's second-oldest district. Also destroyed during WWII, its 18th- and 19th-century buildings have enjoyed an expensive facelift. The great physicist and chemist **Maria Skłodowska-Curie,** winner of two Nobel prizes, was born at ul. Freta 16 in 1867 (see **Museums,** p. 390). Ul. Freta leads to **Rynek Nowego Miasta,** the site of **Kościół Sakramentek** (Church of the Holy Sacrament), which was founded in 1688 to commemorate King Jan III Sobieski's 1683 victory over the Turks in Vienna. Its interior no longer reflects its past glory, but the Baroque dome is a noteworthy sight.

Trakt Królewski (Royal Route) and Park Łazienki

The 4km **Trakt Królewski,** Warsaw's most attractive thoroughfare, begins on **plac Zamkowy** and continues along **ul. Krakowskie Przedmieście.** The "Royal Way," so named because it leads south in the general direction of Kraków, Poland's former capital, is lined with palaces, churches, and convents built when the royal family moved to Warsaw. Traffic and crowds of tourists now detract from its once regal splendor. On the left as you leave plac Zamkowy, **Kościół św. Anny** (St. Anne's Church) dates from the 15th century (open daily dawn-dusk). Farther down the street, the **Adam Mickiewicz Monument** gazes toward plac Piłsudskiego and Ogród Saski (Saxon Garden), which contains the **Grób Nieznanego Żołnierza** (Tomb of the Unknown Soldier). Urns hold earth from the graves of Polish soldiers murdered by the Soviets in Katyń and from battlefields marked by Polish blood. A ceremonial **changing of the guard** takes place at noon on Sundays and national holidays.

Fryderyk Chopin spent his childhood in the neighborhood near ul. Krakowskie Przedmieście, and gave his first public concert in **Pałac Radziwiłłów** (a.k.a. **Pałac Namiestnikowski**), #46/48, the building guarded by four stone lions. The palace needs more active help these days in its new role as the Polish White House, and guards from the Polish military join the faithful felines out front. A block down the road, **Kościół Wizytek** (Church of the Visitation Nuns) once resounded with the romantic ivory pounding of the mop-topped composer. **Pałac Czapskich,** Chopin's last Warsaw home before he left for France in 1830, provided the setting for much of his composing. Now the palace houses the **Academy of Fine Arts** and **Salonik Chopinów** (the Chopins' Drawing Room; tel. 266 251; open Mon.-Fri. 10am-2pm; 1zł, students 0.50zł). Chopin died abroad at the age of 39 and was buried in Paris, but his heart belongs to Poland; it now rests in an urn in the left nave of **Kościół św. Krzyża** (Holy Cross Church). And you thought he left it in San Francisco.

In front of Kościól św. Krzyża, a complex of rebuilt palaces on the left belongs to **Uniwersytet Warszawski,** founded in 1816. **Pałac Kazimierzowski,** at the end of the alley leading from the main entrance to the university, now houses the rector's offices, but was once the seat of the School of Knighthood. Its alumni record includes General Tadeusz Kościuszko, who fought in the American Revolutionary War and later led an unsuccessful revolt against Russia. **Pomnik Mikołaja Kopernika (Copernicus Monument),** a permanent seat for the image of the famous astronomer, and **Pałac Staszica,** the seat of the Polish Academy of Sciences, mark the end of ul. Krakowskie Przedmieście. Trakt Królewski continues as **ul. Nowy Świat** (New World St.). The name of the street dates back to the mid-17th century, when a new settlement was started here, composed mainly of working-class people. It was not until the 18th century that the aristocracy started moving in, embellishing the area with ornate manors and residences. Today, there are wider and busier streets in the city, but none as enjoyable a place for a walk. Trakt Królewski terminates with the **Botanical Gardens** (open daily 9am-4pm; 3zł, students 1zł), on the left side of Al. Ujazdowskie, and with **Pałac Łazienkowski,** summer home of the last Polish king, Stanisław August Poniatowski.

With its swans and majestic peacocks, **Łazienki** (Baths; tel. 621 62 41, ext. 233 or 234) is an appropriate setting for the striking Neoclassical **Pałac Łazienkowski,** also called **Pałac na Wodzie** (Palace on Water). This, like most palaces in the park, is the progeny of benefactor King Stanisław August and his beloved architect Dominik Merlini. Galleries of 17th- and 18th-century art wait inside (open Tues.-Sun. 9:30am-4pm, barring rain; 3.50zł, students 2zł; guided tour in English 20zł). **Stara Pomarańczarnia** (Old Orangery; 1786-88) served not only as a greenhouse for orange trees, but also as a theater and servants' quarters (open Tues.-Sun. 9:30am-4pm; 2zł, students 1zł; guided tour in Polish 8zł, in English 20zł). **Teatr Stanisławowski** celebrated its grand opening on September 6, 1788. In 1791, Stanisław August donated the theater to Wojciech Bogusławski, an accomplished actor, director, playwright, "father of Polish theater," and all-around butt-kicker. Bogusławski accepted the gift and opened the theater to the general public. In the west wing of Stara Pomarańczarnia, the 140 sculptures of **Galeria Rzeźby Polskiej** (Gallery of Polish Sculpture) illustrate the evolution of Polish sculpture from the end of the 16th century through 1939.

It's not just the monuments and museums that attract tourists to Łazienki; the serene greenery makes it an oasis of peace in the busy capital. Leave Warsaw behind, stroll down the shadowed, pebbled park alleys, and relax to the sounds of Chopin, performed in free concerts at **Pomnik Chopina** every Sunday at noon and 4pm from spring to autumn (park open daily dawn-dusk).

Commercial District and Former Warsaw Ghetto

In the center of Warsaw's commercial district, southwest of Stare Miasto, the 70-story "Stalinist Gothic" **Pałac Kultury i Nauki** (Palace of Culture and Science; a.k.a "The Wedding Cake"), ul. Marszałkowska, is a fitting monument to the man—larger-than-life, omnipresent, and tacky. Locals claim the view from the top is the best in Warsaw. Why? It's the only place from which you can't see the building (panorama open daily 9am-6pm; 7.50zł). The palatial eyesore houses over 3000 offices, exhibition and conference facilities, three theaters, a swimming pool with a 10m diving tower, several cinemas, and two museums—**Museum Ewolucji** (Museum of Evolution; tel. 656 66 37) and **Muzeum Techniki** (Museum of Technology; tel. 656 67 47; both museums open Tues. and Thurs. 9am-5pm, Wed. and Fri.-Sat. 9am-4pm, Sun. 10am-5pm; 3zł, students 1.50zł). Below, **pl. Defilad** (Parade Sq.), Europe's largest square (yes, even bigger than Moscow's Red Square), swarms with freelance bazaar capitalists.

Still referred to as "the Ghetto," the modern **Muranów** neighborhood (the name literally means "walled") holds few vestiges of the nearly 400,000 Jews who lived here—comprising one-third of the city's total population—before being deported to death camps during WWII. The **Umschlagplatz,** at the corner of ul. Dzika and ul. Stawki (tram #35 from Marszałkowska,will take you there), was the railway platform where the Nazis gathered 300,000 Jews for transport to the death camps. A large monument, with writing in Polish, Hebrew, and Yiddish, now stands in its place. Early in the occupation of Warsaw, the Nazis decided to confine the Jews to the Ghetto, which they accomplished by building a high wall around the entire neighborhood. Though you won't find it on any map, a small section of the **original ghetto wall** still stands between two apartment buildings on ul. Sienna and ul. Złota, just west of Al. Jana Pawła II and near the Warszawa Centralna station. Enter the courtyard at ul. Sienna 55; the wall is on the left. As the plaque indicates, two missing bricks now compose part of the Holocaust Memorial Museum in Washington, D.C. The ghetto was liquidated in 1943 after its residents, with minimal arms and resources, revolted against their imprisoners. The large **Pomnik Bohaterów Ghetta** (Monument of the Ghetto Heroes) stands in a park on ul. Zamenhofa, a short walk south of the Umschlagplatz. In the western corner of Muranów, **Cmentarz Żydowski** (Jewish Cemetery) stretches for kilometers, a thickly wooded treasure of gravestone craftsmanship (open Mon.-Thurs. 9am-3pm, Fri. 9am-1pm). A living remnant of Warsaw's Jewish life, however, is the beautifully reconstructed **Nożyk Synagogue,** ul.

POLAND

Twarda 6, north of the Pałac Kultury. The complex of buildings surrounding the old synagogue also houses the **Jewish Information and Tourist Bureau** (tel./fax 620 05 56; open Sun.-Fri. daily 9:30am-4pm), which arranges a wide range of English-language tours of Jewish Warsaw, Auschwitz, Treblinka, and Majdanek (US$25-70).

Wilanów and Praga

After his coronation in 1677, King Jan III Sobieski bought the sleepy village of Milanowo, had its existing mansion rebuilt into a Baroque-style palace, and named the new residence Villa Nova (in Polish *Wilanów*). Over the years, a long line of Polish aristocrats made the palace their home. One of the bluebloods, Duke Stanisław Kostka Potocki, thought it might be nice to share it with his subjects—in 1805, he opened it to visitors, thus founding one of the first public museums in Poland. Since then, **Pałac Wilanowski** (tel. 428 101) has functioned both as a museum and as a residence for the highest ranking guests of the Polish state. To get here, take bus #180 or express bus B from ul. Marszałkowska to the end-stop, "Wilanów." (Palace open Wed.-Mon. 9:30am-2:30pm. 3zł, students 1zł. Guides in English 20zł.) The gardens' landscaping will wow even the most experienced topiarist (open Wed.-Mon. 9:30am-2:30pm; 1.50zł, students 0.70zł). **Muzeum Plakatu** (Poster Museum; tel./fax 422 606), next to the palace, displays 50,000 **posters** from the last 100 years (open Tues.-Sun. 10am-3:30pm; 4zł, students 1zł).

The **Praga** neighborhood, across the Wisła from Stare Miasto and connected to it by Most Śląsko-Dąbrowski, offers a Victorian contrast to the more contemporary architecture of the city center. The area along the Wisła north of Al. Solidarności is all green, beginning with the lush **Park Praski** and leading into the **Ogród Zoologiczny** (Warsaw Zoo). One of the more interesting sights is the **Katedra Kościoła Prawosławnego** (Russian Orthodox Church), Al. Solidarności, a five-domed structure with a Byzantine layout and a Renaissance facade. It's generally locked, except during services. The traditional interior is magnificent, including an elaborate iconostasis. From ul. Marszałkowska, take tram #4 to "Dw. Wileński," the second stop over the river. And in case Orthodoxy makes you bargain-hungry, a short walk due south (with the river on your right) will bring you to one of the universe's largest bazaars.

Museums

Muzeum Narodowe (National Museum), Al. Jerozolimskie 3 (tel. 621 10 31). Poland's largest museum. Founded in 1862 as a museum of fine arts, converted into a national museum in 1915. Impressive illustration of the evolution of Polish art. Also houses a Gallery of Medieval Art and a Gallery of European Art, which include Italian works from the 14th-18th centuries, German art from the 15th-16th centuries, and Dutch and Flemish paintings from the 17th century. Open May-Sept. Tues.-Wed. and Fri.-Sun. 10am-4pm, Thurs. 11am-6pm; Oct.-April Tues.-Wed. and Fri.-Sun. 10am-4pm, Thurs. 11am-6pm. 5zł, students 2.50zł. Thurs. free.

Muzeum Wojska Polskiego (Polish Military Museum), Al. Jerozolimskie 3 (tel. 827 47 13). Polish weaponry through the ages. Documents the nation's fight for independence during WWII. Open Wed.-Sun. 10am-4pm; 2zł, students 1zł, Fri. free. Guided tours in English 20zł. Library open Wed.-Fri. noon-3pm.

Muzeum Historyczne Miasta Warszawy (Warsaw Historical Museum), Rynek Starego Miasta 28 (tel. 635 16 25). Chronicles the evolution of style in architecture and clothing from the 13th century to the present. Open Tues. and Thurs. noon-7pm, Wed. and Fri. 10am-3:30pm, Sat.-Sun. 10:30am-5pm. 3zł, students 1.50zł, Sun. free.

Zamek Królewski (Royal Castle), pl. Zamkowy 4 (tel. 657 21 78). **Royal Suites** open to guided tours only; individual sightseeing possible in other parts. 8zł, students 3.50zł. Open Tues.-Sun. 10am-6pm. **Other interiors:** 3zł, students 1.50zł; Thurs. free. English tours of the castle 35zł. On Sun. you can get the whole castle without the tour 10zł, students 4zł. Purchase tickets and reserve guides at the *kasa*, ul. Świętojańska 2 (tel. 657 23 38), across from the castle. Open Tues.-Sun. 10am-4:30pm.

Muzeum Literatury im. Adama Mickiewicza, Rynek Starego Miasta 20 (tel. 831 40 61). Honoring Poland's national poet, the permanent exhibition focuses on Mickiewicz's life and work. The museum also features temporary exhibits and writer's studios of Julian Tuwim, Leopold Staff, and others. Open Mon., Tues., and Fri. 10am-3pm, Wed.-Thurs. 11am-6pm, Sun. 11am-5pm; 3zł, students 2zł.

Muzeum Marii Skłodowskiej-Curie, ul. Freta 16 (tel. 318 092), in the Skłodowskis' former house. Founded in 1967, on the 100th anniversary of Maria's birth, the exhibit chronicles Maria's life in Poland, emigration to France, and marriage to scientist Pierre Curie, with whom she discovered radium, polonium, and wedded bliss. Open Tues.-Sat. 10am-4:30pm, Sun. 10am-2:30pm; 2zł, students 1zł.

Muzeum Fryderyka Chopina in **Zamek Ostrogskich,** ul. Okólnik 1 (tel. 827 4 71, ext. 34 or 35). Portraits, manuscripts, letters, keepsakes, and a piano belonging to the great composer during the last 2 years of his life. Open Mon.-Wed., and Fri.-Sat. 10am-2pm, Thurs. noon-6pm; 3zł, students 2zł.

Muzeum Archeologiczne "ARSENAŁ," ul. Długa 52 (tel. 831 15 37; fax 831 51 95). Among the artifacts are 1500 Roman coins and the armor of Poland's first leaders—the Piast dynasty. Open Mon.-Fri. 9am-4pm, Sun. 10am-4pm. Closed the 3rd Sun. of each month. 1.50zł, students 0.80zł, Sun. free.

ENTERTAINMENT AND NIGHTLIFE

Don't be fooled by people who tell you Warsaw doesn't have much nightlife outside of the **kawiarnie** (cafes) of Stare Miasto and ul. Nowy Świat. While these are excellent places to sit back and relax with a cold glass of *piwo* or a chic cup of *kawa,* the late-night student scene can be incredible, especially on weekends. Don't miss out on the sunrise hike up Al. Niepodległości from one of the student clubs back to the city center. Even if you decide not to party until 4 or 5am, there are plentiful pubs and, in summer, outdoor beer gardens; many offer live music and good, inexpensive grilled food to go with your *EB* or *Żywiec.*

Performances

Classical concerts fill the Gallery of Sculptures in **Stara Pomarańczarnia** near Pałac Łazienkowski on Sundays in June and July. Inquire about concerts at **Warszawskie Towarzystwo Muzyczne** (Warsaw Music Society), ul. Morskie Oko 2 (tel. 496 856; tickets available Mon.-Fri. 9am-3pm and just before concerts). **Pomnik Chopina** (Chopin Monument), nearby in Park Łazienkowski, hosts free Sunday performances by classical artists (May-Oct. noon and 4pm). **Teatr Wielki,** plac Teatralny 1 (tel. 826 32 87), Warsaw's main opera and ballet hall, offers performances almost daily. **Filharmonia Narodowa,** ul. Jasna 5 (tel. 826 72 81), gives regular concerts but is closed in summer. Classical music is also played in Zamek Królewski's **Sala Koncertowa,** plac Zamkowy 4 (tel. 657 21 70; tickets sold Tues.-Sun. 10am-3pm).

Jazz, rock, and blues fans have quite a few options as well, especially in summer. Other than the jazz mecca **Akwarium** (see **Nightclubs,** below), the cafes and pubs of Stare Miasto occasionally fill the restored streets with the sound of music. In summer, **Pałac Pod Blachą,** an open-air beer garden, offers live music nightly until 11pm right next to plac Zamkowy (down the steps in the direction of the river). **Sala Kongresowa** (tel. 620 49 80), in the Pałac Kultury on the train station side, hosts serious jazz and rock concerts. Most popular artists who make their way to Poland end up here. Enter Sala Kongresowa from ul. Emilii Plater.

Pubs

Warsaw's pubs are popular with both trendy locals and visitors looking for a comfortable nook where they can relax and have a relatively overpriced drink (compared to elsewhere in Poland). The extra cost is often made up for by free concerts, however, making the atmosphere livelier and more enjoyable than the cheaper beer gardens.

The Irish Pub, ul. Miodowa 3 (tel. 262 533). The name, decor, and beer are Irish, but the clientele is local. The large Guinness on tap (1L, 23zł) comes in a mug resembling a bucket. Folk and country music nightly at 7:30pm. Open daily 9am-11pm.

Morgan's, ul. Okólnik 1 (entrance on ul. Tamka; tel. 826 81 38), under the Chopin Museum. Irish in the sense that you may find that you're the only one not speaking with an Irish accent (unless, of course, you are). Very comfortable and friendly. Excellent Guinness (0.4L, 10zł). Open daily 3pm until the last guest leaves.

Harenda Pub, ul. Krakowskie Przedmieście 4/6 (tel. 826 29 00), at Hotel Harenda. Decorated like a British social club, complete with leather-and-wood decor and plenty of pictures of the owners in bow ties doing chummy things like taking road trips and going on brewery tours. The friendly crowd usually stays until closing, but don't go for a Polish lesson. 0.5L Żywiec 6.50zł. Open daily 8am-3am.

Nightclubs

These clubs are aimed at a young and energetic crowd. They're very hit-and-miss, usually based on where people feel like meeting for the night. Posters around town have the latest info about special club and disco nights.

Park, Al. Niepodległości 196 (tel. 257 199 or 259 165). This international disco is one of the more popular student hangouts in Warsaw. The name is where to find it; just listen for the loud music through the trees. Tues. Polish rock, 8pm-2am; cover 6zł, students 3zł. Wed. classic rock, 8pm-2am; 6zł, students 3zł. Thurs. metal and punk, 8pm-2am; 6zł/3zł. Fri.-Sat. pop and rock, 9pm-3am; 12zł/6zł. Sun. reggae, 10pm-2am; 6zł/3zł.

Club Giovanni, ul. Krakowskie Przedmieście 24 (tel. 826 92 39), on the premises of Uniwersytet Warszawski, to the right and down the steps as you enter through the main gate. Or enter from the street by way of the narrow, unmarked stairway with the music at the bottom (the one right next to the main gates, which are often closed at night). As far from a disco as it gets. Rock music rules here, but if you want to hear something else, bring your own tapes. Seriously. Popular with a low-key student crowd. Plenty of beer on tap (5zł). A good, friendly, hangout bar at all hours, complete with foosball and comfy leather chairs. Thurs. night live music (and outdoor grill in the summer) only make this place better. Also a good spot for a cheap, more-than-decent meal. Vegetarian pizza 12zł, half-pizza 6zł, quarter-pizza 3zł. Open Mon.-Fri. 10am, Sat.-Sun. 1pm until the last person leaves.

Jazz Club Akwarium, ul. Emilii Plater 49 (tel. 620 50 72). Across from Pałac Kultury. The top spot in the city for live jazz. Drinks and food served. Concerts daily. Various artists—call or stop by for their program; it's posted on the door. The crowd is much older, but the love of be-bopping-good music knows no age limit. Open daily 11am until at least 11pm, depending on the show, Fri.-Sat. until 3am.

Stara Dziekanka, ul. Krakowskie Przedmieście 56. This entirely outdoor club has a permanent awning that protects revelers from the elements. A great place to meet both locals and foreigners and dance in the cool summer night. Grilled food, Żywiec (3zł), and lots of music blend together in a big open-air stir-fry. Picnic tables and stone terraces contrast with the pounding techno and dance mixes, but somehow it works. Open daily 7pm-2am. Cover Sun.-Thurs. 5zł, Fri.-Sat. 10zł.

GAY WARSAW

Unless a tourist has come to Warsaw for a black eye, he or she does not advertise homosexuality. Warsaw is largely a community of conservative businesspeople, and gay clubs are few and ephemeral, but at least they're there. For the latest info, call the gay and lesbian **hotline** (tel. 628 52 22; open Wed. 6-9pm for women, Fri. 3-9pm for men). They'll tell you the best spot to hit and when. Kiosks sell *Inaczej* and *Filo*—magazines that list gay entertainment providers throughout the country.

Między Nami, ul. Bracka 20. A left off Al. Jerozolimskie when coming from the Pałac Kultury. The 2nd restaurant with an outside seating area, on the right. Mixed during the day, mostly gay in the evening. Inside, the decor revives the Communist love of steel structures in a classy way. Salads 6-7zł, 0.3L juice 4zł. Open Mon.-Thurs. 10am-10pm, Fri.-Sat. 10am-midnight, Sun. 4-10pm.

Koźla, ul. Koźla 10/12. One block left from Rynek Nowego Miasta, when facing away from Stare Miasto. No sign outside, but it's the only club on Koźla. Ring the buzzer to be let in. A narrow staircase leads down to a small space that manages to combine the qualities of a beerhouse, a lounge, and a cruise bar. It's been operating since May 8, 1994; if you visit the pub on its birthday, you'll hit a party worthy of Victory Day. Open daily 5pm-2am.

POLAND

Paradise, at the corner of ul. Wawelska and ul. Żwirki i Wigury, in the grounds of the "Skra" sports complex. Disco on Sat. nights. A large, bright dance floor, mellow-out area, and a patio if you need a breather. Men and women. Beer 4zł. Cover 15zł.

■ Near Warsaw: Żelazowa Wola

The birthplace of Fryderyk Chopin, Żelazowa Wola is a must-see on any Chopin fan's itinerary. The cottage is surrounded by a small, maze-like park, and weekly concerts draw music lovers. At one time, the town was the site of a large manor that belonged to the Skarbek family. The composer's father, a Frenchman named Nicolas Chopin, worked as a French tutor in the house of Count Skarbek. There, he met and married Justyna Krzyżanowska, a distant cousin of the count. They had four children—three daughters and Fryderyk, who was born February 22, 1810. The Chopin family did not remain at Żelazowa Wola for very long; they moved to Warsaw in October 1810. The **cottage** (tel. (0494) 223 00) provides an interesting look at early 19th-century life. Although the family's original furniture is lacking, the interior is maintained in the style of the era. Among the mementos on display are the composer's birth certificate and the first *polonaise* he wrote (at the tender age of seven). Every Sunday, and on Saturdays in July and August, music fans gather here to listen to **concerts**—probably the best reason to make the trip. Noteworthy Polish musicians perform Chopin's works for crowds relaxing in the park. The schedule of selected music and performing musicians, posted throughout Warsaw, is always available at the Chopin museum (see **Warsaw: Museums,** p. 391); both change weekly. (Cottage open May-Sept. Tues.-Sun. 9:30am-5:30pm; Oct.-April 9:30am-4pm; 5zł, students 2.50zł. English labels. Concerts held 11am and 3pm.) Concerts are free if you're content to listen from the park benches just outside the music parlor (park admission 1zł, children 0.50zł; recorded tour in English, French, Russian, and other languages 10zł). Seats in the parlor itself cost 20zł.

Three **buses** a day pass through Żelazowa Wola, 53km west of Warsaw, but none of the signs in Warsaw mention it. Rest assured, it is indeed a regular stop on the route to **Kamion,** although it may be a good idea to tell the bus driver that you want to stop at Żelazowa Wola. Buses to and from Kamion are limited, and only the 9:45am bus actually puts you in Żelazowa Wola in time (11:10am) to take it all in (the other 2 arrive after the museum has closed, and there are no direct buses back after 4:30pm). Or, take a **commuter train** from **Warszawa Śródmieście** to the small town of Sochaczew (at least 20 per day, 5.20zł). Sochaczew city **bus** #6 runs to "Żelazowa Wola" at least hourly. Each way, the entire trip costs 6-7zł and takes 1½-2½ hours, depending on transfers. The trip back to Warsaw can be done on the 12:40 or 4:30pm bus directly from Żelazowa Wola, or back through Sochaczew via #6.

MAŁOPOLSKA (LESSER POLAND)

The Małopolska uplands lie in Poland's southeast corner. This ancient province stretches from the Częstochowa-Kraków highlands in the west, strewn thick with medieval castle ruins, to Lublin in the east. After the transfer of the country's capital to Kraków in 1320, the area gained sociopolitical prominence and experienced an economic boom as 14th-century Rothschilds bet their gold on the city's fast development. Kraków, which suffered only minimal damage during WWII, remains Poland's heart and cultural focal point, drawing foreigners and Polish visitors alike; but the smaller towns to the east provide a more tranquil perspective on Polish life.

■ Kraków

Once tucked away behind the walls of Communism, Kraków (KRAH-koof), recently chosen as a cultural capital of Europe, is now a trendy, international city. The Stare Miasto is full of architectural gems, and its ancient cellars are packed with cafes and galleries of all kinds. Although the city suffered little damage during World War II, the specter of destruction is never far removed: the notorious Nowa Huta steelworks in Kraków's eastern suburb are a grim reminder of the Stalinist era, and the Auschwitz-Birkenau death camp lies only 70km to the west. Yet it is perhaps precisely this combination of vitality and darkness that gives Kraków—also home of the country's oldest and best university—its uniquely dynamic atmosphere.

ORIENTATION AND PRACTICAL INFORMATION

The city fans outwards in roughly concentric circles from the huge **Rynek Główny** (Main Market Square), located at the heart of the **Stare Miasto** (Old Town). The green belt of the **Planty** gardens rings the *Stare Miasto,* and the **Wisła** river, snaking through the center, skims the southwest corner of **Wzgórze Wawelskie** (Wawel Hill). The **bus** and **train stations** sit adjacent to each other about 10 minutes northeast of the *rynek.* To reach the center from the stations, head toward Hotel Europejski; take the underpass diagonally across the street to the Planty. Follow **ul. Szpitalna** to the church, then turn right to reach the *rynek.*

Tourist Offices: Dexter, Rynek Główny 1/3 (tel. 217 706 or 213 051; fax 213 036). Pleasant English-speaking staff organizes tours and offers free pamphlets about sights and cultural events. Open Mon.-Fri. 9am-6pm, Sat. 9am-1pm. **Orbis,** Rynek Główny 41 (tel. 224 035). Sells international bus, plane, ferry, and train tickets, including *Wasteels.* Also arranges visits to the Wieliczka salt mines and Auschwitz. English spoken. Open April 1-Oct. 31 Mon.-Fri. 8am-7pm, Sat. 8am-3pm, off-season Mon.-Fri. 9am-6pm.

U.S. Consulate: ul. Stolarska 9 (tel. 221 400). Open Mon.-Fri. 8:30am-5pm.

Currency Exchange: At *kantors,* Orbis offices, and hotels. Rates vary widely. *Kantors,* except those around the train station, usually have the best rates. **Bank PKO S.A.,** Rynek Główny 31 (tel. 226 022; fax 220 083), accepts traveler's checks for a 1.5% commission, gives MasterCard, Visa, and EuroCard cash advances, and has an **ATM.** Open Mon.-Fri. 7:30am-7pm, Sat. 7:30am-1:45pm. To get a better rate, change your traveler's checks into dollars here and then take the cash to a *kantor.* Most *kantors* are open only during business hours, but the **Forum Hotel,** ul. M. Konopnickiej 28 (tel. 669 500) has a 24hr. currency exchange.

American Express: Rynek Główny 41, 31-013 Kraków (tel. 229 180), in the Orbis office and with the same hours (see Tourist Offices, above). Cashes all traveler's checks with no commission, replaces lost checks, holds mail, accepts wired money, and sells traveler's checks. Another branch is located in the Orbis office in the Hotel Cracovia, al. Focha 1, 30-111 Kraków (tel. 219 880; fax 224 981). From the *rynek,* head west on Piłsudskiego and follow it just past the intersection with al. Krasińskiego (about 15min.)—you can't miss the hotel. Open May 1-Oct. 15 Mon.-Fri. 8am-8pm, Sat.-Sun. 8am-4pm; off-season Mon.-Fri. 8am-4pm.

Flights: The newly renovated **Balice airport** (tel. 116 700 for all airlines and info) now provides international flights on major European airlines (Swissair, British Airways, Austrian Airlines, and, of course, LOT). The airport lies 15km west of the center and can be reached from the main train station by bus #208 northbound (40 min.) or express bus D (30min.). Currency exchange booths and car rentals wait for the arrival of the last international flight before closing. Airport usually open 4am-midnight. **LOT** (tel. 952 or 953), ul. Basztowa 15. Open Mon.-Fri. 8am-6pm, Sat. 8am-2pm. **INT Express Travel Agency,** ul. św. Marka 25 (tel./fax 217 906), is registered with most major airlines. Open Mon.-Sat. 8am-8pm.

Trains: Kraków Główny, pl. Kolejowy (tel. 224 182, info 933). To: Berlin (1 per day, 8hr., 106.30zł); Bratislava (1 per day, 7hr., 86zł); Brno (2 per day, 6hr., 77zł); Budapest (1 per day, 11hr., couchette 147zł); Gdańsk (3 per day; 11hr., 32zł; 4 express per day, 10hr., 45zł); Kiev (1 per day, 22hr., 52zł); Lviv (1 per day, 10½hr., 65zł); Prague (1 per day, 8½hr., 120zł); Vienna (1 per day, 9hr., 141zł); Warsaw (9 per day, 4¾hr., 20zł; 14 express per day, 2½hr., 35zł); and Wrocław (14 per day, 4½hr., 21zł). Tickets are sold at train stations and travel offices (see above). Some trains to southeast Polish cities leave from **Kraków Płaszów,** south of the city center. Take tram #3 or 13 away from the *rynek* from the stop on ul. Starowiślna.

Buses: ul. Worcella (info tel. 936), directly across from Kraków Główny. International tickets are sold by **Sindbad** in the main hall (tel. 221 238; open Mon.-Fri. 9am-5pm). To: Budapest (1 per day, 11hr., 45zł); Lviv (1 per day, 10hr., 38zł); Prague (1 per day, 11hr., 190zł); Warsaw (3 per day, 6hr., 28zł).

Luggage Storage: At the train station: 1% of luggage value (average around 6zł) plus 1.50zł per day. Open 24hr. At **PTTK Dom Turysty** (see **Accommodations,** p. 395): 1.50zł per piece per day. Open daily 7am-10pm.

Public Transportation: Buy tickets at kiosks near **bus** and **tram** stops (1zł) and punch them on board. If you're carrying a large backpack, it needs its own punched ticket. It's a good idea to buy a few at a time, as many kiosks close before trams and buses stop running. Tickets can also be bought on board for a slight surcharge. Express buses A, B, and C cost 1.30zł; night buses 2zł. Day passes cost 5zł; weekly passes 12zł. Beware of violating the system—if you're caught, you'll be yelled at and will have to pay a 36zł fine. Multilingual pamphlets about tram and bus transportation are available in kiosks on the far right of the train station.

Taxis: tel. 666 666, 919, 96 33, or 222 222.

Bookstores: Odeon, Rynek Główny 5. English, French, Russian, and Spanish literature. Open daily May-Oct. 9am-midnight, off-season 9am-9pm.

Laundromat: ul. Piastowska 47, on the 2nd floor of Hotel Piast. 2hr. drop-off available. Wash 4zł per load; dry 4zł per load. Open daily 10am-7pm.

Pharmacies: Similarly ubiquitous. After hours, all post lists of open pharmacies.

Medical Assistance: Private doctors at **Profimed,** Rynek Główny 6 (tel. 217. 997), and ul. Grodzka 26 (tel. 226 453). Open Mon.-Fri. 8am-8pm, Sat. 9am-1pm.

Police: tel. 997.

Internet Access: Available at club U Louisa (see **Entertainment,** p. 400). Internet service 3zł per hour, Netscape 5zł per hour. Initial fee of 25zł to set up your own account (not required). Open daily 11am-11pm.

Express Mail: DHL, ul. Balicka 79 (tel. 237 775). **Express Mail Service** available in the main post office (tel. 226 696; open Mon.-Fri. 7:30am-9pm, Sat. 8am-2pm, working Sat. 8am-3pm) and in the branch at ul. Lubicz 4 (tel. 224 026; open Mon.-Fri. 7am-8pm).

Post Office: Main office ul. Westerplatte 20 (tel. 225 163, 228 648, or 222 497; fax 223 606). Open Mon.-Fri. 7:30am-8:30pm, Sat. 9am-2pm, working Sat. 9am-4pm, Sun. 9-11am. **Postal code:** 31-045.

Telephones: At the main post office (open 24hr.), and the office opposite the train station, ul. Lubicz 4 (tel. 221 485 or 228 635). **Phone code:** 012.

ACCOMMODATIONS AND CAMPING

Reservations are prudent at all times of the year, but necessary in summer. Friendly neighborhood room-retriever **Waweltur,** ul. Pawia 8 (tel./fax 221 921), arranges private accommodations (open Mon.-Fri. 8am-8pm, Sat. 8am-2pm; singles 43zł, doubles 75zł). Locals also rent **private rooms;** watch for signs or solicitors in the train station.

Jan-Pol PTTK Dom Turysty, ul. Westerplatte 15 (tel. 229 566; fax 212 726), near the main post office and not far from the train station. Big, brown, and right on the park. The place to meet young travelers (and rowdy school children during the academic year). Only 1 key per room, so the suites usually remain open. Make use of the hotel vault, or cuddle up with your money belt in the low-slung beds. A 5min. walk from the *rynek.* Reception open 24hr.; check-out 10am. Be careful: you may only be allowed to pay for 1 day at a time, and could get turfed out if a tour group comes along. Clean 8-bed dorms around 23zł per person, more in summer.

Schronisko Młodzieżowe (HI), ul. Kościuszki 88 (tel. 221 951), inside the gates of a convent. Take tram #2 (direction "Salwator") from ul. Westerplatte, across from the train station, to the last stop (15min.). Last tram leaves around 10:30pm. Or walk: from the Planty, head down ul. Zwierzyniecka until it turns into ul. Kościuszki—the convent will appear in about 20min. Run by nuns in a heavenly setting on the bank of the Wisła. Schoolgroups in early summer and early fall detract a bit from the hostel's overall serenity. Reception open daily 8am-2pm and 5-11pm. Lockout 10am-5pm. Strict curfew 11pm. 8- to 36-bed rooms. 9zł per person, with HI 7.50zł. Sheets 2.50zł.

Schronisko Młodzieżowe (HI), ul. Oleandry 4 (tel. 338 822). Take bus #119 headed north from the train station, and get off once the main drag turns into ul. Mickiewicza. Oleandry parallels Mickiewicza, so turn right onto R. Ingardena and then left onto Oleandry. It's not far from Hotel Cracovia (see American Express, p. 394) and lies behind Biblioteka Jagiellońska, about a 10-15min. walk from the center. Cheap but dingy. Flexible lockout 10am-5pm. Curfew 11pm. 394 beds. Clean doubles 16zł. 4- to 5-bed dorms 15zł; 6- to 8-bed dorms 14zł; 8- to 16-bed dorms 13zł (only one key per room).

Hotel Wycieczkowy, ul. Poselska 22 (tel. 226 765; fax 220 439), 3 blocks south of the *rynek* off ul. Grodzka. Small, quiet rooms connected by roller coaster hallways. Singles 100zł; doubles 90zł; doubles with bath 140zł; quads 160zł.

Hotel Piast, ul. Piastowska 47 (tel. 374 933 or 372 176). Take tram #4 or 12 west from the train station to "Piastowska." This dorm is the main haunt of foreign students who come from all over the globe to study Polish at Uniwersytet Jagielloński. The only place in Kraków with coin-operated washing machines. Singles 32.10zł first night, additional nights 29zł (only available July-August). Doubles 42.80zł, additional nights 38.60zł; doubles with bath 60zł, additional nights 55.60zł; triples with bath 60.90zł, additional nights 54.60zł.

Camping Krak, ul. Radzikowskiego 99 (tel. 372 122 or 372 957; fax 372 532). Take tram #4, 8, 12, or 40 to "Fizyków" and walk north. Caravans 13zł, cars 9.50zł, tents 9zł. Open May 15-Sept. 30.

FOOD

There are several late-night grocery stores scattered on the outskirts of the *Stare Miasto*, including **Społem,** pl. Kolejowy, across from the train station (open 24hr.). *Obwarzanki* (soft pretzels with poppy seeds), a street-stand specialty, sell for a mere 0.50zł. Most of the eateries listed below lie within a few blocks of Rynek Główny.

Restaurants

Chimera, ul. św. Anny 3, in the cellar and garden (tel. 232 178). The oldest and most famous salad restaurant in town. Especially popular with students. A large plate of up to 6 of their 20 creative and delicious salads costs 7zł, a small one with up to 4 salads runs 5zł; small is large and large is huge. Free live music every evening (outdoor folk music in summer, indoor piano music in winter). Open daily, in summer 9am-when the last person leaves (usually before midnight); in winter 9am-10pm.

Jadłodajnia u Stasi, ul. Mikołajska 16. A one-person operation named after the owner's mom, Pani Stasia. Definitely low-budget. Famous for its traditional Polish food, such as *pierogi z serem* (cheese dumplings; 2.70-3.20zł) and *pierogi z truskawkami* (strawberry dumplings; 1.70-3.70zł). Open Mon.-Fri. 12:45pm until the food runs out—usually between 4 and 5pm. Come by early afternoon for the best selection, but be prepared to wait in line.

Bar Mleczny Barcelona, ul. Piłsudskiego 1, across from the Planty on the west side of the *Stare Miasto*. A bastion of proletarian dining—a full meal for under 3zł. *Riż z jabłkami* (rice with apples) 0.91zł. *Pierogi z serem* (cheese dumplings) 1.64zł. Food may be a little on the greasy side—welcome to Poland. Open daily 8am-6pm.

Cechowa, ul. Jagiellońska 11 (tel. 210 936), 1 block west of the *rynek*. Crowded tables and chairs give the box-shaped room a more homey feel. Try their specialty, *śledź po krakowsku* (Cracovian herring), 3.80zł. Other traditional Polish dishes run 3.50-17zł. Open daily 11am-10pm.

Balaton, ul. Grodzka 37 (tel. 220 469). Its divine Hungarian cuisine always attracts crowds. Main dishes 6-11zł. Menu in Hungarian and Polish; if that leaves you lost, the waitress will recommend the delicious *placki ziemniaczane po węgiersku* (potato pancakes with meat stew; 12zł). Open daily 9am-10pm.

Restauracja Ariel, ul. Szeroka 17 (tel. 213 870), in the old Jewish district of Kazimierz, a 15min. walk south of the *rynek*. Outdoor cafe-style seating and elegant interior with antique-looking furniture. Concerts featuring Jewish, Russian, and gypsy music nightly at 8pm, 15zł. *Lots* of tour groups. Food a creative but inauthentic mix of Polish and Jewish cooking. Gefilte fish 9.90zł. Open daily 10am-midnight.

Cafes

Cafe and Gallery Krzysztofory, ul. Szczepańska 2 (tel. 229 360), in the dim, smoke-filled cellar of the Dom Krzysztofory. A favorite among students and artists. The gallery has new exhibits every 2-3 weeks, and is open Tues.-Sun. 11am-5pm. The cafe also hosts avant-garde theater performances. 3.30zł for 0.5L of *Żywiec* beer. Open daily 11am-midnight; if the door is closed, push on in.

Camelot, ul. św. Tomasza 17 (tel. 210 123). Handcrafted wooden dolls and original paintings by prominent Polish artists decorate the interior. Check out the odd little table sitting on the window sill. Big green salad 10.80zł. *Müsli z jogurtem* (muesli with yogurt) 7zł. Cabaret held in the cellar. Open Mon.-Thurs. 9am-11pm, Fri.-Sun. 9am-12am. Several other cheaper cafes line the rest of św. Tomasza.

Kawiarnia Jama Michalika, ul. Floriańska 45 (tel. 221 561). More than a century old, this is one of Kraków's most famous—and surely best decorated—cafes. Sip espresso (3.10zł), nibble on pastries, and attack elaborate ice cream specialties in this former haunt of the Polish intelligentsia. No smoking. Cabaret in the evenings.

SIGHTS

Unlike Warsaw, Kraków was fortunate enough to be spared destruction in World War II, but the fumes emitted by the postwar Nowa Huta steelworks, located in the city's eastern suburbs, have eroded Kraków's monuments over the last four decades. Designated a UNESCO World Heritage Site in 1978, the city has gradually been able to scrape off the grime, revealing its beauty and character.

Stare Miasto (Old Town)

At the center of the Stare Miasto spreads **Rynek Główny,** one of the largest and most distinctive market squares in Europe. At its northeast corner rises the asymmetrical **Kościół Mariacki** (St. Mary's Church). The church's two towers were built by two brothers with different working styles: one hurried, and the other took his time. The hasty brother realized that the work of his careful sibling would put his own to shame, and committed fratricide in a fit of jealousy. The murder weapon is on display in the Sukiennice (see below), although other legends remember the knife as an instrument once used to cut off the ears of thieves. The richly decorated interior of the cathedral holds a 500-year-old wood altarpiece carved by Wit Stwosz, which was dismantled by the Nazis and rediscovered by Allied forces at the war's end. Now reassembled, it is ceremoniously unveiled at noon each day (cathedral open daily noon-6pm; altar admission 1.50zł, students 1zł). A *hejnał* (trumpet call) blares from the towers every hour, on the hour—its abrupt ending recalls the destruction of Kraków in 1241, when the invading Tartars are said to have shot down the trumpeter in the middle of his song. Polish radio broadcasts the noon call nationwide.

Smack in the middle of the *rynek,* the yellow Italianate **Sukiennice** (Cloth Hall) is as mercantile now as it was when cloth merchants actually used it: the ground floor is lined with stalls selling souvenirs. Upstairs, the **Muzeum Narodowe** (National Museum; tel. 221 166) houses a gallery of 18th- and 19th-century Polish classics (open Tues.-Wed., Fri.-Sun. 10am-3:30pm, Thurs. 10am-6pm.; 3zł, students 1.50zł). During the academic year, students cruise the area and wait for inspiration—or just for their friends—under the **statue of Adam Mickiewicz,** Poland's most celebrated Romantic poet. Across the square stands the lonely **Wieża Ratuszowa** (Town Hall Tower; open Mon.-Fri. 10am-4:30pm, Sat.-Sun. 10am-3:30pm; 1.50-3zł).

Running northeast from Kosciół Mariacki's corner of the *rynek,* **ul. Floriańska** leads to the **Barbakan,** the only remnant of the city's medieval fortifications. Ul. Floriańska was once part of the Royal Tract—the road leading to the castle—and many houses date from the 14th century. At the north end of the street, **Brama Floriańska,** the old gate to the city, is the centerpiece of the only remaining part of the city wall. A local lover of historical monuments convinced someone that the wall would block the disease-carrying north wind, thus rescuing the gate from the 19th-century destruction of most of the wall. A left onto ul. Pijarska from ul. Floriańska takes you to the **Muzeum Czartoryskich,** ul. św. Jana 19 (tel. 225 566), which shelters paintings from the Renaissance to the 18th century, including Leonardo da Vinci's *Lady with an Ermine* and Rembrandt's *Landscape with a Merciful Samaritan* (open Tues.-Thurs. and Sat.-Sun. 10am-3:30pm, Fri. 10am-4:30pm; 3zł, students 1.5zł, Sun. free). A few blocks southwest of the museum, the tiny **Kamienica Szołayskich,** pl. Szczepański 9 (tel. 227 021), which houses religious art of the 15th-18th centuries, was undergoing renovations in summer '97.

Kraków's **Uniwersytet Jagielloński** (Jagiellonian University), more than 600 years old, ranks as the second oldest university in Eastern Europe (after Prague's Charles University). Astronomer Mikołaj Kopernik (Copernicus) and painter Jan Matejko are among its noted alumni. The university's oldest building, the 15th-century **Collegium Maius** at ul. Jagiellońska 15, one block west of the *rynek,* enchants with a Gothic courtyard and vaulted walkway (open Mon.-Fri. 11am-2:30pm, Sat. 11am-1:30pm).

South of the *rynek,* the **Kościół. Franciszkański** (Franciscan Church) on ul. Franciszkańska houses Stanisław Wyspiański's enormous "God the Father" stained- glass window, famous for its rippling colors. Pope John Paul II resided across the street in the **Bishop's Palace** in his former incarnation as Cardinal Karol Wojtyła. A statue in the courtyard commemorates his 60th birthday in 1980. To the south, on ul. Grodzka, the **Kościół św. Piotra i Pawła** (Church of St. Peter and St. Paul) was the first Polish church built in the Roman Baroque style (open Mon.-Sat. 9am-5pm, Sun. 1-5pm). Right next to it, the 11th-century Romanesque **Kościół św. Andrzeja** (Church of St. Andrew) sheltered many of Kraków's citizens as the city burned in the Tartar invasion of 1241. Slightly west of Grodzka, **ul. Kanonicza,** like Floriańska, was once part of the Royal Tract. Several galleries line the path to Wawel, including **Cricot 2,** Kanonicza 5 (tel. 228 332). A museum of the works of an avant-garde group once led by the late Tadeusz Kantor, the funky exhibit features eerie sounds and pieces—costumes, lights, etc.—from avant-garde shows (open Mon.-Fri. 10am-2pm).

Wawel (The Royal Castle)

Zamek Wawelski (Wawel Castle) is one of the finest pieces of architecture in Poland. Begun in the 10th century but remodeled during the 1500's, the castle contains 71 chambers, a magnificent sequence of 16th-century tapestries commissioned by the royal family, and a series of arrases depicting the story of Noah's Ark. The castle is undergoing renovation—not all of the rooms are open to the public. The **Crown Treasury** features swords, including the *szczerbiec* (jagged sword), which was used in the coronations of Polish kings. Another exhibit, the **Oriental Collection,** contains vases and an enormous 17th-century Turkish tent elaborately decorated with appliques. (Tickets available at window inside Wawel; ticket window closes 1hr. before castle. Royal Chambers (5zł, students 2.50zł), Oriental Collection (3zł, students 1.50zł), and Treasury open Tues.-Fri. 9:30am-4:30pm, Sat. 9:30am-3pm, Sun. 10am-3pm. Admission free on Wed. Oct. 1-March 31 exhibits close at 3pm and are free Sat. Visitor's office (tel./fax 220 904) open Mon.-Sat. 8:45am-4pm, Sun. 10am-3pm.)

Poland's monarchs were crowned and buried in the **Katedra Wawelska,** next to the castle. Karol Wojtyła was archbishop here before his move to Rome. The cathedral houses ornate tombs of kings and other dead white males—poets Juliusz Słowacki and Adam Mickiewicz, and Polish and American military leader General Józef Piłsudski. The sarcophagus of King Kazimierz Jagiełłończyk was crafted by Wit Stwosz (the creator of the altar in Kościół Mariacki), while St. Maurice's spear, presented by German Emperor Otto III in 1000 to the Polish prince Bolesław Chrobry (who later became the country's first king in 1024), symbolizes Polish-German friendship. Atop the cathedral, **Dzwon Zygmunta** (Zygmunt's Bell) sounds only on rare occasions, but when it does, its tones echo for miles around the city (cathedral open May-Sept. daily 9am-5pm; off-season 9am-3pm; 4zł). Outside, the **statue of Tadeusz Kościuszko** glorifies the Polish patriot who fought in the American Revolution and organized an anti-Russian revolution in Poland in 1794. The entrance to **Smocza Jama** (Dragon's Cave), home to Kraków's fire-breathing pet, hides in the complex's southwest corner (open May-Sept. daily 10am-6pm; closed off-season; 1.50zł).

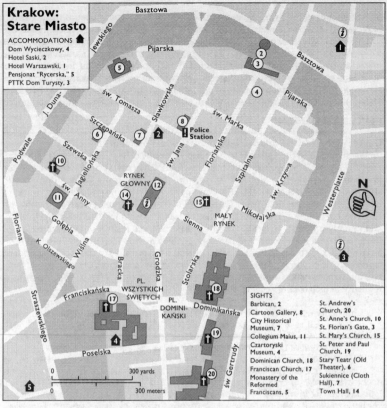

Krakow: Stare Miasto

ACCOMMODATIONS

Dom Wycieczkowy, 4
Hotel Saski, 2
Hotel Warszawski, 1
Pensjonat "Rycerska," 5
PTTK Dom Turysty, 3

Police Station

RYNEK GŁOWNY

MAŁY RYNEK

PL. WSZYSTKICH ŚWIĘTYCH

PL. DOMINI-KAŃSKI

Basztowa
Pijarska
Basztowa
Pijarska
św. Tomasza
Szczepańska
Szewska
Jagiellońska
św. Anny
Gołębia
Wiślna
Bracka
Grodzka
Franciskańska
Poselska
Sienna
Sławkowska
św. Jana
św. Marka
Floriańska
Szpitalna
Mikołajska
św. Krzyża
Westerplatte
Stolarska
Dominikańska
św. Gertrudy
Straszewskiego
k. Olszewskiego
Floriana
Podwale
J. Duna-
Tewskiego

0   300 yards
0   300 meters

N

SIGHTS

Barbican, 2
Cartoon Gallery, 8
City Historical Museum, 7
Collegium Maius, 11
Czartoryski Museum, 4
Dominican Church, 18
Franciscan Church, 17
Monastery of the Reformed Franciscans, 5
St. Andrew's Church, 20
St. Anne's Church, 10
St. Florian's Gate, 3
St. Mary's Church, 15
St. Peter and Paul Church, 19
Stary Teatr (Old Theater), 6
Sukiennice (Cloth Hall), 7
Town Hall, 14

POLAND

Kazimierz (The Old Jewish Quarter)

South of the Stare Miasto lies **Kazimierz,** Kraków's 600-year-old Jewish quarter. Founded in 1335, Kazimierz was originally a distinct town. King Jan Olbrecht decided to move Kraków's Jews there in 1495 in order to get them out of the city proper. The community thrived until 1939—on the eve of the war, 64,000 Jews lived in the Kraków area, many of them in Kazimierz—but Nazi policies forced most of the Jews out, and the rest (15,000) had to resettle in the drastically overcrowded ghetto in the Podgórze district by 1941. All were deported by March 1943, many to the nearby Płaszów and Auschwitz-Birkenau concentration camps. Krakow's Jewish population has risen in recent years, as more and more Poles learn that at least one of their parents was of Jewish heritage; currently, there are between 3000 and 4000 citizens who consider themselves ethnically and culturally Jewish.

To reach Kazimierz, take tram #13 east from pl. Dominikańska, one block south of the *rynek,* and get off when you reach the post office at the intersection of ul. Miodowa and Starowiślna. Ul. Szeroka runs parallel to and one block west of Starowiślna. By foot, the 15-minute walk from the center leads southeast on ul. Sienna, which turns into Starowiślna. Turn right on Miodowa, then take the first left on Szeroka. The beautiful but tiny **Synagoga Remuh** at Szeroka 40 is Kraków's only working synagogue (open Mon.-Fri. 9am-4pm; services Friday at sundown and Saturday morning). The beautiful **cemetery** in back is one of Poland's oldest Jewish cemeteries. Two other (and larger) remaining synagogues testify to the former vitality of Kraków's Jewish community. **Templ Synagoga,** Miodowa 24, was founded by the Association of Progressive Israelis in 1860-62 and features a polychrome ceiling and 36 splendid stained-glass windows (closed to the public). Poland's oldest synagogue,

Stara Synagoga (Old Synagogue), Szeroka 24, houses a small **museum** (tel. 220 962) depicting the history and culture of Kraków's Jews. Particularly fascinating are the photos of prewar Kraków and the appalling sequence of destruction in the 1940s (open Wed.-Thurs. and Sat.-Sun. 9am-3pm, Fri. 11am-6pm; 4zł, students 2zł). The **Jewish Bookstore Jarden,** Szeroka 2 (tel. 217 166), organizes tours, including a two-hour tour of Kazimierz and the Płaszow concentration camp which traces the sites shown in the film *Schindler's List*. Two- to six-hour tours in English (20-70zł, students 15-65zł) depart from the bookstore (open Mon.-Fri. 9am-6pm, Sat.-Sun. 10am-6pm).

ENTERTAINMENT

Dexter (see **Practical Information,** p. 394) offers brochures on each month's cultural activities, and the **Cultural Information Center,** ul. św. Jana 2 (tel. 217 787; fax 217 731), sells a comprehensive monthly guide, *Karnet* (1.50zł), and tickets for upcoming events (open Mon.-Fri. 10am-7pm, Sat. 11am-7pm). Local, international, and student festivals abound in Kraków, particularly during the summer. Some to note are the **International Short Film Festival** (late May), the **Festival of Jewish Culture** (end of June), and the **Jazz Festival** (October/November). Additionally, Kraków will join eight other European cities in an international festival of cultural exchange from 1998 until 2000. Kino Pod Baranani, Rynek Głowny 27 (tel. 230 768) and Kino Mikro, ul. Lea 5 (tel. 342 897) are two of Kraków's more adventurous **independent cinemas.** The center is saturated with pubs and clubs of all sorts. Classical music buffs will appreciate **Filharmonia Krakowska** (tel. 220 958 or 229 477), which performs regularly in its hall at ul. Zwierzyniecka 1.

U Louisa, Rynek Główny 13 (tel. 218 092). Good, loud, live jazz and blues on weekends, as well as a gallery. Cover 3zł. Beer 4-7.50zł; namesake brand 10,5 4.30zł. Also includes a **Cybercafe** (see Internet Access, p. 395). Open weekdays 11am-2am, weekends 11am until the last customer leaves.

Pub Pod Papugami (Under the Parrots), ul. św. Jana 18 (tel. 228 299). Low stools surround peculiar little low-to-the-ground tables. Frequented by a quiet student crowd. Pool 7zł per hour. 0.4L of Guinness 6.80zł. Open daily 4pm-2am.

Jazz Club "U Muniaka," ul. Floriańska 3. Cafe run by well-known Polish jazzman Janusz Muniak, who often invites his friends for jam sessions. Concerts Thurs.-Sat. at 9:30pm. Open daily 5pm-12am, until 1am when there are concerts. The 15zł cover may scare off some.

Student Club, Rynek Główny 8 (tel. 243 902). A student hangout, as the name suggests. Very cheap, laid-back, and simple. No food. *Żywiec* 3zł. Jazz every Tues. and discotheque on weekends. Hours vary daily, but usually open about 9am-2am.

Free Pub, ul. Sławkowska 4, just through the archway and down the stairs on the right. Unmarked and easy to miss. Beer 3.50zł. Crowded after 2am, closes at 6am.

Hadi, ul. Starowiślna 6, in Kazimierz. Mixed gay club open daily. Discotheque from 8pm on weekends.

Spartakus, ul. Konopnickiej 20 (tel. 666 022), just across the bridge on bus #103, 104, 114, or 164, or tram #2. Provides steam bath, Finnish sauna, a fitness center, a sun deck, and a cafeteria for 14zł per day to gay and straight men. Open daily 11am-11pm.

■ Near Kraków

OŚWIĘCIM: AUSCHWITZ-BIRKENAU

An estimated 1.5 million people, mostly Jews, were murdered and thousands more experienced incomparable suffering in the complex of Nazi concentration and death camps that encompassed **Auschwitz** (Oświęcim) and **Birkenau** (Brzezinka). These two names conjure up vivid images of the Nazi death machine, due in no small part to the film *Schindler's List,* which was partially filmed at the camps. Prisoners were first held at the smaller **Konzentrazionslager Auschwitz I,** which was—and still is—located within the limits of the town of Oświęcim. The red brick buildings, originally built as barracks for Polish soldiers, appear eerily normal until the irony of the inscription on the camp's gate—*Arbeit Macht Frei* (Work Makes Free)—slowly becomes clear. In fact, prisoners kept under the horrifying conditions at Auschwitz were far luckier than those who were herded directly to the crematoria at **Konzentration-slager Auschwitz II-Birkenau**—the extermination camp.

Visitors begin tours at the **museum** at Auschwitz. The barracks hold displays detailing the Nazi atrocities, and many of the nations whose citizens were murdered here have erected their own exhibits or memorials. As you walk through the former barracks, separated only by glass sheets from enormous rooms holding remnants from the camp's storehouses at the end of the war—including suitcases, shoes, glasses, and more than 100,000 pounds of slowly decomposing women's hair—the sheer magnitude and terror of the place slams into focus. An English-language guidebook with maps of the camps is sold at the entrance for 2zł. There's at least one English showing per day of a horrifying **film** shot by the Soviet Army, who liberated the camp on January 27, 1945. The black-and-white pictures of the near-dead survivors make it difficult to believe that these were the fortunate ones. Check the schedule at the movie ticket office (1zł). (Museum open daily June-Aug. 8am-7pm; May and Sept. 8am-6pm; April and Oct. 8am-5pm; March and Nov.-Dec. 15 8am-4pm; Dec. 16-Feb. 8am-3pm. Free. Children under 14 are strongly advised not to visit the museum.)

The starker **Konzentrationslager Auschwitz II-Birkenau,** in the countryside 3km from the original camp, is a 30-minute walk along a well-marked route. Between April 15 and September 31, a bus shuttles to this site from the parking lot at the Auschwitz museum (7 per day, 1zł). Birkenau was constructed later in the war when the efficient killing of the Jews, Romani, Slavs, homosexuals, disabled people, and any others the Nazis deemed "inferior" was deemed more important than the benefits of their labor. Begin with the central watchtower, where you can view the immensity of the camp—endless rows of barracks, watchtowers, chimneys, gas chambers, and crematoria. The Nazis tried to destroy the evidence of their mass destruction, and there remain only 45 brick buildings, 27 wooden ones, and what looks like a desolate forest of perfectly spaced brick chimneys. The gas chambers and crematoria are in ruins, having been dynamited by the retreating Nazis; the train tracks that led up to them, however, have been partially reconstructed, and photos of the selection process make it all too easy to imagine the arbitrary system that divided people permitted to work from those headed directly for the gas chamber. In the right corner of the camp lies a pond, still gray from the ashes deposited there half a century ago; fragments of bone can still be found in the area near the crematoria.

Buses run to Oświęcim from Kraków's central bus station (11 per day, 1½hr., 5.40zł; get off at "Muzeum Oświęcim"). **Trains** leave from Kraków Główny (4 per day, 1¾hr., 5zł), although times are not particularly convenient and trains may not be direct. More trains run from Kraków Plaszów, south of the center (see **Kraków: Trains,** p. 394). Tourist offices in Kraków also offer tours that include transportation and knowledgeable guides. From the train station in the town, buses #2, 3, 4, and 5 drop visitors off at the "Muzeum Oświęcim" bus stop. By foot, turn right as you exit the station, go one block and turn left; the road stretches 1.6km to Auschwitz, which will be on the right.

WIELICZKA

A 1000-year-old **salt mine** awaits at ul. Daniłowicza 10 (English info tel. 787 366) in the tiny town of Wieliczka, 13km southeast of Kraków. Pious Poles carved the immense 20-chapel complex, situated 100m underground, entirely out of salt; in 1978 UNESCO declared the mine to be one of the 12 most priceless monuments in the world. The most spectacular of the sculptures is the 180-ft. long and 33-ft. high **St. Kinga's Chapel.** Two tours circulate through the mine: one visits the salt sculptures, and the other covers the **underground museum,** which gives a history of the salt mines and demonstrates methods of salt extraction. The museum tour is more interesting in theory than in practice. (Open daily April 15-Oct. 15 7:30am-6:30pm; Oct. 16-April 14 8am-4pm. Obligatory guided tours 17zł, students 8.50zł, cameras 5zł, videocameras 10zł. English guide available at 12:30pm in June and 5 times daily in

July and August; 21zł per person for English guide.) To save money, pick up the English guidebook for 3zł; its pictures and text will allow you to follow along with the Polish tour. **Orbis** organizes daily trips to the mine (3hr.; 70zł, students 50.50zł); its bus leaves daily at 3:25pm from PTTK Dom Turysty at Westerplatte 15. Or choose a budget option: **trains** also head here from Kraków (1 per hr., 25min., 1.50zł), and private **minibuses** depart from the road between the train and bus stations (every 15min., 1.50zł). Once in Wieliczka, follow the former path of the tracks and then the signs reading *"do kopalni"* (to the mine).

Let Them Eat Salt!

When Kinga, daughter of the Hungarian King Bela, married prince Bolesław Śmiały (the Bold), future monarch of Poland, the princess wanted her dowry to be a present not just to Bolesław, but to all the people of Poland. Upon questioning the delegates of the prince, she discovered that Poles had been supping on soulless stews and enduring flavorless foodstuffs for centuries. The reason? They had no salt. That night a mysterious voice came to Kinga and divulged the whereabouts of a magnificent El Dorado of salt. The next day, she asked her father to give her whatever her ring would touch. He agreed, and Kinga hurled the ring over the mountains separating Poland and Hungary. Upon arriving in Kraków, she ordered workers to start digging in the spot where the ring had fallen—after days of digging, the men found the ring stuck fast in an endless deposit of salt.

TARNÓW

A Roms town before WWII, Tarnów still manages to preserve its Gypsy legacy. Dedicated to "all travelers, past, present and, I hope, future," **Muzeum Etnograficzne,** ul. Krakowska 10 (tel. (014) 220 625), traces the history of Polish Gypsies since 1401, when they first came to the area. WWII saw 35,000 Polish Gypsies perish; today, only 20,000 remain. The museum exhibits a display on their history, art, and culture. In the summer, painted caravans await riders, and the Gypsy flag—a red wheel against a green and blue background—symbolizes the Gypsies' nomadic tradition (museum open Tues. and Thurs. 10am-5pm, Wed. and Fri. 9am-3pm, Sat.-Sun. 10am-2pm; 1zł, students 0.50zł; English brochure 3zł). Tarnów lies 82km east of Kraków, connected to it by **trains** (38 per day, 1-1½hr., 6-9zł) and **buses** (24 per day, 2hr., 10zł), both of which arrive at **pl. Dworcowy,** 15 minutes from the center. From the main bus station, turn right on **ul. Krakowska,** which crosses **pl. Kościuszki** and ends at the *rynek.*

■ Sandomierz

The *małopolski* town of Sandomierz (SAN-do-myezh), chartered before 1241, is immaculately clean, charming, and just about empty. The sights are captivating, and the cafes are great, if you don't mind the eerie feeling of being one of the few people there to enjoy them. Named after Sudomir, its founder, the town suffered destruction by the Tatars in 1241-60 and a Swedish invasion in 1656. Only one fortification remains, but the *rynek*'s 15th-century apartments and the underground system of dungeon-like wine cellars survived. Timely restorations in 1967 kept this medieval operation from sliding into the Wisła.

Orientation and Practical Information Trains roll to Przemyśl (2 per day, 3hr.) and Warsaw (3 per day, 4hr.). **Buses** run to Kraków (2 per day, 4hr., 16zł); Lublin (7 per day, 2½hr., 10zł); and Warsaw (16 per day, 19zł). Taking a bus from one of these major points is by far the easiest means of reaching Sandomierz; from smaller towns, the local tourist office can point out buses that pass through. The **train station,** ul. Lwowska (tel. 832 23 74), sits in the outskirts across the Wisła river. To reach the center from the train, take bus #3 or 11. The **bus station,** ul. 11-go Listopada (tel. 322 302; open daily 4:30am-9pm), northwest of Stare Miasto, is a 15-minute walk from the center or a short ride on bus #10. Ul. 11-go Listopada links the bus station with the main drag, **ul. Mickiewicza.** A left on Mickiewicza leads past a park to **Brama Opatowska** (Opatowska Gate), which ushers you into Stare Miasto. Inside the underpass, a large **PTTK map** marks the way. The **PTTK tourist office,** Rynek 25/26 (tel. 832 23 05; fax 832 26 82), has free maps of the town (open Mon.-Fri. 8am-3pm). Nearby bookstores also sell a handy-dandy map/city guide (2zł). Travel info and bookings are available next door to PTTK at **Orbis,** Rynek 23 (tel. 832 30 40; open Mon.-Fri. 9am-4pm, Sat. 9am-1pm). **Exchange currency** at *kantors,* post offices, and banks throughout town. The **post office** lies at Rynek 10 (open Mon.-Fri. 8am-6pm, Sat.-Sun. 8am-1pm). **Postal code:** 27-600. **Phone code:** 015.

Accommodations and Food Accommodations are centrally located and reasonably priced. **Hotel Dick,** Mały Rynek 2 (tel. 832 35 91), stands erect one block north of the *rynek,* with carpeted rooms, clean communal bathrooms, and an unfortunate name in English (pronounced "ditsk"; singles 37.45zł; doubles 51zł; triples 63zł; quads 74zł; 5-bed dorms 30zł per person). The smaller **Dom Noclegowy,** ul. Zamkowa 1 (tel. 832 22 19), just down the hill from the *rynek,* offers simple singles (30zł), doubles (45zł), and triples (60zł), each equipped with an antique furnace. Bathrooms are communal but decent.

The main eateries in Sandomierz cluster around the *rynek.* **Snack Bar 30,** Rynek 30 (tel. 832 28 38), offers salads (4.50zł per bowl) and pizza (10zł; open daily 10am-10pm). It's a point-and-serve operation, so non-Polish speakers won't be encumbered by unpronounceable words. **Winnica** (Vineyard), Mały Rynek 2 (tel. 832 35 91), serves tasty Polish fare such as *pierogi* (4.20zł) in a traditional setting with a slightly pre-NATO feel (open daily 11am-midnight). For something lighter, the **Kawiarnia "Retro,"** Rynek 5 (tel. 832 28 50), offers an elegant, second-story interior overlooking the *rynek* as well as sweet snacks; the *kawa po sandomiersku*—there's a whipped egg somewhere in there—is delicious (4.18zł; cafe open daily noon-10pm).

Sights The Gothic **Brama Opatowska,** the only remainder of the town's fortifications, marks the entrance to Stare Miasto. Steep stairs head to the top of the gate—and a fantastic view of Sandomierz (open daily 10am-5:30pm; 1.40zł, students 1zł). Ul. Opatowska continues past the gate straight to the spacious, sloping, cobblestone **Rynek Starego Miasta** (Old Town Square). A right on ul. Oleśnicka, just before the *rynek,* leads to the entrance of the mysterious **underground tourist route**—yes, it's actually called that—traveling through stone and brick chambers inhabited by Tatar ghosts. In these 14th-century cellars, wealthy merchants stored grain and wine made from the grapes of the vineyards that covered the sunny slopes surrounding Sandomierz. The guide also recounts the story of the legendary Halina Krempianka, who sacrificed her life to save her hometown from the Tatars (Polish tours every 30min. daily 10am-5:30pm; 3.40zł, students 2zł).

In the middle of the *rynek,* the Renaissance **ratusz** houses a division of the **Muzeum Okręgowe** (Regional Museum), which features a model of 18th-century Sandomierz (open Tues.-Sun. 9am-4pm; 2zł, students 1zł; Sat. free). Ul. Mariacka takes you to the town's grandest monument, the 14th-century **Bazylika Katedralna.** It has retained its Gothic structure, but the interior has been redone in Baroque style (open March-Nov. Mon.-Sat. 10am-12:30pm and 2:30-5pm, Sun. 3-5pm; Dec.-Feb. Mon.-Sat. 10am-noon and 2:30-3pm, Sun. 3-5pm). During the summer, the cathedral hosts weekly organ concerts. Continuing down ul. Mariacka, a right on ul. Zamkowa leads to **Zamek Kazimerzowski.** Built in the 14th century by King Kazimierz Wielki and destroyed by the Swedes in 1656, the castle has recently undergone restoration—only the walls and skeleton reflect the original layout. Inside, the **archaeological exhibit,** ul. Zamkowa 14 (tel. 832 38 68 or 832 38 69), includes an 11th-century chess set (open Tues.-Sun. 10am-5pm; 3zł, students 1zł). Up at the top, the quiet **Kawiarnia Zamek** serves darkness, coffee, beer, desserts, and art (open daily 11am-10pm).

POLAND

■ Kazimierz Dolny

Although the town was established by Kazimierz the Great in the 14th century, it's actually named in honor of Prince Kazimierz the Just, who in 1181 donated the settlement to a nunnery near Kraków. Kazimierz Dolny (KAH-zhee-myezh DOL-nih) burned down twice in the 16th century, Cossacks ransacked it during the 17th, and cholera and Swedes destroyed it during the 18th. When Communists proposed turning this bewitching little community into a huge resort in the 1960s, protests helped avert yet another destruction. The only invader now is the sunset over the Wisła.

Orientation and Practical Information Some buses pass on the way between Puławy and Lublin (1 per hr., 1½hr., 5.20zł), making frequent stops in the countryside; others zoom to Warsaw (7 per day, 3½hr., 10.40zł). When coming from Lublin or Warsaw, Kazimierz will not be posted as the final destination—ask which buses pass through. When leaving Kazimierz by bus, don't assume that the driver will make the detour into the bus station—he or she may stop across the street just off the cobblestone **ul. Podzamcze.** If you've just arrived, continue up the incline to get to the *rynek,* which is on the left. The **PTTK tourist office,** Rynek 27 (tel. 810 046), sells divine little maps of town (2.50zł) and arranges private rooms (open May-Oct. Mon.-Fri. 8am-6pm, Sat.-Sun. 10am-5:30pm; off-season Mon.-Fri. 8am-3pm, Sat.-Sun. 10am-2pm). The **pharmacy** cures at Rynek 17 (tel. 810 120; open daily 8am-7pm). The **post office,** ul. Tyszkiewicza 2 (tel. 810 515; fax 810 500), a block west of the *rynek* (open May-Oct. Mon.-Fri. 8am-8pm, Sat.-Sun. 10am-5pm; off-season Mon.-Fri. 8am-8pm, Sat. 9am-1pm, Sun. 9-11am), offers a **currency exchange** (open Mon.-Fri. 8am-8pm) and **telephones.** There's no bank, so bring some cash. **Postal code:** 24-120. **Phone code:** 081.

Accommodations and Food Rooms in town are fairly limited, especially during summer weekends and during the **Ogólnopolski Festiwal Kapel i Śpiewaków Ludowych** (Festival of Folk Groups and Singers), which takes place during the last week of June. It's especially important to call ahead for reservations during these times. **PTTK** (see above) arranges private singles (14-22zł per person), doubles (13-20zł per person), and triples (12-19zł per person) around town and in the outskirts for a 1zł commission. The clean and conveniently located **Youth Hostel "Strażnica,"** ul. Senatorska 23a (tel. 810 427), sits only one block southwest of the *rynek.* Its 50 beds come in 2- to 10-person rooms (doubles and triples 16zł per person, students 14.50zł; dorms 13zł, students 12zł; sheets 2.50zł; breakfast included). The staff can also provide current information about camping along the Wisła.

A **grocery** lies just south of the *rynek* at ul. Klasztorna 5 (open Mon.-Fri. 6am-7pm, Sat. 6am-3pm, Sun. 9am-2pm). **Restauracja Staropolska,** ul. Nadrzeczna 14 (tel./fax 810 250), a block south of the *rynek,* is the town's culinary legend, serving Polish food at its best in the shade of spruce trees (*barszcz* with meat dumplings 5zł; open daily 11am-10pm). **Bistro "U Zbyszka,"** ul. Sadowa 4 (tel. 810 723), just west of the *rynek* off ul. Nadwiślańska, invites guests to cool off in the pool (2.50zł per hr.), but wait an hour after eating (salads 4zł, *kiełbasa* 6zł; open daily 10am-10pm). An old-fashioned bakery with the freshest rolls in town, **Piekarnia Sarzyński,** ul. Nadrzeczna 6 is a few steps from the *rynek* (bread 4zł, tarts 2.70zł; open daily 6am-8pm).

Sights and Entertainment Hike up to the **castle tower,** which used to alert the residents to passing boats on which they could levy tolls. From this lofty vantage point, you can see not only a long stretch of the Wisła, but also the castle at Janowiec (open Tues.-Sun. 10am-5pm; castle ruins and tower 0.60zł). On your way up or down, stop by the 16th-century **Kościół Farny św. Jana Chrzciciela i św. Bartłomieja** (Cathedral of St. John the Baptist and St. Bartholomew) to survey one of Poland's oldest (1620) and best-preserved organs. **Muzeum Sztuki Złotniczej** (Museum of Goldsmithery), Rynek 19 (tel. 810 289), displays European jewelry, silver and gold religious paraphernalia, and a large collection of Jewish silver dating back to the 15th century. Just southwest of the *rynek*, **Kamienica Celejowska,** ul. Senatorska 11/13 (tel. 810 104), houses a collection of paintings inspired by the town. The **Muzeum Przyrodnicze** (Museum of Natural History), ul. Puławska 54 (tel. 810 326 or 810 341), displays fossils and rocks from the Kazimierz region. (Museums open May-Sept. Tues.-Sun. 10am-4pm; Oct.-April 10am-3pm; admission to each museum 2zł, students 1zł.) Also worth a quick peek is the building that used to house the **synagogue** (1677), east of the *rynek* at ul. Lubelska 2. The synagogue served a community of 3000 Jews, all of whom were sent to death camps during the Nazi occupation; a tablet on the building's east wall commemorates their fate.

▒ Lublin

Despite the slow pace of its surroundings, *Małopolska's* capital is far from dull and anything but provincial. The center of the Polish Reformation and Counter-Reformation in the 16th and 17th centuries, Lublin (LOO-bleen) has long been an incubator of social and religious movements. The Catholic university here was the only university in Poland to maintain its independence from the government during the Communist era. Lublin thus acquired a young, vibrant, bohemian presence. These days many of the city's efforts are aimed at restoring the crumbling architecture to its past glory.

ORIENTATION AND PRACTICAL INFORMATION

The city's main street, **ul. Krakowskie Przedmieście,** runs west from **Stare Miasto** and turns into **Aleje Racławickie** before reaching the **Ogród Saski** (Saxon Gardens) to the north and the **KUL** (Katolicki Uniwersytet Lubelski) to the south. Take bus #5 or 10 to town from the bus station. On foot, head toward the castle and climb **ul. Zamkowa.** After changing names several times, it will emerge through **Brama Krakowska** (Kraków Gate). Take tram #150 from the train station to the city center.

Tourist Office: IT, ul. Krakowskie Przedmieście 78 (tel. 532 44 12), carries maps (4zł) and brochures. Open Mon.-Fri. 9am-6pm, Sat. 10am-2pm. Another tourist office, **Orbis,** ul. Narutowicza 31/33 (tel. 532 22 56; fax 532 15 30), handles international and domestic plane, train, and bus tickets and books hotels. Open May-July Mon.-Fri. 9am-5pm, Sat. 10am-2pm; Aug.-April Mon.-Fri. 9am-5pm.

Currency Exchange: *Kantors* around town have the best rates. **Bank PKO S.A.,** ul. Królewska 1 (tel. 532 10 16), accepts traveler's checks (1% commission) and offers cash advances on MC and Visa. Open Mon.-Fri. 7:30am-6pm, Sat. 10am-2pm. **ATM:** Outside the lobby of the ritzy Orbis Unia Hotel, al. Raclawiekie 12, across from the Ogród Saski. Takes AmEx, Visa, MC, Plus, and Cirrus.

Trains: pl. Dworcowy 1 (tel. 532 02 19, info 933). To Kraków (2 per day, 4hr., 22.80zł) and Warsaw (10 per day, 2½hr., 16.65zł).

Buses: ul. Tysiąclecia 4 (tel. 776 649, info 934) To Warsaw (10 per day, 3hr., 12zł).

Public Transportation: Buy tickets at kiosks. 10min. ride 0.70zł; 20min. ride 0.90zł.

Pharmacy: ul. Krakowskie Przedmieście 49 (tel. 532 24 25). Open 8am-8pm; after hours, ring the bell.

Post Office: ul. Krakowskie Przedmieście 50 (tel. 743 64 00). **Fax** service (fax 532 50 61). Open Mon.-Fri. 7am-9pm, Sat. 8am-9pm, Sun. 10am-5pm. **Postal code:** 20-930.

Telephones: At the post office. Open 24hr. **Phone code:** 081.

ACCOMMODATIONS

Rooms in Lublin are abundant and relatively inexpensive. In the summer, **university dorms** serve as lodging, though they are quite a trek from the center. The tourist offices (see above) have information about these rooms. The helpful staff of **Horyzont** (tel./fax 531 58 46), upstairs in the train station, makes hotel and camping reservations (10zł fee), and speaks good German and a bit of English (open Mon.-Fri. 10am-4pm, Sat. 10am-1pm).

Schronisko Młodzieżowe (HI), ul. Długosza 6a (tel. 533 06 28), west of the center near the KUL. Friendly owners, a clean kitchen, and informal camping facilities. Walk to the end of the Ogród Saski and turn right on ul. Długosza. Lockout 10am-5pm. Curfew 10pm. Triples 10zł per person; dorm rooms 8zł; sheets 3.50zł.

ZNP Dom Noclegowy, ul. Akademicka 4 (tel. 533 82 85), next to the KUL. From the Ogród Saski bus stop, cross the street and follow ul. Łopacińskiego until it turns into ul. Akademicka. Singles 35zł; doubles 44zł; 6-person dorms 18zł per person.

Hotel Lublinianka, ul. Krakowskie Przedmieście 56 (tel. 532 42 61). Centrally located, with well-stocked bar downstairs (singles 47zł, with bath 60zł; doubles 76zł; quads 120zł).

FOOD

Lublin's eateries and grocery stores cluster along and around ul. Krakowskie Przedmieście, with a few scattered around Stare Miasto as well. A **24-hour grocery store, Delikatesy Grota,** ul. Krakowskie Przedmieście 13, seems to specialize in rotisserie chicken and late-night beer runs, but it'll do in a pinch.

Jazz Pizza, ul. Krakowskie Przedmieście 55 (tel. 736 149). Sports walls adorned with portraits of Dizzy Gillespie. Hosts jazz concerts and cooks up one helluva jazzy pizza. (5.50zł plus 1-2zł for extra toppings, salads 3zł). English menu; 15% discount to Canadians, eh. Open Mon.-Sat. 11:30am-midnight, Sun. 3-10pm.

Bar Deli Rood, ul. Krakowskie Przedmieście 21. A modern version of fast food. Salads, soups, and platters (under 6zł). Open Mon.-Sat. 10am-10pm, Sun. 11am-8pm.

Bar Staromiejski, ul. Jezuicka 1, in Stare Miasto. Cafeteria-style food, including soups (1zł) and *pierogi* (2.50zł). Open Mon.-Fri. 8am-5pm, Sat.-Sun. 8am-4pm.

Bar Turystyczny Mleczny, ul. Krakowskie Przedmieście 29. Similar grub, but closer to the center of things. Full meals 3zł. Open Mon.-Sat. 7am-6pm, Sun. 8am-5pm.

SIGHTS AND ENTERTAINMENT

The 19th-century ocher facades of **ul. Krakowskie Przedmieście** introduce the medieval **Stare Miasto.** A stroll east from pl. Litewskim, which showcases an **obelisk** commemorating the 1569 union of Poland and Lithuania and a **Tomb of the Unknown Soldier,** leads to pl. Łokietka and the 1827 **Nowy Ratusz** (New Town Hall), seat of Lublin's government. To the right starts ul. Królewska, with the grand **Katedra św. Jana Chrzciciela i Jana Ewangelisty** (Cathedral of St. John the Baptist and St. John the Evangelist; 1586-96). The cathedral's frescoes and gilded altar are worth a visit.

To the left of the Nowy Ratusz runs **ul. Lubartowska,** the main artery of prewar Lublin's Jewish district. **Plac Ofiar Getta** (Victims of the Ghetto Square), on the left side of the street, centers around the **Monument to the Murdered Jews.** At #10 stands **Bożnica,** the only synagogue in Lublin to survive the war. The early 20th-century synagogue and former rabbinical academy also houses **Izba Pamięci Żydów Lublina,** a museum dedicated to the memory of Lublin's Jewish community (open Thurs. noon-2pm, Sun. 11am-1pm).

Ul. Krakowskie Przedmieście travels straight through pl. Łokietka to the fortified **Brama Krakowska,** which houses **Oddział Historyczny Muzeum Lubelskiego** (Historical Division of the Lublin Museum), pl. Łokietka 3 (tel. 532 60 01; open Wed.-Sat. 9am-4pm, Sun. 9am-5pm; 1zł). Across the gate, ul. Bramowa leads to the **rynek,** lined with early Renaissance houses. In the middle of the *rynek* stands **Stary Ratusz** (Old Town Hall); redone several times, it finally settled for the 18th-century Neoclassical style. A walk along ul. Grodzka leads through the 15th-century **Brama Grodzka** (Grodzka Gate) to ul. Zamkowa, which runs to the massive **Zamek Lubelski** (Lublin Castle). Most of the structure was built in the 14th century by King Kazimierz Wielki, but was restored in the 19th century with a neo-Gothic exterior. During the Nazi occupation, the castle functioned as a Gestapo jail; the prisoners were shot *en masse* when the Nazis had to make a fast retreat. Inside the castle walls, **Muzeum Lubelskie** (tel. 532 50 01) features archaeological and ethnographic displays. Its most prized possession is Jan Matejko's canvas of the signing of the Polish-Lithuanian treaty, which occurred in this castle (open Wed.-Sat. 9am-4pm, Sun. 9am-5pm; 1zł).

Thanks to a large student crowd, Lublin has an impressive number of cafes and pubs and an active music scene. The **Old Pub,** ul. Grodzka 8 (tel. 743 71 27), serves whiskey (2.20-13zł), beer (2-7zł), *wino grzane* (heated wine with spices; 4.50zł), and cappuccino (3zł) on antique sewing machine tables (disco upstairs; open Sun.-Thurs. 11am-10pm, Fri.-Sat. 11am-11pm). The tiny **18 Hester Cafe,** ul. Okopowa 20 (tel. 743 66 70), in a cellar two blocks south of ul. Krakowskie Przedmieście, is packed with and run by students (open Mon.-Fri. noon-midnight, Sat.-Sun. 4pm-midnight). For a little disco-dancin', check out **Graffiti,** at Teatr Scena Ruchu, al. Piłsudskiego 13 (tel. 532 75 42; open Tues., Wed., Sun. 6pm-1am; disco Thurs.-Sat. 6pm-3am; women 4zł, men 6zł, Thurs. free; must be 20 or older). **Hades,** ul. Peowiaków 12 (tel. 532 87 61), is home to a good nightclub, cafe, and restaurant. There's also live music—listen to it backwards (open daily 3pm-midnight; disco Fri. and every day in the summer from 9pm; men 3zł, women free). **Kaprys Music Cafe,** Rynek 17 (tel. 532 36 17), in the heart of Stare Miasto, occasionally has concerts and always has 0.5L of *Żywiec* (3.20zł; open daily 11am-11pm).

■ Near Lublin: Majdanek

The largest concentration camp after Auschwitz, **Majdanek** is all too near Lublin: it stands merely 4km from the city center, a 30-minute walk down the road to Zamość (Droga Męczenników Majdanka; Road of the Martyrs of Majdanek). Approximately 235,000 people died here, including Jews, Poles, Danes, and others transported here from all over Europe. **Panstwowe Muzeum na Majdanku** (Majdanek State Museum) was founded in 1944 after the liberation of Lublin. The Nazis didn't have time to destroy the camp, so the original structures stand in their entirety, including the gas chambers, the crematorium, the third field prisoners' barracks, the watchtowers, the guardhouses, and the electrified barbed-wire perimeter.

A visit to Majdanek begins with the information building (tel. 744 26 47 or 744 19 55; fax 744 05 26), whose staff supplies free information in several languages and shows a 15-minute documentary that includes the first footage taken after the camp's liberation (available in English, last showing 3pm; 2zł per person). Walking through the entire camp takes 1½-2 hours. The route begins with the gas chambers; signs in Polish, English, French, Russian, and German explain Nazi methods of extermination and experiments. Guardhouses 43-45 contain historical exhibitions, including statistical displays, prisoners' clothes, instruments of torture, and a sample of the 730kg of human hair exported from Majdanek to a fabric factory in Germany. Perhaps most stunning of all, guardhouses 52-53 are literally filled with the 800,000 pairs of shoes the Nazis took from victims of Majdanek and neighboring camps. At the end of the path through the camp, the intact ovens sit next to the concrete dome of the mausoleum, a massive mound of ash and human bone. (Museum open May-Sept. Tues.-Sun. 8am-6pm, Oct.-Nov. and March-April daily 8am-3pm; free. Children under 14 not permitted). From Lublin, eastbound **bus** #28 from the train station, **trams** #153 and 158 from al. Racławickie, and southbound tram #156 from ul. Królewska all stop at the huge granite monument marking the entrance at Droga Męczenników Majdanka 67.

■ Zamość

Designed by the Italian architect Bernardo Morando, Zamość sprang up in the 1580s as the dream come true of a young aristocrat, Jan Zamojski. Having studied in Padua, Zamojski wanted to recreate its beauty in his homeland and succeeded in conjuring up a perfect town with a palace, town hall, opulent houses, churches, an academy, and an immense *rynek*. Touted by locals as the "Padua of the North," Zamość is undergoing widespread restoration in an attempt to resuscitate its former beauty.

POLAND

Orientation and Practical Information Turn right outside the **train station,** ul. Szczebrzeska 11, and walk toward the spires of Stare Miasto, or take a city bus. **Trains** (tel. 386 944) run to Lublin (3 per day, 3hr., 9zł) and Warsaw (2 per day, 5½hr., 23zł). **Buses** (tel. 384 986) shuttle faster, also to Lublin (42 per day, 2hr., 6.90zł) and Warsaw (5 per day, 5hr., 23zł). For a **taxi,** dial 395 050. From the **bus station,** ul. Sadowa 6, **city buses** #0, 16 and 22 (0.80zł; 1.60zł at night; half-price for students; get tickets at a kiosk) depart from the same side of the street as the station and circle around Stare Miasto. Otherwise, it's a 25-minute walk along ul. Partyzantów. Bus #0 connects the bus and train stations. The **ZOIT tourist office,** Rynek Wielki 13 (tel. 392 292, fax 708 13), in the *ratusz,* sells maps and brochures about Zamość (0.20-2zł; open Mon.-Fri. 7:30am-5pm, Sat.-Sun. 9am-2pm). **Bank PKO S.A.,** ul. Grodzka 2 (tel. 392 040), cashes traveler's checks and provides MC and Visa cash advances (open Mon.-Fri. 8am-6pm, Sat. 10am-2pm). The **pharmacy,** Apteka Rektorska, dispenses drugs at Rynek 2 (tel. 392 386; open Mon.-Sat. 8am-7pm). The **post office** and **telephones** are at ul. Kościuszki 9 (tel. 385 123; open Mon.-Fri. 7am-9pm, Sat. 8am-1pm). **Postal code:** 22-400. **Phone code:** 084.

Accommodations and Food The hostel-like **Dom Turysty "Marta,"** ul. Zamenhofa 11 (tel. 392 639), is right in Stare Miasto (4-bed dorms 15zł per person). **Ośrodek Sportui Rekreacji,** ul. Królowej Jadwigi 8 (tel./fax 386 011), next to the stadium, offers singles (41zł), doubles (53zł), triples (63zł), and quads (73zł), all with baths. Dorm beds also available (18zł per person). **Camping** facilities can be found down the road at ul. Królowej Jadwigi 14 (tel. 392 499), in a wooded area past the stadium (campsites 2zł per person; tent rental 6zł per night; 4-bed bungalows with bath and fridge 20zł per person).

The culinary experience in Zamość is rather limited. **Ratuszowa,** Rynek 13 (tel. 715 57), in the town hall, serves traditional Polish fare in a relaxed cafe setting. Soups run 2-3zł, while only 14zł will get you the most expensive main dish (open daily 9am-11pm). **Café-Restaurant Muzealna,** ul. Ormiańska 30 (tel. 386 494, ext. 40), is a similar establishment with tasty *pierogi* (5zł) and outdoor dining (open daily noon-midnight). A **24-hour grocery** is at ul. Łukasińskiego 11, but the stores in the town center are better stocked.

Sights and Entertainment The whole town is a monumental sight, with its Renaissance layout, imposing **ratusz,** peaceful cobblestone *rynek,* and surrounding houses with painted facades. Especially worth seeing are the splendidly preserved **Armenian burgher houses,** ul. Ormiańska 22, 24, 26, 28, and 30, in the northeast corner of the *rynek.* House #26 is the headquarters of the **Muzeum Okręgowe** (tel. 386 494), which displays regional art, including Lusatian jewelry from 1000BC (open Tues.-Sun. 10am-4pm; 2zł, students 1zł). A. Allori's *Annunciation* is inside the **Katedra,** ul. Kolegiacka. The region's religious riches—chalices, monstrances, and saints' relics—pack the adjoining **museum** (open May-Sept. Thurs.-Mon. 11am-4pm; 0.50zł). You can also climb the cathedral's belltower for a panoramic view of Stare Miasto (open daily 10am-4pm; 2zł, students 1zł). Diagonally across from the cathedral, **Muzeum "Arsenał,"** ul. Zamkowa 2 (tel. 384 076), houses war trophies and other military artifacts (open 10am-3:30pm; entrance closes at 3pm; 1zł, students 0.50zł). Pool tables abound in the bars, and many residents and tourists head to the *rynek* for an evening *piwo;* unfortunately, the good times begin winding down before midnight. Jazz is available year-round at **Jazz Club Kosz,** ul. Zamenhofa 3 (tel. 386 041); enter from the back of the building (open daily 1pm-1am). At the end of May, jazz musicians from Poland, Ukraine, and Belarus jam for the **Jazz na Kresach** (Jazz in the Borderlands) festival. September gathers jazz singers for the **Międzynarodowe Spotkania Wokalistów Jazzowych.** Every summer, the town echoes with life during **Zamojskie Lato Teatralne** (Theater Summer), when experimental groups perform in theaters and on the streets. Contact **Wojewódzki Dom Kultury (WDK),** ul. Partyzantów 13 (tel./fax 393 887), for info.

■ Łańcut

The palace-castle complex of the luxurious **Zamek w Łańcucie** (Łańcut Castle) entices visitors with a glimpse into the lavish lifestyle of Polish nobility past. But the impressive museum is not all the palace offers; the extensive park grounds surrounding it are a serene and shady setting for walking or relaxing. Founded by King Kazimierz III Wielki in the middle of the 14th century, the town was fortified between 1610 and 1620 by the Lubomirski family, who acquired the castle after the death of Stanisław Stadnicki—the "Devil of Łańcut." The Baroque fortress survived Swedish and Turkish sieges, but failed to please Elżbieta Lubomirska z Czartoryskich, an 18th-century lap dog-loving duchess with French tastes and an eye for fine art. Under her direction, the castle was transformed into an aesthetically amiable edifice. The Potocki family inherited the palace and continued to expand it. Although it was spared damage during WWII, the palace lost its soul when the last Lord of Łańcut fled Poland in 1944, taking 11 railway cars full of valuable artifacts with him. The new government turned the complex into a **museum** showcasing the rooms, furniture, architecture, and artwork of the complex. The ticket office (tel. 20 08; fax 20 12) is next to the tourist office (open April-Sept. Tues.-Sat. 9am-4pm, Sun. and holidays 9am-3pm; Feb.-March and Oct.-Nov. Tues.-Sun. 9am-3pm; 7zł, students 3zł). The guided tour, which is included with admission, outfits visitors with felt-soled shoes before making the rounds of the palace. The tour also includes the **Oranżeria** (Orangery), inside the palace grounds, and the **Powozownia,** the largest display of carriages in Europe. The palace hosts the mid-May **Festiwal Muzyki** and the June **Kursy Interpretacji Muzycznej,** both of which draw international musicians. Outside the palace gates stands a **synagogue,** ul. Paderewskiego, with impressive 18th-century polychromy (open June-Sept. Tues.-Sun. 10am-4pm, or by request; 1zł).

Buses (tel. 21 21) run to Przemyśl (13 per day, 1½hr., 6.80zł). **Trains** (tel. 23 17) zoom to Kraków (9 per day, 2½hr.); Przemyśl (23 per day, 1hr.); and Warsaw (1 per day, 7hr.). From the **bus station,** ul. Sikorskiego, opposite the palace gardens, it's a 10-minute walk along ul. Kościuszki to the *rynek.* Turn right as you leave the station. To get to the palace from the **train station,** ul. Kolejowa, call a **taxi** (tel. 20 00), or head along ul. Żeromskiego, across from the station, then right on ul. Grunwaldzka (30min.). To reach the *rynek,* turn right where ul. Grunwaldzka meets ul. Kościuszki. The **Trans-Euro-Tours tourist office,** ul. Kościuszki 2 (tel./fax 30 16), provides information on hotels, operates charter bus lines, and has a **kantor** (open Mon.-Fri. 9am-5pm, Sat. 9am-1pm). **Postal code:** 37-100. **Phone code:** 017. When calling from outside Łańcut, dial 25 before each number.

The quiet **Hotel Zamkowy,** ul. Zamkowa 1 (tel. 26 71), in the palace park, attracts an international crowd. The rooms are clean and remarkably well-priced (doubles 30-40zł, with bath 60-100zł; triples 45zł, with bath 90zł). **Dom Wycieczkowy PTTK,** ul. Dominikańska 1 (tel. 45 12), occupies the old Dominican monastery. All rooms have been recently renovated and the bathrooms sparkle with Mr. Clean, twice as bald and half as pious (doubles 15zł per bed; dorms 11-14zł per bed). The four basic food groups are all available at the **grocery,** ul. Paderewskiego (open Mon.-Fri. 8am-9pm, Sat. 8am-8pm, Sun. 9am-7pm). **Restauracja Zamkowa,** ul. Zamkowa 1 (tel. 28 05), in the palace, serves up tasty soups (2-5zł) and main dishes (10-17zł) in stately dining halls the color of clear *barszcz* (open daily 9am-10pm; 2zł).

■ Przemyśl

Less than a *złoty's* toss from the Ukrainian border, Przemyśl exhibits an Eastern flair that no other Polish city can match. Travelers headed south occupy hotels around the train station and help each other with linguistic matters. Farther out, in the Old Town, churches stand on every corner, and on Sundays, the city resonates with the sound of Catholic masses broadcasting from the many outdoor loudspeakers.

Orientation and Practical Information The **bus station,** ul. Czarnieck-iego, is across the tracks from the **train station** at pl. Legionów, a five-minute walk from the city center. From the bus station, cross the train tracks through the tunnel marked "Peron 1, 2, 3, 4," and you will emerge at the train station. Take a diagonal right onto ul. Sowińskiego after Orbis, then turn right on **ul. Mickiewicza,** the main road which veers to the right again and becomes **ul. Jagiellońska** after 100m. To reach the *rynek,* head straight from ul. Mickiewicza along the much narrower **ul. Franciszkańska,** bearing left at the fork. **Trains** (tel. 784 031) chug to: Warsaw (5 per day, 7hr., 22.60zł); Kraków (11 per day, 4hr., 20.40-25zł); Lublin (2 per day, 4hr., 19.50zl); Tarnów (14 per day, 3hr., 16.65zł); Ivano-Frankivsk, Ukraine (1 per day, 30zl); and Lviv (2 per day, 4hr., 19.50-27.50zł). The station has **luggage storage** (2.80zł per day). **Buses,** ul. Czarnieckiego (tel. 785 435), travel to Lublin (4 per day, 4hr., 18zł) and Lviv (15 per day, 3hr., 15zł). The Lviv buses are always packed with Ukrainian and Polish merchants. After the *rynek,* the street turns into **ul. Grodzka. PTTK,** ul. Grodzka 1 (tel. 783 274 or 782 725), carries **maps** (3zł) and guides (1.50zł), and gives tips on sightseeing (open Mon.-Fri. 8am-3pm). **Orbis,** pl. Legionów 1 (tel. 783 366), handles international bus tickets; when pressed, they will also offer information on Przemyśl (open Mon.-Fri. 7:30am-7pm, Sat. 8am-3pm). **Bank PKO S.A.,** ul. Jagiellońska 7 (tel. 783 459), handles **traveler's checks** and Visa, MC, and EC cash advances (open Mon.-Fri. 8am-6pm, Sat. 10am-2pm), but *kantors* give better rates on cash. The **pharmacy** sits at ul. Jagiellońska 6 (tel. 782 506; open Mon.-Sat. 7:30am-9pm, Sun. 8am-8pm, but someone is on call 24hr.). The **post office** does the usual at ul. Mickiewicza 13 (tel. 783 270; open Mon.-Fri. 7:30am-8pm, Sat. 8am-2pm, Sun. 9am-11am). **Telephones** (tel. 786 718) are in the post office (open daily 7am-9pm). **Postal code:** 37-700. **Phone code:** 010.

Accommodations and Food To get to **Youth Hostel Matecznik,** ul. Lelewela 6 (tel. 706 145), take bus #2, 2a, or 14 from ul. Mickiewicza toward the center (2 stops). Ul. Lelewela is the second main drag across the river, and Matecznik lies 100m farther on the right, set back from the road. (Singles 11zł, students 9zł; doubles 28zł, students 20zł; triples and quads 13zł per person, students 11zł. 8- to 12-bed dorms 11zł, students 9zł. 20% discount with IFYH or PTSM card. Lockout 10am-5pm. Open year-round. Reserve a week in advance.) The central, carpeted **Dom Wyciec-zkowy PTTK "Podzamcze,"** ul. Waygarta 3 (tel. 785 374), sits down the hill off ul. Grodzka. Rooms are spic and span, but bring toilet paper. (Triples and quads with sink 14zł per person. Doubles 32zł. 19-bed dorms 10.50zł, but the sheets may be shorter than the beds. Reservations recommended.). **Dom Wycieczkowy Prze-mysław,** ul. Sowińskiego 4 (tel. 789 031), stands across from the train station, on a small street off the right side of pl. Legionów. If you don't reserve ahead, Russians and Ukrainians may beat you to these crumbling, overpriced rooms (singles 27zł, doubles 36zł, triples 47zł, quads 63zł, quints 64zł). Management claims there is a shower.

You can buy milk or *wódka* at the **grocery,** pl. Na Bramie 5 (tel. 783 503), between the train station and the *rynek* (open Mon.-Sat. 7am-7pm, Sun. 8am-12:30pm). Cross the bridge to ul. Focha 2 for a vast selection of food and goods at the **Delikatesy** (open Mon.-Sat. 6am-10:30pm, Sun. 8am-10:30pm). You'll find 39 kinds of pizza at **Pizzeria Margherita,** Rynek 4 (tel. 787 347), as well as service you probably weren't expecting. Absorb UV rays in the garden, or relax inside this popular hang-out (small 3.20-5.70zł; large 5.90-11zł; spaghetti 5.60-11.50zł; open daily 11am-11pm). **Polonia Restaurant,** ul. Franciszkańska 35 (tel. 785 778), serves up big food for little prices (cutlets 6-9zł, veggie dishes 2.50-6zł; open Mon.-Wed. 10am-10pm, Thurs.-Sun. 10am-midnight; **disco** once a weekend 6pm-midnight).

Sights The twisting cobblestone streets of the city center and the paths along the river make for nice strolling. The austere **Katedra** on ul. Grodzka and ul. Katedralna was closed for repairs in 1997, but for a Betsey Johnson-esque interior, check out the **church** on ul. Franciszkańska. Above the town, on ul. Zamkowa, stands the white, Renaissance **zamek,** with views of Przemyśl and the river San below (open 10am-

6pm, Oct.-March 10am-4pm; entrance to tower 0.80zł, students 0.40zł). The **Carmelite Monastery,** ul. Karmelicka, boasts Italian-cast bells that ring on the hour; its corresponding **convent** sits up the hill farther on ul. Tatarska.

Down the hill, **Museum Diecezalne,** ul. Śnigurskiego 2, has a room devoted to Polish Catholic, Ukrainian Greek Catholic, and Jewish artifacts. A shrine to Pope Jan Pawel II ends the tour. Monks and nuns run the place; donations are encouraged (open May 3-Oct. 30 daily 10am-3pm). Next door, **Museum Narodowe,** ul. Śnigurskiego 3, houses archaeology exhibits, paintings, and icons (open April-Sept. 9am-6pm; Oct-Mar. daily 10am-4pm, 1zł, students 0.50zł).

ŚLĄSK (SILESIA)

West of Kraków, Śląsk (Silesia) became Poland's industrial heartland when uncontrolled Five-Year Plans tore out the land's coal, iron, and zinc, replacing these resources with heavy pollution. Farther west, Dolny (Lower) Śląsk managed to confine heavy industry, protecting its castles and Sudeten mountain spas. The Śląsk coal mines provided crucial support for the Solidarity movement; after the initial rush, however, they are now experiencing unemployment and stagnation. Fortunately, the heavy influx of German tourists coming to visit—and sometimes to reclaim—the farms and tenement houses of their parents keeps the area economically afloat. Western brand names, from blue jeans to fast food chains, are almost unavoidable.

■ Katowice

Known as an industrial core and magnet for businesses, Katowice (KA-toe-VEE-tseh) is not likely to be anyone's final destination, but most travelers in Poland find themselves in its huge train station at some point. The center's soot-covered architectural splendor, friendly inhabitants, and active nightlife make it a decent place to pass a few hours. Outside the center, the jumble of towering commercial structures vanishes, leaving only pollution and rows of poverty-stricken Soviet-style apartments.

Orientation and Practical Information The **train station,** situated in the heart of Katowice, serves as a major transportation hub, with direct links to: Berlin (2 per day, 9hr., *couchette* 50.31zł); Bratislava (1 per day, 5hr., *couchette* 23zł); Budapest (2 per day, 8hr., 154zł); Cieszyn (1 per day, 1½hr., 12zł); Kiev (1 per day, 24hr., *couchette* 61zł); Kraków (20 per day, 2hr., 7zł); Lviv (1 per day, 12hr., *couchette* 90zł); Prague (2 per day, 7hr., *couchette* 17zł); Vienna (2 per day, 6hr., *couchette* 17zł); and Warsaw (14 express per day, 2½hr., 29.40zł). The **bus station,** only three blocks away on ul. Piotra Skargi (tel. 153 83 14 or 589 917), has connections to many western European countries, including Austria, France, Germany, Great Britain, Italy, Norway, and Spain. **Buses** (red tickets) and **trams** (blue tickets) run throughout the city; buy tickets at kiosks (1.20zł) or on the bus/tram (1.50zł). **Almatur,** ul. 3-go Maja 7 (tel. 598 858 or 596 418; fax 589 782), a two-minute walk from the train station toward the *rynek,* arranges excursions and sells international bus tickets (open Mon.-Fri. 9am-5pm, Sat. 9:30am-2pm). Looming and booming **banks** are everywhere, especially on ul. Warszawska and ul. Mickiewicza. **Bank PKO** gives EuroCard, MC, and Visa advances and cashes traveler's checks. One of their 11 Katowice branches is between the train and bus stations at ul. Chopina 1 (tel. 10 69 75 21; open Mon.-Fri. 8am-6pm, Sat. 9am-1pm). The **post office** is on ul. Pocztowa, which branches off from the *rynek* (open Mon.-Fri. 7am-8pm, Sat. 8am-1pm). **Postal code:** 40-001. The **telephones** within the post office are open 24hr. **Phone code:** 032.

Accommodations and Food The new **youth hostel,** ul. Graniczna 27a (tel. 313 799), is a good 15-minute walk from the center. Or take any tram from the rotunda heading away from the train station to the third stop; the hostel is a few

POLAND

blocks down on the left. The hostel is currently under construction, but should be open in 1998. **Hotels** cost more than they should in this business-saturated town. **Hotel Polonia,** ul. Kochanowskiego 3 (tel./fax 514 051), is relatively cheap (singles 65zł, with bath 76zł; doubles 99zł, with bath 125zł). The smoky, red-and-black decor of **Hotel Centralny,** ul. Dworcowa 9 (tel. 153 90 41), gives it a seedy feel, though the rooms are clean (singles 67zł, with bath 78zł; doubles 108zł, with bath 120zł).

Ul. Stawowa, the tiny street shooting off from the train station, is full of restaurants and fast food. The restaurant in **Hotel Polonia,** a 5-minute walk from the train station, serves inviting and cheap food in a rather bland atmosphere (soup about 1.70zł, average main dish 8zł). For more flavor, go to **Biala Brama,** ul. Chopina 4. Elegantly lined with silver chairs, the cafe offers many different drinks and pastries for reasonable prices (espresso 2.60zł, *adwokat*—cognac and eggs—6zł, liqueur and kiwi juice 5zł; open Mon.-Sat. 10am-8pm, Sun. noon-8pm). A **late-night grocery store** can be found next to the train station—look for Delikatesy signs.

Sights and Entertainment   The **Muzeum Śląskie** (Silesian Museum), ul. Korfantego 3 (tel. 585 661; fax 599 804), houses regional and national Polish painting and historical artifacts. The building was turned into apartments during the Communist era; it reopened in June 1989, but some rooms are still undergoing renovation (open Mon.-Fri. 10am-5pm, Sat.-Sun. 11am-4pm; 5zł, students and children 3.50zł, Sat. free.) Located in a former tenement house, the **Muzeum Historii Katowic,** ul. Szafranka 9 (tel. 156 21 34 or 156 18 10), shows models of the interiors of 19th- and 20th-century middle-class homes (open Tues. and Thurs. 10am-3pm, Wed. and Fri. 10am-5:30pm, Sat.-Sun. 11am-2pm; 2zł, students 1zł). The popular **Park Kultury i Wypoczynku** (Park of Culture and Recreation) lies on the outskirts of Katowice in the suburb Chorzów, about a 20-minute tram ride from the center (#6, 11, or 41 from rotunda, heading toward the left with the train station behind you). The Śląskie Stadium, a zoo, and a planetarium and astronomical observatory are all included in this grand park, one of the biggest in Europe (open 10am-dusk).

The city has a lively nightlife, especially during the academic year. The creaky wooden floors of **Amsterdam Klub Muzyczny,** ul. Słowackiego 13 (tel. 253 81 42), swell with students and others drinking *Żywiec* (0.5L 4zł) and listening to live and recorded jazz, acid jazz, and reggae (open Sun.-Thurs. 4pm-midnight, Fri.-Sat. until about 1am; no cover). The stark but popular **Klub Studencki "Akant,"** ul. Teatralna 9, attracts a mixed crowd, not just students—maybe it's the cheap beer (0.5L *Żywiec* 3.50zł). On Fridays and Saturdays, it turns into a discotheque (open Sun.-Thurs. noon-10pm, Fri.-Sat. noon-2am). For gay nightlife, **Prima,** ul. Węglowa, is the place to be on Friday nights (all other times it's closed). **Tropicana,** ul. Mariacka 14, is also popular among young gays (open nightly).

■ Częstochowa

Częstochowa (CHEN-sto-HO-va) is Poland's Catholic Mecca. Every year, thousands make the pilgrimage to the towering monastery on Jasna Góra to see the most sacred of Polish icons: the *Black Madonna*. Even in this spiritual center, the legacy of Communism is evident: the monastery has a perfect view of towering smokestacks. Despite this reminder of dark days, however, the immaculate, tree-lined streets make Częstochowa warm and welcoming for an international array of visitors.

ORIENTATION AND PRACTICAL INFORMATION

Częstochowa lies about 100km northwest of Kraków. The main **train** and **bus stations,** connected at the south end of the railway station's platform #4, are located close to the town center and linked with **Jasna Góra** to the west by **al. Najświętszej Marii Panny** (NMP; Avenue of Our Lady). From the train station, turn right on al. Wolności to get to al. NMP. The tourist office and the cheapest sleeps gather at the base of the monastery.

Tourist Offices: WCIT, al. NMP 65 (tel. 241 360; fax 243 412). Fanatically orga-nized; provides a free map and detailed info on hotels. Open Mon.-Fri. 9am-6pm, Sat.-Sun. 10am-6pm. **Jasnogórskie Centrum Informacji (IT),** ul. Kordeckiego 2 (tel. 653 888; fax 654 343), inside the monastery near the entrance to the cathe-dral. English-speaking staff sells maps and English guidebooks (5zł), arranges mon-astery tours in English (70-100zł, depending on group size), and makes reservations for Dom Pielgrzyma. Office also has an **ATM** connected to the Visa, MC, and Cirrus networks. Office and ATM open June-Oct. daily 7am-8pm; Nov.-May 8am-5pm.

Currency Exchange: *Kantors* throughout the city. **Bank PKO S.A.,** ul. Kopernika 17/19 (tel. 655 060), several blocks south of al. NMP off ul. Nowowiejskiego. Cashes traveler's checks for 1% commission; MC and Visa cash advances. The **ATM** (24hr.) is connected to Plus and Visa. Open Mon.-Fri. 8am-6pm, Sat. 10am-2pm.

Trains: Częstochowa Główna, ul. Piłsudskiego 38 (tel. 241 337). To: Katowice (36 per day, 2hr., 7.40zł); Kraków (7 per day, 2hr., 19.60zł); Warsaw (7 per day, 3hr., express 18.50zł); and Wrocław (2 per day, 3½hr., 11zł).

Buses: al. Wolności 45/49 (tel. 246 616). Turn left on ul. Wolności when leaving the train station. To: Kraków (4 per day, 3hr., 13zł); Warsaw (4 per day, 4hr., 17.50zł); and Wrocław (5 per day, 4hr., 16zł).

Luggage Storage: At the train station (1.12zł, plus 0.32zł for every 50zł declared). Open 24hr., with 30min. breaks at 6:45am and 6:45pm. Also at the monastery, for a donation. Open June-Oct. daily 6am-6pm; Nov.-May 7am-5pm.

Pharmacy: al. NMP 50 (tel. 246 274). Open Mon.-Fri. 8am-9pm, Sat. 8am-2pm.

Post Office: ul. Orzechowskiego 7 (tel. 241 125 or 242 959), between the bus and train stations. Open Mon.-Fri. 7am-9pm, Sat. 7am-2pm. **Postal code:** 42-201.

Telephones: At the post office. **Phone code:** 034.

ACCOMMODATIONS AND CAMPING

The best deals sit at the foot of Jasna Góra. Higher prices by the train station reflect only the convenient location. Reservations are strongly recommended all year, but are a must for early May and mid- to late August.

Dom Pielgrzyma im. Jana Pawla (The Pilgrim's House), ul. Wyszyńskiego 1/31 (tel. 247 011; fax 651 870), outside the west gate of the monastery. A large operation with homey, spacious, and clean rooms. Very popular; miraculous prices. Religious paraphernalia proliferates. Singles 42zł; doubles 47zł; triples 69zł; all with bath. Quads with sink 48zł.

Dom Pielgrzyma—Hale Noclegowe, ul. Klasztorna 1 (tel. 656 688, ext. 224), just southeast of Jasna Góra's west gate. For the ascetic pilgrim. Clean bedrooms and communal bathrooms, but no hot water. 3- to 10-bed dorms 9zł per person.

Youth Hostel, ul. Jasnogórska 84/90 (tel. 243 121). From al. NMP, go right on ul. Dąbrowskiego, then left on ul. Jasnogórska. At the hostel sign, go to the end of the long alley. Lockout 10am-5pm. Curfew 10pm. 6zł per person. Sheets 1.50zł. Open July-Aug. only.

Camping Oleńka, ul. Oleńki 10/30 (tel. 247 495), across the parking lot from the west gate of the monastery, near Dom Pielgrzyma. A sprawling complex with sur-prisingly clean and comfortable rooms. Kitchen facilities. Tent space 6zł per per-son. Bungalow singles 15zł; doubles 30zł; triples 54zł; quads 72zł; quints 90zł; all with bath. A bring-your-own-tent party. Open year-round.

FOOD

Although food options are not as plentiful as in other cities, no one is going to starve—unless they're fasting. Numerous kiosks sell cheap snacks, including *zapie-kanki*. **Solidom,** al. NMP 75, welcomes shoppers to its hallowed halls of post-Com-munist consumerism (open Mon.-Sat. 6am-9pm, Sun. noon-8pm).

Pod Gruszką (Under the Pear), al. NMP 37 (tel. 654 490), next to Almatur in a little courtyard. Popular student hangout with huge wax-dripping candles adorning tables laden with salads (15-20zł per kg) and *Żywiec* (3zł). More of a cafe at night. Open daily 10am-10pm, sometimes later.

Bar Herbaciarnia, ul. Wyszyńskiego 1/31 (tel. 24 70 11, ext. 288), at Dom Piel-grzyma. Big, simple self-serve main dishes (2-6zł), soups (1zł), and salads (2zł) dished up in a modern dining hall. Open daily 7am-8pm, off-season 7am-7pm.

Klub Muzyczny Stacherczak, ul. Racławicka 3 (tel. 246 235), 1 block off al. NMP at the corner with ul. Dąbrowskiego. Chinese food and music in a posh setting. Main dishes 5-20zł. Open daily 11am-midnight. AmEx, MC, Visa.

Restauracja Cepelianka, al. NMP 64, located in a student center complete with movie theater. A younger crowd, though older patrons feel at home, too. Meals 5-10zł, beer 3zł. Open daily 11am-11pm.

SIGHTS

Klasztor Paulinów (Paulite Monastery), on top of **Jasna Góra** (Bright Mountain), is *the* sight in town. The monastery, which resembles a Baroque fortress, was founded in 1382 by Duke Władysław Opolczyk, who also donated the epiphany-inducing painting *Blessed Mother and Child* in 1384. What the masses of pilgrims travel here to see, though, is the reportedly miraculous **Czarna Madonna** (Black Madonna). A Byzantine icon (ca. 500-700, though some believe it to be a painting by St. Luke), the *Czarna Madonna* was desecrated in 1430 by Hussites and later restored. Two scars said to have appeared on the Madonna's cheek serve as a reminder of the sacrilegious conduct of the Hussites and as proof to the faithful that the miraculous icon could not be destroyed. Legend has it that the icon has also defended Polish troops during bat-tle. The ornate 15th-century **Bazylika** houses the icon inside the small **Kaplica Matki Bożej** (Chapel of Our Lady). Countless crutches, medallions, and rosaries strung upon the chapel walls attest to the faith of the pilgrims in the painting's otherworldly powers. (Chapel open daily 5am-9:30pm. Icon revealed Mon.-Fri. 6am-noon and 1-9:30pm, Sat.-Sun. 6am-1pm and 2-9:30pm. Everything in Jasna Góra is free of charge, but donations are encouraged.)

The monastery also houses a large **treasury** that contains invaluable art works, many of them donations by pilgrims: monstrances, chalices, candelabra, liturgical vestments, and jewelry (open daily 9-11:30am and 3:30-5:30pm). The **Arsenał** exhib-its weapons, military insignia, medals, and orders, including many from World War II (open daily 8-11:30am and 2-5:30pm). **Muzeum Sześćsetlecia** (Museum of the 600th Anniversary) commemorates the founding of the church and monastery and contains an impressive collection of 17th- to 19th-century musical instruments (open daily 11am-4:30pm). A climb up the **tower** (open daily 9am-noon and 2:30-6pm) and a walk around the fortifications afford magnificent views of the region.

The largest pilgrimages and crowds converge on the monastery during the **Marian feasts and festivals.** These include: May 3 (Feast of Our Lady Queen of Poland), July 16 (Feast of Our Lady of Scapulars), August 15 (Feast of the Assumption), August 26 (the Feast of Our Lady of Częstochowa), September 8 (Feast of the Birth of Our Lady), and September 12 (Feast of the Name Mary).

If the heavenly glow of Jasna Góra gets a little too bright, **Katedra św. Rodziny** (Cathedral of the Holy Family) is just on the other side of the train station off ul. Pił-sudskiego. Follow ul. Katedra past Hotel Miły, and the cathedral looms on the right. One of the largest churches in Poland (100m end-to-end), it was erected in 1927 in neo-Gothic style. Facing the left wall as you enter the cavernous interior, note the large plaque honoring Roman Dmowski, the leader of Poland's right-wing nationalists during the interwar period; his image faces (and cringes at) the street named for Józef Piłsudski, his arch-rival.

■ Near Częstochowa: Trail of Eagles' Nests

Just when you've had it up to there with crowded buses, churches, and regional his-tory museums, a trip to the **Trail of Eagles' Nests** reminds you why you love to travel. Along the narrow 100km strip of land known as the **Kraków-Częstochowa Uplands,** numerous crags of Jurassic limestone erupt from rolling green hills. Beginning in the 12th century, **fortifications** were built along the uplands. The natural shape of the limestone was often preserved and incorporated into the design of **castles,** whose perches high on the rocky crags earned them the appellation "eagles' nests." Beginning in the 16th century, the effectiveness of the castles' defenses declined as artillery technology advanced. By the 18th century, most of the fortresses had seriously deteriorated, due to declining economic and political power; many were destroyed by the Swedish invasions. Today, only a few of the castles remain whole, including **Wawel,** in Kraków, and **Pieskowa Skała** just northwest of Kraków. The ruins of the rest still lie along the uplands, waiting to be discovered by trail or by bus.

A **hiking trail** that runs along the entire 100km takes about seven days to walk. **PTTK** in Kraków or Częstochowa can provide **maps.** The trail is marked by red blazes, and maps are regularly posted along the way. The route leads through many small towns where hikers can find tourist info, provisions, and accommodations. The two biggest attractions on the trail, the **ruins at Olsztyn** and the Pieskowa Skała Castle, make easy half-day trips from Częstochowa and Kraków, respectively.

To reach **Olsztyn castle,** take **bus #58** or **58bis** from ul. Piłsudskiego, across from the Częstochowa train station (11 per day, 30min., 1.10zł). Once there, it's hard to miss the ruins, which sit high above the town. The castle, originally constructed in the 12th and 13th centuries, consists of upper and lower parts later flanked by two outer castles. The Swedish army ransacked the complex in 1655, inciting its eventual ruin. In the 18th century, locals appropriated bricks from the partially destroyed castle to rebuild the local church, further reducing the castle's glory. The sole preserved sections are in the **upper castle,** including two **towers.** Ghosts are rumored to haunt the castle; Maciek Borkowic, imprisoned here for his rebellion against King Kasimir the Great, and a young bride lost in the dungeon are the two most haunting apparitions. But if apparitions don't appear, there's always the yellow and purple wildflowers, a view far beyond the towering Jasna Góra, and...mooo...cows.

Wrocław

Wrocław (VROTS-wahv), the capital of Dolny Śląsk, straddles the Odra river. Since the city's elaborate postwar reconstruction (and recent post-Communist restoration), only photographs recall Wrocław's destruction in World War II, when it became *Festung* (Fortress) Breslau under the Nazis, one of the last battlegrounds en route to Berlin. Wrocław charms visitors with its many bridges, lush parks, and 19th-century buildings, all of which give this vast, graceful city an antique feel.

ORIENTATION AND PRACTICAL INFORMATION

The political and social heart of Wrocław is its **rynek.** The **train** and **bus stations** lie 15 minutes southeast of the *rynek;* cheap accommodations cluster by the train station. To get to the *rynek* from the bus station, cross **ul. Sucha,** and go through the station to the main entrance on **ul. Piłsudskiego.** Check out the **map** of the city at the train station's entrance. Then take ul. Piłsudskiego and turn right on **ul. Świdnicka.**

Tourist Office: IT, ul. Rynek 14 (tel. 443 111 or 441 109; fax 442 962). Well-stocked with useful maps (2.50zł). Info in English available. Open in high season Mon.-Fri. 9am-6pm, Sat. 10am-4pm.

Budget Travel: Almatur, ul. Kościuszki 34 (tel. 443 003 or 447 256; fax 443 951), in the student center "Pałacyk." Info about student hostels, ISICs, and international bus tickets. Youth fare bus tickets available here. Open Mon.-Fri. 9am-5pm, Sat. 10am-2pm.

Currency Exchange: At *kantors* throughout the city and in the train station. **Bank PKO S.A.,** ul. Oławska 2 (tel. 444 454), cashes traveler's checks and gives MC and Visa cash advances. Open Mon.-Fri. 8am-6pm, Sat. 10am-2pm. **24-hour ATMs** throughout the city, including pl. Solny 17 (Plus/Visa).

Trains: ul. Piłsudskiego (tel. 688 333). A true traveler's center, with a 24hr. exchange booth, pharmacy, and many eateries. Counters #17 and 18 deal with international links. To: Berlin (3-4 per day, 5½hr., 58.33zł); Budapest (1 per day,

12hr., 100.60zł); Dresden (3 per day, 4½hr., 59.90zł); Kraków (14 per day, 4hr., 21zł); Poznań (18 per day, 1¾hr., 16.65zł); Prague (3 per day, 6½hr., 51.60zł); and Warsaw (9 per day, 5hr., 23.70zł).

Buses: ul. Sucha 1 (tel. 612 299 or 618 122), behind the trains. To: Kraków (destination "Krosno"; 1 per day, 7hr., 26zł); Poznań (2 per day, 3hr., 16zł); and Warsaw (4 per day, 8hr., 29.60zł); also connections to western Europe. Open daily 5am-11pm.

Public Transportation: Trams and **buses.** Tram #0 goes around in circles, so you can never really get lost. Tickets cost 1.20zł (students 0.60zł) per person and per backpack. A 1-day pass is also available (6zł). Purchase tickets at kiosks or, on the weekend, pay on the tram or bus.

Taxis: tel. 919, 633 737, or 210 303.

Luggage storage: At the train station. Open 24hr. 0.73zł per day, plus 0.27zł for every 10zł of declared value.

Pharmacy: ul. Kościuszki 53 (tel. 443 032). Open Mon.-Fri. 8am-9pm.

Medical Assistance: tel. 343 63 69 or 999.

Internet Access: Cyberkawiarnia, ul. Kuźnicza 29a (tel. 723 571 or 447 528; fax 723 058). See **Entertainment,** p. 417.

Post Office: ul. Małachowskiego 1 (tel. 441 717; fax 447 419), to the right when exiting the train station. *Poste Restante* is a few doors down at ul. Małachowskiego 11. Open Mon.-Fri. 7am-8pm, Sat. 9am-3pm. **Postal code:** 50-415.

Telephones: Outside the post office. **Phone code:** 071.

ACCOMMODATIONS

Check with the tourist office for info about renting private rooms.

Youth Hostel (HI), ul. Kołłątaja 20 (tel. 343 88 56), directly opposite the train station on the road perpendicular to ul. Piłsudskiego. Clean, safe, and spacious. Perfect location, too. Lockout 10am-5pm, curfew 10pm. 7-13zł per person.

Hotel Piast, ul. Piłsudskiego 98 (tel. 343 00 33), near the train station. For a quieter stay, request a room that does not face ul. Piłsudskiego. Clean singles 38zł; doubles 70zł; triples 81zł; quads 100zł, all with sinks. Breakfast 9zł.

Hotel Podróżnik, ul. Sucha 1 (tel. 732 845), above the bus station. The visible-from-space-sized rooms may be especially good for families. Doubles with bath 90zł; quads with bath 140zł.

Dom Nauczyciela, ul. Nauczycielska 2 (tel. 229 268; fax 219 502). Take tram #4 from the Hotel Piast stop (direction "Biskupin") or #0 to pl. Grunwaldzki, the 2nd stop after a large bridge. Go left off pl. Grunwaldzki, then turn left again at the gas station. Friendly reception. Singles 37.45zł; doubles 49.22zł; triples 60.99zł; quads 68.48zł; quints 80.25zł.

Camping Stadion Olimpijski, al. Paderewskiego 35 (tel. 484 651). Take tram #17 from the train station and get off at the stadium. 6zł per person; tents 2zł per person; bungalow doubles 24zł; quints 53zł.

FOOD

There are several **24-hour grocery stores: U Pana Jana,** pl. Solny 8/9 (tel. 343 56 85), is convenient to the *rynek*.

Bar Vega, ul. Rynek Ratusz 27a (tel. 443 934). 2 modern, spiffy floors of fast veggie relief. The menus differ by floor—head upstairs for an international flair. Even with a dictionary, the names of the imaginative dishes are hard to decipher—just be adventurous. Full meal under 5zł. Open Mon.-Fri. 8am-7pm, Sat.-Sun. 9am-5pm.

Bar Miś, ul. Kuźnicza 48 (tel. 342 49 63). The polar bear on the sign outside points the way to this bargain cafeteria. The crowds are a sure sign of its popularity. Savor a full meal for 4-5zł. Open Mon.-Fri. 7am-6pm, Sat. 8am-5pm.

Spiż, ul. Rynek Ratusz 9 (tel. 446 856 or 447 225; fax 445 267). Restaurant and microbrewery. Beer lovers lounge in this cool shelter on hot summer evenings. A frothy 0.5L of *Spiż* runs 4.50zł. The menu goes wild with Mexican *platos* (beef tortillas 10zł; gazpacho 5.50zł). Prize-winning ox tongue in beer sauce (10zł). Restaurant open daily noon-midnight; beer cellar open daily 10am-midnight.

Tutti-Frutti, pl. Kościuszki 1/4 (tel. 444 306). Endless list of ice cream desserts (5-12zł) and tortes (3-7zł). Bakery open Mon.-Sat. 9am-8pm, Sun. 9am-6pm. Restaurant open daily 10am-10pm. Take-out ice cream open daily 10am-11pm.

SIGHTS

Wrocław's oldest neighborhood, **Ostrów Tumski** (Cathedral Island), ages peacefully across the river from the center next to the **Ogród Botaniczny** (Botanical Garden), ul. Sienkiewicza 23 (open Mon.-Fri. 8am-6pm, Sat.-Sun. 10am-6pm; 3zł, students 2zł). The stately **Katedra św. Jana Chrzciciela** (Cathedral of St. John the Baptist) gives this section its dignified character. Inside the cathedral, a nun shows off the amazing marble **Kaplica św. Elżbiety** (Chapel of St. Elizabeth; donation requested). Climb up the tower for a phenomenal view of the surrounding churches (open daily 10am-3pm; 2zł, children 1zł). The modern heart of the city, **Stare Miasto,** showcases the Renaissance and Gothic **ratusz** on **Rynek Główny** (Main Market Square) and contains the **Muzeum Historyczne** (tel. 441 434). One exhibit focuses entirely on ul. Świdnicka, a street in central Wrocław so beautiful that the Germans tried to have its stones moved to their soil. Take time to look at the collections of armor and old silver, including an amazing scepter (open Wed.-Fri. 10am-4pm, Sat. 11am-5pm, Sun. 10am-6pm; cashier closes 30min. earlier; 3zł, students 1.50zł; free Wed.).

The **Uniwersytet Wrocławski** occupies much of the city northwest of the *rynek*. A center of Wrocław's cultural life, it contains a number of architectural gems, the most impressive of which is **Aula Leopoldina.** This 18th-century lecture hall, with magnificent ceiling frescoes, is on the second floor of the main University building, pl. Uniwersytecki 1 (open Thurs.-Tues. 10am-3:30pm; 2.50zł, students 1zł).

East of Stare Miasto lies the **Muzeum Panoramy Racławickiej,** ul. Purkyniego 11 (tel. 442 344; fax 336 39). Its 120m by 15m *Panorama Racławicka* depicts the 18th-century peasant insurrection led by Tadeusz Kościuszko against the Russian occupation. Originally painted and displayed in Lviv in 1894, it was transplanted to Wrocław at the end of World War II, along with many of the city's residents. To find the museum, head north from the *rynek* on ul. Kuźnicza and turn right on ul. Kotlarska, which becomes ul. Purkyniego (museum open Tues.-Sun. 8am-5pm; 9zł, students 4zł). Tickets are also valid for the **Muzeum Narodowe** (National Museum), pl. Powstańców Warszawy 5, in the dignified brick building across the street. Check out the medieval Silesian paintings and sculptures, 16th- to 19th-century graphic art, and paintings by Canaletto and Grottger (open Tues.-Wed., Fri., and Sun. 10am-4pm, Thurs. 9am-5pm, Sat. 10am-5pm; 3zł, students 2zł).

The **Cmentarz Żydowski** (Jewish Cemetery), ul. Ślężna 37/39, has recently been opened to the public. Pay your respects to famous citizens such as Ferdinand Lasalle and the family of Thomas Mann's wife (open only Sun. noon; 3zł). To reach the cemetery, take tram #9 from the train station heading away from the center.

Wrocławskie Zoo, ul. Wróblewskiego 1, is famous for torturing its feathered and fuzzy collection less than most zoos in Poland. Take tram #2 or 4 from the train station (dir. "Biskupin") and get off at ul. Wystawowa, next to a massive hall on the left (open daily 9am-6pm; cashier closes at 5pm; 3zł, students 2zł). In northeast Wrocław, the **Morskie Oko beach,** ul. Chopina 27 (tel. 482 717), has kayaks, tennis and volleyball courts, and a weight room (open daily 9am-7pm). An indoor **swimming pool** exudes watery peace at ul. Teatralna 10 (tel. 441 656), in a prewar building in the center of the town. The relaxing **Park Szczytnicki,** with the Japanese house on water, lies in the east part of the city. The gardens were built by Japanese gardeners, just for the hell of it.

ENTERTAINMENT

For up-to-the-nanosecond cultural information, pick up a copy of **Co jest grane** (What's Playing), free at tourist offices. Wrocław is famous for its student and experimental theater; check out the **Grotowski Center,** Rynek-Ratusz 27 (tel. 445 320). The month of May brings the international **Jazz nad Odrą** festival to Wrocław. Tickets are available at clubs **Pałacyk** (see below) and **Rura,** ul. Łazienna 4 (tel. 442 410), Wrocław's resident jazz club. Many student clubs are the place to go for live music.

Szalony Koń (Crazy Horse), Rynek 36 (tel. 441 079), at basement level. In case the posters of Marilyn Monroe and Charlie Chaplin, the albums glued to the wall, or the half-Chevrolet that graces the main room don't clue you in, this place is bad-ass. The barstools are made from saddles, complete with stirrups. A big *EB Czerwone* gives a tasty kick in the head (4zł). Occasional live concerts. Open Sun.-Thurs. 3pm-2am, Fri.-Sat. 3pm until the last guest disintegrates.

Kawiarnia "Pod Kalamburem," ul. Kuźnicza 29a (tel. 447 528), in the theater building in the university area. A decadent, Art Nouveau artists' corner (read: spiffy keen). A large cup of viscous caffeine 3zł. Open Mon.-Sat. 10am-11pm, Sun. 4pm-11pm. Piano concerts every Fri. and Sat. at 9pm. The adjacent **Cyberkawiarnia** (cybercafe; same tel.) provides a variety of teas, coffees, and desserts along with Internet access on new high-speed computers. A great cup of coffee and an hour of Internet use 8zł. Open 10am-10pm.

Night Club "Reduta," ul. Piotra Skargi 18a (tel./fax 723 522), at the end of ul. Teatralna. Popular, in part because there's an outdoor terrace over the main hall, complete with fountain. Cover 10zł. Open nightly 9pm-5am.

Pałacyk, ul. Kościuszki 34 (tel. 38 094). A student disco, cinema, and billiard hall. Movie showings posted in the entrance hall. Billiards open daily 3pm-late. Disco open nightly 9pm-5am. Cover charge Fri.-Sat. 5zł.

Studnia, ul. Szewska 19 (tel. 343 15 13). A small pub near the university that expands its operation to 2 floors when school is in session. *Piast* 2.90zł per 0.5L. Open Mon.-Fri. 4pm-1am, Sat.-Sun. 5pm-midnight. Concerts Oct.-June.

▓ Karpacz

The (non-biting) flies outnumber the (also non-biting) Germans who outnumber the locals in this resort in the Karkonosze mountains. Winter tourists flock for the thrills of skiing, while summer hikers are rewarded with panoramic views above the treeline. Mineral springs and hang-gliding are not far off. The main draw, however, is the raw beauty of the landscape, especially Śnieżka (the highest peak in the Sudety Mountains). If you can stand the unadulterated commercialism of Karpacz, the breathtaking view—even from within the town itself—will be your compensation.

Orientation and Practical Information Since Karpacz's streets are poorly marked and follow the contours of the mountain, it's a good idea to obtain a map and plot your course in advance. The town meanders uphill from the train station along **ul. 3-go Maja.** This main road is concealed from the station by trees and an incline—walk up the concrete stairs and follow the short path to the left. Although there's no main station, **buses** stop at regular intervals along the hill. Get off at the first stop after the **train station** ("Karpacz Bachus") and either go uphill to the Karpacz tourist office or downhill to IT. **Trains** (tel. 619 684) and **buses** both head to Jelenia Góra (3 trains per day, 35min., 2zł; 33 buses per day, 30min., 2.60zł). **Karpacz,** ul. 3-go Maja 52 (tel. 619 547; fax 618 558), exchanges currency, arranges private rooms (20zł), and makes reservations at pensions and hotels (open Mon.-Fri. 9am-5pm, Sat. 9am-2pm). **IT,** ul. 3-go Maja 25a (tel./fax 619 716), speaks German, gives out lots of brochures and maps (3zł), and arranges private rooms (15-25zł per person; open Mon.-Fri. 9am-6pm, Sat. 9am-4pm, Sun. 9am-3pm). Ask at either tourist office about equipment (bikes, skis, rock-climbing, horses) rental or camping. **Bank Zachodni,** ul. 3-go Maja 43 (tel./fax 761 92 52), cashes traveler's checks (US$1.50 commission; open Mon.-Fri. 9am-4pm). There's a **pharmacy,** Pod Złotą Wagą, at ul. 3-go Maja 82 (tel. 619 312; open daily 9am-8pm). The **post office** sends mail at ul. 3-go Maja 21 (tel. 761 92 20; fax 761 95 85; open Mon.-Fri. 7am-9pm, Sat. 9am-3pm, Sun. 9-11am). **Postal code:** 58-540. All **telephones** in Karpacz use magnetic cards, which can be bought at the post office and from most kiosks. **Phone code:** 075.

Accommodations and Food Private rooms proliferate. Pensions start around 15-20zł, including all meals, but hotels can be much cheaper. Unfortunately, some of them are only open part of the year—inquire at the Karpacz tourist office or at IT (see above) for current information. **D.W. Szczyt,** ul. Na Śnieżkę 6 (tel. 619 360), is at the uphill end of town next to Świątynia Wang—take the bus to "Karpacz Wang." At 860m, with views of the valley, Mt. Śnieżka, and the church, these comfortable rooms rule. Make reservations at the Karpacz tourist office (15zł per person). **FWP Piast,** ul. 3-go Maja 22 (tel. 119 244), is downhill across the street from IT. Its spacious singles, doubles, and triples err on the side of brown, but the ping-pong is free (20zł per person, with meals 33zł).

Tourists not pressured into taking meals at their hotel can opt to eat at another pension or at one of the few operations catering solely to the palate. **Astra,** ul. Obrońców Pokoju 1 (tel. 761 93 14), just uphill from IT, serves up large, finger-licking-good meals at slightly high prices. Potato dumplings with meat and salad (6zł), salmon filet with fries and salad (14zł), and spaghetti (7zł) are all reasonable options (open daily 10am-midnight). The grocery store **"Delikatesy,"** ul. 3-go Maja 29 (tel. 761 92 59), stocks everything necessary for a picnic in the mountains (open daily 9am-9pm).

Sights and Hiking Walking to **Świątynia Wang** (Wang Chapel), ul. Śnieżki 8 (tel. 761 92 28), at the upper end of town, takes 1½ hours and limber quads, but the chapel is by far the town's most unexpected and wonderful draw. This Viking church was built in southern Norway at the turn of the 12th century. In the early 1800s, it direly needed restoration no one could afford, so Kaiser Friedrich Wilhelm III of Prussia, out of his love for architecture, had it transported to Karpacz to serve the Lutheran community here. Gaping dragons' mouths, stylized lions, and intricate plant carvings adorn the temple. Organ concerts are held here on Saturday evenings in summer; check the schedule at the ticket office (open in summer Mon.-Sat. 9am-6pm, Sun. 11:30am-6pm; off-season Mon.-Sat. 9am-5:30pm, Sun. 11:30am-1pm; entrance 2zł, students 1zł).

The main question visitors ask is not where you're hiking to, but how you're getting there. Hikers of all ages aim for the crown of **Śnieżka** (Snow Mt.; 1602m), but there are multiple ways of reaching it. Śnieżka and most of the trails lie within **Karkonoski Park Narodowy** (1-day entrance fee 0.50zł, students 0.30zł; 3-day pass 1zł, students 0.50zł). To get to the summit as quickly and painlessly as possible, take the **Kopa chair lift** from ul. Strażacka, just south of ul. Karkonoska, or follow the black trail from Hotel Biały Jar until you see the lift on the left (open daily 8:30am-5:30pm, weather permitting; one-way 7zł, students 5zł; round-trip 10zł, students 8zł). From the top of the chair lift, the hike to the summit takes about one hour. A longer and less crowded trek starts at Świątynia Wang. Follow the blue route up to **Polana** (1080m; 50min.), and then hike up to the scenic **Mały Staw** lake (another 40min.). From here, it's 35 minutes to **Spalona Strażnica** and then an easy 25 minutes to the **Pod Śnieżką** pass (1394m). Ascend to the peak from here (30min.).

Another way to avoid crowds as thick as the swarms of flies involves taking the red path up from behind Hotel Biały Jar's parking circle. One you emerge above the tree line, it's a difficult ascent but still very manageable. The trek to Pod Śnieżką takes 1½ hours, and the summit rises another 20-30 minutes away. Endurance hikers follow the blue trail from Świątynia Wang to Polana, then the yellow path to **Pielgrzymy** (Pilgrims), odd stone formations (1204m; 25min.). Continue along the yellow route to another petrified protrusion at **Słonecznik** (Sunflower; 1423m). Turning left here, the red trail travels to Spalona Strażnica and Pod Śnieżką (1hr.), one mound from Śnieżka.

There are two routes from Pod Śnieżką to the very top. The red "Zygzag" shoots straight up the north side—look for the cobbled path (20-30min.). The blue trail, "Jubilee Way," winds around the peak (30-45min.). Once there, there's a fee to climb to the **observatory,** which looks like it's straight out of *The Jetsons* (1zł, students 0.50zł; open daily 10am-5pm). The lure of most of these hikes lies in the expansive views when above the treeline. Be prepared for strange winds.

■ Jelenia Góra

In Poland's southwest corner, the land buckles along the Czech border to form the Sudety mountains. The crisp air and mineral springs in the Jelenia Góra valley have provided a welcome respite for centuries of city dwellers, including Goethe, Marysieńka Sobieska, and Henryk Sienkiewicz. At the foot of the Karkonosze range (part of the Sudety), Jelenia Góra makes a perfect starting point for treks to loftier hiking and skiing. The renovated turn-of-the-century facades in the town's *rynek* are some of the best-preserved in the region.

Orientation and Practical Information Stare Miasto is ringed by a street that bears the name **ul. Podwale** in the north and west and **ul. Bankowa** in the south. The **train station,** ul. 1-go Maja 77 (tel. 764 69 36), 15 minutes east of town, sees trains off to Warsaw (3 per day, 8hr., 26.40zł) and Wrocław (13 per day, 2½hr., 9.60zł). Most **buses** stop at the train station. The main **bus station,** ul. Obrońców Pokoju 1B (tel. 752 39 36), 10 minutes northwest of town, sends buses to Wrocław (often with a different final destination—check; 4 per day, 3hr.). To get to the center of town, turn right onto ul. 1-go Maja when leaving the train station. Bear (but don't turn) right at the first large intersection, and ul. 1-go Maja will lead you directly to Stare Miasto. The **IT tourist office,** ul. 1-go Maja 42 (tel. 752 51 14; fax 752 40 54), is two streets past that first large intersection with al. Wojska Polskiego. One of the most helpful, friendliest tourist offices in western Poland, it's well-equipped with brochures, maps (2-4zł), and advice. The staff speaks German better than English (open Mon.-Fri. 8am-6pm, Sat. 8am-4pm, Sun. 9am-3pm). **Bank Zachodni,** ul. J. Kochanowskiego 8 (tel. 646 22 59), the second left after the train station, gives Visa cash advances and cashes traveler's checks at 0.5% commission. Western Union money transfers are also possible (open Mon.-Sat. 8am-5pm, Sun. 8am-3pm). A **24-hour ATM** and an **exchange machine** are available at another branch, ul. Bankowa 5/7, just south of the *rynek.* The **post office,** ul. Pocztowa 9/10, lies two minutes south of ul. 1-go Maja, one street past the IT office (open Mon.-Fri. 7am-9pm, Sat. 9am-3pm, Sun. 9am-11am). **Telephones** are next to the post office. **Postal code:** 58-500. **Phone code:** 075.

Accommodations and Food If you're visiting both Karpacz and Jelenia Góra, consider staying in Karpacz, where hotels are cheaper. Jelenia Góra's cramped **Youth Hostel Bartek,** ul. Bartka Zwycięzcy 10, (tel. 752 57 46) is off ul. Kochanowskiego two streets south of the train station (around 6zł per bed). **Hotel Sudety,** ul. Krakowska 20 (tel. 752 93 00), has reasonably priced rooms close to the trains. Go left when leaving the station (singles 32zł, with bath 59zł; doubles 57zł, with bath 96zł; triples 67.42zł; quads 77zł). **Hotel and Camping Park,** ul. Sudecka 42 (tel. 752 69 42; fax 752 60 21), 15 minutes southeast of town on the road to Karpacz, hides in a petite, pretty park (doubles 50zł, triples 55zł; tent sites 5zł per person, tents 7.50zł).

Relax beneath the gleaming white arches of the pl. Ratuszowy arcade at one of the three restaurants rubbing shoulders on the west side of the square. **Pokusa** (Temptation), #12 (tel. 752 53 47), and **Retro,** #14 (tel. 752 48 94), offer traditional Polish food, while **Smok** (Dragon), # 15 (tel. 752 59 28), prepares Chinese dishes. All offer outside dining on the *rynek* (meals at all 3 around 10-20zł; open 10am-10pm). Many cafeteria-type establishments on ul. 1-go Maja provide faster, cheaper options. For a cheapo feast, **Karczma Staropolska,** ul. 1-go Maja 33 (tel. 752 23 50), serves tavern chow (meals 4-8zł; open daily 8am-10pm). Excite your palate with a zesty Hungarian menu at **Tokaj,** ul. Pocztowa 6 (tel. 24 479), across from the post office (main dishes sizzle at 10-20zł; open daily 10am-10pm). **Kawiarnia Hortus,** pl. Ratuszowy 39, brews a great cup o' joe (2-3zł) and chills cool ice cream concoctions (2-5zł; open daily 9am-8pm).

Sights and Entertainment Originally constructed at the turn of the 17th century, after the Thirty Years' War, the market square of **pl. Ratuszowy** had the good fortune to survive World War II without any major damage. Recent renovation has only enhanced the Baroque appearance of the buildings. In the middle of all this, the 1747 **ratusz** displays its unadorned Classicist architecture.

Jelenia Góra's many churches merit an *Amen*. Several steps northeast of the square, the **Kościół św. Erazma i Pankracego** (Church of Sts. Erasmus and Pancras; tel. 221 60) becomes visible at pl. Kościelny 4. This basilica-style church boasts an elaborate 22m by 11m altar. At the intersection of ul. Konopnicka and ul. 1-go Maja, the locked **Kaplica św. Anny** (St. Anne's Chapel) is worth a glance—it originally formed part of the 16th-century town defenses. The 18th-century **Kościół św. Krzyża** (Holy Cross Church), down ul. 1-go Maja, sits in a walled park. Built in the shape of a Greek cross, the 1717 Baroque pulpit is composed of three pieces of limestone. The Michael Roeder **organ** here is one of Poland's largest.

To escape the crowds, an hour-long walk along the green-yellow path away from the bus station leads to the relaxing gorge **Perła Zachodu** (Pearl of the West). Lose yourself in the amazing views over the reservoir.

The 14th-century **Zamek Chojnik,** atop a wooded hill in the suburb of **Sobieszów,** was left in ruins by a 17th-century lightning bolt. The castle tower offers stupendous views of the mountain ranges (open daily 9am-5pm; 1.20zł, students 0.60zł). Hiking opportunities abound; the red trail (45min.) is steeper and rockier than the blue and green routes (both 30min.). To reach the castle, five miles from town, take bus #7, 9, or 15 from the train station or from ul. Bankowa (every 30min., 20min., 1zł—buy the ticket at a kiosk), and get off after the bus turns right at Restaurant Pokusa. Backtrack a bit and follow the signs to Chojnik, across the river and south along dirt paths. If you've planned the trip two weeks in advance, you can stay at **Schronisko PTTK "Chojnik"** (58-570 Jelenia Góra-Sobieszów; tel. 755 35 35), within the castle. The hostel's primary allure is its location (12zł per person; open April 15-Oct. 15). In September, the castle hosts the **Knights' Crossbow Tournament.**

Other local festivals include the May 1st **Antiques and Oddities Market,** which crams pl. Ratuszowy with all sorts of odds and ends sheltered from daylight for centuries. The week-long **International Street Theater Festival** fills the town's narrow streets with open-air performances of juggling and general clowning around in July; for information, contact the **Regional Cultural Center,** ul. Bankowa 28/30 (tel. 752 58 40 or 752 68 18).

WIELKOPOLSKA (GREATER POLAND)

A train ride through the *wielkopolski* lowlands reveals often stunning views of deep green fields and gently rolling hills, as well as a few dense woodlands. The region has its share of sleepy villages and German tourists, and except a few urban pockets, Wielkopolska is as serene as it is culturally rich. At the heart of Poland's religious and political history—which have often gone hand-in-hand—Wielkopolska remains an important attraction for international travelers.

■ Poznań

International trade fairs, a lively music scene, and delectable local food and architecture draw throngs of international businesspeople, musicians, and tourists to Poznań (POSE-nine). Just off the main streets, locals enjoy outdoor meals in the *rynek,* and students seek out good beer in colorful watering holes. Located midway between Warsaw and Berlin, Poznań maintains its unique character after the last photo has been taken and the last briefcase closed.

ORIENTATION AND PRACTICAL INFORMATION

Most of the entertainment, sights, restaurants, accommodations, and services can be found in the central **Stare Miasto.** The main train station, **Poznań Główny,** sits on ul.

POLAND

Dworcowa in Stare Miasto's southwest corner; the **bus station** is 500m down ul. Towarowa. From here, the sights, sounds, and smells of Stare Miasto are either a 20-minute walk or a short bus ride away. On foot, head out of the train station on **ul. Dworcowa** until it ends, then take a right onto **ul. Św. Marcin.** Continue to **al. Marcinkowskiego.** From here, **Stary Rynek,** Stare Miasto's heart, is easily reached by going left, then taking the next right, **ul. Paderewskiego.** Or, catch any **tram** heading down Św. Marcin (to the right) from the end of ul. Dworcowa. Get off at the corner of ul. Św. Marcin and al. Marcinkowskiego for a short walk to the sights.

Tourist Offices: Glob-Tour, ul. Dworcowa (tel./fax 660 667), in the main lobby of the train station. Tourist info in English, maps of Poznań and the region (3-4zł), and a **currency exchange.** Open 24hr. **Centrum Informacji Turystycznej (IT),** Stary Rynek 59 (tel. 852 61 56), in the heart of Stare Miasto. Sells maps of Poznań and surrounding areas (5zł) and provides information in English and German about sights and budget accommodations. Open Mon.-Sat. 9am-5pm. **EUROSTOP** locations are sprouting up around town. The one at ul. Fredry 7 sells ISICs.

Currency Exchange: Bank Polska Kasa Opieki, ul. Św. Marcin 52/56 (tel. 855 85 58), offers excellent rates and cashes traveler's checks (1% commission for Polish currency, 1.5% for foreign). The **ATM** hooks up to Cirrus, MC, Plus, and Visa. There are numerous **kantors** and banks in the city, especially on ul. Św. Marcin.

Trains: ul. Dworcowa 1 (tel. 661 212 or 693 499). To: Berlin (4 per day, 3hr., 93.40zł); Gdańsk (7 per day, 4hr., 22zł); Kraków (6 per day, 6hr., 24.60zł); Warsaw (11 per day, 3½hr., 29.40zł); and Szczecin (11 per day, 3hr., 18.75zł).

Buses: ul. Towarowa 17 (tel. 331 228), near the train station. To Gniezno (41 per day, 40min.-2hr., 4.70zł), and other local towns. Open daily 5:30am-9pm.

Public Transportation: Tram and **bus** tickets are sold in blocks of time rather than per ride. Approximate times are given on the route maps around town (10min. 0.50zł; up to ½hr. 1zł; 1hr. 1.50zł). Students pay half-price. Tickets can be purchased at the Glob-Tour office in the train station or at kiosks. Getting caught empty-handed can result in a fine of up to 50zł. Ticket prices double 11pm-4am.

Taxis: Radio Taxi, tel. 919, 951, 222 222, or 515 515.

Luggage Storage: At the train station. 1zł. Open 24hr.

English Bookstore: Omnibus Bookstore, ul. Św. Marcin 39. Wide selection of paperbacks. Open Mon.-Fri. 10am-7pm, Sat. 10am-2pm.

24-Hour Pharmacy: ul. 23-go lutego 18 (tel. 522 625).

Medical Assistance: ul. Szkolna 8/12 (tel. 852 72 11).

Post Office: ul. Kościuszki 77 (tel. 536 743). Open Mon.-Fri. 6:30am-9pm, Sat.-Sun. 8am-9pm. **Postal code:** 61-890.

Telephones: Everywhere, including outside the main post office. You can also place international calls at the post office. It may be difficult to access some international networks from pay phones. **Phone code:** 0618.

ACCOMMODATIONS

There are three year-round youth hostels. During its fairs (March, June, Oct.), the city fills up quickly with tourists and businesspeople, and most prices rise by at least 10%. Getting a decently priced room without calling ahead at these times is virtually impossible. For **private rooms,** contact **Przemysław,** ul. Głogowska 16 (tel. 658 306; fax 665 163; open Mon.-Fri. 9am-6pm, Sat. 10am-3pm).

Youth Hostel (HI), ul. Berwińskiego 2/3 (tel. 663 680). Take a left out of the train station on ul. Głogowska; ul. Berwińskiego is the second street on the right, about 10min. from the main part of town. Clean rooms in an old school. Wake up to the sounds of children playing. Curfew 11pm. Lockout 10am-5pm. 13.50zł per person, including sheets; HI members 10zł. Reception open daily 5-10:30pm.

Wojewódzki Ośrodek Metodyczny, ul. Niepodległości 34 (tel. 532 251), just a short walk from ul. Św. Marcin (take ul. Niepodległości north about 15min. to the hostel) and Stare Miasto. By bus, take #51 away from the train station to Hotel Polonez and backtrack a block. Spacious rooms on a tree-shaded street. Bathrooms have been known to be less than sparkling. 17zł per person, students 10zł.

Central Poznań

Hotel Wielkopolska, 2
Katedra Piotra i Pawła, 6
Kościół Farny Marii
Magdaleny, 5
Museum of Historic
Musical Instruments, 3
Ratusz, 4
Wojewódzki Ośrodek
Metodyczny, 1

POLAND

Hotel Royal, ul. Św. Marcin 71 (tel. 537 884; fax 517 931), a short walk from the *rynek.* Rooms are on the small side, but prices quite a value for the location. Singles 50zł, 60zł with bath; doubles 80zł.

FOOD

They say food says a lot about a place, and whoever "they" are, they're right about Poznań. Two specialties capture the flavor of this city in edible form: *pyzy,* a cross between noodles and potato dumplings, and *rogale świętomarcińskie,* croissants with various fruit fillings sold by the kilo on November 11, St. Martin's Day. There are several **24-hour grocery stores** around town. Try **Prospero,** ul. Wielka 18 (tel. 523 307), to pick up "just one more" bottle of *Lech Premium,* the local brew of choice (2.50zł), as well as real food.

Cara Mia, Stary Rynek 51 (tel. 523 581). Polish and Italian food, specializing in pizza. Main dishes 9-15zł. Outdoor dining in summer. Open daily noon-11pm.

Bar Mleczny Pod Kuchcikiem, ul. Św. Marcin 37. Traditional Polish food at unbeatable prices. Gorge yourself with a meal of *pyzy* and a bottled Pepsi (3.75zł). Open Mon.-Fri. 8am-7pm, Sat. 8am-4pm, Sun. 10am-4pm.

Cukiernia "U Marcina," ul. Św. Marcin 32 (tel. 526 788). More traditional Polish food at a nice price. Also a small snack bar for a quicker bite to eat. Main dishes 3-5zł. Open Mon.-Sat. 9am-8pm, Sun. 9am-7pm.

Kebap Istanbuł, ul. Głogowska 43 (tel. 663 712), down the street from the train station. Mostly Near Eastern fare (13-17zł). You choose the meat, and they'll cook it for you. Open daily 10am-10pm.

SIGHTS

Poznań seems to be more about "doing" than "looking," but don't let all that action distract you from a number of noteworthy highlights. Downtown, in **Stary Rynek,** opulent 15th-century merchant homes frame the heart of Stare Miasto. Almost all are in fine form, with a rainbow of colors and architectural flourishes worth looking up from your dessert for. They surround the **ratusz,** a multicolored pearl of Renaissance architecture. The original was built in the 13th century and reconstructed by the architect Giovanni Battista di Quadro after a fire. It is deemed to be the finest Renaissance secular monument north of the Alps by whomever decides such things. A portion of the front facade has been restored to its original colorful splendor. Locals and tourists alike consider it to be one of the finest places to sit and eat in the often crowded *rynek.* The *ratusz* houses the **Muzeum Historii Poznania,** Stary Rynek 1 (tel. 525 613; open Mon.-Tues. and Thurs.-Fri. 10am-4pm, Wed. 11am-6pm, Sun. 10am-3pm; 1zł, students 0.60zł, Fri. free; guidebook in English 1zł). In front of the *ratusz* is the menacing **1535 whipping post,** funded by fines paid by maids who dressed too "sharply" for their masters.

Behind the town hall, on the *rynek*'s northeast corner, begins **ul. Żydowska** (Jewish St.), the center of the prewar Jewish district. Its synagogue, built in 1907, was turned into a swimming pool in 1940. On the opposite side of the square, **Kościół Farny Marii Magdaleny,** resplendent with frescoes and pink marble, blesses the end of ul. Świętosławska. It is open to the devout, tourists, and devout tourists during most daylight hours whenever Mass is not being said (at which time two of the three groups above are more than welcome). Organ concerts are held Monday to Saturday at 12:15pm. On a less Catholic note, the **Muzeum Instrumentów Muzycznych,** Stary Rynek 45/47 (tel. 520 857), truly rocks, starring Chopin's own piano and a collection of instruments from Polynesia and Africa, as well as a room full of amazing antique music machines (open Tues. and Sat. 11am-5pm, Wed. and Fri. 10am-4pm, Sun. 10am-3pm; 1zł, students 0.60zł). In the oldest part of town, **Ostrów Tumski,** stands the first Polish cathedral, **Katedra Piotra i Pawła** (Cathedral of St. Peter and Paul), with a ring of 15 chapels. The original building was constructed in 968, soon after the first Polish bishopric was established in Poznań. Burned down in 1945, it was rebuilt after the war in neo-Gothic style. The tombs of two famous Piasts are in the **Kaplica**

Złota (Golden Chapel): Prince Mieszko I (d. 992) and his oldest son, Bolesław Chrobry (the Brave), the first king of Poland (d. 1025). Again, visiting hours are whenever Mass is not going on (daily 9am-4pm).

One of the hardest sights to miss on ul. Św. Marcin provides a glimpse into more recent history. The **park** on pl. Mickiewicz commemorates a clash in 1956 between workers protesting food prices and government troops; 76 people died in the conflict. Two stark crosses are knotted together with steel cable and emblazoned with dates recalling workers' uprisings throughout Poland. An electronic recording tells the story from a console in front of the monument (free, just select your language).

For a quick dip in the hot summer months, go to **Jezioro Maltańskie** (Malta Lake). Take tram #1, 4, 6, or 7 eastbound from the center and get off at ul. Zamenhofa. The year-round artificial **ski slope** here lets you get a jump on ski season.

ENTERTAINMENT

Poznań's lively music and theater scenes change quickly. The monthly **Poznański Informator Kulturalny, Sportowy i Turystyczny (IKS)** contains many useful phone numbers and info in English on all cultural events (5zł; sold at bookstores and some kiosks). All questions about Poznań's music scene can be addressed to the Music Society—**Towarzystwo Muzyczne im. Henryka Wieniawskiego**, ul. Świętojańska 7 (tel. 522 642; fax 528 991), across from Kościół Farny. Posters, pasted all over large stone columns near and along ul. Św. Marcin, alert passersby to local goings-on. Those seeking less formal entertainment (or simply a place to hang out) have options ranging from classy pubs to local yards with kegs and music to neon-and-smoke nightclubs. The *rynek*'s restaurants provide a lively outdoor atmosphere in which to sip cappuccino or gulp beer surrounded by 15th-century wonders.

The Dubliner, ul. Św. Marcin 80/82 (tel. 536 081, ext. 147), located in the Zamek (Poznań Culture Center). The entrance is on al. Niepodległości. A true Irish Pub, run by real Irishmen, offering Irish food, beer, and whiskey, where they teach the Irish saying: "May you be in heaven half an hour before the devil knows you're dead." Pint of Guinness, on tap, in all its opaque magnificence, 9zł. Disco times are announced outside. Open daily 11am-1am.

Dziedziniec Zamkowy, in the courtyard of the Zamek, just past The Dubliner. A spontaneous hangout popular with students. With kegs of 3zł-a-glass beer, loudspeakers, and some benches and trees surrounded by the Pałac Kultury, it's like a backyard party without a house to trash. The variable hours are posted outside.

Stajenka Pegaza (Pegasus's Little Stable; tel. 516 418), corner of ul. Fredry and ul. Wieniawskiego. If you like good beer and sudden musical uprisings, drop by and bring your favorite tape; they'll play it for you. A fun-loving mix of locals and tourists and a number of draft beers make this somewhat out-of-the-way spot one of the places to be, especially on weekend nights. Small *Żywiec* 3zł. Open Mon.-Fri. from 11am, Sat. from noon, Sun. from 3pm, until the last guest leaves, around 2 or 3am.

■ Gniezno

Legend has it that Gniezno (g-NYEZ-no; "nest") was built by Lech, the mythical founder of Poland, as a place to perch. The hamlet is a pocket of tree-lined neighborhoods, tiny shops, and a town square in miniature. The residents took the Pope's visit in June 1997 as an opportunity to repaint, replant, and rebuild, making Gniezno more welcoming and charming than ever. What keeps the tourists (and the Pope) coming is the massive **Katedra Gnieźnieńska,** at the end of ul. Chrobrego, past the *rynek* and a short walk up ul. Tumska. The 14th-century cathedral conceals a history of pre-Christian presence and at least four earlier churches. The first Polish king, **Bolesław Chrobry** (the Brave), was crowned here in 1025, 25 years after Gniezno had become the seat of Polish archbishops. A large, foreboding statue of Bolesław (you'll recognize him from the 20zł note) guards the cathedral on the west side. The bronze 12th-century door presents the life and martyrdom of **Św. Wojciech** in 18 bas-reliefs. His

POLAND

remains compose (and decompose in) various parts of the church. Light coming in at odd angles illuminates the side altars but leaves the main altar, with its ornate spiraling columns, dark and somber. The gratings are as much as 700 years old (church open Mon.-Sat. 10am-5pm, Sun. 1:30-5:30pm; English info available; 2zł).

The serene yard which surrounds the parish buildings leads to the 12th-century **Kościół św. Jerzego** (Church of St. George) and the **Archdiocesan Museum,** ul. Kolegiaty 2 (tel. 263 778), which documents the history of Catholicism in Poland. Especially impressive are the 14th-century ecclesiastical robes, which took more than 20 years to create (open May-Oct. Tues.-Sun. 9am-4pm; 1.50zł, students 1zł).

Gniezno is linked by **train** to Poznań (20 per day, 50min., 10zł) and Toruń (6 per day, 1hr., 8.10zł) and by **bus** (numerous buses daily, 20min.-2hr., 4-6zł). To reach the sights, head straight out of the train station onto ul. Lecha. Make a left onto ul. Chrobrego, and walk 10 minutes to the **rynek,** the center of town. The **Youth Hostel (HI),** ul. Pocztowa 11 (tel. 264 609), near the train station, is connected to the elementary school. Leaving the train station, go right on ul. Dworcowa, which leads to ul. Pocztowa. Be sure to bear left when the road splits to avoid an impromptu tour of the train yards. The pricing is hard to decipher, but clean, spacious one- to eight-bed dorms run 10-21zł (lockout 10am-5pm, curfew 11pm). Provided you don't mind the sound of the motorcycle race course that reaches (literally) to the doorstep, **Hotel Orzeł,** ul. Wrzesińska 25 (tel 264 925), is decent and cheap. Leaving the train station, turn left and walk the two blocks to ul. Warszawa. Take another left, go over the bridge, stay right, and enjoy the next 15 minutes of strolling. Reservations, again, are a good idea (singles start at 30zł; doubles with bath 60zł). Pub-like **Królewska,** ul. Chrobrego 3 (tel./fax 261 497), located in a cellar, boasts sparkling red-and-white tables, a fireplace, and tuxedoed waitstaff serving pork, beef, poultry, and vegetarian options (main dishes 10-15zł; open daily 9am-10pm; menu in Polish, English, and German). Królewska also has a snack bar for a quicker, cheaper meal. For bar food in the 5-10zł range, call on the centrally located **Citybar,** Rynek 15 (tel. 253 535), at any time—it doesn't close. And if you have a moment or an hour, don't pass up a chance to buy some *bułki* (rolls) and wander around the gorgeous park surrounding **Jezioro Jelonek,** just west of the *rynek.*

■ Near Gniezno: Biskupin

The archaeological site on Lake Biskupin contains well-preserved artifacts of an early Iron Age settlement (ca. 1200BC), and features wooden reconstructions of fortifications, roads, and buildings. A daytrip to Biskupin should also include a ride on the **narrow-gauge railway,** complete with coal-powered steam engine. On a sunny day, chug through plains with the breeze in your face for views of farms, wildflowers, lakes, and streams before reaching the Biskupin site, tucked in a wooded area. Even if archaeology doesn't make your clock strike twelve, the ride is not to be missed.

Buses travel from Gniezno to Żnin (1hr., 4zł). Take the 10 or 11am bus in order to have time to see the sights. Żnin can be difficult to reach on weekends and holidays; check with the station the day before your excursion. Once in Żnin, the narrow-gauge steam train to Biskupin can be reached by facing the bus station and going left, then turning right on ul. Dworcowa (9:40am, 12:20pm, 3:20pm, and other times as posted; 4zł). To reach the **ticket booth,** walk across the train tracks and head under the wooden gate (3.50zł, students 2.50zł; English guide 0.50zł). A carved-wood **map** is near the gate. The last train back leaves at 3:26pm.

The archaeological site is best appreciated by first visiting the **museum** in the white building at the end of the entrance road. The museum's **exhibit hall** contains info about Biskupin's culture as well as original tools, personal items, pottery, skeletal remains of Neolithic plant and animal species, and artifacts that show evidence of trade with places as distant as Egypt. The museum also presents human skeletal remains from the Neolithic Period (ca. 10,000BC), and a large chunk of the original settlement. To get to the actual **reconstruction,** head out the front door and back to the main road. Face the ticket booth and go right, following the arrows along a tree-shaded walkway. Visitors lucky enough to be at the reconstruction at precisely 11am will see that yes, indeed, the sun does come a-shinin' in just as the museum said it would. On the right-hand row of houses, park employees wear the closest thing to period dress they could find and demonstrate some of the crafts that were practiced in the Neolithic era to present a model of a more lived-in home. The "Diabel wenecki" ("Venice Devil") braves the little lake every 30 minutes, providing a view of the site from the water (Mon.-Sat. 9am-5pm, Sun. 9am-4pm; 2.50zl at the main gate). Before hopping back on the train, visitors to Biskupin can check out the **experimental archaeology exhibit.** Head back to the museum and go around to the right to get a look at re-created bread ovens and animals that are related to those which inhabitants of Biskupin may have raised or hunted. Even if none of this interests you, go simply to peek at the largest specimen of Polish red cattle you may ever see.

▒ Toruń

Toruń extols itself as the birthplace and childhood home of Mikołaj Kopernik—a.k.a. Copernicus—the man who "stopped the sun and moved the Earth." After strolling through the medieval cobbled streets, visiting the museum, and resting on the promenade along the river, you'll wonder why he ever left. Within the city center, parishioners pray in 500-year-old churches, and children play in the ruins of a Teutonic castle. All the while, life moves on amid the sights and sounds of a town that has matured to a modern city and yet has lost none of its medieval charm.

ORIENTATION AND PRACTICAL INFORMATION

Toruń lies 150km northeast of Poznań. The main **train station, Toruń Główny,** lies across the Wisła from most of the city. Take **city bus** #22 or 27 across the river to reach the center. Buy tickets at any of the little booths outside the station (0.95zł; punch both ends; large luggage requires its own ticket). Toruń has an efficient and expansive public transportation system. To find the **tourist offices,** get off at **plac Rapackiego,** the first stop across the river, and head through the little park area with your back to the bus; they're on your left. To get there on foot, go left on **ul. Kujawska** from the train station, turn right on **ul. 700-lecia Torunia,** and hike over the Wisła. Plac Rapackiego is on the right, after **ul. Kopernika.** The official Toruń tourist information center, **IT,** is located next door to the PTTK. To reach the center from the **bus station,** head away from the buses and through the small park that leads to **ul. Uniwersytecka.** Take a left on ul. Uniwersytecka until it intersects with **Wały Gen. Sikorskiego,** and go right on Sikorskiego until **plac Teatralny.** At plac Teatralny, turn left on **ul. Chełmińska.** Most of the sights are centered around two main areas: **Rynek Staromiejski** (Old Town Square) and **Rynek Nowomiejski** (New Town Square). The two parts of town are divided by **ul. Podmurna.**

Tourist Offices: IT, ul. Piekary 37/39 (tel./fax 621 093). Info on Toruń and Copernicus. Helpful English-speaking staff. Open May-Aug. Mon. and Sat. 9am-4pm, Tues.-Fri. 9am-6pm, Sun. 9am-1pm; Sept.-April closed Sun. **PTTK,** plac Rapackiego 2 (tel. 249 26; fax 282 28). **Maps** and brochures 3-5zł. 2hr. English tour of town 54zł. Open Mon.-Fri. 8:30am-4pm, Sat. 9am-1pm. **Orbis,** ul. Mostowa 7 (tel. 228 73; tel./fax 21 714). Plane and rail tickets. Open Mon.-Fri. 9am-5pm, Sat. 10am-2pm.

Currency Exchange: Bank PKO S.A., ul. Kopernika 38 (tel. 109 15). Cashes AmEx and Visa traveler's checks for 1% commission (min. 5zł). AmEx, MC, and Visa cash advances. Open Mon.-Fri. 8am-6pm. Private *kantors* exchange cash. A **24hr. ATM** at ul. Szeroka 38 is hooked up to AmEx, Cirrus, MC, Plus, and Visa.

Trains: tel. 130 44. To: Warsaw (3 per day, 3hr., 20.40zł); Gdańsk (6 per day, 2½hr., 19zł); Poznań (5 per day, 2hr., 16zł); Szczecin (2 per day, 5hr., 23zł). International *kasa* sells Wasteels and Interrail. Open Mon.-Fri. 8am-5pm, Sat.-Sun. 7am-7pm.

Buses: tel. 228 42. To: Warsaw (5 per day, 17zł); Gdańsk (2 per day, 16.40zł); and Poznań (1 per day, 13zł).

Pharmacies: Apteka Królewska, Rynek Staromiejski 4 (tel. 621 00 17). Open Mon.-Fri. 8am-8pm, Sat. 8am-4pm.
Taxis: Radio Taxi, tel. 91 93.
Post Office: Rynek Staromiejski 15 (tel. 191 00). Open Mon.-Fri. 8am-8pm, Sat. 8am-1pm. **Postal code:** 87-100.
Telephones: At the post office. Open 24hr. **Phone code:** 056.

ACCOMMODATIONS

Toruń has no particular "crunch season"—most visitors seem to be students who simply pile back on the bus at the end of the day. **IT** (see above) has info on accommodations in town and can arrange stays at student hostels (5-12zł per person).

Hotel Polonia, plac Teatralny 5 (tel. 230 28), opposite the municipal theater and down the street from the *ratusz*. Surprisingly large rooms with large beds are in a shady building in a busy part of town. Singles 32zł, with bath 50zł; doubles 42zł.
Hotel Pod Orłem, ul. Mostowa 17 (tel. 210 96; fax 26 397). Huge, comfortable rooms in a quiet corner of the city center. Bathroom facilities a bit spartan. Singles 40zł, with bath 70zł; doubles 50zł, with bath 85zł; triples 80zł, with bath 120zł.
Dom Wycieczkowy, ul. Legionów 24 (tel. 238 55). Take bus #10 outside the Old Town Gate heading away from the river to the 3rd stop. Small, well-kept rooms in a quiet neighborhood a short walk from the center and 3 blocks north of the bus station. Singles 34zł; doubles 42zł; triples 57zł; quads 72zł.

FOOD

Despite the gradual emergence of chains, Toruń has not dropped its centuries-old calling card: **gingerbread** (*pierniki*). Originally sold by Corpernicus's father to put his son through school, it is now offered by the kilo in various forms: covered in chocolate, shaped like Copernicus himself, and myriad other possibilities. Grocery stores in town include **Delikatesy,** ul. Szeroka 29 (tel. 10 540; open Mon.-Fri. 7am-8pm, Sat. 7am-7pm, Sun. 9am-3pm), and **Serdelek,** ul. Szeroka 19 (tel. 27 654; open daily 8am-7pm). The large market **Targowisko Miejskie** sits behind the "Supersam," one block north of the Old Town on ul. Chełminska (open daily 8am-4pm).

Bar Mleczny, ul. Różana 1. This clean, new milk bar serves up primarily vegetarian traditional Polish dishes, as well as a smattering of meat dishes. *Naleśniki,* the house specialty, come with a multitude of fillings. Try them with blueberries and cream (*z jagodami i śmietaną,* 2.80zł). Open Mon.-Fri. 9am-7pm, Sat. 9am-4pm.
Pizzeria Muzyczna "Vir," ul. Browarna 1 (tel. 652 10 14). Perhaps the best pizza in town, in a 3-story loft complete with thick wooden beams, a bar on the 2nd floor, and great pizzas and salads (under 10zł). Occasional concerts at 8pm. Open daily 11am-midnight.
Stołówka Urząd Wojewódzki, plac Teatralny 2 (tel. 182 13). Enter at the Bufet sign and follow the enticing aroma through the underground passageways. A hearty meal for less than 5zł awaits you. Open daily 8am-8pm.
Lotos, ul. Strumykowa 16 (tel. 104 97). Various Far Eastern specialties—Chinese food meets Polish cooks in a setting complete with bamboo and tropical fish tank. Try the "5 Flavored Chicken" (11.60zł) or curried beef (10.20zł). Vegetarian dishes 5-8zł. Open daily 11am-10pm. MC, Visa.
Kopernik Factory Store, ul. Żeglarska 25 (tel. 237 12), and Rynek Staromiejskie 6 (tel. 28 832). Stock up on Toruń's delicious *pierniki* in almost every imaginable form. This place gets mega-crowded, so be patient while visions of gingerbread dance in your head. Open Mon.-Fri. 10am-6pm, Sat.-Sun. 10am-2pm.

SIGHTS

An astounding number of attractions are packed into Toruń's medieval ramparts. **Stare Miasto,** constructed by the Teutonic Knights in the 13th century, saw the birth of renowned astronomer Mikołaj Kopernik (February 19, 1473). His birthplace, **Dom Kopernika,** ul. Kopernika 15/17 (tel. 270 38), has been meticulously restored, and visitors can get a peek not only into the life of Copernicus, but that of 14th-century Toruń in general (open Tues.-Sun. 10am-4pm; 3zł, students 2zł). Dom Kopernika also houses a miniature model of 1550 Toruń (4zł, students 3zł). A traditional 16th-century sound and light show in five languages accompanies your visit (every 30min.).

The **ratusz** (town hall), Rynek Staromiejski 1 (tel. 27 038), stands in the center of the tourist district as one of the finest examples of monumental burgher architecture in Europe. The original Gothic building, which has four wings, was built in the late 14th century, but various elements, such as the turrets, were added throughout the centuries. The town hall now contains **Muzeum Okręgowe** (Regional Museum), where exhibits include the famous portrait of Mikołaj Kopernik from the late 16th century, portraits of wealthy and influential citizens of Toruń, and works of modern Polish art (open Tues.-Sun. 10am-4pm; 3zł, students 2zł). For an additional 2zł (students 1zł), you can climb the medieval 13th-century tower to survey the whole city.

Opposite the *ratusz* stands **Dwór Artusa** (Artus Court), Rynek Staromiejski 5, designed in the 1880s by Rudolf Schmidt. The house was erected on the site of the original Renaissance building—also called Dwór Artusa—which had been the seat of patricians belonging to the Hanseatic League. The building now houses the Toruń Orchestra. **Kamienica Pod Gwiazdą** (House Under the Star), Rynek Staromiejski 35 (tel. 211 33, ext.16), originally a Gothic building, was later redone in Baroque style, with a finely modeled facade decorated with floral and fruit details. During a reconstruction in the late 1960s, fragments of Gothic, late Renaissance, and Classical architecture were uncovered. This odd bird blends well with its equally varied neighbors. Check out the exhibits on the arts of the Far East (open Tues.-Sun. 10am-4pm; 3zł, students 1zł). **Dom Eskenów**, ul. Łazienna 16 (tel. 270 38, ext. 14), exhibits 20th-century Polish painting and military uniforms from medieval times to the early 20th century (open Tues.-Sun. 10am-4pm; 2zł, students 1zł).

The **Ruins of the Teutonic Knights' Castle,** ul. Przedzamcze, continue to fascinate visitors. The 14th-century **toilet tower** served its lords as indoor plumbing and a repository of smelly defense—back in those days, they didn't just *fart* in the enemy's general direction. The 13th-century castle was destroyed by a city-wide burghers' revolt on February 8, 1454. The **Leaning Tower,** ul. Krzywa Wieza 17, is another unique building of Teutonic origin. Built in 1271 by a knight of the order as punishment for falling in love with a peasant girl, the 50-foot tower—the "Leaning Tower of Poland"—now deviates 5ft. from the center at its top.

Among the tall Gothic churches that crop up everywhere, **Bazylika Katedralna pw. św. św. Janów** (Cathedral of St. John the Baptist and St. John the Evangelist) is the most impressive of its kind. Built during the 13th to 15th centuries, it mixes Gothic, Baroque, and Rococo elements. The tower contains Poland's second-largest bell, cast in 1500, and the chapel witnessed Kopernik's baptism in 1473. From here, it's a short walk across the *rynek* to ul. Panny Marii and **Kościół Św. Marii** (Church of the Virgin Mary). It's not open to the public, but it's worth stopping by for the view from the street of the eerily high aisle and stained glass. At the end of a long day, stroll along the **Bulwar Filadelfijski**—named for Toruń's sister city, Philadelphia—among lingering couples who line the stone steps to the river, where outdoor eating spots offer a place to sit and watch the local fishermen wait for a bite.

ENTERTAINMENT

Student life revolves around Miasteczko Akademickie—"little academic town"—reached by bus #15 from ul. Odrodzenia 7 to the end of the line at ul. Sienkiewicza. The entertainment is tucked away just off ul. Gagarina in the neighborhood by the bus stop. In Stare Miasto, music can be found at the **Blue Music Club,** ul. Browarna 1 (tel. 193 20), off Rynek Nowomiejski. The entrance is around the corner from the pizza place next to ul. Wielkie Garbary 1 (open Thurs.-Sat. from 8pm, cover 5zł). For daytime adventures, **Hotel Aeroklub Pomorski,** ul. Bielańska (tel. 224 74; fax 263 29), offers the opportunity to **parachute** or fly **gliders** (430zł per hr. for 3 people, minimum 10min.).

Pub Czarna Oberża (Black Inn), ul. Rabiańska 9 (tel. 109 63). Local students favor this billiards and beer hangout. Impressive selection of imported beer, including Guinness and Kilkenny (7.80zł). *Żubrówka* vodka and apple juice 4.50zł. Open Mon.-Thurs. 1-11pm, Fri.-Sat. 1pm-midnight, Sun. 2-11pm.

Piwnica Pod Aniołem (tel. 270 39), in the basement of the *ratusz*. A slightly older crowd in a much older building. Open Mon.-Fri. 10am-1am, Sat.-Sun. 10am-2am.

Kawiarnia Pod Atlantem, ul. Św. Ducha 3 (tel. 267 39). Feast on coffee, cakes, and ice cream (3-6zł) while seated in truly royal plush chairs. Open daily 10am-10pm.

Kawiarnia Flisacza (tel. 257 51), on ul. Flisacza, overlooking the Wisła. Don't be scared away by the spikes and barbed wire; you're more than welcome to sit here and enjoy cafe treats and a variety of food. Open daily 10am-10pm.

▦ Łódź

It's time to give Łódź (WOODGE) some credit. Its reputation as an industrialized pit has prevented many from discovering the museums, architecture, and—yes—beauty of this much-maligned city. Tourist offices tend to promote the more international Warsaw to the northeast, the more picturesque Toruń to the north, or the more pious Częstochowa to the south. But this 15th-century city, second in size only to the capital, is home to numerous points of interest, including the famous Łódź film school, which has produced such luminaries as Andrzej Wajda and Krzysztof Kieślowski. During WWII, Łódź was the site of the largest ghetto in Europe, and anyone interested in the history of Poland's Jews will not want to miss its sights.

ORIENTATION AND PRACTICAL INFORMATION

The main drag, **al. Piotrkowska**, runs north-south in easy walking distance from both train stations. Lined with restaurants and shops, a large section of the street is pedestrianized from **ul. Traugutta** in the north to **Al. Marsz. Józefa Piłsudskiego** in the south. Accommodations and museums are nearby. From **Łódź Fabryczna,** the main train station, cross **al. Jana Kilińskiego,** the wide street with multiple tram lines, and head toward Dom Kultury. Continue west two blocks to get to ul. Piotrkowska. From the Łódź Kaliska station, walk southeast to the large traffic circle, turn left onto **al. Adama Mickiewicza,** which becomes al. Marsz. Józefa Piłsudskiego, and continue about 15 minutes to the intersection with ul. Piotrkowska.

Tourist Offices: IT, ul. Traugutta 18 (tel. 337 299; fax 339 902), in Dom Kultury, across al. Jana Kilińskiego from Łódź Fabryczna. A very outgoing bunch with information about sights and accommodations. Entrance in the back of the building. Open Mon.-Fri. 8:15am-4:15pm, Sat. 10am-2pm. **Orbis,** ul. Piotrkowska 68 (tel. 363 533 for flight info, 332 114 for buses), does the Orbis thang (travel bookings and accommodations). Open Mon.-Fri. 9am-5pm, Sat. 10am-2pm.

Currency Exchange: *Kantors* bumble around ul. Piotrkowska. **Powszechny Bank Gospodarczy S.A.,** al. Piłsudskiego 12 (tel. 362 886), cashes traveler's checks and give MC and Visa cash advances. Open Mon.-Fri. 8am-6pm, Sat. 9am-1pm.

Trains: Łódź Fabryczna PKP (tel. 935) sees trains off to Warsaw (8 per day, 2hr., express 14.40zł) and Kraków (1 per day, express 22zł). From **Łódź Kaliska** (tel. 934), trains chug to Toruń (8 per day, 16.60zł). Posted train schedules provide info for both stations.

Buses: Łódź Fabryczna PKS (tel. 319 706) is attached to the train station. To: Warsaw (10 per day, 11.50zł); Kraków (7 per day, 21zł); and Wrocław (4 per day, 19zł).

Public Transportation: Trams and buses cost 1zł for a ride of up to 30min., 1.50zł up to 1hr., 2zł for 2hr., and 4zł for a full-day pass. Prices double at night.

Luggage Storage: At Łódź Fabryczna. **Lockers** come in three sizes: A (3zł per day), B (4.50zł per day), and C (6zł per day). There's also a locked storage room (1.12zł plus 0.32zł for every 50zł in declared value, per day); go to *kasa* #9. Open daily 4:30am-6pm and 8-11pm.

24-Hour Pharmacy: Apteka Hepatica, ul. Piotrkowska 35 (tel. 303 539).

Post Office: ul. Tuwima 38 (tel. 301 752). Open 24hr. *Poste Restante* at window #19 (open daily 7am-9pm). **Fax service** (fax 328 208). **Postal code: 95-000.**
Telephones: At the post office. Open 24hr. **Phone code:** 042.

ACCOMMODATIONS

A number of budget options are centrally located around ul. Piotrkowska. Off the south end, **Schronisko PTSM (HI),** ul. Zamenhofa 13 (tel. 366 599), offers clean, comfortable rooms not far from Łódź Kaliska (singles 16zł, dorms 13zł; curfew 10pm; lockout 10am-5pm). By the north end, the super-classy **Youth Hostel (HI),** ul. Legionów 27 (tel. 330 365; fax 302 377) provides newly renovated singles (27zł) and dorms (22zł first night, 18zł each additional night), with a 25% discount for members (curfew 10pm; lockout 10am-5pm). A little farther down the street, the wary budget traveler encounters **Hotel Garnizonowy,** ul. Legionów 81 (tel. 338 023), a large, simple spot (singles 37.45zł; doubles 47.08zł; triples 62.20zł; quads 85.60zł; dorms 21.40zł). It's not uncommon for managers to inflate prices slightly for Western tourists, depending on the establishment and mood.

FOOD

Don't ask why, but pizza is the order of the day—maybe Łódź's student population prefers it. Ul. Piotrkowska abounds with pizzerias where it's possible to get a nutritious, extraordinarily filling meal for under 10zł. **Pizzeria "Solo,"** ul. Piotrkowska 41 (tel. 300 132), serves a large variety of equally large pizzas (less than 10zł), as well as Greek salads (3.50zł; open Mon.-Thurs. 11am-9pm, Fri.-Sat. 11am-10pm, Sun. noon-9pm). **In-Centro Pizza,** ul. Piotrkowska 453 (tel. 369 992), is packed with hungry twenty-somethings. Excellent pizza and not so many tables, so make a friend (open Mon.-Sat. noon-10pm, Sun. 1-10pm). **Bar Mleczny,** ul. Jaracza 7, is home to the typical, cheap, and copious food you'd expect from a milk bar. Try the *naleśniki* with strawberry sauce (2zł; open daily 8am-6pm). A **24-hour grocery** sits next to the Zamenhofa hostel (see above).

SIGHTS

In addition to the colorful, newly restored Baroque facades of ul. Piotrkowska, Łódź is home to several sights of historical and cultural interest. One block northwest of the monument at **plac Wolności,** which crowns the northern end of ul. Piotrkowska, stands the grandiose **Poznański Palace,** named for the family of wealthy Jewish industrialists who lived there in the late 19th and early 20th centuries. The ornate gray building, which should be completely renovated by 1998, now houses **Muzeum Historii Miasta Łodzi** (Łódź Historical Museum), ul. Ogrodowa 15 (tel. 540 323; fax 540 202), which includes permanent exhibitions on the Poznański family and the legendary pianist Artur Rubinstein, a Łódź native. Temporary exhibits in 1997 included a biographical exhibit about the emigre writer Jerzy Kosiński, also a Łódź son (open Mon.-Tues. and Thurs.-Sun. 10am-2pm, Wed. 2-6pm; 2zł, students 1zł, Sun. free; guidebook 10zł). Four blocks south from the palace along ul. Gdańska brings you to **Muzeum Sztuki w Łodzi** (Łódź Fine Arts Museum), ul. Więckowskiego 36 (tel. 326 787), home to works by Picasso, Kandinsky, and other impressive 20th-century artists (open Tues. 10am-5pm, Wed. and Fri. 11am-5pm, Thurs. noon-7pm, Sat.-Sun. 10am-4pm; 3zł, students 2zł, Thurs. free).

Ever wonder where such international film giants as Andrzej Wajda, Krzysztof Kieślowski, and Roman Polański got started? Well, it so happens that all of the above studied at Łódź's famous film school. They're now immortalized in the **Muzeum Kinomatografii,** pl. Zwycięstwa 1, housed in a mid-19th-century mansion on al. Piłsudskiego. Wajda filmed his *Promised Land* here and left his mark in the form of a broken mirror (open Tues.-Fri. 10am-2pm, Sat.-Sun. 11am-3pm; 1zł).

But the most affecting sight in Łódź, and one of the most beautiful, is the sprawling **Cmentarz Żydowski** (Jewish Cemetery), the largest in all of Europe. There are more than 180,000 tombstones, many of them quite elaborate; but because many Jews

POLAND

from the Łódź Ghetto were buried in unmarked graves, the cemetery contains about twice as many graves as stones. Don't attempt the main gate at ul. Bracka; it's generally kept locked for security reasons. Instead, take tram #1, 15, or 19 north to the end of the line (30min.). Continue up the street to the first corner and make a sharp left turn onto the cobblestone ul. Zmienna, and continue until the small gate in the wall. Near the entrance there's a memorial to the Jews killed in the Łódź Ghetto, and signs lead the way to the **Pole Ghettowe** (Ghetto Fields). Further information is available at **Gmina Wyznaniowa Żydowska** (Jewish Community Center), ul. Zachodnia 78 (tel. 335 156; English spoken), which sells an English-language guide (10zł) to other sights of Jewish interest. (Cemetery open Sun.-Fri. 9am-4pm, closed on Jewish holidays. 2zł admission goes toward maintenance; free for those visiting the graves of relatives).

POMORZE

Pomorze, literally "along the sea," sweeps over the murky swamps and wind-swept dunes of the Baltic coast. In the face of shifting sands and treacherous bogs, fishermen built villages here millennia ago. A few hamlets grew into large ports—Szczecin on the lower Odra River, and Gdańsk and Gdynia in the east—but the landscape in between is still littered with coastal lakes, lagoons, small fishing ports, and the mysterious four-faced totems of Pomorze's ancient inhabitants.

■ Szczecin

Strategically situated on the Odra River, the port of Szczecin (sh-CHAY-chin) has witnessed power plays for centuries. All of this grappling has only increased the city's growth, and railways and waterways sprawl for miles around the center. Szczecin's tightly packed downtown has the most to offer—the city's labyrinthine core commands fleets of historic buildings. These and the shipping port's friendly attitude make Szczecin a popular starting point for tourists arriving from across the sea.

ORIENTATION AND PRACTICAL INFORMATION

Szczecin sits near the German border at the mouth of the Odra River, about 65km from the Baltic Sea coast. You'll need a map, so visit a **tourist office.** This is most easily accomplished by getting off the train at the **Szczecin Główny** train station (the bus stop is a block away) and following ul. Owocowa until it turns left and becomes ul. Dworcowa. Al. Niepodległości shoots to the right off ul. Dworcowa's end. Turn right onto ul. Wyszyńskiego; the **CIT** office is two blocks down, on the right. Almost all sights lie in the rectangular area framed by the **Odra** to the east, **ul. Piłsudskiego** to the north, **al. Piastów** to the west, and the connected **ul. Krzywoustego, pl. Zwycięstwa,** and **ul. Wyszyńskiego** to the south. In between are several traffic circles and divided roads that test your sense of direction at every turn.

Tourist Offices: Centrum Informacji Turystycznej (CIT), ul. Wyszyńskiego 26 (tel. 340 440; open Mon.-Fri. 9am-5pm, Sat. 10am-2pm), and **Szczecińska Agencja Turystyczna (SAT),** al. Jedności Narodowej 1 (tel. 339 253; fax 342 581; open Mon.-Fri. 10am-5pm). Both are excellent sources for **maps** (4.50zł), brochures, and accommodations info. Each also sells little tourist books (5zł). Szczin's **Orbis** office, pl. Zwycięstwa (tel. 344 425), is particularly useful if you plan on crossing a border, though it meets the full range of travel needs and even has a **kantor.** Open Mon.-Fri. 10am-6pm, Sat. 10am-2pm. *Kantor* closes 30min. before office.

Currency Exchange: Pomorski Bank Kredytowy S.A., ul. Bogurodzicy 5 (tel. 880 033). Branches throughout the city. Cashes AmEx and Visa traveler's checks and gives AmEx, MC, and Visa cash advances. Open Mon.-Fri. 8am-6pm. *Kantors* all over town exchange currency at better rates.

Trains: Szczecin Główny sits at the end of ul. 3-go Maja; take tram #1 or 3 north to the center. To: Gdynia (3 per day, 5hr., 23.50zł); Poznań (11 per day, 3hr., 13.80zł);

and Berlin (1 per day, 2½hr., express 70.20zł). **Antique steam trains** (*pociągi turystyczne retro*) run weekends. Schedules posted at the train station.

Buses: pl. Tobrucki, 2min. northeast of the train station. Tickets can be purchased either at the station or through Orbis (see above). Frequent daily connections to Świnoujście and Poznań (around 14zł).

Public Transportation: The city's numerous **tram** and **bus** lines run along most major roads. Fares are 0.60zł for up to 10min., 1zł for 10-40min., and 3zł after 11pm. Schedules, route information, and tickets available at kiosks around town.

Taxis: Auto Taxi, tel. 919. **Radio Taxi,** tel. 96 22. **Super Taxi,** tel. 96 66.

24-Hour Pharmacy: ul. Krzywoustego 7a (tel. 336 673).

Post Office: ul. Bogurodzicy 1 (tel. 346 124). Open Mon.-Fri. 8am-8pm, Sat. 9am-2pm. **Postal code:** 70-405.

Telephones: At the post office. Open 24hr. **Phone code:** 091.

ACCOMMODATIONS

For a complete list of summer youth hostels, which tend to be spartan, contact **Almatur,** ul. Bohaterów Warszawy 83 (tel. 346 356). Budget accommodations in Szczecin become harder to find as summer months draw crowds to the city.

Youth Hostel (HI), ul. Monte Cassino 19a (tel. 224 761; fax 225 401). Take tram #1 from the train station or the center to ul. Felczarka. By foot, it's a short hike through downtown along ul. Wojska Polskiego, followed by a right on ul. Felczarka and a left onto ul. Monte Cassino. Often-crowded rooms of up to 12. Lockout 10am-5pm. Curfew 11pm. Singles 18.60zł, members 14,70zł; dorms 14.60zł, members 6.90zł. Sheets 3zł. **Bike rental** (1zł per hr.) and **luggage storage** (1zł per day).

Hotel Piast, pl. Zwycięstwa 3 (tel. 336 622). Central ex-police barracks proclaims "Hotel" in black Gothic letters above the oak-shadowed entrance. Scenic downtown location. Singles 46zł, with bath 54.50zł; doubles 71zł, with bath 92zł.

Hotel Gryf, ul. Wojska Polskiego 49 (tel. 334 566; fax 334 030). Gryf offers some of the best-kept rooms in town for the money, all just 5min. from the sights. Popular with a younger crowd; the friendly atmosphere can't help but rub off. Singles 47zł, with bath 60zł; doubles 80zł, with bath 97zł.

"Foundation in Support of Local Democracy" Hostel, ul. Marii Skłodowskiej-Curie 4 (tel. 704 72). In a white school building marked "Zachodniopomorska Szkoła Samorządu Terytorialnego." Take tram #9 to "Traugutta," continue two blocks, turn left, and walk to the end of the street. Worth the long trek northwest from the center. Singles 25zł; doubles 50zł, with bath 76zł; triples 60zł; quads 80zł.

FOOD

The invasion of Western fast-food chains is in full force, but local food still survives in both kiosks and restaurants. The 24-hour supermarket (hey, a *real* supermarket) **Extra** is centrally located at ul. Niepodległości 27 (MC and Visa). A quick meal can be had at one of the many **bars** around town for under 5zł, including **Bar Turysta,** ul. Obrońców Stalingradu 6 (open Mon.-Fri. 6:30am-7pm, Sat. 8am-4pm, 1st and 3rd Sun. of month 8am-3pm). **Lucynka i Paulinka,** ul. Wojska Polskiego 18 (tel. 346 922), treats browsers downstairs with luxury food items and upstairs with sinful desserts, cups of coffee, and stiffer libations. Desserts and coffee start around 2zł (open Mon.-Fri. 9am-9pm, Sat.-Sun. 10am-9pm; MC and Visa accepted). **Pod Muzami,** pl. Żołnierza Polskiego 2 (tel. 347 209), connects to the expensive Hotel Victoria. Brass mirrors and pink lighting dominate the decor; standard Polish fare runs 10-20zł (open daily noon-5am; dancing with live band every night at 9pm; cover 6zł, Sat.-Sun. 10zł).

SIGHTS

A millennium of history and a legacy of occupation, re-occupation, and invasion have left Szczecin's buildings with more than a few stories to tell. Some original structures remain, but much of the city's beauty lies in its restorations. A relic of the Prussian settlement, the Baroque **Brama Portowa** (Port Gate) marks the downtown area with a Prussian flavor, featuring female figures blowing trumpets, a Latin inscription com-

POLAND

memorating King of Prussia Friedrich Wilhelm I, a panorama of 18th-century Szczecin, and Viadus, the god of the Odra, leaning against a jug from which the river's
waters flow. Originally called the Brandenburg and later the Berlin Gate, it was built
in 1725 and spared during the removal of the city fortifications in 1875 because of its
architectural value. Friedrich Wilhelm would be proud.

Time has not been as kind, however, to some of the other structures in downtown
Szczecin. A block away on ul. Wyszyńskiego, the 13th-century **Katedra św. Jana
Ewangelisty** (Cathedral of St. John) looms over the city. Destroyed during WWII, it
has been carefully restored to its original Gothic shape; however, it still patiently
awaits the restoration of its stained glass windows. For a good example of how Szczecin's past meets its present, head for the 870-year-old **Kościół św. Piotra i Pawła**
(Church of St. Peter and Paul). Visitors can relive the parish's past few decades
through the photo collages inside, which include shots of a visit by the pope. On ul.
Korsarzy, the giant, newly restored **Zamek Książąt Pomerańskich** (Castle of Pomeranian Princes; tel. 347 391) overlooks it all from the site of Szczecin's oldest settlement. The seat of Pomeranian princes until 1630, it later belonged to Swedes,
Prussians, and Germans. These days, it's occupied by an opera and theater group.
The large courtyard is often the site of performances and concerts (open daily 10am-
6pm). Check at the castle for upcoming events. While you're at it, climb the tall
wieża (tower; 2zł) for a panoramic view of the entire region.

Behind the castle bravely stands the abandoned **Baszta Panieńska Siedmiu
Płaszczy** (Maiden's Tower of Seven Cloaks), on ul. Panieńska, the only one of the
medieval fortifications' 37 original towers to survive WWII. Imagining that the cars
speeding along the highway below are fearsome Nordic invaders will give you a good
sense of the tower's historical importance.

Heading back to the market square from the castle leads to the old **ratusz,** built in
1450. Rebuilt after WWII in the original Gothic style, it now houses one of the three
branches of the **Muzeum Narodowe** (National Museum); this one illustrates Szczecin's history from stones to cups and saucers. Another branch—a chronicle of Pomeranian art—is in the Baroque palace of the **Pomeranian Parliament,** ul. Stromłyńska
27/28, north of Castle Hill two blocks west of Kościół św. Piotra i Pawła. (Both open
Sat.-Sun. 10am-4pm, Tues. and Thurs. 10am-5pm, Wed. and Fri. 9am-3:30pm. 1 ticket
good for 3 galleries.)

■ Świnoujście

In addition to the sheer musical pleasure of saying its name (shvee-noh-OOSH-che),
this watery Baltic town also offers beautiful beaches and lush parks. If this weren't
enough, the seaside promenade ul. Żeromskiego is a feast for the senses, as well as a
feast in its own right.

Orientation and Practical Information Świnoujście occupies parts of
two islands, **Wolin** and **Uznam,** linked by a ferry across the **Świna River.** The **train**
and **bus stations** and the international **ferry terminal** are all located on the Świna's
east bank, near the **port** on Wolin Island. **Trains** travel to Szczecin (10 per day, 2hr.,
11.60zł) and Warsaw (2 per day, 8½hr., 38zł). **Polferries,** ul. Dworcowa 1 (tel. 321 30
06), next to the main dock, sends ferries to Copenhagen (2 per day, 9hr., 159zł) and
Malmö, Sweden (2 per day, 10hr., 159zł). **Unity Lines** runs a ferry to Ystad, Sweden
(10pm, 9hr., 155zł). To get to the main part of town, on the west side of the river,
hop on the free **car ferry** (every 20min. 5am-11pm, 1 per hr. midnight-5am) across
the street from the train and bus stations, five minutes up the road from the main
ferry terminal; head left out of the ferry terminal on **ul. Dworcowa.** Once you reach
the other side of the river, disembark, take a left, and check out the map of the city to
get your bearings. **PTTK,** ul. Paderewskiego 24 (tel. 321 26 13), sells 3-4zł **maps**
(open Mon.-Tues. and Thurs.-Fri. 7am-3pm, Wed. 9am-5pm). **Orbis,** ul. B. Chrobrego
9 (tel. 321 44 11), also vends maps, as well as train tickets (open Mon.-Fri. 10am-
5pm). Two km west of Świnoujście, on ul. Wojska Polskiego, there is a pedestrians-

and bicycles-only **border crossing** to Seebad Ahlbeck, Germany. If you want to buy anything at the German market, be sure to change money on the Polish side before you cross. From the Wolin Island side of the Świna, Ahlbeck can also be reached by the **Fehmarn I ferry** (5 per day, round-trip 12zł, children 6zł). **Bank PKO S.A.,** ul. Pił sudskiego 4 (tel. 321 57 33), cashes **traveler's checks,** exchanges money, and produces credit-card cash advances (open Mon. and Fri. 8am-6pm, Sat. 10am-2pm). A **24-hour pharmacy,** ul. Piłsudskiego 23 (tel. 321 25 15), deals most drugs (open daily 8am-8pm; knock after hours). The **post office** is at ul. Piłsudskiego 1 (tel. 321 20 15; open Mon.-Fri. 8am-8pm). **Postal code:** 72-600. **Phone code:** 097.

Accommodations, Camping, and Food Reserve ahead for summer. If you plan to spend a few nights in town, start the room hunt at **Orbis** (see above), which locates **private rooms** (25zł). **Hotel Wisus,** ul. Żeromskiego 17 (tel. 321 58 50), has comfy rooms near the beach (25-30zł per person), as does its neighbor **Hotel Hutnik,** ul. Żeromskiego 15 (tel. 321 54 11)—follow the HI signs (singles 41zł; doubles 73zł; 5% discount for HI members). A short hike from the center and beach, the **Youth Hostel (HI),** ul. Gdyńska 26 (tel. 327 06 13; reception open 6-10am and 5-10pm), has free luggage storage and clean rooms (14-17zł per person, members 8.50-11zł). At **Camping Relax,** ul. Słowackiego 1 (tel. 321 39 12, reservations 321 47 00), tents and sites cost 9zł, or relax in cozy cabins (triples 60-125zł; quads 100-165zł).

Kiosks clamor by the dozen along ul. Żeromskiego. Try the inexpensive and delicious *gofry*—hot Belgian waffles with whipped cream and strawberries. More substantial appetites can find a grilled *kiełbasa* and *piwo* for only 4zł. In the main part of town, stop by **Bar "Neptun,"** ul. Bema 1 (tel. 321 26 43), across from the post office, where you not only feast on inexpensive Polish dishes (7-15zł) and homemade carrot juice, but also get a chance to see the charismatic and multilingual Mr. Tomasz Strybel in action. If your Polish falters, anything from German to Spanish could follow (open daily 8am-10pm). **Restaurant Thang Long,** ul. Rybaka 13 (tel. 321 55 22), serves authentic Vietnamese food prepared by Chef Pham Van Tinh (10-25zł). **Grocery Kama,** ul. Chopina 2 (tel. 327 04 73), features fresh bread, cheeses, and meats (open Mon.-Fri. 7am-9pm, Sat.-Sun. 7am-9pm).

Sights and Entertainment Visitors flock to Świnoujście's main attractions: the shady parks and the Baltic shoreline, with its grassy dunes and relaxed beachcombing. Even before you step off the ferry, it's impossible to miss this town's seafaring side. Colorful tugboats sit at the port, while sailors walk the streets. The **beach** and the **promenade** along ul. Żeromskiego are sights in and of themselves.

As the sun goes down, the kiosks along ul. Żeromskiego transform into locales for good times and cheap beer (0.5L 2.50zł). Crowds of college-age fun-seekers move on from kiosk *piwo* to the **nightclubs,** which are within easy walking distance. For a real culture shock, check out the **Manhattan** nightclub, ul. Żeromskiego 1 (tel. 321 26 11), with its New York City decor (open nightly 9pm-6pm; cover 6zł).

▓ Woliński Park Narodowy

Amid the quickly developing coastal resorts, Woliński National Park protects a pristine tract of Wolin Island that contains glacial lakes, a bison preserve, and breathtaking views of the Baltic Sea. Pine-scented breezes blow through its trails, erasing any memory of civilization, while dense woodland dampens the nearby road noise, leaving silence for the cries of distant eagles. Comforts are not far away, though; a park visit begins in Międzyzdroje, a tiny village on the Baltic Sea.

Orientation and Practical Information Międzyzdroje (MYEN-dzi-ZDROY-eh) can be reached from Szczecin by **bus** or **train** (17 each per day, 1hr. 40min., 13zł); from Świnoujście by train (direction Szczecin, 17 per day, 30min., 2.90zł); or by a special **shuttle bus** (more than 40 per day, 1.80zł). Obtain **maps** (4.50zł), **exchange cash,** and get info about the park, budget travel, and accommoda-

POLAND

tions at **PTTK,** ul. Kolejowa 2 (tel. 804 62; fax 800 86), in the center of town. Go right out of the train station/bus stop and follow ul. Kolejowa to the center. Both the town and the park have very large **maps** posted at regular intervals—day-hikers will do just fine without a copy of their own, given the well-marked trails. The **pharmacy** sits at pl. Zwycięstwa 9 (tel. 801 54; open Mon.-Fri. 8am-8pm, Sat. 8am-3pm). The **post office** is at ul. Gryfa Pomorskiego 2, around the corner from PTTK (open Mon.-Sat. 8am-8pm). **Telephones** are just inside. **Postal code:** 72-510. **Phone code:** 097.

Accommodations and Food Despite Międzyzdroje's rapid development, affordable accommodations still exist. **PTTK** (see above) arranges stays in private rooms (singles 26zł; doubles 50zł; triples 46zł) and runs the well-kept **PTTK Hotel,** in the same building (July-Aug. 44zł per person; Sept.-June 35zł per person). **Camping Gromada,** ul. Bohaterów Warszawy 1 (tel. 807 79, reservations tel. 805 84), has cabins (9-16zł per person) and tent sites (6-9zł) only a few minutes from the beach. All three options lie within walking distance of both the park and town.

Perhaps the most obvious choice for food is the well-stocked **supermarket Stołoda,** ul. Gryfa Pomorskiego 17, near the post office (open Mon.-Sat. 6:30am-9pm, Sun. 8am-6pm). Visitors who have had enough of the outdoors can slip into **Marina,** ul. Gryfa Pomorskiego 4, to feast on local and Italian fare (open daily 9:30am-11pm).

Hiking Although Międzyzdroje is rapidly drawing crowds as a prime beach resort, the true accolades still belong to **Woliński Park Narodowy.** The park is immaculately kept, with three main **hiking trails** (red, green, and blue—marked on trees and stones every 30m); stick to them, or risk an encounter with park officials or worse. All three can be accessed from Międzyzdroje—the red at the northeast end of **ul. Bohaterów Warszawy,** the green at the end of **ul. Leśna** (follow the signs to the bison preserve), and the blue just off **ul. Ustronie Leśne.** Each trail has something to offer for either ambitious or relaxed hikers. Before hiking, a visit to the **Park Museum,** ul. Niepodległości 3, provides information about the area and a preview of nearby wildlife (open Tues.-Sun. 9am-5pm; 2zł, students 1.50zł).

The **red trail** alone makes the trip worthwhile. Part of a longer trek around Wolin Island, the 15km along the Baltic coastline, beginning at the end of ul. Bohaterów Warszawy, make up the prime hiking leg of the trail. Only a short climb from the trailhead, **Kawcza Góra** is the first of the red trail's many scenic outlooks high above the Baltic Sea. The sun on the water dazzles as you step out of the shade. Look closely, and you just might see one of the park's famed eagles (*bieliki*). Snaking along the cliffs, the trail never strays too far from the shoreline, and breezes off the water keep hikers refreshed. The **green trail** (15km), which heads into the heart of the park, offers the greatest variety of terrain and sights. The beginning is a steep climb up ul. Leśna (a left off ul. Norwida coming from the town center, a right coming from the train). Complete with a **bison preserve** (*Rezerwat Żubrów;* open Tues.-Sun. 10am-6pm; 2zł, students 1.50zł) and glacial lakes, the green trail has a slightly different feel from the red—grassy, bushy, forested, and, well, green. With the sea and the construction far removed, this path is also much quieter. Truly adventurous hikers sometimes combine the two trails into one mega-hike (they meet at the end), but even a short jaunt along the green route leads to some fine-looking bison. Rather than heading east-west like its counterparts, the **blue trail** wanders south, covering more than 20km in its course toward the town of Wolin on the island's southernmost point. This traipse heads into the park right off ul. Ustronie Leśne by the train station—go under the bridge and take a right. Despite the path's location near the station, it is less traveled than the other two, a perfect escape from the mobs of tourists in town.

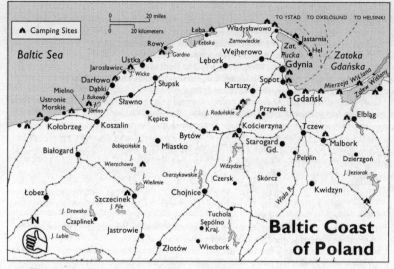

TRÓJMIASTO (TRI-CITY AREA)

Trójmiasto, the tri-city area on Poland's Baltic coast, is rapidly developing into a major tourist destination. The three cities of Gdańsk, Sopot, and Gdynia encompass numerous historic buildings, great restaurants, a wide selection of shops, exciting cultural events and nightlife, and the best beaches in Poland. The area's efficient transportation allows visitors to find a room in one city and see the sights of the other two, as well as daytrip to destinations such as Hel, Malbork, and Frombork.

■ Gdańsk

The strategic location of the city of Gdańsk (gh-DA-insk)—on the Baltic coast and at the mouth of the Wisła—has helped it flourish architecturally and culturally, but also made it the site of many battles. Formerly the German city of Danzig, it saw the first deaths of WWII, which devastated the city. At war's end, Gdańsk threw itself into creating a new national identity while re-creating its previous appearance. This rebirth, though, did not quell the city's combative energy, and it soon served as the birthplace of Lech Wałęsa's Solidarność movement. Now that the 1997 millennium celebration is over, perhaps the swarms of tourists will die down, allowing Gdańsk's charm to shine a little brighter.

ORIENTATION AND PRACTICAL INFORMATION

Gdańsk, Poland's principal port, dips its toes in the Baltic Sea. From the **Gdańsk Główny** train station, the town center lies a few blocks southeast, bordered on the west by **Wały Jagiellońskie** and on the east by the **Stara Motława,** a tributary of the Wisła. To reach **Orbis,** take the underpass in front of the train station McDonald's, go right, and walk until you reach **ul. Heweliusza.** To get to the town center from ul. Heweliusza, go back toward the train station and make a left on Podwale Grodzkie, which becomes Wały Jagiellońskie. Turn left onto **ul. Długa** at the LOT building. Despite the fact that the tourist office is in a neighborhood called **Stare Miasto** (Old Town), the real Old Town is a short walk south, in **Główne Miasto** (Main Town), which contains most points of interest as well as the main avenue, the connected **ul. Dluga** and **Długi Targ.**

POLAND

Tourist Offices: IT Gdańsk, ul. Długa 45 (tel. 319 327; fax 313 008), in Stare Miasto. Distributes info about sights and accommodations. Open daily 9am-6pm. **Orbis,** ul. Heweliusza 22 (tel. 314 425). International and domestic ferry, train, and plane tickets. Also an **AmEx branch office.** Open Mon.-Fri. 9am-5pm, Sat. 10am-2pm.

Budget Travel: Almatur, Długi Targ 11, 2nd floor (tel. 312 931; fax 317 818), in the Główne Miasto center. ISICs and information about youth and student hostels. Open Mon.-Fri. 9am-5pm, Sat. 10am-2pm.

Currency Exchange: At hotels, banks, *kantors,* and certain post offices. The train station has a 24hr. *kantor.* **Bank Gdański,** Wały Jagiellońskie 14/16 (tel. 379 222), cashes traveler's checks for 1% commission. AmEx, EC, MC, and Visa cash advances (no commission). Branch at the train station. Open Mon.-Fri. 8am-6pm. Orbis (see above) exchanges AmEx traveler's checks *sans* commission.

Flights: Rebiechowo airport (tel. 314 026), 22km south. The B bus links to the train station. **LOT,** Wały Jagiellońskie 2/4 (tel. 311 161). Open Mon.-Fri. 8am-6pm.

Trains: Info tel. 311 112. To: Warsaw (July-Aug. 14 per day, Sept.-June 6 per day; 4hr.; 23zł); Kraków (6 per day, 33zł); Berlin (2 per day, 7hr., 85zł); Prague (1 per day, 15hr., 120zł); and St. Petersburg (1 per day, 36hr., 250zł). **Commuter trains** run every 6-12min. to Gdynia (40min., 2.90zł) and Sopot (15min., 2.10zł). Punch your ticket at one of the *kasownik* machines before boarding. Commuter train schedule posted separately from main one.

Buses: Behind the train station through the underground passageway (tel. 321 532). To Malbork (8 per day, 1hr., 4.70zł) and Toruń (2 per day, 4hr., 17zł).

Ferries: Passenger ferries run to Sopot, Hel, and Gdynia (tel. 314 926). To: Oxelösund, Sweden (in high season 1 per day; off-season Mon., Wed., and Fri.; 17hr.; 170.20zł). Book through **Polferries Travel Office** (tel. 431 887; fax 436 574) or **Orbis** (see above). Take the commuter rail to the Nowy Port terminal.

Public Transportation: Gdańsk has an extensive bus and tram system. 1.32zł for 30min, double at night. Pay for large baggage as you would for yourself.

Taxis: It's a bird, it's a plane, it's…**Super Hallo Taxi,** tel. 91 91.

Luggage Storage: At the train station. 0.50zł plus 1% of baggage value. Open 24hr.

English Bookstore: English Books Unlimited, ul. Podmłyńska 10 (tel. 313 373). Watch for a black-and-gold sign. Open Mon.-Fri. 10am-6pm, Sat. 10am-3pm.

24-Hour Pharmacy: At the train station.

Medical Assistance: Ambulance, ul. Nowe Ogrody 1/7 (tel. 411 000). **Private doctors,** ul. Podbielańska 17 (tel. 315 168). A big blue sign on the building says "Lekarze Specjaliści." Visit 24zł. **HIV tests** available. English spoken. Open Mon.-Fri. 7am-7pm. **Emergency doctors,** al. Zwycięstwa 49 (tel. 323 929 or 323 924), or ul. Pilotów 21 (tel. 478 251 or 566 995), in Gdańsk Zaspa. Both are 24hr. facilities that treat foreigners. Calling ahead is recommended. English spoken. Visit 25zł.

Post Office: ul. Długa 22/25 (tel. 389 139). New in 1997. Take a number and wait your turn. *Poste Restante* in the older building two doors down. Open Mon.-Fri. 8am-8pm, Sat. 9am-1pm. **Fax** bureau. **Postal code:** 80-800.

Telephones: Inside and outside the post office. Open daily 7am-9pm. **Phone code:** 058.

ACCOMMODATIONS

With Gdańsk's somewhat limited tourist infrastructure and increasing popularity, it is best to reserve well in advance, especially in summer. **Gdańsk-Tourist (Biuro Usług Turystycznych),** ul. Heweliusza 8 (tel. 312 634; fax 316 301), across from the train station, arranges stays in **private rooms** (singles 30zł; doubles around 50zł; open July-Aug. daily 8am-7pm; off-season Mon.-Sat. 9am-5pm). **Almatur,** Długi Targ 11 (tel. 312 931), directs travelers to student dorms in July and August (25zł per person).

Schronisko Młodzieżowe (HI), ul. Wałowa 21 (tel. 312 313). Cross the street in front of the train station, head up ul. Heweliusza, and turn left at ul. Łagiewniki. Gdańsk's most conveniently located hostel. Escape the kiddie brigade in smaller rooms. Kitchen; showers in basement. Reception on the 2nd floor. It may be the friendliest hostel in Poland, but it's not the tidiest. Lockout 10am-5pm. Curfew 10pm. 12-16zł, students 10-14zł. Sheets 2zł. Luggage storage 1zł.

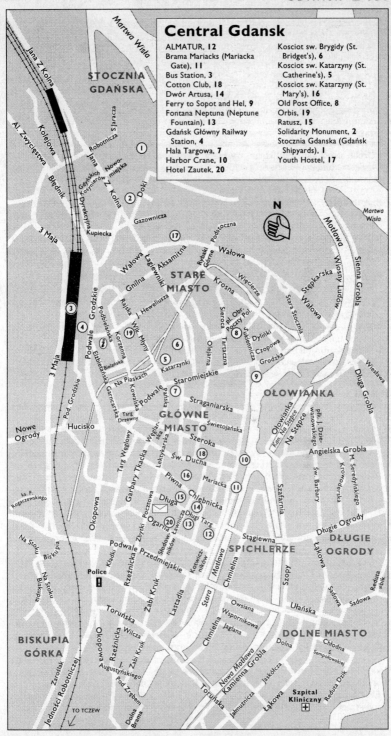

Central Gdansk

ALMATUR, 12
Brama Mariacks (Mariacka Gate), 11
Bus Station, 3
Cotton Club, 18
Dwór Artusa, 14
Ferry to Sopot and Hel, 9
Fontana Neptuna (Neptune Fountain), 13
Gdańsk Główny Railway Station, 4
Hala Targowa, 7
Harbor Crane, 10
Hotel Zautek, 20

Kosciot sw. Brygidy (St. Bridget's), 6
Kosciot sw. Katarzyny (St. Catherine's), 5
Kosciot sw. Katarzyny (St. Mary's), 16
Old Post Office, 8
Orbis, 19
Ratusz, 15
Solidarity Monument, 2
Stocznia Gdanska (Gdańsk Shipyards), 1
Youth Hostel, 17

POLAND

Schronisko Młodzieżowe (HI), ul. Grunwaldzka 244 (tel. 411 660). Take tram #6 or 12 north from in front of the train station to where the tracks form a jug-handle (end of line #6; 30min.). Cross the tracks and follow the path to ul. Grunwaldzka. Immaculate and efficiently run. Reception open daily 5pm-9pm. Lockout 10am-5pm. Curfew 10pm. 12-17zł per bed. Sheets 2.50zł. Luggage storage 1zł.

Hotel Zaułek, ul. Ogarna 107/108 (tel. 314 169). Right off Długi Targ—so it's noisier than the hostels, but the price is tough to beat for the location. The carpetless floors can get chilly, but rooms are clean and beds comfy. Singles 40zł; doubles 55zł; triples 60zł; quads 70zł.

FOOD

For fresh produce of all sorts, try **Hala Targowa,** ul. Pańska, in the shadows of Kościół św. Katarzyny just off Podwale Staromiejskie (open Mon.-Fri. 9am-6pm, first and last Sat. of the month 9am-3pm).

Bar "Neptun," ul. Długa 33/34 (tel. 314 988). Hearty, homestyle meat dishes alongside vegetarian ones in a cafeteria-style setting. A quick, basic break from sightseeing. Full meal 4zł. Open Mon.-Fri. 7am-6pm, Sat. 9am-5pm.

Bar na Rybce, ul. Rybackie Pobrzeże. Moored in the Motława, downstream from the Harbor Crane, this floating restaurant serves fish 'n' beer at great prices. Visit its twin in Gdynia. Open daily 11am-9pm, but the early bird gets...the daily catch.

Pizzeria Napoli, ul. Długa 62/63 (tel. 314 146). Lives up to its "Best in Town" sign, with 30 varieties of tasty pizza (6-20zł) and spaghetti (12-17zł). Take-out and delivery available, but with a prime people-watching location like this one, why go home? Open daily 11am-10pm. AmEx, MC, Visa.

Royal, ul. Długa 40/42 (tel. 315 924). Ideal pastry shop with coffee and drinks. Apple pastry 1.50zł. Open Mon.-Fri. 10am-9pm, Sat. 11am-9pm, Sun. noon-6pm.

U Szkota, ul. Chlebnicka 10 (tel. 314 911). This Scottish restaurant with a history serves up salmon, eel, trout, chicken, and beef (around 15zł). Kilted waiters add to the plaid experience. Open daily noon-midnight.

SIGHTS

Gdańsk was one of the first Polish cities to undergo an exhaustive postwar facelift; only a few buildings have yet to be fully restored. The handsome market square, **Długi Targ,** forms the physical and social center of Główne Miasto, where the original 16th-century facade of **Dwór Artusa** faces out onto **Fontanna Neptuna.** The square hosts local artists and craftsmen, and visitors buy everything from original art to Gdańsk-themed t-shirts. Next to the fountain, where ul. Długa and Długi Targ meet, the 14th-century **ratusz** houses **Muzeum Historii Gdańska.** Don't miss the fantastic Red Chamber, with its ceiling covered in allegorical paintings by Baroque masters. Visit the museum's White and Winter Chambers to read a 1656 letter from Oliver Cromwell to Gdańsk authorities. Another, more sobering, exhibit shows the state of Gdańsk right after WWII—including some of the actual rubble (open Tues.-Thurs. 10am-4pm, Sun. 11am-4pm; 4zl, students 2zl).

One block north of Długi Targ is Gdańsk's grandest house of worship, the 14th-century **Kościół Najświętszej Marii Panny** (St. Mary's). Almost completely rebuilt after its destruction in WWII, the church reigns as Poland's largest brick cathedral. Visitors can climb the 405 steps up the steeple to rise above the din and clatter of the city (open May to mid-Oct. daily 9am-5:30pm; 2zł). In the foreground of the view from the top stands the 14th-century **Kościół św. Katarzyny** (St. Catherine's), ul. Wielkie Młyny, and, behind it, the 15th-century **Kościół św. Mikołaja** (St. Nicholas's). Gdańsk's churches were often visited by Polish monarchs: King Władysław III Łokietek, who unified Polish principalities in the 14th century, supervised court trials in Kościół św. Katarzyny; and King Zygmunt III, who moved the capital from Kraków to Warsaw, received his electorial diploma in Kościół św. Mikołaja.

Ul. Mariacka, behind Kościół Najświętszej Marii Panny, is a tree-shaded cobblestone street that ambles from the church to the river; street musicians playing medieval music complete the mood. After **Mariacka Gate,** the Motława River lies ahead, along with numerous cafes and shops that line **ul. Długie Pobrzeże.** Check out the prices on silver and amber. Going left along Długie Pobrzeże leads toward the huge Gothic **Harbor Crane,** which once set the masts on medieval ships. This crane and the modern warship Sołdek are part of **Centralne Muzeum Morskie** (Central Maritime Museum; tel. 316 938; fax 318 453; open daily 10am-6pm; 2zł, students 1zł).

Attend Sunday Mass at Lech Wałęsa's parish—the simple brick **Kościół św. Brygidy** (St. Bridget's), ul. Profesorska 17, just north of Główne Miasto. Several blocks to the east, on pl. Obrońców Poczty Polskiej, lies the **Stara Poczta** (Old Post Office)—the rallying point for Polish resistance during the German invasion and, since then, a patriotic symbol. *Solidarność* flags fly high once again at **Stocznia Gdańska** (Gdańsk Shipyard) and at the **monument to the 1970 uprising,** pl. Solidarności, just north of the center at the end of ul. Wały Piastowskie. Take a ferry to the island of **Westerplatte** to visit the site of WWII's first shots. Boats leave from outside the Green Gate at the end of Długi Targ (tel. 314 926; March 20-Nov. 15 9 per day; 1hr.; round-trip 18zł, students 11.50zł).

The most beautiful of Gdańsk's many suburbs is **Gdańsk-Oliwa,** with the lush green **Park Oliwski,** ul. Opata Jacka Rybińskiego (open May-Sept. daily 5am-11pm; March-April and Oct. 5am-6pm). Within the park's gates is oldest church in the Gdańsk area, the 13th-century **Katedra Oliwska.** Rest and gaze at the golden stars of the high Gothic cross vaults or, if you arrive in August, when the annual **Music Festival** is held, enjoy the strains of the magnificent 18th-century rococo organ.

ENTERTAINMENT

Of the three cities that line this little stretch of the Baltic Sea, Gdańsk draws the oldest and biggest crowds. The Długi Targ area is packed with tourists taking in the sights, buying amber, or relaxing at a cafe. Even after the last tour bus leaves, though, a handful of **pubs** keep their doors open for some good beer and company. During the first two weeks of August, the **Jarmark Dominikański** street fair erupts in Gdańsk. The **Jantar Jazz Festival,** which visits the city during July and August, ushers in the September **Polish Film Festival,** held in the LOT building next to Hotel Hevelius. Orbis (see **Practical Information,** p. 438) can provide tickets and details.

Żak, Wały Jagiellońskie 1 (tel. 316 125; email magrent@softel.gda.pl), in a multi-turreted mansion close to Główne Miasto, near the traffic circle at the intersection of ul. Hucisko. Gdańsk's one bastion of information on student culture and a most happening place. The best bet on any weekend night. Movie theater (4-5zł), pub downstairs (open daily 2pm-2am), and fashionably downtrodden cafe upstairs with an "English table" on Tues. beginning at 8pm (open daily 2pm-2am). Żak's free magazine describes upcoming events, including the weekend's live music—usually jazz and rock concerts by local bands or well-known stars.

Cotton Club, ul. Złotników 25/29 (tel. 318 813). Head here for jazz, or at least a jazzy atmosphere. Billiards downstairs. Open daily 4pm-late. No cover.

Bar Kubicki, ul. Wartka 5 (tel. 355 460), on the Motława off the north end of Długie Pobrzeże. Good music, beer, friendly staff, and candles to boot. Open daily noon-late.

Irish Pub "Piwnica," ul. Podgarbary. Follow the signs from near the Golden Gate on ul. Długa. The brick and wood setting of this cellar pub is perfect for a bowl of Irish stew (9zł) followed by a glass of "snake mix" (Guinness and cider, 6zł). Also serves a full line of Irish beers and whiskey (3-10zł). Open daily 1pm-midnight.

Palowa, ul. Długa 47 (tel. 315 532), in the basement of the *ratusz.* A popular pseudo-medieval cafe run by the students' union. Tortes from 4zł per slice. Coffee 4-8zł. Mixed drinks 5-15zł. Open daily 10am-10pm.

■ Near Gdańsk

SZTUTOWO

Forty kilometers east of Gdańsk, the tiny village of Sztutowo (shtoo-TO-vo) would be unremarkable were it not for the **Obóz Koncentracyjny Stutthof** (Stutthof Concentration Camp). Though considerably smaller than many of the WWII-era camps around Poland, Stutthof was infamous as a forced-labor, transit, and death camp. Now, the **Muzeum Stutthof w Sztutowie** allows visitors to visit the original site and buildings, including the barracks, the gas chambers, and the crematorium. The large brick building near the entrance, once the home of the Nazi administration, now shows a short film about the camp (1zł; min. 15 people; last showing at 4:30pm; no film Mon.), while the remaining barracks house a Polish-language historical display. One structure to the left of the main gate is filled with shoes. (Museum open daily May-Sept. 8am-6pm, Oct.-April 8am-3pm. Free. Visitors must be at least 14 years old and respectfully dressed.) **Buses** from the Gdańsk bus station run to Sztutowo every hour (4.70zł). Ask the bus driver to drop you off at the "Sztutowo Muzeum" stop; the museum is then just a short walk up **ul. Muzealna,** which is marked by a large stone monument. The main "Sztutowo" bus stop, from which you can catch a return bus, is a 20-minute walk farther down the road from Gdańsk.

MALBORK

One of the many castles belonging to the **Teutonic Knights,** Malbork became the focal point of the Order in the 1300s. The Teutons first came to the region in 1230 at the request of the Polish duke, Konrad Mazowiecki, to assist the nation in its struggle against the heathen Prussians. The Teutons double-crossed the Poles, however, establishing their own state on conquered Prussian soil in 1309, with Malbork as their capital. The great period of Teutonic castle-building lasted until the Order was defeated at the Battle of Grunwald in 1410. Malbork withstood several sieges, but the Poles finally defeated their arch-enemies in 1457 under the leadership of King Kazimierz Jagiellończyk. For the next 300 years, Malbork served as one of the major arsenals and strongholds of the Kingdom of Poland. After Poland's first partition (1772), Malbork was incorporated into Prussia. Heavily damaged during WWII, the fortress was used by the Germans as a POW camp (Stalag XXB). After the fall of the Third Reich, Malbork returned to Poland, and reconstruction continues.

Like most Teutonic castles, Malbork's layout is rectangular. It is unique, however, in that it is a complex of three huge castles. Construction began in the mid-1270s with the monastery that became the **Higher Castle.** It was to contain the main Church of the Virgin Mary, the Grand Masters' burial chapel, the chapter-room, the refectory, the dormitory, the treasury, kitchen facilities, a prison cell, and storerooms. The Higher Castle was surrounded by a system of fortifications, and, from 1335 to 1341, a **tower** and a **bridge** over the Nogat River were incorporated. The most splendid additions to Malbork were those of the Grand Master Winrich von Kniprode, for whom Rhenish architect Nikolaus Fellenstein designed the magnificent **Master's Residence** in the **Middle Castle.** Guest lodgings also lay in this part of the castle, along with the most magnificent hall, the **Grand Refectory,** where great feasts were held. Finally, the 14th and 15th centuries saw the development of the **Lower Castle,** which included an armory, a chapel, an infirmary, servants' quarters, stables, and storerooms. (Open May-Sept. Tues.-Sun. 8:30am-5pm; Oct.-April Tues.-Sun. 9am-2:30pm. 9.50zł, students 6zł. Includes 2½hr. guided tour in Polish. English-speaking tour guides available for 78zł extra.)

Malbork makes a perfect daytrip from Gdańsk by **train** (25 per day, 40min., 7zł) or **bus** (7 per day, 1hr., 4.20zł). With your back to the station, walk right on ul. Dworcowa, then go left at the fork (dir. "Elbląg" on the sign). Go up and around the corner to a roundabout, cross the street at the first crosswalk (before the roundabout), and head toward the Pizza sign. The **Maltur tourist office,** ul. Sienkiewicza 15 (tel. 722 614), sits near the traffic circle (open Mon.-Fri. 10am-4:30pm, Sat. 10am-2pm). To get to the castle, follow **ul. Kościuszki,** and continue as it becomes **ul. Piłsudskiego.** Make a right on **ul. Solina,** and follow it to the castle.

Close to the train station sits the **Youth Hostel,** ul. Żeromskiego 45 (tel. 722 511). Buy a bus ticket at a kiosk and ride bus #6, 7, or 8 one stop or bus #1 or 9 two stops to Wielbark (11zł per person, sheets 5zł; showers, kitchen; English-speaking reception open daily 8-10am and 5-9pm; curfew 11pm). The shiny exterior of **Hotel**

Zbyszko, ul. Kościuszki 43 (tel. 723 394), on the right as you head to the castle, leads to some very nice singles (54zł), doubles (60zł, with bath 78zł), and triples (102zł); all prices include breakfast. **Cafe Zamkowa,** next to the castle entrance, prepares a regal feast amid coats-of-arms (meals 12-20zł, open daily 7am-midnight). **Phone code:** 055.

FROMBORK

Little Frombork is closely associated with the name and work of astronomer **Mikołaj Kopernik (Copernicus),** who lived here from 1510 until his death in 1543. It was in this town that Kopernik conducted most of his observations and research and composed his revolutionary book, the heliocentric *De Revolutionibus Orbium Coelestium.* The tiny waterfront village surrounds a truly breathtaking and well-maintained cathedral complex perched majestically atop a hill. Follow the signs from the train and bus stops to get to the **cathedral.** Once you cross the wooden bridge, the *kasa* on the left (tel. 73 96) sells tickets to **Muzeum Kopernika,** the cathedral, and the **wieża** (tower). The museum houses copies of *De Revolutionibus Orbium Coelestium* and a number of Kopernik's documents, including a scrap of paper that served as his Ph.D. diploma, circa 1503 (open Tues.-Sun. 10am-5:30pm; Oct.-April Tues.-Sun. 9am-3:30pm; 1.20zł, students 0.70zł). Next door in the cathedral itself, the famous 17th-century **organ** has a seven-second echo and impeccable sound quality (open Tues.-Sat. 9:30am-5pm; 1.80zł, students 0.90zł; organ concerts twice daily). A climb up the tower provides a phenomenal view of the cathedral, the town, and the Wisła lagoon (open Mon. 9:30am-5pm, Tues.-Sat. 9:30am-7:30pm; 2zł, students 1.20zł). Underneath the tower is a **planetarium** (tel. 437 392) with six Copernicus-themed shows daily (2zł, students 1.50zł).

Frombork is best reached by **bus** from Gdańsk (5 per day, 2hr., 6.80zł). Bear in mind that the attractions close just as the third bus of the day leaves Gdańsk. Taking the **train** (7.30zł) entails changing in Elbląg, which may take up to four hours, depending on the connection. Once in Frombork, the **train station** and the **bus stop** are along **ul. Dworcowa,** with the docks right behind them. Return bus tickets must be purchased from the driver. In a parking lot opposite the train station stands a wooden hut with the familiar **IT** sign (tel. 75 00; open daily 8am-7pm). The main **tourist office, Globus,** ul. Elbląska 2 (tel./fax 73 54), sits across from the cathedral in the *rynek,* at the end of the path from the train station (open daily 9am-7pm). Both offices have detailed info on local accommodations, the cathedral, and the museum, and can arrange ferry trips to Krynica Morska (a popular beach) and to Kaliningrad.

The **Youth Hostel Copernicus,** ul. Elbląska 11 (tel. 74 53), sits in a quiet wooded area about 400m from the train station. As you leave the station, head right on ul. Dworcowa, and follow the blue and white signs. The white stone building's rooms are clean and adorned with plants and pictures of the great astronomer (8zł per bed, over 26 10zł). Camping is available behind the hostel (4zł). **Dom Wycieczkowy PTTK,** ul. Krasickiego 2 (tel. 72 52), on a hill near the cathedral area, offers singles (18zł, with bath 25.60zł), doubles with bath (40zł), dorms (12zł per person), and a home-style **restaurant** (open daily 7am-9pm). **Phone code:** 055.

■ Sopot

In Poland, many small towns center around one main street. But when that "one main street" leads to some of the best beaches in Poland, a 512m pier, and renowned spas, it's hard not to take notice. With just as much fun in the sun as Gdańsk and a trendier image than Gdynia, beach-goers and music-lovers flock to little Sopot each summer for a dose of seaside R & R. Whether it's on the beach, in a spa, or at the disco, it's all in the name of fun.

Orientation and Practical Information The **commuter rail** connects Sopot to Gdańsk (15min., 2zł) and Gdynia (25min., 1.10zł). Trains run every six minutes during the day and less frequently during the evening; punch tickets in the yellow *kasownik* box before boarding. **Buses** also serve Gdańsk (every 30min., 1.40zł) and Gdynia (10 per day, 3.20zł). **Ferries,** at the end of the pier (tel. 511 293), float to: Hel (3 per day, round-trip 26zł, students 19zł); Gdynia (1 per day, round-trip 18zł, students 13zł); and Westerplatte (1 per day, round-trip 18zł, students 13zł; open daily 8am-7pm). **Ul. Dworcowa** begins at the train station and leads to the pedestrian **ul. Monte Cassino,** which runs along the sea to the **molo** (the 512m pier). **Orbis,** ul. Monte Cassino 49 (tel. 514 142; fax 517 486), sells tickets for trains, planes, ferries, and concerts at Opera Leśna, and is the best place to get info on the Sopot scene. The office also **exchanges currency** and **traveler's checks** (open Mon.-Fri. 10am-6pm, Sat. 10am-2pm). **IT,** ul. Dworcowa 4 (tel. 512 617), in a little wooden house next to the train station, arranges budget accommodations (25-30zł) and sells **maps** of lil' old Sopot (2.70zł) and the tri-city area (5.90zł; open Mon.-Fri. 8:30am-6pm, Sat.-Sun. 9am-2pm). **Bank Gdański S.A.,** pl. Konstytucji 3 Maja 1 (tel. 510 299), opposite the train station, gives AmEx, MC, and Visa cash advances and cashes traveler's checks (open Mon.-Fri. 8am-6pm, Sat. 8am-2pm). **Kantors** hang out near the train station. **24-hour ATMs** along ul. Monte Cassino and at Bank Gdański are connected to AmEx, Cirrus, MC, Plus, and Visa. The **post office** is on ul. Kościuszki 2 (tel. 515 951), the first street on the right heading down ul. Monte Cassino (open Mon.-Fri. 8am-8pm, Sat. 9am-3pm). **Telephones** are inside and outside of the post office (open Mon.-Fri. 7am-9pm, Sat. 9am-3pm, Sun. 11am-6pm). **Postal code:** 81-701. **Phone code:** 058.

Accommodations and Food Sopot is one of Poland's most popular and expensive resorts, so summer reservations are a must. Consider renting a **private room;** stop by IT (see **Practical Information,** above) for help (singles 24zł; doubles 40zł; triples 44zł). To save money and escape the crowds, stay near the **Sopot Kamienny Potok** train station, one stop north of the main Sopot station. This part of town is just as near the sea as the pricier resorts and tends to be less crowded. To *really* save money, however, stay in Gdańsk. **Hotel Miramar,** ul. Zamkowa Góra 21/25 (tel. 518 011; fax 515 164), is not the aqua-green structure you see as you cross ul. Niepodległości (that's the restaurant and nightclub) but the moderately sized brown building behind it. The nice rooms in a park-like area are a a short walk from the beach (singles with bath 95zł; doubles with bath 125zł; triples with bath 190zł; AmEx, MC, Visa). **Camping Nr. 19** is technically at the same address and phone number as Hotel Miramar (see above), but has a separate reception area and entrance, on ul. Niepodległości, about 300m from the end of the path from the Sopot Kamienny Potok train station (go left). It's outfitted with showers and a billiard hall; the 24-hour snack bar "Amigo" is next door (8zł per person; tents 3.50zł; 4-person cabins 50zł).

Fish and beer can be found by the pier. Even though ul. Monte Cassino grows more generic-looking with the continuing invasion of chain restaurants, a few spots stand out. **Bar Rybny Pod Strzechą,** ul. Monte Cassino 42 (tel. 512 476), serves simple but good fish dishes at unbeatable prices (2-7zł; open daily 10am-11pm). Reward the huge sculptures at **La Mela,** ul. Monte Cassino 16 (tel. 511 544), by visiting the popular, sunny interior. A wide selection of Italian dishes, including pizza and lasagna (10-20zł), are available (open daily 11am-9pm). One block south of the pier, **Saigon Restaurant,** ul. Grunwaldzka 8 (tel. 513 374), serves Vietnamese dishes like sweet-and-sour chicken (11.50zł) and crab soup (4.50zł; open daily noon-10pm).

Sights and Entertainment Sopot gained prominence because of its **beach,** which is unavoidable and truly as impressive as they say. The most popular and extensive sands spread at the end of ul. Monte Cassino. This is also where the famous 512m **molo** (pier) begins (Mon.-Fri. 1.20zł, Sat.-Sun. 1.80zł and a smile).

The town is just beginning to realize that the fun doesn't have to end when the tides come in. The number of street-side **cafes, pubs,** and **discos** along ul. Monte Cassino continues to multiply. **Pub FM,** ul. Monte Cassino 36 (tel. 513 359), offers a student crowd its house specialty, *pierogi ruskie* (dumplings with potato and cheese filling; 4.50zł), but most folks come here for the beer and cider (open daily 1pm-1am). The **Loch Ness Pub,** ul. Monte Cassino 45 (tel. 502 840), offers refreshing alternatives to Polish beer, including Guinness (open Sun.-Thurs. 1pm-1am, Fri.-Sat. 1pm-

2am). Discos and nightclubs by the pier are the latest rage. Especially popular are **Fantom** (tel. 512 547; open daily 10pm-6am; cover 5zł) and the misleadingly named **Non-Stop** (open daily 10pm-late; cover 10zł). Both are right next to the pier. The open-air **Opera Leśna's rock and pop music festival** dominates the area in mid-August; call ahead for tickets and info on other festivals and shows (tel. 511 812). Concerts on the pier are frequent in summer; watch for ads for **Amfiteatr na molo** (tickets and info at the pier box office; tel. 510 481). At ul. Ceynowy 5/7, **Sopocki Klub Tenisowy** (tel. 513 569) rents out **tennis** courts (9-22zł per hr.).

■ Gdynia

Young Gdynia (gh-DIN-ya), mostly built only after WWI, is in no hurry to grow up. Although it lacks the history and tradition of Gdańsk and the glitz of Sopot, the town seems more than happy to be a spot for the simpler sides of maritime life: boats, sailors, and fish. Evening strolls along the waterfront show boat-lovers a little slice of nautical heaven; anyone who wants a no-frills visit to seaside life need look no further.

Orientation and Practical Information Despite its small size, the Gdynia Główna **train station** welcomes a large volume of traffic in both trains and **buses**. The **commuter rail,** the cheapest and easiest way to get to Gdańsk (2.90zł) or Sopot (1.10zł), runs from *peron* (platform) one. Punch your ticket in a yellow *kasownik* box before getting on the train. **Trains** run to: Warsaw (14 per day, 31zł); Kraków (5 per day, 30.30zł); Poznań (8 per day, 23.30zł); Szczecin (6 per day, 23.30zł); and Wrocław (6 per day, 26.40zł). **Buses** zoom to: Hel (21 per day, 2hr., 6zł); Świnoujście (2 per day, 8hr., 34zł); and Warsaw (2 per day, 7hr., 25zł). Any of the three roads running away from the station will take you toward the beach and the pier. **Ul. 10-go Lutego** is the most direct. If you end up on **ul. Jana Kolna, ul. Wójta Radtkiego,** or **ul. Starowiejska** (which parallel ul. 10-go Lutego), take a right at the end of the street onto **pl. Kaszubski,** then turn left on ul. 10-go Lutego where it runs into the fountain-filled **Skwer Kościuszki.** For shopping, continue along pl. Kaszubski to **ul. Swiętojańska,** a 3km road full of things to buy and eat. The **beach** is off Skwer Kościuszki. The **tourist office** (tel. 285 378 or 219 225) is in the train station, but somewhat hidden in the back corner of the main lobby by the **bus ticket area.** The friendly staff sells **maps** (4-5zł), helps with accommodations, and maintains computerized lists of all bus connections from the tri-city area to the European Union (open Mon.-Fri. 9am-6pm, Sat. 9am-2pm). The *kantor* in the train station, to the right of the ticket counters, is always open and offers good rates. **Bank Gdański S.A.,** Skwer Kościuszki 14 (tel. 204 135), provides AmEx, MC, and Visa cash advances and cashes AmEx and Visa **traveler's checks** (open Mon.-Fri. 8am-6pm, Sat. 8am-2pm). There are **24-hour ATMs** throughout town. **Ferries** leave from al. Zjednoczenia 2 (tel. 202 642), on Skwer Kościuszki, to: Gdańsk (2 per day, 2hr., 24zł, students 17zł); Hel (5 per day, 1hr., 18zł, students 13zł); Sopot (3 per day, ½hr., 12zł, students 8zł); Westerplatte (2 per day, 1¼hr., round-trip 18zł, students 13zł). **Lion Ferry,** ul. Kwiatkowskiego 60 (tel. 213 623; fax 213 620), sends 1 ferry per day to Karlskrona, Sweden (13hr., 179zł). The **post office,** ul. 10-go Lutego 10 (tel. 218 711), is between the train station and Skwer Kościuszki (open Mon.-Fri. 7am-8pm, Sat. 9am-3pm). **Telephones** are at the post office (open 24hr.). **Postal code: 81-301. Phone code: 58.**

Accommodations and Food Given fast commuter rail service and a slew of cheap sleeps, Gdynia is a good base for the tri-city area. **Turus,** ul. Starowiejska 47 (tel. 218 265; fax 209 287), opposite the train station, finds private singles (25zł), doubles (40zł), and triples (42zł), but only for those staying at least three nights (open Mon.-Fri. 8am-6pm, Sat. 10am-6pm). To reach the **Youth Hostel (HI),** ul. Morska 108c (tel. 270 005), exit the train station through the tunnels under the platforms toward ul. Morska, then take bus #22, 25, 30, 105, 109, or 125 along ul. Morska for 4 stops. The entrance is in the back of the building marked 108b. Rooms are basic and clean. Polish students and HI members get priority (12zł; sheets 2zł; reception open daily 8-10am and 5-10pm). **Hotel Lark,** ul. Starowiejska 1 (tel. 218 046), is at the end of the road that begins to the right of the train station. Only a short walk from the sights and the beach, the decent rooms are comfortable, if a bit dark (singles 57zł; doubles 84zł; triples 98zł; MC, Visa).

One of the most extensive markets in the tri-city, **Hala Targowa** stretches between ul. Jana Kolna and ul. Wójta Radtkiego (open Mon.-Fri. 9am-6pm, Sat. 8am-3pm). You can get everything from fresh fruit, vegetables, and meat to clothes, watches, and books—numerous Russian vendors sell their goods at bargain prices. For a full sensory experience, check out the pungent "hall of fish." As in many seaside towns, there are also **kiosks** and food stands galore along the waterfront **Hala Rybna,** where a full meal can be had for less than 6zł. **Chang-Lin,** ul. Dworcowa 11a (tel. 208 107), a stone's throw from the train station, has a surprisingly extensive Chinese menu, in Polish and English (main dishes around 13zł; open daily noon-11pm). Marooned at Skwer Kościuszki next to the sailboat Dar Pomorza, **Bar na Kutrze** (tel. 243 165) keeps things simple, but tasty, with two choices: fish and beer (meals less than 7zł). Try the Baltic specialty, *dorsz* (open daily 10am-9pm).

Sights The kiosks lining the pier on Skwer Kościuszki give it a carnivalesque atmosphere, and crowds hang around well after mealtimes to relax by the sea. For more seaside views, walk along **Bulwar Nadmorski im. F. Nowowiejskiego.** The stroll also includes a few popular places to sit and watch others do the walking. Check out **Cafe Bulwar,** with its outdoor stage, and the **Contrast Caffè,** with its fishnet and seashell decor—two of the more prominent meeting places. Both await just south of Skwer Kościuszki and stay open until the last guest leaves. Those who feel inspired to get nautical will not be disappointed by the pier. The warship **Błyskawica** docks here, complete with crew (open Tues.-Sun. 10am-1pm and 2-5pm; 2zł, students 1zł). The 1909 sailboat **Dar Pomorza** (tel. 202 371) served as a school at sea for the Polish navy between 1930 and 1981, and has won several sailing competitions (open daily 10am-6pm; admission and guided tour 3zł, students 1.50zł). The boat **Bożena** (tel. 510 685, ext. 206, after 3pm 575 613) gives hour-long tours of Gdynia's port (11 per day, 8am-10pm; tickets 9zł, students 7zł). **Muzeum Oceanograficzne i Akwarium,** at the end of the pier, sheds some light on the surrounding sea, its history, and the multitudes of animals that call it home (open daily 9am-7:30pm; 5zł, students 3zł).

For theatrical entertainment, **Teatr Muzyczny w Gdyni** (ticket info tel. 216 024 or 216 025) puts on several productions at pl. Grunwaldzki 1 (tel. 209 521). Call for schedule information. After the theater, blow on over to disco **Tornado** (tel. 202 305), below the restaurant Róża Wiatrów on the pier (open Fri.-Sat. 9pm-4am; cover Sat. men 10zł, women 5zł).

▨ Hel

Go to Hel—really. For almost a millennium, the sleepy village of Hel has lived off the beautiful fish of the Baltic Sea and the booty from boats stranded on the Mierzeja Helska (Hel peninsula). Recently, the town has awakened to the sound of tourists walking its clean, wide, gorgeous beaches. Hel opens the gates to a day of relaxation, serving up amazing fish and a pleasant change of pace from the crowded resorts.

Orientation and Practical Information Frequent **trains** (9 per day, 2hr., 8zł) and **buses** (1 per hr., 2hr., 6zł) connect Hel to Gdynia. The road is lined with wind-swept dunes and awesome seaside views. The **train station,** as well as one of the town's two bus stops, is a short walk from the main street, **ul. Wiejska.** Take **ul. Dworcowa** to the right (with your back to the station) as it follows a small park to intersect ul. Wiejska, and make a left to head into town. If you take the bus past the train station to the last stop, you'll be dropped off at the other end of ul. Wiejska. Hel can also be reached by **boat** from Gdańsk (1 per day, 2hr., round-trip 35zł, students 24zł); Sopot (in summer 3 per day, 70min., round-trip 26zł, students 19zł); and Gdynia (in summer 4 per day, round-trip 25zł, students 19zł). When Hel freezes over, the ferry no longer runs. It arrives at Hel's dock on **Bulwar Nadmorski,** a block from ul. Wiejska. Tickets are sold in the white kiosk by the ferry landing (tel. 750 437; open daily 9am-5pm). The **PTTK tourist office,** ul. Wiejska 78 (tel. 750 621, ext. 40 01), in a 19th-century fishing hut, is staffed by super-friendly volunteers (the entrance to the office is in the back). Though they mainly organize trips for local youth, they also help find private accommodations and sell maps and brochures (around 4zł; open Mon.-Sat. 10am-2pm). **Exchange currency** at the **post office,** ul. Wiejska 55 (tel. 750 550; open Mon.-Fri. 8am-6pm, Sat. 9am-1pm; *kantor* open noon-6pm). **Telephones** are available inside and outside. **Postal code:** 84-150. **Phone code:** 058.

Accommodations and Food To spend a few days in Hel before you die, contact PTTK (see above); they arrange **private accommodations** (15zł per person). If you have no luck there, get in touch with the director of Muzeum Rybołówstwa (Fishing Museum), Hanna Bulinska, who may be able to put you up in her **pensionat,** ul. Plażowa 5 (tel. 750 848), a large, white stucco house a few hundred meters west of the museum (15zł per person). Private rooms are also offered by many of the shop owners along ul. Wiejska; just look for the *wolne pokoje* signs in the windows. The rooms themselves are fairly standard, but with so few options in town, they can get crowded, especially in summer, when the mainland is jam-packed.

It'll be a cold day in Hel before anyone starves; the town feeds its guests well. Most eateries flank ul. Wiejska. The central **supermarket "Marina,"** ul. Wiejska 70, stocks groceries (open Mon.-Sat. 5:30am-8pm, Sun. 9am-4pm). Restaurants and kiosks focus on either fish or desserts. PTTK runs the tasty and inexpensive **Bar Turystyczny,** ul. Wiejska 78, a.k.a. **Jak U Mamusi** (Like at Mommy's House). This mommy serves tomato soup to fight off colds (2.50zł), grilled sausage to make you big and strong (2.50zł), and salmon to build those brain cells (2.60zł; open daily 11am-6pm). Farther down, **Izdebka,** ul. Wiejska 39—a white-and-brown fisherman's hut built in 1844 with a finely crafted street lantern in front—sells a variety of fresh fish for under 4zł (open daily 10am-8pm). If you're in the mood for dessert, stop for coffee (1-2zł) and sweets (2-4zł) at **Maszoperia,** ul. Wiejska 110 (tel. 750 297), a 200-year-old hut with a traditional half-door. The name of this coffeehouse means "Fisherman's House" in the Kashubian dialect, but even vegans can enjoy the tiny eatery with its shady yard and homey interior. It's a popular meeting place, and if you ask nicely, they may take musical requests (open daily 10am-midnight).

Sights If, like Odysseus, you arrive in Hel by boat, the first thing you'll see after the harbor is Hel's oldest building. Hel's bells top the red-brick **Kościół św. Piotr i Pawla** (Church of St. Peter and Paul) (1417-32), Bulwar Nadmorski, which now houses **Muzeum Rybołówstwa** (Fishing Museum; tel. 750 552). An English history of the church waits just inside by the ticket window. The museum displays nets, canoes, boats, and fishing and boat-building techniques of the last 1000 years. Check out the fishermen's ice skates, the needles used for mending nets, and the giant metal combs used to catch eel. The second floor details the development of Hel and exhaustively describes its role in WWII. (open Tues.-Sun. 9:30am-5:30pm; 3zł, students 2zł). For an extra 1zł, climb the **wooden tower,** which commands a magnificent view of the tri-city area, Hel's harbors, and Hel town.

One of the Baltic Coast's best-kept secrets is the **beach** at the end of ul. Leśna (don't be discouraged by the small patch of sand by the ferry landing—it gets better). Ul. Leśna begins by the fishing museum and runs through a park to the other side of the *mierzeja*. It's a 15- to 20-minute walk through a pleasant pine forest, and it's well worth it. **Ul. Wiejska,** the main artery, has retained much of its old character, thanks to **19th-century fishermen's houses** at #29, 33, 39 and 110. These low-set, cellar-less huts are made of pine and bricks and face the street sideways. Following ul. Wiejska as it turns into ul. Kuracyjna eventually leads to a part of the Hel headland closed to visitors. This is the location of the **Headland Battery,** site of the Polish defense of Hel at the beginning of WWII. Concrete firing positions still exist as evidence of the town's military history.

MAZURY

East of Pomorze, this region of woods and lakes lives up to its nickname: "the land of a thousand lakes." It would not be unfair to add "and a thousand Germans" to this title—the majority of tourists here are Germans who have come to find their roots in this area, which once belonged to the Prussian empire. Mazury is home to about 4000 lakes; the largest, Śniardwy and Mamry, each have an area of more than 100 square km. The myriad of canals, rivers, and streams create excellent conditions for kayaking and sailing. Mrągowo and Augustów are the last outposts of civilization for tourists venturing out into the wild and beautiful waters.

■ Mrągowo

Tiny orange-roofed houses speckle the endless lakes and rivers (once part of a Scandinavian glacier) where Germans and other tourists come to boat, fish, kayak, swim, water-bike, water-ski, and ride horses. Known as Sensburg before 1947, Mrągowo (mrawn-GOH-voh) was named for Celesty Mrongowiusz, a patriot who fought the Germans so his countrymen could continue speaking Polish. His descendants have given up the struggle, and now most respond to *deutsch*. Shops and cafes crowd the central streets, but the hills and valleys swarm with more mosquitoes than tourists.

Orientation and Practical Information The **train station,** on ul. Kolejowa, receives trains from other towns in the Mazury, but try to take a bus to Mrągowo, because the *osobowy* trains that traverse the region are painfully slow. The **bus station** sends buses to Gdańsk (daily at 9:30am, 5hr., 40zł); Warsaw (7 per day, 4½hr., 20.40zł); Olsztyn (21 per day, 1½hr., 5.40zł; switch here for 5 daily buses to Kaliningrad, Russia); and Augustów (2 per day in summer, otherwise change buses in Ełk; 3hr., 5.40zł). The station separates **ul. Warszawska,** a leg of Mrągowo's main thoroughfare, from **ul. Wojska Polskiego,** which leads out of town. With your back to the blue Mrągowo sign, bear right on ul. Warszawska to head into town (5min.). A right turn on **ul. Traugutta** drops down to **Jezioro Czos,** the biggest of the five *mrągowski* lakes. With a little zig, ul. Warszawska becomes **ul. Ratuszowa,** and, after a left-right zag, it reluctantly becomes ul. Królewiecka. A bit farther down on the left, at the corner of ul. Ratuszowa and Mały Rynek, the staff of **Eco-Travel,** Mały Rynek 6 (tel./fax 36 67; open Mon.-Fri. 8am-5pm, Sat. 9am-2pm), not only books rooms (no fee) and changes money, but also speaks English. For **currency exchange,** try one of the many *kantors* or **Bank Gdański S.A.,** ul. Ratuszowa 6 (tel. 29 72 or 44 49; fax 29 62), which also cashes traveler's checks for a 1% commission (minimum charge 2zł) and provides MC and Visa cash advances (open Mon.-Fri. 8am-6pm). The **post office** (tel. 20 11) is at ul. Królewiecka 39 (open Mon.-Sat. 8am-8pm, Sun. 9am-2pm). **Postal code:** 11-700. **Telephones** await inside the post office (open Mon.-Fri. 7am-9pm, Sat. 9am-2pm, Sun. 9-11am). **Phone code:** 08984.

Accommodations and Food The cheapest deal in town is the simple yet clean **Hotel Meltur,** ul. Sienkiewicza 16 (tel. 29 00), which rents out doubles only (37.45zł, with shower 42.80zł, with shower and TV 53.50zł). From the bus station, turn left on ul. Wojska Polskiego, follow it down for 0.5km, and turn right onto ul. Sienkiewicza (10min.). You may want to take a taxi after dark (3zł). Mrągowo's other hotels are all on ul. Jaszczurcza Góra, on the other side of Jezioro Czos. To get to them, turn right from the bus station and head through town until you come to ul. Gizycka, which hugs the lake and eventually leads to Jaszczurcza Góra (50min.). A taxi whisks you there in 10 minutes (4-5zł). **Pensjonat Eva,** ul. Jaszczurcza Góra 14 (tel. 31 16), has rooms with showers and color TVs (singles 80zł; doubles with breakfast 120zł; reception open 24hr.). Eva's neighbors on ul. Jaszczurcza Góra, **Pensjonat To-Tu,** at #26 (tel. 39 77), and **Pensjonat Maria,** at #20 (tel. 39 79), offer similar lodgings at similar prices, right on the shore of Jezioro Czos (closed off-season).

Bars, snack shops, and ice cream joints pepper the town's main thoroughfare. The **Intercommerce supermarket,** ul. Brzozowa 10 (tel. 62 01), has groceries galore (open Mon.-Sat. 6am-8pm, Sun. 9am-1pm). Mrągowo's premier restaurant, **Restauracja Fregata,** is located just left of ul. Ratuszowa near ul. Dolny Zaułek (tel. 22 44), and serves both international *plats* and local dishes. For a taste of the region, try *schab po mazursku* (Mazurian pork; 10.50zł; open daily 9am-9pm).

Entertainment Every July 29 to August 1, an amphitheater on the shore of Jezioro Czos holds a **Country Picnic Festival. Miejski Dom Kultury "Zodiak"** (House of Culture), ul. Warszawska 26 (tel. 30 63), features weekend concerts at 6pm by both amateurs and professionals: Fridays are for rock, Saturdays for folk, and most Sundays for live Polish pop. The main **beaches**—Plaża Orbisu, packed with canoeists, and Plaża Miejska—are both on Jezioro Czos. The coolest late-night draw in town is the curiously named **Bar Lasagna,** ul. Warszawska 7a (tel. 21 15), where locals gather until the wee hours to eat spaghetti (4zł) or *kiełbasa* (2zł) and indulge in Polish beer (3zł; bar open daily 11am-1am). The pub **Olimpia,** pl. Kajki 5 (tel. 23 95), also serves cheap beer (3zł) and has a jukebox. Local hipsters gather at **Milano,** ul. Królewiecka 53 (tel. 20 41), a disco that plays pop, rock, and—yes—Polish hip-hop.

■ Near Mrągowo: Święta Lipka

During the Middle Ages, a Prussian tribal leader was pardoned by the ruling Teutonic knights and expressed his gratitude by placing the Virgin Mary's likeness in a local linden tree. Rumors of miraculous healing and epiphany soon attracted pilgrims to the so-called **Święta Lipka** (Holy Linden)—so many that the Teutonic knights built a shrine to the arbor in 1320. Two hundred years later, the knights razed the Catholic chapel due to a religious reversal and slowed the flow of believers by installing gallows (bodies included) around the tree. The gallows have since rotted away, and nothing deters the annual flocks of Germans who come to visit **Sanktuarium Maryjne** (Sanctuary of Our Lady). Amid lakes, craft shops, and a flower-filled cemetery, the shrine guards an interior as breathtaking as its surroundings. Biblical paintings and a spiky gold re-creation of the miraculous linden adorn the inside. When large crowds gather (i.e., all the time), glistening suns start swirling, baby-faced angels shake their golden bells, the archangel strums her *balalaika,* and golden trumpeters accompany the organ music. **Concerts** are held every Friday at 8pm in July and August. Five **buses** make the 30-minute trip to Święta Lipka on weekdays (2.60zł); two run on weekends. If you miss one of these, take the bus to Kętrzyn (16 per day, 40min., 4zł), and catch one of the many buses that run to Święta Lipka from there.

PODLASIE

This small northeastern region, which has been christened "Poland's green lungs," receives maximum environmental protection. Just a two-hour train ride from Warsaw, Podlasie is decidedly anti-urban, with wide open fields punctuated by Poland's few Russian Orthodox villages and the meandering Bug and Narew rivers. Puszcza Białowieska (Białowieża Forest), once the favorite hunting ground of Polish kings, is now a national park and the habitat of a huge variety of wildlife. The European bison reigns as undisputed king of the forest here, while Białystok, northwest of the preserve, is the region's hip capital.

■ Białystok

Białystok is a trading town, and the multilingual residents won't let you forget it. Located a mere 60km from the Belarusian border, the city is a magnet for hawkers from Poland, Belarus, Lithuania, and Russia who come to exchange their goods at one of the largest markets in Eastern Europe. Despite its location, Białystok is remarkably

POLAND

active, as the traders and a healthy influx of local students add a fairly cosmopolitan flair to this provincial capital. Purported to be the birthplace of the famous *biały* roll, Białystok is the natural launching point for excursions to nearby Tykocin and to Białowieski Park Narodowy.

ORIENTATION AND PRACTICAL INFORMATION

The downtown is organized along **ul. Lipowa,** which leads from the **bus and train stations** east to **Rynek Kościuszki,** the city center, and then on to **pl. Branickich.** If you arrive by train, cross the tracks via the overpass leading to the bus station. From here, with your back to the bus terminal, go left on **ul. Bohaterów Monte Cassino,** then right on **ul. Świętego Rocha,** which leads directly to ul. Lipowa. Follow this street to the *rynek* (15min.). Other major roads are **ul. Sienkiewicza,** which heads northeast and south from the *rynek,* and **ul. Piłsudskiego,** which runs more or less parallel to ul. Lipowa to the north.

Tourist Offices: Orbis, ul. Rynek Kościuszki 13 (tel. 42 16 27). Provides Western Union, cash advances on MC and Visa, and currency exchange, in addition to train and bus tickets. Open Mon.-Fri. 9am-5pm, Sat. 9am-2pm. In the bus station, the kiosk **Mapy** gives out free info and carries a selection of maps (4zł). **PTTK,** ul. Lipowa 18 (tel. 52 25 02 or 52 30 05), sells maps, guides, and train and bus tickets. Also organizes trips to the Białowieża bison reserve. Open Mon.-Fri. 8am-4pm.

Budget Travel: Almatur, ul. Zwierzyniecka 12 (tel. 42 82 09). Sells ISICs and has info on student travel and accommodations. Open Mon.-Fri. 9am-4pm.

Currency Exchange: *Kantors* flank ul. Lipowa. **Bank PKO S.A.,** ul. Sienkiewicza 40 (tel. 43 65 05), cashes all major brands of traveler's checks for 0.5% commission. MC and Visa cash advances at a 2.5% fee. Open Mon.-Fri. 8am-6pm, Sat. 8am-2pm.

Trains: ul. Kolejowa 1 (info 910). To: Augustów (6 per day, 2hr., 13zł); Warsaw (12 per day, 2½hr., 18zł); Gdańsk (2 per day, 7-8hr., 26zł); Vilnius (daily, 9hr., 68zł); St. Petersburg (daily, 26hr., 176zł); and Moscow (daily, 27hr., 176zł).

Buses: ul. Bohaterów Monte Cassino 8 (tel. 224 61, info 936). To: Mrągowo (2 per day, 4hr., 16zł); Augustów (4 per day, 2hr., 9zł); Białowieża (2 per day, 2½hr., 9zł); Warsaw (4 per day, 3½hr., 14zł); Gdańsk (daily, 9hr., 40zł); Minsk (2 per day, 9hr., 40zł); and Vilnius (daily, 9hr., 30zł).

Luggage Storage: At the train station. 4zł. Open daily 8am-6pm.

Pharmacies: Apteka Dyżurna, ul. Lipowa 45 (tel. 42 33 65). Open Mon.-Sat. 7am-9pm, Sun. 10am-5pm.

Post Office: Rynek Kościuszki 13 (tel. 42 42 30 or 42 28 12). Open Mon.-Fri. 8am-8pm. **Postal code:** 15-091.

Telephones: In the post office. Pay phones line ul. Lipowa. **Phone code:** 085.

ACCOMMODATIONS

PTTK (see **Practical Information,** above) directs tourists to the city's best steals. If it's closed, head to ul. Sienkiewicza, north of ul. Lipowa, to find the bargains.

International Youth Hostel (HI), al. Piłsudskiego 7b (tel. 52 42 50). Your basic, crowded hostel offering backpackers a place to crash. Take bus #1 or 18 from the train station or walk: heading toward ul. Lipowa, hang a left on Sw. Rocha and a right on al. Piłsudskiego. The hostel lies behind gray apartment buildings (10min.). The *dyrektor*'s understanding of "curfew" sometimes means sharing drinks with guests into the wee hours. Lockout 10am-6pm. Curfew 10pm. 6- to 14-bed dorms 10.50zł, nonmembers 14zł; students 9zł, student nonmembers 12zł. Sheets 2.50zł.

Hotel Rubin, ul. Warszawska 7 (tel. 77 23 35), in a stylish old building. To get there, walk down ul. Lipowa (15min.), turn left on ul. Skłodowskiej, go up the hill, and turn right on ul. Warszawska, 1 block past the park on your right. Or take bus #2 or 21 from the train station and get off at the first stop on ul. Warszawska (15min.). Caters to Eastern European visitors, though the friendly owners will try to speak your language no matter who you are. Small but clean rooms, communal bathrooms. Doubles 50zł, with bath 120zł; triples 70zł, with bath 135zł.

POLAND

Internat Nauczycielski, ul. Sienkiewicza 86 (tel. 32 36 64), 2 blocks up the street from Hotel Rubin. Enter through courtyard in back. Offers clean rooms and a diligent staff. Tends to fill up on Fri. and Sat., when pedagogical students come to town to study for exams. 2- or 3-bed rooms 20zł per person. 5- or 6-bed dorms 18zł per person. Curfew theoretically 10pm, but negotiable.

FOOD

The city's best eateries are on ul. Lipowa and around Rynek Kościuszki. The brand-new spic-and-span **McDonald's** directly opposite the bus station serves as a reminder that not even eastern Poland is immune to American cultural imperialism. **Supersam,** ul. Skłodowskiej 14, is a full-blown supermarket (open Mon.-Fri. 6am-9pm, Sat. 6am-8pm, Sun. 8am-6pm).

Pizzeria Giorgio, ul. Lipowa 28 (tel. 52 12 42). Saucy pizza and lusty, crusty aromas draw in crowds from the street for mongo treats topped with peppers, olives, and lotsa cheese (7.50-9zł). Open daily 11am-10pm.

Raj Smakosza (Gourmand's Paradise), ul. Malmeda 1 (tel. 42 60 42), on the corner of ul. Lipowa. A white-and-green oasis for weary travelers. Better than the average milk bar, with very tasty food. Fresh green salads 1.50zł, chicken 4.30zł, *bigos* 3.70zł, *chłodnik* 1.70zł. Open daily 7am-8pm.

SIGHTS AND ENTERTAINMENT

Although the interior of **Pałac Branickich** is closed to tourists, this 18th-century mansion, which once belonged to a powerful aristocratic family, is definitely worth a visit. Easily the most impressive building in Białystok, it stands as a Baroque reminder of the city's glorious past. Today, the Versailles-like structure houses a bustling medical school. While the students have the edifice to themselves, you can get far enough in to see their test scores posted inside the door. The **palace park and gardens,** which host occasional concerts, are open to the public. Pass through the main gate on pl. Branickich, and walk down a long alley—they're out back (open April-Sept. daily 6am-10pm, Oct.-March 6am-8pm).

Muzeum Wojska (Military Museum), ul. Kilińskiego 7 (tel. 41 54 48), collects Polish weapons, military dress, and historical records. The rooms bristle with cruel daggers, improbably huge swords, and the arms of Poland's vanquished. The centerpiece is an exhibition of items relating to WWII, specifically the German march across Poland and the subsequent defeat of the Nazis. Posters and placards from the era, many praising the Red Army for its efforts, are among the items on display. Most interesting, though, are the captured German objects, including one dagger with "*Alles für Deutschland!*" inscribed on the blade (museum open Tues.-Sun. 9am-5pm; 2zł, students 1zł; English guidesheets available).

A short walk to the west of the palace, the *rynek*'s **ratusz** originally served as a trade center. In 1940, it was demolished by the Russians, who planned to put a monument to Stalin in its place. This plan never materialized, and the site remained vacant until the present building was constructed in 1958. Inside, the ground floor of **Muzeum Okręgowe** (regional; tel. 42 14 73) contains a **gallery of Polish painting** with a small but impressive collection of Neoclassical, Romantic, Impressionist, and Symbolist paintings. The lower level of the museum hosts a series of visiting exhibitions (open Tues.-Sun. 10am-5pm; 2zł, students 1zł, art students free).

For nightlife, head to one of the many watering holes around Rynek Kościuszki, where locals meet for cheap beer and conversation. **Kawiarnia Ratusz,** at ul. Wyszyńskiego 15 (tel. 45 48 04), located under the white clocktower of the *ratusz,* is popular with locals (open May-Nov. daily 10am-midnight; beer 2.50zł). Jazz concerts in the summer start at 8pm. If you feel like grinding your gears to some techno dance music, visit **Klub Muzyczny Metro,** ul. Białówny 9A (tel. 32 41 54), off ul. Malmeda, where local students pump it up on the dance floor (open Sun.-Thurs. 6pm-2am, Fri.-Sat. 6pm-4am; beer 3.50zł). The pub **Bez Lokalu** (Without a Place), ul. Skłodowskiej 14 (tel. 204 66), also has occasional concerts and gives out info on local student life. For

POLAND

the latest flicks, head to **Kino Ton,** ul. Rynek Kościuszki 2 (tel./fax 43 53 82), which features English-language films with Polish subtitles (open daily noon-midnight). Or, if you fancy being your own James Bond, head to Białystok's recently opened **casino,** inside the **Hotel Cristal** at ul. Lipowa 3 (tel. 42 50 61; fax 42 58 00). Goldfinger will be waiting for you (open daily 8pm-5am; admission 1zł; passport must be shown).

■ Near Białystok

TYKOCIN

For an impressive and sobering reminder of Poland's Jewish past, take an afternoon bus trip to tiny Tykocin, home to one of the most beautiful synagogues in Poland (16 buses per day, 1hr.). Turn left from the central square onto ul. Złota (which becomes ul. Piłsudskiego) to find the renowned **synagoga,** a 17th-century gem enclosed by unassuming walls. Of the three carved wood entrances, only the one on ul. Piłsudskiego is functional. Hebrew prayers and ornamental designs scroll around all four walls of the cavernous interior. During services, rabbis would occupy the central **bimah**—glass cases in front protect one of the synagogue's copies of the Torah. The synagogue once served 2300 Jewish residents of Tykocin, who accounted for almost 70% of the village's population. After the Nazis killed all but 150 of Tykocin's Jews, the temple was abandoned until 1977, when restoration began. Today, not a single Jew is left in Tykocin; the last one left for Israel several years ago.

The synagogue also provides exhibition space for Judaic artifacts—skillfully crafted silver menorahs and paintings chronicling Jewish struggles. The 4zł admission (students 2zł) buys entrance both to the temple and to the regional museum next door, which is housed in the *synagoga*'s Talmudic House and features an interesting array of 17th- to 19th-century Polish household wares, as well as visiting exhibitions. On the other side of town, just past the *rynek,* stands the colossal **Kościół św. Trójcy** (Holy Trinity Church), an 18th-century structure whose two enormous towers overshadow the market square. For a bite to eat, head to **Restauracja Tejsza,** behind the regional museum (open daily 10am-10pm; small meals 6-10zł).

BIAŁOWIESKI PARK NARODOWY

Puszcza Białowieska (Białowieża Primeval Forest), a natural treasure of towering trees and Eastern European bison, sprawls out over oceans of flatland. Exploration begins in the sleepy town of Białowieża. The preserve is reached by following a well-marked 4-5km path from the park entrance (bike rental available; see below). Stay on the trail, lest you catch a park official on a bad day. About 250 of the lumbering bison remain; many of their brethren were wiped out by hungry WWI soldiers. The bison preserve forms a small part of the park that only guided tours may enter.

There are two direct **buses** that go straight to Białowieża from Białystok (2½hr., 9zł), but they run at inconvenient times. An alternative is to hop on one of the frequent buses to Hajnówka (1½hr., 4.80 zł), and change there for Białowieża (45min., 2.50zł). Leave very early, as there may be a wait between buses. From the bus stop and train station, the preserve entrance is over the bridge and up the hill, as is **Hotel-Restauracja Iwa** (tel./fax (0835) 122 60), home of **Guliwer tourist office.** The office arranges three-hour **guided tours** of the park in horse-drawn carts (50zł), rents bikes (1.70zł per hour), and arranges hotel rooms (doubles 55zł, with bath 65zł; triples with bath 76zł; quads without 60zł; office open daily 9am-5pm). Next door, **Dom Wycieczkowy PTTK** (tel. (0835) 125 05; fax 126 24) offers two-hour group **tours** (50zł for a group of 25; English tour 70zł) and rents comfortable rooms (singles 20zł; doubles 32zł, with bath 42zł; quads 60zł; MC and Visa accepted).

KARPATY (THE CARPATHIANS)

The Polish Carpathians attract millions of visitors each year, luring Poles and foreigners alike with great hiking and skiing. Karpaty's varied terrain—from the rounded hills of the Bieszczady in the east and Beskidy in the west to the skyrocketing Tatry in the middle—offers recreational possibilities to satisfy every fancy. With armies of street stalls selling homemade everything, Tatran folk culture hits visitors straight in the face. But to acquaint yourself with the locals' real world, don't confine your stay to touristy Zakopane; explore the gentler, less-frequented slopes in the east and west.

For a map of the Polish and Slovak Tatras, see pp. 654-655 in the **Slovakia** chapter.

■ Sanok

The cultural and economic hub of the Bieszczady, Sanok sits proudly atop a hill, confident in its rich artistic heritage. Under Communism, much of the wealth of rural churches was looted and brought to Sanok. The icon museum houses priceless pieces of local religious art, and the open-air museum recreates village life destroyed by war and time. Sanok is also an ideal base for trips into the nearby mountains.

Orientation and Practical Information The train and bus stations, linked by an overpass, are a 15-minute hike from the *rynek*. **Trains,** ul. Dworcowa (tel. 463 05 16), huff to Kraków (4 per day, 18.30zł); and **buses,** ul. Lipińskiego, puff to Kraków (4 per day, 5hr., 21zł) and Przemyśl (8 per day, 6zł). Buses #3 and 4 will take you near the center from the stations. A detailed map is posted across from the train station. To walk to the center, go left on ul. Dworcowa (facing the map), which will become ul. Kolejowa. Head right at the intersection with ul. Lipińskiego, which becomes **ul. Jagiellońska.** After a steep hill, the latter curves to the right and eventually turns into **ul. 3-go Maja,** which heads straight to the *rynek*. **Ul. Kościuszki** houses banks, grocery stores, and the post office; it jets out where ul. Jagiellońska meets ul. 3-go Maja. **PTTK,** ul. 3-go Maja 2 (tel./fax 463 25 12), sells maps and offers info on sightseeing in the area (open Mon.-Fri. 8am-4pm). On the opposite corner of the block from the PTTK, at the corner of ul. Kościuszki and ul. Grzegorza Sanoka, an **Orbis** office awaits to book your plane and train trips (tel. 463 09 38; open Mon.-Fri. 8am-5pm, Sat. 9am-1pm). **Bank PKO S.A.,** ul. Kościuszki 12, cashes traveler's checks and gives MC and Visa cash advances (open Mon.-Fri. 7:30am-5pm, Sat.9am-1pm). If you're looking to **exchange** cash, *kantors* have the best rates. The **Mountain Rescue (GOPR)** headquarters is at ul. Mickiewicza 49 (tel. 463 22 04). The **post office** sits at ul. Kościuszki 26 (tel. 463 03 82; open Mon.-Fri. 8am-8pm, Sat. 8am-2pm). **Postal code:** 38-500. **Phone code:** 013.

Accommodations and Food Staying overnight in Sanok will cost a bit, but the rooms are all good value for the money. The fastidious owners of **Hotel Jagielloński,** ul. Jagiellońska 49 (tel. 463 12 08), near the station, offer some of the cleanest and most dignified rooms in eastern Poland—spacious and outfitted with Oriental carpets, bathrooms, telephones, and TVs (singles 48zł; doubles 59zł; triples 75zł). Just up the road on the right, **Hotel Turysta,** ul. Jagiellońska 13 (tel. 463 09 22) has large rooms, all with clean bathrooms (singles 45zł; doubles 65zł; triples 80zł). If you've always wanted to know what Communist color coordination was all about, visit **Hotel PTTK,** ul. Mickiewicza 29 (tel. 463 10 13). This hotel offers midget baths in each room and a tourist office. To get here, take bus #0 from the stations and get off when the bus turns onto ul. Mickiewicza (singles 45zł; doubles 58zł). Hotel Błonie's **campground,** Aleje Wojska Polskiego 1 (tel. 463 02 57; fax 463 14 93), a 15-minute walk or a short ride on bus #0 from the train station, is set amid stadium lights to the right of the road and offers sites by the San River (3.40zł per person, tent rental 2.80-3.40zł per night; open June 15-Sept. 15).

Restaurant Max, ul. Kościuszki 34 (tel. 463 22 54), has a large and affordable selection of Polish cuisine (3-12zł; open daily 10am-10pm). **Restauracja Jagiellońska,** at the hotel, is slightly more expensive, but not unreasonable (main dishes 10-20zł). It lures clients with impeccable service (open daily noon-midnight). The **grocery store** with the longest hours is **Delta,** ul. Kościuszki 6 (tel. 463 68 08; open Mon.-Sat. 7am-9pm, Sun. 9am-9pm).

Sights and Entertainment The **museum complex** in the *zamek,* ul. Zamkowa (tel. 463 06 09), is a must. The three-room **Muzeum Ikon** houses 15th to 19th-century Ukrainian icons and religious artifacts from the surrounding region. The adjoining **gallery** exhibits the surrealist works of local painter Beksiński, who is well-known throughout Poland (open Tues.-Sat. 9am-3pm, Mon. 11am-3pm; 2.50zł, students 1.50zł, Mon. free). Sanok's **churches** are also worth peeping into, especially on Sunday, when they get mystical in a drone of ritual chants. The walls of the 14th-century **parish church,** in the *rynek,* still echo with the marriage vows of King Władysław Jagiełło—the founder of one of medieval Europe's most powerful dynasties.

The **skansen,** 2km north of town and across the river San, recreates the village life of the region's main ethnic groups: the Łemks and Boyks. It rates among Europe's best open-air museums. A pleasant walk, the museum can also be reached by bus #3 from the *rynek.* Get off immediately after the bus crosses the river, take a sharp right onto ul. Rybickiego, and follow the signs to the *skansen* (open daily May-Oct. 8am-6pm; April 9am-4pm; Nov.-March 9am-3pm; 3zł). While wandering around the site, make sure to visit the 150-year-old schoolhouse displaying old textbooks and maps.

Park Miejski has outstanding views of the city and the valley. From the *rynek,* go southwest on ul. 3-go Maja, turn right on ul. Piłsudskiego, and follow it until the end. Or, enter the park next to the post office.

From Sanok, buses run regularly to popular **hiking** destinations in the Bieszczady Mountains. The friendly staff at the Hotel PTTK information desk (see above) will eagerly help plan a trip to Ustrzyki Górne, Wetlina, Komańcza, or Jezioro Solina. They have maps, as well as information detailing accommodations and hiking routes. In the winter, cross-country and downhill **skiing** is popular. Not to be missed is the **Bieszczadzki Park Narodowy,** with its well-preserved forests and diverse flora and fauna. Included within the park is the highest peak in the Bieszczady, **Tarnicza** (1346m).

■ Zakopane

Set in a valley surrounded by sky-high, jagged Tatran peaks and soul-stirring alpine meadows, Zakopane (ZAH-ko-PAH-neh), Poland's premier year-round resort, buzzes with hikers and skiers. While prices in the Swiss and Austrian Alps can be higher than even the mountains, meals and lodging here can still be had for a few dollars—and, of course, the views are always free. The streets are lined with local merchants selling everything from leather jackets to Russian army hip flasks.

ORIENTATION AND PRACTICAL INFORMATION

The **bus** and **train stations** lie across **ul. Jagiellońska** from each other, next to the street's intersection with **ul. Kościuszki.** The center lies a 10- to 15-minute walk west along the tree-lined ul. Kościuszki; **ul. Krupówki** is the restaurant and shopping hub. **Łysa Polana,** about 25km from Zakopane, is the closest spot to cross the Slovak border (tel. 661 93 for current border-crossing info; open 24hr.).

Tourist Offices: IT, ul. Kościuszki 17 (tel. 122 11; fax 660 51), at the intersection with ul. Sienkiewicza. Sells maps and brochures and arranges private accommodations in town (20zł per person, 25zł with bath). Open daily 7am-9pm. **PTTK Biuro Usług Turystycznych,** ul. Krupówki 12 (tel. 158 48; fax 124 29). Arranges Tatra excursions. 4hr. guided tours in English 30-150zł, full-day 190-370zł. Open in summer Mon.-Fri. 8am-4pm, Sat. 8am-2pm, Sun. 8am-noon; off-season closed Sun.

Currency Exchange: Bank PKO S.A., ul. Gimnazjalna 1 (tel. 685 05), north of and parallel to ul. Kościuszki, near the bus station. Cashes traveler's checks for 0.5%

commission and offers EuroCard, MC, and Visa cash advances. Open Mon.-Fri. 8am-6pm, Sat. 10am-2pm. **Orbis,** ul. Krupówki 22 (tel./fax 122 38). Cashes traveler's checks at 1% commission and provides MC and Visa Gold cash advances (max. withdrawal 300zł). Open Mon.-Fri. 9am-5pm, Sat. 9am-3pm.

Trains: ul. Chramcówki 35 (info tel. 145 04). To: Bielsko-Biała (dir. "Sucha Beskidzka"; 19 per day, 3½-4½hr., 9.60-14.50zł); Kraków (24 per day, 3½hr., 9.60-14.50zł); and Warsaw (3 per day, 8hr., 15.40-23zł, express 6hr., 30zł).

Buses: ul. Kościuszki 25 (info tel. 146 03). To: Budapest (2 per week, 8hr., DM30-35); Kraków (every 30-90min., 2½hr., 9zł); Poprad, Slovakia (5 per day, off-season 2 per day, 2½hr., 8zł); and Warsaw (1 per day, 8hr., 24-60zł).

Taxis: Radiotaxi, tel. 919.

Bike Rental: Ital-Pol, ul. Piłsudskiego 4a (tel. 144 23). Italian mountain bikes 5zł per hr., 20zł per 4hr., or 25zł per day. Open July-Aug. Mon.-Fri. 10am-6pm. Other bike rental places are on ul. Kościuszski near the center and ul. Piłsudskiego.

Luggage Storage: At the train station, 2.72zł per piece per day (until midnight). Open 24hr. except 1-1:30pm. At the bus station, 1.5zł per piece per day. Open daily 8am-7pm.

Pharmacy: ul. Krupówki 39 (tel. 633 31). Open daily 8am-8pm.

Mountain Rescue Service: ul. Piłsudskiego 63a (tel. 634 44).

Post Office: ul. Krupówki 20 (tel. 638 58). Open Mon.-Fri. 8am-8pm, Sat. 8am-2pm, Sun. 9am-11am. **Postal code:** 34-500.

Telephones: ul. Zaruskiego 1, near the post office. **Phone code:** 0165.

ACCOMMODATIONS AND CAMPING

Since Zakopane sits at the summit of mountain tourism in Poland, it is crowded from July to September, around Christmas, during February, and around Easter. Prices skyrocket in high seasons by 50-100%. **IT** (see **Tourist Offices,** above), is a popular source of private rooms and pensions (20-60zł per person). Or prowl around the town and its outskirts looking for *pokój, noclegi,* or *Zimmer* signs (10-15zł, with some haggling). Hikers often stay in **schroniska** (mountain huts), but call ahead in summer to avoid being stranded in the middle of nowhere.

PTTK Dom Turysty, ul. Zaruskiego 5 (tel. 632 81). A large chalet in the very center of town. Spacious rooms and reasonably clean bathrooms with 24hr. hot water. 4-bed dorms 20zł per person; 6- to 8-bed dorms 16zł per person; more-than-8-bed dorms 14zł. 3zł surcharge for stays of only 1 night.

Schronisko Młodzieżowe (HI), ul. Nowotarska 45 (tel. 662 03). From the bus station, walk down ul. Kościuszki toward town, then take the 2nd right onto ul. Sienkiewicza and walk 2 blocks. The hostel is across the street. Small rooms in a large, loud building. Somewhat clean showers open daily 5-10pm. Curfew 11pm. Doubles 46zł. 4- to 6-bed dorms 17zł per person. Larger dorms 13zł per person. Sheets 3zł. The required HI card may be purchased for US$2 per night, US$9 for one year.

Student Hotel "Żak," ul. Marusarzówny 15 (tel. 157 06), in the south part of town on the Biały Potok stream, close to hiking trails. About 30min. walk from the train and bus stations. Head south on ul. Jagiellońska; after about 15min., turn right on ul. Witkiewicza, which turns into ul. Kazimierza. Take a left on ul. Grunwaldzka, and follow ul. Marusarzówny to the end and around the bend. Small, fresh rooms with thin mattresses. Only 2 toilets and 4 showers for as many as 50 guests, but clean and recently renovated. Hot water, except in the evenings. 6- to 8-bed dorms 12zł per person, with ISIC 9.50zł. Sheets 4zł.

Schronisko Morskie Oko (tel. 776 09), by the Morskie Oko lake (see **Hiking,** below). A gorgeous, clean hostel in an ideal location—you won't mind the trek to the scenic lake. 3- to 6-bed rooms 28zł per person, 14zł in the old part of the hostel. Reception open 8:30am-9:30pm. Reservations a must.

Camping Pod Krokwią, ul. Żeromskiego (tel. 12 256), across the street from the base of the ski jump. From the train station, head south on ul. Jagiellońska; at the church, make a quick right on ul. Witkiewicza and an immediate left on ul. Chałubińskiego. Follow ul. Czecha from the roundabout, and turn right on ul. Żeromskiego. Bungalows 22zł per person, with shower 25zł. Hotel rooms 25zł per person, with shower 30zł. Tents 7-9zł plus 7zł per person, students 6zł.

FOOD

Highlanders sell *oscypek* (goat cheese), the local specialty, on street corners. From a distance, the salty cheese resembles carved wood; up close, it looks like a little roll. Vendors have a poor reputation for refrigeration; watch out for anything that might spoil. For other supplies, head for the grocery store **Delikatesy**, ul. Krupówki 41 (open daily 7am-7:45pm), or its competing neighbor, **Baca** (open daily 7am-10pm).

U Wandy, ul. Sienkiewicza 10. Heading toward the train station from town on ul. Kościuszki, turn right on ul. Sienkiewicza. The restaurant is on the right in a private home. Servings so immense and tasty that guests need help getting up. The small-of-stomach may want half portions. Chicken cutlet 8zł. Open Tues.-Sun. 2-6pm.

Karczma Obrochtówka, ul. Kraszewskiego 10a (tel./fax 639 87). Head up ul. Krupówki, and continue when it merges with ul. 3-go Maja. After passing ul. Makuszyńskiego to the right, ul. Kraszewskiego is the first alley on the left, after an *apteka.* Worth the search for its great kitchen and folk atmosphere, complete with candles and conversation. Soups 4-7zł. Main dishes 4-19zł. Open daily noon-10pm.

Teatralna, (tel. 627 66) ul. Zamoyskiego 1A, up ul. Krupówki toward the mountains. The hanging costumes in this new establishment frequented by actors come directly from the Kraków Theater. Vegetarian (around 5zł), Italian (8-12zł), and Polish food. Open daily 1pm until last guest leaves, sometimes as late as 3am.

SIGHTS AND ENTERTAINMENT

On a rainy day, check out **Stary Kościół Parafialny** (Old Parish Church), ul. Kościeliska, and its nearby cemetery. This small wooden church is the oldest in Zakopane and filled with awe-inspiring woodwork. Even many of the tombstones are made of wood. To find it, take a left at the bottom of ul. Krupówki onto ul. Kościeliska; the church will appear on the right a few minutes later. The **Muzeum Tatrzańskie,** ul. Krupówki 10 (tel. 152 05), across a little footbridge on the left, has exhibitions on the history of Zakopane and the customs of the *górale* (mountain people; open Tues.-Sun. 9am-4pm; 2zł, students 1.20zł; Sun. free; English guidebook 2zł). A branch of the museum at ul. Kościeliska 18 (tel. 136 02) displays examples of the different architectural styles characteristic of Zakopane (open Wed.-Sat. 9am-4pm).

Chata Zbójnicka (Bandit's Hut; tel. 142 17; fax 639 87), ul. Jagiellońska, is by far the best place for raucous and intoxicating mountain nights. Five minutes south of the train station, a gravel path takes off to the left and leads directly up to the music-filled mountain house. The only way to be allowed in is to kick the door loud enough that the doorkeeper decides you're sufficiently hardy to endure an evening in the *chata.* He may tell you to go away on your first try. The more attitude you throw back, the more welcoming he'll be. A folk band provides dance music, and the staff serves a tea so potent its fumes alone will raise your spirits (10zł). Don't be surprised if the waiters tell their guests to serve or cook their own food—or if someone leaves with his tie cut off or with her face smeared with charcoal (open daily 5pm-midnight). For a quieter evening, check out the cafes on ul. Krupówki. At **Piano-Cafe,** ul. Krupówki 63, you can try out the piano, or just sit and talk around the flower-filled tables (0.5L *Żywiec* 3.50zł; open until around midnight).

HIKING

The magnificent **Tatrzański Park Narodowy** (Tatran National Park) provides abundant opportunities for short or long hikes. Entrances to the park lie at the head of each trail (1zł, students 0.50zł; keep your ticket). For dramatic vistas, catch a bus or minibus to **Kuźnice** (every 20min., 1zł), south of central Zakopane. Or walk along ul. Jagiellońska, ul. Chałubińskiego, or ul. Przewodników Tatrzańskich from the train station to catch the 1955m **Kasprowy Wierch** cable car. (Open July-Sept. daily 7am-6:30pm; June 7:30am-6:30pm; March-May and Oct. 7:30am-5:40pm; Dec.-Jan. 8am-4:10pm; Feb. 8am-4:40pm. Round-trip 17zł, students 11zł.) Before hiking, buy the map *Tatrzański Park Narodowy: Mapa turystyczna* at a kiosk or bookstore (see **Essentials: Wilderness and Safety Concerns,** p. 42, for hiking info). For an overview of the Tatras, see the map in the Slovakia chapter.

Dolina Kościeliska (half-day): An easy and lovely hike crosses a valley of Potok Kościeliski. A bus shuttles from Zakopane to Kiry (every 30min., 1.50-2zł), where a green trail takes off south toward Hala Smytnia and continues to Mała Polanka Ornaczańska. One route leads to Jaskinia Mroźna (Frost Cave), about an hour-long excursion. The valley makes a good biking route as well.

Morskie Oko (Sea Eye; 1406m, half-day): The mountain lake Morskie Oko dazzles herds of tourists every summer. Take a bus or minibus from Zakopane's bus station (11 per day, 45min., 3zł) to Polana Palenica (Burnt Clearing), a.k.a. Łysa Polana (Bald Clearing), then hike an easy 9km along the road (2½hr. each way).

Dolina Chochołowska (Mulch Valley; full day): Take the westbound trail from the entry to Dolina Kościeliska, which turns south into Dolina Chochołowska after 3.5km. The trail follows Potok Chochołowski along an easy climb to a clearing.

Giewont (1909m, 4½hr.): Giewont's silhouette looks like a man lying down, hence the mountain's starring role in so in many legends as the "Sleeping Knight." The moderately hard blue trail (6km) leads to the peak. Begin at the lower cable car station in Kuźnice, and follow signs to the peak along Droga Brata Alberta and Piekło (Hell). Chains anchored into the rock help with the final ascent.

Czerwone Wierchy (Red Peaks; 2122m, full day): The red trail leads west from the top of the cable car at Kasprowy Wierch (see above) along the ridge separating Poland and Slovakia. Four of the 7 peaks along the way have paths that allow tired hikers to return to Zakopane. From the last peak, Ciemniak, the trail descends to the exit of Dolina Kościeliska, connected to Zakopane by bus.

Dolina Pięciu Stawów Polskich (Valley of the Five Polish Lakes; full day): One of the most beautiful hikes in the area. The 14hr. summer-only option departs from Kuźnice and leads along the blue path to Hala Gąsienicowa. Refuel here at Schronisko Murowaniec, then continue to Czarny Staw (Black Tarn). On the incline to Zawrat, you'll get to climb hand-over-hand up the chains. In the valley, another *schronisko* waits at Przedni Staw (Front Tarn) to shelter those exhausted by the hike or overwhelmed by the scenery. The blue trail ends 200m north (it sounds easy, but there are several steep climbs and descents) at Morskie Oko, where you can eat, drink, or spend the night (see **Accommodations,** above). From the lake, a road travels down to Łysa Polana, which is connected to Zakopane by bus. A shorter version of the hike (6-8hr.) begins at Łysa Polana. Head in the direction of Morskie Oko (see above). A green path takes off to the right about 45min. into the hike, after the waterfall Wodogrzmoty Mickiewicza. This heads to Dolina Pięciu Stawów Polskich. Once you reach Wielki Staw (Great Tarn), head east towards Przedni Staw and follow the trail to Morskie Oko.

Rysy (2499m, 8hr.): To claim you've climbed Poland's highest peak, follow the red trail from Schronisko Morskie Oko (see **Accommodations,** above) along the east lakeshore and up to Czarny Staw (Black Tarn). The arduous climb to Rysy begins in the tarn's southeast corner. Only for the fittest, and only in good weather.

■ Near Zakopane: Przełom Dunajca

A relaxing trip to the legend-packed Przełom Dunajca (PSHEH-wom doon-EYE-tsa; Dunajec Gorge) suits those no longer craving Tatran thrills. The two- to three-hour float on a wooden **raft** includes a Polish guide in traditional costume who navigates the cliff-bounded waterways, crossing the Polish-Slovak border for 1km of the ride. Look out for the place where the Slovak Robin Hood, Janosik, purportedly jumped 12m from bank to bank. The seven large stone slabs on the hill supposedly represent seven priests who were turned to stone as punishment for their trysts with a holy sister. Around the bend, the nun's silhouette is carved into the cliff.

The rafts travel from Sromowce to Szczawnica (daily May-Oct.). Tickets (bags over 5kg require their own) cost 20zł (May-Aug.) and 18zł (Sept.-Oct.; tel. (0187) 297 21; office open May-Aug. daily 8:30am-5pm; Sept. 8:30am-4pm; Oct. 8:30am-2pm). Direct **buses** go to Sromowce from Zakopane at 9am and 1:45pm (1½hr., 4.80zł). **Minibuses** also make the trip, leaving as soon as they're full (15zł). To catch a direct

POLAND

bus back to Zakopane (4 per day, 2hr., 6.80zł), walk 20 minutes down the riverside road to ul. Manifestu Lipcowego, which runs to the bus terminal.

■ Bielsko-Biała

A composite of two towns that used to belong to two duchies, Bielsko-Biała (BYEL-skoh BYAH-wah) is one of the only places in Poland where two religions—Catholicism and Lutheranism—thrive. Thanks to its history of religious tolerance, Bielsko-Biała, the prewar home of dynamic Jewish and German minorities, has always done well for itself. Today, the city proudly proclaims that it is "traditionally rich" to travelers using it as a base for trips to the Beskidy mountains.

ORIENTATION AND PRACTICAL INFORMATION

Bielsko-Biała has two hearts: the Bielsko castle and center in the west, and the Biała *rynek* in the east, separated by a 10-minute walk along **ul. 11-go Listopada**. The train and bus stations are 15 minutes north of the Bielsko center along **ul. 3-go Maja,** the main thoroughfare. Because of the town's split personality, getting around could cause you to blow a few spark plugs yourself. To get to the Biała *rynek* from the train station, continue down ul. 3-go Maja and turn left down the concrete stairs immediately before **pl. Chrobrego** and the Bielsko *zamek*. This will connect to ul. 11-go Listopada, which crosses the Biała river and eases on down to the Biała center.

Tourist Offices: In-Tour, ul. Piastowska 2 (tel. 122 139; fax 122 406), at the intersection with ul. 3-go Maja. Sells brochures and maps of the city and region (2-6zł). Open Mon.-Fri. 8am-5pm, Sat. 8am-noon. **Orbis,** ul. 3-go Maja 9a (tel. 124 00 or 232 61; fax 207 84). Sells international ferry, bus, and plane tickets; helps find hotels; and gives out maps and brochures. Open Mon., Wed., and Fri. 9am-5pm, Tues. and Thurs. 10am-5pm, Sat. 9am-4pm.

Currency Exchange: Bank PKO S.A., ul. 11-go Listopada 15 (tel. 127 231). Cashes AmEx, Thomas Cook, and Visa traveler's checks at 1% commission (minimum 5zł) and a stiff exchange rate, and offers MC and Visa cash advances. Open Mon.-Fri. 8am-6pm, Sat. 9am-1pm. *Kantors* are concentrated along ul. 11-go Listopada.

Trains: ul. Warszawska 2 (tel. 128 040, info 933), at the north end of ul. 3-go Maja. To: Bratislava (2 per day, 5½hr., 75zł); Katowice (30 per day, 1½hr., 6zł); Kraków (4 per day, 2¾hr., 9zł); Warsaw (5 per day, 6hr., 15zł); Zakopane (2 per day, 7zł).

Buses: ul. Warszawska 5 (tel. 123 125, info 228 25), connected to the train station by an overpass. To Kraków (18 per day, 2¼hr., 8zł) and Oświęcim (4 per day, 4zł).

Medical Assistance: ul. Wyspiańskiego 21 (tel. 122 045).

Post Office: ul. 1-go Maja 2 (tel. 151 001; fax 210 50). Open Mon.-Fri. 7am-8pm, Sat. 7am-1pm. *Poste Restante* at window #9. **Postal code:** 43-300.

Telephones: At the post office. **Phone code:** 033.

ACCOMMODATIONS AND FOOD

PTTK Dom Wycieczkowy, ul. Krasińskiego 38 (tel. 230 19), five minutes from the bus and train stations, rents spacious rooms, some with white-tiled bathrooms. Look for the stately green-and-white building to the left of ul. Piastowska. (Lockout 10am-6pm; curfew 10pm. Doubles 38zł, with bath 55zł; triples 50zł, with bath 80zł; 5- to 7-bed dorms 15zł per person. Sheets included.) **Pod Pocztą** (Under the Post Office), ul. 1-go Maja 4a (tel./fax 124 730), just *past* the post office, maintains decent but dark rooms with sinks and clean communal bathrooms (singles 60zł; doubles 70zł). **Youth Hostel "Bolka i Lolka,"** ul. Komorowicka 25 (tel. 274 66), is a short walk off ul. 11-go Listopada; turn left one street past the main *rynek*. Populated by a younger crowd, these up-to-8-bed dorms sometimes sport a television set (lockout 10am-5pm; curfew 9pm; 12zł per person; sheets 2zł).

Restaurants abound around the central ul. 11-go Listopada, as do grocery stores; one of the larger ones is **Savia,** ul. 11-go Listopada 38 (tel. 233 44; open Mon.-Fri. 6:30am-9pm, Sat. 6:30am-8pm, Sun. 8am-4pm). For a reasonably good meal at the

The Who?

The farther south one travels in Poland, the more likely it is to run into signs advertising Italian clothes, Italian cars, and—most importantly—Italian ice cream (soft-serve, not the *gelati* you loved in Florence). But the Polish word for "Italian," *włoski*—VWO-skee—clearly has nothing to do with Italian. This stems from an ancient case of mistaken identity: the Poles who first came into contact with the distant Italians mistook them for another tribe, and the name sticks to this day, making an order of Italian cuisine a potentially tongue-twisting experience. And if you say "Italian," you'll get a swift correction.

lowest price in the town, try the **Bar Mleczny** at the PTTK hostel (see above). Meals run under 6zł (open Mon.-Fri. 8am-6pm, Sat. 8am-4pm). **Restauracja Starówka,** pl. Smołki 5 (tel. 224 24), off ul. 3-go Maja at the beginning of ul. 11-go Listopada, displays a diverse menu in Polish and English and dabbles in Polish, French, and Chinese cuisines (main dishes 10-20zł; open daily 10am-midnight). **Pizzeria Margerita** (tel. 125 161), ul. Cechowa, off ul. 11-go Listopada, serves up pizzas (5-17zł) and a garden of salads (4zł; delivery available; open Mon.-Sat. from 11am, Sun. from noon).

SIGHTS AND ENTERTAINMENT

Bielsko's modest 14th-century **castle** stands above pl. Chrobrego, though the entrance is located on its south end at ul. Wzgórze 16 (tel. 125 353). Its museum houses a collection of European paintings and sculptures (open Tues.-Wed. and Fri. 10am-3pm, Thurs. 10am-6pm, Sat. 9am-3pm, Sun. 9am-2pm; 1zł, students 0.50zł). The simple, early 20th-century **Katedra św. Mikołaja** (St. Nicholas's Cathedral), pl. Mikołaja 19 (tel. 124 506), just south of the castle, got bumped up from provincial church status only a few years ago, when the Pope transformed the local parish into a bishopric. The grounds of **Kościół Ewangelicko-Augsburski** (Lutheran Church), pl. Lutra 8 (tel. 127 471), just northwest of the castle, feature Poland's only **statue of Martin Luther.** Bielsko's **Stare Miasto,** just west of the castle, is perfect for strolling, with its crowded narrow streets and galleries. The grandest view of all, though, spreads along the main thoroughfare, **ul. 3-go Maja.** The 19th-century architecture on this street has led some to liken Bielsko to Vienna, despite a dreary Communist-era, brownish-gray color darkening many of the facades.

The tall towers of **Kościół Opatrzności Bożej** (Providence Church), ul. Ks. Stojałowskiego 64 (tel. 144 507), south of central Biała, are easily spotted. Peek in at its Baroque interior, and don't miss the small gold pulpit showing Jonah bidding the whale farewell. The **ratusz,** two blocks south of ul. 11-go Listopada next to the Biała stream, is a striking piece of Historicist architecture, modeled after a medieval hall. The portals in the northeast corner of the square merit a closer look.

The repertoire of the experimental **Puppet Theater "Banialuka,"** ul. Mickiewicza 20 (tel. 121 046), off the northwest corner of pl. Chrobrego, ranges from folk tales to classic dramas. (Performances Wed.-Fri. 11am and 1pm, Sun. 4pm; closed during tours and July-Aug; every 8th show intended for adults. Tickets 4zł; ticket counter open Tues.-Fri. 11am-1pm.) Across from the theater, relax at **Café Dziupla,** ul. Mickiewicza 15. This cellar pub offers a pool table as well as drinks (0.5L *Żywiec* 3zł) and music (open Mon.-Fri. 11am-11pm, Sat.-Sun. 4-11pm; live piano music every Thursday at 7pm). **John Bull Pub,** ul. 11-go Listopada 60/62 (tel. 121 661), in Biała's second square just south of its main *rynek,* pours imported British beer (0.4L of John Bull bitter 8.80zł) as well as the locally brewed *Tyskie* (0.4L 3.40zł; open Mon.-Sat. 11am-midnight, Sun. 4pm-midnight).

Just a few kilometers south of Bielsko-Biała lies the sleepy town of Żywiec (ZHIH-vyets), home to Poland's best-known, hardest-hitting signature **brew** of the same name. Because the **Żywiec Brewery** is a long way down ul. Browarna, which often lacks a sidewalk, the fastest, safest way to the miracle factory is to take **bus #1, 5, 10,** or 15 from the bus stop at the entrance to the *rynek* (1zł). **Trans-Trade-Żywiec,** ul. Browarna 90 (tel. (033) 612 701; tel./fax 615 773), is unmistakable—a modern complex of buildings with trucks and trains pouring in and out. Unfortunately, the brewery conducts tours only by special arrangement; call in advance. But if you've come for the drink, the **Piwarnia** (Beer Garden) sells the freshest, cheapest beer in Poland; Żywiec products are sold at manufacturer's cost (0.3L 1.80zł) in a traditional setting (open daily 11am-10pm). After a couple of hours here, the town begins to look pretty. Twenty-two **trains** connect Bielsko-Biała and Żywiec daily (40min., 5.80zł round-trip). The **bus station,** across the street from the train station, sends 11 buses per day to Bielsko-Biała.

■ Near Bielsko-Biała

CIESZYN/ČESKÝ TĚŠÍN

The Olza River divides Polish Cieszyn (CHEH-shin) from Czech Český Těšín (CHESS-kee TEH-shin). Walking across this natural boundary is **the cheapest way to cross the Czech/Polish border.** From the Cieszyn bus station, ul. Korfantego (tel. (033) 520 279), or the train station, ul. Hajduka 10 (tel. (033) 520 108), diagonally across from the buses, it's about a 15-minute walk to the footbridge (Most Przyjaźni) into the Czech Republic. The most direct route is to walk up the short hill to ul. Korfantego and turn right. Take another right onto ul. Jana Michejdy and follow it until it hits ul. Zamkowa; a left here will bring you to the footbridge. Once across the Czech border, continue straight on ul. Hlavní until you reach the railroad tracks, and turn left onto ul. Nadrazni. The **Český Těšín train station** (tel. (0659) 579 41), ul. Nadražní, will be on your right (10min. walk from the bridge). The **bus station** (tel. (0659) 578 41), ul. Jablunkovská, is nearby—cross the train tracks and a main road, and bear slightly toward the right. Buses from Cieszyn head to: Katowice (every hr., 1½hr., 8zł); Bielsko-Biała (every hr., 1hr., 4zł); and Kraków (5 per day, 3hr., 13zł). Trains take off to: Bielsko-Biała (10 per day, 1¼hr., 3.70zł); Kraków (1 per day, 3hr., 9.60zł); and Katowice (1 per day, 1¾hr., 11.10zł). Trains leave Český Těšín to: Brno (4 per day, 3hr., 160kč); Olomouc (4 per day, 1½hr., 56kč); and Prague (4 per day, 5hr., 160kč).

The worn streets of 1000-year-old Cieszyn provide a few options for killing time between bus connections. As the story goes, King Leszko's three sons were united at a **well** in what is now Cieszyn after a long trek. They were so overjoyed to meet that they created a town around the well called Cieszyn ("happy"). From the *rynek,* go down ul. Głęboka, and turn left onto ul. Sejmowa. The first right on ul. Trzech Braci (Three Brothers) will take you down a steep cobblestone hill to the well where the brothers supposedly met. Near Most Przyjaźni stand the remains of Cieszyn's **medieval castle.** After trudging up a wobbly, cobbly hill, you can climb the tower's narrow stairs for an amazing panoramic view of both Poland and the Czech Republic (open daily April-Oct. 9:30am-5pm, Nov.-March 9:30am-3pm; 1zł, students 0.50zł.)

Targowa, ul. Stary Targ 1 (tel. (033) 521 854), has a welcoming blend of tourists and locals. The funky angled chairs give each table some privacy (salads 1.80zł per 100g, *pierogi* 5.50zł). An ideal spot for coffee and sweets, **Corso,** ul. Głęboka 21 (tel. (033) 522 903), has people-watching terrace seats and a sparkling white interior. Tortes 1.50zł (open Mon.-Sat. 9am-7pm, Sun. 9am-9pm).

■ Szczyrk

Gymnastics for the English-speaking tongue (mumble a "sh" sound with an "rk" at the end), Szczyrk's name comes from the sound that the Żylica stream makes as it passes through town—or so say the legends. Offering more hiking, mountain biking, ski jumping, and ski lifts than any other retreat in Poland, Szczyrk is a year-round tourist destination, and the second largest winter resort in the country.

Orientation and Practical Information Szczyrk is tucked away in a valley of the **Beskid Śląski** mountains, the westernmost part of the Carpathians. Frequent **buses** (43 per day, 30min., 2zł) connect the town to Bielsko-Biała. The town stretches for 8km along the **Żylica,** although most services are concentrated in the 2km **centrum.** Bus stops line the main thoroughfare. Take the bus to "Szczyrk Centrum," and then go left on ul. Beskidzka to find the **tourist office,** ul. Beskidzka 41 (tel./fax 178 187). It offers detailed mountain biking and skiing info, as well as **maps** of the town and hiking trails (open Mon.-Fri. 8:30am-4pm, Sat. 10am-2pm). **Exchange currency** at **Bank PKO,** ul. Beskidzka 12 (tel. 178 350; open Mon.-Fri. 10am-4:30pm). There is a **pharmacy** at ul. Myśliwska 11 (tel. 179 166; open Mon.-Fri. 9am-10pm, Sat.-Sun. 9am-7pm). For those whose skills and precautions fail them, **mountain rescue (GOPR)** is reachable at ul. Dębowa 2 (tel. 178 986; emergency 986). **Equipment rental,** including mountain bikes, is available next door at Dębowa 1 (tel. 178 789). A **post office** with ringing **telephones** sits at ul. Beskidzka 101 (open Mon.-Fri. 7am-8pm, Sat. 8am-1pm, Sun. 9-11am). **Postal code:** 43-370. **Phone code:** 033.

Accommodations and Food   Lodgings span the entire range: hotels, hostels, pensions, and private rooms. **Beskidy,** ul. Myśliwska 4 (tel. 178 878), has pleasant rooms that may be guarded by a rather protective dog (9-12zł per person, with shower 16-20zł; prices slightly higher in winter; open daily 10am-5pm). Only a 10-minute walk from the center of town, **Dom Turysty PTTK,** ul. Górska 7 (tel. 178 321; fax 178 979), at the "Szczryk PTTK" bus stop, has two-, three-, and four-person rooms with bath (20zł per person). Farther from the town and the main hiking/skiing trails but connected by frequent buses to "Szczyrk Skalite" is **Camping Skalite,** ul. Kampingowa 4. (Tel. 178 760; reception open daily 8am-7pm. Tent sites 5zł per person; tents 4-6zł; bungalow doubles 32zł, with bath 41zł; triples 41zł, with bath 55zł.)

Unfortunately, Szczyrk's restaurants are largely limited to kiosks. Keep in mind that summer is the off season, so there's less of everything. To stock up on food before hiking or biking, stop by the 24-hour **Delikatesy,** ul. Beskidzka 4 (tel. 178 585).

Sights and Hiking   Although mellow mountains flank both sides of the town, most activity is focused on **Skrzyczne,** the highest peak in the region (1257m), and as unpronounceable as its namesake town. Ski lifts ascend the slopes of Skrzyczne and its neighbor, **Małe (Little) Skrzyczne** (1211m); many well-marked **hiking** and **mountain biking** trails aim for both peaks. For a full view of possible paths, buy a map or check out the boards at the intersection of ul. Górska and ul. Beskidzka. The flatter bike trails are marked by circles; the steeper, hiking-only trails by lines. The longer green trails start by these signs, while the more challenging red and blue trails begin by the "Szczyrk Kolejka" bus stop. Szczyrk is an equal opportunity mountain—even the laziest travelers can appreciate the views from the top. From the base near the "Szczyrk Kolejka" bus stop, a **chair lift** whisks panorama pursuers to their destination. The lift, ul. Myśliwska 45 (tel. 178 620; fax 178 662), has two sections: upper and lower (each 2.50zł, full round-trip 10zł; lift operates daily from 8:30am-5:30pm).

Of the many **caves,** the most famous is **Jaskinia Malinowska** (Malinowska Cave). On the slopes of Malinowska Skała at an elevation of 1005m, the caves contain 132m of passageways—legend has it that a treasure was hidden in this maze by the 16th-century outlaw Ondraszek, so keep your eyes open. The flies don't bite, but they love visitors. Other than them, you may be the only one there. Bring insect repellent and proper equipment. Take the bus to "Szczyrk Salmopol," and then follow the green trail. The green trail from Szczyrk centrum heads to the cave—after passing Skrzyczne, Małe Skrzyczne, Kopa Skrzyczeńska (1189m), and Malinowska Skała (1152m) on the way. Even if a little spelunking doesn't float your boat, the incredible hike over the high trails affords more-than-worthwhile views of heaven. Keep left at the two forks after Skrzyczne and go right (follow the signs) at the third to get to Malinowska Skała. The round-trip hike across the four peaks and back to Szczyrk takes about four hours. Some of the terrain may be muddy. For general info on hiking, see **Essentials: Wilderness and Safety Concerns,** p. 42.

POLAND

Map of Romania showing cities, monasteries, camping sites, and neighboring countries including Slovak Republic, Ukraine, Hungary, Moldova, Yugoslavia, and Bulgaria.

ROMANIA
(ROMÂNIA)

US$1	= 7450 lei (ROL)	1000 lei =	US$0.13
CDN$1	= 5386 lei	1000 lei =	CDN$0.19
UK£1	= 11,851 lei	1000 lei =	UK£0.08
IR£1	= 10,921 lei	1000 lei =	IR£0.09
AUS$1	= 5420 lei	1000 lei =	AUS$0.19
NZ$1	= 4728 lei	1000 lei =	NZ$0.21
SAR1	= 1585 lei	1000 lei =	SAR0.63
DM1	= 4091 lei	1000 lei =	DM0.24
Country Phone Code: 40		**International Dialing Prefix: 00**	

Ruins dating from ancient to medieval times dot Romania's landscape and testify to the country's glorious yet troubled history, while exquisite monasteries from Walachia to Moldavia recall the artistic achievements of those years. Ensconced within the mysterious Carpathian Mountains, the countryside unveils stunning views. On the other side of the country, the Black Sea Coast blends peaceful beaches with fast-action fun in the summer. Romanians go out of their way to make visitors feel at home. In the end, those willing to seek out Romania's treasures rather than focus on the damaging effects of Ceauşescu's Communism are sure to be rewarded.

ROMANIA ESSENTIALS

Americans do not need visas for stays of up to 30 days. Citizens of Australia, Canada, Ireland, New Zealand, South Africa, and the U.K. all need visas to enter Romania. Single-entry visas (US$22) allow for a 60-day visit, and multiple-entry visas (US$68) are good for 180 days; transit visas (US$22) are valid for four days. Obtain a visa at a Romanian embassy (see **Essentials: Embassies and Consulates,** p. 5) or at the border for no additional fee. To apply, submit a passport, payment by money order, and a letter stating the type of visa needed. Get a visa extension at a local police station.

GETTING THERE

You can **fly** into Bucharest on Air France, Alitalia, British Airways, Delta, Lufthansa, Swissair, or TAROM. **TAROM** (Romanian Airlines) is currently renewing its aging fleet; it flies direct from Bucharest to New York, Chicago, and most major European cities. The recent renovation of Bucharest's Otopeni International Airport has improved the notoriously bad ground services, but the airport is still far from ideal.

Trains head daily toward Western Europe via Budapest. There are also direct trains to and from Chişinău, Moscow, Prague, Sofia, and Warsaw. To buy **international tickets** in Romania, go to the **CFR** (Che-Fe-Re) office in larger towns. Budapest-bound trains leave Romania through either Arad or Oradea; when you buy your ticket, you'll need to specify where you want to exit. An ISIC will occasionally get you a 50% discount on domestic tickets, but technically student discounts are for Romanians only.

Buses connect major cities in Romania to Athens, Istanbul, Prague, Varna, and various cities in Western Europe. With private international bus companies, it is generally cheaper to take a domestic train to a city near the border and then catch a bus from there. Since plane and train tickets to Romania are often expensive, buses are often a good, if slow, option. Inquire at tourist agencies about timetables and tickets, but buying tickets straight from the carrier saves you from paying a commission.

GETTING AROUND

CFR sells domestic **train** tickets up to 24 hours before the train's departure. After that, only train stations sell tickets, generally only an hour before the train leaves. There is an info desk at the station where you can ask which counter sells tickets to your destination (staffers occasionally speak English). The timetable *Mersul Trenurilor* is incredibly useful in forming a plan of attack (L5000; instructions in English and French). Schedule info is available at tel. 221 in most cities. **Interrail** is accepted.

There are five **types of trains:** *InterCity* (indicated by an "IC" on timetables and at train stations), *rapid* or *expres* (in green), *accelerat* (red), and *de persoane* (black or blue). *InterCity* trains stop only at major cities such as Bucharest, Cluj-Napoca, Iaşi, and Timişoara, and have three-digit numbers. *Rapid* trains (also 3 digits) are the next fastest; *accelerat* trains also have three digits, but are slightly slower and dirtier. *De persoane* have four digits, are downright slow and dirty, and stop at almost all stations. The even slower *cursă* trains are also indicated by four-digit codes and stop at every single stop. The price differential between **first class** (*clasa-întii,* wagons marked with a "1" on the side, 6 people per compartment) and **second class** (8 people per compartment) is small, but the difference in comfort and security is significant. If you take second class in the summer, be prepared to spend your time hanging out in the hall with everyone else looking for some cool air. Only *de persoane* are well-ventilated, since one window is inevitably open. If taking an **overnight train,** opt for first class in a *vagon de dormit* (sleeping carriage). During holiday periods or for July and August trips to the beach, try to purchase tickets at least five days in advance.

Use the extensive local **bus** system only when trains are not available. Although buses cost about the same as trains, they are usually packed and poorly ventilated. Look for signs for the *autogară* (bus station) in each town.

Domestic **flights**—on Soviet-era An-24 airplanes—connect Bucharest's Băneasa Airport (closer to downtown than Otopeni) to all major Romanian cities. Fares are expensive, but prices are lower than in the EU. TAROM has a good safety record.

Hitchhiking, though popular, remains risky; *Let's Go* does not recommend it. A wave of the hand, rather than a thumb, is the recognized sign. Some Romanians drive vans that become unofficial buses along popular routes. Big trucks are most likely to stop and most likely to be going long distances. Drivers generally expect a payment similar to the price of a train ticket for that distance for providing a lift, although some kind souls will take you for free or accept whatever you can afford. Do not hitchhike at night if you can avoid it.

TOURIST SERVICES

ONT (National Tourist Office) used to be one of the more corrupt government agencies in Romania; it was customary to bribe its employees for any service. The times are changing, though ONT still doesn't always give reliable information about the price and availability of cheap rooms. Branches in expensive hotels are often more useful than the main offices. The chaos that reigns in the Romanian tourist industry means that nobody knows what belongs to whom. ONT acts as one of many **private tourist agencies** providing travel packages for a commission, while at the same time giving "official" tourist information. Hotels and restaurants start up and shut down all the time, and prices change with dizzying speed; double-check all important data directly. **BTT,** the youth travel agency, is designed for groups and will be befuddled by your presence. Your best bet is to find friendly Romanians to help you.

MONEY

The Romanian unit of currency is the leu, plural **lei** (abbreviated L). The most common banknotes are L500, L1000, L5000, L10,000, and the brand-new L50,000. Coins come in L100 and L50 denominations. Pay for everything in lei; whenever someone offers to take U.S. dollars directly, it's usually at a disadvantageous rate.

Because many Romanians stave off the inflation demons by carrying dollars or marks, **private exchange bureaus** litter the country; unfortunately, few take **credit cards** or **traveler's checks.** Know the going rates and commissions before exchanging money. U.S. dollars and Deutschmarks are preferred, though other common currencies can usually be exchanged somewhere. Always keep receipts for money exchanges. **Unofficial currency exchange** is illegal, but getting cheated is more of a risk than getting jailed. Don't hand over your money before you get your lei, and check your bills carefully. **ATMs,** which generally accept Cirrus, MC, Plus, and Visa, give lei at reasonable rates. Most banks cash traveler's checks in dollars or marks, then exchange them for lei, a process that generally incurs high fees.

COMMUNICATION

Orange phones take **phone cards;** all non-orange phones take **coins.** Unless you like the idea of carrying around a kilogram of coins, use a phone card, available at telephone offices in denominations of L20,000 and L40,000. Rates per minute run L4000 to neighboring countries, L6500 to most of Europe, and L11,900 to the U.S. International access numbers include: **AT&T Direct,** tel. 018 00 42 88; **British Telecom,** tel. 018 00 44 44; **Canada Direct,** tel. 018 00 50 00; **MCI WorldPhone,** tel. 018 00 18 00; and **Sprint,** tel. 018 00 08 77. They aren't kidding when they write "not available from all phones." Some phones will also arbitrarily cut off calling card calls after a few minutes. Shop around for the best phone—try the phone office. **Local calls** cost L300-400 and can be made from any phone; **intercity calls** can be made from the new digital phones (orange and blue) or from old phones marked *telefon interurban.* Dial several times before giving up—a busy signal may just indicate a connection problem. It may be necessary to make a phone call *prin comandă,* that is, with the help of the operator at the telephone office. It costs a lot more and is no easy task, but may be the only option in small towns. At the phone office, write down the destination, duration, and phone number for your call. The clerks shout your telephone destination in the most incoherent way possible, so stay nearby. Pay up front, and always ask for the rate per minute. At the post office, request *avion* for **airmail,** which takes one to two weeks to reach the U.S.

LANGUAGE

Romanian is a Romance language; those familiar with French, Italian, Spanish, or Portuguese can usually decipher public signs. In Transylvania, **German** and **Hungarian** are widely spoken. Throughout the country, **French** and **Russian** are common second languages for the older generation, **English** for the younger. English-Romanian dictionaries are sold at book-vending kiosks everywhere. Spoken Romanian is a lot like Italian, but with two additional vowels: "*ă*" (pronounced like "u" in "cut") and the interchangeable "*â*" or "*î*" (like "e" in "winter"). The other two characters peculiar to the Romanian alphabet are "*ş*" ("sh" in "shiver") and "*ţ*" ("ts" in "tsar"). At the end of a word, "*i*" is rarely pronounced. "*Ci*" sounds like the "chea" in "cheat," and "*ce*" sounds like the "che" in "chess." "*Chi*" is pronounced like "kee" in "keen," and "*che*" like "ke" in "kept." Don't forget to roll, roll, roll your r's!

HEALTH AND SAFETY

> **Emergency Numbers: Police:** tel. 955. **Ambulance:** tel. 961. **Fire:** tel. 981.

Most **public restrooms** lack soap, towels, and toilet paper. Reflecting a decline in public services, many restrooms on trains and in stations smell as if they haven't been cleaned in years. Worse yet, attendants charge L300-500 and give you only a square of toilet paper. Pick up a roll at a newsstand or drug store. It's also possible to find relief at most restaurants, even if you're not a patron.

Beware the adrenaline-high **drivers** in congested Bucharest. Whether they're paved or not, roads in Romania tend to be littered with holes, and unlit carriages and carts compound the danger of road transportation in the country.

Stash basic medicines in your backpack; any given drugstore (*farmacie*) may not have what you need. *Antinevralgic* is for headaches, *aspirină* or *piramidon* for colds and the flu, and *saprosan* for diarrhea. Condoms (*prezervative*) are available at all drugstores and at many kiosks. **Feminine hygiene** products are sold in big cities.

ACCOMMODATIONS AND CAMPING

While some **hotels** charge foreigners 150-300% more than locals, lodging is still less expensive than in Berlin or Vienna—just don't expect the same quality. As a general rule, one-star hotels are iffy, corresponding to a mediocre European youth hostel; those with two stars are decent; and those with three are good but expensive. In some places, going to ONT (in resorts, the *Dispecerat de Cazare*) and asking for a room may get you a price up to 50% lower than that quoted by the hotel. This arrangement allows hotels to fill unsold rooms and ONT to earn a nice commission.

Private accommodations are generally the way to go, but hosts rarely speak English; be aware that renting a room "together" means sharing a bed. Such rooms run L40,000-50,000 per person, possibly including breakfast and other amenities. See the room and fix a price before accepting. Many towns allow foreign students to stay in **university dorms** at insanely low prices. Ask at the local university rectorate; ONT *may* be able to help. **Campgrounds** are crowded and their bathrooms redefine the word "foul." Relatively cheap **bungalows** are often full in summer.

FOOD AND DRINK

Romanian food is fairly typical of Central Europe, with a bit of Balkan and French thrown in. Romanians rarely eat out, which explains the relative scarcity of restaurants. An average homemade dish is usually better than a similar dish cooked at 90% of Romanian restaurants, so try to wrangle a dinner invite. In the mountains, shepherds will often sell you fresh cheese, sometimes for a pack of cigarettes. Try a private bakery for the best *pîine* (bread). *Lapte* (milk) is rather fatty; powdered milk is available in many shops. On the street, you can find cheap *mititei* (a.k.a. *mici*—garlicky barbecued ground meat) or Turkish-style kebabs, but beware the long-languishing meat some vendors attempt to sell. Ice cream (*înghețată*) is cheap and tasty. Harder to find, but worth the effort, are the sugary *gogoși* (fried doughnuts).

Lunch usually starts with a soup, called *supă* or *ciorbă* (the latter is saltier and usually better), followed by a main dish (usually grilled pork, beef, or chicken) and dessert. Soups can be very tasty; try *ciorbă de perișoare* (with vegetables and ground meatballs), *ciorbă de văcuță* (with vegetables and beef), *ciorbă de fasole* (with beans), or *ciorbă de burtă* (with tripe). Pork comes in several varieties, of which *mușchi* and *cotlet* are the best quality. Vegetarians will probably want to stick to salads, which are usually good and cheaper than meat anyway. For dessert, *clătite* (crepes) or *papanași* (doughnuts with jam and sour cream) can both be fantastic if they're fresh. Specialties include *mămăligă* (cornmeal served with butter, cheese, and sour cream) and delicious *sarmale* (ground meat in grape or cabbage leaves).

In restaurants, note that some prices are per 100g rather than per portion. If you order certain meats, such as chicken, there is no way to predict how many grams you will actually receive and, therefore, how much you will have to pay. *Garnituri*, the extras that come standard with a meal, usually have a price for each and every item—including a dollop of mustard! Generally speaking, if the waiters put it in front of you, you're paying for it, so make sure you know all the prices beforehand.

CUSTOMS AND ETIQUETTE

It is customary to give inexact change for purchases, especially those under L100. "Non-stop" cafes and kiosks can be found in all cities, but this doesn't necessarily mean they're open 24 hours; shops close arbitrarily when attendants run errands, wash the floor, or go home early. Be wary of weekend **business hours**—many banks and businesses may be closed on Friday afternoons. **Churches** are open most of the day, and you'll find more people praying than taking pictures. Services are lengthy (4hr. on Sun.), but people quietly come and go at all times. At small churches, services are often heralded by someone walking around the church hitting a board to scare away evil spirits.

Romanians take pride in their country's tradition of **hospitality.** Most will be eager to help, offering to show you around town or inviting you into their homes. When you're visiting, bring your hostess an odd number of flowers. Romanian **men** are generally fairly respectful of women. When giving directions, it's normal for a man to lead you by the arm or with a light hand on the back. If he puts his arm around your waist, however, he wants something. **Disabled travelers** may be dismayed to find that very few establishments are wheelchair-accessible. Even if a hotel has an elevator, there are usually a few steps before the building's entrance.

Homosexuality has been legal in Romania only since 1996, and public display of affection for gays is still illegal. Keep in mind that outside the major cities, many Romanians hold conservative attitudes toward sexuality, which may translate into harassment of gay, lesbian, and bisexual travelers. Consequently, homosexuals in Romania are well-hidden, and gay hangouts are ephemeral, if they exist at all. Romanian women often walk arm-in-arm or hand-in-hand without anyone batting an eye.

NATIONAL HOLIDAYS

Romanians observe: January 1-3, New Year's; April 12, Catholic Easter; May 1, May Day; December 1, Union Day; December 25-31, Christmas.

LIFE AND TIMES

HISTORY

The area that is now Romania has been inhabited by a variety of peoples since around 2000BC. Greek historian Herodotus recorded the presence of two major tribes, the **Getae** and the **Dacians,** by the 5th century BC. After a bloody war from 101 to 106, Emperor Trajan conquered Dacia. The Dacian leader, Decebalus, resented Roman control as much as he welcomed Rome's artisans. The Roman administration retired in 275 in the face of attacks from the east, but the colonists stayed, as did their effect on the Romanian language—the only Latin-based Eastern European language.

Over the course of the next eight centuries, the region was invaded by Visigoths, Huns, Avars, Slavs, Bulgars, and Magyars, and was subject to the **First Bulgarian Empire** between the 8th and 10th centuries, when Eastern Orthodox Christianity was introduced. During the 11th century, **Transylvania** was absorbed into the Hungarian empire. **Walachia,** the first Romanian state (called Muntenia or Țara Româneasca by the Romanians), was established south of the Carpathians in the early 14th century. **Moldavia,** east of the Carpathians, followed in 1349. Walachia's Mircea cel Bătrân fought off the 14th-century invasions of the **Ottoman Turks.** For nearly 30 years, **Ștefan cel Mare** (Stephen the Great; 1457-1504) of Moldavia resisted the likes of Mohammed the Conqueror of Constantinople and repulsed attacks of Moldavia's Christian "allies." After his death and the fall of Budapest in the 15th century, however, Walachia and Moldavia became Turkish vassals. **Mihai Viteazul** (Michael the Brave), ruler of Walachia, conquered Transylvania and Moldavia in 1600, but the union didn't survive his murder the next year.

Surrounded by the Austro-Hungarian Empire to the west, the Poles and Lithuanians to the north, the Russians to the east, and the Ottomans to the south, Romania was a battleground for the superpowers until the 1800s. Moldavia and Walachia effected their union in **1859** by simultaneously electing **Alexandru Cuza** to be their prince. Yet, faced with a divided country and possible dissolution, he was forced to abdicate in 1866 in favor of newly elected foreign Prince **Carol Hohenzollern-Sigmaringen** (prince 1866-81; King Carol I 1881-1914). Carol stamped out corruption, built the first railroads, and built up the army that in 1877 finally won independence from Turkey. With the disintegration of the Austro-Hungarian Empire after its defeat in WWI, Romania managed to double its territory, gaining Transylvania (from Hungary), Bukovina (from Austria), and Bessarabia (from Russia). **December 1, 1918,** the date of the union, is Romania's National Day. Romania's population also doubled, gaining substantial minority groups, including Hungarians in Transylvania and Jews in Bessarabia.

> Forced to choose between the Stalinist USSR and Nazi Germany, Romania's dictator, General Antonescu, picked the latter.

Greater Romania's size was short-lived, however. The country looked toward western powers to help it defend itself, but France and Britain seemed indifferent to Romania's economic plight, and the signing of the German-Soviet Nonaggression Pact at the beginning of **WWII** signaled no help there. Between June and September of 1940, the USSR reclaimed Bessarabia and northern Bukovina, Hungary took Transylvania, and Bulgaria took southern Dobrogea. Squeezed between the Stalinist USSR and Nazi Germany, Romania's dictator, **General Antonescu,** chose the latter. In 1944, **King Mihai** orchestrated a coup, herded up over 50,000 German troops, and attempted to surrender to the Allies. Romania's fate, however, had already been decided by the Big Three, and the Soviets soon infiltrated the government, arrested hundreds of citizens, and forced the king into exile. The **Romanian People's Republic** was proclaimed on December 30, 1947.

Opposition was violently suppressed in the **postwar era.** More than 200,000 Romanians died in jails or labor camps during the purges of the 1950s; farms were forcibly collectivized. In 1965, **Nicolae Ceaușescu** became the leader of the Communist

ROMANIA

Party. Although he tried to lessen Romania's dependence on Moscow—which earned him the praise of NATO—he pursued ruthless domestic policies. Industrialization created useless, polluting factories. To cover foreign debt, Ceaușescu exported basic products, creating chronic domestic shortages. The average Romanian lacked food and heat, and electric power was randomly cut off. In the 80s, Ceaușescu began to "systematize" villages—demolishing them and transplanting the people into urban, concrete-block nightmares.

By the late 80s, Ceaușescu had turned Romania into a police state, but in **1989,** the country erupted in a **revolution** as ruthless as the man it pulled down. The revolt started as a minor event in Timișoara, when the dreaded *Securitate* (Secret Police) arrested a popular Hungarian priest. Riots soon ripped around the country, and clashes with security forces in Bucharest on December 21-22 brought thousands of protesters into the streets. Ceaușescu and his wife were arrested, summarily tried, and executed on Christmas Day. Meanwhile, protesters and the army battled the *Securitate* for control of the national television system. Many claim this revolution was actually a carefully prepared coup, citing the subsequent deaths of almost everyone who came in contact with the Ceaușescus during their arrest.

The enthusiasm that followed these December days didn't last, as power was seized by **Ion Iliescu's National Salvation Front,** composed largely of former Communists. Iliescu was himself a high-ranking Communist official whom Ceaușescu pushed into minor positions for his pro-Russian leanings. Despite his past, Iliescu won the 1990 presidential elections with 70% of the vote and slowly began to reform the system. In June 1990, Iliescu garnered international condemnation after calling miners to repress student demonstrations in Bucharest; for three days, the miners terrorized the city, beating anyone resembling a protester.

LITERATURE

Think of Romania and literature, and what pops to mind is the tale of Count Dracula. Though it may have Romanian roots, Bram Stoker and his vampire-obsessed imitators do not. The identification, however, is not entirely inappropriate, as Romanian literature has throughout its history taken its cue from other cultures.

The 17th century saw the flowering of the Romanian historiographic tradition, although several prominent examples were written in languages other than Romanian, including the Moldavian **Miron Costin's** verse history of Moldavia in Polish and Prince **Dmitri Cantemir's** Latin histories of the region. During most of the 18th century, Ottoman oppression quashed Romanian literary activity. Toward the end of the century, however, Romanian literature was reawakened. **Alecu Văcărescu** fathered the Romanian lyric tradition. **Ienachiță,** Alecu's father, wrote the first grammar of the language, Alecu's son **Iancu** is considered by some the father of Romanian poetry, while **Nicolae** was also a noted poet.

The **Pașoptisti,** the French-influenced generation of the 1840s, enthusiastically cultivated a wide range of new genres; **Grigore Alexandrescu's** fables and satires stand out among them. Building on the Pașoptist tradition, the next generation—clustering around the literary magazine *Junimea*—penned the great classics of Romanian literature. Turning to German culture as a model, the Junimea writers combined cosmopolitan awareness with a preoccupation with defining Romanian national identity in literature. **Mihai Eminescu,** the Romanian national poet—often called the "Great Lost Romantic"—brought Romanticism to an unprecedented peak. His monumental poem *Luceafărul* combines the reinterpretation of cosmological myths and discussions about immortality with delicate terrestrial love scenes. The Junimea generation also fostered Romania's most celebrated dramatist and satirist, **Jon Luca Caragiale,** and greatest story-teller, **Jon Creangă,** as well as one of Romania's first great women poets, **Veronica Micle,** Eminescu's beloved.

The interwar years saw praiseworthy novels of every type. **Hortensia Papdat Bengescu** wrote family novels with an emphasis on women's lives. **Carmil Petrescu** focused on the "problem of the intellectual" in *Patul Lui Procust (Procust's Bed)*. Critic **G. Câlihescu** wrote the experimental, style-conscious novel *Enigma Otiliei*, while **Liviu Rebreanu** became Romania's most important Realist writer. The lyric poem, Romania's strongest tradition, was represented by writers like Rilke-influenced **Lucian Blaga,** poet and mathematician **Ion Barbu, G. Bacovia**—an original Symbolist—and, most of all, **Tudor Arghezi.** History of religion, philosophy, and literary theory met in the works **Eugène Ionescu,** one of the world's best absurdist dramatists, **Emil Cioràn,** a celebrated essayist and stylist in France, and **Mircea Eliade,** an important religious historian. Another member of this generation, **Constantin Noica,** became, through his philosophical writings, a major intellectual figure. The absurd is a category often revisited in Romanian literature by **Tristan Tzara,** founder of French Dadaism, and the most revolutionary of the interwar prose writers—**Urmuz.**

Sucked into the Soviet sphere in the wake of WWII, Romanian writers exchanged their long-standing allegiance to Western models for the shopworn hackery of **Socialist Realism.** Writers such as **Arhezi** were denied the right to publish, while others, including **M. Sadoveanu** and **C. Petrescu,** changed poetics to suit this new tone. **Marin Preda,** who later died under mysterious circumstances, became a celebrated novelist, and **Nichita Stânescu** opened a new age in Romanian lyric poetry.

> **Though the story of Dracula may have Romanian roots, Bram Stoker and his legions of vampire-obsessed imitators do not.**

Since 1989, much of the work of censored writers as novelist and poet **Ana Blandiana** and **Mircea Cârtărescu** has been published and is starting to gain international recognition. In 1992, Cârtărescu's *Visul* (*The Dream*) was nominated in France for the Médicis Prize as well as for "The Best Foreign Book of the Year." The work of some intellectuals imprisoned by Communists during the 50s has also appeared since 1989. **Nicolae Steinhardt** recounts the spiritual ascension of a man enduring some of the most cruel and anti-human prisons of the 20th century in *Jurnalul Fericiru.*

ROMANIA TODAY

In the first democratic transfer of power in Romania's history, **President Emil Constantinescu** replaced the Communist Ion Iliescu in November 1996. A reformist from the Romanian Democratic Convention party (CDR), Constantinescu has pledged an era of reform. He hopes to repair the economy by opening Romania up to capital markets and by lifting barriers on international investment, and promises to bring to trial those responsible for the numerous bouts of political violence that marred Romania's first post-Communist years. The parliamentary elections of 1996 overthrew the leftist coalition of Nicolae Vacaroiu, which had attracted the concern of Western governments with its slowly paced reforms, and replaced it with a new liberal coalition under the leadership of **Prime Minister Victor Ciorbea.** Prosperity, however, may still be far away; ragged beggars in front of flashy shop windows remind visitors that Romania has a long and painful climb ahead. In the 1997 NATO expansion negotiations, France supported admitting Romania into the military alliance but was rejected by a United States fearful of the financial implications. Nonetheless, French President Jacques Chirac has predicted that Romania will be invited in by 1999.

Bucharest (București)

Bucharest (București; BOO-coo-resht) bears the scars of Romania's political struggles. Settled continually since Neolithic times, the capital derives its name from an ancient shepherd named Bucur. First mentioned in a 1459 document signed by Vlad Țepeș (a.k.a. Vlad the Impaler), the city spent centuries as just another stop on the road from the Balkans to Central Europe before becoming the capital of Muntenia. As the capital of unified Romania in 1859, Bucharest garnered such titles as "Little Paris" and "Pearl of the Balkans" for its boulevards, parks, and fine Neoclassical architecture. Today, the metropolis is a somber ghost of its former self; relatively untouched by war, this city has been destroyed in times of peace. Ceauşescu's government demolished many historic neighborhoods, replacing them with concrete blocks. However, instead of the impersonal skyscrapers typical of other major cities, parks and historic buildings, many of which are currently undergoing face-lifts, dot the cityscape.

ORIENTATION AND PRACTICAL INFORMATION

Bucharest lies some 60km from the Danube in south Romania. The main streets all radiate from the center. After exiting Gara de Nord, the main **train station,** head left and then take a right on **Calea Griviţei.** Continue east on Calea Griviţei and go right on **Calea Victoriei** to reach the sights. Or walk another four blocks on **Str. Biserica Amzei,** the continuation of Griviţei, to **Bd. Magheru** near Piaţa Romană (which becomes Bd. Bălcescu and Bd. Brătianu), the main artery. It's also possible to take the Metro or trolley #79 from the station to **Piaţa Romană,** where Bd. Magheru begins. The English-language *Nine O'Clock* (daily) and *România Liberă* (weekly) are both free in major hotels. **Maps** difficult to find elsewhere in Romania are sold by the barrel in Bucharest, especially by the street vendors in Piaţa Universităţii.

Tourist Offices: For reliable help, go to the main **ONT** office, Bd. Magheru 7 (tel. 614 07 59). From Piaţa Romană, walk down Magheru; ONT is on the right behind a line of trees. Offers **maps** (L2000), tours, and info on sights and accommodations across Romania, as well as **private rooms** (US$20 per person in the center, $15 on the outskirts). The office has a **Europcar rental** desk and an **exchange office** (with bad rates). Open Mon.-Fri. 8am-8pm, Sat. 8am-3pm, Sun. 8am-1pm. Major hotels also have tourist info desks. Get a free **map** at most major hotels.

Embassies: Canada, Str. Nicolae Iorga 36 (tel. 222 31 78), near Piaţa Romană. Open Mon.-Thurs. 8:30am-1pm and 2-5pm, Fri. 8:30am-1pm. **Russia,** Şos. Kiseleff 6 (tel. 617 13 19). Open Mon., Wed., and Fri. 9am-1pm. **South Africa,** Str. Grigore Alexandrescu 86 (tel. 746 85 81). Open Mon.-Fri. 9am-2pm. **U.K.,** Str. Jules Michelet 24 (tel. 312 03 03; fax 312 02 29). Open Mon.-Thurs. 8:30am-1pm and 2-5pm, Fri. 8:30am-1:30pm. Citizens of **Australia, Ireland,** and **New Zealand** should contact the U.K. embassy. **U.S.,** Str. Tudor Arghezi 7/9, a block behind Hotel Intercontinental. For services, go to the adjacent consulate at Str. Snagov 26 (tel. 210 40 42, after-hours tel. 210 01 49; fax 211 33 60). Open Mon.-Thurs. 8am-11:30am and 1-3pm, Fri. 8-11:30am.

Currency Exchange: Avoid changing money on the street by going to one of the many currency exchange offices. Banks will usually extract a ridiculous commission (US$5 min. on traveler's checks). For a better rate, try the **O.K. exchange bureaus,** 16 N. Bălcescu (open "non-stop"; credit cards 9% commission, traveler's checks 7%) and Bd. Magheru 33 (open Mon.-Fri. 8:30am-9:30pm, Sat. 8:30am-8pm; credit cards 9%, traveler's checks 4%). The ubiquitous **IDMs** also take checks and cards, but at almost L1000 less per dollar than O.K. **ATMs** are at major banks, including **Bancorex,** near Piaţa Victoriei and Universităţii.

American Express: Represented by Marshall Tourism, Bd. Magheru 43, 1st floor, #1 (tel. 223 12 04). Replaces lost cards and checks, but cashes traveler's checks only in an emergency. Open Mon.-Fri. 9am-5pm, Sat. 10am-noon.

Flights: Otopeni Airport (tel. 230 00 22), 16km outside of the city, for international traffic. Bus #783 to Otopeni leaves from Piaţa Unirii every 1-2hr.; if you're coming from the airport, buy tickets on board (L3000) or get a magnetic card strip in the center. Coming from Otopeni, buses stop near Hotel Intercontinental on Bd. Magheru. **Băneasa Airport** (tel. 232 00 20), connected with Piaţa Romană by bus #131 (L1000) and Gara de Nord by bus #205, handles domestic flights. Buy **international tickets** at the **CFR/TAROM office,** Str. Domniţa 10 (tel. 646 33 46; see **Trains,** below). The TAROM office at Piaţa Victoriei (tel. 659 41 85), sells domestic and international tickets. Both open Mon.-Fri. 7am-7pm, Sat. 7:30am-1pm.

Trains: Gara de Nord (tel. 57 76) is the principal station. **Obor** (tel. 152), accessible by trolley #85 from Gara de Nord or #69 from Piaţa Universităţii, and **Băneasa** (tel. 48 27), accessible by bus #301 from Piaţa Romană, are secondary stations that may be useful for travel to and from the Black Sea Coast. **Tickets** can be purchased in advance at **CFR,** Domniţa Anastasia (tel. 614 55 28). From Piaţa Universităţii, head

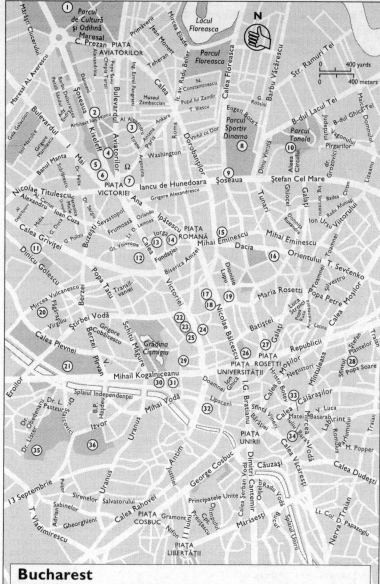

Bucharest

1 Village Museum
2 Russian Embassy
3 Ministry of Foreign Affairs
4 Geological Museum
5 Romanian Peasant Museum
6 Museum of Natural History
7 Government of Romania
8 Dynamo Stadium
9 Emergency Hospital
10 Bucharest Circus
11 North Railway Station
12 Art Collections Museum

13 Goethe Institute
14 Canadian Embassy
15 British Council
16 French Library
17 Romanian Development Agency
18 Romanian Atheneum
19 State Ownership Fund
20 National Military Museum
21 Opera House
22 National Art Gallery
23 Great Palace Hall
24 Senate

25 Natl. Agcy. for Privatization
26 National Theatre
27 American Library
28 Italian Library
29 Palas
30 Ministry of Justice
31 City Hall
32 National History Museum
33 Caritas
34 Jewish Theatre
35 Progresul Arena
36 Casa Republicii

ROMANIA

How to Have a Pleasant Time in Gara de Nord

You may hear a number of scary stories regarding Gara de Nord. In reality, it's no better or worse than major transportation hubs throughout Europe, but here are some extra safety tips that will help you handle the station like a pro.

1. Know where you're going. The station is shaped like a T. To get to the second class ticket counters from the main entrance, head straight and take the right branch; the second-class area is at the far end to the right. The less crowded first-class ticket counter is on the right side of the entrance corridor. The information booth is at the intersection of the T.

2. Don't carry money in an easy-to-swipe place. Pickpockets are common.

3. Do *not* spend the night here! If you've run out of money, go home!

4. Don't be afraid to ask for help. This is Romania, after all, and people are always happy to help. If you are having communication problems, at least one of the illegal money changers in front of IDM Exchange will speak English. Just don't exchange money with them. IDM is on the left side of the entrance corridor.

5. Don't take a taxi, unless you really know what you're doing (see **Taxis,** below). Drivers will overcharge you from the station; take the Metro instead.

---

west on Bd. Carol I toward Bd. Kogălniceanu. Turn left on Str. Brezoianu and then left on Domnița Anastasia. Domestic tickets sold on the ground floor, international and TAROM on the 1st floor. Open Mon.-Fri. 8am-7pm, Sat. 8am-noon. Learn the phrase *"Un bilet pentru…"* (One ticket to…). To: Budapest (6 per day, 13hr., L220,000); Chișinău (1 per day, 13hr., L73,000); Istanbul (1 per day, 18hr., L215,000); Kiev (1 per day, 17hr., L300,000); Sofia (2 per day, 10hr., L160,000).

Buses: Filaret, Piața Gării Filaret 1 (tel. 336 06 92), and **Rahova,** Șos. Alexandriei 164 (tel. 220 44 10), are in the south suburbs; **Obor** and **Băneasa** train stations also host bus stations. For international buses, ask about departures at the main office. The **Toros** bus line (tel. 638 24 24), right outside Gara de Nord, sells tickets to Istanbul leaving from Gara de Nord (3 per day, Sat. 1 only; 12-15hr.; L200,000). For buses to Athens, try **Liotsikas,** Bd. Cantemir 25 (tel. 330 46 46; 3 per week, 20hr., $50). Offices for destinations in Western Europe cluster around Piața Dorobanților along Str. Sofia. International buses tend to be good and cheap—better than a train!

Public Transportation: Buses, trolleys, and **trams** cost L800. Punch your ticket when getting on the bus. If caught without a punched ticket, you'll pay a hefty fine. Buy tickets at a kiosk before you get on—not all buses sell them on board. **Express buses** generally only take magnetic cards (L4000 round-trip), except #783. Unlimited day passes are available for all regular transportation lines (L5500) but not at all ticket kiosks. Buses are packed on busy routes—people literally hang out the doors. Hold on to valuables! The **Metro** offers less crowded, reliable service to all major points in Bucharest (runs daily 5am-midnight). Magnetic strip cards cost L1800 for 2 trips, L7500 for 10 trips, or L3500 for a day pass.

Taxis: tel. 953. Expect to pay at least L1500 per km. Try to hail "state taxis" with the number 053 on the rear passenger door. Arrange the *prețul* (price) before accepting a ride. Taxi drivers have long been overcharging foreigners; they can now do it legally by setting the meter on *"Tarif #2."* Try to negotiate a fixed price (L20,000-30,000 is probably the best you'll get)—the driver is likely to pocket the money.

Car Rental: Avis (tel. 312 20 43), in Hotel București, a little north of the national Art Museum on Calea Victoriei. Rents cars starting from US$33 per day plus US$0.33 per km and US$17 insurance.

Hitchhiking: *Let's Go* does not recommend hitchhiking. Those hitching north take bus #783 to the airport. Those heading to the Black Sea and Constanța hop on tram #14 from Piața Sf. Gheorghe, near Piața Universității on Bd. I.C. Brătianu. At the end of the line, they switch to bus #146 to get farther. To Giurgiu and Bulgaria, people take the Metro to Eroii Revoluției and hop on bus #275 to the end of the line. To Pitești and western Romania, travelers take the Metro to Industriilor, then get on bus #150 (dir. "Sat. Rudeni") and get off when it looks like a good hitching spot.

Luggage Storage: Gara de Nord has one for foreigners and one for locals—so much for the "mixed luggage keeps the peace" theory. L1800-4000. Open 24hr. Storage is on the left wall as you enter the main entrance.

Bucharest Metro

- Yellow Line
- Blue Line
- Red Line
- Orange Line
- Terminus
- Street
- Waterway

24-Hour Pharmacies: Şos. Colentina 1 (tel. 635 50 10), by the Bucur Obor Metro stop, and in Gara de Nord (tel. 222 91 55). Ring the bell at night. Info tel. 065.

Medical Assistance: Spitalul de Urgenţă, Calea Floreasca 8 (tel. 230 01 06). Near the Ştefan cel Mare Metro station.

Express Mail: DHL, Calea Victoriei 63 (tel. 312 26 61), behind Hotel Bucureşti in the same office as a travel agency.

Internet Access: Raffles, Calea Victoriei 25 (tel. 311 26 82), just south of Bd. Carol I. L6500 per 30min. Open Mon.-Fri. 10am-6pm, Sat. 10am-2pm. **Internet Cafe,** Bd. Carol I 25. From Piaţa Universităţii, head east on Bd. Carol I until Piaţa Rosetti. Use the Internet on the ground floor (L7000 for 15min.; L12,500 for 30min.).

Post Office: Str. Matei Millo 10 (tel. 613 03 87). From Piaţa Universităţii, walk west on Bd. Carol I, turn right on Calea Victoriei, and turn left at the tall telephone office. Open Mon.-Fri. 7:30am-8pm, Sat. 7:30am-2pm. *Poste Restante* is 3 doors down, next to Hotel Carpati. **Postal code:** 70154.

Telephones: Orange **card phones** allow international calls from throughout the city. Try the train station and near the **telephone office,** Calea Victoriei 37. Open 24hr. Use the side entrance on the same street as the post office. You can also order collect or operator-assisted calls. For directory assistance, dial 930. **Phone code:** 01.

ACCOMMODATIONS

The ONT office on Bd. Magheru can arrange **private rooms** or **hotel** accommodations. Men hanging out by the hotels in front of Gara de Nord offer rooms at L40,000-50,000 per person. For tried-and-true private accommodation, ask about private rooms at the hotel or cafe-bar near Hard 'n' Heavy Cafe. During the school year (early Sept. to late June), Romanian students will often share their drab rooms. Try the **dor-**

mitories of the **Polytechnic Institute** near the Semănătoarea Metro. The hotel situation is not rosy; good hotels are worth the money, rat-holes cost more than they should, and it's hard to find decent rooms for less than L100,000-200,000 per person.

Hotel Cerna, Str. Golescu 29 (tel. 637 40 87). A surprisingly nice hotel next to Gara de Nord. Exit the station and turn right. Small but pleasant rooms come with or without decent bathrooms. Singles L48,000, with bath L120,000; doubles L85,000, with bath L160,000; apartments L250,000.

Villa Helga Youth Hostel, Str. Salcâmilor 2 (tel. 610 22 14). Friendly and funny staff provides beds, free laundry, and Romanian cigarettes. Hang out with English-speakers in the TV room. US$12 per bed. Meet staffers at Gara de Nord or take bus #86, 79, or 133 from Piaţa Romană to Piaţa Galaţi (east along Bd. Dacia), then take a right on Str. V. Lascăr, a hard left on Str. Viitorului, and a right on Str. Salcâmilor.

Hotel Triumf, Şos. Kiseleff 12 (tel. 222 31 72; fax 223 24 11). Feel like a noble at this hotel in the heart of embassy row. Balconies have an excellent view of the gardens. Singles with shower L250,000, with bath L270,000; doubles with shower L360,000, with bath L390,000. L20,000 breakfast credit included. Laundry service available. Take bus or trolley #131, 205, 301, or 331 (from Piaţa Lahovari) to Arcul de Triumf and walk south on Şos. Kiseleff; the hotel is on the left. MC, Visa.

Hotel Bucegi, Str. Witing 2 (tel. 637 52 25), across from Hotel Cerna and Gara de Nord. Small, dark rooms with okay bathrooms. Singles with shower L40,000; doubles with sink L70,000, with bath L80,000; triples L90,000; quads L90,000.

Hanul Manuc, Str. Iuliu Maniu 62-64 (tel. 613 14 15; fax 312 28 11). From Unirea and McDonald's in Piaţa Unirii, head straight along the north side of Piaţa Unirii on Str. Halelor and take the first right. This former monastery, founded in 1808, offers its guests tranquility in the center of Bucharest. Comfy rooms, all with bath. Singles L236,000; doubles L435,000. AmEx, Visa, MC. Call ahead.

FOOD

Open-air markets offering all manner of veggies, fruits, meat, and cheese abound in Bucharest—good ones are at Piaţa Amzei, Piaţa Matache, and Piaţa Latina. To reach **Piaţa Amzei** from Piaţa Romană, head down Str. Mendeleev (between Bd. Dacia and Bd. Magheru) and turn right. **Piaţa Matache** is easily reached from Gara de Nord: head left, then right, down Calea Griviţei, and the second street on the right leads to the market. From Piaţa Universităţii, hop on trolley #66, 69, 70, 85, 90, or 92 east to **Piaţa Rosetti;** or, with your back to Hotel Intercontinental, turn left and walk east on Bd. Carol I for 10 minutes to reach **Piaţa Latina.** Markets are open daily but tend to be slower on Sundays. There's a **covered market** at Piaţa Dorobanţilor (open Mon.-Sat. 8am-8pm, Sun. 8am-2pm), reachable from Piaţa Romana by buses #131 and 301. **Grocery stores** are also plentiful—**Vox Maris Supermarket,** at Piaţa Victoriei, is open 24 hours. For excellent **bread and pastries,** check out one of the Turkish bakeries or **Ana,** Str. Radu Beller 6 (tel. 230 67 00) or Calea Dorobanţilor 134 (tel. 230 57 32), both near Piaţa Dorobanţilor (open Mon.-Sat. 8am-8pm, Sun. 9am-noon). When eating in a restaurant, be sure your cheap, delicious lunch isn't transformed into an outrageous rip-off. Ask to see the menu, and check the math.

Cafe de la Joie, Str. Lipscani 80-82 (tel. 312 29 10). This French-style bistro delights with Art Nouveau decorations and an abundance of salads (L10,000). Located in the Old Town; the address is somewhat misleading. From Piaţa Universităţii, walk down Bd. I.C. Babtianu and turn right on Str. Lipscani. Take the next left; the cafe is marked by a "bistro" sign. Open Mon.-Sat. 6pm until 2 or 3am.

Club Art Papillon, Str. Matei Voievod 66A (tel. 642 55 37). From Piaţa Universităţii, walk east on Bd. Carol I, which becomes Bd. Republicii and then Bd. Pache Protopopescu. Turn right on Str. Matei Voievod and left at the fork; Papillon is on the right (20-30min.). Trolleys #86 from Piaţa Romana and #90 from Universităţii head down Matei Voievod. An artsy hangout with wicker chairs and musical entertainment during the school year. Meat main dishes under L10,000. Open 24hr.

Pescarul (The Fisherman), Bd. N. Bălcescu 9 (tel. 650 72 44), across the street from Hotel Intercontinental at Piaţa Universităţii. Almost goes overboard with the sailor atmosphere—there's even a boat sticking out of the wall. Delicious full meals L30,000-40,000. Open Mon.-Sat. 10am-11pm. Visa. The bar/coffeehouse hybrid next door hosts a **disco** after 8pm (L5000 cover, L10,000 Sat.).

Casa Oamenilor de Ştiinţa (COŞ), Piaţa Lahovari 9 (tel. 211 19 99). From Piaţa Romană, head east on Bd. Dacia until the first intersection with Str. Dorobanţilor. COŞ is on the opposite side of Hotel Dorobanţi in Piaţa Lahovari. Dine outside in a shady, fountain-filled garden or inside amid Baroque opulence. Meals L50,000-70,000, drinks included. Open daily noon-midnight.

Carul cu Bere, Str. Stavropoleos 5 (tel. 613 75 60). The facade earned a place in ONT's souvenir photo album, and the interior ain't too shabby, either. Chicken soup *à la greque* L4500. Meals up to L40,000. Folklore performances nightly at 8pm. Open daily 10am-1am. MC, Visa.

SIGHTS

Piaţa Universităţii, home to the **National Theater,** is in the heart of downtown. Demonstrators perished fighting Ceauşescu's forces here on December 21, 1989, the day before his fall. In spring 1990, students protesting the new ex-Communist leaders occupied the square and declared it a "Neo-Communist-free zone"; for almost two months they held daily meetings that gathered tens of thousands of people, with many of Romania's top intellectuals speaking from the university balcony. After President Iliescu called the protesters *golani* (hooligans), the crowd sang "*Imnul Golanilor*" ("Hymn of the Hooligans") daily. Demonstrations were smothered in June 1990 by the brutal three-day intervention of a few thousand miners brought in by the government. Crosses commemorating the martyrs line the center of the square, and defiant anti-Iliescu graffiti decorates university walls and the **Architecture Institute,** across from Hotel Intercontinental in the small Piaţa 22 Decembrie 1989.

From Hotel Intercontinental, head straight down Bd. Brătianu to get to the **Bucharest History Museum** (closed for renovations in summer 1997). A few hundred meters farther down on the left lies **Sf. Gheorghe** (St. George's Church), built in 1700 after Constantin Brîncoveanu, the prince of Bucureşti and enemy of the Turks. The interior is under restoration, but don't miss **Kilometer Zero** in the courtyard, from which all distances in the country are measured. Farther down on the right begins famous **Str. Lipscani,** named after the Leipzig merchants who did business here before today's Gypsies and Turks. Turn right onto Str. Lipscani to get to Calea Victoriei, or continue on Bd. Brătianu up to **Piaţa Unirii,** past **Sf. Ion (St. John's Church)** on the left. The inside of this 1774 church is chiseled into rock. Farther down, the *piaţa* is home of Communist Romania's biggest supermarket, Unirea, now converted into the Romanian version of a **shopping mall.**

Ceauşescu drastically rearranged Piaţa Unirii but spared **Dealul Mitropoliei,** the hill on the southwest side, diagonally opposite Unirea. Head up Str. Dealul Mitropoliei to find the headquarters of the Romanian Orthodox Church, in one of the largest **cathedrals** in Romania (open Mon.-Sun. 8am-7pm). Within, on the left, St. Demetrius refuses to rot under a regal shroud. Before the altar on the right, the seat of the patriarch (Romania's Pope) mirrors the seat on the left where the king of Romania, Mihai I, would sit were he in town. In addition to the **Patriarchal Palace,** the cathedral also flanks the former Communist Parliament building. This impressive Baroque construction now belongs to the church and periodically hosts free religious concerts. At the base of the hill stretches Bd. Unirii, formerly "Victory of Socialism Boulevard." Turn left down Bd. Unirii from the Dealul to reach the world's second-largest building (after the Pentagon), **Palatul Parlamentului;** it even has several floors underground. Formerly, this building was Casa Poporului (People's House). This designation is not a source of national pride, as Ceauşescu demolished several historic neighborhoods and spent billions of dollars on the private palace he called the country's "civic center." Ceauşescu also shored up the shores of the **Dîmboviţa,** but, strangely, wasn't able to make the river any bigger.

Bucharest's oldest buildings are northwest of Piaţa Unirii, in the triangle between the river, Bd. Brătianu, and Bd. Kogălniceanu. Behind Hanul Manuc are the ruins of the old princely court, **Curtea Veche,** a former home of Vlad Ţepeş (currently under restoration). From Bd. Brătianu, head west on Str. Lipscani, the somewhat deteriorated center of the old city, to reach Calea Victoriei. Turn left and left again on the side street Stavropoleos to find the 1724 **Stavropoleos Church,** whose name means "town of the cross." Inside, amid smoke-blackened frescoes, is the throne of Prince Mavrocordat, ruler of Walachia in the 1700s (open Wed.-Mon. 8:30am-6pm).

Museums abound in Bucharest. In the Old Town, at the corner of Str. Stavropoleus and Calea Victoriei, **Muzeul National de Istorie a României** (History Museum of Romania), Calea Victoriei 12 (tel. 615 70 55), traces Romanian history from prehistoric times to 1922. The treasures include the famed *cloşca cu pui de aur* (golden hen and chicks). Many believe that the Soviets, who grabbed the collection after WWI, returned copies and kept the originals. Most of the US$500 billion collection has yet to be returned (open Wed.-Sun. 10am-5pm; L3000, students L1500). Head up Calea Victoriei from the museum to reach **Piaţa Revoluţiei** (also called Piaţa Palatului). The Royal Palace, former residence of Romania's kings, is now **Muzeul Naţional de Artă** (National Art Museum), Calea Victoriei 51-53 (tel. 613 30 30). Rumor has it that *Securitate* forces shot at many paintings at point-blank range. The permanent collection is in the part of the museum closed for renovations, with the rest of the museum housing temporary exhibits (open Wed.-Sun. 10am-6pm; L3000, students L1500, Wed. free). Across the street, the polished facade of the grandiose **Bibliotecă** recovers from 1989 tank fire. To the left of the Bibliotecă, behind the tiny park, the elegant **Ateneul Român** is also under restoration. The country's premier classical music hall, it was built in 1888 according to the plans of a French architect. The concert hall's fresco depicts Romanian history from Dacia to WWI, and the flower chandelier is the only one of its kind in Europe. Unfortunately, due to restoration work, visitors will temporarily have to forgo seeing the interior.

North, **Muzeul Colecţiilor de Artă,** Calea Victoriei 111 (tel. 650 61 32), groups several private collections of Renaissance and Romanian paintings as well as some temporary exhibits. The quickest way to this museum is to follow Bd. Dacia west from Piaţa Romană to Calea Victoriei (open Wed.-Sun. 10am-6pm; L3000, students L1500, Wed. free). A 10-minute walk from the museum is **Piaţa Victoriei,** the site of several turbulent demonstrations in 1990. On the north side of the square, by the intersection with Bd. Dacia, is **Muzeul de Istorie Naturala Grigore Antipa** (Antipa Museum of Natural History), Şos. Kiseleff 1 (tel. 650 47 10). The collection of stuffed animals from around the world impresses, but tourists will probably find the Romanian displays more interesting; there's even a mini-cave that recreates the country's stalactite- and stalagmite-filled natural wonders. In summer 1997, only the Romanian fauna exhibit was open during renovations (open Tues.-Sun. 10am-6pm; L1000, students L500). Next door, **Muzeul Ţăranului Român** (Peasant Museum) is the best museum in Europe, according to the 1996 award plaque in the foyer. The remains of a wooden church and religious items indicate that the museum has shed Ceauşescu's shackles (open Tues.-Sun. 10am-6pm; L3000, students L1000). Although it's no substitute for the countryside of Moldavia or Maramureş, the open-air **Muzeul Satului** (Village Museum; tel. 222 91 10) does an excellent job of recreating peasant dwellings from all regions. The museum is in part of Herăstrău park, along Şos. Kiseleff (open daily in summer 9am-7pm, off-season 8am-4pm; L1000). Take bus #131, 205, 301, or 331 to the Muzeul Satului stop, then backtrack a few meters.

On the other side of town, **Muzeul Naţional Cotroceni** (tel. 221 12 00) offers a tour of the royal apartments. Originally built as a monastery, Cotroceni became home to Romania's crown prince Ferdinand. Despite a 1977 earthquake, the museum is in good shape thanks to renovations by Ceauşescu, who wanted to make the building into a hotel for diplomats. Check out the lovely Rococo flower room, the table where Mihai I signed his abdication in 1947, or see, from a distance, the current home of the president of Romania. Call ahead to join a mandatory tour (open Mon.-Fri. 9am-4pm; L20,000, temporary exhibits L8000; English book L20,000; English pamphlet L1000). To reach Cotroceni from Politehnica Metro, head east on Bd. Iuliu Maniu and continue on Şos. Cotroceni; the entrance is on the right.

Visitors to Romania's history museums are often dismayed to find that exhibits presenting the last 50-80 years are non-existent. Not so with **Muzeul de Istorie a Comunitaţilor Evreieşti din România** (Jewish History Museum of Romania), Str. Mămulari 3 (tel. 615 08 37). The ground floor focuses on the history of Romania's Jewish community, while the first floor displays Jewish cultural contributions. The altarpiece of this former synagogue consists of a number of boxes detailing the Holocaust in Romania, which cut the country's Jewish population to 14,000. Ask the English-speaking attendant to explain anything you don't understand (open Wed. and Sun. 9am-1pm; L2000; photos L1000). To reach the museum, head up Bd. Corneliu Coposu from Piaţa Unirii (near Unirea). Take the first right across a parking lot between Unirea and the KMO store, and turn left at the very end of the street.

North of Piaţa Universitaţii, the avenue that connects it to Piaţa Romană (Bd. N. Bălcescu, then Bd. Magheru) was once the Bucharest equivalent of the Champs-Elysées. Turn left on any of the streets that lead to the parallel **Calea Victoriei;** it too was beautiful in the good old days and is making a comeback today. From Piaţa Victoriei, Bd. Lascăr Ctargiu leads to Piaţa Romană, while Şos. Kiseleff and Bd. Aviatorilor lead north; these are Bucharest's most fashionable streets and are rife with beautiful embassies. Near Parcul Herăstrău on Şos. Kiseleff stands **Arcul de Triumf,** built to celebrate Romania's independence from Turkey in 1877. Ten minutes north rises **Casa Presei** (Press House), constructed in the 50s as a copy of Moscow University; many newspapers have offices here. Both sights are accessible by the same buses that go to Muzeul Satului. The sidestreets between Piaţa Victoriei and Calea Dorobanţilor, with names like Paris, Washington, and Londra, brim with villas and houses typical of the beautiful Bucharest that was, and show how even an occasional Communist-era building can be integrated beautifully into a neighborhood. From Piaţa Victoriei, head up Str. Paris behind the fabulously ugly government building, then wander as you will (just don't get lost!) to see Bucharest as it should be.

Bucharest is replete with parks that compensate in part for its urban wastescape. Ten minutes west on Bd. Carol I from Piaţa Universitaţii are the **Cişmigiu Gardens,** one of Bucharest's oldest parks, filled with elegant alleys and a small lake. Nearby is "lovers' way," shaded by a canopy of trees, and a "writers' circle" with busts of many of the country's literary heroes. From March to October, you can burn off calories by renting a **paddle boat** on the lake (daily 8am-8pm, L1500 per hr., L1500 deposit). Across from Cotroceni palace, the **Botanical Gardens,** Şos. Cotroceni 32, offer a peaceful retreat at a site where demonstrators gathered during the 1848 revolution (open daily 8am-8pm; in winter 9am-4pm; L1000, pamphlet in English L2000; ticket booth closes 30min. before park). A 15-minute walk north along either Şos. Kiseleff or Bd. Aviatorilor from Piaţa Victoriei is the beautiful **Herăstrău Park** (take the Metro to Piaţa Aviatorilor). The park has a big lake with **rowboat** and **jet-ski rentals,** a small amusement park, several restaurants, and tennis courts. For boats (open 9am-8pm; L15,000 per hr., L15,000 deposit) and lake tours, head left (west) around the lake. For jet-skis (L5000 per min.), turn right. Across the lake, peacocks occasionally venture onto paths. The bars also provide ample opportunity to rub elbows with locals. Well-groomed **Cişmigiu Park** is, along with Herăstrău Park, the focal point for much of the city's social life. Elderly pensioners, young couples, football players, and chess whizzes abound. Exit Herăstrău park on the west near the amusement park and boat rental, turn left and take your first right to get to the **Ştrand,** a sporting place that includes tennis courts (L20,000 per hr.) and a swimming pool (open May-Sept. 15 7am-6pm; L8000, weekends L10,000; students L3000).

ENTERTAINMENT

Bucharest hosts some of the biggest **rock festivals** this side of Berlin; guests include rising indie groups as well as falling stars like Michael Jackson. Tickets are cheap. Inquire at the tourist office, and keep your eyes peeled for posters. **Cinemas** show mostly American movies with Romanian subtitles. Many have a very relaxed atmosphere; moviegoers often sit at cafe tables while watching the film. For the cinema experience, stick to the establishments that cluster on Bd. Magheru and on Bd. Kogălniceanu (what Bd. Carol I becomes west of Piaţa Universităţii), which show new movies first. Ticket prices are generally around L6000.

Performances

Concerts, plays, and operas in Romania tend to be less expensive than movies (the season runs from Sept. to mid-June). **Atheneul,** Piaţa Revoluţiei (tel. 615 00 26), holds excellent concerts at affordable prices. Also check out **Opera Română,** Bd. M.L. Kogălniceanu 70 (tel. 613 18 57), at the Eroilon Metro, and **Teatrul de Operetă,** Nicolae Bălescu 2 (tel. 613 63 48). Next door, huge banners hanging from the **Teatrul Naţional,** Bd. N. Bălcescu 2 (tel. 613 91 75), in Piaţa Universităţii, announce the season's plays. Also famous are **Teatrul C.I. Nottara,** Bd. Magheru 20 (tel. 659 31 03), and **Bulandra Teatrul Mic,** Str. Constantin Mille 16 (tel. 614 70 81; season ends July 15). Near Piaţa Amzei is the privately owned **Masca,** Str. Biserica Amzei 5 (tel. 230 02 75). Bucharest also boasts Europe's only state Jewish theater—**Teatrul Evreiesc,** Str. Iuliu Barasch 15 (tel. 323 45 30); performances are sometimes staged throughout the summer. The shows are in Yiddish, though the simultaneous headphone translations into Romanian should make everything clear—if you speak Romanian, that is. A state circus, **Circul Globus,** Alcea Circului 15 (tel. 210 41 95), keeps everyone smiling but goes on tour in the summer. Tickets are usually sold starting on Saturday for the following week's performances at each theater's box office; they go quickly, so plan ahead (generally L5000-15,000). Most shows are in Romanian. Tickets are also available one hour before showtime. If a performance is sold out, ask to speak to the manager; he or she may be able to provide you with house seats.

NIGHTLIFE

Pack a map and cab fare—streets are poorly lit, and buses are unreliable. Bars and nightclubs crawl with the *nouveau riche* and foreign businesspeople. Bucharest also suffers from summer disease: clubs and popular hangouts slow down or close while everyone heads on vacation. Bars proliferate, some in luxury hotels. Try the expensive **Dubliner Irish Pub,** Bd. N. Titulescu 18 (tel. 222 94 73), which has Guinness and English-speaking waiters and patrons (open daily noon-2am).

Club A, Str. Blanari 14 (tel. 615 68 53). From Piaţa Universităţii, walk down Bd. Brătianu and take the 3rd right; Club A is on the right. Rumor has it that the vice-consul at the American Embassy is in one of the bands here. Tues. jazz, Wed. blues, Thurs. alternative, Fri.-Sat. disco, Sun. oldies. Cover L4000, Fri.-Sat. L6000, women free weekdays. Open Tues.-Sun. 9pm-5am. Closed in summer.

Martin (tel. 230 32 43), at the intersection of Calea Dorobanţilor and Bd. Iancu de Hunedoara, a 10min. walk from Piaţa Victoriei. Or take bus #131, 301, or 331 to "Perla." Cinema by day, best disco in town at night. Cheap beer, rave music, and the occasional late-night jam add to the great atmosphere. Open Thurs. and Sun. 9:30pm-5am, Fri.-Sat. 10pm-5am; cover on weekends L10,000. MC, Visa.

Laptărie, at the National Theater. Enter where the theater and the operetta buildings meet and take the elevator to the top. A terrace and bar entertain the cool crowd. In winter, jazz concerts (L10,000-25,000) replace the summer attraction of movies shown out on the terrace (L2500). Terrace open in summer daily 9:30pm until 2 or 4am; bar open 10am-2am in winter.

Cafe Indigo, Str. Eforie 2 (tel. 312 63 36). From Piaţa Universităţii, walk west on Bd. Carol I, turn left on Culea Victoriei, and take the next right on Str. Eforie. Jazz and blues make noise here every weekend during the school year, while a movie theater showing classic films operates during the day. Light meals around L10,000. Open 24hr.

Hard 'n' Heavy, Str. Gabroveni 14 (tel. 615 08 12), down the street from Cafe de la Joie. Rock music draws those who've come to drink, dance, or hang out in the Old Town. L8000 drink minimum. Open Tues.-Fri. and Sun. 8pm-3am, Sat. 8pm-5:30am.

Casa de Cultura Studentcasca, Calea Plevnei 61 (tel. 615 25 42). Take the Metro to Eroilor and exit toward Spitalul. Cross the river and continue straight on Str. Ştirbei Vodă; the first right is Plevnei. Nicknamed Preoteasa (Priestess), it grinds with students. The disciples of this Priestess speak in tongues—notably English. Very slow in summer. Cover on Sat. L10,000, students L5000. Open Fri.-Sun. 9:30pm-5:30am.

■ Near Bucharest: Snagov

If you crave a quick break, take a daytrip to **Snagov,** a tiny village about 50km north of Bucharest. In summer, hordes descend upon **Snagov Park** (5km west of Snagov town), where you can swim in the brownish lake, try your hand at waterskiing (L50,000), or hire a boat to take you to **Snagov Monastery.** Here, allegedly, lies the grave of the infamous Vlad Țepeș; but it's difficult to identify a body without a head (which is supposedly in Turkey). Having learned his methods as a hostage in Turkey in his youth, the so-called **Count Dracula** earned his reputation by impaling the heads of the Turkish police (and lots of other people) and then using them as decorative touches along the walls of his capital. His methods successfully repelled a full-scale Turkish invasion. Vlad rebuilt the Snagov monastery and added a jail for prisoners accused of high treason, which held a veritable *Who's Who* of Romanian heroes during the 1848 revolution. Today, only the church remains, and it's undergoing restoration. Ask the nun and priest who live on this lonely island to let you in (L5000; English pamphlet L4000). **Trains** head for Snagov only on the weekends; two leave Bucharest in the morning and two return in the evening (80min., L3400). Unfortunately, the train is not close to either the lake or the monastery. Some hitch from the train or from Bucharest, but you can avoid the hassle by going on the tour organized by Villa Helga (see **Bucharest: Accommodations,** p. 474; US$9).

TRANSYLVANIA

Though the name evokes images of a dark, evil land of black magic and vampires, Transylvania (*Ardeal*) is actually a region of green hills and mountains descending gently from the Carpathians to the Hungarian Plain, dotted with German- and Hungarian-speaking villages. This is Romania's most Westernized region, due to geography and the influence of Austrian rule and ethnic minorities. Cities are cleaner, services better, and waiters friendlier. Even the speech is slower and more musical, with a few regional expressions such as "*fain*" (good, fine, or cool) and the Austrian "*Servus!*" (hello). Despite pride in being *Ardeleni,* locals believe in a unified Romania. But the friendly feeling is not always mutual, and some Romanian jokes portray Transylvanians as slow and stupid (e.g., "A Transylvanian shepherd sitting on the grass was asked if he was sitting and thinking. He replied, 'No, I'm only sitting'"). Unlike the jokes, Transylvanian cities are anything but dull—narrow cobblestone streets wind through tilted medieval houses, stern Gothic churches, and rococo palaces.

▒ Cluj-Napoca

Cluj-Napoca (CLOOZH na-PO-ka) lies on the Someșul Mic river below the hills of Feleac and Făgeti. Transylvania's unofficial capital and largest student center is over 70% Romanian, but includes a vocal Hungarian minority. Cluj's name reflects its rich heritage—Napoca from the city's Roman name, Cluj (derived from Klausenburg) from medieval German domination and life under the Habsburgs. Massive renovation of historic buildings is largely completed, and a renewed interest in monument construction and ancient archaeology brings Cluj once again into full splendor.

ORIENTATION AND PRACTICAL INFORMATION

About 200km from Bucharest and 135km from the Hungarian border, Cluj is well connected by bus and train to many Romanian cities. From the **train station,** the **bus station** is a quick walk to the right and another right across a bridge. Buses #3 and 4, left and across the street from the train station, run to Piața Mihai Viteazul (round-trip

L1700). Continue along the road past McDonald's and turn right on Bd. 21 Decembrie 1989 to reach the center. By foot, cross the street and head down Str. Horea, which changes to Str. Gh. Doja after crossing the river. At the end of Str. Gh. Doja spreads the main drag, **Piaţa Unirii.**

Tourist Office: KmO, Piaţa Unirii 10 (tel. 19 11 14). Open Mon.-Fri. 8am-6pm, Sat. 10am-2pm. **OJT Feleacul,** Str. Memorandumului (tel. 19 69 55), 3 blocks from Unirii. City map in front. Open Mon.-Fri. 8am-8pm, Sat.-Sun. 9am-1pm. Check with either to arrange a group tour of Cluj or to **exchange currency.** OJT sells maps (L4000) and can get hotel rooms at cheaper prices, both within Cluj and beyond. Either office may be able to provide a private room (US$7-18) or a bed in a dorm.

Currency Exchange: Bancă Transilvania, Bd. Eroilor 36 (tel. 19 31 90), off Piaţa Unirii. Transforms traveler's checks directly into lei at 0.75% commission (L2000 minimum). Open Mon.-Fri. 9:30am-1pm.

Flights: TAROM, Piaţa Mihai Viteazul (tel. 43 26 69). To Bucharest (3 per day except Sun., 1hr., US$45). Open Mon.-Fri. 7am-7pm, Sat. 9am-1pm.

Trains: CFR (tel. 19 24 75), Piaţa Mihai Viteazul. Open Mon.-Fri. 7am-7pm. To: Alba Iulia (5 per day, 2-3hr., *accelerat* L15,100); Braşov (4 per day, 4hr., *accelerat* L21,800); Bucharest via Sighişoara and Braşov (4 per day, 7hr., *accelerat* L27,700); Budapest (3 per day, 5-7hr., L161,000); Sibiu (2 per day, 4hr., *accelerat* L15,100); Iaşi via Suceava (4 per day, 9hr., *accelerat* L27,700); and Timişoara (5 per day, 5hr., *accelerat* L21,800).

Buses: Str. Giordano Bruno 3 (tel. 43 52 78), near the train station. To Budapest (leaves Mon.-Tues. and Thurs.-Fri. 7am, returns Tues.-Wed. and Fri.-Sat. 11am, 9hr., L70,000) and Sibiu (1 per day, 3-4hr., L24,000).

Taxis: Pritax, Str. Dorobanţilor 3 (tel. 19 27 27). L1000 per km. Other companies are Mesagerul (tel. 19 26 26), or City (tel. 16 66 66). Be wary of unofficial cabs.

Express Mail: DHL, Bd. Eroilor 10 (tel. 19 06 92; fax 19 04 81), across the street from the cathedral. Open Mon.-Fri. 9am-4:30pm.

Post Office: Str. Gh. Doja 33. Open Mon.-Fri. 7am-8pm, Sat. 7am-1pm.

Telephones: Behind the post office (tel. 12 48 24). Phones open daily 7am-10pm; fax/telex Mon.-Fri. 7am-9pm. The phone building in Piaţa Unirii is open Mon.-Fri. 7am-9pm. **Phone code:** 064.

ACCOMMODATIONS

Lodging in Cluj is expensive, and private rooms are hard to come by.

Hotel Central-Melody, Piaţa Unirii 29 (tel. 11 75 65). Restaurant, sidewalk cafe, game room, and a very risqué nightly cabaret show (11pm-midnight). Singles L72,000; clean doubles L120,000, with bath L164,000; triples L165,000, with bath L210,000. Breakfast included.

Hotel Piccolia Italia, Str. Racoviţă 20 (tel. 13 61 10), next to Restaurant Casa Alba. Small hotel offers fairly spacious and inviting rooms with TV and use of a fridge. Singles L120,000; doubles L140,000. Reserve 2 days in advance.

Hotel Topaz, Str. Albinii 10 (tel.41 40 21; fax 41 40 66). Take bus #3 to "Abinii." Brilliant white exterior and clean rooms with shower, phone, and color TV. Singles L189,000; doubles L204,000. Breakfast included. Reserve 1-2 weeks ahead.

Camping Făget (tel. 19 62 27), 7km from the city towards Bucharest. Tiny bungalow doubles L60,000; quads L90,000. Tent space L11,000 per day per person. Very communal showers, restaurant, and small grocery nearby. Open May 1-Nov. 1.

FOOD

Cluj has an extremely rapid turnover of establishments; local students might provide some hints. Don't miss the chocolaty *Doboş Cluj,* a local specialty cake (L2300). A big indoor/outdoor **market** invades Piaţa Mihai Viteazul daily as long as it's light out, and sometimes even when it isn't. **Sora,** Bd. 21 Decembrie, across from Hotel Melody, will keep you supplied with food (open Mon.-Fri. 7am-8pm, Sat. 7am-3pm; smaller section open 24hr.).

Mary's, Str. Pavlov 27 (tel. 19 19 47), the continuation of Str. Gh. Barițiu. Go with someone you like. Candlelit mauve decor or leafy terrace; music requests accepted (bring tapes). Laid-back waitstaff. Meat main dishes under L17,000. Open daily noon-midnight. Reservations recommended.

Restaurant Panoramic, Str. Șerpuitoare 31 (tel. 43 20 80). If you climb Cetățuie Hill for the panoramic view, follow the gravel path behind Hotel Transylvania away from the cross monument to reward yourself with a hearty dinner in this stylish spot. Soup with dumplings, cream, and lemon L5160. English/Romanian/French menu. Open Mon. 3pm-midnight, Tues.-Sun. noon-midnight.

Restaurant Casa Alba, Racovița 22 (tel. 43 22 77), last hard right off Str. Horea before the river. Set in an old-style villa, the purple salon and terrace offer scrumptious food. Beef with mushrooms L19,200. Smaller dishes such as spaghetti and *cașcaval* (cheese) under L10,000. Open daily 7am-10pm. MC, Visa.

SIGHTS

Most strolls begin in **Piața Unirii,** where the 80m Gothic steeple of the Catholic **Biserica Sfântul Mihail** (Church of St. Michael) offers a magnificent view of the city. Ancient frescoes discovered during 1993 renovations now shine anew (services daily 6:15 and 7:30am, Sun. at 7, 8:45, 10, and 11:30am, and 6pm). Near the cathedral stands the **equestrian statue of Mathias Rex** (Matei Corvin), perhaps the most argued-over statue in Eastern Europe. Erected in 1902 when Transylvania was still part of the Austro-Hungarian Empire, this statue of the half-Romanian Cluj-born king who ruled Hungary from 1458 to 1490 once stood for harmony between Romania and Hungary, but has come to symbolize ethnic tension. In 1933, historian Nicolae Iorga added an inscription to the pedestal denying that King Mathias had conquered Transylvania; Hungarians deleted the inscription in 1940; the Communists diplomatically labeled the monument in Latin; and in 1992, nationalist Mayor Funar had Iorga's words reinscribed. Though UNESCO protects the statue, the quarrel continues. Archaeological excavations here and in Piața Muzeului also reflect the desire to glorify Romania's Roman past.

Around the square stand several palaces, most built between the 17th and 19th centuries by Hungarian nobles. The fanciest is **Bánffy Palace,** Piața Unirii 30 (tel. 19 69 53), home to the **Muzeul Național de Artă** (Art Museum), which focuses on Romanian art (open Wed.-Sun. 10am-5pm; L3000). At Piața Unirii and Bd. Eroilor, a bell tops the new **Monument of the Memorandum.** The Memorandum was an 1891 petition sent to the emperor by Romanians claiming national rights. At the corner of the Piața and Str. Memorandumului, walk about 50m down Str. Matei Corvin to see the **Casa natală a lui Matei Corvin,** where Mathias Rex is said to have been born, now home to the Art School. The adjacent streets allow for a medieval stroll. From Piața Unirii, head to **Piața Avram Iancu,** along either busy Str. 21 Dec. 1989 (commemorating the victims of the 1989 revolution) or Bd. Eroilor. In the square is the Byzantine-Romanian **Catedrala Arhiepiscopală** (Orthodox Cathedral), built in 1933 (open Tues.-Fri. and Sun. 6am-8pm, Mon. and Sat. 6am-1pm and 5-8pm). The newly built **statue of Avram Iancu** in front is one of Mayor Funar's favorite projects; it replaced a Soviet tank. The **Teatrul Național și Opera Română** (National Theater and Opera), also in the square, imitates Paris's Garnier Opera House. During the season (Oct. 1-June), performances run about 2-3 times per week. Buy tickets at Piața Ștefan cel Mare 14 (tel. 19 53 63; open Mon.-Fri. 11am-5pm; best seats L5000, students L2500). Tickets for Hungarian opera (Sept.-June) are sold at Emil Isaac 26-27 (tel. 19 34 68) at the end of Str. G. Barițiu (L5250, students L3150).

In Piața Muzeului, a 13th-century Franciscan **monastery** is home to the Music High School. Head toward Casă lui Matei Corvin, turn left, then turn right again onto Str. Franklin Delano Rooswelt (*sic!*). The **Biserica Franciscanilor** (Franciscan Church) is still open for business; its Baroque interior belies its foundation on a Roman temple site. The **Carolina Monument,** next to the archaeological excavation in Piața Muzeului, used to grace Piața Unirii, but was moved to make room for Mathias Rex's statue. Opposite is the **Muzeul de Istorie** (History Museum), Str. Constantin Daicoviciu 2, with a 17th-century printing press and a flying machine built by a Cluj University professor in 1896 (open Tues.-Sun. 10am-4pm; L1000). The **Muzeul Etnografica al Transilvaniei,** Str. Memorandumului 21 (tel. 19 23 44; open Tues.-Sun. 9am-5pm; L1500, students L1000), displays Romanian, Hungarian, and Saxon objects. To get to the museum's outdoor counterpart, cross the street, catch bus #30, and go four stops. Backtrack a bit and take the first left (open May 1-Nov. 1 Tues.-Sun. 10am-6pm; L1500). On the way up, you'll pass **Pădurea Hoia,** a forest where UFO enthusiasts gather each year on June 23 to commemorate a UFO sighting here.

The student area lies south of the main square, down Str. Universitații. Turn left on Str. Mihail Kogălniceanu to find the 15th-century **Protestant Church,** Kogălniceanu 21, which often hosts organ concerts. In front stands a replica of the statue of St. George slaying a dragon (the original is in Prague). Many of the townsfolk took refuge in this church when the town was attacked; in fact, halfway around the left wall of the church, above the secret escape door, is a partially buried cannonball. A few steps up lies **Bastionul Croitorilor** (Tailor's Bastion), one of the few remnants of the medieval defense wall. In front of the bastion, a statue of **Baba Novac** commemorates the 1601 slaying of a general in the army of Mihai Viteazul. His Houdini-esque escape from a Turkish prison is legendary. The small **Orthodox Church**—the first Romanian Orthodox church in Cluj—is off Universitații; turn right on Str. Avram Iancu, and then left on Str. Bisericii Orthodoxe. The Ottomans did not permit Romanians to build an Orthodox church of stone until 1795, and then only outside the city walls.

North of Piața Unirii, a short walk down Str. Gh. Doja leads to Piața Mihai Viteazul, named after the king of Muntenia who unified the Romanian principalities in 1600. Walk east on Str. G. Barițiu, cross the river to the right, and climb **Cetățuie Hill;** a dazzling view awaits. Down the hill and across the river lies the majestic but narrow **Parcul Central** (rowboats in the little lake available daily 8am-8pm; L3000 per person per 30min.). The **Grădină Botanica** (Botanical Garden) might be the most relaxing and beautiful in Romania. From Piața Unirii, take Str. Napoca to Piața Păcii, then head left up to Str. Republicii. There's a Japanese garden with a pond and bridge, a Roman garden, greenhouses with waterlilies and palm trees (open daily 9am-6pm), and an ivy-clad tower (open daily 9am-7pm; L2000, map L1000). An often-crowded pool by the park and Hotel Sport cools heads from June to Sept. 15 (open daily 9am-7pm; L2000).

ENTERTAINMENT

Bars and clubs in this youthful city are plentiful, but not always full in summer, as the local students glut the sea-bound trains as soon as the school year ends in mid-July.

Diesel, Piața Unirii 17 (tel. 19 84 41), right across from Biserica Sfântul Mihail. Sweep by the black rococo tables and ancient half-wall and descend to the centuries-old cellar. The thick vaults delineate more intimate rooms with minute black chairs and tables for sitting and drinking. The piano in the bar room pounds out the fact that yes, this *is* a jazz bar. Occasional concerts. Open 24hr.

Itali Gali (tel. 42 68 93), on Calea Floreți. A newly opened dance club that draws all the business from its competitors. L5000 cover; women L3000; women free Sun. Open Thurs.-Fri. and Sun. 10pm-3am, Sat. 10pm-4am.

Apollo, Str. Sindicatelor 7 (tel. 19 41 38). From OJT, walk straight to Str. Emil Isaac and turn left on Sindicatelor. Struggling to be the best disco in the city. Cover L3000. Large indoor dance floor open Thurs.-Sun. 4pm-4am.

■ Near Cluj: Apuseni Mountains

BELIȘ

The tiny, restful lake resort at **Beliș,** deep in the wilds of the **Munții Apuseni** (Apuseni Mountains), was all the doing of a dam downstream, which created the artificial lake **Făntinele.** It's even possible to see a church steeple under the lake's surface when the water level falls. The resort entertains year-round with hiking, skiing, and water sports. More **hiking** awaits on the south side of the Apuseni; buy **hiking maps** (L1600) at the reception of pricey hotel **Statiunea Fântânele** (tel. 43 22 42). **Pensiunea Geo-molean** (tel. 25 15 30) is expensive, but a good value: included in the price of a room are home-cooked meals and rides—on horses, in a motorboat, or in a romantic carriage (US$25-30 per person). The budget **Popasul Turistic "Brădet"** has doubles and triples (L20,000 per person) and tiny cabana beds (L15,000 per person). It's open only in summer, and there's only one shower, but guests may use the kitchen facilities. **Huedin** is the closest train station to Beliş (11 per day, 1hr., L3300). A bus makes the 35km trek to the resort (Mon.-Fri. 4 per day, Sat.-Sun. 2 per day; L4500). From the station, turn right and head straight parallel to the tracks to reach the bus.

SCĂRIŞOARA

Some of the world's richest stalagmite formations hang from Scărişoara's **peştera ghetarul** (ice cave). Visit the cave in spring, before the ice topology melts. Take the **bus** from Cluj to **Cîmpeni** (3 per day, 3hr., L19,000). You'll need to get to the village of Gîrda (many hitch) to find a guide. Then follow the unpaved road along Valea Bis-trii (Bistra River Valley; 17km). Shortly after passing the river's source and hitting a fork in the road, the path merges with the red-stripe trail, which travels west to the cave. After 14km, it intersects an unpaved road that leads to Beliş (22km north) and Poiana Horea (7km north). To the south lies Albac (14km). Continue west another 12km to reach the cave. Bring money; you may need up to US$10 for a guide.

Cetate Ponorolui lies a day's hike from Scărişoara on the Karstic-Padiş plateau. An underground river with lakes and 100m-tall caverns runs under these three cliffs. The surrounding region of Podiş rewards the determined tourist with unspoiled beauty—serene streams, hidden caves, and dazzling views. **Maps** of the hiking trails are available in Beliş, or visit **Rural Eco-Tours Agro-Montan (RETAM)**, Str. Libertătii 3 (tel./fax 43 03 30), for information on cycling, hiking, and accommodations in the mountains. RETAM also organizes tours (US$10-26 per day).

■ Alba Iulia

Alba Iulia (AL-bah YOO-lee-ah), the historic capital of Transylvania, reflects its regal status in almost every building in the old citadel. Churches, museums, and monuments testify to a 2000-year history going back to the early Dacians. A bit more recently, King Ferdinand and Queen Maria were crowned here on October 15, 1922, sealing Romania's unification.

Orientation and Practical Information Trains arrive from Bucharest (3 per day, 6hr., L26,000); Cluj (4 per day, 2hr., L11,000); Sibiu (1 per day, 5hr., L8400); and Timişoara (2 per day, 5½hr., L16,600). **Buses** (tel. 81 29 67) also head for Sibiu (1 per day, 2hr., L8500). The **train station** is a 15-minute walk from the center. A mini-van at the station (dir. "Cetatea") runs to Piaţa Iuliu Maniu or the Cetatea (L800). By foot, walk straight out of the train station. When you reach the intersection where five roads meet, take a soft right, then walk five blocks. Take a left on **Str. Mihai Viteazul** to reach the Cetatea, or turn right to reach the town center. Str. Mihai Viteazul becomes **Str. Primăverii**—cross the park diagonally to reach the hotels and tourist services in **Piaţa Iuliu Maniu. OJT Societatea Cetatea,** at #22 (tel. 81 32 06), sells maps (L1500; open Mon.-Fri. 8am-3:30pm). On weekends, try next door at Hotel Transilvania. **Hotel Parc** has good rates for currency exchange (open Mon.-Fri. 8am-8pm, Sat. 9am-1pm). The **post office,** Piaţa Eroilor 2 (tel. 81 12 34), is behind the statue of Remus and Romulus (open Mon.-Fri. 7am-7pm, Sat. 8am-noon). **Telephones** are inside (open daily 7am-9pm). **Postal code: 2500. Phone code: 058.**

Accommodations and Food Mini-Hotel, Str. Mihai Viteazul 6 (tel. 81 37 78), maintains a number of doubles with modern communal bathrooms right at the first portal to the Cetatea (L50,000). On the other side of the Cetatea, **Hotel Cetatea,** Str.

Unirii 3 (tel. 81 17 80), spoils its clients with bar, restaurant, laundry service (additional charge), and bright rooms with shower (singles L123,000; doubles L228,000; triples L249,000; L15,000 breakfast credit included; EC/MC/Visa).

Eateries and groceries line **Piața Iulia Maniu** and its park. **Rosu și Negru,** Piața Iulia Maniu 14, crams every food product known to man in its small space. The **Mini-Hotel's restaurant** serves up myriad salads, pizza (L4000-7,000) and *clatite* (crepes) in what would otherwise be a small, upscale salon (open 24hr.). **Eden Restaurant** (tel. 81 06 99), although in a less-than-Edenic spot between the train and bus stations, is full of locals. It is also possible to see the food before you order (sandwiches and main dishes L3000-8000; open daily 8am-3pm and 8-10pm).

Sights Str. Mihai Viteazul leads to the heart of **Cetatea (Citadel) Alba Carolina.** After the citadel's first sculpted gate, a brick ramp continues to the demolished second portal. The moat is a grassy field and the drawbridge a road, but it doesn't take much to imagine the stronghold as it was centuries ago. The **white obelisk** at the top of the ramp honors Horea, Cloșca, and Trișan—martyred leaders of the 1784 peasant uprising against a Hungarian overlord. The stairs to the left after the ornate arch lead to the jail and to a great view. Two blocks up the fortress's central road, the **statue of Mihai Viteazul,** the king who briefly united the Romanian principalities in 1600, comes into view. A right off Str. Mihai Viteazul at the monument leads to the **Muzeul Unirii** (Museum of Unification; tel. 81 33 00), which traces the development of Alba Iulia from the Dacians to contemporary times. The **Sala Unirii** (Unification Hall), garnished on the outside with a row of busts, centers around the table on which the unification charter of Transylvania and Romania was signed (open Tues.-Sun. 10am-5pm, ticket office closes at 4:30pm; L1200; Sala Unirii L800 extra; students 50% off).

The 1246 **Catedrala Romano-Catolica** rises on Str. Mihai Viteazul. The temple contains the tombs of the Huniade family, including Ion, "the White Knight of the Christians," who checked the 15th-century Ottoman invasions. Although the church's organ concerts occur at unpredictable times, the rosewood sculptures in the alcoves are a consistent attraction (open Sun.-Fri. 8am-5pm; services Mon.-Sat. 7am, Sun. 8am, 10am, and 6pm). The **Catedrala din Alba Iulia** (Orthodox Cathedral), ahead to the right behind some orangey-brown columns, is usually referred to as the **Catedrala Încoronării** (Coronation Church), since it was built for the coronation of King Ferdinand and Queen Marie. The cathedral was constructed on the site of the Roman Apulum fortress (open Mon.-Sat. 7am-9pm, Sun. 6:15-9pm; services Mon.-Sat. 7am, 8am and 6pm, 5pm in winter; Sun. 8am, 10am, and 6pm, 5pm in winter). On the far side of the citadel from the Mihai Viteazul statue, the **Biblioteca** (Batthyaneum Library), Str. Bibliotecii 1 (tel. 81 19 39)—officially open only to scholars—contains Charlemagne's **Codex Aureus** (810), a work of gold-ink calligraphy.

WESTERN CARPATHIANS

■ Timișoara

In 1989, 105 years after becoming the first European city illuminated by electric street lamps, Timișoara (Tee-mee-SHWAH-rah) ignited a revolution that lit up the country and left Communism in cinders. Romania's westernmost city, Timișoara has always fostered Romania's cultural and economic change, embracing the future with little hesitation.

ORIENTATION AND PRACTICAL INFORMATION

Timișoara lies only 75km from the Hungarian border. By train, get off at **Timișoara Nord** rather than **Timișoara Est.** Trolley #1 runs from the station to the center; get off when you see the multicolored Catedrala Mitropolitană. Tram #11 (L800) runs by

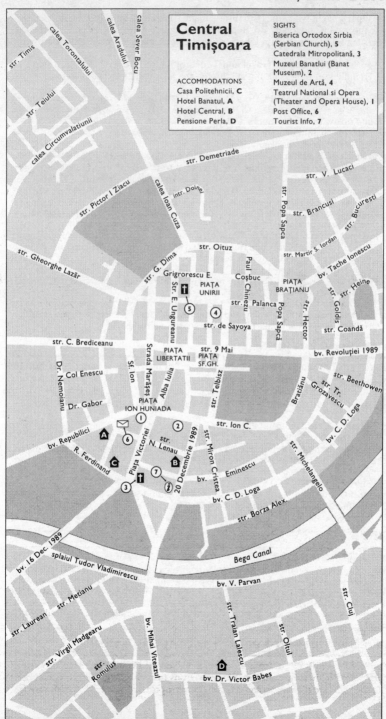

Central Timișoara

ACCOMMODATIONS
Casa Politehnicii, **C**
Hotel Banatul, **A**
Hotel Central, **B**
Pensione Perla, **D**

SIGHTS
Biserica Ortodox Sirbia (Serbian Church), **5**
Catedrala Mitropolitană, **3**
Muzeul Banatului (Banat Museum), **2**
Muzeul de Artă, **4**
Teatrul National si Opera (Theater and Opera House), **1**
Post Office, **6**
Tourist Info, **7**

ROMANIA

the **Opera;** alight when the tram turns left and backtrack a little. By foot, turn left outside the station and follow **Bd. Republicii** east, until you reach the opera. To the left, **Str. Alba Iulia** leads to **Piaţa Libertaţii;** to the right, **Piaţa Victoriei** gathers crowds.

Tourist Office: Colibri Travel and Tourism, Bd. C. D. Loga 2 (tel./fax 19 40 74). Friendly staff offers old, but still useful, free maps and specializes in tours. Open Mon.-Fri. 9am-5pm.

Currency Exchange: IDM, Str. 9 Mai (tel. 13 27 41, ext. 126), on the ground floor of the Bega supermarket next to Hotel Continental. From Piaţa Libertaţii, take a right and follow the trolley tracks 4 blocks. Advances on AmEx, Diners Club, MC, Visa, and more without commission, but at bad rates. Open Mon. 10am-5:30pm, Tues.-Fri. 8am-7:30pm, Sat. 9am-1:30pm.

Trains: CFR Agentie de Voiaj, Bd. Republicii 1, 2nd floor (tel. 19 18 89), sells tickets. Open Mon.-Fri. 8am-8pm. To: Bucharest (6 per day, 7hr., L51,000 for *rapid*); Budapest (2 per day, 5hr., L180,000); and Belgrade (2 per day, 4hr., L52,000).

Taxis: Bimbo Taxi (tel. 953 or 18 24 88). L1250 per km. Despite the name, you only get one kind of ride in these cabs. Available 24hr., baby.

English Bookstore: Mihai Eminescu, Măceșilor 2 (tel. 19 41 23), in the main square near Restaurant Bulevard. Open Mon.-Fri. 9am-6pm, Sat. 9am-1pm.

Internet Access: Computer Club, on al. Studenţilor. Cross the Bd. Michelangelo bridge, turn left on Bd. Vasile Parvan, and take your 3rd right. A path on your left leads to al. Studenţilor. Full internet access L7000 per hour. Open Mon.-Sat. 9am-midnight, Sun. 9am-11pm.

Post Office: Str. Piatra Craiului, off Bd. Republicii and Piaţa Victoriei. Open Mon.-Fri. 7am-8pm. **Postal code:** 1900.

Telephones: Walking toward Catedrala Mitropolitană from the Opera, take the 1st left after passing the Romulus and Remus statue. The phone office is 30m ahead on the right. Open daily 7am-1pm and 2-9pm. **Phone code:** 056.

ACCOMMODATIONS

Hotels in Timişoara tend to be old but decent. Private rooms are hard to find, but students might get lucky in the dorms on Bd. Victor Babeş. Cross the bridge following Str. R. Ferdinand, continue down Str. Mihai Viteazul, and take a left on Bd. Dr. Victor Babeş. A *căminaul* (dorm) is open to visitors in July and August (US$1 per night).

Politehnicii, Str. Ferdinand 2 (tel. 19 68 50). Decent rooms in a good location. Doubles L60,000, L80,000 with bath. L7000 breakfast credit included.

Hotel Banatul, Bd. Republicii 3-5 (tel. 19 19 03; fax 19 01 30). Decent but dark rooms with confidence-inspiring bathrooms. Singles with sinks L25,000, with bath L45,000; doubles L42,000, with private shower L70,000; triples L63,000, with shower L105,000.

Hotel Central, Str. Lenau 6 (tel. 19 00 91), behind Muzeul Banatului. Funky old chairs on every floor. Clean rooms with TV, telephone, and wall tapestries. Doubles with bath L120,000. Breakfast included.

FOOD

Food is plentiful and fairly inexpensive in Timişoara. An **outdoor market** sits at the corner of Str. C. Brediceanu and Str. Paris, three blocks from Piaţa Libertaţii (open daily 8am-8pm, but slower on Sun.). Take a left on Str. C. Brediceanu and follow the trolley tracks, passing a sidewalk shrine to a 1989 martyr. Grocery stores and 24-hour snack shops abound in the Piaţa Victoriei area.

Braseria Opera (tel. 19 07 90), next to the Opera. Grill-pizzeria with reproductions of turn-of-the-century paintings on the walls. Waitresses in short red skirts bear dishes and desserts named after operas while the latest Euro beat plays in the background. Thick-crust pizza L8800-19,100. Open daily 9am-midnight.

Restaurant N-Z, Str. Alba Iulia 1 (tel. 19 39 77). This young and modern restaurant welcomes customers with Western music and a pictoral guide to the menu. Meaty main dishes less than L15,000, but sometimes you pay by weight, so watch out. Open Mon.-Fri. 9am-10:30pm, Sat.-Sun. 11am-10:30pm.

SIGHTS AND ENTERTAINMENT

The tourist hub revolves around the **Teatrul Naţional şi Opera Româna Timişoara** (Theater and Opera House), at the intersection of Piaţa Victoriei, Bd. Republicii, and Piaţa Ion Huniade. Nearby, the old **Castelul Huniazilor** houses the **Muzeul Banatului** (Banat Museum), which traces Timişoara's history. A comprehensive display of artifacts extends from pre-history to 1989, but mysteriously skips about 50 years following WWII (open Tues.-Sun. 10am-4:30pm; L800, students L400, disabled free). **Catedrala Mitropolitană,** across the square from the Opera, captures the contemporary historian's interest. Built 1936-46, the cathedral, with a Byzantinesque rainbow-tiled roof and 8000kg bells, was a gathering place for protesters during the uprising against Ceauşescu. The wooden *troika* across the street and plaques at the entrance record the sacrifices made by young revolutionaries. Inside, candles keep their memory alive (doors open all day; services Mon.-Fri. 6pm). A small museum in the basement displays religious objects and art (open Wed.-Sun. 10am-1pm; free). **Biserica Reformată Tökes,** Str. Timotei Cipariu 1, birthed the 1989 revolution, but aside from a marble plaque commemorating the event, there's not much to see. From Catedrala Mitropolitană, follow Bd. 16 Decembrie 1989, cross the bridge, and take the third left; the entrance is 5m to the left. After going back across the bridge, the first left traverses **Parcul Central** (Central Park). A right at the staid Communist **Liberation Monument** to Romania's WWII dead leads to Piaţa Victoriei. The inscription on the monument reads, "For the liberty and independence of the country."

Str. Alba Iulia travels from Piaţa Victoriei past numerous shops to **Piaţa Libertăţii,** the city's geographic center. The old **town hall,** Piaţa Libertăţii 1, houses the Art School. Fashioned as a Baroque-Renaissance mix in the 1700s, it's the oldest edifice in Timişoara. On the left, Str. Ungureanu runs under the clock towers of the mustard-colored 1743 **Biserica Ortodox Sirbia** (Serbian Church), Str. Ungureanu 12 (open Mon.-Fri. 8-9am, Sat. 4-6pm, Sun. 10am-noon). Behind the church, **Piaţa Unirii** basks in the presence of the **Old Prefecture,** the Baroque facade of which reveals a building in utter disrepair. The quiet square's **Domul Romano-Catolic** (Catholic Cathedral), which looks better thanks to an edict on its walls decreeing vandalism a crime, has survived many a war and revolution since its construction in 1754. Do *not* drink the water from the central fountain.

Play video games and send email to your beloved at **Computer Club** (tel. 199 747), on al. Studentilor in the Student Quarter (see **Practical Information: Internet Access,** p. 486). **Club 30,** Piaţa Victoriei 7, is a dark and smoky place to sit, drink, and listen to jazz (Thurs. and Sun.) and other live music (open daily 10pm-3am). **Discoland** (tel. 198 008), near the Opera, reigns as the largest and probably most popular disco in town (open daily 10pm-4am; cover L10,000). The **Opera** ticket office is just up from the building, on Str. Mărăşeşti (open Tues.-Sun. 10am-1pm and 5-7pm; tickets around L8000, students half-price). If you're eager for a swim, check out a **Bază de Agrement** along the river (entrance to the pools L2000-7000).

■ Oradea

Only 20km from Romania's northwest border, Oradea (oh-RA-day-ah) is rich in boutiques and hotels that thrive on trainloads of tourists making one last stop in Romania on their way to Hungary. Oradea's impressive architecture combines with the natural wonders in the surrounding area to attract visitors.

Orientation and Practical Information Trains run from Bucharest (2 per day, 11hr., *accelerat* L34,000), Budapest (4 per day, 5hr., L172,000), and Timişoara (5 per day, 3hr., *accelerat* L16,000). A private **bus** also runs from Budapest (4-5 per day, 4½hr., L140,000). Take bus #12 from Piaţa Unirii to the bus station. At the train station, Bagaje de Mână **stores luggage** around the clock (L1800). The kiosk across the street sells tickets (L800) for the **trolley** heading down **Str. Republicii** to the center (3 stops). On foot, walk past the **taxis** (tel. 14 44 44), then turn left on Str. Republicii. Take a soft right at the major intersection with a McDonald's. In the first block on the left of this Rococo promenade, in addition to selling some books in English, **Libraria Tineretului** (tel. 41 86 50) has an overly detailed **map** (L10,000; open Mon.-Fri. 8am-8pm). **Banca Nationala a României,** Parcul Traian 8, exchanges traveler's checks. From Str. Republicii, take a left onto the main street, **Parcul Traian,** at Globus Hamburger Center (open Mon.-Fri. 8-11am). **CFR travel agency** is at Str. Republicii 2 (open Mon.-Fri. 7am-7pm). Across from the beige church is a **24-hour pharmacy,** Str. Republicii 33. The **post office,** Str. Roman Ciorogaru 12, lies to the right off Str. Republicii (open Mon.-Fri. 8am-8pm; Cokes L1000). The **telephone center** hides in the alleyway across from CFR near the intersection of Str. Republicii and Piaţa Ferdinand (open Mon.-Fri. 7am-9pm). **Postal code:** 3700. **Phone code:** 059.

Accommodations and Food High prices don't always mean exquisite rooms. **Hotel Parc,** Str. Republicii 5 (tel. 41 46 99), offers a welcoming foyer and clean rooms (singles L50,000; doubles L100,000, with bath L130,000; breakfast included). **Hotel Astoria,** Str. Teatrului 2 (tel. 13 05 08), provides decent rooms with passable bathrooms (singles L45,000; doubles L80,000, with shower L110,000).

Dim, intimate lights warm the cellar-restaurant **Knights of Malta,** Str. I. Vulcan 5 (tel. 43 78 18), where the emblem of the knights dominates a wall. The closest it gets to Malta, though, is pasta (spaghetti L11,000; open daily 11am-midnight). Try the cholesterol-stuffed *gogoşi* (battered, fried sweets with powdered sugar; L1000) at **Patiseria Trei Zorele,** in Piaţa Regele Férdinand I (open Mon.-Fri. 7am-6pm). The seldom-frequented **Restaurant Oradea** (tel. 13 43 39), an easy walk from the CFR office, preserves a baroque atmosphere while "classical" music plays in the background—not bad for a quiet tea for two (meals around L12,000; open daily 9am-1am).

Sights Str. Săvineştilor, off Str. Republicii near the train station, leads to the open gates and gardens of the **Muzeul Tării Crişurilor,** a mammoth palace-*cum*-museum with exhibits of art, history, and Romanian and Hungarian ethnography, as well as its very own set of mammoth bones (open Tues., Thurs., and Sat. 10am-3pm, Wed., Fri., and Sun. 10am-6pm; L5000, students L2500). Left of the museum, a gracious **park** attracts mostly adults with swings, rose bushes, benches for two, and a fountain.

Most of the other sights are in Piaţa Unirii, across the river from Piaţa Regele Ferdinand I. When crossing, check out the very Hungarian white **Church of St. László,** built to celebrate Oradea's liberation from Ottoman rule. Facing the church is the impressive **Primaria** (town hall). In the center of Piaţa Unirii is an equestrian bronze of **Mihai Viteazul.** At the far right end of Piaţa Unirii on Str. Iuliu Maniu rises **St. Nicholae Orthodox Cathedral,** formerly of Catholic persuasion. **Biserica cu Luna** occupies the opposite side of the square. The 18th-century church has a Baroque exterior and a surprisingly un-Orthodox interior decor, with the saints painted in correct perspective and proportion (open daily 7am-7pm). A unique mechanism halfway up the clocktower illustrates the phases of the moon and is supposedly never adjusted by human hands. Back across the river, the **theater** in the middle of the *piaţa* is a small-scale replica of the Vienna Opera, built by the same architect in 1900. Tickets to the theater and philharmonic are available at the **Agenţie Filharmonic şi Teatrală,** Str. Republicii 6 (open Mon.-Fri. 10am-4pm, Sat. 10am-1pm).

TRANSYLVANIAN ALPS

The Southern Carpathians have protected the inhabitants of Muntenia from almost every invader. The citadels and castles along the former frontier recall those who tried to exert power over this difficult region. The striking peaks now serve a more recreational cause; their unspoiled wilderness, pristine streams, and wildlife make the mountains a hiker's paradise.

■ Sibiu

Founded by German colonists in the 12th century, Sibiu (SEE-bee-oo)—one of Romania's oldest cities—is a town of medieval monuments. Considered the strongest fortress in all of Transylvania, not even Ceaușescu's "systematization" could infiltrate its walls. German and Hungarian influences have left their cultural mark.

ORIENTATION AND PRACTICAL INFORMATION

To reach the center from the train station, walk 10 minutes up **Str. Generalu Magheru** (continue left at the fork) to **Piața Mare,** marked by a statue of Gheorghe Lazăr, founder of the Romanian schools. The 18th-century **Catedrala Romano-Catolica** separates Piața Mare from **Piața Mică.** From Piața Mare (a.k.a. Piața Republicii), continue straight up **Str. Nicolae Bălcescu** to **Piața Unirii.** This *piața* is only a few minutes away from the train station by **trolley** T1 or T2 (L1600 for 2 trips); get off when you see Dumbrava department store or Hotel Bulevard. Go through the underpass to Hotel Bulevard, then turn right on Str. Nicolae Bălcescu, site of many useful offices.

Tourist Office: Prima Ardeleanu, Piața Unirii 1 (tel. 21 17 88). This office may aid your stay in Sibiu by giving you old, but still applicable, maps. It can also set you up in a private room (L40,000-60,000 per night). Open daily 8am-5pm.

Currency Exchange: EDF Asro, Str. N. Bălcescu 41 (tel. 21 50 57), by the sign for the Trans Europa travel agency. Enter the alleyway, go up the 1st stairs to the left, and take a left at the landing. Exchanges currency and cashes traveler's checks for a reasonable commission (L1000 per L20,000). Open Mon.-Fri. 9am-5pm, Sat. 9am-3pm. More services for extra lei offered by **IDM,** Piața Mică. AmEx traveler's checks; EC, MC, and Visa cash advances. Open Mon.-Fri. 8am-8pm, Sat. 9am-2pm. An **ATM** accepting Cirrus, EC, MC, and Visa lies opposite CFR.

Trains: CFR, Str. N. Bălcescu 6, next to Hotel Împaratul Romanilor, sells train tickets. Open Mon.-Fri. 7am-7:30pm. To Bucharest (9 per day, 5hr., L21,800 for *accelerat*) via Brașov.

English Bookstore: Thausib, in Piața Mică (tel. 21 57 74). Open Mon.-Fri. 9am-6pm, Sat. 10am-3pm.

Express Mail: DHL, Str. N. Bălcescu 10 (tel. 21 15 67). Open Mon.-Fri. 9am-5pm.

Internet Access: PVD-Net Group, Str. N. Bălcescu 5 (tel.21 67 71; http://pvd-net.logicnet.ro). Full internet access (telnet, www, and email) L6500 for 30min., L10,000 for 1hr.). Open Mon.-Fri. 9am-6pm.

Post Office: In the light-blue building at the corner of Str. Metropoliei and Str. Poștei. From Piața Unirii, walk up Str. Tribunei and turn right on Str. Metropoliei. Open Mon.-Fri. 7am-8pm, Sat. 8am-noon. **Postal code:** 2400.

Telephones: Across the street from DHL (see above). Open Mon.-Sat. 7am-7pm. **Phone code:** an acrobatic 069.

ACCOMMODATIONS

Sibiu offers quality lodging for decent prices. Ask at the tourist office about **private rooms** (L40,000-60,000).

Hotel La Podul Mincunilor, Str. Azilului 1 (tel. 21 72 59). Walk down the stairs from the Podul Mincunilor (see **Sights,** below), and take the 1st left onto Str. Azilului; the hotel is 30m down on the right. Knock on the shutters if the gate is closed. A washing machine comes with 1 room; TV and a shower or bath (reliable hot water!) is standard for all 3 rooms. Singles L80,000; 2-4 bed rooms L120,000.

Hotel-Bar Pensiune (Hotel Leu), Moș Ion Roată 6 (tel. 21 83 92), near Turnul Scărilor. The "Lion Hotel" is painted a pinkish-tan with emblems that fit the name. Count Dracula somehow sneaked into the hallway, too. Liveable doubles and quads with communal toilets and showers L50,000 per person.

Hotel Bulevard, Piața Unirii 2/4 (tel. 21 60 60; fax 21 01 58). Ideal location. Clean, modern rooms with bath and nonstop hot water. Friendly staff. Singles L85,000; doubles L145,000. Breakfast included. Add L20,000 for a fridge in the room and a TV with more than 20 channels.

FOOD

Food is available all over the city at negligible cost. Facing Hotel Bulevard from Dumbrava, take a right onto Bd. Spitalelor, then another right at the bus stop stuffed with street vendors to reach an **outdoor market.** Fruit-, vegetable-, and flower-sellers start business as early as 7am. The market winds down around 7pm, but you can find something to munch on 'round the clock at **Juventas Non-Stop,** Str. N. Bălcescu 40.

Crama Sibiul Vechi (Wine Cellar of Old Sibiu), Str. Papiu Ilarian 3 (tel. 43 19 71), below street level by the phone office. Carved-wood chairs and handwoven table-cloths. Busy waiters clad in black-and-white vests serve filling meals (L20,000) with enough booze to intoxicate an elephant. Open daily noon-midnight, with live folk music 7pm-midnight.

Împaratul Romanilor, Str. N. Bălcescu 4 (tel. 21 65 00), in the similarly named hotel. Pricey and prissy with starched white tablecloths. Patrons may choose one of the meals prepared in 45 seconds or *file de porc surprise* for L18,000. Delicious *clatite* (crepes) L2600-7000. Menu and diet-menu available in English, German, and French. A live band will sometimes play an evening tango, but the dance floor is under-utilized. Open daily 7am-midnight. MC, Visa.

Cofetăria Perla, Piața Mare 6 (tel. 21 71 15). Good desserts, but better known for its special orders. Delicious fruit tarts and baklava go for L1500. Open Mon.-Fri. 8am-9pm, Sat.-Sun. noon-9pm.

SIGHTS AND ENTERTAINMENT

Piața Mare, which once hosted myriad festivals and an occasional public execution, constitutes the center of Sibiu's old town. The *piața* lies in the shadow of the massive **Biserica Romano-Catolică,** a beautifully restored 18th-century monument built by the Austrians after they conquered Transylvania in a failed attempt to re-convert the Saxons to Catholicism (open irregularly). The **Ethnographic Museum,** Piața Mică 11, displays a collection of objects from central Africa in addition to two temporary exhibits. The museum even boasts a 2500-year-old mummy (open in summer Tues.-Sun. 10am-6pm, off-season Tues.-Sun. 9am-5pm; L10,000). The affiliated shop on Str. Avram Iancu 2-4 vends ceramics and costumes for reasonable prices (hand-painted eggs L9500). After reaching Piața Mica from Piața Mare, head right until you see a small bridge, **Podul Mincunilor** (Bridge of Lies). Legend has it that youths and maid-ens would meet up in the square, declare their undying love, and agree on another rendezvous. Since few couples ever saw each other again, the bridge became known as an instrument of untruth, although why it should take the blame is beyond us.

The towering 1520 **Cathedrala Evanghelică,** on the nearby **Piața Huet,** features many figurines and coats-of-arms carved on its interior walls (open Mon.-Sat. 9am-12:30pm; summer organ concerts Wed. at 6pm.) To the right is the 13th-century guardhouse **Turnul Scărilor** (Tower of the Stairs), Piața Huet #3, now a private residence. The ornate **Muzeul Brukenthal** in Piața Mare is still worth a visit, although some of its finest paintings were stolen in the 1960s. The gallery on the second floor has strong Dutch and Italian art collections; Transylvanian painting decorates the first floor (open Tues.-Sun. 9am-5pm, ticket booth closes at 4:30pm; L6500, students L3000). Take a left upon leaving to find the second museum named for former Transylvanian governor Samuel von Brukenthal. The Gothic **Brukenthal History Museum,** Str. Mitropoliei 2, displays Dacian anthropological finds, as well as royal medalia, the costume of the Order of Mihai Viteazul, armored suits, and two-handed swords, and lances suspended from the ceiling (open Tues.-Sun. 9am-5pm; ticket booth closes at 4pm; L5000, students L2500). Down Str. Mitropoliei, Romania's second-largest **Catedrala Ortodoxă** is a quarter-scale copy of Istanbul's St. Sophia. Unlike its Turkish counterpart, however, Sibiu's cathedral is in excellent condition and is still used for its original purpose (open 6am-8pm daily).

Every May and June, Sibiu warms up for Romania's biggest **jazz festival. Teatru Radu Stanca,** next to the Dumbrava department store on the way to the open-air market, sometimes shows plays or American movies, and hosts an international **the-**

ater festival in June. Cinema Tineretului, Str. Odobescu 4 (tel. 21 14 20), shows many American movies during the day (11am-5pm, L5000) and turns into an attractive disco at night. **Discoteca Piramid** offers booze, billiards, and Egyptian decor (open 9pm-4am; cover L10,000 after 10pm; women free weekdays).

■ Near Sibiu

PĂLTINIŞ

In the **Munţini Cibinului** (Cibin Mountains), 35km from Sibiu, Păltiniş (pall-tee-NEESH) is Romania's oldest (1894), highest (1440m), and possibly smallest mountain resort. Its beautiful location, fresh air, and numerous hiking opportunities have made Păltiniş a favorite of everyone from modern Romanian philosophers to Nicu Ceauşescu (son of the former dictator and Sibiu party-boss). In winter, Păltiniş becomes a major **ski** center. In summer, many businesses shut down, as visitors largely consist of either day-trippers or those destined for loftier locales along the *trasee turistice* (trails). Open year-round, the **red dot trail** leads northwest toward **Cheile Cibinului** (gorges; 5km). The **red cross/red stripe trail** (4hr. round-trip) follows an unpaved road for part of the way to **Vf. Bătrâna** (Old Woman's Peak; 1911m). Staying on the red stripe trail for 25km (7hr.) to **Cindrel Peak** (2244m) is a more difficult, but more visually rewarding, experience (trail open only in summer). Philosopher **Constantin Noica's grave** is at **Schit Church,** 2km from Păltiniş on the road to Sibiu. The house where he spent his last years, **Casa Noica,** reveals more (tel. 138; open Mon.-Thurs. 10am-4pm, Fri. noon-6pm, Sat. 8am-noon, Sun. 6-8pm; free). Head right after leaving Hotel Cindrel, pass the orange building, and continue down the gravel road. Take the next left and follow the trail until you reach Noica's *casa*.

On the main street, the kiosk in front of **Gasthaus zum Hans** sells **hiking maps** (open Tues.-Sun. 10am-6pm). Climb the stairs by the post office and keep heading up to find **Hotel Cindrel** (tel. 21 32 37), which features well-kept rooms with showers, TVs, and great views (doubles L100,000; EC and MC accepted; reception open until midnight). The hotel/restaurant **Cabana Turiştor** (tel. 21 23 24) on the main road near the post office, offers the same amenities, *sans* cable, at a lower altitude (doubles L56,000 per person; triples L54,000 per person). For other accommodations options, ask the post office operator, who will direct you to a villa or private room (L30,000-40,000). Stock up on food in Sibiu before coming to Păltiniş; there's no grocery store, and only one restaurant opens for dinner—the Cabana Turiştor (main dishes L4000-9000; restaurant open daily 8am until last guest leaves, usually 10pm-midnight). The main street **post office** has a **telephone center** that dials and rings daily 8am-8pm. **Phone code:** a titillating 069.

A comfortable **bus** connects Sibiu's train station ro Păltiniş (3 per day, 1hr., L5000, pay the driver). Ask for "mah-SHEE-nah de pahl-tee-NEESH." Sibiu's **Agenţia de Turism—Păltiniş** (tel. 43 28 53), in Piaţa Unirii, has bus schedules. If you missed it in Sibiu, the schedule is also posted at the post office in Păltiniş. Ride the bus to the **ski lift** (open in winter 9am-5pm; 8min.; round-trip L6000). Follow the signs here to start hiking the red triangle, red cross, or blue dot trails. To get to the main street, trace the ski lift and turn right. Continue on the main street to get to the red dot trail.

FĂGĂRAŞ MOUNTAINS

Romania's highest, longest, and most spectacular, the Făgăraş mountain ridge extends more than 60km, from the Olt Valley to the Piatra Craiului mountains. Wildflower-scented meadows, cloud-bathed summits, and views of Walachian plains and Transylvanian hills cure all fatigue. Be sure to bring adequate supplies (compasses are hard to find) and a good map. Look for a rudimentary map in Păltinis and Sibiu, or pick up *Drumeţi În Carpaţi* in Bucharest or Bran (about L15,000). The hiking season lasts from July to mid-September, but the mountains are never crowded. Prepare for harsh weather. The ridge can be traversed in seven days; the usual route is from west to east, starting in Transylvania. It is possible to sleep in a *cabana,* but be prepared to camp if necessary. *Cabana* facilities vary; some may offer just sleeping sacks (L15,000 per person), while others offer doubles with baths (L40,000-100,000). Call **Cabana Salişte** in Sibiu (tel. 21 17 03) to make reservations for two of the more upscale cabanas. Cabana Sur, on the red triangle path, has burned down.

Countless itineraries are possible, but most start in the Olt Valley on the railroad from Sibiu to the south. A majority of hikers enter the ridge at **Lac Avrig,** a glacial lake reachable by the red cross and blue dot trails, or the **Şaua Puha** (Puha Saddle). Both are accessible from **Avrig** on the Braşov-Sibiu train line (8 per day, 1hr., L3700 for *accelerat*). Plan a full day to reach the ridge. **Custura Sărăţii** (1hr. east of Şaua Puha) is the ridge trail's most spectacular and difficult portion; for two hours you'll cling to rocks on a path sometimes less than a foot wide, surrounded by cliffs on both sides (an alternate path lets the less daring avoid this route). Many end their hike with a descent into the **Sîmbăta Valley** (red triangle trail); the ridge ends at Cabana Plaiul Foii near the Piatra Craiului mountains, about 30km from Braşov. To get down to the valley, however, you may have to backtrack to find a suitable descent trail. Nobody should hike in the Făgăraş alone. See **Essentials: Wilderness and Safety Concerns,** p. 41, for some tips on keeping healthy while hiking.

▒ Curtea de Argeş

Hiding in the foothills of the Muntii Făgăraş, Curtea de Argeş (CURT-a DAR-jesh) preserves many buildings that date back to the town's 14th-century heyday as Walachia's capital. Noted for its monastery, the resting place of numerous Romanian monarchs, Curtea also serves as an excellent base for adventurers seeking **Count Dracula's real castle,** Cetatea Vlad Ţepeş, 27km away. A bus from the station in Curtea de Argeş (take a right from the train station) takes you most of the way to the castle (direction "Căpăţineni," 4-7 a day, 30min.; L5000). From here, continue on foot 500m along the main road, until you see the Cetatea Poienari sign. The steps leading to the castle are appropriately torturous, zig-zagging endlessly up the mountain (a good 20min.). Don't fear if you lose sight of both the start and end of the trail: you're not lost, and the insects and goats will keep you company. The partially restored ruins eventually emerge from the clouds. Here, Vlad Ţepeş and his successors were bold enough to sleep 30ft from their prisoners (open Tues.-Sun. 8am-5pm, L2000). A short illustrated guide in English is available (L6000). Those looking for a less exhausting trip to the castle can take a taxi (L50,000-60,000 round-trip).

Back in town, the story of the **monastery** is no less gruesome than that of Vlad Ţepeş. In 1512, Voievode Neagoe Basarab directed Master Manole to build the most beautiful church the world had ever seen. The best craftspeople were assembled to carry out his command, but work stalled halfway through—everything accomplished during the day was mysteriously destroyed at night. The builders redoubled their efforts, but the pattern continued. The solution finally came to Manole in a dream: unless human blood coursed through the church's stones, it could not possibly surpass all others. Since few visitors traveled through town, the workers decided to entomb the first of their wives to arrive at the site the next morning. Only honest Manole did not inform his wife of the danger. She was buried within the walls of the monastery. As the men placed the last tiles on the roof, Basarab asked the workers whether they could ever build another church so beautiful. All answered that they could, and would, build another even more splendid. Furious that his church might be outdone, the prince removed all the ladders and scaffolding, leaving the craftsmen to die on the roof. Neagoe Basarab, as well as many other famous crowned heads—King Carol I, Queen Elizabeth, Queen Maria, and King Ferdinand—have all found eternal peace in the monastery, along with Manole's wife. Across the street, a spring, the **Fântâna lui Manole** gushes on the site where Manole, Icarus-like, crashed on wings fashioned to help him escape from the monastery. To reach the monastery from the train station, turn left and head right up the cobblestone Str. Castenilor. Take a right at the park, then a left onto the main **Str. Basarabilor.** Yellow and blue signs point the way to "Mânăstirea Curtea de Argeș." At the fork well past the hotel, take a right (monastery open daily 7:30am-7pm; L1000).

Trains run from Bucharest to Pitești (1½-2hr.); change here for Curtea (7 per day, 1hr., total trip L10,200). Along the way to the monastery, a **tourist office** (open Mon.-Fri. 8am-6pm) and **currency exchange** (open Mon.-Fri. 8am-4pm) await inside Hotel Posada, Str. Basarabilor 27 (tel. 71 18 00; fax 71 18 02). The name of this conveniently located hotel commemorates the battle during which King Charles Robert of Hungary unsuccessfully attempted to annex Walachia (singles L125,000, with bath L250,000; doubles with bath L230,000; inconsistent hot water; breakfast included). Dine at Posada or the terraced **Restaurant Manole** (tel. 71 17 44), across from the monastery. *Mititei* (L1250)—a grilled, garlicky beef patty—should be eaten with mustard and washed down with beer. Live music most nights (open 10am-midnight).

■ Brașov

One of Romania's most beautifully restored cities, Brașov (BRA-shohv) rises from the foot of **Muntele Tâmpa,** providing a base for excursions to the Carpathian mountains. Founded by Saxons in the 14th century, Brașov grew in commercial importance, thanks to its strategic location overlooking the main pass across the mountains. It eventually evolved into a crucial transportation hub between Bucharest and Western Europe, with a correspondingly diverse population of Romanians, Germans, and Hungarians. The Communist era belched forth industrial mammoths on the periphery, but mercifully spared the city center.

Orientation and Practical Information Trains to Bucharest, some originating in Budapest, leave up to 22 times a day (2am-9pm, 2½-4hr., L1400 for *accelerat*). Train info can be found at **CFR** on Str. Republicii (open Mon.-Fri. 7am-7:30pm, Sat. 9am-1pm). To get to town from the station, ride bus #4 (direction "Piața Unirii"; L1600) to the main **Piața Sfatului** (10min.); descend in front of **Biserica Neagră,** a big, dark Gothic church. By foot, cross the street and walk straight down Bd. Victoriei; then follow Str. Mihail Kogălniceanu right around the civic center until it ends. At the fork, take the soft right on **Bd. 15 Noiembrie** (becomes **Bd. Eroilor**) and turn left on Str. Republicii or Str. Mureșenilor (2km). To get to the main **bus station** from Piața Sfatului, go right on Str. Mureșenilor, and turn left onto Bd. Eroilor. Buy bus tickets at the booths on the elevated sidewalk (open Mon.-Fri. 5:30am-11:30pm, Sat.-Sun. 6:30am-10:30pm). **Odeon Travel,** Str. Mureșenilor 28 (tel. 14 28 40), offers info about transportation and hotels (open Mon.-Fri. 9am-2pm and 5-8pm, Sat.9am-1pm). Ask here about buses to London or Frankfurt (Wed., Thurs. and Sat.; a hideously long time; L590,000). Hotel Aro-Palace, Eroilor 9, sells **maps** (L3000). From Piața Sfatului, walk on Str. Mureșenilor until it intersects Bd. Eroilor at the park, and turn right. An **ATM** rests peacefully two doors down from the hotel (Cirrus/EuroCard/MC/Plus/Visa). **Exchange currency** at any bureau in the central *piața*. **IDM** (tel. 14 21 13), in the circular building at the intersection of Bd. Eroilor and Str. Republicii, changes AmEx and EuroCard **traveler's checks** and gives cash advances on Diners Club, MC, and Visa (open Mon.-Fri. 8am-8pm, Sat. 9am-6pm, Sun. 9am-2pm). A 24-hour **pharmacy,** Aurofarm, is at Str. Republicii 27 (tel. 14 35 60) near the big Bayer sign. Despite its address, the **post office,** Str. Nicolae Iorga 1 (tel. 41 51 64), is actually on Bd. Eroilor between Str. Mureșenilor and Str. Nicolae Bălcescu. **Postal code:** 2200. **Telephones** are nearby on Bd. Eroilor (open daily 6:30am-10pm). **Phone code:** 068.

Accommodations and Food If you have no luck with the **private room** hawkers at the train station, visit **EXO,** Str. Postăvarului 6 (tel. 14 45 91). From Piața Sfatului, walk 15m on Str. Republicii and go right on Diaconu Coresi. The next left is Postăvarului. EXO finds rooms starting at L20,000 per person (open Mon.-Sat. 11am-8pm, Sun. 11am-2pm). **Hotel Postăuarul,** Politehnicii 62 (tel. 14 43 30), offers spacious singles with toilet and sinks. The hallway showers are far from grungy (L79,300; doubles L110,000, with bath L122,000; triples L165,900; breakfast included).

A daily **outdoor/indoor market** on Str. Nicolae Bălescu, two blocks from the intersection with Bd. Eroilor, provides a cheap and eye-catching selection of fruits, vegetables, and other fresh and packaged foods. Good luck figuring out the cheese (open Mon.-Fri. 7am-7pm, Sat. 7am-2pm). **Crama,** Piaţa Sfatului 12 (tel. 14 39 81), in the 16th-century Hirschner house, welcomes guests with folk costumes hanging on the walls next to stuffed game. Eat meat main courses (from L9000) while watching traditional dances (open Tues.-Sun. 7pm-2am; Visa accepted). **Restaurant Intim,** Str. Mareşenilor 4 (tel. 14 17 46), goes for the intimate feel with drawn curtains and red upholstered walls. It serves breakfast (under L6000) as well as lunch and dinner to a diverse clientele (English menu; open daily 8:30am-10pm).

Sights and Entertainment Piaţa Sfatului and Str. Republicii are perfect for a stroll, and many historical sights even have signs in English. The central *piaţa*'s ornate **Orthodox Cathedral** was built in 1896 of marble and delicate gold. The **History Museum** on the square used to be the city hall and courthouse; legend holds that the condemned had to jump from the tower to their deaths. The small museum holds archives and artifacts of Braşov and nearby regions (open Tues.-Sun. 10am-6pm; L4000, students L1000). Beyond the square along Str. Gh. Bariţiu looms the Lutheran **Biserica Neagră** (Black Church), Romania's most celebrated Gothic church. It received its name after being charred by fire in 1689. Keep your grubby hands away from the church's 17th- and 18th-century Anatolian carpets, or pay a US$100 fine (open Mon.-Sat. 10am-3:30pm; L1000; no photos).

The city gate, **Poarta Schei,** was built in 1828 to separate the old German citadel from the Romanian *schei*—a quiet area of old-style houses. From the main square, follow Str. Apollonia Hirschner and turn right onto Str. Poarta Schei. Behind the *poarta,* Str. Prundului leads to Piaţa Unirii and its two attractions: the black-towered, icon-filled **Biserica Sfîntu Nicolae,** and **Prima Şcoala Românescă** (Romania's First School) built in 1495, which has French and Romanian signs (open 9am-5pm, L4000, students L1000). The **Ethnographic Museum,** Bd. Eroilor, exhibits Transylvanian folk costumes and ceramics and sells folk crafts (guides in English, French, and German available, L5000; open Tues.-Sun. 10am-6pm; L1500, students L750). To see the mountains without too much exertion, **telecabina** (cable cars) climb up Muntele Tâmpa from Aleea T. Brediceanu (round-trip L5000; open daily 10am-7pm). To climb a road less traveled, trails on Aleea T. Brediceanu lead to the surprisingly majestic **Weaver's Bastion** and other **medieval ruins.**

Braşov is home to a number of cultural activities; check the posters around town for upcoming events. **Operas** tend to be low on production but big on opera; tickets are sold on Str. Republicii at Agenţia Teatrală de Bilete (tel. 14 41 38; open daily noon-4pm; L6300, students L3150). For more physical entertainment, check out **Disco Club Rok 92** (tel. 41 25 31) on Str. A. Hirscher off Piaţa Sfatului. Dance to a DJ or live music under black lights (open 10pm till 4-6am; men L1000, women free). In late summer, Piaţa Sfatului hosts the international music festival **Cerbul de Aur** (Golden Stag), which in the past has featured the likes of Ray Charles and MC Hammer.

■ Near Braşov

BRAN

It's a dark and stormy night in the 19th century. As rain crashes down on the roofs of Bran and lightning illuminates its looming castle, an unknown chariot navigates the Bran pass, the tight road between the old principalities of Transylvania and Walachia. This chariot was long thought to have belonged to Bram Stoker, who was said to have been so impressed by the scene that he wrote a book about it: *Dracula,* which was soon to become the root of the vampire myth and its zillions of re-interpretations. Unfortunately, this myth is no more true than the vampire story itself; Stoker, in fact, never visited Romania. The book also put Romania on the map for most Westerners as a backwards and superstitious country. In reality, **Vlad Tepeş Dracula** (literally

Vlad the Impaler, son of Dracul), had little to do with either this overly restored edifice or vampires. As Prince of Walachia (reigned 1448, 1456-62, and 1476-77), he was charged with protecting the Bran pass, which played a crucial role during the Middle Ages in the development of Romanian trade.

The castle at Bran, which overlooks the pass, bears only a physical resemblance to the castle in Stoker's novel; Tepeş actually resided in a castle near Curtea de Argeş (see p. 492). Despite its lack of vampiric significance, the castle contains a number of interesting exhibits, including an **ethnographic village** (with rather poor English and French translations) and **museum** featuring Bran's economic, rather than mythic, importance (L15,000, students L10,000; open Tues.-Sun. 9am-5pm). **Hiking maps** are available near the entrance to the castle complex (L10,000-15,000). Follow the yellow triangle, red cross, or red stripe trails on Str. Valeriu Lucian Bologa to Omu peak (6-7hr.; see **Sinaia,** p. 496). In an **emergency,** call Safeguard Braşov (tel. 11 65 50).

To get to Bran from Braşov, take bus #28 (direction "IAR Caminul") to "Gară Bartolomeu" (5min.; L1600), where the **bus** to Bran departs (hourly, fewer on weekends; 45min.; L4500). To get to the castle, head down the main road (Str. Principal) back towards Braşov and take the first right. Castel Magazin, on this corner, **exchanges money** (open Tues.-Sun. 10am-4pm). To find the **tourist office,** Bran Imex, 395 Dr. Aurel (tel. 23 66 42), follow the main road away from Braşov and take a right on Str. Aurel Stoian (open daily 8am-6pm). The **post office** (open Mon.-Fri. 8am-6pm) and the **telephone office** (open Mon.-Fri. 7:30am-8pm, Sat. 8am-2pm) lie further down Str. Principal beyond the castle museum. **Phone code:** 068.

The locals take their town's pop culture appeal in stride. The **Cabana Bran Castle** (tel. 23 64 04) provides cheap sleeps (4-bed rooms L40,000 per person), but you have to cross a stream to get there. Head down Str.Str. Aurel Stoian, turn left across the street from the building with the blue Stomatologue sign, and follow the gravel path up to the left. The tourist office arranges private rooms (doubles with bath US$9). **Dracula Market,** at the intersection of the main road and Str. Valerin Lucian Bologa, is where Dracula goes food shopping (open daily 8am-6pm; no blood for sale). **Bella Italia** (tel. 23 64 88), on the road leading away from Braşov, offers *calzones* minus the red stuff—that is, tomato sauce (L12,000)—and *spaghetti alla Napoleana* (L4700). A tall glass of beer (L4000) would appeal even to a blood drinker (open Tues.-Sun. 1-10pm). Only non-vampires can boogie down at **Disco Bar Dracula,** near the Cabana Bran Castle (open Fri.-Sat. 11pm-5am, Sun. 6pm-midnight).

POIANA BRAŞOV

About 13km from Braşov, this mountain niche has long been vying with Sinaia for the title of Romania's best resort. The beautifully green, open area among the mountains is perfect for **hiking** or **skiing.** Trails here are accessible to the average hiker, and **Mt. Postăvarul** (1802m) has super-fab views. Centrul de Echitatie (tel. 26 21 61), by the road to Braşov, instructs aspiring **equestrians** and thrills with ponies, carriage rides, and horses (open daily 8am-8pm). In summer, swimming, tennis, and track facilities draw visitors to the town. In winter, in addition to 10 **downhill ski runs,** Poiana Braşov offers **cross-country skiing** and **ice skating.** Ski schools and rentals abound near the *telecabinas* (cable cars): *telecabina* Poiana-Kanzel, behind Hotel Teleferic, and *telecabina* Capra Neagra, behind Hotel Sportul (L15,000 round-trip; open daily in summer 8am-6pm, in winter 8am-4pm).

Buses for Poiana Braşov leave from the bus station in Braşov on Bd. Eroilor (2 per hr., 6:30am-midnight; L2100). Ask for "maşina de Poiana," or find bus #20 at the far end of the bus platform. Once in Poiana Braşov, examine the map signs where the bus leaves you. Poiana Braşov's **tourist office** (tel. 26 23 89) offers great one-day excursions (US$7-30), including a trip to Bran castle (US$7), and can help find rooms in local hotels (open Mon.-Fri. 8am-3pm). Skimpy **maps** are available at *telecabina* Capra Neagra (L500). **Currency exchange** bureaus are located in hotels. The white **Complex Favorit** plays host to a **post office** (open Mon.-Fri. 9am-4pm), a **telephone office** (open Mon.-Fri. 7am-7pm, Sat. 7:30am-1:30pm), and a **pharmacy** (open daily 10am-6pm). To get to Complex Favorit from the bus station, turn away from the mountain, and take the street veering to the right from the bus parking lot. **Postal code:** 2209. **Phone code:** 068.

Lodging prices swell during peak seasons (July 15-Sept. 15 and Dec. 20-late March). *Cabanas* are cheaper than hotels. **Cabana Cristianu Mare** (tel. 18 65 45) is serviced by *telecabina* Poiana-Kanzel. Both the view and the non-stop hot water elicit sighs of delight (clean doubles, triples, and 8-bed rooms for L30,000 per person). Call ahead for reservations. **Coliba Haiducilor** (The Outlaw's Hut; tel. 26 21 37), cloistered in the woods behind Hotel Teleferic, gets all its food from its own farm. There's a balcony and patio with bright wooden tables and a view of the forest (salads and meat dishes L13,000-20,000; open daily noon-midnight).

■ Sinaia

Romania's most celebrated year-round alpine resort, Sinaia (see-NAY-ah) made its mark as a favorite getaway of Romania's first royal family in the late 1800s. The resort, with its elegant villas and park, still retains an aristocratic aura. The palace and monastery combine with slopes and hiking trails to draw tireless sightseers, skiers, and hikers, who mingle with friendly locals and the occasional black-clad monk. Wedged into the Prahova valley, flanked by the Bucegi mountains on both sides, and home to important relics of Romania's past, Sinaia offers the best of Romania.

Orientation and Practical Information Trains run to Bucharest almost every hour (2hr., L11,000 for *accelerat*). From the station, cross the street, climb the stairs, and take a left onto a cobblestone ramp at the first landing. Climb the first steps and take two left turns to **Bd. Carol I,** the main street. Large hotels, including the Hotel Palace (see **Accommodations,** below), provide **tourist info.** The Palace also offers a **currency exchange** (open daily 8:30am-11pm) and a **laundry** (open daily 8am-4pm). **Commercial Bank,** a block past Hotel Montana, Bd. Carol I 49, has it all: traveler's check exchange (Mon.-Fri. 8am-noon), credit card advances, an **ATM** (Cirrus/Plus/MC), and a steep commission. **Telecabinas** (cable cars) whisk you to Cota 1400 (elevation 1400m) from behind Hotel Montana (Mon.-Fri. 8:30am-4pm, Sat.-Sun. 8am-5pm; 8min.; one-way L4,000). From Cota 1400, take another *telecabina* to Cota 2000 (Mon.-Fri. 8:45am-3:45, Sat.-Sun. 8:30-4pm; 7min.; one-way L3000). In an emergency, contact the **mountain rescue** squad, Bd. Carol I 47 (tel. 31 31 31). With your back to Hotel Montana, the **post office** is across the street and to the left (open Mon.-Fri. 7am-8pm, Sat.-Sun. 8am-noon). A **telephone office** and train ticket information booth are in the post office. **Postal code:** 2180. **Phone code:** 044.

Accommodations and Food Locals await tourists at the train station with offers of *o cameră* (private rooms; US$5-10). On the trail, stay in a mountain *cabana* (L250,000). Sinaia's priciest hotels, which are geared towards foreigners, offer many amenities, but prices go hiking mid-summer and during winter holidays. **Complex Economat** (tel. 31 11 51), in the park of Castelul Peleș, offers surprisingly decent prices for its three-star hotel (excellent singles L80,000; doubles with bath L150,000; L5000 discount for students and the disabled). Redeem your L10,000 breakfast credit at the welcoming but pricey **restaurant** downstairs (dishes up to L38,000; open Mon. noon-10pm, Tues.-Sun. 7am-11pm). **Hotel Palace** (tel. 31 20 51) lies at Str. Octavian Goga 11. Instead of making a left onto Bd. Carol I, keep to the right and wind around the park. The hotel is the imposing white building on the right. Reservations are essential (singles start at L155,000; doubles L205,000; L15,000 breakfast credit included; up to 50% discount for stays of more than 1 night). **Hotel-Restaurant Furnica,** Str. Furnica 50 (tel. 31 18 50; singles L100,000, doubles L120,000), offers a tasty selection of meats (up to L10,000), soups (from L1500) and salads.

Sights and Hiking The construction of **Castelul Peleș** (Peleș Castle) was begun in 1873 when Carol Hohenzollern-Sigmaringen was merely a prince; upon its completion 10 years later, he moved in as the king of newly independent Romania (open

Wed.-Sun. 9am-3pm; L30,000). Although this immense summer residence reflects its German roots, it also holds the Florentine Room, with miniature bronze copies of Michelangelo's *Dawn* and *Dusk* from Lorenzo di Medici's tomb; the tapestry-lined Turkish room, for smoking *sheesha*; and the armory, which contains more than 4000 pieces of European and Asian weaponry from the 14th-18th centuries. The well-informed tour guides speak English, French, German, and Spanish. Crown Prince Ferdinand's residence, **Pelişor,** also hides on the estate (open Wed.-Sun. 9am-4pm; L20,000, an extra L5000-10,000 may get you in with a smaller group). Built at the turn of the century, Pelişor boasts a number of dissonantly converging styles, including a sitting room covered in gold leaf. **Mânăstirea Sinaia** (monastery) hosts an active group of Orthodox monks. Founded in 1695, the monastery is open free of charge.

The *telecabina* (cable car) to Cota 1400 leads to alpine **hikes** and summer **hanggliding. Ski slopes** descend from Cota 2000, which can be accessed by *telecabina* or, in winter, *teleschi* (ski lifts). Along the Bucegi range, the **yellow stripe trail** leads obsessive hikers on a strenuous six-hour climb from Cota 2000, past **Babele** (2200m; accessible by cable car—see Buşteni, below), to the highest peak of the Bucegi—**Omu** (2505m). The Babele rocks are said to represent two *babe* (women). From Cabana Babele, the mountain cabin, follow the **red cross trail** to the 42m **Crucea Eroilor** (Heroes' Cross, a.k.a. Crucea Caraiman; 1hr.), a monument to Romanians killed in WWI. Flashlight-equipped spelunkers follow the **blue cross trail** to **Cheile Peşterii,** a pitch-black but easily reached cave. Remember that cable cars stop running weekdays at 4pm. Detailed maps of the trails of Sinaia, Buşteni, and Predeal are available for L850-1500 at the hotels. Most trails are inadvisable in the winter and are recommended only for "well-trained tourists" in summer. If you prefer dancing to hiking, disco at the **Blue Angel** (tel. 31 26 17), across from Hotel Montana, to all kinds of music (open daily 9pm-4am; cover Tues.-Sun. L5000, Mon. free). Women have a high probability of getting in free.

■ Near Sinaia: Buşteni

Hikers seeking a quick trip to the natural sights of the Bucegi range should jump on the first choo-choo and head for the *telecabina* in Buşteni, two train stops from Sinaia (14 trains per day, 10 min., L1100). A less frequent bus also makes the trip (L1200). Opposite the train station stands a small stone **church** built by King Carol I in 1889. To hit the Bucegi trails, take a left onto the main road and walk past **Hotel Caraiman,** Bd. Libertaţia 89 (tel. (044) 32 01 56; doubles with bath L80,000). At the Hotel Silva sign take a right and head for them there hills. The *telecabina* to Babele (L10,000, 15min., Mon.-Fri. 9am-3:45pm, Sat.-Sun. 9am-4:45pm) hides behind the hotel. After Babele, the *cabina* continues on to Cheile Peşterii (see **Sinaia: Sights,** p. 496). Buşteni is also a good jumping-off point for a number of short, easy hikes, including the **blue triangle** path (3hr.), which starts from the Buşteni train station. Pick up supplies and a **hiking map** in Sinaia before heading on to Buşteni.

▓ Sighişoara

Sighişoara (see-ghee-SHWAH-rah) is perhaps the least spoiled and most enchanting medieval town in Transylvania. Surrounded by mountains and crowning a green hill, its gilded steeples, old clocktower, and irregularly tiled roofs have largely survived centuries of attacks, fires, and the ever-present threat of floods. The **Cetatea** (Citadel), built by Saxons in 1191, is preserved as a living museum. Still, beautiful and relaxing Sighişoara is small and won't keep you busy for more than a day. Enter the Cetatea through the **Turnul cu Ceas** (Clock Tower), off Str. O. Goga. The **history museum** inside this old tower displays artifacts and furniture since Roman times. Climb to the top to see the clock's mechanism and an expansive view of the area (tel. 77 11 08; open Tues.-Fri. 9am-5:30pm, Sat.-Sun. 9am-3:30pm; L3000, students L1500). Nearby, the three-room **Museum of Medieval Armory** offers a small exhibit on Vlad Ţepeş (son of Vlad Dracul) and arms from all over the world (open Tues.-Sun.

ROMANIA

10am-3:30pm; L2000; students L1000). From the clock tower, walk straight past Vlad Dracul's house and take a left at Str. Şcolii to reach the 175-step **covered wooden staircase** (built 1662) leading to the old Saxon **church** (closed for renovations). At the top of the stairs, go down to the right to find the affiliated graveyard—definitely the type you wouldn't want to get caught in late at night (open May-Oct. daily 8am-8pm, Nov.-April 9am-4pm). The inscription on the cemetery gate reads: "Whoever you are, know you enter a cemetery." Oh, the wisdom of the ancients... **Biserica Mânăsterii,** by the clock tower, offers a brochure in English about Sighişoara's churches (open Mon.-Sat. 10am-6pm).

Trains run to Bucharest (13 per day, 4½hr., L19,300 for *accelerat*) and Cluj-Napoca (4 per day, 2½-3hr., L18,000). **Store luggage** at the train station (L1800-3600; open 24hr.). To reach the center, take a right on **Str. Libertaţii,** go left on **Str. Gării,** veer left at the Russian cemetery commemorating the victory over fascism, turn right and cross the footbridge over river **Târnava Mare,** and walk down the street behind Sigma, Str. Morii. A right at the fork leads to Str. O. Goaga and the Cetatea, a left to main **Str. I Decembrie 1918. OJT Agenţie de Turism,** Str. 1 Decembrie 1918 10 (tel. 77 10 72), helps find rooms in hotels, organizes tours, and sells English maps (L3000; open Mon.-Fri. 9am-5pm, Sat. 9am-2pm). **IDM exchange office** (tel. 77 19 62), at #9, accepts AmEx, MC, Visa, and other traveler's checks (open Mon.-Fri. 8am-8pm, Sat. 9am-1pm). Further down, as Str. 1 Decembrie 1918 becomes Piaţa H. Oberth, lies the almighty **post and telephone office** (post open Mon.-Fri. 7am-9pm; telephones daily 7am-9pm). **Postal code:** 3050. **Phone code:** 065.

At the train station, a young man speaking English may offer you a room at his summer youth hostel. **Bobby's Hostel,** Str. Tache Ionescu 18 (tel. 77 22 32), could use some improvement in the bathroom department (ask about hot water availability), but the company will likely be great—young people from all over stop here (doubles L80,000; large 11-bed dorms L35,000; sheets included). The hostel is officially open only between July 1 and August 30, but Bobby may sneak you in if you come off-season. **Hotel-Restaurant Non-Stop** (tel. 77 95 01), near the train station, has beautiful rooms and bathrooms (doubles L70,000; breakfast included). In the Cetatea, try **Restaurant Cetatea,** Piaţa Cositorarilor 5 (tel. 77 15 96); its claim to fame is that the father of Vlad "Count Dracula" Ţepeş might have once lived there. Watch out: no menu means high prices for good meals (soup L7500, beef main dishes L20,000-30,000; restaurant open daily noon-7pm, bar open noon-6pm). Restaurants downtown serve Italian food at high prices. **4 Amici,** Str. Morii 7 (tel. 77 25 69), serves pizza and other Italian fare (L5400-18,000) Listen to music while watching the pizza man at work, or peruse the Italian magazines left on the tables (open daily noon-midnight). The grocery stores along Str. 1 Decembrie 1918 will satisfy any lingering need.

NORTHERN ROMANIA

Nestled up against Ukraine and Hungary, the Maramureş region of northern Romania had its heyday during WWII, when the area supplied oil to the German armies. Nowadays, few visitors find reason to venture into the area's rolling hills, but those who do will be rewarded with the peaceful, little-seen traditions of village life.

■ Sighetu-Marmaţiei

The northern village Sighetu-Marmaţiei (see-GHEH-too mar-MAH-tsee-ay; or just Sighet) blends small shops stocking imported goods with towering church steeples on its main street. Meanwhile, streets on the periphery seem like they belong in a rural hamlet, as locals wear a modern version of the traditional costume. **Memorialul Victimelor Comunismului şi al Rezistenţei** (Memorial to the Victims of Communism and the Resistance), on Corneliu Coposu, has earned worldwide acclaim and UNESCO patronage. The silent walls of the jailhouse-turned-museum witnessed the death of the Romanian elite, as the Communist Party imprisoned countless professors, doctors, ministers, generals, and other intellectuals opposed to the Red wave. A partial list of those exterminated between 1952 and 1955 hangs on the facade of this sobering sight (open Tues.-Sun. 9:30am-1pm and 3-5pm). The museum is off Str. Bogdan Vodă near the *Primaria* (town hall). The decaying Communist-era **Holocaust Memorial** (down Str. A. Muresan off Pța. Libertătii) commemorates the 38,000 Maramureș Jews killed by Hitler. The **Muzeul de Arhitectura și Artă Populară** (Outdoor Folk Architecture Museum), Str. Bicazului, on the Dobăieș Hill, is reachable from the center by bus #1 (2 per hr., L1500). When you see Școala #5 on your right, get out and continue down the road. Near the old tracks, turn left up Str. Muzeului. The museum looks like an ideal village, with the most beautiful peasant houses in Maramureș transplanted here; make sure the guide doesn't forget to open the houses. The interiors reveal intricately furnished rooms embellished with handmade carpets, covers, and more (open Tues.-Sun. 10am-6pm; L3000, students L1000).

The scenic **train** ride from Cluj (1 per day, 4½hr., L15,600) is worth every *leu;* daily trains run to Bucharest (11hr., L31,300) and Timișoara (10hr., L17,500). To reach the **tourist office,** walk three long blocks down Str. Iuliu Maniu away from the train tracks and take a left before the yellow church. **OJT tourist office,** Piața Libertății 21 (tel. 31 28 15), sells **maps** of the region (L2000; open Mon.-Thurs. 8am-4pm, Fri. 8am-2pm, Sat. 9am-1pm). **Bancă Comercială,** Str. Iuliu Maniu 32, accepts Visa and cashes all kinds of traveler's checks at 1.5% commission (US$5 minimum; open Mon.-Fri. 8-11:30am and 12:30-2:30pm). The **post office** is at Str. Bogdan Vodă—cross the square from OJT and take a left (open Mon.-Fri. 7am-8pm, Sat. 8am-noon). Continue down the street and turn left at the garden with a statue to find the **telephone office,** Str. Dragos Vodă 2 (open daily 7am-9pm). **Phone code:** 062. **Postal code:** 4925.

Ask at the tourist office about **private rooms** (L30,000-50,000). When it comes to true budget accommodations, **Mini-Hotel Magură,** Str. Iuliu Maniu 44, across from the train station, is probably your best bet; the communal bathroom is decent (singles L50,000; doubles L60,000). A 20-minute walk down Str. Mihai Eminescu (continue straight at the yellow church) leads to the city's only park, where **Hotel Marmația** (tel. 31 22 41) rents rooms with showers and TV (singles L74,000; doubles L116,000; breakfast included). In the center, tons of little eateries and patisseries offer a variety of yummy things at low prices. For a real restaurant experience, **Restaurantul Curtea Veche** (tel. 31 14 36), facing the ever-present yellow church, serves traditional Romanian meals (L15,000-25,000).

■ Near Sighetu-Marmaţiei: Săpânţa

Maramureș, the northwest region of Romania, is known for its stunning wood-carving and reverence for secular traditions. Here, you'll see many people making and wearing folk costumes, especially on Sundays and during feasts and holidays. With its colorfully decorated houses and craft traditions, the village of **Săpânţa** (suh-PUN-tsah) well illustrates the way modern changes give new life to an old culture. The town, on the Satu Mare-Sighet road, has gained renown for its **Cimitirul Vesel** (Merry Cemetery), in which brightly colored gravesite crosses include funny paintings and poems about the deceased. Most verses begin *"Aci eu mă odihnesc/...mă numesc"* (Here is where I now remain/... is my name) and proceed to poke fun at death (open April-Sept. daily 8am-8pm; L2500). On the street passing the cemetery on the right, the tiny **Casă Memorialā Ion Stan Pătraș** (House of Ioan Pătraș) contains fancy chairs, plates, and mini-tombstones made by this *auteur* of Cimitirul Vesel (open daily 7am-10pm; L3000). At the entrance to the cemetery, the locals hanging out shooting the breeze offer cheap **rooms** in their houses (L40,000).

Buses connect Săpânța to Sighetu-Marmaţiei (7 per day, Sat. and Sun. 3 per day, 30min., L3000). Be sure to get off at the center rather than at the Săpânța sign. From the bus stop, walk a few feet along the bus route, and take the first left. Follow the road to the S-turn flanked by the church and cemetery.

ROMANIAN MOLDOVA AND BUKOVINA

Eastern Romania, which once included the neighboring Republic of Moldova, extends from the Carpathians to the Prut River. Moldavia, as this region was then called, saw its greatest glory in the 15th century under the rule of Ştefan cel Mare (1457-1504). Today it's somewhat underdeveloped, largely because any attempts at improvement were thwarted by Soviet repression. The northern landscape rolls into green, gentle hills that contain some of Romania's most beautiful churches and villages. Iaşi, the 19th-century capital, remains culturally rich. Farther north, Bukovina is home to unique painted monasteries and old-style hospitality.

■ Iaşi

The intoxicating perfume of lindens in summer is as omnipresent as church steeples in Iaşi (ee-AHSH). During the second half of the 19th century, this city was Romania's second administrative and first cultural center. Its spiritual life revolved around the Junimea society, founded by the country's top writers, nobles, and intellectuals. They looked westward, filling Iaşi with Neoclassical homes and palaces. These buildings, remarkably well-preserved after 45 grinding years of Communism, draw throngs of tourists to the city's clean, modern streets.

ORIENTATION AND PRACTICAL INFORMATION

To reach Iaşi's center, walk up the slope leading away from the stations, take a right on **Str. Arcu** (which becomes **Str. Cuza Vodă** from Piaţa Unirii onward), and follow the tram tracks. After a block, you'll hit **Piaţa Unirii,** equally accessible via tram #1 or 3 (L1700 round-trip) from directly in front of the train station, across the street from Vama Veche (Old Customs Tower). Be forewarned; ticket checkers are super-diligent, so stamp your ticket right away.

> **Tourist Offices: Libraria Junimea,** Piaţa Unirii 4 (tel. 11 46 64). Next door to CFR. Sells hard-to-find **city maps** (L6000). Open Mon.-Fri. 10am-6pm.
> **Currency Exchange: IDMs** litter the city—the most central is at Piaţa Unirii 12 (tel. 21 72 26), in Cinematograf Victoria. Changes AmEx, MC, Visa, and Australian traveler's checks, and gives cash advances on MC and Visa, though at unfavorable rates. Open Mon.-Fri. 8am-8pm, Sat. 9am-1pm.
> **Trains:** Str. Silvestru. To: Bucharest (5 per day, 6hr., *accelerat* L27,400); Chişinău (1 per day, 6hr., L22,000); Moscow (Wed., Fri., and Sun., 6-7hr., L454,400); and Timişoara via Cluj-Napoca (4 per day, 16hr., *accelerat* L39,800). **CFR,** Piaţa Unirii 9/11 (tel. 14 76 73). Open Mon.-Fri. 8am-8pm.
> **Buses:** Str. Arcu (tel. 14 65 87). To: Braşov (1 per day, 7hr., L35,000); Chişinău (5 per day, 4hr., L31,000); and Ungheni (2 per day, 2hr., L10,000).
> **Taxis: Ro-Taxi** (tel. 21 72 72). L1000 per km.
> **Luggage Storage:** At the train station. L1800 per day. Also at the bus station. L1000.
> **Post Office:** Str. Cuza Vodă 3 (tel. 11 59 85). Open Mon.-Fri. 7am-8pm, Sat. 8am-noon. **Postal code:** 6600.
> **Telephones:** Str. Lăpuşneanu 17. From Piaţa Unirii, walk to Hotel Traian, and go down Str. Lăpuşneanu past the hotel on the right; the office is behind a tiny church. Open daily 7am-9pm. **Phone code:** 032.

ACCOMMODATIONS

Finding private rooms is an inexact science; try wandering around the center looking like a needy tourist. Or call Mrs. Dincă, Str. Cuza Vodă 6, Bl. Plomba, et. 1, apt. 5 (tel. 11 57 67); she has a room downtown (full board available).

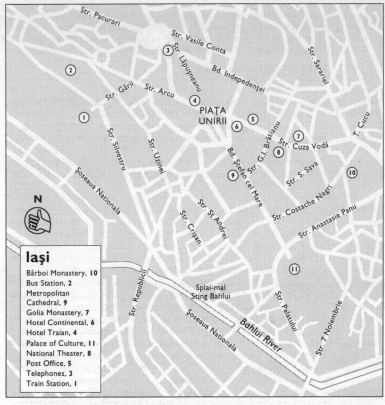

Iaşi

Bărboi Monastery, 10
Bus Station, 2
Metropolitan
Cathedral, 9
Golia Monastery, 7
Hotel Continental, 6
Hotel Traian, 4
Palace of Culture, 11
National Theater, 8
Post Office, 5
Telephones, 3
Train Station, 1

Hotel Continental, Str. Cuza Vodă 4 (tel. 11 43 20). Great location. Modest rooms with TV, phone, and fridge. Singles L56,000, with TV, etc. L76,000; doubles L96,000, with TV L130,000; triples L144,0000.

Hotel Traian, Piaţa Unirii 1 (tel. 14 33 30). Rococo rooms with pastel silk-covered furniture echo the exterior architecture. Comfort level ranges from Type A to C. Class B (shower, but no TV): singles L88,000; doubles with bath L140,000; triples with bath L198,000. L15,000 breakfast credit included. Visa.

Hotel Conest, Str. Maşinii 4 (tel. 23 07 00). Take tram #1 or bus #9 from the center toward Podul Ros; after passing the river, get off at the traffic circle and continue down Str. Nicolina. Stay on the left sidewalk instead of following the road as it rises to cross the train tracks. Then head diagonally across the intersection to the hotel. Diligent security guards. Doubles L70,000, with bath L96,000; triples L96,000. Breakfast included. Ask about the hot water schedule.

FOOD

For groceries, try the modern **Rodex,** Str. Arcu 3/5, in the basement under the TAROM office (open 24hr.). The **market** is at Piaţa Mihai Viteazul near the intersection of Str. Copou and Bd. Independenţei. Or grab cheap food at the traffic circle near Hotel Conest.

Pizzeria Metro, Str. Ştefan cel Mare 7, between the Mitropolitan Cathedral and Trei Ierarhi. Cool, clean, intimate eatery. A variety of 9-inch pies (L13,000) and good service. Or take a square piece o' pie with you (L5000). Open daily 8am-midnight.

Bolta Rece (Cold Ceiling), Str. Rece 10 (tel. 11 25 67). Walk down Str. Cuza Vodă past Hotel Continental and take the first left (at the Philharmonic) onto Str. Brăte-

ROMANIA

anu. At Bd. Independenţei, continue almost straight across the street, then turn left onto Str. Rece after the green-towered Sf. Teodor church. Head for the basement if you're seeking the atmosphere of the famous pub where great writers once got drunk. Tasty food and drink (meals L20,000-30,000). Open daily 8am-midnight.

SIGHTS AND ENTERTAINMENT

Monuments line both sides of Str. Ştefan cel Mare, which runs from Piaţa Unirii to Piaţa Ştefan cel Mare, dominated by the massive neo-Gothic **Palatul Culturii.** The palace, marked by a clocktower that plays the 1859 union of Moldova and Walachia song—*Hora Unirii*—contains four museums: **Muzeul de Istorie** (History Museum), **Muzeul de Etnografie a Moldovei, Muzeul de Artă,** and **Muzeul Ştiinţei şi Tehnicii** (Polytechnic Museum). The ethnographic wing starts on the second floor with agricultural instruments, including waterwheels and wooden olive-oil machines. The art wing exhibits Italian and Dutch Renaissance works, and **Sala Voivozilor** (Voivodes' Hall) displays portraits of Romanian rulers from Traian to King Carol II. The polytechnic wing, on the first floor, teems with centuries-old music boxes, phonographs, and the first automatic (but hand-powered) piano. The archaeological wing showcases a rich display of the 5000-year-old Cucuteni culture, characterized by pottery with swirl motifs. Although the recently reopened history museum examines ideas the Communists ignored, such as the origins of Christianity in Romania, the exhibits still end with WWII. (All museums open Tues.-Sun. 10am-4:30pm. History and ethnographic museums each L2000; art and science L3000. Students 50% off.)

In front of the palace, at Str. Anastasia Panu 65, sits **Sf. Nicolae-Domnesc** (St. Nick's), built in 1492 by Ştefan cel Mare and renovated in 1900 by Carol I (open daily 6-11am and 5-7pm). A few meters up Str. Ştefan cel Mare on the left stands the gorgeous **Trei Ierarhi** church, the exterior walls of which display Moldavian, Romanian, and Turkish patterns in raised relief. Gold covered the exterior until invading Tatars melted it down in 1653; the interior retains its original gold sheen. In 1821, the flag of the Eteria, a secret society for the liberation of Greece from Turkey, was sanctified here (church open daily 9am-noon and 3-7pm). The **monastery,** home to the country's first printing press and later a school, displays valuable manuscripts, books, icons, and tapestries (open daily 10am-9pm; L1000, students L500).

Past the **Primaria** (city hall) and the 1894 **Teatrul National,** a statue commemorates the theater's founder, Vasile Alecsandri, a leader of the 1848 revolution and an important literary and political figure. The box office, Str. Ştefan cel Mare 8 (tel. 11 48 49), beyond the 1833 **Mitropolia Cathedral,** sells opera and theater tickets (open Mon.-Fri. 10am-1pm and 5-6:30pm, Sun. 10am-noon; tickets up to L8000, students half-price; season runs Sept.-July). Nearby rise **Sf. Gheorghe** and **Mitropolia** (the Orthodox equivalent of a bishopric), with paintings by Gheorghe Tattarescu. From Piaţa Unirii, walk four blocks up Str. Cuza Vodă to the late 17th-century **Golia Monastery,** an imposing monument (gates lock at 7:30pm). Cross the street and run the gauntlet of minimarts to the **Mănăstirea Bărboi tower,** Str. Bărboi 12, with a Greek interior dominated by a huge golden iconostasis (open daily 8am-7pm).

Where Golia meets Bd. Independenţei, crawl up Str. Sărăriei—*uphill,* that is—for a half-hour to the famous **Bojdeuca** (Hut), Str. Simion Băruţiu 4, where writer **Ion Creangă** spent his last years. Creangă was born a peasant and pursued a career as a priest until he was expelled for shooting crows in the churchyard. He turned to writing and became famous in the Junimea circle for his storytelling. His most important work, *Aminitiri din copilarie (Memories of my Boyhood),* depicts life in his native village. Follow Str. Sărăriei past #120 and follow the signs "Bojdeuca" (open Tues.-Sun. 10am-5pm; L1000). On March 1, huge parties honor Creangă's birthday.

From the *Bojdeuca,* walk a few yards up Str. Sărăriei, turn left on Str. Ralet, and continue on Str. Berthelot. The last house on the right before Bd. Copou is that of **General Berthelot,** sent by the French government to help the Romanians in WWI. (The government had moved to Iaşi while Bucharest was occupied by the Germans.) At the end of Str. Berthelot, turn right on Bd. Copou. The Neoclassical **Alexandre Ioan Cuza University,** on the left, was built between 1893 and 1897 from the plans of French architect Le Blanc. Uphill on Bd. Copou lies **Copou park,** reachable by bus #35 from Piaţa Unirii. The park, arranged by prince Mihail Sturza in 1836, is famous for the **Mihai Eminescu linden,** the tree that shaded Romania's greatest poet as he wrote. Eminescu, who was born in Bukovina (which at the time belonged to Austria), studied in Vienna and Berlin and returned to Iaşi for a few years before moving to Bucharest. Statues of several writers and satirists, including Creangă, Eminescu, and Veronica Micle, line a nearby promenade. The new **Eminescu Museum** features pictures of the poet and some of his documents (open Tues.-Sun. 10am-5pm; L1000). Farther up Bd. Copou, more parks flank both sides of the street.

The late 17th-century **Mănăstirea Cetăţuia** perches on a hill 4km south of the center. Intended as an imitation of Prince Duca's Biserica Trei Ierarhi, it boasts panoramas to match. Head for Hotel Conest, then follow the Nicolina bridge toward the train tracks. Follow the tracks to the left to the bell-tower of **Mănăstirea Frumoasa** (Beautiful Monastery). Cross via the walkway underneath the railroad tracks to get to the front gate. You'll see Mănăstirea Cetăţuia in the distance; head up the hill.

For a change of pace, lounge by the **pool** at Piscina Moldova (tel. 14 22 25), an indoor pool open year-round, except in August (open Mon.-Thurs. 2-6pm and 7-11pm, Fri.-Sun. 9am-1pm, 2-6pm, and 7-11pm; L10,000). From Palatul Culturii, take a right on Str. Anastasia Panu; the *piscina* will be on the right. Travelers may be able to swing a few unofficial minutes of Internet time at **COPA,** Str. Moara de Foc 35, 8th floor (tel. 25 29 10). Much English is spoken here, but the lone computer is often booked. In summer, stroll by **Bahlui River** (10min. south of the Palace of Culture), where touring frog choirs often perform. If there's a disco-lover in you, head toward **Rosu şi Negru,** heavily frequented by local university students (open daily 10pm-3:30am; cover L4000, free Mon.). Catch bus #42, 43, 44, 45, or 46 from Pţa. Mihai Viteazul, get off at Tudor Vladimirescu, and head across the street and around to the right of the building.

■ Suceava

Although Suceava (soo-chay-AH-vah) initially may not impress as a beautiful city, it serves as a useful base for exploring Bucovina's monasteries. Moldova's capital under Ştefan cel Mare, the "Athlete of Christ," the town-citadel opened its gates to Mihai Viteazul in 1600, completing his conquest of the Romanian provinces.

Orientation and Practical Information Suceava lies 100km northwest of Iaşi near the foothills of the Carpathians. There are two **train stations:** the main **Suceava,** Str. Iorga 7, Cart. Burdujeni (tel. 21 38 97), and **Suceava Nord,** Str. Gării 4 Cart. Iţcani (same tel.). **Trains** run to Bucharest (8 per day, 6hr., *accelerat* L27,700), Iaşi (4 per day, 2½hr., *accelerat* L11,500), and Timişoara (4 per day, 12-13hr., *accelerat* L37,100). Buy tickets at **CFR,** Str. Bălcescu 8 (tel. 21 43 35; open Mon.-Fri. 7am-8pm; international tickets 8:30am-2:30pm). To get downtown from the Suceava train station, take **trolley** #2 (15min., L1600 round-trip) to the *centru* (or **bus** #1 from Suceava Nord). Get off where unimpressive ruins surround a beige stone tower (6 stops). **Buses** run to Chernivtsi, Ukraine (Cernăuţi; 8 per day, 3hr., L40,000) and Iaşi (1 per day, 3hr., L22,000) From the **bus station,** Str. Alecsandri 2 (tel. 21 60 89), head right, then take a left at the traffic circle onto Str. Bălcescu. **ONT,** Str. Bălcescu 2 (tel. 22 12 97; fax 21 47 00), in the main square, has one of Romania's nicest tourist-office staffs. It offers old maps (free), arranges car tours of the monasteries (US$60 per day, driver included), and books rooms (open Mon.-Fri. 8am-3pm, Sat.-Sun. 8am-2:30pm). **Exchange currency** or cash AmEx, EC, MC, Thomas Cook, or Visa traveler's checks at **IDM,** Str. Ştefan cel Mare 20a (tel. 22 79 67). From ONT, take the first left after CFR; it's on the left at the corner (open Mon.-Fri. 9am-6pm, Sat. 9am-1pm). An **ATM** at Bancă Comercială al Romănie, next to the history museum, happily accepts Cirrus, MC, Plus, and Visa. The **post office,** Str. Dimitrie Onciul, is in a low brick building (open Mon.-Fri. 7am-8pm, Sat. 8am-noon). **Telephones** (Str. Meseriasilor) are on the first side street to the right after CFR, walking up Str. Bălcescu from ONT (open daily 7am-10pm). **Postal code:** 5800. **Phone code:** 30.

Accommodations and Food ONT (see above) can arrange hotel rooms at the discounted price of US$12 a night. Ask at **Bucovina Estur,** Str. Ştefan cel Mare 24 (tel. 22 32 59), across the piaţa from ONT, about private rooms in Suceava and the area (US$15 per night). The surprisingly nice **Hotel Autogară** (tel. 21 60 89), above the bus station, may not be in the loveliest neighborhood, but features sunny new doubles with private bathrooms that put posher hotels to shame (singles L35,000; doubles L70,000). Uphill from Suceava station, **Hotel Socim,** Str. Jean Bart 2h (tel. 25 76 75), has bearable rooms (singles L45,000; doubles with bathroom L60,000; quads L60,000; apartment for two L70,000). On Str. Petru Rareş between Str. Alecsandri and Str. Ştefan cel Mare, the huge covered **market, Piaţa Agroalimentar,** complements bakeries and convenience stores (open daily during daylight hours). Delicious *mititei* occasionally grill just behind the market. Step down into the **cramă** (wine cellar) in front of the fortress, where huge wooden wine barrels and long benches covered with woolen hand-woven *cergi* set the ideal atmosphere for hearty, cholesterific grilled specialties (full meal L15,000; open daily 9am-11pm).

Sights The ruins of **Cetatea de Scaun** (Royal Fortress) spread in **Parcul Cetăţii,** east of Piaţa 22 Decembrie. Take a left on Bd. Ipătescu, a right on Str. Cetăţii (a gravel path), walk down the hill, and go up the path. This neat ruin is in excellent shape, despite the fact the Ottomans ordered it demolished. The fortress was built around 1388, when Prince Petru Muşat I of Moldavia moved his capital here; Ştefan cel Mare added 3m-thick walls. The defenses resisted the 1476 siege of Sultan Mahomed II, conqueror of Constantinople, but not the 1675 Ottoman attacks. Climbing on the buildings is not a good idea (open daily 8am-9pm; L2000). From the cafe in front of the fortress, follow the fence into the woods and take a right to reach a park with strollable gardens and a 22m **statue of Ştefan.** More medieval ruins molder in neighboring hills. The road to Rădăuţi leads north to the rhombus-shaped **Cetatea Scheia.** The **Complexul Medieval Zamca** is a bit of a trek away, on the other side of the city. Catch bus #29 or, from the main square, walk west on Str. Bălcescu, take Str. Vodă at the traffic circle, turn right on Str. Enescu, then left on Str. Zamcii. This trapezoidal Armenian fortress built in 1606 combines Gothic, Classical, and Ottoman elements.

Back in town, check out the **Istoricul Mânăstirii Sf. Ioan cel Nou.** From the main square, turn right on Bd. Ipătescu, then left on Str. Ioan Vodă cel Viteaz. The church has a very dark interior (open daily 5:30am-8:30pm). Thousands come from Bucovina for the June 24 **city festival Sânzăiene**—a celebration of the local **Sf. Ioan cel Nou** (St. John the New)—in which the mummified remains of the saint are removed from the monastery's church and paraded in a religious procession. According to legend, John was decapitated at Cetatea Alba and brought back to Suceava by Prince Alecsandru cel Bun. The **Muzeul Bucovinei Secţia de Istorie** (History Museum), Str. Ştefan cel Mare 33 (tel. 21 64 39), contains a French wax reconstruction of Ştefan cel Mare's throne room. The exhibit moves from 300,000-year-old mammoth bones to the vestiges of the archaeology gold mine at Cucuteni to the Daco-Roman era, and includes numerous paintings, coins, and wares; notice especially the green glass signifying the mixing of Dacians (who did not know how to make glass) and Romans (who did). Ask for the museum brochure (L2000); it has a great town **map** (museum open Tues.Sun. 10am-6pm; L8000.)

■ Near Suceava: Bukovina Monasteries

Bukovina's painted monasteries, hidden among green hills and rustic farming villages, have witnessed many attacks over the centuries and endured early Communist-era policies that forcibly ended the monastic life of many a monk in favor of "reintegration." Built 500 years ago by Ştefan cel Mare and his successors, the exquisite structures serenely mix Moldavian architecture with Byzantine, and Romanian soul with

Christian dogma. Most of the monasteries are small, with stone walls and wooden roofs, surrounded by living quarters for friendly monks or nuns and heavy stone walls that never managed to discourage looters. Unfortunately, getting to the monasteries by relying solely on public transport may seem like a trial of faith. When you finally reach these little slices of heaven, boys and girls, wear long sleeves and a long skirt or pants or you may soon be sporting borrowed skirts over your shorts. Smoking is prohibited, as is photography of the monks and nuns.

VORONEȚ AND HUMOR

Albastru de Voroneț (Voroneț Blue) is a phrase that haunts Romanian imaginations, from schoolchildren to experts feverishly looking for a modern equivalent of its 15th-century paint. The *albastru* that brought the monastery its legendary fame is also the source of its prolonged restoration, since most work has to be postponed until *albastru de Voroneț* is produced once more. Voroneț's **frescoes** are just incredible, and the *Last Judgment* mural a masterpiece. The damned wear the faces of Moldavia's enemies, the blessed look ethnically Moldavian, and angels sport regional musical instruments. God sits above Jesus at the very top of the wall, and angels roll up the Zodiac around him, demonstrating the passing of earthly time. *Jesse's Tree,* on the south wall, displays the genealogy of Jesus, while the north wall depicts scenes from Genesis and Adam's pact with the Devil. The church was built in 1488 by Ștefan cel Mare, supposedly on the advice of St. Daniel. The gold-covered iconostasis is made from *tiza* wood, which can last up to 1000 years (open daily 8am-8pm; entrance L5000; photography L10,000). To reach Voroneț from Suceava, take a **train** to **Gura Humorului** (most any Cluj/Timișoara train will do; 4 per day, 1hr., L5300) or **bus** (2 per day, 1hr., L6000). Or try a bus to Vatra Dornei that stops in Gura Humorului. From Gura Humorului, catch the **bus** for Voroneț (Mon.-Fri. 4 per day, 10min., L1500). To find the bus, walk straight out of the train station and turn right on Ștefan cel Mare. Or, to walk to the monastery, keep going, and after less than 1km, take a left onto Carterul Voroneț, which leads south toward Voroneț (5km). Finding a private room in Gura Humorului is as easy as breathing; approach anyone near the monasteries (up to L50,000 per person).

   Humor, which dates from 1530, is about 6km north of Gura Humorului. The south wall depicts the Virgin Mary's life. A fresco based on a poem by the patriarch of Constantinople represents her saving Constantinople from a Persian attack in 626. With an eye towards contemporary threats, the artist substituted Turks for Persians and added weapons typical of the 16th century. He painted himself in as a cavalier running a Turk through with his spear. The open porch provides an opportunity to study a *Last Judgment* fresco up close (open daily 8am-8pm; L5000). Getting to Humor is no joke: **buses** leave from Gura Humorului (see Voroneț, above; Mon.-Fri. 5 per day, L2000). By foot, take a right on Ștefan cel Mare from the train or bus station and walk to the heart of Gura Humorului. At the fork, near a park on the right, follow the soft left 6km to the monastery.

MOLDOVIȚA AND SUCEVIȚA

Moldovița is the largest of the fortified painted monasteries, and its frescoes are among the best-preserved. Built in 1532 and painted in 1537, it has another *Last Judgment,* another *Jesse's Tree,* and a monumental *Siege of Constantinople*. The siege of 626, painted on the exterior wall to the right of the entrance, depicts the ancient fortress in an uncanny 16th-century light. The monastery was closed from 1785 until 1945, and the north wall is badly weathered. Elaborately carved grapevine columns painted with gold jut out from the iconostasis. As in most of the monasteries, the founder is painted "*al fresco*" inside the nave, presenting the church to Jesus. The museum houses the original wooden (now seatless) throne of Prince Petru Rareș, founder of myriad monasteries. Opposite the throne in the main room is the *Pomme d'Or* prize awarded to Bukovina in 1975 in recognition of its touristic and artistic importance. Be sure to see the massive **religious tome** donated by Catherine the

Great. (Monastery admission L5000; photography L15,000. Guidebook in French, English, and German L2500.) From Suceava, take a **train** to Vama (1½-2hr.) and switch for the train to Vatra Moldoviței (3 per day, 5th stop, 35min., L6300 for whole trip), 2km east of Moldovița. **Buses** also run from Suceava through Vama to Vatra Dornei (Mon.-Fri. 3 per day, Sat.-Sun. 2 per day, 1¼hr., L7500).

Sucevița is beautifully set in fortified hills, where its white walls shine on sunny days, making it look more like a citadel than a monastery. The frescoed south wall presents a *Genealogy of Jesus* and a *Procession of Philosophers,* which portrays Pythagoras, Socrates, Plato, Aristotle, and Solon in Byzantine cloaks. Plato is carrying a small coffin of bones on his head. The shade of green you see is unique to Sucevița. Unlike the north faces of the other monasteries, Sucevița's is well-preserved; souls climb a heavenly ladder of 30 rungs, each rung representing a virtue and a sin. The west wall remains unpainted—the artist fell from the scaffolding, and his ghost supposedly prevents completion. The black stone head under the arch represents a woman who hauled stone for the construction with her oxen for 30 years. Inside, a *Last Judgment* decorates the wall under the balcony's Zodiac ceiling, next to an illustration of the martyred **Sf. Ioan cel Nou** returning from Cetatea Alba. The pro-nave depicts the deaths of 420 Orthodox saints, while the chamber contains an iconostasis carved from *tiza* wood. The **tomb room,** painted with scenes from Jewish history, houses the tombs of the **Movila** dynasty. A tiny door on the left leads to an emergency hiding place for relics and precious icons. The nave depicts scenes from the life of Jesus, and the altar boasts two iconostases. The museum in one of the old towers displays intricate tapestries, religious icons, and books (open daily 6am-10pm; L5000).

Sucevița lies 29km north of Moldovița (see p. 505). From Suceava, catch the **train** to Rădăuti (7 per day, 1hr., L2600). Turn left from the train station and follow the road right to reach the bus station, from which **buses** run to Sucevița (Mon.-Fri. 5 per day until 5pm, Sat.-Sun. 3 per day until 3pm, 30min., L3500). It is also possible to take the Moldovita-Rădăuți bus between the Sucevița and Moldovița monasteries.

PUTNA

Immaculately white and beautiful in its simplicity, **Sfânta Mănăstire Putna** deceptively appears to be the newest of the monasteries. Only one tower has survived the ravages of history, which included fires, earthquakes, and attacks; not even the frescoes remain. The complex encompasses the marble-canopied **tomb of Ștefan cel Mare** (among others) and an interesting **museum,** and boasts the only collection of recorded music of the monasteries (L8000 per cassette). In the church, Ștefan decays down on the right; his sons occupy the nearer tombs. Built in 1469, Putna was the first of 38 temples founded by Ștefan, who built one church after each battle he fought. Ștefan left Putna's location up to God: he climbed a nearby hill marked by a cross, to the left of the monastery, and shot an arrow into the air. A piece of the oak it struck is on display at the museum, along with a number of manuscripts and religious garb (open daily 9am-7pm). Quiet **lodging** can be found near the monastery along the main road in dubious two-bed bungalows (L25,000-40,000); you can also camp out (L10,000). If spending a few more lei doesn't scare you, check out **Cabana Putna** off the main road—it's got a decent bathroom, inviting rooms (doubles L100,000; breakfast included), and a happenin' bar-restaurant (soup L7500, meals less than L21,000). There are good **hiking trails,** but, alas, no map. Tourists flood Putna on **July 2**—St. Stephen's Day. For the scenic ride to Putna, catch direct **trains** from Suceava, 75km southeast (6 per day, 2½hr., 5600 lei). The last train leaves Putna in late afternoon. The monastery lies 2km from the train station. Exiting the platform, take a right and then a left at the first intersection, and keep walking.

About 7km from Sucevița on the road to Putna/Rădăuți, you'll pass through the potter's village of **Marginea,** famous for its black pottery with carefully carved designs. The studio is open to visitors, especially to ones who buy pots at the incredibly low prices (L3000-30,000). **Atelièr Ceramică** is right by the road—just watch for the huge signs (open daily 7am-7pm). Next to the studio, a village house playing the role of a shop sells stunning handmade folk costumes and carpets. Bidding for the big stuff starts at L300,000, but feel free to haggle. Hard currency, as in US$ or DM, works wonders too. Buses from Rădăuţi to Suceviţa or Moldoviţa (see above) head through Marginea (10min., L2000).

NEAMŢ AND SECU

Fields of clovers and buttercups cradle **Mănăstirea Neamţ**, 12km northwest of Târgu Neamţ. A throne worthy of Conan the Destroyer looks upon a 6th-century *Madonna and Child* known as "the miracle-worker." Presented to Alesandru cel Bun in 1424 by the Byzantine Empire, the icon was nearly lost in a Turkish attack. Legend has it that the Madonna's piercing eyes paralyzed the Turk who stole it, and he, stricken, swore to renounce Allah if the icon saved him. He died a monk at Mănăstirea Neamţ. Be sure not to miss the chandelier holding eight ostrich eggs—symbols of eternal life. On the path to the church sits a placard indicating where the bones of a saint were discovered in 1986. The monks first decided to excavate this spot because small stones supposedly stood up whenever a non-Christian walked by. The covered remains of the saint are on display inside the church (open daily 8am-8pm; L6000; no photos). The **museum,** once home to the calligraphy school that nurtured Moldova's first historians, contains icons, priestly garb (nice hat!), and Dimitrie Cantemir's 1825 *Descriptio Moldoviae* (at 45cm by 32cm, the biggest printed Old Romanian book). A **grocery store** sells goodies 2km away, but most bring food from Târgu Neamţ, which is on the Suceava-Buzău-Bucharest **train** line: switch at Paşcani (1hr. from Suceava) onto a train to Târgu Neamţ (4am-8:30pm, 5 per day, 50min., L6300). **Buses** from Suceava also head straight for the center of Târgu Neamţ (3 per day, 2½hr., L8000). Getting between the **bus** and train stations is tricky; ask a cabbie to take you to the *autogară* (up to L16,000), or head for Str. Cuza Vodă. Catch the bus at the *autogară* to Mănăstirea Neamţ (Mon.-Fri. 6 per day, Sat.-Sun. 4 per day, 30min., L3600). The monks can offer you a place to stay nearby in dorm rooms with shared bathrooms. Prices are negotiable—so negotiable that you may even get in for free. Stay for the monasterial ambience, not the rooms.

BLACK SEA COAST

The land between the Danube and the Black Sea has weathered a troubled history. Conquered by the Turks in the 14th century, it remained part of the Ottoman Empire until 1877, when it was ceded to Romania as compensation for losing part of Moldavia to its treacherous ally Russia. Beautiful beaches stretch to the south, while the interior, made up of valleys and rocky hills, holds Roman, Greek, and early Christian ruins, and produces some of Romania's best wines. Crowds packed the littoral in the past, but now prices are too steep for many Romanians, particularly during high season (July-Aug.). Accommodations prices drop L40,000 at other times of the year.

For a map of the Black Sea Coast area, see p. 123 in the **Bulgaria** chapter.

■ Constanţa

Though Ceauşescu's grandomania made Constanţa (con-STAN-tsa) into one of the largest—though largely unused—ports in Europe, the city started out 2500 years ago as the simple Greek port of Tomis. A crossroads between East and West, the town has served as home, place of exile, or conquest for many, including Germans, Turks, and Romans (it's named for the daughter of Emperor Constantine). This is one of Romania's largest cities, and generally just a place to catch buses to the resorts, but you may stumble across traces of eclectic charm in the dust- and sea-scented city center.

Orientation and Practical Information Constanţa, 225km from Bucharest, is north of the Black Sea resorts. **Trains,** which are packed in summer, head for

ROMANIA

every corner of the country, largely via Bucharest (up to 27 per day, 2½hr., *accelerat* L17,000). Buy tickets in advance, and remember that a seat reservation is required for a *rapid* or *express*—only on the *accelerat* can you squeeze in the hallway. From Bucharest, try early-morning trains from Obor or Baneasă if you don't have a reservation. Constanța's main **train** and **bus stations** are near each other, but northbound buses leave from **Autogară Tomis Nord** (from the train station, ride 5 stops on tram #100, then head left). To get downtown from the train station, take trolley #40 or 43 and get off where Bd. Tomis intersects Bd. Ferdinand ("Stație Continental"; 4 stops). Buy tickets (L1700 round-trip) from the kiosks in front of the station, or find an official RATC booth and get a day pass (L3400). Warning: ticket checkers are diligent. Cash **traveler's checks** (6% commission) or get a **cash advance** on Visa (10%) at the **Trans Danubius** tourist office, Bd. Ferdinand 36 (tel. 61 31 03; open Mon.-Sat. 9am-7:30pm, Sun. 9:30am-1pm). The agency offers tours of the Danube Delta (1 per week, US$63), and sells tickets for the much-advertised **Constanța-Istanbul boat** (May-Sept. Mon. and Fri. 4pm; leaves Istanbul Tues. and Sat. 11pm; 6hr., US$55). They can also swing you a car (with driver) for US$0.35 per km, insurance and gas included. **Internet access** is available at **Space Games,** Bd. Ștefan cel Mare 76 (tel. 65 54 06; L2000 to send email, L4000 to receive; open daily 10am-9pm). At Bd. Tomis and Ștefan cel Mare are the **post office** (open Mon.-Fri. 7am-8pm, Sat. 9am-1pm) and **telephones** (open Mon.-Sat. 7am-10pm). **Postal code:** 8700. **Phone code:** 041.

Accommodations and Food While it's hard to find a cheap inn here, it isn't so difficult as elsewhere on the coast. The seaside **Hotel Palace,** Str. Remus Opreanu 5 (tel. 61 46 96), invites you to linger in classic rooms with bath, TV, phone, and fridge (singles L128,800; doubles L182,000; triples L273,000; L28,000 breakfast credit included; laundry service available). The **restaurant** offers a beautiful terrace view of the sea (open daily 7am-midnight). **Hotel Astoria,** Str. Mircea cel Batrîn 102 (tel. 61 60 64), also offers decent rooms with bath and TV near the water (singles L190,000; doubles L250,000; quads L340,000; L15,000 breakfast credit included). To reach the hotel, continue on Bd. Ferdinand away from the train station and turn left when you hit the water; it's just past Hotel Sport. **Private rooms**—many within five minutes of the Mamaia beach, though a bit far from Constanța's center—provide an affordable alternative. **Cazare la Particulari,** Str. Lăpaișneanu (tel. 64 28 31), can find you singles (L70,000) or doubles (L100,000). Take tram #100 to the end of the line from the train station, and look for Restaurant Nord on the right (open mid-June to mid-Sept. Mon.-Sat. 8:30am-5:30pm, Sun. 8:30am-1pm).

From Stație Continental, head left down Bd. Tomis to find **UFO International,** Bd. Tomis 17, which sets fast food in a spacious black and metallic interior (meals under L10,000; open Mon.-Fri. 10am-8pm, Sat.-Sun. 10am-midnight). At the corner of Bd. Tomis and Ferdinand, the **Grand supermarket** has it all non-stop. An outdoor **market** features the usual produce, cheeses, and meats near the intersection of Ștefan cel Mare and Str. Mihăileanu. Head back toward the train on Bd. Ferdinand past the Trans Danubius office and go right on Str. Mihăileanu (open daily dawn to dusk).

Sights and Entertainment Escape innumerable gray apartment blocks by exploring the **Old Town.** From Stație Continental, turn left down Bd. Tomis to get to the center. The main attraction of **Muzeul de Artă Populară,** Bd. Tomis 32 (tel. 61 61 33), is the peasant glass icon exhibit (open daily 9am-8pm; in winter Tues.-Sun. 9am-5pm; L2000; English/French catalogue L10,000). Turn right off Bd. Tomis before reaching Muzeul de Artă Populară to find **Muzeul Marinei Romane** (Naval History Museum), Str. Traian 53 (tel. 61 90 35), which stockpiles instruments, uniforms, documents, and models that dazzle even experts. An ancient tree-trunk canoe and Greek frigate are moored here (open Tues.-Sun. 10am-6pm; in winter 10am-5pm; L3000).

Continue down Bd. Tomis, following it until it curves left and ends in Piața Ovidiu to reach the **statue of Ovid,** who penned some of his most famous poems while in exile here. He was ostensibly exiled for writing *The Art of Love*—but the real reason may have been his affair with Emperor Augustus's daughter. **Muzeul de Istorie**

Naționalǎ și Arheologin, Piața Ovidiu 2 (tel. 61 45 83), displays several items from the Roman past, and recounts the 19th-century War of Independence (from Turkey) with a particular flair (open daily 9am-8pm; in winter Tues.-Sun. 9am-5pm; L5000; pictorial guide in English L5000). To the left of the museum, behind the Roman columns, are **excavations** of a Roman port with the **world's largest floor mosaic,** preserved from the 4th century BC and discovered only in 1959—walk behind the museum to better admire it and the brickwork (same hours as museum; L5000).

Off Piața Ovidiu on Str. Arhiepiscopiei, the **mosque** is one of the few reminders of Turkish domination and has one of the largest **oriental carpets** in Europe (maybe to cover the mosaic?), woven in the 18th century on the Danube island of Ada-Kaleh. The 50m **tower** (140 steps) offers a bird's-eye view of the town. Built in 1730, the mosque was reconstructed by King Carol I in 1910. If you come for services (Fri. 1pm), wash your hands, feet, and face in the courtyard (open June-Sept. daily 9:30am-5:30pm; L2000). The less religious might prefer to relax among 2000-year-old Greek amphorae and Roman sarcophagi in the shade of the **archaeological park** that lines Bd. Ferdinand opposite Trans Danubius.

Closer to the sea are **Catedralǎ Ortodoxa Sf. Petru și Pavel,** Str. Arhi Episcopiei 25, built in 1877, following Romania's independence from Turkey (open daily 7am-7pm), and a beautiful, statue-lined waterfront promenade. To the left, the **statue of poet Mihai Eminescu** gazes dreamily toward the sea. Behind him on Str. Remus Opreanu is the tiny **Farul Genovez** (Genoa Lighthouse), built in 1861. Continue down the boardwalk to find boats waiting to sail away. Take a short tour of the sea (L10,000 per person, if enough people show up), or charter a yacht for a few hours. It's cheaper for large groups; bargain directly with the owners.

Near Lacul Tǎbǎcǎriei at Bd. Mamaia 255 (tel. 64 70 55), a **planetarium** and a **delfinarium** (dolphin show) coexist. Take trolley #40 or 41 from Bd. Ferdinand and get off after crossing the tram tracks at the "Delfinariu" stop (5 shows daily 11am-7pm; off-season 11am-4pm; L4000). Near Catedralǎ Ortodoxa along the water, the asymmetrical Baroque **Cazino,** Str. Libertǎții 48 (tel. 61 74 16), was built in 1910 and still smacks of the cosmopolitan high-life. You might just want to look at the restaurant and the terrace view rather than eat there; meals hit L100,000 (open daily 10am-midnight). In the summer, the nearby resorts steal Constanța's disco thunder. The young and restless hang out on the stretch of beach below Hotel Sport and Hotel Palace.

■ Near Constanța

The coast to the south of Constanța is lined with sandy beaches and 70s-revival tourist resorts. The resorts are rather interchangeable; nearly all have the requisite amusement parks and campsites. The season runs from June 1 to September 15; you may find everything closed if you arrive at any other time. The peak of the season, July and August, means heavy crowds and the highest prices. **Buses** run south from Constanța in the direction of Mangalia (3 per hr. until 7:30pm, 40km, L3500). More comfortable private minibuses to Mangalia usually cost L5000, but hit L10,000 in the evening after the trains and buses stop running. Minivans connect the constellation of resorts near Mangalia late into the night (L2000). **Trains** are frequent, slightly slower, and a bit less expensive (4am-10pm). All of the resorts on the coast have the same **postal** and **phone codes** as Constanța (8700; 041).

MANGALIA, 2 MAI, AND VAMA VECHE

The **railway** terminus of Mangalia sees scores of trains dump beachgoers onto the sunburnt streets of this large haven of Communist architecture (up to 18 per day from Constanța, 1hr., L4400; **luggage storage** L1800-3600). You may get an offer for a **private room** here for as low as L30,000. Most Constanța-Mangalia (L5000) and Olimp-Mangalia (L2000) **buses and minivans** stop here and turn around. If you're on a budget, Mangalia is ideal—you can grab groceries at the green **covered market** on Str. Rozilor (walk down the side street, Str. Ion Creangǎ, leading away from the station 1 block and take a left; market open daily 6:30am-8:30pm), then hightail it south

6km to **2 Mai** or 11km to **Vama Veche.** These less-touristed villages offer tent space and **private accommodations** (L40,000-50,000; set the price before you move in). A few Coca-Cola signs predict that 2 Mai's beauty might not outlive the first stage of Romanian privatization, but Vama Veche remains untouched. Most young people **camp** at the south end of the nude beach in 2 Mai (tent space L7000 per person; parking L1000). Every night, they light campfires and play guitars. 2 Mai is popular among intellectuals, artists, and free-spirited students, but those over 30 are not unknown here. Dine at the definitely "in" **Şuberek's** (pizza L8000, Turkish pie L1500; open daily 8pm-6am). Another **campground** (tents L10,000 per person; parking L2000), with a beach overlooked by industrial cranes, lies in the north part of 2 Mai, a block away from the bus #14 stop. Get to 2 Mai by the occasional **minivan** from Mangalia (L2000) or catch bus #14 from Mangalia (8 per day 6am-8:30pm, L1400). At Vama Veche, **camp** on the quiet beach (L8000 per person; parking L2000). Besides hitch-hiking, the only way to get to Vama Veche is **bus** #14 (see above; L1800).

EFORIE NORD, EFORIE SUD, AND COSTINEŞTI

Closest to Constanţa are **Eforie Nord** and **Sud,** the first Black Sea resorts. Although they're beginning to show their age, they're still large and popular, and are especially renowned for the mud baths near **Lake Techirghiol.** The lake water is rumored to be so salty you can't sink (do not test this rumor by purposefully trying to sink!). In Eforie Nord, **Hotel Bega** (tel. 74 14 68) *almost* overlooks the sea (singles L104,000; doubles L130,000). **Hotel Apollo,** near the center, offers more drab doubles (L110,000). Continue away from the center on the seaside Bd. T. Vladimirescu and turn left after Maxim Disco to find **Camping Meduza,** Str. Sportului (tel./fax 74 23 85; tents L7000 per person). Reach the Efories from Constanţa by **train** (up to 18 per day, 20min., *accelerat* L2600), or take **bus** #12 (L1800).

South of the Efories, **Costineşti,** the coastal hot-spot, gets wonderfully crowded with young people. Some hitch the 4km from the bus stop; others take **bus** #12 (L3200). The **train** drops you even closer; get off at Costineşti Tabără and circle right around the lake to the entrance. After trains stop running (around 8 or 9pm), there's no easy way to leave this isolated resort. **Hans Exchange,** at the entrance, takes Visa and MC as well as traveler's checks at slightly unfavorable rates (6% commission; open daily 10am-10pm). **Albatros** (tel. 73 40 15), straight ahead, provides decent doubles overlooking the sea (L32,000 with bath). The super-budget *căsuţe* (little houses) run L24,000-32,000 (2 beds). Along the town's main street, which parallels the sea, travelers may get lucky by following *Camere pe închiriat* (rooms for rent) signs. One **cafeteria** advertises its cakes with the slogan "*Prăjituri foarte proaspete. Serviţi cu încredere.*" ("Very fresh cakes. Eat confidently.") **Grocery stores** gather near the train station and on the main street, as do unofficial backyard campgrounds.

Overlooking the sea, **Disco Tineretului** occasionally hosts live bands and features kick-ass UV/laser lights, but the main activity at this mostly teenage outdoor club is dancing (open nightly 9:30pm-4am; cover L10,000). Renting a **boat** for a spin around the lake is also popular in the evening.

VENUS, SATURN, AND NEPTUN

Venus rose from the foam of Saturn's seas to create one of the best **beaches** on the coast. Across the highway from the great beach sandwiched between Venus and Saturn lies a popular **free camping** zone. Venus wins a prize for having the most diverse set of rides in its amusement park. Staying in Saturn is fairly inexpensive: at the height of the season, stay at a one-star hotel (doubles L72,000; triples L96,000); a two-star hotel (singles L64,000; doubles L80,000; triples L105,000); or in small two-bed *căsuţe* (L36,000). Camping is even cheaper (L7000 per person).

Alternatively, some vacationers accept offers of **private rooms** (usually around L40-60,000). Dancers strike out under a mirrored ball at **Bowling Saturn** (tel. 75 17 40), the least expensive but certainly not the only **disco** in town (open nightly 9pm-5am; L3000). Chow at **Grădina de Vară** (tel. 75 18 92) amid billiards, video games, and loud music (meals under L30,000; open daily 9am-midnight). For Saturn, take the train to Mangalia, head toward the covered market (see above), and continue straight a block. From Saturn, it's a short walk through the resort to nearby Venus.

Neptun, site of Ceauşescu's summer villa, is one of the more highbrow resorts, with carriage rides, modern amenities, and probably the best eateries on the coast. Up to 16 trains per day run to Neptun from Constanţa (50min., *accelerat* L3700). Exchange **traveler's checks** at **Bancă de Comerţ Exterior** (tel. 73 19 34; 1.5% commission). **Phones** ring at the Neptun **post office** (post open Mon.-Fri. 7am-8pm, Sat. 8am-2pm; phones open daily 6am-10pm). The **Dispecerat de Cazare** (housing office; tel. 73 13 10; fax 63 90 02), in the Topkapî shopping center, helps find rooms, often at prices lower than hotels' (singles in 2-star hotel US$12, 3-star hotel US$18; 10% commission; May-Sept. open 24hr.). The women lurking on the sidewalk near Topkapî will find you a private room (L50,000-60,000) for a 10% commission. Two-star hotels, such as **Apollo** (tel. 73 16 16), and **Romanţa** (tel. 73 10 23), offer clean, spacious rooms with showers (singles L152,000; doubles L240,000). **Sat de Vacanţa** (tel. 73 12 20) has wood and plaster houses as well as tent lots (2-bed wood with running water L49,000; 2-bed plaster with shower L72,000; tent space L23,000 per person).

Feast on grilled sturgeon with potatoes and quality wines while enjoying folk dance shows in the shade of the verdant trees at the **Rustic** (tel. 73 10 26). Reserve with your hotel's tourist office or directly with the restaurant (main dishes under L20,000; show L15,000; open daily 9am-3pm and 8pm-2am). There are a few **grocery stores** on the main street. **Disco Rainbow** (tel. 73 18 12) is a haven for young folks looking for a good time (open daily 9pm-5am; cover L10,000).

■ Danube Delta

After winding through eight countries, the Danube empties into the Black Sea at the complex, enormous (almost 2000 sq. mi.) biosphere known as the Danube Delta. This region provides a refuge for more than 300 species of birds and 110 types of fish, as well as Europe's only pelican colony. The delta is overgrown with more than 1000 species of plants, including the insatiable, carnivorous *Aldrovanda*. Villagers are tapping the delta's resources, and the expanding tourism has begun to affect the most traveled parts of the region. Yet the maze of lakes, channels, islands, tropical woods, and dunes has remained mostly pristine, due in part to its UNESCO designation as a "Reservation for the Biosphere," and is a great site for fishing, boating, or simply observing an intricate ecosystem.

Because of the difficulty of finding cheap transportation around the area, Tulcea (once the Greek colony of Aegyssus) is the best place to start exploring the delta, but not necessarily a town where you'll want to spend much time. Arrive in Tulcea early in the morning on a weekday to have the best chance of getting on a boat going somewhere. Scheduled ferries are few and far between to Galaţi and Brăila (Fri.-Sat. 12:15pm, 3½hr., L50,000) or Crişan and Sulina (Mon., Wed., Fri., and Sat. 1:30pm, 3hr., L50,000, returning the next morning). The **Tulcea Tourism Agency** (tel. (040) 51 66 04) arranges outings to the delta (US$30 per day) and provides fishing licenses (US$10 per day; open Mon.-Sat. 9am-6pm). **Hotel Egreta,** Păcii Str. 2 (tel. (040) 51 71 03), offers blissfully bug-free rooms with phone and TV (singles L200,000; doubles L260,000; Visa, MC). The affiliated tourist agency arranges tours and sells maps (L5000; open Mon., Wed., and Fri. 8:30am-8:30pm, Tues. and Thurs. 5:15am-8:30pm, Sat. 5:15am-1pm, Sun. 9am-4pm). For a more riverine experience, check out one of the **floating hotels** at the port near Hotel Delta (rooms L30,000-75,000).

From Tulcea, you can rent a boat and attempt to navigate the delta yourself, but it may be worth the money to sit in on an **organized tour,** which Tulcea Tourism Agency (see above) and Constanţa's Trans Danubius (see p. 507) both arrange. Another possibility is to find a **fisherman** willing to show you around. If you're anxious about paddling yourself, **rowers** usually wait at the docks, but it generally costs the same as going with a guide. Prices vary, but be ready to shell out L200,000-300,000 for three hours with an experienced guide—if you're lucky, he'll even speak a few words of English. Save yourself heaps of cash by traveling with a group. A popular destination within the delta is **Crişan,** reachable by **ferry** or boat from Tulcea. One caveat—the mosquitoes are huge and the water and food supplies may be small. Another option is to continue past Crişan on the ferry to the town of **Sulina,** which has lost some of the popularity it enjoyed during the Communist regime. Though not as inexpensive as it was during its heyday, its riverfront promenade and fine sand still make it a romantic spot. It's also a good location to rent a private **boat** to explore the less traveled parts of the delta. There are no budget hotels in Sulina, but **private accommodations** (L30,000-40,000) should be available. People will probably be waiting for tourists at the port; look for *Zimmer Frei* signs.

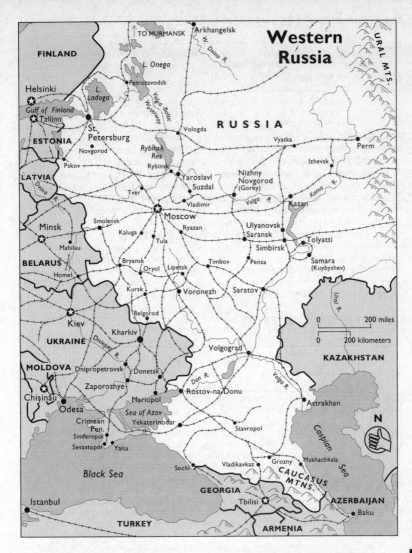

RUSSIA (РОССИЯ)

US$1 = 5843R (Rubles)	1000R = US$0.17
CDN$1= 4224R	1000R = CDN$0.24
UK£1 = 9295R	1000R = UK£0.11
IR£1 = 8566R	1000R = IR£0.12
AUS$1 = 4251R	1000R = AUS$0.24
NZ$1 = 3608R	1000R = NZ$0.27
SAR1 = 1243R	1000R = SAR0.81
DM1 = 3209R	1000R = DM0.31
Country Phone Code: 7	International Dialing Prefix: 810

As of January 1, 1998, the ruble will be redenominated, with three zeroes taken off the end. One U.S. dollar will equal approximately six new rubles. All prices in *Let's Go* are listed in old rubles.

> *It is a riddle wrapped in a mystery inside an enigma.*
> —Winston Churchill on Russia (1939)

Many Russians claim they no longer recognize today's Russia, but Churchill is as right today as he was more than 50 years ago. The country is certainly moving toward Westernization, but this drive is slowed by romantic nostalgia for the Soviet past. Though considered a world superpower, Russia is more of a chaotic bazaar, with its own ever-changing rules and frustrations. Rapid economic change and the collapse of a legal infrastructure have led to a rise in poverty and a growing discontent with the new system. As a result, many Russians have started to lend political support to old Communist leaders, making restructuring even more difficult. The collapse of the Soviet Union has allowed Russia's vast patchwork of autonomous regions and minority nationalities to fray, while a generation gap continues to grow between the Old and the New Russians—yet the country endures with unique resourcefulness. Remaining proud of its well-preserved heritage, Russia generates new popular culture at unprecedented speeds, mixing intimate debates around the kitchen table and a crawling economy with rocking politics and wild rave parties.

RUSSIA ESSENTIALS

Russian visas require an invitation stating itinerary and dates of travel and are thus inherently difficult to get without a Russian connection. Fortunately, the following organizations specialize in supplying invitations and/or visas for individual tourists, but some require that you book accommodations for your stay in Russia with them. Prices vary dramatically, so shop around.

Host Families Association (HOFA), 5-25 Tavricheskaya, 193015 St. Petersburg, Russia (tel./fax 812 275 19 92; e-mail hofa@usa.net). Arranges homestays in more than 20 cities of the former Soviet Union. Visa invitations available for HOFA guests to Russia, Ukraine, and Belarus. Singles US$30, doubles US$50. Occasional 20% discounts for non-central locations and Russian-speaking students.

IBV Bed & Breakfast Systems, 13113 Ideal Dr., Silver Spring, MD 20906, USA (tel. (301) 942-3770; fax 933-0024). Visa invitations with accommodations booking.

Red Bear Tours/Russian Passport, also known as **Russia-Rail Internet Travel Service,** Suite 11A, 401 St. Kilda Rd., Melbourne 30004, Australia (tel. (3) 98 67 38 88; fax 98 67 10 55; toll-free in Aus. (800) 33 30 31; email passport@werple.net.au; http://www.travelcentre.com.au or www.russia-rail.com). Provides invitations to Russia and the Central Asian Republics, provided that you book accommodations with them. Also sells rail tickets for the Trans-Siberian/Manchurian/Mongolian and Silk routes and arranges assorted tours.

Russia House, U.S., 1800 Connecticut Ave. NW, Washington, D.C. 20009 (tel. (202) 986-6010; fax 667-4244). **Russia,** 17 Leningradsky Prospekt, Moscow 125040 (tel. (095) 250 01 43; fax 250 25 03). Provides invitations and visas for Russia, Ukraine, and Belarus.

Russian Youth Hostels, Estonia: Estonian Youth Hostels Association, Tatari 39-302, EE0001, Tallinn (tel. (2) 646 14 57; fax 646 15 95). In **Finland:** SRM—Finnish YHA, Yrjönkatu 38B, Helsinki 00100 (tel. (090) 694 03 77). In **Germany:** DJH—German YHA, Tempelhofer Ufer 32, D 1000 Berlin 61 (tel. (030) 264 95 20).

St. Petersburg International Hostel (HI), 3rd Sovetskaya ul. 28, St. Petersburg, Russia 193036 (tel. (812) 329 80 18; fax 329 80 19; email ryh@ryh.spb.su; http://www.spb.su/ryh). Arranges visa invitations, registers you once you get to Russia, and sells air and train tickets.

Traveller's Guest House, 50 Bolshaya Pereyaslavskaya, 10th floor, Moscow, Russia 129401 (tel. (095) 971 40 59 or 280 85 62; fax 280 76 86; email tgh@glas.apc.org). Arranges visa invitations, will register you once you arrive in Russia, make reservations, and get train tickets.

If you have an invitation from an authorized travel agency, apply for the **visa** in person or by mail at a Russian embassy or consulate (see **Essentials: Embassies and Consulates,** p. 5). Bring a photocopy of your invitation; a photocopy of the front pages of your passport; a completed application (available from an embassy or consulate); three passport-size photographs; a cover letter stating your name, dates of arrival and departure, cities you plan to visit in Russia, date of birth, and passport number; and a money order or certified check for the amount of the visa fee to the embassy or consulate nearest you (single-entry visas US$40 for 2-week processing, US$50 for 1-week service, US$120 for service in 3 business days; double-entry visas US$80/100/120 respectively). If you have even tentative plans to visit a city, have it put on your visa; it's also a wise idea to get a visa for longer than you actually plan to stay. It's OK to enter Russia through a city not on your visa. Many organizations (hotels, etc.) will **register your visa** for you on arrival, but if this service is not provided, go to the central OVIR (ОВИР) office (in Moscow called UVIR—УВИР) to register; many ignore this step, but it's the law. This is also where you can attempt to extend your visa—a bureaucratic hassle; it's better to get a long one before you go.

GETTING THERE

Flying on British Airways or Delta to St. Petersburg or Moscow is the most direct way to reach Russia (student fares sometimes available). **Rail travel** from European capitals to Moscow and St. Petersburg is cheaper. Find out if you are going through Belarus, for which you may need a transit visa; sometimes you can get by with only a Russian visa. If you wait until you reach the border, it may be more expensive, and you risk not returning to your train in time. (The Warsaw-Tallinn express goes through Lithuania instead.) Finnord **buses** leave for St. Petersburg four times per day from Lahti, Finland, and are cheaper than trains.

One day the customs officials will tear your pack apart, the next they'll just nod and dismiss you. Always be polite. If you fly in, especially with a group, your baggage will probably not be inspected. You may encounter more difficulty if you arrive by train or car. If you have doubts about anything, bring plenty of documentation or check with the Russian embassy before you go. Politely answer the border officials' questions, but do not offer any information for which they don't specifically ask.

You cannot bring rubles into or out of the country. At the border, you'll be given a **Customs Declaration Form** to declare all your valuables and foreign currency. Don't lose it. Everything listed on the customs form must be on your person when you leave the country. You may not export works of art, icons, old samovars (pre-electric models), or antique books—technically, anything published before 1945. Keep receipts for any expensive or antique-looking souvenirs.

GETTING AROUND

In summer 1996, the U.S. State Department issued a warning about the overnight train between Moscow and St. Petersburg. See **Essentials: Before You Go,** p. 15, for info on how to find the latest travel advisories.

Be flexible. Expect airport delays, tour cancellations, cold showers, and bathrooms *sans* toilet paper. The rules have changed so often, and so differently in different locations, that no one really knows what they are anymore. As a result, an authority figure can choose whatever version suits him or her best. While argument is often futile, at times battling the Russian sense of arbitrary confusion with your own sense of confusion can be beneficial *and* the only way to become tolerant of and accustomed to the chaos. Station clerks might have a panic attack if you try to ask where you should be buying tickets. Go instead to the "Справочное Бюро" (Information) window or the designated Intourist *kassa*. You'll probably have to pay for any information they give you (up to 6000R), and the clerks aren't likely to be friendly. As elsewhere, apologetic politeness can take you farther in your pursuits than angry frustration.

Foreigners are officially required to buy **internal plane and train tickets** at inflated Intourist prices. The actual enforcement of this rule varies. The law requires you to show your *dokumenty* (документы; passport) when you buy train and plane tickets. This makes it nearly impossible to get the Russian rate. With the help of a Russian friend, you may be able to circumvent this, but be warned: your name is printed on your ticket, which will be checked against your passport on board—though bribery may help. If you buy your train tickets at the station like everyone else, you run the risk of only getting a third-class seat. You can buy train tickets originating in a different city, but it is best to use the Moscow or St. Petersburg central ticket offices and buy round-trip tickets from these two cities.

Trains tend to be the cheapest way to get around. The only credit card accepted is AmEx; otherwise all fares must be paid in rubles. Train cars are divided into many classes. The most expensive are luxury two-bed "SV" (СВ) compartments, cozy four-bed *"koupé"* (К), and open-car *platskartny* "P" (П). Women traveling alone might want to consider buying tickets for all the beds in a *koupé* for safety reasons, although the more economical *platskartny* could also be safe because of its very lack of privacy (i.e., you don't risk being behind a closed door with unsavory people). There are also different types of trains: *firmenny* (фирменный) offers a safer, more comfortable ride, and the "er" and "more" are reflected in the price; *skory* (скорый; express) is slightly less expensive, makes the fewest stops, and takes the least amount of time to get to the final destination; and *passazhirsky* (пассажирский; passenger) tends to be the slowest, with messy bathrooms and an often rugged crowd. *Elek-trichka* (**commuter rail,** marked on signs as пригородные поезда; *prigorodnye poezda*) has its own platforms at each station; buy tickets at the *kassa*. These trains are often packed, especially on weekends, so expect to stand.

Russia boasts an extensive **bus** network and a vast, not-so-reliable **air** system monopolized by **Aeroflot,** which is marked by its aging fleet and history of disasters. Nascent Aeroflot alternative **Transair** services only select cities. **Buses** are slightly less expensive and less crowded than trains; they are a good option for shorter distances. On the Hungarian **Ikarus** buses, you'll get a seat assignment in a fairly comfy reclining chair. You can often store luggage in the undercarriage for a fee (5000-25,000R).

Within Russian cities, overcrowded **buses, trams, trolleys,** and (in major metropoles) unbelievably efficient **metro** systems ferry citizens quickly and cheaply. In the metro, buy *zhetony* (жетоны; tokens) at the *kassa,* then drop them into machines that let you onto escalators. Magnetic strip cards have recently been introduced on the metro; you can buy one for 10 rides or more. There are regular buses and more comfortable express buses (marked with "Э"). On the express buses, pay the driver (usually 2500R); otherwise, buy bus tickets at newsstands or in special kiosks and punch them on board. *Do not* buy them from the *babushki* at metro stations (they may be fake or invalid). Don't try to ride for free, especially in city centers; the system is very energetic in searching out free riders, particularly during the last week of the month, and fines are high (8900-25,000R). Metro stations are labeled only in Cyrillic; if you don't read Russian, you can usually recognize stations by memorizing the first and last letters. When two lines intersect, there is often a different station name for each line. You'll want to know the words *vkhod* (вход; entrance), *vykhod* (выход; exit), *vykhod v gorod* (выход в город; exit to the city), and *perekhod* (переход; transfer to another line). Metro stations are marked above ground by a capital "М." Try to acquire the newest city map possible—stations and street names have been changing wildly in recent years.

Hailing a **taxi** is indistinguishable from hitchhiking, and should be treated as such. Most drivers who stop will be private citizens trying to make a little extra cash (despite the recent restriction on this technically illegal activity). Those seeking a ride should stand off the curb and hold out a hand flat, palm down, no thumb; when a car stops, riders tell the driver the destination before getting in. He will either refuse the destination and speed off, or nod his head, at which point haggling begins. Either the driver or hopeful rider will ask the *Skolko?* (How much?) question, which can lead to either a blunt refusal or negotiations. Meters are non-operational. Non-Russian speakers will get ripped off unless they manage a firm agreement on the price—sign language works too. While this informal system might seem dicey, official labeled taxis can be expensive and dangerous, with reports of kidnappings and muggings.

TOURIST SERVICES

"Tourist" centers may not parallel those in other countries—no maps, brochures, no help. Russian tourist centers exist to make money on tours and tickets, not to help confused tourists. If you start asking questions about the city, the staff may get upset, as they prefer to work with large companies sending groups. Even though we list tourist offices in this chapter as we do elsewhere in the guide, remember that, with rare exceptions, they are travel agencies, not founts of information. Yet trying won't hurt, and polite, even apologetic, inquiries can yield unexpectedly fruitful results.

MONEY

In August 1997, President Boris Yeltsin announced that the **ruble** would be redenominated on Jan. 1, 1998. The exchange rate for new bills was predicted at approximately six rubles to the U.S. dollar, so in effect three zeros are being lopped off the end. The change will occur over the next two years, as old bills are gradually removed from circulation.

Government regulations require your passport at exchanges. Find an *Obmen Valyuty* (Обмен Валюты; currency exchange) sign, hand over U.S. dollars—many places will change Deutschmarks, and some also accept French francs and British pounds—and receive your rubles. *Do not exchange money on the street.* You'll have no problem changing rubles back at the end of your trip (just keep exchange receipts), but the exchange rate is unstable, so it's best not to change large sums at once.

ATMs (банкомат; *bankomat*) are moving into most major cities, and big establishments now accept major **credit cards.** Main branches of banks will usually accept **traveler's checks** and give cash advances on credit cards—Visa is best. If you keep American currency on hand, be aware that most establishments do not accept crumpled, torn, or written-on bills of any denomination.

Apart from the vast range of prices for the same services in different cities and establishments, prices can be quoted in all sorts of "units"—rubles, US$, Finnish Marks, etc., but only rubles are accepted for payment. To explain the policy of overcharging foreigners, one theory argues that foreign prices are "real value" prices, and it's Russian citizens who get the discounts.

COMMUNICATION

Old local **telephones** in Moscow take special tokens, sold at metro *kassy;* in St. Petersburg, they take metro tokens. However, these old public phones are gradually becoming obsolete; the new ones take phone cards, are good for both local and intercity calls, and often have instructions in English. Phone cards are sold at central telephone offices and newspaper kiosks. You can make **intercity** calls from private homes, telephone offices, your hotel room, or *mezhdugorodnye* (междугородные) phone booths. It will take awhile, but you can usually get through. Dial 8, wait for the tone, then dial the city code.

Direct **international** calls can be made from telephone offices and hotel rooms: dial 8, wait for the tone, then dial 10 and the country code. You cannot call collect, unless using AT&T service (same access number as listed below), which will cost your party dearly (US$8 first min.; US$2.78 each additional min. to the U.S.). Prices for international calls vary greatly from city to city, from 9000R per minute (to the U.S.) up to 25,000R. To make calls from a telephone office, you can buy tokens or phone cards, or simply prepay your calls (depending on the city) and use the *mezhdugorodnye* (междугородные) telephones; be sure to press the *otvet* (ответ; reply) button when your party answers, or you will not be heard. If there are no automatic phones, you must pay for your call at the counter and have it dialed for you by the operator. Several hotels in Moscow now have direct-dial booths operated by a special card or credit card. The cost is astronomical (at least US$6 per min. to the U.S.). For **AT&T Direct,** dial 155 50 42 in Moscow and dial 325 50 42 in St. Petersburg; **Sprint,** dial 155 61 33 in Moscow. When calling from another city, dial 8-095 or 8-812 before these codes; you pay for the phone call to Moscow or St. Petersburg in addition to the international connection. For **Canada Direct,** dial 810 80 04 97 72 33 in Moscow. Calling into the country is much less frustrating. Most countries have direct dial to Moscow and St. Petersburg. For other cities, go through the international operator.

There is neither rhyme nor reason to the former Soviet Union's **mail service.** Delivery can take from two weeks to eternity. Domestic mail will usually reach its destination; from abroad, send letters to Russian recipients via friends who are traveling there, and do the same to get mail out. Airmail, if you want to risk it, is *avia* (авиа). **AmEx** card- and traveler's check-holders can receive letters (but not packages) at the AmEx bureaus in Moscow and St. Petersburg; this strategy is usually more reliable than Russian mail. They will hold your mail for 30 days. **DHL** operates in Moscow, St. Petersburg, Novosibirsk, Nizhny Novgorod, and Petrozavodsk. Central post offices are now equipped to send and receive **faxes. Email** offers an instant and free connection to selected universities and institutes inside the country; ask student friends about setting up a trans-oceanic connection. The youth hostels in Moscow and St. Petersburg also offer email services.

Most hotels stock *Time, Newsweek,* and the *International Herald Tribune* (US$2), as well as the local English-language newspapers *Moscow News* and *St. Petersburg Times.* If you plan on being in Russia for an extended period, a short-wave radio is invaluable. The BBC World Service comes in at around 1508MHz in west Russia.

LANGUAGE

Take some time to familiarize yourself with the **Cyrillic** alphabet. It's not as difficult as it looks and will make getting around and getting by immeasurably easier. For more info on the Slavic script, see p. 797. Though more and more people speak **English** in Russia, come equipped with at least a few helpful phrases. See the **Glossary,** p. 811. Note that улица (*ulitsa;* abbreviated ул.) means "street", проспект (*prospekt;* пр.) means "avenue", площадь (*ploshchad;* пл.) means "square", and бульвар (*bulvar;* бул.) is "boulevard". Apart from learning Russian numbers, practice the word *tysyacha* (plural *tysyach;* тысяча, тысяч; thousand(s)): since all prices are in thousands, this word is extremely useful when shopping or haggling. Once you get the hang of the alphabet, you can pronounce just about any Russian word.

HEALTH AND SAFETY

Emergency Numbers: Fire: tel. 01. **Police:** tel. 02. **Ambulance:** tel. 03.

Russian bottled water will be mineral water; you may prefer to boil or filter your own, or buy foreign **bottled water** (the Finnish kind is cheap) at a supermarket. Water in much of Russia is potable in small doses; however, water in Moscow and St. Petersburg should be boiled. A gamma globulin shot will lower your risk of hepatitis. Check the expiration date before buying any packaged snack. Men's **toilets** are marked with an "М", women's with a "Ж"—the 500-5000R charged for public toilets generally gets you a hole in the ground and a measured piece of toilet paper; get into the habit of carrying your own T.P. If either the color or the texture of local brands does not appeal to your sense of comfort, Western-type supermarkets sell pink and blue Finnish kinds. It's okay to drop into a hotel or a restaurant just to use their toilet.

Reports of **crime** against foreigners are on the rise, and it is important to remember that as a foreigner, you are a walking target—more so in Moscow and St. Petersburg than in small towns less used to tourists. Although it is hard to look Russian, try not to flaunt your true nationality. Your trip will be that much more pleasant if you never have to file a crime report with the local *militsia,* who will not speak English and will probably not help you. Reports of mafia warfare are scaring off tourists, but unless you bring a kiosk for them to blow up, you are unlikely to be a target.

For **medical emergencies,** leave the country or get to a St. Petersburg or Moscow clinic for foreigners. Local ambulance drivers will speak no English. Get traveler's health insurance before you leave (ISIC provides some coverage; see **Essentials,** p. 19); you can use one of the foreign clinics here, or even be evacuated.

ACCOMMODATIONS AND CAMPING

American-style **youth hostels** have begun to appear in St. Petersburg and Moscow. Some arrange visas. Reserve well in advance, especially in summer. Hotels offer several classes of rooms. "Lux," usually a two-room double with TV, phone, fridge, and bath, is the most expensive. "Polu-lux" is a one-room single or double with TV, phone, and bath. Rooms with bath and no TV, if they exist, are cheaper. The lowest price rooms are *bez udobstv* (без удобств), which means one room with a sink. As a rule, and in small cities in particular, only cash is accepted as payment. Many hotels have restaurants on the ground floor, often the best eatery in town; all have at least a buffet or cafeteria—probably the worst food in town. In Russia, hot water—even all water—is sometimes turned off for pipe repair and conservation. In parts of south Russia, water gets turned on only once every two weeks due to shortages.

University dorms offer cheap rooms; some take in foreign students for about US$10 per night. The rooms are liveable, but don't expect sparkling bathrooms or reliable hot water. Make arrangements with an institute from home.

FOOD AND DRINK

Russian cuisine is a conglomeration of dishes both delectable and disgusting, where a tasty borscht can come in the same meal as a bit of *salo* (pig fat). The largest meal of the day, *obed* (обед; lunch), is eaten at around noon or 1pm and includes *salat* (салат), usually cucumbers and tomatoes or beets and potatoes with mayonnaise or sour cream; *sup* (суп; soup), either meat or cabbage; and *kuritsa* (курица; chicken) or *myaso* (мясо; meat), often called *kotlyety* (котлеты; cutlets) or *beefshteaks* (бифштекс). Ordering a number of *zakuski* (закуски; Russia's answer to Spanish *tapas*) instead of a main dish can save money and add variety. Dessert is *morozhenoye* (мороженое; ice cream) or *tort* (торт; cake) with *cofye* (кофе) or *chai* (чай; tea). Russian **cafes** (кафе) offer food for lower prices; often the tables have no chairs. A *stolovaya* (столовая; cafeteria) may be unsanitary. You'll be charged extra for bread, water, and disposable forks, plates, and cups.

One can find basic Russian eats on the street, from stores, or at the market. In the store category, **dietas** (диета) sell goods for people on special diets (such as diabetics); **produkty** (продукты) and **gastronom** (гастроном) offer a variety of meats, cheeses, breads, and packaged goods. The larger **universam** (универсам) simulates a supermarket in its variety. The **market** (рынок; *rynok*) sells abundant fruits and vegetables, meat, fresh milk, butter, honey, and cheese. Wash and dry everything before you eat it—Russian farmers use pesticides liberally. Milk may not be pasteurized. **Bakeries** (булочная; *bulochnaya*) sell fresh black and white bread daily and, sometimes, sweet rolls, cakes, and cookies.

The **kiosks** found in every town are mini-convenience stores, selling soda, juice, candy bars, and cookies; all you have to do is point at what you want. You'll see a lot of the much-consumed *shashlyki* (шашлыки; barbequed meat on a stick) and *kvas* (квас), a fermented dark-brown drink (see **"Just for the Taste,"** p. 694). Kiosks often carry alcohol; imported cans of beer are safe (though warm), but be wary of Russian labels—you have no way of knowing what's really in those bottles. Buy booze in a foreign grocery store. *Zolotoye koltso, Russkaya,* and *Zubrovka* are the best vodkas; *Stolichnaya,* considered the best vodka in the world, is mostly made for export.

Moskovskaya is another known name, and generic brands will get the job done. Among local beers, *Baltika* (Балтика) is the most popular and arguably the best. It's okay to drink beer on the street or in a park. If you opt for *Baltikas,* numbered 1 through 7, here is the system: *Baltika* 1 is the lightest (10.5%) and *Baltika* 7 is the strongest (14%). *Baltikas* 4 and 6 are dark. The rest are lagers: 3 and 4 are the most popular options; 7 is extreme.

Vendors do not provide **bags** for merchandise. You can usually buy plastic bags in stores, the market, and on the streets, but to ensure that you won't have to carry around a smelly fish in your hands all day, bring your own bag or paper. The actual process of **purchasing** might be extended, especially in the older, typically Soviet stores. In stores, decide what you want, then go to a *kassa* and tell the person working there the item, the price, and the *otdyel* (отдел; department) from which you are buying. The person there will take your money and give you a receipt. You then take the receipt back to the *otdyel,* give it to the person working there, and they will give you what you want—finally.

CUSTOMS AND ETIQUETTE

Decades of collective lifestyle forced people very close together, so that the notion of personal space is almost nonexistent in Russia. People pack tightly in lines and on buses and tolerate the discomfort with stoic patience. To pack in or out of an over-crowded bus, tram, or Metro car requires forceful shoving, which is the rule of the game on public transportation. On public transportation, it's polite to give your seat to the elderly, pregnant women, and women with children. For men, it's gallant to yield your seat to a woman. It's okay for everybody (including fragile *babushky*) to push and shove if polite requests don't get you anywhere. On trains, on even the hot-test day of the summer, you'll find the windows closed "for the winter" (no, there is no air-conditioning, either). If you luck out with a single window that does open, Russians will close it anyway—for the national fear of drafts.

Tipping is not expected, but with the frightful way foreign tourists throw money around, it may soon be. Most establishments, even train ticket offices, close for a **lunch break** sometime between noon and 3pm. Places tend to close at least 30 minutes earlier than they should, if they choose to open at all. 24-hour stores take a lunch or "technical" break and a day off.

The concept of **sexual harassment** hasn't reached Russia yet. Local men (and not necessarily drunkards) will try to pick up women and will get away with offensive language (if not the deed). The routine starts with an innocent-sounding "*Devushka...*" (young lady); just say "*Nyet*" (No) or simply walk away. Locations and intensity of pursuit vary, with intentions ranging from playfulness to physical abuse. And no, they don't wear deodorant—it's considered fine for Russian men to smell.

The laws outlawing **homosexual** acts were taken off the books about seven years ago, but Russia is still not very tolerant of gays, lesbians, and bisexuals. In Moscow and St. Petersburg, a gay scene is starting to spring up.

Because of the recent influx of imports, token packs of cigarettes and ballpoint pens are no longer accepted as currency and don't make very good **gifts** for Russians. When visiting friends, bring flowers, cookies, or candy. A bottle of imported wine is a very special gift. Russians tend to dress up to go visiting, even is just across the street. Visiting a museum in shorts and sandals is disrespectful (they will give you a very hard time at the Hermitage). Many locals say that criminals spot foreigners by their sloppy appearances, so dress up, don't smile when stared at, and don't address people by their last names (for polite requests, use first and middle names).

NATIONAL HOLIDAYS

Russians celebrate: January 1, New Year's Day; January 7, Orthodox Christmas; February 23, Defenders of the Motherland Day; March 8, International Women's Day; March/April, Orthodox Easter; May 1-2, Labor Day; May 9, Victory Day; June 12, Independence Day; November 7, Great October Socialist Revolution.

LIFE AND TIMES

HISTORY

The East Slavs, ancestors of the Russians, began migrating from Central and Eastern Europe to present-day Russia around the **6th century** AD. At least as important in the development of Russia, however, were the **Varangians**, a Scandinavian tribe that led extended raids down the river routes toward Baghdad and Constantinople. Between 930 and 1000, the region was under the complete control of Varangians from Novgorod, who developed the trade route from the Baltic to the Black Seas—thus establishing the basis of the economic life of what would become Kievan Rus and, eventually, Russia. The tenth-century Varangian **Prince Svyatoslav** led victorious campaigns against the Khazars and the Volga Bulgars. His son **Vladimir,** who established a dynastic system, extended the realm to include the Don, Dnieper, Dniester, Neman, western Dvina, and upper Volga rivers. He was also responsible for officially adopting **Christianity** in 988, encouraged by followers of the missionaries **Cyril and Methodius,** who also introduced the Cyrillic alphabet.

In the 1100s, **Vladimir Monomakh** founded the city of Vladimir to the north of Kiev and moved the capital from Kiev to Vladimir in 1169, when Vladimir became the main center of economic activity. **Mongols** (also known as **Tatars** or the **Golden Horde**) came in 1236 and conquered the Russian lands by 1240. Russia remained somewhat isolated from the rest of Europe for 240 years, developing in a direction that would for many centuries make Russia a stepsister to other European countries. Cities had to pay protection money to their Mongol overlords, Eastern Orthodoxy flourished, and trade links multiplied. Many Kievan arts continued, however, including literature, architecture, and icon-painting, and there was little Tatar influence in religion or intellectual life. The Lithuanian-Polish Empire became interested in Russian territory but was defeated by the Mongols in 1370. In 1380, Grand Prince Dmitri attempted an uprising against the Mongols, which was brutally repressed.

> **Ivan the Terrible expanded Russia westward, but also alienated his generals and killed his oldest son and heir with his own hands.**

Ivan III (the Great) finally threw off Russia's Mongol yoke and set out to make Moscow a dominant power, conquering Novgorod and other neighboring principalities. **Ivan IV (the Terrible)** was the first ruler to have himself formally called "tsar." He conquered neighboring Kazan and expanded into the European sphere, but also alienated his generals, suffered severe skeletal deformation, and killed his oldest son and heir with his own hands, a move that clipped the continuity Russia always fell short of enjoying. Ivan's second son, **Fyodor I,** was too weak to rule the empire, and Fyodor's brother-in-law, **Boris Godunov,** became the actual ruler. When Fyodor died childless in 1598, Boris became tsar of Russia, thus putting an end to the Rurik dynasty. Conspiring against Godunov, the Russian **boyars** (nobles) brought forward a pretender named Dmitry, who claimed he was the son of the deceased Fyodor I. After Godunov's mysterious death, the *boyars* succeeded in making the **"False Dmitry"** tsar. What followed was a decade of unprecedented instability and chaos, with the *boyars* continually striving for more power and control over the numerous tsars. Finally, in 1613, **Mikhail Romanov** was chosen as tsar, beginning the Romanov dynasty that ruled until the Bolshevik Revolution of 1917.

Romanov **Peter the Great,** who became Tsar in 1682, dragged Russia toward Europe. He became known as the "Westernizer of Russia," although he was not intent on Westernization *per se,* but rather simply opposed to all things Russian. Peter created his own elite and built a trading capital on the Baltic. He killed innumerable workers in the process, hung the opposition, traipsed around Europe causing even more damage than the average *Let's Go* traveler, and in general precipitated a permanent crisis of cultural identity. He died in 1725, without a male successor. This ushered in a period of tsars and tsarinas under the control of the nobles until the advent of **Catherine the Great.** The meek, homely daughter of an impoverished Prussian aristocrat, Catherine came to Russia to marry Elizabeth's nephew, Peter III. Shortly after Peter became tsar, Catherine overthrew him in a coup. Along with her political advisor, **Grigory Potemkin,** she expanded her empire to include the north shore of the Black Sea, Crimea, and the steppes beyond the Urals and along the Caspian Sea.

In the late 1800s, famine, peasant unrest, and a wave of strikes culminated in the failed **1905 revolution.** Although Tsar **Nicholas II** established a progressive congressional body, the *Duma,* and made attempts to address the demands of the people, **WWI,** along with the intrigue that developed between his wife Alexandra and her advisor **Rasputin,** forced his abrupt abdication. The organizational genius **V.I. Lenin,** leader of the Bolsheviks, steered the bloodless coup of October 1917 to success. Thus began the great failed experiment. After the Bolshevik revolution came the **Civil War,** in which the White Army, backed by foreign powers, struggled with Bolshevik troops. A period of social liberation followed the Red Army's victory. 1922 witnessed the birth of the **Union of Soviet Socialist Republics (USSR),** but Lenin died in 1924 without naming a successor. **Joseph Stalin** succeeded in eliminating his rivals, **Trotsky,** Zinovev, and Kamenev, and in 1929 became the sole leader of the Communist Party. The first wave of political executions and **Socialist Realist** intellectual stifling began soon after. Five-year economic plans, forced collectivization of Russia's farms, and the creation of Siberian labor camps formed the basis for Stalin's totalitarian regime. Priority was given to national defense and heavy industry, which led to shortages of consumer goods. Numerous purges resulted in millions of casualties.

> Vladimir Ilich Lenin steered the bloodless October 1917 coup to success. Thus began the great failed experiment.

In international affairs, Stalin was able to find only one chum—**Hitler.** After trusting the Nazi dictator's promises of conquering the world together, the USSR entered **WWII** unprepared. The Soviet Union won only thanks to the icy winter of 1943-44, which proved too much for the unprepared, frostbitten German army to endure.

In 1949, the Soviet Union formed the **COMECON,** which incorporated all the Eastern European countries, reducing them to satellite states and linking them inseparably to the Party's headquarters in Moscow. After Stalin's death in 1953, **Nikita Khrushchev** emerged as the new leader of the Union. In his 1956 "secret speech," he denounced the terrors of the Stalinist period, and a political and cultural **"thaw"** followed in the early 60s. In 1964, Khrushchev was ousted by **Leonid Brezhnev,** who stayed in power until 1983, overseeing a period of monstrous political repression. **Yuri Andropov** and **Konstantin Chernenko** followed him in humorously quick succession. The geriatric government finally gave way to the 56-year-old, controversial **Mikhail Gorbachev** in 1985. As the decline of the aging elite consumed political circles, the army became frustrated with its losses in the war with Afghanistan. Gorbachev's political and economic reforms were aimed at helping the country regain the status of a superpower. Reform began with the slow steps of **glasnost** (openness) and **perestroika** (rebuilding). The state gradually turned into a bewildering hodgepodge of semi-anarchy, deepening economic crises, and cynicism. Ironically, Gorbachev was the architect of his own demise. Despite his great popularity abroad (and the 1990 Nobel Peace Prize), discontent with his reforms and a failed right-wing coup in August 1991 led to his resignation, the dissolution of the Union, and **Boris Yeltsin's** election as President of Russia. Fragments of the Soviet Union have remained together under the **Commonwealth of Independent States,** but other areas have gone their own way.

LITERATURE

Christianity, that source of most early European writings, gave to Russia both an alphabet (Cyrillic), and a literary language **(Old Church Slavonic).** But the language was not their own, and though **Archpriest Avvakum** wrote his autobiography in colloquial Russian, most literature was strictly religious. Commoners preserved poetry and folklore orally in epic **byliny,** while the elite wrote religious works and political propaganda praising the Muscovy princes.

In the 17th century, commerce between Russia and the West increased, and new ideas—religious, technological, and social—followed flourishing trade routes. Peter the Great embraced all this novelty, ordering the mass translation of western technical manuals. To expedite practical affairs, he relegated Old Church Slavonic to the clergy, and replaced Old Church characters with a simplified **civic alphabet.** In 1757, **Mikhail Lomonosov,** a scientist who was also one of the first Russian poets, wrote a grammar that systematized the colloquial language into a literary medium. As Peter emulated Western Europe in technology, Russian writers derived inspiration from French writers. In fiction, **Nikolai Karamzin** mastered the "sentimental" trend in *Letters of a Russian Traveler,* and in *Poor Liza* completed Lomonosov's reform by making the gentry's everyday speech the literary medium.

Some contend that the greatest year for Russian literature was 1799, when of **Aleksandr Sergeyevich Pushkin** was born. In his 38 short years, the "Russian Shakespeare" mastered European literary technique, added his own brand of Russian spice, and became not only the greatest Russian poet, but also the central figure in all of the nation's literature. Published in 1825, *Eugene Onegin* was his greatest novel. Though his sympathy with dissenters evident in this and other works created a stir with the Russian secret service, Tsar Nicholas, who had close ties with Pushkin's family, protected him. Unfortunately, the tsar's control did not extend to affairs of love; Pushkin died in a duel over his flirtatious wife's honor. **Mikhail Lermontov** became heir to Pushkin's literary legacy. Exiled to the Caucasus for a lament he wrote on Pushkin's death, Lermontov published *A Hero of Our Time* in 1840. A year later, at age 26, he too was killed in a duel. Another follower of Pushkin, **Nikolai Gogol** (1809-52) wrote the satirical *The Government Inspector,* the first major Russian play, and *Dead Souls,* whose satirical attitude toward life greatly influenced Dostoevsky.

It seems that in order to become a great writer in the 19th century, a stint in prison was required. **Ivan Turgenev** made the mistake of praising Gogol in an obituary, and yet another eulogizer was arrested. The tsarist government had other reasons for incarcerating the author; his most famous work, *Fathers and Sons,* spoke of challenging authority, and the hero, Bazarov, came to symbolize nihilism. The style of Russia's most philosophically and spiritually intense writer, **Fyodor Dostoevsky,** was greatly influenced by his experiences of a mock execution and imprisonment in Siberia, traces of which can be seen in his works *Crime and Punishment* and *The Brothers Karamazov.*

> **As Trotsky put it, writers didn't have to be Marxists, but did have to be "fellow travelers."**

Russian writers had borrowed many literary ideas from the West, which led to criticism that the country's literature represented a backwards nation mooching the thoughts of other countries. **Lev Tolstoy,** with his cutting psychological analysis and extensive use of the Russian idiom in *War and Peace* and *Anna Karenina,* convinced most that Russian literature was not only branching in original directions but also creating new work that could teach other European writers. Two other authors who helped create a distinctly Russian literature were **Anton Chekhov** (1860-1904), author of *The Three Sisters* and *The Seagull,* and **Maksim Gorky** (1868-1936), author of *Mother* and *The Lower Depths.* The latter grew up a member of the proletariat, and, as a Bolshevik sympathizer, helped establish a role for literature in the new order that followed the revolution. Lenin tolerated literary objectivity, and works like **Mikhail Sholokhov's** famous *And Quiet Flows the Don* were published.

The Revolution of 1917 led to chaos in the literary world. The printing of books stopped, while political poetry readings exploded. Many fled the country. **Vladimir Mayakovsky,** the revolution's first mouthpiece, committed suicide, as did **Sergei Esenin.** Authorities persecuted **Anna Akhmatova** into silence, and banned the great satirist, **Mikhail Bulgakov,** author of *Master and Margarita.* As Trotsky put it, writers didn't have to be Marxists, but did have to be "fellow travelers."

Largely championed by Gorky in the 1930s, **Socialist Realism,** a mix of historical fiction and cheerleader patriotism, became the model for party-authorized artists. After the war, freedoms that the state had allowed to boost embattled spirits were restricted, and most progress in the arts stopped. Following Stalin's death in 1953, Khrushchev came to power, and the literary structures thawed somewhat. The regime established official writers' journals—a good way of tracking literary dissidents. Unlike most authors, **Boris Pasternak** did not emigrate and suffered state persecution for such works as the world-famous *Dr. Zhivago.* Rejected in the USSR for its unbiased analysis of the civil war, the book was published instead in Milan. After Khrushchev's fall in 1964, controls became tighter, and previously tolerated authors like **Aleksandr Solzhenitsyn,** who published the accusatory *One Day in the Life of Ivan Denisovich* in 1963, couldn't get anything else to press. Solzhenitsyn received the Nobel prize in 1970, but in 1974, with *The Gulag Archipelago,* he joined **Vladimir Nabokov** (of *Lolita* fame) in exile. He returned to Russia in 1994.

In 1986, *glasnost* saw the circulation of previously banned books. Of recent fame are **Viktor Yerofeev** for *Russian Beauty,* translated into 27 languages, and **Tatyana Tolstaya** for *On the Golden Porch,* published in the west in 1989.

RUSSIA TODAY

The war in **Chechnya,** renewed after a Chechen offensive on Yeltsin's inauguration day, ended with the August 31, 1996 signing of a treaty brokered by National Security Adviser Aleksandr Lebed with little to no input from the ailing President **Boris Yeltsin.** The agreement postponed any permanent decision on Chechnya's independence until December 31, 2001, but it is well worth noting that the chief rebel negotiator, **Aslan Maskhadov,** was elected president of the republic in January 1997. Although Maskhadov fiercely promotes Chechen independence, leaders in Moscow claimed to welcome his election, stating that it would promote the resolution of the Chechnya conflict. Plans for negotiations between Russia and the republic, however, were indefinitely suspended in July 1997.

> President Yeltsin's decision to redenominate the ruble in 1998 was seen to reflect a new confidence in Russia's economy.

While trying to construct a new Russian economy, Yeltsin must engage in a power struggle with the Russian Parliament, which includes such figures as right-wing nationalist **Vladimir Zhirinovsky.** At the same time, in the name of democracy, Yeltsin has at times assumed (or tried to assume) near-dictatorial prerogatives. Yeltsin won the 1996 presidential election easily, but his health remains unstable. The accidents that plagued the space station **Mir** in spring and summer 1997 served further to demoralize the nation, as did the admission of Poland, Hungary, and the Czech Republic to NATO in the face of strong Russian opposition. Nonetheless, Yeltsin's decision to redenominate the ruble in 1998 was seen as reflective of a new confidence in Russia's economy. The monthly inflation rate has decreased to nearly 1%.

Moscow (Москва)

Moscow is huge, apocalyptic, and compelling. Founded by Yuri Dolgoruki in 1147, the city's early peak came in 1571, when it had over 100,000 citizens and was one of the world's largest settlements. Originally built up by Ivans the Great and Terrible, Moscow reigned as Russia's capital until 1714, and again after 1917, when it became the site of some of the 20th century's most watched political maneuvering. Home to one in 15 Russians (and 80% of Russia's wealth), the city throbs with energy and noise. Stalinist edifices provide a gray backdrop for the vibrant colors of churches and monasteries. Behind anonymous walls, apartments full of books and beloved knick-knacks shine like pools of light at the end of the dank hallways of crumbling buildings. Out on the street, Moscow is a haphazard and anarchic conglomerate of peasant villages—a bazaar where careerists selling Japanese televisions out of a truck stand next to grandmothers offering up the potatoes and dill they've been growing at their *dachas*. Moscow is Russia's center of change, and provides the visitor with a dizzying view of the country's possibilities. You may not love it—you may even hate it—but you won't regret you came.

ORIENTATION AND PRACTICAL INFORMATION

A series of concentric rings radiates from the **kremlin** (кремль; *kreml*). The outermost ring road forms the city boundary, but most sights lie within the inner **Sadovoe koltso** (Садовое кольцо; Garden Ring). **Krasnaya ploshchad** (Красная площадь; **Red Square**) and the kremlin mark the city center. Nearby begin Moscow's popular shopping streets: **Novy Arbat** (Новый Арбат), running west parallel to the Metro's blue lines, and **ul. Tverskaya** (Тверская), extending north along the green line. Ul. Tverskaya was formerly called ul. Gorkovo (Горкого); the upper half, which leads to the Garden Ring, is now known as **ul. Pervaya Tverskaya-Yamskaya** (Первая Тверская-Ямская). If you familiarize yourself with the Cyrillic alphabet and orient yourself by the **Metro**, it's difficult to get lost. An extensive city **map**, including all public transportation routes and a street index, is sold at many kiosks for around 25,000R. Many are outdated, so be sure to check that a recent year is clearly marked. See this book's **color insert** for maps of the Metro and the city.

Useful Organizations

Tourist Offices: Snag a free city **map** (with Metro map on back) at a major hotel, such as the Olympic Penta Hotel at M4, 5: Prospekt Mira. **Intourservice Central Excursion Bureau,** Nikitsky per. 4a (Никитский; tel. 203 75 85; fax 200 12 43). M1: Okhotny Ryad. **Moskovsky Sputnik,** Moskovsky спутник), Maly Ivanovsky per. 6, kor. 2 (Малый Ивановский; tel. 924 03 17). M5, 6: Kitai Gorod. Student travel, visas, and tickets. Open Mon.-Fri. 9am-1pm and 2-6pm, Sat. 9am-1pm and 2-5pm.

Tours: Main office of **Intourist,** ul. Mokhovaya 13 (Моховая; tel. 292 12 78). Arranges English-language tours of the Armory Chamber and Kremlin (Mon.-Wed. and Fri.-Sun. at 11am, US$20) and sightseeing tours by bus (daily at 2:30pm, US$10). **Moskovsky Gorodskoy Bureau Exkursy** (Московский Городской Бюро Экскурсий; City of Moscow Bureau of Excursions), ul. Rozhdestvenka 5 (Рождественка; tel. 921 15 08). Excellent 1½hr. bus tours of the main sights (Russian only). Tours leave from the northeast corner of Krasnaya pl., between the Lenin Museum and GUM; look for the person with the microphone (daily 9am-8pm; 25,000R).

Budget Travel: Student Travel Agency Russia (STAR), 50 Bolshaya Pereyaslavskaya, 10th fl. (tel. 913 59 52; fax 280 90 30; email star@glas.apc.org), in the same building as Traveller's Guest House. Discount plane tickets, Interrail and Eurobus passes, ISICs, worldwide hostel booking. Open Mon.-Fri. 10am-6pm.

Passport Office (ОВИР/OVIR): ul. Pokrova 42 (Покрова). Most hotels register you automatically and give you a card to prove you're staying there.

Embassies: Australia, Kropotkinsky per. 13 (Кропоткинский; tel. 956 60 70). M3: Smolenskaya. Open Mon.-Fri. 9am-12:30pm and 1:30-5pm. **Belarus,** ul. Maroseyka 1716 (Маросейка; tel. 924 70 31; fax 928 64 03). **Canada,** Starokonyushenny per. 23 (Староконюшенный; tel. 241 50 70). M1: Kropotkinskaya. Open Mon.-Tues. and Thurs.-Fri. 8:30am-1pm and 2-5pm. **China,** ul. Druzhby 6 (Дружбы; tel. 938 20 06; fax 938 20 05; consular section tel. 373 58 35; fax 373 77 25). **Estonia,** Maly Kislovy per. 5 (tel. 290 50 13; fax 202 38 30). Consular section located at Kalzhny per. 8 (Калжни; tel. 291 46 36). M3: Arbatskaya. Open Mon.-Thurs. 10am-noon. **Ireland,** Grokholsky per. 5 (Грохольский; tel. 288 41 01). M4,5: Prospekt Mira. Open Mon.-Fri. 9:30am-1pm and 2:30-5:30pm. **Lithuania,** Borisoglebsky per. 10 (Борисоглебский; tel. 291 15 01; fax 202 35 16). M3: Arbatskaya. Open Mon.-Fri. 9-11:30am. **Mongolia,** consular section at Spasopeskovsky per. 711 (Спасопесковский; tel. 241 15 48; fax 291 61 71). **New Zealand,** ul. Povarskaya 44 (Поварская; tel. 956 35 78). M4, 6: Krasnopresnenskaya. Open Mon.-Fri. 9am-5:30pm. **South Africa,** Bolshoy Strochinovsky per. 22/25 (Большой Строчиновский; tel. 230 68 69). Open Mon.-Fri. 9am-5pm. **U.K.,** nab. Sofiskaya 14 (Софиская; tel. 956 72 00; fax 956 74 20). M1, 3, 8: Borovitskaya. Open Mon.-Fri. 9am-5pm. **Ukraine,** Leontevsky per. 18

(Леонтевский; formerly ul. Stanislavskovo), off ul. Tverskaya (tel. 229 10 79, visa tel. 229 69 22). M3: Tverskaya. Lines tend to be long and visas can take up to a week to process, so come early. Open Mon.-Fri. 9:15am-12:30pm. **U.S.,** Novinsky 19/23 (Новинский; tel. 252 24 51, emergency tel. 230 20 01). M6: Krasnopresnenskaya. Open Mon.-Fri. 9am-6pm.

Currency Exchange: Banks at almost every corner; check ads in English-language newspapers. The pamphlet *Moscow Express Directory,* updated biweekly and free in most luxury hotels, lists the addresses and phone numbers of many banks, as well as places to buy and cash traveler's checks. **Sberbank** (Сбербанк), pr. Mira 41/1 (Мира; open Mon.-Fri. 9am-7pm, Sat. 9am-6pm), and numerous other locations, cashes AmEx, Thomas Cook, and Visa traveler's checks and issues EC, MC, STB, and Visa cash advances for 3% commission. Steer clear of the banks around the Arbat, which often charge 5% commission. Nearly every bank and hotel has an **ATM.** A particularly useful and reliable one stands in the lobby of the Central Telegraph building (Cirrus/MC/Plus/Visa). **AmEx ATM** in the lobby of the AmEx office. Money can be withdrawn in dollars or rubles. Beware of ATMs randomly stuck to the sides of buildings on the Arbat; not only do they work irregularly, but standing out in the middle of a busy street to get your money isn't very wise.

American Express: ul. Sadovaya-Kudrinskaya 21a, Moscow 103001 (Садовая-Кудринская; tel. 755 90 00; fax 755 90 04). M2: Mayakovskaya. Take a left onto ul. Bolshaya Sadovaya (Большая Садовая), which becomes ul. Sadovaya-Kudrinskaya. Travel assistance for all; banking services for members. Mail held for members and traveler's-check holders. Open Mon.-Fri. 9am-5pm, Sat. 9am-1pm.

Western Union: Rossyski Credit (Российски Кредит), Usacheva 35 (Усачева; tel. 119 82 50), left entrance. M1: Sportivnaya. Exit to the right; it's on the right, next to the Global USA Shop. Open Mon.-Fri. 9am-8pm, Sat. 9am-4pm.

Express Mail: DHL, Radisson-Slavyanskaya, Berezhkovskaya nab. 2 (Бережковская; tel. 941 87 40). M3: Kievskaya. **GUM (ГУМ) business center** (бизнес-центр), 2nd floor (tel. 921 09 11; fax 921 46 09). Open Mon.-Sat. 8am-8pm. **Main Office,** Trety Samotechny per. 11/2, 3rd floor (3-ий Самотечный; tel. 956 10 00; fax 974 21 06). M4, 8: Novoslobodskaya. Open Mon.-Fri. 8am-5pm.

Post Offices: Moscow Central Telegraph, ul. Tverskaya 7, a few blocks from the kremlin. M1: Okhotny Ryad. Look for the globe and the digital clock out front. **International mail** service open Mon.-Fri. 8am-2pm and 3-9pm, Sat. 8am-2pm and 3-7pm, Sun. 9am-2pm and 3-7pm. Address mail: "Москва 103009, До востребования (POSTE RESTANTE), GALBRAITH, Kate." **Faxes** and **telegrams** at window #1; immediate fax windows #7 and 8. Telegrams to the U.S. about 2500R per word. Faxes 12,000R per page to Europe, 18,000R to the U.S., and 42,000R to Australia and Africa. Open daily 8am-9:30pm. **Poste Restante** also at the **Gostinitsa Intourist post office,** ul. Tverskaya 3/5, 2nd fl. Address mail "PATEL, Riaz, До востребования, K-600, Гостиница Интурист, ул. Тверская 3/5, Москва." Window #32 sends letters, but not packages, abroad. To mail **packages,** bring them unwrapped to the Intourist post office or to Myasnitskaya 26 (Мясницкая); they will be wrapped and mailed while you wait. Intourist post office open Mon.-Fri. 9am-noon and 1-7pm, Sat. 9am-noon and 1-5pm. Regular letters (4500R) theoretically take 3 weeks; special delivery (заказное; *zakaznoe*; 10,000R) takes 1 week. **Postal code:** 103009.

Telephones: Moscow Central Telegraph (see **Post Offices,** above). To **call abroad,** go to the 2nd hall with telephones. Collect and calling card calls not available. Prepay at the counter for the amount of time you expect to talk. You will then be given the number of a stall from which to dial directly. Use the **international telephone cabinets** (международные телефоны; *mezhdunarodnye telefony*). To get a refund if you do not reach your party, you must stand in line again at the same counter. Depending on the time of day, calls to Europe run about 6300R per min.; to the U.S. and Australia about 14,700R; to Africa 17,550R. Open 24hr. Major hotels have direct-dial international phone booths at exorbitant rates (US$6-15 for 1min. to the U.S.). International calls can also be placed from private homes (dial 8-10-country code-phone number). For calling card access numbers, see **Russia Essentials: Communication,** p. 517. **Local calls** require plastic tokens (жетоны; *zhetony*), sold at some Metro stations and kiosks (1500R). **Phone code:** 095.

Transportation

Flights: International flights arrive at **Sheremetyevo-2** (Шереметьево-2; tel. 956 46 66 or 578 91 01). M2: Rechnoy Vokzal. Take the van under the автолайн sign in front of the station (every 10min. 7am-10pm, 20min., 10,000R). 24hr. Most domestic flights and many flights within the ex-USSR originate at **Vnukovo** (Внуково; tel. 436 21 09), **Bikovo** (Биково; tel. 558 47 38), **Domodedovo** (Домодедово; tel. 323 85 65), or **Sheremetyevo-I** (tel. 578 23 72). Buy tickets in *kassy* at the **Tsentralny Aerovokzal** (Центральный Аэровокзал; Central Airport Station), 2 stops on tram #23 or trolley #12 or 70 from M2: Aeroport. Check the express-bus schedules posted outside the station. Taxis to the center charge more than you ever dreamed possible, up to 400,000R—if you're not using public transportation, make sure you know how to bargain (in July 1997 you could get it down only to US$40-50). Agree on a price *before* you get into the cab.

Foreign Airline Representatives: Air France, ul. Korovy Val 7 (Коровий Вал; tel. 234 33 77; fax 234 33 93). Open Mon.-Fri. 9am-6pm. Also at Sheremetyevo-2, 6th floor (tel. 578 31 56). Open Mon.-Sat. 5:30am-11pm, Sun. 1-6pm. **British Airways,** Krasnopresnenskaya nab. 12, 19th fl., #1905 (tel. 258 24 92; fax 258 22 72). Open Mon.-Fri. 9am-5:30pm. **Delta,** Krasnopresnenskaya nab. 12, 11th fl., #1102a (tel. 258 12 88; fax 258 11 68). Open Mon.-Fri. 9am-5:30pm, Sat. 9am-1pm. **Finnair,** ul. Kuznetsky Most 3 (Кузнецкий мост; tel. 292 17 62; fax 292 49 48). M6: Kuznetsky Most. **Lufthansa,** Olimpysky pr. 18/1 (Олимпийский; tel. 975 25 01; fax 971 67 84), in Hotel Olympic Penta. M4, 5: Prospekt Mira. Open Mon.-Fri. 9am-5:30pm.

Trains: tel. 266 93 33; for booking and delivery of tickets tel. 266 83 33. Unless traveling in the Moscow region, all foreigners are required to purchase tickets for *mezhdugorodnye* (междугородные; intercity) trains from an official government agency such as Intourist or its affiliates (this rule may change in the near future). To buy a ticket, bring your passport to the *Tsentralnoe Zhelezhnodorozhnoe Agenstvo* (Центральное Железнодорожное Агентство; Central Train Agency), to the right of Yaroslavsky Vokzal (M4: Komsomolskaya). Purchase your tickets at window #10 or 11. A complete schedule of train stations, trains, destinations, and departure times is posted on the left side of the hall. *Kassy* open daily 8am-1pm and 2-7pm. If you have to catch a train and the Central Train Agency is closed, go to the 24hr. Intourist *kassy* on the 2nd floor of Leningradsky Vokzal (entrance #3, windows #20 and 21). They are supposed to sell tickets to St. Petersburg only, but have been known to bend the rules when everything else is closed. Buy tickets for the **Trans-Siberian** a few days in advance to ensure that you get a berth; otherwise you will be out-elbowed by hefty Mongolian traders and their families. Your ticket has your surname on it and tells you at which *vokzal* (вокзал; station) to catch your train. Platform numbers are announced when the trains arrive. Tickets for *elektrichki* (local trains) should be bought at the *prigorodnye kassy* (пригородные кассы; local ticket booths) in each station. Moscow has nine train stations, arranged around the circle line (кольцевая линия; *koltsivaya linia;* M4) of the Metro:

Leningradsky Vokzal (Ленинградский), Komsomolskaya pl. 3 (tel. 262 42 81 or 262 91 43). M1, 4: Komsomolskaya. To St. Petersburg, believe it or not.

Kazansky Vokzal (Казанский), Komsomolskaya pl. 2 (tel. 266 28 43), opposite Leningradsky Vokzal. To the east and southeast, including Volgograd, Kazan, Rostovna-Donu, and central Asia.

Yaroslavsky Vokzal (Ярославский), Komsomolskaya pl. 5 (tel. 266 05 95). To Siberia and the Far East. The starting point for the legendary Trans-Siberian Railroad (see **Trans-Siberian Railroad,** p. 562).

Paveletsky Vokzal (Павелетский), Paveletskaya pl. 1 (tel. 235 68 07) and **Kursky Vokzal** (Курский), ul. Zemlyenoy Val 29, 1 (tel. 266 48 20). To Crimea, eastern Ukraine, Georgia, Azerbaijan, and Armenia.

Rizhsky Vokzal (Рижский; tel. 924 57 62), Rizhkaya pl. To Rīga, Latvia (3 per day, 16hr.), and Estonia.

Belorussky Vokzal (Белорусский; tel. 251 60 93), pl. Tverskaya Zastava. To: Warsaw (5 per day, 24hr.); Minsk (10-12 per day, 9-13hrs.); and Kaliningrad (3 per day, 26hr.).

Kievsky Vokzal (Киевский; tel. 240 11 15), pl. Kievskovo Vokzala. To Bulgaria, Romania, Slovakia, and Ukraine.

Train and Airplane Tickets: Intourtrans Glavnoe Zhelezhnadarozhnoe Agenstvo
(Главное железнадарожное Агенство; Main Ticket Office), Maly Kharitonevsky per. 6
(Малый Харитоньевский; formerly Griboyedova; tel. 262 06 04). M5: Turgenevskaya.
Take a right off ul. Myasnitskaya (Мясницкая) and walk into the ancillary building on
the right. Main ticket office in Moscow for foreigners and international and domestic tickets. Open daily 8am-1pm and 2-7pm. Also in **Gostinitsa Intourist.** Same
hours as main office, but limited ticket availability. Foreigners are required to purchase tickets from Intourist or one of its government affiliates, though the lesser
hassle and shorter lines make this office tempting.

Public Transportation: The **Metro** is large, fast, and efficient—a work of art in
urban planning. It stops within a 15min. walk of any place in town and is a continual reminder that 13 million people do live in Moscow; all 13 million of them ride
the Metro. Passages to different lines or stations are indicated with a blue-and-white
sign of a man walking up stairs. A station that serves more than one line will generally have more than one name, although there are exceptions. Trains run daily 6am-
1am. Rush hours are 9-10am and 5-6pm. Buy light-green tokens (2000R) from the
kassy inside the stations; long lines form during rush hours. **Bus** and **trolley** tickets
are available in gray kiosks labeled "проедные билеты" and from the driver (1500R).
Be sure to punch your ticket when you get on, especially in the last week of the
month when ticket cops come out—the fine for not doing so is 10,000R. *Edinye
bilety* (единые билеты; monthly passes) let you ride on any form of transportation
(180,000R). Buy them after the 20th of the preceding month. Monthly Metro
passes are more cost-effective (90,000R). Purchase either from the *kassy*. Metro
maps are on the wall inside the entrance to every station; also consult the maps (in
both Latin and Cyrillic) in the front and back of this book.

Taxis: If you don't speak Russian, it's nearly impossible to get a fair rate. Ask around
for the going rate (3500R per km during summer 1997) and agree on a price before
you set off. Taxi stands are indicated by a round sign with a green T. Ordering one
over the phone (tel. 927 00 00) entails a 20,000R surcharge. Meters tend to be
purely ornamental, although a new law decrees that they must be used. Make sure
the driver turns it on. Try to avoid taxis unless you know Moscow.

Car Rental: Alamo, pr. Mira 43 (tel. 284 37 41; fax 284 43 91; email alm@centro.ru).
M4, 5: Prospekt Mira. Minimum 3-day rental includes insurance and unlimited mileage (US$90 per day). **Hertz,** ul. Chernyakhovskovo 4 (Черняховского; tel. 151 54 26;
fax 956 16 21; email hertz.mos@co.ru). Opels US$113 per day, with unlimited mile-
age and insurance. **Budget,** ul. Verkhnaya Radishchevskaya 16, kor. 1, room #8
(Верхняя Радищевская; tel. 915 52 37; fax 915 59 40). Fords US$113 per day, unlim-
ited mileage, insurance included. Open Mon.-Fri. 9am-7pm.

Other Practical Information

English-Language Press: Two free English-language daily newspapers are easy to
find in hotels and restaurants across the city. *The Moscow Times* (more widely read
and distributed) and *The Moscow Tribune* have foreign and national articles,
sports, and the like for news-starved travelers. Both also have weekend sections
(Fri. in summer, Sat. off-season) that list exhibitions, theatrical events, English-language movies, and housing and job opportunities. The *Moscow Business Telephone Guide* and *What and Where in Moscow*, both free, are excellent info
resources if you don't want to shell out 150,000R for the quarterly *Information
Moscow* (useful only if you are actually living here). Foreign publications such as
Time, Newsweek, and *The International Herald-Tribune* (25,000-30,000R) are
available in foreign supermarkets and major hotels. For 1- or 2-week-old magazines
at a lower price, check the stands at the bottom of ul. Tverskaya near the kremlin.

Cultural Centers: The Western powers have all ganged up, putting their cultural
centers in the same building: the **Foreign Library,** ul. Nikoloyamskaya 1, 3rd floor
(Николоямская). M4, 7: Taganskaya. The **American Cultural Center** (tel. 956 30 22
or 215 79 85) has a library full of reference materials. Open Mon.-Fri. 10am-8pm.
The **French Cultural Center** (tel. 915 36 69; open Mon.-Fri. 1-6pm) and the **British Council Resource Centre** (tel. 915 35 11; open Mon.-Fri. 10am-8pm) are next
door. Bring your passport, you expat, you!

Photocopies: For a complete list, check under "copy services" in *Moscow Business Telephone Guide,* free in most luxury hotels. **Intergraphics** (Интерграфикс), ul. Marksistskaya 5 (Марксистская; tel. 222 39 82; fax 232 93 64). M1, 4, 6: Taganskaya. Stamps, passport photos, color copies, and color laser printing. Copies 500R per page, lower for large orders. Open Mon.-Fri. 9am-6pm. AmEx, Diners Club, EC, MC, Visa. **Alphagraphics** (Алфаграфикс), Leningradsky pr. 53 (tel./fax 258 75 00), in the northeast part of town. M2: Aeroport. Same services at comparable prices. Open Mon.-Fri. 9am-9pm, Sat. 9am-6pm. AmEx, Diners Club, MC, Visa.

Internet Access and Computer Services: MicroAge, Leningradsky pr. 53 (tel. 258 75 85; fax 258 75 77), in the same building as Alphagraphics (see **Photocopies,** above). Computer use US$6 per hr. Addicts can Telnet to email accounts back home or set up their own accounts here (US$15 per month). Laser printing US$0.30 per page. Software in English and Russian sold, including Windows 95, Microsoft Office, Word, and Excel. Open Mon.-Fri. 9am-8pm, Sat. 9am-6pm. Visa, AmEx, Diners Club, MC accepted. **Partiya Internet Cafe** (Партия), Volgogradsky pr. 1 (Волгоградский). M6: Proletarskaya. US$3 per hr. Open daily 10am-8pm.

English-Language Bookstores: Angliskaya Kniga (Англиская Книга), ul. Kuznetsky Most 18 (tel. 928 20 21). M6: Kuznetsky Most. Moscow's largest selection of English books, imported straight from Britain. Savvy enough to carry *Let's Go.* Friendly staff, decent selection, especially in 19th-century classics and Russian/ Soviet studies. Open Mon.-Fri. 10am-7pm, Sat. 10am-6pm. AmEx, EC, MC, Visa accepted. **Shakespeare and Company,** Pervy Novokuznetsky per. 5/7 (tel. 231 93 60). M2: Novokuznetskaya. Carries books from *The New York Times* bestseller list. Need we say more? Open Mon.-Sat. 9am-6pm.

Laundromat: Traveller's Guest House (see **Accommodations,** p. 515) does your laundry for 25,000R per load. **California Cleaners,** Leninsky pr. 113/1 (tel. 956 52 84), and 12 other locations around Moscow. For free pickup and delivery call 497 00 05 or 497 00 11. Wash and dry 20,000R per kg, with ironing 30,000R per kg.

24-Hour Pharmacies: Leningradsky pr. 74 (Ленинградский; tel. 151 45 70). M2: Sokol. **Kutuzovsky pr. 14** (Кутузовский; tel. 243 16 01). M3: Kutuzovskaya. **40-Letia Oktyabrya pr. 4,** bldg. 2, (40-летия Октября; tel. 350 05 94). M9: Lyublino.

Medical Assistance: American Medical Center, Vtoroy Tverskoy-Yamskoy per. 10 (2-ой Тверской-Ямской; tel. 956 33 66; fax 956 23 06). M2: Mayakovskaya. American joint venture offering walk-in medical care for hard currency (US$215 per visit). Most experienced Western medical clinic in Moscow. Pharmacy and X-ray on premises. Monthly membership US$55, students US$45. Open Mon.-Sat. 9:30am-7pm; call for after-hours service. **Mediclub Moscow,** Michurinsky pr. 56 (Мичуринский; tel. 931 50 18 or 931 53 18). M1: Prospekt Vernadskovo. Private Canadian clinic offering full-scale emergency service. Medical consultations $90-120. Payment in rubles or by credit card only (Diners Club, EC, MC, Visa). Open Mon.-Thurs. 9am-8pm, Fri. 9am-6pm, Sat. 10am-2pm.

Dentists: Intermedservice, ul. Tverskaya 3/5, 20th fl., room 2029 (tel./fax 956 84 93), in Gostinitsa Intourist. M1: Okhotny Ryad. Swiss-Belgian-Russian venture offering basic dental care. Open Mon.-Fri. 9am-5pm. **U.S. Dental Care,** ul. Shabolovka 8, kor. 3 (Шаболовка; tel. 931 99 09). M4, 5: Oktyabrskaya. U.S. dental venture. Open Mon.-Sat. 7am-9pm.

Emergencies: Fire, tel. 01. **Police,** tel. 02. **Ambulance,** tel. 03. Call your embassy for passport and visa problems. Call 299 11 80 to report offenses *by* the police. **Lost children:** tel. 401 99 82. **Lost credit cards:** tel. 956 90 06 for AmEx, tel. 956 34 56 for Diners Club, MC, and Visa. **Lost property:** Metro, tel. 222 20 85; other transport, tel. 923 87 53. **Lost documents:** 200 99 57.

The Third Most Expensive City in the World?

Foreigners and Russians alike have recently been complaining of Moscow's rising prices—especially in real estate—which are being pushed to new limits by "New Russians" who can afford new Western goods. On a ratings scale that recently measured the "expensiveness" of 100 cities around the world, New York City was rated 1.00 and Washington, D.C. got 0.92. But Moscow came out a surprising 1.50, behind only Kyoto (1.55) and Tokyo (1.60), thus making it the third most expensive city in the world. Боже мой!

ACCOMMODATIONS

Just about everything can be found in Moscow these days, except budget accommodations. The pickings are slim, and whatever options do exist tend to be run-down and grossly overpriced. In summer, make sure to reserve at least a week ahead. Numerous women standing outside major rail stations rent **private rooms** or **apartments** (as low as 60,000R per night; don't forget to haggle); just look for the signs advertising rooms (сдаю комнату; *sdayu komnatu*) or apartments (сдаю квартиру; *sdayu kvartiru*). If you're interested in a **homestay**, book it in advance (see **Russia Essentials**, p. 514). The establishments below are as cheap as it gets in the capital.

Traveller's Guest House, ul. Bolshaya Pereyaslavskaya 50, 10th fl. (Большая Переяславская; tel. 971 40 59; fax 280 76 86; email tgh@glas.apc.org). M4, 5: Prospekt Mira. Walk north along pr. Mira, and take the 3rd right on Banny per. (Банный). At the end of the street, hang a left; TGH is the white 12-story building across the street. The only hostel-like accommodation in Moscow, of which the management is clearly aware. *The* place to meet other budget travelers and get travel advice. **Trans-Siberian tickets** sold with a US$20 service charge, but it beats waiting in line all day at the *kassy*. The travel agency STAR, also on the 10th floor, serves as the Moscow affiliate of Council and STA, offering discounted plane tickets and railpasses. Kitchen facilities. Laundry service (25,000R for a 3-5kg bag, 1- to 2-day service). Airport pickup and dropoff (US$30-45). Visa invitations for Russia (US$35). Phone-cards for calls abroad sold (100,000R and up). TGH T-shirts (45,000R). Check-out 11am. Dorm beds 105,000R. Singles 210,600R; doubles 280,800R. Reserve at least 1 week ahead; retain copies of all reservation forms and receipts. *The Moscow Times* free. MC, Visa.

Galina's Flat, ul. Chaplygina 8, #35 (Чаплыгина; tel. 921 60 38), in a beautiful old neighborhood. M1: Chistye Prudy. Leaving the Metro, head down bul. Chistoprudny (Чистопрудный) past the statue of poet Griboedov (Грибоедов), and take the 1st left onto Kharitonevsky per. (Харитоньевский) just after the blue Kazakh Embassy, and then the 2nd right on Chaplygina. Go through the courtyard (under the blue sign designating the address), hang a right, and enter the building where you see the Уникум sign over the doorway; the flat is on the 5th floor on the right-hand side. Galina and her sidekick Sergei welcome you to their homey Russian apartment, a palace of coziness by Russian standards. Easygoing atmosphere. Hot showers. Kitchen facilities. Safe location. Only 8 beds, so call ahead. 5-bed dorm US$8; double US$10 per person. If an 8th person arrives, an extra cot will appear.

Gostinitsa Tsentralnaya (Гостиница Центральная), ul. Tverskaya 10 (tel. 229 89 57), next to Pizza Hut. M2,6,8: Pushkinskaya. Standard Russian hotel with downstairs guard and floor women to keep your key. Much cheaper than other centrally located hotels. All rooms have sinks; bath and toilet off the hall. Singles US$37; doubles $50 (prices listed in US$, but you still pay in rubles). MC, Visa.

American Academy of Foreign Languages, ul. Bolshaya Cheryomushkinskaya 17а (Большая Черёмушкинская; tel. 129 43 00; fax 123 15 00). M5: Akademicheskaya. From the Metro, turn left at the Ho Chi Minh statue and walk 15min. on ul. Dmitriya Ulyanova (Дмитрия Ульянова), then turn left on Bolshaya Cheremushkinskaya. Or take infrequent buses #218, 142, or 67, which stop across the street from Ho Chi Minh, down ul. Dmitriya Ulyanova to the 3rd or 4th stop ("Fabrika"). Trolley #26 also runs to the hotel from the M5: Shabolovskaya stop; get off at "Shveinaya Fabrika Moskva" (15min., 1500R). Bed in a triple or quad 55,000R; in a more spacious double 75,000R; 2-room "lux" suites 400,000R; "half-lux" suites 300,000-340,000R. Cash only. At the so-called American Academy of Foreign Languages, even some English is spoken.

Prakash Guesthouse, ul. Profsoyuznaya 83, Kor. 1 (2nd entrance), 3rd fl., (Профсоюзная; tel. 334 82 01; fax 334 25 98). M5: Belyaevo. From the Metro, take the exit nearest the last car of the train and go all the way to the right of the *perekhod* (tunnel), exiting from the last stairway on the left-hand side. The guest house is in the 4th building on your right, the first 16-story structure you see. Enter from 2nd entrance, to the right of the main entrance. If you call ahead, they'll meet you at the Metro. Friendly if far away accommodation, catering to Indian guests. Reception open daily 7am-11pm; call ahead if you're arriving earlier or later. Shower, toilet, and telephone for local calls in each room. Singles US$30; doubles US$40. Breakfast US$5. Dinner US$10. Cash only.

FOOD

Eating out in Moscow *can* be incredibly expensive, but it doesn't *have* to be. Prices are ridiculous along the main tourist streets and near big hotels, but walking just one block off the roads most traveled can make all the difference. Many restaurants list prices in dollars, but do so only to keep from having to constantly change their menus to keep up with inflation; payment is usually in rubles. Russians tend to eat late in the evening, so you can avoid crowds by eating earlier. Reservations are a good idea for the more popular restaurants, particularly on weekends. **Cafes,** substantially cheaper than restaurants, often serve better food, offering one or two well-prepared dishes rather than a selection of mediocre ones.

The Chains (or, How Uncle Sam Won the Cold War)

McDonald's (Макдоналдс, not that you need the Cyrillic). Ronald now has six golden arches in Moscow; ul. Bolshaya Bronnaya 29 (Большая Бронная; M6: Pushkinskaya) and ul. Arbat 50/52 (Арбат; M3: Smolenskaya), are the most popular. Big Mac 11,000R. Large fries (большая порция картофель-фри; *bolshaya portsiya kartofel-fri*) 8000R. Open daily 8am-midnight.

Pizza Hut (Пицца Хат), ul. Tverskaya 12. M6: Pushkinskaya. Armed guards protect the upscale interior—complete with requisite salad bar and Americans. Small cheese 29,300R. Medium veggie 71,000R. Apple pie 7900R. Outside counter sells 10,800R slices. Open daily 11am-11pm. AmEx, MC, Visa.

Baskin Robbins, on the Arbat, at Gostinitsa Rossiya, and in bright pink kiosks all over Moscow. The not-always-31 flavors are losing their appeal, due to the high prices and influx of other ice cream. Tiny scoop 7000R. Open daily 10am-9pm.

Russkoe Bistro (Русское Бистро). Moscow's homegrown answer to McDonald's, with locations all over town (particularly near the Pushkinskaya Metro, where you can see *three* of them at once). Soups 5000R, salads 8000R, meat rolls 3000R. Open daily 10am-midnight.

Krasnaya Ploshchad (Near the Kremlin)

Moscow Bombay, Glinishchevsky per. 3 (Глинищевский; tel. 292 97 31; fax 292 93 75), just off ul. Tverskaya. M6: Pushkinskaya. English menu reveals a full page of veggie options (US$6.75). Tandoori chicken US$9. *Naan* US$2. Reservations recommended, especially on weekends. Open daily noon-midnight.

Zakuska na Khudozhestvennom (Закуска на художественном) ul. Kamergersky Proezd 5/7 (Камергерский проезд; tel. 229 10 60). M6: Pushkinskaya. Wicked cheap cafe north of Tverskaya. *Pelmeni* 6600R. Chicken 6000R. Open daily 10am-8pm.

Rostik's (Ростик'с), on the 2nd floor of GUM department store, at the end nearest Kazansky Sobor. Moscow's answer to KFC, only here the birds are roasted. 2 pieces of chicken with roll 18,900R. Fried fish 19,300R. Shakes 9000R. English menu. Order and pay at one of the *kassy,* then go get your food. Take-out available. Open Mon.-Sat. 8am-8pm, Sun. 11am-6pm.

Dieticheskaya Stolovaya (Диетическая столовая), ul. Bolshaya Dmitrovska 11 (Большая дмитровска; tel. 22 09 04). M6: Pushkinskaya. Specializing in food for those with special dietary concerns, like diabetics, but offers simple, cheap, and good food to all. Full meal around 10,000R. Open daily 10am-8pm.

Copacabana Cafe, on the 2nd floor of GUM. Some call it the hottest spot north of Havana—it calls itself Brazilian, but the food is standard quasi-foreign-cafe fare. Hot sandwiches and some salads for 15,000-20,000R. Ice cream sundaes 7300-21,500R. Open Mon.-Sat. 8am-8pm, Sun. 11am-6pm.

La Cantina (Ла Кантина), ul. Tverskaya 5 (tel. 292 53 88), on the right of Gostinitsa Intourist. M1: Okhotny Ryad. The small booths, long bar, and mural of the "Moscow honky-tonk" spell a carefully designed Mexican restaurant with a Russian flavor. Popular with tourists craving Spanish guitar bands. Nachos and chili 45,000R. Large chicken enchiladas a whopping 85,000R. Open daily 8am-midnight.

Russky Suvenir (Русский Сувенир; Russian Souvenir), Petrovka per. 23/10 (Петровка). M6: Pushkinskaya. Inside, it looks like a log cabin with folk paintings of roosters and maidens. Waiters wear traditional Russian clothing. Tender beef in a pot 30,000R. *Shchi* (cabbage soup) 21,000R. *Kvas* 2400R. Open Mon.-Fri. noon-11pm.

Blinchiki (Блинчики), a kiosk on Strasnoy bul. (Страстной), off ul. Tverskaya diagonally opposite McD's. Scrumptious apricot-filled *bliny* 3000R. The long line at midday means this is the real thing. Open daily 8am-8pm.

Cafe Oladi (Оладьи), ul. Pushkinskaya 9 (tel. 916 26 59), just past the Tchaikovsky Conservatory. The eponymous dish consists of small, sweet pancakes with jam or sour cream (7000R). Yum! Open daily 9am-8pm.

Around the Arbat

Cafe Margarita (Кафе Маргарита), ul. Malaya Bronnaya 28 (tel. 299 65 34), at the corner of Maly Kozikhinsky per. (Малый Козихинский). An artistically painted door leads to this super-trendy cafe opposite the Patriarch's Ponds, where Bulgakov's *Master and Margarita* begins. Enjoy the house specialty—tomatoes stuffed with garlic and cheese—or just sip a cup of tea and watch the artsy gossip and smoke the afternoon away. *Lobio* 20,000R. *Bliny* with mushrooms 36,000R. Open daily 1pm-midnight. Live piano music after 7pm (cover 15,000R).

Praga, Arbat 2 (tel. 290 31 37), near the corner of Novy Arbat. M3: Arbatskaya. Creator of the infamous "Praga" chocolate torte sold all over Moscow, the bakery to the right of the restaurant sells scrumptious goodies for a few thousand rubles. Open daily 9am-8pm.

Evropeiskoe Bistro (Европейское Бистро), Arbat 16 (tel. 291 71 61). Look for the orange-and-blue awning. Reasonably priced joint that serves "Eurofood"—Russian cuisine under a fancier name. Try the *Evromix* salad (Евромикс; 26,700R) or the *Evropizza* (Европицца; 26,800R) for a quick fill. Open daily 8am-midnight.

Mzury Gryzinsky Restoran (Мзиури), Arbat 43 (tel. 244 00 24). M3: Smolenskaya. Located downstairs in the Georgian Cultural Center, the blue-tiled walls and hand-woven carpets make you feel like you're in the heart of Tblisi. *Shashlyk* 40,000R. *Chkhakhokbili* (Чхохбили; chicken in tomato sauce) big enough to feed 3 people 150,000R. Georgian national dish *Khachapuri* (Хачапури; cheese baked in dough) 25,000R. Live Georgian music Tues.-Sun. after 7pm. Open daily noon-midnight. **Wax Exhibit** on 2nd floor displays political leaders, from Edvard Shevardnadze to Yeltsin and Clinton (15,000R). **Section Disco and Bar,** a Turkish disco in the same building, rocks to pop, funk, and reggae (open daily 4pm-6am; Sun.-Thurs. no cover, Fri.-Sat. 50,000R for striptease).

Italian Bar, Arbat 49 (tel. 241 43 42). Although this restaurant serves pricey fare, you can have a seat at the snack bar outside and watch the hordes tramp past. Cappuccino 24,000R. Sandwich 30,000R. Pizza 30,000-42,000R. Open daily noon-2am.

Near the Pushkin Museum of Fine Arts

Patio Pizza, ul. Volkhonka 13a (Волхонка; tel. 201 50 00), opposite the museum. M1: Kropotkinskaya. This place rocks, and everybody knows it—come before 7pm to avoid the lines. Spacious and light, with fast service. International clientele. The food and prices, not the buzzing atmosphere, are the draw. Delicious thin-crust pizzas and desserts please the palate without excessively lightening the wallet. Well-stocked salad bar 40,000R. Pizzas 50,000R. Lasagna 55,000R. Chocolate mousse or sinful nutcake 30,000R. Open daily noon-midnight. AmEx, MC, Visa.

Krisis Genre, Bolshaya Vesinaya per. 22/4 (Большая Весиная; tel. 243 86 05), on the corner of per. Ostrovskovo (Островского), in an abandoned-looking apartment building. M1: Kropotkinskaya. Walk through a small opening in a gate across from the Danish Embassy on Ostrovskovo per. into the courtyard—it's the 3rd door on the right. A small cafe near the Arbat catering to pensive artsy types—bring your *Crime and Punishment.* Main dishes 21,000-31,000R. Bloody Mary 10,000R. Coffee 6000R. Open Tues.-Sun. noon-1am.

Mama Zoya's, Sechenovsky per. 8 (Сеченовский; tel. 201 77 43). M1: Kropotkinskaya. Hearty, inexpensive Georgian cuisine and gypsy dancers who take requests. Extremely popular. Main dishes 20,000-28,000R. Open daily 11am-10pm.

West of Gorky Park

Guria, Komsomolsky pr. 7/3 (Комсомольский; tel. 246 03 78), on the corner of ul. Frunze, opposite St. Nicholas of the Weavers. M1, 4: Park Kultury. Walk through a courtyard to the left. Delicious Georgian fare for some of the city's lowest prices. One of the hottest eateries for both locals and foreigners. Vegetarian meal of *lobio* (beans), *khachapuri,* salad, and Georgian yogurt 20,000R. *Satsivi* (turkey in walnut sauce) 13,000R. English menu. BYOB. Open daily 11am-10pm.

U Pirosmani (У Пиросмани), Novodevichi proezd 4 (Новодевичий; tel. 247 19 26; fax 246 16 38), across from Novodevichy Convent, with one of Moscow's best views. M1: Sportivnaya. Turn left, and walk straight until you see the pond; the restaurant is on the left. Specializing in delicately spiced Georgian cuisine, it's a cut above the rest for flavorful dishes served with panache. Clinton ate here in spring '96. *Lobio* US$3. *Khachapuri* US$2. *Baklazhany* (eggplant) US$6. Reserve for dinner. Open daily noon-11pm. AmEx.

Near M2: Mayakovskaya

Tram, ul. Chekhova 6 (Чехова; tel. 299 07 70). M6: Pushkinskaya. Directly below the LENKOM theater, this drama-themed establishment serves above-average Russian food at below-average prices. Busy, but worth the wait. Borscht 6000R. Open 24hr.

American Bar and Grill, ul. Tverskaya-Yamskaya 3211 (Тверская-Ямская; tel. 251 79 99), directly opposite M2: Mayakovskaya. Wait can be up to 2hr.; most crowded 1-3pm. Despite the *faux*-American decor, the menu and prices are truly American. A good place for noisy fun—the bar is a scene in itself. New England clam chowder US$6. Chips and salsa US$4. BBQ ribs US$7. Cheesecake US$8. Budweiser US$4. American breakfast served daily 4am-11am; bottomless cup of coffee or tea included. Open daily noon-5am. AmEx, MC, Visa.

Starlight Diner, ul. Bolshaya Sadovaya (Большая Садовая; tel. 290 96 38). M2: Mayakovskaya. Another location at ul. Korovy Val 9 (tel. 230 32 68). M4: Octyabrskaya. Cheaper than the American Bar and Grill, this "diner" is straight outta Jersey—and it's got the decor to prove it. Burgers US$5. Open 24hr.

Near the Traveller's Guest House

Zaydi i poprobuy (Зайди и попробуй; Drop in and Try), pr. Mira 124 (Мира; tel./fax 286 81 65). M5: Rizhskaya, then take the trolley a couple of stops north. Entrance on Malaya Moskovskaya ul. (Малая Московская). Drop in you do, since the restaurant is below street level, through a dim entrance hall. The interior pleases with bright tablecloths and murals. The food is your favorite Russian cuisine, well prepared. Borscht 9000R. Main dishes 35,000R. Open daily 11am-11:30pm.

Kombi's, pr. Mira 46/48. M4: Prospekt Mira. Other locations at ul. Tverskaya-Yamskaya 32/1 (M2: Mayakovskaya) and ul. Tverskaya 4 (M1: Okhotny Ryad). Clean sandwich shop with subs (12,500-21,000R), salads (6000-15,000R), and milkshakes (9000R). The closest you'll ever come to a New York deli in this part of the world, and even that's stretching it. English menu. Open daily 9am-10pm.

Near Krasnaya Presnya

Cafe Kitayskoy Kukhni (Кафе Китайской Кухни; Cafe of Chinese Cooking), ul. Krasnaya Presnya 30 (Красная Пресня; tel. 252 33 84). M6: Ulitsa 1905 goda. Turn left from the Metro stop; it's on the left, marked by yellow lettering that lights up at night. A small, dark cafe that looks just like so many others across the city. The difference is that it serves cheap Chinese food. Not all of the menu is translated into English, so look at what the Russian customers get and point. Fried emperor's chicken 21,000R. Boiled rice 2000R. Dumplings 24,000R. Open daily 10am-10pm.

Santa Fe, ul. Mantulinskaya 6 (Мантулинская; tel. 256 14 87). M6: Ulitsa 1905 goda. A hefty walk—exit onto ul. 1905 goda from the Metro, follow it straight to the Mezhdunarodny, and take a right. The restaurant is on the left. The New Mexican decor and bustling foreignness of this place make it a yummy oasis even for the budget traveler. Service with a smile. Black bean soup US$7. Cajun burger US$15. Large desserts US$8-22. Open Sun.-Thurs. noon-2am, Fri.-Sat. noon-3am. AmEx, MC, Visa.

Zhenya's Place (Женино Место), ul. Kolumbiskaya 95 (Колумбиская; tel. 38 25 43 63). M2: Kakaya Nyeisvestnaya. *Über*-intellectual restaurant and cafe that serves the best borscht this side of the Volga (16,000R). Ivy-League educated owner Zhenya may be a bit arrogant, but he's been to Ulaan Baatar! Try *mesyats slishkom pozdno* (месяц слишком поздно), a jumpin' central Asian dish (600R). Service may be *extremely* slow. Open Mon.-Fri. 9-11pm, Sat. 6-8am.

Markets

As Georgians, Armenians, Uzbeks, and peasants from all over cart their finest produce to Moscow, your best bet for fresh fruits and vegetables is a market. A visit is worthwhile just for the sight of sides of beef, piles of tomatoes, peaches, grapes, jars of glowing honey, and huge pots of flowers crowded together in a visual bouquet. The central market (M8: Tsvetnoy Bulvar), next to the Old Circus, has reopened after a recent reconstruction. The alternative is the Rizhsky Market (M5: Rizhskaya). Exit the Metro and keep turning left until you see it. Otherwise, impromptu markets spring up around Metro stations; some of the best are at Turgenevskaya, Kuznetsky Most, Aeroport, Baumanskaya, and Oktyabrskoye Pole. In general, people appear with their goods around 10am and leave by 8pm, though stragglers stick around until around 10pm. Produce, sold by the kilogram, is far cheaper than in the grocery stores.

Supermarkets

The number of supermarkets increases just as the need for them decreases—many of the goods sold here can be found more cheaply in kiosks and in even smaller markets selling Russian and foreign foods. Yet little beats the convenience of knowing you can find everything you need in one place. Listed below are a few of the largest:

Eliseevsky Gastronom (Елисеевский), ul. Tverskaya 14 (tel. 209 07 60). Moscow's most famous grocery reflects the economic situation of the times. These days, the shelves are packed with foreign goods, the lines are long, and the prices are lower than in the hard-currency supermarkets. This landmark is endowed with stained glass, high Baroque ceilings, and high-flying chandeliers. Open Mon.-Fri. 9am-9pm, Sat. 8am-7pm.

The Arbat Irish House, Novy Arbat 11, 2nd fl. (Новый Арбат; tel. 291 76 41). M3: Arbatskaya. Also a clothing-electronics store, with an Irish pub to boot. Open daily 9am-9pm, Sun. 10am-8pm. Well-stocked Russian supermarket **Novoarbatsky Gastronom** is downstairs. Open Mon.-Sat. 8am-10pm, Sun. 9am-9pm. MC, Visa at both.

Gastronom Tsentralny, ul. Bolshaya Lubyanka 12/1 (Большая Лубянка), behind Lubyanka Prison. This 24hr. supermarket has all kinds of food, with a 20% elevation in price 10pm-7am—you pay for that midnight snack. Clean and cheery, but considered expensive by locals. AmEx, Diners Club, MC, Visa.

Dorogomilovo (Дорогомилово), ul. Boshaya Dorogomilovskaya 8 (Большая Дорогомиловокая). M4: Kievskaya. Left of McDonald's, across the park from Kievsky Vokzal. Considered the least expensive of the new supermarkets stocking Western foods. Such necessities as salmon (25,000R), yogurt (1700-2400R), and Minute Maid orange juice (12,000R). Open Mon.-Sat. 9am-9pm, Sun. 9am-7pm.

Stockmann, M2,4: Paveletskaya. Facing the station on the opposite side, walk left 2 blocks, past the *bliny* stand on your left; the glassed-in store is behind the white curtains. Finnish grocery emporium accepting **credit cards only.** *PC Magazine, Time,* and *The Economist* sold here. Open daily 9am-9pm.

Diplomat, ul. Bolshaya Gruzinskaya (Большая Грузинская; tel. 251 25 89). M4: Belorusskaya. Department store stocked with fresh produce from all over the world. Open Mon.-Sat. 10am-8pm.

SIGHTS

Moscow's sights reflect the city's strange history: the visitor can choose among 16th-century churches or Soviet-era museums, but there's little in between. Russia's capital also suffers from the 200 years when St. Petersburg was the tsar's seat—there are no grand palaces, and the city's art museums pale in comparison to the Hermitage. Tourists will notice that the political upheaval of the last decade has taken its toll on the museums dedicated to Lenin, Marx, and Engels, which are closed indefinitely while their political significance is reassessed. Yet the "political reconstruction" of the capital has also led to physical renovation, and the city seems to be constantly under construction, with new buildings going up practically overnight. In the wake of Moscow's 850th anniversary celebration, a massive restoration and reconstruction effort has left some sights temporarily out of commission. Despite the fact that 80% of Moscow's pre-revolutionary splendor was torn down by the Soviet regime, the capital still packs enough sights to occupy you for a week.

Krasnaya Ploshchad (Красная площадь; **Red Square**)

There is nothing red about it; *krasnaya* meant "beautiful" long before the Communists co-opted it. Krasnaya pl., a 700m-long lesson in history and culture, has been the site of everything from a giant farmer's market to public hangings, from political demonstrations to a renegade Cessna's landing. On one side, the **kremlin** stands as both the historical and religious center of Russia and the seat of the Communist Party for 70-odd years; on the other, **GUM,** once a market, then the world's largest purveyor of grim Soviet consumer goods, has become a bona fide shopping mall. At one end, **Pokrovsky Sobor** (Покровский Собор; St. Basil's Cathedral), the square's second oldest building, rises high with its crazy-quilt onion domes; at the other the **History** and **Lenin Museums** are both closed for ideological repair. Lenin's historical legacy has come into question, and his name and face are coming down all over Moscow. The Party, so to speak, is finally over. But Lenin's mausoleum still stands in front of the kremlin, patrolled by several scowling teenage draftees. Moscow's mayor has built a church to block the largest entrance to the square, ensuring that Communist parades will never again march through. Begin your visit here; tradition has it that first-time visitors must enter with their eyes closed to get the full effect.

Kreml (Кремль; **Kremlin**)

Like a spider in her web, the kremlin sits geographically and historically in the center of Moscow. Here Ivan the Terrible reigned with his iron fist; here Stalin ruled the lands behind the Iron Curtain. Napoleon simmered here while Moscow burned, and here the Congress of People's Deputies dissolved itself in 1991, ending the USSR. But despite the tremendous political history of the one-time fortress, the things to see here are largely churches. Buy tickets at the *kassa* in Aleksandr Gardens, on the west side of the kremlin, and enter through Borovitskaya gate tower in the southwest corner. Shorts and large bags are not allowed; there is a check-room (for your bags, not your shorts; 1000R). Much of the kremlin is still government offices; the watchful police will blow whistles if you stray into a forbidden zone.

Follow the people with cameras to **Cathedral Square,** where the most famous gold domes in Russia rise. The first church to the left, **Blagoveshchensky Sobor** (Благовещенский собор; Annunciation Cathedral), guards the loveliest iconostasis in Russia, with luminous icons by Andrei Rublev and Theophanes the Greek. Originally only three-domed, the church was elaborated and gilded by Ivan the Terrible. The second, southeast entrance is also his work; four marriages made Ivan ineligible to use the main entrance. Across the way, the square **Arkhangelsky Sobor** (Архангельский Собор; Archangel Cathedral) gleams with vivid icons and frescoes. But this temple has a more morbid attraction; it is the final resting place for many tsars prior to Peter the Great. Ivans III (the Great) and IV (the Terrible) are behind the south end of the iconostasis; Mikhail Romanov is in front of it.

The center of Cathedral Square is **Uspensky Sobor** (Успенский собор; Assumption Cathedral), where Ivan the Terrible's throne still stands by the south wall. The icons on the west wall are from the 15th century; the others are from the 1640s. Napoleon, securing his excellent reputation with the Russians, used the place as a stable in 1812. To the east of Uspensky Sobor rises **Kolokolnya Ivana Velikovo** (Колокольня Ивана Великого; Ivan the Great Belltower). Its tower is visible from 30km away thanks to Boris Godunov (the one pre-Peter tsar not buried in the kremlin—he's in Sergievsky Posad), who raised the tower's height to 81m. The ground floor has exhibits from the kremlin's collection. Behind the Assumption Cathedral stands the **Patriarshy Dvorets** (Патриарший Дворец; Patriarch's Palace), site of the Museum of 17th-

RUSSIA

Kremlin

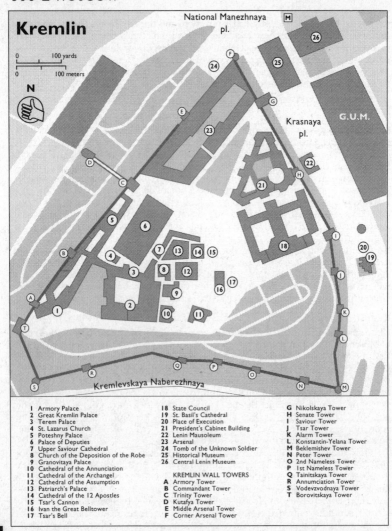

National Manezhnaya pl.

Krasnaya pl.

G.U.M.

Kremlevskaya Naberezhnaya

1 Armory Palace	18 State Council	G Nikolskaya Tower
2 Great Kremlin Palace	19 St. Basil's Cathedral	H Senate Tower
3 Terem Palace	20 Place of Execution	I Saviour Tower
4 St. Lazarus Church	21 President's Cabinet Building	J Tsar Tower
5 Poteshny Palace	22 Lenin Mausoleum	K Alarm Tower
6 Palace of Deputies	23 Arsenal	L Konstantin-Yelana Tower
7 Upper Saviour Cathedral	24 Tomb of the Unknown Soldier	M Beklemishev Tower
8 Church of the Deposition of the Robe	25 Historical Museum	N Peter Tower
9 Granovitaya Palace	26 Central Lenin Museum	O 2nd Nameless Tower
10 Cathedral of the Annunciation		P 1st Nameless Tower
11 Cathedral of the Archangel	KREMLIN WALL TOWERS	Q Tainitskaya Tower
12 Cathedral of the Assumption	A Armory Tower	R Annunciation Tower
13 Patriarch's Palace	B Commandant Tower	S Vodevaznaya Tower
14 Cathedral of the 12 Apostles	C Trinity Tower	T Borovitskaya Tower
15 Tsar's Cannon	D Kutafya Tower	
16 Ivan the Great Belltower	E Middle Arsenal Tower	
17 Tsar's Bell	F Corner Arsenal Tower	

Century Russian Applied Art and Life, and **Sobor Dvenadtsati Apostolov** (Собор Две-надцати Апостолов; Church of the Twelve Apostles), built by Patriarch Nikon in the 17th century as revenge against Ivan the Terrible's extravagant Sobor Vasiliya Blazhennovo.

Behind Arkhangelsky Sobor, the **Tsar-kolokol** (Царь-колокол; Tsar Bell), the world's largest, has never rung and never will: an 11.5-ton piece cracked off after a fire in 1737. Also open to visitors, the **Oruzheynaya i Vystavka Almaznovo Fonda** (Оружейная и Выставка Алмазного Фонда; Armory Museum and Diamond Fund; tel. 221 47 20) lies just to the left as you enter. All the riches of the Russian Church, and those of the state not in the Hermitage, can be found in these nine rooms. Room 3, on the second floor, holds the legendary **Fabergé eggs**—each opens to reveal an impossibly intricate jewelled miniature. Room 6 holds thrones and other royal necessities: crowns and dresses (Empress Elizabeth is said to have had 15,000 gowns, only one of which is on display). Room 9 contains royal coaches and sleds—Elizabeth (not one for understatement) had her sled pulled by 23 horses. The Diamond Fund (tel. 229 20 36), in an annex of the Armory, has still more glitter, including a 190-carat diamond given to Catherine the Great by Gregory Onov, a special friend of hers. That's all of the kremlin you can actually go into, except for the **Kremlin Palace of Congresses,** the square white monster built by Khrushchev in 1961 for Communist Party Congresses. It's also a theater, one of the few open in summer for concerts and ballets. (Kremlin open Fri.-Wed. 10am-4pm. 12,000R, students 6000R; includes tour. Diamond Fund US$17. Armory free.)

Near the Kremlin

Aleksandrovsky Sad (Александровский Сад; Aleksandr Gardens) is more than just the place to buy kremlin tickets; this pleasant garden is a cool green respite from central Moscow's carbon monoxide fumes. At the north end, at the **Mogila Neizvestnovo Soldata** (Могила Неизвестного Солдата; Tomb of the Unknown Soldier), an eternal flame burns in memory of the catastrophic losses the country suffered in WWII, known in Russia as the Great Fatherland War. Twelve urns containing soil from the Soviet Union's "Hero Cities"—the ones that withstood especially heavy casualties—stand there as well. It used to be the trendy spot to get your picture taken on your wedding day—that and Lenin's mausoleum.

    Gosudarstvenny Universalny Magazin GUM (Государственный Универсальный Магазин ГУМ; State Department Store; tel. 221 57 63), built in the 19th century, was designed to hold 1000 stores, and its arched wrought-iron-and-glass roofs resemble a 19th-century train station. During Soviet rule, going to the GUM was a depressing experience; the sight of 1000 empty stores is pretty grim. These days, however, it has been completely renovated and is a shopping mall of which any American metropolis would be proud. Most stores quote prices in US$ or DM, although you can pay in rubles. Gucci and Pierre Cardin already have stores here, and Calvin Klein and Turkish designer Mine Nisanci are opening up stores in 1998. Enter by the History Museum. (GUM open Mon.-Sat. 8am-9pm, Sun. 11am-7pm.)

    There is perhaps no more familiar symbol of Moscow than **Pokrovsky Sobor** (Покровский Собор; St. Basil's Cathedral; formerly known as Собор Васили Блажного, *Vasiliya Blazhnovo*; that's right, the one pictured on the cover of this guide). Completed in 1561, it was commissioned by Ivan the Terrible to celebrate his 1552 victory over the Tatars in Kazan. The nine main chapels are named after the saints' days on which Ivan won his battles, but the cathedral itself used to bear the moniker of a holy fool, Vasily—anglicized to Basil—who correctly predicted that Ivan would murder his own son. Before the Kazan victory, Vasily died and was buried in the church that once stood on this ground. The grand cathedral that replaced it has seen the addition of a few minor domes since Ivan's time, as well as the innovative 17th-century colorful patterns for which the domes are known. The interior is filled with intricate, but reconstructed, frescoes. Downstairs sits an exhibit on the history of the church and Ivan's campaign against the Tatars, all in Russian. (Open Wed.-Mon. 10am-4:30pm. 25,000R, students 15,000R. Buy tickets from the *kassa* to the left of the entrance, then proceed upstairs.)

    Kazansky Sobor (Казанский Собор; Kazan Cathedral) stands on the opposite end of the square. This orange-and-gold birthday-cake church has been reopened for services after being completely demolished in 1936 to make way for May Day parades. The interior is much plainer than that of most Russian churches, and the iconostasis is free of gold Baroque madness. There is a healthy mix of tourists and worshippers, so don't worry too much about the myriad of rules on the door (open daily 8am-7pm; services at 8am and 5pm).

    In the glory days, **Mavzoley V.I. Lenina** (Мавзолей В.И. Ленина; Lenin's Tomb), a squat red tomb in front of the kremlin, was guarded by fierce goose-stepping guards, and the line to get in was three hours long. The guards have now been replaced by one bored cop, and the line has completely vanished—making getting in, at least when it's open, a cinch. No photos are allowed of Vlad's embalmed remains, and backpacks and bags must be checked at the cloakroom in Aleksandrovsky Sad.

Entrance to the mausoleum also gives access to the **kremlin wall,** where Stalin, Brezhnev, Andropov, Gagarin, and John Reed, author of *Ten Days that Shook the World,* among others, are buried (open Tues.-Thurs. and Sat.-Sun. 10am-1pm). As you admire the mausoleum on your stroll around Krasnaya pl., note the balcony on top, where Russia's leaders stood during May Day and November 7 parades. Rumor has it that the plushest bathroom in Moscow is hidden somewhere in the back. Unfortunately, it has not yet been opened to the public.

Art Museums

Since the most recent revolution, **Muzey Izobrazitelnykh Iskusstv im. A.S. Pushkina** (Музей Изобразительных Искусств им. А.С. Пушкина; Pushkin Museum of Fine Arts), ul. Volkhonka 12 (tel. 203 95 78), M1: Kropotkinskaya, is becoming better organized, with new buildings to house its large collection of European Renaissance, Egyptian, and Classical art. Russia's second most famous art museum (after St. Petersburg's Hermitage), the Pushkin was founded in 1912 by poet Marina Tsvetaeva's father, who wanted his art students to have the opportunity to see Classical art in the original. It gained the majority of its impressive exhibits after the revolution ensured that no museum would be one of private possessions. The Egyptian art on the first floor and the French Impressionists (mainly Monets) on the second are understandably major pilgrimage areas, but as the museum frequently rotates its large collection, spending time in each section is probably more advisable. Although not as daunting as many museums of its caliber, this one still requires a day. Each floor has a detailed plan, and audio tours (30min., 15,000R) help guide the way (open Tues.-Sun. 10am-7pm, *kassa* closes at 6pm; 40,000R, students 20,000R). The aquamarine building to the left of the main entrance houses the three-floor **Museum of Private Collections,** which exhibits famous foreign and Russian art from the 19th and 20th centuries. The museum began when Ilya Siberstein donated his collection to the state, and asked that it be placed in the old Prince Yard Hotel, frequented by Ilya Repin and Maxim Gorky. The exhibits are not chronological, but focus on the private individual collector—a sign that even museums here are changing. Your ticket from the main building will get you in here as well, but keep in mind that the Private Collection closes at 5pm, not 7pm.

Located in Moscow's inner south section of churches and 18th-century manor houses, **Tretyakovskaya Galereya** (Третьяковская Галерея), Lavrushensky per. 10 (Лаврушенский; tel. 230 77 88), M7: Tretyakovskaya, exhibits some of the most important Russian paintings and sculptures, as well as a magnificent collection of icons. The icons have been the subject of some debate recently, as many of the churches from which they were taken wish to reclaim them. Although the collection contains a number of modern works (including Malevich's infamous *Black Square*), the museum's Mona Lisa equivalent is the 12th-century Vladimir icon *God and Mother,* taken from Constantinople. The icon hung for centuries in the Kremlin's Uspensky Sobor, and allegedly protected Moscow from the Poles (open Tues.-Sun. 10am-8pm; 36,000R, students 18,000R).

Moscow boasts an impressive collection of other museums of national and international significance; the more renowned ones are listed below. **The Moscow Metro,** one of the most beautiful in the world, is worth a tour of its own. All stations are unique, and those inside the ring line are elaborate, with mosaics, sculptures, and crazy chandeliers. It's only 2000R—and with trains coming every two minutes, you can stay as long you as like, with no *babushka* in the corner to yell at you. Stations **Kievskaya, Mayakovskaya,** and **Ploshchad Revolutsii** (with a statue on each step) are particularly good, as are **Novoslobodskaya, Rimskaya,** and **Mendeleevskaya.** Note the atomic-model light fixtures in the Mendeleevskaya station (open daily 6am-1am).

Gosudarstvennaya Tretyakovskaya Galereya (Государственная Третьяковская Галерея; State Tretyakov Gallery), ul. Krymsky Val 10 (Крымский Вал; tel. 928 41 06). M1, 4: Park Kultury. Directly opposite the Gorky Park entrance, on the right side. Built to house newer works and exhibitions of Russian art, it shares a building with the **Central House of Artists;** the Tretyakov is the building in back, with an entrance to the right side. Comprehensive Russian art exhibits: the ground floor usually hosts contemporary art, while the 2nd floor is devoted to showcasing different 19th-century artists. The top floor contains the permanent exhibit, a huge retrospective of Russian art from the 1910s to the 30s, which intelligently describes the development of Socialist Realism. Open Tues.-Sun. 10am-8pm. *Kassa* open until 7pm. 25,000R, students 12,000R; Russians 6000R, Russian students 2000R. Behind the gallery to the right lies a makeshift **graveyard for fallen statues.** Once the main dumping ground for decapitated Lenins and Stalins, now it contains plaques and neat pathways to ease your journey among sculptures of Gandhi, Einstein, and Niels Bohr, among others. Stalin himself, nose broken, lies uncomfortably on his elbow, and the unfortunate Khrushchev's head rolls in the grass. In the background, notice the enormous Christopher Columbus-like statue of Peter the Great; a bronze atrocity, it is one of Moscow's most controversial monuments.

Tsentralny Dom Khudozhnika (Центральный Дом Художника; Central House of Artists; tel. 238 96 34), ul. Krymsky Val 10. M1, 4: Park Kultury. Houses numerous small exhibits. Cutting-edge Russian art as well as fast-changing progressive historical exhibits. Consult *The Moscow Times* for info, or go to the auction hall and start a private collection of your own. Open Tues.-Sun. 11am-8pm. 15,000R.

Manege (Манеж), Manezhnaya pl. (Манежная; tel. 202 89 76). M1: Okhotny Ryad. A big yellow building with white columns. This one-time riding school for the military is now the Central Exhibition Hall, and often features interesting modern Russian exhibits. Enter from the north end, on the square. Open Wed.-Mon. 11am-8pm; *kassa* closes 1hr. before exhibitions.

Vse-rossysky Muzey Dekorativno-Prikladnovo (Все-российский Музей Декоративно-Прикладного; All-Russia Museum of Decorative and Applied Folk Art), Delegatskaya ul. 3 (Делегатская; tel. 923 77 25; fax 923 06 20), just north of the Garden Ring. M8: Tsvetnoi Bulvar. This is what the junk they sell on the Arbat is supposed to look like. The 1st building, where you buy your tickets, contains rooms of fine- quality painted and lacquered wood, 17th- and 18th-century textiles, and samovars. The 2nd, ul. Delegatskaya 5, is more interesting—the 1st room juxtaposes traditional Russian peasant costumes of the last century against what the St. Petersburg glitterati were wearing in the same period. Open Sat.-Thurs. 10am-4pm; *kassa* closes 3pm. Closed last Thurs. of every month. 7000R, students 3000R.

Muzey Narodnovo Iskusstva (Музей Народого Искусства; Museum of Folk Art), ul. Stanislavskovo (tel. 290 52 22). M6: Pushkinskaya. No sign on the door; the large black doors are the entrance to this 1-room museum. The exhibit changes continually, with the right half of the room simply for display and the left half for sale. Open Sun.-Tues. 11am-5:30pm. 5000R, students 2500R. Art from 10,000R.

Historical Museums

Muzey Revolyutsii (Музей Революции; Museum of the Revolution), ul. Tverskaya 21 (tel. 299 67 24; fax 299 85 15). M6: Pushkinskaya. Housed in the former mansion of the Moscow English club, this museum actually covers everything *since* the revolution, although it often has exhibits from previous centuries. Amazingly, this Soviet archive has progressed with the times, adding statistics on the ill effects of socialism (in 1989, 40% of pensioners earned less than 60 rubles per month), as well as eclectic documents on subjects such as 80s rock bands. Even their beat-up trolley has a recent story to tell: it was the one damaged in the August 1991 coup that clinched Yeltsin's support. But it's the museum shop on the 1st floor that reflects a revolutionizing Russia. One of the best places to buy Soviet medals, this store also stocks old posters and T-shirts with slogans like "The Party is Over" or "Хард Рок Кафе." Museum open Tues., Thurs., and Sat. 10am-6pm, Wed. 11am-7pm, Sun. 10am-5pm. 10,000R, English tour 150,000R.

Muzey Istorii Moskvy (Музей Истории Москвы; Museum of the History of Moscow), Novaya pl. 12 (Новая; tel. 924 84 90). M5, 6: Kitai-Gorod. A Soviet-era museum where they still turn the lights on as you go through. The collection consists of anything old and pretty enough to display. The ground floor houses archaeological finds from the area and old maps and plans, showing how Moscow expanded from the kremlin. Upstairs are 19th-century knick-knacks and Lev Tolstoy's desk chair. Open Tues., Thurs., and Sat.-Sun. 10am-6pm, Wed. and Fri. 11am-7pm. 20,000R.

Tsentralny Muzey Vooruzhennykh Sil SSSR (Центральный Музей Вооруженных Сил СССР; Central Museum of the Armed Forces of the USSR), ul. Sovetskoy Armii 2 (Советской Армий; tel. 281 48 77; fax 281 77 35). M4: Novoslobodskaya, then walk down ul. Seleznevskaya (Селезневская) to the square and go left; the museum is a block down on the right. Military paraphernalia from WWII; the most interesting is the milepost 41 marker from the Moscow-Leningrad highway, the closest the Nazis ever got to Moscow. Lots of tanks, guns, and propaganda posters. Open Wed.-Sun. 10am-5pm, closed 2nd Tues. and last week of each month. 20,000R.

The White House, M4: Krasnopresnenskaya. You can't visit this symbol of the 1993 political upheaval. But since you've probably already seen it on TV, stroll by and see what it's like in times of relative peace. Yeltsin climbed atop a tank here, brandishing the flag of the Russian Federation, and declared himself the only legitimate ruler of the country. Not long after, Yeltsin switched positions when he bombarded an anti-reformist Parliament with cannonfire during the October 1993 coup. The building has since been renovated, but if you look closely you can still see bullet holes in the fence. From the Metro station, take a left and follow the trail of red ribbons and makeshift monuments.

Borodino, Kutuzovsky pr. 38 (tel. 148 19 65). M3: Kutozovskaya, then 10min. to the right down Kutozovsky pr. A giant statue of Commander Kutuzov stands in front of the large circular building that houses the Borodino panorama and museum. Commemorating the bloody battle with Napoleon in August 1812, the 360° painting and accompanying exhibitions usually require you to wait in line along with the others eager to enter this bizarre memorial. Open Sat.-Thurs. 10am-4pm. 15,000R.

Houses of the Literary and Famous

Russians take immense pride in their formidable literary history, preserving authors' houses in their original state, down to half-empty teacups on the mantelpiece. Each is guarded by a team of fiercely loyal *babushki*. Plaques on buildings throughout the city mark where writers, poets, artists, and philosophers lived and worked.

Lev Tolstoy Estate, ul. Lva Tolstovo 21 (Льва Толстого; tel. 246 94 44). M1, 4: Park Kultury. A hefty walk down Komsomolsky pr. toward the colorful Church of St. Nicholas of the Weavers; turn right at the corner on ul. Lva Tolstovo. The estate is 3 blocks up on the left. The author lived here winters 1882-1901. He spent the summers at Yasnaya Polyana (a beautiful daytrip 200km south reachable only by car), which may explain why he kept the large garden overgrown and wild; the current curators have left the lush dark green foliage as unkempt as in Tolstoy's day. One of the most perfectly preserved house-museums in Moscow—it seems as if the author and his family have just stepped out for a walk and will be back at any moment. Tolstoy was apparently a man of habit; he always drank barley or acorn coffee, dined at 6pm every evening, and wrote *The Resurrection* in the study here between exactly 9am and 3pm every day. But the personalities of Tolstoy's children, many of whom died young, are present in the house too, providing a more comprehensive understanding of the author as a father. Helpful explanations of each of the rooms are provided in English. See the bicycle Papa Tolstoy learned to ride at the age of 60. The *kassa* is to the right of the entrance gate or, if that is closed, in the yellow house down a path to the left inside the entrance. Open in summer Tues.-Sun. 10am-6pm, *kassa* open until 5pm; off-season 10am-3pm; closed last Fri. of the month. 20,000R, students 10,000R, Russians 5000R.

Alexei Tolstoy Museum-Apartment, ul. Spiridonovka 4 (Спиридоновка, tel. 290 09 56), M6: Pushkinskaya or M3: Arbatskaya, next to Gorky's apartment. Alexei Tolstoy lived here from 1941-1945, shortly after winning the Stalin Prize for his novel *Peter the Great.* Grander than most museums with its collection of classical paintings and chandeliers. Placards in English explain each room, as do the *babushki* standing guard. Open Thurs. and Sat.-Sun. 11am-5:30pm, Wed. and Fri. 1-5:30pm. 10,000R, students 6000R.

Muzey Tropinina (Музей Тропинина), Shchetininsky per. 10 (Щетининский; tel. 231 17 99). M8: Polyanka. A superb 19th-century building owned by the serf Tropinin, chock-full of paintings by Russian artists. Often has exhibits on Russian 19th-century life. Open Mon. and Thurs.-Fri. noon-6pm, Sat.-Sun. 10am-4pm. 5000R.

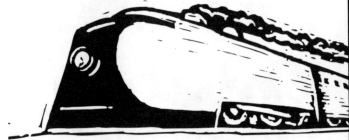

Bakhrushin Theater Museum, ul. Bakhrushina 31 (Бахрушина; tel. 233 44 70). M2, 4: Paveletskaya, and turn left (across the street from the station). One of the numerous theater museums in Moscow, it celebrates one of Russia's great art forms with a chronologically arranged permanent exhibit of costumes, dressers, programs, photos, and other intricately crafted theatrical creations. The pamphlet at the desk tells you, in English, all you need to know. Open Mon., Thurs., and Sat.-Sun. noon-7pm, Wed. and Fri. 1-8pm. *Kassa* closes 1hr. before the museum.

Gorky's Apartment, ul. Malaya Nikitskaya 6/2 (Малая Никитская; former Kachalova; tel. 290 51 30). M6: Pushkinskaya. A pilgrimage site more for its architectural interest than for its collection of Maksim Gorky's possessions. Designed by Shekhtel in 1906, this house is one of the best examples of Art Nouveau you'll find. The main staircase is modeled to project the feeling and movement of waves on the sea. Open Wed. and Fri. noon-5pm, Thurs. and Sat.-Sun. 10am-6pm, closed last Thurs. of the month. Tours 30,000R.

Chekhov's House Museum, ul. Sadovaya-Kudrinskaya 6. M6: Barrikadnaya. Chekhov lived here from 1886 until 1890, both writing and receiving patients—but you won't get as much of a feel for the author/doctor as he did for the Russian psyche. Open Tues., Thurs., and Sat.-Sun. 11am-6pm, Wed. and Fri. 2-8pm. *Kassa* closes 1hr. earlier. Closed last Fri. of each month.

Muzey Evgeny Evgenevich, pr. Marshala Zhykova 20/45 (Маршала Жыкова; tel. 319 19 73). M6: Polezhayevskaya. From the Metro, take bus #43 or 65 to the 3rd stop, and walk up 50m and in a bit from the street to find the building. Located near the once-fashionable Serebriny Bor (Silver Forest) neighborhood which housed Communist party *apparatchiks,* the museum consists of the small two-room apartment where the novelist was born. Although his works never received the worldwide attention he had hoped for, some nevertheless consider Evgenevich to be the "Russian Joyce." Evgenevich compared himself to rival Vladimir Nabokov, as his family also fled the Bolshevik regime—then he wound up at Oxford, while Nabokov attended the rival institution. An English brochure (5000R) explains the chronology of the writer's life, outlining the particulars of his travels in Russia and Europe which eventually led to the publications of "Я и мигрант" (*Migrant and Me*), his magnum opus. Open Mon.-Tues. and Thurs.-Fri. 9am-6pm, Sat. 9am-4pm. *Kassa* closes 1hr. earlier. Closed last Fri. of each month. 25,000R, students 10,000R.

Dom-muzey Shalyapina (Дом-музей Шаляпина; Shalyapin House-Museum), Novinsky bul. 25 (Новинский; tel. 252 25 30 or 252 62 36). M6: Barrikadnaya. This tastefully furnished house where opera singer Shalyapin hung his hat from 1910 until 1922 was donated by the musician's son to serve as a museum; it is better known as a concert hall for fall and winter performances. Open Tues. and Sat. 10am-6pm, Wed.-Thurs. 11:30am-7pm, Sun. 10am-4pm. 5000R, English tours 35,000R.

Muzey-dom Stanislavskovo (Музей-дом Станиславского; Stanislavsky Museum-House), Leontevsky per. 6 (Леонтьевский; formerly Stanislavskovo; tel. 229 24 42). M6: Pushkinskaya. Walk down ul. Tverskaya, and take a right on ul. Leontevsky. The respected theater director held lessons in his home, the rooms of which have different themes. More interesting than his upstairs apartment, however, are the collections of costumes in the basement used for famous productions of Gogol's *Government Inspector* and Shakespeare's *Othello.* The *babushki* will proudly explain the director's importance and point out the vase offered to Stanislavsky by Isadora Duncan. Open Thurs. and Sat.-Sun. 11am-6pm, Wed. and Fri. 2-9pm, closed last Thurs. of each month. 5000R, with Russian tour 30,000R.

Literaturny Muzey Pushkina (Литературный Музей Пушкина; tel. 201 32 56), ul. Prechisterka 12/2 (Пречистерка; formerly Kropotkinskaya), at the corner of Khrushchevsky per. (Хрущевский). M1: Kropotkinskaya. In case you haven't experienced Pushkin-worship first-hand, this carefully tended museum will convince you that Pushkin is indeed much beloved. If the 1st editions Pushkin owned don't thrill, his doodles should amuse. Unfortunately, it was closed in 1997 for renovations. Usually open Wed.-Sun. 10am-6pm, closed last Fri. of the month.

Muzey Gertsena (Музей А. И. Герцена), Sivtsev Vrazhek per. 27 (Сивцев Вражек; tel. 241 58 59), on a side street parallel to Arbat. M3: Arbatskaya. Take a left off Arbat one street before the graffiti wall, then turn right at the 1st street and look left. Residence of philosopher-novelist A. Gertsen from 1843-46. A fairly typical and well reconstructed 19th-century mansion with much of Gertsen's furniture and unique portraits. Gertsen wrote the novels *The Thieving Magpie, Doctor Krovpo,* and *Who Is to Blame* in the 3 years he lived here. Open Tues., Thurs., and Sat.-Sun. 11am-6pm, Wed. and Fri. 1-6pm. 5000R.

Muzey Gogolya (Музей Гоголя), Nikitsky bul. 7 (tel. 291 12 40). M3: Arbatskaya. It's actually only 2 small rooms inside a library. But at least it provides a glimpse of the brilliant 19th-century writer's life and a look at his meager possessions—without costing a ruble. Open Mon.-Thurs. noon-5:45pm.

Dom-muzey Lermontova (Дом-музей Лермонтова; Lermontov House-Museum), ul. Malaya Molchanovka 2 (Малая Молчановка; tel. 291 52 98), off Novy Arbat. M3: Arbatskaya. Russia's much-loved and respected poet lived in this small house— appropriately preserved and guarded. Enter through the white gate to see another example of fairly well-to-do 19th-century life. Open Tues., Thurs., and Sat.-Sun. 11am-5pm, Wed. and Fri. 2-5pm.

Art Galleries

Moskovskaya Galereya (Московская Галерея), ul. Kuznetsky Most 11 (tel. 925 42 64). M6: Kuznetsky Most, then turn left. Not to be confused with the much larger **House of Artists** across from Gorky Park, this is a gallery of contemporary art, and unlike most museums, offers a picture of Russian cultural achievement that hasn't been spoiled by some state planner—it's what people are doing here, *now.* Four large rooms, informally hung with the latest stuff. Works include sculpture, prints, lithographs, and paintings. Buy tickets at the *kassa* in the art supply store. Open Mon. and Wed.-Sun. noon-6:30pm; 3000R.

Exhibition Hall of the Russian Academy of Art, ul. Prechistenka 21/12 (tel. 201 74 25). M1: Kropotkinskaya, near the Pushkin Literary Museum. A well-visited exhibit hall that displays the work of trendy artists, including some from the Soviet period. Exhibits change periodically. Open Wed.-Fri. noon-8pm, Sat.-Sun. 10am-6pm. *Kassa* closes an hour earlier. 5000R, students 2000R.

MARS Gallery, ul. Malaya Filevskaya 32 (Малая Филевская; tel. 146 20 29; fax 144 84 26). M3: Pionerskaya. Widely known for contemporary and avant-garde art. Check *The Moscow Times* for exhibits. Open Tues.-Sun. noon-8pm.

Universal Art Gallery, Petrovsky bul. 14 (tel. 202 46 68), on the premises of the modern Drama Academy. M8: Tsvetnoy Bulvar. Impressive collection of Russian Impressionism and Realism from the 1930s-60s, including works by Radimov and Ioganson. Paintings and graphics by Socialist Realists. Open Tues.-Sun. 2-8pm.

Irida, Prospekt Mira 68 (tel. 971 03 28). M5: Rizhkaya. Paintings, tapestries, ceramics, clothing, *matryoshka* dolls—you name it—all by Russian *women* artists. Open daily 11am-7pm.

Monasteries, Churches, and Synagogues

If the grime and bedlam get to you, escape to one of Moscow's hidden parks, churches, or monasteries. Before the Revolution, the city had more than 1000 operational churches; today, fewer than 100 still stand. Among the most famous is **Novodevichy Monastyr** (Новодевичий Монастырь; tel. 246 85 26; M1: Sportivnaya). Take the exit out of the Metro that does not go to the stadium, then a right on that street. The convent is several blocks down on the left. You can't miss the high brick walls, golden domes, and tourist buses. Tsars and nobles kept the coffers filled by exiling their well-dowried wives and daughters here when they grew tired of them. Buried within the monastery's walls are some well-known 16th-century Russians, but all the truly famous folks are entombed at the cemetery next door. Just wandering around the grounds is rewarding on a pleasant day, but a few of the buildings are also open. The **Smolensky Sobor** (Смоленский Собор; Smolensk Cathedral), in the center of the convent, shows off some Russian icons. Unfortunately, due to staff shortages, it is closed in rainy weather. Other buildings of interest include **Uspenskaya Tserkov** (Успенская Церковь; Assumption Church; tel. 246 85 26), to the right of Smolensky, and a small three-room **exhibit hall** at the far end of the grounds. Entrance to the grounds is 2000R; to buy tickets to the other buildings, stop by the white *kassa* on the left once you enter the gate. (Open Wed.-Mon. 10am-5pm; closed 1st Mon. of each month. 25,000R. Avoid Sun., when tour buses hog the place.)

Turning right and down the street, the convent's **kladbishche** (кладбище; cemetery) cradles the graves of Gogol, Chekhov, Stanislavsky, Khrushchev, Shostakovich, Mayakovsky, Bulgakov, and other luminaries. The tombstones are often highly creative representations—visual or symbolic—of the deceased. Once closed to prevent too many from flocking to Khrushchev's tomb (straight through the entrance at the back of the cemetery), it is now open to the public. The writers are conveniently clustered near each other. When tombstone shopping, Bulgakov's wife saw the stone and knew immediately this would be perfect for her deceased husband. Upon buying it, she learned it had originally been considered for Gogol, whom Bulgakov greatly admired. Buy tickets at the small kiosk across the street from the entrance; a useful map (7000R, Cyrillic only) of the cemetery is also sold here (open daily 10am-6pm).

Danilovsky Monastery (M8: Tulskaya), is home to the head of the Russian Orthodox Church, the Patriarch. Although the grounds and building are stunning, there is little but the exterior to see. A map on the left side of the entrance explains the different buildings, and it's worth a visit simply to see the long-robed monks scurrying about their business. The Patriarch's office is hard to miss, due to an enormous mosaic of a stern-looking man watching over the visitors to his domain. The monastery itself is a montage of pastels, with buildings freshly painted in soft pinks, yellows, and blues. Entrance is free; simply turn right from the Metro, and you can't miss the whitewashed walls and turrets (open daily 6am-7pm; services Mon.-Fri. 7am and 5pm, Sat.-Sun. 9am and 5pm).

Donskov Monastery (tel. 452 16 46; M5: Shabolovskaya), the least famous of Moscow's monasteries, is, as a result, the most authentic, and incredibly serene. From the Metro, head right on Shabolovka until the second street, then turn right again. Since the fall of Communism, the red-brick Donskov has gained a congregation, but not quite its 1591 prestige. Still, on Russian Orthodox holidays the monastery teems with life, and on other days it sits peacefully in the golden sunlight. The church straight ahead from the entrance is cased in clearly painted frescoes, while the smaller church to the right is also operational, but, due to its greater age, less ornate (open daily 7am-7pm; services daily at 8am and 5pm; women should cover their heads).

The **Moscow Choral Synagogue,** Bolshoy Spasoglinishchevsky per. 10 (Большой Спасоглинищевский; formerly ul. Arkhipova; tel. 923 96 97; M5, 6: Kitai-Gorod), is large, airy, and lovely. Head north on Solyansky Proezd (Солянский Проезд), then take the first left. The synagogue, first constructed in the 1870s, is a pleasant respite from ubiquitous onion domes. It functioned during Soviet rule, though KGB agents stationed across the street were instructed to take pictures of anyone entering (later to be used as negative evidence), thus preventing all but the boldest of Moscow's Jews from participating in services. Today more than 200,000 Jews officially live in Moscow, and services are increasingly well-attended, especially on holidays. The interior of the synagogue has two prayer rooms; the main room is marked by 10 chandeliers and a patterned square ceiling that protects the upper level, where women must sit. The graffiti occasionally sprayed on the building serves as a reminder that Russian anti-Semitism is not dead. Regular services are held every morning and evening, presided over by Swiss rabbi Pinchas Goldsmith. Sabbath services are held Saturday mornings at 9am. Otherwise, the synagogue is open daily 9:30am-6pm. A small restaurant on the premises serves kosher food (open Sun.-Mon. 9am-6pm).

The **Spaso-Andronikov Monastyr** (Спасо-Андроников), at Andronevskaya pl. (Андроневская; M7: Ploshchad Ilicha) on the banks of the Yauza river, which branches off from the Moscow river, preserves life-size 16th-century icons and a biblical text from the 14th century. The monastery itself dates from the 1360s; master of iconography Andrei Rublyov was once a monk here and is buried inside. The tiny **Muzey Andreya Rubleva** (Музей им. Андрея Рублева), across the street through the park (tel. 278 14 89), showcases several beautiful icons but, strangely, nothing by Rublyov. (Open Mon.-Tues. and Thurs.-Sun. 11am-6pm, closed last Fri. of the month. *Kassa* closes 5pm. 35,000R, students 7000R, free last Thurs. of the month.)

An 18th-century ecclesiastical gem, **Tserkov Ioanna Voina** (Церковь Иоанна Воина; Church of St. John the Warrior), ul. Bolshaya Yakimanka 54 (Большая Якиманка; formerly Dimitrova; M4, 5: Oktyabrskaya), takes its name from the patron saint of the tsar's musketeers (open Tues.-Fri. 8am-7pm, Sun. 7am-7pm; services Tues.-Sun. at 5pm). The city's inner south region is speckled with numerous churches, sometimes boarded up. **Yelokhovsky Cathedral,** ul. Spartakovskaya 15 (Спартаковская; M3: Baumanskaya), is Moscow's largest and perhaps most beautiful operational church. Built in 1845, only the gilded interior outshines the brilliant turquoise exterior. The cathedral has the grand honor of being one of the main administrative locations of the ever-growing Russian Orthodox Church (open daily; call for service times).

Nikolskaya Tserkov v Khamovnikakh (Никольская Церковь в Хамовниках; Church of St. Nicholas of the Weavers) is one of Moscow's better-known churches, mainly because it's very hard to miss. Located at the corner of Komsomolsky pr. and ul. Frunze (Фрунзе) across from the popular Cafe Guria (M1, 4: Park Kultury), it looks like Hansel and Gretel's witch designed it, with deliciously artificial green-and-orange trimming. Enter off ul. Frunze to witness the low ceilings and colorful interior (open Mon.-Sat. 8am-7pm, Sun. and holidays 7am-7pm; service begins at opening).

Finally, you can't leave Moscow without visiting what is surely the city's most controversial landmark, the enormous, gold-domed **Khram Khrista Spositelya** (Храм Христа Спосителя; Cathedral of Christ the Savior; M1: Kropotkinskaya), between ul. Volkhonka (Волхонка) and the Moscow river. These days, it's visible from just about anywhere in the western part of the city. Believe it or not, the city government of Moscow, led by Mayor Yury Luzhkov, constructed the cathedral that stands here today in a mere two years, on the site of the former **Moscow swimming pool.** Nicholas I had originally placed a cathedral on this spot to commemorate Russia's victory over Napoleon, but in 1934 Stalin had it dynamited so that he could erect a "Palace of the Soviets," which he wanted to be the tallest building in the world, on the spot. The so-called "Palace" was to be topped with a 100m statue of Lenin (the world's tallest statue). The ground on which the great building was to stand ultimately proved to be too soft to hold a building of such weight, and after Stalin's death Khrushchev abandoned the project and instead turned the site into the Moscow outdoor swimming pool. Although 20,000 people per day used the pool, in the early 90s it was discovered that vaporization from the heated water damaged paintings at the nearby Pushkin Museum, so the pool was closed. In 1994-95 a controversy erupted over what was to become of the site; the Orthodox Church and Moscow's mayor finally won out to raise funds to build the US$250 million cathedral that stands there today. As for where they got the money—well, let's just say it was a miracle.

Regions for Walking

The **Arbat** (M3: Arbatskaya), a pedestrian shopping arcade, was once a showpiece of *glasnost* and a haven for political radicals, Hare Krishnas, street poets, and *metallisti* (heavy metal rockers). Now, it boasts a McDonald's, a Baskin Robbins, and a Benetton. With these forerunners of capitalism, this formerly infamous street has lost much of its uniqueness and political significance. You can still buy Russian souvenirs, from amber to *matryoshka* dolls, but the commercial aspect once so unique has spread across the city. Midway up, on a sidestreet, is a graffiti wall dedicated to rocker Victor Tsoi of the Soviet group Kino, who served as an idol to many young Russians before his death in a car crash three years ago.

Intersecting but almost parallel with the Arbat runs **Novy Arbat,** a thoroughfare lined with foreign businesses (such as the Arbat Irish House), and massive Russian stores like the famous **Dom Knigi,** a giant bookstore, and **Melodiya,** a top record store. Halfway up ul. Tverskaya from Krasnaya pl., **Pushkinskaya pl.** (M6: Pushkinskaya) is Moscow's favorite rendezvous spot. Amateur politicians gather here to argue and hand out petitions, while missionary groups evangelize. All the major Russian news organizations are located in this region, perhaps one of the reasons the square is the center of free speech—though as the eight-story **Izvestia,** the formerly Communist-controlled newspaper, peers disapprovingly at Moscow's golden arches nearby, the changes are not so easy to read. Everything on the square is large—from the golden arches to the **Kinema Rossiya,** Moscow's largest movie theater, which brought *Terminator* to the masses. Follow ul. Bolshaya Bronnaya, next to McD's, down to the bottom of the hill, turn right, and follow ul. Malaya Bronnaya to **Patriarshy Prud** (Патриарший Пруд; Patriarch's Pond), where the action of Mikhail Bulgakov's *The Master and Margarita* begins. This region, known as the Margarita, is popular with artsy students and old men playing dominoes by the shaded pond.

Soviet and Old Russian architecture have their showdown on **ul. Razina** (Разина), one left turn past St. Basil's. The on- and off-ramp of the **Rossiya,** the world's largest hotel, snakes around a series of lovely churches. Turn right out of GUM down **Nikolskaya ul.** to reach **pl. Lubyanka,** currently site of the headquarters of the KGB and formerly of a huge stone Felix Dzerzhinsky, the organization's founder.

On the square's northeast corner sits **Muzey Mayakovskovo** (Музей им. В. В. Маяковского; Mayakovsky Museum), Lubyansky proezd 3/6 (Лубянский; tel. 921 93 87; fax 928 60 92), a fascinating achievement in Futurist museum design. Chairs sit at an angle and hang from walls. Convoluted red metal in the shape of fire climbs the spiral staircase; green paint spills everywhere. Look for the bust of Mayakovsky surrounded by huge crimson metal shards; the museum hides in the building behind it. The avant-garde poet and artist lived here in a communal apartment from 1919. His room is preserved at the top of the building, the eye in the storm of steel girders and shards of glass, chronicling his initial love affair with the revolution (Communist propaganda wallpapers the museum) and his travels abroad. Mayakovsky shot himself in this flat in 1930, for unknown reasons. (Open Fri.-Tues. 10am-6pm, Thurs. 1-9pm. *Kassa* closes 1hr. earlier. Closed last Fri. of the month. 3000R, guided tours well worth the 2500R in Russian, not necessarily the 70,000R in English.)

Moscow State University (МГУ; *Em Ghe Oo*), a hefty walk from M1: Universitet, lies within a single Stalinist edifice. To fully appreciate its size, you must go inside, which means persuading a student to take you. If you're desperate for expat company, hang out in the neighborhood: you're bound to run into some of the foreigners who here come to "study." Near MSU, in **Lenin Hills** (a leafy enclave overlooking the city center), is one of the city's best viewing areas, from which you can see the **Luzhniki Sports Complex,** the **Lenin Stadium**—site of the 1980 Olympics—and all of Moscow. It's also one of Moscow's premier make-out spots, despite the camera-toting tourists and kitsch vendors.

The recently-opened **Park Pobedy** (Парк Победы; Victory Park; M3: Kutuzovskaya), is a popular gathering point. The entire park and its museum was built as a lasting monument to WWII, in which 27 million Russians perished. The main square showcases stones, each inscribed with a year in which the Soviet troops fought in the war (1941-45). The stones lead to a fountain and to the gigantic semi-circular **Muzey Otechestvennoy Voyny** (Музей Отечественной Войны; Museum of the Great Fatherland War), ul. Bratya Fonchenko 11 (Братя Фонченко; tel. 449 80 44), which is devoted to documenting Russia's plight in WWII. Downstairs, six large rooms reconstruct battle scenes in 3-D imagery. Start with the Berlin room on your right and make your way to the Moscow room; the room showcasing the war in Leningrad is particularly life-like and impressive. Upstairs, a Pantheon-like room commemorates the USSR's "13 Hero Cities." On the ground level, hundreds of books record the names of the Soviet Union's war dead. The enormous wings of the museum are not yet open to the public, although even without them this may be the world's largest WWII museum (open Mon. and Wed.-Sun. 10am-6pm, *kassa* open until 5pm; closed last Thurs. of the month; free). In the park behind the WWII museum is **Muzey Voynye Tekhniki** (Музей Войные Техники; Museum of War Technology), an outdoor display of several WWII fighter planes and helicopters, including an American Douglas DC-3 that was given to the Russians. On your way back, peek into the 1995 gold-domed **Khram Chest Georgiya Pobedanostsa** (Храм Честь Георгия Победаносца; Church of St. George the Victorious), which commemorates those who died in battle.

ENTERTAINMENT

Moscow is a large, fast-paced city, with the entertainment options to prove it. Renowned theaters, opera, and ballet provide a healthy injection of culture, while parks, baths, and green outskirts prescribe a relaxing dose of thought-free repose. Going out to the **theater** can be a particularly rewarding experience, especially now that humor is no longer a commodity of the state; educated Muscovites pride themselves on their city's superb collection of theaters. Unfortunately, summer in Moscow is the wrong season for theater. The Russian companies not on vacation are usually on tour, and the only folks playing in Moscow are touring productions from other cities, which, with the exception of St. Petersburg, tend to be of lesser quality. Starting in September and running well through June, however, Moscow boasts some of the world's undisputed best theater, ballet, and opera, as well as excellent orchestras. If you buy tickets far enough in advance and don't demand front row center, you can attend very cheaply. All theaters have a model in the lobby so you can identify your seats before you buy your ticket. Tickets can usually be purchased from *kassy* located inside the theater (open noon until right before the performance starts at 7pm).

Scalpers and Intourist often snatch up tickets to performances at the Bolshoy and the Tchaikovsky Concert Hall, so if you have no luck at the box office, hang out outside the theater. Scalpers look around a lot and ask if tickets are needed with the not-so-subtle "*Bilety nada?*" or "*Bilety nyzhny?*" ("Need tickets?"). Haggle over what you think may be a fair price. Always check back at the *kassa* to be sure you are not paying too much. At the *kassa,* ask for the cheapest tickets, "*samiy dishoviy.*" These usually go for 5,000-75,000R at the Bolshoy Theater and 5000-20,000R at the Tchaikovsky Concert Hall.

Bolshoy Teatr (Большой Театр; tel. 292 00 50; fax 292 90 32). M2: Teatralnaya Pl. Literally "The Big Theater." Both the opera and ballet companies are still good, despite multiple defections abroad, and the theater itself is pure pre-revolutionary elegance. Champagne and caviar served at intermission under crystal chandeliers—pretend you're Anna Karenina or suave Vronsky. Daily performances Sept.-June at 7pm. Tickets 5000-75,000R, premieres 20,000-100,000R.

Maly Teatr (Малый Театр; tel. 923 26 21), just north of the Bolshoy on Teatralnaya pl. The "Small Theater" shows a different production every night, mostly Russian classics of the 19th and 20th centuries, including Tolstoy and Chekhov. Difficult for those who don't speak Russian, but fun for those who do. *Kassa* open Tues.-Sun. 12:30-3pm and 4-7:30pm. Daily performances at 7pm. Tickets 3000-20,000R.

Moscow Operetta Theater, ul. Boshaya Dmitrovka 6 (tel. 292 63 77), just east of the Bolshoy. Completes the M2: Teatralnaya theater triumvurate. Famous operettas staged year-round. Performances begin at 7pm. Tickets 5000-35,000R.

Tchaikovsky Conservatory's Big and Small Halls, ul. Gertsena 13 (tel. 229 81 83). M6: Pushkinskaya. Centrally located and big. *Kassa* in big hall open daily noon-7pm. Concerts almost daily at 7pm plus Sun. at 2pm. Back-row tickets for the small hall (малый зал; *maly zal*) just 5000R. During intermission, locals are known to sneak into the grander big hall (большой зал; *bolshoy zal*) to admire its pipe organ and chandeliers. Scalpers may lie and say no tickets are available when the *kassa* will sell them more cheaply.

Leninsky Komsomol (LENKOM) (tel. 299 96 68), ul. Malaya Dmitrovka. M6: Pushkinskaya. Director Mark Zakharov is well-known in Russia and attracts crowds to see dramas such as *Figaro* and *Chaika* and bright, sensational shows in the style of Broadway musicals. Performances every other day at 7pm. *Kassy* open daily 1-3pm and 5-7pm. Tickets around 15,000-50,000R.

Taganka Theater (tel. 915 12 17). M4, 6: Taganskaya. Directly across the street from the ring line exit. This avant-garde theater is the only reason to come to this oppressive square on the loud and dusty Garden Ring. Shows renowned for their satirical value. Closed in summer. *Kassa* open in winter daily 1-3pm and 5-7pm.

Mossoviet Theater, Bolshaya Sadovaya ul. 16 (tel. 299 20 35). M2: Mayakovskaya. Head director Pavel Khomsky stages popular dramas, including adaptations of Dostoevsky, Oscar Wilde, Andrew Lloyd Webber, Flaubert, and Bulgakov. Perfor-

Tusovka (too-SOV-ka)

Tusovka is a word that even Russians are be unable to define precisely, yet it's a widely used, handy expression to describe any cool gathering, from a night at a club to an art exhibition, from a street festival to a private party. *Tusovka* implies a get-together with roaming, gawking and talking, shoulder-rubbing and shoving, raving and dazing; it involves a common interest (or semblance thereof), a shared space, and a fair amount of people (no, public transportation doesn't count). It most frequently occurs at clubs and cafes, once in a while in museums. *Tusovka* can be "*klassnaya,*" "*krutaya,*" "*klyovaya*"—all different shades of "cool." At its origin sometime in the late 80s, *tusovka* referred to informal, independent, alternative, subversive, and often bohemian gatherings. These days, even conventional newspapers advertise the groovy gigs under the heading "*tusovki,*" and the casual invitation, "Let's go to a *tusovka,*" promises a hot event and cool atmosphere.

mances daily at 7pm. Tickets 10,000-40,000R, and often available. *Kassa* open daily noon-5pm.

Sovremennik (Современник), Chistoprudny bul. 19a (tel. 921 64 73). M1: Chistye Prudy. Shakespeare, Shaw, Chekhov, and Gurkin. All shows begin at 7pm. Tickets 5000-50,000R.

Stanislavsky Theater, ul. Tverskaya 23 (tel. 299 72 24). M2: Tverskaya. Named for the famous director. Mostly avant-garde productions. Closed in summer. *Kassa* open in winter daily noon-7pm.

Moscow State University Student Theater (МГУ), ul. Bolshaya Nikitskaya 3 (tel. 203 66 12). Performances vary wildly, but not prices—usually under 25,000R.

Children's Musical Theater, pr. Vernadskovo 5 (Вернадского; tel. 930 70 21). M1: Univesitet. Popular with the kiddies, and you'll be able to understand it, too. *Kassa* open daily noon-3pm and 4-6pm.

Luzhniki Dvorets Sporta (Дворец Спорта; Sports Palace), Luzhnetskaya nab. 24 (Лужнетская; tel. 201 09 55). M1: Sportivnaya. Seats 103,000 people. Site of 1980 Olympics. Rock concerts held here when they can't fit in Moscow Dinamo Stadium, north of town.

Circus

Great Moscow Circus, pr. Vernadskovo 7 (tel. 930 02 72). M1: Universitet. Used to be the greatest show on earth, then all the big stars defected, so it's the greatest show in Moscow. Performances Tues.-Fri. at 7pm, Sat.-Sun. at 11:30am, 3, and 7pm. *Kassy* open daily 11am-3pm and 4-7pm. Tickets start at 20,000R and can be purchased from "Театры" kiosks. Children under 6 free.

Old State Circus, Tsvetnoi Bulvar 13 (tel. 200 68 89). M8: Tsvetnoi Bulvar. Turn right and walk half a block; it's on the right, newly renovated. Traditional street circus. Usually has animal acts in the first half and a glittery acrobatic performance in the second. Perfect for non-Russian speakers. Eager scalpers outside, so comparison shop. Don't miss the motorcycle acrobat act of Oleshchenko and Shavro or Piotr Prostetsov's trained dogs. Performances Mon. and Wed.-Fri. at 7pm, Sat. at 8 and 7pm, Sun. at 1, 3, and 7pm. Closed on Tues. *Kassa* open daily 11am-7pm. Tickets 9000-20,000R.

Parks

From M1, 4: Park Kultury, cross the **Krimsky most** bridge to **Gorky Park,** or from M4, 5: Oktyabrskaya, enter through the main flag-flanked gate on Krimsky Val. In summer, droves of out-of-towners and young Muscovites promenade, relax, and ride the roller coaster at Moscow's **amusement park.** In winter, the paths are flooded to create a park-wide **ice rink.** A ride on the large **ferris wheel** in the center of the park affords a 360° look at the tallest of Moscow's landmarks: all the Stalinist sister buildings can be seen from the top (park open daily 11am-2am; general admission 10,000R. 150,000R for 12 rides).

Izmaylovsky Park (Измайловский Парк) is, not surprisingly, at M3: Izmaylovsky Park—go left and follow the hordes. The main reason to come this far out of the center is not the park but the colossal weekend market, called "Vernisazh" (Вернисаж). Arrive late Sunday afternoon, when people want to go home and are willing to make a deal. And comparison shop—the first painted box you see will not be the last, guaranteed. *Everything* is sold here, from carpets and samovars to military uniforms, pins, and old Soviet money. There are jewelry, shawls, old books, tacky and cool t-shirts, and Russia's favorite form of folk art: variations on the theme of painted wood—boxes, eggs, spoons, cutting boards, all decorated with designs and flowers. And, of course, the ubiquitous *matryoshki*—nesting dolls that used to be painted with pretty girls' faces, but now come in other themes. Find the tiniest Soviet premier, the seventh dwarf, and the shortest Chicago Bull. Some stalls even take orders; delivery in a week (open daily 9am-5:30pm).

Another respite from Moscow's chaos is the tsars' **Kolomenskoe Summer Residence**, on a wooded rise above the Moskva River at M2: Kolomenskaya. Follow the signs to "к музею Коломенское." Walk about 400m south on ul. Novinka (Новинка) past *Kinoteatr* (Кинотеатр), and go right just before the long fence. Peter the Great's 1702 log cabin and Bratsk Prison, where the persecuted Archpriest Avvakum wrote his celebrated autobiography, have been moved here from Arkhangelsk and Siberia respectively. The **Kazan Church** (tel. 112 03 42) holds services at opening and closing (open Mon.-Fri. 8am-1pm and 6-8pm, Sat.-Sun. 8am-8pm). At the complex's edge, overlooking the river, stands the 16th-century **Uspenskaya Sobor** (Assumption Church), the first example of a brick church built like a traditional wooden building (St. Basil's is a rather more famous example). Note the gold double-headed eagle at the top of the entrance gate: this emblem of the Romanovs, made of plastic, was installed in 1994. Red-coated guards with handy axes and swords patrol the grounds. (Grounds open daily 7am-10pm; free. Museums open Tues.-Sun. 11am-6pm; 4000R; buy tickets at the *kassa,* not at the expensive tour bureau.)

Serebryany Bor (Серебряный бор; Silver Pine Forest) is the cheapest and fastest way to get into the countryside and relax. Take trolleybus #20, which starts at M1: Okhotny Ryad and stops at Pushkinskaya pl. (in front of *Izvestia*) and Mayakovskaya pl. on its way straight up ul. Tverskaya, to the very last stop (50min.). Join the groups of Russians heading to this gorgeous natural park and island. The 2.5 sq. km are crisscrossed with paths, making it possible to explore the countryside before taking your picnic down to the riverside and sunbathing. It is, understandably, one of Moscow's favorite weekend afternoon spots—*shashlyk* stands and other signs of civilization cater to the frolicking urbanites. Much-loved by the tsars, the region now belongs to the bathing-suit-clad masses.

VDNKh (ВДНХ) lies, surprise surprise, near M5: VDNKh. Go left out of the Metro toward the pavilions. The **Vystavka Dostizhenii Narodnovo Khozyaystva** (Выставка Достижений Народного Хозяйства; Exhibition of Soviet Economic Achievements) has changed since its original conception. Now that it has been fairly conclusively demonstrated that there were no Soviet economic achievements, this World's Fair-esque park filled with pavilions (each in a more garish architectural style than the last) has become, ironically, a large department store. Pavilions proclaim "Atomic Energy" and "Education" right above signs reading "Stereos" and "Shoes." It's a fun place for a midday walk, and open-air concerts make it a good picnic spot. At the far end is the **Cosmos Pavilion,** where you can see the rocket that launched Sputnik (shops open around 10am until dark). **Zoopark** (Зоопарк; tel. 255 53 75) lies on both sides of ul. Bolshaya Gruzinskaya (Большая Грузинская; M6: Barrikadnaya). Come see animals that are generally too big for the cages provided for them, and watch Russian children feed cotton candy to everything within reach. It's a somewhat depressing experience, but popular among young Muscovites nonetheless (open Tues.-Sun. 9am-8pm; *kassa* closes at 7pm; 5000R.)

Although Moscow is filled with serene green areas, one of the largest and most popular with small children is **Krasnaya Presnya** (Красная Пресня; M6: Ulitsa 1905 goda). Walk down ul. 1905 goda until the Mezhdunarodny and turn right to find the leafy oasis, with scattered small playgrounds and wooden houses.

SHOPPING

The phrase "If you can't buy it in New York, it probably doesn't exist" can now be applied to Moscow, too. Everything is sold here, from exercise machines to French perfume, but most imports will cost a bundle. As if GUM and all the Univermags were not enough, the monstrous crater now on Manezhnaya pl., next to the kremlin, the destruction and construction of which can be viewed from a special ramp, will soon become a massive shopping complex. Typical gifts, like *matryoshka* dolls and amber, are most easily found at large markets like Izmaylovsky Park (see **Parks,** above), where they are slightly cheaper, and in tourist haunts such as the Arbat. The hidden treasures usually lie buried in local gift shops, where Russians buy cheap but beautifully crafted presents for their friends. At the **Melodiya** record store, Novy Arbat 40, you can find hard-to-get Russian classics and records by popular artists, often cheaper than in the U.S. (tapes 8000R, CDs 37,000-50,000R; open Mon.-Sat. 9am-8pm). The towering **Dom Knigi** (Дом Книги), Novy Arbat 22, is worth visiting if only to gain an understanding of the Russian love of books. Tourists and Russians alike scour the shelves for a wide variety of literature, but only the maps are in English (open Mon.-Fri. 10:30am-7:30pm, Sat. 10am-6pm). Just north of Lubyanka pl., **Torgovy Dom Biblio-Globus** (Торговый Дом Библио-Глобус), Myasnitskaya 6, is a privatized bookstore that also sells imported office supplies and electronic equipment. Art books and Russian literature, ancient and classic, can be found at excellent prices (open Mon.-Fri. 10am-7:30pm). **Global USA Superstore,** ul. Usacheva 35 (Усачева; 254 56 57; M1: Sportivnaya), stocks electronics, clothing, some food, *The Moscow Times,* and *The International Herald-Tribune* (open daily 10am-8pm).

NIGHTLIFE

Moscow's nightlife is the most kickin' action this side of the Volga, and certainly the most varied—not to mention expensive and dangerous—in Eastern Europe. While Moscow may not be New York or London, it certainly thinks it is—and it's got the cover charges to prove it (usually 100,000R). Restaurants often transform themselves into dance clubs after dark, while the casinos in this casino capital sometimes stay open 24 hours. Check the weekend editions of *The Moscow Times* or *The Moscow Tribune* for music festival listings (the annual jazz festival thrills Moscow every summer) and club reviews. *The Moscow Times'* Friday pull-out section, *MT Out,* provides an excellent synopsis of each week's events, as well as up-to-date restaurant, bar, and club reviews. Cheaper and more popular bars on isolated streets may show a better time than the dark, half-empty, elegant, and expensive "bars" close to the center, which mainly cater to "New Russians" or to no one at all.

Bars

Krizis Zhanra, per. Ostrovskovo 22/4 (Островского; tel. 241 29 40). M1: Kropotkinskaya. It's set back from the street a bit; look for the door with the light. Crammed with students and artsy types; it can often be hard to find a seat. One of the best places in Moscow to grab a beer (*Corona* 14,000R). Great, inexpensive food. Extremely popular with local and foreign students who know Moscow. Live concerts begin at 9pm. Arrive early. Open daily 11am-11pm.

Shamrock Bar, Novy Arbat 13 (tel. 291 76 81). M3: Arbatskaya. A total scene on weekend nights, this place overflows with large groups of Americans, Irish, and Russians. Chicken wings 25,000R. Bud 17,500R. Guinness 27,000R. Open Sun.-Thurs. 10am-1am, Fri.-Sat. 10am-5am. AmEx, Diners Club, MC, Visa.

Rosie O'Grady's, ul. Znamenko 9/12 (Знаменко; tel. 203 90 87). M8: Borovitskaya. Go right out of the Metro, then right on ul. Znamenko. Rosie's is on the left, at the corner of ul. Marxa i Engelsa. Friendly Irish staff and largely expat clientele. Loud and cheerful. Pub food and drinks, all somewhat pricey. Pint of Guinness 32,000R. *Corona* 23,000R. Sandwiches 19,000R. Open daily noon-1am.

John Bull Pub, Kutuzovsky pr. 4 (tel. 243 56 88). M4: Kutuzovskaya. Take a left; it's behind the Ukraine hotel. An English pub with US$5 draft beers. Chinese, Russian, and pub food. Main dishes US$6-30 with 50% discount noon-3pm. Lounge and conference room for private meetings or parties. Live pop bands, karaoke, blues, and jazz nights. Always some English-speaking staff. Open Sun.-Wed. noon-1am, Thurs.-Sat. noon-3am. AmEx, Diners Club, MC, Visa.

Moosehead Canadian Bar, ul. Bolshaya Polyanka 54 (Большая Полянка; tel./fax 230 73 33). M4: Dobryninskaya. Take a right coming out of the Metro, and hop on trolley #8. Indoor and outdoor bars with live music on weekends and a full menu of food, beer, and mixed drinks. The bartenders will make anything you request. *Tuborg* on tap (26,500 per pint). Chicken fingers 37,000R. Moose steak US$25. Moosehead burger and fries 45,000R. Come in for breakfast (a hearty Canadian one 45,000R) or stay till then. Happy hour Mon.-Fri. 6-8pm with Coors 2-for-1. Open Mon.-Fri. noon-5am, Sat.-Sun. 10am-5am.

Bednye Lyudi (Бедные Люди; Poor Folks), ul. Bolshaya Ordynka 11/6 (Большая Ордынка; tel. 231 33 42). M7: Tretyakovskaya. Loud hangout for young Russians and students from overseas, but the cheap food (under 15,000R) and great beer (you name it, they have it) draw *bednye studenty* to this bunker of a hangout. Open Mon.-Thurs. 5pm-5am, Fri.-Sun. noon-5am.

Trety Put (Третий Путь), ul. Pyatnitskaya 4 (Пятницкая; tel 231 87 34). M7: Fretyakovskaya. Welcome to your Greenwich Village loft-turned-nightclub and -bar, featuring a number of little rooms where you can watch videos, play chess, or dance to psychedelic music. Live house, techno, and experimental music. Young grunge and alternative crowd. Cover hovers around 20,000R. Open daily 9pm-2am.

The Hungry Duck, ul. Pushechnaya 9 (Пушечная; tel. 923 61 58). M1, 6: Kuznetsky Most. The younger crowd comes here to be seen when they're too drunk to see for themselves. Packed crowd, some with some clothes, some without some clothes. Most happenin' pick-up joint in the city. Live music on weekends. Free on weekdays, 30,000R cover on weekends. Open daily noon until the last drunk leaves.

Propaganda, Bolshoy Zlatoustinsky per. 7 (Большой Златустинский; tel. 924 57 32). M5, 6: Kitai-Gorod. Popular expat dance bar that also caters to a Russian grunge scene. Homey atmosphere and good, cheap beer (15,000R). No cover. Open Sun.-Thurs. 11am-2am, Fri.-Sat. 11am-6am.

Sports Bar, Novy Arbat 10 (tel. 290 43 11). M3: Arbatskaya. Next to Melodiya and across from the Irish Bar. The 2 floors fill up fast for big games; otherwise, the 2nd floor is the place to be with pool tables, darts, and mafiosi with cellular phones. A true paradise for Eurosport lovers: 8 TVs at the bar and a large screen so you can catch it from every angle. The disco is one of the city's most popular. Live bands from 9-11pm. Bottled beer 24,000R, draft 34,000R. Tonya Harding and O.J. Simpson burgers. Open daily 9:30am-midnight. Happy hour 5-8pm with "cheap" beer on special. 30,000R cover on weekends. AmEx, Diners Club, MC, Visa.

Clubs

Master, ul. Parlobskaya 6 (Парлобская; tel. 237 17 42). M4: Dobryninskaya. Mostly filled with student types, but New Russians are learning the ins and outs of techno, too. Come on Fri., when it's packed. Upstairs is hard-core techno, downstairs, commercial techno. If techno ain't your thing, this ain't the place for you. Cover 50,000R for women, 100,000R for men. Open daily 9pm-8am.

Treasure Island, ul. Bolshaya Yushunskaya 1a (Большая Юшунская; tel. 292 12 82), inside Hotel Sevastopol. M2: Kakhovskaya (a leg of the Metro in the south of Moscow). It's time to ditch the smoldering center and its smelly fumes and head out to the 'burbs. *Deep* in southern Moscow. Worth the effort for the circus-like, Broadway-inspired light show, cheap drinks, and more attractive babes with glow-in-the-dark crosses than at Berlin's Love Parade. Cover 100,000R. Open daily 10pm-6am.

Club Loutch, Pyaty Monetchikovsky per. 3 (Пяты Монетчиковский; tel. 231 94 63). M4: Paveletskaya. Formerly the happenin' club Ptyuch, this newest venue is reputedly funded by Boris Berezovsky, Russia's first billionaire; it's next to his mansion, anyway. Saturdays are best, featuring erotic rave dancing, Dr. DJ Pavlov, and none of those teenage hipsters who like to frequent the techno joints. Cover 100,000R after 11pm. Open 10pm-6am.

GAY AND LESBIAN NIGHTLIFE

A mere seven years ago, homosexuality in Russia was illegal, but now Moscow's gay community is increasingly coming out of the closet. Nevertheless, it is still not safe to appear openly gay, and nightclubs have experienced occasional police raids. Many gay establishments are unmarked, while others have instituted a card-pass system for admission. Although those who run Moscow's gay clubs take safety very seriously, they are not at all averse to admitting tourists of all orientations to the clubs. A phone call to a club should be enough to secure a pass; or call Oleg (tel. 211 87 79), a very friendly guy with tons of information about the gay scene. Some useful groups are: **Treugolnik** (Треугольник; general tel. 932 01 00), a gay and lesbian social and lobbying organization, and **AIDS Infoshare Russia** (tel. 110 24 60). Both carry info on gay and lesbian life in Russia and the former Soviet Union.

Tikhi Krig (Тихи Криг; The Quiet Circle), ul. Tryetovo Yamskovo Polya 14/16 (Третого Ямского Поля; tel. 947 97 51). M4: Belorusskaya, across the street from the Golden Palace Casino. Opened summer 1997. A laid-back establishment known as "a quiet spot for all orientations." Open 24hr.

Tri Obezyany (Три Обезяны; Three Monkeys), Trubnaya pl. 4 (Трубная; tel. 208 46 37). M8: Tsvetnoi Bulvar. Pleasant decor and absence of techno music ensure a good time, although, like Russia itself, it's difficult to get in without an invitation. Call Sergei (tel. 242 45 72) to get a pass. Cover 60,000R. Fri. and Sat. are best; Sat. is lesbian night. Open daily 6pm-9am.

Chance (Шанс), ul. Volocharskovo 11/5 (Волочарского; tel. 956 71 02), in Dom Kultury Serp i Molot (Дом Культуры Серп и Молот). M7: Ploshchad Ilicha. Walk down ul. Sergia Radonezhskovo all the way through the third open driveway on your right. When you come to a road where the tram tracks turn, walk up the stairs. It's on top of the hill, straight ahead. 3 bars and aquariums—some with naked men in them. Although the club is popular with everyone and the crowd is a mixture of ravers, punks, students, and New Russians, it's 90% gay. Downstairs is dance music, upstairs is Russian pop. Plush sofas ensure you get to know even those who are too timid to dance. Cover 30,000-100,000R, depending on the night, your gender, and how late you arrive. Open daily 11pm-6am.

Imperia Kino, ul. Povarskaya 33 (Поварская; tel. 290 44 89; M6: Barrikadnaya). Moscow's one and only official lesbian club. The large dance floor is a comfortable place for showing what you've got, to a background of house, techno, soft rock, and Russian love songs.

Banana (Банан), ul. Baumanskaya 50/12 (tel. 267 45 04). M3: Baumanskaya. Underground club east of the city center, with glow-in-the-dark decor. Music is a good mix, with occasional lapses into technomania. Hot in '97; come here to meet gay Russian men. Membership technically required for admission, but tends to be lenient. Cover for non-members 50,000R. Open daily 10pm-10am.

■ Near Moscow

SERGIEV POSAD (СЕРГИЕВ ПОСАД)

Possibly Russia's most famous pilgrimage point, Sergiev Posad attracts wandering Orthodox believers with a mass of churches huddled at its main sight—**Troitsko-Sergieva Lavra** (Троицко-Сергиева Лавра; St. Sergius's Trinity Monastery). During Soviet times, Sergiev Posad was called Zagorsk, and the town is still called this by many locals; don't be thrown off. At approximately 60km from Moscow, it's the closest town on the Golden Ring to the capital. After decades of state-propagated atheism, the stunning monastery, founded in the 1340s, has again become a religious center, and monks pace the paths between the colorful collection of churches and gardens. The patriarch of the Russian Orthodox Church, also known as the Metropolitan, resided here until 1988, when he moved to the Danilovsky Monastery in Moscow (see **Monasteries, Churches, and Synagogues,** p. 542). Although entrance into the *lavra* (the highest monastic order) is free, there are separate fees for the wall's ramparts, the folk art exhibit, the art museum, and the historical museum. Each church is exquisite, but Russian Orthodoxy's opulent colors come out in the **Trinity Cathedral,** where the numerous covered heads and quickly crossing hands entrance the visitor as much as the gilded Andrey Rublev icons. The **Chapel-at-the-Well** has an appropriately superstitious history—one day, a spring with magical healing powers allegedly appeared inside a tiny chapel in the monastery. Old women still come here with empty bottles to carry the holy water home. Next door, **Uspensky Sobor** (Успенский Собор; Assumption Cathedral), was modeled after the eponymous cathedral in Moscow's Kremlin. Outside the door on the left is the grave of Boris Godunov, who, among other things, has the distinction of being the only Russian tsar not buried in Moscow's kremlin or St. Petersburg's St. Peter and Paul Cathedral. The **Khudozhestvenny Muzey** (Художественный Музей; art museum), at the back of the complex, contains numerous icons, but many have been returned to their original churches (open Tues.-Sun. 10am-6pm; 27,000R, Russians 5000R).

Elektrichki (commuter trains) run to Sergiev Posad from Moscow's Yaroslavsky Vokzal (every 30-40 minutes, 30min., 8000R). Departure times are listed on a white board immediately outside the *prigorodnye kassy* (пригородные кассы; suburban cashiers), where the tickets are sold. Any train with the end destination "Sergiev Posad" or "Aleksandrov" (Александров) will get you there. The announcement boards in front of the trains often do not work, though; tiny strips on the sides of the trains show their destinations.

■ Smolensk (Смоленск)

Since Smolensk's founding in 863, the Tatars have sacked it, Moscow and Lithuania fought over it, Poland snatched it, Napoleon stormed it, and the Soviet state demoralized it. Abroad, the town is known best for one of the Soviet Union's most infamous wartime crimes—the Katyn massacre. Only in 1990 did Russian authorities admit that 4000 Polish officers were killed by the Soviet troops to whom they had surrendered in nearby Katyn Forest in 1940; prior to this, their deaths had been blamed on the Nazis. Today most travelers pass through Smolensk on their way from Poland to Moscow without actually ever setting foot in it; but the city, with its long history and daytrip amount of sights, is certainly worth a peek.

Orientation and Practical Information Smolensk is one of the few hilly towns in Russia, thanks to the Dnieper River's eroding currents. Old city walls surround the center on the **south bank,** the location of all sights and hotels. A **train station** (tel. 215 20), north of the river, sends trains to Moscow (10-12 per day, 6-7hr., 56,000R) and Minsk (6 per day, 5hr., 47,000R), as well as destinations west such as Berlin, Prague, Rīga, Vilnius, and Warsaw. For Kiev, take a bus from the **bus station,** just north of the train station, to Bryansk, north of the Russian-Ukrainian border (5-6 per day, 5hr.), and a train from there. Try to get your tickets beforehand, as lines tend to be long. Across the river, **Kolkhoznaya pl.** (Колхозная) hosts a farmer's market. **Ul. Bolshaya Sovetskaya** (Большая Советская) leads from the square to the center, up the hill past **Uspensky Sobor** (Успенский Собор; Assumption Cathedral). Trams #1, 4, and 7 run up ul. Bolshaya Sovetskaya to the center. The local branch of **Intourist,** ul. Konyonkova 3 (Конёнкова; tel. 314 92), near Gostinitsa Tsentralnaya, sells **maps** (7000R) and arranges tours (20,000-30,000R; open daily 9am-1pm and 2-6pm). **Store luggage** downstairs at the train station for 10,500R per bag (open 24hr. except noon-2pm and 1-3am). **Exchange currency** at *Obmen Valyuty* (Обмен Валюты) on the corner of ul. Lenina (Ленина) and ul. Bolshaya Sovetskaya (open Mon.-Sat. 10am-2pm and 4-8pm). The **central post office** can be found at ul. Oktyabrskoy Revolutsii 6 (Октябрьской Революции; open Mon.-Fri. 8:30am-6:30pm, Sat. 9am-3pm). **Telephones** at the train station serve intercity connections (open 24hr. except short mealtime breaks). **Phone code:** 08100.

Accommodations and Food All of Smolensk's hotels double their rates for foreigners, but prices are comparable with each other. **Gostinitsa Tsentralnaya** (Центральная), ul. Lenina 2/1 (tel. 317 54), is true to its name, right near the Glinka Garden and about 10min. from Uspensky Sobor. It's been recently renovated, so all rooms have baths and amenities (singles 190,000R; doubles 380,000R; 20,000R charge for reservation). To reach **Gostinitsa Rossiya** (Россия), ul. Dzerzhinskovo 23/2 (Дзержинского; tel. 339 70), take tram #3 from the train station and get off at "Спартак" (Spartak Stadium). This monster of a hotel has all the conveniences (singles 188,000R; doubles 228,000R; including bath, toilet, phone, TV, and hot breakfast).

Dark cafes squat on ul. Bolshaya Sovetskaya and ul. Lenina. The border town's large **market** (Заднепровский рынок; *Zadneprovski rynok*), ul. Belyaeva (Беляева) across the river directly downhill from the Assumption Cathedral, offers meat inside, and fruit and veggies outdoors (open daily 7am-3pm). **Holstein 777** (tel. 308 30) is on ul. Bolshaya Sovetskaya just south of ul. Lenina—look for the Holstein Beer sign. This private-venture cafe—seemingly the only one of its kind in Smolensk—has American music, foreign beer, and fairly high prices, but better food than the hotel restaurants (main dishes 20,000-50,000R; coffee 6000R; *Holstein* 16,000R; open daily noon-4am). **Restoran Rossiya** (Ресторан Россия), on ul. Dzerzhinskovo in the eponymous hotel, is lighter than most hotel eateries, with cloth napkins and flowers on the tables in a grand hall. Prices are reasonable, except for the 5000R live-music cover at dinner, which you may want to avoid anyway (open daily 7-10am and noon until the wee hours of the morning).

Sights and Entertainment The spectacular green-and-white **Uspensky Sobor** (Успенский собор; Assumption Cathedral), one of Russia's largest, rises from Smolensk's highest hill. A flight of stairs leads from ul. Bolshaya Sovetskaya to the cathedral and the eye-crushing views from its terrace. A cathedral in one form or another has stood on this site since 1101. The latest model was completed in the early 18th century, and its gilded interior is said to have so impressed Napoleon that he forbade his men from pillaging it. To the right as you enter, up a flight of steps, a 16th-century copy of St. Luke's *Virgin with Child* has returned after being stolen in 1923. Even today, masses of the devout ply it with candles in hope of the occasional miracle. (Open Mon.–Sat. 8am-8pm, Sun. 7am-9pm. Services Mon.-Sat. 9am and 6pm, Sun. 7am and 6pm; no photographs; men must enter bare-headed.)

Apart from Uspensky Sobor, the city's most striking architectural landmark are the 6km-long, 15m-high walls of the **Smolensk Kremlin**, which serve as a reminder of the many invaders the town has withstood. While the walls can be seen from many points in the city, the one spot you can actually scale a **tower** is off ul. Oktyabrskoy Revolutsii, to the left. The three towers on ul. Timiryazeva (Тимирязева) can be climbed, and a walk along the battlements provides a beautiful panorama (try to ignore the Brezhnev flats).

The second floor of **Istorichesky Muzey** (Исторический Музей; History Museum), ul. Lenina 8 (tel. 338 62), is basic town-history fare: archaeological finds from the area, some 13th-century graffiti, 15th- and 16th-century icons, and local textiles and handicrafts. These last are unusually pretty—Smolensk is a huge flax-growing region, and as a result, home to skilled weavers and embroiderers (open Tues.-Sun. 10am-6pm; 2000R, students 1500R). For more on Smolensk flax, visit **Vystavka Smolensky Lyon** (Выставка Смоленский Лён; Smolensk Flax Exhibition), on ul. Bolshaya Sovetskaya, in the pink Troitsky Monastyr (Троицкий монастырь; Trinity Monastery). This three-story exhibit shows every aspect of Smolensk's main trade in full detail, with a Soviet touch. Two floors have photographs and models of linen-producing equipment of earlier times; the results—folk dresses—hang in the final room. The top floor is a bit anomalous, with exhibits of cooperative #2031's model worker #3567 illustrating the brilliant success of mass-produced Soviet clothing; no final display is needed for this, though—you can see it on the old women on the street (open Tues.-Sun. 10am-6pm; 2000R, students 1500R).

Muzey Velikoy Otechestvennoy Voyny (Музей Великой Отечественной Войны; World War II Museum) is located at ul. Dzerzhinskovo 4a (tel. 331 19). Walk past the busts of Soviet war heroes flanking the path to the main museum—yet another proof of the devastation WWII wreaked on Russia. The personal possessions of Nazi soldiers are included here alongside photographs of Smolensk's young men who died in the Great Fatherland War. The sign "Ещё не кончилась Война" over the main exhibit means "the war still hasn't ended," which, although referring to the situation at the time, could just as easily be about Russia's attitude toward WWII today. Only for hardcore WWII buffs (open Tues.-Sun. 10am-5pm; 2000R, students 1000R).

GOLDEN RING (ЗОЛОТОЕ КОЛЬЦО)

To the north and west of Moscow lie a series of towns known as the Golden Ring (Zolotoye Koltso), with ancient churches and kremlins widely considered to be Russia's most beautiful. These towns gained importance in the 12th century as power shifted north with the weakening of Kiev. Vladimir and Sudzal were once Russian capitals and shine today as main attractions on Ring tours; Yaroslavl was the capital of its own principality in the 13th century. Today, the Golden Ring's architectural monuments and the towns' slower pace of life make a visit worthwhile.

■ Yaroslavl (Ярославль)

Yaroslavl (YAH-roh-SLAH-vl) acquired its wealth from 16th-century trade with the Middle East and the West, though even in its early days it rejected outside influence, setting a bear on Prince Yaroslav the Wise when he considered settling down on this spot. The citizens have fought as fiercely to keep out Soviet architectural monstrosities. With wide leafy boulevards, romantic river-view walks, numerous parks, and proximity to Moscow, Yaroslavl offers any tourist the best of two worlds—a provincial Russian feel with the comforts of a capital city.

ORIENTATION AND PRACTICAL INFORMATION

Yaroslavl lies on the **Volga's** west bank, 280km northeast of Moscow. It straddles the **Kotorosl** river, with most of the sights and churches off the north bank. Locals call the corner where the Kotorosl meets the Volga "*strelka*" (стрелка; the promontory). Many bus lines originate from **pl. Volkova** (Волкова). Ul. Kirova (Кирова) runs east out of this square towards the Volga. Ul. Komsomolskaya (Комсомольская) and ul. Pervomayskaya (Первомайская) lead south to **Moskovsky pr.** (Московский) and **Moskovsky Vokzal** (Московский Вокзал). The train station you will probably use, however, is **Glavny Vokzal** (Главный Вокзал). In an attempt at avoiding name-change confusion, street signs often list a whole genealogy of names, resulting in corners adorned with up to four different name plates. **Maps** (a whopping 18,000R) are available at most kiosks. It's best to avoid Yaroslavl around June 20th—or book way ahead: this is Commencement Day for the town's two military academies.

> **Tourist Office: Intourist,** Kotoroslnaya nab. 11a (Котоcrecльная; tel. 22 93 06; fax 30 54 13), on the 1st floor of Gostinitsa Yubilenaya. English-speaking staff provides a rare deal: they can **book accommodations** for 150% of the Russian rate.
> **Currency Exchange:** In the post office (open Mon.-Fri. 9:30am-1pm and 1:30-4:30pm) or at **Intermedbank** (Интермедбанк), ul. Sverdlova 18 (Свердлова). Open Mon.-Fri. 9am-9pm, Sat. 9am-6pm. No bank in town takes traveler's checks.
> **Trains:** Foreigners must get their tickets (bring your passport) at the Intourist *kassa* #4 in the advance ticket office (кассы предварительной продажи железнодорожных билетов; *kassy predvaritelnoy prodazhy zheleznodorozhnykh biletov*), pr. Lenina 11a (Ленина). Take trolley #1 to "Городской вал" (Gorodskoy val). At the lights ahead take a right, and at the next light take a sharp left. Open Mon.-Sat. 9:15am-1pm and 2-6pm. Find out from which station your train departs; there are several.

To get to **Glavny Vokzal** (info tel. 29 21 11), take trolley #1 to the last stop on ul. Svobody (Свободы). Trains leave for Moscow (9 per day, 5hr., 40,000-52,000R) and St. Petersburg (3 per day, 14hr., 72,000-94,000R). 24hr. **lockers** at station. Trains for Nizhny Novgorod (2 per day, 8hr., 52,700R), as well as daily trains to Moscow and St. Petersburg, depart from **Moskovsky Vokzal,** Moskovsky pr., across the Kotorosl. Take bus #5 or 9 from just below pl. Volkova. *Kassa* #4 open 24hr. You are best off, though, buying a round-trip ticket from Moscow.

Buses: Avtovokzal across from Moskovsky Vokzal. Tickets are available 15-20min. before departure, once the bus arrives in the station. To Vologda (1 per day, 5hr., 45,900R).

Ferries: To the north of the river on Volzhskaya nab. (Волжская), downstairs. Hydrofoils leave infrequently to Golden Ring town Kostroma (1hr., 15,600R), as well as to Kazan (48hr., 131,000R); Moscow (36hr., 93,000R); and Volgograd (5 days, 247,000R). Schedules are posted at the station, or call 22 42 50 or 25 43 25.

Public Transportation: Yaroslavl's local transportation system is excellent, with trolleys and buses stopping every 2min. Trolley #9 runs up and down Moskovsky pr. through pl. Volkova to Leninsky pr. (Ленинский). Trolley #1 travels from the center to Glavny Vokzal. Buy tickets (1000R) at the light-blue kiosks next to main stops labeled "яргортранс продажа проездных документов," or from the conductor for a 1000R surcharge. Since the fine for being caught without a ticket is only 8000R, many locals don't bother buying them.

Post Office: Bogoyavlenskaya pl. (Богоявленская; tel. 22 37 28), across from the monastery (take trolley #9). **Fax,** telex, and a photocopier. Open Mon.-Sat. 8am-8pm, Sun. 8am-6pm. **Postal code:** 150000.

Telephone Office: In same building as the post office. Prepay at the counter, and get a booth. Three tones mean the call has yet to go through. Press the "ответ" (*otvet*) button when someone answers. Buy tokens for local and intercity calls (400R and 3000R); for the latter, use phones labeled "междугородный автомат" (*mezhdugorodny avtomat*), which malfunction as a rule. Open 24hr. **Phone code:** 0852.

ACCOMMODATIONS

Yaroslavl has always been popular among Russians and foreigners, and its hotel prices are correspondingly high. Most hotels are of the large, pre-*perestroika* Intourist variety. Consequently, the staff is more likely to speak English, but accommodations will be more expensive and not necessarily better.

Gostinitsa Yaroslavl (Ярославль), ul. Ushinskovo (Ушинского; tel. 30 50 75). Large and central. Impeccably neat, sparsely furnished rooms and friendly service. No personal bathrooms, but the communal toilets (without seats) are remarkably clean. Checkout noon. Singles with TV and phone 193,000R; doubles 286,000R; triples 296,000R. It pays to reserve through Intourist: they knock the rates down to 140,000R for singles and 196,000R for doubles.

Gostinitsa Kotorosl (Которосль), ul. B. Oktyabrskaya 87 (Б. Октябрьская; tel. 21 24 15; English info 21 15 81). One stop on tram #3 from Glavny Vokzal. Intourist rates: singles with shower and toilet 175,000R; doubles 300,000R.

Gostinitsa Yubileynaya (Юбилейная), Kotoroslnaya nab. 11 (Которосльная; tel. 22 41 59; English info 22 45 94). From pl. Volkova, walk down Komsomolskaya ul. to pl. Bogoyavlenskaya (Богоявленская), past the Church of the Epiphany on the left and turn right. Intourist's first choice and thus home to many tour groups, this 7-floor hotel is comfortable nonetheless. English spoken. Private bathrooms. In summer, ask for a room on the back side; front ones have an attractive view but get incredibly hot. Intourist rates: singles 205,000R; doubles 330,000R. Breakfast included.

FOOD

Yaroslavl is not Moscow or St. Petersburg—it doesn't have a McDonald's or favorites that locals brag about, so stock up on fruits and vegetables at the **tsentralny rynok** (центральный рынок), ul. Deputatskaya 1 (Депутатская; open Mon.-Sat. 8am-6pm, Sun. 8am-4pm). The central and crowded **gastronom** on Kirova 13 sells just about everything else (open daily 8am-noon and 1-11pm). Two Western-style grocery stores at ul. Ushinskovo 10 and 12 offer vegetarian possibilities (open daily 8am-11pm).

Staroye Mesto (Старое Место), ul. Komsomolskaya 3, off pl. Volkova. Comfortable booths in a cellar room await through a beaded curtain and down a flight of stairs. Russian meals from a short but delicious menu. Vegetable salad 12,000R. Chicken Kiev 23,000R. Open daily noon-10pm.

Cafe Lira (Кафе Лира), Volzhskaya nab. 43 (tel. 22 21 38), 1 block south of the river station. Main dishes 15,000-23,000R. Try *zhyulen s gribami* (жюльен с грибами; creamy local mushrooms in a ceramic bowl; 18,000R). Open daily noon-11pm.

Chayka (Чайка), pr. Lenina 24 (tel. 23 46 91). Cheesy Chinese restaurant serving a wide variety of surprisingly good salads, soups, and main dishes with a somewhat Far Eastern feel. Chinese meals—including vegetarian options—30,000-60,000R. Euro dishes 30,000-50,000R. Open daily noon-11pm.

SIGHTS AND ENTERTAINMENT

Spaso-Preobrazhensky Monastyr (Спасо-Преображенский Монастырь; Monastery of the Transfiguration of the Savior), pl. Bogoyavlenskaya, has been guarding the banks of the Kotorosl since the 12th century. The high white walls of this fortified monastery surround a number of buildings and exhibitions, which, frustratingly, all have separate entrance fees. Enter the grounds through **Svyatye Vorota** (Святые Ворота; Holy Gate), on the side facing the Kotorosl. The most popular attraction, the **zvonnitsa** (звонница; belltower) in the rear entrance, offers a spectacular panorama of the town (7000R). The 15th-century **cathedral** in the center, on the other hand, is usually passed over by visitors who head left to **Medveditsa Masha,** an eight-year-old Russian bear found as a cub and installed in the monastery. Masha more than pays for her supper, delighting tourists by posing for cameras. She looks cuddly, despite being kept in an iron cage little more than six times her size.

The most appealing exhibits within the monastery complex include the **Drevnerusskoe i Narodno-Prikladnoe Iskusstvo** (Древнерусское и Народно-Прикладное Искусство; Old Russian and National-Applied Art exhibit), devoted to national crafts and icons of the Yaroslavl school (7000R); **Pamyatniki Spasskovo Monastyrya** (Памятники Спасского Монастыря; Monuments of the Transfiguration Monastery), which describes the history of medieval structures on the monastery's land (6000R); and **Ekspozitsiya Slovo o Polku Igoreve** (Экспозиция Слово о Полку Игореве; Igor Exhibition; 6000R), dedicated to the discovery and publication of one of the first literary productions of Old Russia, which dates back to the 12th century and was found on the grounds of the monastery in the late 18th century. (Monastery grounds open daily 8:30am-7pm. Free with purchase of tickets to museums, 2000R for entrance just to the monastery. Exhibitions open Tues.-Sun. 10am-5:30pm. *Kassa* closes at 4:30.) Unrelated to the monastery except by proximity, a groomed **beach** on the Kotorosl competes for popularity on hot days with its more cultured neighbor.

Across from the monastery, the large red-brick **Tserkov Bogoyavleniya** (Церковь Богоявления; Church of the Epiphany), pl. Bogoyavlenskaya, requires an entrance fee, but it's worth it to see the one frescoed room and a small exhibition of fragments of frescoes recovered from destroyed Yaroslavl churches. The main room has an ornately carved Baroque iconostasis and wooden benches. Concerts are often held here at 6pm—ask at the monastery. The antechamber allows you to examine the frescoes up close. (Open Wed.-Mon. 10am-5pm. 6000R, students 2000R; photography pass 10,000R. Knock on the door if the church seems closed.) Across the park from the bottom right-hand corner of the monastery, **Tserkov Arkhangela Mikhaila** (Архангела Михаила; Church of the Archangel Michael) has red brick and green domes similar to those at Tserkov Bogoyavleniya, and contains additional frescoes by local artists (open daily 9am-8pm; services Sat., Sun., and holidays 9am and 5pm). Yaroslavl's most beautiful church, **Tserkov Ilyi Proroka** (Церковь Ильи Пророка; Church of Elijah the Prophet) lies on Sovetskaya pl. (Советская) at the end of ul. Kirova. Built in the 17th century in traditional Yaroslavl style, this church is replete with glowing original frescoes, although the iconostasis is a partial restoration (open Thurs.-Tues. 10am-1pm and 2-6pm; 8000R, Russians 4000R; photos 10,000R; services Sun. 8:30-11am). The view alone vindicates a visit to **Tserkov Spasa na Gorodu** (Церковь Спаса на Городу; Church of the Savior On-the-City). Continuing along the same road is the *strelka,* where the Volga and Kotorosl rivers meet. A garden has been built at the spot; bring a picnic lunch.

The **Khudozhestvenny Muzey** (Художественный Музей; Art Museum) has two branches. The first, **Muzey Metropolichi Palaty** (Метрополичьи Палаты), Volzhskaya nab. 1 (tel. 22 34 87), displays the best of Yaroslavl's icons and attracts the majority of the Volga-cruising tourists with its busy exhibition-sale of traditional crafts. The modern branch, in the former Governor's house at Volzhskaya nab. 23 (tel. 30 34 95), displays 18th- to 20th-century Russian paintings and sculpture in several media (both open Sat.-Thurs. 10am-5:30pm; *kassy* close at 4:30pm; 10,000R). The nearby **Muzey Istorii Goroda Yaroslavlya** (Истории Города Ярославля; Museum of the History of Yaroslavl), at Volzhskaya nab. 17/2 (tel. 22 25 40) where it intersects Sovetsky per., is a small museum filled with engravings, furniture, photos, and clothes from numerous eras of Yaroslavl's history. The modern period exhibit focuses on the family that inhabited this building, down to their school textbooks and baby baskets (open Thurs.-Mon. 10am-6pm; *kassa* closes at 5:30pm; 5000R, students 2000R). The tiny **Muzey Muzyka i Vremya** (Музыка и Время; Music and Time Museum), Volzhskaya nab. 33, is housed in a restored 19th-century brick house. This private museum encourages you to interact with its artifacts: you can play a clavichord and listen to an old Victrola (open Tues.-Sun. 10am-7pm; 10,000R, students 5000R; organized tours in Russian or English 15,000R).

Nightlife here involves much Russian pop. The dances at **Club Yuta** (Клуб Юта), ul. Respublikanskaya (Республиканская; tel. 32 97 86), in Gostinitsa Yuta, last from 9pm to 2am (open Thurs.-Sun.; cover 20,000R for men, 10,000R for women). The well- advertised but hard to find—it's downstairs—**Dzhoypati** (Джойпати), ul. Naberzhnaya 2 (Набержная), has longer hours and caters to a younger and wilder crowd (open daily 10pm-5am; cover 15,000R for men, 10,000R for women). In the summer, many locals find it too hot to be cooped up in a club and instead drive to Volzhskaya nab., open their car doors, blast the radio, and simply stroll on the street.

■ Vladimir (Владимир)

Once the capital of Russia and the headquarters of the Russian Orthodox Church, Vladimir (vlah-DEE-meer) suffered at the hands of the Tatars in the 13th century, and eventually fell to Moscow in the early 1300s. Until that time, it rivaled Kiev in size and splendor. Since Vladimir became a province, its importance has declined, but the city has held on to some of the Golden Ring's most attractive churches.

Orientation and Practical Information Trains run from the station on Vokzalnaya ul. (Вокзальная) to Moscow's Kursky Vokzal (8 per day, 3hr., 35,000-60,000R) and Nizhny Novgorod (1 per hr., 4hr., 74,100R). **Buses** for Yaroslavl (daily, 6hr., 45,200R) and Suzdal (every hr., 4700R) depart across the street from the train station. **Store luggage** at the bus station (open daily 7:30-11:30am and 12:30-7:30pm; 3000R) or the train station (open 24hr.; 8900R). Nearly everything of interest to tourists is along **ul. III Internatsionala** (III-его Интернационала), a five-minute walk uphill from the train station. Vladimir's tourist office, **Excursionnoe Byuro** (Экскурсионное Бюро), ul. III Internatsionala 43 (tel. 22 42 63), arranges English-language tours of Vladimir (66,000R plus 8000R per person; 45,000R plus 4000R for students) and Suzdal (77,500R plus 8000R per person). The bulletin board outside lists events and exhibits (open Mon.-Thurs. 8:30am-5:30pm, Fri.-Sun. 8:30am-3pm). For **currency exchange,** go to any *Obmen Valyuty* (Обмен Валюты) or any major bank on the main street. The train station contains a 24-hour **telephone office** that serves only Russian cities. A 60,000R telephone card is required to use these phones (good for about 15min. to Moscow or St. Petersburg). For **international calls,** head to Peregovorny

Punkt (Переговорный Пункт), Gorkovo 60 (Горкого; take trolley #10 to pl. Lenina; open 24hr.). **Postal code:** 600003. **Phone code:** 0922. For 5-digit numbers, add an extra "2" on the end.

Accommodations and Food

Uphill on the left path from the train station, **Gostinitsa Vladimir** (Гостиница Владимир), ul. III Internatsionala 74 (tel. 22 30 42) rents clean rooms with sink, TV, and an occasional chair (bed in a triple 53,000R; singles 80,000R, with bath 180,000R; doubles 120,000R, with bath 260,000R). The next-door **grocery** is well-stocked (open Mon.-Fri. 9am-8pm, Sat. 9am-7pm, Sun. 9am-5pm). **Cafe Blinchiki** (Кафе Блинчики), ul. III Internatsionala 28 (tel. 22 36 91), sits directly opposite the trading arcades in a large square. Steaming hot *bliny* come with lots of fillings and toppings; *blinchiki* stuffed with meat, cottage cheese, or honey cost 2400-3800R (open daily 10am-6pm). Unlike many a Russian eatery, **Cafe Slavianka** (Славянка), ul. III Internatsionala 24 (tel. 22 35 32), can call itself a "restaurant," cooking up yummy mushrooms (20,000R), sauteed eggplant (16,000R), and "Slavyansky Syurpriz" (Славянский Сюрприз; Slavic Surprise; 28,000R). Guitar music plays nightly in the tavernish little room (open daily noon-1am).

Sights and Entertainment

The 1197 **Dmitrievsky Sobor** (Дмитриевский Собор; St. Dmitry's Cathedral) is the only surviving building of Prince Vsevelod III's palace. Painstakingly carved in stone, the cathedral's outer walls display the stories of Hercules, King David, and Alexander the Great, but locked doors prevent visitors from viewing the Byzantine frescoes inside, as a major restoration project is underway. Vladimir's **Uspensky Sobor** (Успенский Собор; Assumption Cathedral), to the right of the Dmitrievsky Sobor, once guarded the famous Mother of God icon, which is now in Moscow's Tretyakov Gallery (see **Moscow: Sights,** p. 538). Fortunately, its interior still includes frescoes by the renowned artists Andrei Rublyov and Daniil Chiorny. Looming large and white at the top of a small hill, the cathedral was begun in 1158, and in 1189 received four more domes and two more aisles (open Tues.-Sun. 1:30-5pm; 5000R). Between the two cathedrals, the **Muzey-Zapovednik** (Музей-Заповедник; Museum-Preserve), ul. III Internatsionala 58 (tel. 22 24 29), has a picture gallery displaying paintings from the 18th to the 20th centuries (open Tues. and Fri. 10am-4pm, Wed.-Thurs. and Sat.-Sun. 10am-5pm), but the sculpture park in front with statues of Snow White and the seven dwarves is what makes it unique. The **Muzey Istorii Vladimirskovo Kraya** (Музей Истории Владимирского Края; Museum of the History of Vladimir), ul. III Internatsionala 64 (tel. 22 22 84), stocks its first floor with three-foot mammoth tusks, roosters in relief, and locks larger than most faces. The second floor keeps the tinies: statuette candle-sticks, old photos of Nicholas II, and a 1912 issue of *Pravda* (open Tues. and Fri. 10am-3:30pm, Wed.-Thurs. and Sat.-Sun. 10am-4:30pm, closed last Fri. of the month; 7000R). Next door are the remains of the **Rozhdestvensky Monastyr** (Рождественский Монастырь; Nativity Monastery), Aleksandr Nevsky's former burial site. Peter I schlepped the poor guy's remains to Petersburg in the 1600s; the town was left with just an empty coffin (open only for worship daily 4-5pm).

Zolotye Vorota (Золотые Ворота; Golden Gate; tel. 22 25 59) stands triumphantly in the middle of ul. III Internatsionala, separating the center from the rest of town. Climb to the top for a view of Vladimir's central street through the low windows. The gate's interest value lies in its age—from the 12th century (open Mon. and Wed. 10am-4pm, Thurs.-Sun. 10am-5pm, closed last Fri. of the month; 7000R).

The church-like brick building beyond Zolotye Vorota houses an exhibit of **crystal and lacquer crafts,** a large room filled with gorgeous gadgets from the surrounding region (tel. 248 72; open Mon. and Wed. 10am-4pm, Thurs.-Sun. 10am-5pm, closed last Fri. of the month; 7000R). The **Vystavka Starovo Vladimira** (Выставка Старого Владимира; Exhibit of Old Vladimir; tel. 254 51), in a water tower near the gates, displays regional archaeological finds (open Wed.-Thurs. 10am-4pm, Fri.-Sun. 10am-5pm, closed last Thurs. of the month; 7000R). Down the hill to the right of the exhibit, behind the gates, an out-of-place monument demonstrates what can be done with U.S. investments in Russia. The weirdly familiar low fence, encircling lawn, and attached garage decorate the **Amerikansky Dom** (Американский Дом; American House)—it looks like it ought to be inhabited by Boris and Natasha Cleaver, but actually houses an English language school.

Vladimir is most famous for its **choirs.** Eduard Markin's Boys' Choir holds Saturday concerts of old Russian hymns and folk songs in an old church on ul. Georgievskaya (Георгиевская; tel. 22 54 95), a rock road rolling off ul. III Internatsionala around building 26. The Zavazalskovo Choir (Хор Завазальского) performs on Thursdays in the Planetarium building, which was formerly the Nikolo-Kremlevskaya church. Call Aleksandr Nikolsky of the Vladimir Music Society for more information (tel. 22 31 60).

■ Suzdal (Суздаль)

Set in fertile countryside with lazy streams and dirt roads, miraculous Suzdal (SOOZ-dull; pop. 10,000) looks much as it always has. Colorfully painted wooden houses and churches charm visitors, but just as the town withstood decades of Communism, it now stands strong against the current tourist hordes as a historically protected landmark. Until the 12th century, Suzdal's **kremlin** ruled over the Rostov-Suzdal principality. Although lush countryside now drowns the fortress's imposing power, inside, the star-studded blue domes of the **Rozhdestvensky Sobor** (Рождественский Собор; Nativity Cathedral) still dazzle. Brightly colored frescoes and ornately carved arches decorate the early 13th-century church. Unfortunately, the cathedral is rarely open to visitors, as even the mildest changes in humidity can damage the frescoes. The **Krestovaya Palata** (Cross Hall), once used for receptions, now houses a small museum of paintings and objects of everyday religious use. The **Muzey Drevnerusskoy Zhivopisi** (Музей Древнерусской Живописи; Museum of Old Russian Painting) displays icons of the Suzdal school from the 15th to 17th centuries (museums and cathedral open Wed.-Sun. 10am-6pm, closed last Fri. of the month; 7000R for each sight; photography pass 8000R). When the weather is good, a *troyka* trots around the ramparts for 10,000R per person (Sat.-Sun. noon-5pm).

Most churches and monasteries stand near Suzdal's main axis, **ul. Lenina** (Ленина). Thanks to heavy fundraising by Ivan the Terrible, among others, the **Spaso-Evfimiev Monastyr** (Спасо-Евфимиев Монастырь; Monastery of St. Euphemius the Savior), on ul. Lenina, is Suzdal's largest monastery. Inside is the 16th-century **Preobrazhensky Sobor** (Преображенский Собор; Transfiguration Cathedral). Built in the 1590s, the cathedral boasts colorful frescoes by the artist Gury Nikitin. Examine the before-and-after frescoes—a vibrant upper-level and original untouched lower. The bells in the adjacent belfry give a daily concert every hour between 11am and 5pm. Across from the belltower, the early 16th-century **Uspenskaya Tserkov** (Успенская церковь; Assumption Church) holds an exhibition of Russian books dating back to the 15th century (complex open Tues.-Sun. 10am-5pm, Wed.-Thurs. 10am-4pm, closed last Thurs. of the month; 4000R, cathedral 4000R extra, museum 7000R extra). The **Muzey Drevyannovo Zodchestva i Krestyanskovo Byta** (Музей Деревянного Зодчества и Крестьянского Быта; Museum of Wooden Architecture and Peasant Life), across the river from the kremlin, is a bunch of 18th-century wooden houses and churches, complete with scythe-bearing peasant re-enacters (open May-Sept. Wed.-Mon. 9:30am-4:30pm, closed last Fri. of each month; grounds 3000R, buildings 8000R). The 17th-century **Aleksandrovsky Monastyr** (Александровский Монастырь; Aleksandr's Convent), ul. Gasteva (Гастева), off ul. Engelsa, stands on the grounds of a long-gone 13th-century church built by the legendary Aleksandr Nevsky.

Vasilevskaya ul. (Васильевская) runs from ul. Lenina to the **bus station,** which sends buses to Vladimir (every hr., 50min., 4700R). The **Glavny turistsky kompleks** (GTK; главный туристский комплекс; main tourist complex) is a 40-minute walk from the center. Go north on ul. Lenina to the yellow belltower, and turn left. Follow this road as it curves, and take a right when you come to a fork. The **Intourist** office inside GTK speaks Russified English and sells **maps** of Suzdal (5000R; open Mon.-Fri. 9am-5pm). The complex's lobby also houses the **post office** (open daily 8am-8pm). **Postal**

code: 601260. The **telephone and telegraph office,** ul. Lenina 110, operates directly across from the yellow belltower (open 24hr. with a 1-2pm break)—only calls within Russia can be made from here. For international calls, trot back to the expensive credit-card phone at the GTK lobby. **Phone code:** 9231.

When you see the hotel prices in Suzdal, you'll be glad you're taking the bus back to Vladimir. The only reasonable option is **Rizopolozhenskaya Gostinitsa,** on the territory of the Rizopolozhensky monastyr. The hotel offers shabby but clean rooms (singles, doubles, and triples 45,000R per person). Long fed on annual inundations of foreign tourists, Suzdal has more upscale Russian restaurants than cities 10 times its size. **Pogrebok** (Погребок), Kremlyovskaya ul. 3 (Кремлёвская; tel. 247 32), off ul. Lenina, serves reasonably priced local specialties in clay pots (7000-15,000R). Wash it all down with the mildly alcoholic honey drink *Medovukha* (7000R per jug; open Tues.-Sun. 10am-6pm).

■ Vologda (Вологда)

Deep in the north forests churns Vologda (VOH-lug-duh), self-proclaimed home of the world's best butter and lace. Although it lies beyond the boundaries of the Golden Ring, tourist-free Vologda, with its silver-domed churches and ornately carved wooden houses, nevertheless shares the richness of old Russian architecture with the more celebrated towns of Yaroslavl and Suzdal. Vologda is the same age as Moscow—both cities were founded in 1147—and in summer 1997 the town received a major face-lift as an 850th birthday present. A large trading city before the opening of the Baltic Sea to Russians, today this town along the sleepy Vologda river is a site of provincial peace and slow-paced economy.

Orientation and Practical Information Trains leave from pl. Babushkina (Бабушкина; info tel. 72 06 73) to Moscow (12 per day, 11hr., 70,000R) and St. Petersburg (12 per day, 12hr., 73,000R). Next to the train station, **buses** (info booth tel. 72 04 52; station open daily 5:30am-9pm) chug to places not worth going, except for Kirillov (5 per day, 3hr., 23,000R) and Yaroslavl (2 per day, 4½hr., 45,000R). **Store luggage** at the train station (lockers 8900R; open 24hr.). Vologda is a small town, with everything you could need within a few blocks of **ul. Mira** (Мира). The town's **center** lies 10 minutes from the train station down ul. Mira. **Exchange currency** (US$ only) on the 1st floor of Vologdabank (Вологдабанк) at ul. Mira 36; bring your passport (open daily 9am-1pm and 2-3pm). Public transportation consists of old, crowded, and frequent **local buses** (buy 1500R tickets from conductor; buses labeled "Центр" or "#1" run to the center). A **post office,** pl. Babushkina 1, lies next to the bank (open Mon.-Fri. 8am-noon and 1-7pm, Sat. 8am-noon and 1-5pm). **Postal code:** 160001. **Telephones** operate in the train station (open 24hr.). **Phone code:** 8172.

Accommodations and Food Choices are slim, but mercifully affordable. Hot water is often not available for one summer month, ironically, for "sanitation reasons." Always bring toilet paper. Prices are identical for Russians and foreigners, although foreigners are charged a one-time "room tax" (around 17,000R). The pastel **Gostinitsa Spasskaya** (Гостиница Спасская), ul. Oktyabrskaya 25 (Октябрская; tel. 72 01 45), welcomes guests to its bright, carpeted, spacious rooms. The place caters to businesspeople and has office equipment for rent (faxes, photocopiers, laminators!), as well as excellent service and clean rooms (singles with bath 90,000R, with TV and telephone 140,000R; doubles with bath 140,000R, with the goods 200,000R). A currency exchange and restaurant are on the premises. The budget **Gostinitsa Vologda** (Гостиница Вологда), ul. Mira 92 (tel. 72 30 79), is spotlessly clean with a friendly staff, and contains a good restaurant and buffet. Tiles are chipped in the hall bathroom; there's no toilet paper, seat, or—at times—soap; but at least the toilets have doors (singles with TV and telephone 80,000R, with bath 116,000R; doubles 109,000R, with bath 200,000R; showers 8000R).

RUSSIA

Several **markets** sit on ul. Mira, including an open-air fruit and veggie market behind ul. Mira 20-22. Take a left on the pedestrian shopping street off ul. Mira, then a quick right behind #20 (open daily 9am-4:30pm). The selection of cafes and restaurants in Vologda is far from rich, but most places feature an attractive *kompleksny obed* (комплексный обед; lunch special), usually served until 6pm. **Cafe Lukomorye** (Кафе Лукоморье), ul. Lermontova 4 (Лермонтова), is one of the most charming options for either lunch or dinner. Turn right past ul. Mira 1 and stay right as the road curves; it's the big faux-diner building with a painting of a slick car on the side. Inside, the cheery cafe plays upbeat tunes and serves delicious veggie salads (6000-7000R), ice cream with syrup (4000R), and tea (200R). *Kompleksny obed* (fixed menu) is 19,000R; the paintings on the wall are also for sale (open Mon.-Fri. 10am-11pm, Sat.-Sun. 10am-2am). The recently opened **Pizzeria**, ul. Orlova 6 (Орлова), by the kremlin, is a convenient stop while sightseeing; it features cheap pizzas with all imaginable sorts of toppings (5000-6000R; open daily 11am-10pm).

Sights and Entertainment Follow the gold and silver domes to get to Vologda's sightseeing center at Kremlyovskaya pl. (Кремлёвская)—the 16th-century **Arkhiereysky Dvor** (Архиерейский Двор; Archbishop's Courtyard), commonly referred to as the Vologda kremlin. Most structures within the walls of this fortification have been converted into museums. The **Ekonomichesky Korpus** (Економический Корпус; Economist's Quarters), the town's first civil building, houses an exhibition of 17th- to 19th-century silver, and the Baroque **Iosifovsky Korpus** (Иосифовский корпус) houses Vologda's **Istoriko-Arkhitekturny i Khudozhestvenny Muzey** (Историко-Архитектурный и Художественный Музей; Museum of History, Art, and Architecture). The main exhibit combines temporal and natural history, with stuffed ducks quacking next to samovars against a backdrop of World War II posters. Outside of the kremlin's gates stands Vologda's gem: the massive, multi-domed **Sobor Sofysky** (Собор Софийский; Sofia's Cathedral). Built from 1568 to 1570, it merits a look for the stunning, newly renovated frescoes painted by artists from Yaroslavl. The 1869 gold-domed **kolokolnya** (колокольня; belltower), to the left of the cathedral, rings its own bells every 15 minutes. To the left of the *kolokolnya* stands the Baroque **Voskresensky Sobor** (Воскресенский Собор; Assumption Cathedral), housing the **Vologodskaya Oblastnaya Kartinnaya Galereya** (Вологодская Областная Картинная Галерея; Vologda Regional Art Gallery), dedicated to 17th- to 19th-century Russian art. A branch devoted to Western art lies at ul. Orlova 15 (all museums and cathedrals open Wed.-Sun. 10am-5pm; each 5000R). By the river, to the right of Sobor Sofysky, a monument honors poet **Konstantine Batyushkov,** Pushkin's teacher.

A promenade through town leads to Vologda's most unique attraction—its **19th-century wooden houses.** The most significant ones along Oktyabrskaya ul. (Октябрская) are labeled. To reach **Spaso-Prilutsky Monastyr** (Спасо-Прилуцкий Монастырь; tel. 77 41 75), take bus # 103 from the end of ul. Mira to the last stop (15min.). Begun in 1371, this monastery—which reopened in 1991 after being closed for 70 years—is a not-too-removed escape into the countryside. The monastery basks on the banks of the Vologda, and the earthen ramparts provide a perfect place to enjoy a riverside lunch. To arrange a tour in Russian (10,000R per person), call ahead; otherwise, only a small central yard and gift shop are accessible to visitors. (Monastery open daily 7am-9pm. Morning liturgy 7-9:30am; evening services 5-8pm. Main church only open during services. Donations requested.)

■ Near Vologda: Kirilla-Belozersky Monastery
(Кирилла-Белозерский Монастырь)

This 14th-century monster of a monastery puts the smaller, poorer one in Vologda to shame, and is even worth the three-hour bus ride to **Kirillov** (Кириллов; 5 per day, 23,000R; last bus leaves Kirillov 7pm) from Vologda, especially if the weather is good. Get off the bus at central Kirillov, one stop before the bus terminal; watch for the white stone mass on your right and hop out there. According to legend, St. Kiril

RUSSIA

founded the monastery when the Virgin Mary came to him in a vision and showed him the towers of a new monastery. Enter through the Kazan Tower and proceed along the road between the remains of the so-called *ostrog* (острог; stockaded town) and the new town until you reach **Svyatye Vorota** (Святые Ворота; Holy Gate), the entrance to the monastery proper. In the monastery's museums, you can admire the luxurious clothes and icons and historical Russian folk valuables. The most interesting exhibitions include: 15th-century Russian icons (14,000R); two 16th-century iconostases in the St. John's and Transfiguration churches (both 4500R); folk arts and ceramic toys (7000R); and the monastery's walls and towers (3000R; Russian tours 75,000R for groups of 15 or fewer; to arrange a tour, call 314 79; monastery open Tues.-Sun. 9am-5pm). In summer, the grassy shore of **Lake Beloye** outside the monastery walls turns into an improvised beach. The water might be too cold for swimming, but the view is peaceful and relaxing. Kirillov's only lunch spot is **Restaurant Rus** (Русь), two blocks to the right of the monastery at ul. Uritskovo 8 (Урицкого). Service is excruciatingly slow, but you can get a wholesome three-course meal for under 15,000R (open Tues.-Sun. noon-11pm).

THE TRANS-SIBERIAN RAILROAD

The most legendary train route in the world, the Trans-Siberian Railroad snakes its 9289km way across two continents and eight time zones. The term "Trans-Siberian" actually does not refer to a single train, but to three sets of rail tracks and the numerous trains that run along them. The **Trans-Siberian** line links Moscow and Vladivostok, the **Trans-Mongolian** connects Moscow with Beijing via Ulaan Baatar, Mongolia, and the **Trans-Manchurian** line heads directly to Beijing. For a long time, many of the cities along the railways were closed to foreigners—now, however, they're yours to enjoy. Or just pull back the curtains and watch endless rivers, chiseled mountains, minute wooden cottages, and kilometers of grazing cows go by. Russian stations may not provide service with a smile, but fellow railers will chat about the changing times and where to get the cheapest goods. They might even ask you to join in a round of the card game *durak* (fool); if you don't want to look like one yourself, check out **"Playing the Fool,"** p. 585.

Departing All Trans-Siberian **trains** depart from Moscow's **Yaroslavsky Vokzal** (M4: Komsomolskaya). The better long-distance trains, called *fermeny* (private), offer cleaner facilities but also cost as much as 50,000-150,000R more than regular *skory* (fast) trains. If your journey is longer than 24 hours, paying extra is worth the price. From Moscow, the *fermeny* trains are: train #2 (*Rossia*) departing for Vladivostok at 2:15pm on odd days; train #10 (*Baikal*) to Irkutsk and Lake Baikal, departing at 9:20pm on odd days; train #4 (*The Chinese Train*) to Beijing via Ulaan Baatar, the cleanest and best train, departing Tuesdays at 8pm; train #20 (*The Russian Train*) to Beijing on the Trans-Manchurian line, departing Fridays at 8:25pm; and train #6 to Ulaan Baatar, departing Wednesdays and Thursdays at 8pm. *Fermeny* trains usually have a plaque on the side of each car stating the train's name.

Costs The cost of your journey depends on the agency that books your ticket. Prices can as much as triple, depending on the combination of types and categories of trains. It is more expensive to get off and on again at different cities than to travel non-stop between two destinations, as you must buy separate tickets at each departure point. The least expensive way to get tickets is to buy them yourself from **Tsentralnoe Zheleznodorozhnoe Agenstvo** (Центральное Железнодорожное Агенство; Central Train Agency) in Moscow (see p. 527). The agency sells *fermeny* tickets to all destinations, including Irkutsk (1,013,000-1,105,000R), Vladivostok (1,972,000R), and Beijing (Trans-Mongolian line 898,000R; Trans-Manchurian 940,000R). For a US$20 commission, the **Traveller's Guest House** in Moscow (see p. 530) will buy a

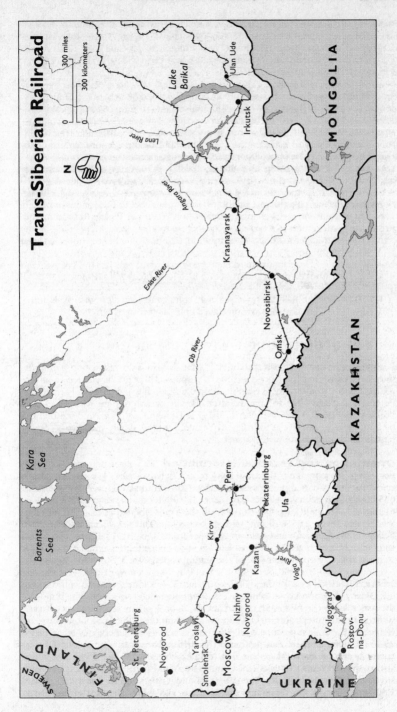

Trans-Siberian Railroad

300 miles

300 kilometers

N

MONGOLIA

KAZAKHSTAN

RUSSIA

UKRAINE

FINLAND

SWEDEN

Lake Baikal

Ulan Ude

Irkutsk

Lena River

Angara River

Krasnayarsk

Enise River

Novosibirsk

Ob River

Omsk

Perm

Yekaterinburg

Ufa

Kirov

Kazan

Volga River

Kara Sea

Barents Sea

Nizhny Novgorod

Yaroslavl

Volgograd

Rostov-na-Donu

St. Petersburg

Novgorod

Smolensk

Moscow

ticket for you to spare you the endless wait in line. The hostel offers first- and second-class fares to Irkutsk (1st class US$364, 2nd class US$196), Vladivostok (1st class US$638, 2nd class US$335), Beijing (Trans-Mongolian: 1st class US$322, 2nd class US$194; Trans-Manchurian: 1st class US$282, 2nd class US$191), and Ulaan Baatar (1st class US$282, 2nd class US$191).

Logistics You may need **visas** to enter both China and Mongolia; the Chinese visa is best obtained in Moscow, while a Mongolian visa can be picked up in Moscow, Irkutsk, or Ulan Ude. Two attendants—*provodnik* (male) or *provodnitsa* (female)—sit in each train wagon to make sure all goes smoothly; they also offer tea (1000R) more cheaply than the restaurant car. Try to avoid being put you into the first or last *coupé* in the wagon; these neighbor the toilets and, especially on non-*fermeny* trains, the stench can become unbearable after several days of travel (on *fermeny* trains they are cleaned several times per day). Always carry your own toilet paper. A posted schedule in each wagon lists arrival times for each *stoyanka* (стоянка; stop). When the train stops for longer than 15 minutes, locals come out to hawk food to passengers. The **restaurant car** is changed at each border, so you'll have Russian food in Russia, Mongolian food in Mongolia, and Chinese food in China. Depending on the train, Moscow and Perm are separated by about 22 hours, another 6½ hours gets you to Yekaterinburg, and 23 hours more stand between you and Novosibirsk. From Novosibirsk, it's 32 hours more to Irkutsk. Another 8 hours gets you to Ulan Ude, and it's a mere day from there to Ulaan Baatar, which is 36 hours from Beijing.

> The Trans-Siberian Railroad traverses eight time zones, but all train arrivals and departures are listed in Moscow time at stations, as well as in *Let's Go.*

■ Yekaterinburg (Екатеринбург)

Both the birthplace of Yeltsin and the site of the Romanovs' assassination, Yekaterinburg has intimately experienced the end of empires. Although the city feels a bit like the end of the world, on this train it's only the beginning—of Siberia. Founded by Peter the Great in 1723 and named after his wife, Yekaterinburg was renamed in honor of Bolshevik Yakov Sverdlovsk in 1924. Though most locals and train timetables still refer to the city as Sverdlovsk, Yekaterinburg is slowly shedding its Soviet past and returning to imperial elegance.

Orientation and Practical Information Set your watch two hours forward from Moscow time. The **train station,** ul. Chelyuskintsev (Челюскинцев), sends trains to: Moscow (12 per day, 29hr., 359,000R); Irkutsk (1-3 per day, 2½ days, 675,000R); Novosibirsk (4-7 per day, 22hr. 320,000R); and Vladivostok (1 per day, 5½ days, 1,205,000R). Passing through on the Trans-Siberian lines are: train #2 to Vladivostok (even days 7:49pm); train #4 to Beijing (Thurs. 12:22am); train #20 to Beijing (Sun. 12:44am); and train #6 to Ulaan Baatar (Fri.-Sat. 12:22am). Foreigners can purchase tickets at *kassa* #2 in the ticket salon on the third floor; take the circular steps all the way on the left side of the station (open 24hr.). **Store luggage** in the basement (7,000-10,000R; open 24hr.). You can take a **shower** (2000R) at the rest area near track #1; look for the Душ (*dush*) sign. Two kilometers south of the station lies **Glavny pr.** (formerly ul. Lenina), Yekaterinburg's main street, off which most of the major sights can be found; take trolley #1, 8, or 9, or any bus with "пр. Ленина" written on it. American citizens can seek assistance at the **U.S. Consulate,** ul. Golgolya 15, 4th floor (Голголья; tel. 56 47 44; fax 56 45 15; emergency tel. (8 3439) 05 15 06; open Mon.-Fri. 8am-4:30pm). The **British Consulate** is next door. **Change currency** at **Most Bank** (Мост Банк), ul. Mamina-Sibiryaka 145 (tel. 55 55 09), which also cashes traveler's checks (2% commission) and gives commission-free cash advances (open Mon.-Thurs. 9am-12:30pm and 1:30-4pm, Fri. 9am-12:30pm and 1:30-3pm). Outside is a 24-hour Cirrus/MC/Plus/Visa **ATM.** The **post office,** Glavny pr. 39 (tel. 51 22 42), allows you to **fax**, telex, and even send **email** (open Mon.-Fri. 8am-8pm, Sat.-Sun. 8am-6pm). The **telephone office** (телефоный пункт), ul. Tolma- chova 23, is just around the corner (open daily 5am-2am). **Postal code:** 620151. **Phone code:** 3432.

Accommodations and Food Foreigners pay double the Russian price for accommodations, but there are still cheap rooms if you're willing to settle for mini- mum comfort. **Gostinitsa Bolshoy Ural** (Гостиница Большой Урал), ul. Krasnoarmey- skaya 1 (Красноармейская; tel. 55 68 96), behind the gray opera house on pr. Lenina 46a, offers the barest rooms, but at least they have hot water (bed in 4-person room 25,000R; singles 100,000R; doubles 11,000R; bring toilet paper). Take bus #31 from the train station or any trolleybus down ul. Lenina to "Operny Teater." **Hotel Evrasia** (Евразия), pr. Lenina 40 (tel. 51 57 58; fax 51 81 55), down the street from the opera house, has similarly unluxurious amenities. (Singles 100,000R; doubles 150,000R; bed in a triple 50,000R. Toilet paper? Keep dreaming.)

Babushki haggle at **Chayny market** (Чайный), across from the train station. The restaurant **Harbin** (Харбин), ul. Kubishina 39 (Кубишина; tel. 61 75 71), south of town, serves possibly the best Chinese food in Russia. To get there, take bus #23 or trolley bus #15 from the train station to the circus (Цирк; *tsirk*; open daily 1-4pm and 6-11pm). For cheaper options, check out the cafes on pr. Lenina, especially those hid- ing around the bridge.

Sights and Entertainment Yekaterinburg demonstrates its former imperial majesty through its museums. **Muzey Izobrazitelnikh Iskusstv** (Музей Изобрази- тельных Искусств; Fine Arts Museum), per. Voevodina 5 (Воеводина; tel. 51 03 05), just off Glavny pr. by the bridge, boasts a bevy of busts, bears, and belligerent bulls carved in black stone (open Wed.-Sun. 11am-6pm; 8000R, students free). Diagonally across Pokrovsky pr., the excellent **Istoriko-Kraevedchesky Muzey** (Историко-крае- ведческий музей; Historic-Regional Museum), ul. Malisheva 4b (Малишева; tel. 51 47 93), charts the history of the Ural region and the Yekaterinburg *oblast* with photos and Soviet propaganda posters. A fascinating exhibit devoted to the Romanovs resides on the second floor (open Mon. and Wed.-Sun. 11am-6pm; closed last Mon. of each month; 5000R, students free). In this new era of political freedom, the small **Muzey Politicheskoy Istorii** (Музей политической истории; Political History Museum) Voznesenski pr. 26 (Вознесенски; formerly Karla Libknekhta, Карла Либкнехта; tel. 51 22 40), off Glavny pr., explodes with political satire blasting Boris Yeltsin. The requi- site folk art and wax figure museum awaits upstairs (open Tues.-Sat. 10am-5:30pm; 2000R, students 1000R; free last Wed. of each month; tours in Russian 10,000R). Directly across the street on Voznesenski pr., a roof without walls marks the spot where a firing squad ended the line of **Romanovs** (unless you believe in Anastasia) in 1918. It is rumored that Yeltsin was ordered to bulldoze the house on this spot when he was Sverdlovsk's Communist party boss. Nearby sits the light-blue **Khram Vozhneseniya Gospodya** (Храмъ Вожнесения господя; Ascension Church; tel. 51 64 07), on Vozhneseniya gorka (open daily 8am-8pm). The town's residents gather on lazy afternoons in the two main squares. **Istorichesky Skver** (Исторический Сквер), along the canal leading to **Gorodskoy Prud** (City Pond), is where the city began in 1723. Today, it's the site of numerous monuments and museums. Slightly to the west, **pl. 1905 goda** guards the requisite statue of Lenin and the enormous (and very Soviet) city hall where Yeltsin worked before being called to Moscow in 1985.

At the east end of the ul. Lenina stands the mammoth, gray **Ural State Technical University** (Уральский Государственный Техниуеский Университет), ul. Mira 19 (tel. 44 85 99). Founded in 1924 and formerly known as the Ural Polytechnical Institute, this is the Harvard of the Ural region and the *alma mater* of Yeltsin (class of '56). Take tram #8, 13, 15, or 18 from pl. 1905 goda to get to the university.

For **entertainment**, head to the **Opera and Ballet Theater** (Оперный Театр и еалет), Glavny pr. 46a (*kassa* open daily 10am-7pm; performances start at 7pm; tick- ets 10000R). The **Circus**, on Sibirsky pr. (Сибирский), near the Harbin restaurant,

RUSSIA

sends in the clowns, as well as the bears, monkeys, snakes, and horses (Fri., Sat., and Sun. 2pm; *kassy* open daily 9am-6pm; 10,000R; kids 5 and under free).

■ Novosibirsk (Новосибирск)

Born only a century ago, the young city of Novosibirsk (pop. 1.5 million) has grown faster than any other in Siberia, and now competes with Moscow and St. Petersburg in both population and political power. The region's biggest city, Novosibirsk lies at the geographical center of Russia, and makes a good stopover for those who wish to experience urban life in the middle of Siberia.

Orientation and Practical Information Novosibirsk is three hours ahead of Moscow time. The **train station,** ul. Shamshurina, sends trains to: Moscow (5-6 per day, 3 days); Yekaterinburg (7-8 per day, 280,000R); and Krasnoyarsk (5-6 per day, 150,000R, 13hr.). Novosibirsk is also the starting point for the **Turkistan-Siberian** railway, which connects Siberia with Central Asia; trains leave for Almaty, Kazakhstan (1 per day, 38hr.) and Bishkek, Kyrgyzstan (3-4 per week, 51hr.). The following Trans-Siberian services stop in Novosibirsk (in Moscow time): train #2 to Vladivostok (odd days 5:10pm, 4 days); train #4 to Beijing (Thurs. 9:12pm); train #20 to Beijing (Sun. 9:45pm); and train #6 to Ulaan Baatar (Fri.-Sat. 9:12pm). **Luggage storage** is in the train station (12,000R; open 24hr.). The **Metro** connects the city center, **pl. Lenina,** to the train station at stop "Гарина-Михайловского" (Garina-Mikhailovskovo). From the train station, walk out into the city and then underground where you see the "M." Take the Metro one stop to Sibirskaya (Сибирская), then walk upstairs to change stations; one more stop takes you to pl. Lenina (1000R). The Sibirskaya Metro is close to the circus, the Ascension Church, the market, and the stadium. Buy a **map** (20,000R) at **Tsentralny Dom Knigi** (Центральный Дом Книги), Krasny pr. 29 (open Mon.-Sat. 10am-2pm and 3-7pm). **Sibirsky Bank** (Сибирский Банк), ul. Lenina 4 (tel. 22 42 94), seems to be the only bank willing to give Visa cash advances (3% commission) or cash **traveler's checks** (2% commission). It also sends money via **Western Union** (open 10am-1pm and 2-4pm). There is a **pharmacy** at ul. Chaplygina 58 (tel. 23 32 07), at the corner of Krasny pr. across the street from St. Nicholas's Church (open daily 8am-7pm). The **post office,** ul. Sovietskaya 33 (tel. 22 05 83), is a philatelist's dream (open Mon.-Fri. 8am-7pm, Sat.-Sun. 8am-6pm). The **telephone office,** ul. Lenina 5 (tel. 22 02 28), is up the block and to the left (calls to Moscow 3400R per min.; open 24hr.). **Postal code:** 630099. **Phone code:** 3832.

Accommodations and Food Hotel prices come as big as the city, though a few mid-range options do exist. **Hotel Tsentralnaya** (Центральная), ul. Lenina 3 (tel. 22 72 94; fax 22 76 60), has clean, comfortable rooms and is about as central as you can get. Take the Metro to "Pl. Lenina" or trolleybus #25 from in front of the train station five stops to "Conservatoria" (singles 100,000R; doubles 220,000R). **Hotel Novosibirsk** (Новосибирск; tel. 20 11 20; fax 21 65 17), across from the train station, offers rooms with phone, fridge, and dynamic views of the city (singles 150,000R; doubles 240,000R; 16,700R surcharge for 1st night; 8350R for passport registration).

A large **market** covers nearly as much area as the stadium it borders on ul. Krylova (Крылова; open daily 8am-7pm). **Gastronom,** Krasny pr. 30, offers indoor shopping (open daily 8am-8pm). In the *Tsentralny Kompleks* mall (Центральный Комплекс), on the corner of ul. Lenina and Krasny pr., **Cafe Virineya** (Виринея) sells small pizzas (8000R) and meat-filled *piroshki* (4000R; open daily 11am-5pm and 6-10pm).

Sights and Entertainment The well-known opera and ballet theater companies on pl. Lenina leave for the summer. Nonetheless, traveling troupes come around in July and August, as do art exhibits. The popular **Novosibirskaya Kartinnaya Galereya** (Новосибирская Картинная Галерея; Novosibirsk Picture Gallery), Krasny pr. 5 (tel. 22 20 42), features a permanent exhibit of Russian artists of the 18th to 20th centuries (20,000R, students 10,000R). Across the street, **Soyuz Khudozhnikov** (Союз

Художников; Union of Artists' Gallery), Sverdlova 13 (tel. 23 44 38), exhibits the work of local artists (open Mon.-Fri. 10am-5pm; 2000R). Up Krasny pr. from the galleries, the tiny, golden-domed **Chasovnya vo imya Svyatitilya Nikolaya** (Часовня во имя Святитиля Николая; St. Nicholas's Church) supposedly sits smack dab in the middle of Russia (open daily noon-5pm). The larger **Khram Vozneseniya Gospodnya** (Храм Вознесения Господня; Ascension Church), on ul. Gogolya (Гоголя), flaunts a heavenly blue ceiling with classical paintings and a dazzling white and gold iconostasis (services Mon.-Fri. 9am and 5pm, Sun. 7am, 10am, and 5pm). **Kraevedchesky Muzey** (Краеведческий Музей; Regional Museum), Krasny pr. 19 (tel. 21 70 31), displays Russian pottery and other items from the Novosibirsk *oblast* (open Mon.-Fri. 10am-6pm; 5000R, students 1000R). **Tsentralny Park** (Центральный Парк) entertains kiddies with logwood playgrounds, a ferris wheel, and swings (5000R for 5min.). Novosibirsk's young set meets at the hip **Club 888,** on the other side of the river at M: Studenticheskaya; take a right upon exiting the Metro and another right behind the first building on your immediate right (open daily 8pm-4am).

■ Irkutsk (Иркуцк)

A Siberian trading post for three centuries, Irkutsk is one of the few eastern metropoles that sprang up *before* the Trans-Siberian's tracks were laid. A bazaar for fur-traders and a den for desperate gold-diggers, Irkutsk developed as a feisty mix of high culture and window-smashing brawls. The pit of unchecked capitalism said *"nyet"* to the Revolution in 1917, welcomed the retreating White troops, and only turned Red in 1920. Today, long-tempered by the shackles of a restrictive regime, Irkutsk has lost much of its fire, although nearby Lake Baikal beckons with wilds of its own.

Orientation and Practical Information Set your watch five hours forward from Moscow time. The Angara River bisects the town; the old city center and all the sights lie on the right bank, while the train station and some budget accommodations are situated on the residential left bank. The **train station,** on ul. Vokzalnaya (tel. 43 17 17 or 29 65 01) sends locomotives to: Moscow (1-3 per day, 3½ days, 1,127,000R); Novosibirsk (2-3 per day, 33hr., 463,600R); Ulan Ude (4-5 per day, 8hr., 193,500R); Vladivostok (1-2 per day, 3 days, 943,000R); and Ulaan Baatar (1-2 per day, 36hr., 330,000R). The following Trans-Siberian trains pass through (in Moscow time): train #2 to Vladivostok (odd days 1:19am); train #4 to Beijing (Sat. 4:04am, 600,000R); train #6 to Ulaan Baatar (Sun. and Mon. 4:04am, 330,000R); and train #20 to Beijing (Tues. 4:55am, 650,000R). Foreigners are required to purchase tickets from the **Intourist** *kassy* (tel. 28 28 20) on the station's second floor. **Luggage storage** is in a silver building beyond the red house to the left of the train station (5400-12,600R).

There is no official tourist office, but the 24-hour **Irkutsk-Baikal Travel Office,** inside Hotel Intourist, ul. Gagarina 44 (tel. 29 01 95; fax 29 03 14), is the next best thing. The agency sells **maps** and **tickets** for planes, trains, and the theater, and hands out free info about Irkutsk (English, French, and German spoken; open 24hr.). The travel office to the left of the reception desk **changes money** (24hr.), and you can send **email** from the Intourist Business Center (tel. 29 00 55; fax 29 03 14), on the hotel's third floor (US$3 per page). Irkutsk may be big, but only **Vneshtorgbank** (Внешторгбанк), ul. Sverdlova 40, room 201 (tel. 24 16 72), gives cash advances (MC and Visa; 1-2% commission) and changes **traveler's checks** (2% commission plus US$0.50 per check; open Mon.-Fri. 9:30am-3:30pm). The **Mongolian consulate,** ul. Lapina 11 (tel./fax 34 21 43 or 34 24 47), can arrange **visas.** (No invitation needed for 7-day tourist visa; 72hr. service US$25, 24hr. service US$50. Transit visa available with ongoing train ticket and valid Chinese visa for US$20. Consulate open Mon.-Sat. 9am-1pm and 2-6pm.) The main **post office,** ul. Stepana Rezina 23 (Степана Резина; tel. 33 26 92), accepts *Poste Restante* (16,500R; open Mon.-Fri. 8am-8pm, Sat.-Sun. 9am-6pm). The **telephone office** is at ul. Proletarskaya 11 (Пролетарская; tel. 34 36 36), across from the circus (open 24hr.). **Postal code:** 664000. **Phone code:** 3952.

Accommodations and Food **Amerikansky Dom** (Американский Дом), ul. Ovstrovskovo 19 (Островского; tel. 43 26 89; tel./fax 33 13 22), is owned by Lida Sclocchini, the Russian widow of the man from Philadelphia whose early-80s love affair was the basis for *From Russia With Love*. With the train station behind you, follow the tram tracks up the hill to your left and veer to the right where the tracks fork to the left; from here, walk up two blocks, take a right, and then take the first real left on the semi-paved road that leads up the hill. Ul. Ostrovskovo (unmarked) is about 400m ahead on the right, on the street below the main drag at the top of the hill; Amerikansky Dom is 30m down on your right (15-20min.). Alternatively, take a taxi from the station (20,000-30,000R). From ul. Lenina, on the right bank of town, bus #11 (dir. "ul. Chaikovskovo") runs to the "Magazin" stop; descend the hill and take the first left to reach ul. Ostrovskovo. The clean, American-style house has hot water and only seven beds; reserve in advance (bed and breakfast US$20; laundry US$5; Mongolian visas arranged). **Hotel Rus** (Гостиница Русь), ul. Sverdlova 19 (tel. 24 27 15), features clean, carpeted rooms with private toilets and hall showers (doubles 200,000R; single bed in a double 100,000R; breakfast included).

One of the town's many **supermarkets** (супермаркет) stocks meats and cheeses at ul. Stepina Razina 12 (open Mon.-Sat. 9am-2pm and 3-7pm, Sun. 11am-2pm and 3-7pm). The **central market** hawks fresh fruit, veggies, and meat (open daily 8am-8pm). Any form of transport that reads "рынок" (*rynok*) leads to the market. **Cafe Sport Express** (tel. 33 48 30), on ul. Stadion Trud, in the large stadium, serves killer *pelmeny* (13,200R), as well as a variety of other inexpensive and delicious dishes (open daily 10am-9pm). **Cafe Karlson** (Кафе Карлсон), ul. Lenina 15 (tel. 33 30 97), serves tough and juicy *langet* (лангет; pork; 13,200R), hearty salads, and *Beck's* beer (15,700R; open daily 11am-midnight).

Sights and Entertainment Irkutsk's most illustrious residents were the Decembrists, who arrived as exiles in the 19th century. Prince Sergey **Trubetskoy's house-museum** (Музей Трубецкого), ul. Dzerzhinskovo 64 (Дзержинского; tel. 27 57 73), exhibits his books, furniture, tapestried icons, silverware, and photos of his jail cell (open Mon. and Thurs.-Sun. 10am-6pm; *kassa* closes at 5:30pm; 15,000R, students 4000R). Another Decembrist *dom*, **Muzey-Dekabrista Volkonskovo** (Музей-Декабриста Болконского), ul. Volkonskovo 10 (tel. 27 57 73), waits on a dusty side street just off of ul. Timiryazeva (Тимирязева; open Tues.-Sun. 10am-6pm; *kassa* closes at 5:30pm; 15,000R, students 4000R). To get there, take trams #1-4 to "Dekabersky Sabitiye" and walk around the big domed church. Near the river, **Kraevedchesky Muzey** (Краеведческий Музей; Regional Museum), housed in a pink Victorian building at ul. Karla Marxa 2 (tel. 33 34 49), exhibits furs, skis, Buddhist masks, drums, woven icons, music shells, and pipes of local Siberian tribes. Antique clothes and furniture in old Russian styles wait next door (open Tues.-Sun. 11am-6pm; 15,000R). **Khudozhestvenny Muzey Imeni Sukacheva** (Художественный Музей Имени Сукачева; Sukachev Art Museum), ul. Lenina 5 (tel. 34 42 30), houses Chinese vases, Siberian paintings of the 16th-20th centuries, and a display of the works of the *peredvizhniky* (traveling artists; open Wed.-Sun. 10am-6pm; 20,000R). The elegant gold-columned iconostasis in **Znamenskaya Manastyr** (Знаменская Манастырь), north of the town center on ul. Angarskaya (Ангарская), is brightened by a golden chandelier-lit interior. Take trolley #3 or buses #8, 13, or 31 to the first stop past the northern bridge, or walk along ul. Frank Kamenetskovo (Франк Каменецкого), bear right at the fork, and carefully cross the street to the blue-green domes (open daily 8:30am-8pm; services daily 8:30 and 11am). **Bogoyavlensky Sobor** (Богоявленский Собор; Epiphany Church), to the west (open daily 8:30am-5pm), and **Spasskaya Tserkov** (Спасская Церковь; Savior's Church), to the north, have both recently reopened. Irkutsk's light blue **synagogue,** on ul. Karla Libknekhta 23 (Карла Либкнехта; tel. 27 53 67), off of ul. Karla Marxa, holds services Saturdays at 10:30am (open Mon.-Fri. 10am-5pm). A **mosque** rises high at Karla Libknekhta 86.

At night, many youth head to the aptly-named **Ostrov Unosty** (Остров Уности; Youth Island), across the bridge near the regional museum. Although swimming is prohibited, rented **canoes** and **water-skis** ply the waters. The white spiky building hosts discotheques (Fri. and Sat. 11pm-3am; cover 15,000R).

■ Lake Baikal (Озеро Байкал)

A natural freak, a clear-blue oddity, mighty Baikal defies the definition of "lake," diving into the realm of fantasy. At 1637m, it is the **deepest freshwater body of water** in the world—those gaping jaws guard one-fifth of the earth's unsalted water. Twenty-five million years old, it is also the world's most ancient lake (most aren't older than 100,000). Surrounded by snow-capped peaks, its deep blue waters teem with species found nowhere else in the world—translucent shrimp, oversized sturgeon, and deep-water fish that explode when brought to the surface. The *nerpa* freshwater seal lives 3000km from its closest relative, the Arctic seal, and no one knows quite how it got here. One deep-water fish has evolved into a gelatinous blob of fat—so fatty, in fact, that locals stick wicks in the lipidinous lumps and use them as candles.

Baikal's **shores** are no less fascinating than its waters. Reindeer, polar foxes, wild horses, brown bears, wild boars, and nefarious Siberian weasels hide in the forested surrounding mountains, while glacial lakes melt into ice-cold waterfalls. Wooden villages and Buryat *ger* (tent) communities border the edges. Painted rocks and "wishing" trees strung with colored rags recall the locale's shamanistic heritage, and the Buryat region to the northeast counts 45 Buddhist monasteries. Deserted gulags (where many lamas and shamans spent their last days under an atheist regime) pepper the outskirts.

In **winter** the lake freezes, and ferry routes become roads for trucks. During the Russo-Japanese war (1904-05), the army even built train tracks over the ice in order to get troops to the front lines faster. No engine ever made it across, however; the first train car fell through the ice and started the watery graveyard of trains, trucks, and other vehicles that now lies at the lake's bottom.

The human touch has not always been kind to Baikal's gentle ecology. Intense fishing has decimated some species, and pollution from upriver cities and shoreside factories has begun to disturb the balanced ecology. One of the lake's greatest threats could be the **Irkutsk dam,** located 5km south of Irkutsk proper. Hundreds of rivers feed into Baikal, but only one, the Angara, flows out. Legend has it that poppa Baikal once threw a rock at his errant daughter Angara in an attempt to steer her back from falling in love with a chap named Yenisey, whom he didn't like. He failed for millennia, but with the Irkutsk dam, mighty dad might be getting his wish. Unfortunately, the dam has raised water levels, which is slowly ruining the shallower feeding grounds of Baikal's famous trout (*omul*).

Getting to Lake Baikal can be a tricky matter, as most of the lake's shoreline is inaccessible by public transportation. Make sure you bring along food and have plenty of time to spare if you plan to camp and hike along the lakeshore. The most popular destination for day-trippers is the village of **Listvyanka** (Листвянка), situated on the lake at the mouth of the Angara River, 69km southeast of Irkutsk. **Buses** (5 per day, 80min., 18,000R) run to Listvyanka from Irkutsk's bus station, on ul. Oktyabrskaya Revolutsiye 11 (tel. 27 24 11). A quicker and more interesting way to get to Listvyanka is to take a **hydrofoil** from Irkutsk's "Raketa" terminal (tel. 23 80 53), on ul. Solnichnaya, south of town (2-3 per day, 1hr., 23,000R). From ul. Lenina in Irkutsk, take bus #16 or trolleybus #5 to the terminal (20min., 2000R).

Listvyanka itself (pop. 2500) is a tourist-friendly town where meandering cows battle tourists and their cars for control over the one and only real street, ul. Gorkovo (Горково), which runs from the boat dock to the ritzy Hotel Baikal, where Yeltsin and German Chancellor Helmut Kohl stayed during their trip to Lake Baikal in 1993. **St. Nicholas's Church,** ul. Kylekova 88 (tel. 571), built in gratitude for a miraculous ship rescue, sits off in the hills with a dark green dome. Backtrack from the boat terminal and turn right when you see the stream. The cows may moo and follow you unless you moo back. Plain white walls and detailed, golden-framed icons wait inside the church (open Mon.-Fri. 10am-6pm; services Sat.-Sun. 8:30am-noon and 1-7pm).

Housing options are not hard to find. Several of the homeowners on **ul. Chipaeva** (Чипаева), the first right off the main street heading away from the boat docks, rent out rooms in their *dachas*. The owners of **Traktir** (Трактир), ul. Chipayeva 24, will put you up in their gorgeous wooden house (US$25 per person, breakfast included) and let you use their *banya* (bathhouse). Listvyanka's cheapest overnight option is the *babushka*-run **Listvyanskoe Lesinchestvo** (Листвянское Лесинчество), in a wooden house with bright red signs out front. The old ladies who run the place sell brochures and **maps** (10,000R) of Lake Baikal and the surrounding area (beds 83,000R). The **post office** is a minute's walk away at ul. Gorkovo 49 (open Mon.-Fri. 8:30am-1pm and 3-5:30pm, Sat. 8:30am-noon; closed last Thurs. of each month).

In recent years, authorities and international organizations have begun initiatives to preserve the region. **Barguzinsky Zapovednik** (Баргузинский Заповедник; Barguzinsky National Reserve), on Baikal's east shore, was Russia's first national reserve. **Pribaykalsky Natsionalny Park** (Прибайкальский Национальный Парк) encompasses much of the lake's west coast, and is the closest reserve to Irkutsk. When fog doesn't obscure the forest tops, views spread over pine-trees and crystal clear water. Some days, visibility is better in the water (30m) than on land. **Olkhon Island,** also part of the park, is a prime spot for seal watching.

■ Ulan Ude (Улан Удэ)

Capital of the Buryat Republic and epicenter of Russian Buddhism, Ulan Ude's surreal offerings include the biggest bust of Lenin known to man, which graces the main square. Visitors won't find many Russians here, however—only Asian Buryats who speak fluent Russian and practice Buddhism and Shamanism rather than Russian Orthodoxy. Founded as a Cossack fort on the Slenga River in the 18th century, the town—originally called Verkhnyudinsk—served as a trading center for caravans traveling between Russia and China. Renamed Ulan Ude (Buryat for "Red Uda," one of its two rivers) in 1934 in a Soviet attempt to recognize the Buryat people, the city is much more Asian than Irkutsk. The *datsan* (Buddhist monastery) in Ivolga, 28km away, provides reason enough to stop in Ulan Ude en route to Ulaan Baatar.

Orientation and Practical Information Ulan Ude, five hours ahead of Moscow time, is in the same **time zone** as Mongolia and all of China. The **train station,** just off ul. Revolutsiy 1905-a goda (tel. 34 25 31), lies north of the city center, and sends trains to: Moscow (1-3 per day, 8hr., 1,250,000R); Irkutsk (4-5 per day, 8hr.,193,300R); Vladivostok (1-2 per day, 64hr., 832,000R); Ulaan Baatar (1 per day, 24hr., 231,000R), and Beijing (2 per week, 560,000R). Ulan Ude is the last (or first, depending on the direction you're traveling) major Russian city on the Trans-Mongolian line. The following Trans-Siberian **trains** pass through the city (in Moscow time): train #2 to Vladivostok (odd days at 9:00 am); train #4 to Beijing (Sat. at 11:49am); train #20 to Beijing (Tues. at 12:36pm); and train #6 to Ulaan Baatar (Sun.-Mon. at 11:49am). Foreigners are required to purchase tickets from the Intourist *kassa* on the second floor of the station; look for the door with the Международные Кассы sign. **Luggage storage** is in the red building to the right of the station (small bags 5400R, backpacks 12,600R). Ulan Ude's main square, **pl. Sovyetov** (Советов), lies 0.5km south of the station; take bus #10 or #36 to reach it (1500R). The main artery, **ul. Lenina,** runs south from pl. Sovyetov. Forget about cash advances in Ulan Ude, but **Buryatsky Bank Sberbanka Rossiye** (Вурятский Банк Сбербанка России), ul. Lenina 49 (tel. 21 65 58), exchanges traveler's checks (4% commission) and various foreign currencies (open Mon.-Thurs. 8:30am-1pm and 2-4pm, Fri. 8:30am-3pm). A **pharmacy** can be found at ul. Lenina 29 (tel. 21 24 37; open daily 8am-2pm and 2:30-8pm). Mail postcards of Buddhist shrines from the **main post office,** ul. Lenina 61 (tel. 21 51 31). **EMS** is at counter #6 (open Mon.-Fri. 8am-7pm, Sat.-Sun. 9am-6pm). The 24-hour **telephone office** is at ul. Barsoyava 25 (Барсоява; tel. 21 36 24 or 21 24 63), behind the train station (to Moscow 6000R per minute, to the US 9800-19,600R per minute). **Postal code:** 670000. **Phone code:** 3012.

Accommodations and Food The best budget hotel is **Hotel Barguzin** (Баргузин), ul. Sovietskaya 28 (tel. 21 57 46). Take bus #36 from the train station and ask the driver for the hotel by name; or take bus #10 to pl. Sovietov, walk two blocks down ul. Lenina, and make a right on ul. Sovietskaya. There's no hot water, but if you smile and wheedle, the friendly staff might sneak you a room at the Russian rate (singles 88,000R, with TV 93,000R; doubles 59,000R per bed; triples 44,000R per bed). The hotel's **snack bar** is open 24 hours. **Hotel Oden** (Одон), ul. Gagarina 43 (Гагарина; tel. 24 34 80), has bare rooms with few amenities (40,000-60,000R per person). Exit the train station going right and take the first left on ul. Yerbanova (Ербанова), and then the second left onto ul. Gagarina. Numerous small **cafes** line ul. Lenina. **Kinsburger** (Кинсбургер), ul. Lenina 21 (tel. 21 52 53), serves a decent hamburger (7000R) and *Buryat krokyet* (крокет; 7000R), a dumpling filled with potatoes, lettuce, and some meaty stuff they call *farsh* (open daily 8am-1am).

Sights and Entertainment Begin your tour of Ulan Ude at the city's main square, **pl. Sovyetov,** which is crowned by an unbelievably enormous figurehead of Vladimir Ilyich Lenin. It's so big that it's even listed in the *Guinness Book of World Records* as the largest bust in the world (Dolly Parton might disagree). The Soviet-era buildings built around pl. Sovyetov house Buryat Republic government offices. At the southwest corner of the square stands the yellow **Buryat State Academic Theater of Opera and Ballet** (Бурятский Государственный Академический театр оперы и балета), a classical-style building with two horsemen perched on top to guard the front entrance; the steps on the theater's rear side afford stunning views of the downtown area and the surrounding mountains (theater performances premiere Oct.-May at 7pm; inquire at the *kassy* about obtaining tickets).

The recently opened **Muzey Istorii Buryatii** (Музей истории бурятии; Museum of Buryat History), ul. Profsoyuznaya 29 (Профсоюзная; tel. 21 65 87), off ul. Kommunisticheskaya by Hotel Buryatia, was first founded in 1923, but closed down, supposedly for renovation, in 1980. True renovations began only after Ulan Ude celebrated the 250th anniversary of Buddhism in Russia in 1992, and it finally reopened to the public in May 1997. Today the museum showcases the marvelously intricate iconographic tapestries of **Boatogalay Dugarov,** Buryatia's most famous artist. Pictures depict Dugarov with his son, also an artist of Buddhist iconography, and his mentor, with whom he built the Temple of Great Liberation, a Buddhist shrine in northern Italy. Though the display is currently contained in only four rooms, the museum plans to open exhibits on two more floors by the end of 1997 (open Tues.-Sun. 10am-6pm; 10,000R, students 3000R).

Walking four blocks south on ul. Kommunisticheskaya brings you to ul. Kirora (Кирова), and the local **Iamrim** (ламрим; Buddhist shrine). Walk past the black gate and ask to take a peek inside. The immediate neighborhood of 18th- and 19th-century **wooden houses** is the oldest part of town. The crumbling 18th-century **Odigitrysky Sobor** (Одигитрийский Собор), at the southern tip of ul. Lenina, houses perhaps the best collection of Buddhist artifacts in Russia; unfortunately, the cathedral is closed and the dusty collection is not currently open to the public; but if you plead, the Buryat *babushka* guarding the front door may be kind enough to show you around. If all goes according to plan, the collection, which was assembled from artifacts recovered from *datsans* closed by the Soviets, should move to a more permanent home in Muzey Istorii Buratii (see above) by 1998.

The two most interesting sights lie outside the city limits. The **Ethnografichesky Muzey** (Етнографический Музей; tel. 33 57 54), 10km north of the city center, can be reached by bus #8 from in front of Hotel Baikal (Байкал) at pl. Sovyetov (every 30min., 2000R). Ask the driver to drop you off at "Etnographichesky Muzey," then walk about 1km down the road that veers left from the bus stop (15min.); the museum will appear beyond a green fence on your right. The museum is an open-air complex of reconstructed buildings meant to depict the lifestyles of people in the Baikal and Buryat region. The "Buryat complex" consists of several **ger** (traditional Buryat tent-homes, also known as yurts), and the "Russian old-life complex" features an almost perfect copy of a wooden Russian country church (open Tues.-Sun. 9am-6pm, *kassa* closes at 5pm; 20,000R, Russians 5000R, students 3000R).

The most beautiful building in the Buryat region is in the hamlet of **Ivolga** (Иволга), 28km west of Ulan Ude. In the middle of the hills stands **Datsan-Ivolga,** a large Buddhist monastery complete with a yellow, curved roof, a white picket fence with Buddhist prayer drums, and a slew of Mongolian-trained Buddhist **lamas.** Built in 1972, the shrine served as the center of Buddhism in the former Soviet Union. In the main temple are several Buddhist scriptures handwritten in Tibetan and Sanskrit, and a display of gifts. Around the edge of the complex are 120 prayer drums, each filled with a sacred scripture. The lamas' houses are behind the complex. From the bus station in Ulan Ude, take **bus #130** (every 25-30 min) to Ivolga and walk 3km to the *datsan* (free; visit in the morning or early afternoon).

THE VOLGA REGION (ПОВОЛЖЬЕ)

The longest river in Europe, the 3700km Volga is Russia's main trade artery, linking Moscow with five seas and oceans. The fertile threesome of the Volga, Don, and Oka rivers gave birth to Russian civilization around the 7th century. The Slavs prospered here until the first wave of Mongol invasions forced them north. But even northern forests and powerful fortresses provided insufficient protection, and they were soon overrun—within half a century, the Russians were able to push back south to Azov and reclaim their ancestral lands. *Povolzhye* (literally "along the Volga") includes primarily the territories of the middle and lower Volga. Previously closed to foreign visitors, the cities of Nizhny Novgorod, Kazan, and Ulyanovsk are mostly significant as trade and industrial ports, yet have wildly different historical origins.

■ Nizhny Novgorod (Нижний Новгород)

According to a Russian proverb, St. Petersburg is Russia's head, Moscow its heart—and Nizhny Novgorod its pocket. Once peripheral to the Russian state, but now a center of privatization, Nizhny Novgorod (NEEZH-nee NOHV-guh-rud, formerly Gorky) is Russia's third largest city, with a population of 1,500,000. Founded in 1221, the city has established itself over the last two centuries as the center of the Russian economy, with the Nizhny Novgorod Trade Fair its main claim to fame. The Soviet-strangled Trade Fair was resuscitated in the early 1990s as part of economic reforms introduced by the former governor, who became vice prime minister of Russia in May 1997. Nizhny opened its gates to foreigners in 1991, welcoming tourists with smiling, industrious citizens more optimistic about their future than most Russians.

ORIENTATION AND PRACTICAL INFORMATION

Central Nizhny has two levels: the lower one includes the river station and **ul. Rozh-destvenskaya** (ул. Рождественская), and the upper, larger level boasts the Gorky museums, the **kremlin,** and the art museums. The main pedestrian street, **ul. Bolshaya Pokrovskaya** (Большая Покровская; formerly Sverdlova), runs from the kremlin to **pl. Gorkovo** (пл. Горького), and is lined with stores, restaurants, and cafes. **Verkhne-Volzhskaya nab.** (Верхне-Волжская наб.), originating near the kremlin, rises up to the top of a cliff overlooking the river. The **Nizhny Novgorod Trade Fair,** on the bank of the Oka near pl. Lenina (Ленина), is also a useful reference marker.

Tourist Office: Intourist, pl. Lenina, in Tsentralnaya Gostinitsa (Центральная Гостиница), Rm. 814. Open when they want to be. Plane and rail bookings.

Currency Exchange: Gostinitsa Oktyabrskaya (Октябрьская), Verkhne-Volzhskaya nab. 5. Cashes traveler's checks at 6% commission, and gives cash advances on Eurocard and MC. Open daily 8:30am-1pm and 2-6pm. Take your Visa card to **Inkom Bank** (Инком Банк), Varvaskaya 32 (Варваская; tel. 37 94 42). Open Mon.-Sat.

Kharkiv · Kupyansk · Don R. · Frolovo · N

UKRAINE · Severodonetsk · Millerova · Dubovka · Volgograd · KAZAKHSTAN

Chur R. · Cherny-shkovsky · Kalach-na-Donu · Volzhskiy · Krasnoslobodsk · Shungay

Kramatorsk · Lugansk · Kamensk-Shakhtinskiy · Morozovsk · Krasnoslobodsk · Akhtubinsk

Artemovsk · Gorlovka · Gukovo · Tsimlyanskoye Vdkhr.

Konstantinovka · Novoshakhtinsk · Shakhty · Tsimlyansk

Donetsk · Makeyevka · Novocherkassk · Kotelnikovo · Volga R. · Kopanova · Yenotayevka

Mariupol · Taganrog · Rostov-na-Donu · RUSSIA · Krasny Yar

Berdyansk · Azov · Port-Katon · Zernograd · Proletarskaya · Astrakhan

Primorska (Nogaysk) · Yeysk · Kushchevskaya · Salsk · Manich R. · Elitsa · Kirovsky

Azovskoye More (Sea of Azov) · Kanevskaya · Staraminskaya · Belaya Glina

Primorsko-Akhtarsk · Timashevsk · Tikhoretsk · Kaspijskoye More (Caspian Sea)

Slavyansk-na-Kubani · Korenovsk

Kerch · Taman · Temryuk · Ust-Labinsk · Armavir · Stavropol · Neftekumsk

Anapa · Krymsk Abinsk · Yekaterinodar · Maykop · Nevinnomyssk

Novorossiysk · Gelendzhika · Khadyzhensk · Mineralnyye Vody

Tuapse · Yessentuki · Pyatigorsk · Mozdak · Kizlyar

Chornoje More (Black Sea) · Krasnaya Polyana · Karachayevsk · Kislovodsk · Terek R.

0   100 miles   Sochi · Adler · Dombai · Teberda · Tyrnyauz · Malgobek · Kaspiysk

0   100 kilometers   Gagra · C A U C A S U S · Nalchik · Grozny · Makhachkala

Sukhumi · Mt. Elbrus 5633m · Mt. Kazbek 5047m · Mt. Tebulos 4492m

Ochamchira · GEORGIA · Derbent

Southern Volga Region and Caucasus · Poti · Kutaisi · Chiatura · Tskhinvali

Kobuleti · Chashuri · Gori · Tbilisi · Rustavi

Batumi · TURKEY · ARMENIA · AZERBAIJAN

8:30am-1pm and 2-8pm. An **ATM** (банкомат) at Bolskaya Pokrovskaya 24 accepts Plus, Cirrus, Visa, and MC.

Trains: Moskovsky Vokzal (Московский Вокзал), across the river from the kremlin. Trains to Kazan (1 per day, 9hr., 73,000R) and Moscow (3 per day, 8hr., 84,000R), via Vladimir (4hr., 55,000R).

Buses: Coming out of the train station, the *avtovokzal* (автовокзал) is a 5min. walk to the left. Buses are generally more crowded than trains. To Moscow (4 per day, 9hr., 93,000R) and Vladimir (6 per day, 5hr., 53,000R). Open daily 6am-10:30pm.

Ferries: Nizhne-Volzhskaya nab. (Нижне-Волжская; tel: 34 04 25). Prices ascend by quality category (1-3, depending on what level of the deck you want to be on). To: Kazan (4pm, 19hr., 82,400-609,500R); Moscow (noon, 6 days, 142,300-1,520,800R); Volgograd (4pm, 90hr., 213,400-1,579,200R); and Yaroslavl (noon, 20hr., 82,400-609,500R). Open daily 7am-6pm.

Public Transportation: Nizhny is clearly laid out but bigger than most Russian towns; you'd do well to use public transportation and confine your travels to central Nizhny. A 1-day pass for buses and express buses (denoted by "э" after the number) costs 2000R at blue booths labeled "проездные карточки" (*proezdnye kartochki*); a 5-day pass is 9500R. On trams and trolleys, pay the conductor or driver 1000R. Taxi-buses (marked with a "T" prefix) are 2500R. Most destinations are marked on the front of the bus. Any bus or trolley labeled "Московский Вокзал" goes across the river to the train station and stops at the ferry station and Tsentralnaya Gostinitsa. Any bus or tram with "#1 Минина" on the side goes to the town center. Public transportation runs until 11:30pm, which may explain why the restaurants and bars on Bolshaya Pokrovskaya close at 11pm.

Taxis: Most taxis never turn on their meters, but the "official" prices are posted on the sides of the cabs: 3000R initial charge plus 3000R for each km. Be prepared to be asked how much you expect to spend; approximate the mileage and haggle.

Luggage Storage: 24hr. lockers 8900R; special coins sold. Turn the four buttons on the inside of the locker to pick a combination. Put the coin in the slot and close.

Post Office: ul. Bolshaya Pokrovskaya 56, at pl. Gorkovo. Open 8am-8pm. **Postal code:** 603000.

Telephones: Next to the post office at pl. Gorkovo 1. Pay at window #4. Receipt lists your booth number. Dial 8; wait for the tone; then dial 3 when you hear an answer. Local calls are free. To the U.S. 19,600R per min. 8am-8pm, 9800R per min. 8pm-8am. Open Mon.-Sat. 8am-10pm, Sun. 8am-6pm. **Phone code:** 8312.

ACCOMMODATIONS

Most hotels in Nizhny Novgorod gladly accept foreigners, although each has its own approach to the pricing system. Foreigners are generally charged 150-200% more than Russians, although some of the ritzier establishments, such as the overpriced Oktyabrskaya, have become more egalitarian—maybe someday the rest will follow.

Gostinitsa Volzhsky Otkos (Гостиница Волжский Откос), Verkhne-Volzhskaya nab. 2a (tel. 39 19 71; fax 36 38 94). Facing the kremlin, walk toward the right and turn right at the river. A large, gray hotel right on the Volga in a quiet neighborhood, easy walking distance from the center, but far from the train station. Friendly and happily free of discrimination against foreigners. Singles 100,000R; doubles 250,000R, with view of Volga 300,000R.

Gostinitsa Tsentralnaya (Центральная), ul. Sovetskaya 12 (Советская; tel. 34 59 34), 10min. from the train station and next door to the Trade Fair. Spectacular view of the Oka. Singles with bath, TV, telephone, and refrigerator 264,000R; doubles 442,000. 24hr. room service available from the decent restaurant downstairs.

FOOD

The recent private enterprise explosion has brought a slew of new cafes to town. Many flank ul. Bolshaya Pokrovskaya. Do-it-yourselfers go to the **Torzhok grocery store** (Торжок) on Bolshaya Pokrovksaya near ul. Piskunova (Пискунова; open 24hr.), or the **Dmitrievsky grocery store** (Дмитриевский) on Piskunova (open daily 8am-8pm). The **Mytny Rynok** (Мытный Рынок), between #2 and 4 on Bolshaya Pokrovskaya, vends fruits and vegetables in the summer (open daily 6am-7pm).

Cafe Arlekin (Кафе Арлекин), Bolshaya Pokrovskaya 8A (tel. 33 99 07). A decent selection of moderately priced salads (around 10,000R) and soups (7600-8600R). Try the special *pelmeni* with mushroom sauce (11,000R). Open daily 10am-10pm.

Gardinia (Гардиния), Verkhne-Volzhskaya nab. (tel. 36 41 01), near the art museum, a 5min. walk along the cliff. Large outdoor fast-food joint with flowered umbrellas and a mongo model airplane, started by an American and frequented by wealthy Russians. Chicken filet 25,500R, cabbage salad 10,000R. Also fried potatoes, onion soup, spaghetti, and—Barbie dolls at the adjacent toy store (75,000R!). Open daily 10am-10pm. Visa accepted.

Russkye Pelmeni (Русские Пельмени), Bolshaya Pokrovskaya 24 (tel. 33 21 07). *Pelmeni* served in bouillon or with cheese, sour cream, or butter—all for less than 7000R. *Bliny* 2700R. Cold borscht 4600R. Open daily 10am-9pm.

Houston Bar & Café (tel. 36 02 00), across from the Gardinia and Gostinitsa Oktyabrskaya. Well-to-do Americanophiles, good food, good hours, and an English-speaking owner and menu. Every meal includes veggies and fries. Main dishes 18,000-50,000R, drinks 5000-25,000R. Open Mon.-Fri. 1pm-2am, Sat.-Sun. noon-2am. Visa accepted.

SIGHTS AND ENTERTAINMENT

Nizhny Novgorod's importance as a border town is most visible at the **kremlin.** Resting atop one of Russia's few hills, the fortress surveys a vast expanse, making the town a perfect bastion against the armies of Genghis Khan. The kremlin's eight-

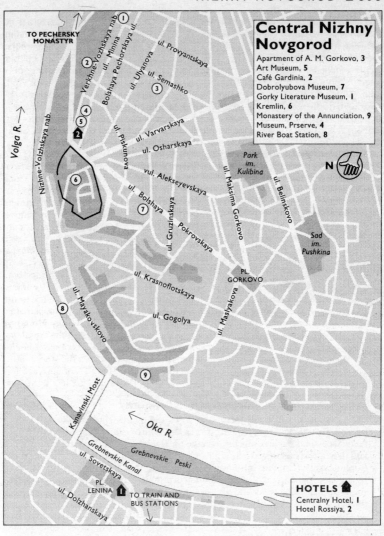

Central Nizhny Novgorod

Apartment of A. M. Gorkovo, 3
Art Museum, 5
Café Gardinia, 2
Dobrolyubova Museum, 7
Gorky Literature Museum, 1
Kremlin, 6
Monastery of the Annunciation, 9
Museum, Prserve, 4
River Boat Station, 8

TO PECHERSKY MONASTYR

Volga R. →

Verkhne-Vozhskaya nab.
ul. Minina
Bolshaya Pechorskaya ul.
ul. Ulyanova
ul. Provyantskaya
ul. Semashko
Nizhne-Volzhskaya nab.
ul. Piskunova
ul. Varvarskaya
ul. Osharskaya
vul. Alekseyevskaya
ul. Bolshaya
ul. Gruzinskaya
Pokrovskaya
ul. Maksima Gorkovo
Park im. Kulibina
ul. Belinskovo
Sad im. Pushkina
ul. Krasnoflotskaya
PL. GORKOVO
ul. Gogolya
ul. Masyakova
ul. Mayakovskovo
Kanavinski Most.
Oka R.
Grebnevskie Kanal
Grebnevskie Peski
ul. Sovetskaya
ul. Dolzhanskaya
PL. LENINA
TO TRAIN AND BUS STATIONS

HOTELS
Centralny Hotel, 1
Hotel Rossiya, 2

meter-thick walls still serve as a defense: the premises house a bank, an art museum, the local governor and mayor's offices, and the 1631 **Arkhangelsky Sobor** (Архан-гельский Собор; Archangel Cathedral), now a museum of the city's history (closed for repairs in summer 1997). The courtyard boasts an impressive collection of WWII-era tanks and other military vehicles. All can be climbed—pretend you're Patton.

The **Khudozhestvenny muzey** (Художественный музей; Art Museum), within the kremlin walls, exhibits Russian art from the 15th to 20th centuries. The works from before the 17th century, largely church art, are labeled in English as well as in Russian. Art from the 18th and 19th centuries includes portraits of tsars and other Russian VIPs; Russian artist Repin adds some color with, among other works, a vivid sketch of Ivan IV embracing his son after dealing his fatal blow. Russian peasants make a showing in Brueghelistic candor. To find the museum, bear right after entering the kremlin and head back to the large white building. (Open Wed.-Mon. 10am-5pm; 20,000R, students 10,000R. Photography permit 100,000R.)

The best part of the **Literaturny muzey imeni Gorkovo** (Литературний музей им. А. М. Горького; Gorky Literary Museum), ul. Minina 26 (tel. 36 65 83), is the building housing it—a 19th-century mansion complete with mirrors, cherubs, velvet wallpaper, and carved dark wood. The inside supposedly shows the literary and cultural achievements of Gorky's contemporaries, with a sprinkling of his handwriting specimens. A photo of 19th-century Nizhny lends some historical perspective (open Wed.-Sun. 9am-5pm; 3000R; guided tours 2000R per person). To visit the **Kvartira A. M. Gorkovo** (Квартира А. М. Горького; Gorky's Apartment), ul. Semashko 19 (Семашко; tel. 36 16 51), turn right off Verkhne-Volzhskaya nab. one street after Gostinitsa Oktyabrskaya, and keep walking for a couple of blocks; the museum is on the right. Gorky lived here from 1902 until 1904 (open Tues.-Wed. and Fri.-Sun. 9am-5pm).

The **Muzey Sakharova** (Музей Сахарова; Sakharov Museum), pr. Gagarina 214 (Гагарина; tel. 66 86 23), is reachable by trolley #13 from pl. Minina or bus #43 from the Trade Fair down pr. Gagarina to "Музей Сахарова" (about 30min. from pl. Gorkovo). Cross the street, and it's just to the right. The Nobel Laureate and physicist Andrei Dmitryevich Sakharov lived on the first floor of this typically Soviet apartment block while in internal exile from 1980 until 1986. Guards watched his every movement, and he was forbidden to have visitors or even a telephone in his apartment (open Sat.-Thurs. 9am-5pm; 4000R; call to reserve English tours, 8000R).

There are two monasteries in Nizhny. The operational **Blagoveshchensky Muzhskoy Monastyr** (Благовещенский Мужской Монастырь; Annunciation Monastery), is up the hill a short distance from where ul. Rozhdestrenskaya ends and the bridge over the river begins. The monastery was founded in 1221; it reopened in 1993 after a period of sad Soviet dilapidation. Most of the surviving structures date back to the 17th century. The **cathedral** and **church** are open to the public, while the **planetarium** is a remaining sign of the Soviet use of sacred spaces. **Pechersky Monastyr** (Печерский Монастырь), on the lower banks of the Volga, is closed, but the crumbling building and overgrown foliage are welcomingly mind-numbing. Take bus #24 or 74 to "*avtovokzal*"; then walk all the way down the street across from the stop.

The tourboat **Moskva** (Москва), docked across from the Hotel Tsentralnaya, offers 2-hour rides around the Volga and Oka rivers (6700R). Departures are nightly at 6pm.

Watch Out for Grandma

They push harder than anyone on the buses and metro. They bundle up to the ears on even the hottest days in scarves and winter coats, then strip down to teeny-weeny bikinis and sunbathe on the banks of the Neva. They are *babushki*, and they mean business. Technically, *babushka* means grandma, but under the Communist system, Russians began using it as a generic term for elderly women. In any case, be warned: if a *babushka* gets on the metro, no matter how hardy she looks, and how weak and tired you feel, surrender your seat, or prepare for the verbal pummeling of a lifetime.

■ Kazan (Казань)

Dating from the 14th century, Kazan (kah-ZAHN) is one of the oldest Tatar settlements in Russia. But in 1552, Ivan the Terrible annexed it to Russia after a devastating siege. Today Kazan is the capital of the Republic of Tatarstan, which declared its autonomy from Russia in 1990. Suspended between the Muslim East and the Christian West, the city is remarkable for the surprisingly harmonious coexistence of the Russians and the Tatars, who respectively comprise 54% and 40% of the population. The green, white, and red Tatarstan flag shares space with the Russian flag, while all streets and stores display bilingual signs.

ORIENTATION AND PRACTICAL INFORMATION

Kazan, a city of a little more than a million inhabitants, lies on the east bank of the **Volga** at the point where the river turns from east to south. Moscow is 700km to the west, Ulyanovsk 172km to the south. The city straddles the **Kazanka** (Казанка) river, which feeds into the Volga from the northeast. The streets of the old city on the south bank of the Kazanka splay out from the 16th-century **kremlin. Ul. Baumana** (Баумана), the main shopping street, links the kremlin with **ul. Kuybysheva** (Куйбышева), the city's commercial center. **Maps** are available in the lobby of Gostinitsa Tatarstan (Гостиница Татарстан), pl. Kuybysheva 2, for 5000-10,000R. To reach the center from the **train station,** catch tram #2 or 4 in front of the main building. From the **river station** (речной вокзал; *rechnoy vokzal*), take trolley #2 or tram #7.

Tourist Office: Intourist (Интурист), ul. Baumana 9, 2nd floor of Hotel Kazan (tel. 32 41 95). No maps, no free info—just tours for prices we aren't allowed to know for "commercial reason." Open Mon.-Fri. 9am-1pm and 2-6pm.

Currency Exchange: Spot an "Обмен Валюты" sign to change your US$ or DM. Cash only. Rates vary little, and there is generally no commission.

Trains: ul. Said-Galieva (Саид-Галиева; tel. 39 23 00). Connections to: Moscow (1 per day, 13hr., 96,000R); Nizhny Novgorod (1 per day, 9hr., 74,000R); Volgograd (1 per day, 37hr., 120,000R); and St. Petersburg (1 per day, 28hr., 166,000R). Buy all tickets on the 2nd floor, and check out the computerized info booths. Another ticket office is at ul. Galiaskara Kamala (Галиаскара Камала), around the corner from the Aeroflot office (see above; open daily 8am-noon and 1-7pm).

Public Transportation: Trams, trolleys, and **buses** are cheap, frequent, and crowded. The faster the vehicle moves, the more packed it will be. You may be able to breathe on a tram. Tickets (800R) can be purchased individually or in strips of 10 from the driver, or from light-blue kiosks at the stations and pl. Kuybysheva. Tickets are sometimes collected as you exit. Billboard maps of the tram and trolley routes are posted at the river station and in pl. Kuybysheva.

Taxis: Many drivers are private citizens trying to make a few dollars. They habitually triple their rates for foreign passengers. Negotiate for 5000R per km.

Ferries: ul. Portovaya (Портовая; tel. 32 07 05). Ferries (теплоходы; *teplokhody*) leave for Moscow (every other day, 179,000-1,329,900R) and all points along the Volga. Cheap, fast **hydrofoils**—*rakety* (ракеты) and *meteory* (метеоры)—cover shorter routes at least once per day (Nizhny Novgorod, 54,000R). Departures are often early in the morning.

Luggage Storage: In the train station. 8900R per day. Open 24hr.

Post Office: ul. Lenina 8 (Ленина). Use the hall on the left for **faxes** and letters (window #6). Photocopying also available. Open Mon.-Fri. 8am-1pm and 2-7pm, Sat.-Sun. 9am-6pm. **Postal code:** 420111.

Telephones: Mezhdugorodny telefon (Междугородный телефон), ul. Pushkina 15 (Пушкина). Order international calls 1-2hr. ahead. Open 24hr. **Phone code:** 8432.

ACCOMMODATIONS

The Tatarstan authorities have ruled that foreigners pay roughly 150% more than Tatars for hotel rooms. Don't take it personally: hotel owners will reassure you that Latvians, Lithuanians, Estonians, and Moldovans suffer the same fate. Moreover, only two hotels in town will take foreigners. With a struggle, foreign students at Russian universities can pay the lower rate. Bring your student card and a letter from your institution. **Hotel Tatarstan** (Татарстан), Pushkina 4 (tel. 32 69 79), offers singles with TV, refrigerator, telephone, and bath for 180,000R. Prices should rise drastically over the next two years, when one floor of the hotel will be remodeled and reserved for foreigners. The best deal in town is with **Ida Pergishina** (tel. 37 41 55). For around 65,000R, you can stay in one of her four rooms with bathroom and phone at ul. Kachalova 77 (Качалова), about three stops from the center on any tram line. Call her—she'll come and pick you up if you're not too far away.

FOOD

There's a reason for the name "Steak Tartar." Red meat rules in Tatarstan, so the health-conscious must resign themselves to the **farmers' market** (колхозный рынок; *kolkhozny rynok*) on ul. Gabdully Tukaya (Габдуллы Тукая), one stop on tram #2, 4, or 7 from the end-stop at the train station, or three stops on tram #2 or 4 from pl. Kuy-bysheva in the direction of the train station. Arrive early and don't forget to haggle (open Tues.-Sun. 6am-6pm).

Dom Chaya (Дом Чая), ul. Baumana 64. Flowery cows, velvet cats, and outrageous tapestries of peasant life line the booths. Service is languid, but this is definitely the best budget option for local flavor. A multi-course meal of local specialties costs 25,000R. Open daily 9am-8pm.

Cafe Blinnaya (Кафе Блинная), ul. Baumana 47. *Bliny* are the specialty here, served with butter, honey, sour cream, or meat (1700-3500R). Small variety of salads and soups (1000-2750R). Open daily 7am-3pm and 4-8pm.

Cafe Vechernee (Кафе Вечернее), ul. M. Dzhalilya 14A (M. Джалиля). This Western-style bar just off ul. Baumana offers a variety of sandwiches (3000-8000R) and a changing main course of the day (18,000-21,000R). Vast selection of beer, wine, and vodka (drinks 8600-16,200R). Open daily 1pm-1am.

SIGHTS AND ENTERTAINMENT

To celebrate the destruction of the Mongol kremlin, Ivan the Terrible built the white-washed **kremlin** that now presides over Kazan. The main entrance at the end of ul. Kremlyovskaya (Кремлёвская) leads to the government offices, which are closed to the public, and to the **Blagoveshchensky sobor** (Благовещенский собор; Annunciation Cathedral), designed by Pskov masters Ivan Shiryaev and Postnik Iakovlev in 1561, which now holds state archives. Archbishops of Kazan are buried in the vault underneath. Unfortunately, the cathedral is currently undergoing restoration and is closed to visitors. Across the square from the entrance to the kremlin, the **Tatarstan Museum,** Kremlyovskaya 2 (tel. 32 09 84), displays an exhibit on the early history of Kazan, as well as local arts and crafts (open Tues.-Sun. 10am-5pm; 3000R).

One block down ul. Kremlyovskaya and downhill to the right, the 18th-century **Petropavlovsky sobor** (Петропавловский собор; Peter and Paul Cathedral) commemorates Peter the Great's 1722 visit to Kazan (entrance on ul. M. Dzhalilya). Its Baroque octagonal central tower looks all the more colorful against the spare white walls of the nearby kremlin. The interior, featuring a 25-meter iconostasis, somehow survived decades of Bolshevik plundering, including a brief stint as a pool hall, before being returned to the Orthodox Church in 1989. Pick up your copy of *Popery and its Struggle against Orthodoxy* on your way out, but leave quietly since this is a func-tional church—women should wear skirts and head coverings (open daily 7am-noon and 3-7pm). A short walk further down ul. Kremlyovskaya brings you to the campus of **Kazan State University.** A rare beardless statue of Lenin, easily recognizable by his trademark pout, honors the university's favorite expellee.

Pl. Svobody (Свободы) lies at the intersection of ul. Karla Marxa and Pushkina; here stands the pillared **Tatarstan Theater of Opera and Ballet** (tel. 38 46 08; box office open Mon.-Fri. 10am-7:30pm, Sat.-Sun. 10am-2pm and 3-7:30pm; 4 performances per week at 11am or 6pm; tickets 5000-20,000R). Two 200-year-old **mosques** stand on the banks of the first of three Kaban lakes along ul. Kayuma Nasyri (Каюма Насыри), but they're closed to tourists. A large **park,** which includes a circus and stadium, sits on the shore of the Kazanka. The tall red-brick tower on ul. Baumana near pl. Kuyby-sheva, currently occupied by an eyeglass repair shop and two kiosks selling under-wear and circus tickets, tops the **Tserkov Bogoyavleniya** (Церковь Богоявления; Revelation Church). Services are held weekends and holidays at 8am in the building behind the tower.

■ Ulyanovsk (Ульяновск)

Twenty-five years ago, Soviet authorities threw their hearts, bulldozers, and concrete mixers into the construction of a memorial zone commemorating the birthplace of Vladimir Ilich Ulyanov, a.k.a. Lenin. What resulted was a monument to the man and the failed system. The Lenin memorial complex, as well as the city that houses it, serves as a peculiar mausoleum of Soviet culture—Ulyanovsk (ool-YAH-novsk) is one of the only towns in the former Soviet Union to preserve all of its Communist-era names. A short walk east from ul. Goncharova down any cross street leads to the main Lenin sights. The first stop is **Dom-muzey Lenina** (Дом-музей Ленина; Lenin's House), ul. Lenina 68 (tel. 31 22 22), next door to Ulyanovskturist. You'll have to put on leather overshoes so as not to soil the holy ground. The restored house holds a grand piano and other bourgeois items (open Sun.-Mon. and Wed.-Fri. 9am-4:30pm; 2000R, students 1500R). Vladimir Ulyanov was actually born in a house on **100th Anniversary of Lenin's Birth Square** (100-летия со дня рождения В. И. Ленина; 100-*letiya so dnya rozhdeniya Lenina*). The **birthplace** contains furniture typical of the period; the **kvartira-muzey** (квартира-музей; room-museum) is just a collection of family photographs. The surrounding concrete **Lenin Memorial** building (tel. 39 49 41) holds a concert hall and a rich collection of Bolshevik memorabilia, culminating in a glittering shrine to Ilich himself (open Tues.-Thurs. and Sat.-Sun. 9am-5pm, Fri. 9am-4pm; 1000R, students 500R). At the south end of the square, the **Classical Gymnasium,** Kommunisticheskaya 2 (Коммунистическая; tel. 31 28 68), graduated Vladimir Ulyanov, son of the regional school superintendent, at the top of his class. Note the glowing recommendation letter from the school director, whose son, Aleksandr Kerensky, went on to lead the Provisional Government that Lenin deposed in October 1917 (open Tues.-Sat. 9am-5pm, Sun. 9am-4pm; 1000R, students 500R). The adjacent **Park Druzhby Narodov** (Парк Дружбы Народов; Friendship of the Peoples Park) was constructed by teams from each of the 15 (former) Soviet republics.

Trains (tel. 37 07 07) chug to Moscow (3 per day, 17hr., 156,700R), Volgograd (4 per week, 15hr., 138,000R), and Kazan (2 per day, 6½hr., 45,000R), but most tourists stop off during a **ferry** ride along the Volga. The dock is south of the center off ul. Kirova (Кирова; tel. 31 85 32). Take tram #1 or 4 from the center to the river station (речной вокзал; *rechnoy vokzal*), and walk (15min.) down ul. Minaeva (Минаева) to the left of the tram. A short walk west along ul. Lenina takes you to **Ulyanovskturist** (Ульяновсктурист) at #78 (tel. 32 64 12), which may or may not have a tourist **map** to give away (open Mon.-Fri. 8am-noon and 1-4:30pm). **Inkombank** (Инкомбанк), Goncharova 26, accepts most traveler's checks and changes money (open Mon.-Sat. 9am-12:30pm and 1:30-3pm). **Cafes** line ul. Goncharova and ul. Karla Marxa (Карла Маркса). **Cafe Uyut** (Кафе Уют), ul. Karla Marxa 5, serves homemade *pelmeni* (3400R) and pizzas (4500R; open daily 10am-7:30pm). **Postal code:** 432000. **Phone code:** 8442.

■ Volgograd (Волгоград)

Memories of World War II still haunt Volgograd (VOHL-guh-grahd). Here, in what was then Stalingrad, the remnants of the Nazi Sixth Army surrendered to Soviet troops on January 31, 1943. The 200-day battle, perhaps the war's worst, left 91% of the city in ruins and an estimated two million dead. Apparently the only way to compensate for such losses was to rebuild the entire city as a monument to the fallen—statues and plaques commemorating the battle fill Volgograd's wide streets. The war will always be at the forefront here, but the warm southern sun and the cool breezes off the Volga create a pleasant venue for absorbing the city's powerful history.

ORIENTATION AND PRACTICAL INFORMATION

Crescent-shaped Volgograd stretches around a bend in the Volga, 800km south of Ulyanovsk and 1000km southeast of Moscow. The **Volga-Don Canal,** which begins in Volgograd's southernmost region, links the city with Rostov-na-Donu, 500km to the west, and with the Azov and Black Seas beyond. The main hotels and the majority of the restaurants and shops lie between the train and ferry stations. From the train station, head for the neon **Gostinitsa Intourist** (Гостиница Интурист) sign atop a large building. This hotel stands in central **pl. Pavshikh Bortsov** (пл. Павших Борцов), and wide, tree-lined **alleya Geroev** (аллея Героев; Avenue of Heroes) leads from here to the river. **Mamaev Kurgan** (Мамаев Курган), home to Volgograd's most impressive sights, is a 100m-high hill that rises 2km north of the city center. A kiosk in the basement of the train station sells city **maps** (5000R).

Tourist Office: The bureau in **Gostinitsa Intourist**, ul. Mira 12 (Мира; tel. 33 14 68), carries no maps but does have at least 5 women on duty who will gladly help you (all at once). They also have a quasi travel agency offering information about **flights** (but not buses or trains). Open daily 9am-12:30pm and 1:30-6pm.

Passport Office (OVIR): Registration is theoretically required for stays of longer than 3 days, but enforcement is spotty and the passport office is impossible to find. Gostinitsa Intourist registers you automatically.

Currency Exchange: 1st floor of Gostinitsa Intourist. 1% commission. Open daily 9am-1pm and 2-8pm. **TSUM** (ЦУМ) department store, floor 2½; store located behind the Intourist. Also 1% commission. Open Mon.-Sat. 9:30am-1pm and 2-5:30pm. **Inkombank** (Инкомбанк), ul. Barrikagy 39 (Баррикаты). Visa cash advances; AmEx, Thomas Cook, and Visa traveler's checks with 2% commission. Take trolley-bus #8 to pl. Titova (Титова), go uphill, and then right.

Trains: Volgograd-I (tel. 005), northwest of pl. Pavshikh Bortsov. To: Moscow (2 per day, 24hr., 165,000R); Astrakhan (1 per day, 14 hr., 65,000R); and Rostov-na-Donu (1 per day, 15hr., 150,000R).

Buses: Avtovokzal Tsentralny (Автовокзал Центральный), ul. Bolonina 11 (Болонина; tel. 37 72 28). Cross the tracks behind the train station, take a right down the steps on the right side of the bridge, and go down the first road on the other side—don't go all the way across the bridge. To: Astrakhan (3 per day, 12hr., 79,000R); Pyatigorsk (1 per day, 12hr., 110,000R); and Rostov-na-Donu (4 per day, 14hr., 90,000R).

Ferries: Rechnoy vokzal (Речной вокзал), nab. 62-y Armii (62-й Армии; tel. 44 52 09), near the foot of the steps at the end of alleya Geroev. "Hard class" is a bed in a quad on the lower deck; "2nd class" is a bunk-bed double on the middle deck; and "1st class" is a double with a basin. 3 boats per week to Moscow (1 week; hard class 150,000R, 1st class 650,000R) and Nizhny Novgorod (5 days; hard class 98,000R, 1st class 447,000R). 1hr. boat rides (5000R) leave from near the river station on summer afternoons. On weekends, annoy local fishermen on the 1hr. disco cruise (5000R). Ticket office open daily 8am-5pm. Boats run only after June 1.

Public Transportation: The **metrotram** (метротрам) runs north from the center along pr. Lenina (Ленина). It travels underground in the center, but otherwise resembles a tram more than a metro. Tickets (1000R) are sold at kiosks by above-ground stops and at ticket counters underground. The stop closest to alleya Geroev is "Комсомольская" (Komsomolskaya). **Buses** link the train station with the city's south and west regions. The buses are heavily patrolled, so be sure to buy your ticket (1000R, not available at smaller stops) before you board. Don't be surprised if the *kassa* (касса) looks closed—just shove your money in and a hand will take it. The metrotram and buses theoretically run 'til midnight, but are scarce after 10pm.

Luggage Storage: Kamera khraneniya (Камера хранения), in the basement of the train station. 8900R per day. Open same hours as train station.

Pharmacy: Apteka (Аптека), alleya Geroev 5 (tel. 36 19 75). Open daily 8am-8pm.

Post Office: pl. Pavshikh Bortsov (tel. 36 10 78), opposite Gostinitsa Intourist. Open Mon.-Fri. 8am-8pm, Sat.-Sun. 8am-6pm. Postcards show a sign above that used to read "V. I. Lenin's ideas are alive and will triumph." *Poste Restante* at window #11. Telephone desk open daily 9am-9pm. **Postal code:** 400066.

Telephones: Phones take *zhetony* (жетоны; tokens), sold at the post office (1000R). To make a long-distance call or send a fax, use the **Mezhdunarodny Telefon** (Международный Телефон) office located in the central post office, to the right. Calls to the U.S. cost 14,700R per minute. Hours same as post office. **Phone code:** 8422.

ACCOMMODATIONS

Despite its large student community, Volgograd does not offer much in the way of accommodations for visitors. The larger, centrally located hotels are inordinately expensive, while budget rooms are on the fringe of town and hard to find. So decide whether you're paying or hiking, and choose from the following:

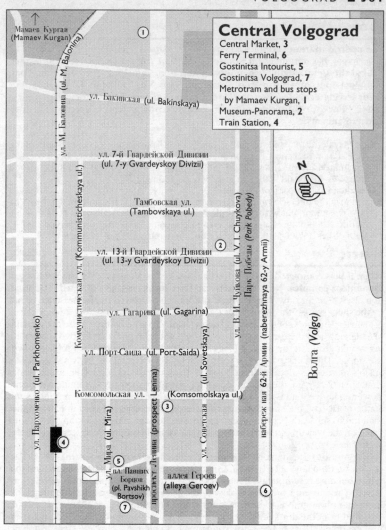

Central Volgograd

Central Market, **3**
Ferry Terminal, **6**
Gostinitsa Intourist, **5**
Gostinitsa Volgograd, **7**
Metrotram and bus stops
 by Mamaev Kurgan, **1**
Museum-Panorama, **2**
Train Station, **4**

Gostinitsa Uyut (Уют), ul. Kanunnikova 7a (Канунникова; tel. 36 54 28). Hiking. Take the metrotram to its southernmost stop, and follow the crowd upstairs. Branch off on a path to the right, near the top of the stairs, cross the tracks, and follow this road till it dead-ends. Take a left, continue 3 blocks, and then right on ul. Kanunnikova. Three blocks ahead, and the hotel is behind the institute on the right. Bare rooms with hall bath (no shower), but by far the cheapest sleep in town. Singles 56,000R; doubles 90,000R.

Gostinitsa Intourist, ul. Mira 14 (tel. 36 45 53; fax 33 91 75). Paying. An unusually worthwhile Intourist hotel owned by its employees, who fully intend to bring the service up to world standards. The rooms are clean, the staff polite, and the hot water reliable. Singles US$36, US$65 with shower; doubles US$50, US$80 with shower. AmEx, Diners Club, MC, and Visa accepted.

Gostinitsa Volgograd, ul. Mira 12 (tel. 36 17 72; fax 33 99 24). Paying! Across the square from the Intourist and mirroring it in appearance. All rooms have showers. Singles 310,000R; doubles 400,000R.

FOOD

The **central market** (центральный рынок; *tsentralny rynok*), ul. Sovetskaya 17 (Советская), has entrances on Komsomolskaya ul. (Комсомольская) and pr. Lenina, behind the Central Bank (open in summer Mon. 7am-4pm, Tues.-Sat. 7am-7pm, Sun. 7am-5pm; off-season Mon. 7am-4pm, Tues.-Sat. 7am-6pm, Sun. 7am-5pm). **Cafes** serving alcohol, coffee, and ice cream abound near alleya Geroev on pr. Lenina and ul. Chuykova (Чуйкова), but there are far more monuments in Volgograd than sit-down restaurants.

> **Kafe Mayak** (Кафе Маяк), nab. 62-y Armiya 1 (62-й Армии; tel. 36 36 36), south of the river station in a short but conspicuous lighthouse. Interior elegantly decorated, but limited menu. *Salat* 7250-16,900R. Main courses 20,000-30,000R. Seafood *shashliks* 44,000-68,000R. Open daily noon-midnight.
>
> **U drakona** (У дракона), pr. Lenina 12 (tel. 36 78 94). Squeezed between a cafe and a casino at the intersection of pr. Lenina and alleya Geroev. It's supposed to be a Chinese restaurant, but with the purple-palace decor and the waitresses in tight, shimmering white blouses and short black skirts, you'd think they only served cheese. Main dishes 25,000-50,000R. Open daily noon-4pm and 6pm-midnight.

SIGHTS

When it was completed in 1967, Russians flocked to Volgograd's **Mamaev Kurgan monument complex**. New revolutions and new problems have directed their attention elsewhere for now, but first-time visitors will be moved by the presence (if not by the sheer size) of the Mat Rodina (Мат Родина; Motherland) statue.

Mamaev Kurgan's strategic peak changed hands 13 times in the course of the Battle of Stalingrad, and the earth became so clogged with shrapnel that for two years nothing would grow on the mound. Today, trees dedicated to individual soldiers cover the slopes. The stairs to the peak teem with graffiti shouting the Party's slogans, like Stalin's murderous dictum "Ни шаг назад!" (Not a step back!). Farther up, statues of stoic Soviets carrying their wounded silently say more than any Communist rhetoric. Towering above it all is the 52m-tall **Mat Rodina** statue. She vaguely resembles the Statue of Liberty, but she leans forward in motion, and with sword in hand (rather than torch) she leads her troops into battle. The Russian soldiers guarding the eternal flame on the way up put on an impressive gun-twirling routine. Metrotram runs here, as do buses #8, 9, 12, and 13.

In contrast to the memorial complex, the dramatic **Muzey-Panorama** (Музей-Панорама), ul. Chuykova 2 (tel. 34 67 23), located between pl. Lenina and the river in a white building resembling a nuclear power plant with a lid on top, is pure Soviet kitsch. The museum presents a blow-by-blow account of the Soviet counterattack, including photographs, uniforms, guns, and Communist Party membership cards retrieved from the dead. Supposedly the scene from the top of Mamaev Kurgan during one crucial day's fighting, the panorama is a polemic against Western historians who downplayed the Red Army's role in the defeat of Nazism (open Tues.-Sun. 10am-5pm, closed last Fri. of each month; 5000R). A gutted **mill,** preserved to demonstrate the wartime destruction, crumbles by the Muzey-Panorama. Across the street stand the remains of **Dom Pavlova** (Дом Павлова), where Sgt. Yakov Pavlov and 23 soldiers held out for 58 days against ceaseless German attacks.

After all that war and history, the centrally located **Muzey Izobrazitelnikh Iskusstv** (Музей Изобразительных Искусств; Fine Arts Museum), pr. Lenina 21 (tel. 36 39 06), may provide a much-needed break from reality (open Thurs.-Tues. 10am-5:30pm; 3000R). To beat the heat, hang out on the south edge of the city by the mouth of the **Volga-Don Canal,** guarded by a dapper Lenin on one side and a bare pedestal where Stalin once stood on the other. Near the triumphal arch of the canal's first lock, local teenagers jeer and spit at passing cruise ships. Those nostalgic for Five-Year Plans can admire the city's industrial megaliths on hour-long **boat rides,** which include a close-up view of the massive hydroelectric power plant north of the city.

ENTERTAINMENT

With streets thronged by students during the day, you'd expect Volgograd to be jumpin' at night. Unfortunately, it's likely to be just you and the monuments. What action there is can be found by the river, just north of the ferry station, as makeshift stages occasionally pop up and local bands attempt to cover American music. Don't expect too much: a rendition of Michael Jackson's "Bad" acquires a new dimension when performed by drunk Volgograd youths. The **stadium**, one stop before Mamaev Kurgan, hosts Russia's top-league **soccer** team; game announcements are posted outside. The **New Experimental Theater (NET)**, pl. Pavshikh Bortsov, boasts an internationally known troupe who put on old favorites like *Romeo and Juliet* (*kassa* open Wed.-Sun. 2pm-7pm; tickets 90,000-130,000R). The marble-pillared **Planetarium**, ul. Gagarina 14 (Гагарина; tel. 36 41 84), has astronomy for children and adults, as well as films of the city's reconstruction (shows Tues.-Sat. 10am, noon, 2, and 4pm; 10,000R). The **Teatr Kukol** (Театр Кукол; Puppet Theater), pr. Lenina 15 (tel. 33 06 49), stages performances mainly for children (shows Sat.-Sun. 11am; 3500R; *kassa* open Tues.-Fri. 11:30am-2pm and 3-6pm, Sat.-Sun. 10am-1:30pm and 2:30-5pm). Stop at the big top, **Volgograd Tsirk** (Волгоград Цирк; circus), ul. Krasnoznamensk (Краснознаменск; tel. 36 31 06; daily shows; 10,000R). To reach the **beach** on the vast Volga's other side, take a quick ferry to **Krasnoslobodsk** (Краснослободск) from terminal #12 at the river station (1 per hr. 6am-10:30pm, 12min., 5000R).

■ Astrakhan (Астрахань)

Since this century's wars didn't get to Astrakhan, the city looks much like it did two hundred years ago, when it thrived as a trading post between Kazakhstan and the Caucasus. The Communist touch was particularly gentle on this city, and so the regime did not especially dampen Astrakhan's bazaar-like atmosphere. This poverty-stricken, many-faced port is struggling to hold on to its glory as the last outpost of civilization before the Caspian Sea consumes the mighty Volga.

ORIENTATION AND PRACTICAL INFORMATION

The diverging branches of the Volga river delta make Astrakhan a difficult place to navigate, but you can almost always see the **kremlin**, so when in doubt, head for it. To get to the center from the train station, take bus #5 or 13, or tram A, 1 or 2. To walk, head south along **ul. Pobedy** (ул. Победы) and turn right onto **ul. Sverdlova** (Свердлова) after the river **Kutum** (Кутум). You'll arrive at the northern tip of the kremlin. The kremlin's walls are bordered by **ul. Zhelyabova** (Желябова) to the west and northwest, **ul. Oktyabrskaya** (Октябрьская) to the east, and **pl. Lenina** (пл. Ленина) to the south. The central **ul. Sovetskaya** (Советская) runs perpendicular to **ul. Kirova** (Кирова), and ends at the kremlin's east wall. The areas around the kremlin and along the river near the ferry station are the only parts of the city in which Astrakhan manages to hide its poverty.

Tourist Office: Intourist (Интурист), ul. Sovetskaya 21 (tel. 24 63 44). Head down Sovetskaya away from the kremlin, 5 blocks past the gun-wielding Communist, to the large white building. Go right in the first door on the right inside the arch. They can arrange fishing trips or other excursions to the delta. Open daily 10am-5pm.

Passport Office (ОВИР): ul. Kirova 5 (tel. 22 66 28). Go around the corner of the building, enter through the last door on your right, and go up to the 4th floor. You should register, unless your hotel has done it for you. Open Mon.-Fri. 2-5pm.

Currency Exchange: ul. Babushkina 60 (Бабушкина; tel. 24 70 98). Head north on Kirova, then take a right on Babushkina. Four blocks ahead on the right you'll find the only place for Visa cash advances (3% commission). Expected to provide MC and AmEx services by fall '97. English spoken. Open Mon.-Fri. 9am-1pm, 2pm-6pm.

Trains: Privokzalnaya pl. (Привокзальная). To Moscow (1 per day, 35hr., 150,000R).

Buses: Beautiful building south of the kremlin, across the canal. To: Moscow (1 per day, 24hr., 230,000R); Pyatigorsk (1 per day, 12hr., 116,800R); and Volgograd (2 per day, 12hr., 96,500R).

Public Transportation: Useful only to get from the train station to the city center. Pay on the bus (1200R).

Ferries: on the bank southwest of the kremlin. Three different tour options (8000R-15,000R). The longest goes to the mouth of the Caspian Sea (but not across). Open 6:30am-8pm.

Luggage Storage: Available at both the train and bus stations, for 8900R and 6000R respectively.

Post Office: (tel. 22 99 77) corner of Kirova and ul. Chernyshevskovo (Черныш-евского). Open Mon.-Sat. 8am-10pm, Sun. 10am-5pm. **Photocopies:** 700R. City **maps** also available here. **Postal code:** 414000.

Telephones: International telephone office just beyond the post office, under the bridge and up the stairs to the right. Open Sun.-Fri. 8am-10pm. **Phone code:** 8512.

ACCOMMODATIONS AND FOOD

As in many other Russian cities, Astrakhan's hotels are often foreigner *un*friendly. Expect to pay frustrating tourist prices, unless you have not only a good accent, but also fake papers.

Gostinitsa Lotos (Лотос), ul. Kremlevskaya 4 (Кремлевская; tel. 22 95 00) to the right of the ferry station. Rooms lined with thin carpets showing scars of fun had by American magnates, but clean with spacious beds. Overhead showers, and a view of the Volga. Singles 128,400R; doubles 186,300R per bed. Call to reserve.

Gostinitsa Corvet (Корвет), ul. Boyeval 50a (Боевал; tel. 34 03 78). Take bus #18 to "Zhilgorodok" (Жилгородок), and head right. Plush rooms with shower, but you're only getting what you paid for. Singles 200,000R; doubles 300,000R.

Gostinitsa Gavan (Гавань; tel. 24 68 42). From the bus station, cross the canal and turn left. Five minutes ahead, take a right on ul. Karla Marxa (Карла Маркса), and round the bend on the right. Or take bus #4 to Karla Marxa. Sympathetic to weary foreigners, but a Russian roommate can help. Singles with cold shower 116,000R.

Astrakhan is hailed as the black caviar capital of the world, but don't count on finding any in its restaurants. Do, however, expect to see enough **ice cream** stands to impress even Ben and Jerry. **Fruit and vegetable** stands cluster around the western wall of the kremlin. Cafes abound along the river, most with grills flaming and beer flowing. **Cafe U Perepravy** (Кафе у Переправы), under the colored tent right on the water, serves up a mean meat roll for only 3000R (open noon-11pm). If you can't handle the mosquitoes by the river, **Cafe Lebed** (Кафе Лебедь), ul. Zhelyabova (желябова), southwest of pl. Lenina across the small lake, will fill you up for under 20,000R, view of swans included (open 10am-midnight; live music after 8pm).

SIGHTS AND ENTERTAINMENT

The prominent **Astrakhansky Kreml** (Астраханский Кремль; kremlin) is the city's main landmark. Built during 1582-89, it later picked up some towers, a **church,** and a **torture chamber** for bad people. It houses an art school, so don't be shocked if someone asks you to pose—it's not the KGB. For tours, go to the **Tower Museum** (tel. 22 54 44) in the opposite corner of the courtyard from the church (admission 2000R, tours 5000R; open Tues.-Sun. 10am-5pm). Also be sure to check out the beautiful **rose gardens** below the kremlin in pl. Lenina. Perhaps the single most impressive building in the city is the green-and-beige **cathedral** across the canal from Gostinitsa Gavan. Gaze from afar, because closer up you'll see that the practical Soviets turned this beautiful building into the bus station.

The **Istoriko-arkhitekturnyi muzey** (Историко-арkhитектурный музей; Museum of Architectural History), Sovetskaya 15 (tel. 22 78 75), a large red building 4 blocks straight out of the kremlin's front door, has an impressive collection of miniature **model ships,** oddly enough (14,000R; open daily 10am-5pm). The **Teatr Kukol**

(Театр Кукол; Puppet Theater; tel. 24 50 08) ul. Fioletova 12 (Фиолетова) is geared mainly toward children, but the bar next to the ticket counter might make it fun for you as well. Morning shows 4000R, evening 10,000R.

During the warmer months, Astrakhan's **nightlife** centers around the river. The overlapping sounds of **live music** from nearly every cafe blend into a lively hum. Get a mug of the smooth and eponymous local brew, *Piva Astrakhana* (available at several kiosks scattered among the cafes, 2000R), and take your pick. If you want to showcase your dance moves, hop on over to the **Kangaroo Club**, ul. Volodarskovo 13 (Володарского; tel. 22 92 50). It's connected via a restaurant to **Club Prazdnik** (Праздник, Holiday), and 15,000R will get you in the door to the complex. Things get going around 10pm and usually go on until 4am. The clubs nearer to the kremlin cater to an older crowd—mostly mafiosos and others leading the thug life.

Playing the Fool

Russians do it *all* the time. Whoa! Easy there, Ivan! We're not talking about that whole "Communism" misunderstanding, nor even all that silly vodka. No, we mean **Durak** —Russian for "fool"—the favorite (and damn near only) Russian card game. The game is so popular, in fact, that most card decks sold in Russia only have 36 cards—for Durak you don't need the cards below 6, and it's assumed that's all you'll be playing. So the next time you're riding the Russian rails and someone greets you with "Durak," don't get upset. They're not questioning your intelligence—they just want you to play the fool.

■ Rostov-na-Donu (Ростов-на-Дону)

For millennia, European merchants traveled to the mouth of the Don to trade with the tribes of southern Russia's plains. In 1749, the tsarist government decided to cash in on such commerce by establishing a customs post on the site of modern Rostov. Commerce and agriculture have attracted communities of Armenians, Greeks, and, most recently, Koreans to the area. Ever since the Chechen Communists decided to relocate (after some "persuasion" from the Russian mafia), ethnic tensions have been less of a problem.

ORIENTATION AND PRACTICAL INFORMATION

Rostov-na-Donu rises over the north bank of the Don, 1000km south of Moscow and 400km southwest of Volgograd. The Don feeds into the Taganrog Bay and the Azov Sea 35km west of the city. The Rostovskaya *oblast* (region) shares a long border with Ukraine, the east edge of which is directly north of the city. The main street of Rostov's central grid, **ul. Bolshaya Sadovaya** (Большая Садовая), starts at the **train station** and parallels the river to the **Park of the October Revolution.** Rostov's quieter east region was, until 1928, the separate Armenian city of Nakhichevan-na-Donu. It still has a large Armenian community and several active Armenian Orthodox churches. The other main street, **Budennovsky pr.**, starts at the **river port** and climbs past the **Central Market** and across ul. Bolshaya Sadovaya. From the **train station,** take bus #12 to get to the city center.

Tourist Offices: The service bureau of **Gostinitsa Intourist,** Bolshaya Sadovaya 115 (tel. 65 90 66; fax 65 90 07), is willing to help you even if you're not staying at the hotel. They organize group and individual tours and sell brochures (5000-10,000R). Open daily 9am-5pm.

Passport Office (ОВИР): ul. Abaroni 8 (Абарони; tel. 39 23 70). Registration not compulsory if you've registered elsewhere in Russia. Tourist hotels automatically register you, and bus and train station hotels will give you a card that proves you're staying there. That's a good thing, too, because the ОВИР office is only open Wed. and Fri., 11am-noon.

Currency Exchange: Gostinitsa Intourist (see above) has a 24hr. exchange bureau that cashes AmEx and Thomas Cook traveler's checks and gives Visa cash advances at a 2% commission. An **ATM** in the lobby is the only one in town (Visa only).

Trains: The **vokzal** (tel. 67 02 10) is at the westernmost stop of tram #1 and bus #12. Make sure your tram is *"pro Rossi,"* meaning it does not enter Ukraine, unless you have a Ukrainian transit visa. To: Kiev (1 per day, 23hr., 210,000R); Moscow (1 per day, 25hr., 160,000R); Sochi (4 per day, 16hr., 85,000R); and Volgograd (1 per day, 15½hr., 60,000R). The *elektrichka* (commuter train) leaves from **Prigorodny vokzal** (tel. 38 36 00), across the tracks and 2 blocks to the right of the main station. To: Novocherkassk (9 per day, 1½hr., 5000R); Taganrog (9 per day, 1½hr., 5000R); and Tanais (9 per day, 1hr., 3000R).

Buses: pr. Siversa 1 (Сиверса; tel. 32 32 83), opposite the trains. To: Azov (every 20min., 1 hr., 6500R); Simferopol (every other day, 12hr., 130,000R); Volgograd (4 per day, 10-12hr., 100,000R).

Public Transportation: Trams, trolleys, buses (1000R), and **express buses** (1500R) run daily roughly 5am-1am, but get spotty on the outskirts around 8pm, and in the center after 11pm. The comfortable express buses, imported from Germany and Sweden, stop on request only.

Luggage Storage: In the train station. 8900R. Open 24hr.

Post Office: Soborny per. 24 (Соборный; tel. 66 72 09). From the Central Market, walk away from the train station, and go left at the Russian Orthodox church. Open Mon.-Sat. 7:30am-7:30pm. **Postal code:** 344007.

Telephones: Local phones take tokens (1000R) available at the post office and at **Mezhdugorodny Telefon** (Междугородный Телефон), pl. Lenina 99, adjacent to Gostinitsa Tourist, which is also the place to make international calls. Open daily 8am-10pm. One minute to the U.S. 19,000R. **Phone code:** 8632.

ACCOMMODATIONS

The best budget accommodations in Rostov are the **hostels** at the train and bus stations. The tower portion of the **train station** has a bath and shower in every room, with reliable hot water (80,0000R per person). The hostel at the **bus station** (tel. 32 66 63) has a similar arrangement, but the loudspeaker from the station could get a little annoying (70,000R per person).

Gostinitsa Moskovskaya (Московская), ul. Bolshaya Sadovaya 62. Right in the city center, on the 2nd floor of a beautiful building in need of a paint job. Ask for the cheapest room or they'll try to give you a "lux" suite you don't need. Singles 112,000R; doubles 124,000R.

Gostinitsa Rostov (Ростов; tel. 39 16 66), Budennovsky pr. 59. Take bus #6 north from the center until you see the hotel on the left. Singles with shower and phone 125,000R; doubles 215,000R.

FOOD

Rostov is at the center of Russia's wheat-growing region, so try the local baked goods—especially the pastries sold at street stands along **ul. Bolshaya Sadovaya.** The wine cellar **Solntse v bokale** (Солнце в бокале; Sun in a Wineglass), Budennovsky pr. 25 (tel. 66 45 51), sells regional wines for 18,000-22,000R per bottle (watch out for the sparkling ones). Most cafes are on ul. Bolshaya Sadovaya. The central market, Budennovsky pr. 18, is impressive and hectic; it sells the usual staples, plus Korean noodles and fresh fish (open daily 6am-8pm; usually closes earlier on Sun.).

Cheburechnaya (Чебуречная), Voroshilovsky pr. 20 (Ворошиловский; tel. 64 09 78). Despite the odd bamboo walls and decor, this is Russian food. Borscht 5000R, namesake *cheburechnaya* (meat-filled pastry) 3000R. Open 9am-11pm.

Cafe Russky Chai (Русский Чай; Russian Tea), ul. Bolshaya Sadovaya 74 (tel. 66 46 19). Serves up substantial quantities of Russian fare (cutlet 8000R, *plov* 8000R) to accompany its signature beverage (900R). Open daily 8am-10pm.

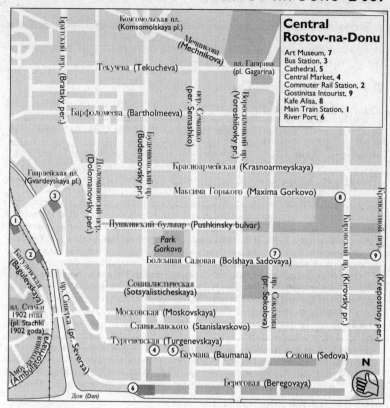

Central Rostov-na-Donu

Art Museum, 7
Bus Station, 3
Cathedral, 5
Central Market, 4
Commuter Rail Station, 2
Gostinitsa Intourist, 9
Kafe Alisa, 8
Main Train Station, 1
River Port, 6

Cafe Randevu (Кафе Рандеву), ul. Bolshaya Sadovaya 53. A popular—nay, even romantic—streetside spot to sit and sip a beverage in the afternoon shade of a concrete block. Open daily 11am-11pm, indoor section open until midnight.

SIGHTS AND ENTERTAINMENT

The 1860 **Cathedral of the Birth of the Holy Mother of God,** next to the Central Market on ul. Stanislavskovo, is a startling sanctuary of peace amid the frenzied clamor of the market below (open daily 7am-7pm). To reach the 1783 Armenian Orthodox **Surb-Khach,** ul. Myasnikyana (Мясникяна), now bizarrely stranded amid a bowl of Soviet-style apartment blocks, take express bus #77 from the central market to "Космонофт." It's the isolated green dome up the hill to the right. The **museum** inside has artifacts and writings in Russian and Armenian, with one panel of English explanation (open Tues.-Sun. 10am-7pm). The monument at **Zmeyskaya Balka** (Змейская Балка; Snake Hollow), in the northwest of the city, marks the spot where 27,000 citizens of Rostov were shot by the occupying Nazis. Despite nearby signs promising that "Not a single one will be forgotten," there is no mention that more than half of those killed were Jewish, and the complex has fallen into a state of disrepair—which makes it perhaps all the more moving. Take bus #6 from the city center, and get off after you see the statues on the left.

Park Gorkovo, on Bolshaya Sadovaya near Budennovsky pr., is a common spot for evening activities. At the north end of the park, the **Kinoteatr Podina** puts on weekend jazz concerts (Fri. and Sat. 6:30-10:30pm, 15,000R) and shows movies nightly. At the center, an **amusement park** spins and twirls (swings 2000R, bumper cars 3000R; open Tues.-Sun. 10am-10pm). Don't miss the mosaics in the underpasses, which depict classrooms full of children raising their hands and other scenes of idyllic Soviet life. The only dance action in town is found in the **Python** (Питон; tel. 38 47 06), located to the left of Hotel Tourist in pl. Lenina. It's definitely a step above the average hotel bar (open nightly 8pm-3am, cover 30,000R on weekends).

■ Near Rostov-na-Donu

STAROCHERKASSK (СТАРОЧЕРКАССК)

Cherkassk, now **Starocherkassk,** was the capital of the Don Cossacks from 1644 to 1806, during which time it played a role in nearly all of Imperial Russia's major peasant uprisings. Pushkin's visit here inspired *The Captain's Daughter* and a several-volume history of the Pugachev rebellion. Now a pleasantly stagnant *stanitsa* (farming village) on an island upstream of Rostov, its center has been preserved as a **museum of Cossack life and history** (open daily 9am-5pm; 3000R). Bring your own lunch.

The older houses are constructed in typical Cossack style, with high cellars to protect the residents from the annual floods and meter-thick walls to defend against less frequent human attacks. The active nine-cupola **Voskresensky sobor** (Воскресенский собор; Resurrection Cathedral) dates from 1706 and contains biblical frescoes that are incomprehensible in parts due to age and neglect. By the cathedral's doors hang the chains with which authorities dragged legendary **Stepan Razin,** the most famous of Russia's Cossack rebels, to Moscow to be executed in 1671. After the suppression of Razin's revolt, the previously independent Cossacks were forced to pay homage to the tsar (open Thurs.-Tues.). In front of the cathedral lie the gateposts and weighing scales from the marketplace of Azov, trophies of the Cossack occupation (1637-1644). Nearby stands the house where **Kondratii Bulavin,** another rebel leader, was murdered by treacherous Cossacks in 1708. His body—minus head and hands—was displayed in Azov as a warning to would-be revolutionaries. About 7km from the center are the ruins of the star-shaped **Petrine fort.** Buses from Rostov to Starocherkassk leave only from the old bus station (tel. 51 08 67) in the northeast corner of town. Take tram #1 from the market to "Старого Автовокзал" (4-6 buses daily; 9,600R).

NOVOCHERKASSK (НОВОЧЕРКАССК)

Novocherkassk became the Cossacks' capital in 1806, after they gave up attempts to protect Cherkassk from flooding. Strategically located on a hill between the Aksai and Tuzlov Rivers, the city overlooks the surrounding steppe, and continues to house Cossacks and a large contingent of Russian troops. During World War II, the Nazis left the city largely intact in recognition of anti-Soviet collaboration. From the bus station, walk out and cross the street. Soviet propaganda, including the classic novel *And Quiet Flows the Don* by Mikhail Sholokhov, portrayed the Cossacks as active supporters of the Bolshevik Revolution, but in fact Novocherkassk was one of the centers of White counter-revolutionary opposition during the Civil War. Bus #1 will take you to the **Voznesensky Katedralny Sobor** (Вознесенский Катедральны собор; Ascension Cathedral), in the cobblestone pl. Yermaka (Ермака). Envisioned by the ataman Matvey Platov as a Russian version of St. Peter's in Rome, the cathedral—Russia's third largest—ended up taking a century to build because the cupolas kept falling down. Now the cathedral is in a dismal state of disrepair. Inside are monuments to Cossack heroes in the defeat of Napoleon.

Next to the cathedral in pl. Yermaka is a **statue of Yermak Timofeevich,** who conquered Siberia for the tsar in the late 16th century. The original design of the monument had the tsarist two-headed eagle at Yermak's feet, but the authorities in St. Petersburg worried that the Cossacks might get the wrong idea and ordered the eagle removed. Apparently, the Cossacks got the idea anyhow, and the better part of the **Muzey Istorii Donskovo Kazachestva** (Музей Истории Донсково Казачества; Museum of the History of the Don Cossacks), down pr. Platova (Платова) from the cathedral, celebrates the Cossacks' insurgent ways. The bronze statue of an austere Stepan Razin, who was by all accounts a bad-ass (see **Starocherkassk,** above), leads the way to a collection of dangerously accessible chain armors, shields, and swords. "I came to give you freedom," Razin reportedly said. At each display, Marx and Lenin express their admiration for the Cossacks' resolve to fight for liberty. In the opposite room, the tsars are good guys again, as the feats of the Cossacks in wars with Napoleon are given their due. The museum also contains archaeological finds from Tanais. (Open Tues.-Sun. 10am-5pm; 1000R if you can avoid the 800% tariff on foreigners; call (252) 241 14 in advance for a 30,000R group tour in English.) **Buses** (8 per day, 1hr., 8000R) and the *elektrichka* (9 per day, 1½hr., 5000R) connect the town to Rostov. Sit on the train's right side for better views of the Don Steppe.

TANAIS (ТАНАИС)

Tanais is a **museum** and **archaeological dig** at the site of a 2000-year-old Greek colony. Founded in the 3rd century BC, the colony grew into a major trading center between Greeks and nomadic steppe tribes. In return for olive oil, wine, cloth, and pottery, the Greeks bought fish, wheat, cattle, wool, and slaves. The city was destroyed and rebuilt several times before its abandonment in the 4th century AD.

Archaeologists first took interest in the **ruins** more than 170 years ago, initially sending the most important finds to museums in Moscow and St. Petersburg. Systematic excavations began in 1955; every summer since, students from Moscow and Vladimir have come to work on the dig, enduring the scorching sun and Neolithic living conditions. Only a fraction of the city has been uncovered, but archaeologists have already learned much about life and commerce in the city from the wealth of inscriptions, pottery, ornaments, and human remains they have unearthed. Many of the students on hand speak English, and are happy to share their knowledge with curious visitors. The on-site **museum** displays finds from the last 40 years, including elegant amphorae from the Mediterranean, statuettes of Greek gods, bronze oil-lamps, glass vials, and a pair of ancient handcuffs. A couple of the ancient buildings have been reconstructed to aid the imagination, but otherwise the original walls and foundations speak for themselves (museum open in summer 10am-4pm; 4000R; closed off-season). The *elektrichka* runs here from Rostov (9 per day, 1hr., 3000R).

TAGANROG (ТАГАНРОГ)

Boasting a remarkable number of midday drunks and a vigilant militia, Taganrog would be noteworthy if only because its most conspicuous monuments are not devoted to Communists. Instead, the **birthplace of Anton Chekhov** devotes its myths to the great playwright and short story master. The best place to begin your tour of Anton's old haunts is (surprise!) ul. Chekhova (Чехова). There you'll find **Domik Chekhova,** ul. Chekhova 69, where Chekhov cried his first tears in 1860 (open Tues.-Sun. 9am-4pm, 2000R). Take the tram (1000R) from there to "Spartovsky" (Спартовский) to get to the **Literary Museum,** ul. Oktyabrskaya 9 (Октябрьская). In the school where Chekhov studied, the museum contains reconstructed classrooms and a large collection of manuscripts, letters, journals, and early editions of Chekhov's works, interspersed with choice quotes from the famous *literati* Lenin and Marx (open Tues.-Sun. 10am-6pm; 2000R). **Lavka Chekhovykh** (Лавка Чеховых), ul. Sverdlova 100 (Свердлова), was the Chekhovs' home and shop from 1869 to 1874. The front-room grocery store—which illicitly doubled as a pharmacy—has been restored (with emblematic food items). The rest of the house has been reconstructed according to Chekhov's reminiscences, including paintings by Anton's brother (open Tues.-Sun. 10am-5pm; 4000R). To get to Taganrog, take the *elektrichka* (9 daily, 1½hr., 5000R) to the end of the line (that's Taganrog II—don't get off at Taganrog I).

THE CAUCASUS (КАВКАЗ)

> *"The air is pure and fresh as a child's kiss, the sun is bright, the sky is blue. What more can one wish? What need have we here of passions, desires, regrets?"*
> —Mikhail Lermontov, *A Hero of Our Time*

Lermontov wasn't alone in his wish to possess the soaring peaks and soothing waters of the Caucasus. Since prehistoric times, this region bordering the Black Sea has been a meeting place for traders, tribes, and tourists—in fact, Lermontov first saw the *Kavkaz* as a visitor to a Black Sea spa. The three wars that have ravaged the area over the past five years are just the aftershocks of centuries of conflict among local groups. For the past 200 years, the ruling Russian regime has manipulated and exterminated the peoples of this diverse and uneasy region. Lermontov's novel was inspired by his service in the Russian army, which brutally subdued a unified Caucasian force in 1859. Rule under the Soviet regime was no kinder. Resentment, engendered by Stalin-era deportation and Russification and nurtured by recent political oppression, boiled into guerrilla warfare in 1991. Today the passions, desires, and regrets of the region's peoples make headlines, but the sun is just as bright and the sky as blue as it was for Lermontov and the traders who sailed into port centuries ago.

■ Pyatigorsk (Пятигорск)

Foreigners are just beginning to discover the North Caucasus, a vacation mecca that Russians have treasured for centuries. Allegedly magical springs found in these mountains have been used to cleanse the body and soul of many a weary traveler—and to clear the minds of Russia's greatest writers. Pyatigorsk is the biggest of the five cities in the area at the base of the mountains, and is probably the most convenient place to start a trek into the Caucasus. It is still a resort town, as it has been since the late 18th century, but the student population is beginning to turn it into an exciting place.

ORIENTATION AND PRACTICAL INFORMATION

Pyatigorsk lies reverently at the foot of **Mt. Mashuk** (933m) and 10km south of the Beshtau peaks. The city's center lies around **Park Tsvetnik** (Парк Цветник), which merges right into some of the major sights of Mt. Mashuk. Get there by tram #4, stopping at "Tsvetnik." This is the city's center as far as interest and food go. The two train stops in Pyatigorsk are the main **Pyatigorsky vokzal**, and **Lermontovskaya** (Лермонтовская), which will bring you closer to the university, motel, and most of the **Lermontov historical sites** around the base of Mt. Mashuk.

Tourist Office: Bureau Puteshestviye (Бюро Путешествие, ul. Kraynevo 74 (ул. Крайнего; tel. 500 54). With the post office behind you, go down the hill 5 blocks and enter through the lime-green gate on the right. Arranges trips to local mountains, including Elbrus (Эльбрус), for 100,000R. Tours available in English. Open Mon.-Fri. 10am-6pm.

Budget Travel: Pyatigorsk State Pedagogical University has several mountain campsites which are the best way to see the Caucasus without spending a fortune. These sites are in limbo, though, due to safety concerns along the Georgian border. For the latest information, contact Aleksander Grankin, head of the Student Union (tel. 920 21), or visit the 6th floor of the university, across the square from the "Universam" (Универсам) tram stop on the #4 line. When operational, these sites run from 30,000-50,000R.

Passport Office: At the police station, ul. Rudennova 1 (Руденнова). Open Mon.-Sat. 8am-4pm.

Currency Exchange: Major banks line pr. Kirova (пр. Кирова). The **Intourist** (tel. 593 40) cashes traveler's checks (2% commission), but offers no credit card or ATM services. Open 9am-noon and 1-6pm.

Trains: Long-distance tickets are available at **Pyatigorsky vokzal.** Get there by taking tram #2 down the hill to the "Vokzal" stop. Daily to: Kiev (33hr., 177,000R); Sochi (13hr., 70,000R); and St. Petersburg (46hr., 250,000R). The *elektrichka* (electric commuter rail) runs to Kislovodsk (every 40min., 1hr., 3200R), and Min-Vody (every 30min., 45min., 2400R one-way). Trains run 5am-midnight.

Buses: Glavny autovokzal provides intercity travel, and can be reached by taking tram #1 or 4 to "Kraynevo" and walking down the hill across from the post office for 10min. Daily to Astrakhan (14hr., 75,000R) and Rostov (18hr., 110,000R). Buses to the local mountains leave from **Gorachevsky autovokzal,** at tram #4's last stop, "Ludmila" (Лудмила). To Chegett, a prime spot for basing a trek (20,000R).

Public Transportation: Buses are rare and lame in Pyatigorsk, but **tram #4** rules. It runs from the Lermontovskaya train station to the Gorachevsky bus station, stopping at Park Tsvetnik, the University ("Universam"), and the lower market. Tram #4's first cousin, **tram #2,** ain't half bad either—it runs between the two train stations. All trams are 1000R; pay on board.

Luggage Storage: In Pyatigorsky vokzal. Walk past the outdated automated lockers to the window with the living, breathing person. Open 24hr. 8000R per piece.

Post Office: ul. Kraynevo 53. Tram #4: "Kraynevo." Open 8am-7pm. **Postal code:** 357500.

Telephones: Tokens for local phones are 1000R. International and intercity calls can be made from **Mezhdugorodny Telefon** (Междугородный Телефон), ul. Kraynevo 54, across the street from the post office. Open 24hr. **Phone code:** 86533.

ACCOMMODATIONS

The tourist office (see above) may be able to find you a homestay, but the University dorm facilities are the true gem in Pyatigorsk accommodations.

Pyatigorsk State Universitiy Dorm #4, up ul. 295 Strelnoy Divizii (295 Стрельной Дивизии) from the Lermontovskaya rail stop toward the Lermontov Duel Site. Ask for the *kommandant,* Galina Maksimovna. They may put you in a suite with other students, but you can help them with their English homework in exchange for the party low-down. And besides, it's only 10,000R per night!

Avtomotel, ul. 295 Strelnoy Divizii 15 (tel. 920 22) across the street and up a bit from Dorm #4, opposite the stone gates marking the entrance to the Lermontov Duel Site. Clean but aging, especially in the bathroom, where the hot water might be sporadic. Doubles only, but with TV, fridge, and bath, and you may get it all to yourself. 64,000R, plus 4200R for the first night.

Gostinitsa Beshtau (Бештау; tel. 996 52), ul. Bulvarnaya 17 (Бульварная), "Universam" on tram #2 or 4. Slightly more expensive, but rooms have private showers. English spoken. Singles 70,000R; doubles 120,000R.

FOOD

Quality fruits and vegetables abound in the **market,** just up ul. Kraynevo from the post office. Being "non-Russian" is currently in vogue among Pyatigorsk's sit-down establishments. Worried you're missing out on Russian culture, you say? Well…don't look a gift horse in the mouth.

Cafe Tals, (Кафе Талс), ul. Kalinina 85 (Калинина; tel. 574 60). Think you're tough, do ya? Well, step up to the bar—and order yourself a sweet roll and some OJ. This little European bakery cafe cooks up bread in ways you never thought possible, all right before your eyes in old-school ovens. Great selection of juices as well (2000R). Closes somewhat early, so ideal for a sticky-sweet breakfast (500-2000R), or try a meat roll for a light lunch (3000R). Open 8am-8pm.

Pizza Roma, with 2 locations (a chain!): pr. Kalinina 2 (tel. 519 28), down the hill from the gate to the Duel Site, and ul. Kirova 29a, in front of the "Tsvetnik" stop on tram #4. The proprietors researched American pizzerias to develop these clones. Pricey, but worth it; their creative slogan says it all—"We are the Best." Small cheese 20,100R, large 43,700R. Hamburger 7000R. Open 10am-10pm.

Cafe Na Stipendiyu (Кафе На Стипендию; tel. 935 92), on the corner of ul. Bulvarnaya opposite the "Universam" stop on trams #2 and 4. Remarkable salads and desserts compensate for an average meal selection. The place to get that caviar you've been craving since Astrakhan (38,900R). Main dishes 9000-15,000R. Lots of students. Open 10am-10pm.

SIGHTS AND ENTERTAINMENT

Pyatigorsk is perhaps most famous for being the site of the Russian writer Lermontov's death. Here, he was challenged to a duel by a Major Martinov, the ostensible cause of which was a witty epigram in which Lermontov wrote something like "The Major's saber hangs down to his knees." It is a matter of some historical debate whether there was a government or other conspiracy, or whether the Major was just very touchy about his saber. Without walking to the barrier, Lermontov fired into the air. The cowardly scoundrel of a major in turn walked up to the barrier and killed Russia's greatest living writer. The series of events eerily resembled both Pushkin's duel and that of Lermontov's fictional character Pechorin. To get to the **Duel Site,** walk up the hill from Lermontovskaya station, past the university dorms, and through the stone gates across the street. There is a well-labeled map at the park entrance that shows the duel site location, as well as the locations of other attractions around Mt. Mashuk. The road around the base of the mountain makes for a pleasant 3- to 4-hour hike, and passes everything worth seeing.

Two kilometers into the trip are the **Gates of Love,** a graffiti-ridden stone arch rumored to secure a lifetime of love to those who pass under it. Twenty minutes beyond that is **Proval,** a light blue, sulfur-stinky spring that was one of Lermontov's old stomping grounds. Pyatigorsk's springs are said to have **magic healing powers.** They may, for example, cure a digestive tract that has been grumpy since one's arrival in a land where little is safe to eat or drink. There is no longer a bridge over the spring (a man and his cow allegedly fell through and broke it), but the cave entrance is open daily 8am-5pm. **Spring #24** is across the street and down the stairs from the cave, and offers cold, albeit sulfurous, **free water** (open 7-8am, 1-1:30pm, and 5-6pm, so time your trip right, and bring a cup!). If you want to enjoy Proval or the springs without the accompanying hike, take bus #1 or 15 to "Proval."

Walking up the hill from Proval and branching left at the red and white sign will take you down the mountain to the **Akademichskaya Galereya** (Академическая Галерея), through the white arch and on the left. 3000R gets you into the exhibition (open daily 10am-6pm). The Aeolian harp, famous from Lermontov's *A Hero of Our Time,* can be found in the lookout tower to the left and above the archway.

Park Tsvetnik can be approached by walking down the stairs from the Academichka or by taking tram #4 to "Tsvetnik." In the park lies the **Teatr Muzikalinoi Komedii** (Театр Музыкальной Комедии; Theater of Musical Comedy), ul. Kirova 17 (tel. 522 21), which puts on nightly shows for 20,000-25,000R (ticket window open 10am-7pm). Continue down the hill to the gardens in front of the light blue **Lermontovnaya Galereya** (Лермонтовная Галерея), and see if you can go "Deep Blue" on one of the many old men playing chess on the benches. At the base of the park stands the Lermontov Statue, and a right on ul. Karla Marxa (Карла Маркса) will take you to his house, **Domik Lermontova** (Домик Лермонтова), ul. Lermontova 4 (tel. 527 10; open Wed.-Mon. 10am-5:30pm; 6000R).

For activities that involve **no Lermontov whatsoever:** A **cable car** travels to the top of Mt. Mashuk, offering a view of snow-capped peaks (open 10am-5pm; 6000R each way). Bus #15 stops right under the cable. The **amusement park** in Park Kirova is ideal for those traveling with children (and, of course, for the young at heart). A wild spinning ride resembling astronaut proving-ground equipment costs 5000R—you must be as tall as Lermontov to ride (park open daily 10am-9pm).

Unless you crash a dorm party, the best **nightlife** in town is on top of the Gostinitsa Bestayu (see **Accommodations,** p. 591), in a mixed gay/straight club called **Seventh Heaven.** They haven't yet thought of charging a cover, and they couldn't care less if you BYOB (open 10pm-2am, best on Thurs.-Sat. nights).

■ Near Pyatigorsk: Kislovodsk (Кисловодск)

"The air of Kislovodsk prepares you to love." It is unclear whether Lermontov meant that the city's air prepares you to love its many shirtless, elderly inhabitants—either way, this small-scale resort, one hour southwest of Pyatigorsk on the *elektrichka*, makes for an excellent daytrip or stepping-off point for a mountain adventure. Kislovodsk is smaller and slightly more upscale than its sister city, and most of the town's action centers around the many **sanatoria** capitalizing on its natural springs. Downtown sights center around the **Narzan Gallery and Springs,** which you can find by taking the underpass across from the station, going down the hill on the cobblestone street, and taking a left at the bottom. The Gallery is the tan-colored castle on your right, and it is the area's most famous **natural spring** (open 7-9am, noon-2pm, and 4-6pm). The water is free—but bring a cup. Numerous artists display their work (mostly landscapes of the local mountains) just outside the gallery doors. **Hiking trails** into the Mt. Maloe Sedlo region begin in a park just beyond the Gallery; the paths are surprisingly well-marked. Trail #3 leads to a **cable car** that travels to the mountaintop (10,000R round-trip; open daily 10am-1pm and 2-6pm). After dark, the park is considered dangerous, and most of its gates close at 10pm.

Continuing down the cobblestone road (instead of turning left at the Gallery) and following it down the hill to the right will lead you to Kislovodsk town center, such as it is. Numerous **currency exchanges** line the streets, but none offers credit card or traveler's check services. Restaurants in Kislovodsk are geared toward the geriatric set, and priced accordingly. A small **bakery** across from the gallery, at ul. Kominterna 1 (Коминтерна), whose sign reads simply ХЛЕБ, is a great place to catch a snack before returning to Pyatigorsk's more reasonable prices (fresh rolls 1000-2000R; open 9am-8pm daily). And of course, there's always ice cream. Budget accommodations would be out of the question in this spa haven if it weren't for the **Kislovodsk Bureau of Journey and Excursion (KBJE),** which is on a mission to attract a younger, budget-minded crowd to the area. Located at ul. Dzerzhinskovo 24 (Дзержинского), to the right of the **Hotel Kavkaz,** KBJE can arrange centrally located private rooms for under 20,000R a night, as well as tours and excursions to local hiking and camping hotspots (25,000-60,000R). Those interested in tours should call five days in advance (tel. 365 68; fax 762 07). Take bus #4 from the train station up the hill to the "Hotel Kavkaz" stop. The city **postal code** is 357700; the **phone code** is 86537.

■ Sochi (Сочи)

In an earlier era, admirers dubbed Russia's Black Sea coast the "Caucasian Riviera," but Sochi now aspires to be the next Miami. The warm, opaque waters of the Black Sea, the subtropical climate, and the pebble beaches marred only by an occasional concrete slab make this resort a perpetual favorite among Russian vacationers. Once a bastion of the aged and decrepit, Sochi is increasingly attracting hip-hoppety youngsters and foreigners, and its facilities reflect it. Open late, incredibly modern, and preferring Latin over Cyrillic, Sochi is not the place to experience Russian culture—which may be precisely why so many Russians want to be here.

> The nearby mountains give the resort potential for a scenic adventure, but they also signal that the border with Georgia's breakaway republic, Abkhazia, is near. The crowds have returned to Sochi, but border guards with machine guns still keep many of the most beautiful mountain hikes and coastal cruises off-limits. If you do decide to savor the natural surroundings, take a guide. See **Essentials: Safety and Security**, p. 14, for more information.

RUSSIA

ORIENTATION AND PRACTICAL INFORMATION

Greater Sochi extends 145km along the Caucasian coast of the Black Sea, from Tuapse to the border of Abkhazia. The city center is roughly 1400km south of Moscow, on the same latitude as Marseille. North of the center are the resort towns of Lazarevskoye and Dagomys; south are Khosta and Adler. The central section of the city, draped around several hills, bears little relationship to the two-dimensional grid shown on tourist maps. **Ul. Gorkovo** (Горького) links the train and bus stations with the seashore, and **Kurortny pr.** (Курортный) runs along the coast from the **Park Riviera** (Парк Ривьера) toward the airport in Adler, crossing ul. Gorkovo at Gostinitsa Moskva and passing most of Sochi's sanatoria. **Ul. Moskovskaya** (Московская) runs from the train station past Gostinitsa Chaika to the Sochi river. **Ul. Vorovskovo** (Воровского) is the first left after Gostinitsa Chaika off ul. Moskovskaya.

Tourist Offices: The bureau in the Gostinitsa Moskva (see **Accommodations,** p. 595) offers mountain excursions, but they are impractically expensive for individual tourists (150,000R and up). Booths along the beach offer cheaper daytrips (50,000R), but they're not much better than what you could see on your own using public transportation (and a certain yellow book).

Passport Office (ОВИР): ul. Gorkovo 60 (tel. 99 97 69). Registration is desirable but not compulsory if you've registered elsewhere in Russia. Most hotels will register you automatically. Open Mon., Wed., and Sat. 9am-1pm, Tues. and Fri. 3-6pm.

Currency Exchange: Exchange booths everywhere. The ultra-modern Lazurnaya Hotel (Лазурная), pr. Kurortny 103, gives Visa cash advances and cashes traveler's checks at 5% commission. Take bus #4 or 17 from the train station. Open 24hr.

Trains: Zheleznodorozhny vokzal, ul. Gorkovo 56 (tel. 92 30 44, reservations tel. 92 31 17). Foreigners must buy tickets on the lonely 2nd floor of the adjacent round building at *kassa* #12 (and pay for the privilege; open daily 8am-1pm and 2-7pm). To Moscow (1 per day, 40hr., 215,000R)—choose one via Aiksi (Аикси), Russia, not Kharkiv, Ukraine, or risk meeting dollar-hungry border officials. To Kiev (3 per week, 40hr., 179,000R) and Rostov-na-Donu (2 per day, 12hr., 85,000R).

Buses: Avtovokzal, ul. Gorkovo (tel. 99 65 69), next to the train station. Shuttles to Adler and Dagomys leave every 30min. from the circle in front of the bus station. Bus numbers vary, so look at the sign in the front window. Pay the driver (6000-10,000R depending on time of day). Schedules are posted inside the station, but to take a long-distance bus, your best bet is to find out the approximate time of departure and look for the appropriate bus behind the station.

Public Transportation: Buses are 1500R and very useful for travel between the city center and the beach areas. Bus #7 goes from the station past the central hotels. Bus #4 travels from the station to the waterfront. Both scarce after dark.

Ferries: Port service has been cut back during an ambitious renovation project. Call 996 62 55 for most recent info. To İstanbul (2 per week, 10hr., 650,000R).

Taxis: Well-marked by orange and white signs.

Luggage Storage: In the walkway below the **train station.** Open 7am-7pm.

Post Office: ul. Vorovskovo 1 (tel. 92 20 15), corner of Kurortny pr. **Poste Restante** and **Express Mail Service** (tel. 92 28 10) in window to the right of building. Open Mon.-Sat. 8am-8pm, Sun. 8am-6pm. **Postal Code:** 354000.

Telephones: Public phones are both free and reliable. **Mezhdugorodny Telefon** (Междугородный Телефон), ul. Vorovskovo 6, opposite the post office, places long-distance calls, makes **photocopies,** sends **faxes,** and has a 24hr. currency exchange (with a fair rate). Open 24hr. **Phone code:** 8622.

ACCOMMODATIONS

The moment you step off the bus or train in Sochi, you're bound to be accosted by a mob of grandmas requesting the honor of your presence in their domiciles. Be aware, however, that the nice old lady you meet at the train station may not be the one who owns the room she's advertising, but rather just a field agent for those higher up the *babushka* chain of command. It's best simply to get a phone number and an address and check the place out for yourself. Expect to pay 50,000-70,000R a night; most expect at least a 2-night stay. Elderly landladies are often happy to prepare meals and do laundry at mutually agreeable rates. Keep in mind, though, that a nosy *babushka* is almost as bad as a parent. If hanging with the geriatric set is more than you can handle, the most reasonable hotels are:

Gostinitsa Primorskaya (Приморская), Sokoglova 1 (Сокоглова; tel. 92 57 43), between Kurortny pr. and Leningrad beach. A palatial, old, yellow-and-white building with basic salmon rooms. Singles 80,000R; doubles 105,000R. 1st-floor shower is hot but costs 6000R. Fills up quickly; reservations recommended.

Gostinitsa Chaika (Чайка), ul. Moskovskaya 3 (tel. 92 14 36), across from the train station. Big rooms with a view (of the train station). Private showers with sporadic hot water. Singles 96,000R; doubles 156,000R.

Gostinitsa Magnolia (Магнолия), Kurortny pr. 58 (tel. 92 92 92). Two adjacent hotels under one manager. Basic but liveable singles with sink, fridge, phone, hall toilet, and hot shower 130,000R; doubles 200,000R.

FOOD

A **market** at the corner of ul. Moskovskaya and ul. Konstitutsii (Конституции) presents a wealth of ready-to-eat Caucasian delicacies as well as excellent Georgian bread and fresh fruits. Except for a few stragglers, it generally closes by 9pm. Expensive cafes line the beach, most serving mock American fare. **Cafe California** (Кафе Калифорния; tel. 92 32 67) takes you back to Vermont with Ben and Jerry's ice cream (3000R per scoop; open daily 9am-midnight). For a taste of the local specialty, spicy Caucasian food, try the **Shashlychnaya Akhun Cafe,** at the base of the tower on Gora Akhun (see **Sights,** below), For around 25,000R, they'll serve up Georgian salads and meat kebabs (open daily 9am-10pm). To taste local fare without climbing a big hill, head to **Cafe Natasha** (Кафе Наташа), right behind the post office at ul. Varovskovo 3 (Варовского). Fresh Georgian bread accompanies their spicy meats and beans. Meals are generally under 15,000R (open daily 8am-midnight).

SIGHTS AND ENTERTAINMENT

First and foremost is the **beach** and its human attractions. More and more unclothed youths mix with the traditional geriatric crowd to people Sochi's beaches, but then you didn't come here to walk alone along the Black Sea shore. If you did, head north along the coast, or try the emptier and cleaner private hotel beaches, which are emptier because they charge admission (15,000-20,000R). Rent a wooden *lezhak* (лежак; lounge chair; 5000R), jet skis (150,000R per 10min.; open daily 9am-8pm), and paddleboats (30,000R per hr.). Near the ferry terminal is a **waterslide park,** "Аква Парк Маяк" (open daily 9am-8pm; 90,000R).

The city's remarkable **dendrary** (дендрарий; arboretum), Kurortny pr. 74 (tel. 92 36 02), contains 1600 types of plants from around the world (open daily 9am-12:45pm and 1:45-4pm). Take bus #11 to "Svetlana" (Светлана). A cable car takes visitors from Kurortny pr. to an observation post at the top of the park, from which you can walk back down through the park. **Park Riviera,** ul. Yegorova 1 (Егорова), on the south side of the ferry terminal across the Sochi river, begins with a massive mosaic of Vlad's goateed mug in hellish reds. It's a pretty park full of evergreens, outdoor cafes, marble statues of deer, and the occasional war monument. Enterprising folks sell ice cream, toys, and semi-pornographic paintings to strolling vacationers. The **observation tower** at the peak of **Gora Akhun,** an 8km walk or taxi ride from Sputnik International Tourist Center on the road to Adler, affords a panoramic view of Sochi, Khosta, Adler, the foothills of the Caucasus, and, of course, the Black Sea (open Wed.-Mon. 10am-5pm). Taxis are hard to find at the top, so be prepared to walk down. For rainy days, Sochi boasts a **Muzey istorii goroda-kurorta** (Музей истории города-курорта; Museum of the History of the Resort-City), ul. Ordzhonikidze 29 (Орджоникидзе; tel. 92 23 49; open 9am-5pm; 5000R) and an unremarkable **khudozhestvenny muzey** (художественный музей; art museum), Kurortny pr. 51 (tel. 99 99 47; open Tues.-Sun. 10am-5:30pm; 5000R).

The city has a flourishing cultural life, with a major annual **independent film festival** the first 10 days of June and an **art festival** in September. During the peak tourist season in July and August, theater troupes, orchestras and rock bands come from all over Russia to play for the vacationing elite. The **Zimny Teatr** (Зимний театр; Winter Theater), ul. Teatralnaya 2 (Театральная; tel. 99 77 06), down ul. Teatralnaya from Kurortny pr., holds frequent concerts and shows (usually 40,000-80,000R), some featuring the philharmonic (tel. 99 77 51; tickets 20,000R). There are also several outdoor **letnie teatry** (летние театры; summer theaters), among them one in the Frunze Park at ul. Chernomorskaya 2 (Черноморская; tel. 99 77 72). Many of the small **bars** lining the beach have live music after dark, but those who need an entire building to contain their dance moves will be comforted by the presence of **Discoclub Cascad** (Дискоклуб Каскад), on pr. Kurortny between the sea port and the Magnolia. This two-story house of techno opens nightly at 9pm and charges a 30,000R cover (but you get a "free" half-bottle of champagne with your paid entrance). The weekly *Sochi* newspaper, available at kiosks, lists some coming attractions (in Russian), or you can try calling Galina Korneeva, deputy head of the Department of Culture and Tourism (tel. 92 43 17); her husband, Sasha Korneev, is a local impresario.

THE NORTHWEST (СЕВЕРО-ЗАПАД)

Lakes and monasteries shine like cool diamonds in the frigid forests of Russia's northwest territory. Once Russia's sole access to the open sea, the region acquired castles and palaces befitting its service to the empire. Many now decay in romantic abandon, but the northwest's greatest prize—the grad that Peter built—stands as a living monument to the Tsar's love of the far north.

■ St. Petersburg (Санкт-Петербург)

Founded by Peter I (the Great) in 1703, Russia's new capital—won from the Swedes during the Northern War—was created atop a drained swamp on the Gulf of Finland, a task that drove thousands of laborers to early deaths. It was to this young city that westward-looking tsars tried to drag Russia from Byzantium, and in its streets that Pushkin and Dostoevsky wrote their great works. The year 1917 brought an end to an empire and its imperial city—Petrograd, known as "the cradle of the October Revolution," subsequently deferred to Moscow in affairs of state. After Lenin's death in 1924, the city that had been Petrograd (changed from the German-sounding "Sankt Peterburg" during WWI to foster patriotism in the Russian Army) became Leningrad, a name now associated with the tragic 900-day Nazi siege that killed a million of its residents. The population did not recover until the '60s; even today, almost every family remembers victims. Despite such tragedy, enchanting St. Petersburg has persisted as Russia's cultural capital, home to an internationally renowned ballet company, one of the most prestigious art museums in the world, and a thriving alternative scene.

ORIENTATION AND PRACTICAL INFORMATION

St. Petersburg (often called "Petersburg" or simply "Peter") is a six-hour train ride east of Helsinki and nine hours northwest of Moscow. It sits at the mouth of the **Neva river** (Нева) on the **Finsky Zaliv** (Финский Залив; Gulf of Finland). Several canals run roughly parallel to the river, and the main thoroughfare is **Nevsky pr.** (Невский пр.), which runs from the **Admiralteystvo** (Адмиралтейство) on the river to **pl. Vosstaniya** (пл. Восстания) and **Moskovsky vokzal** (Московский вокзал; Moscow Train Station) before veering south to **Aleksandro-Nevskaya Lavra** (Александро-невская Лавра; Aleksandr Nevsky Monastery). Across the river and to the north of the Admiralteystvo is **Petropavlovskaya Krepost** (Петропавловская Крепость; Fortress of Peter and Paul), the historic heart of the city. The area including Nevsky pr. and the **Hermitage** (Эрмитаж) is mainland St. Petersburg; the rest of the city consists of islands, the two largest being **Vasilevsky** (Васильевский) and **Petrogradsky** (Петроградский). The **Metro** is an efficient and convenient way to get around the center, although packed at rush hour. In the center, **trolleybuses** have more frequent stops; #5, 7, and 22 go up and down Nevsky pr. The city makes promenading a pleasure, and most major sights are close to one another. Free English-language newspapers, including *The St. Petersburg Times, Pulse,* and *Neva News,* list current entertainment and sightseeing options and are available at hostels and in major hotels. Travelers should also pick up a copy of the info-stuffed *Traveler's Yellow Pages for St. Petersburg.*

Useful Organizations

Tourist Offices: Sindbad Travel (FIYTO), 3-ya Sovetskaya ul. 28 (3-я Советская; tel. 327 83 84; fax 329 80 19), in the International Hostel. Geared toward students and budget travelers. Issues ISICs (35,000R) and GO25 cards (45,000R) and arranges plane, train, bus, and ferry tickets, as well as escorted package tours and adventure trips. 10-80% discounts on plane tickets. Open Mon.-Fri. 9:30am-5:30pm. **Ost-West Contact Service,** ul. Mayakovskovo 7 (Маяковского). Free info on practically everything, from clubs to train schedules to pharmacies. Very professional and knowledgeable staff arranges visas, homestays, boat and bus tours, and theater tickets. English and German spoken. Open Mon.-Fri. 10am-6pm, Sat. noon-6pm.

Consulates: Canada, Malodetskoselsky pr. 32 (Малодетскосельский; tel. 325 84 48, fax 325 83 83). M1: Tekhnologichesky Institut. Open Mon.-Fri. 9am-1pm and 2-5pm. **U.K.,** pl. Proletarskoy Diktatury 5 (Пролетарской Диктатуры; tel. 325 60 36; fax 325 60 37). M1: Chernyshevskaya. Open Mon.-Fri. 9:30am-5:30pm. **U.S.,** ul. Furshtatskaya 15 (Фурштатская; tel. 275 17 01, 24hr. emergency tel. 274 86 92; fax 213 69 62). M1: Chernyshevskaya. Open Mon.-Fri. 9:15am-1pm and 2-5:30pm. **Aussies** and **Kiwis** should contact their embassies in Moscow but can use the U.K. consulate in an emergency.

Currency Exchange: Обмен Валюты (*Obmen Valyuty*) signs everywhere. The black market no longer exists. **Central Exchange Office,** ul. Mikhailovskaya 4 (Михайловская; tel. 110 49 09), off Nevsky pr. across from Grand Hotel Europe. M3: Gostiny Dvor. All major credit cards and traveler's checks accepted at 3% commission. Expect a long wait. Shorter lines for cash and AmEx traveler's checks. Open Mon.-Fri. 9am-1:30pm and 3-6pm, Sat.-Sun. 9:30am-2pm and 3-6pm. Keep your exchange receipts if you plan to change rubles back into hard currency.

ATMs (Bankomat, Банкомат): All accept Cirrus, EC, MC, Most, Plus, and Visa. At **Nevsky pr. 27/29** (M3: Gostiny Dvor) and **Nevsky pr. 153** (M3: pl. Aleksandra Nevskovo; open 9:30am-7:30pm). Also in **Passazh** (Пассаж) department store, Nevsky pr. 48; across from the main entrance to M3: Gostiny Dvor; and in **Hotel Astoriya** (Астория) on Isaakievskaya pl. (Исаакиевская).

American Express: ul. Mikhailovskaya 1/7, St. Petersburg 191073 (tel. 329 60 60; fax 329 60 61), in Grand Hotel Europe. Books domestic and international flights, replaces lost and stolen AmEx cards, and refunds and sells traveler's checks. Cardholders can cash personal checks and receive mail—no packages. Send mail: c/o American Express, P.O. Box 87, SF-53501, Lappeenranta, Finland. Open Mon.-Fri. 9am-5pm, Sat. 9am-1pm.

Internet Access: International Youth Hostel (HI), 3-ya Sovetskaya ul. 28 (3-я Советская; tel. 329 80 18; fax 329 80 19; email ryh@ryh.spb.su; http://www.spb.su/ ryh). Receive email (free) or send it (18,000R for 30min.; available after 6pm). See also **Accommodations,** below.

Express Mail: DHL, Izmaylovsky pr. 4 (Измайловский; tel. 326 64 00; fax 326 64 10). Packages and letters to the U.S. in 2 working days. Holds mail and packages and provides courier pickup service. Up to 200g to the U.S or Canada costs 278,400R; to the U.K. 285,400R. Open Mon.-Fri. 9am-6pm, Sat. 10am-4pm. **Branch office** in the Nevsky Palace Hotel, Nevsky pr. 57 (tel. 325 61 00; fax 325 61 16). Open Mon.-Fri. 9am-6pm. **Westpost,** Nevsky pr. 86 (tel. 275 07 84; fax 275 08 06), in Dom Aktyora (Дом Актёра). Sends and receives letters and packages to and from any country. A letter up to 20g to the U.S. costs 11,500R; a package up to 2kg costs 354,500R. Also rents postal boxes. Open Mon.-Fri. 10am-8pm, Sat. noon-6pm.

Post Office: ul. Pochtamtskaya 9 (Почтамтская). From Nevsky pr., go west on ul. Bolshaya Morskaya, which becomes ul. Pochtamtskaya. It's about 2 blocks past

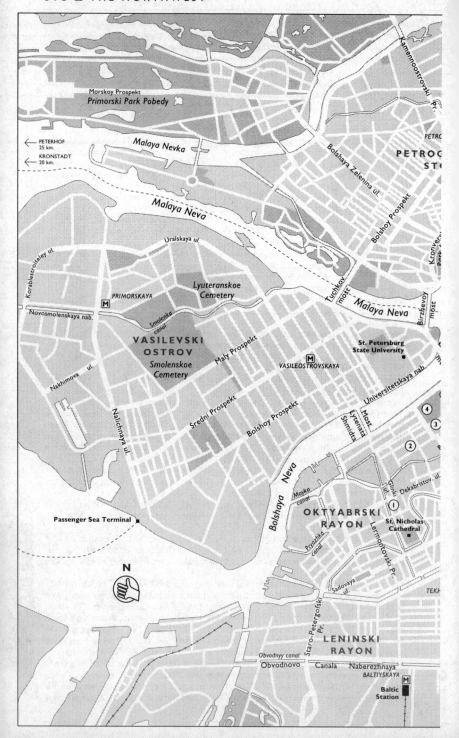

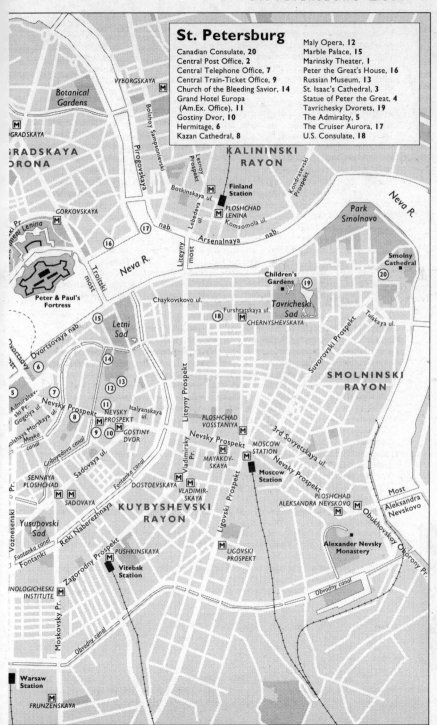

St. Petersburg

Canadian Consulate, 20
Central Post Office, 2
Central Telephone Office, 7
Central Train-Ticket Office, 9
Church of the Bleeding Savior, 14
Grand Hotel Europa
 (Am.Ex. Office), 11
Gostiny Dvor, 10
Hermitage, 6
Kazan Cathedral, 8

Maly Opera, 12
Marble Palace, 15
Marinsky Theater, 1
Peter the Great's House, 16
Russian Museum, 13
St. Isaac's Cathedral, 3
Statue of Peter the Great, 4
Tavrichesky Dvorets, 19
The Admiralty, 5
The Cruiser Aurora, 17
U.S. Consulate, 18

Isaakievsky Sobor on the right, just before an overhanging arch. Come here to change money or to make intercity or international calls. Mailing services are not reliable for international letters and parcels, but can be used fairly confidently for mail within the former Soviet Union. Letters within Russia 950R, international airmail 3500R for letters, 2500R for postcards. **EMS** (Russian Express Mail) open Mon.-Fri. 9am-5pm. Post office open Mon.-Sat. 9am-7:30pm, Sun. 10am-5:30pm. For *Poste Restante*, address mail: "<u>SABATINI</u>, Bernardo, До Востребования, 190 000 Санкт-Петербург, Главпочтамт, Russia." Held for up to 1 month.

Telephones: Central Telephone and Telegraph, Bolshaya Morskaya ul. 3/5 (Большая Морская). Face the Admiralteystvo, and it's right off Nevsky pr. near Dvortsovaya pl. For intercity calls, use one of the *mezhdugorodny* (междугородный) phone booths; they take special grooved *zhetony* (жетоны; tokens) sold across from the booths (2400R). Or prepay your phone call in the *kassa* in the 3rd hall; they will give you change if you haven't used up all the time. Instructions in English available. When making long-distance calls, dial 8 and wait for the tone before proceeding. When your party answers, push the little round button bearing an arrow for a few seconds (there are good pictograms on the phones). Open 24hr. **Intercity calls** can also be made from any public phone on the street that takes phone cards (21,000R for 25 units, 126,000R for 400 units; 1 unit=1min. for local calls; 54 units=1min. to U.S.). Cards can be purchased at the Central Telephone Office or at newspaper kiosks, and are good for both local and intercity calls. Certain phones also take Metro tokens for local calls. For **AT&T Direct,** call 325 50 42; you can also use this service to call collect. **St. Petersburg Center of Business Communications** (tel. 312 20 85; fax 314 33 60). Shares space with the Central Telephone Office and offers express mail, computer rentals, typewriting, and printing. Open daily 9am-9pm. **Phone code:** 812.

Transportation

Flights: The main airport, Pulkovo (Пулково), has 2 terminals: Pulkovo-1 for domestic and Pulkovo-2 for international flights. From M2: Moskovskaya, take bus #29 for Pulkovo-1 (30-40min), and bus #13 for Pulkovo-2 (25-30min.). Hostels can usually arrange for you to be taken (or met) by taxi. **Air France,** Bolshaya Morskaya 35 (tel. 325 82 52). Open Mon.-Fri. 9am-5pm. **British Airways,** Nevsky pr. 57 (tel. 325 62 22). Open Mon.-Fri. 9am-5:30pm. **Delta Airlines,** Bolshaya Morskaya 36 (tel. 311 58 19 or 311 58 20). Open Mon.-Fri. 9am-5:30pm. **Finnair,** Malaya Morskaya 19 (Малая Морская; tel. 315 97 36 or 314 36 45). Open Mon.-Fri. 9am-5pm. **Lufthansa,** Voznesensky pr. 7 (Вознесенский; tel. 314 49 79). Open Mon.-Fri. 9am-5:30pm. **SAS/Swissair,** Nevsky pr. 57 (tel. 325 32 50). Open Mon.-Fri. 9am-5pm.

Trains: St. Petersburg has 4 main railway stations that handle both local and overnight trains. Carefully check your ticket to see from which station your train leaves.
Varshavsky Vokzal (Варшавский Вокзал). M1: Baltiskaya. To: Rīga (1 per day, 20hr., 257,900R); Tallinn (1 per day, 9hr., 127,000R); and Vilnius (1 per day, 15hr., 193,800R).
Vitebsksky Vokzal (Витебский Вокзал). M1: Pushkinskaya. To Kiev (1 per day, 27hr., 243,000R) and Odesa (1 per day, 36½hr., 316,200R).
Moskovsky Vokzal (Московский Вокзал). M1: Pl. Vosstaniya. To: Novgorod (every other day, 5hr., 104,000R); Moscow (15 per day, 6-8½hr., 245,000R); and Sevastopol (1 per day, 38hr., 362,100R).
Finlyandsky Vokzal (Финляндский Вокзал). M1: Pl. Lenina. To Helsinki (1 per day, 5½hr., 310,000R).
Tsentralnye Zheleznodorozhnye Kassy (Центральные Железнодорожные Кассы; Central Ticket Offices), Canal Griboedova 24. Open Mon.-Sat. 8am-8pm, Sun. 8am-4pm. Foreigners must purchase domestic tickets at **Intourist** windows #100-104 on the 2nd floor; intourist international tickets at windows #90-99. If you simply want information on prices, go to ticket window #90; 3000R per question. There are also Intourist offices at each train station. For **schedule and fare information** in Russian, call 168 01 11 or 162 33 44.
Buses: nab. Obvodnovo Kanala 36 (Обводного Канала). M4: Ligovsky pr. Take tram #19, 25, 44, or 49 or trolley #42 from the Metro 1 stop until just across the canal. Facing the canal, walk right along it for 2 long blocks. The station is on your right; enter through the back. Often cheaper and more comfortable than trains if you are

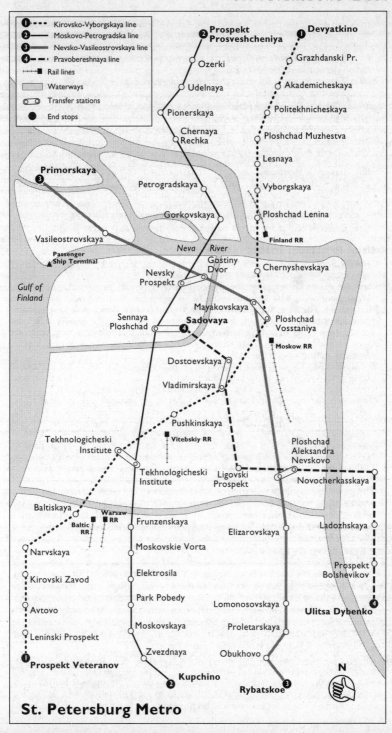

St. Petersburg Metro

Legend:
- ❶ ····· Kirovsko-Vyborgskaya line
- ❷ —— Moskovo-Petrogradska line
- ❸ ▬▬ Nevsko-Vasileostrovskaya line
- ❹ – – Pravobereshnaya line
- ⊢⊣■ Rail lines
- Waterways
- ⊙⊙ Transfer stations
- ⬤ End stops

❷ **Prospekt Prosveshcheniya**
❶ **Devyatkino**
Grazhdanski Pr.
Ozerki
Akademicheskaya
Udelnaya
Politekhnicheskaya
Pionerskaya
Ploshchad Muzhestva
Chernaya Rechka
Lesnaya
❸ **Primorskaya**
Petrogradskaya
Vyborgskaya
Ploshchad Lenina
Gorkovskaya
Finland RR
Vasileostrovskaya
Passenger Ship Terminal
Neva River
Chernyshevskaya
Gostiny Dvor
Gulf of Finland
Nevsky Prospekt
Mayakovskaya
Sennaya Ploshchad
❹ **Sadovaya**
Ploshchad Vosstaniya
Moskow RR
Dostoevskaya
Vladimirskaya
Pushkinskaya
Ploshchad Aleksandra Nevskovo
Tekhnologicheski Institute
Vitebskiy RR
Tekhnologicheski Institute
Ligovski Prospekt
Novocherkasskaya
Baltiskaya
Warsaw RR
Frunzenskaya
Baltic RR
Elizarovskaya
Ladozhskaya
Narvskaya
Moskovskie Vorta
Kirovski Zavod
Elektrosila
Prospekt Bolshevikov
Avtovo
Park Pobedy
Lomonosovskaya
Leninski Prospekt
Moskovskaya
Proletarskaya
Ulitsa Dybenko ❹
❶ **Prospekt Veteranov**
Zvezdnaya
Obukhovo
❷ **Kupchino**
Rybatskoe ❸

N

RUSSIA

traveling during the day. Buy tickets the day you leave to avoid a 2000R surcharge for advance booking. Only one-way tickets sold. Station open daily 5:30am-midnight. Advance ticket booth open 8am-2pm and 3-8pm. To Tallinn (2 per day, 6½hr., 92,500R) and Tartu (1 per day, 8hr., 89,000R). Baggage costs extra, depending on destination (2000-5000R).

Public Transportation: Buses, trams, and **trolleys** run fairly frequently, depending on the time of day. Read the list of stops posted on the outside of the bus. Trolleys #1, 5, and 22 go from pl. Vosstaniya to the bottom of Nevsky pr., near the Hermitage. Buses are often so packed that you might have to jump off and on again at every stop to let people out. The **Metro** (Метро) is a comprehensible, efficient, and safe method of exploring the city (open daily 5:30am-12:30am). Four lines run from the outskirts of the city through points in the center. The driver announces the station at which you are arriving *as well as* the next station and the possible line change. A Metro *zheton* (жетон; token) costs 1500R and also works in some phone booths for local calls. Bus, tram, and trolley *talony* (талоны; tickets) cost 1000R; you can buy them from the driver. Be sure to punch your ticket, as the fine for not doing so is 8300R (not to mention great humiliation), and they do check. A 125,000R **monthly transportation card** is good for unlimited public transportation; purchase one at any Metro station during the first days of the month.

Other Practical Information

Laundry Service: Pick-up next-day laundry service tel. 560 29 92. 40,000R for 4.5kg, plus 40,000R for delivery. Only Russian spoken.

Film and Photo Developing: 1hr. photo Triokom, Nevsky pr. 20 (tel. 311 99 74). Photo developing 4400R per roll plus 1400R per print. 1 roll of Kodak 24,000R.

Pharmacies: The 24hr. **supermarket** at pl. Vosstaniya (see **Food,** p. 603) sells shampoo, Kleenex, and toothpaste, as well as tampons and pads. The *apteka* at Nevsky pr. 22 stocks Russian and Western medicines (including giardia cure Tinidazole), as well as lotions, cosmetics, and tampons. Open Mon.-Fri. 8am-9pm, Sat.-Sun. 24hr. At night, enter through the back.

Bi-Gay-Lesbian Organizations: Gay and Lesbian Association **KRYLYA** (КРЫЛЬЯ; wings; tel. 312 31 80; email krilija@ilga.org) is the city's principal officially recognized organization. Information, help, accommodations. English spoken.

Medical Assistance: American Medical Center, ul. Serpukhovskaya 10 (Серпуховская; tel. 326 17 30; fax 326 17 31), near M1: Tekhnologichesky Institut. Western doctors and bills in English. **Polyclinic #2,** Moskovsky pr. 22 (tel. 316 38 77), and **Hospital #20,** Gastello ul. 21 (Гастелло; tel. 108 40 90), treat foreigners.

Emergencies: Fire: tel. 01. **Police:** tel. 02. **Ambulance:** tel. 03. Police and ambulance drivers do not speak English. If you are a victim of a crime, report it immediately to the local police station—bring a Russian speaker—and to your consulate.

The pipes and drainage system in St. Petersburg have not changed since the city was founded, so there is no effective water purification system, making contact with giardia very likely. Always boil tap water, dry your washed veggies, and stock up on bottled water. For more info, see **Essentials: Health,** p. 17.

ACCOMMODATIONS

Nowhere is Russia's constantly changing political and economic situation more visible to the tourist than in the accommodations scene. Where once travelers were assigned a hotel by Intourist, now they can choose among deluxe new joint ventures, old Intourist dinosaurs, **hostels,** and **private apartments.** *St. Petersburg Press* lists apartments for rent, both long- and short-term; pick up a free copy in the Grand Hotel Europe or at one of the hostels. The International Hostel's *The Traveler's Yellow Pages* has current listings of accommodations options.

Russian-speakers may want to consider a **homestay,** which can be arranged by the **Host Families Association** (HOFA; tel./fax 275 19 92; email alexei@hofak.hop.stu.neva.ru), based at the St. Petersburg Technical University. They provide B&B in apartments close to the city center or less than 1km from a metro station, with an English-speaking family. The most economical B&B package includes only room and breakfast: if your host meets you at the station or treats you to a homemade dinner, expect to be charged extra. Also available: deluxe B&B (includes dinner) and full service (all meals and car) packages. HOFA can also provide tours and theater tickets. Given two to three weeks notice, the association will find you a bed in any major city in the CIS (singles 173,000R; doubles 288,000R; 20% discounts for non-central locations and families with poor English.)

Both members of the national **Russian Youth Hostels Association (HI)** in St. Petersburg accept reservations by phone and offer services such as procuring and registering visas, booking train tickets, and providing rides to the airport. They also sell maps and bottled water.

International Youth Hostel (HI), 3-ya Sovetskaya ul. 28 (3-я Собетская; tel. 329 80 18; fax 329 80 19; email ryh@ryh.spb.su; http://www.spb.su/ryh), in a restored 5-story building in the city center near M1: Pl. Vosstaniya. Walk from the metro along Suvorovsky pr. (Суворовский) for 3 bocks; turn right on 3-ya Sovetskaya ul. In a quiet and pleasant neighborhood. Clean with basic Soviet furnishings. Kitchen, laundry service (23,000R for 4kg of laundry), cybercafe (see **Internet Access,** p. 597), TV, and VCR. Tickets for ballet, theater, trains, etc.; city tours also offered. Films in English on weekends at 8pm. "Crazy Bus Project" lets you visit 4 night-clubs for 85,000R; call 310 08 72. Check-in by midnight. Check-out 11am. 2- to 5-bed dorms. 109,000R, ISIC holders 104,000R, HI members 97,800R. Breakfast and sheets included. Reservations (recommended in summer) can be made from all over the world (U.S. tel. (310) 379-4316; fax 379-8420; email 71573.2010@compuserve.com; U.K. tel. (0171) 836 1036). MC and Visa accepted for reservations from abroad only. The hostel is a member of the International Booking Network (IBN), so you can book all other IBN hostels from here or vice versa.

Hostel "Holiday" (HI), ul. Mikhailova 1 (Михайлова; tel./fax 542 73 64). M1: Pl. Lenina. Exit at Finlyandsky Vokzal and turn left on ul. Komsomola (Комсомола), then right on ul. Mikhailova. Just before the river, turn left into a courtyard, then right. A "YH" adorns the wall ahead of you. The door stays locked (there's a code for guests); ring the bell. Entrance on the 3rd floor. Same basic services as the International Youth Hostel. The bar has an incredible view of the Neva and Petropavlovsky Sobor. Open 9am-midnight. Check-out 11am. 3- to 5-bed dorms 104,400R per person. Doubles 417,600R. Breakfast and sheets included. Dinner 40,000R.

Hotel Olgino (Отель Ольгино), 18 Primorskoye Shosse (Приморское Шоссе; tel. 238 36 71; fax 238 34 63). M2: Chernaya Rechka, then bus #110 (20-25min.). Campsite and recently renovated hotel just outside the city. Sauna (200,000R for 2hr.) and horse rentals. Camping 40,000R; parking 11,500R; showers and kitchen on site. Singles 201,000R; doubles 172,500R. Three-meal packages additional 69,000R.

Dvorets Molodezhi (Дворец Молодежи; Palace of Young People), ul. Professora Popova 47 (Профессора Попова; tel. 234 32 78; fax 234 98 18). M2: Petrogradskaya, then bus #25, 71, or 134. Hardly a palace, despite the pompous Soviet name. Rooms with bath, TV, and phone for travelers of all ages. Winter garden, 2 cafes, restaurant, and swimming pool (open Sept.-May). Singles 150,000R; doubles 240,000R. Home to a famous billiards club (pool 50,000R per hr.; darts 30,000R per hr.; open daily noon-6am).

FOOD

On the surface, Russian menus vary about as much as Stalinist architecture, but many restaurants guard top-secret methods of preparing old favorites, and some boast their own specialties. Even in highly touristed regions, menus are often exclusively in Cyrillic. Because of the small number of really good restaurants and the small size of most of these establishments, the top restaurants fill up fast. Make reservations (usually on the same day) by phone, especially if you speak Russian and are patient; otherwise go in person. Getting to restaurants often requires a good walk. A number of "ethnic" restaurants, beyond Chinese and Indian, offer cuisines from all over the former Soviet empire. Breakfast and late-night snacks are difficult to find—most places are open 11am-11pm. Hotels, supermarkets, and bakeries are off-hours options.

RUSSIA

Fast Food

Skazka (Сказка; Fairy Tale), Nevsky pr. 27. M3: Gostiny Dvor. Combines the traditional Russian treat *bliny* (блины) with amicable Western service and unbeatable prices. Try *bliny* with cabbage and mushrooms (6500R) or with cheese and ham (7500R), or go for the delicious dessert *skazka (bliny,* bananas, and ice cream; 15,000R). Eat in or take out. Open 24hr.

Minutka (Минутка), Nevsky pr. 20. A light and clean fast-food shop with large sandwiches for not-so-large prices. Tuna sandwich 33,500R; mushroom 25,500R. Salads 17,000-23,000R. Grab a cookie for 3000R. Open daily 10am-10pm.

Carrol's (Карролс), ul. Vosstaniya 3/5, ul. Marata 2, Nevsky pr. 45, Kamennoostrovsky pr. 31/33. A Finnish-owned chain that serves tasty hamburgers (9900-16,300R), french fries (6500R), and sodas (5000R). Open daily 9am-11pm.

Russian Cuisine

Green Crest (Грин Крест), Vladimirsky pr. 7 (Владимирский). M1: Vladimirskaya/M4: Dostoevskaya. "Ecological oasis in this gastronomical desert," reads the welcoming sign at the door. Indeed an oasis for vegetarians: 12 varieties of fresh salads, picturesquely displayed. Get them by scoops (100g for 4600R). Mushroom pizza 16,500R. No smoking. Open daily 10am-10pm.

Bistro (Бистро), ul. Malaya Morskaya 14. A little cafe on the way to Isaakievsky Sobor from Nevsky. Good Russian food at good Russian prices, with an eye-pleasing display that works better than any menu. *Bliny* with meat 7000R; salad 3000-12,000R; pastries 1500R. Open Mon.-Sat. 10am-9pm, Sun. 10am-8pm.

Pelmennaya "Alina" (Пельменная "Алина"), Suvorovsky pr. 3. About a block from the Russian Youth Hostel. This simple cafe serves the cheapest hearty food in town. Borscht 5300R; salad 2800-5100R; *pelmeny* 5700R. Open daily 10am-9pm.

Vetal (Веталь), Admiralteysky pr. 8. Go left 1 block at the bottom of Nevsky pr. An exquisitely beautiful traditional Russian restaurant. Hearty food and a location ideal for an after-dinner stroll down Nevsky or through the Hermitage. 7 kinds of *pelmeny* for 14,500-18,000R. Stuffed peppers 16,000R; stuffed tomatoes 13,000R. Open daily 11am-midnight.

Ethnic Cuisine

Tblisi (Тблиси), ul. Sytninskaya 10 (Сытнинская; tel. 232 93 91). M2: Gorkovskaya. Follow the wrought-iron fence that wraps around Park Lenina until you see the Sytny (Сытный) market. Tblisi is just around the corner. Or, take a left off Kronverkskaya ul. (Кронверкская). A cooperative that has maintained its atmosphere since 1987. A wide selection of sumptuous Georgian appetizers (*satsivi;* chicken in walnut sauce, 20,000R) and hot dishes (*tolma;* meat wrapped in grape leaves, 17,000R; *lobio;* beans with walnut spices, 17,000R). Excellent but pricey Georgian wine (60,000R per bottle); ask the staff to recommend one. Lunch specials daily noon-5pm (25,000R). English menu. Open daily noon-11pm.

Tandoor (Тандур), Voznesensky pr. 2 (tel. 312 38 86). On the corner of Admiraleysky pr., 2 blocks left from the bottom of Nevsky pr. For a treat, head here, if only to see adorable Russian boys in Indian costume, complete with gold shoes. This tidy, tasteful restaurant with red carpeting and mournful music presents well-prepared, fairly authentic cuisine, thanks to an Indian chef and manager. The unfamiliar odor of good food wafting onto the street will lure you in if this description hasn't. Many vegetarian options 34,500-57,500R; *lassi* 11,500R; *naan* bread 5800R. Main dishes 57,000-103,500R. Lunch special (noon-4pm) 86,300R. English menu. MC, Visa, AmEx, Diners Club. Open daily noon-11pm.

Yan Tsin (Янь Цзин), ul. B. Morskaya 14 (Б. Морская; tel. 110 69 97), M2: Nevsky Prospekt. Despite the eclectic decor and music, the cuisine is authentic North Chinese. Soups 12,000R; boiled or fried dumplings 20,000R; fried rice 12,000R; vegetarian main dishes 26,000-38,000R; seafood plates 80,000-118,000R. English menu, friendly Western service. Open noon-2am.

Cafes

Cafes have traditionally played a large role in the culture of St. Petersburg, when the likes of Dostoevsky and Lenin met to discuss revolutions over coffee and cakes. Later, sterile and faceless Soviet-era cafes accommodated the emerging alternative culture, which now flourishes in nightclubs. Today's cafes are mostly mainstream, holding only vague echoes of intellectual and cultural debates. Ranging from dirty little holes in the wall to stylish coffee-and-chat houses, cafes in St. Petersburg often cater to smaller budgets, so you can eat cheaply and mingle with natives.

Idiot (Идиот), nab. Moyki 82 (Мойки; tel. 315 16 75), about 200m along the Moyka from Isaakievskaya pl. A tasteful, elegant cafe that reproduces the atmosphere of the Silver Age salon, complete with turn-of-the-century decor. Comfy couches invite leisurely reading; books are available in the entrance hall (English titles 17,000R each). Homemade *pelmeny* with mushrooms, potatoes, or cabbage (25,000R). Happy hour 6:30-7:30pm: 2-for-1 beer or wine. Open daily noon-11pm.

The Brooklyn Bridge Cafe, nab. Moyki 106, near Teatralnaya pl. and Novaya Gollandia island, in the Lesgafta Institute (follow the bright orange sign). Graffitied wall and Manhattan "view." Designed as an alternative to New Russians' hangouts, it caters to students and artists. Darts with beer prizes. Cheapest Guinness in town (20,000R per pint); *Baltika* on tap (10,000R); *medovukha* (light alcoholic honey drink). Huge homemade pizzas (10,000R; toppings 1500R); breakfast specials (12,000R). Happy hour 5-8pm. Open daily 10am-10pm.

Kafe Kolokolchik (Кафе Колокольчик; Little Bells), per. Krylova 1 (Крылова), at the corner of ul. Sadovaya. Enter through the fancy iron gates. Art-filled interior. Salads (5000R); *borscht* (3500R); chicken or fish main course (7000R); coffee (2000R); beer (5000R). Open noon-4pm and 5-9pm.

Lyagushatnik (Лягушатник; Frog's Pool), Nevsky pr. 24. All-time favorite ice cream parlor. The predominantly green decor explains the name. Ice cream of all sorts (8800-10,000R); Turkish coffee (3500R). Open 10am-11pm.

Supermarkets

St. Petersburg's supermarkets offer quality imported products, but charge for the convenience. Most open at 11am, take a 1-2pm break for lunch, and close at 8 or 9pm, but a few 24-hour stores exist.

Supermarket, (Супермаркет), Nevsky pr. 48, inside the Passazh building (Пассаж). M3: Gostiny Dvor. Open Mon.-Sat. 10am-9pm, Sun. 11am-9pm.

Eliseevsky (Елисеевский), Nevsky pr. 56, across from pl. Ostrovskovo. Both a gastronomical and decorative delight. Fancy stained glass and elaborate chandeliers elegantly frame Russian delicacies. Open 9am-1pm and 2-9pm.

Babylon Super, Maly pr. 54/56 (Малый; tel. 230 80 96), off Bolshoy pr. M2: Petrogradskaya. Open Mon.-Sat. 10am-9pm, Sun. noon-8pm.

Markets

Markets stock fresh produce, meat, cheese, honey, and the occasional prepared dish or two, but are more expensive than state-owned stores. They are a truly Russian experience and require energy on the part of all involved. Sellers easily spot foreigners, and many will try to cheat you; watch out for fingers on the scales and count your change. If you are not satisfied, simply walk away; a simple *nyet* will do wonders to bring the price down. Bargaining is what these places are all about; they're bazaars, not Safeways, after all. Don't forget to bring bags and jars. The **covered market,** Kuznechny per. 3 (Кузнечный), just around the corner from M1: Vladimirskaya, and the **Maltsevski Rynok,** ul. Nekrasova 52 (Некрасова), at the top of Ligovsky pr. (Лиговский; M1: Pl. Vosstaniya), are the biggest and most exciting. **Kondratevsky Polyustrovsky Rynok,** Polyustrovsky pr. 45 (Полюстровский), M1: Pl. Lenina, bus #37 or 106, is a pet market on weekends (all markets open Mon.-Sat. 8am-7pm, Sun. 8am-4pm; closed one day each month for cleaning).

SIGHTS

St. Petersburg is a city obsessed with glory days. Citizens speak of "before the Revolution" as though it had occurred only a few years ago and of dear old Peter and Catherine as though they were first cousins. The museums scattered throughout the city are architectural monuments rich in history, but visiting them reveals as much about the city's present as its past.

Hermitage

Originally a collection of 225 paintings bought by Catherine the Great in 1764, the **State Hermitage Museum** (Эрмитаж) rivals both the Louvre and the Prado in architectural, historical, and artistic magnificence. Housed at Dvortsovaya nab. 34 (Дворцовая; tel. 110 96 57), the Hermitage is the world's largest art collection.

After commissioning the building of the Hermitage in 1769 and filling it with works of art, Catherine II (the Great) wrote of the treasures, "The only ones to admire all this are the mice and me." This, to the public's great fortune, is no longer true, since the collection was made public in 1852. The **Zimny Dvorets** (Зимний Дворец; Winter Palace), commissioned in 1762, reflects the extravagant tastes of the Empress Elizabeth, Peter the Great's daughter, and the architect Rastrelli. By the end of the 1760s, the collection amassed by the enlightened empress had become too large for the Zimny Dvorets, and Catherine appointed Vallin de la Mothe to build the **Maly Hermitage** (Малый Эрмитаж; Small Hermitage)—a place in which she could get away by herself or with one of her lovers. The **Veliky Hermitage** (Великий Эрмитаж; Big Hermitage) and the **Hermitazhny Teatr** (Эрмитажный Театр; Hermitage Theater) were completed in the 1780s. Stasov, a famous imperial Russian architect, built the fifth building, the New Hermitage, in 1851. The tsars lived with their collection in the Zimny Dvorets and Hermitage complex until 1917, after which the museum complex was nationalized.

The museum consists of five buildings: the **Zimny Dvorets,** the **Maly Hermitage,** the **Veliky Hermitage,** the **Hermitazhny Teatr** (often closed), and the **Novy Hermitage** (Новый Эрмитаж; New Hermitage). Buy an English floor plan near the ticket booth (500R), or consult those found on each level. The rooms are numbered, and the museum is organized chronologically by floor, starting with **Egyptian, Greek,** and **Roman** art on the ground floor of the Maly and Veliky Hermitages, and **prehistoric artifacts** in the Zimny Dvorets. On the second floors of the Hermitages are collections of 17th and 18th century **French, Italian,** and **Dutch** art. In rooms 226-27, an exact copy of **Raphael's Loggia,** commissioned by Catherine the Great, stands just as in the Vatican.

Room 189 on the Zimny Dvorets's second floor, the famous **Malachite Hall,** contains six tons of malachite columns, boxes, and urns. If you wondered why the revolution occurred, the decadence of this home might explain. The Provisional Government of Russia was arrested in the adjacent dining room in October 1917. On the third floor of the Zimny Dvorets (the only building with three floors) are **Impressionist, Post-Impressionist,** and **20th-century** European and American art. If you're running late, visit them first—the museum closes starting at the top. (Open Tues.-Sun. 10:30am-6pm; cashier and the upper floors until 5pm. 60,000R, students free, Russians 15,000R; cameras 20,000R.)

In June 1997, the museum received a US$1.6 million grant from IBM to provide wider electronic access to the Hermitage treasures for Internet visitors all over the world. Project "Hermitage-IBM" is to be completed by fall 1998. Also planned is an ambitious expansion of the Hermitage's facilities that will allow the museum to exhibit four times as much art as it does now. It would be impossible to absorb the whole museum in a day or even a week—indeed, only 5% of the 3-million-piece collection is on display at any one time. Rather than attempting a survey of the world's artistic achievements, pick a building or a time period on which to focus. Lines can be long, so come early or on a weekday. Allow three to four hours to see the museum. It's easy to latch onto a tour group, especially if you understand Russian.

Isaakievsky Sobor (St. Isaac's Cathedral) and Environs

An awe-inspiring view of the city's rooftops awaits from the dome of **Isaakievsky Sobor** (Исаакиевский Собор; tel. 315 97 32), a massive example of 19th-century civic-religious architecture designed by Frenchie Auguste de Montferrand. On a sunny day, the 100kg of pure gold that coats the dome shines for miles. Not a cheap thrill, considering that the cost of building this opulent cathedral was well over five times that of building the Zimny Dvorets; 60 laborers died from inhaling mercury fumes during the gilding process. The job took 40 years, due in part to Montferrand's lack of experience and in part to a superstition that the Romanov dynasty would fall with the cathedral's completion. The cathedral stood finished in 1858, the Romanovs fell in 1917, and while we're about it, Rasputin was probably a charlatan, but that's all water under the mystic bridge. Although the interior flabbergasts visitors for the first few minutes, after getting used to the grandeur of the place, the details merit a look. Some of Russia's greatest artists have worked on the murals and mosaics inside. Because the cathedral is technically a museum, the paintings have their titles explained in English. Still, the cathedral holds religious services and is packed with *babushki* at Easter. It's dedicated to St. Isaac, the saint with the great fortune to have his birthday coincide with Peter the Great's (May 30th). The chips in the marble columns outside appear courtesy of German artillery fire during the siege of Leningrad. (Museum open Thurs.-Tues. 10am-6pm; Colonnade—the climb to the top—open 10am-5pm. The *kassa* is to the right of the cathedral. 46,000R, students 23,000R, Russians 10,000R. Colonnade 17,500R, students 5500R.)

Despite the fact that the Nazi air force chose the cathedral as "reference point #1" during WWII, the starving citizens of Leningrad planted cabbages in the square directly in front, while in an admirable display of restraint, they never touched the unique collection of seeds from all over the world stored in the Vavilov Institute of Plant Breeding on the other side of the square. Photographs of the cabbage field are displayed at the "Leningrad During the War Years and the Siege" exhibition in Rumyantsev House, Angliskaya nab. 44 (Английская; tel. 275 72 08), along the embankment, five minutes from the Admiralteystvo heading away from the Hermitage. Every St. Petersburg inhabitant will tell you to visit this museum, which makes the devastating effects of WWII painfully clear (open Mon. and Thurs.-Sun. 11am-5pm, Tues. 11am-4pm; 15,000R, Russians 2000R). A blue-and-white sign at Nevsky pr. 14, close to the Admiralteystvo, is another reminder of the tragic fate of the city during the 900-day siege. It reads, in translation, "Citizens! During artillery bombardments this side of the street is more dangerous."

Nevsky Prospekt and Environs

The Prospekt begins at the **Admiralteystvo** (Admiralty), whose golden spire, painted black during WWII to disguise it from German artillery bombers, towers over the Admiralty gardens and Dvortsovaya pl. The height of the tower—one of the first buildings in the young Petersburg of 1705—supposedly allowed Peter to supervise the continued construction of his city. He also directed Russia's new shipyard and navy from its offices. The gardens, initially designed to allow for a wider firing range when defending the shipyard, hold the statues of important Russian literary figures.

On the river side of the Admiralteystvo stands Etienne Falconet's **Bronze Horseman**—symbol of the city and its founder's massive will. Catherine the Great commissioned the meaning-laden statue as a "gift" to her father-in-law in 1782. It shows the famous Peter mounted on a rearing horse crushing a snake, which symbolizes both Sweden, which Peter I defeated in the Northern War, and the "evils" of Russia over which he triumphed. The horse stands on a rock from the site outside of St. Petersburg where Peter first surveyed the city, and the wave behind him represents the sea (St. Petersburg was Russia's first seaport to the west).

Dvortsovaya Ploshchad (Дворцовая Площадь; Palace Square), the huge windswept expanse in front of the Zimny Dvorets, has witnessed many turning points in Russia's history. Here, Catherine took the tsar's crown after she overthrew her husband, Tsar Peter III. Here, Nicholas II's guards fired into a crowd of peaceful demonstrators on "Bloody Sunday" in 1905. And here, Lenin's Bolsheviks seized power from Kerensky's provisional government during the quasi-mythical storming of the Winter Palace in the Revolution of 1917. Today vendors peddle ice cream and carry-out portraits, as the angel at the top of the **Aleksandryskaya Colonna** (Александрийская Колонна; Aleksandr Column) waits for another riot. The column commemorates Russia's defeat of Napoleon in 1812. The inscription on the Hermitage side reads "To Aleksandr I from grateful Russia"; the angel's face is said to resemble the tsar's. The column itself weighs 700 tons, took two years to cut from a cliff in Karelia, and required another year to bring to St. Petersburg. With the help of 2000 war veterans and a complex pulley system, it was raised in just 40 minutes and now sits on a pedestal, held there only by its massive weight.

The landmark Art Deco bookstore, **Dom Knigi** (The House of Books), Nevsky pr. 28 (tel. 219 94 43), was the Russian headquarters of the Singer Sewing Machine company before the revolution. The globe at the top is that company's emblem. The store has lost most of its former glory—only the first two floors are open—but it's worth a visit. There is a good selection of English, German, and French titles on the ground floor, where you can also buy computer software and expensive office supplies. Upstairs, stock up on reasonably priced posters, art books, and cards; maps are also sold here (open Mon.-Sat. 9am-8pm).

The colossal edifice across the street from Dom Knigi, modeled after St. Peter's in Rome but designed and built by Russian architects (and left to decay by the Soviets) is the **Kazansky Sobor** (Казанский Собор; Kazan Cathedral; tel. 311 04 95). Formerly the **Museum of the History of Religion and Atheism,** but now the **Museum of the History of the Russian Orthodox Church,** its gold cross was restored in 1994. The cathedral was originally created for the purpose of housing **Our Lady of Kazan,** a sacred icon now lost. The few icons, robes, and Bibles are displayed in glass cases, dwarfed by the interior of the cathedral—the real reason to pay the entrance fee. As one last attraction, Marshal Mikhail Kutuzov, a famous Russian officer who defeated Napoleon in 1812, is buried here. Since entering through the front or the main side door would be contrary to the "Russian Rule of Appearances" (the more dilapidated the outside, the more you appreciate the inside), a small door around to the left is actually the museum entrance. (Open Mon.-Tues. and Thurs.-Fri. 11am-5pm, Sat.-Sun. 12:30pm-5pm; *kassa* closes at 4:30pm. 17,000R, students 8500R. Russians 3500R, students 2000R. Morning services 9am, Sun. 10am.)

The colorful **Spas Na Krovi** (Спас На Крови; Church of the Bleeding Savior, a.k.a. the Savior on the Blood; tel. 315 97 32), on the Griboyedov canal, sits on the site of Tsar Aleksandr II's bloody 1881 assassination. The church, under repair for the past 20 years, is scheduled to reopen in August 1997; it will hold a museum of mosaics. The minutely detailed mosaics on the exterior also merit a close look. The adjacent chapel houses various temporary exhibitions (open 11am-7pm, 35,000R). Farther down, at Nevsky pr. 35, stands the pale yellow **Gostiny Dvor** (Гостиный Двор; Merchants' Arcades). Built in the 18th century as St. Petersburg's main marketplace, the fine building, undergoing restoration, is now the city's largest department store (open Mon.-Sat. 9am-9pm, Sun. 11am-8pm). **Ploshchad Ostrovskovo** (Островского), just off Nevsky pr., a minute away from M3: Gostiny Dvor, is one of the richest squares in the city. It holds a monument to Catherine the Great, surrounded by principal political and cultural figures of her reign: her favorite, Potemkin; Marshall Suvorov; Princess Dashkova; poet Derzhavin…To the right is the St. Petersburg main public library, decorated with sculptures and bas-reliefs of philosophers and writers of ancient times. The oldest Russian theater, Aleksandrovsky (Александровский), built by architect Rossi in 1828, is behind Catherine's monument. The first production of Nikolai Gogol's *The Inspector General* was staged here in 1836. On ul. Zodchego Rossi (Зодчего Росси, Architect Rossi St.), behind the theater, is the **Vaganova School of Choreography,** which graduated such greats as Vaslav Nizhinsky, Anna Pavlova, Rudolf Nureyev, and Mikhail Baryshnikov.

Dvorets Sheremetevykh (Дворец Шереметьевых; Sheremetev Palace), nab. Fontanki 34 (tel. 272 38 98), a block from Nevsky pr., was constructed at the beginning of the 18th century as a residence for Peter the Great's marshal Boris Sheremetev. The palace underwent numerous alterations throughout the 18th century, and after the Revolution, it briefly housed the Museum of Russian Everyday Life before falling into neglect and decay. Major restorative work has been underway since 1990; the two rooms currently open to visitors contain a permanent exhibition on music in St.

Petersburg. Occasional concerts take place in the palace's music room October to May (palace open Wed.-Fri. 2-6pm, Sat.-Sun. noon-6pm; closed last Wed. of the month; 20,000R, Russians 3000R; concerts 5000R).

Ploshchad Vosstaniya (Восстания; Uprising Square) is the halfway point of Nevsky pr., marked by Moskovsky Vokzal. Some of the bloodiest confrontations of the February Revolution took place here; the Cossacks turned on the police during a demonstration in this square. The obelisk in the center was erected in 1985, replacing a statue of Tsar Aleksandr III removed in 1937. Across from the train station, a green building bears the words "Город-герой Ленинград" (Leningrad, the Hero City), in reference to and remembrance of the crippling losses suffered during the German siege.

Aleksandro-Nevskaya Lavra (Aleksandr Nevsky Monastery)

At the far end of Nevsky pr., directly opposite M3, 4: Pl. Aleksandra Nevskovo, **Aleksandro-Nevskaya Lavra** (Александро-невская Лавра), is a major pilgrimage spot and a peaceful place to stroll. The monastery derives its name and fame from Prince Aleksandr of Novgorod, whose body was moved here by Peter the Great in 1724. In 1797, it received the highest monastic title of "*lavra,*" bestowed on only four Orthodox monasteries. Placement of the dead has always been a concern of Russian Orthodoxy; not only are cemeteries of major importance and gravestones carefully sculpted, but the most desired burial place is under the entrance to the church (the more people walk over your grave, the less your soul will suffer in purgatory). This belief was apparently not in vogue when Peter established Aleksandro-Nevskaya Lavra, for many of the tombs in the monastery's two cemeteries are way too massive to walk over. A cobblestone path lined with souvenir-sellers and beggars connects the monastery's cathedral and two cemeteries. The graveyard on the left is the 1716 **Lazarevskoye Kladbishche** (Лазаревское Кладбище, Lazarus Cemetery), the city's oldest. Going around the edge of the cemetery to the left leads to the plain black tomb of **Natalya,** the wife of Aleksandr Pushkin. Smack in the tiny cemetery's middle lie the graves of two famous St. Petersburg architects: **Andrei Voronikhin,** who designed the Kazansky Sobor, and **Adrian Zakharov,** architect of the Admiralteystvo. In a surprising concession to non-Russian-speaking tourists, most of the graves have plaques in English.

Across the way, on the right side as you walk in, the **Tikhvinskoye Kladbishche** (Тихвинское Кладбище, Tikhvin Cemetery) is not as old, but is larger, and its ground holds more famous names. The most important is **Fyodor Dostoevsky** (who could only afford to be buried here thanks to the Russian Orthodox Church). The grave can be found around to the right, fairly near the entrance, strewn with flowers. Continuing along the cemetery's right edge, you arrive at the cluster of famous musicians: **Mikhail Glinka,** composer of the first Russian opera and a contemporary of Pushkin's; **Mikhail Balakirev,** left of Glinka, was a teacher of **Rimsky-Korsakov** and instrumental in gathering this group of musicians together in life. Balakirev's famous pupil's grave is easily recognized by its unfriendly angels and white marble Orthodox cross; many are drawn to **Borodin's** grave by the gold mosaic of a composition sheet from his famous *Prince Igor;* **Mussorgsky, Rubinstein,** and **Tchaikovsky** are in magnificent tombs next to Borodin. Once Tchaikovsky's homosexuality was discovered and publicized, the conservative Conservatory deemed it more appropriate that the unfortunate musician commit suicide and end his brilliant career than disgrace its hallowed halls. Whether the composer truly complied or was murdered is, like most of Russian history, still unclear, but black angels watch over his tomb. However, it would have been easy for Tchaikovsky to kill himself; drinking a glass of St. Petersburg water would have done it—there was a deadly plague loose at the time. The tomb to the left of the entrance is that of **Stravinsky.**

The **Blagoveshchenskaya Tserkov** (Благовещенская Церковь; Church of Annunciation), farther along the central stone path on the left, was the original burial place of the Romanovs, who were then moved to Petropavlovsky Sobor (exhumation is possibly the only Russian government activity as popular as rewriting history). The church is currently under renovation. The **Troitsky Sobor** (Троицкий Собор; Trinity Cathedral), at the end of the path, is a functioning church, teeming with priests in black robes and workmen crossing themselves. The large interior contains many altars and icons. It is often possible to join English tours at the monastery; while the herd mentality may annoy you, the guides are often very knowledgeable. (Services in the cathedral Mon.-Sat. 6am, 10am, and 5pm; Sun. 7am, 10am, and 5pm. Admission free during services. Lazarevskoye open Fri.-Wed. 11am-4pm; Tikhvinskoye open Fri.-Wed. 11am-6pm. One ticket gives entrance to both; 8000R, students 4000R. Photography 4000R; video 8000R; map of Tikhvinskoye 2000R.)

Smolny Institute and Cathedral

Bus #136, 134, or 46 from the stop across the street from M1: Chernyshevskaya chugs to the **Smolny** (Смольный) complex. Once a prestigious school for aristocratic girls, the **Smolny Institute** earned its place in history when Trotsky and Lenin set up the headquarters of the **Bolshevik Central Committee** here in 1917 and planned the Revolution from behind its yellow walls. Now it is the municipal office of St. Petersburg. The gate buildings at the end of the drive read, from left to right, "First Soviet of the dictatorship of the proletariat" and "Proletarians of all nations, unite!" Farther down, again from left to right, are busts of Engels and Marx. A visit to the legendary Lenin's study inside can be arranged by phone only (tel. 276 14 61). Next door rises the blue-and-white **Smolny Sobor** (Смольный Собор; Smolny Cathedral), notable for combining Baroque and Orthodox Russian architectural styles. The church now functions as an exhibition and concert hall (performances Sept.-May). Climb to the top of a 68m high bell tower and survey Lenin's—er, Peter's—city (open Fri.-Tues. 11am-6pm, Wed. 11am-5pm; *kassa* closes 45min. early; 15,000R, photography 20,000R).

Petropavlovskaya Krepost (Peter and Paul Fortress)

Across the river from the Hermitage, the walls and golden spire of **Petropavlovskaya Krepost** (Петропавловская Крепость; tel. 232 94 54) beckon. Turn right exiting M2: Gorkovskaya on Kamennoostrovsky pr. (Каменноостровский), the street in front of you (there is no sign). Follow the street to the river, and cross the wooden bridge to the island fortress. In summer, locals sunbathe standing up; in winter, walruses and masochists in Speedos swim in holes cut through the ice. Construction of the fortress began in May 1703, a date now considered the birthday of St. Petersburg. Originally intended as a defense against the Swedes, it never saw battle because Peter I defeated the northern invaders before the bulwarks were finished. With the Swedish threat gone, Peter turned the fortress into a prison for political dissidents; sardonic etchings by inmates now cover the citadel's stone walls. The fortress currently houses a gold-spired cathedral that gives the complex and several other museums its name. Purchase a single ticket for all museums at the *kassa* on the right just as you enter. (Open Thurs.-Mon. 11am-5pm, Tues. 11am-4pm; closed last Tues. of each month. 17,000R, students 8500R. Russians 5000R, students 2500R, children 1500R.)

Inside, the icons of **Petropavlovsky Sobor** (Петропавловский Собор; Peter and Paul Cathedral) are currently under restoration, but you can see the graves of almost every tsar since Peter the Great, whose coffin still bears fresh flowers (open Thurs.-Mon. 10am-5:40pm, Tues. 10am-4:40pm). Just outside the church, Mikhail Shemyakin's controversial bronze statue of Peter the Great at once fascinates and offends Russian visitors with its scrawny head and elongated body. **Nevskie Vorota** (Невские Ворота; Nevsky Gate) stands beyond the statue, to the left. Here, prisoners were sent to their executions. Plaques on the wall mark the water level of the city's worst floods. **Trubetskoy Bastion** (Трубецкой Бастион), in the fortress's southwest corner, is a reconstruction of the prison where Peter the Great imprisoned and tortured his first son, Aleksei. Dostoevsky, Gorky, Trotsky, and Lenin's older brother also spent time here (same hours as museum).

Letny Dvorets (Summer Palace)

The **Letny Sad i Dvorets** (Летний Сад и Дворец; Summer Garden and Palace), a lovely place to rest and cool off, lie behind the Russky Muzey and directly across the river from Petropavlovskaya Krepost. Two entrances at the north and south lead to long paths lined with replicas of Classical Roman sculptures and busts. In the northeast corner of the Garden, Peter once kept his small **Letny Dvorets** (tel. 314 03 74). Peter lived downstairs, surrounded by heavy German furniture and lots of clocks, while upstairs resided his kids and wife Cathy, who upon his death became Russia's first tsarina. Individuals must join a tour (and it'll be in Russian). Buy your ticket, and wait outside until they invite you in. The **Chayny Domik** (Чайный Домик; Tea House) and **Kofeyny Domik** (Кофейный Домик; Coffee House), also in the Garden, hold temporary exhibitions. (Garden open summer daily 8am-11pm; off-season 8am-7pm. Palace open Wed.-Mon. 11am-6pm; closed the last Mon. of the month. 20,000R, students 10,000R. Tea and Coffee Houses 2000R each.)

Marsovo Pole (Марсово Поле; Mars Field), so named because of military parades held here in the 19th century, extends next to the Letny Sad. The broad, open park is now a memorial to the victims of the Revolution and the Civil War (1917-19). There is a monument in the center with an eternal flame. Don't walk on the grass; you'd be treading on a massive common grave.

Petrogradskaya Storona (Петроградская Сторона; Petrograd's Side)

Domik Petra Pervovo (Домик Петра Первого; Peter's Cabin), Petrovskaya nab. 6 (Петровская; tel. 232 45 76), as you exit the fortress, sits right along the river. From M2: Gorkovskaya, walk to the river, turn right and go two blocks down the road. The small brick house, set back in a park on the left, contains a log cabin—the first building constructed in St. Petersburg. It was the home of Peter I while he supervised the construction of the city; it's now a shrine, with all the furniture as it was and Peter's compass still on his desk. (Open Wed.-Mon. 10am-5pm, closed last Mon. of the month. 15,000R, students 7000R. Cameras 8000R, videocameras 15,000R.)

Continue along the river past Peter's Cabin to the cruiser **Avrora** (Аврора). Initially deployed in the Russo-Japanese war, the ship later played a critical role in the 1917 Revolution when it fired a blank by the Zimny Dvorets, scaring the pants off Kerensky and his Provisional Government. Inside are exhibits on revolutionary and military history (open Tues.-Thurs. and Sat.-Sun. 10:30am-4pm; free).

Vasilevsky Ostrov (Васильевский Остров; Vasilevsky Island)

Menshikov Palace, Universitetskaya nab. 15 (Университетская; tel. 213 11 12), is reachable by M3: Vasileostrovskaya, but it's better to cross the bridge north of the Admiralteystvo and walk left; the palace is a yellow building with a small courtyard. Aleksandr Menshikov was a good friend of Peter I and governor of Petersburg. Peter entertained guests here before he built the Letny Dvorets, and then gave it to the Menshikovs, who employed Catherine I as a serving-girl before she became Peter's second wife. The museum displays a "Russian Culture of Peter's Time" exhibition, with fragments of original 18th-century interiors and Dutch tiles (open Tues.-Sun. 10:30am-4:30pm; 30,0000R, students 6000R).

Oktyabrsky Rayon (Октябрьский Район; October Region)

Petersburg's romantic quarter sees canal Griboedova meander through quiet neighborhoods with leafy parks. On the outer borders of the *rayon,* the large park **Yusupovsky Sad** (Юсуповский Сад), named after the prince who succeeded in killing Rasputin only after poisoning, shooting, and ultimately drowning the resilient monk, provides an island for peaceful picnics. In the district's center is the Nikolsky Cathedral and, visible from there, **Teatralnaya Pl.'s** Mariinsky Theater.

The **Large Choral Synagogue of St. Petersburg,** Lermontovsky pr. 2 (tel. 114 11 53), is St. Petersburg's only functioning synagogue and Europe's second-largest (morning and evening services daily—call for times). Although the grounds are not well-kept, once you enter (not through the original main door, but to the left) you may find an English-speaking guide. The synagogue celebrated its 100th anniversary on December 8, 1993 and has only around 70 regular members. In 1893 it had 5000; the decline is a sign of the persecution and emigration of Russian Jews. Make sure that the knowledgeable guides show you the wedding hall (open daily 9am-9pm).

It's easy to spot **Nikolsky Sobor** (Никольский Собор; St. Nicholas's Cathedral), a magnificent blue-and-gold structure in striking 18th-century Baroque style. Turn right off ul. Sadovaya across the canal onto ul. Rimskovo-Korsakovo (Римского-Корсакого), near the Marinsky Theater and Conservatory. The entrance is directly across from the spectacular bell tower, whose bells are supposed to have special mystic powers. Inside, the smell of burning wax is particularly potent due to low ceilings (services daily at 10am and 6pm).

Kalininsky Rayon (Калининский Район; **Kalinin Region**)

To truly understand St. Petersburg's obsession with WWII, come to the remote and chilling **Piskarovskoye Memorialnoye Kladbishche** (Пискаровское Мемориальное Кладбище; Piskarovskoye Memorial Cemetery). Close to a million people died during the 900 days that the German army laid siege to the city; this cemetery is their grave. An eternal flame and grassy mounds marked with the year are all that mark the dead. The place is nearly empty, yet the emotion is palpable—this is the grave of a Hero City. The monument reads: "No one is forgotten; nothing is forgotten." Stop at M1: Ploshchad Muzhestva (Площадь Мужества) and go left to the street. At the corner, cross Nepokorennykh pr. (Непокоренных) in front and catch bus #123 from the shelter. Ride about six stops (7-10min.). On the right will be a large flower shop and on the left the cemetery, recognizable by a low granite wall and two square stone gate buildings, each with four columns.

A Museum-goer in Russia

Russians have always prided themselves on high museum culture, the famed Hermitage in St. Petersburg being the ultimate symbol of classical art appreciation. Yet Russia has not always been so high-cultured; the tradition of museum-going started in the early 18th century with Peter the Great's collection of curiosities and monstrosities, the **Kunstkamera.** To lure the reluctant public to his horror show of bottled two-headed fetuses, stuffed eight-legged cows, and live human freaks, Peter offered a glass of vodka to each guest. After his death, the wax figure of the tsar himself welcomed visitors to the Chamber of Curiosities. Now the themes of Peter the Great are back again; an epidemic of wax museums, dedicated to the notorious, the curious, and the ugly, is sweeping through Russia's cultural capital. Rembrandt competes with Rasputin, and ultimately loses, as Russians stream to the dark caves of pop panopticons, bypassing the enlightened temples of high culture.

MUSEUMS

There are essentially four kinds of museums in St. Petersburg: big, famous ones; fast-disappearing Soviet shrines; re-created homes of cultural figures; and churches, monasteries, and cemeteries. The first are a must, despite high foreigner prices and large tour groups. The second appeal largely to lovers of the absurd. The third are pilgrimage sights where you can see (and say you saw) this or that famous author's pen and toothbrush, but are less revealing if you don't read Russian. The fourth are monuments and memorials to the WWII dead, as well as to the often sorrowful history of religion in Russia.

Russky Muzey (Русский Музей; Russian Museum; tel. 219 16 15; fax 314 41 53). M3: Gostiny Dvor. In the yellow 1825 Mikhailovsky Dvorets (Michael Palace), next to Pushkin's monument. Go down ul. Mikhailova past the Grand Hotel Europe. Enter through the basement in the right corner of the courtyard; go downstairs and turn left. The second-largest collection of Russian art, after Moscow's Tretyakov Gallery (see **Moscow: Art Museums,** p. 538). The first public museum of Russian art (1898). Chronologically arranged collection: 12th- to 17th-century icons, 18th- and 19th-century paintings and sculpture. Russian folk art. Benois Wing with modern art and often-controversial exhibitions, such as "The Color Red in Russian Art." Open Wed.-Mon. 10am-6pm; *kassa* closes at 5pm. 48,000R, students 24,000R. Russians 8000R. Cameras 25,000R.

Muzey Etnografii (Музей Этнографии; Ethnographic Museum), Inzhenernaya ul. 4, bldg. 1 (tel. 210 43 20). Next to the Russky Muzey. Hands-on exhibitions of the traditions, crafts, arts, and cultures of the 15 former Soviet republics. Open Tues.-Sun. 11am-6pm; *kassa* closes at 5pm. 20,000R, students 10,000R. Russians 6000R, students 1500R.

Muzey Antropologii i Etnografii—Kunstkamera (Музей Антропологии и Этнографии—Кунсткамера; tel. 218 14 12). Facing the Admiralteystvo from across the river. A natural history museum with a ghoulish twist. "Lives and habits" of the world's indigenous peoples, and Peter's anatomical collection, featuring severed heads and deformed fetuses, homage to the then-modern art of formaldehyde preservation. Top-floor gallery of Lomonosov, a well-known scientist and the founder of Moscow University. Eclectic collection includes Peter I's dining room table, busts of Voltaire, and a mosaic portrait of Peter the Great. Open Fri.-Wed. 11am-4:30pm. 15,000R, students 10,000R. Russians 5000R. Cloakroom 1000R.

Muzey Teatralnovo i Muzykalnovo Iskusstva (Музей Театрального и Музыкального Искусства; Theater and Music Museum), pl. Ostrovskovo 6, 3rd fl. M3: Gostiny Dvor. Posters, programs, set designs, elaborate costumes. Tickets to concerts and lectures (2000-20,000R) in the small concert room sold at entrance. Open Thurs.-Tues. 11am-6pm, Wed. 1-6pm. 15,000R, students free.

Gosudarstvenny Muzey Istorii Peterburga (Государственный Музей Истории Петербурга; State Museum of the History of St. Petersburg), inside Petropavlovskaya Krepost (see p. 610). Paintings, clothing, posters, sewing machines, and phonographs from the late 19th century. Open Thurs.-Mon. 11am-6pm, Tues. 11am-5pm; closed last Tues. of each month.

Muzey Politicheskoy Istorii Rossii (Музей Политической Истории России), ul. Kuybysheva 2/4 (tel. 233 70 52). M2: Gorkovskaya. Head down Kronverksky pr. toward the mosque, then turn left on Kuybysheva. In the mansion of Matilda Kshesinskaya, Marinsky Theater's prima ballerina and lover of Nicholas II. Soviet propaganda, focusing on the 1905 and 1917 revolutions. Printing press, revolutionary items, and other artifacts carefully displayed. Open Fri.-Wed. 10am-6pm. 12,000R, students 6000R. Russians 3000R.

Intererny Teatr (Интерьерный Театр, Interior Theater), Nevsky pr. 104, 4th fl. (tel. 273 14 54 or 275 58 64). M3: Mayakovskaya. Witty carnival project exhibits, ranging from stage costumes for Catherine the Great and Lenin to theatrical models of architectural landmarks, such as the Bronze Horseman and the Kunstkamera building. A fun way to see the city's architectural and political history. Open Tues.-Sun. 10am-6pm. 5000R, students 3000R. Tours 10,000R.

Muzey Pushkina (Музей Пушкина), nab. Reki Moyki 12 (Реки Мойки; tel. 311 38 01), just off Dvortsovaya pl. on the canal, the yellow building on the right. Former residence of Russia's adored poet—most Russians consider Pushkin as good as or greater than Shakespeare. Personal effects of the poet, and many drafts and sketches (Pushkin loved to draw funny-looking people in his margins). In the library, where Pushkin died, the furniture is original, and the clock is stopped at the time of his death; the poet was fatally wounded defending his unfaithful wife's honor in a duel with a Frenchman who had begun to court her (some believe that the affair was contrived by Tsar Nicholas I, who did not approve of Pushkin's poetics). Whether you are a Pushkin lover, or just hope to gain a little more insight into the nation's greatest obsession, this small and elegant museum is an hour wellspent. Enter through the courtyard; the *kassa* and museum entrance are on the left. Open Wed.-Mon. 11am-6pm, closed last Fri. of the month. 12,000R includes a tour in English, students 6000R.

Dom Dostoevskovo (Дом Достоевского; Dostoevsky House), Kuznechny per. 5/2 (Кузнечный; tel. 164 69 50), around the corner to the right from M1: Vladimirskaya. Where Dostoevsky wrote *The Brothers Karamazov;* his notes and bills, on display, are in perfect order, thanks to his wife and secretary, Anna. The area resembles Dostoevsky's St. Petersburg, though die-hard *Crime and Punishment* fans should check out Sennaya pl. (Сенная)—the actual setting of the book's grisly murder. Museum organizes expensive neighborhood tours. Open Tues.-Sun. 10:30am-6:30pm; *kassa* closes at 5:30pm, closed last Wed. of month. 16,000R, students 8000R. Russians 4000R, Russian students 2000R. Film versions of Dostoevsky's novels shown Sat.-Sun. at noon. 4000R, students 2000R.

RUSSIA

Muzey Anny Akhmatovoy (Музей Анны Ахматовой), Fontanki 34 (tel. 272 22 11). Enter at Liteyny pr. 51, through an archway; keep left and follow the signs. Personal possessions of the poet whose Soviet-era writings made her a national heroine. Open Tues.-Sun. 10:30am-5pm, closed last Wed. of each month. 4000R, students 2000R. Russians 2000R.

Muzey Kirova (Музей Кирова), Kamennoostrovsky pr. 26/28, 5th fl. (tel. 346 02 17). M2: Petrogradskaya. 10min. walk to the right of Metro exit. Kirov headed the Leningrad Communist Party from 1926 until his mysterious death in 1934. His hunting trophies populate his re-created home. Lower floor full of Stalins, most donated by the executioner himself. Open Thurs.-Tues. 11am-6pm; closed last Tues. of each month. 15,000R, students 8000R.

Artillerysky Muzey (Артиллерийский Музей; tel. 238 47 04). M2: Gorkovskaya. One of the oldest museums in the city; opened in 1756, moved to its present site in 1868. Housed in an old arsenal. Lots of cannons, including the toy one little Peter the Great played with, and tanks in the courtyard. Open Wed.-Sun. 11am-5pm; closed last Thurs. of each month. 15,000R, students 7500R, cameras 15,000R.

Muzey Arktiki i Antarktiki (Музей Арктики и Антарктики; tel. 113 19 98). M3: Mayakovskaya. On the corner of Kuznechny per. and ul. Marata (Марата). Model ships, nautical instruments, and everything else Arctic expeditions could have used. Foxfurs and stuffed wolves glorify humankind's invasion of the wild. Environmental disasters in the region not on display. Open Wed.-Sun. 10am-5pm; *kassa* closes at 4pm; closed last Sat. of each month. 10,000R.

ENTERTAINMENT

St. Petersburg's famed White Nights lend the night sky a pale glow from mid-June to early July. In summer, couples stroll under the illuminated night sky and watch the bridges over the Neva go up at 1:30am. Remember to walk on the same side of the river as your hotel—the bridges don't go back down until 3-4am. For those more familiar dark nights, St. Petersburg offers ample activities, generally at little cost.

Classical Music, Opera, and Ballet

The city of Tchaikovsky, Prokofiev, and Stravinsky continues to live up to its reputation for classical performing arts; it is easy to get 5000R tickets to world-class performances. The Mariinsky Ballet, one of the world's best companies and the place where Russian ballet won its fame, often has inexpensive tickets available. Sprinkled across the city are a few large concert halls. During the third week in June, when the sun barely touches the horizon, the city holds a series of outdoor evening concerts as part of the **White Nights Festival.** Check kiosks and posters for more info. Theater season ends around the time of this festival and begins again in early September, but check for summer performances at ticket offices at Nevsky pr. 42, across from Gostiny Dvor, or from kiosks and tables near Isaakievsky Sobor and along Nevsky pr. It may be more productive to go to the *kassa* of the theater where the performance will be held. A monthly program in Russian is usually posted on kiosks throughout the city.

In general, theaters start selling tickets 20 days in advance; good seats sell out fast, but cheap ones are often still available on the day of the performance. A model of the seating arrangement is always displayed. *Yarus* (ярус) are the cheapest seats, and if you come in close to the start of a performance, a *babushka* who works there might let you sneak into this section for free. Scalpers often sell tickets in front of the theater; this is generally safe, but check the date on the ticket. Intourist buys out many of the better seats, but charges exorbitant prices. Performances often start a few minutes late. Russians dress up for the theater and consider the foreigner who arrives for a performance of *Uncle Vanya* in everyday clothes an insult to their culture.

For the most part, Russian singers, dancers, and orchestras are at their best when they perform Russian pieces. While the Maly Opera's rendition of *La Traviata* may be the worst Italian opera you've seen, Tchaikovsky's *Queen of Spades* (Пиковая Дама; *Picovaya Dama*) may well be the best staging and performance of Russian opera you will ever experience. Likewise, choose Prokofiev over Strauss when seeking a powerful and emotional orchestral event.

Mariinsky Teatr (Мариийнский Театр), Teatralnaya pl. 1 (tel. 114 43 44). M4: Sado-vaya. Walk 10min. along canal Griboyedova, then turn right onto the square. This imposing aqua building is one of the most famous theaters for ballet in the world. Pavlova, Nureyev, Nizhinsky, and Baryshnikov all started here, where Tchaik-ovsky's *Nutcracker* and *Sleeping Beauty* premiered. The ballet goes on tour for 2 months in the summer, and good seats are mostly sold out, but it's worth a try. For 2 weeks in June, the theater hosts the **White Nights Festival**, for which tickets are easier to get. Tickets (8000-50,000R) start selling 10 days in advance. Evening per-formances at 6:30pm. *Kassa* open Wed.-Sun. 11am-3pm and 4pm-7pm.

Maly Teatr (Малый Театр), also known as Mussorgsky Theater, pl. Iskusstv 1 (Искусств; tel. 219 19 78), near the Russky Muzey. Second to the Mariinsky for opera and ballet, but opens July-Aug. when the Mariinsky is closed. Similarly impressive concert hall, and excellent performances of Russian ballet and opera. Tickets sold 20 days in advance. Ticket for foreigners up to 125,000R, Russians 5000-30,000R. *Kassa* open daily 11am-3pm and 4-8pm. Documents checked at the *kassa* and at the door.

Shostakovich Philharmonic Hall, Mikhailovskaya ul. 2 (tel. 311 73 33), opposite the Grand Hotel Europe. M3: Gostiny Dvor. Large concert hall with both classical and modern concerts. Acoustics are not perfect, due to its former use for Boyar Council meetings, which had no need for such subtleties. Tickets from 4000R, depending upon the concert and day. The Philharmonic tours for most of the summer.

Akademicheskaya Kapella (Академическая Капелла), nab. Reki Moyki 20 (tel. 314 10 48). M2: Nevsky Prospekt. Small hall for choirs, solos, and small orchestras. Con-certs at 7pm. Prices from 3000R. *Kassa* open daily noon-3pm and 4-7pm.

Glinka Maly Zal, Nevsky pr. 30 (tel. 312 45 85). Part of the Shostakovich Philhar-monic Hall, but better acoustics than in the main hall. Tickets from 20,000R, depending upon the concert and day. *Kassa* open daily 11am-3pm and 4-8pm.

Conservatoriya (Консерватория), Teatralnaya pl. 3 (tel. 312 25 19), across from Mari-insky Teatr. M4: Sadovaya. Often excellent student ballets and operas performed here. Evening performances start at 6:30pm, Sat.-Sun. at 6pm. Matinees at noon. Tickets 5000-20,000R. *Kassa* open daily noon-6pm.

Theater, Puppets, Circus, and Cabaret

Russian plays in Russian are generally better than Shakespeare in Russian. The Rus-sian circus, while justly famous, is not for animal rights activists. In fact, even those who come garbed in fur coats and hats may want to run home and throw red paint on themselves after seeing a bear whipped into walking a tightrope. Nonetheless, the circus can be amusing and, of course, you don't need to speak Russian to enjoy it.

Aleksandrinsky Teatr (Александринский Театр), pl. Ostrovskovo 2 (tel. 312 15 45). M3: Gostiny Dvor. Turn right on Nevsky pr., then right at a park with Catherine's statue. Ballet and theater—mostly classics like *Hamlet* and *Cyrano de Bergerac*. The theater attracts some of Russia's most famous actors and acting companies. St. Petersburg citizens wait in line for hours for certain Moscow troupes performing Chekhov in the building built by Rossi in 1832. Summer ballet season starts July 25. Performances at 11am and 7pm. Tickets 5000-15,000R, available 20 days in advance. *Kassa* open daily 11am-7pm.

Bolshoy Dramatichesky Teatr (Большой Драматический Театр), nab. Reki Fontanki 65 (Реки Фонтанки; tel. 310 92 42). M3: Gostiny Dvor. Conservative productions of Russian classics. Tickets 2000-20,000R. *Kassa* open daily 11am-3pm and 4-6pm.

Teatr Marionetok (Театр Марионеток), Nevsky pr. 52 (tel. 311 19 00). Puppet and marionette shows. Mostly for children. Shows start at 11am and 2pm. Closed July-Aug. Tickets from 3000R. *Kassa* open Tues.-Wed. and Fri-Sun. 10:30am-4pm.

Tsirk (Цирк; Circus), nab. Fontanki 3 (tel. 210 43 90), near the Russky Muzey. M3: Gostiny Dvor. Russia's oldest circus. With the exception of a cool live orchestra, it has the requisite exploited animals and other trappings of a good Russian circus. Tickets from 7000R. Matinees at 11:30am, afternoon shows at 3pm, evening shows at 7pm. *Kassa* open daily 11am-4pm.

Music Hall (tel. 233 02 43), in Aleksandrovsky Park. M2: Gorkovskaya. A fully decked-out (plumes and all) Russian cabaret. A very cheesy experience. Tickets from 10,000R; shows at 7pm. *Kassa* open daily noon-7pm.

Yubileyny Sports Palace, Pr. Dobrolyubova 18 (Добролюбова, tel. 238 40 49), equally far from M3: Vasileostrovkaya and M2: Gorkovskaya. Occasional rock concerts; tickets from 30,000R. And, of course, sports events.

Shopping

The best place to go for souvenirs is Nevsky pr., just beyond Gostiny Dvor toward the Admiralteystvo. If you speak Russian, use it—you're less likely to get ripped off. Comparison shopping is a good idea, too. Even the black market has fixed prices. Or try actual stores, where posted price tags can't sucker foreigners. Some of the most common traditional Russian treasures found are woolen flower-print scarves, *matryoshka* dolls (dolls within a doll), *samovars*, blue-and-white china from Gzhel (make sure it says Гжель on the bottom), and semi-precious stones from the Urals. The factory where Russian tsars stocked their shelves, **Leningradsky Farforovy Zavod** (Leningrad Porcelain Factory), still fashions affordable teacups.

Souvenirs: The outdoor **markets** on either side of Nevsky pr. just beyond Gostiny Dvor have the widest selection of both classical and tacky Russian souvenirs (for example, *matryoshka* dolls painted with characters ranging from *Aladdin* and *The Little Mermaid* to Yeltsin and Lenin). Or try the open-air **souvenir fair** on kan. Griboedova (кан. Грибоедова) behind Spas Na Krovi. Geared toward tourists, with English spoken. Prices tend to be reasonable, and Russian-speakers can often bargain them down. Stands usually open 11am-8pm. Watch your moneybelt and keep an eye out for thieves. There are also a few **souvenir shops** where more interesting items can be found, often for better prices—though books tend to cost more than in the U.S. **Museum gift shops** are a good place to find things, too—often they stock a small selection of lacquer boxes and amber jewelry.

Crafts and Antiques: Antikvariat Rus (Антиквариат Русь), Kamennostrovsky pr. 17 (Каменностровский). Silver candlesticks, *samovars*, old books, paintings, and silver tea-glass holders for reasonable prices. Walk 4 blocks north of Kamennoostrovsky pr. from M2: Gorkovskaya. Open Mon.-Sat. 11am-2pm and 3-7pm.

Bookstores: Dom Knigi (Дом Книги; open daily 9am-8pm; see p. 608) and **Dom Voyennoy Knigi** (Дом Военной Книги; open Sun.-Fri. 10am-7pm, Sat. 10am-6pm), Nevsky pr. 22. Books, office supplies, and souvenirs, as well as maps and dictionaries. **Isskustvo** (Исскуство), Nevsky pr. 16. Art books, jewelry, and an eclectic assortment of CDs (30,000-80,000R). Open daily 10am-2pm and 3-7pm.

Music: Saigon (Сайгон), Nevsky pr. 49/2. Formerly the center of alternative music culture, Cafe Saigon has become a cool music store, selling Russian and Western CDs (45,000-120,000R) and videos (25,000-32,000R). Open 10am-10pm.

Nightlife

During the pre-Gorbachev era, Petersburg was the heart of the underground music scene, and this is still evident in the number of interesting clubs. There are plenty of expensive dance clubs for Russian "businesspeople," too, but better evening fare can be found tucked away in former bomb shelters, often off the main drag. Be careful going home late at night, especially if you've been drinking—loud, drunk foreigners might as well be carrying neon signs saying "rob me!" Clubs last no longer than college relationships, though during the brief period of fresh excitement they attract most of the cool St. Petersburg crowd. The HI hostels can recommend the newest places, or check the Friday issue of *St. Petersburg Times* and *Pulse* for current events.

St. Petersburg Rock Club (Рок Клуб), ul. Rubinsteyna 13 (Рубинштейна). M1: Vladimirskaya; M4: Dostoevskaya. In the courtyard and through the right door on the far wall. Soviet rock superstars like Kino and Igry got their starts in this dingy old building. Popular hangout for musicians and a fashionable young crowd. During the day, a music store operates inside (CDs 20,000R). Tickets to concerts available in the club or in music stores like Saigon (see above). Open Mon.-Thurs. noon-11pm, Fri.-Sat. noon-1am. Cover 15,000-30,000R, depending on the show.

Tunnel (tel. 238 80 75), in an old bomb shelter. No address—it's a bomb shelter, after all. Located on Lyubyansky per. (Любянский) between ul. Blokhina (Блохина) and Zverinskaya (Зверинская). M2: Gorkovskaya. Techno and dancing? This is the place. Very young crowd. Cover 30,000R. Open Fri.-Sat. midnight-6am.

Jungle, ul. Blokhina 8 (tel. 238 80 33). New gay club on the Petrogradskaya Storona. No sign—spot the aquamarine door and go upstairs. Admittance based on membership, but foreigners are welcome. You may wish to call in advance. Bring your ID—no one under 17 is allowed, though exceptions are not uncommon. Erotic and drag shows starting at 1:45am. Cover midnight-12:15am and 4-6am 20,000R; 1-4am 50,000R. Open Fri.-Sat. midnight-6am.

Fish Fabrique, ul. Pushkinskaya 10 (Пушкинская). M3: Mayakovskaya. Deliberately mutilated interior reproduces the atmosphere of a bomb shelter on the 4th floor of a former apartment building. Soft neon lights, artsy crowd, bohemian feel. Live rock concerts and theme music nights. Open Wed.-Thurs., Sun. 7-11:30pm, cover 10,000R; Fri.-Sat. 9pm-5:30am, cover 20,000R. One floor down is the New Academy of Fine Arts—the center of the contemporary alternative visual arts scene, founded by local legend Timur Novikor. Gallery open Fri.-Sun. 5-8pm.

Griboyedov (Грибоедов), Voronezhskaya ul. 2A (Воронежская; tel. 112 25 65). M4: Ligovsky Prospekt. Green lantern above the door announces this literally underground, stylish new club. Techno and acid jazz, art exhibitions, video screenings. Lounging, aloof, artsy crowd. Open Thurs.-Sun. 11pm-6am; cover 30,000R.

The Shamrock, ul. Dekrabristov 27 (Декрабристов; tel. 219 46 25). Across from the Mariinsky in Teatralnaya pl. A shining example of Ireland's second largest export, this authentic Irish bar is a fun place to down a beer or two (or three). Western music and a young, but not seedy, crowd. Pint of Guinness or Kilkenny 28,000R. Hearty pub food. Open daily noon-2am. MC and Visa.

Jazz Philharmonic Hall, Zagorodny pr. 27 (Загородный; tel. 164 85 65). M1: Vladimirskaya. Mainstream and Dixieland jazz venue organized by local jazz celebrity David Goloshchyokin. Nightly concerts at 8pm. Tickets 20,000-50,000R, depending on the program (sold 2-8pm in the *kassa*). Open nightly 7-11pm.

■ Near St. Petersburg

Ride the suburban *elektrichka* trains any spring or summer weekend day to witness the Russians' love of the countryside. Most Russians own or share a *dacha* outside the city and go there every weekend; families crowd outgoing trains loaded down with groceries, pets, and perhaps lumber for a new construction project. The tsars were no different; they, too, built country houses, and several of these palaces have been restored to their original glamour. These make particularly good daytrips from St. Petersburg when one more stroll along Nevsky makes your butt itch. Although Peterhof and the Catherine Palace in Pushkin have small cafes nearby, they are grossly overpriced, so do as the Russians do and bring a picnic lunch to eat in the idyllic parks. And wear a jacket if your destination is Peterhof—the grounds abut the Gulf of Finland and the garden can get quite windy.

The three palaces stand on what was German territory during the siege of Leningrad in 1942-44. All were burned to the ground during the Nazi retreat, but Soviet authorities provided the staggering sums of money necessary to rebuild these symbols of the tsars and of rich cultural heritage during the postwar reconstruction.

PETERHOF (ПЕТЕРГОФ)

Formerly known as Petrodvorets (Петродворец), this is the most thoroughly restored of the palaces. The entire complex at Peterhof is 300 years old, and many of the tsars added to it or expanded existing palaces. **Bolshoy Dvorets** (Большой Дворец; Grand Palace; tel. 427 95 27) was Peter's first residence here, but his daughter, Empress Elizabeth, and then Catherine the Great greatly expanded and remodeled it. The rooms have been completely returned to their previous glory, reflecting the often conflicting tastes of various owners of the palace and the diverse interior fashions from early Baroque to Neoclassicism. A palace tour is worthwhile.

Golden cherubs guard the ceremonial stairs to the palace. Just before the throne room, the pompous **Chesma Gallery,** a chamber larger than most one-family homes, depicts the Russian victory over the Turks at Chesma Bay in 1770. Aleksandr Orlov supposedly arranged for a frigate to be exploded in front of the painter to ensure the authenticity of the images. Farther along, two Chinese studies flank a picture gallery that contains 360 portraits of the same eight women dressed in different outfits of authentic 18th-century silk, all by the Italian Pietro Rotari. Apparently his widow, strapped for cash, sold the whole lot to Catherine the Great. The last room on the tour—**Peter's study,** lined with elegantly carved oak wood panels—is a rest for the eyes after all the glittering frou-frou. Much of the room inexplicably survived the Nazi invasion—the lighter panels are reconstructions, some of which took 1½ years to complete. (Palace open Tues.-Sun. noon-12:30pm, 1-2:30pm, and 4:15-5pm; closed last Tues. of each month. 46,000R, students 23,000R. Cameras 15,000R, videocameras 40,000R. All handbags must be checked; 500R.)

Below the Grand Palace, the **Lower Gardens** are less well-kept but more extensive than the Upper Gardens. To the right, a **Wax Museum** contains figures of the residents of Peterhof (open daily 9am-5pm; 17,000R, students 8500R). From the Wax Museum and the nearby quay, the view up the cascade with the Grand Palace as a backdrop stuns. Look the other way to see the shores of Finland across the Gulf of Finland. Follow the sound of children's shrieks and giggles to the **"joke fountains,"** which, activated by one misstep, suddenly splash their unwitting victims. (All parks open daily 9am-9:30pm; entrance 22,000R. Fountains flow May-Sept. daily 11am-8pm, Sun. until 9pm.)

On the other side of the garden stands **Monplaisir,** the house Peter actually lived in (the big palace was only for special occasions). Smaller and less ostentatious than its neighbors (he was the tsar with good taste), it is graceful and elegant. Note the fairy-tale decor of the study, which combines the Chinese technique of lacquer painting with the spirit of Russian national art. Long, marble-floored galleries flank the main wing. The place is peaceful even on the busiest Saturdays (open Thurs.-Tues. 10:30am-5pm; closed last Thurs. of each month; 33,000R, students 17,500R). Next door is **Ekaterininsky Korpus** (Екатерининский Корпус, the Catherine Building), where Catherine the Great lay low while her husband was (on her orders) being overthrown (open Fri.-Wed. 10:30am-5pm; closed last Fri. of each month; 17,000R, students 8500R; photography 7000R, videocameras 20,000R).

The **Hermitage Pavilion** is tucked away in the woods of the eastern section of the lower park, symmetrically opposite Monplaisir. A big hall on the first floor displays 124 paintings by 17th- and 18th-century European painters. The kitchen affords a behind-the-scenes look at gala receptions, displaying 18th-century kitchenware in an authentic setting (open Thurs.-Tues. 10:30am-5pm; closed last Thurs. of each month; 17,000R, students 8500R).

The fastest and most exciting way to get to Peterhof during the summer is to take the *meteor* (метеор, hydrofoil) from the quay on Dvortsovaya nab. (Дворцовая) in front of the Hermitage (every 30min. from 9:30am, 30min., 40,000R; for return trip check schedule in Peterhof). Peterhof is also an easy trip by **elektrichka** (every 15min., 40min., one-way 4000R, round-trip 8000R) from the Varshavsky vokzal, M1: Baltiskaya (Балтийская). Buy round-trip tickets from the ticket office (Билетные Кассы) in the courtyard—ask for "NO-vyi Peter-GOFF, too-DAH ee oh-BRAHT-nah." Find Novy Peterhof (Новый Петергоф) on the map in the center of the courtyard at the train station, pick a train going beyond it, then find the right track. Get off at Novy Peterhof, and either walk left down the road for about 15 minutes or take any bus from the station to the stop after the cathedral (1000R). The crowds are heaviest on weekends.

TSARSKOYE SELO (ЦАРСКОЕ СЕЛО)

About 25km south of the city, Tsarskoye Selo ("Tsar's Village") surrounds Catherine the Great's summer residence, a gorgeous azure, white, and gold Baroque palace overlooking sprawling, English-style parks. The area was renamed "Pushkin" during the Soviet era—most Russians and train conductors still use that name. Built in 1756 by the architect Rastrelli before he went to work on the Winter Palace, this opulent residence was remodeled by Charles Cameron under the orders of Catherine the Great; she had the good taste to remove the gilding from the facade, desiring a modest, little "cottage" where she could relax. The Baroque Palace, named **Ekaterininsky Dvorets** (after Elizabeth's mom, Catherine I) was largely destroyed by the Nazis; each room exhibits a photograph of it in a war-torn condition. The **Amber Room** suffered the most; its walls were stripped and probably lost forever (one rumor places the hidden furnishings somewhere in Paraguay). A sign in the room reads: "Ruin of the Amber Room is loss of all of mankind. You sacrifice us—we atone for our common duty to the world culture." While the English leaves much to be desired, the idea is clear—even the exorbitant entrance fees don't suffice to completely repair these mansions. Despite this, many of the salons, especially the huge, glittering **Grand Hall** ballroom, have been magnificently restored. Elizabeth used to hold costume parties here. Today there is ample space for you to waltz around—even in *tapochki*. North of the main staircase the other stark rooms wait, one displaying a number of exquisite artifacts from East Asia. Tag along with one of the many English-speaking tours (tel. 466 66 69; open Wed.-Mon. 10am-5pm, closed last Mon. of every month; 40,000R, students 20,000R, Russians 10,000R; photography 20,000R).

Although the Ekaterininsky Dvorets alone is worth the trip, many bring a picnic and take the time to wander through the surrounding parks (open 10am-8pm; 12,000R, students 6000R; after 6pm entrance to park is free). Aleksandr I's palace, though closed to the public, stands guard over a wild forest, and the rest of the 1400-acre **Catherine Park** is a gardener's paradise—a melange of English, French, and Italian styles. The **Great Pond** is the centerpiece of the English park; it is possible to rent **rowboats** here in summer. To the east lies the Italian-landscaped park where Catherine would ramble with her dogs. Some believe Catherine loved Muffy and Fido (or the Russian equivalent) more than her children; they now rest in dog peace under the **Pyramid.** Numerous other architectural curiosities pepper the park. The **Ruined Tower** was built pre-ruined (saving later invaders the trouble). Next to Catherine's Palace, the **lycée** schooled the likes of Pushkin (tel. 476 64 11; open Wed.-Mon. 10:30am-4:30pm; 10,000R, 12,000R with a tour, students 5000R, 6000R with a tour). Pushkin, then 12, was one of the *lycée*'s first students, and his cubbyhole can still be seen, along with the classrooms, laboratory, and music rooms.

Although Pushkin and Pavlovsk can be combined in one day, a leisurely visit is more enjoyable. Take any *elektrichka* from Vitebsky vokzal (M1: Pushkinskaya). To buy your ticket, go to the right of the station to a gray bunker-like building. Ask for "Detskoe Selo" or "Pushkin" (one-way 3000R, round-trip 6000R). Ask for "too-DAH ee oh-BRAHT-nah" if you want a ticket for the way home, too. Don't be worried that none of the signs say Pushkin; all trains leaving from platforms 1-3 go through there. It's the sixth stop, recognizable both by the number of people who get off and because it is the first platform that looks like a station (30min.). The conductor should mumble "Pushkin" at some point before you arrive. Once at the station, it's a 15-minute walk or 10-minute ride on bus #371 or 382 (1000R) almost to the end (you're less likely to get lost on the bus). There will be a yellow building on the left; the palace is barely visible through the trees on the right.

SHLISSELBURG (ШЛИССЕЛЬБУРГ)

About 35km east of St. Petersburg is the medieval fortress Shlisselburg, also known as Oreshek (Орешек; a tough nut). The fortress played a key role during the Swedish campaign of Peter the Great, who appropriately named it Shlisselburg, the key-city, but it has fallen into touristic decay since the state subsidies were cut off. Yet the ruins of Shlisselburg hide centuries of history, as well as remarkable architecture; absorb it all leisurely in a tourist-free setting.

Orientation and Practical Information Shlisselburg is located on a small island at the estuary of the Neva river. To reach the fortress, catch the **express bus** #575 from M4: Ulitsa Dybenko; buy the ticket from the conductor (every 30min., 1hr., one-way 8000R, weekends 12,000R) or take bus #440 across the street from M3:

Prolitarskaya (110min., one-way 8000R). Ride past the "Shlisselburg" stop to the last stop—"Петрокрепость" (Petrokrepost). From the bus station, walk across the bridge and make a left, heading toward the river. Then turn right at the statue of Peter the Great that stands in a shady little cove. On your left awaits the **ferry** (6 per day, last ferry from the fortress leaves at 4:30pm, 3min., round-trip 6000R). The fortress opens in summer—i.e., when the water isn't frozen (daily 9am-4:30pm; 6000R, students 4000R). No **food** is sold on the island, but there are a cafe and restaurant on the way to the river station across the bridge to the right. The cafe at ul. Zhuka 2 (Жука) sells cheese and salami sandwiches (300R); the restaurant Alians (Альянс), ul. Zhuka 1, offers veggie salads (3000R), stuffed tomatoes (5000R), and *pelmeni* (6000R; open 11am-7pm and 8pm-1am).

Sights The merchants of Novgorod built the original fortress in 1323, calling it "Oreshek" after the island Orekhovy (Ореховый; nut island), and used it as a trading outpost. When the pier burned down in 1352, the clever Novgorodians replaced it with a stone structure. Oreshek became a strategic military point in the 15th century, was rebuilt from scratch as a fortress with six towers and drawbridges, and would ultimately spend most of the 17th century under Swedish control. October 1702 saw the forces of Peter the Great retake the fortress and rename it Shlisselburg. In a legendary letter, Peter wrote: "Tough was this nut indeed, but luckily we cracked it; our artillery worked true wonders." From this point on, it was the central base for Peter I's war expeditions against Sweden.

As with many fortresses, later in the century the fortified island became a prison for political undesirables—intellectuals, writers, and revolutionaries. Continuing around to the left through an archway leads to a small courtyard and the **Old Prison,** built in 1789. Between 1826 and 1834, the Old Prison held members of the Decembrist group that, in 1825, attempted to overthrow the tsarist regime. From 1884 to 1906, it held death-row revolutionaries—perhaps most significant was **Aleksandr Ilich Ulyanov,** elder brother of Vladimir Iliyich Ulyanov, a.k.a. **Lenin.** Aleksandr was a member of the terrorist political faction that led the assassination of Tsar Aleksandr III; he was executed at Shlisselburg on May 8, 1887, and his death marked the beginning of his younger brother's deep resentment toward the tsarist government. Inside the Old Prison is a **museum** that details the building's history. The **3rd Cell** shows the fine amenities each Decembrist received, while the even grimmer **4th Cell** depicts what later revolutionaries endured. Yet the first prisoners of Shlisselburg were members of the royal family; in the early 18th century, the displeased Peter sent his first wife Evdokiya Lopukhina and his sister Maria Alekseevna here.

Ahead of the main yard and to the left stands the **New Prison** (1884), darker and danker than even the Old Prison. It too houses a **museum** displaying photographs and living conditions of inmates. The far right door in the courtyard leads outside the fortress walls. (If the door is closed, ask the *babushka* attendant to unlock it.) From here opens a magnificent view of Ladoga Lake. During the siege of Leningrad, the only road connecting the city with the mainland, known as "The Road to Life," ran across Ladoga. Ships in the summer and trucks during the winter (when Ladoga froze) carried ammunition and food supplies to the besieged city. Outside, an Orthodox Cross marks the **communal grave** shared by soldiers of the Northern War and WWII. Toward the left around the perimeter stands the **overseer's building,** built in 1911 and bombed completely by the Nazis during WWII. Beyond that, the 1911-vintage **Fourth Prison** building held revolutionaries until the revolution of 1917, at which point all the prisoners of Shlisselburg were freed. An **exhibition and monument** to the battle at Shlisselburg during WWII marks the middle of the yard. The Nazis attempted to obliterate the fortress, leaving only the sad remains of the day. To the right of the monument you can see a fragment of the 14th century Novgorodian fortress—a precious archaeological find excavated in 1969.

■ Novgorod (Новгород)

Founded in the 9th century by Prince Rurik, Novgorod blossomed during the Middle Ages, at one time reaching almost double its current population. One legend tells of how the town saved itself from the Suzdal army by hanging an icon on the town's gates. When the Virgin's likeness began to cry, the besieging army fled in terror. And although the fierce Novgorodians also managed to fend off the Mongols, they lost their independence to Moscow when Ivan III and Ivan the Terrible subjugated the city. Novgorod's kremlin, Russia's oldest, was the first architectural landmark the country renovated after WWII. Many of the 140 churches and 50 monasteries built between 1100 and 1500 have survived to this day. Bigger and more thoroughly restored than Pskov, Novgorod makes a good introduction to early Russia.

ORIENTATION AND PRACTICAL INFORMATION

Novgorod has two centers—the **kremlin** on the west side of the river, and **Yaroslav's Court** on the east. There are some hotels on the east side, notably the Rossiya and the Sadko, but the **train station, bus station, telephone office,** and **hostel** rest on the west side. The west is laid out like a spider web, with the kremlin in the center. **Pr. Karla Marxa** (Карла Маркса) runs from the train station to the earth walls that surround old Novgorod; turn left here for the hostel. There are usually good fruit stands on this corner. From the walls, **ul. Oktyabrskaya** (Октябрьская, formerly ul. Sovetskaya) runs to pl. Pobedy (Победы) and the kremlin. Purchase **maps** at **Gostinitsa Intourist,** from the kiosk at the kremlin's east side, or in the St. Petersburg youth hostel (17,000R). Be warned: the latest edition, from 1994, only partially reflects the numerous changes in street names. Novgorodians use the old and new names interchangeably, and two street signs often adorn the same corner.

- **Tourist Offices:** ul. Meretskovo 2 (Мерецкого), on the left side of the square in front of the kremlin. English tours of Novgorod (54,000R per person) and kremlin (36,000R). No maps or brochures. Open 9am-6pm.
- **Currency Exchange:** ul. Velikaya 16 (Великая), inside Hotel Intourist. Changes money from "any" hard currency. Also in banks throughout the city—spot the "Обмен Валюты" sign.
- **Trains:** Straight ahead at the end of pr. Karla Marxa. To: St. Petersburg (2 per day; 5hr., 45,400R); Moscow (1 per day, 8hr., 117,300R). More expensive than the bus, but a lot more comfortable. For all tickets, go to Intourist *kassa* #1. Open 24hr.
- **Buses:** End of pr. Karla Marxa, to the right as you face the train station. It's a small white building labeled "Автостанция." Station open 5am-10pm. Daily buses run to: Moscow (10hr., 84,000R); St. Petersburg (3½hr. when the driver is in a good mood, 49,500R); and Pskov (4½hr., 44,000R; one leaves in the early morning and arrives at midday). The departure listings indicate the direction, the time of departure (отправление из Новгорода), and the duration of the trip.
- **Luggage Storage:** In the train station (5400R per day). Open 24hr. Also in the bus station (3000R). Open daily 5am-10pm.
- **Post Office:** ul. B. Sankt Peterburgskaya 9. Open Mon.-Fri. 9am-2pm and 3-8pm, Sat. 9am-7pm. **Postal code:** 173001.
- **Telephone Office:** pl. Pobedy, corner of ul. Gorkovo (Горького) and ul. Oktyabrskaya. Phones on the right are for direct calls. Prepay your call at the *kassa* and get a booth number. You'll receive change if not all the time has been used. For international calls use either direct dial or advance booking (the wait for international calls can be an hour). 1min. to Moscow 2100R, to the U.S. 14,700R. Or call **AT&T Direct** in Moscow (see p. 517) or a similar service. Open 24hr. Tokens for local calls 600R; for intercity calls 2100R. **Phone code:** 8160.

ACCOMMODATIONS

Novgorod's accommodations provide a wide variety of comforts and prices. The hostel, a Russian dorm turned cheap hotel, is the most viable option for budget travelers, but a few other old hotels offer reasonable rates.

Gostinitsa Roza Vetrov (Гостиница Роза Ветров), ul. Novo-Luchanskaya 27 (Ново-Лучанская; formerly Komsomolskaya; tel. 720 33). A Russian Youth Hostel affiliate. From the station, take a left onto Oktyabrskaya (Октябрская). Continue around left where the road turns into ul. Aleksandra Germana (Александра Германа). Then take a right onto ul. Novo-Luchanskaya. The hostel is on the right; the entrance is on the small street before it. This converted dorm has shabby but clean, bright, and airy rooms with firm beds on the 2nd floor (as you enter, keep going right until you reach the staircase). Staff speaks some English. Kitchen with facilities. Private or semi-private baths with shower, sink, and toilet. Blocks of 2 rooms for 5 people: a double and a triple in one suite share toilet and bath. Bed in a double 50,000R, in a triple 40,000R. Deluxe singles (with phone, shower, and fridge) are 140,000R, deluxe doubles 200,000R. Reserve through the St. Petersburg International Youth Hostel or the Russian Youth Hostel Association. Small cafeteria sells soups, salads, and main dishes for 8,000-10,000R (open daily noon-4pm and 6-11pm).

Gostinitsa Sadko (Садко), ul. Fyodorovsky Ruchey 16 (Фёдоровский Ручей; formerly Gagarina; tel. 753 66). The corridors are well-lit; rooms include a proper shower as well as TV and phone. Singles 120,000R; doubles 180,000R; triples 240,000R. Reservations recommended.

Gostinitsa Rossiya (Россия), nab. Aleksandra Nevskovo 19/1 (Александра Невского) at ul. Bolshaya Moskovskaya (Большая Московская, previously Lenina; tel. 341 85). Across from the kremlin—the view is its best feature. Clean and spacious rooms with soft beds. Each room has a toilet and "shower" (a spray fixture attached to the wall). Singles 140,000R; doubles 180,000R. Merciful rates for foreign students: singles 70,000R; doubles 90,000R; triples 120,000R. Baggage check available.

FOOD

The few eateries with any kind of ambience cater to tourists and raise their prices accordingly. *Shashlyky* and *sloyki* (слойки, a delicious pastry with jam) are available at a stand outside the kremlin; if it's sunny, picnic on a bench or by a lake. A well-stocked grocery store, **Vavilon** (Вавилон), ul. Oktyabrskaya 10, is another alternative to fancy dining in Novgorod (open daily 8am-11pm).

Detinets (Детинец; tel. 746 24), in a stone tower of the kremlin; follow the signs. Rough brick walls, medieval atmosphere, real candles in the fancy chandeliers, and traditional Russian cuisine, all in an old church. Tour groups fill the place; reservations recommended. Second-floor restaurant; downstairs bar serves jolly *medovukha,* an alcoholic honey drink, for 5300R per mug. *Golubtsy* (stuffed cabbage) 23,900R, mushrooms with *smetana* 20,900R, and *shchi* (delicate cabbage soup) 8500R. Open daily 11am-11pm.

Pri Dvore (При Дворе), ul. Oktyabrskaya 3 (tel. 743 43). Within 5min. of the kremlin and the hostel. Yummy *shashlyky* grilled outside (9,000R), extensive Russian menu indoors. Lower prices noon-4pm: stuffed summer squash 8000R, *bliny* with meat 6500R, cod with sour cream 9100R. After 6pm, veggie salads go for 5000-8000R, seafood salads 12,000R, *pelmeni* with mushrooms 18,000R, chicken Kiev 25,000R. Live music Wed.-Mon. nights. Umbrella-shaded courtyard bar open daily noon-11pm. Restaurant open noon-4pm and 6-11pm.

Skazka (Сказка, fairy tale), ul. Meretskovo 13 (tel. 771 60). From the square in front of the kremlin (interchangeably called pl. Pobedy (Victory), Kremlyovskaya (Kremlin), and Sofyskaya (St. Sofia), go left through the park about 150m; the restaurant occupies the corner of ul. Meretskovo and ul. Chernyshevskovo (Чернышевского). Modern establishment serving traditional Russian cuisine and playing modern Russian pop at night. Veggie salads 12,000R, soups 5000-6000R, *pelmeni* with mushrooms 18,000R, mushrooms with sour cream 18,000R. Open daily noon-midnight. Reservations recommended. In the **dessert hall,** snack on sandwiches or hot dogs (2500-6000R) or indulge in ice cream desserts (5770R). Open 11am-10pm.

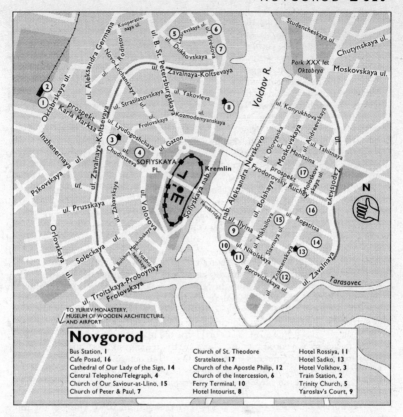

Novgorod

Bus Station, 1
Cafe Posad, 16
Cathedral of Our Lady of the Sign, 14
Central Telephone/Telegraph, 4
Church of Our Saviour-at-Llino, 15
Church of Peter & Paul, 7
Church of St. Theodore Stratelates, 17
Church of the Apostle Philip, 12
Church of the Intercession, 6
Ferry Terminal, 10
Hotel Intourist, 8
Hotel Rossiya, 11
Hotel Sadko, 13
Hotel Volkhov, 3
Train Station, 2
Trinity Church, 5
Yaroslav's Court, 9

SIGHTS AND ENTERTAINMENT

Entering the **kremlin** from the lakeside affords a panoramic view of the fortress's massive brick walls and the sandy lakeshore spotted in summer with sunbathers, as well as the **Novgorod horseman,** which commemorates the city's survival through the ages. Originally designed for Moscow after WWII, the statue was given to Novgorod after the capital rejected it. Nearby, you can see the excavation of the 12th-century city, revealing 28 layers of history. The kremlin walls (3m thick, 11m high), punctuated by nine towers, were first built in the 11th century; the fortress was originally known as *detinets,* a small kremlin. Wandering through the oldest kremlin in Russia is free, as are most of the interesting sights (kremlin open daily 6am-midnight). To the immediate right of the lakeside entrance, an array of bells stand at the base of the **belfry.** Continuing to the right past the sounds of a music school, walk straight to **Sofysky Sobor** (Софийский Собор; St. Sophia's Cathedral), the religious pinnacle of any trip to Novgorod. The oldest stone building in Russia, this 11th-century Byzantine cathedral is most imposing from the outside, where the Swedish west doors depict intricately carved scenes from the Bible. The dark interior obscures the few icons which remain (most are in the museum). With the exception of the inside of the dome, all the frescoes were painted fresh in the 19th century. Notice the golden dove on one of the cupolas—according to legend, as long as the dove remains, there will be peace in the city, and as long as Sofysky Sobor stands, Novgorod will withstand all troubles (open daily 8am-8pm; services 10am and 6pm; free). The **Concert Hall and Philharmonia** in the kremlin hosts recitals (25,000R; *kassa* open Mon.-Fri. 2-7pm, Sat. noon-5pm).

RUSSIA

Behind the cathedral are the **chasovnya** (часовня; clock tower) and the **Granovi-taya Palata** (Грановитая Палата; Faceted Chamber). The tower's bell used to call citizens to meetings of the *veche* (city council)—a partially democratic government. The Ivans quickly did away with both the bell and the *veche*. The Chamber, next door, contains many precious religious artifacts, but you need a guide to enter—buy your ticket at the museum and wait for a group to gather or arrive (open Thurs.-Tues. 10am-6pm, closed last Fri. of the month; 12,000R, students 6000R). In the park's center, the **Tysyachiletie Rossii** (Тысячилетие России; Millennium of Russia Monument), built in 1852, is one of three identical bell-shaped monuments. The second stands in St. Petersburg in a park off Nevsky pr., the third in Kiev. Taking a minute to encircle this bronze depiction of all Russian history is bound to be less painful than it was to go through it—as shown by the numbers of fallen men holding daggers. The old favorites, Rurik, Prince Vladimir of Kiev, and Peter the Great are all here—as well as the hordes of others being smushed by a gleeful Dmitry Donskoy. The sculptural group atop the bell represents kneeling Russia's 988 adoption of Christianity.

Directly behind the monument, the town's large **museum** conveys the full duration of Novgorod's history. Starting on the ground floor with thin arrowheads and birch-bark inscriptions from the 12th century, move on through delicately carved 14th-century combs and amulets. The rubles from the period, long and heavy metal rods, look like they'd do a lot to improve the Russian economy today. Also on the ground floor are recreations of Novgorodian life through the centuries—with the requisite red rooms on the Soviet period. The second floor holds famous icons, including the one that saved the town from the Suzdal army. Lamentably, the 20th-century art isn't much to look at (open Wed.-Mon. 10am-6pm, closed last Thurs. of each month; 12,000R, students 6000R, photos 15,000R, video 35,000R).

Across the footbridge from the kremlin and to the right, **Yaroslavovo Dvorishche** (Ярославово Дворище; Yaroslav's Court) is the old market center and the original site of the palace of Novgorod princes. There are the remains of the 17th-century waterfront arcade, several churches from the 13th to 16th centuries, and the market gatehouse, which is now a museum. In **Tserkov Uspenia** (Церковь Успения; Assumption Church), they kept the silver standard of a ruble and a barrel of honey as a standard for one pound.

The **Yuriev Monastyr** (Юриев Монастырь), dating from 1030, is one of the three working monasteries that surround Novgorod. It is striking for its location, in the middle of broad and windy marshes; it also has an excellent view on Lake Ilmen, the site of the 9th-century Rurik's court, from which the state of Russia originated. Take bus #7 (1000R) from pl. Pobedy to the airport. Go left at the fork around a small church to see the monastery in front. The central **Georgievskaya Tserkov** (Георгиевская Церковь; St. George's Church), dating to 1119, contains 16th-century icon paintings and a unique round *kafedra* (кафедра; pulpit) in the center. The church has been heavily reconstructed; some work is still going on (8000R, students 4000R, photography 10,000R). Four monks live on the monastery's premises, and most buildings are closed to the public. Women are required to wear skirts (you can rent one for 2000R). On the way out notice the bright blue cupolas of **Khristovozdvizhenskaya;** golden stars symbolize the monastery's high status (monastery open Wed.-Mon. 7am-9pm). About 1km west, the **Muzey Derevyannovo Zodchestva** (Музей Деревянного Зодчества; Museum of Wooden Architecture) is a collection of houses and churches from the surrounding towns, some dating from the 16th century (bus #7, as above; open Thurs.-Tues. 10am-6pm; 10,000R, students 5000R; cameras 6000R).

■ Pskov (Псков)

Since its first mention in the chronicles in 903 and until 1721 (when Peter I opened the "Window on the West" elsewhere), Pskov was an important border and trading town, and still has the fortress walls to prove it. Thanks to energetic restoration, the 18-foot-thick limestone monsters are ready to withstand more sieges. The site of

Nicholas II's abdication in March 1917, Pskov lets you savor history better than Russia's amnesiac metropoles.

ORIENTATION AND PRACTICAL INFORMATION

Pskov's main axis is **Oktyabrsky pr.** (Октябрьский пр.), with Gostinitsa Oktyabrskaya, the telephone office, and the post office all within five minutes of each other. It runs into the main square, **Oktyabrskaya pl.** (Октябрьская пл.), where it intersects **ul. Sovetskaya** (ул. Советская), which runs up to the kremlin in the town's north end. The **Velikaya** (Великая) and **Pskova** (Пскова) Rivers intersect just north of the kremlin. Across the Velikaya is Gostinitsa Sputnik, and farther along **Rizhsky pr.** (Рижский) sits Gostinitsa Rizhskaya. The old outer town walls run for 9km along the river and along **ul. Sverdlova** (Свердлова) by Pskov's two big parks. **Vokzalnaya ul.** (Вокзальная), where the bus and train stations are, intersects with the end of Oktyabrsky pr. to the right as you exit either station.

Tourist Offices: Intourist, Rizhsky pr. 25, 3rd floor, rm. 330 (tel. 46 75 13 or 46 17 63; fax 44 74 33), in Gostinitsa Rizhskaya, 10min. from Oktyabrskaya pl. over the bridge. Or take bus #17, 2, or 14 (1500R). Arranges city tours in English; 115,000R without transportation, 230,000R with car or bus. Open Mon.-Fri. 9am-6pm. City maps are rare in Pskov—some were spotted in Gostinitsa Sputnik last year. A **tourist bureau** (tel. 219 06 or 239 88), at the entrance to the kremlin on the right, provides information. Open Mon.-Fri. 9am-1pm and 2-5:30pm.

Currency Exchange: Oktyabrsky pr. 15. Open Mon.-Fri. 8am-1pm and 2-7:30pm, Sat. 9am-2:30pm. Or head to any other bank decorated with an Обмен Валюты sign.

Trains: Buses #1, 2, and 17 end their routes at the train station. Daily trains to: Moscow (12hr., 100,000R); St. Petersburg (7hr., 50,000R); and Tallinn (6½hr., 80,000R). Ticket office open 24hr.

Buses: The bus is the best way to get in and out of Pskov, unless you're going to Moscow. To: Novgorod (2 per day, 4hr., 45,000R); Pechory (8 per day, 1½hr., 11,000R); and St. Petersburg (2 per day, 6hr., 64,300R). Different *kassy* sell tickets for different destinations, indicated above the windows. *Kassy* open 8am-1pm and 2-7pm. Bus station open 5am-10pm.

Public Transportation: Buses #1 and 17 leave from in front of the train station, turn right after the bus station, and go through the center of town. Bus #17 stops in front of Gostinitsa Rizhskaya. Bus #1 stops near Gostinitsa Oktyabrskaya. Buy tickets from the bus conductor (1500R).

Luggage Storage: In the train station (6400R per day). Open 24hr.

Post Office: On the north side of pl. Oktyabrskaya. Open Mon.-Fri. 8am-8pm, Sat.-Sun. 8am-1pm and 2-5pm. **Postal code:** 180004.

Telephones: Oktyabrsky pr., in a large gray building opposite the proud statue of Kirov between ul. Nekrasova (Некрасова) and ul. Gogolya (Гоголя). Prepay intercity and international calls, get a booth number, receive change if not all the time is used (2000R per min. to St. Petersburg, 9800R per min. to the U.S.). Office open 24hr. **Faxes, email,** and **photocopying** 10am-7:30pm. **Phone code:** 81122.

ACCOMMODATIONS

Options for overnight stays are slim. Intourist's old Rizhskaya, Hotel Sputnik, and Hotel Oktyabrskaya fall within budget. For a bit more, **HOFA** (see **St. Petersburg: Accommodations,** p. 602) provides homestays (170,000R per night).

Gostinitsa Rizhskaya (Гостиница Рижская), Rizhsky pr. 25 (tel. 623 01), 10min. from the bridge near Oktyabrskaya pl. Or take bus #17. Huge and clean. Well-kept rooms, squishy beds, soft blankets. English spoken. Small bathtub, shower, and toilet in each room. Singles 210,000R; doubles 360,000R. TV, phone, and fridge extra.

Gostinitsa Oktyabrskaya (Октябрьская), Oktyabrskaya pr. 36 (tel. 399 12), 5min. from Oktyabrskaya pl. past a park on the left (check out the monument to Pushkin and his nurse in the park: Russians do love their Pushkin, and Pushkin loved his nurse). Or take bus #1. The barest essentials for a correspondingly low price. Some

English spoken. Reception open 24hr. Small, musty rooms with firm beds and clean sheets. Sink with cold water only included. The one toilet for the long hallway is clean but may be malodorous; showers on each floor 2000R. Singles 140,000R; doubles 140,000R; triples 180,000R.

Gostinitsa Turist (Турист), ul. Paromenskaya 4 (Пароменская, former Krasnoznamenskaya; tel. 44 51 50). Economical and typically Soviet—the best budget option in Pskov. Perfectly located across the river from the kremlin right on the bank of River Velikaya. Clean, if somewhat shabby, doubles and triples with toilet and shower but without phone or TV. 80,000R per person. Call to reserve. Small buffet at reception sells soft drinks and beer. Restaurant offers a limited but decent menu: veggie salads (well, your Russian regulars: tomatoes and cucumbers) 1500-3130R, soups 2100R, fried chicken 9500R. Open 8-11am, noon-4pm, and 6-11pm.

FOOD

If you eat solely at the Russian restaurants here, you will enjoy a salty, fatty, potato-oriented diet. Foodstuffs available in kiosks consist of mostly cookies and candy bars. A wise idea is to mix and match, supplementing everything with fruit or cucumbers bought at the **Tsentralny Rynok** (Центральный Рынок; Central Market) or on the street: in summer, fresh fruits and vegetables are widely available, as well as honey, cheese, and a variety of meat. There is also a buffet (Буфет) with a small variety of pastries. The market is off pr. Karla Marxa (Карла Маркса) down a dirty, narrow street about 50m past a church that's being renovated. Behind a fence, it's the large building labeled "РЫНОК" in huge letters (opens at 8am). A supermarket, **Rostek-Market** (Ростэк-Маркет), is at Oktyabrsky pr. 16. This "24hr" store closes for "technical break" daily between 2:30 and 3pm and for most of Monday, but it's well-stocked with local and imported goodies at acceptable prices.

Cafe Cheburechnaya (Кафе Чебуречная), Oktyabrsky pr. 10A, in a yellow clapboard building; enter from back. This Georgian cooperative is your best bet for food in Pskov. Cheerful and well-lit, with a TV that's always on, it specializes in *chebureki:* greasy, but tasty, meat pies in yummy dough (3000R.) Salads (3500R) and shish kebabs (9000R) also served. Open 11am-6pm.

Uyut (Уют; Comfort), behind Cafe Cheburechnaya. Russian cafe with a comfortable darkish interior serving the basics: salads (10,000-12,000R), sandwiches (5000-6000R), *pelmeni* old Russian style (18,000R). plus an extensive drink list. Nightly variety show (midnight-1:30am; 10,000R). Newly acquired computer provides **Internet access** (prices to be established). Open daily 11am-5am.

Olympia (Олимпия), Oktyabrsky pr. 30A (tel. 397 31). New restaurant geared toward foreigners. Dark velvety decor, soft carpets, neat paintings on the walls. Extensive, delicious menu. Bean salad (11,700R), marinated chicken with tomatoes (13,000R), chicken stroganoff in sour cream (25,300R), pork stewed in beer (31,900R). Live music and dancing Wed.-Sun. Open daily noon-midnight.

SIGHTS

Although many 15th- and 16th-century walls and towers can be seen along the river and ul. Sverdlova, the oldest (13th-century) are north, around the **kremlin** and Dovmontov Gorod—the small, popular area that also encompasses **Troitsky Sobor** (Троицкий Собор; Holy Trinity Cathedral).

In **Dovmontov Gorod** (Довмонтов Город), named after Prince Dovmont, the foundations of nine churches, all built between the 12th and 15th centuries, can still be seen—the ruins aren't much to look at, but the idea of the once-thriving religious center is impressive (kremlin area open 24hr.; English-language group tours 230,000-280,000R). Through an archway, past the beggars who line the cobbled path, is the pinnacle of Pskov's many churches. The gild-domed **Troytsky Sobor,** founded in the 10th century by Saint Olga (who married Prince Igor of Kiev and was Russia's first Christian monarch, later canonized) on her way to nearby Novgorod, is actually the fourth cathedral to stand on this spot. The current structure was built in 1699 and is covered with 17th-century frescoes that exemplify the Pskovian school of icon painting (those closest to the ceiling are the oldest and most valuable). The feeling of being in another time is awe-inspiring: from the beggars to the bearded priests to the windy courtyard to the man sweeping the tiles of the church for hours, this sacred place seems arrested at the turn of the 18th century. (Church open 8am until the end of the evening service. Services daily 8-11am and 6pm-late, presided over by bearded priests in flowing gold and blue robes. Free; donation appreciated.) Walking back out into the green courtyard, pass through an archway to a spot overlooking the intersection of the Velikaya and the Pskova. Looking out over the wide rivers, high grass, and yellow flowers, rural Pskov appears for the moment to have survived every effort at modernization, as if guarding the myth of old noble Russia.

The **Pogankiny Palaty i Muzey** (Поганкины Палаты и Музей; Pogankin Palace and Museum) sits on Komsomolsky per. (Комсомольский), at the corner of Sovetskaya ul. Enter through the new wing—quickly walk past Soviet art and history and the glares of the guards through the courtyard to the main house. Originally the home of a wealthy 17th-century merchant, it holds an exhibit on Pskov's history, including the Dovmont sword that was passed on to each new prince, unique icons depicting 16th-century Pskov, and silver artwork (open Tues.-Sun. 11am-5pm; closed last Tues. of the month; 14,000R, students 10,000R; tour in English 100,000R).

Mirozhsky Monastyr (Мирожский Монастырь) lies along the Velikaya, across the southernmost bridge and to the right. **Spaso-Preobrazhensky Sobor** (Спасо-Преображенский Собор; Transfiguration Cathedral), dating from 1156, enjoys particular fame; its spectacular art-book-like frescoes are typical of the Pskov region. The place is certainly worth a visit, if only to impress your Russian friends, who hold it in understandably high esteem (open Tues.-Sun. 11am-5pm; 10,000R, students 7000R; tour in English 80,000R). Pskov has more **churches** than restaurants and hotels combined. Unfortunately, most desperately need repair and are closed to the public. The recently reopened **Uspeniya s Paromenya** (Успения с Пароменья; Assumption Church), across the Velikaya and near Hotel Sputnik, is exemplary of restoration craftsmanship. A couple of old churches, including the 16th-century **Nikoly-na-Usokhe** (Николы-на-Усохе), are scattered around the main Oktyabrskaya pl. To see the interior of a typical Pskov church in all its splendor, head to Pechory.

■ Near Pskov: Pechory Monastyr

If you happen to be in Pskov overnight, **Pechory Monastyr** (Печоры Монастырь; Pechory Monastery) is a good excursion for the next day; you can go in the morning and be back in time for the night train to Moscow or St. Petersburg or the afternoon bus to Novgorod. Buy a ticket to Pechory at the bus station (11,000R) and then one back again to Pskov as soon as you arrive (schedules vary). The monastery is to the right at the end of Yurevskaya ul. (Юревская). Go left out of the station, then make the first right. Founded in 1473, the monastery particularly flourished in the 16th century, when, inhabited by 200 brothers, it doubled as a fortress. Today the complex is home to around 60 monks. Go through the main entrance past the begging and praying people and take the path on the left leading inside and down. Straight ahead is the gem of the complex, the yellow and white **Uspensky Sobor** (Успенский Собор; Assumption Cathedral). The door on the left leads to the sacred caves, where monks and hermits are bricked up in the walls (services daily 6am and 6pm; caves closed to visitors except at 9:30am, after morning service).

Next to Uspensky Sobor is a whitewashed belfry with a golden-winged angel adorning the facade. A few steps down, the beautiful flower garden surrounds a sacred water fountain that is the site of regular pilgrimages (besides being sacred, the water is safe to drink). On your way out notice the golden-domed 1827 **Mikhaylovskaya Tserkov** (Михайловская Церковь; St. Michael Church), beyond the "no entrance" (Нет Входа) sign. (Open daily 9am-5pm. Free; donations appreciated. Call 215 93 to arrange a tour of the monastery. Tours in English or German 200,000R; with caves and secret garden arboretum 100,000R extra. Photography permit 25,000R from "guard" at entrance. Women must wear scarves and skirts.)

KARELIA (КАРЕЛИЯ)

Forested Karelia, an autonomous region of the Russian Federation, spreads between St. Petersburg and the Arctic Circle. Among the region's 60,000 lakes are Ladoga and Onega, the largest in Europe and second in Russia only to Siberia's mighty Baikal. Karelians, Finnish by stock, speak a dialect closely related to the Finnish language, and consider themselves autonomous from and more cultured than the Russians. Signs, often in Russian and Finnish, give the capital, Petrozavodsk, a mildly international feel, subdued by the distinctly Soviet reality that they name.

■ Petrozavodsk (Петрозаводск)

Easily accessible by night train from St. Petersburg, and with clean(er) air, small, quiet, streets, and (relatively) well-kept buildings, Petrozavodsk is Russia's answer to a waterfront New England town—down to the Ben & Jerry's store in the center. Founded in 1703, the same year as St. Petersburg, Petrozavodsk (Peter's Factory) was originally a foundry and armaments plant. Later, tsars exiled misbehaving intellectuals and disfavored politicians here. Now, the fountain-filled city is mostly a stopping point for an ice-cream cone, some rest, and a quiet stroll on Kizhi Island, though President Yeltsin's happy vacation in the area during the summer of 1997 might increase the Karelian capital's touristic popularity.

Orientation and Practical Information Frugal-minded Petrozavodsk has not undergone the widespread and high-priced street-name changing that makes Moscow and St. Petersburg lessons in pre-Revolutionary Russian history. However, some streets are different from the ones on the maps, so be alert. **Pr. Lenina** (Ленина), the main road down the center of town, runs from the train station to **Lake Onega.** It's a pleasant walk, or take trolley #1 (1500R, pay the conductor) to the embankment. Everything necessary is within two blocks of this main road. The **train station** stands at the head of pr. Lenina, which runs into pl. Lenina. From there, take pr. Marksa (Маркса) to the **ferry dock** to reach Kizhi. **Trains** chug to Moscow (4 per day, 8-11hr., 179,200R) and St. Petersburg (2-3 per day, 9hr., 104,000R). Buy tickets in the Intourist *kassa.* Try to buy tickets for the train that starts or ends in Petrozavodsk to or from St. Petersburg, or you run the risk of riding with drunken sailors from Minsk. The train from St. Petersburg leaves from Moskovsky Vokzal (Московский Вокзал; Moscow Station) daily at 9:50pm. There's **luggage storage** in the train station (8900R per day, open 24hr.). **Intourist,** pl. Lenina (tel. 77 63 06), in Gostinitsa Severnaya, triples as a **currency exchange** (open Mon.-Sat. 10:20am-1pm and 2-7pm) and source for train tickets if the *kassy* by the station are out. Intourist also offers guides to the city (70,000R) and **tours** (min. 15 people) of **Martsialnye Vody,** Russia's first mineral spa, and a nature reserve at **Kivach** (office open Mon.-Fri. 9am-1pm and 2-5pm). Currency exchange offices also line pr. Lenina (usually open Mon.-Sat. 10am-6pm). **Knizhny Dom** (Книжный Дом; House of Books), pr. K. Marksa 14, sells city **maps** and postcards (open daily 9am-8pm). On pr. Lenina, pass Gostinitsa Severnaya, take a right on ul. Andropova, and a left on Sverdlova (Свердлова) to reach the **post office,** ul. Sverdlova 29, where **EMS** (Russian Express), photocopying, **email,** and currency exchange are available (open Mon.-Fri. 8am-8pm, Sat. 9am-6pm). **Telephones** reside next door at ul. Sverdlova 31 (open 24hr.). Prepay for intercity calls at the *kassa,* get a booth, and receive change if not all paid-for time has been used. International calls can be ordered in advance, or purchase a phone card for 126,000R (this buys a 14min. call to the U.S.) and use any phone in the office or on the street for international calls. The **DHL** office is located at ul. Andropova 15, 5th floor (tel. 77 65 00 or 77 65 78). US#15; **Postal code:** 185035. **Phone code:** 814.

Accommodations and Food As Karelia considers itself an independent territory, anyone not holding a Karelian passport will pay higher prices. The prices quoted below are for non-Karelians and non-Russians, and, as always, are subject to the ever-fluctuating ruble. A pretty, old, red building on the outside, **Gostinitsa Severnaya** (Гостиница Северная), pl. Lenina (tel. 77 49 67), offers the Russian standard-issue, hospital-green corridors and old women cleaning with wet rags inside. The clean, airy rooms have TV and phone, and some English is spoken. (Singles 52,000R, with sink 75,000R, with bath and toilet 130,000R; doubles 96,000R, with sink 140,000R, with bath and toilet 260,000R. Reservations recommended.) Pink, 10-story **Gostinitsa Karelia** (Карелия), nab. Gyullinga 2 (Гюллинга; tel. 55 73 58 or 55 88 97), has small rooms with TV, telephone, and primitive but functioning bathrooms. Walk five minutes from the ferry dock, head down pr. Marksa from pl. Lenina, and turn right on ul. Lunacharskovo (Луначарского). Pass the fountain, and take the first left directly overlooking the water. So popular with Finnish tourists that all prices are listed in Finnish Marks (singles 164,250R, doubles 219,000R, triples 295,600R; breakfast 20,000R, lunch and dinner 35,000R).

Petrozavodsk has the usual collection of grimly basic (and basically grim) Russian restaurants—the glorious exception being **Ben & Jerry's**, Krasnaya ul. 8 (Красная; tel. 77 45 34), on the corner of ul. Andropova, where you can get Vermont's finest for rubles. From the train station, walk down pr. Lenina, then go left on ul. Antikaynena (Антикайнена), and take the first right past the market onto Krasnaya ul. The ice cream and cones are made on the premises (small cone 3500R, large cone 4500R; open Tues.-Sun. 10am-8pm). Take a left as you face the ferry dock to reach **Restoran Petrovsky** (Ресторан Петровский), ul. Andropova 1 (tel. 77 09 92), just off pr. Marksa. Low vaulted ceilings, whitewashed walls, high-backed chairs, earthenware on the tables, and wrought iron gates separating different rooms recreate the austere atmosphere of Peter the Great's time, while the small bar features reindeer decor (salads 2000-10,000R, baked fish 12,500R, *myaso po-petrovski*—мясо по-петровски—juicy meat in a clay pot 16,500R; open daily noon-5pm and 6pm-midnight). Smoke-free Georgian **Shashlychnaya Kavkaz** (Шашлычная Кавказ), ul. Andropova 13/16 (tel. 77 09 45), at the corner of pr. Lenina, is decorated with pine tables, ironwork, and a fireplace. *Kharcho* (харчо; spicy meat and rice soup; 4000R), *shashlyk* (13,800R), and trout baked in sour cream (15,800R) are among the specialties (open daily 11am-4pm and 5-10pm). **Magazin Tsentralny** (Магазин Центральный), pr. Lenina 26, sells a range of breads, cheeses, fruits and vegetables, packaged goods, meat, and yogurt; it doubles as a pharmacy, selling shampoos, tampons, and medicine (open daily 8am-midnight). A **23¾-hour grocery store** is at pl. Gagarina, on the corner of pr. Lenina, near the train station (closed daily 9-9:15pm).

Sights The city's charm derives from the **waterfront** on Onega Lake between pl. Lenina and the ferry dock. Views and sculptures are both spectacular; note in particular the delightfully freakish sculpture "The Fisherman," designed by American Rafael Consuegra (1991), and the wish-fulfillment tree adorned with brass bells and a white plaster ear next to a sign reading "Whisper one wish." The waterfront becomes the main entertainment scene on summer nights, when open-air bars and restaurants selling beer and *shashlyki* pop up along the water to nourish strollers. For insight into the unique Karelian double culture, check out **Karelsky Kraevedchesky Muzey** (Карельский Краеведческий Музей; Museum of Local Karelian Culture), pl. Lenina 1 (tel. 77 27 02 or 77 94 79; open Sat.-Thurs. 10am-5:30pm; 15,000R, tour in English 90,000R, photography 10,000R). To learn more about why the town's founder deserves the title "the Great," take a spin through the new **Museum of Peter the Great,** located by the ferry port, near its eponym's statue (due to open by 1998).

One of the few working churches in Petrozavodsk, **Krestovozdvizhenskaya Tserkov** (Крестовоздвиженская Церковь) is on ul. Volkhovskaya 1 (Волховская), at the corner of ul. Pravdy. Head to the west end of ul. Kirova, cross the bridge by pl. Kirova, turn left, and go right at the fork. The yellow-and-white church with bright blue cupolas and an elaborate iconostasis and dark, peaceful, extremely wooded cemetery are on the left (worth the long walk only if you love churches). On the way to the church, on pl. Kirova, you'll pass a typical example of high Stalinist architecture, the **Muzykalny i Russky Dramatichesky Teatry** (Музыкальный и Русский Драматический Театры; Musical and Russian Drama Theaters; 1955). Meanwhile, restorations on the famous **Sobor Aleksandra Nevskovo** (Собор Александра Невского; Alexander Nevsky Cathedral), pr. Uritskogo 32, are going well; the golden cupolas already shine, and the interior will soon reopen to praying and touring folks.

■ Near Petrozavodsk: Kizhi (Кижи) and Valaam (Валаам)

Kizhi, 70km northeast of Petrozavodsk, is a undisturbed island that has served since 1966 as an outdoor museum of 18th-century wooden architecture. An ancient pagan ritual site that drew Russian Orthodox colonizers in the 12th century, the 5km-long island still shimmers with mysticism. Covered in tall grass and Queen Anne's lace, with lovely green hills napping around the placid lake, Kizhi is essentially a nature reserve. Wooden buildings, most of them moved from the nearby villages around Lake Onega, dot the south part of the hushed island. You must pay to enter this open-air "museum," but once on the premises, you are free to explore both the architecture and the natural beauty of what the Karelians call "our Greece." The striking **Pre-obrazhenskaya Tserkov** (Преображенская Церковь; Church of the Transfiguration) and its 22 domes, all in unpainted wood, are visible from afar. Unfortunately, the iconostasis inside cannot be viewed: entry is prohibited due to everlasting (and futile) restoration works. Despite UNESCO protection, not one expert has figured out how to restore the church, built in 1714 without a single nail. Another church, the child-size 14th-century **Church of the Resurrection of Lazarus,** was moved here from the former Murom monastery and may be the oldest wooden building in Russia. Although the churches are closed, you can enter a *banya* (Russian sauna), a barn, and three peasant houses, preserved in their pristine, fairy-tale beauty.

The house of **"Wealthy Peasant Oshevnev"** (1876) was built to accommodate 22 people, and is stuffed with plenty of peasant possessions. Attached in back is a covered courtyard of the "koshel" (carrying box) type—a conventional way to expand living quarters. Beware: don't smack your head on the doorways of the small dark interior. The houses of **"Average Peasant Yelizarov"** and **"Poor Peasant Shchepin"** are strikingly similar to Oshevnev's, but with fewer possessions inside. A leisurely walk, including a relaxing picnic, should take about three hours—exactly the length of time between a ferry's arrival and departure (open daily noon-7pm; 54,000R, tour 18,000R per person; Russians 18,000R, Karelians free).

To catch the **ferry** from Petrozavodsk, follow ul. Lenina from the train station. Then walk down the hill to the waterfront path, and follow it around to the right. Buy tickets in the white building on the right. Walk through the second door of the building to get to the ferry *kassa* (building open 7:30am-8pm). The regularly scheduled boats to Velikaya Guba (Великая Губа), beyond Kizhi, leave at 1 and 6pm, returning at 3:30 and 8:30pm; boats also leave for Kizhi directly (at noon and 12:30pm), but these are mostly on weekends and often full. Double-check the departure times in Kizhi, or you risk an oversaturation of air, museum, and nature (mid-May to mid-Nov. or until the lake freezes over; 1¼hr.; round-trip 40,000R).

Once a refuge for Russian monks and now a famous **nature reserve,** accessible only by tourist boats, **Valaam Island** offers a romantic escape from urban everyday-ness amid granite cliffs, pine trees, and clear waters. Currently Karelian, the island has changed its "nationality" several times since the 13th century, when a Russian Ortho-dox **monastery** was founded here. Destroyed by the Swedes four centuries later, the monastery was "resurrected" (and used as a prison) by Peter the Great in 1715 after his victory over Sweden. By the end of the 19th century, Valaam possessed an awe-inspiring five-domed **cathedral** of the transfiguration, as well as a whole range of agri-cultural and church buildings. In 1917 the island became a Finnish territory, but was regained by the Soviets at the end of the war with Finland in 1940. At that point, the monks packed up their sacred possessions and left the island for Finland, leaving the remnants of the monastery for tourists. Convoluted history aside, Valaam is all about awe and aura; go there to wonder and wander in transcendental peace.

Unless you particularly care for Petrozavodsk, it might be more rewarding to take a boat trip to Kizhi and Valaam **directly** from St. Petersburg. Lake cruises leave every three days and take three to four days to visit Valaam in Lake Ladoga and Kizhi in Lake Onega. **Sindbad Travel** in St. Petersburg (see p. 597) sells vouchers for these very popular excursions (double cabin on the lowest deck, with showers but no windows, is 1,140,000R for a 3-day journey, 1,392,000R for a 4-day journey).

THE KALININGRAD REGION (КАЛИНИНГРАДСКАЯ ОБЛАСТЬ)

History and fate have conspired to leave the Kaliningrad region (*Kaliningradskaya Oblast*) part of Russia. Once the headquarters of Russia's Baltic Sea Fleet, Kaliningrad was left behind when the Soviet Union unraveled, an island of armed, confused Russians severed from the Motherland by three new sovereign nations: Latvia, Lithuania, and Belarus. The region's separation anxiety dates back to its history as the German province of East Prussia. Though still a part of Germany during the interwar period, Kaliningrad was thrust into isolation by Poland's acquired "corridor to the sea"; at the end of World War II, the area was captured by the Soviets. Today, Kaliningrad has become a home for 40,000 ethnic Germans who were deported to Siberia by Stalin in the 40s and 50s and have come seeking refuge from the harshness of the Russian Far East while they wait to be granted political asylum in Germany.

▓ Kaliningrad (Калининград)

Sovietization was accomplished so completely after the Red Army's 1945 occupation that a contemporary observer would hardly suspect that Kaliningrad was a German city for 700 years. Home to philosopher Immanuel Kant, former Königsberg (King's City), appropriately named for its importance in Prussia, was virtually razed during World War II. The erstwhile German inhabitants have all disappeared—killed in conflict, deported to Germany, or exiled by Stalin to Siberia. For security reasons, the city, named after Stalin's henchman Mikhail Ivanovich Kalinin (who himself never set foot in the city), was only opened to tourists in 1991; before that it held 200,000 Russian soldiers and sailors and the Soviet Baltic Fleet. Amid the westernization in other Baltic states, Kaliningrad remains an island of confusion, edging economically ahead of the rest of Russia, but lagging far behind its Eastern European neighbors.

ORIENTATION AND PRACTICAL INFORMATION

From the bus and southern train stations, both situated on **pl. Kalinina** (пл. Калинина), the main artery, **Leninsky pr.** (Ленинский пр.), runs north across the **Pregolya river** (Преголя) and **Kneiphof Island,** site of the **cathedral,** past the hideous House of Soviets to **Tsentralnaya pl.** (Центральная), where it veers left to extend to its terminus, **pl. Pobedy** (Победы). From here, **pr. Mira** (Мира) points west past the zoo, while **ul. Chernyakhovskovo** (ул. Черняховского) travels east toward the central market and the amber museum. Obtainable at many bookstores and kiosks, the **map** "План города для туристов" (*Plan goroda dlya touristov*; city plan for tourists; 15,000R) provides information about museums and sights.

Tourist Office: Gostinitsa Kaliningrad (Гостиница Калининград), Leninsky pr. 81, on the north end of Tsentralnaya pl., contains the bare-bones tourist service **Noktyurn** (Ноктюрн; tel./fax 46 95 78), to the left of the lobby. Helps with the most basic questions. Open Mon.-Sat. 8am-6pm.

RUSSIA

Consulates: Lithuania, Sovietsky pr. 49 (Советьский; tel. 27 32 17). **Poland,** ul. Kutuzova 43/45, 3rd fl. (Кутузова; tel. 27 42 92).

Currency Exchange: Kiosks with "Обмен Валюты" signs dot major downtown intersections, including a stand conveniently located across pl. Kalinina from the bus terminal. **Investbank** (Инвестбанк), Leninsky pr. 28 (tel. 43 11 62), immediately to the right of Hotel Kaliningrad (see above). Accepts AmEx traveler's checks and gives Visa and MC advances, both for a 2% commission. Branch offices are starting to appear throughout Kaliningrad. Open Mon.-Sat. 9:30am-1pm and 2-4pm.

Trains: Yuzhny Vokzal (Южный Вокзал; South Station; tel. 49 99 91 or 49 26 75), on the south side of pl. Kalinina, handles international connections. Open 4am-midnight. To: Moscow (1 per day, 22hr., 236,000R); St. Petersburg (odd days, 22hr., 158,000R); Vilnius (1 per day, 8hr., 130,000R); and Warsaw (Mon. only, 8hr., 117,000R). Trains no longer go to Rīga. International cashier open 8am-1pm and 2-8pm. **Severny Vokzal** (Северный Вокзал; North Station; tel. 49 26 75), north of pl. Pobedy, behind the big pink building that used to be the KGB headquarters, sends trains to Baltic Coast cities. To Svetlogorsk (10 per day, 1hr., 6000R) and Zelenogradsk (6 per day, 35min., 4800R).

Buses: pl. Kalinina, immediately east of Yuzhny Vokzal (tel. 44 36 35). To: Gdańsk (2 per day, 4½hr., 38,000R); Hrodna, Belarus (1 per day, 10hr., 46,000R); Klaipėda (4 per day, 3½hr., 31,000R); Warsaw (Mon.-Sat. 2 per day, 8-9hr., 64,000R); Minsk (3 per week, 12hr., 72,000R); and Vilnius (2 per day, 8hr., 49,000R). *Kassa* open 5:30am-2pm and 3-11:30pm. Some Polish buses are at the *Kyonigavto* desk (Кёнигавто; tel. 44 65 10). Open Mon.-Sat. 6am-10pm, Sun. 6am-6pm.

Public Transportation: The transportation system in Kaliningrad is undergoing a massive overhaul. Slower, public **trams** transverse the city (800R); **buses,** which are now privatized, will speed your journey (1000R). Many lack numbers, so look for your destination written on the front. Trams #2 and 3 run from pl. Kalinina to pl. Pobedy via pl. Tsentralnaya, connecting the southern and northern train stations, while tram #1 runs east to west from beyond the zoo toward the market. Pay the *konduktor* (*not* the driver) on board.

Taxis: In every major square, especially at the train stations, zoo, and pl. Pobedy. Agree on a price before setting off.

Pharmacy: Apteka (Аптека), Leninsky pr. 63/67 (tel. 43 27 83). Fairly current compared to other stores in the city, which isn't saying much. Open daily 8am-8pm.

Express Mail: UPS, ul. Chernyakhovskovo 66 (tel. 43 46 84). Open Mon.-Fri. 9am-6pm.

Post Office: Out of the way at ul. Leonova 22 (Леонова; tel. 21 52 33), a right off pr. Mira, way past Gostinitsa Moskva (open Mon.-Fri. 9am-6pm, Sat. 10am-6pm). *Poste Restante* at window #21. **EMS** at window #8 (tel. 27 34 95). **Branch office** at ul. Krasnooktyabrskaya 6/12 (Краснооктябрьская; tel. 44 33 15), to the right of Leninsky pr. before the river. Shorter lines. **Postal code:** 236 000.

Telephones: ul. Leonova 20, through the back entrance to the post office. **Faxes.** Open 7am-10pm. **International Telephone Center** (tel. 45 15 15; fax 46 95 90), inside Hotel Kaliningrad, on the left as you enter. 1min. connection to Moscow to reach AT&T or MCI operator costs 3000R; **internet access** should be available soon. Open daily 7:30am-11pm. **Phone code:** 0112.

ACCOMMODATIONS

The budget tourist industry hasn't really hit Kaliningrad yet, so don't expect an overabundance of accommodations. The new hotels being built are geared toward attracting New Russians and foreign businesspeople, and may be a bit expensive for budget travelers. If the options below aren't appealing, take a train to Svetlogorsk, a sea-side holiday town just 30 minutes north of the city. There, hotels and sanatoria abound, and many are eager to accept foreigners.

Gostinitsa Kaliningrad (Гостиница Калининград), Leninsky pr. 81 (tel. 46 94 40), on the north side of Tsentralnaya pl. The fanciest digs in town. Also houses a tourist bureau, exchange office, phone center, and a business center, which plans to offer internet access in 1998. Singles 270,000R; doubles 390,000R. Reception open 24hr.

Gostinitsa Kyonigavto (Кёнигавто), Moskovsky pr. 184 (tel. 46 76 52; fax 46 07 22), on the right side of the street heading away from the city center. Take any bus to

"Московский проспект" (Moskovsky pr.) from Yuzhny Vokzal. Clean, newly remodeled rooms, each with its own bathroom, TV, and shower. Owner speaks German with a sexy Russian accent. Reception and bar open 24hr. Parking 10,000R. Singles 200,000R; doubles 222,000R.

Gostinitsa Moskva (Москва), pr. Mira 19 (tel. 27 20 89), a few blocks past pl. Pobedy, on the left. Take any tram in the direction of "Парк Калинина" (Park Kalinina) and ask the driver where to get off. Where Russians from other parts of the country stay when they're in town. Communication center on the 1st floor is more convenient than the nearby post office. Somewhat musty rooms; iffy hot water. Singles 120,000R, with shower 125,000R; doubles 160,000R, with shower 200,000R; triples 150,000R, with shower 160,000R.

Gostinitsa Patriot (Патриот), ul. Ozernaya 25a (Озерная; tel. 25 50 23 or 27 94 50). Take tram #10 or bus #37. Set amid Soviet-style apartment blocks, this is the cheapest place in town—if you can bear it, that is. Don't forget to bring toilet paper. No hot water. Singles 100,000R; doubles 160,000R.

FOOD

Though new restaurants are slowly appearing in Kaliningrad, most cater to foreign businesspeople and *nouveau riche* Russians, and are either low in quality or high in price. For groceries, head to the **tsentralny rynok** (центральный рынок; central market) at ul. Chernyakhovskovo's intersection with ul. Gorkovo (open daily 9am-6pm). The market was built for a 1930s trade exhibition, but currently merchants from Baku and their fruits cram its huge halls. **Universam** (Универсам), Moskovsky pr. 83 (tel. 43 26 77), does a reasonable impersonation of a supermarket (open daily 9am-10pm). A number of small *produkty* (продукты) stands have been cropping up as food becomes more available; they don't usually stock much, but they'll do in a pinch.

Pri Svechakh (При Свечах; In Front of the Candles), on the terrace of the Dramatichesky Teatr (tel. 21 77 71). The best outdoor cafe in the city. Relax and watch the city rush by over a cold *EKU Pils* (10,000R) and sandwiches (6000-8000R).

Stary Gorod (Старый Город), Leninsky pr. 21; entrance on the side. Packed with Russians and other hungry folks who come for the big portions rather than the atmosphere. Salads 2000-5000R, main dishes around 10,000R. Open daily 9am-11pm.

Restoran Moskva (Ресторан Москва; tel. 27 27 07), in Gostinitsa Moskva. Breathtakingly Soviet, deep-red interior with weird stained glass is the main attraction besides low prices. They carry only a few of the items on the menu, so ask first. Beef stroganoff 10,100R; steaks 12,300R. Open daily noon-5pm and 6-11pm.

The Smak (Смак), Moskovsky pr. 127 and Sovietsky pr. 12, among other locations. Lips smack for the tasty, cheap burgers (6700R) spewing from these Dutch fastfood stands littering the city (look for a yellow awning). Large fries 4300R. Usually open daily 9am-8pm.

SIGHTS

Kaliningrad's former pride and joy is the old **Cathedral** (director tel. 21 25 83), which now ages on the large Kneiphof Island in the middle of the Pregolya river. A fire in 1544 damaged the cathedral; funds are now actively being sought to build a new roof and restore the towers, but the scarred, burnt-out shell stands as both a reminder of the city's German heritage and a monument to the Russian conquest of the city. The plastic surgery currently in progress supplies the old church with a third symbolic role: reflecting the heavy flow of German tourist money into the city. Inside, you can see the vandalized and eroding tombs lining the cathedral's walls, or climb the mythical steps made famous in the fairy tales of German Romantic writer E.T.A. Hoffmann (cathedral open daily 9am-5pm; 1000R, foreigners DM1). The Kaliningrad Symphony occasionally holds concerts here; inquire within. Walk around (outside) to the back of the cathedral to find the immaculately kept grave of **Immanuel Kant** (1724-1804), the German philosopher who spent his entire life in Königsberg and taught at the local university. Kant's grave is enclosed with pink marble colonnades, probably to protect him from the busloads of German tourists who arrive daily to see it. Behind the cathedral, not far from Kant's remains, is a monument erected in 1991 by Prussian-born Germans to **Julius Rupp** (1809-1884), one of Königsberg's famous pastors, whose house once stood on this spot. Rupp founded a new, unofficial religious order which he called *Druzya Sveta* (Друзья Света; Friends of the Earth), and which stood for harmony of all peoples and all religions. Though Rupp was chastised for his views in the 19th century, he remained one of Königsberg's influential thinkers, eventually passing on many of his beliefs to German artist Käthe Kollwitz, his niece.

North of the cathedral, Leninsky pr. expands into **Tsentralnaya pl.,** another spot endowed with Soviet significance. Since 1255, when Teutonic knights first arrived in the area, a castle guarded the hill east of the square. As part of the concerted effort to turn Königsberg into a truly Soviet city, the 700-year-old Königsberg Castle was blown up in 1962 and replaced by Kaliningrad's **Dom Sovetov** (Дом Советов; House of Soviets), an H-shaped monstrosity that, after 35 years, has yet to be completed. Save some film for this poured-concrete paean to soulless Soviet architecture. The nearby **Khudozhestvennaya Galereya** (Художественная Галерея; Gallery of Artists), Moskovsky pr. 60/62 (tel. 46 72 49), displays the works of local artists and contains rotating exhibits on the history of the *oblast* (open Tues.-Sun. 11am-7pm; 10,000R).

Ul. Shevchenko (Шевченко), which runs on the north side of the Dom Sovetov, rapidly changes into ul. Klinicheskaya (Клиническая) and begins to snake around the east edge of **Prud Nizhny** (Пруд Нижний), the smaller of the city's two lakes. Halfway up is the **Istoriko-Khudozhestvenny Muzey** (Историко-Художественный Музей; Museum of History and Art), Klinicheskaya 21 (tel. 45 39 02). The second floor is devoted to the heroic Soviet army and its conquest of the depraved German city of Königsberg in 1945. There is also a newer, less bombastic display on the Afghanistan War. Rotating exhibits of modern artists from the former Soviet Union comprise the third floor (open Tues.-Sun. 11am-6pm; 10,000R). Further north, ul. Klinicheskaya ends across from the **Muzey Yantarya** (Музей Янтаря; Amber Museum), pl. Vasilevskovo (Васильевского; tel. 46 12 40). Located in one of Königsberg's seven remaining **City Gates,** this is perhaps the city's finest and most interesting museum. Nearly 90% of the world's amber comes from nearby Yantar, much of it smuggled out illegally every year, and these are the best specimens of the lot. The museum's three floors display amber crowns, jewelry boxes made for Catherine the Great, one of the world' largest single pieces of amber (weighing in at 4kg., 280g), and even the poor insects who met their fate inside various pieces of amber as they hardened (open Tues.-Sun. 10am-6pm; *kassa* closes at 5:30pm; 5000R, foreigners 10,000R, students 3000R). Amber souvenirs are sold downstairs, but better prices can be found elsewhere.

Off Leninsky pr., on ul. Universitetskaya (Университетская), the garden of the University of Kaliningrad confronts the **Muzey Blindazh** (Музей Блиндаж; Bunker Museum; tel. 43 05 93), a network of rooms from which the Nazis directed their defense of Königsberg before the city was finally conquered by Soviet forces on April 9, 1945. The museum presents the capture of the city in great detail; unlucky Room 13 has been left exactly as it was when the city's commander signed it over to the Red Army (open daily 10am-5:30pm; 10,000R, Russians 3000R). Leninsky pr. leads to **Pl. Pobedy** (Victory Square), in the middle of which stands a 7m **statue of Lenin,** one of the last monuments from the Soviet era still standing. Two blocks left of the statue, at Sovetsky pr. 3-5, in a glorious pink-and-white Prussian building, were housed the former Kaliningrad headquarters of the **KGB.**

Wrestling baby bears welcome you to the **zoo** (tel. 21 89 24), on pr. Mira, across from Gostinitsa Moskva; their older relatives have learned to do tricks for tourists offering food (against the rules, of course). Once among the top five zoos in Europe, it celebrated its 100th anniversary in 1996. You'll see a lot of empty cages, but also some animals and a pleasant, if labyrinthine, park (open 9am-9pm; 5000R). The stadium across from the zoo is home to Kaliningrad's beloved soccer team, Baltika.

ENTERTAINMENT

The **Teatr Kukol** (Театр Кукол; Puppet Theater; tel. 21 29 69) in the **Kalinin Park of Culture and Rest** (ПКиО; *PKiO*) is two stops past the zoo on tram #1 or 4; trolleybus #3, 4, or 6; or bus #3, 5, 14, or 105. The turn-of-the-century **Luise Church,** named for the Prussian queen, also caters to the kindergarten crowd (box office open Mon.-Fri. 10am-5pm). You can find frequent **organ concerts** in the large brick church at ul. B. Khmelnitskovo 63a (Б. Хмельницкого), several blocks northeast of Yuzhny Vokzal. Prices and times fluctuate; check posters for more information. There's also the **Dramatichesky Teatr,** pr. Mira 4 (Драматический Театр; tel. 21 24 22), housed in a Weimar-era residence east of the zoo. Ask the friendly director Anatoly Kravtsov for a tour of the remarkable building (open daily 9am-9pm; tickets to performances run 10,000-15,000R). The German government has recently built a cultural center for the large number of ethnic Germans who have arrived in Kaliningrad from central Asia. **Deutsch-Russiches Haus** (Немецко-Русский Дом), ul. Yaltinskaya 2a (Ялтинская; tel./ fax 46 96 82 or 45 06 31), off Moskovsky pr., offers German-language drama, German courses, and other events for anyone interested in the history of German-Russian relations (open Tues.-Sat. 9am-6pm).

Nightlife in Kaliningrad is slowly reviving. At **Diskoteka Vagonstra** (Дискотека Вагонстра), on ul. Radishcheva (Радищева) in a cavernous, unmarked gray building, *mafiosi* shimmy with students and soldiers till dawn. Take tram #1 or 4 five stops past the zoo, and follow ul. Vagonstroitelnaya (Вагонстроительная), the street immediately behind the tram as you get off. The first street on the right is ul. Radishcheva.

■ Near Kaliningrad: Svetlogorsk (Светлогорск)

The premier resort for fashionable Königsbergers, Svetlogorsk, formerly known as Rauschen, escaped the heavy hand of Soviet architecture and still retains much of its old German flavor, with tree-lined streets and turn-of-the-century villas set on high, coast-hugging dunes. Banana sellers set up shop on the long, narrow stretch of beach, while plump Russians test the frigid Baltic waters. **Buses** run to Svetlogorsk from Kaliningrad's bus terminal (every 20min. 7am-9:45pm, 1hr., 5000R), while **trains** depart from Severny Vokzal (10 per day, 1hr., 6000R). There are two train stations in Svetlogorsk, located 2km apart, although not all trains stop at the second one. Both stations offer luggage storage (open 5:20am-8:50pm; 8900R). The second station, **Svetlogorsk II,** on ul. Lenina (Ленина), is much closer to the beach; an old-fashioned **chairlift** whisks you to the sand (chairlift open Fri.-Sun. 10am-7pm; 2000R). The last train to Kaliningrad leaves nightly at 8:40pm. If you happen to get off at **Svetlogorsk I,** head left behind the station and then turn right onto a broad paved road; after walking through the small forest, take the first paved left, which will lead down a hill and over a yellow bridge to **Kaliningradsky pr.** (Калининградский). From here, continue up the hill and take the left fork to tree-lined **ul. Gagarina** (Гагарина), where the city center begins. **Ul. Oktyabrskaya** (Октябрская), seemingly lined with more eateries than there are in all of Kaliningrad itself, leads to the center of town, and down to the beach. Off Gagarina is the **post office,** ul. Ostrovskovo 3 (Островского; tel. 32 17; open Mon.-Fri. 8:30am-5pm, Sat. 8:30am-2pm). **Postal code:** 238 550. Next door is a **currency exchange** (open Mon.-Fri. 9am-1pm and 2-4pm). The **telephone office** is in the same building (tel. 32 10; fax 46 32 74; open 24hr.). **Phone code:** 02533.

Gostinitsa Troyka (Гостиница Тройка), Kaliningradskaya 77a (tel. 330 63 or 330 81) has bright rooms with tall ceilings, big windows, a toilet, and even a lukewarm shower (doubles 80,000R; triples 120,000R; quads for students 160,000R). **Baltika** (Балтика), ul. Vereshchagina 8 (Верещагина; tel./fax 30 82), caters to Westerners only. From Svetlogorsk I, head down ul. Lenina past the stadium (doubles with shower and toilet from 120,000R). Named after Pushkin's imaginary forest, **Bar Ulukomorya** (Бар Улукоморья), Oktyabrskaya 20, serves traditional Russian meals for traditional Russian vacationers (under 10,000R; open daily 9am-7pm). **Bar Skorpion** (Бар Скорпион), ul. Lenina 31a (tel. 61 09), to the right of the Svetlogorsk II station, serves tasty *shashlyki* (шашлыки) for 19,800R (open daily 10am-11pm). A **Mini Market** (Мини Маркет) is at Oktyabrskaya 10, at the corner of ul. Gagarina, (open daily 8am-11pm). Svetlogorsk's first (and only) nightclub, **Kolosseo,** on Kaliningradsky pr. next to Svetlogorsk II, was formerly a *shashlik*-serving emporium. Now it's a combination disco, bar, and casino where locals flock to boogie-woogie (open Thurs.-Sat. 10pm-5am).

SLOVAKIA
(SLOVENSKO)

US$1	= 35Sk(Slovak koruny)	10Sk =	US$0.29
CDN$1	= 25Sk	10Sk =	CDN$0.39
UK£1	= 56Sk	10Sk =	UK£0.18
IR£1	= 52Sk	10Sk =	IR£0.19
AUS$1	= 26Sk	10Sk =	AUS$0.39
NZ$1	= 22Sk	10Sk =	NZ$0.45
SAR1	= 7.48Sk	10Sk =	SAR1.34
DM1	= 19Sk	10Sk =	DM0.52
Country Phone Code: 421		**International Dialing Prefix: 00**	

Survivor of centuries of nomadic invasions, Hungarian domination, and Soviet industrialization, Slovakia has emerged as an independent country. With rocky mountains
to the north and forested hills in the center, Slovakia is covered with natural wonders—it's no surprise that hiking and skiing have become national pastimes. Castle
ruins, relics of the defenses against Tatars and Turks, dot the countryside, and in
smaller towns, even suburban factories have not compromised the old-time atmosphere. So for a lesson in isolated rurality, take a deep draught of Slovak wine, put on
some hiking boots, and enjoy the freedom.

SLOVAKIA ESSENTIALS

Americans and South Africans can visit Slovakia visa-free for up to 30 days; Canadians
and Irish, 90 days; and Britons, 180 days. Citizens of Australia and New Zealand need
a 30-day visa (single-entry US$21; double-entry US$32; multiple-entry US$52 for 90
days and US$93 for 180 days; transit US$21). Apply in person at an embassy or consulate, or by mail; processing takes two days. Submit your passport, cash or money

order for the fee, as many visa applications as planned entries, and two passport photos for every application. For a list of Slovak embassies and consulates, see **Essentials: Embassies and Consulates, p.** 5. For a visa extension, go to the local office of Alien and Border Police.

GETTING THERE AND GETTING AROUND

International bus and rail links connect Slovakia to all of its neighbors. Large train stations operate **BIJ-Wasteels** offices, which offer 20-50% discounts on tickets to European cities (but not Prague) for those under 26. **EastRail** is valid in Slovakia; **Eurail** is not. As everywhere, you need to pay a supplement to take an InterCity or EuroCity fast train, and if there's a boxed R on the timetable, a *miestenka* (reservation; 7Sk) is required. International ticket counters are marked with multilingual signs.

Larger towns on the **railway** possess many *stanice* (train stations); the *hlavná stanica* is always the main one. Smaller towns have only one, and teensy-weensy villages usually have just a decaying hut that posts an illegible schedule and shelters drunks. Tickets must be bought before boarding the train, except in the tiniest towns. **ŽSR** is the national train company; every information desk has a copy of **Cestovný poriadok** (58Sk), the master schedule. *Odchody* (departures) and *príchody* (arrivals) are on the left and right of schedules, respectively, but don't always believe information about platforms—check the station's display board for the right *nástupište*. Reservations are sometimes required and often recommended for *expresný* trains and first-class seats, but not for *rychlík* (fast), *spešný* (semi-fast), or *osobný* (local) trains. Trains usually run on time. Station **lockers** are fiddly; instructions probably won't be in English. Insert a 5Sk coin, choose your own personal code on the *inside,* insert your bag, and try to shut the door. If it does not lock, have a fit, and try another locker. Attempt 10 times. If you fail, go to the luggage window. To reclaim your bag, arrange the outer knobs to fit your personal code. Sometimes the aging circuit takes a few seconds to register and open. Left luggage offices are easier and sometimes cheaper (3Sk).

In many hilly regions, **ČSAD** or **SAD buses** are the best and sometimes the only way to get from A to B. Except for very long trips, buy the ticket on the bus. Schedules seem designed to drive foreigners batty with their many footnotes; the most important are as follows: **X,** weekdays only; **a,** Saturdays and Sundays only; **r** and **k,** excluding holidays. **Numbers** refer to days of the week on which the bus runs—1 is Monday, 2 is Tuesday, and so forth. *Premava* means including; *nepremava* is except; following those words are often lists of dates (day first, then month). In the summer, watch out for Sts. Cyril and Methodius Day, July 5.

The rambling wilds and ruined castles of Slovakia inspire great **bike** tours. The Slovaks love to tramp on two wheels, especially in the Tatras, the foothills of West Slovakia, and Šariš. **VKÚ** publishes accurate maps of most Slovak regions (65Sk, in German 85Sk), with color-coded trails.

TOURIST SERVICES

The main tourist information offices form a loose conglomeration called **Asociácia Informačných Centier Slovenska (AICES),** complete with distinctive green logo. The offices are invariably on or near the town's main square, and the nearest one can often be found by dialing 186. English is often, but not always, spoken here; accommodation bookings can usually, but not always, be made; and the staff is usually, but not always, delightful. **SATUR,** the Slovak bit of the old Čedok, seems more interested in flying Slovaks abroad on package tours, but may be able to help Anglophone travelers. **Slovakotourist** is thinner on the ground, but can be very useful.

MONEY

After the 1993 Czech-Slovak split, Slovakia hastily designed its own currency, which is now the country's only legal tender. One hundred **halér** make up one Slovak **koruna** (Sk). Keep your exchange receipts to change Slovak korunas back into hard currency. **Všeobecná Úverová Banka (VÚB)** operates offices in even the smallest towns and cashes **traveler's checks** for a 1% fee. Most offices give **MC** cash advances and have Cirrus, EC, MC, and Visa **ATMs**, called **Bankomats.** Many **Slovenská Sporitelňa** bureaus handle **Visa** cash advances and have Visa **ATMs.**

COMMUNICATION

The **mail** service in Slovakia is efficient and modern. Almost every *pošta* (post office) provides **Express Mail Services,** but to send a package abroad, a trip to a *colnice* (customs office) is in order. *Poste Restante* mail with a "1" after the city name will arrive at the main post office. Local **telephone** calls cost 2Sk; drop the coin in after you've been connected. The phone is likely to eat your money and do nothing. Buy a phone card instead (100Sk). Even in small towns, **cardphones** are common now, and although they sometimes refuse your card, they're much better than the coin-operated variety. Long-distance access numbers include: **AT&T Direct,** tel. 00 42 100 101; **British Telecom Direct,** tel. 00 42 104 401; **Canada Direct,** tel. 00 42 100 151; **MCI WorldPhone,** tel. 00 42 100 112; **Sprint,** 00 42 187 187. Slovakia's only **English-language newspaper,** the weekly *Slovak Spectator* (24Sk), is published in Bratislava and geared toward a business audience, but it has some listings and publishes an annual glossy *Spectacular Slovakia* brochure (75Sk) for tourists. Other English-language finds are likely to be dreary government propaganda sheets. **Rádio Tatry** has thrice-daily English bulletins on mountain conditions, at 7:20am, 9:20am, and 8:20pm, on 102.5FM.

LANGUAGE

Slovak is a tricky Slavic language. It's closely related to **Czech,** but the two are not identical. Any attempt to stumble through even a few words will be appreciated. **English** is not uncommon in Bratislava, particularly among the young, but people outside the capital are more likely to speak **German,** and you may not find any English-speakers, even in the tourist office. **Russian** is understood, but not always welcome. When speaking Slovak, the two golden rules are to pronounce every letter—nothing is silent and it's all phonetic—and to emphasize the first syllable. Accents on vowels affect length, not stress. Flick the "r" off the top of your mouth.

HEALTH AND SAFETY

> **Emergency Numbers: Fire:** tel. 150. **Ambulance:** tel. 155. **Police:** tel. 158.

Tap water varies in quality and appearance—sometimes crystal clear, sometimes chlorine-cloudy—and may cause a modicum of abdominal discomfort. Bottled water is available in grocery stores. A reciprocal agreement between Slovakia and the U.K. entitles Brits to free medical care here. Drugstore (*drogerie*) shelves heave with Western brand names; obtaining supplies shouldn't be hard.

ACCOMMODATIONS AND CAMPING

Foreigners will often pay up to twice as much as Slovaks for the same room—just get used to it. Finding cheap accommodations in Bratislava before the student dorms open in July can be hard, and you can't always count on being able to stay where you planned in the Tatras, but on the whole it's not difficult to find accommodations. Call ahead, but don't expect an English-speaker to answer the telephone. The tourist office, **SATUR,** or **Slovakotourist** can usually help. **Juniorhotels (HI),** though uncommon, are a step above the usual hostel. In the mountains, **chaty** (mountain huts/chalets) range from plush quarters for 400Sk per night to a friendly bunk and outhouse for 100Sk. **Hotel** prices fall dramatically outside Bratislava and the High Tatras, and hotels are rarely full. **Pensions** (*penzióny*) are generally less expensive than hotels and, especially when family-run, often nicer. Two forms of *ubytovanie* (lodging) cater mainly to Slovaks and offer super prices for bare-bones rooms: **stadi-**

ums and sport centers often run hotels on the lot for teams and fans (the requisite ground-floor pubs are always hoppin'); **workers' hostels** generally offer hospital-like rooms and no pub. **Campgrounds** lurk on the outskirts of most towns, and many offer bungalows for travelers without tents. Camping in national parks is illegal.

FOOD AND DRINK

Slovakia rose out of its 1000-year Hungarian captivity with a taste for paprika, spicy *gulaš*, and fine wines. The good news for vegetarians is that the national dish, *bryndzové halušky*, is a plate of dumpling-esque pasta smothered in a thick sauce of sheep or goat cheese. The bad news is that it sometimes comes flecked with bacon. The Slovaks like their dumplings (*knedliky*), but—unlike in the Czech Republic—it's often possible to escape from them and have potatoes (*zemiaky*) or fries (*hranolky*) instead. Slovakia's second-favorite dish is *pirohy*, a pasta-pocket usually filled with potato or *bryndzou* cheese, with bits of bacon on top. Also popular is *pstruh* (trout). *Kolačy* (pastry) is often baked with cheese, jam, or poppy seeds and honey.

Fine white wines are produced in the Small Carpathians northeast of Bratislava, especially around the town of Pezinok. *Riesling* and *Müller-Thurgau* grapes are typically used; quality varies greatly. *Tokaj* wines are produced around Košice. You can enjoy any of these at a *vináreň* (wine hall). *Pivo* (beer) is served at a *pivnica* or *piváreň* (beerhall). Slovakia produces several brandies: *slivovica* is plum, *marhulovica* is apricot, and *borovička* is juniper-berry.

CUSTOMS AND ETIQUETTE

Tipping is common in restaurants; most people round up to a convenient number, and 8-10% is generous. Tip by refusing change as you pay. Most **museums** close Mondays, and **theaters** take a break during July and August. Like Poland and unlike the Czech Republic, Slovakia is an intensely Roman Catholic country, and social mores are often quite conservative. Although **homosexuality** is legal, a gay couple walking down the street might encounter stares or insults; usually everyone is so shocked, though, that no one interferes. **Ganymedes,** the national gay organization, runs hotlines around the country, but few employees speak English. **Grocery store attendants** will accost you if you don't grab a basket by the entrance. And, more often than not, restaurant **toilets** will be locked with the key (*kluč*) hanging up by the bar.

NATIONAL HOLIDAYS

January 1, New Year's and Independence Day; January 6, Epiphany; April 10, Good Friday; April 13, Easter Monday; May 1, May Day; May 8, Liberation Day; July 5, Sts. Cyril and Methodius Day; August 15, Assumption Day; August 29, Anniversary of Slovak National Uprising; September 1, Constitution Day; September 15, Our Lady of Seven Sorrows; November 1, All Saint's Day; December 25, Christmas.

LIFE AND TIMES

HISTORY

The Slovaks have never been very powerful, but they do have a distinct history. Settled by **Slavs** in the 6th and 7th centuries, Slovakia was incorporated into the Greater Moravian Empire in the 870s, along with Bohemia, South Poland, and what is now West Hungary. Following a Magyar invasion in 896, Slovakia was assimilated into the **Kingdom of Hungary.** In the wake of economic devastation caused by Tatar attacks in the 13th century, a Hungarian king invited German **Saxons** to help develop the area of the kingdom inhabited by the Slovaks. For a few decades at the start of the 14th century, a local ruler, **Matús Čák,** effectively controlled Slovakia, but the Hungarian monarchy quickly regained control, ruling Slovakia for 200 years.

After the Ottomans defeated Hungary in the 1526 **Battle of Mohács,** Slovakia became a bulwark of the West against the Turks as the Hungarians moved their capital to Bratislava in 1536. The **Habsburg** emperors, who ruled Hungarian Slovakia between 1526 and 1918, eventually freed all of Hungary from Turkish occupation, and began to redevelop the region by 1700. **Lutheranism** and **Calvinism** had become popular among the German, Slovak, and Magyar communities of Slovakia, particularly in the East. The Habsburgs proceeded to restore **Roman Catholicism** in the lands, leading to religious wars in 1603 and 1669-71.

In the 19th century, various national movements emerged in the Kingdom of Hungary, led by **L'udovít Štúr.** The tumultuous **Revolution of 1848** in Hungary brought little change to Slovakia but disaster to its Hungarian overlords. After the Austro-Hungarian *Ausgleich* (Compromise) of 1867, Hungary regained control over Slovakia, which remained one of the most submerged nations in the Austro-Hungarian Empire; without even its own province, it lived under direct Hungarian rule. Ignoring the wise advice of Hungarian intellectuals, the Hungarian government, particularly under Tisza (1875-90), intensified the policy of Magyarization, forcing many Slovaks to leave their homeland and alienating those who remained.

The Slovak national movement continued to blossom through the turn of the century, but the "Czecho-Slovak National Committee," which had met in Pittsburgh during **WWI,** opted for a joint Czecho-Slovak state. On October 28, 1918, six days before Austria-Hungary sued for peace, Slovakia was attached to Bohemia, Moravia, and Sub-Carpathian Ruthenia to form **Czechoslovakia,** a new state in the heart of Europe, with its capital at Prague. The state made a good start, repelling an invasion of Slovakia by the Hungarian communist **Bela Kun** in 1919 and securing the withdrawal of Romanian troops from Ruthenia. It became a **liberal democracy** on an American model and one of the world's wealthiest nations. Czechoslovakia was the only state in Central or Eastern Europe that did not descend into fascist, authoritarian, or communist rule. Though the policies of the Czechs toward the German and Slovak minorities were relatively liberal, however, they were often not liberal enough for Slovak nationalist parties, who resented what they regarded as Czech domination.

In the preamble to **WWII,** Hitler made Czechoslovakia an early target. Abandoned by the British and French in the **Munich Agreement** of September 1938, which urged Czechoslovak President Beneš to accede to German demands for the Sudetenland, Slovaks urgently called for autonomy. In October 1938, Slovakia was proclaimed an autonomous unit within a federal Czecho-Slovak state, known as the short-lived **Second Republic.** But by March 1939, the democratic state buckled under German pressure, when German troops invaded Bohemia and Moravia. As Hitler occupied Prague, Slovakia emerged as a collaborative Nazi puppet "independent state" under **Monseignor Tiso.** Authoritarian Hungary took advantage of the difficult position of the formerly prosperous, democratic state, helping itself to the province of Ruthenia. Resentment against Tiso and the Nazis caused the two-month **Slovenské Národné Povstanie** (SNP; Slovak National Uprising), which began in August 1944. Originally organized against Tiso, the uprising became anti-Nazi when Hitler ordered the military to occupy Slovakia after partisans shot a German general.

> In 1918, Slovakia joined with Bohemia, Moravia, and Ruthenia to form Czechoslovakia, a new state in the heart of Europe.

After WWII, Slovakia joined the reconstituted democratic Czechoslovakia. Postwar Czechoslovakia expelled members of Slovakia's Hungarian and Saxon communities and was forced to cede Ruthenia to the Soviet Union. **Communists,** lead by **Klement Gottwald,** won 36% of the vote in 1946, which made them the largest single party and allowed them to form a left coalition. In February 1948, the Popular Front government fell apart and the Communists mounted a Soviet-backed coup. In theory, the 1948 constitution guaranteed Slovakia equal rights, but Slovaks felt oppressed by a Czech-dominated government. The Stalinist regime that emerged in Czechoslovakia remained subservient to Moscow until Slovak **Alexander Dubček,** the First Secretary of the Czechoslovak Communist Party, introduced his **"Prague Spring"** reforms in

1968. Soviet tanks crushed Dubček's allegedly disloyal government, and the country returned to totalitarianism in 1969. With the defeat of the reformist regime, Slovakia was given increased autonomy in an effort to prevent such dissent from recurring, and Bratislava was made a "capital city" in 1969. Rural Slovakia underwent heavy industrial development. After the Soviet invasion, the Communists remained in power in Czechoslovakia until the **Velvet Revolution** of 1989. **Václav Havel** was appointed President and the government set about introducing a pluralistic political system and a market economy. In this atmosphere of increased freedom, and encouraged by Czechs perceiving the Slovaks as being resistant to rapid economic liberalization, Slovak nationalism began to gain ground and ultimately triumphed in the **1993 Declaration of Independence.** Less than four years after Czechoslovakia had played a crucial role in burying the Soviet empire, the state ceased to exist, making a truly independent Slovakia a reality for the first time.

LITERATURE

Slovak began to emerge as a literary language only in the 18th century, and even then only because a temporary decline in literary Czech left room for Slovakia to produce its own locally colored devotional texts. Early examples of the Slovak novel, such as **Ignác Bajza's** *René* (1785), represented a Slovak version of Czech rather than a distinct language. Slovak literature has often attempted to define itself through overtly nationalist themes, however. **Ján Holly's** lyrics and idylls of the late 18th century celebrate the Slovak land and people, and, like many subsequent Slovak works, owe a tremendous debt to indigenous folk poetry. Yet the work of Holly and his contemporaries still relied on a Czech-influenced version of West Slovak dialects.

> "The Untilled Field," full of exploited peasants and greedy capitalists, yields to the predictable excesses of the leftist political novel.

Literary Slovak as an independent tradition began with the 19th-century linguist, patriot, and nationalist **L'udovít Štur.** Štur's "new" language—based on the Central Slovak dialects and more widely accepted than any previous attempt at standardization—inspired a string of nationalist poets. Foremost among these was **Andrej Sládkovič,** author of the national epic *Marína* (1846). Slovak writers' nationalist passions may be surpassed only by their amorous ones. Sládkovič's contemporary, the poet and revolutionary **Janko Král,** launched an enduring tradition of Slovak Romanticism with his ballads, epics, and lyrics, a tradition followed by the rustic Slavophile poets **Vajansky** and **Hviezdoslav.**

As the Slovak nation came of age in the wake of WWI, Slovak literature also reached maturity. Besides the established nationalist and romantic themes, more cosmopolitan influences began to appear in Slovak writing: **E. B. Lukáč** introduced Symbolism to the Slovak tradition, Surrealism found a champion in **Rudolf Fabry,** and **Laco Novomeský** complemented his career as a Communist journalist with early poetic endeavors at so-called **Socialist Realism.** The long-established primacy of poetic forms also began to give way to novels and short stories. As in poetry, rustic themes and the life of the village took center stage, often as an object of celebration, but increasingly as the butt of scorn and ridicule. **Janko Jesenký** savaged the tin-pot regional poo-bahs of the new Slovak administration after WWI in his two-part satirical novel *Demokrati (The Democrats)*, deromanticizing the small-town experience and portraying villagers as shallow, petty, Magyarized hypocrites.

The succession of the nominally independent, Nazi-puppet Slovakia, and its reabsorption into a Communist Czechoslovakia, did little for the country's literature. If the thought of reading a self-styled Slavic Zola who makes his model's political overtones seem subtle doesn't appeal to you, be sure to avoid the ham-handed novels of **Peter Jilemnický.** *Pole neorane (The Untilled Field)* succumbs to the predictable excesses of the leftist political novel, with its set full of exploited peasants and greedy capitalists straight out of a Leninist version of Central Casting. You'll fare no better with the stiff anti-fascist, anti-Clerical cant of **František Hečko.** While authoritarianism helped produce Kafka, Hašek, Kundera and Havel in the Czech Republic, it is an enigma that similar repression appears to have stifled Slovak literature. With its newfound independence, perhaps Slovakia will experience a literary renaissance.

SLOVAKIA TODAY

Coming out of the 1993 Velvet Revolution with only 25% of former Czechoslovakia's industrial capacity and even less of its international reputation, Slovakia has had more trouble adjusting to the post-East-Bloc world than its former partner. Premier **Vladimir Mečiar** of the Movement for a Democratic Slovakia Party (HZDS) has accumulated power by returning to the political patterns of the past, ignoring the parliament and free market reforms, and keeping industry under state control. Opposition leaders are hampered by the lack of a strong parliament. There has been tension with the sizable Hungarian minority, provoked by Mečiar's insistence that Slovak be the only official language. Moreover, some Slovaks are having second thoughts about independence, particularly as the standard of living continues to lag behind that of the Czech Republic. The coalition government, consisting of HZDS, an extremist Communist party, and an extremist right-wing party, has garnered harsh criticism from Western governments for its anti-democratic behavior. Despite Mečiar's promises that his nation is approaching stability, potential investors and allies are wary of dealing with Slovakia until it emerges from its current political and economic funk. In 1997's NATO enlargement discussions, not only was Slovakia not offered membership, it did not even warrant the promise of future consideration that Slovenia and Romania received.

> Tension with the Hungarian minority is not improved by the premier's insistence that Slovak be the only official language.

Bratislava

After 80 years of playing second fiddle to starlet Prague, this burgeoning city of half a million has been thrust into a new role as the capital of Slovakia. Although much of the population lives in the grim housing projects surrounding the center, the marvelously compact (and pedestrianized) historic center—where the Austrian Empress held court during the 18th century *and* where the rulers of Hungary were crowned—is where visitors will spend most of their time. Lightly touristed in comparison with Vienna and Prague, this thriving new capital merits a visit.

ORIENTATION AND PRACTICAL INFORMATION

Bratislava lies on the banks of the **Dunaj** (Danube), a proverbial stone's throw from the Austrian and Hungarian borders. Don't get off at the **Nové Mesto train station,** which is much farther from the center than **Hlavná stanica** (main station). From the station, take tram #1 to **nám. SNP,** the administrative center. From the bus station, take bus #107 to **nám. J. Štúra,** by the river. The Dunaj runs east-west across Bratislava. The city's south half consists of little more than a convention center, an amusement park, and miles of postwar high-rises. **Most (Bridge) SNP,** which connects the two sections, becomes the highway **Staromestská** to the north. The **castle** towers on a hill to the west, while the city center stands between nám SNP and the river.

Tourist Offices: Bratislavská Informačná Služba (BIS), Klobučnicka 2 (tel. 533 37 15). Sells maps (30Sk), gives city tours, and books rooms. Open Mon.-Fri. 8am-7pm, Sat.-Sun. 8:30am-1:30pm. Branch in **train station annex** open daily 8am-6pm.
Embassies: Canada (honorary consulate), Kolárska 4 (tel. 361 277; fax 361 220).Open Mon. and Wed. 3-5pm. **South Africa,** Jančova 8 (tel. 531 15 82; fax 531 25 81). Open Mon.-Fri. 9am-noon. **U.K.,** Panská 16 (tel. 531 96 32; fax 531 00 02). Visa section open Mon.-Fri. 9-11am. Other sections by appointment only. **U.S.,** Hviezdoslavovo nám. 4 (tel. 533 08 61; fax 533 5934). Open Mon.-Fri. 8am-4:30pm.

Bratislava

Bratislava Castle, **6**
Franciscan Church, **2**
Michael Tower, **1**
Old City Hall, **4**
Primate's Palace, **3**
Slovak National Gallery, **7**
Slovak National Museum, **8**
St. Martin's Cathedral, **5**

The nearest embassy for Australians and New Zealanders is in Vienna. In an emergency, they should contact the British Embassy, as should Irish citizens.

Currency Exchange: Všeobecná Úverová Banka (VÚB), Gorkého 9 (tel. 515 79 76; fax 515 80 90). Cashes traveler's checks and handles MC and Visa cash advances. Open Mon.-Wed. and Fri. 8am-4:30pm, Thurs. 8am-3pm. A machine at Mostová 6 changes US$, DM, and UK£ into Sk at 3% commission. **ATMs** accepting Cirrus, EC, and MC are at Primaciálne nám. and at the train and bus stations. There's also one for Visa at the train station.

American Express: At **Tatratour,** Františkánske nám. 3, Bratislava 81101 (tel. 533 55 36; fax 533 55 38). Cashes (2% commission) and sells (1% commission) traveler's checks, and holds mail. Open Mon.-Fri. 10am-6pm, Sat. 9am-noon.

Flights: Ivanka **airport** (info tel. 577 33 53), 8km northeast of city center. Take bus #24 to or from the train station. Most use the much larger airport in nearby Vienna. The following carriers have local offices: **Austrian Airlines** (tel. 531 16 10), **British Airways** (tel. 399 801), **ČSA** (tel. 361 038), **Delta** (tel. 533 47 18), **LOT** (tel. 364 007), **Lufthansa** (tel. 367 814), and Slovak **Tatra Air** (tel. 236 227).

Trains: Bratislava Hlavná stanica (info tel. 204 44 84), north of town center. Go up Štefánikova, right onto Šancová, and left up the road that goes past the waiting buses. International tickets at counters #9-16. **Wasteels** office at front of station has cheap tickets for those under 26. Wasteels open Mon.-Fri. 8:30am-4pm. To: Berlin (2 per day, 11hr., 2699Sk, Wasteels 1993Sk); Budapest (10 per day, 3hr., 378Sk, Wasteels 435Sk); Kraków (2 per day, 8hr., 1022Sk, Wasteels 527Sk); Prague (9 per day, 5hr., 228Sk); Vienna (4 per day, 1hr., 220Sk); and Warsaw (1 per day, 8hr., 1284Sk, Wasteels 742Sk).

Buses: Mlynské nivy 31 (info tel. 542 22 22), east of the center. Take bus #210 from train station or 30 or 38 from the river. To: Budapest (1 per day, 5hr., 330Sk); Prague (10 per day, 4½hr., 240Sk); and Vienna (9 per day, 1½hr., 320Sk). Check ticket for bus number (*č. aut.*); several different buses may depart simultaneously.

Hydrofoils: Lodná osobná doprava, Fajnorovo nábr. 2 (tel. 363 522; fax 536 22 31), along the river. A scenic alternative to trains for Danube destinations. To: Vienna (1-2 per day in summer, 1½hr., round-trip 330 Austrian Schillings (AS), one-way 210AS; Budapest (1-2 per day in summer, 4hr., round-trip 1000AS, one-way 680 AS). Book tickets at least 48hr. in advance. 30% student discount. Also to Devín castle (3 per day, round-trip 60AS, one way 30AS). Credit cards accepted.

Public Transportation: All daytime trips on **trams** or **buses** require a 7Sk ticket sold at kiosks or the dusty orange automats found at most, but not all, bus stations. Night buses marked with black and orange numbers in the 500s require 14Sk. Most trams pass by nám. SNP; most buses stop at the north base of Most SNP. The fine for joyriding is 700Sk; authorities *do* check. Tourist passes sold at some larger kiosks (1-day 35Sk, 2-day 65Sk, 7-day 105Sk).

Taxis: Try BP (tel. 303 111), Fun Taxi (tel. 377 777), or Otto Taxi (tel. 531 42 00).

Hitchhiking: Those hitching to Vienna cross Most SNP and walk down Viedenská cesta. This road also travels to Hungary via Győr, though fewer cars head in that direction. Hitchers to Prague take bus #104 from the center to the Patronka stop. Hitching is legal and common, but not recommended by *Let's Go.*

Luggage Storage: Fiddly lockers at the train and bus stations. 5Sk.

English Bookstore: Big Ben Bookshop, through the arch at Michalská 1 (tel. 533 36 32; fax 533 36 92). Open Mon.-Fri. 9am-6pm, Sat. 10am-1pm. **Interpress Slovakia,** on the corner of Sedláska and Michalská in the center. An extensive selection of foreign press. Open Mon.-Sat. 7am-10pm, Sun. 10am-10pm.

Laundromat: INPROKOM, Laurinská 18 (tel. 363 210). Same-day express service 7-48Sk per garment; slower service 4-30Sk. No self service. Open Mon.-Fri. 8am-6pm.

Gay Help Line: tel. (090) 53 61 13 23. Open Tues. and Thurs. 6-8pm.

24-Hour Pharmacy: The most central one is at nám. SNP 20 (tel. 363 731), although it's not really on the square at all: find it on the corner of Gorkého and Laurinská.

Post Office: Nám. SNP 35 (tel. 533 1241). *Poste Restante* at counter #6. Open Mon.-Fri. 7am-8pm, Sat. 7am-6pm, Sun. 9am-2pm. **Postal code:** 81000 Bratislava 1.

Telephones: 2nd floor of the post office, above the "Telefón Telegram" entrance. Open Mon.-Fri. 7am-9pm. Office at Kolárska 12 open 24hr. **Phone code:** 07.

ACCOMMODATIONS AND CAMPING

Bratislava's tourist agencies seem to requisition everything but retirement homes and orphanages to accommodate the summer rush of Vienna-bound crowds. During July and August, a dozen dorms open up as hostels. But unless the avaricious *ubytovanie* (accommodation) companies start kicking out students before the end of classes, good deals will be hard to come by in June. Most cheap beds are near the station on the northern side of town, a 20-minute walk from the town center. **BIS,** in the center or at the station, provides addresses for private rooms (singles 400Sk; doubles 600Sk).

Pension Gremium, Gorkého 11 (tel. 321 818; fax 533 06 53). Sterling showers and stuffed chairs in the heart of the city. A popular cafe will feed you downstairs. Singles 800Sk; doubles 1300Sk. Breakfast included. Only a few rooms, so call ahead.

Youth Hostel Bernolak, Bernolákova 1 (tel. 397 723; fax 397 724). From the train station, take bus #22, 23, or 210, or tram #3. From the bus station, take bus #37 or trolley #210 to "Račianské Mýto." Friendliest hostel in town; best English, too. Spacious singles 440Sk; doubles 520Sk; triples 600Sk; all with showers and toilets. 10% discount with Euro26, HI, or ISIC. Disco downstairs. Open July-Aug.

YMCA na Slovenska, Karpatská 2 (tel. 398 005). Walk down the long lane from the train station and turn left on Šancová. Old, terraced building. Sterile, spacious rooms with less sterile showers. Student bar and cinema keep things hopping. 9am check-out. Doubles 400Sk; triples 600SK; quints 1000SK.

Youth Hostel, Wilsonova 6 (tel. 397 735). Same directions as for YH Bernolak—Wilsonova runs parallel to Bernolákova. Rooms remarkable only for their cheapness. 2- to 4-bed dorms 150Sk per person, 30% discount with Euro26, HI, or ISIC. Open July-Aug. 9am checkout.

Autocamping Zlaté Piesky, Senecká cesta 2 (tel. 257 373), in suburban Trnávka. Take tram #2 or 4 or bus #118 to the last stop and cross the footbridge. Campground and bungalows are down by the lakeside, far out of town. 90Sk per person, 80Sk per tent; different kinds of bungalows for 650Sk and 900Sk. Cheaper if you're Czech and/or Slovak.

FOOD

Besides burgers, Bratislava's restaurants serve the region's spicy meat mixtures with west Slovakia's celebrated **Modra** wine. Offering escape from both cost and confusion is **Tesco's Potraviny** (grocery store), Kamenné nám. 1 (open Mon.-Wed. 8am-7pm, Thurs. 8am-8pm, Fri. 8am-9pm, Sat. 8am-5pm, Sun. 9am-5pm). A **market** at Žilinská 5, near the train station, vends flowers and vegetables (open Mon.-Sat. 6am-4pm). A **late-night deli** operates at Špitalská 45.

Prašná Bašta, Zámočnícka 11 (tel. 334 957). Turn right off Michalská just before the tower. Weird mannequin statues and wooden beams frame the vaulted interior. Garlicky chicken thighs (88Sk), sheep's cheese gnocchi (49Sk), fine onion soup (22Sk), and generous glasses of wine (9Sk). English menu. Open daily 11am-11pm.

Veľkí Františkání, Františkánske nám. 10 (tel. 533 30 73), around the corner from Hlavné nám. Dishes range from bean soup (25Sk) to plates of roast duck that fly off into Sk infinity. The candle-lit wine cellar (*Rizling Rýnsky* 90Sk) is the restaurant's focus. The atmosphere heats up at night, when folk musicians play and Slovaks sing along. Music nightly; 25Sk cover. Open daily 10am-10:30pm.

Cafe London, Panská 17 (tel. 331 793), in the British Council's courtyard. Serves up Anglophile nostalgia with generous portions of quiche (63Sk) and chicken salad, tuna, and roast beef sandwiches (39-72Sk). Bratislava's English congregate here, but they're a nice bunch. Open Mon.-Fri. 9am-9pm.

Corleone's, Hviezdoslavovo nám., on the north side. Italian *trattoria*. Delicious pizzas—an offer you can't refuse (mostly 69-139Sk). Open daily until midnight..

You Want Fries with That?

The only thing less comprehensible than a Slovak menu is a Bratislavan menu at one of the city's ubiquitous burger stands. A cheeseburger costs less than a *hamburger so syrom* (hamburger with cheese) because, as the stand owner will explain with humiliating logic, a cheeseburger is made of cheese—only cheese. A *pressburger,* named after Bratislava's former moniker Pressburg, consists of bologna on a bun, and hamburgers are actually ham. Everything comes boiled (except the cheese) and stuck on a roll with diced cabbage, onions, and sauce.

SIGHTS

Stará Bratislava (Old Bratislava)

From **nám. SNP,** which commemorates the bloody and unsuccessful Slovak National Uprising against the fascist Slovak state, and which—together with the adjoining Kamenné nám—is the heart of the modern city, a walk down Uršulínska leads to **Primaciálne nám.** To the left, on Klobučnícka, is the main tourist office, and a CD shop that is also the entrance to a museum devoted to the composer **Hummel** (open Tues.-Sun. noon-5pm; 10Sk). On the square itself, the Neoclassical **Primaciálny Palác** (Primate's Palace) dates from 1781. In 1805, Napoleon and Austrian Emperor Franz I signed the Peace of Pressburg (the German name for Bratislava) here, two weeks after the decisive French victory at Austerlitz, just outside Brno. Buy tickets on the second floor and go up to the third to see the **Zrkadlová Sieň** (Hall of Mirrors), where it all happened, as well as some rather ponderously decorated hallways, paintings, and tapestries (open Tues.-Sun. 10am-5pm; 20Sk). The **Muzeum Histórie Mesta** (Town History Museum) is in the **Stará radnica** (Old Town Hall), accessible from Primaciálne nám. You don't need a ticket to see the wonderful 1:500 model of Bratislava just inside. The rest of the collection includes a battery of untranslated Slovak notices describing the medieval town and a series of galleries full of objects illustrating Bratislava's development (tel. 333 401; open Tues.-Sun. 10am-5pm; 25Sk, students 10Sk). The distinctive yellow tower of the Stará radnica fronts onto **Hlavné nam.**, one side of which is being wholly reconstructed. Tourists drift through all day, sometimes pausing to enjoy the brass bands that play in the square on summer evenings.

South of Hlavné nám., long, wooded **Hviezdoslavovo nám.** spreads along Rybárska brána. The square is really a park surrounded by 19th-century architecture and dominated at its eastern end by the 1886 **Slovenské Národné Divadlo** (Slovak National Theater). Mostová runs past the **Reduta,** home of the Slovak Philharmonic, into nám. L'udovíta Štura, which celebrates the man who codified the Slovak language in the 19th century, helping to distinguish it from Czech. A left along the Dunaj leads to the **Slovenské Národné Muzeum** (Slovak National Museum), Vajanského nábr. 2 (tel. 533 39 85) which houses the region's archaeological finds, including casts of local Neanderthal skeletons (open Tues.-Sun. 9am-5pm; 20Sk). Going right along the river takes you past the four-story **Slovak National Gallery,** Rázusovo nábr. 2 (tel. 533 4276), which displays excellently preserved examples of Slovak Gothic and Baroque sculpture, frescoes, and paintings (open Tues.-Sun. 10am-5pm; 25Sk, students 5Sk).

Heading back into the center, a left down Panská leads past **Lekáreň Gyógyszertár Apotheke Salvator** (Salvator Pharmacy), which, decorated with 19th-century cupids and lobsters, resembles a shrine more than a drugstore. Father along is the **Dóm sv. Martina** (St. Martin's Cathedral), a fairly unspectacular Gothic church where the kings of Hungary were crowned for three centuries. Next to Sv. Martina, the freeway travels south to the SNP suspension bridge, its reins held by a giant flying saucer (admission 10Sk). On the northern side of the bridge, the road zooms over what used to be **Schlossberg,** the old Jewish quarter, bulldozed in the name of "progress." Over the road from the cathedral, the **Múzeum Židovskej Kultúry** (Museum of Jewish Culture), Židovská 17 (tel. 631 85 07), preserves valuable fragments of a vanished population (open Sun.-Fri. 11am-5pm; 30Sk). From the cathedral, go down Kapitulská, right onto Prepoštská, and left onto Michalská, a busy pedestrian street guarded by the **Michalská brána** at the north end. Trot up to the top (open Wed.-Mon. 10am-5pm; 20Sk).

Go through the tower's gateway, out of the Old Town, and onto **Hodžovo nám.,** a noisy nightmare of traffic and congestion. Up Staromestská at Konventná 13/15, the former **Evangelical Lyceum** has played a significant role in Bratislava's intellectual life, producing several renowned historical figures. Among its students were Slovak leaders Štúr, Kollár, and Šafárik, Swabian writers Eduard Glatz and T. G. Schröer, Hungarian poets Petőfi and Jókai, and Czech historian František Palacký. On the north side of Hodžovo nám., **Grassalkovičov palác** (Grassalkovich Palace), at #1, is the grandest of the city's many grand Hungarian aristocratic residences. Street lamps and a modern fountain disturb the white Baroque facade's composition, now being restored to serve as the seat of Slovakia's president. Behind the castle, the **Grassalkovich Gardens** offer escape from the noisy chaos of the square.

Bratislavský Hrad (Castle)

From the banks of the Danube to the center's historic squares, the four-towered *Bratislavský hrad* remains a visible landmark. Of strategic importance for more than a millennium, the castle's heyday was in the 18th century, when Austrian Empress Maria Theresa held court here. The castle was burned down in 1811 and bombed out during WWII, so what the visitor sees today is largely Communist-era restoration. The view of the Danube passing from Austria through Slovakia and into Hungary is impressive. There's also a **Historické Múzeum** (open Tues.-Fri. 9am-5pm, Sat.-Sun. 10am-6pm; 30Sk).

ENTERTAINMENT AND NIGHTLIFE

For film, concert, and theater schedules, pick up a copy of *Kám v Bratislave* at BIS. Although it's entirely in Slovak, the info is easy to decipher. **Slovenská Filharmonia** plays regularly at Palackého ul. 2, which fronts onto Mostová; the box office (tel. 533

33 51) is around the corner on Medená (open Mon.-Fri. 1-5pm). The Filharmonia and most theaters take their vacations in July and August. Tickets to the **Národné Divadlo** (National Theater) are sold at the box office at Laurinská 20 (open Mon.-Fri. noon-6pm; around 50Sk). A dozen **cinemas** are scattered across the city; listings are in *Kám,* but it's almost all Hollywood.

Danglár, Hviezdoslavovo nám. 18. Francis Bacon-esque prints adorn this basement pub's walls, where a lively, studenty Slovak crowd knocks back 23Sk beers as moody rock pounds away. Open Mon.-Fri. 4pm-2am, Sat. 6pm-2am, Sun. 5pm-1am.

U angelo (tel. 321 572), on Laurinská. Small, tightly packed bar where even Cupid wall art can't detract from a stylish atmosphere. Beer 29Sk, wine 15Sk, cocktails 44-79Sk. Open Mon.-Sat. 9am-midnight, Sun. 5pm-midnight.

Dubliner, on Sedlarská, just off Hlavné nám. Bratislava's *ersatz* Irish pub has wobbly wooden tables, a leaky roof, and a tremendously lively atmosphere as it fills up after dinner. And instead of the tired old 1916 proclamation, an *Irish Post* front cover from 1939 charting Hitler's grab for Czechoslovakia is well worth a look. Expensive Guinness and Kilkenny; you're better off with *Staropramen* (30Sk). Open Mon.-Sat. 10am-1am, Sun. noon-midnight.

Mamut, Cintorínska 32 (tel. 321 151). The mammoth was a huge and distinguished prehistoric beast. This one's just huge. One of Europe's largest beerhalls is redis-covering itself as a trashy casino complex. Jazz or country band Thurs.-Sat. Pint of *Budvar* 20Sk. Open daily 10am-midnight, beer garden 11am-11pm.

■ Near Bratislava

DEVÍN CASTLE

Slovakia's best-loved castle ruins perch on a promontory 9km west of Bratislava. Slavs first fortified the rock during the 800s under the Great Moravian Empire's King Rat-islav, but the Magyars soon dismantled his state and claimed the hills. Devín remained a Hungarian stronghold guarding the Danube until Napoleon's troops sacked it and left the castle's winding walls to crumble. Decades later, the stones became a roman-tic symbol of Slovakia's past glory and its future independence. Under the Commu-nists, the castle grew to symbolize totalitarianism, sheltering sharpshooters who were ordered to fire at anyone walking along the beach. Although the militiamen have left, vultures have made Devín's watchtower into a hunting lodge, and carry away unwary tourists in their deadly talons. A **museum** exhibits archaeological tidbits. From the Danube just below Bratislava Castle, take bus #29 to Devín village. The parking lot at the end of Brigádnická leads to the castle (tel. 473 01 05; open May-Oct. Tues.-Fri. 10am-5pm, Sat.-Sun. 10am-7pm; 30Sk).

TRNAVA

Slovakia's oldest town—Trnava (truh-NA-va) received its charter in 1238—is home to a remarkable collection of (mostly Baroque) churches. As the Turks moved onto the Danube's plain, the Hungarians moved their great institutions westward. The Diet went to Bratislava, but the Archbishopric of Esztergom came here in 1543. The town became a center of the Counter-Reformation, and a Jesuit university was founded here in 1635. As the Turks were pushed back, the university moved to Buda in 1777, and the archbishop went back to Esztergom in 1820. But the buildings from the days when Trnava was known as the Slovak Rome remain, making the town an ideal day-trip from Bratislava. The churches don't post regular opening hours—if you find one locked, hang around for a bit, and someone may appear to let you in. To guarantee seeing everything, visit on Sunday.

Churches surround the main **Trojičné nám.,** where the **tourist office** (tel. (0805) 511 022) lurks on the ground floor of the **Mestská veža** (municipal tower; open Mon.-Fri. 8am-6pm, Sat.-Sun. 10am-6pm). Several meters to the north is the 18th-cen-tury Jesuit **Kostol Najsvätejšej Trojice** (Church of the Holiest Trinity), which boasts half a dozen richly gilded Baroque altars. Go west to the more classical Franciscan

Kostol sv. Jakuba (St. James's Church), erected 1689-1717. A walk south, down Hlavná, goes past the small **Kostol sv. Heleny** (Church of St. Helen), a 14th-century Gothic church with a more recent interior. Heading east takes you to **Dóm sv. Mikuláša** (St. Nicholas's Cathedral); its Gothic basilica dates from 1421, twin steeples from 1567, and interior furnishings from the 17th and 18th centuries. Heading back toward the main square and right onto Hollého leads to the most impressive of the lot, the barrel-vaulted **Katedrálny chrám sv. Jána Krstiteľa** (Church of St. John the Baptist). The 1670 Baroque altar fills the eastern end with over two dozen carved figures. From Dóm sv. Mikuláša, there's a great view of the huge **Družba estate** through the 13th-century town walls. Then go right past **Kapitulská's** striking facades to the **Západoslovenské múzeum** (Western Slovakia Museum), which has fine permanent and temporary exhibitions (open Tues.-Sun. 10am-6pm).

Trnava is on the main Bratislava-Košice line, so fast **trains** (35min.) stop every hour or two, with slower trains (50min.) plugging some of the gaps (24Sk). The tourist office can book accommodations, but the cheapest beds are a 20-minute walk from the center. From the station, go right over the long pedestrian bridge through the gardens at the far end, and turn left onto **Hlavná**. This street leads to the main square, on which sit the **post office** (open Mon.-Fri. 7am-7:30pm, Sat. 8am-noon) and a **Chinese restaurant,** on the second floor of the horrific Dom Kultúry (lunchtime menu 60Sk; open daily 10am-10pm). Get groceries from **Danipek,** Hlavná 33 (open Mon.-Fri. 6am-12:30pm and 1:30-6pm, Sat. 6am-noon).

CENTRAL SLOVAKIA

Rail connections are poor but journeys spectacular in the hills of central Slovakia, where medieval towns once mined the richest gold and silver deposits in Europe. Nestled between Bratislava and the snow-capped Tatra mountains, this territory was violently contested during the anti-fascist Slovak National Uprising (SNP) of 1944.

■ Banská Bystrica

The hills around Banská Bystrica (BAN-ska bis-TREE-tsah) are clearly visible from the old town center, a bright, bustling, car-free square, where a rock fountain contentedly burbles and only a stark shiny obelisk commemorating Stalin's armies gives any clue that this was part of the old Eastern bloc. Two museums flesh out the history of the town—originally a medieval silver mine, and, more recently, the epicenter of the Slovak National Uprising—and a clutch of galleries, churches, cafes, and Renaissance buildings make Banská Bystrica ideal to visit en route to or from the Tatras.

Orientation and Practical Information The railway lines around Banská Bystrica provide gorgeous rides around the hills and valleys—it's just a shame the connections are so lousy. **Trains** (tel. 74 21 32) run to Bratislava (2 per day, 4hr., 128Sk) and Košice (1 per day, 4hr., 150Sk). **Buses** (tel. 74 54 79) go to Bratislava (20 per day, 4hr., 130Sk) and Liptovský Mikuláš (7 per day, 2hr., 53Sk). The bus terminal is next door to the train station, where **24-hour luggage lockers** cost 5Sk. To get to the town center, follow the underpass under the highway on the far side of the bus station from the train station. A walk up **Kukučinova** and a left onto **Horná** at the pyramid brings you to **nám. SNP.** The 20-minute walk can be avoided by taking the **city bus** (5Sk) from the bus station, which goes left along **Štefánikovo nábrežie,** past the Communist-era Hotel Lux block, and then along the edge of the center. Get off here and walk up one of the intersecting roads to nám. SNP. **Kultúrne a Informačné Stredisko (KIS),** nám. S. Moyzesa 26 (tel./fax 543 69; email pkobb@isternet.sk), just off the eastern end of nám. SNP, has leaflets about cultural events, free maps, and info on Banská Bystrica's accommodations (open May 15-Sept. 15 Mon.-Fri. 9am-7pm, Sat. 9am-1pm, off-season Mon.-Fri. 9am-5pm). **VÚB,** nám. Slobody 1 (tel. 720 11 11) and Dolná 17 (tel. 72 39 00) off nám. SNP, **exchanges currency** and cashes traveler's checks. There's a Visa **ATM** outside the tourist office. Several **pharmacies** operate around nám. SNP, sometimes posting addresses of late-closing places in the window. The **post office** is at Horná 1 (tel. 75 26 37), just off nám. SNP (open Mon.-Fri. 8am-8pm, Sat. 8am-noon, Sun. 8-10am). A Visa **ATM** and a **card phone** stand outside; coin-operated phones are inside the building. **Postal code:** 97400. **Phone code:** 088.

Accommodations and Food Summer visitors should ask **KIS** (see above) about temporary **hostel** arrangements. The agency can also secure **private rooms. Hotel Národný dom,** Národná 11 (tel. 72 37 37; fax 72 57 86), off nám. SNP, is admirably central and congenially carpeted, and thoughtfully provides its guests with small metal shoehorns. There's a casino and cafe in the building, and the opera house is next door (singles 400Sk; doubles 600Sk; triples 800Sk; all with shower except for two triples at 600Sk). Just around the corner, **Hotel Passage Urpín,** Jána Cikkera 5 (tel. 724 556; fax 723 831), is another acceptable, cheapish central hotel. (Singles 430Sk, with shower and toilet 470Sk. Doubles 600Sk, with shower and toilet 680Sk. Triples 900Sk. Quads with shower 1400Sk. Major credit cards.)

Top of the pops for food is **Copaline Baguette,** Dolná 1 (tel. 725 868), which stuffs fresh French bread with ham, cheese, eggs, and tomatoes—just point at the *sendvič* you want (35-50Sk), and try the yummy chocolate *puding* (14Sk) while you're at it. Come for breakfast to beat the lines, although lunch is worth the wait (open Mon.-Fri. 6:30am-midnight, Sat.-Sun. 8am-midnight). For a meal in a traditional Slovak underground bunker, **Slovenská pivnica,** Lazovná 18 (tel. 537 16), off nám. SNP, has *hotové jedlá* (40-54Sk) and *halušky* dishes (32-60Sk; open daily 11am-10pm). There's a **supermarket** at Kapitulská 12 (open Mon.-Fri. 8am-6pm, Sat. 8am-noon).

Sights and Entertainment A cluster of the town's oldest buildings stands on or behind nám. Š. Moyzesa. The tourist office is on the ground floor of the old **Barbakan** fortification; next door, the restored **Pretórium** building (tel. 72 48 64)—once the town hall—displays three floors of avant-garde art (open Tues.-Fri. 10am-6pm, Sat.-Sun. 10am-4pm; 20Sk, students 10Sk). Behind these two, the Romanesque **Kostol Panny Márie** (Church of the Virgin Mary) sports a fine Baroque barrel ceiling and holds an even finer Gothic altarpiece by Majstr Pavel of Levoča. Next door, **Kostol sv. Kríža** (Holy Cross Church) has a decent Gothic interior, but is often locked.

Wandering back onto **nám. SNP,** be sure to admire the tilt of the leaning *hodinová veža* (clock tower) at the eastern end. The **Stredoslovenské múzeum** (Museum of Central Slovakia), nám. SNP 4, has a historical collection nicely presented in a restored Renaissance house, with an English-language sheet to accompany your visit (open Sun.-Fri. 9am-noon and 1-5pm). At the far end of the square, the 14th-century **Bethlenov dom,** Dolná 8 (tel. 72 41 67), offers more space for temporary art exhibitions (open Tues.-Fri. 10am-6pm, Sat.-Sun. 10am-4pm).

Two exhibitions away from the square deserve visits. **Skuteckého dom,** a restored 19th-century neo-Renaissance villa at Horná 55 (tel. 42 54 50), displays the state's collection of paintings by local artist Dominik Skutecký (1849-1921), a dogged realist in the age of Impressionism whose *Chess Players* and *Self-Portrait* are strikingly good (open Tues.-Sun. 10am-5pm; 20Sk, students 5Sk; ask the staff to lend you the glossy English catalog). Then there's the **Múzeum Slovenského Národného Povstania** (Museum of the Slovak National Uprising), in the oddly shaped building in the gardens of Kapitulská, which runs out of nám. SNP. Banská Bystrica was the rebels' headquarters during the eight weeks of fighting that began when Nazi forces entered puppet ally Slovakia's territory on August 29, 1944. The museum charts the course of the failed insurrection and the grim Nazi reprisal attacks against civilians that followed, as well as setting the SNP in the wider context of WWII, the "independent" Slovak state of Josef Tiso, and the deportation of the Slovak Jews organized by his regime. No English help is given, but a rough knowledge of WWII's development helps make a sense of the exhibits (open Tues.-Sun. 9am-6pm; 20Sk, students 10Sk).

In mid-June, the town hosts **Pivinex,** a celebration of beer, wine, and folklore. At **Piváreň Perla,** Horná 52, copper vats of *Perla* stand bubbling right behind the bar while Slovak men chain-smoke in front of it. Both barflies and businessfolk enjoy the quality microbrew (12Sk) on communal tables and benches. Don't be shy about scooting in (open Mon.-Sat. 8am-10pm). The town's well-known **Rázcesti puppet theater** is at Kollárova 18 (tel. 245 67; box office open Mon.-Fri. 7am-3pm; tickets 30-50Sk; closed July-Aug.). Many young people spend evening hours in the park surrounding the SNP Museum, where small children idly handle machines of war.

■ Near Banská Bystrica: Banská Štiavnica

Perched on a hill in the Štiavnica highlands, the monuments of Banská Štiavnica (BAN-ska shtee-ahv-NEE-tsa) testify to the town's past as a medieval gold-mining center and a bastion against the Turks during the 16th century. **Trojičné nám.,** at the town's heart, has a whopping big **plague column,** erected in 1764 to mark the plague of 1710. There's a somewhat dull **collection of rocks** at Trojičné nám. 6, and a much better art gallery two doors up, **Galéria národného umelca Josefa Kollára,** Trojičné nám. 8 (tel. 234 31). The historical collection is mediocre, but the two permanent exhibitions of the work of Edmund Gwerk and Josef Kollar make the visit worthwhile. (Open May-June and Sept. Tues.-Sun. 8am-4pm; July-Aug. Tues.-Sun. 9am-5pm; Oct.-April 8am-3pm. Tours on the hour, but no one minds if you wander through on your own. 20Sk, students 10Sk.) Up the hill at Starozámocká 11 (tel. 321 13), the **Starý zámok** (Old Castle) dominates the town. Tours leave hourly (from 9am-4pm) to visit the Romanesque funeral chapel and the ossuary.

Follow Sládkoviča just up from the **radnica** (town hall—check out the backwards-running clock) as it bends away to the left. You'll pass below the town's 17th-century **Klopačka** (Knock-tower); its resonant board once summoned miners to work at 5am. The building is now home to an exhibition about Slovak mining techniques (same hours as gallery above; 10Sk, students 5Sk). Sládkoviča ends by the Piargska brána (Piarg gate), and behind the nearby church stands the **Nový zámok** (New Castle; tel. 215 43), built in 1571 as a watchtower against Turkish invasions. Following the Turkish wars, it survived 200 years as a gunpowder storehouse and now houses statues of Turks, a model of a Turkish living room, weapons, and unobstructed views of the countryside from the top floor. Tours in Slovak (every 45min.) are accompanied by a written translation in English. (Open July-Aug. Tues.-Sat. 8am-4:30pm, Sun. 10am-4:30pm; May-June and Sept. Tues.-Sat. 8am-4pm, Sun. 10am-4pm; Oct.-April Tues.-Sat. 8am-3pm. 20Sk, students 10Sk.) Past Piargska brána, Sládkoviča becomes Hellova, and 1km or so along the road lies the **Banské Múzeum v Príroda** (Open-Air Mining Museum; tel. 229 71). The above-ground exhibit (free) is mildly interesting, but the star attraction is the journey along 1-2km of medieval mining tunnels. (Open May-Sept. Tues.-Sun. 8am-4pm; Oct.-Nov. 8am-3pm; last entry at 2pm. Tours start when 15 people have congregated. 30Sk, students 15Sk.)

Buses drive six times a day (4 per day on weekends) between Banská Bystrica and Banská Štiavnica (1hr., 33Sk), ending their trip a 20-minute walk away from the sights. The **tourist office,** Radničné nám. 1 (tel./fax 218 59), in the *radnica,* sells maps of the city (15Sk), books rooms, and plans tours of the area (open Mon.-Fri. 8am-6pm). A few pensions offer rooms, which might come in handy if the last weekend bus (at 1:45pm) leaves without you. **Postal code:** 969 00. **Phone code:** 0859.

■ Liptovský Mikuláš

Despite a history dating to 1286 and fame in Slovak folklore as the place where popular hero Juraj Janošik—who stole from the rich to give to the poor (sound familiar?)—was stuck on a spike in 1713, Liptovský Mikuláš (LIP-tov-skee mee-koo-LASH) is an ungripping town with a drab modern center. The nearby Nízke Tatry (Low Tatras), however, are much less crowded than their taller Carpathian cousins farther north, and only a short (and frequent) bus ride away from Liptovský Mikuláš.

Orientation and Practical Information Liptovský Mikuláš is best approached by train. The **train station** (tel. 228 42) lies on Stefanikova, and the **bus station** (tel. 236 38) is the asphalt lot directly outside. **Trains** run to Poprad (many per day, 40min.-1hr., 28-44Sk); Košice (12-15 per day, 2hr., 100Sk); and Bratislava (12-15 per day, 4hr., 158Sk). **Buses** run to Poprad (5 per day, 1-2hr., 46Sk). The **town center** is an easy 10-minute walk from the bus and train terminals. Follow Stefanikova towards the gas station at the bus station's far end, then turn right onto Hodžova. The town's main square, **nám. Mieru,** lies just past the post office and the tourist office, **Informačné Centrum,** nám. Mieru 1 (tel. 224 18), on the northern side of the square in the Dom Služieb complex. The staff speaks a little English, sells local hiking maps (ask for VKÚ sheet 122; in Slovak 64Sk, in German 85Sk) and foreign newspapers, and sorts out accommodation bookings and bicycle rental. (Open mid-June to mid-Sept. Mon.-Fri. 8am-7pm, Sat. 8am-2pm, Sun. noon-7pm; mid-Sept. to mid-June Mon.-Fri. 9am-6pm.) **VÚB,** Štúrova 19 (tel. 223 57), exchanges currency and has a **24-hour ATM** for Cirrus, EC, and MC (bank open Mon.-Wed. and Fri. 8am-noon and 1-5pm, Thurs. 8am-noon and 1-3pm). A machine **exchanges currency** at Štúrova 1. **Store luggage** in the lockers at the train station (5Sk). There's a **pharmacy** in Dom Služieb around the corner from the tourist office (open Mon.-Fri. 8am-5pm). The **post office,** Hodžova 1, is off nám. Mieru (open Mon.-Fri. 8am-7pm, Sat. 8am-noon). Coin and card **phones** stand outside. **Postal code:** 03100. **Phone code:** 0849.

Accommodations and Food Finding a bed shouldn't be a problem. Ask the tourist office if local **worker's hostels** are taking tourists, or about **private rooms.** Otherwise, dead-central **Hotel Kriváň,** Štúrova 5 (tel. 522 414; fax 242 43), is a good bet, offering clean, compact singles (220Sk), doubles (440Sk), and triples (590Sk), with baths, showers, toilets, and TVs in (slightly) more expensive rooms.

Get chocolate bars and other nourishment for hiking at the *potraviny* in the **obchodný dom** in the **Prior** building on nám. Miera (open Mon.-Fri. 8am-7pm, Sat. 7am-2pm). There are few good places for cooked food. **Liptovská Izba,** nám. Osloboditeľov 21 (tel. 51 48 53) has fine Slovak meals: *hotové jedlá* (40-65Sk), vegetarian *bryndzové halušky* (40Sk), or meaty *bravčovy rezeň na šampionoch* (80Sk), washed down with wine (24Sk per glass) in the all-wooden dining room (open Mon.-Sat. 10am-10pm, Sun. noon-10pm).

Sights The **Múzeum Janka Kráľa,** nám. Osloboditeľov 31 (tel. 225 54), presents an excellent survey of the town's history, starting with a prehistoric skull and ending with the liberation of the town in April 1945. An English guidebook (30Sk) is a handy companion (open June-Sept. Tues.-Fri. 9am-4pm, Sat.-Sun. 10am-5pm; off-season closed Sat.; 15Sk, students 10Sk). Also on nám. Osloboditeľov, **Kostol sv. Mikuláš** (Church of St. Nicholas) has stood since 1280. Statues of 19th-century nationalists and the saint himself surround the church. **Stará Evanjeliká Fara** (Old Evangelical Parsonage), Tranovského 8 (tel. 225 46), tries to convince visitors that Woodrow Wilson's Fourteen Points date back to the 1848 petition "Requirements of the Slovak Nation" (open Tues.-Fri. 8am-2pm, Sat.-Sun. by request in Múzeum Janka Kráľa; 10Sk, students 5Sk). **Židovská synagogá** (Jewish synagogue), on Hollého south of nám. Miera, has by its door a wrenching bronze memorial to the 885 Jews of Liptovský Mikuláš murdered by the Nazis: their names are recorded in the Múzeum Janka Kráľa.

Early July brings huge crowds to **Východna,** 20km east of Liptovský Mikuláš, for its **Folklore Festival,** a four-day drunken celebration of music, dance, and story-telling. If you're planning to stay in Liptovský Mikuláš, book rooms in advance, as the festival coincides with the Feast of St. Cyril and St. Methodius (July 5), and thousands of Slovaks descend on the region. For information, contact Regionálne Kultúrne Stredisko, Tranovského 2, 03180 Liptovský Mikuláš (tel. 229 80; fax 229 81).

■ Near Liptovský Mikuláš: Nízke Tatry

Liptovský Mikuláš is frequently used as a base for hiking in the **Nízke Tatry,** or Low Tatras. Despite their name, these mountains are not to be underestimated: "low" though they may be, their peaks still reach well above the tree line. If your first instinct is to get to the top of the tallest peak in the area—**Mt. Ďumbier,** at 2043m— here's one way to do it. Catch an early bus from platform 11 at Liptovský Mikuláš's bus station to **Liptovský Ján** (20min., 8Sk) and hike the blue-marked trail up the Štiavnica river and onto the **Ďumbierske sedlo** (saddle) by **Chata generála M.R. Štefanika** (Gen. M.R. Štefanika hut; about 4hr.). Then follow the red path up to the summit (1hr.). Doubling back, but following the signpost to **Chopok,** leads along the ridge to the neighboring peak (1½hr.). At the hut there, **Kammená chata,** you might be able to snag a bed (110Sk) as well as *Martiner* draft beer (25Sk) and a mug of tea (10Sk). From Chopok, it's an easy walk down to the bus stop at Jasná, but you may prefer to ride down on the chairlift (June-Aug. every 30min. until 4:40pm, Sept.-Nov. and mid-Feb. to mid-May until 4:20pm, mid-Dec. to mid-Feb. until 3:30pm; 80Sk). With **VKÚ sheet 122** (available at the tourist office in Liptovský Mikuláš; see p. 651), it's possible to compose endless hiking variations on the Chopok-Ďumbier theme; all the trails are well-marked and easy to follow. Buses go from Liptovský Mikuláš (15 per day, 30min., 12Sk) to the "Jasná" stop at Hotel Ski, 1km before Jasná, where signs point toward the chairlift up the mountain.

Demänovská ľadová jaskyňa, an **ice cave** midway between Liptovský Mikuláš and Jasná (15min. by bus from Liptovský Mikuláš, direction Jasná; 6Sk), is yet another treasure. Get off the bus at Kamenná chata, and follow signs 15 minutes up the hill to a valley view. The ice cave features bones from Ice Age bears and signatures of more recent 18th- and 19th-century visitors. The last part of the tour brings visitors to a frozen waterfall draped beneath bleached stone. (Open mid-May to mid-Sept. Tues.-Sun. 9am-4pm. Tours leave every 1-2hr.; contact the tourist office in Liptovský Mikuláš for info. 40Sk, students 20Sk.)

Also ask at the Liptovský Mikuláš tourist office (see p. 651) for info about watersports, paragliding, horseback-riding, climbing, and **bike rental** (250-300Sk per day) in Demänovská valley. Guidebooks with cycling tours (Slovak 39Sk, German 49Sk) include easily decodable maps. Windsurfing, boating, canoeing, and swimming— often with instruction—are available at **Autocamping Liptovský Trnovec,** 6km from Liptovský Mikuláš on Liptovský Mara, the local artificial lake. Again, ask the tourist office for details.

VYSOKÉ TATRY (THE HIGH TATRAS)

Spanning the border between Slovakia and Poland, the jagged Vysoké Tatry are the tallest peaks in the entire Carpathian range, rising sharply from the plain to the summits at 2500m. Millions of visitors pack the slopes each year, coming for the winter sports—the region is bidding for the 2006 Olympics—or the summer hiking trails that run over the saddles, through the valleys, and up to some of the highest peaks. While the resort towns are hardly exciting, nothing is more gripping than a good set of mountains, and these are some of Europe's finest. Budget accommodations are still easy to find—including cheap beds in the mountain *chaty* (huts)—and a ridiculously cheap mountain railway means it often doesn't matter where you stay.

■ Poprad

Poprad was born when Czechoslovakia glued together four sleepy mountain villages with drab apartment blocks. It's not a pretty place, but super transport lines to the Vysoké Tatry and the towns of the Spiš region, together with a looser accommodation scene than is found in the mountain resorts, work to make Poprad a good place to stay. Most travelers just pause here to change trains on the way to the Tatras, which rise sternly on the far side of the railroad tracks.

Orientation and Practical Information Trains (tel. 72 18 30) leave from the north edge of town to: Košice (every 1-2hr., 70min., 70Sk); Bratislava (12 per day, 4hr., 178Sk); and Kežmarok (9 per day, 30min., 7Sk; take train bound for Plavec). *Tatranská Elektrická Železnica* (*TEŽ*; electric train) connects Poprad with the Tatran resorts (about 1 per hour, up to 18Sk depending on destination), but buses are generally quicker and more frequent, if less fun. Buy tickets from the fairly user-friendly machines. **Buses** (tel. 233 90; information open Mon.-Fri. 7am-3pm), near the train station at the corner of Wolkerova and Alžbetina, head to: Zakopane in the Polish Tatras (3 per week, more in season, 2hr., 70Sk); Banská Bystrica (12 per day, 2½hr., 99Sk); Košice (10 per day, 2hr., 70Sk); and surrounding resorts. To get from the bus station to the tourist office in **nám. sv. Egídia,** walk behind the station on **Wolkerova,** pass through the lower floor of the train station, and follow the green "Centrum" signs through the park and then down **Mnoheľova. Popradská Informačná Agentúra,** nám. sv. Egídia 114 (tel. 186 or 721 700; fax 721 394), speaks some English and sells maps—including VKÚ sheet 113 of the Vysoké Tatry (64Sk)—and two useful English language guidebooks, *Everyman's Guide to the High Tatras* (12Sk), and *The Tatras and Surroundings* (66Sk), which is glossy and has a train and bus timetable attached. The staff has info about all sorts of recreation, and can also book accommodation anywhere in the region. (Poprad private rooms and some of the cheaper mountain *chatas* run DM10-15. Office open Mon.-Fri. 8am-7pm, Sat. 9am-1pm.) **Tatratour,** nám. sv. Egídia 19 (tel. 637 12; fax 638 89) is the local **American Express** representative, accepting traveler's checks at 2% commission (open Mon.-Fri. 9:30am-6pm, Sat. 9am-noon). **VÚB,** Mnoheľova 9 (tel. 605 1111), cashes AmEx and Visa traveler's checks at 1% commission (open Mon.-Wed. and Fri. 8am-noon and 1-5pm, Thurs. 8am-noon and 1-3pm). Cirrus/MC **ATMs** are around the corner and all over town; a Visa ATM is on the corner of nám. sv. Egídia and 1 Maja, where there's also a **currency exchange machine** to turn hard Western bank notes (including Czech *koruny*) into softish Slovak *koruny* (1% commission, min. 20Sk). **Luggage storage** at the station is 5Sk for a locker or 3Sk per day at the 24-hour office (closed for lunch noon-12:45pm). A **pharmacy, Lekáreň Altea,** heals at nám. sv. Egídia 29 (tel. 724 222; open Mon.-Fri. 7:15am-7:30pm, Sat. 8am-noon). The **post office** is at Mnoheľova 11 (tel. 640 02; open Mon.-Fri. 7am-6pm, Sat. 8am-11am). **Postal code:** 05800. **Phone code:** 092.

Accommodations and Food Poprad eagerly accommodates the annual tourist hordes with **booking agencies** on every block and **pensions** around every corner. Most places are decent—it's really just a matter of the age of the carpet and the softness of the toilet paper. **Domov Mládeže,** Karpatská 9 (tel. 634 14), is a large workers' hostel that doubles as a tourist hostel in summer. Walk down Alžbetina as it runs away from the station, then go right onto Karpatská. Basic furnishings, nice bedding, and clean washing facilities are offered at an absurdly low price (1- to 4-bed rooms 130Sk per person, 200Sk for only one night). Between the bus and train stations, **Hotel Európa,** Wolkerova 3 (tel. 72 18 83), rents out rooms with ghastly wallpaper and Čedok logos on the bedding. It's comfortable enough, if you can sleep through the rumbling trains and don't mind the communal bathrooms (singles 400Sk; doubles 550Sk; triples 850Sk). Tower block **Hotel Gerlach,** Hviezdoslavovo 2 (tel. 721 945; fax 636 63), off Mnoheľova, is similar to Hotel Európa, but quieter, and includes a pizzeria with a panorama on the 8th floor (open daily 7am-11pm) and a pool table in the bar (singles 350Sk; doubles with bath 790Sk; triples 900Sk).

Eateries range from expensive ethnic restaurants and Slovak sit-down establishments to cheap bistros and stand-up sausage kitchens. Try a pint of a local brew—*Spiš* this or *Tatranské* that. There's a daily fruit, vegetable, and flower **market** on Joliota Curiého, off the main square, and a **supermarket** on the top floor of the department store next to the tourist office (open daily until 7pm). Local restaurants

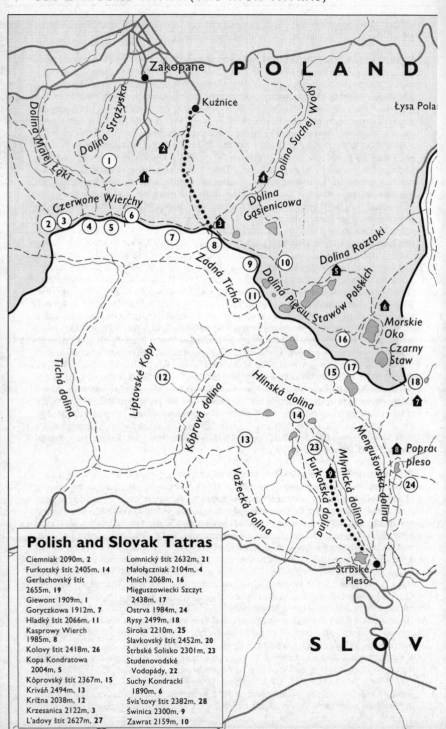

Polish and Slovak Tatras

Ciemniak 2090m, **2**
Furkotský štít 2405m, **14**
Gerlachovský štít 2655m, **19**
Giewont 1909m, **1**
Goryczkowa 1912m, **7**
Hladký štít 2066m, **11**
Kasprowy Wierch 1985m, **8**
Kolový štít 2418m, **26**
Kopa Kondratowa 2004m, **5**
Kôprovský štít 2367m, **15**
Kriváň 2494m, **13**
Krížna 2038m, **12**
Krzesanica 2122m, **3**
L'adový štít 2627m, **27**

Lomnický štít 2632m, **21**
Małołączniak 2104m, **4**
Mnich 2068m, **16**
Mięguszowiecki Szczyt 2438m, **17**
Ostrva 1984m, **24**
Rysy 2499m, **18**
Siroka 2210m, **25**
Slavkovský štít 2452m, **20**
Štrbské Solisko 2301m, **23**
Studenovodské Vodopády, **22**
Suchy Kondracki 1890m, **6**
Śvis'tový štít 2382m, **28**
Świnica 2300m, **9**
Zawrat 2159m, **10**

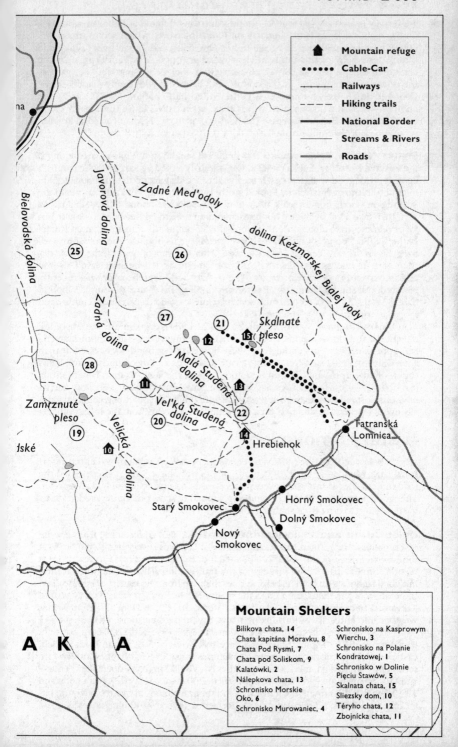

Mountain refuge

●●●●● **Cable-Car**

┼┼┼┼ **Railways**

- - - - **Hiking trails**

▬▬▬ **National Border**

——— **Streams & Rivers**

▬▬▬ **Roads**

Bielovodská dolina

Javorová dolina

Zadné Med'odoly

dolina Kežmarskej Bialej vody

25

26

Zadná dolina

27

21

15

Skalnaté pleso

12

28

Malá Studená dolina

11

13

Zamrznuté pleso

Vel'ká Studená dolina

22

19

20

14

Tatranská Lomnica

Velická dolina

10

Hrebienok

ślské

Starý Smokovec

Horný Smokovec

Dolný Smokovec

Nový Smokovec

AKIA

Mountain Shelters

Bilikova chata, 14
Chata kapitána Moravku, 8
Chata Pod Rysmi, 7
Chata pod Soliskom, 9
Kalatówki, 2
Nálepkova chata, 13
Schronisko Morskie Oko, 6
Schronisko Murowaniec, 4

Schronisko na Kasprowym Wierchu, 3
Schronisko na Polanie Kondratowej, 1
Schronisko w Dolinie Pięciu Stawów, 5
Skalnata chata, 15
Sliezsky dom, 10
Téryho chata, 12
Zbojnícka chata, 11

are heavily geared toward tourists—good value can be found at **Panorama Pizzeria** on the eighth floor of Hotel Gerlach, on Hviezdoslavovo, which serves pizzas (46-60Sk), heavily cauliflowered veggie dishes (19-35Sk), and Tatran beer (17Sk), and offers a fine view of the Tatras in clear weather (open daily 7am-11pm). Dining choices at **Egídius** (tel. 72 28 98), on Mnohelova, include the outdoor beer garden, the downstairs restaurant, or the upstairs candlelit cafe with funny-shaped chairs. Cabbage and sausage soup (20Sk) and grilled half-chicken (125Sk) are good choices—wash it all down with wine (28Sk; open daily 11am-11pm; major credit cards accepted). **Balkan Espresso** (tel. 636 86), nám. sv. Egídia near Zdravotnícka, serves up chocolate- and cream-flavored joy (6-10Sk; open daily 8am-9pm).

Sights Nám. sv. Egídia boasts a few medieval buildings; the most eye-catching is the fortified **Kostol sv. Egídia** (St. Egidius Church), erected by Saxons in the late 13th century, with good wall frescoes. If they've finished digging up the road outside, you might be able to get in. Central Poprad is otherwise very dull, but a little corner of the Spiš region is a 15-minute walk away in nearby **Spišská Sobota;** follow Štefánikova east, then take a left by the ice hockey stadium on unmarked Kežmarská (or take **bus** #2 or 3 in the same direction). All major sights, including the medieval Saxon **Kostol sv. Juraja** (St. George's Church) that gave the village its original name of **Georgensberg,** lie on the tiny, central **Sobotské nám.** After 45 years of neglect, the whole district, with its understated elegance and painted houses, has been declared historic and is currently under restoration. The Renaissance **watchtower** was recently restored, but still shows its age. **Podtatranské Múzeum** (Tatra Museum), Sobotské nám. 33 (tel. 72 13 23), reconstructs some old interiors and displays local crafts (open Mon.-Sat. 9am-4pm; 10Sk, students 4Sk).

At **Vináreň sv. Juraj,** Sobotské nám. 29 (tel. 72 14 11), drink in the shadow of the old church and, on weekends, enjoy the live music (open Tues.-Thurs. 3pm-2am, Fri.-Sat. 5pm-5am, Sun. 4pm-midnight). Many hotels have ground-floor bars. **Surprise City Club,** Štefánikova 4 (tel. 634 45), offers billiards and disco under black lights (open nightly 2pm-4am). For unpretentious noise, the **Beat Club** at Hotel Europa can't be—er—beat (open Tues.-Sat. 8pm-3am; small cover Fri.-Sat.) The city and its environs host **folklore festivals** at least once a month, with something going on virtually every weekend in summer; get a free schedule of events from the tourist office.

Starý Smokovec

Starý Smokovec (STAH-ree SMO-ko-vets) is the Vysoké Tatry's most central resort town, and, founded in the 17th century, one of the oldest. Cheap sleeps down the road in next-door Horný Smokovec makes it easily accessible to the budget traveler. The wooden church and Hotel Grand give a touch of style; otherwise, modern tastelessness plays to crowds of shuffling tourists.

Orientation and Practical Information TEŽ **trains** arrive from Poprad (every 30min.-1hr., 30min., 10Sk) and Tatranská Lomnica (every hr., 15min., 6Sk) at the town's lowest point, south of Hotel Grand. **Buses** (tel. 29 84) to many Tatra resorts stop in a parking lot just east of the train station. There are no street names, but good signposts on corners help, as does the **map** from the **tourist office**. Head up the road from the trains, then cross the main road veering left. The friendly staff of **Tatranská Informačná Kancelária** (tel. 34 40; fax 31 27), in Dom Služieb, provides weather info and sells various hiking maps, including the crucial **VKÚ Sheet 113** (64Sk in Slovak, 85Sk in German; open Mon.-Fri. 8am-noon and 12:30-6pm, Sat.-Sun. 8am-noon and 12:30-4pm). **Slovenská Sporiteľňa** (tel. 24 70), also in Dom Služieb, cashes traveler's checks and has two machines outside: one changes foreign currency (1% commission, min. 20Sk), the other is a Visa **ATM** (bank open Mon., Thurs., and Fri. 7:30am-noon and 12:30-3:30pm, Tues. 7:30am-noon, Wed. 7:30am-noon and 12:30-5pm). **VÚB,** around the left side of the shopping block above the bus stop, has a Cirrus/MC **ATM.** A **funicular** runs to Hrebienok (every 30-40min., one-way 40Sk, round-trip 50Sk). For equipment and guides, **T-ski** (tel. 42 32 00), in the ski lift station, offers everything from ski classes to river-rafting trips, and rents **bikes** (250Sk per day, afternoon 180Sk), **skis** (190-390Sk), and mountain **guides** (from 1500Sk per day; open daily 9am-5pm). There's a pharmacy, **Lekáreň U Zlatej Sovy** (tel. 42 21 64), on the second floor of Dom Služieb (open Mon.-Fri. 8am-noon and 1-4:45pm, Sat. 8am-noon). A **post office** (tel. 42 24 71) lies near the train station (open Mon.-Fri. 8am-4:30pm, Sat. 8-10am). **Postal code:** 6201. **Phone code:** 0969.

Accommodations and Food Along the road running east out of Starý Smokovec, the hamlet **Horný Smokovec** has plenty of options for the budget traveler. It's home to **Slovakoturist** (tel. 42 20 31), where the English-speaking staff books **mountain chaty** (350-450Sk), **private rooms** (250-300Sk), and cottages for six to eight people (about 2200Sk). Farther along the road (or two stops on the TEŽ toward Tatranská Lomnica), down a short path through the trees, is **Hotel Junior Vysoké Tatry** (tel. 42 26 61; fax 42 24 93), an admirable hostel with compact rooms and a disco club. (Singles 320Sk; doubles 610Sk; triples 760Sk during hiking or skiing seasons; beds 200Sk per person with ISIC or HI card. Breakfast included.) In Starý Smokovec itself, the not-so-young **Hotel Plesnivec** (tel. 25 35; fax 29 93), near the lift station and even higher than Hotel Grand, rents aging rooms with communal bathrooms (370SK per person).

There's a **grocery** in the shopping block above the bus station (open Mon.-Fri. 7:45am-7pm, Sat.-Sun. 8am-3pm), or try **Tatranská Kuracie,** just across the road from the grocery, which serves *Maďarský guláš* (69Sk) and the stuffed meat *Špecialita kúria* (112Sk; open daily 10am-8pm).

Hiking The funicular to **Hrebienok** (1285m) leads right to the heart of hiking country; alternatively, it's a 30-minute hike up the green trail through the pines. An easy 20-minute green trail from Hrebienok leads to the foaming **Studenovodské Vodopády** (Cold Waterfall). The eastward blue trail descends from the waterfall through the towering pines to **Tatranská Lomnica** (1½hr.). The long, red "*Tatranská magistrála*" trail travels west from Hrebienok to the chalet **Sliezsky Dom** (1670m; 250Sk per person), to **Chata Kapitána Moravku** (also 250Sk per person) on the shore of **Popradské Pleso.** From here, the red trail continues to **Štrbské Pleso.** A more daunting blue trail goes north from the *magistrála* to climb one of the highest Tatran peaks, the stony **Slavkovský Štít** (2450m; about 8hr. round-trip from Hrebienok; for advanced hikers only).

The *magistrála* also heads north from Hrebienok to **Skalnaté Pleso,** which has a nearby *chata* (see **Tatranská Lomnica: Sights and Hiking, p. 658**). The gentle two-hour climb takes in some excellent views. Take the green trail to Studenovodské vodopády, change to the blue, and at the old cabin foundation, head up the red. The hike to **Malá Studená Dolina** (Little Cold Valley) is also fairly relaxed; take the green trail from Hrebienok through barren landscape to **Téryho Chata** (2015m; 4hr.; 150Sk per person, though there may be an obligatory meal plan).

An intense six-hour hike leads through the immense **Veľká Studená Dolina** (Big Cold Valley) to **Zbojnícka Chata** (1960m; beds 170Sk). From Sliezsky dom, take the green trail to **Zamrznuté Pleso** (Cold Lake; 2047m), change to the blue towards the *chata,* and follow the crashing **Veľký Studený Potok** (Big Cold Stream), which will drop you off at Studenovodské vodopády. From here, the green trail returns to Hrebienok. Trails are open July-September only.

■ Near Starý Smokovec: Štrbské Pleso

Having hosted the "Interski" Championship in 1975, Štrbské Pleso (SHTREB-skay PLAY-so) has joined Poprad in a bid for the 2006 Winter Olympics. For the moment, the hotels and ski-jump towers that rose during the 70s clutter the placid **Štrbské pleso** (Lake Štrbské), while gaggles of schoolkids add screams and whistles to the mess. Then again, one can't hope to enjoy the Tatras' most-beloved ski resort alone. The town is the range's highest settlement and a great starting point for hikes.

Just one lift works in the summer, hoisting visitors up to **Chata pod Soliskom** (1840m), in a rocky loft overlooking the lake and the expansive plains behind Štrbské Pleso. A small restaurant under the lift station at the top, **Bivak Club,** offers tea (15Sk), shots of liquor (30-40Sk), and Tatran fast food: soup (30Sk), sausage with bread and mustard (35Sk), and, of course, beer (25Sk). The lift is 10 minutes up the road from the trains (June-Sept. 8am to mid-afternoon; June and Sept. 40Sk one-way, 60Sk round-trip; July-Aug. 60Sk/90Sk). Once at the top, hike to the peak of **Predné Solisko** (2093m); otherwise the only route is the blue path back down to Štrbské Pleso.

Two magnificent day hikes start from Štrbské Pleso—both involve stretches with chains. The yellow route, marked one way only, heads out along **Mlynická Dolina** (valley) and visits five tarns (mountain lakes) and **Vodopád Skok** (Skok Waterfall), crossing **Bystré Sedlo** (saddle; 2314m) and circling the **Štrbské Solisko** peak (2302m) before returning to Štrbské Pleso (about 7hr.). The second hike takes you to the top of **Rysy** (2499m), on the Polish-Slovak border, which is Poland's highest peak and the highest Tatra you're allowed up without a guide. From Štrbské Pleso, follow the *magistrála* to **Chata Kapitána Moravku** (1500m; 250Sk per person), take the blue trail up the side of the valley, and then the red for the ascent of Rysy, past the lakes, **Zabie Plesá,** to **Chata pod Rysmi** (2250m; 120Sk per person), where there is free hot tea for anyone who brings up 5kg of supplies from Chata Kapitána Moravku. Rysy's peak is 40 minutes from the *chata;* allow a good seven hours for the round-trip, and be careful on the descent.

The first stretch along the *magistrála* from Štrbské Pleso to **Popradské pleso** (1¼hr.) attracts all levels of hikers. Before reaching the lake, it branches into two trails: the green runs to the *pleso* along the rambling **Hincov Potok** (stream), while the red continues parallel to it with a view of the stream's valley. **Chata Kapitána Moravku,** at the top, offers lakeside grogs.

From the *chata,* the 15-minute yellow trail (open July-Oct.) leads south to **Symbolický cintorín** (1525m). Built 1936-40 by the painter Otakar Štafl, the cemetery serves as "a memorial to the dead, and a warning for the living." Painted crosses, metal plaques, and broken propeller blades find a serene home on the side of mountain **Ostrva** (1984m). The trail ultimately ends at a paved blue path. The tired can descend the lacking-in-views blue trail down to a TEŽ stop (45min.), but backtracking to Štrbské Pleso is far more interesting. The *magistrála* trail continues from the *chata* for hours along scenic ridges to **Hrebienok** (see **Starý Smokovec: Hiking,** p. 656). There's a bit of a climb up to **Sedlo pod Ostrvou** (1959m), but it levels off after that.

TEŽ **trains** leave hourly from Štrbské Pleso for Starý Smokovec (40min., 14Sk) and Poprad (70min., 18Sk), but the rare **buses** shuttle to Poprad faster (50min., 18Sk). Budget travelers should leave the town before dusk, since hotel prices beat the town's altitude. For food supplies, the **grocery** in the Obchodny Dom building by the station is open daily 8am-7pm.

■ Tatranská Lomnica

With snow as deep as Štrbské Pleso's, and sleeps as cheap as Smokovec's, Tatranská Lomnica (ta-TRAN-ska lom-NEE-tsa) is becoming increasingly popular as the Vysoké Tatry's budget ski resort. During summer, however, few hiking trails lead directly from this town, and the ear-popping lift to Lomnický Štít is the town's only attraction.

Orientation and Practical Information Buses are the best way to get here from Poprad (every ½-1hr., 30min., 12Sk). **TEŽ trains** (tel. 967 884) run from Starý Smokovec and Štrbské Pleso. With no street names and buildings somewhat scattered, this village can be confusing, but all the vital services are within spitting distance of the train station. **Tatratour** (tel. 967 204; fax 967 992), in a small corner on the second floor of Obchodný Dom Javor, by the tracks, has skeletal information on the town's hotels (open Mon.-Fri. 9am-noon and 12:30-5:45pm). An **information**

board about halfway between the train stop and Hotel Lomnica, away from the tracks, displays the location of hotels, pensions, and restaurants, and has a free phone to call for reservations and neat buttons to press to find out whether rooms are available. **Currency exchanges** pop up around town, including **Slovenská Sporiteľňa** (tel. 96 72 59; fax 96 76 67), in the woods behind the train station, which cashes traveler's checks and has a 24-hour Visa **ATM** (open Mon. and Thurs.-Fri. 7:45am-3pm, Tues. 7:45am-1pm, Wed. 8am-5pm). **Poľhobank**, right on the track across from the railroad station, has a Cirrus/EC/MC **ATM**. In Slalom Restaurant, on the main road near the train stop, **WR Šport** (tel. 46 81 43) rents bikes (250Sk per day), in-line skates (150Sk per day), skateboards (100Sk per day), and skis (open daily 8am-8pm). The **post office** (tel. 96 72 00) lies behind the train station (open Mon.-Fri. 7:30-11:30am and noon-4pm, Sat. 8-10am). **Postal code:** 05960. **Phone code:** 0969.

Accommodations and Food Follow the road southeast out of Tatranská Lomnica, to where the campsites lurk on the edge of the National Park. The large **Eurocamp FICC** (tel. 46 77 41; fax 46 73 46), 4km from town, has its own train stop (1 train per hr. or so, 4Sk), and offers sterile doubles with communal bathrooms (570Sk), 100 spacious bungalows with spotless showers (quads 1600Sk), and tent sites (90Sk per person; campsite open June-Sept.). A sports store on the grounds **rents bikes** (220Sk per day), in-line skates (40Sk per day), and skis (150Sk per day; open daily 8am-8pm). A grocery store, disco, restaurants, bar, and movie theater mean that you want for nothing. A 10-minute walk away from the mountains from the Eurocamp FICC stop, **Športcamp** (tel. 46 72 88) offers tiny, shiny lacquered-wood rooms with shared showers (170Sk per person), and tent sites (68Sk per person; reception open daily 6am-10pm). If you don't have a tent, don't feel bad—try the orange **Penzión Bělín,** in the center of the town (tel. 46 77 78). Follow the green walkway from the station for two minutes through the gardens, and a sign will point you right (singles 170Sk; doubles 340Sk; triples 750Sk).

There's a fine **supermarket** just behind the main station building (open Mon.-Fri. 7:45am-7pm, Sat.-Sun. 8am-3pm). Of the town's restaurants, **Reštaurácia Júlia** (tel. 46 79 47), 200m below the station (follow the sign) is an attractive option, with garlic and egg soup (20Sk) and garlicky pork chops (105Sk). Vegetarians or those who can't cope with garlic can take refuge in a large plate of *halušky* (50Sk; open daily 11:30am-9:30pm).

Sights and Hiking Get tickets early for the remarkable lift up to **Lomnický Štít** (2634m), the Tatras' second-highest peak. Follow the signs around town to the *lanova draba,* mini-cabins that ride up to the crystal-clear glacial lake of **Skalnaté Pleso** (1751m; 150Sk one-way; tickets on sale around 7am), where a cable car ascends to the summit (a steep 300Sk each way) for a staggering view of just about everywhere. The craggy mountain peak has good picnic spots; at the lake, **Skalnata Chata** is an admirable refreshment stop. A second lift also plows the Tatranská Lomnica-Skalnaté Pleso furrow, with its lower terminal just below Grand Hotel Praha (runs 7am-4pm, July-Aug. until 6:15pm; 15 ascents each day).

Hiking is generally better from Starý Smokovec or Štrbské Pleso, but a few full-day hikes are accessible from Tatranská Lomnica's lift—a trail from **Skalneté Pleso** toward Lomnická vyhliadka and then to **Zamkovské Chata** (1hr.; beds 220Sk) brings hikers to **Malá Studená Dolina** (valley) and **Téryho Chata** (2hr.; beds 150Sk). Beyond, the yellow trail branches left toward Priečne sedlo and **Zbonjnícka chata** (beds 170Sk) at the head of **Veľká Studená Dolina** (2hr.). This leads back toward civilization in the form of Hrebienok (3hr.) and its funicular down to Starý Smokovec. This is an ambitious hike—bring water, warm clothes, and a VKÚ map; start early; and pay attention to weather. The blue trail from Tatranská Lomnica to **Vodopády Studeného Potoka** (cold waterfalls) and back to Tatranská Lesná is gentler.

SPIŠ

Tourists know Spiš (SPISH) only as neighbor of the Tatras and home of Kežmarok. But to the east, flatter land leads to tiny towns where villagers walk their cows and the lawnmower has not yet replaced the scythe. In the minds of romantics, the white sprawling ruins of Spišský hrad rule the region, and Levoča, home of the world's tallest Gothic altar, bustles with the wealthy merchants who placed it there. For centuries an autonomous province of Hungary with a large Saxon population, Spiš made its last bid for independence in 1918, and the Germans were evicted in 1945, but the towns, churches, and ruins that remain are well worth a day or two.

■ Kežmarok

Prosperous Kežmarok (KEZH-ma-rok) has always been marked by conflict: the townsfolk against the rulers in the castle, the Catholics against the Protestants, and everybody against neighboring Levoča. As late as 1918, the townsfolk proclaimed their own republic, but were quickly incorporated into the new Czechoslovak state. These struggles threw up Kežmarok's finest buildings—three remarkable churches and the old castle—making the town a pleasure to visit. Cheap accommodations and a train line to Poprad make it a feasible base for exploring the nearby peaks of the Vysoké Tatry.

Orientation and Practical Information Trains run to and from Poprad (12 per day, 20min., 7Sk) from the stately, bright yellow station (tel. 32 89) northwest of town. **Buses** arrive next door under blue and yellow canopies—eight daily to Levoča, 10 to Starý Smokovec, 20 to Tatranská Lomnica, and lots and lots to Poprad (30min., 10Sk). Cross the river by the bridge farther over to the left, and follow MUDr. Alexandra to the main **Hlavné nám.,** where the Baroque tower of the *radnica* rises above two-story dwellings. Hiding in an alcove at Hlavné nám. 46, the Anglophone staff of the **tourist office** (tel./fax 40 47) sells a handy **map** of town (5Sk) and books accommodations (private rooms from 150Sk, pensions 15-16DM; open Mon.-Fri. 8:30am-5pm, Sat. 9am-2pm). **Slovenská Sporiteľňa,** MUDr. Alexandra 41 (tel. 30 41), **exchanges currency** commission-free and has a Visa **ATM** outside (open Mon., Thurs., and Fri. 7:15am-3:30pm, Tues. 7:15am-1pm, Wed. 7:15am-4:30pm). A Cirrus/MC **ATM** waits outside the **VÚB bank** on Hviezdoslavova, off Hlavné nám. There's a **pharmacy** nearby, Lekáreň Luna, Hviezdoslavova 9 (open Mon.-Fri. 7:30am-5pm, Sat. 8am-noon). The **post office,** Mučeníkov 2 (tel. 52 28 22), lies past the VÚB, where the street changes to Mučeníkov. It's hidden behind a row of trees (open Mon.-Fri. 8am-noon and 1-7pm, Sat. 8am-noon). **Postal code: 06001. Phone code: 0968.**

Accommodations and Food There shouldn't be a problem finding cheap accommodations in Kežmarok, and the tourist office (see above) is always there to help. **Penzión No. 1,** Michalska 1 (tel. 46 00), is family-run and couldn't be more welcoming. Turn left out of the station and it's the first building you come to, with comfy rooms and a big, friendly dog, too (doubles and triples 150Sk per person). Receptionists have been replaced by security heavies at the ski-lodge **Hotel Štart** (tel. 52 29 15; fax 52 29 16), off Pod lesom behind the castle (wood-paneled singles 160Sk; doubles with bath 440Sk). A cheap Slovak meal can be had at the improbably named **Restaurant Tiffany,** Hlavné nám. 40. *Maďarský guláš* with *knedle* (that's Hungarian goulash and dumplings; 37Sk) and the sausage starter *Bratislavské párky* (20Sk) are among the options, as is *Kamzík* beer (0.5L 12Sk; open Mon.-Sat. 8am-10pm, Sun. 9am-9pm). Groceries punctuate the town center; the most interesting is the tofu propaganda center **Enzym,** Hradné nám. 20 (open Mon.-Fri. 9am-noon and 1-5pm).

Sights and Entertainment From the main Hlavné nám., a walk down Hviez-doslavova leads to Kežmarok's highlight, not the mighty Nový Evanjelický Kostol (New Evangelical Church), but its much smaller next-door neighbor, the **Drevený Atikulárny Kostol** (Wooden Articulated Church). Three constraints governed its construction in 1717: anti-Protestant regulations required the church to be outside the town walls, hence the location; to be built without a foundation, hence the sinking feeling; and to be paid for out of parish funds alone, hence the decision to build entirely out of wood. The astonishing Baroque interior of yew and lime bursts with imaginative talent; even the nails are wood, and the porthole-shaped windows are the mark of the Swedish sailors who helped to build it. When the church sank too low for comfort, local Protestants erected the colossal **Nový Evanjelický Kostol** alongside, a mesmerizing mix of Romanesque, Byzantine, Renaissance, and Middle Eastern elements. The strict interior symmetry explains the presence of two pulpits. The Kežmarok-born Imre Thököly, exiled to Turkey for fighting the Habsburgs, now rests in peace in his own private vault. (Both churches open June-Sept. daily 9am-noon and 2-5pm, Oct.-May Tues. and Thurs. 10am-noon; tour 20Sk, students 10Sk.)

In the middle of the Old Town, **Kostol sv. Kríža** (Church of the Holy Cross) dominates nám. Požiarnikov. Open by request at the priest's office (opposite the back entrance to the church), the interior boasts several 15th-century Gothic altars, two organs, and some rather fine frescoes. The church was built to be a Catholic bastion against Protestantism, but turned Protestant, and then mercurially reverted to Catholicism. Next to the church is the extremely elegant 1591 **zvonica** (watchtower), the most famous landmark in Kežmarok (closed to the public).

Hlavná and Nová culminate at the impressive **Kežmarský hrad** (castle), Hradné nám. 42 (tel. 41 53). Owned by the powerful Habsburgs, Thurzos, and Thökölys, and often at war with the town, the 15th-century fortification fashionably confounds styles by wearing a fine Renaissance decor on its stocky Gothic body. Its large, empty tower was the 16th-century prison of Beata Laska, the owner of the castle, whose trip to the Vysoké Tatry—the first ever recorded—angered the husband she left behind. The courtyard contains the foundations of the 13th-century Saxon church and is worth a look. The boring and compulsory guided tour in Slovak around the **Kežmarok Múzeum** (tel. 26 18) makes the trip inside the castle less attractive, although you do see an old pharmacy interior, an exhibit devoted to pioneer radiologist Dr. Alexander, and a fine 1657 baroque chapel at the end. (Open May-Sept. Tues.-Fri. 9am-5pm with tours every 30min. except at 12:30pm, Sat.-Sun. 9am-5pm with tours on the hour except at noon; Oct.-April Tues.-Sat. 9am-5pm, with tours on the hour except at noon. 20Sk, students 10Sk.)

The *hrad* hosts a party every night at the **Castellan Club** (tel. 27 80), in the castle wall at the head of Starý Trh, underneath the castle. Shake down under disco lights, shoot some pool, or just watch the fish behind the bar (open Sun.-Thurs. 8:30pm-3am, Fri.-Sat. 8:30pm-5am; free for women, small cover for men).

■ Levoča

The wealth of medieval Levoča (LEH-vo-cha) was due to its position on the Hungarian trading routes coupled with the "Law of Storage," the imperial concession that forced merchants passing through to stay 14 days and offer all they had for sale at wholesale prices. To this commercial prosperity was added artistic distinction in the early 16th century, when Majster Pavol's workshop pioneered an expressive style of wood-carving and erected the world's tallest Gothic altar in Chrám sv. Jakuba (St. James's Church). Today's town feeds off this illustrious past—modernity somewhat passed it by—with two kinds of visitors: tourists inspecting the walled medieval center, and Catholics assembling for the annual Festival of Marian Devotion in early July.

Orientation and Practical Information Relegated to a sidetrack on Slovakia's railway system, Levoča is reached most easily by bus. The **bus station** (tel. 51 22 30) rarely opens its info booth, but departure times are listed on a large billboard.

Buses hop to Košice (8 per day, 2hr., 62Sk); Poprad (frequent, 30min., 18Sk); and Prešov (hourly, 2hr., 128Sk). Turn right out of the bus station, right again along the main road, and duck under the arch that appears on the left to walk up to **nám. Majstra Pavla,** the center of everything. There's an infrequent **local bus** (5Sk) that covers the same distance by a much more circuitous route. The helpful **tourist office,** nám. Majstra Pavla 58 (tel. 37 63), has lots of information about both Majstr Pavol and the town, and can book *penzión* accommodations (300Sk per person; open Mon. 9am-5pm, Tues.-Fri. 9am-6pm, Sat.-Sun. 9:30am-5:30pm). The small **VÚB,** nám. Majstra Pavla 28 (tel. 51 43 16), changes traveler's checks at 1% commission (open Mon.-Wed. and Fri. 8am-noon and 1-4:30pm, Thurs. 8:30am-2pm). Its Cirrus/MC **ATM** is across the square in the corner by Uholná. **Slovenská Sporiteľňa,** nám. Majstra Pavla 56, has a Visa **ATM.** There's a **pharmacy** at nám. Majstra Pavla 13 (tel. 51 24 56; open Mon.-Fri. 7:30am-5pm, Sat. 8am-noon). The **post office** is at nám. Majstra Pavla 42 (tel. 24 89; open Mon.-Fri. 8am-noon and 1-4:30pm, Sat. 8-11:30am). **Telephones** stand outside. **Postal code:** 05401. **Phone code:** 0966.

Accommodations and Food Except for the first weekend in July, when around 250,000 pilgrims come to town, finding accommodations shouldn't be a problem. The tourist office can book local pensions (see above) and has a list of nearby campsites. Cheaper hotels lie outside the medieval center, but not too far. For **Hotel Texon,** Francisciho 45 (tel. 51 44 93), catch the local bus and hop off when you see the white Obchodné centrum Texon building. The modern hostel's rooms are nicely carpeted, with Majster Pavol pics on every wall. Every two rooms share a bathroom (180Sk for 1-2 nights; 150Sk for longer stays; reception is more a concept than a place—wander around until you find the friendly staff). **Hotel Faix,** Probstner-ova cesta 22 (tel. 51 23 35), lies by the town wall, an easy five-minute walk from the bus station. The aging doubles (480Sk, with shower 720Sk) are a better value than the singles (440Sk, with shower 680Sk). Two floors share one bathroom.

There's a **grocery** at nám. Majstra Pavla 45 (open Mon.-Fri. 6am-7pm, Sat. 6am-1pm, Sun. 7am-noon). **U 3 Apoštolov,** nám. Majstra Pavla 11 (tel. 51 23 02), is wildly popular, serving *Apoštolská špecialita* (a meaty stew stuffed into a potato pancake; 117Sk) and other *levočské* and *spišské* dishes (40-150Sk), as well as *Zlatý bažant* beer (19Sk). The menu has English translations (open Mon.-Sat. 9am-10pm, Sun. 10am-10pm; AmEx/MC). With a photo of the restaurant's spiritual leader above the door, **Vegetarián,** Uholná 3 (tel. 51 45 76), offers a cheaper lunchtime alternative, with four veggie dishes served up each day (35-42Sk) with soups (6-8Sk) and salads (7-8Sk). The cafeteria-style service makes deciphering a Slovak menu unnecessary (open Mon.-Fri. 11am-3pm).

Sights Levoča's star attraction is the 14th-century **Chrám sv. Jakuba** (St. James's Church), which contains the tallest Gothic altar in the world, a staggering 18.62m, and the result of 10 years' work by—predictably enough—Majster Pavol, from 1507-1517. Highlights are the depiction of the Last Supper, the 2.5m statues of James, Mary, and John the Evangelist, and the smaller Church Fathers above. To the left of the altar, a medieval mural depicts the seven deeds of bodily mercy as well as the seven deadly sins. Another mural presents the sad tale of St. Dorothy. Thrust into a pagan land, she was given the choice of heathenry with a rich husband or chaste Christianity with a torturous death. What could she do? She was a saint, after all. Unfortunately, she never found the ruby slippers, and the mural shows her terrible fate. Putting 2Sk into the "Automatic Info" box will get you five minutes of commentary on the sculptures in English or Hungarian. (Church open Sun.-Mon. 1-6pm, Tues.-Sat. 9am-6pm; closes at 4pm in winter. 20Sk, students 10Sk.)

Three branches of the **Spišske Múzeum** are dotted around the main square. By far the best is in **Dom Majstra Pavla** at #20, with an exhibition on the master's work that contains high-quality facsimiles of much of his best stuff and allows you to get much closer to the amazing Last Supper than you can in the church itself—anguished Judas at the front has his pouch of silver draped over his shoulder. An English tour is offered, but is not compulsory. Pay 5Sk more and the staff will let you into Levoča's **Klietka Hanby** (Cage of Shame), the oversized birdcage in the square where women of supposedly loose morals were pilloried in the 16th century. The **radnica,** in the middle of the square, is more interesting for its architecture than for the exhibit of armor and local crafts it houses. According to legend, the white lady now painted on one of the doors betrayed the town by giving the city's keys to her lover—an officer in the invading Hungarian army. The museum staff will try to show you a 20-minute video about Levoča's history—it's in English and perfectly watchable, and might persuade you the town's more than a one-majster show. The third part of the **Múzeum,** at #40, is an only moderately interesting collection of local painting and woodwork. (All museums open May-Oct. Tues.-Sun. 9am-5pm, Nov.-April Tues.-Sun. 8am-4pm, with a 30min. lunch break; each is 15Sk, students 5Sk.)

Three km from Levoča and clearly visible from the town, the neo-Gothic **Bazilika Panny Marie** (Basilica of the Virgin Mary) stands on top of Mariánská hora, attracting 250,000 pilgrims in the first weekend in July for a festival of Marian devotion which culminates in a Sunday morning 10am Mass—led by the Pope himself in 1995.

Spišské Podhradie and Žehra

There's nothing to see in Spišské Podhradie (SPISH-skay pod-HRA-dyeh) itself, but on the hills above the valley are two of Slovakia's finest monuments. West of town, walled **Spišska Kapitula,** the region's religious capital, contains **Katedrála sv. Martina** (St. Martin's Cathedral), with some fine medieval frescoes. The clergy were driven out by scientific socialists in 1948, but have since recolonized the place. **Spišský hrad,** central Europe's largest castle, sprawls in magnificent white over the mountain opposite. There's been a fortified settlement here for 2000 years, but today's ruins are 12th- to 15th-century, the remains of the Hungarian castle that dominated the Spiš region until it burned down in 1780. Many paths lead to the castle, but perhaps the most satisfying is the little-worn, grassy 2km trek from the left side of the town's cemetery. Watch out for cow patties. It's a good walk, but the ruins are much less interesting once you get inside, and the small museum collection is dull. The view from the top turret, on the other hand, is not a little spectacular (open May-Oct. daily 9am-6pm; foreigners 40Sk).

The real highlight of the day is the church at **Žehra,** about 4km away. From the castle entrance, descend to the parking lot and hike along the marked trail leading out the other side, past the limestone crags and down into the wide valley. **Kostol Svätého Ducha** (Church of the Holy Spirit) is easy to spot, with its onion-shaped dome on top of the tower, and is filled with remarkable 14th-century frescoes uncovered in the 1950s. The church is usually locked, but the priest, at house #87 nearby, will open it up for visitors. It's about 6km along the road back to Spišské Podhradie.

Buses head to Poprad (hourly or so until 9pm, 1hr., 45Sk), Levoča (hourly until 9:30pm, 20min., 10Sk), and Prešov (12 per day until 7pm, 1½hr.). If you really want to stay here overnight, **Areatour,** Marianské nám. 22 (tel. (0966) 81 11 54), can find local accommodations (open Mon.-Fri. 7:30am-4pm). Marianské nám. has little to offer in the way of restaurants, so try the **potraviny** (grocery), at #4 (open Mon.-Fri. 5:30am-7pm, Sat. 5:30am-2pm, and Sun. 7:30am-4pm). **VÚB,** Marianské nám. 34 (tel. 81 11 49), exchanges traveler's checks (open Mon.-Wed. and Fri. 8am-noon and 1-4:30pm, Thurs. 8:30am-2pm). The **post office** is at Marianské nám. 1 (open Mon.-Fri. 7:30am-noon and 1-5pm, Sat. 8-11am). **Postal code:** 5304. **Phone code:** 0966.

Slovenský Raj

South of Poprad and on the other side of the Nízke Tatry lies the Slovenský Raj (Slovak Paradise) National Park. Fast-flowing streams have carved deep ravines into the limestone hills, and the whole region is smothered in pine forests and liberally marked with summer hiking trails and winter cross-country ski routes.

Orientation and Practical Information Nestled in a gorge on the shores of the man-made lake Palcmanská Maša, Dedinky (pop. 400) is the largest of the towns on the Slovenský Raj's southern border. The easiest way to get there is to catch the **bus** from Poprad (10 per day, 1hr., 24Sk) heading for Rožňava, which stops at the **Dobšinská ľadová jaskyňa** (see below), then at **Stratená** (see below), and then at a junction 2km south of Dedinky. The sign pointing to Hotel Raj shows the road to take; then look for the yellow-marked trail that leads to the village. There is a train station near the village, but **trains** really only shunt along the obscure Margecany-Červená skala branch line. Dedinky's **post office** is behind the wooden tower near the bus stop (open Mon.-Fri. 7:30am-3:30pm, Sat. 7:30-8:30am). **Postal code:** 4973. **Phone code:** 0942.

Pick up a copy of **VKÚ sheet 124,** one of the excellent green maps, at a tourist office or bookshop before entering the region. If there's been a third edition for 1998, get that one, otherwise the 1995 edition should be fine (about 60Sk in Slovak, 85Sk in German). A **chairlift** runs from Hotel Priehrada up to Chata Geravy (hourly; June Mon. 9am-3pm, Tues.-Sun. 9am-4pm; July-Aug. Mon. 9am-3pm, Tues.-Sun. 9am-4:30pm; Sept.-May daily 9am-2:45pm; round-trip 60Sk; one-way 40Sk). **Geret Tours** (tel. 73 10 16; open daily in summer 9am-6pm), along the town's only road, rents four-person **rowboats** (30Sk per hr.) and two-person **paddle boats** (40Sk per hr.). Street **bikes** are 20Sk per hour; mountain bike tours cost more, as the park only permits off-road cycling with a proper guide—the happy chappies at Geret have a photo-catalogue of tours, and 500Sk or so will hire the necessary bikes and guide.

Accommodations and Food It's a good idea to book ahead in July, August, and January. In Dedinky, **Hotel Priehrada** (tel. 982 12; fax 982 21) deals out dated rooms with a view of the lake (200Sk per person; shared bath and toilets), and books *chaty* behind the hotel, which are just as clean (180Sk; lower prices Sept. to mid-Dec. and April-June). It also has a preposterously cheap **campsite** in front of the lake (20Sk per tent per night, 10Sk per person). **Penzión Pastierňa**, Dedinky 42 (tel. 17 81 75), where the green trail descends into the village, has good rooms (250Sk) and a restaurant downstairs serving the usual Slovak fare—meaty dishes (56-90Sk), *halušky* (59Sk), and red wine (23Sk per glass). The chairlift from Dedinky will take you to **Chata Geravy,** which is a great point for starting hikes, and also has small rooms with huge pillows. (Rooms 150Sk; with half-pension 300Sk; with full-pension 400Sk; book rooms at Hotel Priehrada before going up. Guests at the *chata* get a special rate on the chairlift: 30Sk round-trip.) In addition, almost every home in Dedinky doubles as a **pension** (about 200Sk per person). Solo travelers be warned: owners may be reluctant to take just one, but keep looking. Nearby **Stratená,** a one-road town surrounded by jagged cliffs and usefully on the bus route, is home to several room-renting families (again around 200Sk per person), as well as to **Chata Stratenká,** Stratená 51 (tel. 981 67), where rooms are 200Sk, bathrooms are shared, and the restaurant downstairs closes early (8pm in July-Aug., otherwise 6pm) but fills you up fairly cheaply. Stock up on those necessary carbs at the **grocery** in Dedinky (open Mon.-Fri. 7am-6pm, Sat. 7am-5pm, Sun. 9am-5pm), or at the one at the base of the ice cave trail (see below), which also operates a **buffet** with soup and bread to warm you up after the icy cave (grocery open Mon. 7:30am-noon, Tues.-Fri. 7:30am-5:30pm, Sat. 8:30am-4pm).

Sights and Hiking Almost 150,000 cubic meters of frozen water survive from the last Ice Age in the 19km stretch of **Dobšinská ľadová jaskyňa** (ice cave). The 30-minute tour covers only 475m of the cave, but that's enough to inspire awe at the ice monster lurking below, with hall after hall of frozen columns, gigantic ice wells, and hardened waterfalls. The blue trail from the parking lot is 20min. long and gets quite steep. (Open mid-May to June Tues.-Sun. 9:30am-2pm; July-Aug. 9am-4pm, Sept. 9:30am-2pm. Hourly Slovak tours 60Sk, students 55Sk; English 100Sk, students 85Sk.)

This is a national park, so camping and fire-lighting are prohibited. Cascade trails are marked one-way—you can go up, but not down. Some trails are closed November to June to those without certified guides. Don't worry about red marks on trees unless you want to chop them down.

Biele Vody (White Waters, 1½hr.): This is the trail in all the pictures. The hike, heading up to one of the park's many rapids, involves ladders and is one-way, so there's no turning back even for bad cases of vertigo. From Hotel Priehrada in Dedinky, take the red trail to Biele Vody. The blue cascade trail will be on the left. Chata Geravy (see Dedinky) waits at the top, and the green trail leads back down, or ride the roller-coaster lift.

Havrania skala (Crow's Cliff, 2½hr.): From Stratená, the green train leads up the hill to the spring **Občasný prameň** in an hour, or from Chata Geravy it's 1½hr. through hillside meadows along the yellow trail. From the (underwhelming) spring, a 30min. climb up the steep, earthy yellow trail leads to the gorgeous lookout over almost everything on top of Havrania skala. The yellow trail continues downhill, a steep hour-long descent, to meet the road just west of Stratená—turn left when you hit tarmac.

Vemký Sokol (6-8hr.). A more demanding hike leads into the heart of Slovenský Raj and up its deepest gorge. Follow the road west from Stratená or east out of Dobšinská ľadová jaskyňa. At the head of the big U-bend, take the green trail running north, over the Sedlo Kopanec (991m) and along the stream. Turn right onto the road and take the red path to the bottom of the gorge. The one-way yellow trail leads up the ravine, criss-crossing the mountain stream. Your feet will get wet and muddy; the logs are slippery; and some of the walkways encourage belief in a Supreme Being. From the top, the red path returns to Chata Geravy and the descent to Dedinky. Hugely satisfying. Those who don't like wet feet can follow the red trail from the bottom of the gorge to the top around the northern edge (30min. longer).

ŠARIŠ

Tucked in east Slovakia, Šariš is still struggling to deal with many of the political events of the last 80 years. The deeply religious majority never really liked the Communists, but the current wave of fierce capitalism still strikes them as a little too gung-ho. Nonetheless, Košice did rule all of Czechoslovakia for three months in 1945, and long before the revolution, Šariš boiled as a hotbed of anti-Habsburg revolt. For many years a borderland against Turkish invasions, the region and its sleepy towns still stand behind bastions built to repel the Saracens. Even Košice, Slovakia's second city, seems to run on a slower speed. German-speaking tourists are fewer here, with English in the running for second language; mostly, though, it's you and the locals.

■ Košice

Though the medieval gold merchants who founded Košice (KO-shih-tseh) would wince at the blast furnaces and steel foundries that have replaced their fine metal shops, the town's Gothic and Renaissance center has managed to survive fires, revolutions, an Ottoman invasion, and the city's intense industrial development. Eastern Slovakia's cultural and political heart now pulses with the lively conversations of theater-goers and the ribald jokes of wine-lovers.

ORIENTATION AND PRACTICAL INFORMATION

Košice's Staré Mesto lies close to the train station. To get to the central **Hlavná** and the tourist office, exit the station and follow the "Centrum" signs across the park to **Mlynská,** which intersects Hlavná at Dóm sv. Alžbety.

Tourist Offices: Metské Informačna Centrum, Hlavná 8 (tel. 186; fax 622 69 38). Provides maps of the city center (26Sk), the whole town (75Sk), and nearly anywhere else in Slovakia; books rooms; and advertises Košice's numerous cultural events in a monthly pamphlet (4Sk). Open June-Sept. Mon.-Fri. 8am-6pm, Sat. 9am-1pm; Oct.-May Mon.-Fri. 9am-5pm, Sat. 9am-1pm. **Tatratour,** Alžbetina 6 (tel. 622 48 72), near the cathedral. This local **American Express** representative arranges pension stays (600Sk per person). Open Mon.-Fri. 9am-5pm.

Currency Exchange: VÚB branches are liberally sprinkled throughout the city; the one at Hlavná 8 (tel. 622 62 50), right next to the tourist office, cashes traveler's checks and exchanges currency, both at 1% commission. Cirrus/MC-linked **ATMs** spit money in front of many VÚB branches, including Hlavná 8.

Trains: Predstaničné nám. To: Bratislava (every 2hr., 5hr., 226Sk); Prague (7 per day, 9hr., 403Sk); Budapest (3 per day, 4hr., 470Sk); Kraków (3 per day, 6hr., 543Sk); Lviv, Ukraine (1 per day, 6-8hr., 800Sk); and Kiev (1 per day, 12hr., 818Sk).

Buses: Next to the train station. Buses are bumpier and more expensive than trains, but sometimes faster for local trips, and always more scenic. To Brno (4 per day, 10½hr., 325Sk). Trips as far as Poland, Germany, and even Italy also possible.

Public Transportation: Trams and **buses** cover the city and its suburbs. Tickets cost 6Sk at kiosks and little orange boxes at bus stops (exact change required).

Taxis: Rádio Taxi (tel. 18 83). **Lucky Taxi** (tel. 633 00 00). **CTC** (tel. 189).

Luggage Storage: At the train station. 5Sk per bag. Open 24hr.

24-Hour Pharmacy: Toryská 1 (tel. 42 94 91).

Post Office: Poštová 20 (tel. 622 77 25). Open Mon.-Fri. 7am-7pm, Sat. 7am-2pm. **Postal code:** 4001. **Phone code:** 95.

ACCOMMODATIONS

Although accommodations generally cost more in Košice than in smaller towns, a few hotels and *penzións* are manageable. The tourist office has a list of possibilities, but prices may be old. In July and August, student dorms are the cheapest option (about 60Sk per night). Check with the tourist office for more information.

Pension Rozália, Oravská 14 (tel. 633 97 14). From the station, take tram #6 to "Amfitéater" (about 20min.) and walk up Stará spišská cesta, which is behind you near the amphitheater. A 10min. trek leads through a gentle suburb gushing with greenery and birdsong. Oravská appears on the right; ring the bell at #14. Small rooms with windows overlooking a garden. 200Sk per person. Call ahead.

Hotel Strojár, Južná Trieda 93 (tel. 544 06; fax 544 07). Tram #3 heads directly from the train station to "Hotel Strojár" (5min.). This renovated hotel boasts nearly spotless rooms, firm beds, and a congenial manager. Every 2 rooms share a bathroom. Singles 210Sk, with sheets 350Sk; doubles 600Sk; triples 840Sk.

Hotel Európa, Protifašistických Bojovníkov 1 (tel. 622 38 97), across the park in front of the train station and bridge. A posh 19th-century hotel whose bathroom tiles seem to have been around since the Hungarian occupation. Communal toilets and one shower room for both women and men. Singles 330Sk; doubles 570Sk; triples 770Sk. Apartments with private bath and fridge-equipped living room 1200Sk.

FOOD

Eateries flood the city center, but it quickly becomes apparent that most restaurant-goers live on a liquid diet of coffee, beer, and wine. A restaurant where people are actually eating merits a second look. For complete self-service, try the **Tesco's** at Hlavná 109 (open Mon.-Fri. 8am-10pm, Sat. 8am-5pm, Sun. 8am-4pm).

Ajvega, Orlia 10 (tel. 622 04 52), off Mlynská. Veggie pasta, pizza, soups, and salads. The *Maxi Zelo* (60Sk) defies the Slovak notion of "1 salad, 1 vegetable" with tomatoes, peppers, cucumbers, and carrots all in one bowl. If there are no free tables on the ground floor, go up 2 flights. Open daily 11am-11pm.

Lampáreň, Hlavná 115 (tel. 622 49 95). Solid, tasty dishes (50-116Sk). Don't be fooled if the hallway to this dim, smoky cellar is dark. Around 10pm it turns into a rather stunted disco—you might want to go somewhere else for fun. Open Mon.-Tues., Thurs., and Sun. 11am-1am, Wed. and Fri.-Sat. 11am-2am.

Pizzeria Venezia, Mlynská 20 (tel. 622 47 61). Best pizza in town, and one of the only places to get late-night food. Pizza 89-99Sk; spaghetti 96Sk. Open daily 10am-midnight.

Aida, Poštova 4. Draws the crowds from the streets for sweets (7-10Sk) and fabulous ice cream (3Sk per scoop). Open daily 8am-10pm.

SIGHTS AND ENTERTAINMENT

The streets of Košice's Staré Mesto provide a few full days of good walking tours. Bulbous **Hlavná** marks the heart of historic Košice. At the street's widest point, **Dom sv. Alžbety** (Cathedral of St. Elizabeth) towers above the city. Originally designed as a high-Gothic monument, this confused cathedral has undergone repeated renovations and now stands as a cool conglomeration of almost every style known to Western architecture. In 1900, restorers built a crypt under the cathedral's north nave. Transported from Turkey in 1906, Košice's prodigal son, **Ferenc Rakóczi II,** stirs up much less trouble in a sarcophagus. The cathedral's little brother next door, **Kaplnka sv. Michala** (Chapel of St. Michael), serves as a mortuary (closed to the public). Outside, a relief of St. Michael weighs the souls of the dead. On the other side of the cathedral, **Urbanova veža** (Urban's Tower) houses the city's **metallurgical museum,** featuring cast-iron bells, pewter doorknockers, and golden candlesticks (closed in 1997). The tower's exterior arcade is decorated with tombstones, some dating to Roman times.

Built of stones discarded from Dom sv. Alžbety, the 19th-century **Jakabov palác,** Mlynská 30, off Hlavná, served as the temporary home of Czechoslovakia's president during spring 1945. Off Mlynská, Puškinova leads to the closed **synagogue.** A strikingly graphic memorial to local Jews deported to concentration camps hangs outside. North of the cathedral on Hlavná, on the other side of the fountain (which dances to music in the afternoons and evenings), stands the stately neo-Baroque **Štátne divadlo** (state theater), built at the turn of the century. The tiny stream gliding down the center of Hlavná and bubbling into a fountain near the theater was recently added.

Farther north, the 14m **Morový Stĺp** (Plague Column) commemorates the devastating plague of 1710. Running off Hlavná near the theater, Univerzitná leads to two museums, **Miklušova väznica** (prison) and **Rakóczi's House,** both at Hrnčiarska 7. The ticket office for both lies behind the gate at Hrnčiarska. All browsing is loosely guided, but not necessarily in English. Housed in the former city jail, **Miklušova väznica** reveals everything you ever wanted to know about life behind bars during the 17th-19th centuries—prisoner graffiti, death verdicts, and torture instruments. The tour leads through reconstructed prison chambers, many with unflattering sketches of the executioners, and photo collections of actors demonstrating the various methods of torture and annihilation. So as not to torture the prison's delicate floors, visitors are asked to put on slippers (one size fits all...small feet). **Rakóczi's House** is a shrine to Rakóczi Ferenc II, Hungary's anti-Habsburg national hero. The museum contains furniture and an entire room from Rakóczi's home in Turkey, where he died in exile. Check out the guest book for the number of Hungarian visitors. (All museums open May-Sept. Mon.-Fri. 9am-5pm and Sun. 1-5pm; Oct.-April Tues.-Fri. 9am-5pm and Sun. 9am-1pm. 20Sk, students 10Sk.)

Hlavná eventually ends at Hviezdoslavova between the two main buildings of the **Východoslovenské Múzeum** (East Slovak Museum), Hviezdoslavova 3 (tel. 622 30 61). Inside the building to the right, recent history shines with examples of the region's folk and religious art, such as dancing saints, gigantic Jewish wedding rings, and a life-size sculpture of a knight on horseback descending upon a peg-legged beggar. To the left, prehistoric remnants illuminate the saga of the Celts, Germans, and Slavs who settled the region. After the upper floors, the museum's pride awaits downstairs behind a two-ton door. In 1935, while laying foundations for a new finance headquarters at Hlavná 68, workers discovered a copper bowl filled with 2920 gold *tholars* and a Renaissance gold chain over two meters long. The vault displays them, along with a 1992 discovery (open Mon.-Sat. 9am-5pm, Sun. 9am-1pm).

Information and tickets for Košice's **philharmonic** and four **theaters** are available at the Hlavná 8 tourist office. Beer and wine halls are plentiful in the town center. The intimate **Tokaj Vináreň,** Poštová 3, serves Slovak wine by the glass among wine barrels and vines, but focuses on selling by the bottle (open Mon.-Fri. 9am-6pm, Sat. 8am-noon). You'll hear little jazz in the **Jazz Club,** Kovasća 39 (tel. 622 42 37), but crowds fill its damp and dark cellars while the walls resound with disco, oldies, Latin American music, and more (beer 12-20Sk; cover 20Sk, 50Sk when there's live music; open 7pm-late). Satisfying a little-known Slovak fetish for bluegrass, live music plays for line-dancers on weekend nights at **Country Club Diera,** 14 Poštová (tel. 622 05 51). Bartenders serve tequila shots and seven types of whiskey behind pictures of Annie Oakley and Davy Crockett. Luckily, the beer isn't American (open Mon.-Thurs. 11am-3am, Fri. 11am-4am, Sat. 3pm-3am, Sun. 3pm-1am). For unadulterated disco and 30Sk beers, head for **Hacienda,** Hlavná 65 (open daily 9pm-3am; cover 40Sk, weekdays 30Sk, women free Mon. and Wed., students free Tues.).

■ Prešov

In Prešov (preh-SHOVE), cultural mish-mash is as common as good beer. Large contingents of Magyars, Gypsies, and Rusins (a very small Slavic minority) maintain their diverse traditions, while clean-cut couples, black-clad widows, and Catholics flaunting their Sunday best underscore the town's rural intimacy. Beware: Prešov shuts down almost entirely on weekends.

Orientation and Practical Information Prešov's stem, **Košická,** sprouts straight out of the train station, blooming into **Masaryková,** then **Hlavná.** At the town square, Hlavná splits into two branches that re-merge after enveloping Kostol sv. Mikuláša. Northbound **buses** and **trams** (all except #19 and 31) travel between the station and the center; take the underpass under Masaryková and purchase a 6Sk ticket from the orange automats. Automats stand at most bus or tram stops (exact change required). It's about a 20-minute walk along Košická from the train and bus station to the center. **Metské Informačna Centrum,** Hlavná 67 (tel. 14 69 09), provides town and hotel info (open Mon.-Fri. 7:30-11:30am and 12:30-4:30pm, even Sat. 9am-noon). **Exchange currency** at **VÚB,** Masaryková 13 (tel. 333 61), which accepts AmEx traveler's checks (1% commission) and gives MC and Visa advances (open Mon.-Thurs. 8am-noon and 1:30-5pm, Fri. 8am-noon). **Istrobanka,** Hlavná 75, has good rates and an **ATM** that takes EC and MC (open Mon.-Fri. 8am-4pm). **Trains** (tel. 73 10 43) travel to Košice (around 19 per day, 50min., 18Sk) and Bratislava via Kysak (8 per day, 4½hr., 212Sk). **Buses** (tel. 72 45 91 or 72 35 11), opposite the train station, travel to Košice (1-2 per hr., 30-45min., 24Sk); Poprad (1-2 per hr., 1½hr., 65Sk); and other *šarišské* towns. The **post office,** Masaryková 2 (tel. 326 43), sits slightly south of the city center (open Mon.-Fri. 8am-7pm and Sat. 8am-1pm). Coin and card **telephones** stand outside. **Postal code:** 08001. **Phone code:** 91.

Accommodations and Food Many inexpensive rooms hide in Prešov's southwest suburb, and since tourists aren't common, vacancies are. **Turistická Ubytovaňa Sen,** Vajanského 65 (tel. 73 31 70), offers a few refreshing rooms; definitely call in advance (140Sk per person). The well-swept doubles at **Penzion Lineas,** Budovatelská 14 (tel. 72 33 25, ext. 28; fax 72 32 06), include toilets and baths (430Sk). From the station, walk toward the town center, take the first left on Škultétyho, and a left again at Budovatelská. The disco next door runs nightly until 6am, but doesn't disturb sleepers. **Student dorms** are the cheapest option during July and August (60Sk per person), though the warden will probably only speak Slovak. One sits right across from Penzion Lineas at Budovatélská 31 (tel. 72 44 72).

Prešov boasts a wellspring of high-quality restaurants, but only a trickling have low prices. For do-it-yourselfers, there's a **Tesco's** at Legionarov 1, where Hlavná turns into Masarykova (open Mon.-Fri. 8am-7pm, Sat. 8am-4pm, Sun. 8am-1pm). **Florianka,** Baštová 32 (tel. 734 083), sits next door to Slovakia's best hotel and restaurant management school, which has made this former firehouse its training ground. Sip *Šariš* beer (200Sk) near the old pushcart firetruck outside or enjoy hot meals (30-100Sk) in the restaurant's blazing red interior. The student chefs score high marks on food, service, and English-language ability (open Mon.-Fri. 11am-9:30pm). Saving the day on weekends, **Bagetèria,** Hlavná 36 (tel. 73 26 02), serves baguette sandwiches with and without meat (15-90Sk; open Mon.-Fri. 6am-10pm, Sat.-Sun. 7:30am-10pm). Cafe/restaurant **Edan,** Hlavná 9 (tel. 73 37 04), is a bit more expensive, but tasty. If you're feeling adventurous, try the local specialty—so-called bull's testicles (120Sk). More conventional meals include veggie options (70-120Sk; open Mon.-Fri. 10am-midnight, Sat. 1-11pm). Down the street from Bagetèria, **Veliovič Cukráreň,** Hlavná 28, supplies sweets (6-10Sk), hefty desserts (banana splits 40Sk), and cappuccino (15Sk; open daily 8am-9pm), while **Adria,** up past Kostol sv. Mikuláša at Hlavná 121, serves truly scrumptious ice cream (only 3Sk per scoop).

New York, Paris, Prešov

At first glance, it may seem that one of these things is "not like the others." Prešov's residents proudly broadcast, however, that the 49th parallel runs right through the city's Hlavná ul., placing it on a direct line with the City of Light and the City That Never Sleeps. Souvenirs and advertising pair New York with the Statue of Liberty, Paris with the Eiffel Tower, and Prešov with a bottle of beer. It seems, however, that the person who dreamed up this bit of geographical trivia might have had a few too many of those bottles of beer: while Prešov and Paris are indeed in cosmic alignment, New York hovers around the *41st* parallel.

Sights and Entertainment Hlavná's Renaissance houses stand back in deference to the town's older **Kostol sv. Mikuláša** (St. Nicholas's). The Gothic cathedral's distinctive turrets attest to Saxon influence in Prešov during the late Middle Ages. The church opens its doors only irregularly at times other than services; long skirts and pants will spare you glares. Beside the church at Hlavná 86, the 16th-century **Rákoczi Palace,** with its attic gable of plants and saints, houses the **Vlastivedné múzeum** (City Museum; tel. 734 708). The lacework inside is impressive; the exhibition on fire moves quickly from making it in the Stone Age to fighting it in more recent eras, finishing up with several great old firetrucks parked behind the museum (open Tues.-Fri. 10am-5pm, Sat.-Sun. 11am-3pm; 20Sk, students 10Sk). Farther down the street, at #62, stands the 19th-century **Ruský Dom** (Rusins' Clubhouse), the community center for this tiny minority group. A second-floor office sells books on Rusin history and culture, as well as the local Rusin newspaper. The hammer-and-sickle-adorned column outside seems even more anachronistic than the statue of Neptune near it. The latter was given to the town by a Jewish merchant in the 19th century as thanks for allowing him to settle in Prešov. Perambulate down to the Greek Orthodox **Katedrálny chrám sv. Jána Krstiteľa** (St. John's Cathedral), at the base of Hlavná, to peek at the breathtaking altar. On the west side of Hlavná, the restored Gothic **Šarišská galéria,** Hlavná 51 (tel. 72 54 23), features Slovak art (open Tues., Wed., and Fri. 9am-5pm, Thurs. 9am-6pm, Sat. 9am-1pm, Sun 1:30-5:30pm; 6Sk, students 2Sk, Sun. free).

Heading west from the town hall on Hlavná, the narrow, medieval **Floriánova** leads to **Brána sv. Floriána** (St. Florian's Gate), a remnant of Prešov's early Renaissance fortifications. In northwest Staré Mesto, at Švermova 56, money ran out for the renovation of the ornate **synagogue's** exterior, but if you can get in, the well-maintained interior is worth it. Constructed in 1898, the synagogue served Prešov's Jewish community until World War II. A **monument** erected in 1991 commemorates some 6000 Prešov Jews who fell victim to the Nazis and the Tiso regime; the current Jewish community numbers only slightly over 100. The synagogue houses the **Múzeum Judaík** (tel. 73 16 38; open Tues.-Wed. 11am-4pm, Thurs. 3-6pm, Fri. 10am-1pm, Sun. 1–5pm; Slovak tours 10Sk, students 5Sk; in German 20Sk, students 10Sk).

There's a surprising amount of nightlife in this placid town—see for yourself at any of Prešov's numerous pubs, *vinareňs,* and nightclubs. For relaxation before the revelry, the town also has two theaters and a fine **Múzeum Vín,** Floriánova ul. (tel. 73 31 08). This demure drinking establishment in the basement of the *radnica* serves a variety of Slovak, Moravian, and Hungarian wines (5-10Sk each) in the degustation room; guests are allowed to visit the museum's stocks. A 1763L wine barrel and 1.2m double-barreled-shotgun wine bottle wait at the end (open Mon.-Fri. 9am-6pm, Sat. 8am-noon; 10Sk). **Piváreň Smädný Mních,** Svátoplukova 1 (tel. 72 37 89), on a side passage, features the "Thirsty Monk" (13Sk) and many happy locals. Just don't try swinging on the wagon-wheel chandeliers (open Mon.-Thurs. 11am-11pm, Fri. 11am-1am, Sat.-Sun. 3pm-midnight). The town's best open-air beer garden, **Zahradný Dvor,** Hlavná 64 (tel. 723 538), serves *Šariš* for a mere 11Sk. The tables are wood, and so are the gnarly branching sun shades (open Mon.-Sat. 8am-10pm). For some disco fun, the red-lighted **Alpha,** Kováčska 3 (tel. 72 52 52), is the place to be. Dress up and dress tight (open Thurs. and Sun. 8:30pm-4am, Fri.-Sat. 8:30pm-4:30am).

▓ Bardejov

For the last 500 years, the monuments of Bardejov (bar-day-YOV) have been dancing with disaster. The troubles began in 1494 when the vault of Kostol sv. Egídia collapsed only months after its construction. Turkish armies, an earthquake, and three fires subsequently left the town in ruin, but the citizens have kept coming back with a vengeance. Bardejov's most recent restoration won a UNESCO heritage gold medal in 1986. The strangely empty town now seems so perfectly medieval that one expects to see the ghosts of Bardejov's merchants milling about the quiet square.

Orientation and Practical Information The quickest way to enter and exit Bardejov is by **train:** to Košice (around 30 per day, 2hr., 40Sk) via Prešov (1hr., 15min., 22Sk) and Kraków (1 per day, 6¼hr., 585Sk). The **bus station,** next to the train station, sends buses to Poprad (15 per day, 2½hr., 68Sk); Košice (around 10 per day, 1¾hr., 53Sk); and local towns. From the **train station,** go left and take the path leading into the stone fortification. Continue straight, then turn left onto ul. Stocklova and take a quick right onto ul. Poštova to reach the center, **Radničné nám.** The **tourist office,** Radničné nám. 21 (tel./fax 72 60 72), beckons with its green and white "I"; its staff sells more than 10 different guides about the region, and also assists in finding rooms (open daily May-Oct. 15 9am-6pm; off-season 8am-4pm). **Exchange currency** at **VÚB,** Kellerova 1 (tel. 722 671), which cashes AmEx and Visa traveler's checks at 1% commission and has a Cirrus/EC/MC **ATM** (bank open Mon.-Thurs. 8am-noon and 1:30-5pm, Fri. 8am-noon; ATM open daily 6am-10pm). **Polhobanka,** Dlhý rad 17 (tel. 74 67 45), does Visa cash advances (open Mon.-Fri. 8am-2:30pm). The **post office** is at Dlhý rad 14 (tel. 72 26 62; open Mon.-Fri. 7:30-11:30am, Sat. 7:30-9:30am). Phone cards are sold in the outer foyer (open Mon.-Fri. 7am-6pm), and **telephones** stand outside. **Postal code:** 08501. **Phone code:** 0935.

Accommodations and Food Fearing Staré Mesto's fortifications or taxes, inexpensive hotels wait outside the city walls. Popular among teenage Slovaks, **Športhotel,** Katuzovovo 31 (tel.72 49 49), is 10 minutes away from the train station. Turn right from the station and follow Slovenská; make a left on Kúpelná, and, after 200m, a right on Kellerova (the street isn't clearly marked, but you'll see a bridge immediately when you turn). Take the first left after the bridge and the hotel will appear on the right. Airy rooms with toilet and shower glow with the handiwork of the hotel's maids (290Sk per person). **Hotel Toplá,** Fučíkova 25 (tel. 72 40 41), looks a bit grim from the outside, and the bathrooms don't smell of roses, but the rooms themselves are pretty and clean, and cheaper than the ones in the center. From the train station, walk slightly left toward town and then take the first right onto Nový Sad, which becomes Fučíkova (singles 415Sk; doubles 430Sk; triples 545Sk).

Restaurants in Bardejov are affordable, but few rise above the rabble of snack bars and drab beerhalls. **U Zlatej Koruny,** Radničné nám. 41 (tel. 72 53 10), is one exception, serving a wide variety of wines, as well as elegant main dishes (35-120Sk), soups (10-20Sk), and—get them while you can—salads (10-30Sk; open Sun.-Thurs. 9am-10pm, Fri.-Sat. 9am-11pm). **Reštaurácia Na Bráne** (tel. 72 23 48), at the end of Hviezdoslavova, tends a bit more toward the drab beerhall-esque look with its smoky interior, but the food (main dishes 25-80Sk) is simple and good (open May-Sept. Tues.-Sun. 8:30am-noon and 12:30-5pm; off-season Tues.-Sat. 8am-noon and 12:30-6pm).

Serve yourself at **Supermarket Centrum,** Slovenská 11, across from the train station (open Mon.-Fri. 6am-6pm, Sat. 5:45-11:45am).

Sights Bardejov may be the only town in Šariš in which the square's centerpiece isn't a church. The maple tree at the south end is a gift from the USA, brought in 1991 by the illustrious former U.S. vice-prez Dann Kwuayle. The **radnica** (town hall), Radničné nám. 48 (tel. 74 60 38), now serves as one of the town's museums, displaying historic trinkets—including the key to the city, which the mayor's wife allegedly passed to her treacherous Turkish lover in 1697. Accompanied by harpsichord music, the tour leads past ancient steins and a slingshot that makes the story of David and Goliath believable. The **Ikony** exhibition, Radničné nám. 27 (tel. 72 20 09), houses a huge collection of Orthodox icons. The display "Nature of Northeastern Slovakia" in the **Prírodopisné Múzeum** (tel. 72 26 30), on Rhodyho, will interest anyone who loves stuffed animals or loves to stuff 'em. All museums (including Bardejovské Kúpele; see below) join under the auspices of Šarišske Múseum, the office headquarters of which, at Radničné nám. 13 (tel. 60 38), should not be mistaken with the actual exhibitions. (Museums open May-Oct. 15 Tues.-Sun. 8:30am-noon and 12:30-5pm; off-season Tues.-Sun. 8am-noon and 12:30-4pm; 25Sk, students 10Sk.)

   Kostol sv. Egídia (Church of St. Aegidius), behind the town hall, contains 11 Gothic wing altars crafted between 1450 and 1510. In the 17th century, iconoclastic Calvinists took over the town and the church. Fortunately, they compromised with the town's merchants and let the altars stay as long as they remained shut. The biggest and most valuable is the 15th-century **Nativity Altar** (open Mon.-Fri. 9am-5pm, Sat. 10am-3pm, Sun. 11am-3pm; 20Sk, students 10Sk). Up a hill to the east of town, **Kostol sv. Kríža** (Church of the Holy Cross) stands watch over Bardejov's cemetery. A forest path leads past 14 stark Stations of the Cross before reaching the weed-over-run graveyard. A full panorama of Bardejov's valley stretches below, but watch out for the stinging nettles. One of Bardejov's **bastions,** in the town's southeast corner, first served as a crossroads beacon and later as the local beheading stock. The tourist office has pamphlets on all the **walking tours** possible around Bardejov and its 14th-century towers.

   About 5km from Bardejov, **Bardejovské Kúpele** works wonders with water cures and pure country air. Actual curing stations are off-limits, but several free fountains run with the spa's acidic water. The complex is an awkward collection of 18th- and 19th-century buildings in need of a paint job and more recent (and less ornate) hotels, all tied together by sidewalk and fountains. The spa reached its height in the late 18th and early 19th centuries, when Elizabeth, the wife of Austrian Emperor Franz Joseph, Alexander I of Russia, Emperor Joseph II of Austria-Hungary, and Napoleon's second wife, Maria Luisa, all came for cures. WWI and the end of the Empire cut off the spa from the Hungarian aristocrats who had come in search of the great outdoors with the comforts of home. On the resort's outskirts, Slovakia's oldest folklore exhibition sits in a hectare replica of Šariš village life. In summer, the **skansen** (or Múzeum Lůdovej) hosts regular folk festivals and craft days (tel. 72 20 72; open May-Sept. 9:30am-noon and 12:30-6:30pm). To get to Bardejovské Kúpele, take **bus** #1, 2, 6, 7, 10, or 11 to the end of the line (20min.).

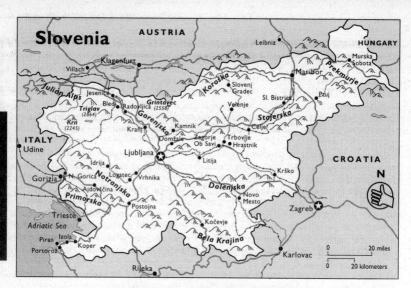

SLOVENIA (SLOVENIJA)

US$1 = 170Slt	100Slt = US$0.59
CDN$1 = 123Slt	100Slt = CAD$0.81
UK£1 = 270Slt	100Slt = UK£0.37
IR£1 = 249Slt	100Slt = IR£0.40
AUS$1 = 124Slt	100Slt = AUS$0.81
NZ$1 = 108Slt	100Slt = NZ$0.93
SAR1 = 36Slt	100Slt = SAR2.77
DM1 = 93Slt	100Slt = DM1.07
Country Phone Code: 386	**International Dialing Prefix: 00**

Slovenia, the most prosperous of Yugoslavia's breakaway republics, has reveled in its independence, modernizing rapidly as it turns a hungry eye toward the West. For a country half Switzerland's size, Slovenia, on the "sunny side of the Alps," is extraordinarily diverse: in a day, you can breakfast on an Alpine peak, lunch under the Mediterranean sun, and dine in a vineyard on the Pannonian plains. Painters, bring extra amounts of green and white: Slovenia's pine-covered hills and mountains which irresistibly attract hikers in the summer and skiers in the winter, won't disappoint you.

SLOVENIA ESSENTIALS

Australian, Canadian, Irish, New Zealand, U.K., and U.S. citizens can visit visa-free for up to 90 days, but South Africans need visas (US$35 for 3-month single-entry and transit; US$70 for 3-month multiple-entry). Apply by mail or in person in your home country (see **Essentials: Embassies and Consulates,** p. 5). Processing takes a few days, and requires your passport and the fee in the form of a money order.

GETTING THERE AND GETTING AROUND

Slovenia is easily accessible by car, train, or plane. There are three international **airports:** commercial flights all arrive at the **Ljubljana Airport** in Brnik, which has regular bus service to the city center 25km away. The reformed national carrier **Adria Airways** flies to European capitals and Tel Aviv. A regular **hydrofoil** service also runs between Venice and Portorož.

Ljubljana has many international rail links. **Trains** are cheap, clean, and reliable. You can usually find a seat on local trains, though it's best to avoid peak commuting hours around Ljubljana. For most international destinations, a 20% discount is available for travelers under 26; check at the Ljubljana station (look for the **BIJ-Wasteels** logo). Round-trip tickets are 20% cheaper than two one-way tickets. Most stations have luggage storage. "*Vlak*" means train, "*prihodi vlakov*" means arrivals, and "*odhodi vlakov*" means departures. Schedules usually list trains by direction.

Buses are roughly 25% more expensive and usually slower, but run to some otherwise inaccessible places. Tickets are sold at the station or on board; put your luggage in the passenger compartment if it's not too crowded. For those traveling by **car,** the **Automobile Association of Slovenia's** emergency telephone number is 987. *Let's Go* does not recommend **hitchhiking** as a safe means of transportation. However, hitchers report success going from major cities to major tourist resorts, although they advise avoiding the busy seasons (Dec.-Jan. and July-Aug.).

TOURIST SERVICES AND MONEY

Tourist offices are located in most major cities and tourist spots. The staff are generally helpful, speak English and German, provide basic information, and assist in finding accommodations. Most businesses are open Monday-Friday 8am-7pm, and Saturday 8am-noon. Many restaurants are also open Sundays.

The national **currency** is the Slovenian **tolar** (Slt). Hard currency prices tend to be stable, but are usually set in Deutschmarks (DM) rather than US$. **Exchange offices** abound. **Banks** are usually open Monday-Friday 8am-5pm and Saturday 8-11am. Rates vary, but tend to be better in major cities. Some establishments charge no commission (a fact reflected in the rates). Banks and the vast majority of shops and restaurants accept major **credit cards,** including AmEx and Diners Club, but the most widely endorsed is MasterCard/Eurocard, followed by Visa. There's a 20% **value-added tax,** but for purchases over 9000Slt, the tax is refundable at the border (ask the store salesperson for a tax-free check). **ATMs** don't exist outside major cities.

COMMUNICATION

Postal facilities and services are reliable. **Post offices** are usually open Monday-Friday 8am-7pm and Saturday 8am-noon, with night and Sunday service in larger cities. To send letters via airmail, ask for *letalsko*. While at the post office, purchase a **magnetic phone card** (750Slt per 50 impulses, which yields 50 local calls or 1½min. to the U.S.). For **MCI WorldPhone** call 080 88 08. Similar services for other phone companies are not yet available, but should be sometime in 1998. Operators will assist in connecting calls if you dial 90 in Ljubljana, Kranj, Maribor, and Nova Gorica, and 900 in other Slovene cities. Calling the U.S. is expensive (over US$6 per min.).

English-language press is available in all larger cities. Slovenia receives **satellite programs** in English, and **Radio Slovenia** releases English-language news, weather, and traffic updates (nightly at 10:30pm, Program 1, AM 326.8, 918kHz).

LANGUAGE

Slovene, a Slavic language, employs the Latin alphabet. Most young people speak at least some **English,** but the older generation is more likely to understand **German** (in the north) or **Italian** (along the Adriatic). Many cities along the Italian border are officially bilingual. The tourist industry is generally geared toward Germans, though most tourist office employees speak English.

When speaking Slovene, "*č*" is pronounced "ch," "*š*" is "sh," and "*ž*" is pronounced is "zh." "*R*" is at times a vowel (pronounced "er"), while "*v*" and "*l*" turn silent at the strangest times (see the Slovenian glossary, p. 812).

HEALTH AND SAFETY

> **Emergency Numbers: Police:** tel. 113. **Fire:** tel. 112. **Ambulance:** tel. 94.

Slovenia's **climate** varies by region: mediterranean near the Adriatic, alpine in the mountains, moderately continental on the eastern plains, and pleasant everywhere in summer, though snow may strew the Alps as late as June. A Slovene proverb says that if it *doesn't* rain on May 15, it *will* rain for 40 days afterwards, but don't use this as a reason to avoid spring visits—even the groundhog isn't always right.

Crime rates, especially for violent crime, are very low in Slovenia. Even in the largest cities, friendly drunks and bad drivers are the greatest public menace. The occasional unwanted ogles and pick-up lines do occur.

ACCOMMODATIONS AND CAMPING

At the height of the tourist seasons, prices are steep, services slow, sights crowded, and rooms scarce. The seaside, packed as early as June, causes claustrophobia in July and August. Tourists also tend to swarm to the mountains during these months, and student rooms are generally available late June to early September. **Hotels** fall into five categories (L (deluxe), A, B, C, and D) and tend to be expensive. **Youth hostels** and **student dormitories** are cheap, but are generally open only in summer. Usually, the best option is to rent **private rooms**—prices vary according to location, but rarely exceed US$30, and most rooms are good. Inquire at the tourist office, or look for *Zimmer* or *sobe* signs on the street. **Campgrounds** can be crowded, but are generally in excellent condition. Bungalows are rare.

FOOD AND DRINK

The best bet for mouth-watering, homestyle cooking is a *gostilna* or *gostišče* (interchangeable words for a restaurant with a country flavor, although a *gostišče* usually also rents rooms). A good national dish to start with is *jota,* a potato, bean, and sauerkraut soup. *Svinjska pečenka* (roast pork) is tasty, but **vegetarians** should look for *štruklji*—large, slightly sweet dumplings eaten as a main dish. Slovenes also have good desserts; one of their favorites is *potica,* which consists of a sheet of pastry that is spread with a rich filling and rolled up. The most popular filling is made from walnuts, though poppy seeds and fruit are both tasty.

The country's **wine** tradition, dating from antiquity, was fostered during the Middle Ages by monks and feudal lords. Look for familiar grape varieties on the label. *Renski Rizling* and *Šipon* are popular whites. Slovenia produces many unique red wines, including the light *Cviček* from the central region and the potent *Teran,* bottled on the coast. The art of brewing is also centuries old in Slovenia; good beers include *Laško* and *Union.* For something stronger, try *Žganje,* a strong fruit brandy. The most enchanting alcoholic concoction is *Viljamovka,* distilled by monks who know the secret of getting a full pear inside the bottle.

CUSTOMS AND ETIQUETTE

Slovenians welcome foreigners to their country with open arms. If you are fortunate enough to be invited into someone's home, remember to bring an odd number of **flowers.** At restaurants and cafes, the bill is never split; one person pays the whole bill, and any evening up can be attended to later. **Tipping** is not expected, though rounding the bill up will be appreciated. In general, **business hours** are Monday to Friday 8am to 5pm, Saturday 8am to noon. Though anti-gay acts are rare, the attitude towards **homosexuals** generally ranges from unsure to unfriendly. Tap **water** is drinkable everywhere.

NATIONAL HOLIDAYS

Slovenians observe: January 1-2, New Year's; February 8, Prešeren Day; April 27, Day of Uprising (WWII); May1-2, Labor Day; May 22, Whit Sunday; June 25, National Day; August 15, Assumption Day; October 31, Reformation Day; November 1, All Saint's Day; December 26, Independence Day.

LIFE AND TIMES

HISTORY

Slovenes are descendants of west Slavic tribes who migrated to the Eastern Alps in the 6th century, absorbing the existing Romano-Celtic-Illyrian cultures. In 623, the Slavs broke free from the rule of the Avar khans, and a Slavic kingdom emerged under **Samo** (623-658), which fell to the Franks after 748. Though the Slavs were assimilated into the Magyar and Bulgarian tribes, the tribal duchy of Carinthia—precursor of modern Slovenia—survived.

Following the fall of the Frankish Empire in the 10th century, Slovene lands were given to the **German kingdom** and divided into Carinthia, Carniola, and Styria. The Slovenes were given a secondary place as serfs in the German kingdom, labeled "Wends." The German kingdom was not secure, however, and the territory occupied by Slovene speakers changed hands frequently, falling briefly under Slavic rule in the 13th century, when **Otakar II** of Bohemia attempted to establish a Slavic empire. However, after Otakar's 1278 defeat, Styria fell to the **Habsburgs;** Carinthia and Carniola followed in 1335. Habsburg rule, although occasionally stifling, allowed Slovenes to reach relatively high levels of both literacy and technological development, as well as early integration into a market economy. The last half of the 19th century nonetheless saw a growing hunger for a Slovene national identity, marked by the formation of political parties and the spread of the use of the Slovene language.

During **WWI,** Slovene politicians pressed for the creation of an independent state of south Slavs, which was to consist of present-day Slovenia, Croatia, and Bosnia-Herzegovina. In 1918, the Kingdom of Serbs, Croats, and Slovenes (renamed **Yugoslavia**— Land of the South Slavs—in 1929) was officially created, with the capital in Zagreb, and thus Slovenia ceased to be a part of the Austro-Hungarian empire. The new state was too weak, however, to withstand the attacks of Hitler's armed forces during **WWII.** When Yugoslavia fell in 1941, Slovenia was partitioned among Germany, Italy, and Hungary. After the German attack on the Soviet Union in summer 1941, Christian Socialists and other left-wing groups joined the Yugoslav **partisan army** of **Josip Broz Tito.** Led by the Communist party, the army was eventually recognized by the British and Americans as an ally against Hitler, and as such, was supplied with arms to continue their fight.

In 1945, partisans occupied all of Yugoslavia, and once again the state came into being, this time with Tito in command in the new capital, Belgrade. Tito liquidated Slovene politicians and leaders who failed to cooperate with the Communists; tens of thousands of Slovene patriots were murdered at Kočevje. The 50th anniversary of this mass murder was commemorated in 1995, thus ending five decades of silence. From 1948, as a rift formed between Tito and Stalin, Yugoslavia introduced certain features of a market economy. Slovenia was soon acknowledged as its most Western and economically strong republic. Upon Tito's death in 1980, confusion invaded the scene of a seemingly peaceful and stable country. Long-suppressed **ethnic conflicts** re-emerged and threatened to shake the foundations of the entire state. Yugoslavia was comprised of several large ethnic groups with little in common, other than the fact that they were all descendants of Slavic tribes and happened to occupy neighboring territories. The efforts of the Communist party to find

> Serbia had no border claims against the Slovenes, and no large Serbian minority lives in Slovenia (unlike the situation in Bosnia).

a leader to replace Tito failed. Without the fear of a strong hand in Belgrade, opposition speedily emerged in Slovenia, as well as in the other republics.

In April 1990, Slovenia held the first contested multiparty elections in Yugoslavia since before WWII, bringing to power a center-right coalition that called for independence. On June 25, 1991, Slovenia seceded from the federation. The Yugoslav army responded with force, but after 10 days of violent clashes, it gave up the fight; Serbia, the driving force behind Yugoslavia and the conflict, had no border claims against the Slovenes, and no large Serbian minority lives in Slovenia (as opposed to Bosnia). The final steps to independence were the new Slovene **constitution** of December 1991 and its recognition by the European Community in 1992.

LITERATURE

The earliest surviving examples of the Slovene language are preserved in the *Brizinski spomeniki* (Freising Manuscripts), a collection of confessions and sermons in the Latin alphabet, dating from around 1000. The spread of Protestantism throughout the Habsburg empire encouraged the development of religious literature, such as the 1584 translation of the Bible by **Jurij Dalmatin.** Concurrently, **Adam Bohorič** produced the first Slovene grammar. During the Enlightenment and Revival period (1768-1848), **Marko Pohlin,** an Augustinian monk, rose as a leading literary figure, writing a Slovene grammar and dictionary and a bibliography of Slovene literature. At the same time, **Jernej Kopitar** initiated early attempts to standardize and codify the Slovene language, while **Matija Cop** was active in publishing literary periodicals in Slovenia; the first Slovene-language newspaper came out in Ljubljana in 1843. The early 19th century's greatest poet was France Preseren, who was instrumental in establishing a modern and expressive literary Slovene. During this time and throughout the later Realist period (1848-1899), writers such as **Fran Eriavec** focused on folkloric themes with a patriotic flavor; the first Slovene novel, *Deseti brat* (*The Tenth Brother*), by **Josip Jurčič,** was published in 1866.

Despite the Romantic themes of nationalism and freedom from foreign influence, Western European ideas seeped in during the first half of the 20th century, and shaped the Slovene Modernist and Expressionist movements. Modernism flowered in prose in **Ivan Cankar's** 1904 *Hisa Marije pomocnice* (*The Ward of Our Lady of Mercy*) and his 1907 *Hlapec Jernej in njegova pravica* (*The Bailiff Yerney and His Rights*), while Expressionism showed the social and spiritual tensions brought on by WWI, in the poetry of **Tone Seliskar, Miran Jarc,** and **Anton Vodnik,** as well as in the plays of **Slavko Grum.** The advent of Soviet **Socialist Realism** crushed many of the modern and avant-garde trends that had diversified the Slovene literary movement. Slovene writers, as elsewhere in the East Bloc, lost a great deal of freedom, and were restricted to Communist allegories guised in the themes of war, patriotism, and peasant life. Disillusionment was the theme of **Bozo Vodusek's** caustic sonnets, while other lingering effects of WWII could be seen in poet/dramatist **Matej Bor's** 1958 *Sel je popotnik skozi atomski vek* (*A Wanderer in the Atomic Age*). **Cene Vipotnik, France Balantič,** and especially **Jože Udovič,** all contributed to Slovene literature's continued growth. At the end of the 70s, a number of Slovenian writers, including **Vitomis Zupan, Igor Torkar,** and **Jože Snoj,** came out with books that dealt with Stalinism in Slovenia. The post-modern trend of the 80s showed up in the so-called **"Young Slovenian Prose"** movement, which had its strongest representation in short prose pieces. Today, Slovenian literature is widely translated, especially into German, and enjoys a level of activity rivaling the past.

> The advent of Soviet Socialist Realism crushed many of the avant-garde trends that had diversified the Slovene literary movement.

SLOVENIA TODAY

On July 12, 1995, the European Commission approved Slovenian associate membership in the EU. The terms were favorable, but problems may arise because of the stipulation that Slovenia revise the 1975 Osimo Agreements with Italy. The required change could lead Slovenia to reject EU membership as it might allow the reacquisition of Slovene lands by Italians forced out after WWII; in any case, accession is not likely to happen until 2003. Currently, the **Liberal Democratic Party** (LDS; made up of former Communists), in coalition with two smaller conservative parties, holds the power in the **Skupšcina Slovenije** (Assembly of Slovenia), with **Janež Drnov** of the LDS as Prime Minister. **Milan Kučan's** five-year term as President ends in fall 1997. Slovenia has gained membership in international organizations such as the Council of Europe, the IMF, the World Bank, the World Trade Organization, and the Central Europe Free Trade Area, while NATO admission looks to be possible in the not-too-distant future. Though the process of economic reform is far from over, the pains of transition have so far been easier to bear here than in many parts of Eastern Europe; Slovenia's per capita GNP is far above that of most Eastern European countries.

Ljubljana

Slovenia's proud, vivacious capital is a city of culture and exquisite warmth. Yet most of all, it is a city of romance. As legend has it, even monuments fall in love with each other in Ljubljana (lyoob-LYAH-nah). The view from the castle hill demonstrates why the name of the city is only one vowel away from the Slovene word for "beloved" (*ljubljena*). The Baroque monuments and Art Nouveau facades may best be viewed from the castle, but the city is best felt in the streets, where business people, politicians, and intellectuals mingle along the banks of the green Ljubljanica river.

ORIENTATION AND PRACTICAL INFORMATION

The **train** and **bus stations** are on **Trg Osvobodilne Fronte (Trg O.F.)**, north of **Stari Grad** (Old Town). To reach the central square, proceed perpendicular to Trg O.F. along **Resljeva cesta,** bear right on **Trubarjeva cesta,** which leads to **Prešernov Trg.** After crossing the **Tromostovje** (Triple Bridge), Stari Grad emerges at the castle hill's base; the tourist office is the first building on your right.

Tourist Office: Tourist Information Center (TIC), Stritarjeva 1 (tel. 133 01 11; fax 133 02 44). The friendly staff offers free maps and excellent brochures. Open Mon.-Fri. 8am-7pm, Sat.-Sun. 9am-5pm.

Budget Travel: Erazem, Trubarjeva cesta 7 (tel. 133 10 76), in the Stari Grad. Geared toward students. ISICs (650Slt), FIYTOs (700Slt), tickets, and info.

Embassies and Consulates: Australia, Trg republike 3 (tel. 125 42 52; fax 126 47 21). Open Mon.-Fri. 9am-1pm. **U.K.,** Trg republike 3 (tel. 125 71 91; fax 125 01 74). Open Mon.-Fri. 9am-noon. **U.S.,** Pražakova 4 (tel. 30 14 27; fax 30 14 01). Open Mon., Wed., and Fri. 9am-noon.

Currency Exchange: Currency exchanges (*menjalnična*) abound. **Ljubljanska Bank,** Beethovnova 7, at the corner of Čankarjeva, has good, commission-free rates and cashes AmEx and other traveler's checks. Open Mon.-Fri. 8:30am-noon and 2-4pm, Sat. 9am-noon.

American Express: Atlas, Trubarjeva cesta 50, 1000 Ljubljana (tel. 131 90 20). Holds mail, but doesn't cash traveler's checks or wire money. Open Mon.-Fri. 8am-4pm, Sat. 8am-noon; AmEx services available weekdays only.

Flights: A shuttle (500Slt) makes the trip from the central train station to the **airport,** 26km away in Brnik (tel. (64) 22 27 00). **Adria Airways,** Gosposvetsta 6 (tel. 31 33 12); **Austrian Airlines,** Dunajska 107 (tel. 168 40 99); **Lufthansa,** Gosposvetska 6 (tel. 32 66 69); **Swissair** in Hotel Lev, Vošnjakova 1 (tel. 31 76 47).

Trains: Trg O.F. (tel. 131 51 67). To: Budapest (2 per day, 10hr., 5370Slt); Munich (2 per day, 6hr., 8468Slt); Trieste (4 per day, 3hr., 1350Slt); Venice (3 per day, 6hr., 3000Slt); Vienna (2 per day, 6hr., 6300Slt); Zagreb (10 per day, 2½hr., 1220Slt).

Buses: (tel. 133 61 36) next to the trains. To: Budapest (Tues., Thurs., Fri. 1 per day, 8hr., 4350Slt); Munich (Tues.-Thurs. and Sat. 1 per day; Sun. 3 per day, 6hr., 5250Slt); and Zagreb (5 per day, 3hr., 1680Slt).

Public Transportation: Buses run until midnight. Drop 100Slt in change in the box beside the driver, or buy 65Slt tokens at post offices and newsstands. One-day, weekly, and monthly passes are sold at **Ljubljanski Potniški Promet,** Celovška 160 (tel. 159 4114).

Taxis: call 97 00 through 97 09.

Laundromat: Alba, Wolfova 12 (tel. 21 44 04). Open Mon.-Fri. 8am-6pm.

Pharmacy: Lekarna Miklošič, Miklošičeva 24 (tel. 31 45 58). Open daily 24hr.

Medical Assistance: In case of emergency, call **Bohoričeva Medical Centre,** Bohoričeva 4 (tel. 323 060), or **Klinični center,** Zaloška 7 (tel. 133 62 36).

Internet Access: Connect during the day at **K-4** (see **Entertainment,** p. 680).

Post Office: Slovenska 32. Open Mon.-Fri. 7am-8pm, Sat. 7am-1pm. *Poste Restante* received at Pražakova 3 (tel. 31 45 84), 3 blocks south of the train station in a tall yellow building. Open Mon.-Fri. 7am-8pm, Sat. 7am-1pm. **Postal code:** 1106.

Telephones: 24hr. phones in front of the post office. **Phone code:** 061.

ACCOMMODATIONS AND CAMPING

There are several choices in Ljubljana, but don't expect any Eastern European bargains. On top of higher prices, there is a nightly **tourist tax** (approx. 2DM). Most prices are quoted in Deutschmarks. **TIC** (see **Practical Information,** above) will attempt to find a private single (DM20) or double (DM30-50).

Dijaški Dom Tabor, Vidovdanska 7 (tel./fax 32 10 60). From the stations, head south along Resljeva, then east on Komenskega. Athletic facilities and overall cleanliness, but shared showers and toilets. 180 beds in doubles and triples. Checkout 11am. DM26, with ISIC DM22. Breakfast included. Open June 25-Aug. 25.

Dijaški Dom Ivana Cankarja, Poljanska 260-28 (tel. 133 52 74). From the stations, go south along Resljeva, then east on Poljanska. Close to civilization, but farther from transportation. Less popular but of only slightly lesser quality than Dom Tabor. DM20 per person. Open June 25-Aug. 25.

Park Hotel, Tabor 9 (tel. 133 13 06; fax 32 13 52), near Dom Tabor. Socialist look inside and out. Most rooms have showers and toilets, but are poorly maintained. Singles 4930-6130Slt; doubles 6260-7660Slt. 20% student discount. Breakfast included.

Autocamp Ježica, Dunajska 270 (tel. 168 39 13; fax 168 39 12). Take bus #6 northbound from Slovenska ulica. Tall trees and green grass greet campers. Swimming and tennis. 920Slt per person plus 160Slt per night. Open year-round.

FOOD

About 30 meters below the aristocratic tranquility of Ljubljanski Grad lies something a bit more vivacious and a whole lot more concrete. Along the foot of the hill, bargain restaurants and colorful cafes line Mestni and Stari trg, while Vodnikov trg, near the cathedral, hosts a huge **outdoor market** (open Mon.-Sat. until 2pm). In general, most restaurants in Ljubljana offer pretty cheap daily *menüs,* which consist of soup, salad and a main dish (500-1000Slt).

Vodnikov hram, Vodnikov trg 2. Serves traditional, hearty fare in surroundings suffused with stained wood and antiques. Cheap dishes include *golaž* (beef or pork stew; 480Slt) and *pasulj z mesom* (beans with meat; 500Slt). Open Mon.-Fri. 5:30am-8pm, Sat. 5:30am-3pm.

Gostilna Pri Pavli, Stari trg 21. Serves *zrezek* (schnitzel, 1100Slt) and *golaž* (550Slt). The daily *menü kosilo* (800Slt), an even better deal includes a meat dish (often stuffed pepper). Domestic beer 200Slt. Open Mon.-Fri. 7am-10pm, Sat. 7am-3pm.

Šestica, Slovenska 40 (tel. 21 95 75). Enchanting garden restaurant. Excellent Slovene food and wines at slightly higher prices (main dishes 850-1600Slt). Also serves as an exhibition space for the works of modern Slovenian painters.

SIGHTS

The best way to learn about the city may be to meet in front of the **rotovž** (city hall), Mestni trg 1, for the two-hour **walking tour** in English and Slovene (June-Sept. daily at

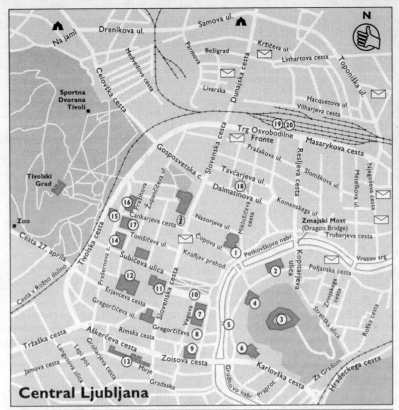

Central Ljubljana

Bus Station, 19
Kongresni Trg
  (Congress Square), 10
Levstikov Trg (Levstik Square), 6
Ljubljanski Grad (Castle), 3
Mestni Trg and Stari Trg
  (Town Square and Old Square), 5
Miklošič Park, 18
Moderna Galerija
  (Museum of Modern Art), 15
Narodna Galerija
  (National Gallery), 6

Narodni Muzej
  (National Museum), 14
NUK- National and University
  Library, 8
Opera, 17
Prešernov Trg (Prešeren Square), 1
Roman Wall, 13
Rotovž (Town Hall), 4
SAZU (Slovene Academy of
  Arts and Sciences), 7

Stolnica (Cathedral), Škofijski
  Dvorec (Bishop's Palace)
Semeniše (Seminary), 2
Train Station, 20
Trg Francoske Revolucije
  (French Revolution Square), 9
Trg Republike (Republic Square
  and Parliament Building), 12
Uršulinska Cerkev
  (Ursuline Church), 11

5pm; Oct.-May Sun. at 11am; 700Slt). In front of the *rotovž* spurts a fantastic fountain, wrought by the great local master Francesco Robba in 1751, embellished with allegorical sculptures of three rivers—the Ljubljanica, Sava, and Krka. **Ljubljanski Grad** (Ljubljana Castle) is just a short hike up the hill. The castle dates from at least 1144, and today hosts several museums and galleries. The castle's main asset, apart from its recently renovated medieval architectural splendor, is the view of Ljubljana that it offers. To see the whole city at once, climb the tower (200Slt; open daily 10am-dusk).

A short walk form the *rotovž* across the **Tromostovje** (Triple Bridge) brings you to the main square, **Prešernov trg.** Christened in honor of the great Slovene poet France Prešeren, the square contains a Neoclassical **Frančiškanska cerkev** (Franciscan Church) built in the 17th century. Native sculptor Francesco Robba crafted the impressive altar inside in 1736. The Tromostovje, is an attraction in itself. In the 1930s, revered architect Jože Plečnik modernized the old **Špitalski Most,** supplementing the stone construction with two footbridges; his handiwork transformed the bridge into one of Ljubljana's most admired architectural jewels.

To the left of the Triple Bridge is the **Zmajski Most** (Dragon Bridge), built in 1901 to replace the old wooden "Butcher's Bridge." Originally named after the Emperor Franz Joseph, the locals never accepted it as such; the dragons of Ljubljana's coat of arms, which adorn the bridge, give it the current name. Across the bridges, the **stolnica** (cathedral) occupies the site of an old Romanesque church dedicated by the boatmen and fishermen of Ljubljana to their patron St. Nicholas. Today's cathedral dates from the early 18th century; little original artwork remains, but visitors can still admire the 15th-century Gothic *Pietà*, the impressive triple organ, and the gold trim suffusing every shadow in the church with a mellow light.

Trg Francoske Revolucije (French Revolution Square) and its environs were once occupied by the Teutonic Knights; the neighborhood **Križanke,** the Slovene translation of their name, still commemorates them. In the square, the Knights set up a monastery, which was abandoned in the 18th century and subsequently deteriorated. It was restored under Plečnik's guidance, and now hosts music, theater, and dance performances for the **Ljubljana International Summer Festival** (mid-July to Sept.).

North of the library, Baroque **Kongresni trg** is named after the Congress of the Holy Alliance, convened in 1821 by the Austrian emperor, the Russian tsar, and the Neapolitan king. South of the square stands **Ljubljana University.** Westward, across Slovenska cesta, **Uršulinska Cerkev** (Ursuline Church) is nicknamed Holy Trinity Church because of the statues outside; these stone replicas replace the original wooden ones placed here in 1693 when the plague spared Ljubljana, which are now in the City Museum.

Ljubljana's plentiful **museums** cluster around the Slovene **Parliament** buildings, near Trg Republike. **Narodni Muzej** (National Museum), Muzejska 1 (tel. 21 88 86), exhibits collections on archaeology, culture, and history. The nearby **Moderna Galerija,** Cankarjeva 15 (tel. 21 41 06), displays the works of 20th-century Slovene artists. Every odd-numbered year, it also hosts the **International Biennial of Graphic Art,** the largest such exhibition in the world. To the left of Moderna Galerija stands **Narodna Galerija,** Cankarjeva 20 (tel. 21 97 16), which houses the creations of Slovene artists from the Middle Ages to the present. (All open Tues.-Sat. 10am-6pm, Sun. 10am-1pm; 500Slt, students 300Slt). Near the museums, across from Tivolska cesta, **Tivoli Park** possesses some of Ljubljana's prettiest strolling grounds, as well as excellent jogging paths. It's also home to **Tivolski Grad** (Tivoli Castle), built by Jesuits in the 17th century, and the **International Center of Graphic Art.**

ENTERTAINMENT

Cankarjev Dom hosts the **Slovene Symphony Orchestra** and well-known jazz musicians from around the world, while **Tivoli Hall** is the venue for rock concerts, hockey, and basketball. Information on these events, as well as ballet, opera, theater, and special museum exhibitions, can be found in the *Where To?/Events* brochure, published monthly and available at tourist offices. If nothing suits your fancy, join Ljubljana's large student population at the excellent cafes or bars lining the streets of the Old Town, or in the dance clubs near the modern high-rises. Many of the city's events are organized under the auspices of several long festivals. The **Slovene Days of Music Festival** takes place at the end of April. The beginning of June is reserved for the **International Wine and Viticulture Fair,** while the middle of the month echoes with the sounds of the **International Festival of Alternative and Ethno Music.** July and August bring many international stars to the **International Summer Festival** and **Festive December** rings out the year.

K-4, Kersnikova 4 (tel. 131 32 82). A different program every night, from folk to techno. Remodeled every year and always hip. Sunday is gay night. Open nightly 10pm-4am. Cover 200-1000Slt. Students get 40% off. During the day (9am-10pm), K-4 provides the only **Internet** access in Ljubljana.

Eldorado, Nazorjeva 6. The Aztec tomb interior transforms daily from a Mexican restaurant (11am-5pm) to a flashy nightclub (10pm-4am) with go-go dancers, concerts, and cultural events. Cover Fri.-Sat. 1000Slt (includes 500Slt worth of drinks).

Jazz Club Gajo, Beethovnova 8. Alternates live music with nights of classic jazz. Even if you don't like jazz, you won't want to miss the orgasmic jazz-juice. Open Mon.-Fri. 10am-2am, Sat.-Sun. 6pm-midnight. No cover.

■ Near Ljubljana: Postojnska Jama (Postojna Cave)

Like a poodle guarding the gates of heaven, the town of Postojna is a proud keeper of one of the most amazing works of nature in Europe: the two-million-year-old Postoj-naska jama. A 15-minute walk northwest of the town brings you to the **jama** (cave), Janska cesta 30 (tel. 25 041). Follow the signs from the center of town or ask anyone. Tours of the cave last an hour and a half; part is on foot and part by train (in English, French, Italian, and German; 1960Slt, students 800Slt. Tours leave May-Sept. on the hour; Oct.-April on even hours). Bring a jacket or rent a cloak for 100Slt; the temperature in the cave is a constant 8°C. The tour passes through only 20% of the cave's 27km, but that's more than enough to wow visitors with plant-like columns, curtains of stone, gorges, rivers, and multi-colored stalactites. The final "hall" you enter hosts frequent musical performances by Slovene groups.

The town is reachable via **bus** (1hr., 650Slt) or **train** (1hr., 550Slt) from Ljubljana, or you can come up from the coast at about the same price. The caves will probably only be a daytrip, but if you choose to stay, drop by **Kompas Postojna,** Titov trg 2a (tel. 242 81) in the city's center, which should be able to find a room for about 1800Slt (open Mon.-Fri. 8am-8pm, Sat. 9am-1pm).

About 9km from Postojna is **Predjamski grad** (Predjama Castle), carved into the face of a huge cliff (open Mon.-Sat. 10am-5pm; 500Slt, students 250Slt). On the last Sunday in August, a colorful knights' tournament takes place in front of the castle. Local buses are rare; if you're motorized, follow the signs from the cave. Otherwise, hitchers report success, but, as always, exercise extreme caution.

JULIJSKE ALPE (THE JULIAN ALPS)

Mix a few crystal-clear mountain lakes, a pound of Magic Mountain Mix©, a pound of Fabulous Forest Fixative©, and a pint of emerald green river water. Add a handful of warm, hospitable people and a pinch of neat little villages. Bake for two hours. Finally, garnish with expensive hotels, happy skiers, healthy hikers, content eaters, blissful drinkers, and hard-core athletes. Serve warm in summer, ice-cold in winter.

▓ Bled

Imagine Bled as a postcard: green alpine hills, snow-covered peaks in the distance, and an opaque green lake, with a stately castle surveying it all. It's no wonder that people have been coming to **Blejsko Jezero** (Lake Bled) for centuries to recuperate in warm spas or lose themselves in the romance of a warm summer evening. The nature around the lake has inspired architects and city planners in the past century to try to match its beauty with their creations. Today, this internationally known resort is a paradise, but maybe a slightly too perfect one: even the swans seem to have had a haircut recently.

Orientation and Practical Information Trains stop in **Lesce,** 5km from Bled on the Ljubljana-Salzburg-Munich line (1hr., 420Slt). From there, take one of the frequent **commuter buses** (10min., 160Slt) to Bled. These stop on **Ljubljanska,** the main street, and at the main **bus station** (closer to the youth hostel and the castle). Or, arrive directly by bus from Ljubljana (hourly, 1½hr., 800Slt). Bled is spread around the lake, with most buildings clustered along the east shore. Ljubljanska leads straight to the water. For tourist info, visit **Turistično društvo,** Cesta svobode 15 (tel. 74 11 22; fax 74 15 55), and pick up a copy of the *Bled Tourist News,* which will be an excellent illustrated addendum to your yellow Bible (open Mon.-Sat. 8am-6pm,

Sun. noon-4pm). **Currency exchanges** have bad rates and extract large commissions, so discard dollars in Ljubljana. If you must change money, try **Kompas Bled,** Ljubljanska cesta 4 (tel. 74 15 15; fax 74 15 18), which cashes traveler's checks with a 3% commission (open Mon.-Sat. 9am-8pm, Sun. 8am-noon and 4-7pm). The **post office** stamps letters at Ljubljanska 10 (tel. 74 16 01; open Mon.-Sat. 7am-noon). **Postal code:** 4260. **Phone code:** 064.

Accommodations and Food All accommodations prices are quoted in DM, but you can pay in Slt. **Private room** prices vary according to season. **Kompas Bled,** (see above) seeks out singles for DM20-31 and doubles for DM34-52 per person (tourist tax DM1.5 per night). Stays of less than three nights cost 30% more. Finding a private room yourself may save money; look for *sobe* signs, particularly on Prešernova cesta. The newly renovated **youth hostel,** Grajska cesta 17 (tel. 782 30), is a bright supernova in the backpacker's dark sky. Everything from the stylish wooden furniture to the private bathrooms and showers is brand new. To find this jewel, walk up the hill of Grajska cesta from the bus station; it's 100m past the "Grad 1004" cafe. (DM20 with ISIC, FIYTO, GO25, or PZS-IYHF, prices 20% higher with no student ID; all meals served, DM6 each.) **Camping Zaka-Bled,** Cesta svobode 13 (tel. 74 11 17; fax 74 22 88), sits in a beautiful valley on the opposite side of the lake. Refrigerators, electrical connections, sand volleyball, tennis and basketball courts, a store, a restaurant, and a beach are all available—but, alas, no bungalows (checkout 3pm; DM12 per person; tourist tax DM1; open April-Oct.).

As long as you don't require a lakeside restaurant, prices aren't much higher than in the rest of Slovenia. **P-hram,** Cesta Svobode 19a, serves Slovene main courses for 650-950Slt—including delicious *kranjska klobasa* (Carniolan sausage; 700Slt; open daily 9am-9pm). Locals justly recommend **Gostilna pri Planincu,** Grajska cesta 8 (tel. 74 16 13), visible from the bus station. This 1903 restaurant serves main dishes (900-1200Slt) till 10pm, and pizzas (600-850Slt) till 10:30. The bar stays open until midnight. If all else fails, **minimarket Špecerija,** Ljubljanska 4, provides rolls, ham, beer (150Slt), and more (open Mon.-Sat. 7am-8pm, Sun. 9am-noon).

Sights The lake made the town famous, not vice versa. A stroll around the lake's 6km perimeter should take about two hours. The **island** in the center holds the **Cerkev Marijinega vnebovzetja** (Church of the Assumption), which has stood there since the 9th century. Though today's structure actually dates from the 17th century, a unique pre-Romanesque apse remains. There are a multitude of ways to approach the heart of the lake. Boat rental costs only 1000Slt per hour. You can also travel via **gondola** from the shore near the town (roundtrip 1½hr., 900Slt). You could even swim, although entering the church in Speedos is hardly kosher. Dive in from a beach without a No Swimming sign; look for other swimmers, who tend to hang out on the west shores. Warm in summer, the water becomes a huge ice-skating rink in winter.

Over 100m above the water perches the perfect medieval **castle.** Just start walking toward it; you can't miss the signs. Castle admission also gets you into an excellent **museum** with art, furniture, weapons, and prehistoric artifacts. You may, however, be content just to sit on the terrace and admire the superb view (open daily Feb.-Nov. 8am-7pm; Dec.-Jan. 8am-4pm; 300Slt).

You don't have to be surrounded by turrets and tourists to see the lake from far above. Numerous **paths** snake from the lake into the neighboring hills. The best one can be found by walking around the lake until the castle and the island are aligned—the path across the street takes about 45 minutes to climb. **Mountain bikes** of assorted quality can be rented at the Kompas Bled tourist agency (see **Orientation and Practical Information,** above; 900Slt per ½-day, 1300Slt per day).

From mid-June to September, **concerts** and traditional cultural activities take place on the island, on the promenade, and in the hotels. The Tourism Association and tourist agencies (see **Orientation and Practical Information,** above) carry a free monthly brochure of events. For such an enchanting place, the nightlife is, surprisingly, not. The **casino** near the waterfront is a sure bet (open nightly 6pm-2am). Across the hall are a late-night **restaurant** (open nightly 6pm-1am) and a **dance floor** that has seen better days, but still has a regular band to crank out slow-dancing favorites—bring a date. The younger crowd tends to find itself at the **Royal Club,** on the ground floor of the huge shopping complex on Ljubljanska cesta. A cafe by day, it's less than exciting by night, but at least the 500Slt cover charge can be redeemed in alcohol (open daily 10pm-4am).

■ Bohinjsko Jezero (Lake Bohinj)

Though only 30km southwest of Bled, Bohinjsko Jezero (BOH-heen-sko) is worlds away from its sophisticated cousin. Protected by virtue of its position within the borders of **Triglav National Park,** this glacial lake, together with its surrounding wildflowers, waterfalls, and windy peaks, stands at the center of Slovenia's alpine tourism universe. Some come for the (unmotorized) water sports, but most are here to ascend the heights and experience warm mountain hospitality on their return.

Orientation and Practical Information One **train** per day arrives in Bohinjska Bistrica, 6km from the lake, from Ljubljana directly (2hr.), and four more come via Jesenice (you may need to change trains). The **bus** to the lake stops in front of the train station in Bohinjska Bistrica. Buses to "Bohinjsko Jezero" generally finish their routes in Ribčev Laz; the stop after the sign is more central. Buses marked "Bohinj Zlatorog" take you through Ribčev Laz to the village on the west end of the lake, and occasional buses climb all the way to the trailhead for the Savica waterfall (see **Sights and Hiking,** below). You can also take the bus directly from Bled (hourly, 1½hr., 380Slt) or Ljubljana (hourly, 3hr., 850Slt); these will drop you off at the lake. You should find everything you need in **Ribčev Laz,** on the water's edge—just ask at the **tourist office,** Ribčev Laz 48 (tel. 72 33 70; fax 72 33 30; open daily July-Aug. 7am-9pm; Sept.-June Mon.-Sat. 8am-8pm, Sun. 9am-3pm). Drop by the **Šport Klub Alpinum,** Ribčev Laz 50 (tel. 72 34 41; fax 72 34 46), near the church, to rent a high quality **bike** (DM5 per hr.; DM12 per ½-day; DM21 per day), get gear for **rafting, kayaking,** and **canoeing,** find **guides,** or get a **fishing license** (lake DM50 per day, DM125 per week; river DM95 per day, DM465 per week; open daily 9am-7pm). **Fishing equipment** can be rented at Pension Rožič, 100m up the road from the tourist office. Šport Klub Alpinum also offers **paragliding** trips (parachuting off the mountaintops; DM65 per jump). The **post office,** Ribčev Laz 47, also **exchanges money** (open Mon.-Fri. 8am-7pm, Sat. 8am-noon). **Postal code:** 64265. **Phone code:** 064.

Accommodations and Food The tourist office (see above) finds singles for DM13-19 and doubles for DM22-32 (prices are 25% higher from the 2nd Saturday in July to the 4th Sat. in Aug.; tourist tax DM2; 30% mark-up for stays under 3 days). **Avtokamp Zlatorog,** on the west side of the lake, has spaces for DM16 (July-Aug.) and DM10 (May-June and Aug.-Sept.); children under 14 pay half-price.

The smell of sizzling fresh fish entices visitors into expensive, but worthy, local restaurants. **Restaurant Triglav,** Stara Fužina 23, brings in enough tourists to offer an affordable daily *menü,* with soup, main course, salad, and dessert (1100Slt). To find it, cross the bridge next to the church on Lake Bohinj, and walk 10 minutes to the next village—the view of the lake from the terrace beats even the prices (open daily 11am-11pm). **Restaurant Rožič,** Ribčev Laz 42, offers a combination of the traditional Slovenian peasant cuisine and Balkan grill. Rožič's daily tourist *menü* (1000Slt), pizza (800Slt), and pasta (700Slt), are better than what's offered by other restaurants around the lake. The **Mercator supermarket,** Ribčev Laz 49, is by the tourist office (open Mon.-Sat. 7am-9pm, Sun. 7am-1pm).

Hiking and Sights Hiking is plentiful around Lake Bohinj, but there are a few rules of the road of which you should be aware. Trails throughout Slovenia are marked with a white circle inside a red circle; look for the blaze on trees and rocks. A bend in the trail may be marked by a bent red line. When trails separate, a sign *usually* indicates which one is headed where. In Slovenia, hikers always greet each other on the path. As old-timers will remind you, the person ascending the path should speak up first; respect belongs to those who have already conquered the hill, not to those puffing their way up. **Mountain bikes** are not allowed on the trails, but they can be fun on the *gozdna pot* (forest roads) and specially marked *poljska pot* (rough dirt roads). See **Essentials: Wilderness and Safety Concerns,** p. 42, for general info about hiking and safety.

Any number of trips can be made from the shores of Bohinj, from the casual to the nearly impossible. For a little guidance, English copies of *An Alpine Guide,* listing the region's best hikes of every difficulty, are free at the tourist office (see **Orientation and Practical Information,** above). Several good **maps** (around 1200Slt) are also available; the ones that cover the most area without losing detail (1:50,000) are *Triglavski Narodni Park* and *Gorenjska,* which includes the area around Bled.

The most popular and accessible destination is **Slap Savica** (Savica Waterfall). If you begin at the trailhead (a bus stops here), the hike is only 20 minutes. Just follow the signs—and the people. From Ribčev Laz, it's a three-hour hike. You can either follow the scenic road or a more peaceful trail through the woods. After the road curves around the lake's southeastern promontory, the trail cuts off to the left, rejoining the main road later. Travelers report some success hitchhiking to the trailhead as well. Once there, it's a 300Slt fee to continue on to the powerful 60m waterfall. After you've seen it, you can return the way you came, or along a trail that skirts the north side of Lake Bohinj. Look for its entrance across the street from the lower of Savica's two mountain huts, and keep to the westbound trail.

If, instead of turning west here, you follow the signs north toward the **Črno Jezero** (Black Lake), you will come to another alpine gem in liquid form (30min.). The hiking is very steep here; be extremely cautious. Shortly after reaching the ridge line, a trail to the right (*Dol Pod Stadorjem*) leads northwest to **Planina Viševnik.** Turn south from this peak to **Pršivec** (1761m; 2½hr.), where the view of the lake is breathtaking. Return the way you came, or follow the trail east to return along the ridge to **Stara Fužina** and Ribčev Laz (2½hr.). If you opt for the latter, be advised that for the first hour and a half, the only shade along the way will be that provided by your hat.

The more traditional way to reach Pršivec is from Stara Fužina. Leave Ribčev Laz along the road to the north, then follow signs to **Hudičev Most** (Devil's Bridge), built by Mr. Devil himself (Italian builder Diavollo). You'll have to pass through a closed gate, which is perfectly legal as long as you're not behind a steering wheel. Shortly after passing the bridge (don't cross it!), you'll come to a crossroad. Continue following the leftmost road (not the trails along the river), and then the marked carriage road that turns into the woods on the left. **Vogar** peak is now about an hour to the west. The path veers off of the plateau twice, so the views are breathtaking for most of the hike. Keep to the left at the junctions to reach Pršivec (4hr.). Again, there are no trees along the way, so bring a hat.

Coming to a Head...or Three

Slovenia's highest peak, Mt. Triglav (2864m) may not seem like much of an ascent until you realize that, on a clear day, the sea is visible from the summit. Originally worshiped by pre-Christian Slovenes, the mountain is now a symbol of the country's identity. Since 1778, Slovenes have been climbing to the top of "Three Heads." The three-peaked contour was the symbol of the Liberation Front when Slovenia was occupied during WWII, and today can be seen on the national flag and coat of arms. Politicians make the hike to show off their national spirit. If you reach the summit, you will be treated like a hero on your return: it's the one way of truly becoming a Slovene. Don't forget to leave your name in the book at the top. A good route up Mt. Triglav begins at Bohinjsko Jezero. Some have done it in one day, but two days provide for a safer and more enjoyable journey. For 1000Slt, *How to Climb Triglav* details all the options.

While resting between hikes, you can take in a bit of culture. The key to the 15th-century **Church of John the Baptist** on Lake Bohinj can be found at the tourist office. The **Alpine Highlander Museum** (tel. 72 30 95), 1.5km north in Stara Fužina, exhibits materials from the life of a 19th-century highlander. You may even be able to get a taste of local food (open Tues.-Sun. 10am-noon and 5-7pm; 150Slt; if no one's around, the curator is Mrs. Renata Mlakar at Stara Fužina 179, tel. 72 30 95). A few kilometers to the east in **Studor** sits a century-old peasant house at #16, now a museum; contact Grega Resman, Studor 14a (tel. 75 35 22).

▓ Bovec

Though surrounded by towering peaks, the small town of Bovec (BO-vets) receives its temperate air from the Adriatic Sea. Don't think for a minute, though, that the crowds of Austrians and Italians are here to relax. In the winter, Bovec is one of Slovenia's premier ski resorts, and in the summer, the wild rapids of the aquamarine Soča river draw people here to kayak. If you don't have your own equipment, this can be an expensive venture: **Soča Rafting,** in the centrally located **Hotel Alp** (tel. 19 62 00; fax 19 62 02), charges DM49 for a rafting trip, including all necessary clothing and transportation (1½hr.). For one day, a complete kayak kit costs DM37, and you'll have to get yourself (and the boat) to the river and back (open daily 9am-6pm). Agencies with similar prices abound; many also offer **mountain bikes** (DM18 per day), **bungee jumping, hydrospeeding** (a sort of jet-powered bodyboard; DM50 per day), and the like. Panoramic flights are available from the nearby airport (1500-7700Slt).

Those with tight budgets need not despair. **Hiking** is wonderfully uncrowded here, as few people see the mountains for the river. Pick up the free *Bovec z Okolico* (Bovec and Surroundings) and a well-marked **map** (630Slt) at Avrigo Tours (see below). Walk downstream about 5km, or take any of the buses headed toward "Pod Čela" to Log Čezsoški, then walk downstream a few minutes more. Here, you can admire the spectacular **Slap Boka** (Boka Falls); at 106m high, and a third as wide, it is the largest falls in Slovenia. The hour-long hike to the falls is not easy, but well worth the effort. Signs point the way, but if you take the trail to **Pri Boki,** farther down the road, you'll end up farther away. Other popular hikes head up the gorge of the **Koritnica river,** 4km to the northeast.

Bovec can be reached by **bus** from Ljubljana (5 per day, 4½hr., 1800Slt). There are two routes; if possible, arrive by the **Vršič Pass** (open July-Aug. only). After winding between some of Slovenia's highest peaks, the bus stops on the 1600m-high pass for 30 minutes to allow travelers—and the bus—a rest. The trip ends in Bovec's main square. **Avrigo Tours** (tel. 861 23; fax 860 64), across the street from the bus depot, serves as the nearest thing to a tourist office. Besides giving info, they can find **private rooms** (singles 1900Slt; doubles 3400Slt; tourist tax 200Slt; 30% charge for stays under 3 nights; open daily 8am-8:30pm, Sun. 9am-noon). To find a room on your own, head down the main street, then check on the small sidestreets. On the way, you'll pass **Alpkomerc,** the city's main grocery store (open Mon.-Wed., Fri.-Sat. 7am-8pm, Thurs. 8am-noon). If you want your food cooked for you, try **Letni Vrt,** by the bus stop, with the most multilingual menu this side of the Danube. The prices are right (pizzas 500-650Slt, large salads 500Slt, items from the grill 700-1000Slt). **Gostilna Sovdat** and the grill **Martinov Hram,** two minutes up the road from the bus stop, are slightly more expensive. The **Elvis Club,** right next to Letni Vrt, unlike the King himself, is surprisingly lively; everyone between the ages of 14 to 40 ends up here to drink, dance, or simply stand around (beer 300Slt; open nightly 10pm-4am; no cover). Up the street from Mr. Presley, the **post office** has **telephones** (open Mon.-Fri. 8am-6pm, Sat. 8am-noon). **Postal code:** 86000. **Phone code:** 065.

THE SLOVENIAN COAST

Though Slovenia has only 40km of the Adriatic coast, this stretch of green bays, little seaside resorts, and recreational beaches has developed a personality all its own. Tourists with cash to spare head straight for the smaller towns, where palm trees and fishing boats dot the shore.

■ Portorož

Mediterranean-style terraces and red-roofed houses march down to the diamond-clear sea. No Slovenian would admit to loving the commercial waterfront of Portorož (port-oh-ROZH), with its hotels, souvenir shops and shoreline spread with sand, but on a hot day, half the country seems to be here. **Buses** arrive from Ljubljana and Postojna (12 per day, 2½hr., 1500Slt from Ljubljana). **Trains** arrive in nearby Koper from Ljubljana (4 per day, 2½hr., 900Slt); a bus connects you to Portorož (2 per day, ½hr., 220Slt). Thomas Mann wrote that Venice should be entered only by sea; to comply, a **catamaran** makes the Portorož-Venice trip (May to mid-Sept. Wed. and Sat., 1½hr., 110DM). Most streets start from **Obala,** the waterfront boulevard, and head uphill. The bus station is just meters from the sea; across the street stands the main **tourist office,** Obala 16 (tel. 74 40 15; fax 74 70 13), with free **maps** and pamphlets (open July-Aug. daily 8am-10pm, Sept.-June Mon.-Sat. 8am-noon and 4-7pm, Sun. 8am-noon). The folks at **Slovenija Turist**—face the sea and turn left on Obala—rent **scooters** (half-day DM30, full-day DM50; open Mon.-Sat. 8am-8pm, Sun. 9am-3pm). Next door, **Publikum Menjalnica** is a decent place to **exchange money** (open daily 8am-12:30pm and 4:30-10pm). **Postal code:** 6320. **Phone code:** 066.

As a rule, hotels and **pensions** are expensive and crowded, although prices drop drastically off-season. **Private accommodations,** offered by the tourist office, remain the least expensive option. (July-Aug. singles DM30; doubles DM40-50; DM2 tourist tax; 50% surcharge for stays of less than 3 days. Off-season prices 33% lower.) To find a room on your own, look for *Sobe* or *Zimmer* signs. **Lucija,** a nearby **campground,** is accessible by bus from the station (every 20min., 120Slt.). It offers minigolf, rowing, sailing, surfing, swimming, tennis, and waterskiing facilities (tel./fax 710 27; DM10 per night, DM3 per person; hot water DM1).

A large number of interchangeable restaurants gobble up patrons on the coastal side of Obala. One stand out is **Portorožka Restavracija,** next to the bus station. Enjoy the outdoor terrace and vast selection (soups 250Slt, omelette 500Slt, spaghetti 550Slt; open daily 9am-10pm). To economize, try **Mercator Degro,** the large supermarket by the bus station (open Mon.-Fri. 7am-8pm, Sat. 7am-7pm, Sun. 8-11am).

■ Piran

Only 3km from Portorož, tiny Piran is just as touristed, but wears its hangers-on more charmingly. The peninsula, filled with narrow stone streets and gaily shuttered houses, still feels like medieval Venice, under the rule of which Piran flourished. Follow the wharf to the central square, which is dominated by a **statue** of the famous Piran-born violinist and composer Giuseppe Tartini. The narrow streets near the center merit a look, as does the charming, though old, **aquarium** in the central square. A short walk uphill, is Piran's most prominent church, the Baroque-Renaissance **Crkva sv. Jurja** (Church of St. George; first built c.600, rebuilt in the 14th century). Take a break from the midday sun to admire the church's cool, quiet interior. The tower is closed, but the terraces afford an amazing view of the sea. A walk along the quay brings you to the odd old **church-cum-lighthouse** at the end of the peninsula.

To book a **private room,** visit **Turistburo,** Tomažičev trg 3 (tel. 74 63 82; fax 74 60 95. Singles DM26-29; doubles DM44-49; tourist tax DM2; 50% surcharge for stays less than 3 nights. Off-season prices 30% cheaper. Breakfast DM6). **Penzion-Val,** Gregorčičeva 38a (tel. 754 99; fax 74 69 11), near the lighthouse, is clean and offers meals (DM27 per person, including breakfast; half pension DM36, full pension DM42, vegetarian meals on request; 10% more for less than 3 nights; 10% student discount). Those expecting sandy beaches will be disappointed, but the concrete quay serves the purpose of a beach well enough. Numerous waterfront restaurants ensure that the beauty of the vista is matched by the excellence of the meal. At **Pavel's** (tel. 74 71 01), main dishes range from spaghetti to schnitzel (650-1500Slt; open Mon.-Sat. 11am-11pm). Twelve **buses** per day head from Ljubljana through Postojna to Piran and Portorož (2½hr., 1500Slt). You can also get to Piran from Trieste by bus (6 per day, 1hr.). The nearest **train station** is on the outskirts of Koper. **Trains** arrive from Ljubljana (4 per day, 2½hr., 900Slt), and a bus connects to Portorož (2 per hr., 30min., 120Slt). Once there, catch a bus (2 per hr., 100Slt) or the casino minivan (every 15min., 150Slt) to Piran.

SLOVENIA

UKRAINE (УКРАЇНА)

US$1	= 1.87hv (hryvny)	1hv =	US$0.54
CDN$1	= 1.34hv	1hv =	CDN$0.74
UK£1	= 3.00hv	1hv =	UK£0.33
IR£1	= 2.75hv	1hv =	IR£0.36
AUS$1	= 1.36hv	1hv =	AUS$0.73
NZ$1	= 1.18hv	1hv =	NZ$0.85
SAR1	= 0.40hv	1hv =	SAR2.52
DM1	= 1.02hv	1hv =	DM0.98
Country Phone Code: 380		**International Dialing Prefix: 810**	

Compared to many of its more Westernized neighbors, Ukraine is anarchic and dour. Foreign tourism is practically non-existent in this huge and diverse land; one need not seek to depart from any beaten path because—aside from an ugly and expensive Intourist trail—there is none. This does mean a lack of comforts, but more importantly, it means that when traveling in Ukraine, you will see people, not just touristy roads and souvenir shops. Museums cost nothing and are empty; medieval castles are still huge, dark, and unsupervised; and cobbled roads remain unpaved. Sometimes the most obnoxious discos lurk in opulent buildings, conjuring visions of ancient barbarians. The ascent of the new rich has pushed some prices well above the normal standard of living, creating a split between the ritzy world of plenty, which Ukrainians expect foreigners to be part of (and pay for), and the impoverished world of want inhabited by the majority of the Ukrainians themselves. There are treasures here, but you'll have to find them yourself, because Ukraine, with enough problems of its own, isn't inclined to play host.

UKRAINE ESSENTIALS

Foreign travelers arriving in Ukraine must have a **visa,** which requires an **invitation** from a citizen or official organization, or a tourist voucher from a travel agency. Regular single-entry visa processing for Americans at an embassy or consulate (see **Essentials: Embassies and Consulates,** p. 5)—with invitation in hand—takes up to nine days (mailing time not included; enclose pre-paid FedEx envelope to speed the return) and costs US$50 (double-entry US$80). Three-day rush service—available for citizens of Australia, Canada, Great Britain, Ireland, New Zealand, and South Africa, but *not* the U.S.—is US$80 (double-entry US$120). You should submit a completed visa application, an invitation or confirmation from a hotel in Ukraine, your passport, one passport-size photo, and payment by money order or cashier's check.

If you arrive in the **Kiev airport** without a visa, you can get a tourist voucher-*cum*-invitation, which will allow you to then buy a visa. This will allow you to proceed through **customs**: declare all valuables and foreign currency above US$1000 (including traveler's checks) in order to settle your tab when leaving the country. The process takes several hours. Anyone planning to work in Ukraine must have an additional letter stating the purpose of the work; the letter has to come from an official Ukrainian agency, even if you will be working for a foreign company. See **Russia: Essentials** for a list of organizations that arrange invitations and visas.

Upon arrival in Ukraine, you should check into a hotel or register with the hall of nightmares that is the **Office of Visas and Registration** (ОВИР), in Kiev at bulv. Tarasa Shevchenka 34 (Тараса Шевченка), or in police stations in smaller cities, within your first three days in the country; visas may also be extended here. Your visa not only lets you into the country, but also allows you to leave; DO NOT LOSE IT. Once you leave Ukraine, your visa becomes invalid. If you have a double-entry visa, you will be given a re-entry slip (въезд; *vyezd*) upon your first arrival. Keep this with you—it's your ticket back into the country. A copy of your invitation and letters of introduction should be carried with you at all times, lest you be harassed by bored police officers.

GETTING THERE

Air Ukraine International (U.S. tel. (312) 337-0004; Kiev tel. 216 67 30 or 221 83 80; fax 216 82 25) flies to Kiev, Lviv, and Odesa from a number of European capitals, as well as from Chicago, New York, and Washington, D.C. Air France, ČSA, Lufthansa, LOT, Malév, SAS, and Swissair also fly to Kiev, generally once or twice a week. **Trains** are much cheaper, and run frequently from all of Ukraine's neighbor states. When coming from a non-ex-Soviet country, prepare for a two-hour stop at the border while the wagons get their wheels changed. **Buses** are a pain, unless you're traveling short distances. Taking a bus from Przemyśl (Poland) to Lviv saves money and time (no wheel changes) and allows you to do a lot of shopping on board; the frequent connection is mobbed by Ukrainians running small-scale trade trips to and from Poland's east border. **Ferries** across the Black Sea have now been reduced to a few routes from Odesa and Yalta to Istanbul.

GETTING AROUND

Trains go everywhere, and offer dirt cheap comfort. Unfortunately, getting **tickets** can drive people batty. For long-distance travel, try to buy tickets two to three days in advance. If you're leaving from a town that's not the start of the train route, however, you'll only be able to obtain same-day tickets. Often a sales clerk will declare that there are no more places when in fact only the two upper classes are full—ask about the other classes as well. Otherwise, try again later at the Intourist office or at the ticket window when tickets are "re-distributed." As one Intourist agent put it, "All the tickets are trapped in a bag—once in a while, someone opens it and lets them out." It's also possible, but risky, to ask the conductor to seat you. Ask: "Мне нужно место; мы можем договориться?" (mnye NOOZH-no MYE-stoh; myh MOH-zhem doh-goh-REET-sah?—I need a place; can we work something out?). Generally, the conductor will charge the cost of the ticket, pocket the money him- or herself, and find you a seat. Otherwise, those who positively need a ticket that day turn to the **scalpers** in the main ticket hall, who ask: "Вам нужен билет?" (Vahm NOO-zhen bee-LYET?—Do you need a ticket?). Scalpers generally charge anywhere from a little to a lot more than the ticket should cost. The tickets they offer are usually valid—check by showing one to a cashier and asking "Когда поезд приходит?" (koh-GDAH POH-ezd pree-KHO-det?—When does the train arrive?). Most towns also have a **central ticket bureau** with an Intourist window. The lines are long and the cashiers are unpredictable, but they are usually close to the center.

Your **ticket** is labeled across the top with the train number, the date and time of departure, the car number, and class. A few lines down you can find your seat (место; *myesto*). If you've planned far enough ahead to have a choice of **class**, there are four to choose from. At the top is *lyuks* (люкс), or *2-myahky* (мягкий; 2-person soft)—a place in a two-bunk cabin in the same car as second-class *koupeyny* (купейний), which has four bunks. Both classes have the same type of beds: almost comfortable, with a roll-up mattress and pillow. The next class down is *platskartny* (плацкартний), an open car with 52 shorter and harder bunks. Places 1-37 are most stable. Places 34-37 are next to the unnaturally foul bathroom. Places 38-52 are on the side of the car—during the summer, the upper-side bunks get hotter than any other spot in Ukraine. Women traveling alone can try to buy out a *lyuks* compartment to avoid nasty drunks, or can travel *platskartny* with the regular folk and depend on the crowds to shame would-be harassers into silence. Avoid the *obshchy* class, where chickens taken to market might lay an egg on your seat when you get up to use the loo. It's a good idea to bring some food and drink to share with others on long journeys. In the upper classes, the car monitor will rent out **sheets** for around 5hv; in *platskartny,* most monitors don't care if you bring your own sheets for the roll-up mattress, but some grumpy ones won't let you use the mattress unless you've paid for sheets.

Except in Kiev, where **platform** numbers are posted on the electronic board, the only way to figure out which platform your train leaves from is by listening to the distorted announcement. In large cities, trains arrive some time before they are scheduled to depart, so you'll have a few minutes to show your ticket to fellow passengers, look helpless, and say "платформа?" (plaht-FORM-ah?). When tripping between Lviv and Kiev, choose trains #92 (to Kiev) and 91 (to Lviv)—both have special "Grand-Tour" cars (Гранд-Тур) that offer still greater coziness (60hv).

Buses are a bit more expensive, but the best way to travel short distances. In large cities, buy tickets at least the night before at the regular ticket-windows. In smaller cities, the *kasa* will start selling tickets only an hour before the bus departs. Sometimes, they'll direct you to buy the ticket from the driver, but always try the *kasa* first. Each platform has its buses posted.

River transport is infrequent, but some routes do exist. Kiev hydrofoils go only as far as Chernihiv. The port agents know more than the Intourist offices, which feign ignorance of the existence of boats.

Taxis overcharge everyone, especially foreigners; agree on a price before getting in. State taxis (recognizable by their checkered signs) wait for passengers at taxi stands throughout cities. Unregulated "private transport" or "gypsy cabs," hailed by holding the hand at a downward salute, are probably the cheapest and most convenient way to travel short distances within a city. Potential passengers ask "Сколько?" (SKOL-koh?—How much?); the driver will say, "SKOL-koh dahsh?" (How much will you give?) Figure out how many kilometers away your destination lies, and haggle. In summer '97, the accepted price of a ride was 0.80-1hv per kilometer, but this changes with the petrol prices. *Let's Go* does not recommend such private transport as a safe means of travel.

TOURIST SERVICES

The breakup of the Soviet Union technically brought about the demise of the official state travel agency, **Intourist**, which was responsible for foreigners traveling to Ukraine. They still have an office in almost every city, sometimes under another name, and offer hard-to-find train tickets, but are used to dealing with groups, not individual travelers. Be sure to smile a lot, speak slowly, and be persistent. Smaller tourist offices, if you can find them, may be more helpful and have cheaper services. Don't be surprised if they don't have any maps or speak any English.

MONEY

On September 2, 1996, Ukraine decided to wipe the extraneous zeros off most prices by replacing the **karbovanets** (Krb; a.k.a. kupon) with a new currency, the **hryvnia** (hv; гривна; pl. hryvny); each hryvnia is worth 100,000 karbovantsi. Beware of individuals who might still try to hand over karbovantsi as change. Hotels usually request hryvny, and only occasionally ask for dollars. International train tickets are usually sold partly in hryvny, partly in dollars. **Exchanging** dollars and Deutschmarks is fairly simple, since Ukrainians frequently use the two currencies themselves; it can be done at Обмін Валют (*Obmin Valyut*) kiosks. Other currencies pose difficulties; **traveler's checks** can be changed into dollars at small commissions in many cities in Ukraine, although this can be a long process, and the banks that cash the checks may have limited hours. **X-Change Points** is another Renaissance thinker in the Dark Ages of Ukrainian finance—they have **Western Union** and can give Visa cash advances (currently available in Kiev, Odesa, Yalta, Uzhhorod, Dnipropetrovsk, and Lviv). Some other banks in big cities will give EC, MC, and Visa cash advances for a high commission; this, too, will probably take a long time. The lobbies of fancy hotels usually exchange dollars at lousy rates. **Private money changers** lurk near legitimate kiosks, devising brilliant plans for taking your money. DO NOT exchange money with them. It's illegal, and they might slip you a wad of useless karbovantsi.

COMMUNICATION

Mail is cheap but slow; allow a minimum of two to three weeks from Kiev to any foreign destination. From other cities, it may never arrive, or even be picked up. You can theoretically drop pre-stamped mail in any "почта" (*pochta*) box, but taking it to the post office yourself is a good idea. The easiest way to mail letters is to buy pre-stamped envelopes at the post office. **DHL** is available in Kiev, Odesa, and Lviv.

Telephones are struggling out of the Stone Age. Order international calls at the post office by writing down the number and country you're calling; there is usually a minimum of three minutes per call, but you're not charged if no one's home. When the call is ready, five to 25 minutes later, you'll be pointed to the right booth. **Utel** (Ukraine telephone) has begun producing electronic **phonecards** available in 10hv, 20hv, and 40hv denominations. They work out to be more than the average post office minute, but are significantly less of a hassle. You can take advantage of Utel's new technology to make **collect calls** from some phones. Dial 27 10 36, and ask for an "ITNT" (a.k.a. AT&T) operator. **AT&T Direct** is available from Utel or private phones. Utel charges 2hv for the connection; the number is (8) 100 11—wait for another tone after the 8. To reach **MCI**, call (8) 100 13; **Sprint** is (8) 100 15. Utel phones can be found in expensive hotels, city telephone centers, and sometimes in expensive restaurants. From private or Utel phones, the international dialing prefix is 810. Order intercity calls at the post office and pay up front; in some cities, payphones marked "міжміський" (*mizhmisky*) work with tokens. At some post offices you will be handed a **plug** when you pay for the first three minutes; insert it into the upper left corner of the front of the phone to get a dial tone, then dial (city code plus number). **Local calls** cost 10-30hv in most cities from any gray payphone. In Kiev, only phone cards are accepted, and can be bought at post offices, the train station, the phone office, and some kiosks. In Lviv, buy **tokens** at the post office or at kiosks. When calling abroad from a hotel, ask the operator to connect you to Utel, which will connect you to an Anglophone operator.

LANGUAGE

Your trip will go more smoothly if you can throw around a few words of **Ukrainian** or **Russian** (see **Glossaries: Ukrainian,** p. 814, and **Russian,** p. 811). In Crimea and most of east Ukraine, Russian is more common than Ukrainian; even in Kiev, most people speak Russian (although all official signs and announcements—such as on the Metro—are in Ukrainian). In west Ukraine, Ukrainian is preferred, and **Polish** is both more accepted and better understood than Russian. The Ukrainian alphabet resembles Russian (see **The Cyrillic Alphabet,** p. 797); however, there are character and pronunciation differences. The most notable additions are the "і" (*ee* sound) and the "ї" (*yee* sound)—the "и" is closest to "s*i*t." The rarely used "є" sounds like "ye" in "yep!" The "ґ" (hard "g") has been reintroduced since independence but is not yet widely used, and the "г," pronounced "g" in Russian, comes out like an "h." "R"s are rolled, though not flamboyantly.

HEALTH AND SAFETY

> **Emergency Numbers: Fire:** tel. 01. **Police:** tel. 02. **Ambulance:** tel. 03.

In every interaction with a Ukrainian who's not after your green bills, you'll be told to keep your foreign profile low, watch your belongings, and not make easy acquaintances, especially on the street. Although **crime** is a widely advertised problem, the risk isn't much greater than in the rest of Eastern Europe. Try to blend into the local look (see **Customs and Etiquette,** p. 694), and you'll be able to give that extra unstolen dollar to a beggar upon leaving. Travelers who have been harassed by the police say it's possible to get back on the law's good side with the aid of a US$20 bill. It's a wise idea to **register** with your embassy once you arrive in Ukraine. Besides making the process of recovering a lost passport much quicker, the embassy staff may be able to offer important information on travel or the situation in Ukraine.

Authorities recommend boiling water for 10 minutes before drinking it, although buying bottled water seems even more sensible. Fruits and vegetables from open **markets** are generally safe, although storage conditions and pesticides render thorough washing absolutely necessary. Meat purchased at public markets should be checked very carefully and cooked thoroughly; refrigeration is a foreign concept and insect life thrives. Embassy officials declare that Chernobyl-related **radiation** poses only a minimal risk to short-term travelers, but the region should be given a wide berth. For more on Chernobyl, see p. 56. Public restrooms range from yucky to scary. Pay **toilets** (платный; *platny*) are cleaner and might provide toilet paper, but bring your own anyway . Public toilets are normally porcelain holes in the ground; due to weak flushing power, there is usually a wastebasket for toilet paper.

Pharmacies are quite common, and medications prescribed by local doctors are usually available. Aspirin is the only available painkiller, but plenty of cold remedies and bandages are at hand. In large hotels, imported medications may be available for hard currency. **Sanitary napkins** (гігієнічні пакети; hee-hee-eh-NEE-chnee pak-YET-ih) and **condoms** (презервативи; prey-zer-vah-TIV-ih) are intermittently available at kiosks.

Women traveling alone are likely to be harassed in one way or another. Ukrainian women never go to restaurants alone, so expect to feel conspicuous if you do, even at midday. Small cafes and cafeterias are safer options; even hotel restaurants may be dangerous. If need be, turn to an older woman for help in an uncomfortable situation; her stern rebukes will usually be enough to embarrass the most persistent jerks.

There is not much racial diversity in Ukraine today. The openness of the university system to African and Arab students used to bring, if not a sizable non-Caucasian population, than at least one that has accustomed locals to complexions other than their own. Outside university cities, **discrimination** might be more prevalent.

ACCOMMODATIONS AND CAMPING

Not all hotels accept foreigners, and those that do often charge them many times what a citizen would pay. Hotels fall into two categories, **"hotels"** and **"tourist bases"**—called "Турбаза" (TOOR-bah-zah), which usually form part of a complex targeted at motoring tourists, but are otherwise nearly indistinguishable from hotels. Though room prices in Kiev are astronomical, singles run anywhere from 5hv to 90hv throughout the rest of Ukraine. The phrase "самое дешёвое место" (SAHM-ah-yih dih-SHOHV-ah-yih ME-stoh) means "the cheapest place." Approaching cautiously, looking innocent, and not interrupting the receptionists' conversation can also lower the price. The more expensive hotels aren't necessarily nicer, and in some hotels, lone women may be mistaken for prostitutes. Most cities have cheap hotels above the train stations—these are usually seedy and not always the safest of places.

Tourism is slow, so hotels usually have room. Hand your passport over to the **administrator** (администратор), who will ask your *familiya* (фамилиа; last name), where you arrived in the country, and how long you are staying. They may hold on to your passport during your stay, although you can get it back if you politely suggest you'd rather keep it with you. You will be given a *vyzytka* (визитка; hotel card) to show to the hall monitor (дежурная; *dezhurnaya*; or чергова; *cherhova*) to get a key; surrender it on leaving the building. Conditions are usually adequate, although you will need your own **toilet paper** (buy it at kiosks or markets). Hot water is a godsend when you find it; some places have no water at all for a few hours every day. Valuables should never be left unattended; ask at the desk if there's a **safe.**

Private rooms can be arranged through overseas agencies or bargained for at the train station. Prices run 2-5hv per person, but conditions are quite variable, and the room always sounds better at the station. During the summer months, **university dorms** might put you up for a couple of nights, depending on whether the *kommandant* likes you. Come during business hours to see this powerful bureaucrat. A bed usually costs 2-4hv. Most cities have a **campground** on the edge of town. The old Soviet complexes can be quite posh, with saunas and restaurants. Space in an electrified bungalow runs 10-20hv per night; tent space and use of facilities run 5-15hv. Free camping is illegal, and enforcement can be merciless.

FOOD AND DRINK

New, expensive restaurants (main dishes 15-60hv and up) are popping up to accommodate the few Ukrainians who can afford them. There are few choices between these and the cheap, sometimes risky bars and *stolovayas*. You can lose big eating at an overpriced restaurant, with the meal entering into a pitched battle with your stomach; or you can emerge triumphant, getting fresh beef-and-vegetable borscht, *kotleti* (cousin of the hamburger), and *kartoshka* (mashed potatoes) for under 2hv at a *stolovaya*. Look around you when you enter restaurants—if people are eating, you should, too. If not, they know something you don't. The more liquor a cafe serves, the worse its food. The famed **stolovaya** (столовая), **yidalnya** (їдальня), and **cafeteria** (кафе) are dying bastions of cheap, hot food. There is usually a choice of two soups, two main dishes, and some *kompot* (a homemade fruit drink); pick up your tray, point to what you want, and pay your bill (usually about 1-2hv) at the cashier. The busier it is, the fresher the food. Non-fresh *stolovaya* food can knock you out of commission for hours, while a delicious *stolovaya* meal is a triumph of the human spirit. **Vegetarians** can fill up here, although cucumbers, tomatoes, and carrots can begin to grate. Most restauranteurs' reactions to vegetarians are hostile, and the meat-free menu rarely has more than 'shrooms (гриби; *hribi*).

Produce is sold by the kilogram in jam-packed **markets** that fill enormous warehouses. Bring your own bags or buy them at nearby kiosks. Markets are open daily, usually by 7am, and close no earlier than 5pm. **State food stores** are classified by content. *Hastronom* (Гастроном) sells everything, but concentrates on packaged goods. *Moloko* (Молоко) offers milk products. *Ovochi-frukty* (Овочі-фрукти) sells fruits and vegetables, often preserved in large jars. *Myaso* (Мясо) provides meat, *Hlib* (Хліб) bread, *Kovbasy* (Ковбаси) sausage, and *Ryba* (Риба) fish. You must usually pay the cashier for the item you want (just tell her the price), point out the counter where you're about to obtain the merchandise, retrieve a receipt, and only then trade the receipt for the item (this also goes for the state department stores, Универмаг; *Unyvermah*). In the suburbs, there is one store per designated region, labeled simply Магазин (*mahazyn*; store). Kiosks often have the same products as expensive Western stores, only for much cheaper (this applies only to non-perishables, however; dairy and meat products are probably not refrigerated in kiosks).

Liquor is available everywhere and is very cheap. A half-liter bottle of *Stolichnaya* costs about 3hv and is generally tastier than the moonshine (*samohonka*) Ukrainians might offer you in their homes. The quality of **beer** depends on the hardships it went through on its way to you. *Obolon* (оболонь) is the most popular, but Lviv's *Zoloty kolos* (Золотий колос) and *Lvivske* (Львівське) outdo it quality-wise. Don't miss out on *kvas* (квас), an unholy and delicious mix of fermented bread and water poured for pennies from huge barrels in the street. For more information on exactly *was ist kvas,* see **"Just for the Taste,"** below. At mealtime, don't count on free water. Few eateries carry water at all; those that do charge more for it than for juices.

CUSTOMS AND ETIQUETTE

A variety of attitudes has arrived in Ukraine. **Smiling** was positively out before, but now being "nice" is riding a high wave, relatively speaking. Even parties to which a foreigner might be invited assume a serious air from the start. Arrive bearing flowers, vodka, or pastries for the hosts, and a grin for the other guests, but expect chitchat to soon evolve into political discussions. Unless you know the situation in Ukraine well, confine your comments to the beauty of the countryside and the weather. Don't defend your liberal views even it kills you not to do so. Topics such as abortion and **homosexuality,** although not taboo, usually provoke a negative reaction. Dinners can last long into the evening; if you try to leave early, you may offfend your hosts.

Although locals don't usually leave **tips,** most expats give the waitron 10% of the meal's price for a beer or two. Often, the server will collect the tip him- or herself simply by giving no change after he takes your money.

Sporty, sturdy backpacks give away your foreignness, as do sloppy T-shirts, jeans, and sneakers. Women and girls are often quite dressed up; shorts, if worn at all, are fancy and normally accompanied by dress shoes.

NATIONAL HOLIDAYS

Ukraine observes: January 1, New Year's; January 7, Orthodox Christmas; March 8, International Women's Day; April 19, Orthodox Easter; May 1-2, Labor Day; May 9, Victory Day (1945); August 24, Independence Day (1991); October 28, Liberation Day (1944).

Just For the Taste

When the sun is high and the steppe is hotter than a parking lot in the middle of the Sahara, Aussies thirst for a Fosters, Czechs for a Pilsner, and Dakotans for a Bud, but a true Ukrainian won't have anything other than a ladle of **kvas** (квас). In Kiev you'll see it served from siphons, and in the provinces from rusty cisterns. The taste—kind of like beer without the hops—varies depending on the container, but it all comes down to acidic bread bubbles; the drink is based on a sourdough solution that rushes tingling into your bloodstream. It's so addictive that Kiev drinks *kvas* all summer, even in the rain, when groups of young tots, middle-aged shoppers, and teenagers in love huddle around toothless tap-masters, all trying to fit under a leaky umbrella.

LIFE AND TIMES

HISTORY

The **Scythians** plied the steppe during the first millenium BC, terrorizing their neighbors with brilliant archery and horsemanship. These semi-nomadic raiders, who only occasionally penetrated Ukraine proper, were in turn replaced by invaders from Central Asia and the Baltic region. While the Crimea and the Black Sea Coast were settled by **Greeks** and **Romans,** the Scythians of the steppe were succeeded by Sarmatians and **Goths,** the latter occupying the entire area from 250AD. The **Huns** rode out of Mongolia in the 370s, replacing the Goths and settling in the south for 300 years.

Recorded Ukrainian history did not begin until the **Kievan Rus** dynasty sprang from the infiltrations of Viking (Varangian) and Baltic fur traders into the Dnipro River region in 882. They grew wealthy from the newly opened north-south fur trade among Constantinople, Novgorod, and the Baltic trading organizations. Though the Kievan aristocracy were Varangian Swedes, they created the first Slavic state and, more importantly, the first Slavic culture, adopting Cyril and Methodius's Cyrillic alphabet as well as the **Christian** religion. Prince **Volodymyr the Great** (I) welcomed missionaries from Constantinople, and was baptized in 988. With the conversion came an influx of Byzantine ideas and culture, which so enraptured Kievan Rus that it attempted to conquer its southern neighbors three times. Volodymyr's son **Yaroslav** promoted architecture, art, music, and particularly the development of written Old Church Slavonic. Kievan Rus declined after Yaroslav's death, however, and the empire splintered as succession problems, meddling Byzantines, and slowing trade depleted its coffers.

Following the empire's collapse, its territory—which included not only modern-day Ukraine but also Belarus, Novgorod, and Vladimir-Suzdal—was divided between nomadic Cumans and Patzinaks and leftover Varangian parcels. The **"Golden Horde,"** Genghis Khan's Mongol army, moved in the 1230s, establishing khanates—the power bases in the area. **Batu,** Genghis Khan's grandson, conquered Kiev in the famous 1240 sack of the city. His death halted the seemingly inevitable penetration of the continent and allowed the khanates to splinter. The Crimean peninsula, however, was ruled by a khanate until 1783.

> The 19th-century Ukrainian nationalist movement was led by the poet Taras Shevchenko, who created a vision of a free Ukraine.

By the mid-14th century, Ukraine was being ruled simultaneously by the Tatars, the grand duchy of Lithuania, and the kingdom of Poland. The **Cossacks,** armed bands on horseback, became the indigenous power structure, and supported themselves by renting their services to the Polish and Lithuanian kings, who had the native Cossacks ward off excursions from Constantinople and **Muscovite Russia.** The fiercely independent Cossacks revolted, however, in response to Polish expansion into their territory. The famous rebellion led by *hetman* (commander-in-chief) **Bohdan Khmelnitsky** defeated a Polish force and reclaimed Kiev and Lviv. An agreement with Moscow helped ward off Polish domination, and the Cossacks led the Muscovite expansion into Siberia. A treaty of 1667, however, divided Ukraine between Russia and Poland, and indigenous culture was suppressed by both powers. Under the **Russian empire,** most of Ukraine was reorganized into Russian provinces; Jews were restricted to the Right Bank, which became known as the **Pale of Settlement.** Odesa grew into a large metropolis and Jewish center, but Jews throughout Ukraine were increasingly victimized by **pogroms** and other types of persecution.

Ukrainian nationalism resurfaced in the 19th century, led by the poet and painter **Taras Shevchenko,** who sought to revitalize the Ukrainian language and create a vision of Ukraine as a free and democratic society. Shevchenko was arrested and exiled to Central Asia for his pains, and in 1863, Aleksandr II issued a decree banning publication in Ukrainian and, in 1876, stage performances and public readings in the language. This repression served only to fan the flames of Ukrainian nationalism, and the movement culminated with the Central *Rada* (council) in Kiev declaring Ukrainian independence in 1917, taking advantage of the tsar's political weakness. The **Bolsheviks** set up a rival government in Kharkiv and seized complete power during the Russian Civil War (1918-20). Under Communist rule, Ukraine was fully incorporated into the **Soviet Union,** answerable in all realms to Moscow. However, the nationalist movement endured, drawing strength from Soviet mismanagement and collectivization, Stalin's forced famine of 1932 (which claimed 7 million lives), hatred of Nazi invaders and Russian settlers, the long-standing ban on the teaching of Ukrainian in Soviet schools, and the Chernobyl disaster of 1986.

Ukraine pulled out of the Soviet Union on December 1, 1991, following an overwhelming vote by 93% of its population for complete **independence.** At the same time, the nation became the beneficiary of a sizeable nuclear arsenal, a portion of the Soviet Black Sea fleet that was under dispute until 1995, and Europe's second largest army. Another legacy of Soviet rule is the foreign conquests, which until recently threatened Ukraine's existence; in the 1994 **presidential elections,** 90% of the Crimean voters supported Prime Minister **Leonid Kuchma** and his promises to cooperate with Russia, while 94% of Lviv's population opted for **President Leonid Kravchuk**'s more nationalist agenda (although he was once Ukraine's head Communist ideologue). Kiev sided with Kravchuk 60-35%. Kuchma won, but has essentially followed in Kravchuk's footsteps. There were riots in Crimea at the end of June 1995, and the issue of police and mafia cooperation is increasingly contentious.

LITERATURE

Ukrainian literature has traditionally looked to diverse sources, finding inspiration in canonical classics and lesser known Polish, Czech, and Slovak texts. Many Ukrainian writers have also emigrated, making it tricky to sort out exactly who can claim them. Needless to say, Russia tends to assert its prerogative when it comes to authors of international repute, e.g. Mikhail Bulgakov and Aleksandr Pushkin.

The first "Ukrainian" literature consisted of the outpourings of the Kievan Rus dynasty. Written in Old Church Slavonic, translations initially constituted the mainstay of the textual supply. Original texts soon sprung up in the **Monumental Style** of the 11th to 13th centuries—works embellished by epithets and alliteration. The documents, infused with an attitude that Communists later attempted to impress upon unwilling Ukrainian comrades, concentrated upon exalting the unified Russian state.

In the 12th century, a new **Ornamental Style,** replete with symbolism and hyperbole, was added to the mix. As the empire was losing strength, Ukrainian writers became disillusioned with the reality of the world and despaired of achieving a harmonious kingdom on earth. The most important endeavors of this era were the **Paterikon** of the Kiev-Pechersk Monastery—an epistolary novel that even the most expert 18th-century English practitioners would be proud of—and *Slavo o polku Ihorevi* (*The Song of Igor's Campaign*), a largely symbolic epic in the courtly tradition. This work is still famous today, and Vladimir Nabokov rendered it in English in 1960. The promise of new literary terrain that these texts displayed was squashed, however, when the Lithuanian-Polish alliance subsumed the territory Ukraine already possessed.

After a long stretch of semi-dormancy, Ukrainian literature re-emerged in the 17th and 18th centuries. Since the country was still politically disparate, these works were sometimes written in Polish or Latin. Emblematic and figured verses, as well as parodic poetry, appeared in print everywhere. One of the most significant exponent of these pieces was **Ivan Velychkovsky.** A new genre emerged—drama, which blossomed into a vital form with historical and morality plays. While some plays were comic, the *intermedia* performed alongside and supplied by authors like **M. Dovhalevsky** and **George Konysky** provided repositories for most of the humor. The most accomplished contemporary author, **Ivan Kotliarevsky** (1769-1838), virtually created the language of the Ukrainian vernacular. In his comic travesty of Virgil's *Aeneid,* called the *Eneïda,* Kotliarevsky not only incorporated all sorts of common Ukrainian idioms, but even transformed the heroes into Cossacks. Imagine Aeneas's horror!

Focusing on ethnography and the creation of scholarly histories of Ukraine, the Romantic movement rediscovered folk tales and added a national element to the newly developed Ukrainian style. Kharkiv, home to **Izmayl Sreznevsky** (1812-80), **Levko Borovykovsky** (1806-89), **Amvrosy Metlynsky** (1814-70), and **Mykola Kostomarov** (1817-85), was an important literary center. Soon the center of Romanticism shifted to Kiev, where Kostomarov, **Panteleymon Kulish** (1819-97), and **Taras Shevchenko** (1814-61), probably the most

> In his comic travesty of Virgil's "Aeneid," Kotliarevsky transformed the heroes into Cossacks. Imagine Aeneas's horror!

famous individual in Ukrainian literature, joined the Brotherhood of Sts. Cyril and Methodius, which was devoted to furthering Ukrainian national identity. In *Knyhy bytiya ukrainskoho narodu* (*Books of Genesis of the Ukrainian People*), Kostomarov expresses the belief that his society, though temporarily incapacitated, will rise again as part of a pan-Slavic union. Shevchenko's brilliantly crafted poems, which sometimes resemble folk songs, speak of Ukrainian autonomy and history, idealizing the Cossack period. Kulish was a novelist who emphasized Ukraine's disparate groups in his portrait of the nation. His novels include *Mykhailo Charnyshenko* and *Chorna Rada* (*The Black Council*).

The Realist period that followed Romanticism also drew from folk sources. Ethnographism infiltrated into naturalistic novels and stories, where conflicts occur between various Ukrainian classes such as the Cossacks and the *chumaks* (exalted wagoners). **Marko Vovchok** (the pseudonym of **Maria Vilinska-Markovych;** 1833-1907) treated the serfs' plight and the oppression foisted on her country by the Russians. Composed in a vernacular style, her tales were recommended by Shevchenko as a way to learn Ukrainian and its idioms. Contemporary poets included **Stepan Rudansky** and **Leonid Hlibov,** while **Ivan Nechuy-Levytsky** and **Panas Myrny** ranked among the novelists. The greatest Realist of the late 1800s was **Ivan Franko** (1856-1916), a poet and novelist who drew from the thematic stash of other European writers and experimented with psychological portraits.

Franko provided a bridge to Modernism, which blossomed in early 20th-century Ukraine. In prose, **Mikhail Kotsiubinsky** (1864-1913) wrote *Fata Morgana,* a study of village life from a subjective and personal vantage point. **Lesya Ukrainka** (1871-1913) proved Ukraine's foremost figure in this period. Having begun with exotic lyrics, she then adopted universal and psychological themes, and eventually developed the verse drama, in which she embraced subjects from various periods and cultures in an attempt to tear the country away from cultural self-absorption.

Stalin's purges from 1933 to 1938 resulted in the imprisonment or execution of many of Ukraine's finest writers. After WWII, experimental schools were suppressed by Russian forces. The Symbolist movement was best embodied by poet **Paul Tychyna,** Futurism was founded by **Michael Semenko,** and Neoclassicism represented by **Maksym Rylsky.** Today, as Ukraine feels its way out of a dire economic situation, it simultaneously endeavors to acquire a new literary life.

UKRAINE TODAY

Over the last two years, Ukraine's relationship with Russia has become somewhat more stable. The two nations initialed a Treaty of Friendship and Cooperation in 1995, but final signatures never materialized, due to disagreements over dual citizenship and control of the Black Sea Fleet. These issues were resolved in June of that year; Russia got control of Sevastopol as a naval base, and received 86% of the fleet. The nation's more serious problem is its shattered economy. Some estimates put unemployment at 40%, as factories stand still, agriculture tries to rid itself of Communist collectivization and psychology, and technological industries attempt to cope with the "brain drain." Perhaps most devastating, however, is the Communist work ethic—the old joke that "they pretend to pay us, and we pretend to work," is still valid as salaries remain unpaid, and workers at hotels, train stations, and stores behave correspondingly. But there appears to be light at the end of the ex-Soviet tunnel, with the economy expected to pull slowly out of its massive recession. In September 1996, a new currency, the **hryvnia,** was introduced to slash five zeros off the previous karbovanets. Inflation was down to 40% in 1996, and reached only 5% in the first half of 1997.

Democracy has yet to arrive in any real sense, however. With a powerful left-bloc opposition in parliament, it is difficult for President **Leonid Kuchma** to implement radical reforms. In June 1996, the parliament approved a new constitution, calling for the introduction of a **Senate** in March 1998 elections. The country plans to resist greater CIS integration and to seek EU membership. The 1999 presidential elections are already shaping up; Kuchma has announced that he will seek a second term, and former prime minister Yevhen Marchuk—dismissed in May 1996—will oppose him. For the budget traveler, although this near anarchy does not make for a smooth trip, it does mean the possibility of seeing a nation in crisis as it attempts to find a place in a world that has left it behind.

Kiev (Київ)

> ...Most often of all I soothe my aged imagination with pictures of gold-domed, garden-cloaked and poplar-crowned Kiev.
> —Taras Shevchenko (from exile)

Laboring under Moscow's shadow, Kiev is not only having a hard time trying to divert tourists south, but is also struggling to recoup its Ukrainian character after a long stint as Russia's third city. With an economic crisis raging around the country and many regions' eyes turned to the capital for help, Kiev cannot find the time to care for itself. Artfully sculpted houses need more than a touch-up to regain their past glory—many are already gutted and abandoned. Mothers begging money for their sick children in Metro stations cannot afford the threepenny rolls that bundled-up country women sell beside them. Meanwhile, a gaudy rich caste glories in its opulent couture and German cars. Kiev needs years to return to the magnificence of which Shevchenko spoke, although tourists will find sights worth a prolonged stop.

ORIENTATION AND PRACTICAL INFORMATION

Although the city straddles the Dnipro River (Дніпро), almost all the attractions and services lie on the right (west) bank. The **Metro's** three intersecting lines—blue (MB), green (MG), and red (MR)—cover the city center but leave most of the outskirts to trolleys and trams. The **train station** is at MR: Vokzalna (Вокзальна). Two stops away is the **Khreshchatyk** (Хрещатик) stop and street, a broad and busy postwar boulevard. Parallel and up from vul. Khreshchatyk runs **Volodymyrska vul.** (Володимирська), brimming with history. **Bulv. Shevchenka** (Шевченка) and **vul. Khmelnytskoho** (Хмельницького) run perpendicular to these. The center of Kiev is vul. Khreshchatyk's **Maydan Nezalezhnosti** (Майдан Незалежності), a fountain-filled fun spot next to the post office. You can buy **maps** (3-5hv) here or in any kiosk.

Tourist Offices: Intercity Travel, vul. Hospitalna 4, #304 (Госпітальна; tel. 294 31 11; fax 220 54 46), on the 3rd floor of Hotel Rus (Готел Рус). As close to a tourist office as you get in Kiev. English spoken. *Kiev Pocket* guides—well worth the 10hv—sold in the downstairs lobby. Open Mon.-Fri. 9am-8pm, Sat. 10am-4pm. The lobby of **Hotel Kyivska** (Київська, formerly Hotel Intourist), behind Hotel Rus at vul. Hospitalna 12, stocks *The Kiev Post*—an English newspaper with the latest info on the city and where to have fun. Also sold in expensive restaurants. Both hotels are at M: Respublikansky stadion (Республіканський стадіон). After emerging from underground, cross the plaza bearing left around the stadium fence; take the elevator past the stadium's ticket office up the hill, and the hotel will be in front of you.

Embassies: Australia, vul. Kominternu 18 (Комінтерну; tel. 225 75 86). Open Mon.-Thurs. 10am-1pm. **Belarus,** vul. Sichnevoho Povstaniya 6 (Січневого Повстанія; tel. 290 02 01). **Canada,** vul. Yaroslaviv Val 31 (Ярославів Вал; tel. 212 35 50). Open Mon.-Tues. and Thurs.-Fri. 8:30am-noon. **Latvia,** vul. Desyatynna, 4/6 (Десятинна; tel. 229 23 60). **Russia,** pr. Kutuzova 8 (Кутузова; tel. 294 79 36 or 294 63 89). Open Mon.-Thurs. 9am-6pm, Fri. 9am-5pm. **U.K.,** vul. Sichnevoho Povstaniya 6 (tel. 290 73 17; fax 290 79 47). Open Mon.-Fri. 9am-noon. **U.S.,** vul. Y. Kotsyubinskoho 10 (Ю. Коцюбинського; tel. 244 73 49; emergency tel. 216 38 05). From Maydan Nezalezhnosti, take trolley #16 or 18 from the top of the square to the 4th stop, and walk down between the Nike and the fruit store. Open Mon.-Fri. 2-5pm. If you're going to your own country's embassy, don't be intimidated by the line for visas—simply show your passport and the security guard will point the way. If you have a passport or visa problem, ask for the *konsulstvo.*

Currency Exchange: *Obmin-Valyut* (Обмін-Валют) windows on every street and alley. They usually take only US$ and DM. No traveler's checks or credit card advances—those are handled by many banks, which offer slightly worse rates. New booths that cash traveler's checks and give Visa and MC advances are appearing, but usually have bad rates or rob you with high commissions. **Legbank** (Легбанк), vul. Shota Rustaveli (Шота Руставелі). From M: Palats sportu (Палац спорту), go northwest on vul. Rognydinska (Рогнидінська) and turn right on Rustaveli. Some of the best rates and lowest commissions (3% for MC and Visa; 2% for traveler's checks if amount is over US$250, otherwise flat US$5 commission). Open Mon.-Sat. 9am-7pm. **NIKA** (НІКА), bulv. Shevchenka 2 (M: Khreshchatyk), a Legbank booth, is located in the center. Open daily 10am-8:30pm with a lunch break. There were no **ATMs** in summer '97, but they may appear soon.

Western Union: vul. Priorizna 17 (Пріорізна; tel. 229 52 36), off Khreshchatyk. Open Mon.-Fri. 9am-7pm, Sat.-Sun. 11am-4pm.

Flights: Kiev-Boryspil Airport (Київ-Бориспіль), 30min. (by car) east of the capital. Cash-only exchange office. 25hv-per-person **buses** leave from the front of the terminal at 2:20 and 3pm and drop passengers off at Hotels Dnipro and Rus. Cheaper is the city bus or a *marshrutne taksi* (маршрутне таксі)—both dump the newly arrived at MR: Livoberezhna (Лівобережна) for a mere 2.5hv (every 2hr.). Buy your ticket on the bus. If you must take a **taxi,** 120hv should be haggled down to 55-60hv, though natives can get it down as low as 20hv. Private company **Taksys** (Таксис; tel. 295 95 08) charges 40hv.

Airline Offices: Air Ukraine, pr. Peremohy 14 (Перемоги; tel. 216 70 40 or 276 70 59). **Austrian Airlines, SAS,** and **Swissair,** Bolshaya Vasilkovskaya 9/2 (tel. 244 35 40 or 244 35 41), inside the blue-fenced Makulon, corner of vul. Khreshchatyk and bulv. Shevchenka. **British Airways,** bulv. Shevchenka 10 (tel. 246 43 98). **Malév,** Volodymyrska vul. 20 (tel. 229 36 61). Open Mon.-Fri. 10am-5pm. Inside Hotel Khreshchatyk at vul. Khreshchatyk 14-16 are: **Air France** (tel. 229 13 95; fax 229 73 80; open Mon.-Fri. 9am-5pm); **ČSA** (tel. 228 02 96; open Mon.-Fri. 9am-5pm); **LOT** (tel. 228 71 50; open Mon.-Fri. 9am-5pm, Sat. 10am-2pm); and **Lufthansa** (tel. 229 62 97; fax 229 29 72; open Mon.-Fri. 9am-5:30pm). Most of these airlines have offices in Boryspil Airport (tel. 296 75 29) as well.

Trains: Kyiv-Passazhyrsky (Київ-Пассажирський; schedule info tel. 005), Vokzalna pl. MR: Vokzalna or tram #2. **Tickets** can be purchased at Intourist window #10 on the 1st floor. Open daily 8am-1pm, 2-7pm, and 8pm-7am. Beware any clerk who demands payment in U.S. dollars at an unreasonable price. There are also potential ticket-buying intermediaries on the main floor. **Advance-Ticket Kasas,** bulv. Shevchenka 38. MR: Universytet (Університет); cross and go left down Shevchenka. No passport required, but the long lines and many lunch breaks mean at least an hour's wait. Open Mon.-Fri. 8am-7pm, Sat.-Sun. 9am-6pm. Kiev is one of the few places in Ukraine where there's no shame in going through **Intourist** (see **Tourist Offices,** above). Scalpers toss 4-6hv on top of the ticket's real price, but they may have tickets that no one else has. Locals ask a clerk to check if the ticket is valid before handing over the money. *"Pro-VER-teh, po-ZHA-lus-tah, EH-tot bee-LYET VAZH-ny"* means "Please, check if this ticket is valid." If Intourist or the *kasy* claim

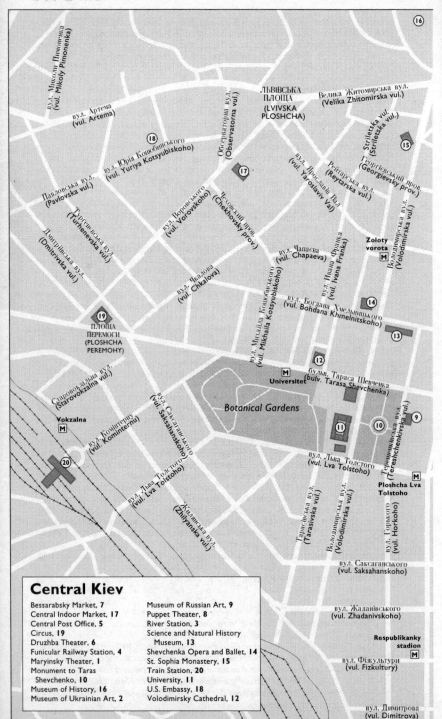

Central Kiev

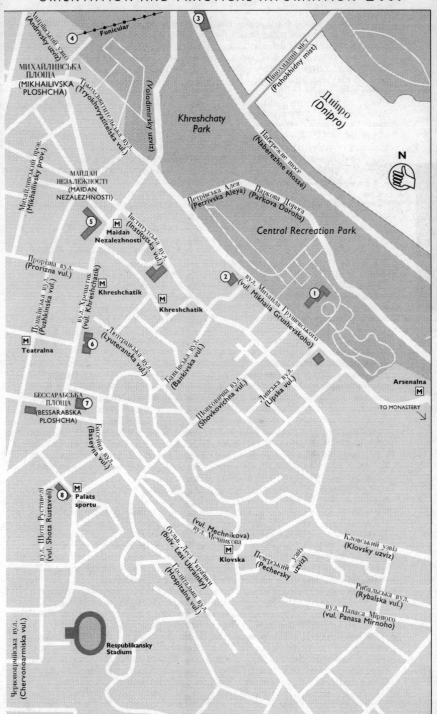

not to have tickets, don't despair—check again the day of the train, 6 and 2 hours ahead (no, it does *not* make sense). To: Ivano-Frankivsk (1 per day, 16hr., 17hv); Kamyanets-Podilsky (1 per day, 11hr., 13hv); Lviv (5 per day, 12hr., 16hv); Odesa (6 per day, 19hr., 16hv); Simferopol (3 per day, 18hr., 21hv); and Uzhhorod (3 per day, 19½hr., 22hv). For **international tickets,** you will need to present your passport so they can charge you a higher price. Witness: Bratislava (daily, 18hr., 108hv); Bucharest (daily, 17hr., 110hv); Budapest (daily, 12hr., 149hv); Minsk (daily, 12-13hr., 33hv); Moscow (6 per day, 15-17hr., 43-61hv); Prague (daily, 34hr., 149hv); and Warsaw (2 per day, 15hr., 66hv).

Buses: Tsentralny Avtovokzal (Центральний Автовокзал), Moskovska pl. 3 (Московська; tel. 265 04 30). Long-distance destinations. To: Kharkiv (2 per day, 17hv); Minsk (2 per day, 21hv); and Moscow (2 per day, 42hv). **Darnytsa** (Дарниця), pr. Gagarina (Гагаріна; tel. 559 46 18), sends buses to Dnipropetrovsk (9hr., 18hv) and Pereyaslav-Khmelnitsky (1½hr., 3hv). **Pivdenna** (Південна), pr. Akademyka Hlushkova 3 (Академика Глушкова; tel. 263 40 04), connects to Odesa, and **Podil** (Поділ), vul. Nyzhny Val 15a (Нижній Вал), sends buses to Crimea. From M: Kontraktova pl. (Контрактова площа), take a short walk northwest along vul. Konstyantynivska (Констянтинівська) and hang a left onto vul. Nyzhny Val.

Hydrofoils: Richkovy Port (Річковий Порт), on Pochtova pl. (Почтова; tel. 416 12 68). M: Pochtova pl. Boats brave the Dnipro's waves only as far as Cherkassy (2 per day, 3 on Sat.; 5½hr.; 9.70hv). Only the 7:30am boat stops in Pereyaslav-Khmelnitsky (2¼hr., 6.25hv); it leaves for Kiev at 4:30pm.

Public Transportation: Kiev's **Metropoliten** is clean and efficient, but it does not reach the university dorms. Local maps color-code the Metro lines, though the cars and stations are all gray. Buy tokens at the "Каса" (*Kasa*) for 0.30hv or a monthly pass from a numbered kiosk for 10hv. Monthly passes are good on all forms of public transportation. If you buy a pass, slide it through the slot on top of the turnstile to enter. You might get hit by the jaws of doom, but ignore them and go on. Guards watch all the time—you won't get away with anything. Check the map *before* you go down the escalator. At the bottom, the order of stations is posted on each side. The stations signs are all in Cyrillic—consult your handy *Let's Go* subway map. People may seem rude and in an unnecessary hurry to get on the train, but when the unforgiving doors slam on you, you'll understand. "Перехід" (*perekhid*) indicates a walkway to another station, "вихід у місто" (*vykhid u misto*) an exit onto the street, "вхід" (*vkhid*) an entrance to the Metro, "нема вхіду" (*nema vkhidu*) no entrance. Tickets for **trams, trolleys,** and **buses** are sold at numbered kiosks (0.30hv) and must be punched on board. If there's a conductor on board (identifiable by badge and tickets in hand), you can buy a ticket from her/him. Be sure to do this right away to avoid the 6hv fine (or jail!) for not having a ticket. Transport runs 6am-midnight, but some buses travel later. Trolleys and buses with identical numbers may have very different routes.

Taxis: Foreigners are overcharged; avoid taxis if you can. Otherwise, give the driver an address *near* your hotel; he won't assume so quickly that you're a foreign businessperson on an expense account. **State taxis** (tel. 058) are more consistently priced and are identifiable by the checkered sign on top. The private company **Taksys** (Таксис; tel. 295 95 08) is a little bit cheaper at 0.36hv per min. 6am-11pm and 0.40hv per min. 11pm-6am. 40hv to the airport. **Private cars** that function like taxis are cheaper; people normally agree on a price before getting in and use their judgment as to how safe it is. The signal for a ride is an arm held down at a 45° angle. *Let's Go* does not recommend such private transport as safe.

Luggage Storage: There are several luggage rooms at the train station, so remember where you left your bags. 2hv. Open daily 8am-noon, 1-7:30pm, 8pm-midnight, and 1-7:30am. Hotels charge more, but are safer; you don't have to be a guest. **Hotel Rus** (see **Tourist Offices,** p. 698) charges 3hv per bag per night. Open 24hr.

English Bookstore: Znaniya (Знания), blvd. Khreshchatyk 44 (tel. 224 82 19), has the widest selection, including classics and modern stuff. Open Mon.-Fri. 10am-7pm. It also has a **photocopier** (0.15hv per page). Also inside **NIKA,** bulv. Shevchenka 2. MBR: Khreshchatyk or Teatralna (Театральна). Books, papers, magazines, *Kiev City Guide.* AmEx, MC. Open Mon.-Sat. 9am-9pm, Sun. 9am-8pm.

Kiev Metro

Героив Днипра (Meroiv Dnipra)
Мінська (Minska)
Оболонь (Obolon)
Петрівка (Petrivka)
Тараса Шевченка (Tarasa Shevchenka)
Контрактова плоша (Kontraktova ploshcha)
Поштова плоша (Poshtova ploshcha)
Майдан Незалеж ности (Maidan Nezalezhnosti)
Хрещатик (Kreshchatik)

Дніпро (Dnipro)

Лісова (Lisova)
Чернігівська (Chernihivska)
Дарниця (Darnitsya)
Лівобереж на (Livoberezhna)
Гідропарк (Hidropark)
Дніпро (Dnipro)
Арсенальна (Arsenalna)

Бортничі (Bortnichi)
Проспект (Prospekt Bazhana)
Осокорки (Osokorky)
Славутич (Slavutich)

Львівська брама (Lvivska brama)

Святошин (Svyatoshin)
Нивки (Nivki)
Берестейська (Beresteyska)
Шулявська (Shulyavska)
Політехнічний інститут (Politekhny institut)
Вокзальна (Vokzalna)
Університет (Universitet)
Театральна (Teatralna)
Золоти ворота (Zoloty vorota)
Плоша Льва Толстого (Ploshcha Lva Tolstoho)

Видубичі (Vidubichi)
Друж би Народів (Druzhby Narodiv)
Печерська (Pecherska)
Клопська (Klovska)

Республіканський стадіон (Respublikansky stadion)
Палац спорту (Palats sportu)

Палац "Україна" (Palats "Ukraina")

Либідська (Libidska)

〰️ Red line
▬ Blue line
〰️ Green line
■■■■■■ Under construction
◯ Transfer station

N

UKRAINE

24-Hour Pharmacy: Apteka, corner of vul. Khmelnytskoho and vul. Ivana Franka (Івана Франка), sparkles with cleanliness and carries high-quality products. Open 24hr.; ring the bell 8pm-8am. **Hotel Kievska** and **Hotel Rus** (see **Tourist Offices,** above) also have well-stocked hard-currency pharmacies in their lobbies.

Gay Information: Check out the monthly publication *Odyn z nas* (Один з нас; tel. 435 64 36; fax 228 72 72). Call for info in Russian and Ukrainian.

Medical Assistance: Emergency Care Center, vul. Mechnikova 1 (tel. 22 42 02 or 227 92 30), also has a **dental clinic** (tel. 227 42 40). The new **American Medical Center,** vul. Berdicherska 1 (tel. 211 65 55; fax 211 65 57), will cost you dearly.

Express Mail: DHL, vul. Vasilkivska (Босильківська; tel. 264 72 00) at Holosiivska pl. (Голосіївська). MB: Libidska (Либідська), on the 1st floor of Pushkinska 42/4 (Пушкінська). Open Mon.-Fri. 9am-7pm, Sat. 10am-1:30pm. **UPS,** vul. Mechnykova 20 (Мечникова; tel. 290 00 00 or 290 10 19). Open Mon.-Fri. 9am-6pm.

Post Office: vul. Khreshchatyk 22, next to Maydan Nezalezhnosti. *Poste Restante* at counters #26-27. Pre-stamped airmail envelopes (1.28hv at counters #10 and 14) are the easiest way to send international mail. Otherwise, the staff weighs and stamps letters at the entrance behind the fountain. Info at counter #10 (no English spoken). To mail packages, enter on the Maydan Nezalezhnosti side. At counter #10, an **email** message can be typed for you and sent for 0.80hv per kilobyte (approximately 1 page). Administrator speaks some English; ask about *elektronna pochta.* Open Mon.-Sat. 8am-8pm, Sun. 9am-7pm. **Postal code:** 252 001.

Telephones: Myzhmisky Perehovorny Punkt (Мижміський Переговорний Пункт), at the post office, or **Telefon-Telefaks** (Телефон-Телефакс), around the corner (entry on Khreshchatyk). Some phones require that you dial an initial "8." To: Moscow 0.45hv per min.; U.K. and Ireland 2.79hv; U.S. 4.64hv; Australia and New Zealand 7.43hv; South Africa 6.50hv. State the number of minutes you want and pay up front. Both offices open 24hr. When making an international call from a private phone, dial 8, wait for a tone, then dial 10, country code, city code, and number. Calls within Kiev require phone cards (0.50hv). **Utel phone cards** are available in denominations of 10hv, 20hv, and 40hv at the post office and upscale hotels. Utel phones can be found in the post office, the train station, hotels, fancy restaurants, and Dim Ukrainski (Дім Український), across from Hotel Dnipro. **Phone code:** 044.

ACCOMMODATIONS AND CAMPING

Hotel prices in Kiev will seem rude at best. However, Kiev's large student population has to live somewhere. The setbacks are that "somewhere" ranges from somewhat distant to very distant, you never know who your roommate might be, and the *kommandant* may refuse to house a foreign tourist. **Diane Sadovnikov**—a former missionary living and working here—and her husband, Yuri, arrange accommodations and a few other services, such as airport drop-off/pickup (US$35-45), invitations (US$30), phone calls, and faxes (office: tel./fax 516 05 48; home: tel. 558 10 58; email 76745.1766@compuserve.com; office open 9am-5pm). Located right near MR: Darnitsa, they can arrange lodging in a private apartment (45-75hv per person), place you with a family, or help make hotel/dorm reservations (possibly at a discounted rate). It's best to fax her a month in advance. Another possibility in a pinch is Eric, the owner of **Club Sofia** (see **Nightlife**, p. 711), who will try to find you a cheap private room for a night or two.

Grazhdanski Aviatski Institut Student Hotel, vul. Nyzhinska 29E (Нижінська; tel. 484 90 59). From behind MR: Vokzalna, ride 5 stops on tram #1 or 7 to "Граматна" (*Hramatna*). Walk back a block, swing a right onto vul. Nyzhinska, and cross the first intersection diagonally into the block complex. Pass the first house, turn left, and walk along the wavy path until "Гостиница ФПК" appears above the entrance to the building 29E, on the right. Singles 13.20hv (1 night 17.80hv). Doubles 11hv per person (1 night 16.50hv). Communal showers. Cafeteria nearby (see p. 705).

Hostinitsa Universytetsky (Університетський), vul. Lomonosova 81 (Ломоносова; director tel. 266 74 44). At MB: Libidska, go right, then left, through the tunnels to get to bus #38. Take it to the end at "Ковалевської" (*Kovalevskoy*), then go a little farther to the two 9-story buildings. 30min. from center. *Avtosvit* (Автосвіт) minibuses also go back and forth, but won't stop unless you flag them down (0.50hv). Call before 5pm and ask for the director. Ask if you can have a room, give him your name, and tell him when you're coming. Upon arrival, insist on speaking with him, not the secretary. Refer to your phone call. Doubles with shower, kitchen, and balcony 66hv, without TVs and fridges 40hv. No English spoken.

Hostinitsa Druzhba (Дружба), bulv. Druzhby Narodiv 5 (Дружби Народів; tel. 268 33 87; fax 268 33 00). MB: Libidska. Go left, then right, in the Metro tunnels. Once above ground, go straight for 100m and turn left before the overpass onto the major road. The hotel is 100m up on your left. Small, shabby, but clean rooms. Short and narrow beds. The cheapest hotel in Kiev, the bathrooms work, and it's on a Metro line. Call ahead and confirm reservations by fax. 3-bed room 55hv per person; doubles 132hv, with shower 162hv. Not always hot water. Be persistent, as they might not mention the cheapest rooms they have available.

Hostinitsa Bratyslava (Братислава), vul. Malyshka 1 (Малишка; tel. 551 76 44). M: Darnytsya (Дарниця). Go left and left again in the Metro tunnel. Head right across the park, and Bratyslava is the concrete beast to the left. The inside is not as Socio-Real as the outside, though the beds are short and narrow. They claim to sterilize toilets after each guest moves out—we can't confirm, but bathrooms are clean. Singles with bath US$54; doubles with bath US$75. AmEx, EC, JCB, MC, Visa.

Taras Shevchenko University Dorms, vul. Lomonosova 37 (director tel. 266 47 64). MB: Libidska, then bus #38 (see directions to Hostinitsa Universytetsky, above) to "Гуртожиток" (*Hurtozhitok*), the 10th stop. Director's office in dorm #2. Same headache as at the Universytetsky, but you're dealing with a different institution. If you can't reach the director, call the dean (*prorektor*) at 266 20 96. Small 2- to 3-bed dorms 1.50hv per person. You probably won't want to take a shower here.

Motel-Camping "Prolisok," pr. Peremohy 179 (tel. 444 12 93). From MR: Svyatoshin (Святошин), take trolley #7 west to "Автостанція Дачна" (*Avtostantsiya
Dachna*), and then go 2km down the highway. Dim, comfy motel doubles 107hv.
Tent space 8.80hv per person. A restaurant, sauna, and trailer parking attract foreign truck drivers. Utel phone on premises. EC, MC, Visa.

FOOD

The number of people in Kiev's restaurant equals the number of coins in locals' pockets—very few. In fact, anticipate undisturbed solitude as you visit the capital's eating
dens. The places that are high-priced even by Western standards cater to foreigners
and the few Ukrainians who can afford them. Locals choose Kiev's specialty drinks
over munchies: *Stolichnaya* vodka, *kava no-skhidnomu* (кава по-східному; eastern-
style coffee), and good-old *kvas* (квас), which vendors sell (0.30hv per 0.5L) in the
most-touristed areas—i.e., Khreshchatyk and Podil, where the majority of the restaurants are found. Meals cost 12hv and up, with a few exceptions. **Mini-Menu** fast-food
bars and markets sell cheaper food, but the former are Western junk, and the latter
sell provisions requiring a kitchen for consumption. The *hastronom* (гастроном;
supermarket) is ubiquitous, usually closing around 7pm. Western-style **supermarkets**
have sprung up everywhere in the center, though they can be good for refrigerated
meat and some other rarities, many of the same items can be found at kiosks and *has-
tronomy* for much lower prices. **7/24,** vul. Baseyna 1/2 (Басеина; tel. 221 58 57),
behind Bessarabsky Rynok, is open 24/7, and accepts EC, MC, and Visa. **Teatralny**
(Театральный), vul. Khmelnystkoho 30/10 (tel. 228 62 65), has similar attributes.

Restaurants

Stary Agat (Старий Агат), vul. Sahaydochnoho 6 (Сагайдочного). M: Poshtova ploshcha. Walk right as you face the funicular. Hungry tourists dine in a white-washed
room at lunchtime and a dusky boudoir (in which stained glass provides the only
light) at dinner. Cheap! Filling *kievskie bitki s garnirom* (cutlets with french fries
and veggies) for just 4.50hv. Open daily 10am-midnight.

Montannya Snack (Монтання Снак), vul. Volodymyrska 68 (tel. 221 70 45). MB:
Ploshcha Lva Tolstoho. Go west on Tolstoho and take the 2nd left on Volodymyrska. Filled with expats and locals. Lebanese dishes in "sandwich" or "meal" format—the first in pita with paper, the second on plate with veggies. Chicken
shwarma sandwich 5hv. Delicious veggie falafel plates with garlic mayonnaise
sauce 4.30hv. Hummus, too. Open Mon.-Fri. noon-11pm, Sat.-Sun. noon-midnight.

Pizza Lola (Піша Лола), vul. Lva Tolstoho 3 (Лва Толстого; tel. 224 74 23). MB:
Ploshcha Lva Tolstoho. Follow the street for 2min., and Lola's in the basement on
the left. Full of molten cheese, these Ukrainian pizzas put Italy to shame. Four
wooden tables inside to support your personal circle of joy (additional seating outside). One-person cheese pizza 7.50hv, with 2 toppings 9hv. 0.5L beer 3.50hv.
Soda water 0.50hv. Open daily 11am-9pm, in summer until 10pm.

Stolovaya (Столовая), Kudravsky Uzviz 7 (Кудравський Узвіз; tel. 417 10 48). Good,
hearty Ukrainian food for next to nothing. Potato soup and bread 0.38hv; *kasha*
(buckwheat), a tomato and cucumber salad, and *kefir* 1.50hv. Not many choices,
but everything's fresh. Open noon-3pm only. Expect lines.

Pantagruel (Пантагрюэль), vul. Lysenko 1 (Лисенко; tel. 228 81 42), right next to MG:
Zoloty Vorota. Delicious, authentic Italian food prepared by a genuine Italian chef in
this low-key little cellar. Rigatoni with tomato and basil (8.50hv); spaghetti with pep-
peroni sauce (9.50hv), and other main dishes (16-22hv). Live music Fri.-Sat. 8-10pm.
Open Sun.-Thurs. 11am-11pm, Fri.-Sat. 11am-2am. English-language newspapers sold.

Yidalnya Kmutsya (Ідалыя Кмуця), prosp. Kosmonavta Komarova (Космонавта Комарова), at vul. Hramatna. Close to the Student Hotel (see p. 704 for directions). The
yidalnya occupies the 3rd floor of the tile-and-dirty-glass building. Fill a tray with
kasha, rolls, eggs, and chicken (about US$1). Then join the students and blue-col-
lar workers stuffing themselves. Open daily 8am-5pm.

Kentucky Beirut Chicken, bulv. Shevchenka 5 (tel. 229 02 94). Yup! A KFC imitation with Lebanese ownership. The higher prices are due to the Middle Eastern
cabbage and sour cream salad. Chicken burgers with fries (3.45hv); chicken Ken-

tucky-style (6.50-10hv). English menu. Call for take-out or delivery (but pay for the inflated price of the taxi). Open 11am-11pm. MC, Visa.

McDonald's, at Khreshchatyk Metro, Lukianivska Metro, and Sevastopolska pl. All opened within the last year, offering the usual comforting or horrifying (depending on how you look at it) food and atmosphere. Hamburgers are cheap (1.25hv). Khreshchatyk Metro branch open Mon.-Thurs. 7am-midnight, Fri.-Sun. 7am-1am.

Cafes

Kavyarnya Svitoch (Кав'ярня Світоч), vul. Velika Zhitomirksa 8a (tel. 228 33 82). On the right as you follow the street from Mikhailivska pl. This famous Lviv confectioners' opened its Kiev outlet in 1995; the cafe's next door. *The* place for black coffee (1hv) accompanied by a toothsome chocolate (0.20-0.45hv). Popular with students. Open daily 9am-9pm.

Vechirny Kyiv (Вечірній Київ), vul. Khreshchatyk 15, in the *pasazh.* Some call its ice cream the best in Kiev. Walnuts and apricots in their creamy 'n' frozen state do wonders for the palate. All natural. 100g scoop 2.13-2.58hv. Outdoor patio for seeing and being seen. Open daily 11am-4pm and 5-10pm.

Cafe U Georga (Кафе У Георга), vul. Khreshchatyk 10. MBR: Maydan Nezalezhnosti. The main street's best grotto for a lunchtime shot of vodka (1hv). A semicircular counter, no tables, loud music about love and San Francisco, and sober, vodka-loving regulars. If vodka sounds too scary, order an eastern coffee (0.70lv) and chat with the barperson about your low tolerance. Open daily 10am-10pm.

Markets

Ukraine is all-European with its continental love of fresh food, even though swarms of flies share the love. The French have their *marchés,* the Kievans their *rynki.* Same continent, same difference.

Bessarabsky Rynok (Бессарабський Ринок; tel. 224 89 34), at the intersection of vul. Khreshchatyk and bulv. Shevchenka. The best of the Ukrainian bazaar-chic sprawl out their goodies here. Anything sells—soap, knitting needles, plum preserves. Come just for the Ukrainian countryside spirit in the middle of Kiev. Open Mon. 7am-5pm, Tues.-Sun. 7am-7pm.

Volodymyrsky-Kolhospny Rynok (Володимирский-Колгоспний Ринок), vul. Chervonoarmyska, between vul. Telmana (Тельмана) and vul. V.-Libidska. MBG: Palats Ukraina (Палац Україна). Even larger than the Bessarabsky. Same deals: flowers, provisions, clothes, tapes, and unhappy furry animals. Open daily 10am-7pm.

Kolhospny Rynok (Колгоспний Ринок), vul. Vorovskoho (Воровського) and vul. Obervatorna (Обсерваторна). 80s Europop stars on tape, food, shoes, and Asian remakes of the most American symbol: the T-shirt. Bargains and bizarre items can be found at the row of kiosks upstairs. Open daily 10am-7pm.

SIGHTS

A millennium as Ukraine's capital has left Kiev with a store of historical sights. Many of these mementos are now crumbling, which only gives the downtown districts a more deep-down aura of decadence. Renovations are underway, and in five years, the naturally weathered beauty may get a facelift and lose itself in thick polish.

Vul. Khreshchatyk and Environs

Downtown Kiev centers around **vul. Khreshchatyk,** a broad commercial avenue largely built after WWII as a monument to Soviet-style bigness. The street begins at the intersection with bulv. Shevchenka, where **Lenin** gazes serenely into the future, surrounded by inspirational sayings—one of the rare Communist monuments in Kiev that has not been desecrated. Across the street, the blue-fenced complex at Chervonoarmyska vul. 9/2 was once the residence of top party officials; now it's the residence of choice for foreign businesspeople and ambassadors. On the opposite corner, **Bessarabsky Rynok** (see **Markets,** above) is one of the most ornate of its kind. Walking along vul. Khreshchatyk, check out the **central department store**

TSUM (ЦУМ), Khmelnytskoho 2 (it's on the corner), where everything is sold in a terrifically confusing jumble of counters (open Mon.-Sat. 9am-8pm).

Continuing up vul. Khmelnytskoho, you'll reach the recently built and highly nationalistic **Muzey Literatury Ukrainy** (Музей Літератури України), on the left at #11 (open Mon.-Sat. 9am-5pm; 0.40hv, students 0.30hv, children 0.20hv; guides in Ukrainian 10hv), and the **Opera House,** farther up the street on the right. The museum traces Ukrainian literature from its inception to the present, quoting Ivan Franko and Taras Shevchenko the entire way. English-speaking guides are available only through Intourist for an exorbitant rate, but the museum staff will happily explain everything in Ukrainian. Down the street, **Dramatichny Teatr** shows Ukrainian productions nightly (*kasa* open 10am-3pm and 4-9pm).

Back on vul. Khreshchatyk, the **archway** to vul. Lyuteranska (Лютеранська) leads to a quiet, residential neighborhood along a street lined with pretty stone facades. The next archway leads to Kiev's most cosmopolitan area, a *pasazh* with fancy, high-priced cafes and bars. Suddenly, you arrive at **Maydan Nezalezhnosti,** or "Independence Plaza" (formerly October Revolution Sq.). This is the very center of town; book vendors, occasional musicians, angel-headed hipsters, and others taking a breather fill the terrace around the large fountains. It was the site of the 1905 uprising and of the execution of Nazi war criminals; the **statue of the little guy with a halo and crooked sword** (a.k.a. Archangel Michael), was unveiled in 1996.

Veer to the right past the square onto vul. Instytutska (Інститутська)—another fancy-facade-filled promenade. Just to the left as Instytutska starts its ascent glows the bright-yellow **Palats Kulturny** (Палац Культурни; Palace of Culture), today one of Kiev's biggest concert halls and a Neoclassical rival to the equally eye-catching Rococo **Natsionalny Bank Ukrainy** (Національний Банк України), also on the left. Tracing back from the bank and rocking your way to the left down vul. Baykova (Байкова) leads to another of Kiev's architectural landmarks—**Budynok Horodetskoho** (Будинок Городецького; Horodetsky Building), vul. Bankivska 10 (Банківська; tel. 291 57 91). Its sadistic gargoyles make Gotham's Penguin and friends look like Barbies. When open, the galleries inside are worth seeing. Men and women gather here to debate away the evening over tankards of beer or *kvas;* right-wing, left-wing, and tourist propaganda is sold along the fountain walls; and the occasional street performer pleases crowds. At night, the Metro stop underneath shelters Kiev's best street musicians.

Continue along vul. Khreshchatyk to reach **Ukrainsky Dim** (Український Дім; Ukrainian House; tel. 229 82 87) on the left, across from Hotel Dnipro. Formerly the Lenin Museum, this stepchild of Communist architecture now houses commercial and cultural exhibitions, a carnival of kiosks and concerts (open Tues.-Sun. 11am-6pm). Up the stairs is **Khreshchaty Park.**

Khreshchaty Park

Referred to by locals as the "Yoke," the silver croquet wicket that towers over the park is the **Arch of Brotherhood,** a monument to Russian-Ukrainian union. The park is actually a series of parks, many of which have excellent views. To the left as you go through the Yoke is Prince Volodymyr holding up a cross, overlooking the river where he had the whole city baptized in 988 despite freezing temperatures. Go right at the arch and into the park for the monument to **brave soccer players.** As the story goes, invading Nazis discovered that one of their prisoners was a member of the Dynamo Kiev soccer team; they rounded up the other players and arranged a "death match" against the German army team. Despite their weakened condition and a referee dressed in a Gestapo uniform, the Dynamo team won the match 3-0. They were immediately thrown into a concentration camp, where most of them perished in front of a firing squad. Farther still stands the **Maryinsky Palace,** built by Bartolomeo Rastrelli, the same guy who designed Kiev's St. Andrew's Church and much of St. Petersburg. The palace was built just for Tsaritsa Elizabeth's visit in the 1750s (closed to the public). Across from the lovely garden (also closed) stands a statue of the Ukrainian poet and revolutionary **Lesya Ukrainka,** gazing sensitively at the splendor of aristocrats and pondering the plight of Ukrainian workers. The park then moves towards the Arsenalna Metro stop, but if you resist its rigid paths, you might find the **grave of Prince Askoldel,** who was murdered by the usurping Prince Oleg in 882.

Bulv. Tarasa Shevchenka

A walk past Lenin's metal figure takes you up a street that is simultaneously pleasant and shady, and broad and busy. The boulevard is dedicated to the poet Taras Shevchenko, whose paintings and poetry re-invented the Ukrainian tongue in the mid-19th century. Banished in 1847, he never returned to Kiev. At #12 stands the **Taras Shevchenko Museum** (tel. 224 25 56), one of the largest and most beautiful literary museums in the former USSR, which contains a huge collection of Shevchenko's sketches, paintings, and prints, as well as some of his correspondence and poetry. Exhibits are labeled in Ukrainian and Russian. (Open Tues.-Sun. 10am-5pm; closed last Fri. of the month. 1hv, students 0.30hv; English tours 20hv, students 10hv.) On the left side of the street, inside one of Kiev's many parks, a famous **monument** to the hero stands at least 1½ times taller than Lenin's paltry form. His namesake **university,** on the park's other side, still leads independent thought in Ukraine. Farther up stands the many-domed ochre **Volodymyrsky Cathedral,** bulv. Tarasa Shevchenka 20, built to commemorate 900 years of Christianity in Kiev. The interior blends Byzantine styles with Art Nouveau.

Mikhailivska Ploshcha and Environs

A funicular (see p. 709) ascends the steep hill west of M: Poshtova, landing next to the recently up-graded **Mikhaylivska pl.** (Михайлівська). The sprucing up accompanied a new statue of snow-white Princess Olga surrounded by death-white St. Cyril, St. Methodius, and virtuous St. Andrew the (Orthodox) Apostle. The 10th-century Kievan Rus's overlady posed here petrified as early as 1911; she has since had many ups and downs, but hopes to hang onto her current upright elegance.

A left on vul. Tryokhsvyatytelska (Трьохсвятительська) as you're walking from the funicular leads to several interesting churches. First on the left sits the petite, whitewashed, and onion-domed **Khram Svyatoho Apostola Ioana Bohoslava** (Храм святого апостола Іоана Богослава; Church of the Holy Apostle John). Entrance is *gratis,* but many visitors buy a small candle (0.20hv) from the priests at the door. The dark church shelters richly colored, gilded icons (open daily 8am-8pm). Continuing down the street on the right, the stolid **Kostyol sv. Aleksandra** (Костьол св. Олександра; Church of St. Aleksandr) mixes serenity with multilingual holy chatter, offering masses in seven languages (open daily 7am-8pm; English mass Sun. 8pm).

Dandy back to Olga through **Volodymyrska Hirka** park, full of tiny pavilions, panoramic viewpoints over the Dnipro, and sculptures by folk artists. This is also a favorite gay cruising spot. Behind Olga to the right, the small Desatynna takes off to the beginning of **Volodymyrska vul.** Nearby lies **pl. Khmelnytskoho,** a square of gorgeous 18th- and 19th-century buildings surrounding the monument to **Bohdan Khmelnitsky,** another national hero, frozen while checking his horse in mid-gallop. Across the *ploshcha* towers the enormous, elaborate **St. Sophia Monastery Complex,** Volodymyrska vul. 24. This is what tourists come to Kiev to see: golden onion domes, decorated facades, and exquisite Byzantine icons from the 11th century. The monastery was the cultural center of Kievan Rus and the site of its first library, and is still the focal point in the increasingly complex question of Ukrainian nationalism. In July 1995, the Uniate Church wanted to bury its patriarch here, a request the government turned down. When the funeral procession led by the Ukrainian nationalist militia attempted entry into the complex, they were violently denied by the police. (Open Fri.-Tues. 10am-5:30pm, Wed. 10am-4:30pm. Foreigners 6hv, Ukrainians 2hv, students 1hv. Architectural museum within an additional 1hv, students 0.50hv, as are exhibitions. 1hr. tours are 10hv for foreigners and 3hv for students.). Down Volodymyrska vul. 300m stand the **Zoloty Vorota** (Золоті ворота; Golden Gates), which are actually made of wood and stone. They have stood here since 1037, marking the entrance to the city and separating it from the wilds outside. A museum devoted to the gates is housed inside them (open May-Oct. 10am-5pm; 2hv, students 1hv).

Andrivsky Uzviz and the Podil District

The easiest way to see the cobblestone **Andrivsky uzviz**—a winding road lined with cafes, souvenir vendors, and galleries—is to ride up and walk down. A **funicular** carries couch *kartoshki* up Andrivsky uzviz from MB: Poshtova every five minutes (daily 6:30am-11pm; 0.30hv). Look for signs saying "Виставка" (exhibition). Be prepared to bargain if you want to buy anything. Next to the entrepreneurs selling real Ukrainian pipes and Soviet Army hats, some independent galleries show the newest and boldest work Ukrainian visual artists have to offer, but most just sell touristy paintings of the street's looming, beautiful **St. Andrew's Cathedral** (closed for renovations). The edifice in question gazes proudly down on its street; you can learn about it and the avenue below at the **Andrivsky Uzviz Museum** at #22 (tel. 416 03 98; open Wed.-Sun. 11am-7pm; 1hv). Before starting the climb down, ascend the **Castle Hill Steps,** at the crossroads of Desatynna, Andrivsky, and Volodymyrska, where the best photos of the cathedral can be taken. Once atop the steps, wander around the grounds on which **Desatinna Tserkva** (Десятинна Церква; Tithe Church) used to convert pagan Kievans to Christianity in the 10th century. The oldest stone church of Kievan Rus (ca. 989-96), it endured for centuries only to be deliberately destroyed in 1937. Now only the stone foundations trace the architectural plan. Next to them, the gray **Natsionalny Muzey Istorii Ukrainy** (Національний Музей Історії України; National Museum of Ukrainian History), vul. Volodymyrska 2 (tel. 228 65 45) is worth a stroll, housing exhibits from the Stone Age to the present. Out front lie the very foundations of the Old City, preserved under glass. Tours are available in Ukrainian and German (open Thurs.-Tues. 10am-6pm, closed last Thurs. of each month; 2hv, students 1hv). Back on Andrivsky uzviz, past the museum, **Bulgakov's House** at #13 (tel. 416 31 88) tells you all you need to know about the *White Guard*—but is only worthwhile if you've read the book. (Open Thurs.-Tues. 10am-6pm; 2hv, students 1hv. 45min. tour in English, German, or French 5hv.)

Andrivsky uzviz spills out onto **Kontraktova pl.**—the center of **Podil,** Kiev's oldest district. Its collection of beautiful—though disintegrating—facades is colored by small **churches** of all faiths. In the *ploshcha*'s north corner lies the **Kiev-Mohyla Academy,** the oldest university in this part of the world. Closed by the Communists, it graduated its first class in 1996 after reopening in 1992. Ramble around, and chances are you'll bump into an American exchange student, or at least English-speaking Ukrainians. Not far from the *ploshcha* is the **Chernobyl Museum,** Provulok Zhorevii, 1 (tel. 417 54 22). Powerful imagery conveys the magnitude of the disaster. Ask about the video replaying the explosion, usually shown only during tours (open Mon.-Sat. 10am-6pm, closed last Mon. of the month).

Babyn Yar and St. Cyril's

The moving WWII monument at **Babyn Yar** (Бабин Яр) commemorates the place where victims of the Nazis were buried starting in September 1941. Although the plaques state that 100,000 Kievans died here, current estimates double that figure. Many of the victims, most of them Jews, were buried alive. Take trolley #27 eight stops from MB: Petrivka or trolley #16 from Maydan Nezalezhnosti (about 10 stops, depending on the optional stops). The monument—a large group of carved figures—stands in the park near the TV tower, at the intersection of vul. Oleny Telihy (Олени Телiги) and vul. Melnykova (Мельникова).

From Babyn Yar, four stops on trolley #27 northeast (catch it on the same side of vul. Telihy as Babyn Yar) towards MB: Petrivka take you to **Kyrylivska Tserkva** (Кирилівська Церква; St. Cyril's Church), the multi-domed shelter of Kiev's best frescoes. From the trolley stop, ascend the stairs to your right. An English version of the church's history is available inside (open Sat.-Wed. 10am-6pm, Thurs. 10am-5pm. 5hv; Ukrainians 2hv, students 1hv.)

Lavra and Environs

Kiev's oldest and holiest religious site is the mysterious **Kievo-Pecherska Lavra** (Києво-Печерська Лавра; Kiev-Pechery Monastery), which deserves a full day of exploration. From MR: Arsenalna, turn left as you exit and walk 20 minutes down vul. Sichnevoho Povstaniya. Trolleybus #20 can also take you here (2 stops going left from the Metro, toward the river). Once the center of Orthodox Christianity, its monks were subsequently mummified and entombed in the **caves**—the most interesting part of the complex. Buy a candle (0.30-0.40hv) as you enter if you want to see anything. Women should cover their heads and shoulders; men should wear pants. When in the caves, you're only allowed to look at the monks whose palms are facing up (open Wed.-Mon. 9-11:30am and 1-4pm). Random people offer tours of the underground as you enter the complex, but the rotting remains are self-explanatory: these people were holy, so they get to be covered with gold-threaded fabrics after death. There are numerous churches, gardens, and museums on the grounds, as well as the Italian Embassy. Most noteworthy are the 18th-century **Velyka lavrska dzvinytsya** (Велика лаврська дзвіниця; Great Cave Bell Tower), from which you can get a fantastic view of the river and apartment blocks on the horizon mingling with golden domes (open daily 9:30am-8pm; 2hv, students 1hv), and the 12th-century **Troitska Nadzramna Tserkva** (Тройцька надзрамна церква; Holy Trinity Church), which serves as the entrance to the monastery. The church's interior (take a left upon entering) contains some beautiful frescoes, a 600kg censer, and the **Uspensky ruiny** (Успенськи руїни), the ruins of the 1073-78 Assumption Cathedral, which was destroyed many times, most recently by the Nazis. The monastery, which was a fortress and has 2m-thick walls to prove it, is also a nice place just to perambulate. As some museums require a separate ticket, seeing everything can become quite expensive. Museums that the ticket can be used for include **Muzey Knygy y Knygopechataniya** (Музей книги и книгопечатания), detailing the history of book and printing development in Ukraine, and **Muzey Istoricheskikh Dragotsennostey** (Музей исторических драгоценностей; Museum of Historical Treasures), which displays all sorts of precious stones and metals, both ancient and modern (open Wed.-Mon. 9:30am-4pm), and the Great Cave Bell Tower. The large ticket shows a map of the complex, though the labels are in Cyrillic only. (Open daily 9:30am-7pm; in winter until 6pm. Ticket for all churches and exhibitions (but no museums) 7hv, students 3hv; Ukrainians 4hv, students 1hv. Ticket for churches and some museums 9hv, students 4hv; Ukrainians 5hv, students 1hv. **Jewelry Museum** 3hv, students 1hv. **Miniatures Museum** 2hv, students 1hv. English guides 2-3hv; private tours 45hv.)

Farther along the same road is the hideously static metal **Motherland,** a.k.a. huge lady with a little sword. The sword used to be bigger, but was shortened when the monks raised a stink about it being higher than the bell tower. The statue, which celebrates the WWII victory, was designed by the wife of the sculptor of the Volgograd Motherland statue (see p. 582). Plans to tear down the tin lady and replace her with a monument to the victims of Chernobyl have not yet come to fruition, but the statue might fall of her own accord due to poor construction. Beneath the metal mama lies **Muzey Velykoi Vitchyznenoi Viyny** (Музей Великої Вітчизненої Війни; Museum of the Great Patriotic War), Sichnevoho Povstaniya 33 (tel. 295 94 57), which illustrates the stages of WWII with panoramas, videos, pictures, weapons, and information on concentration camps and the resistance (2hv, students 1hv; Russian or Ukrainian tours 10hv, students 5hv).

ENTERTAINMENT AND NIGHTLIFE

Sports and the Outdoors

During the soccer season (late spring until autumn), don't miss **Dynamo Kiev,** one of the top teams in Europe. Check with the *kasa* at the Respublikansky Stadium, vul. Chervonoarmyska (MB: Respublikansky stadion).

On hot summer days, locals hang out at **Hidropark** (Гідропарк; MR: Hidropark), where you'll find an **amusement park** and **beach** on an island in the Dnipro. The farther from the Metro you go, the cleaner it is. Tucked in a corner near the bridge, **Venice Beach of Ukraine** is where young buffs lift spare automobile parts to keep in shape. The beach has showers, toilets, and changing booths, yet no one seems to charge admission. **Rent boats** at *Otdykh na vode—Fregat* (Отдых на воде—Фрегат), on the east shore of Hidropark, near the Metro bridge (boat or waterbike 3hv per hour; open daily 9am-8pm; last rental 6pm). The free beach is also a hot pick-up spot for the college-age crowd.

The daily and weekend **bazaars** in the summer at Respublikansky Stadion and Vokzalni are an experience in themselves, even if you don't buy any of the myriad sodas and cigarettes hauled here from all over the former Soviet Union. Everything is wholesale—buy in bulk and start your own kiosk. On the last weekend in May, the festival **Kiev Days** takes place, and Andrivsky uzviz is jam-packed with *shashlyk* stands, orchestras, and craftspeople of all sorts who gather from kilometers around.

Performances

Most of Kiev's theaters close in summer. For **tickets,** check with any *teatralna kasa* (театральна каса; open Tues.-Sun. 9am-5pm; tickets 8-10hv). Most shows are in Ukrainian or Russian. Every March, however, international troupes come for a two-week **theater festival,** where you can hear *Macbeth* performed in Austrian or *Master and Margarita* in Australian. **Kinopanorama,** S. Rustaveli, 19 (tel. 227 11 35), shows movies in English.

Philharmonic, Volodimirsky uzviz 2 (tel. 229 62 51). Classic and classical.

Shevchenka Opera and Ballet Theater, Volodymyrska vul. 50 (tel. 224 71 65 or 229 11 69). MRG: Teatralna. Huge and imposing. Several shows each week at noon and 7pm. Ticket office open Tues.-Sat. noon-2pm and 4-7:30pm, Sun. 11am-1:30pm.

Opereta (Оперета), vul. Chervonoarmyska, corner of vul. Zhylyanska (Жилянська). MB: Respublikansky stadion. Favorites by Kalman, Lehar, and Strauss.

Kyivsky Molody Teatr (Київський Молодий Театр; Kiev Youth Theater), vul. Prorizna 17 (tel. 224 62 51). Possibly Kiev's best, but can get expensive. Irregular performances.

Teatr Russkoy Dramy im. Lesy Ukrainky (Театр Русской Драмы им. Леси Украйнки; Lesya Ukrainka Russian Drama Theater), vul. Khmelnytskoho 5 (tel. 224 90 63). Classic and experimental Russian repertoires. Tickets sold Thurs.-Tues. noon-3pm and 4-7pm, Wed. noon-3pm and 4-6pm.

Puppet Theater, vul. Shota Rustaveli 13 (tel. 220 90 65), in an active synagogue. For adults and children.

Koleso, Andrivsky uzviz 8 (tel. 416 05 27). MB: Kontraktova Ploshcha. Theater and cafe. Ticket office open show days 5:30-7pm. Schedule posted outside.

Ivan Franko Ukrainian Drama Theater, pl. Ivana Franka 3 (tel. 229 59 91). Serious, popular, cheap, and mainly Ukrainian works.

Nightlife

Perhaps it is the foreboding presence of the many cathedrals, or the fact that by midnight many people are too drunk to walk, but the capital simply doesn't live up to its big-city billing when it comes to nightlife. Although the scene is improving, young residents still take their bottles of *Stolichnaya* to the beautiful dark parks, to Maydan Nezalezhnosti, where the fountains light up to the sounds of spontaneous jazz,or back home to drink around the kitchen table. What nightlife there is generally belongs to the BMW owner and the foreigner.

Club Sofia, vul. Sofiivska, 7 (Софіївська; tel. 229 88 16), off Maydan Nezalezhnosti. An exception to the above rule. Unofficially "Eric's Bar," this smoky cellar will already be jam-packed with young artists, intellectuals, foreigners, and Ukrainians of all sorts early in the evening. Be sure to greet owner Eric, as everyone else does; he may even be able to hook you up with a cheap private apartment—call the club and ask for him or his wife, Violeta. 0.5L *Obolon* 4hv. Open daily noon-1am.

The Cowboy Bar, vul. Khreshchatyk 15 (manager's tel. 244 34 64), in the *pasazh.* A piece of Ukraine-imagined America on Kiev's Euro-chi-chi street. Raw, unpainted wood filled with cigarette smoke and live blues, jazz, and country music nightly after 9pm. Behind the bar, where *Obolon* flows (0.33L 3hv) for those who can get through the stone wall of people, a "Wanted" poster promises a reward for the capture of "Robber boss Wild Bill." Open daily 6pm-6am.

Rock Cafe (Рок Кафе), vul. Horodetsky 10. M: Maydan Nezalezhnosti. Walk 300m along the street to the right of the giant steps; the cafe is on your right. Easygoing coffeeshop where unpretentious expats hang with their local acquaintances, but evolves into a busy bar at night. Coffee or ½-glass of sparkling water 3hv—you should know by now that in Kiev, you gotta pay to be hip. Outdoor seating. Pool 3hv per game. Open daily 11am-3am.

Dancing

Kiev's most popular discos pale next to the shining stars of Moscow, but keep your ears open for occasional **raves. Disco Bar Viola,** vul. Chervonoarmyska 35, is probably the cheapest club around, with a different flavor each night (rave, jazz, Latin, disco, etc.). It attracts a young, alternative crowd (open daily 6pm-6am; cover 5hv; free Sun.). The hot new **Dinamo Luks Disco,** vul. Hrushevsky 3 (tel. 229 28 84), is right in the center. Bring your money (Fri.-Sat. men 30hv, women 15hv) and your disco-going clothes, and don't arrive before 11pm. Discos **2000, Flamingo, Club Hollywood,** and **River Palace** are havens for those in the fast lane who can afford the 20-30hv covers. Dress up or you *will* be kicked out.

Gay and Lesbian Entertainment

The gay scene in Ukraine has failed to take off the same way it has in Moscow. Yet gay nightlife, previously limited to private parties and irregular club venues, is slowly starting to flourish. The safest and most popular **cruising area** is the so-called "Walk of Shame," which runs along the M: Khreshchatyk-Bessarabska pl. promenade from Bessarabsky Rynok to the recently opened McDonald's near the Metro. There used to be a gay cafe in the spot where the McDonald's is, but now McD's itself has been dubbed "gay McDonald's" by some. The bread store across Khreshchatyk from the Bessarabsky Rynok is known as a place to meet gay men. In the summer, the scene is revived substantially, thanks to Hidropark; follow the mob to **Molodizhny Plyazh** (Youth Beach). There, buy a 1hv boat ride to the beach opposite, where the crowd is mixed and clothes are optional. There's also an all-gay beach nearby, but it's muddy. *Odyn z nas* (Один з нас), a gay magazine with all sorts of literature, struggles to publish on a monthly basis (tel. 435 64 36; fax 228 72 72). The **lesbian** movement is still very underground; the mixed beach is a girl's only option.

■ Near Kiev: Pereyaslav-Khmelnitsky (Переяслав-Хмельницький)

Once the Cossacks' favorite military base, Pereyaslav witnessed the signing of both the Russian-Ukrainian 1654 agreement, which allied Ukraine with Russia, and, five years later, a treaty that gave the Russian tsar control over the country. Perhaps angry about the town's role in their subordination, Ukrainians neglected Pereyaslav over the next 300 years. Unsurprisingly, the town has been trying to hang on to its past glory—its noble heritage proven by ornate cupolas rising above the greenery of parks. The most obvious attempt at historic preservation is the "Museum of Folk Architecture," an outdoor museum (*skansen*) dedicated to the evolution of Ukrainian villages, from thatched roofs and ornate houses to Socialist Realist monuments dedicated to the peasant spirit. Blind-ended paths that go off from the loop in different directions lead to the most grandiose sights: icon-filled churches, windmills, and *kulak* homes. Many houses keep collections of old instruments, ceramic art, or vehicles, each home guarded by a stately or scythe-bearing watchperson. Although not every old domicile and vegetable garden is worth a stop, two sights are a must. Just to the left of the entrance extends a **Socialist-Realist park**, with sculptures, mosaics, and bas-reliefs spiked with pre-WWII airplanes, trucks, and tractors. The second sight sits on an island set in the skansen's pond. A pagan temple stands watch over a meadow that seems made for that brown-bag lunch you brought from Kiev. (Museum open Thurs. and Sat.-Tues. 10am-5pm, Fri. noon-5pm; half closed Tues., the other half Thurs. 1hv, students 0.50hv, guided tour 2hv.)

The bright cupola rising above Pereyaslav proper belongs to **Voznesensky Monaster** (Вознесенський Монастерь). Since 1975, it has functioned as the **Diorama-Muzey Boi za Dnipro v Rayoni Pereyaslava-Khmelnytskoho** (Діорама-Музей Бої за Дніпро в Районі Переяслава-Хмельницького; Diorama-Museum of the Struggle for the Dnipro in the Region of Pereyaslav-Khmelnitsky). The 0.50hv entry (students 0.20hv) is a small price for the thrill you get inside; the diorama (a three-dimensional semi-panorama) almost makes you almost feel as if you're in the trenches (open Thurs.-Tues. 10am-5pm). A stride further down vul. Khmelnytskoho, on the left, **Muzey Kobzarstva** (Музей Кобзарства) displays more *kobzas* than you're ever seen in your life. What's a *kobza*? you might ask. It's like a mandolin, but with 50 or so strings. When the musician makes a mistake, he or she may blame it on the instrument. (Museum open Thurs.-Tues. 10am-1pm and 2-5pm. Foreigners 2hv, Ukrainians 0.40, students 0.20hv. Tours 2hv.) From the museum, go back up vul. Khmelnytskoho, turning left on vul. Moskovska (Московська), the other sight-studded street in town. At the end of the street, **Mykhaylivska tserkva** (Михайлівська церква) exhibits a **Muzey Odyahu** (Музей одягу; Costume Museum). The costumes are extensive, but the blue interior walls, ceiling frescoes, and the tiny monastery garden are most worth the walk and fee (0.50hv, students 0.20hv; open Thurs.-Tues. 10am-5pm).

The **hydrofoil** from Kiev (2 per day, 3 on Sat., 2¼hr., 7hv—it's the 3rd stop) drops visitors off 1km south of the *skansen*. From the river station, turn left, then right onto the main road, and left onto the tree-lined alley that leads to a cupola-studded horizon. The avenue leads to the *skansen*'s gates. You must go through the village-life museum to reach Pereyaslav-Khmelnitsky proper. Stay on the main dust road and bear right onto its descending branch. Exit through the museum gates, bear right towards the little river, and walk along it to the bridge on the left. Take the overpass and turn right on **vul. Lenina** (Леніна); its second major intersection is with **vul. Khmelnytskoho** (Хмельницького), the slowly pulsating aorta of Pereyaslav. **Pl. Vozzyednannya** (Возз'єднання), the town's softly beating heart, is to the left. To reach the **bus station,** walk left on vul. Khmelnytskoho and continue as the street turns first left, then right (20min.). There are many buses to Kiev's Darnitsy station, since most travelers coming should stop here (1½hr., 3hv). Buy a ticket at the "Мижміська каса," window #2. If the clerk refuses to take the money and blurts out something in Ukrainian, don't despair—she or he is telling you to pay the driver.

EASTERN UKRAINE (СХІД УКРАЇНИ)

Stalin continues to haunt Eastern Ukraine. The country's largest cities lie here, and the region boasts the world's most polluted city: Kharkiv, whose rivers are a prime holiday spot for colonies of cholera. Still, you're likely to pass through on the way to Crimea. If so, a stop in Dnipropetrovsk will be least likely to endanger your health, and will allow you a glance of the ex-USSR's Five-Year-Plan heritage.

■ Dnipropetrovsk (Дніпропетровськ)

A city of currency exchanges, more than a million inhabitants, and major river and rail junctures, Dnipropetrovsk has an eclectic charm that just barely keeps it from becoming a gloomy metropolis. Originally Katerinoslav, for its 1784 founder Catherine II, Dnipro has been open to individual foreign travelers only since 1990. Now the city can be a fine stop on the way…elsewhere.

Orientation and Practical Information About 600km southeast of Kiev and equally north of Simferopol, Dnipropetrovsk sits on both sides of the **Dnipro**

river as it turns right. Most essentials are on **pr. Karla Marxa** (пр. Карла Маркса), which begins as you bear right from the train station and continues to the top of a hill at **Oktyabrska pl.** (Октябрьська). A left on ul. Lenina (Леніна) will take you to the **tourist office** at #8 (tel. 45 15 09; open Mon.-Fri. 8:30am-5:30pm). Yogi Berra once said: "If you can't find a **currency exchange** in Dnipropetrovsk, you ought to have your head examined." **Privatbank,** vul. Serova-Naberezhna, 5b (Серова-Набережна), office #33 (tel. 78 11 35), sucks cash from your Visa (3% commission); and at 5a, office #12 (tel. 41 32 31), exchanges traveler's checks (2% commission; open Mon.-Fri. 9am-noon and 1-5pm). **Trains** run to: Moscow (2 per day, 19hr., 33hv); Odesa (2 per day, 14hr., 9.5hv); Simferopol (1 per day, 12hr., 8hv); and Rostov-na-Donu (every other day, 13hr., 18hv). **Buses** chug from the station at ul. Kurchatova 6 (Курчатова; tel. 78 40 90) to Odesa (1 per day, 10hr., 24hv) and Kiev (1 per day, 10hr., 22hv). **Luggage storage** is in the basement of the train station (1.20hv; open 8am-midnight). Faxes, fun, and phone cards await at the central **post office,** pr. Karla Marxa 62 (open Mon.-Sat. 8am-8pm, Sun. 8am-7pm). *Poste Restante* is at window 12. **Telephones** are next door (4.65hv per minute to your loved ones in the U.S.; open 7:30am-11pm). **Postal code:** 320 000. **Phone code:** 0562.

Accommodations and Food Accustomed to hosting dangerous CIA agents trying to get a look at the latest in Soviet missile systems, Dnipro's hotel technology doesn't yet have a place in its heart for tight-budget travelers. The hotel on the fifth floor of the **bus station** offers the only cheap rooms in town. In a cruel twist of irony, they have only *hot* water (singles or doubles 4hv per person). The **Tsentralny** (Центральний), pr. Karla Marxa, 50 (tel. 45 03 47), charges a bundle for its short-bedded rooms (singles 68hv; doubles 115hv). The **Astoria** (Асторія), at Karla Marxa, 66 (tel. 44 23 04), has only doubles (62hv; with shower 110hv)

The **central market,** at the intersection of pr. Karla Marxa and ul. Gorkovo (Горького), on tram-line #1, opens daily 6am-5pm. Bread and drinks are also sold at the market next to the Tsentralny. A brand new **supermarket** at ul. Pastera, 2 (Пастера, tel. 78 70 32) is well-stocked with foreign goods (open daily 7am-7pm). The restaurant scene is dismal, but the small **cafeteria** at ul. Shmidta, 7 (Шмідта), has *shashliks* at reasonable prices (4hv; open Tues.-Sun. 8am-1pm and 2-6pm). Take bus А or Б from the train station.

Sights and Entertainment Tram #1 heads up the hill to Oktyabrska pl. The yellow building on Lomonosov's right is the **Istorichny muzey** (Історичний музей; Historical Museum), pr. Karla Marxa, 16, with displays on the history of the city, lots of Cossack revolutionary items, and pictures of Cossacks you wouldn't want to meet in a dark alley (open Tues.-Sun. 10am-5pm; 1.50hv). Through the museum and past some displayed artillery is the **Preobrazhensky sobor** (Преображенский собор; Transfiguration Cathedral), a slim structure only one-sixth of its intended size—Catherine II didn't cough up quite enough hryvny. The interior is simply designed, with stellar artistry in light hues (open daily 7am-noon and 3-6pm). This is also one of the few buildings in town that doesn't house a currency exchange. Across the square and down the hill stands the peachy gate to **Park Shevchenko** (Парк Шевченко). The beautiful building on the right used to be **Palats Potomkina** (Палац Потомкина; Prince Potomkin's Palace), but is now a center of student cultural life. Continuing down the hill and across the bridge will bring you to **Komsomolsky Island,** the city's most popular park. Paddle boats can be rented to the right of the bridge (5hv per 30min.).

Back in the center of town, an impressive **Holy Trinity Cathedral** rises from behind the concrete buildings of pl. Lenina. At the end of trolley line #4 at pr. Kalinina, 66 (Калініна), a large church is now a **House of Organ Music** (tel. 52 30 05), with several shows a month (*kasa* open daily 2-5:30pm). Surprisingly, Dnipro has several nightclubs worthy of your moves, as well as a local eponymous brew that tastes distinctly related to Guinness. **King Kong** (Кинг Конг), in Park Shevchenko, is popular with the student crowd. It's in the round concrete building by the river, above the restaurant **Mayak** (Маяк; open Wed.-Sun. nights; cover 5hv). **Plotina** (Плотина; tel. 45

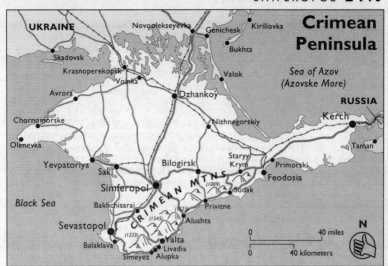

Crimean Peninsula

UKRAINE

Novoolekseyevka · Genichesk · Kirillovka

Skadovsk · Bukhta

Krasnoperekopsk · Voinka · Valok

Avrora · Dzhankoy · Sea of Azov (Azovske More)

Chornomorske · Nizhnegorskiy · RUSSIA · Kerch

Olenevka · Taman

Yevpatoriya · Saki · Bilogirsk · Staryy Krym · Primorski · Feodosia

Simferopol · CRIMEAN MTNS (1009) · Sudak

Black Sea · Bakhchisarai · (525) · Privitne

Sevastopol · (1545) · Alushta

Balaklava · (1233) · Yalta · Livadia

Simeyez · Alupka

N

0 — 40 miles

0 — 40 kilometers

UKRAINE

42 19), pr. Karla Marxa, 97, is in Park Globy (Парк Глобы). Take tram #1 to the Park and follow your ears (cover 10hv; women free Mon.-Wed.).

CRIMEA (КРИМ).

Turn your watch forward one hour from Kiev time for the Crimea (GMT+3)

The Crimean peninsula has been inhabited since antiquity—most recently by Russians. Tsars' palaces stand alongside the sanatoria and resorts that in the past half-century have served the ailing proletariat of colder climes. The peninsula has drawn people to its shores for a simple reason—it is beautiful.

■ Simferopol (Сімферополь)

God made Crimea, and all Simferopol got was a lousy train station. The mountains here are no match for Yalta's, and Sevastopol got the best of the Black Sea, so it's no wonder locals seem resentful that Simferopol's sole purpose is to serve as a thoroughfare to points south. Originally the site of the Scythian city of Neapolis, and subsequently a Tatar town, Simferopol is the hub where all Crimean roads meet. Outside of the train and bus bazaar, the peninsula's capital is calm and lazy, with beautifully manicured parks doing all they can to make up for a relative lack of natural splendor.

ORIENTATION AND PRACTICAL INFORMATION

Bul. Lenina (бул. Леніна) runs on both sides of the park leading from the train station to the city center, which lies approximately at the intersection of **ul. Karla Marxa** (ул. Карла Маркса) and **pr. Kirova** (пр. Кірова). **Trolley #2** travels from the station to the center along **ul. Rosy Lyuksemburg** (Розы Люксембург). Be aware that ul. Lenina in the city center is not the same as bul. Lenina along the park.

Tourist Office: In Hotel Ukraina (Україна) at ul. Rosy Lyuksemburg, 9. Kiosks marked "Экскурсия" organize guided excursions; kiosks are also a source of **maps.**

Currency Exchange: Plenty of "Обмен-Валют" from the train station onward. **Thomas Cook,** ul. Rosy Lyuksemburg, 17 (tel. 29 00 21), cashes traveler's checks (3% commission).

Trains: ul. Gagarina (Гагарина), reachable by trolleys #1, 2, 5, and 6. All times on schedule given in Kiev time (1hr. ahead). To: Kiev (2 per day, 16hr., 22hv); Lviv (1 per day, 31hr., 20hv); Minsk (1 per day, 35hr., 41hv); Moscow (2 per day, 26hr., 45hv); and Odesa (1 per day, 14hr., 13hv). The **elektrichka** (electric train) runs to Sevastopol via Bakhchisarai (every 2hr., 2hr., 1.30hv). Ticket window behind main station building.

Buses: The station is reachable by trolley #1, 2, or 6 (20min. from the train station). Buy tickets at least a day ahead, or ask the driver for standing room. To Feodosia (4 per day, 3hr., 5.90hv). Closer destinations via the regional station next to the train station. To Bakhchisarai (4 per day, 1hr., 1.50hv).

Public Transportation: Trolley is the best way to **Yalta** (2½hr., 4.20hv), departing next to the train station (several per hr. 5:30am-11pm). Walking out of the main building of the station, the ticket window is 50m ahead on the left. Windows #1 and 2 for Yalta.

Taxis: Stands are all over town. Private drivers hawk rides to Feodosia, Kerch, and Yalta. Fares increase exponentially if they learn you're a Brit or a Yank.

Luggage Storage: Between the train and trolley stations, downstairs. 1.50hv per bag for 12hr. Open daily 8am-9pm.

Post Office: ul. Rosy Lyuksemburg, 1. Open Mon.-Fri. 8am-8pm, Sat.-Sun. 8am-6pm. The train station also has a small 24hr. post office. **Postal code:** 333000.

Telephones: At the post offices. 1min. to U.S. 4hv. Open 24hr. **Phone code:** 0652.

ACCOMMODATIONS

The best place to sleep in Simferopol is on the train out of town. Local hotels are ridiculously overpriced, so look for private rooms hawked at the train station, or simply avoid having to spend the night.

Turbaza "Tavraya" (Турбаза "Таврая"), ul. Bespalova, 21 (Беспалова; tel. 23 20 24), 2 stops on trolley #2 after the bus station or a 25min. ride from the trains to "Таврая"—walk up. Recently furnished rooms, older bathrooms. Late-night bar. Singles with shower, TV, and fridge 28hv; doubles 54hv.

Ukraina (Україна), ul. Lyuksemburg, 7 (tel. 51 00 62); take trolley #2 from the train station. This aging but central hotel has high ceilings and a nice courtyard. Singles with sink, TV, and phone US$18; equally well-outfitted doubles 55hv.

Moskva (Москва), Kievska ul., 2 (Київська; tel. 23 21 42), at the "Hotel Moskva" stop on trolley #2. Simferopol's largest hotel. Decent rooms, peeling paint. Singles with bath, TV, and telephone 50hv; similar doubles 80hv.

FOOD

The **central market** at the intersection of pr. Kirova (Кирова) and ul. Kozlova (Козлова) is the place to stock up on groceries and a good way to see the city at work. There are also markets around the train and bus stations. All sell the local specialties, including small shrimp eaten from a piece of newspaper rolled into a cone (about 2hv). These should be eaten only when fresh—and can only be sold with a permit that proves this. The hotel restaurants and cafe-bars that abound along ul. Karla Marxa and ul. Pushkina serve mostly hot dogs and other foods for the unadventurous—but then, if you were truly unadventurous, you wouldn't be in Ukraine. The only noteworthy restaurant in town is **Restoran Latysh** (Латыш, tel. 27 88 63) ul. Ushinskovo 6 (Ушинского) in the city center. Look for the big star of David. You guessed it—they specialize in kosher food (main dishes 2hv-7hv; open noon-midnight).

SIGHTS AND ENTERTAINMENT

The city's major historical landmark is the **Neapol Skifsky** (Неаполь Скіфський; Neapolis archaeological site), a vast excavation of the former Crimean capital reachable by bus #4 from the train station. Sit on the wind-swept cliffs and look out on the "new"

> ### Who Owns Crimea?
>
> In the 5th century BC, Herodotus first recorded that Scythians and Greeks dwelled in Crimea, but invaders have continuously made their way across the isthmus to join the sun-bathing population. The Sarmatians followed the Scythians in the 4th century, and were subsequently supplanted by the Romans, Ostrogoths, Huns, Slavs, Khazars, and Varangians. The peninsula fell under Byzantium until the great Batu Khan (grandson of Genghis) took the region and opened Crimea to trade. Pleased with the land, many Mongols settled and became the indigenous Crimean Tatars.
>
> Crimea remained autonomous until Russia annexed it in 1783 and refurbished it as beach resort extraordinaire. The Crimean War, in 1854, saw France and Britain clash with Russia over the city of Sevastopol. The Russians evacuated, leaving the Tatars to revive their national heritage, language, and culture. In 1917, the Tatars put together a *Kurultay*—Tatar National Constituent Assembly—which declared their autonomy against the will of the Bolsheviks. Russia soon regained control and paid its citizens to settle. The new settlers eradicated the reigning elite, and on the night of May 18, 1944, Stalin had the entire Crimean Tatar population, largely collaborating with the Germans, loaded into train cars and shipped to Uzbekistan.
>
> Crimea was officially made part of Ukraine in 1954 as a "gift" from Khrushchev; now it seems a costly gesture. Russians continue to flood the resorts; they don't want to give up Crimea, but neither does Ukraine, which now reaps the financial rewards. The Tatars have also returned *en masse* over the past five years, demanding their land. Despite such turmoil, Crimea's beauty remains: tall mountains frame a view of lush forests and the light blue sea.

city, but watch out for broken glass. Most of Neapolis's loot, however, is contained in the **Krimsky Kraevedchesky Muzey** (Крімский Краеведческий Музей; Regional History Museum), at the intersection of ul. Pushkina (Пушкина) and ul. Gogolya (Гоголья; open Wed.-Mon. 9am-5pm; 2hv). The **Gorky theater**, ul. Pushkina 15, presents frequent shows (*kasa* open daily 10am-8pm; tickets 2-10hv depending on seat location). The church-crazy and mosque-mad should take a stroll past pl. Radyanska (Радянська) onto ul. Lenina. Take a right onto ul. Proletarska (Пролетарська). On your right, the **Petronavlivska tserkva** (Петронавлівська церква; Church of Sts. Peter and Paul) is complete with the requisite bell tower. Church #2, **Svyatotroitska katedra** (Святотроїцька катедра; Holy Trinity), also stands on the right. The **mosque** sits off ul. Proletarska on ul. Kurchatova (Курчатова), in a small neighborhood of Tatars.

For something a little less reverent, the danceclub **Cosmos** (Космос) is expected to reopen in summer 1998 after undergoing renovations. The nightclub **Flamingo** (tel. 27 89 98), ul. Odesskaya 2 (Одесска), near pl. Lenina, plays the usual techno, but caters to an older-than-student "more serious" crowd (no cover; open noon-1am). The city's **parks** are a joy, well-maintained and full of people. Try the central parks near ul. Pushkina or the *Detsky Park* (Детский Парк; Children's Park), on ul. Shmidta (Шмідта) via trolley #2 or 4, which has mammoth concrete jungle gyms.

■ Near Simferopol

BAKHCHISARAI (БАХЧИСАРАЙ)

Among the dry, solemn cliffs of the Central Crimean steppe, the ancient town of Bakhchisarai quietly guards its secrets. An outpost of the Byzantine Empire at the end of the 6th century and subsequently the seat of Crimean Tatar power, the town is currently occupied primarily by blackberry sellers. Bakhchisarai's **Khansky Palats** (Ханський Палац) was first built in the early 16th century by the second Crimean khan. It has been razed, re-created, and refined many times since then, and the additions are its true attraction. The palace encompasses numerous small rooms and a **courtyard** where the khan's harem hung out. Bought on the free (though black) market, these wives came cheaper than an official wife; since they were illegal, their movement was restricted. You'll also find the **Fountain Courtyard,** which contains the **Golden Fountain** and the famous **Fountain of Tears.** According to legend, the fount was built by a khan who had fallen in love with a fatally ill slave, and who desired company in his weeping. Pushkin made the fountain famous in his poem *Bakhchisaraisky Fontan* (Бахчисарайский Фонтан). Two roses are retained in perpetuum for the fountain to shed tears on. The **Khudozhestvenny muzey** (Художественный музей; Art Museum) sits in the back left corner of the main courtyard. Entrance into the courtyard is free, and a 4hv ticket gets you into the museum and the "special" places of the palace (open Thurs.-Mon. 9am-5pm).

A right from the palace and a 2km walk leads to the **Uspensky Pecherny Monastir** (Успенський Печерний Монастир; Assumption Monastery), currently undergoing reconstruction. Carved out of a cliff in the 15th century, it became the center of Orthodox Christian life in Crimea. Regardless of your religious affiliation, you'll appreciate its incredible view of the valley. The mysterious and ancient **cave town of Chufut-Kale** (Чуфут-Кале) lies 1km farther along the road and up the hill to the left. Built towards the end of the 6th century by order of Byzantium, it subsequently became the first capital of the Crimean Khanate. From this almost impenetrable location, the khans could jeer at potential invaders and shower them with hot oil. After the capital was moved to Bakhchisarai in the early 16th century, the Muslim population left and only Karaite Jews and Armenians stayed, at which point the fortress was renamed Chufut-Kale (Jews' Fortress). The cave complex near the South Gate is a Christian monastery. The architecture of nearby 15th-century **kenassas** (prayer houses) resembles that of synagogues (admission to monastery and Chufut-Kale 3hv).

Close and well-connected to Simferopol, Bakhchisarai makes an ideal daytrip. The *elektrichka* is the cheapest and fastest transport (every 2hr., 45min., 1.10hv); several daily buses also make the trip (1hr., 3hv) from Simferopol's main bus station. From the train station, walk to the top of the hill and catch any bus (0.20hv) going left to get to the palace. Buses do not run noon-4pm, so be prepared for the 30-minute walk (turn left at the hilltop, bear right at the fork, and just keep walking).

FEODOSIA (ФЕОДОСІЯ)

If you didn't think the smooth rocks of Yalta felt much like a beach, head east. Outside the ancient slave-trading town of Feodosia, a 16km stretch of bronzed sand speckled with tiny, smooth bits of seashell creates a shoreline that has attracted vacationers from Roman times to the present. A right out of the bus station on pr. Lenina will take you to a site of ancient Roman ruins, but Feodosia's main attraction is the **beach.** Cross the street, head right 50m, and cross the bridge over the tracks to get a gander at what you came for: the big, bad Black Sea. Going left will take you to a free beach, or pay 4hv for fewer crowds. From the bus station, city **buses #2** and 4 head into town, where Russia's premier collection of **I. K. Aivazovsky's works** is on display. He was by all accounts a strange man, particularly toward the end of his life, when he grew sideburns that made Pushkin's look like a phase in junior high. His most famous work, *Poseidon's Journey on the Sea,* is among the displays (open Thurs.-Mon. 10am-5pm, Tues. 10am-2pm; 4hv at the *kasa* across the street). If you'll be staying the night in Feodosia, the **Astoriya** (Астория; pr. Lenina 9; tel (065 62) 323 16) is your only option (singles 34hv; doubles 50hv). Reservations are a good idea during the summer. The only escape from hot dog-vending kiosks is the **Cafe Assol** (Ассоль) at the intersection of ul. Libnekhta (Лібнехта) and Halereina ul. (Галерейна), which serves Russian meat rolls (3hv) and soups (2hv; open daily 9am-11pm). **Buses** travel to Feodosia from Simferopol's main bus station (6 per day, 3hr., 5.90hv), with Kerch (Керч) as their final destination. Buses back to Simferopol leave Feodosia every 1½hr. until about 8pm; buy tickets (4-6hv) from the driver.

■ Sevastopol (Севастополь)

The Black Sea cuts an inlet into the southwestern tip of Crimea, forming a perfect natural harbor. Positioned at this ideal spot, Sevastopol had no choice but to become a focal point in world history. Russia and Ukraine still quarrel over who owns the city's Black Sea Fleet, and young sailors with shaved heads from both countries throng the streets. Fortunately, you don't have to swab decks or shave your own head to enjoy Sevastopol's historical venues and bustling boardwalk.

Orientation and Practical Information Downtown Sevastopol begins on a hill above the harbor. **Ul. Bolshaya Morskaya** (Большая Морская) follows the slope past the main sights to the boardwalk; **ul. Lenina** (Ленина) runs parallel along the docks. **Primorsky bul.** (Приморский), site of the main park and monuments, runs along the waterfront. City maps are hard to come by—perhaps they assume you're a mariner able to chart your course by the stars. The **tourist office** at Gostinitsa Krym (Крым) and **booths** along the boardwalk offer high-priced excursions around the city and on the water (20hv and up). Most sights can be seen on foot, though, so avoid the bus tour. Lots of military hang around in town, so you'd better register at the **passport office (ОВИР),** ul. Pushkina 12 (Пушкина), if your hotel doesn't do it for you (open Mon.-Fri. 9am-6pm). **Exchange cash** everywhere, particularly around the waterfront, but **traveler's checks** can be cashed only at the post office (2% commission). The **elektrichka** (electric train) runs to Simferopol (every 2hr. 6am-8pm, 2½hr., 1.30hv); the station can be reached by bus #7 from the city center (open 5am-10pm). Buses run from the **Avtovokzal**, ul. Revyakina (Ревякина); take bus #7 one stop past the train station. Four buses head daily to Simferopol (2hr., 3hv) and Yalta (2½hr., 4.60hv). **Local buses** are crowded, but convenient and cheap (0.20hv). Bus #7 connects the stations to the city center; #12 runs between the waterfront and the center. **Store luggage** in the bus station (1hv per day). A clean and professional **pharmacy** is at ul. Lenina 34 (open Mon.-Sat. 8am-7pm, Sun. 10am-4pm). Take bus #12 to "Pobeda" (Победа) to reach the **post office,** ul. Bolshaya Morskaya 21 (open 8am-6pm). **Telephones** are next door (open 7am-10pm; 4.65hv per minute to the U.S.). **Postal code:** 335011. **Phone code:** 0692.

Accommodations and Food The best bet in town is the unassuming **Komnata Otdikha** (Комната Отдыха; Room of Rest), located on the 3rd floor of the small building behind the main train station. Knock at the top of the staircase (doubles 3hv per person). If no rest can be found here, try **Gostinitsa K.Ch.F** (the sign just reads Гостиница), ul. Ostryakova 72 (Острякова, tel. 57 13 00). Take trolley bus #12 to "Kinoteatr Moskva" (Кинотеатр Москва) and continue on foot one block. The hotel is affiliated with the military, so all foreigners *must* register first with ОВИР (singles 28hv; doubles 42hv). The cheapest of Sevastopol's big hotels, but still pricey for foreigners, is **Gostinitsa Krym** (Крым), ul. 6 Bastionnaya 46 (6 Бастионная; tel. 52 22 53). Take trolley #7 or 9 to "Bolshaya Morskaya," then #5 to the hotel (doubles 60hv). Fruits and vegetables are available at the **market** on ul. Partizanskaya (Партизанская), down the hill from pl. Revolyutsii (Революции). Waterfront cafes, all nearly identical, abound along Primorsky bul. For some good conversation, try **Restoran Dialog** (Диалог; tel. 45 56 55), ul. Bolshaya Morskaya, near the post office. The place to find that Snapple you crave, as well as salads (1-2hv) and grilled chicken (4hv; open 10am-midnight).

Sights and Entertainment Trace Sevastopol's proud naval heritage, from Peter the Great to the present, at the **Muzey Flota** (Музей Флота), ul. Lenina 11 (tel. 52 22 89; 5hv, students 2hv; open daily 10am-5pm). Naval "history" can also be seen in the city's port, but you'd better not joke about that within earshot of the sailors—those rusty, decrepit rigs are their real ships. The **Akvarium-Muzey** (Аквариум-Музей) on Primorsky bul., is the premier exhibit of Black Sea life (open daily 10am-6pm; 3.50hv, students 1.50hv).

Sevastopol's nightlife centers (you guessed it) around the waterfront. Cafes and bars along the boardwalk blast live music to make you forget how much you paid for your drink (typically 6hv and up). For dancing action, avoid the techno-blaring "ring" at the end of the boardwalk (if for no other reason than that everyone else is avoiding it—and you know you hate to dance alone). Instead, go bang heads with the grunge crowd at **Bunker** (Бункер), ul. Marata 5 (Марата; tel. 52 01 28)—look for the fiery orange sign at the end of the alley off ul. Lenina, then walk down the spooky hallway. Cover and hours vary depending on live music schedule, so either call ahead or stop by and ask in the afternoon (typically 2-5hv).

■ Yalta (Ялта)

Yalta is all about class—and we're not talking about the struggle of the proletariat here. The cloud-topped mountains form a semi-circle around the aged city before disappearing into the most beautiful of seas; even the all-night discos blaring techno merely dull the sheer physical grandeur. The tsars who created this resort may not have been enlightened, but they knew how to relax. The city's old wooden houses sit on hills, and everything converges at the beachfront promenade, where buskers compete with America-worshipping consumerism for the hearts of vacationers. Yalta's prices are still cheap by European standards, but are slipping out of reach for many former Soviets. Although the scene is currently dominated by foreigners, you can be sure that Yalta's essence—aged, dignified, and just plain cool—will endure.

ORIENTATION AND PRACTICAL INFORMATION

Yalta spreads along the coastline; pedestrian **nab. Lenina** (Ленина) runs from one end of town to the other. **Trolley #1** circles the city from the bus and trolley stations. Get off at **Sovetskaya pl.** (Советская), and walk 100m down **Moskovskaya ul.** (Московская) to get to the sea. The intersection of Moskovskaya and nab. Lenina is **pl. Lenina,** featuring a statue of everyone's favorite revolutionary. A left here leads to the old quarter, whose main streets are **ul. Roosevelta** (Рузвельта) and **ul. Drazhinskovo** (Дражинского).

Tourist Office: Intourist, ul. Drazhinskovo, 50, in the Hotel Yalta, gears its expensive English-language tours to large groups, but does have good city **maps** (5hv). Open 9am-5pm. All of the sights in and around Yalta can easily be seen without the help of the numerous, overpriced excursion bureaus lining the waterfront (contrary to what they'll tell you).

Currency Exchange: A window in the post office deals with everything: exchange, Visa cash advances (3% commission), and all kinds of traveler's checks (2% commission). Open 8am-8pm. A 24hr. exchange is located at the corner of ul. Roosevelta and ul. Sverdlova (Свердлова).

Buses: The **bus station** is located at Moskovskaya ul., 57 (tel. 34 20 92). To: Simferopol (every 20min., 2hr., 4.20hv); Sevastopol (2 per day, 2hr., 4.60hv); and Feodosia (3 per day, 5hr., 9.80hv). Across the street is the **trolleybus station,** which has slightly slower (2½hr.), but more comfortable, trolleys going to Simferopol and Simferopol airport every 20min. (4.20hv; pay on board).

Water Shuttles: Hourly to Alupka (1hr., 3hv) and Lastivchine Gnizdo (30min., 2hv). Buy tickets from window #3 on the pier, in front of the Casino Diana; otherwise you may end up buying a more expensive "excursion" with an additional 8-10hv tour fee, rather than just a regular ticket.

Public Transportation: Trolleys run in the city; #1 is the most useful. Buy tickets (0.20hv) on board.

Luggage Storage: At the bus station. 0.90hv for 12hr. Open 8am-8pm.

24-Hour Pharmacy: Botkinskaya ul., 3 (Боткинская). Ring the bell from 8pm-8am.

Post Office: pl. Lenina. *Poste Restante* and photocopiers (0.20hv per page) are around the corner of the building. Open daily 8am-8pm. **Postal code:** 334200.

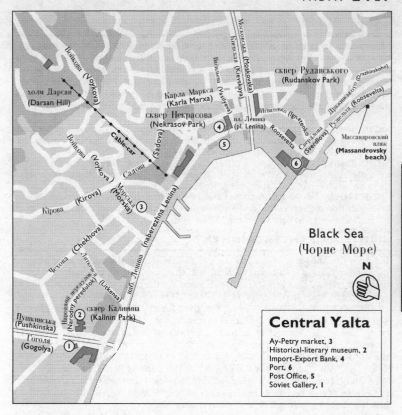

Central Yalta

Ay-Petry market, **3**
Historical-literary museum, **2**
Import-Export Bank, **4**
Port, **6**
Post Office, **5**
Soviet Gallery, **I**

Telephones: Moskovskaya ul., 10 for international and intercity calls. 4.80hv per minute to the U.S. Tokens for local calls (0.25hv) sold at the post office. **Phone code:** 0654.

ACCOMMODATIONS AND CAMPING

The prices at Yalta's beachside hotels have increased dramatically and might continue to do so; the lone traveler will have difficulty getting a place in a double. Book ahead. Bus station *babushki* often offer unbeatable deals on **private rooms**.

Gostinitsa Krym (Крым), Moskovskaya ul., 1/2 (tel. 32 60 01). Small but clean rooms with hall shower and bath. Price can't be beaten for a downtown hotel. Singles 19hv; doubles 28hv. 5hv first-night registration fee.

Massandra (Массандра), ul. Drazhinskovo, 48 (tel. 35 25 91), at the edge of the old quarter. Recently renovated. Doubles with sink 27hv; with shower, telephone, and fridge 54hv.

Motel-Camping Polyana Skazok (Поляна Сказок), ul. Kirova, 167 (Кірова; tel. 39 52 19). Take bus #11, 26, or 27 from the bus station to "Поляна Сказок"; it's about a 20min. walk uphill from there through winding, blackberry-lined roads. A real class-act campground in a charming high-altitude setting, with showers and kitchen facilities. Tents are 5hv per person; bungalows for 2 are small but cheap at 18hv. Rooms in the motel (doubles only) are 65hv.

FOOD

Many **restaurants** along nab. Lenina also serve food with their liquor. Unfortunately, most of the sit-down venues have realized they can charge hungry tourists an awful lot. Seek refuge in the city's **cafeterias** and **stolovayas;** they are the last bastions against the hot dog and pizza "invasion" plaguing Ukrainian eateries. A well-stocked **Gastronom** (Гастроном), nab. Lenina, 4, sells bread for pennies, and there is a **general market** at the corner of Moskovska ul. and ul. Karla Marxa (daily 8am-6pm).

Cafe Siren (Сирень), ul. Roosevelta, 6. Freshly prepared Russian food, just like your grandmother used to make, if your grandmother was Russian. Borscht, *kasha, kakdet*, and some *kompot* 3-4hv. Open daily 8am-8pm.

Cafe Krym (Крым), Moskovska ul., ½. Get in, eat, get out. Do not pass Go. Do not collect 3hv (price of full meal, tops). Simple Russian food, very similar to Siren but without all the "frills." Open daily 7am-8pm.

Cafe Marina (Марина), behind the Casino Diana at the base of the cable car. Slightly better than the cafe-clones along nab. Lenina, due to its pleasant location and lower prices (meat rolls 3hv). Open daily 10am-3am.

SIGHTS AND ENTERTAINMENT

If **Anton Chekhov** is your deity of choice, Yalta is Mecca. The author lived here for the last five years of his life, and from the wealth of monuments and plaques, you can practically retrace his every step. On nab. Lenina at the entrance of Gurman, you can see where he once slept, and on ul. Litkensa (Литкенса) stands the **school** where he taught. At ul. Kirova 112, you can explore the **house** he built, the garden he planted, and the museum his sister dedicated to him. Bus #8 takes you there every 40min. from "Кинотеатр Спартак" (*Kinoteatr Spartak*) on Pushkinskaya ul. (Пушкинская; museum open Tues.-Sun. 10am-5pm; 2hv). Non-literary artsy types will appreciate the old **Soviet Gallery** at ul. Gogolya 1, next to Hotel Oreanda (open Tues.-Sun. 10am-6pm; 3hv), and the **Art Gallery,** across the street at Pushkinska ul., 5a (open Wed.-Sun. 11am-7pm; 2hv). Having sufficiently refined your taste, you can now stop at **Crimea Wines,** on nab. Lenina underneath the "Marino" sign in the Casino Diana building (tastings daily at 2, 3:30, 4:30, and 6pm; 8hv).

Yalta's parks are among the peninsula's most sumptuous. In **Primorsky (Seaside) Park Gagarina,** at the southwest end of nab. Lenina, you can find an **Exotic Fish Aquarium** (open daily 10am-7pm; 2hv). On Moskovska ul., halfway between the bus station and the city center, lies the **circus,** which puts on a nightly show (May-Oct. only; Thurs.-Sat. 5pm, Sun. 3pm. *Kasa* open Tues.-Sun. 10am-5pm; 5hv). If you aren't feeling childish enough yet, **Polyana Skazok** (Поляна Сказок; Fairy-Tale Meadow), next to the campground, takes characters from Russian and Ukrainian fairy tales and immortalizes them in larger-than-life figures (open daily 8am-8pm). A number of **hiking trails** head from Yalta to the **Uchan-Su Waterfall** and other natural wonders. Consult the campground staff for advice. Lazier visitors use the **chairlift** to get to a high-altitude shrine to Zeus, where the jolly Greek stares out to sea. The lift lifts you from behind Casino Diana (June-Oct. daily 10am-8:30pm; 1.50hv).

Yalta is a resort town, but the nightlife is sorely lacking—unless you're into endless hours of video poker or strolling down the boardwalk in your tightest clothing. Cafe bars line nab. Lenina and are the site of what nightlife does exist. Most are open until around 2am and charge 3hv for a beer. The nightclub **Saturn** (Сатурн), in the Kinoteatr Saturn in Sovetskaya pl., plays techno that you can hear from two blocks away (cover 5hv for the fellas; ladies get in free). The **Rock and Roll Store/Bar,** at the end of Pushkinska ul. near the "Кинотеатр Спартак" stop, might be playing good rock music, but then again it might not. At least it's not techno…(beer 5-8hv).

■ Near Yalta

HURZUF (ГУРЗУФ)

Eighteen kilometers from Yalta proper, the streets are narrower and the houses older. Hurzuf is a quieter version of Yalta, replacing man-made tourist attractions with jagged cliffs and rocks jutting dramatically out of the sea. **Chekhov** built his dacha where he could see it all, and it's now a museum. Young **Pushkin** spent two months here, long enough to be worthy of a monument, too. Hurzuf's true charm, however, hides in the narrow streets winding among small old buildings, the cliffs, and the sea. The **Pushkin Museum** is located within a sanitorium, and can only be seen as an "excursion" through **Krym Tur** (Крым Тур), Podvoyskovo 9 (Подвойского; tel. 36 37 53), right in the center of town (museum open Wed.-Sun. 10am-5pm; 2hv). The **Chekhov Museum** is on ul. Chekhova, a small road on the right of Leningradskaya ul. (Ленинградская, open Wed.-Sun. 10am-6pm; 1hv).

Farther along Leningradskaya, the Pionersky Camp contains a tunnel through a cliff, allowing a view of everything. Ask to see the *"tunel v skalë"* at the gate in the middle of the black iron fence on the right, then follow the path to the right to the tunnel entrance. To get to the rocks rising from the sea, one of which houses a **bar**, rent a **paddleboat** (5hv per hr.) on the embankment. Bus #31 goes from Yalta (every 40min., 50min., 0.60hv).

LIVADIA (ЛІВАДІЯ)

An hour's hike or a 10-minute shuttle ride away, Livadia was the place where Yalta's renown began as a resort town, and where it reached history-book levels with the imprecisely named **Yalta Conference.** Churchill, Roosevelt, and Stalin met for a week in February 1945 at **Tsar Nicholas II's summer palace** (built in 1911) to finalize postwar territorial claims. Secretly, the Russians committed to enter the war against Japan after the German defeat (which Stalin did two months after the German surrender; although the bomb was dropped before Soviet troops could be engaged), and Roosevelt and Churchill agreed to send back all captured Soviet troops (though they knew the men would be considered traitors). Some considered the conference a great cave-in on FDR's part, particularly regarding the Soviet presence in Eastern Europe; others, like the ideologically confused tour guides, think the conference guaranteed "50 years of peace."

Shuttle #5 from "Кинотеатр Спартак" (*Kinoteatr Spartak*) in Yalta stops every 40-50 minutes across the park from the **Veliky Palats** (Великий Палац; Great Palace) where it all happened. The second floor has been converted into an exhibition hall and the **Nicholas II museum,** but the rest has been preserved in memory of the conference. The exquisite marble and wood interior, and the view from Nicholas's windows, amply demonstrate that the tsar had it good (open Thurs.-Tues. 10am-5pm; 5hv). The surrounding **park** is also nice—elevators take you down to an ordinary **beach,** if seeing the tsar's "dacha" has made you want to jump.

LASTIVCHINE GNIZDO (ЛАСТІВЧИНЕ ГНІЗДО)

Built in 1911 for a rich German who apparently wanted to get richer on postcards, the fragile Lastivchine Gnizdo (Swallow's Nest) **castle** perched upon a cliff looks like it might crumble into the sea at any moment. It won't be taking any tsars or counts with it, though, as it's now an expensive "Italian" restaurant with a view. Since the castle is itself largely a part of the spectacle, the best viewing site is on a nearby platform—that's where the true postcard photographers go. Some use the gaps in the fencing to sneak onto the **Sanatorium Zhemchuzhina beach** and swim out to the rock, but stay safe; every now and then, a big wave smashes an unlucky swimmer against the rocks. To reach the castle, take one of the **ferries** leaving hourly from Yalta's pier 7 (30min., 2hv), or **bus #27** from the bus station (0.60hv). The bus is only slightly faster and a lot less pleasant. Get off at the "Sanatorium Zhemchuzhina" or

UKRAINE

"Sanatorium Paris" stop. The path leading down is between the two. The last ferry back to Yalta departs at 6pm, the last bus at 8:30pm. Several cafes serve *shashliks* and chicken. From Lastivchine Gnizdo, both the ferry and the bus continue to **Alupka.**

ALUPKA (АЛУПКА)

Alupka is home to the most extravagant *dacha* in Greater Yalta—**Palats Vorontsova** (Палац Воронцова), still an active compound, built by the wealthier-than-thou regional governor, Count Mikhail Vorontsov. Construction of the palace took over 30 years and was completed in 1841. You can walk around the grounds for free (daily 9am-5pm), but to get inside and see how rich people used to decorate their abodes, you pay 4hv (open Tues.-Sun. 9am-5pm). The north of the palace faces **Mt. Al-Petry,** and is correspondingly somber. The south, facing the sea, has a bizarre and magnificent facade. Six lions—a truly impressive marble one by the Italian master Leone Bonani, and five goofy-looking ones by his students—guard a marble portico with an Arabic invocation to Allah. What this is doing at the center of Vorontsov's palace is not exactly clear. Apparently, the English architect who designed the palace thought the Black Sea here looked a lot like the Indian Ocean, and copied the design of an Indian mansion and its inscription. The story has it that when Tsar Nicholas I came to the palace, he was offended at the presumptuousness of its extravagance. Vorontsov merely pointed to the lettering, explaining to the tsar that, after all, all praise is due to Allah. In any case, it looks better than a Communist slogan. One kilometer back in the direction of Yalta, a **cable car** sends you up the face of the cliffs and into the clouds. Enjoy the view on the way up, because unless it's an exceptionally clear day, you won't be able to see more than 20m once you are in the clouds (cable car operates 10am-4pm Fri.-Wed.; 8hv round-trip).

ODESHCHINA (ОДЕЩИНА)

South of Kiev and west of Crimea spreads the Ukrainian steppe and wooded half-steppe. While other regions of the East Slavic diaspora shook themselves free of the Mongol yoke in the 15th century, this area languished under various overlords (most notably the Ottoman Turks) until the end of the 18th century, when fellow Slavs from Moscow and St. Petersburg brought liberation. Along with Russian rule came a curious mix of Russian and French culture, plus the influence of the Jews, who were herded from all over Russia into this small corner.

■ Odesa (Одеса)

Built by the Russians under French influence but located in the Jewish area of settlement, Odesa (Russian Одесса; Odessa) got its money from Catherine and Vorontsov and its attitude from the Jews, the Turks, and the Black Sea. During WWII, it was not the Germans who occupied most of Odesa, but rather the less destructive Romanians, and the city survived with relatively little damage. Although Odesa lays some claim to Pushkin, Isaac Babel—the city's true literary son—earned this title with colorful chronicles of the Jewish mob in Odesa's Moldavank region. Today, Ukraine's biggest port makes good use of its position as a "window on the West." With beautiful beaches, ever-flowing vodka, and discos till dawn, the party town of the former USSR revels against a beautiful Baroque backdrop.

ORIENTATION AND PRACTICAL INFORMATION

Odesa lies on a 50km strip along the Black Sea. Its central section is bounded by the **train station** to the south and the **port** to the north. All streets, many recently renamed, are labeled in both Ukrainian and Russian, but most maps are only in Russian. Occasional signs are in Ukrainian. For verbal queries, you're still better off with Russian, since no one in Odesa speaks Ukrainian. *Let's Go* lists Russian names. The

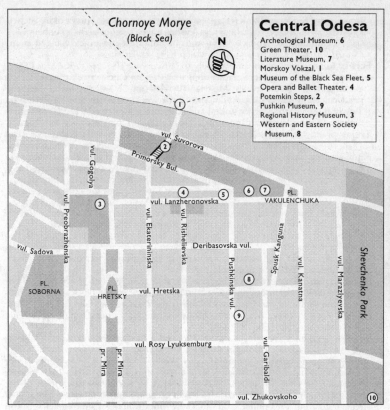

Central Odesa

Archeological Museum, 6
Green Theater, 10
Literature Museum, 7
Morskoy Vokzal, 1
Museum of the Black Sea Fleet, 5
Opera and Ballet Theater, 4
Potemkin Steps, 2
Pushkin Museum, 9
Regional History Museum, 3
Western and Eastern Society
  Museum, 8

UKRAINE

main street, **ul. Deribasovskaya** (Дерибасовская), is partially closed to traffic. Coming out of the train station, walk right across the park to the stop opposite Spartak stadium (Спартак), and take trolley #5 or 9 to the center. The terminus is **pl. Grecheskaya** (Греческая), a block south of ul. Deribasovskaya, also reachable by tram #2, 3, or 12 from the station. Heading toward Shevchenko Park, it crosses **ul. Pushkinskaya** (Пушкинская). A right onto ul. Pushkinskaya from ul. Deribasovskaya leads to the train station, and a left ushers you onto the tree-lined **Primorsky bul.** (Приморский), favored for its panoramic views of the sea. **Maps** are available at Hotel Krasnaya (Красная; 5hv).

Tourist Office: Intourist, ul. Pushkinskaya 17 (tel. 25 24 58 or 22 31 43), in the lobby of Hotel Krasnaya. Trolleys #1 and 4 run here from the train station. Primarily useful for train tickets. Open daily 9am-5pm. The less hectic **Director's Office** upstairs has plenty of advice on Odesa's sights. Some English spoken. Tours of the catacombs and other attractions are available (US$12). Same hours as Intourist.

Office of Visas and International Registration (ОВИР): Krasny Pereulok 5 (Красный Переулок; tel. 25 89 74). You must **register here** (US$10) and keep the registration card for the border guards when leaving Ukraine. If not, you may not be able to leave the country without paying the border guards a heavy "fine."

Tourist Police: Sped-Sluzhba (special service), ul. Zhukovskovo 42 (Жуковского; tel. 28 22 66), at the intersection with ul. Preobrazhenskaya (Преображенская; formerly Советской Армии). On the 2nd floor, to the left. Deals with crimes by and against foreigners, but don't expect to find any knights in shining armor.

Currency Exchange: First Ukrainian Bank, in Morsky Vokzal (Морский Вокзал; sea port). Changes traveler's checks. Open Mon.-Fri. 9am-5:30pm, Sat. 10am-1pm.

Downtown, **Ridvenny Bank** (Ривгенний; tel. 23 08 28), on the corner of ul. Shchepkina (Щепкина) and Preobrazhenskaya, cashes traveler's checks for an unbelievable US$10 commission. Open 9:30am-4pm. US$ and DM can be exchanged at any *Obmin Valyut* (Обмін Валют), all of which have similar rates.

Flights: Russian and Ukrainian planes fly to Moscow for US$160, to Kiev for US$85. Several airlines offer direct connections to European cities; check their offices in the airport for current prices. **Austrian Airlines** (tel. 25 33 78) goes to Vienna (6 per week); **Lufthansa** flies to Frankfurt (2 per week; an insane US$796). **Kiyaviya Travel** (Київавія), in Morsky Vokzal and at Preobrazhenskaya 15 (22 09 59) offers flights on lots of European and former-Soviet airlines. Open Mon.-Fri. 8am-7pm.

Trains: pl. Privokzalnaya (Привокзальная), at the south end of ul. Pushkinskaya. Tram #2, 3, or 12 runs along ul. Preobrazhenskaya to the west end of ul. Deribasovskaya. Buy international (non-former-USSR) or advance tickets in the *Mizhnarodny Zal* (Мижнародний Зал; International Room), to the left as you enter the building. Open 8am-noon and 1-7pm. Or get them at the **Central Ticket Bureau,** ul. Srednefontanskaya (Среднефонтанская). Take bus #136 or 146, or cross the park and take the more frequent tram #17 or 18 to "Sredni Fontan" (Central Fountain) and look for the large Центральные Железнодорожные Кассы sign (*Tsentralnye Zheleznodorozhnye Kassy*). If the computer is working, the **Intourist office,** in Hotel Krasnaya, can also help. To: Kiev (1 per day, 12hr., 17hv); Lviv (1 per day, 15hr., 15hv); Simferopol (1 per day, 13hr., 11hv); Chişinău (2 per day, 6hr., 7.50hv); Moscow (2 per day, 26hr., 45hv); Rīga (47hr., 60hv); and St. Petersburg (1 per day, 35hr., 46hv). **Schedules** posted in the main hall.

Buses: ul. Dzerzhinskovo 58 (Дзержинского). Take tram #5 from the train station or 15 from downtown. Both drop you off 4 blocks north of the bus station. Buy tickets at the station at least the night before, or get a standing-room ticket from the driver. To: Kiev (3 per day, 11hr., 19.50hv); Simferopol (1 per day, 8hr., 20hv); and Chişinău (every 2hr., 6hr., 8.50hv).

Ferries: Schedules are unpredictable. **Morskaya Passazhirskaya Kassa** (Морская Пассажирская Касса), Potomkintsiv pl. 1 (Потемкинцев; tel. 24 01 95), at the top of the Potemkin Stairs. To: Istanbul (every Wed., 2 days, 330hv) and Yalta (1 per month in summer, 80hv). Open Mon.-Fri. 9am-5pm, Sat.-Sun. 10am-2pm. **Morsky Vokzal** (Морский Вокзал), ul. Suvorova, 6 (Суворова), at the bottom of the Potemkin Stairs. Posh and filled with travel agencies, tour companies, a couple of restaurants, and a telephone card vendor. A window in the main terminal tells you which companies are going where. To the left of the main dock, charter ferries cruise by the beaches around Odesa. Tickets also sold on board.

Public Transportation: The train station and pl. Grecheskaya are main end points. Info in Russian available inside train station (1hv per question). **Trams** and **trolleybuses** are free, but beware of pickpockets. Public transportation runs 7am-midnight. **Buses** (50-60 kopecks) are next to impossible to figure out. Your best bet is to ask people which bus goes where you want to go.

Taxis: Marshrutne (taxis; 1hv) take the same routes as trolleys, but are faster. Private cars are cheap but risky.

Pharmacy: Apteka "Help," ul. Sadovaya 21 (Садовая). Open daily 8am-8pm. Ring the doorbell for late-night emergencies.

Medical Assistance: Polyklinik, Primorsky bul. 12 (tel. 22 43 87), inside the courtyard, first door on right. Reception on 3rd floor. Treats foreign patients for hard currency and other ailments.

Express Mail: DHL, ul. Rishelevskaya 27 (Ришельевская; tel. 24 42 69; fax 21 71 79). Open Mon.-Fri. 9am-6pm. Also in Morsky Vokzal.

Post Office: ul. Sadovaya 10. Open Mon.-Sat. 8am-8pm, Sun. 8am-6pm. *Poste Restante* at counter #17. Pre-stamped airmail envelopes (конверт с марками; *konvert s markami*) at counter #19. **Postal code:** 270 000.

Telephones: At the post office. International and intercity calls to the left as you enter. State the number of minutes you want (at least 3min.) and pay first (to the U.S. US$2.50 per min.). Open 24hr. Local calls require *zhetony* (tokens), sold at the post office (0.24hv). **Utel phone cards** at window #24. **Phone code:** 0482.

ACCOMMODATIONS AND CAMPING

There are a few cheap choices: you can **camp** or hole up in a **bungalow** at the campground on the edge of town; you can check into a **hotel,** a crumbling remnant of a glorious marble past; or you can stay in a **private room.** The last is by far the cheapest (US$3 per person and up), but you'll be lucky to get anything near the center. Train-station hawkers are recognizable by their signs—some variation on Сдаю комнату. Ask "*Skolko?*" (Сколько; how much?). Bargain for a better price than the US$10 the *babushki* will start at, and don't pay until you see the room. Collateral is often required for keys during July and August. An equally cheap and less restrictive option is to throw yourself at the mercy of the **dormitories.** Facilities are generally bare bones, but you might get your own room and even meet some students. If the English-speaking assistant dean is in at the **Odesa State University,** Dept. of Foreign Students, ul. Mayakovskaya 7 (Маяковская; tel. 23 84 77), off ul. Preobrazhenskaya in the center, you're in luck. If not, the main dorms are at ul. Dovzhenko (Довженко), the fifth stop of trolley #7 south from the left side of the train station. Or take trolleys #5 or 9 from pl. Grecheskaya. *Obshchezhite* #8 (общежите; dorm; tel. 68 05 60), behind the second big apartment building on the left side of the street, holds the *kommandant*'s office (open Mon.-Fri. 9am-5pm). Don't come on the weekend expecting a room (beds around 10hv per person).

Prices are iffy in the downtown **hotels**—make sure a ghost television or refrigerator isn't added to your bill. Truly budget-minded travelers request *samoye deshovloye mesto* (the cheapest place), which lands you in a triple or quad. Take tram #3 or 12 from the train station to the downtown hotels near pl. Grecheskaya.

Tsentralny (Центральний), ul. Preobrazhenskaya 40 (tel. 26 84 06). The tall marble staircase and elegant lobby complement the fine location. Rooms are spacious and bright, but aging. Singles 28hv, with bath 52hv; doubles 40hv, with bath 76hv. Showers on the first floor 1hv.

Pasazh (Пасаж), ul. Preobrazhenskaya 34 (tel. 22 48 84). This fairly charming hotel is next to the real Pasazh. Pleasant, boxy little rooms. Singles 35hv, with shower 60hv; doubles 60hv, with bath 70hv; triples 68hv, with bath 90hv.

Spartak (Спартак), ul. Deribasovskaya 25 (tel. 26 89 24). Old and grand, trying to regain respectability. Large, sparsely furnished rooms. Bed in a double 20hv, with shower 42hv. Single with shower and telephone 42hv. Doubles with sink 60hv, with shower, TV, telephone, and fridge 80hv. Bare bed double 42hv.

Camping "Delfin" (Кемпинг "Дельфін"), dor. Kotovskovo 307 (Котовского; tel. 55 50 52). From train station, take trolley #4 or 10 to the terminus (a small loop in the road) and transfer to tram "любой" (#7); get off 20min. later at "Лузанівка" (*Luzanivka*) and continue 500m. Far even for a campground, but the friendly staff, cheap restaurant, sauna, bar, and private beach make up for it. Bungalows 40hv per person. Cottages 46hv per person. Tents 14hv per person.

FOOD

Odesa is blessed with good restaurants, a market, and cafes that go beyond "hip" into the realm of "meta-hip." *Odesky* eateries have a thing for the subterranean. Options line ul. Preobrazhenskaya south of ul. Deribasovskaya. The **Privoz mega-market** (Привоз), Privoznaya ul. (Привозная), near the train station, provides more food than the port can handle, as well as anything else you could want.

Alye Parusa (Алые Паруса), ul. Ekaterinskaya 14 (Екатеринская), corner of Deribasovskaya. An air-conditioned break for vegetarians tired of cucumber and tomato salads. Main dishes start at US$3. Open daily 9am-midnight.

Kartoplyanki (Картоплянки), ul. Ekaterinskaya 3. A busy, friendly Ukrainian eatery with excellent food; point to what you want. Potato-and-mushroom something is the specialty. Main dishes US$1-2. Open daily 9am-9pm.

Cafe na Grecheskoy (Кафе на Греческой), ul. Grecheskaya 11, downstairs. Where the hyper-cool sip foreign liquor, discuss shopping, and look disdainfully at the regular folk enjoying juicy cutlets (US$2). Open Mon.-Sat. 10am-10pm.

SIGHTS

Ul. Deribasovskaya is not just the center of town—it's a center of street culture, where jazz musicians play, mimes tailor their performance to the wishes of the most generous donor, open-air cafes attract young hipsters, and dozens of artists offer to draw your portrait (or caricature) for the price of a chocolate bar. At **Gorsad,** the west end of ul. Deribasovskaya, artists display their achievements and sell elegant handiwork. Across the street is the famous **Gambrinus** (see **Entertainment,** p. 730). From ul. Deribasovskaya's west end, cross ul. Preobrazhenskaya to see the **statue of Mikhail Vorontsov,** Odesa's powerful governor during the 1820s. Although the statue is ultra neat-o, it's a poor substitute for the cathedral that used to stand here, which was destroyed in 1936 in an effort to quell the ecclesiastico-political forces that threatened Soviet rule. The square is still called **Soborna pl.** (Cathedral Square); you can see pictures of the church in the **Oblastny istoriko-kraeznavchy muzey** (Обласний историко-краєзнавчий музей; Regional History Museum), ul. Gavarina, 4 (Гаварина; tel. 25 52 02; open Sat.-Thurs. 10am-5pm; 2hv).

A block to the left on ul. Preobrazhenskaya is the superbly aromatic **flower market,** where old women advise young men which flowers to buy for their sweethearts. At the other end of the Deribasovskaya pedestrian zone, turn left on ul. Rishelevskaya to find the **Opera and Ballet Theatre,** an imposing edifice that towers over the surrounding gardens. The nearby **Muzey morskovo flotu** (Музей морского флоту; Museum of the Black Sea Fleet), ul. Lanzheronovskaya, 6 (Ланжероновская; old Lastochkina; tel. 24 05 09), displays dozens of models of old ships in what was once a 19th-century aristocrat club (open Fri.-Wed. 10am-3pm; 1hv; Russian tour 5hv). At #4, check out the **Arkheologichny muzey** (Археологічний музей), housing artifacts found in the Black Sea region that date back to ancient Greek and Roman times. Especially worth a look is the collection of gold coins stored in a basement vault (open Tues.-Sun. 11am-6:30pm; 2hv). The facade looks out upon a copy of the famous *Laocoön* sculpture and a garden. At #2, the **Literaturny muzey** (Літературний музей; tel. 22 32 13), situated in an early 19th-century palace, offers a fascinating account of the city's rich intellectual and cultural history through its books, prints, and photographs. The collection includes the famous letter from Vorontsov asking that Pushkin be sent out of Odesa "for his own development" because he was "getting the idea that he is a great writer." Exhibits are labeled only in Russian, but English-speaking guides are available (open Tues.-Sun. 10am-6pm; 2hv, students 1hv; guide 20hv).

Retrace your steps and take a right at the Arkheologichny muzey onto shady **Primorsky bul.,** the most popular spot to stroll and people-watch. The statue of **Aleksandr Pushkin** has its back unceremoniously turned to the city hall, since the local government refused to help fund its construction. On either side of the city hall are the figures of **Fortuna,** goddess of fate, and **Mercury,** god of trade, Odesa's two symbols. Strolling down Primorsky bul., you'll come upon the statue of the **Duc de Richelieu,** the city's founder, whose concrete stare looks down toward the **Potomkinski skhody** (Потьомкінські сходи; Potemkin Stairs) and toward **Morsky Vokzal,** renovated by the Italians and graced by a hideous golden baby in the parking lot. Director Sergei Eisenstein used the stairs in his epic 1925 film *Battleship Potemkin,* originating the oft-imitated visual cliché of a baby carriage loose on an incline, and the name stuck. The tired can take the **escalator** back up.

Facing the sea, a left at this point will bring you to a **monument** commemorating the actual mutiny on that famous ship. At the end of Primorsky bul. is the unrestored **Palace of Vorontsov** (c. 1826), now a club for schoolchildren. To your left is the long white **Mother-in-Law Bridge,** built, they say, so an elderly lady could more easily visit her son-in-law, a high-ranking official in the local Communist party. For some more beautiful buildings, head back down ul. Gogolskaya—farther along, the repressive **House of Scientists** houses a club for the intelligentsia.

At the end of Primorsky bul., take a right at ul. Pushkinskaya and head down one of Odesa's most beautiful streets. At ul. Pushkinskaya 9, drop by the **Muzey zapadnovo i vostochnovo iskusstva** (Музей западного и восточново искусства; Western and Eastern Art Museum) for the 1856 exterior, rather than for the collection (open Thurs.-Tues. 11:30am-5pm; 2hv). Farther along, at #13, **Literaturno-memorialny muzey Pushkina** (Літературно-меморіальний музей Пушкіна; tel. 24 92 55) commemorates the writer. The 1821 building's noteworthy facade faces away from the sea to avoid salt-air damage (open 10am-5pm). Finally, the **Filarmoniya** (Филармония), built in 1894-99, looks out sternly from the corner of ul. Pushkinskaya and ul. Rozy Lyuksemburg (Розы Люксембург). It's one of only two surviving opera houses constructed with special 19th-century acoustics (the other is Milan's La Scala). A bit further down, the large, gray **Brodsky Synagogue** used to be the center of Odesa's large Jewish community, but today contains an archive. A left at the Filarmoniya leads toward **Park Shevchenko,** a vast stretch of greenery that separates the city from the sea; at the entrance stands a **monument** to the poet Taras Shevchenko.

When Odesa was being built, the nearest rock source was directly underground, which led to the creation of the world's longest series of **catacombs.** During the 2½-year Nazi occupation, the **resistance** was based here, and the city has set up an excellent **museum** in their honor. Due to people getting lost in the extensive network of caves, all of the entrances but one have been closed, and you must be with a tour group to enter. The subterranean museum re-creates the resistance camp—the well, bathrooms, and sitting room (with a picture of Stalin that tourists used to tear down constantly as *perestroika* progressed)—where 30 men and women held out for six months against German attacks. At Guard Point #1, soldiers had to sit in two-hour shifts in complete darkness to wait for German attackers. Graffitoed rocks have been transported from the original site—one declares "Blood for blood; death for death." This understated and haunting complex is one of the most moving WWII memorials in the former USSR. For tours in Russian or Ukrainian, contact the **Ekskurzi Byuro** (Екскурзи Бюро), on the corner of Preobrazhenskaya and Malaya Arnantskaya (Малая Арнантская; tel. 25 28 74), or latch onto one of the Russian tours leaving intermittently from the train station. Intourist (see **Practical Information,** p. 725) can get you an English-speaking guide and car (US$12 per person).

Far from the busy commercial center of Odesa lies the **Memorial Complex of the 411th Battalion,** one of the more entertaining monuments. All of the typical armaments of the Soviet forces are here in their colorful glory, spread out over a large park. You'll think the guns and torpedoes are impressive until you get to the other end of the park and see the tanks (even the turrets move), the bomber, and, yes, the battleship, carried here in pieces by tractor-trailer. The best part is that they're all free for you to climb on, in, and around. The rocky **coast** is also a short walk away, and worth a visit to see the cliffs surrounding this area. At high tide, the sea provides its own brilliant, violent spectacle. The complex is on ul. Amundsena (Амундсена), reachable from the train station by bus #108 or 127 or tram #26 (30min.).

ENTERTAINMENT

After some beers at Gambrinus, afternoon philosophizing is best done on Primorsky bul. or ul. Deribasovskaya, especially in Gorsad—the art hangout and bazaar. Saturdays afford a better catalogue of wedding-dresses than any fashion mag, as newlyweds have their pictures taken.

Performances

Teatr Opery ta Baleta (Театр Опери та Балета), at the end of ul. Rishelevskaya, has shows nightly. Odesa's elite arrive in their most dashing attire. Saturday and Sunday matinees begin at noon, evening performances at 6pm. Buy tickets a day in advance, or at least that morning, from the ticket office to the right of the theater (open daily 8am-8pm; tickets 1-5hv, US$3-35 when a major act comes to town). **Zeleny Teatr** (Зеленый Театр; Green Theater) performs in Park Shevchenko on summer weekends at 6pm. For tickets, go to the **Central Theater Office** (Центральная Театральная Касса),

UKRAINE

ul. Deribasovskaya 10 (open daily 11am-5pm). The **Filarmoniya ticket office** (tel. 21 78 95) is in the Filarmoniya (open 11am-7pm; season Sept.-June; tickets 1-10hv).

Shopping

Commerce is what port towns are all about, and Odesa is no exception. First and foremost is the fabulous **Privoz market,** left of the train station on Privoznaya ul. Several acres large, the market supplies just about everything you can imagine. Roughly speaking, fruit and vegetables are in the middle, milk products are in the northeast corner, and hardware and clothes around the edges. Keep your hands on your wallet—snatch-and-run theft is rampant (open daily 8am-6pm). Odesa's **Tsentralny Universalny Magazin** (TsUM; ЦУМ), ul. Pushkinskaya 21, is another shopping haven (open daily 9:30am-7:30pm). Along ul. Rishelevskaya, the **state department stores** sell everything from cloth to low-priced cassette tapes. The city's fanciest **boutiques** cluster around Sadovaya ul. Look for signs saying Магазин and an English word or woman's name—the best ones are below street level. Many require payment in U.S. dollars, and most are closed on Sundays. Also try the **Pasazh** (Пасаж), next to Hotel Pasazh, a passageway leading from ul. Preobrazhenskaya to ul. Deribasovskaya; it's filled with expensive shops and fashion-conscious shoppers. **Gorsad,** on ul. Deribasovskaya, is the best place for souvenirs, but for something a little more classy, try **Gallery Liberti** (Либерти), Lanzheronovskaya 24a (Ланжероновская; tel. 22 48 67), a treasure trove of antiques, paintings, icons, painted eggs, gemstones, and other Ukrainian and Russian *objets d'art* at eye-poppingly affordable prices.

Beaches

The farther from the center you go, the cleaner the beaches are, but they still don't hold a candle to the ones in Crimea. Most are reachable by either public transportation or walking. **Delfin** (Дельфін), on the edge of the park, and **Arkadiya** (Аркадія), the city's most popular, with wide stretches of sand, can be reached by trolley #5 or bus #129. To the south, **Zoloty Berig** (Золотий Беріг; Golden Shore) is farther away, but boasts the most impressive sea and surf. Trams #17 and 18 stop here, as well as at **Chayka** (Чайка) and **Kurortny** (Курортний) beaches. The beach of the proletariat, **Chornomorka** (Чорноморка), lies just outside a high-rise monstrosity of a neighborhood. Take tram #29 to the terminus and keep going. Tram #5 stops at **Lanzheron** (Ланжерон), the beach closest to central Odesa, and at **Vidrada** (Видрада), with its pleasant **forest road** leading into town through Park Shevchenko.

Nightlife

The party town of the former USSR truly never sleeps. The restaurants, cafes, and bars on Deribasovskaya hop all night with beer, vodka, and music ranging from Eurotechno to Slavic folk. For younger and more light-footed entertainment, discos around Arkadia (trolley #7 from the train station, #5 from pl. Grechskaya), such as bul. Frantzsusky's **Cosmo** and **Rio,** should fill the bill. The following are a few time-honored watering holes.

Gambrinus (Гамбринус), downstairs at the intersection of ul. Zhukova (Жукова) and ul. Deribasovskaya. The dark, spacious interior resembles a Bavarian beer hall, and it's far too cool to be hip. Two gifted old guys provide the tunes, while you drink decent draft beer (0.5L 5hv) and munch on the excellent *zakuski* (snacks). A historical landmark that used to be the center of Odesa's cultural scene before the Revolution, it is also an excellent place to party. Open daily 10am-11pm.

Bar Valday (Бар Валдай), Potomkintsiv pl. 3. A younger scene. The average backpacker is rarely cool enough to enter; worth a shot only if you've packed enough black clothes. Food US$5 and up. Open daily 9am-midnight.

Kafe Bar (Кафе Бар), at Dvorets sporta (Дворец спорта; Sports Palace) on pr. Shevchenko (Шевченко). A hip spot, packed even on weeknights. Definitely hot, but its style may be a bit cramped by the 2 highrise apartment buildings under construction on either side. Dance the night away in the parking lot with club kids and *mafiosi* alike. Open nightly 10pm-4am.

WESTERN UKRAINE (ЗАХІД УКРАЇНИ)

Western Ukraine is trying to act cosmopolitan, tear Ukraine out of Moscow's grip, and move it closer to capitalist Europe. Unlike parts of eastern Ukraine, the language and culture here are definitively Ukrainian—and the people are proud of it. Among tiny, almost primitive villages, you'll find many castles—remnants of the border towns that over the centuries defended the interests of Poland, Turkey, and Russia. Locals unaccustomed to tourists are equally likely to stare at you in disbelief or invite you into their homes.

■ Kamyanets-Podilsky (Кам'янець-Подільський)

Raised on a calcium rock some 500m above the Smotrych River canyon, Kamyanets-Podilsky (ka-mee-NYETS po-DILL-skee) has succumbed to invasion only twice during its near-millennium of existence. The town's two narrow bridges, which deny entrance even to lumbering tractors, have most recently protected Kamyanets' rich architecture from the concrete blocks of Soviet "progress." If Ukraine ever lifts its visa requirements, the stronghold will indubitably surrender to a third attack—that of tourists bound for a historical preserve that may rival Venice as an architectural masterpiece set amid natural wonders.

Orientation and Practical Information The small **city center** lies about a 30-minute walk from the train station, which is at Privokzalna, 1 (Привокзальна). **Trains** puff to Kiev (2 per day, 12hr., 12hv) and Chernivtsi (1 per day, leaves at 1:16am, 4.50hv). **Chervonoarmyska vul.** (Червоноармійська, some remaining signs proclaim Красноармейская) runs straight from the train station toward town, where it crosses **vul. Hrushevska** (Грушевська; formerly ul. Lenina). Cross vul. Hrushevska at the end of Chervonoarmyska vul., and **bus** #5 will take you to the center. On foot, head past the buses to the *rynok* (ринок; market; open daily 7am-6pm, except for selected Mon.). Behind the *rynok,* the **bus station** sends travelers to Chernivtsi (1 per hr. 7am-8pm, 4.30hv), Khotyn (4 per day, 1.15hv), and other local towns. A right here, and you're on pedestrian **vul. Saborna** (Саборна)—a typical small-town boulevard lined with *stolovayas,* **currency exchange** booths, and people selling cigarettes and Pepsi. **Pl. Saborna** lies about halfway down. At its far end in Hotel Ukraina (Україна); on the second floor, **Avitsenna-Transit tourist office** (Авіценна-Транзит; tel. 323 00) sells a useful set of brochures about the town (3-4hv) and throws postcards of the Khotyn castle into the bargain. The couple that runs the place also organizes tours (10hv per person in English; open Mon.-Fri. 9am-1pm and 2-6pm and Sat.-Sun. 9am-1pm and 6pm-midnight). From Hotel Ukraina, a left on vul. Lesi Ukrainky (Українки), then a right onto vul. Knyaziv Koriatovychiv (Князів Коріатовичів) leads to the scenic bridge across the **Smotrych River** (Смотрич) and finally to the Old Town. Before the bridge on vul. Koriatorichiv, **Ukrsotsbank** (Укрсоцбанк) exchanges U.S. dollars (open Mon.-Fri. 8:45am-1pm and 2-6pm). The **post office** (open Mon.-Fri. 8am-7pm, Sat. 8am-5pm) and the **telephone** bureau (open 24hr.) sit near the Hotel Ukraina. **Postal code:** 281 900. **Phone code:** 03849.

Accommodations and Food Hotel Ukraina, vul. Lesi Ukrainky, 32 (tel. 391 48), directs the tourist from its trippily be-muraled lobby to small rooms with huge baths and frequent hot water. Hot water is always available for one hour in the communal shower room (doubles with sink 12.20hv, with bath 16.67hv; triples 15.60hv). The owners can help find **dorm rooms** during July and August.

Vul. Saborna is gagged up by buck-a-meal **stolovayas**. In the center of the Old Town, **Mriya's** (Мрія) solid cafeteria food fills the hungry traveler (cutlet with potatoes 1hv, bread 0.03hv; open Mon.-Fri. 8am-7pm, Sat.-Sun. 8am-4pm). En route to the castle, **Pid Bramoyo** (Під Брамою; tel. 215 88) serves Armenian as well as Ukrainian foot in front of the old Armenian gate (*piloff* 4hv, caviar sandwich 2.50hv). Stop by at least to peek into the vaulted stone interior decorated with wrought-iron chandeliers and say "wow" (open daily 9am-9pm; the cook takes a 2-3pm lunch break). The outdoor **Cafe Orion** (Оріон), vul. Troitska, 1 (Троїтська), has fresh vegetable salad (0.75hv), fruit salad (1.50hv), and Hungarian beer (1hv; open summer only 11am-11pm). **Stara Fortetsya** (Стара Фортеця), bulv. Skhidny, 1 (Східний), next to a rotund defense tower, dwells in the grandiose interior of an old home that used to be a synagogue—winding wooden staircase, balcony, and ceiling-high wall paintings included. After crossing the bridge, swerve left onto vul. Zarvanska (Зарванська), then corner another left, a right, and a left to descend straight down to the *fortetsya*. The smiling waitron offers advice on putting together a more-than-filling meal (3.50-5hv)—and you may need help deciphering the handwritten Russian menu. The terrace seats afford an imposing vista over the Smotrych canyon. At night, the restaurant turns into a **disco** (open daily for food 11am-7pm; disco open daily 7pm-6am; cover 3hv, 10hv during strip shows).

Sights Kamyanets-Podilsky's small and eerily quiet city center contains several bona-fide "monuments to architecture" (according to those plaques the Soviets stuck on buildings of any age). Crossing the bridge, bear slightly right into a narrow cobblestone alley, vul. Petropavlivska (Петропавлівська). Walk along vul. Tatarska to get to the beautiful, 15th-century, Roman Catholic **Kafedralny Petropavlivsky Kostyol** (Кафедральний Петропавлівський костьол; St. Peter and Paul Church), vul. Tatarska, 20, flanked by an 18th-century tower. Its elegantly understated (or looted) interior contains several delicately carved marble figures, including a shrine to the Virgin Mary on the right as you enter. Outside, a **Muslim minaret,** from the cathedral's stint as a mosque during the Turkish occupation, is topped with a golden Madonna that overlooks the entire town—the Poles placed it there on Vatican's orders in 1756, as if to say "Ha, ha!" to the Turks. The partition of Poland began shortly thereafter.

Past the cathedral, a large square on the left contains the 16th- to 18th-century **Budinok Ukrainsko-Polskoho Mahystratu** (Будинок українсько-польського магіс-трату; Ukrainian-Polish Magistrate's House), the large building with the clock tower. Next door stands the 16th-century **Dominikansky Kostyol** (Домініканський костьол; Dominican monastery), complete with fortified walls to keep out the infidels. A fire gutted the complex after it had almost been renovated, but its burned shell still merits a look. Beyond this is a large cobblestone square with some old houses—most notably, at the opposite end of the square, a 16th-century **Armenian merchant's house.** A right at the square is the Roman Catholic **Trynitarsky Kostyol** (Тринітарський Костьол; Trinitarian Church), with an inscription that boldly and honestly proclaims "Всё так не будет" ("Everything will not be like this"). Beyond this, an ancient Turkish bridge takes you to the multi-towered **fortress,** the most famous of the town's aged structures. It was originally built of wood in the 11th century. The 15th-century residents finally realized that was pretty silly, and rebuilt it with stone. The exterior is impressive as you cross the bridge, the interior wonderfully unsupervised. Some stroll about what's left of the walls; others pick apples from the trees in the courtyard. It's all quite medieval. (Open Sat.-Thurs. 8:30am-5pm, Fri. 8:30am-4pm; ethnographic museum in the castle walls closes one hour early; 1hv, students 0.50.)

A number of curious defense bastions await by the Smotrych. At vul. Tatarska's north end, past the Petropavlivsky church, **Staropochtovy Uzviz** (Старопочтовий узвіз; Old Postal Road) drops down on the left to lead past the **Bashta Stefana Batoriya** (Башта Стефана Баторія; Stefan Batory Tower)—named after a victorious Polish king. Its stone **Vitryana Brama** (Вітряна брама; *Windy Gate*) is famous for knocking off Peter the Great's hat. The **Polska Brama** (Польська брама; Polish Gate) lies a bit farther on. Together with the **Ruska Brama** (Руська брама; Ruthenian Gate), the gate was an inventive form of defense, providing for the flooding of the canyon in case of attack. Vul. Ruska (Руська), offering a view of the town from the position of an invader, winds along the river. To reach the peaceful Armenian quarter, wander east, then north (away from the castle), and take a sharp left after crossing under the bridge onto **vul. Dobha** (Добга). A 345° right onto vul. Virmenska (Вірменська) at vul.

Greetings from Let's Go Publications

The book in your hand is the work of hundreds of student researcher-writers, editors, cartographers, and designers. Each summer we brave monsoons, revolutions, and marriage proposals to bring you a fully updated, completely revised travel guide series, as we've done every year for the past 38 years.

This is a collection of our best finds, our cheapest deals, our most evocative description, and, as always, our wit, humor, and irreverence. Let's Go is filled with all the information on anything you could possibly need to know to have a successful trip, and we try to make it as much a companion as a guide.

We believe that budget travel is not the last recourse of the destitute, but rather the only way to travel; living simply and cheaply brings you closer to the people and places you've been saving up to visit. We also believe that the best adventures and discoveries are the ones you find yourself. So put us down every once in a while and head out on your own. And when you find something to share, drop us a line. We're **Let's Go Publications,** 67 Mount Auburn St., Cambridge, MA 02138, USA (email: fanmail@letsgo.com; http://www.letsgo.com). And let us know if you want a free subscription to *The Yellowjacket,* the new Let's Go Newsletter.

When in 172-1011,
do as the 172-1011's do.

All you need for the clearest connections home.

Every country has its own AT&T Access Number which makes calling from overseas really easy. Just dial the AT&T Access Number for the country you're calling from and we'll take it from there. And be sure to charge your calls on your AT&T Calling Card. It'll help you avoid outrageous phone charges on your hotel bill and save you up to 60%.* For a free wallet card listing AT&T Access Numbers, call 1 800 446-8399.

I t ' s   a l l   w i t h i n   y o u r   r e a c h .

http://www.att.com/traveler

Dobha's end runs back to the center past a few churches: **Blahovishchenska Tserkva** (Благовіщенська церква; Church of the Annunciation) and **Mikolaivaivska Virmenska Tserkva** (Миколаївська вірменська церква; Armenian Church of St. Nicholas).

■ Near Kamyanets-Podilsky: Khotyn (Хотин)

The history of **Khotyn Castle** (ho-TEEN) is tied closely to that of Kamyanets. The Turkish invasion of Central Europe, assisted by the seizure of the Kamyanets castle, suffered a setback with the Turks' loss at Khotyn. The Polish-Lithuanian army, led by Hetman Jan Sobieski, defeated the Turks so orgiastically that the *hetman* went on to be elected the next bearer of the Polish-Lithuanian Crown. The Khotyn castle is still hanging on, despite the 1944 Communist invasion of Romanian Bukovina and its appropriation into the Ukrainian SSR. All that stands now are the crumbling remains of the old fortress and a closed church overlooking a river. You're on your own to wander through the grounds, with the occasional cow or cowherder for company (castle open daylight hours; 0.50hv, students 0.30hv; English guidebook 1.50hv). Pack a picnic lunch, jump onto a **bus** from Kamyanets or Chernivtsi (4-6 per day, 1½-3hr., 1hv) and head for this romantic riverbank hideaway. From Khotyn's bus station, walk right onto vul. Shevchenka (Шевченка) and follow this dirt road as it winds through the town and down a hill beyond it. Corner a right, head past the statue, and the fortress will be in sight (40min.).

■ Chernivtsi (Чернівці)

From the late 1700s this city was part of the Austro-Hungarian Empire, but since 1940 Chernivtsi (chair-niv-TSEE) been as red as Yeltsin's nose. Now, smooth BMWs bump over its cobbled streets, and its glorious facades must maintain their beauty among gaudy print shirts. Declared a commercial city by the Soviet Union, today this capital of the Bukovina region holds both newly thriving businesspeople and buildings that crumble as the city's impoverished majority struggles with daily existence. Come here for a pleasant stroll in Habsburg brilliance, or for a view of cultural dissonance at the bizarre confluence of two collapsed empires.

ORIENTATION AND PRACTICAL INFORMATION

Chernivtsi, just 40km north of Romania, climbs up from the **train station.** Across the street from the station, **trolleys** #3 and 5 shuffle their way to the center of town (2 stops). By foot, it's a 20-minute walk: turn left, then take a right onto **vul. Holovna** (Головна; formerly Lenina), which heads straight and then gently to the right into the **city center,** located at **Tsentralna pl.** (Центральна) at vul. Holovna's intersection with Ruska vul. (Руська). Vul. Holovna bears left toward the Bukovina Stadium, **Park Shevchenka,** and the **bus station** (a 30min. walk from the center, or take trolley #3).

Tourist Offices: Intourist, vul. Komarova, 13a (Комарова; tel. 475 55), in Hotel Cheremosh (Черемош), one stop by tram or bus or a 15min. walk from the bus station down the street intersecting Holovna. Open 8:30am-6pm.

Currency Exchange: At numerous Обмін Валют (*Obmin Valyut*). **Ukrinbank** (Укрінбанк), vul. Holovka, 89 (Головка). Gives cash advances and cashes traveler's checks (high commission). **Aval Bank** (Аваль), in Hotel Tourist, vul. Chervonaoarmiska 184 (tel. 789 24), also cashes traveler's checks. Open Mon.-Fri. 9:30am-1pm.

Trains: vul. Gagarina, 38 (Гагаріна). **Advance tickets** (more than 24hr. ahead) must be bought at vul. Holovna, 128. From the train station, trolleys #3 and 5 head along vul. Holovna and then continue to Park Shevchenka, Hotel Bukovina, and, 2 stops later, the advance train ticket office. To: Lviv (2 per day, 5hr., 13hv); Kiev (daily, 14hr., 25hv); and Uzhhorod (daily, 14hr., 30hv). Good luck getting information at tel. 424 10, or reserving (yeah) your tickets at tel. 055.

Buses: vul. Holovna, 219 (tel. 416 35). To: Kamyanets-Podilsky (hourly 8am-8pm, 2½hr., 4.25hv); Khotyn (6 per day, 1½hr., 3hv); Suceava, Romania (13 per day, 10hv); Bucharest (1 per week, 29hv); Chişinău, Moldova (3 per day, 9hr., 14.50hv).

Public Transportation: The trolley conductor charges 0.25hv and can be found sitting in the back on an elevated chair, probably screaming.

Taxis: tel. 051 and 052. A taxi from the bus or train station to Tsentralna pl. shouldn't cost more than 4hv, though drivers will start haggling from 7hv.

Post Office: vul. Khudyakova, 6 (Худякова; tel. 235 63), 50m from Hotel Verkhovina. *Poste Restante* at window #5. Open Mon.-Sat. 8am-2pm and 3-8pm, Sun. 8am-2pm and 3-6pm. **Postal code:** 274 000.

Telephones: Myzhmisky telefon (Мижміський телефон), vul. Ryazanska, 5 (Рязанська), near Hotel Verkhovina. Pay at the counter, announce the city you're calling, and get a booth assignment. Open daily 8am-11pm. **Utel** phones are here and at Hotel Chermosh. **Phone code:** 03722.

ACCOMMODATIONS AND FOOD

Chernivtsi's boastful nicknames, which proclaim it a little Paris, Vienna, or Lviv, have apparently gone directly to the hotel industry's head; prices are high, but conditions don't correspond. Women may not want to stay in hotels here alone. **Private rooms** are occasionally available; Intourist (see above) may be able to help. Since Chernivtsi lies close to the border, hotels ask all guests to register with the public administration before letting a room. **VVIR** (ВВІР) is on vul. Suchavska (Сучавська), at the corner of Shuptetskoho (Шуптецького). From pl. Tsentralna, head along vul. Holovna toward the train station and hang the first right onto vul. Sheptutskoho. The VVIR is down the street on the left, in a blue building; enter from vul. Suchavska. (Open Mon.-Fri. 9am-6pm, but if you arrive on the weekend someone might be around. Get your hotel card from the establishment where you want to stay before coming here.)

Hotel Kyiv (Київ; tel. 224 83), vul. Holovna, 46. Central, well-furnished, livable rooms, though you might see a cockroach or two. Rather small, with interesting smells. Singles with TV and fridge 49hv; doubles with shower 63hv. If you're friendly and persistent, you might be able to bargain. In summer, there's no hot water, and no water at all 10pm-6am. Front doors are kept wide open all night. Women traveling alone may not feel comfortable here.

Hotel Verkhovina (Верховіна; tel. 227 23), Tsentralna pl., 7, at the Адвокат sign. Couldn't be more central unless it moved into the theater. The staff will probably send your rich foreign self up to the Kyiv, which is actually a bit cheaper. Doubles 70hv, with shower 90hv. Prices may be negotiable. Hot water is nonexistent during the summer—even cold water is sporadic. Even more people seem to hang out around the entryway here than at the Kyiv, and they stay all night.

Cafes and **pizzerias** line vul. Holovna and the streets leading away from Tsentralna pl., especially vul. Kobylyanskoi (Кобилянської). None, however, is really worth mentioning. On vul. Ukrainska, by the Armenian Church, clean **Cafe Maestro** (Кафе Маестро) boils up rich soups for under a buck (try the *shchy*; щи; 1.35hv) and fries up meat cutlets (3.60hv). Similarly priced vegetarian main dishes (mostly mushrooms) are also available (open daily noon-11pm).

SIGHTS AND ENTERTAINMENT

Chernivtsi's principal sights are its aged cobbled streets and the elaborate 18th- and 19th-century facades that overhang them. Stroll about at your leisure, but don't forget to have a gander at the **university** at the end of vul. Universytetska (Університетська; take a right at Tsentralna pl. from the train station; vul. Ruska becomes vul. Ryazanska which becomes vul. Universytetska). Intricate, symbolic designs cover the tiled roofs of these stunning, well-maintained buildings, and it's hard to imagine anyone working or studying in their majestic interiors. The **theater** is one of Ukraine's most beautiful houses of drama, with busts of Pushkin, Goethe, and the rest of the gang. Go just past Tsentralna pl. from the train station and then head right. The *kasa* is to the right as you face Shakespeare (open daily 11am-2pm and 5-7pm). During the city's golden age, the garden below the theater was a pool that provided fresh fish for local restaurants. Now it's a popular strolling area. The cute wooden 1607 **Mykolaivska Tserkva**

(Миколаївська церква; St. Nicholas's Church), vul. Sahaydachnoho (Сагайдачного), has recently been renovated after a fire partially consumed it during disputes over whether it should be Russian Orthodox or Uniate. **Pravoslavny Sobor** (Православний собор; Orthodox Cathedral) at **vul. Kobylyanskoy,** the main ivy-colored promenade off pl. Tsentralna, has also recently been restored. Inside, frescoes await avid eyes (open daily 10am-7pm). Farther down on the left, **Virmenska Tserkva** (Вірменська церква; Armenian Church), serves as a hall for organ and chamber music concerts (tickets 6.80hv). Not far from the center, parallel to vul. Holovna, is **Kafedralny Sobor** (Кафедральний собор; Cathedral), nicknamed "*Pyany Sobor*" (Пяный Собор; Drunk Cathedral) because of its distorted domes. On vul. Holovna, across from the entrance to Park Shevchenka, stands a statue of the poet **Paul Celan,** who was born in Chernivtsi back when it was Czernowitz.

As the sun starts to set, locals move out of pl. Tsentralna's beaches and hang out at pl. Teatralna (Театральна), near the theater. **Bar Teatralny** (Бар Театральний), on the south side of the square, gathers a mix of the rich and artful who refresh themselves with gallons of juice and soda. To assert your independent personality, get a cup of caffeine (0.50hv; open daily noon-11pm with a break 4-5pm). You probably won't want to walk by yourself at night along the dimly lit streets.

■ Ivano-Frankivsk (Івано-Франківськ)

Founded in 1661 as the Polish town Stanisławów, Ivano-Frankivsk (ee-VAH-no fran-KEEVSK) lies nestled in the Carpathians along the Bystritsa River. The town—centrally located between Lviv and the mouth of the Danube—was held by Austria from 1772 to 1919, at which point it was turned over to the Soviet Union. A major student hangout, Ivano is even more intellectual than trendy Lviv; but its architecture merits visiting as much as its cafe scene.

Orientation and Practical Information Trains, pl. Pryvokzalna (Привокзальна; tel. 21 22 23 or 21 20 05), whiz to: Kiev (daily, 17hr., 17hv); Chernivtsi (hourly, 3½hr., 3.60hv); Lviv (hourly, 3½hr., 9hv); Odesa (odd days, 22hr., 27hv); Uzhhorod (odd days, 10hr., 12hv); Brest (even days, 17hr., 30hv); Moscow (daily, 40hr., 68hv); and Przemyśl (daily, 6hr., 29hv). **Luggage storage** is 7hv. **Buses,** next door (tel. 238 30), go to Chernivtsi (3½hr., 6.30hv) and Lviv (3½hr., 6hv). **Local transportation** consists of buses and trolleybuses (0.20hv). The 15-minute walk from the train and bus stations past shaded lanes and turn-of-the-century buildings to the center goes by quickly. Head straight from the train station on **vul. Hrunvaldska** (Грунвальдська), which turns into **vul. Hrushevskoho** (Грушевського), and turn right on **vul. Melnychuka** (Мельничука) to reach **pl. Rynok** (пл. Ринок), the old city center. A few streets farther lies the new center of the city—**pl. Vychevy** (Вичеви), from which the pedestrian street vul. Nezalezhnosti (Незалежності) shoots off. The welcoming tourist agency **Auscoprut,** vul. Hrunvaldska 7-9 (tel. 223 21 49; fax 223 14 02), resides in the posh Hotel Roxolana, just five minutes from the train and bus stations. The English-speaking staff gives town info and guided tours, and has some printed material in English for sale. The **maps** (1.44hv) may be out of date, but the current **yellow pages,** sold in kiosks everywhere, has an updated map in the front (agency open Mon.-Fri. 9am-6pm). For **currency exchange,** kiosks—which change dollars, marks, and hryvny—are your best bet. **Ukrainsky Bank,** on vul. Komarova (Комарова; tel. 314 83) will change AmEx, MC, and Thomas Cook **traveler's checks** with a 3% commission. MC, and Visa **advances** are possible with a minimum of US$100 (3% commission). A **24-hour pharmacy** is at vul. Belobederska 2 (Белобедерська; tel. 425 20). The **post office** is at vul. S. Striltsiv 13 (С. Стрільців; open Mon.-Fri. 8am-8pm, Sat. 8am-6pm, Sun. 9am-5pm). Go around the corner to the pl. Vichevy entrance for *Poste Restante* and to send packages. Across the square, **Tsentralny Mizhmisky Perehovorny Punkt** (Центральний Міжміський Переговорний Пункт), vul. Vitovskoho 2 (Вітовського; tel. 241 25 or 220 99), charges 4hv per minute for calls to Australia and New Zealand, 3.50hv to Africa, 2.50hv to the U.S. and Canada, and 1hv to the U.K. (open 7am-11pm). **Utel phones** are located in Hotels Roxolana, Ukraina, Dnister, and Tourbaza Prykarpattya. **Postal code:** 284000. **Phone code:** 803422.

Accommodations and Food Several lodging options exist here besides the ritzy Roxolana. **Hotel Dnister** (Дністер), vul. S. Striltsiv 12 (tel. 235 33), centrally located to the right of pl. Vychevy, offers clean rooms and hot water, though the mattresses sag almost to the ground (singles 33hv; doubles 53hv, with shower 60hv; triples 62.50hv; quads 72hv; hearty breakfast included). Be persistent if they give higher prices—they may not tell you about the cheaper rooms. Fresher air and a friendlier environment can be found at **Tourbaza Prykarpattya** (Турбаза Прикарпаття), vul. Hetmana Mazepy 140A (Гетмана Мазепи; tel. 302 98). It's on the outskirts of town, but reachable by bus #14 or 8 from the train station (15-20min.). Get off after you see a lake on your right. The rooms are fresh and clean (singles 33hv; doubles 54hv; quads 64hv). Quads are unavailable during the summer, when children from Chernobyl are brought in to breathe Ivano-Frankivsk's fresh air. **Hotel Kyiv** (Київ), vul. Nezalezhnosti 4 (tel. 249 56), right in the middle of things, looks like it might disintegrate under your eyes, but is the cheapest around. Take the lift to the fourth floor to find the plain and shabby rooms (singles 20hv; doubles 32hv; quads 48hv) There's no hot water in summer, and probably no showers ("under repair" in summer '97).

Though many restaurants lie near the center, few offer an improvement on the old Soviet-style options. Grocery stores and the market may be your best bet. A small, Western-style convenience store, **Orelya** (Ореля), sits at vul. Hrushevska 20 (open 8am-9pm), and a slightly more expensive 24-hour grocery is near Hotel Ukraina. The enormous, cheap **market** begins every day around 8am and runs to about 6pm. Sundays are the main days, and it's best to get there after noon (things are cheaper). An exception to the restaurant rule is **Cafe Zavyvanets** (Завиванець), pl. Rynok 12, with its fresh, cheap *pelmeni* (1hv; open daily 11am-10pm). A tiny **cafe** across from the post office serves fresh *pierogi* (0.34-0.49hv).

Sights and Entertainment The architecture alone makes Ivano-Frankivsk worth a visit. Vul. Shevchenka contains some of the oldest, richest, and most beautiful homes. Each aged house and street in the center has a history (which you can read about in the Auscoprut tourist office if you know Ukrainian). Right in the heart of pl. Rynok stands the 1666 **ratusha** (town hall). Now the **Kraeznavchy Muzey** (Краєзнавчий Музей; Regional Museum) sits inside these aged walls, exhibiting the 800-year-old sarcophagus of King Yaroslav Osmomsyl. The changing exhibitions often feature local paintings, as well as old furniture and customs of the city (open Tues.-Sun. 10am-5pm; 2hv; Ukrainians 0.40hv, students 0.20hv). **Dom 6,** in pl. Rynok, began as a reading room on November 9, 1884, with a woman, E. Zhelehivsky, at its head; on December 9, the first meeting of the **Society of Ukrainian Women** took place. Around the corner, **Derzhavny Khudozhny Muzey** (Державний Художній Музей; Museum of Sacred Galician Art) resides in a Ukrainian Greek Catholic Church. The museum displays the chronological development of Galician art, focusing on icons from the 16th through 19th centuries. Ancient books, paintings, and sculptures also line the walls (open Sun.-Thurs. 10am-6pm; 0.50hv, students 0.20hv). At the other end of the same square stands an impressive **church** rich with icons. First the Ascension Church, then Greek, it changed to Russian Orthodox in 1955, and only in 1990 returned to Ukrainian Greek Catholicism. Behind the Galician art museum lie the ruins of an old **brewery,** which made *Stanislabeer* until 1939. The round-domed **Ukrainian Orthodox Church,** a block away from the opposite side of pl. Rynok, was originally an Armenian Church. Nearby, a square and statue are dedicated to the Polish poet **Adam Mickiewicz.** Farther out of the center, behind the theater, lies an extensive **park,** formerly a cemetery. In 1917, some graves were transplanted, but many, especially those belonging to Jews, were destroyed.

Intricate rugs, embroidered clothing, carved wooden boxes, and other souvenirs can be found at the **flea market** (базар). Don't be afraid to bargain (open daily about

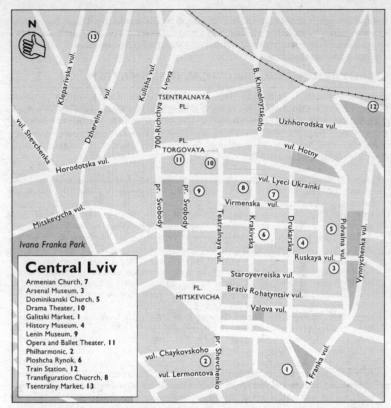

Central Lviv

Armenian Church, 7
Arsenal Museum, 3
Dominikanski Church, 5
Drama Theater, 10
Galitski Market, 1
History Museum, 4
Lenin Museum, 9
Opera and Ballet Theater, 11
Philharmonic, 2
Ploshcha Rynok, 6
Train Station, 12
Transfiguration Chucrch, 8
Tsentralny Market, 13

8am-6pm; best selection on Sun.; prices lower in the afternoon). The surrounding towns sell similar goods at similar (if not lower) prices.

Ivano-Frankivsk supplies evening entertainment in the spring at **Ukrainsky Muzychno-Dramatychny Teatr** (Український Музично-Драматичний Театр), vul. Nezalezhnosti 42, and **Philharmonia** (Філармонія), vul. Lesya Kurbasa 3 (Леся Курбаса; 5-30hv). Most other entertainment ends early. Students and musicians gather for coffee at the **Blues Cafe** (Блуз Кафе), across from the Medical University, vul. Lesi Ukrainy 5 (Лесі Українки). The owner has his own jazz/blues band, and members of the Ukrainian techno group Fantan II are regulars here.(0.5L beer 1.80hv; open Mon.-Fri. 10am-11pm, Sat.-Sun. 2-11pm). All different sorts of people fill the picture-clad walls of **Cafe Maestro** (Маестро), vul. Vahilevycha 81 (Вагілевича). In evenings, the rattle from the TV, crowded tables, and heat from burning lights give the place a lively, yet subdued feel (bottle of beer 2.20-2.80hv; open 11am-midnight). The mushroom tents and outdoor dance floor (not to mention cheap beer) entice many on warm summer days to **Kafe Pid Lylykom** (Під Лиликом), vul. Shevchenka 12. Students, artists, and Ukrainian hippies all hang out in this sometimes rowdy cafe (open Mon.-Fri. 10am-11pm, Sat.-Sun. noon-11pm).

■ Lviv (Львів)

Dear Abby,
Divorced from Poland in 1945 after 600 years of ups and down, I just went through a breakup with the USSR, for whom I had cooked and slaved for over 45 years. I'm living with my mother now, old Kiev, but we don't even speak the same language! In

spite of my age, I feel ready to be conquered by the world. My Polish half-sister, Kraków, tells me that living with tourists creates all sorts of ills, but I just want to be loved, admired, and remembered. Why won't someone enter my gates?

Worthy and waiting, Lviv.

ORIENTATION AND PRACTICAL INFORMATION

The center of town is **pl. Rynok** (Ринок), the old market square. Around it a grid of streets forms the **Old Town,** and along the west side, **pr. Svobody** (Свободи) runs from the Opera House to **pl. Mitskevycha** (Мішкевича). Many hotels are on this strip. Tram #1 runs from the main train station to the Old Town's center, tram #6 to the north end of pr. Svobody. Tram #9 goes from the Old Town to the station. Otherwise, it's a hefty 40-minute walk.

Tourist Offices: The **Hotel George service bureau** (see **Accommodations,** p. 739) plans guided **tours** (55hv for 1-3 people; 80hv for a group of about 10) in various languages, including English, and has a lot of info about the city. They offer a small **map** free and an up-to-date, detailed one for 2hv. Open Mon.-Fri. 9am-5pm. It's much less of a hassle to get train tickets or schedule flights in the **travel office** (tel. 72 67 40) across the hall, though it may cost a few extra hv. English spoken, unlike at the train station. Buy tickets to destinations within Ukraine a week in advance here; international ones can wait until the day before. Open daily 9am-noon and 2-6pm. For other questions, the staff of the friendly service desk of the **Grand Hotel** speaks English and will think you're staying in their hotel if you do too. Grand's city **tours** cost 20hv per hr. for 1-3 people; they **rent cars** with drivers at 36hv per hr. for the first 2hr., 27hv per hr. thereafter.

Currency Exchange: The **Hotel George exchange** cashes **traveler's checks** and gives Visa and MC cash advances at 3% commission. (It's best to get US$ or DM and then exchange it at better rates elsewhere.) Open daily 9am-5pm. **Avalbank** (Авальбанк), vul. Slovatskoho 1 (Словацького; tel. 27 14 20), in the post office, cashes AmEx and Thomas Cook traveler's checks and provides MC, Visa, and EC cash advances at 4% commission. Open Mon.-Fri. 9am-1pm and 2-5pm. **Western Union: X-Change Points,** on the 2nd floor of the post office. Open Mon.-Fri. 8:30am-1pm and 2-6pm, Sat. 8:30am-1pm and 2-6pm, Sun. 8:30am-1pm.

Trains: pl. Vokzalna (Вокзальна; tel. 748 20 68 or 005), at the end of Vokzalna vul. Bus #18 heads to the bus station. **Tickets** available at Intourist windows #23-25 on the 2nd floor and at the Hotel George service bureau, which might be more helpful. To: Kiev (7 per day, 11-16hr., 17-25hv); Ivano-Frankivsk (1 per day, 4hr., 9hv); Odesa (1 per day, 14hr., 25hv); Uzhhorod (2-3 per day, 12-20hv); Bratislava (1 per day, 18hr., 79hv); Budapest (1 per day, 14hr., 104hv); Kraków (8hr., 39hv); Moscow (4 per day, 29hr., 67hv); Prague (1 per day, 21hr., 124hv); Przemyśl (3 per day, 3½hr., 15-18hv); and Warsaw (odd dates, 13hr., 48hv).

Buses: The **main station,** at vul. Stryska (Стрийська; tel. 63 24 73), on the outskirts of town, has extensive regional service and international service to Poland. From town, take trolley #5. From the station, bus #18 goes to the train station, where trams into town are frequent. To: Ivano-Frankivsk (every hr. until 5pm, 3½hr., 6hv); Kraków (3 per day, 7-9hr., 20hv); Lublin (3 per day, 6hr., 14hv); Przemyśl (almost every hr., 4hr., 11hv); and Warsaw (2 per day, 10hr., 20hv). The **second station,** vul. Khmelnytskoho 225 (tel. 52 04 89), can be reached by bus #4 from vul. Shevchenka. Buses to Brest (2 per day, 8hr., 16hv) and Olesko leave from here. **Station #3** is on vul. Petlyury 3 (Петлюри; tel. 62 64 49), and **#4,** with buses to Zhovkva, is at vul. Bazarna (Базарна; tel. 33 80 55). For long-distance destinations, buy tickets a day in advance. Buses are frequently delayed at the border; trains are often quicker. Buy tickets for Polish destinations at window #1 in advance; take a same-day risk at window #2; or buy advance tickets at vul. Voronovo 5 (Вороново; tel. 72 19 91or 72 76 43) behind Hotel George. Open 9am-3pm and 4-6pm

Public Transportation: Buy tickets (0.30hv for **trams** and **trolleys,** 0.40-0.50hv for **buses**) on board from the conductor (not the driver). Controllers are vigilant and ready to slap freeloaders with that 5hv fine. Some kiosks sell a recent public transit **map.** Tram lines are marked in brown, trolley in red, and bus in blue.

Luggage Storage: Hotel George's 2hv per bag per 24hr. Safer than at the stations.

24-Hour Pharmacy: Apteka #23 (Аптека), vul. Zelena 33 (Зелена).

Express Mail: DHL, vul. Tarnovskoho 100 (Тарновського; tel. 75 48 66). Free pick-up. Open Mon.-Fri. 9am-6pm. Ukrainian **EMS** at the post office.

Post Office: vul. Slovatskoho 1 (tel. 72 39 43), a block from Park Ivana Franka, to the right as you face the university. *Poste Restante* on the 2nd floor—get a piece of paper and head to window #4 on the 1st floor. Open Mon.-Fri. 8am-8pm, Sat. 8am-6pm, Sun. 8am-2pm. **Postal code: 290 000.**

Telephones: vul. Doroshenka 39 (Дорошенка), around the corner from the post office. Order your call at the booth to the right as you climb up. For local and inter-city calls, buy *zhetony* (жетоны; tokens) at the telephone office or at kiosks. Pick up the phone, wait for the dial tone, and drop in your *zheton* only when the person answers, or risk losing it forever. Intercity calls can be made only from the tele-phone office or from telephones that say "Мижміські" (*mizhmisky*; intercity). Office open daily 7am-11pm. Sending **faxes** (fax 76 15 85) costs US$0.35 per page. **Utel** cards available at Hotels George, Sputnyk, Lviv, and Karpaty, the telephone center, and the post office. **Phone code:** 0322.

ACCOMMODATIONS

Reflecting increasing numbers of tourists, Lviv has renovated some old Intourist haunts. A few years ago, the Grand Hotel opened its gleaming salons to the public, but not to the budget traveler (216hv per person)—although you might want to check out its downstairs bathroom. Prices are rising, and there's a double standard for foreigners, but the city is much more affordable than Kiev. Many student dorms open up in July and August—the best way to get in is to go through Hotel George's service bureau (call in advance).

Hotel George (Готель Жорж), pl. Mitskevycha 1 (tel. 72 59 52). Take tram #1 from the train station to "Дорошенка" (*Doroshenka*). If you've been traveling at all in Ukraine, you might think this beautiful turn-of-the-century hotel is a miracle. At the city's center, it is both part of the scenery and the perfect place from which to enjoy it. English-speakers are included among its friendly staff, and the recently restored, well-swept building costs a measly 90% extra for foreigners (compared with the usual 300-600%). Large singles with desk, coffeetable, telephone, sink, and clean communal shower cost US$17, with bath US$56. Equally luxurious dou-bles with sink and telephone US$23, with bath US$59. Payment in US$ only. Decent breakfast included. Part of the Lviv experience—and just think what a place like this would cost in Kraków.

Hotel Karpaty (Карпати), vul. Kleparivska 30 (Клепарівська; tel. 33 34 27). From the Opera House, walk straight and take a right onto vul. Kleparivska. Continue straight past *tsentralny rynok* until you see the hotel on your right (about a 20min. walk). Tram #4 from vul. 700-richna Lvova also stops near the hotel. Clean, pleasant rooms. Singles 48hv; doubles 60hv. Bring your own toilet paper.

Hotel Sputnyk (Спутник), vul. Knyahyni Olgy 116 (Княгині Ольги; tel. 64 58 22; fax 64 15 23). A 15min. ride from the city center (tram #3 to the last stop). You may suffer from culture shock shuttling between here and the old part of town, but the facilities are wonderfully modern. Plus, it's practically next door to the concrete Універмаг (*Univermag*) department store, an architectural wonder of its time. All rooms have bath. Singles 57.30hv; doubles 68.40hv. Breakfast included.

FOOD

Pl. Rynok is the restaurant and cafe center; the most convenient (and expensive) **market** is **Galytsky Rynok** (Галицький Ринок), behind the flower stands across from St. Andrew's Church, a block from Hotel George. Fresh berries, honey, and vegeta-bles line the path to the market (open in summer daily 7am-6pm). A little farther out is the cheaper and bigger **Tsentralny Rynok** (Центральний), known as **Krakivsky Rynok** (Краківський) by locals. There are several 24-hour grocery stores: **Mini Market,** vul. Doroshenka 6 (Дорошенка; tel. 72 35 44), is a block from the Grand Hotel.

Restaurants

Lviv is full of quick eateries serving Ukrainian fast food (beef and potatoes, borscht, etc.). There are also several elegant restaurants that serve cuisine on a jarringly lower level than their atmosphere would suggest. New places of both kinds are popping up everywhere; though prices are going up, it's worth exploring.

Mediviya (Медівия), vul. Krakivska 17 (tel. 72 91 41), not far from pl. Rynok. The wooden picnic tables in this small room are often full of people. Fresh Ukrainian food at low prices. *Chanakhy* (Чанахи; bean soup with potatoes and meat) 1.56hv; *pelmeni* (пельмені) 1.40hv. On a cold and rainy day, it's nice to have some tea with honey (*chay z medom;* чай з медом; 0.40hv) or a honey dessert. Open daily 10am-10pm.

Acropolis (Акрополіс), vul. Shota Rystaveli 2 (tel. 76 20 82). Follow vul. I. Franka until it intersects with vul. Zelena (Зелена); Shota Rystaveli shoots off Zelena. This sparkling new establishment is a favorite among both vegetarians and carnivores. They may say they don't serve veggie dishes, but just point to what you want. Main dishes 2.68-5.06hv. *Lakhma* (Лахма) 5.06hv, *moussaka* 3.95hv. Open daily 10am-10pm.

Skifiya (Скіфія), vul. Lermontova 8 (Лермонтова). No seating, but delicious veggie pitas are 2.60hv (unless you specify, this means everything from apples to cabbage to corn). Other pitas 2.60-4.60hv; gyros 5.10hv. The other location at Shevchenka 10 (through a grocery into the cellar) has seating in a bar.

Cafe Castellari (Кафе Кастелларі), vul. Vinnichenka 6, at the start of vul. Lichakivska (tel. 76 58 32). Thin-crust pizzas (6-8hv) are big enough for two—and you can take leftovers with you. Descend below the people-watching spot into this black-and-white joint. Salads 2hv, juices 0.70hv. Take-out, delivery. Open daily 10am-10pm.

Lisova Pisnya (Лісова Пісня), vul. Sichovykh Striltsiv 5 (Січових Стрільців). Close to the university, "Forest Song" is run mostly by students, making it a trendy place for some potato *deruny* (деруни) with pork (3.08hv), a late-night cup o' borscht (борщ; 1.25hv), or a teatime cappuccino (1hv). Open daily 10am-11pm.

Cafes

Reflecting its Polish and Austro-Hungarian heritage, Lviv is a city of coffee and cafes; there are even songs about it. Most are meant for people having a cup o' joe with friends, and a few have their own particularly trendy atmosphere. If a cup of cappuccino costs more than 0.80hv, you're being charged Intourist prices.

Italysky Dvoryk (Італійський Дворик), pl. Rynok 6. Step into the Italian courtyard, where Lviv's coolest residents sip coffee or juice among Renaissance statues and their own personal arches. It's the courtyard of a 16th-century Italian merchant's house, and a museum upstairs contains his richy-rich stuff. Not Lviv's best coffee, but undoubtedly its best coffee setting. Coffee 0.70hv. Open daily 10am-7:30pm.

Bernardinsky Dvoryk (Бернардинський Дворик), behind St. Andrew's Church. Stuck into a defensive well, this cafe hums with life all day. Near darkness envelops the low rumble of conversation, and in winter a fire blazes. Coffee 0.80hv. Open Mon.-Fri. 11am-11pm, Sat.-Sun. noon-11pm.

Mandriki (Мандрікі), vul. Hnatyuka 4 (Гнатюка). Good coffee (0.60-0.80hv), folksy modern carvings, and oak tables. Open daily 10am-4pm and 5-9pm.

The Press Club, pl. Soborna 3 (Соборна). Despite being "in" with the journalist crowd, this spot remains an unpretentious, central location for a light noontime salad (0.85hv) or a late wake-up coffee (0.60hv). Open daily 10am-10pm.

SIGHTS

Lviv is not for the goal-oriented tourist. A gander about the Old Town's cobblestone alleys will lead past towering spires, hunched-over homes, and architectural styles spanning the centuries. The tour begins on pr. Svobody, where the dazzlingly complex exterior of the **Teatr Opery ta Baletu** (Театр Опери та Балету) is surpassed only by its interior, complete with gilded sculpture. It opens onto a pedestrian mall that runs down the middle of pr. Svobody. Exiting the theater, a walk down the boulevard's right side leads past shops and hotels, lodged in the facades of old Polish apartments. On the left, at pr. Svobody 20, **Natsionalny Muzey** (Національний Музей) commands attention, if only for its impressive front. Part of the town's original **city walls and gates** still stand next to the museum. The main gallery offers two permanent exhibits and a changing one (usually of modern foreign art). The collection includes several rooms of 14th- to 19th-century icons and two wings of Ukrainian paintings (open Sat.-Thurs. 10am-5:30pm. 1hv, students 0.50hv, students free Mon.).

A third of the way up pr. Svobody, at #15 (corner of vul. Hnatyuka), **Muzey Etno-hrafii** (Музей Етнографії) harbors an exhibit of Ukrainian dress, archaeological artifacts, painted eggs, and embroidery; it's worth a look inside, if only for the fabulous marble staircase and lofty decorated ceilings (open Wed.-Sun. 11am-7pm, off-season 10am-7pm; 0.50hv, students 0.20hv; exhibitions 1hv; tours 3hv, students 1.50hv). Turn off onto vul. Hnatyuka, and at the fork in the road head left to **Park im. Ivana Franka** (Парк ім. Ивана Франка), which fronts on **Lviv University**. Franka looks kindly down on the students; the ones who walk all the way uphill through the park will be rewarded by the beauteous, ochre-walled, gold-studded **Sobor sv. Yura** (Собор св. Юра; St. Yura Cathedral). The interior of this 18th-century wonder should soon match the beauty of its outer surface; it's currently under renovation (open daily 7am-1pm and 3-8pm). Toward the train, the church you pass on the tram is **St. Elizabeth's Cathedral.** Constructed by Poles when they first settled in Lviv, its spires purposefully reach higher than St. Iura's domes to assert the dominance of Polish Catholicism over Ukrainian Orthodoxy.

Strolling back on pr. Svobody eventually leads to the **Mickiewicz statue,** which honors the Polish poet and patriot and serves as a site of concerts, crowded political discussions, and the occasional Hare Krishna sing-along. Turn left at the Ukraine movie theater and head toward the stone-gray 17th-century Bernardine Monastery, now the Greek Catholic **Church of St. Andrew.** The church boasts a cavernous interior covered in frescoes and a massive altar of rich gold and black granite. To reach the heart of the city, make a sharp left here and take one of the narrow streets leading up to **pl. Rynok,** the historic market square, which presents a collage of richly decorated four-story merchant homes dating from the 16th-18th centuries. The square gazes lovingly at the **ratusha** (town hall), a 19th-century addition. Its corners are guarded by statues of Diana, Venus, Neptune, and patron of Greek love Cupid.

There are enough museums around the square to provide you with cocktail party banter for a year. Several are under the umbrella of the **Istorychny Muzey** (Історичний Музей). The one at pl. Rynok 4 recounts the history of Lviv during the World Wars. The adjoining **Italian Courtyard,** pl. Rynok, 6, presents military clothing, paintings, and other household treasures of the Italian *mascalzone* (rascals) who lived here in the 16th century (both open Thurs.-Tues. 10am-6pm; separate tickets for each exhibition, from 0.30-1hv). The Istorychny Muzey continues at Rynok 24, where one can see various medieval artifacts. **Apteka-Muzey** (Аптека-Музей; Pharmacy Museum), vul. Drukarska 2 (Друкарська), occupies Lviv's oldest drugstore and sells bottles of iron-fortified "wine" designed to cure all ills; ask for the *vino* (open Mon.-Sat. 9am-7pm, Sun. 10am-5pm; 0.20hv). Glean knowledge to stun the artsy crowd at **Muzey Mebliv i Portselyany,** on the second floor at #10 (Музей Меблів і Порцеляни; Museum of Furniture and Porcelain; open Thurs.-Tues. 10am-5pm; 0.50hv, students 0.20hv).

"Beeznesmen"

Wild rumors of the Ukrainian (and Russian) mafia loom large in other parts of the world, and the truth is that the mafia is a strong presence. The average traveler minding his or her own business, however, shouldn't be affected (unless his or her business is starting his or her own business). A tip for spotting these law-evading folk: if you see a man wearing sunglasses and a suit and talking on a cell phone get out of a BMW, you shouldn't jump to conclusions in this PC age, but you can conjecture that this "beeznesman" may perhaps have some, er, connections...

Lviv is jam-packed with beautiful examples of ecclesiastic art and architecture; if you're going to get churched-out anywhere, this is the place. The best time for a tem-

UKRAINE

ple tour is between 5 and 7pm, when the often-shut doors open up for the prayer-thirsty faithful. When casting a glance inside, remain respectful of those who came here for spiritual inspiration—don't walk around, don't talk, and don't take pictures, please. Just beyond the gaze of trident-armed Neptune is pl. Katedralna (Като-дральна), where the main attraction is the Polish **Katolitsky Sobor** (Католицкий собор; Catholic Church; open Mon.-Sat. 6am-noon and 6-8pm, Sun. and holidays 6am-3pm and 5:30-8pm). The huge, decorated columns and dark, apocalyptic frescoes make this one of Ukraine's most awesome cathedrals. The church contains four altars along each nave and a ninth one to the right of the main altar, each worth a lengthy *tête-à-tête*. Next door stands a small Renaissance chapel, **Kaplytsa Boimiv** (Каплиця Боїмів), which is the only example of Lviv's religious architecture that's more a tourist attraction than a house of worship. The chapel was ordered by a rich Hungarian merchant, Boim, and contains the rotted skeletons of 14 members of his family. Gaze up at the ceiling for a head-spinning view of the dome's spiral decorations. In the upper-left corner hangs Mr. Boim's emblem. Lacking noble origins, he bought himself the title of consul, which gave him the right to an "emblem" (some info in English; open daily 10am-5pm; 0.50hv, students 0.20hv). From Diana's column on pl. Rynok, follow vul. Ruska (Руська) east to the massive **Uspenska Tserkva** (Успеньська церква; Assumption Church). Here, more so than in Catholic temples, cameras are a no-no. Every icon was painted by a scholarly and saintly monk. The out-of-place befriezed main altar is a reminder of from when the Russian Orthodox church suffered a brief spell under Greek Catholic supervision. Next to the church, **Bashta Kornyakta** (Башта Корнякта; Kornyakt's Tower) hoists a bell 60m above ground.

To the left and back as you leave the church gates, the Dominican Monastery has been converted into **Muzey Istorii Relihii** (Музей Історії Релігії; Museum of the History of Religion), which depicts different religions of the world. The masterfully carved wooden figures are worth a look (open Fri.-Wed. 10am-6pm; organ concerts some weekends). If you head right as you leave the Assumption Church, you'll find **Mitsky Arsenal** (Міський арсенал), vul. Pidvalna 5 (Підвальна). On display are iron examples of the many implements humans have employed to kill each other (open Thurs.-Tues. 10am-5pm; 1hv, students 0.50hv).

Back on pl. Rynok, prowling north past the pharmacy museum along vul. Krakivska (Краківська), then bearing right on vul. Virmenska (Вірменська), lands you at the barricaded **Virmensky Sobor** (Вірменьський собор; Armenian Cathedral). It seems so out of place that one would never guess it has stood here since the 14th century. At the top of vul. Virmenska 35, the new **Kulturno-Mystetsky Tsentr "Dzyha"** (Культурно-Мистетський Центр "Дзига"; Art-Cultural Center "Dzyha"; tel. 72 74 20), holds funky exhibits of mostly contemporary art—sculptures, paintings, photos, and prints (open 10am-7pm; 1hv). Once a week (usually Sat. or Sun.), concerts are held here; look for notices in the building. Down the hill, a passage runs from vul. Virmenska to vul. Lesy Ukrainky (Леси Українки) between the church and the bishop's hearth, letting the wanderer peek into the ecclesiastic back alleys. On Lesy Ukrainky, a left steers you to **Preobrazhenska Tserkva** (Преображенська церква; Transfiguration Church), one block away at vul. Krakivska 21, a more modern building popular for weddings. Turn left as you exit the church, walk a few blocks, and take a right up the stairs to the ochre **Kostyol Marii Snizhnoi** (Костьол Марії Сніжної; Church of Our Lady of the Snow). Catch an evening or morning service (Mon.-Sat. 7:15am and 7pm; Sun. 9am and 7pm) to glimpse the elaborate altar.

To the left of the Snow Lady runs a path to the old market square. Across and to the right stands **Kostyol sv. Ioana Khrestytelya** (Костьол Св. Иоана хрестителя; Church of St. John the Baptist). Carefully preserved since the 13th century, it's one of the best postcard scenes in the city, and also serves as the **Museum of Old Lviv** (open Tues.-Sun. 11am-7pm; 0.50hv, students 0.30hv). Vul. Uzhhorodska (Ужгородська) climbs to the right around the miniature church all the way up to **Vysoky Zamok** (Высокий Замок; High Castle Hill), where the television tower now stands. A right at the restaurant guides the camera-toters to a panoramic viewpoint above the Old Town. Farther east, take tram #2 or bus #7 from Mytna (Митна), or walk along vul. Lychakivska to vul. Krupyarska (Крупярська). Head up the street on the left to the outdoor **Museum of Architecture,** also known as **Shevchenkivsky Hay** (Шевченківський Гай). Lying on a vast park, the museum harbors a collection of wooden houses brought here from all around western Ukraine (open Tues.-Sun. 11am-7pm; 0.60hv, students 0.45hv).

Back on vul. Lychakivska, head down vul. Mechnykova (Мечникова) to the white-washed chapel and **Lychakivsky Tsvyntar** (Личаківський Цвинтар; Lychakivsky Cemetery). Inside Lviv's most famous necropolis, the tombs of Polish nobles lie beside the simple graves of local residents. Hidden from the sun by a heaven of trees, Lychakivsky's paths provide a pleasant, if unorthodox, strolling ground. For a most instructive visit, follow Mechnykova down past the large empty space to the main gate. Upon entering, follow the path that takes off to the right at a 135° angle to visit the graves of Ukraine's most famous artists. On its left side, a hammer-armed Stakhanovite decorates the eternal bed of **Ivan Franko** (Іван Франко)—a nationalist (or patriotic, depending on how you look at it) poet. Across the path from Franko sleeps **Lyudchenko** (Людченко), Melopmene's favorite composer. Up and to the left of the footway, a statue of a gorgeous man playing a stone lyre attempts to revive the golden voice of **Solomiya Kruzhelnytska** (Соломія Кружельницька), in whose honor Lviv holds the November opera festivals. The last individual grave lies close by, the sepulcher of **Volodymir Yvasyuk** (Івасюк), an all-around artist, marked by the standing figure of a young hunk looking for inspiration. At his tomb, take a right off the alley to reach the rows of graves of Ukrainian, Polish, and foreign soldiers who died defending Lviv during 1918-19. The central arch hails them with a stereotypical Latin motto: *Morti svnt vt liberi vivamvs*—"they died so we may live free." South of the center, tram #2 returns to town; from downtown, take #4. Both the museum and the cemetery are located within **Znesinnya** (Знесіння), an old part of Lviv that dates back to 4000-2000BC. Now it's a large park, including, among other things, beautiful streams and mountains and several factories. **Strysky Park** (Стрийський Парк) is splendidly manicured, with swans and a greenhouse. Vul. Ivana Franka courses south to vul. Striska, which borders the garden.

ENTERTAINMENT

Lviv goes to sleep by midnight only because it starts celebrating by 8pm (or even earlier). Pr. Svobody fills up after lunch with sexagenarians singing wartime and harvest tunes to accordion accompaniment. By eight, sounds of light jazz from sidewalk cafes start filling the avenue, coffeehouses cloud up with smoke, and auditoriums echo with arias or tragic monologues. Only here can you taste all this for pennies, so don't let the contentment of a Hotel George room immerse you in inertia; go out and turn contentment into pleasure.

Performances

Renowned opera, experimental drama, cheap tickets, and an artistic population make Lviv's performance halls the second most frequented institution—after cafes. Theaters post their schedules by the front entrance, although many host only irregular performances in the summer. Tickets range from 2 to 5hv, so now is the time to get that front-row seat that Broadway's neoned playhouses put out of reach. Purchase tickets at each theater's *kasa* or at the **teatralny kasy** (театральни каси; ticket windows) on pr. Svobody 37 (open Mon.-Sat. 11am-2pm and 4-7pm).

Teatr Opery ta Baletu (Театр Опери та Балету), pr. Svobody 1—by now you know exactly where it is (tel. 72 85 62). Catch a Verdi or a Rossini for 5hv on the first balcony. Great space, great voices, great sets—a paradise in gilded Eden.

Philarmoniya (Філармонія) vul. Tchaikovskoho (Чайковського), around the corner from the George. Less frequent performances than the Opera, but with many renowned guest performers, usually from Kiev or Russia. Tickets 2-5hv.

Ukrainsky Teatr Marii Zankovetskoi (Український Театр ім. М. Заньковецької), pl. Svobody 26 (tel. 72 07 51). Famous throughout the land, this home of drama produces the compositions of Ukrainian dramaturgs—classical and experimental alike.

Lvivsky Dukhovny Teatr "Voskresinnya" (Львівський Духовний Театр "Воскресіння"), pl. Peremohy (Перемоги), at the end of vul. Hnatyuka that heads from the Ethnographic Museum on Svobody. Although in Ukrainian, Voskresinnya presents 20th-century works—from Chekhov to Beckett—that many might have already seen performed in English. This will be more than a repeat experience in Slavic, though, as the theater's fame rests on the innovation of its shows.

Nightlife

After singing all day in the streets and coffee-ing up in the java houses, at night Lviv sits down in its squares and patios for yet another sing-along or final cup. For an evening free of partisan arias, stop for a shot of whatever at a club-cafe, or swig some steins at Zoloty Kolos. The closest **gay** life comes to being "organized" is the cruising area on pr. Svobody—from the Opera to the Shevchenko statue. Check for notices in the basement of the puppet theater.

Club-Cafe Lyalka (Клуб-Кафе Лялька), vul. Halytskoho, 1 (Галицького), below the Teatr Lyalok (Puppet Theater). The jovial doorman will give you information (in Ukrainian or Polish) on the other cool hangouts in the city. Downstairs, artsiness fights artfulness for supremacy. Shabbily dressed artfuls do shots while arguing with the sophisticated black-clad wine-sippers. A rarely cleaned wall of posters advertises past and future concerts; speakers exude soft Italian rock or Australian pop; graffitoed bedsheets hang from the ceiling, while colorful modern art bespatters the poster-free walls. There's even a tiny dance corner that fills with people on Fri., Sat., and Sun. (disco nights). 200mL wine 3hv. Coffee 0.60hv. Open Mon.-Thurs. 11am-11pm, Fri.-Sun. 11am until 1 or 2am. Cover 2hv disco nights.

Club-Cafe za Kulisamy (Клуб-Кафе за Кулісами), vul. Tchaikovshovo 7, on the second floor of the Philharmonic. Entrance to the left, but not well-marked. A bastion of bearable background music. Sounds of practicing philharmonic artists fly in through the windows by day. Hard liquors and suds available, but they somehow seem out of place—it's java and Marlboro all the way. Even mellower than Lyalka. Coffee 0.70hv. Open daily noon-midnight.

Zoloty Kolos (Золотий Колос), vul. Kleparivska 18 (Клепарівська; tel. 33 04 89). The USSR's best brewery continues to bubble-up the ex-USSR's best beer. Bottles (0.80hv) stand at the entry to the spacious, cobblestone-walled cellar, or you can enjoy your hops 'n' malt in the cafe (0.65hv). When *Zoloty Kolos* is unavailable, the weaker but equally tasty *Lvivske Pivo* foams. Open daily 10am-11pm.

■ Near Lviv: Olesko (олесько)

The 14th-century **zamok** (castle) at Olesko, 70km from Lviv, has been destroyed repeatedly, yet still sits majestically atop a hill overlooking fields and more fields. With a packed lunch bag, the daytrip from Lviv is well worth it. A **museum** inside the castle holds 15th- to 18th-century wooden sculptures, icons, paintings, and battle tapestries. (Museum open Tues.-Sun. 11am-5pm; 2hv, students 1hv. Ukrainian tours 10hv, students 5hv). Perhaps even more interesting is the castle itself. In the cellar, you can see a split in the walls, one of the only reminders of the destruction caused by a 19th-century earthquake (some cracks were as large as 3m). The dim and damp walls of the cellar also hide an empty **treasury** and an old **well** that was 42m deep before the earthquake. Across from the museum, the 18th century **Monastyr Ordena Kaputsyn** (Монастирь Ордена Капуцинъ; Capuchin Church and Monastery), belongs to the castle museum, but is closed. **Buses** arrive from Lviv's bus station #2 (4 per day, 1½hr., 3hv). Bus #14 from the center will bring you to the castle, which is north of the city's center. Turn left from the bus station and head straight to the church; turn left, and go straight again. The 15-minute walk leads right through the rooster-filled town. Six buses per day go back to Lviv; the last one is at 4:45pm.

■ Uzhhorod (Ужгород)

The trip from Kiev or Lviv to anywhere in southeastern Europe leads through rolling pine-covered hills carved by cold crystal streams. Unlike the Caucasus' jagged peaks, the quiet Carpathian Mountains slowly lumber from one gentle ridge to another. A true border town, 4km from Slovakia and 25km from Hungary, Uzhhorod (oozh-HOAR-rod) subsumes the ethnic mix into its small and pleasant Old Town, a remnant of 800 years of Austro-Hungarian rule. On the city's outskirts, ugly industrialization, a remnant of 50 years on the very edge of the Soviet Union, is stagnating. It's gotten too big to be quaint, and now locals from several countries sit along the banks of the barely flowing Uzh River and wonder what a Habsburg would do in their position.

Orientation and Practical Information   Uzhhorod lies on both banks of the **Uzh** (Уж) River. The **train** and **bus stations** are both on the south side, which was developed more recently. From the train station, cross the street, pass the bus station (on the left), and head down broad **pr. Svobody** (Свободи). At pl. Kyryla i Mefodia (Кирила і Мефодія), Hotel Zakarpattya's **Intourist** (tel. 325 72) sells international train tickets to Budapest (daily, 5hr., 54hv); Prague (daily, 14hr., 96hv); and Belgrade (7hr, 120hv). Intourist also **exchanges** small amounts of cash. Domestic tickets can be purchased at the **train station** to Kiev (2 per day, 18hr., 19hv) and Lviv (3 per day, 7hr. or overnight, 9.50hv). Many **buses** (1hr., 2.35hv) and trains (2hr., 3.50hv) run daily to Mukacheve—bus tickets are harder to obtain than train tickets. Take a right at the big hotel to get to the river and the **town center.** Cross the street after the bridge to get to the **Ukraine Export-Import Bank** (tel. 335 41), pl. Petefi, 19 (Петефі), which cashes traveler's checks at 2% commission (open Mon.-Fri. 9am-noon and 1-3pm). Take a left after the bridge and head down nab. Nezalezhnosti (Незалежності) for the long-distance **telephones** at #6 and Utel phones (open daily 24hr.). Past this, around the corner, is the **post office** (open Mon.-Fri. 9am-6pm, Sat. 9am-5pm), and its pride and joy, the **X-Change Point,** which offers **Western Union** services, cashes traveler's checks, and gives Visa/MC/EC/JUB cash advances at 5% commission (open Mon.-Fri. 8am-6pm). **Postal code:** 294 000. **Phone code:** 03122.

Accommodations and Food   It's a hike from the train station, but **Turbaza Svitanok** (Турбаза Світанок), vul. Koshytska, 30 (Кошицька; tel. 343 09), is undoubtedly the best bet for the budget traveler in Uzhhorod. Head across the river and take a left on the main street running parallel to the river. The *turbaza* lies about seven minutes up the fourth street to the right; signs should point the way. Not only will they lodge and feed you, but this is the main **tourist office** for treks into the Carpathians (1 bed in a double with shower 24hv, 12hv if you talk to the director first; sporadic hot water; meals 1.40-2.30hv). Another branch is at the Kostrina settlement—**Turbaza Dubovy Hay** (Турбаза Дубовий Гай; tel. 372 35), an hour and a half away by commuter rail, by Mt. Krasya (Красиа; 1036m). All of Uzhhorod's *yidalnyas* offer the same uneventful meals. The more populated the cafe, the fresher the *pelmeni*...or the cheaper the vodka.

Sights   Uzhhorod's three main tourist attractions have considerably congregated right next to one another. Head right and up just after Hotel Korona. The huge and majestic Neoclassical exterior of **Kafedralny Sobor** (Кафедральний собор; Cathedral) is on your left. Farther along, a small **zamok** (замок; castle) contains some statues and a museum, and provides pretty views of surrounding foothills. The castle joined the 1704 Transcarpathian revolt against the Habsburgs, which ended rather predictably (open Tues.-Sun. 9am-5pm; 60hv, students 30hv). Across the way, the **Muzey Narodnoi Arkhitektury i Pobutu** (Музей народної архітектури і побуту; Popular Architecture and Life Museum), an open-air museum at vul. Kapitulna 33 and 33a (Капітульна), contains a dozen original wood and stone huts typical of the region, as well as a wooden church built without nails. It's a delightful place for a picnic with the Habsburg family (open Wed.-Mon. 9am-5pm; 0.70hv, students 0.30hv).

YUGOSLAVIA
(ЈУГОСЛАВИЈА)

US$1	= 4.85DIN (dinar)	1DIN =	US$0.21
CDN$1= 3.51DIN		1DIN = CDN$0.29
UK£1	= 7.72DIN	1DIN =	UK£0.13
IR£1	= 7.11DIN	1DIN =	IR£0.14
AUS$1 = 3.53DIN		1DIN = AUS$0.28
NZ$1	= 3.08DIN	1DIN =	NZ$0.33
SAR1	= 1.03DIN	1DIN =	SAR0.97
DM1	= 2.66DIN	1DIN =	DM0.38

Country Phone Code: 381 **International Dialing Prefix: 99**

Yugoslavia has been born again three times: in 1929, 1946, and most recently in 1992, after four of its six constituent republics peeled away to independence. Serbia and Montenegro are the only two remaining countries in this Serb-dominated republic, along with the semi-autonomous provinces Vojvodina and Kosovo. The towns that hide in Yugoslavia's hills are more accustomed to economic hardship than tourist visitation, and Belgrade has gone gray trying to recover from years of international economic embargo. A visit to Yugoslavia is politically compelling, if nothing else.

YUGOSLAVIA ESSENTIALS

Visas are required of nationals from Australia, Canada, Ireland, New Zealand, South Africa, the U.K., and the U.S. Visa processing usually takes seven working days. Citizens of Ireland and Great Britain must bring letters of invitation to support their applications. Tourist visas cost US$20 for Americans, US$22 for others, and should be paid for either by money order or certified check. Do not expect to obtain a visa at the border. At the Yugoslav border, you will be asked to declare the amount of cash you are bringing into the country; keep the receipt. Upon leaving the country, the amount of cash you carry out cannot exceed the amount on the entry receipt. Due to border tensions, crossing from Serbia to Croatia is difficult, but Yugoslavia is accessible through Hungary, Romania, Bulgaria, Greece, Macedonia, and (allegedly) Albania.

GETTING THERE AND GETTING AROUND

Belgrade is the main entry point to Yugoslavia, accessible by plane, train, bus, or car. **Yugoslavia Airlines** (JAT) flies into Belgrade, as do numerous European carriers, including Lufthansa, British Airways, Swissair, Air France, and LOT airlines.

If traveling to Serbia or Montenegro by land, be prepared for significant delays at the **border,** where papers are sometimes painstakingly checked. **Trains** are designated *brzi* (fast) or *putnički* (slow). Reservations for couchettes or **international trains,** which come from Budapest, Thessaloniki, Skopje, Sofia, Istanbul, and elsewhere, are generally required, but if the train is not full, they can be made shortly before departure. Given the mountainous layout of Yugoslavia, **buses** are more convenient and reach farther than trains; they are also less expensive. **Car** travel is difficult, especially since few rental companies exist, Yugoslavs are crazy drivers, and the many windy roads are not in good repair. **Hitchhiking,** while sometimes practiced by locals, is not recommended by *Let's Go.* **Ferries** run from Bar, Montenegro to Bari, Italy; to get to Dubrovnik, one must float to Italy and back to circumvent the closed border between Croatia and Yugoslavia.

TOURIST SERVICES AND MONEY

With the exception of the tourist center in Belgrade, most tourist offices are geared toward organizing tours for locals going abroad—while friendly, the staff can offer little info to international travelers. Most brochures are long out of date, and the thin trickle of tourists is little incentive to update.

Yugoslav **dinars** come in denominations of one, five, 10, and 20 dinars; they are subdivided into the para (100 para = 1 dinar). While all transactions are legally supposed to take place in local currency, many establishments will not refuse Deutschmarks. Banks, hotels, or unofficial street exchange booths (especially in Belgrade) offer **exchange services;** remember to get rid of excess dinars before you leave. Bring enough cash to cover your trip; restocking is difficult, and can be done only in Belgrade. You can cash **AmEx** checks at several banks in Belgrade, but you will get the cash in dollars not dinars, and sometimes banks run out of dollars. Credit cards are about as useful as a cup of decaffeinated coffee when you're tired.

COMMUNICATION

Mail to or from the U.S. takes 10 days to two weeks, and slightly less time to Europe. *Post Restante* services are available in Belgrade only; mail will be held for up to one month. Post offices are identified by the yellow **PTT** (ПTT) signs.

Telephones are coin- or card-operated; telephone **coins,** available at the post offices, are cheaper and more convenient, since telephone cards can be used only in post office booths and expire quickly. The only place to make an **international call** is at the main post office in Belgrade. Go to the desk and ask to make an international call; they will monitor the number of minutes, and you pay at the end. It is not possi-

YUGOSLAVIA

ble to make **collect calls** from Yugoslavia. To make an AT&T credit card call from Yugoslavia, dial 0801, and the area code and number you are trying to reach—but don't count on success. You can dial **information** in Yugoslavia at tel. 988.

LANGUAGE

Serbian, the dominant language in Serbia and Montenegro, is written in both Cyrillic and Latin script, as opposed to Croatian and Bosnian, which use only Latin characters. Newspapers are published in both scripts. Serbian, Croatian, and Bosnian are quite similar, having split only recently due to national pressures. However, the dialect in Serbia also differs from that used in Croatia and Bosnia in being of the *ekavski* family, as opposed to the *jekavski* family; words in Serbian often omit the "*j*" found in their Croatian or Bosnian correlatives. Hence, the Serbian word *cvet* (flower) is *cvijet* in Croatian and Bosnian. To make matters more complicated, the Serbs of Montenegro tend to use the *jekavski* dialect. Certain words also differ from country to country: coffee is *kafa* in Serbia and Bosnia, but *kava* in Croatia; bread is *hleb* in Serbian, *hljeb* in Bosnian, and *kruh* in Croatia. Many people also speak **German** and **English,** but you can't count on it, especially at smaller establishments.

HEALTH AND SAFETY

> **Emergency Numbers: Fire:** tel. 91. **Police:** tel. 94.

Although Serbia and Montenegro were calm during summer 1997, unrest could surface in any part of the country. Travelers are advised to avoid demonstrations and areas of heavy police concentration. U.S. citizens should register with their embassy immediately upon arrival, and all citizens should register with the local police within a few days. Petty crime is quite low—a side benefit, perhaps, of political dictatorship—but be on guard, especially near transportation terminals or in the city centers.

While physicians in Belgrade may be quite well-trained, Serbia and Montenegro lack Western **medical** facilities. You will need to pay cash for any medical treatment, and do not expect to get prescriptions filled at pharmacies.

ACCOMMODATIONS AND CAMPING

State-run hotels dominate the accommodations scene in Serbia and Montenegro; you will be required to leave your passport at the desk when you register, but it will be returned when you leave. Though most hotels are virtually empty, prices remain inexplicably high; the laws of supply and demand have made little impression. Yugoslavia's train and bus stations have surprisingly few advertisers for **private rooms;** renting them may be illegal, and citizens fear the consequences of opposing the government. **Camping** is an option along the Danube and the Adriatic coast.

FOOD AND DRINK

Food in Serbia and Montenegro includes the usual Balkan specialties: *čevapčići,* grilled lamb rolls; *ražnjići* (skewered pork and veal, grilled with peppers and onions); *pljeskavica* (hamburger steak); *punjena tikvica* (zucchini stuffed with minced meat and rice); and other *meso-* (meat)-laden foods. Vegetarians will find it challenging to eat out; make picnics with *hleb* (bread) and *sir* (cheese). *Kajmak* is a creamy Balkan cheese. Seafood, such as fried carp (*šaran*), is readily available, particularly along the Montenegran coast. *Kafa* (Turkish coffee) is a staple of *kafanas* (cafes), as is *pivo* (beer); look for *Bip* beer near Belgrade. *Dingac* and *Postup* wines are specialties of Montenegro. And of course, any proper Balkan dining experience must conclude with a shot of *šljivovica* (plum brandy).

CUSTOMS AND ETIQUETTE

Most shops and offices take a rest day on **Sunday.** As in the rest of the Balkans, Yugoslavs dress stylishly. Girls and young women in particular display the latest fashions when going out. **Tipping** is expected, especially from foreigners; the amount depends on you.

NATIONAL HOLIDAYS

Yugoslavia takes a break on: January 1, New Year's Day; January 7, Orthodox Christmas; May 1, Labor Day; April 27, Constitution Day; July 7, Independence Day (Serbia); and July 13, Independence Day (Montenegro).

LIFE AND TIMES

HISTORY

Yugoslavia's turbulence is not merely a modern phenomenon: long before the Slavic tribes arrived, Yugoslavia passed from the **Illyrians** to the **Celts** in the early centuries BC, and finally to the **Romans.** In 395AD, the land of present-day Serbia was incorporated into the **Byzantine Empire,** while areas to the west (present-day Croatia) went to the **Western Roman Empire.** When the Slavs finally arrived in the 6th and 7th centuries, a divide was already in place between Catholic west and Orthodox east; this divide was strengthened when **Saints Cyril and Methodius** mass-converted the Serbs to Orthodoxy.

After breaking away from Byzantium in 969, Serbia was reincorporated into the Empire in the 11th century and, hobbled by factional infighting, reluctantly remained subjugated, though dominated by the Serbian **Nemanjić** dynasty in the 12th century. In 1217, under Serbian ruler **Stefan Dušan,** Serbia came into its own as a powerful medieval kingdom, establishing the Serbian Orthodox Church in 1218 and conquering Belgrade for the first time in 1248.

Serbian history came to a head on June 28, 1389, in the **Battle of Kosovo Polje** (Field of the Blackbirds), when the Ottoman Turks wiped out a mighty Serb army led by Tsar Lazar, the last Serb prince. The defeat led to almost 500 years of Ottoman domination. Tsar Lazar built a church at the Kosovo battlefield before sending his troops into battlefield, and the site retains religious import to this day: the holiest Serbian monasteries are established here, and the desire to avenge that defeat lingers in Serbian national consciousness. The battle saga has become a Serbian national anthem (see **Literature,** p. 751). Notably, the 500-year Ottoman domination did not result in mass conversions of Serbs to Islam, as it did in neighboring Bosnia; Serbia remains an **Orthodox** state to this day. Ottoman domination did not extend quite as firmly to the hilly outpost of Montenegro. Consequently, Montenegro, hitherto undistinguished from Serbian lands, was able to develop an identity as a separate principality, employing a *vladika* (prince-bishop) system of rule.

> During the Balkan Wars, Montenegro remained relatively peaceful, but Serbia was obviously flexing its muscles.

As the centuries wore on, the sultan's power weakened, and the Ottoman Empire declined, the Serbs increasingly chafed under Turkish domination. The resentment formed the basis for an **1804 revolt** against the Ottomans. Led by **Prince Obrenović,** the Serbs finally drove out the Turks in 1815. Although the prince turned into a despot and was duly exiled in 1842, a bronze statue of him still adorns Belgrade's main square. Autonomy had been gained, but it was not until the **Congress of Berlin** in 1878 that full independence was achieved.

Led by newly independent Serbia, the South Slavs of the Balkans felt an increasing drive to South Slav unity during the late 19th and early 20th centuries. The **First Balkan War,** waged in 1912, pitted Serbia against the weakened Ottoman Turks for control of Macedonia and Kosovo; the Serbs eventually won. The **Second Balkan War** soon followed, in which Bulgaria contested the Serbs and Greeks for control of Macedonia. The war ended triumphantly for Serbia when Romania came to Serbia's aid. Montenegro remained relatively peaceful during the Balkan Wars, but Serbia was clearly flexing its muscles.

YUGOSLAVIA

> ### "Charge the Turks and Crush Their Army"
>
> Thus commences the epic rendition of the **Battle of Kosovo,** the most famous of all Serbian oral epics. In close to 2000 lines (its exact length depends on the singer), *Kosovo* recounts the 1389 defeat of the Serbs at the hands of the Ottoman Empire, which ushered in almost five centuries of Turkish rule. It may seem strange to immortalize a defeat, but *The Battle of Kosovo* emphasizes the valor of the Serbs, the resourcefulness of Serb leader Tsar Lazar, and the bravery of Miloš Obilić, who forfeited his own life to cross to the Ottoman side and kill the hapless sultan. During the recent war, the epic was brought back as a Serbian rallying cry, calling on Serbs to avenge the defeat at Kosovo by attacking the Bosnian Muslims.

South Slav restiveness was one of the factors that sparked **WWI:** in 1914, Gavrilo Princip, a Serb from Belgrade and a member of the nationalist Young Bosnians group, assassinated the Austrian archduke Franz Ferdinand as he was visiting Sarajevo (see **Bosnia: History,** p. 73). About a month after the incident, Austria-Hungary declared war on Serbia, and the Great War officially began. The state entity that grew out of WWI was the **Kingdom of Serbs, Croats, and Slovenes,** a realization of the eponymous "Yugoslav" objective—South Slav unity. Ruled by the Serbian dynasty **Karadjordjević,** the state incurred resentment because it was viewed as Serb-dominated—a chronic source of frustration as the century wore on. In an attempt to obviate the divisive issue ethnic identities, the kingdom was renamed **Yugoslavia** in 1929.

On April 6, 1941, Hitler's troops bombed Belgrade, setting the stage for the Axis occupation of Yugoslavia during **WWII.** Italy took control of Montenegro, while Serbia remained as a puppet state. Yugoslavia dissolved into factional fighting, with the pro-Communist Partisan guerillas, opposed to the Axis, led by **Josip Broz Tito,** of half-Croat, half-Slovene heritage. A pro-Serb group called the **Četniks** fought the pro-fascist, mostly Croat Ustaše group, which operated wartime concentration camps that killed hundreds of thousands of Serbs. In the final tally, approximately 1,700,000 Yugoslavs died in the conflict—one tenth of the population. Yugoslavia emerged after WWII as a nation of six republics (with Kosovo and Vojvodina as autonomous provinces within Serbia) held together by the Partisan war hero and powerful leader **Tito.** Unwilling to let Yugoslavia become a Soviet satellite, Tito practiced his own brand of Communism and quickly earned the enmity of Soviet leader Josef Stalin, who expelled Yugoslavia from Comintern in **1948.** Tito ruled this unwieldy pot of nationalities with an even hand. Yugoslavia took until 1974 to officially establish its **constitution,** which gave power and some autonomy to each of the six republics and to Kosovo and Vojvodina.

When Tito died in 1980, his carefully balanced state began to flail due to ethnic tensions, inflation, debt, and other woes. Less than a year after Tito's death, riots broke out in **Kosovo,** whose 90% Albanian population sought to become the seventh republic of Yugoslavia rather than remain a Serbian province. When the Serb-controlled Yugoslav national army crushed the protests, the stage was set for a decade of unrest. Consolidation of Serb power within the Yugoslav government was the particular agenda of Serbian President **Slobodan**

> **Serbia and Montenegro, along with Kosovo and Vojvodina, are the remaining constituents of "rump Yugoslavia."**

Milošević, who came to power in the late 80s. Milošević, of Montenegran parentage, rose through the ranks of the Communist party, then converted ardent Communism into equally ardent nationalism. Sensing that Milošević sought to convert Yugoslavia into "Greater Serbia," other ethnic groups took alarm. Riots again broke out in Kosovo in 1989 (the 600th anniversary of the Battle of Kosovo Polje; see **"Charge the Turks,"** above), when the Yugoslav government passed a resolution severely restricting Kosovo's autonomy. Finally, on **June 25, 1991, Slovenia** and **Croatia** declared independence from Yugoslavia. The Yugoslav National Army (JNA) promptly invaded Slovenia, but fighting lasted only 10 days before Yugoslavia was forced to recognize the nation's independence. Fighting dragged on into 1992 in Croatia, but the Croats too eventually repulsed the attacks. **Bosnia** followed suit by declaring its independence in April 1992, and the war shifted into Bosnian territory. Backed by Milošević, the Bosnian Serbs embarked on a savage, ultimately unsuccessful four-year siege of Sarajevo. Serbia and Montenegro were left, with Kosovo and Vojvodina, as the remaining constituents of "rump Yugoslavia."

LITERATURE

The prevailing illiteracy of peasant society under the Ottoman Empire inhibited the development of written Yugoslav literature, but a strong tradition of oral epics emerged to take its place. To this day, Serbian men can be seen gathered around a bard spinning a tale of past national glory, accompanied by a *guslar* instrument.

> **To this day, Serbian men can be seen gathered around a bard spinning a tale of past national glory.**

The **Romanticism** sweeping Europe in the early 19th century found expression in Serbian poetry, and coincided with rising Balkan nationalism of the period. **Petar Petrovic Njegoš,** acclaimed as the greatest Serbian poet of all time, was actually from Montenegro. Much of his mid-19th century writings, including *Gorski Vijenac* (The Mountain Wreath), a poetic chronicle of Montenegro's struggle against the Ottoman Empire, discuss Montenegro. Another notable 19th-century figure is **Vuk Karadžić,** a Romantic author whose work touched on the themes of patriotism, human emotions, and nature that weave through other contemporaneous Serbian literature.

As Serbian nationalism grew stronger in the late 19th century, literature increasingly reflected political developments. Romanticism transformed into **Realism** in the years following the 1878 Congress of Berlin, when Serbia officially gained independence. Shifting away from a preoccupation with national and social problems, literature increasingly focused on the plight of the peasant, and the short story became a more popular form. **Pan-Slavic influences,** particularly from the Russian populist movement, entered into Serbian literature. Many Serbian writers were educated in France, causing French Symbolist influences to appear in Yugoslav poetry. The Communist years after WWII bred further explorations of political themes in both Yugoslav fiction and nonfiction. **Milovan Djilaš** wrote *Besuda Zemlja* (Without Justice); this critique of the Communist regime predictably earned him a prison sentence. Perhaps the most famous of all Yugoslav writers was Ivo Andric, the Nobel Prize-winning author of *Bridge on the Drina, Travnik Chronicles,* and other works that examine the mix of ethnicities in Yugoslavia.

Like their neighbors in ex-Yugoslavia, writers from Serbia and Montenegro have also stepped up their literary efforts since the recent war. Nationalism has greatly influenced writers such as **Dobrica Cosič,** a best-selling author of political novels. **Slobodan Selenic** explores similar themes in his novels, which include *Premeditated Murder.* Nationalism is countered, however, in the works of a group of cosmopolitan writers who look to Kafka and Borges for their inspiration. The leading figure of this group, Danilo Kiš (author of *A Tomb for Boris Davidovich*), died in 1989, but the tradition is carried on by writers such as David Albahari. These writers focus on issues of writing itself, and the challenges of urban intellectuals across Eastern Europe.

YUGOSLAVIA TODAY

Slobodan Milošević, who has held power in Serbia for ten years, got the strongest challenge to his political career during mass street protests in Belgrade in late 1996 and early 1997. The protests began after Milošević annulled the results of elections in November 1996, which gave victories to the opposition parties. Thousands of students, organized by the opposition coalition **Zajedno** (Together), marched daily through the streets of Belgrade and other towns, protesting the annulment: at its peak, the movement numbered 200,000 marchers. On January 14, 1997, Milošević yielded to the protests and reinstated the election results. The protestors, while elated, kept to the streets in the hopes of bringing down the president; they faded after time and Milošević, while weakened, remains in control.

In July 1997, up against a two-term constitutional limit as President of Serbia, Milošević ran for President of Yugoslavia, with the intent of transferring power to this erstwhile ceremonial post. (The vote for Yugoslav president was suspiciously advanced a week to prevent the restive Montenegrin contingent from voting by confusing them.) Resentful of Milošević's move to the federal Yugoslav presidency, Montenegro has made noises of succession.

Economic sanctions instituted against Serbia in 1992 were lifted in November 1996, bringing some measure of relief to Yugoslavia. The international community remains wary of Milošević, however, regarding him as the key influence behind **Radovan Karadžic,** the former Bosnian Serb leader indicted for war crimes. Plagued by economic problems and political uncertainty, Yugoslavia still struggles to retain its legitimacy as a federation of Serbia, Montenegro, Kosovo, and Vojvodina.

Belgrade (Београд)

The Slavs' "White City" has actually taken on a hint of gray after many invasions. Ruled by the Byzantines, the Bulgarians, and then the Austro-Hungarians, Belgrade asserted itself briefly in the 15th century as the capital of Serbia before falling again to the Turks. Ottoman control lasted until 1867, when the keys to the city were delivered to Knez (Prince) Mihailo. Four centuries of Eastern influence was gone within four decades; at the turn of the 19th century, Belgrade had a modern European look. Today, Belgrade is a busy metropolis, its center reminiscent of Rome or Paris, while the outer sections are very Balkan in atmosphere. New Belgrade, across the Sava, is a Socialist expanse of gray apartment blocks. The city is clean and well taken care of, but residents complain of the continuously worsening economic situation and the huge population of war refugees. Nevertheless, Belgrade's locals are proud of their city, and welcome foreigners warmly.

ORIENTATION AND PRACTICAL INFORMATION

The neighborhoods and suburbs of metropolitan Belgrade sprawl across the intersection of the **Danube** and **Sava** Rivers; **Stari Grad** (Old Town), the quintessence of Belgrade, lies in the eastern corner formed by the two rivers. **Novi Beograd,** which includes old Zemun, is across the Sava to the west. The main **train station** and central **bus station** sit next to each other near the Sava in Stari Grad, close to the city center. From the small park-like area in front of the train station, **Bul. Nemanjina** runs all the way up to **Trg Dimitrija Tucovića**—more commonly called **Trg Slavija.** The large boulevards **Srpskih Vladara** (formerly Maršala Tita) and **JNA** also feed into Slavija.

To reach the city center from the train station, take the first left after Hotel Beograd off Nemanjina onto **Balkanska** and continue up into **Terazije,** the city's heart. The traffic arteries **Srpskih Vladara, Bul. Revolucije,** and **Rpizrenska,** which becomes **Brankova** after Zeleni Venac, and leads into Novi Beograd, crisscross Terazije. At its northern end, Terazije splits into three streets: **Smemska,** sharply to the left, leads to **Zeleni Venac**—a large market area; to the right is Kolarčeva, a short street ending in **Trg Republike,** which holds the grandiose National Theater and National Museum; and in the center is the longer, pedestrian **Kneza Mihaila,** which leads to the famous **Kalemegdan** fortress, now a park. Embassy-filled **Bul. Kneza Miloša** runs southwest to northeast, crossing Nemanjina, Srpskih Vladara, and Revolucije, after which its name changes to Takovska; the main **post office** is found here. Kiosks at the train station, in the city center, and at busy intersections carry **maps** of Belgrade (15dn), which use the Latin alphabet. The *Beograd Street Finder* (35dn) may confuse more than help.

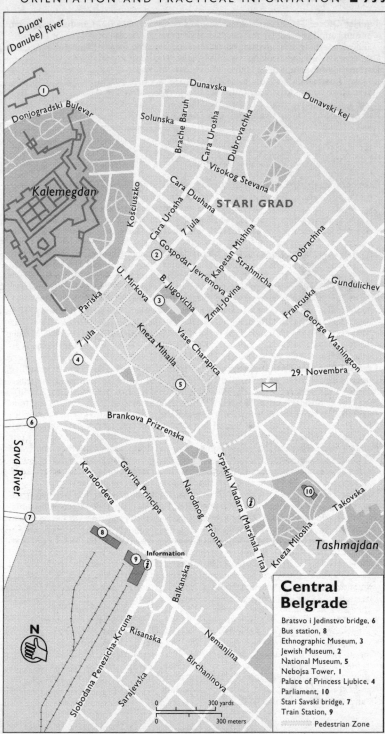

Dunav (Danube) River

Donjogradski Bulevar

Nebojsa Tower (1)

Kalemegdan

Kościuszko

Dunavska

Solunska

Brache Baruh

Cara Urosha

Dubrovachka

Dunavski kej

Visokog Stevana

Cara Dushana

STARI GRAD

Cara Urosha

7 jula

Gospodar Jevremova (2)

Kapetan Mishina

Strahmicha

Dobrachina

Gundulichev

U. Mirkova

B. Jugovicha

Zmaj-Jovina

Francuska

George Washington

Pariska

Ethnographic Museum (3)

Vase Charapica

7 jula

Kneza Mihaila

(4)

(5)

29. Novembra

Sava River

(6)

Brankova Prizrenska

Karadordeva

Gavrita Principa

Narodnog Fronta

Srpskih Vladara (Marshala Tita)

(i)

(10)

Takovska

(7)

Kneza Milosha

Tashmajdan

(8)

Balkanska

(9) Information (i)

N

Slobodana Penezicha-Krcuna

Risanska

Sarajevska

Nemanjina

Birchaninova

0   300 yards

0   300 meters

Central Belgrade

Bratsvo i Jedinstvo bridge, **6**
Bus station, **8**
Ethnographic Museum, **3**
Jewish Museum, **2**
National Museum, **5**
Nebojsa Tower, **1**
Palace of Princess Ljubice, **4**
Parliament, **10**
Stari Savski bridge, **7**
Train Station, **9**

Pedestrian Zone

YUGOSLAVIA

Tourist Office: TIC (Tourist Information Center; tel. 635 622), in the pedestrian underground passage at the north end of Terazije. Excellent source of city info. English-speaking staff gives out brochures and detailed maps of Stari Grad. Accommodations info and booking. Open Mon.-Fri. 9am-8pm, Sat. 9am-4pm.

Embassies: Albania, Kneza Miloša 56 (tel. 646 864; fax 642 941). Open Mon.-Fri. 9-11am. **Australia,** Čika Ljubina 13 (tel. 624 655; fax 628 189) just off Kneza Mihaila; very close to the American Cultural Center. Open Mon.-Fri. 8:30am-4:30pm. **Bulgaria,** Birčaninova 26 (tel. 646 222). Single-entry visa US$55, transit US$45, double transit US$65. Open 10am-1pm. **Canada,** Kneza Miloša 75 (tel. 644 666; fax 641 343). Open Mon.-Fri. 8am-noon and 1-4pm. **New Zealanders** should contact their embassy at Bundeskanzler Platz 2-10, 53113 Bonn, Germany (tel. (49) 228 228 070; fax (49) 228 221 687). **U.K.,** Generala Ždanova 46 (tel. 645 055; fax 659 651). Open Mon.-Fri. 8:30am-noon. **U.S.,** Kneza Miloša 50 (tel. 645 655; fax 644 053). Open Mon.-Fri. 8am-3:30pm.

Currency Exchange: Dinars may not always be available, and Yugoslavian banks don't cash AmEx checks in hard currency, but you can try to change your AmEx checks commission-free (although at a low rate) at **Beobanka,** Kneza Mihaila 22 (tel. 623 032). Open Mon.-Fri. 8am-7pm, Sat. 9am-3pm. **Komercialna Banka** (tel. 335 087), at the corner where Srpskih Vladara and Revolucije flow into Terazije, charges a 7% commission for amounts under US$350 and 1.5% above that. Open Mon.-Fri. 8am-8pm, Sat. 9am-3pm. **Unofficial exchangers** masquerade as ticket sellers around bus stops in Trg Slavija and the central bus station; be alert for the word *devize* (currency). Unofficial exchange rate shouldn't be more than 4dn for 1DM.

Flights: Aerodrum Beograd (tel. 601 555, tourist info ext. 2980, general info ext. 2580), 25km west of Belgrade. **JAT** (Yugoslav Airlines; tel. 450 584; fax 450 562), Svetog Save, next to Hotel Slavija (open 24hr.). **Airport buses** from JAT office, Fontana, Hotel Slavija, and the main train station. Branch at Srpskih Vladara 18 (tel. 642 773; fax 642 534). Discounts for those under 25. **British Airways,** Kneza Mihaila 30/IV (tel. 328 13 03; fax 639 629). Open Mon.-Fri. 9am-4:30pm. **Lufthansa,** Terazije 3/VII (tel. 322 49 74; fax 322 50 09). Open Mon.-Fri. 8:30am-4:30pm.

Trains: Glavna Železnička Stanica (Main Train Station; tel. 688 722). Ticket office open daily 7am-midnight. To: Bar (4 per day, 8hr., 119dn); Novi Sad (7 per day, 1½hr., 13dn); Skopje (3 per day, 9hr., 140dn); and Sofia (3 per day, 10hr., 130dn).

Buses: Autobuska Stanica "Beograd" (Bus Station; tel. 636 299), next to the train station. To: Novi Sad (1¾hr., 25dn); Niš (3¾hr., 48dn); Priština (7 per day, 5hr., 60dn); Budva (6 per day, 12 hr., 95dn); Sarajevo via Pale (4 per day, 8hr., 55dn); Skopje (6 per day, 7hr., 76dn); and Sofia (2 per day, 8hr., 103dn).

Public Transportation: Extremely comprehensive. 15dn ticket valid for 6 rides sold at kiosks. Same tickets valid for buses, trolleys, and trams. Fold and stamp ticket on board. Controllers are rare, but the fine for riding ticketless is 100dn. After 11pm, all schedules are reduced, and some lines stop running completely.

Luggage storage: (гардероба; *garderoba*). At the **train station,** 5dn per bag; passport required. Open 24hr. At the **bus station,** 12dn per bag. Open daily 6am-10pm.

English Bookstore: PROEX Bookshop, 1300 Kaplara 1, sells foreign books. Open Mon.-Fri. 9am-9pm, Sat. 9am-3pm.

Cultural Centers: American Cultural Center, Čika Ljubina 19 (tel. 645 655 ext. 236; tel./fax 630 011). **Email** access for members only. No membership required for library access. **British Council Library,** Kneza Mihaila 48. Membership required to check out materials, but non-members may use them inside. Open Mon., Wed., and Fri. 11am-4pm, Tues. and Thurs. 2-7pm.

Pharmacy: "I Maj" Pharmacy, Srbskih Vladara 9. Open 24hr.

Express Mail: DHL, O. Venac 26 (tel. 328 17 47). Open Mon.-Fri. 8am-4:30pm.

Post Office: Takovska 2. Open Mon.-Sat. 8am-8pm. *Poste Restante* at window #2. Address mail: GERHART, Samantha, c/o *Poste Restante* 11101, Belgrade 1, Yugoslavia. Mail held up to 1 month. **Faxes** at 459 557 or 459 266. **Postal code:** 11101.

Telephones: Public **telephone coins** available at post office (5 impulses, or 3min., 1.3dn) and kiosks (5 impulses 2dn). **Telephone cards** can be used almost exclusively in post offices. Grade A (100 impulses; 18dn), B (200; 29dn), C (300; 43dn), and D (400; 55dn). Collect calls are not possible. Phones in post office open daily 7am-10pm. **Phone code:** 011.

ACCOMMODATIONS AND CAMPING

Most big hotels in Belgrade are still state-owned and overpriced. There are no hostels around, and no agencies that find private accommodations. Chances are also very slim that you'll be approached by people offering a room.

Taš, Beogradska 71 (tel. 324 35 07). About 2km from the bus station, reachable by tram #2 or 7. Get off before Pravni Fakultet, on your right next to Hotel Metropol; Taš is on the left past the park (watch for the sign). Street is noisy, but the decent rooms with private showers are relatively quiet. Doubles only. 148dn per bed.

Beograd, Balkanska 52 (tel. 645 178 or 645 361; fax 643 746). A 2min. walk from the train and bus stations. Rooms somewhat nicer (and pricier) than at Taš. Singles with shower 160dn, with bath 180dn. Breakfast included.

Camp Košutujak, Kneza Višeslava 17 (tel. 555 127). In a refreshing park area about 8km from the city center, accessible by bus #23 or 53 from the train station. Bungalow doubles DM60. Tents DM10 per person. Reception open 24hr.

Pionirski Grad, Kneza Višeslava 27 (tel. 542 166; fax 559 538). Several km past Camp Košutujak; take bus #23 or 53. Student camp that tries to be a hostel, too. Bed DM35, full board DM80. Reception open Mon.-Fri. 7am-9pm, Sat. 8am-6pm.

DOM Hotel, Kralja Milutina 54 (tel. 684 841 or 641 459; fax 683 872). Off Nemanjina near Trg Slavija. Neat rooms, some with fridges. Singles 180dn; doubles 300dn. Breakfast included.

FOOD

Belgrade's gastronomical center is the area called **Skadarlija,** where classy locals dine to a background of live bands playing traditional tunes in the restaurants that line pretty, cobbled Skadarska (10min. northeast of Trg Republike). Common folk can get the cheaper version of this romantic dining experience at the bottom end of the street, where cafes and stands sell inexpensive sandwiches and other grilled foods. The best hamburger and pizza stands are in Trg Slavija (slice or burger 5dn).

Pivnica Aleksandar, Cetinjska 15 (tel. 322 74 01). Gets crowded quickly, as the quality of service is comparable to that in Skadarlija, but less snobbish. A mixed crowd sits on the wooden benches under huge straw umbrellas. 1kg of roasted ribs 35dn. Chicken wings 33dn per kg. Open daily 10am-11pm.

Grmeč, Makedonska 32 (tel. 322 78 74). Cozy restaurant featuring excellent Yugoslavian cuisine. *Teleca čorba* (veal soup) 6dn. *Vešalica na zharv* (roasted and flaming meat) 17dn. Open daily 8am-11pm.

Šumatovač, Makedonska 33 (tel. 322 11 79). Serves all sea specialties. Fresh fish from the Adriatic flown in daily. Fish soup 10dn. Octopus salad 45dn. Lobster 300dn per kg. Air-conditioned and chic. Open daily 7am-1am.

Zlatno Burence (Golden Cask), Žil Verna 10 (tel. 686 040). Charming and comfortable locale with a fireplace. Portraits of Serbian kings adorn the wall. *File "Burence"* (pork) 40dn. Open daily 8am-11pm; closed every other Sun.

Brod Restoran "Sent Andreja," Kej Osloboðenja bb (tel. 106 954). A Chinese restaurant with Chinese cooks (and real meals for vegetarians!). Expensive, but 10% discounts for larger groups. Beijing duck 168dn. Braised shrimp with meat 98dn. Open daily 10am-midnight.

Restoran Šaran (Carp; tel. 618 235), up past Sent Andreja on the left. Lovely courtyard hedged with spruced shrubs. *Šaran prženi* (fried carp) 20dn for 250g. Grilled sturgeon 110dn per kg. Staff speaks German; menu is in English. Open 8am-11pm.

Cafe Guli, Skardarska 13. Different funky cocktails every night. Modern art on the walls must mean it's avant-garde; the menu is as difficult to interpret as the paintings. The small, ivy-covered terrace is a lovely spot to sip a cappuccino (7dn). The cool time to come is Fri. or Sat. night. Open daily 11am-1am.

Ruski Zar, Obiličev venac 29 (tel. 633 992), in the pedestrian zone downtown. A shrine to the Russian emperors, whose portraits hang on the walls. Prices reflect name and location much more than quality. Banana split 20dn. Soda 10dn.

SIGHTS

In Trg Republike stands **Narodni Muzej** (National Museum; tel. 624 322). Buses #31 and 75 stop in front of its entrance on Vase Čampića. Founded in 1844, this museum is one of the oldest cultural institutions in Serbia. Its focus is on the material art and culture from the first years of civilization in the area until the middle of the 20th century, but it also has a collection of foreign art, dominated by French Impressionists (open Tues.-Wed. and Fri.-Sat. 10am-5pm, Thurs. noon-8pm, Sun. 10am-2pm). In front of the museum, around the 1882 **statue of Knez Mihailo,** skateboarding youngsters exhibit an astonishing lack of concern for their bodily safety. Past the fountains across the square begins **Kneza Mihaila,** a commercial street lined with shops, offices, stores, restaurants, and galleries. This is the place to come, shortly before noon or at night, for the best people-watching in the city—besides the promenading Belgradians, you'll see plenty of street singers and sidewalk artists.

Out of the square, at Sima Markovića 8, lies **Konak Knjeginje Ljubice** (Night-quarters of Princess Ljubice; tel. 638 264). Dating from 1831, the princess's residence is in what is today one of the oldest Serbian parts of Belgrade, Kosančićev Venac. Erected on the orders of Prince Miloš, the *konak* is typically Balkan, with touches of Western Baroque. Inside is 19th-century furniture, carpets, and garments. The *konak*'s basement—a former Turkish bath—holds temporary exhibitions of paintings, sculptures, and other works by Yugoslavian artists (*konak* open Tues.-Fri. 10am-5pm, Sat.-Sun. 9am-4pm; 5dn admission includes English brochure). **Murej Srpske Pravoslavne Crkve** (Museum of the Serbian Orthodox Church), 7. Jula 5, near the *konak,* is a small place on the second floor of the building, which also houses the episcopal administration—ask for directions at the entrance or follow the signs. On display here are 16th-century church items such as prayer books, icons, and mantles, as well as the **first printed book** in Belgrade—the 1552 gospel (open Tues.-Sat. 8am-2pm, Sun. 11am-3pm; 1dn).

Opposite Kolarčev N.U., on a street parallel to Kneza Mihaila, is the **Etnografski Muzej** (Ethnographic Museum), Studentski Trg 13 (tel. 328 18 88, ext. 185). Exhibits represent Serbian folk culture of the 19th and 20th centuries. At 7. Jula 71a is **Jevrejski Istorijski Muzej** (Jewish Historical Museum; open Tues.-Sun 10am-12pm). Continuing down the street and taking the first left leads to **Bajrakli Džamija,** Tevremova 11, the only mosque in Belgrade, dating from 1690 (open daily until 11pm, when the last prayer is sung).

Probably the most notable landmark in Belgrade is the well-preserved ruin of the huge fortress **Kalemedan**. It consists of two parts—the Upper and Lower Cities. The Upper City is now a well-lit and extremely popular park, while the Lower City, a hangout for gangs and other undesirables, should be avoided at night. The views of the Danube and the old city of Zemun from the tall walls are perhaps the fortress's greatest attraction, but the complex also holds two small, functioning chapels, a zoo (10dn, children 5dn), and two museums. **Vojui Muzej** (Military Museum) sells a comprehensive guide to its collection (10dn)—reading the whole thing is practically equivalent to a degree in Serbian military science. All kinds of weapons are exhibited here; some, like the corroded spears, date back to Roman times. Uniforms and maps of battles are also shown, and even a bronze statue of proud **Tito** (open 10am-5pm; 4dn). The museum's outdoor section is a playground for small green tanks and heavy weaponry, mostly from WWII. At night, couples cuddle in the shadows of the machines of destruction. Near the military museum is **Muzej Šumarstva i Lova** (Gallery of the Natural History Museum), which both exhibits and sells jewelry and artwork made out of Pacific seashells (necklaces 30dn, rings 40dn; museum open Tues.-Sun. 9am-9pm; 2dn).

Other worthwhile places to visit lie across the Sava River in Novi Beograd and Zemun. A must is **Muzej Savremene Umetnosti** (Museum of Contemporary Art), Ušće Save bb (tel. 145 900 or 145 944), a five-level, concrete, crystal-shaped building with a permanent exhibit encompassing the entire 20th century. The first level is reserved for temporary exhibitions of current artists; recent guests have included painter Petar Dobrovič, sculptor Olga Jevrič, and the German Bauhaus (open Wed.-Mon. 10am-6pm; free). Buses #15 and 84 cross the bridge "Bratsvo i jedinstvo" and stop in front of an alley leading through a park and up to the museum.

The old town of **Zemun,** northwest along the Danube and now part of Belgrade, is very quiet and looks more like a provincial zone than a part of a big metropolis. The houses were built in the Austro-Hungarian style, and many of the narrow cobbled streets are impassable by car. Bus #88 goes to Zemun from Stari Beograd. At Sindelićeva 20 lies **Trag,** a small bookstore/art gallery (open Tues.-Sun. 10am-2pm and 7-9pm). Farther up Sindelićeva and to the left is **Kula Sibinjanin Tanka,** a tall tower now occupied by a cafe. From the narrow terrace on the second level, you can see all of Belgrade and beyond. The cafe sports a cool blue-velvet interior and extends into the courtyard around the tower. All kinds of alcohol and soft drinks are served (open daily 12pm-2am). Eighteenth-century Orthodox **Sveti Nikola,** a.k.a. **Nikolajevska Crkva,** sits at the base of Sindelićeva. Among this church's treasures are the relics of St. Andrea (St. Peter's brother), which rest under one of the icons on the left; an exquisite iconostasis fashioned by Bimitrie Bačević in 1762; and 1868 wood-carvings by Zivko Petrović (open daily 9am-1pm and 5-7pm; Sun. service at 10:30am).

In the summer, since many Belgradians can't afford trips to sea resorts, **Ada Ciganlija** is the natural magnet. It resembles an island, with artificial pebble beaches and a big park in which people bike, rollerblade, and play soccer, basketball, and volleyball. The beach is packed, except for the farthest end, which is reserved for nudists. Cafes are everywhere (cappuccino 7dn). **Bike** (12dn per hr.) and **waterwheel** (15dn per hr.) rentals are available.

ENTERTAINMENT

Narodno Pozorište (National Theater), Trg Republike 2 (tel. 620 946), is a prominent building in the city center. Completed in just two years (1868-69), its interior was decorated by Viennese artists. The theater has lived through several restorations, most recently in 1989, and it now features nightly entertainment—from ballet to comedy. Unfortunately, Narodno Pozorište closes its doors from July 1 to September 1; the rest of the year, buy tickets from the ticket booth inside (open daily 10am-2pm and 3pm until show begins, usually 8 or 9pm; big stage 15-30dm, small stage 15dm). **Bilet Servis** (Ticket Service), Trg Republike 5 (tel. 628 342), sells a valuable bi-weekly English publication detailing all the current cultural events in Belgrade (12dn; open Mon.-Fri. 9am-9pm, Sat. 9am-3pm).

The **concert hall** in **Kolarčev N.U.,** Studentski Trg 5, is on a street parallel to Kneza Mihaila. Classical music is performed by both local and foreign orchestras; the program is different every night—check the schedule inside. Tickets (20-30dn) are sold up until an hour before concerts (hall closed July 1-Sept. 15).

Plato is the name of the pedestrian-only space opposite the entrance to the American Cultural Center, where Čika Ljubina feds into Kneza Mihaila. Several cafes are located here; they're open daily from 9am until midnight, and frequented by university students. Live jazz music can be found here almost every night. During the day, **Akademija,** Raičev 10 (tel. 637 723), operates as an offbeat cafe, serving alcohol and soft drinks (open daily 9am-11pm). From 11pm until early in the morning, the cafe's basement turns into what the iron front door says: "Peace// Anarchy // Freedom." In this underground world, semi-drunk DJs spin the tunes out of a prison cell with a barred window. Rock or blues, the music shakes the intestines (cover 5dn; Fri.-Sat. 10dn for men).

KST (Club of Technical Students), Bulevar Revolucije 73, gets its name from its location—the basement of the Technical University building. This is among the liveliest places in Belgrade. In the corridors outside the dance room, cigarette smoke and neon lighting create a vaguely mystical atmosphere. **Dom Omladine Beograda,** Makedonska 2 (tel. 324 82 02), collects a crowd too cool to dance, despite the huge dance floor. In summer 1997, Dom Omladine hosted **Rockfest**—a festival to which many hot Yugoslavian rock groups were invited (open daily 10pm-2am; cover 10dn). **K Club Restaurant,** 1300 Kaplara (tel. 636 793), attracts a crowd of older and more sedate twenty- and thirty-something regulars. Neon blue lights infiltrate the darkness while Yugoslavian rock music keeps conversations private (open daily 10am-2am).

■ Near Belgrade: Novi Sad (Нови Сад)

Novi Sad is the capital of Vojvodina, the northernmost region of today's Yugoslavia. Sprawled along the banks of the Danube, the city was founded at the end of the 17th century as a settlement for craftsmen, tradesmen, and farmers. In the past, Novi Sad was said to be a microcosm of Yugoslavia, because it was home to people of many nationalities: Serbs, Croats, Hungarians, and others. Today its low-rise buildings and long, straight streets evoke a feeling of untroubled space and freedom.

Orientation and Practical Information The bus and train stations sit adjacent to each other along Bulevar Jaše Tomića, on the other side of which stands **Hotel Novi Sad.** Trains (info tel. 443 200 or 338 438) go to: Belgrade (1.5hr., 13dn); Budapest (176dn); Istanbul (22hr., 322dn); Skopje (9hr. 173dn); Sofia (11hr., 161dn); Subotica (2hr., 16dn); and Thessaloniki (17hr., 233dn). The *Balkan Express* leaves Novi Sad at 6:46am and reaches Belgrade at 8:21am, Sofia at 8:05 pm, and Istanbul at 8:30am on the following day. Many buses (info tel. 333 777; open daily 5:30am-8pm) run daily to Belgrade (1½hr., 29.50dn) and Subotica (1½hr., 26.50dn). There's **luggage storage** at the train station (24hr., 5dn per piece) and the bus station (daily 5am-9pm; 10dn per piece). Buy a **city map** (6dn) from a kiosk within the train station. **City buses** run to the center; purchase 3dn tickets from kiosks or on board. Alternatively, walk down Kisača, which flows into Pašićeva and then becomes Svetozara Markovića, at the end of which there is a church on the left. From the church, you can take a left onto **Dunavska** or a right onto **Zmaj Jovina**—both pedestrian-only streets. The **tourist office** is at Dunavska 27 (tel. 421 811; fax 514 81). The helpful staff speaks English (open Mon.-Fri. 8am-8pm, Sat. 8am-2pm). **Karic Bank,** Njegoseva 11, off Zmaj Jovina after the big Catholic church, cashes AmEx **traveler's checks** whenever the manager is present to authorize the transaction. Zmaj Jovina eventually leads to the **central post office,** on Bulevar Mihajla Pupina (open Mon.-Fri. 7am-8pm, Sat.-Sun. 7am-2pm). **Telephones** are inside (open Mon.-Fri. 7am-10pm, Sat.-Sun. 7am-11pm). **Postal code:** 21 000. **Phone code:** 21.

Accommodations and Food The oldest and probably best place to stay is **Hotel Vojvodina,** Trg Slobode 2 (tel. 622 122), in the heart of Novi Sad very close to the Catholic church on Zmaj Jovina. Rooms are good and the English-speaking reception is open 24 hours (singles 150dn; doubles 200dn). The more luxurious and expensive **Hotel Novi Sad,** Bulevar Jaše Tomica bb (tel. 442 511; fax 443 072), stands opposite the bus and train stations (singles 207dn; doubles 234dn).

Cheap eats can be had at all hours at **Grill II,** Modene 1, just off Zmaj Jovina. **UTR 5+,** Jevrejska 35 (tel. 618 424), is the first of several pizza places sitting next to each other, and may be a good option for vegetarians (small veggie pizza 21dn, large 26dn; open daily 8am-midnight). At the end of the pizza cluster is **Casa Mexicana,** Jevrejska 35 (tel. 248 32), with main dishes exceptional as much in taste as in price (around 50dn). Vegetarian burritos are 53dn. Mexican tunes play amid cool wooden tables and big sombreros; the clientele, not surprisingly, is rather upscale (open daily 9am-midnight). The strictly-for-carnivores restaurant of **Hotel Turotava-Varadin** occupies a separate building within the remains of the fortress in Petrova-Radin town (tel. 433 009). *Natur šnida* (pork) is 20dn, *jagnjeće pečenje* (roasted lamb) goes for 30dn, and *pileće pečenje* (roasted chicken) is 25dn. If you eat outside, you'll have to sit on white plastic chairs, but the panoramic view from the stone terrace should compensate (open daily 9am-midnight).

Sights The most exciting sight is the well-preserved **Fortress Petrovardenska,** built when Novi Sad was part of the Austro-Hungarian empire. The entrance is up the steps that start next to the church on Černiševskog str. right off the central bridge.

From the fortress, the view is uplifting. Tours of the underground tunnels can be arranged (tel. 433 613 or 433 145; tours Mon.-Sat. 9am-4pm). **Prirodnjáćka Izložba** (Natural Exhibition), Turdava 3, is a small museum-gallery on the premises of the fortress that exhibits taxidermized animals (open daily 9am-5pm; 3dn). **Galerija SULUV,** Bulevar Mihajla Pupina 9 (tel. 249 91), presents a new exhibition of works by Vojvodina artists every two weeks. **Muzej Vojvodine,** Dunavska 35-37 (tel. 420 566), next to a small park, is the best museum in town. The exhibits comprise everything related to Vojvodina, including sections on ethnology and applied art (open Tues.-Fri. 9am-5pm, Sat.-Sun. 9am-2pm; 3dn, students 1dn).

KOSOVO (КОСОВО)

A semi-autonomous province in the south of Serbia, Kosovo has stirred up more political trouble than its small size ever warranted. Nine out of ten Kosovars are ethnically Albanian, restive subjects of a regime dominated and policed by Belgrade. The Serbs cherish Kosovo as a font of their national mythology; it was the site of the fateful 1389 Battle of Kosovo Polje, in which the Serbs succumbed to the Turks in a battle immortalized in a ballad (see p. 750). Serb-Albanian apartheid is entrenched in every civil sector, from different schools to proud language usage. Visitors should keep in mind that Kosovo's **borders** with Albania and Croatia are closed, a symptom of the broader obstacles facing any traveler here.

▨ Prizren

A walk through Prizren (PRIZ-ren) is like a walk through the fabric of space-time: ancient citadels in ruins, churches in mid-restoration, and Turkish mosques rising up from the town's streets give evidence of the varied cultures that have influenced settlement across the centuries. Prizren was once famous for its gifted craftsmen, masters of 130 different handicrafts and renowned throughout the Ottoman Empire for their filigree; today, artisans can still be found making jewelry and weapons in the traditional manner, along the streets of town center.

Orientation and Practical Information The **train station,** at the end of town on the road to Peć, is a neglected building used almost exclusively for freight traffic, although a few passenger cars go to Kosovo Polje, near Priština. Fortunately, **buses** (tel. 311 52) from the nearby bus station run to many cities of Yugoslavia: Belgrade (14 per day, 5hr., 64din); Peć (10 per day, 1½hr., 17din); Priština (20 per day, 1½hr., 17din); and Titograd (1 per day, 8hr., 60din), as well as to Skopje, Macedonia (3 per day, 2hr., 50din). There's no **luggage storage** in either station.

Public transportation is only a dream, but the town is small and there's little need for even a **taxi,** unless you're in a hurry (DM2 to start, then DM1 per km). For town info, try the English-speaking staff at the private tourist bureau **Prizrenturs,** Rr. Vidovdanit 34a (tel. 446 83), on a busy main street along the river near town center (open daily 8am-midnight). The only bank cashing **traveler's checks** is **Vojvobanska Banka,** right across the old Turkish bridge in the hub of Prizren. They ask 1% commission and impose a one-day wait for processing transactions (AmEx only; open Mon.-Fri. 7am-7pm, Sat. 8am-3pm). The **post office** is also downtown, near Theranda Hotel (no *Poste Restante;* open Mon.-Sat. 7am-7pm). **Postal code:** 38400. **Phone code:** 29.

Accommodations and Food Due to a political climate that fosters a very suspicious police force, locals are generally unwilling to offer private accommodations. The cheapest place to stay is **Motel Putnik** (tel. 431 07; fax 415 52), at the end of town along the road to Vrbnica, near the Bistrica river. From the bus station, take a right on Rr. Metohijska; follow it to the intersection with a small traffic island. The left-hand road leads downtown, the right-hand one goes to Motel Putnik (119din per person). The more expensive option is **Theranda Hotel** (tel. 222 92), which occupies a massive, easily seen building downtown (singles 150din; doubles 220din).

The tranquil and meditative surroundings—steep hills of rocks on one side and woods on the other, with the river mere steps away—assuage one's spiritual hunger, while the flavorful dishes sate the more prosaic hunger of the stomach, at **Kafe-Restoran Mullini,** at the end of town on the way to Macedonia (tel. 245 56; open daily 8am-11pm). Its locale is known as the Marash complex, after a famous nearby tree touted by locals as the biggest in the Balkans. **Kafe-Restoran Tabahana,** next to the river and close to the fountain square, looks upscale, but the amiable staff will serve common folk as well. *Medaljon* (meat and mushrooms) and *parahaje* (dried meat) cost 25din each; a glass of *Metohijski Rizling* wine is also 25din. Hamburgers are sold everywhere for 5din; their meat is incomparably better than that of any fast food chain. And for the salvation of vegetarians, **traveling markets** visit Prizren frequently, offering fresh fruit and vegetables.

Sights and Entertainment Perhaps that should read "Churches and Mosques." **Bogorodica Ljeviška** (Virgin Ljeviška) church was built in 1307 by King Milutin Nemanjič on the site of a 9th-century Byzantine basilica. With the church's 1756 conversion to a mosque, many of its frescoes were destroyed; luckily, fully one-third have now been rescued (open daily 7am-6pm). After two years of restorations, the 1561 **Sinan Paša Mosque** is again open for visits (following prayers at noon, 4pm, and 7pm). Higher up toward the citadel is the small church **Sveta Nedelja,** built in the 14th century for the mother of mythical hero Krali Marko—a man who, legend claims, not only defeated but also humiliated many a Turk. Continuing up, you'll reach what's left of the 14th-century Orthodox **monastery Sveti Spas.** The small chapel is open only for services and religious holidays, but the remainder of the monastery can still be visited. Finally, on the very top of the hill, crumbling ruins valiantly continue the watch that an intact citadel once kept over Prizren valley. Every year on March 21 or 22, genuine **dervishes** perform miraculous tricks here—Prizren was the dervish center of the former Yugoslavia.

In the evenings, the youth of Prizren head for downtown, crowding the cafes along the river and gathering in groups on the fountain square. Nightlife here, however, tends to burn out soon after midnight.

Not All Dervishes Dance

A dervish is a member of an order of Muslim mystics, believers who attempt to find divine truth through direct personal experience of God. Islamic mysticism is called Sufism in the West, and its followers also known as "the poor" (*fuqara,* plural of Arabic *faqir,* in Persian *darvish,* whence the English "fakir" and "dervish"). Sufism, originating as a reaction against early Muslim worldliness, involves following *tariqah* (the path) toward the goal of *haqiqah* (reality), with the focus on *ma'rifah* (interior knowledge of the divine), rather than on strict adherence to religious laws. In the 12th century, disciples began to gather around Sufi masters (*shaykh*s), and *tariqah* came to mean first the *shaykh*'s entire ritual system (which was followed by his community or mystic order), and then the order itself. The dervish's main ritual is the *dhikr,* which consists of the repeated recitation of a devotional formula in praise of God in order to attain an ecstatic state. This may involve dancing, which begins with rhythmic revolutions to musical accompaniment. Heads thrown back, the dervishes raise their right palms and keep their left hands down—symbolically giving and taking—and whirl faster and faster, striving for a trance-like loss of self and union with God. The *dhikr* ceremony always ends with prayer and a procession. Today, there are hundreds of orders of dervishes, with a membership in the millions.

■ Peć (Peja)

Peć (PEHCH), or Peja (PEY-uh), as the Albanian locals will correct you, is a small town of about 60,000 inhabitants, mostly Albanian. Locals in traditional dress fill the Oriental-style bazaar while the mountains of Rugovska Klisura, excellent for hiking, prop up the sky in the background.

Orientation and Practical Information Beware: as of summer 1997, the border with Croatia was officially closed, making it impossible to get to Dubrovnik through Herceg Novi. The **bus station** is located on Nemanjina, about 1km from the town center. Many buses run daily to Priština, a transportation hub for the rest of Yugoslavia. There is also a bus to Herceg Novi through Budva, via Priština (daily at 7:30pm, 9hr., 82din). The **train station** is about 500m away from the bus station. Head down, away from the mountains, and go about 100m, then take a right; follow that road until you reach the station (on the left). As in Prizren, the traffic is almost exclusively freight trains. There is no **luggage storage.**

You can find **Kosmet Tours** at Nemanjina 102, and **Putnik Tourist** further down toward the town center. They're primarily travel agencies for locals, but may be able to answer questions about the town. **Yugobanka,** close to Hotel Metohija, changes currency but doesn't cash traveler's checks, blaming the embargo for this failing (open Mon.-Fri. 7am-7pm, Sat. 7am-4pm). Opposite Metohija is the **post office** (no collect calls or *Poste Restante;* open Mon.-Fri. 8am-8pm, Sat.-Sun. 9am-4pm). **Postal code:** 38300. **Phone code:** 39.

Accommodations and Food **Motel Jusaj,** Rr. Buriqa 48 (tel./fax 211 49), is your best bet. Opposite the train station, it offers mostly doubles, but single travelers aren't charged extra (DM15 per person). The mountain view makes decent rooms wonderful; the only disadvantage is that all five rooms on each floor share a single shower and stand-up toilet. Reception is on the second floor; enter through the first-floor restaurant. Across the street sits the new privately owned **Hotel Dypon** (tel. 315 93). A bed for the night is DM40-50, depending on how desperate or gullible you look. But the rooms are perfect and so is the mountain view.

Restoran Stari Most (Old Bridge), 150m downstream from Hotel Metohija, straddles the Bistrica River. The prospect of the mountain is grand, as are the prices for standard local fare (namesake dish *Stari Most* 30din; open Mon.-Sat. 7am-10pm). **Food stores** are generally open 6am-10pm, and 5din sandwiches—with meat that'll make carnivores drool more than Pavlov's dogs—are available everywhere.

Sights and Entertainment The oldest mosque in town is **Quarši Djamija,** found in the old-town quarter on Xhemajl Školozi, near the intersection of Nemanjina and Krala Petrar (open for visits after the 1pm and 7pm prayers). About 2km from Peć, along the river, stands the **Patrijaršija Monastery.** Take Boro Vukmirovig from behind Radio Metohija (downtown), going west out of town. You'll see the hospital on the right. The monastery is 500m farther; follow the signs. Today the headquarters of all Serbian Archbishops and Partiarchs, the monastery was the center of Serbian spiritual and cultural life in medieval times. The complex presents four churches, some with frescoes dating back to the 8th century (free; dress appropriately).

Those who need beer after the rigors of the day can find what they crave at **Bocacho,** Rr. Burqičvić 56. The bar's a bit small for the live Albanian folk bands that play there, but the crowd is local and enthusiastic, and *Extra Pečko pivo* is just 6din. From Hotel Metohija, head toward the mountains, take a right after Cafe-Pizzeria Mozart, and look for the small, corner bar on the left. **Ok,** just along the river to the left of Metohija, is the favorite nightspot of the Albanian young and beautiful. Live bands cover songs you'll recognize for an audience more likely to be holding conversations than dancing (open 8am-11pm; cover 5din).

■ Near Peć: Visoki Dečani Monastery

One of Serbia's most beautiful monasteries, Visoki Dečani was intended to be a mausoleum for the nation's kings. Built while the medieval Serbian state was at its apogee by two rulers of the Nemanič Dynasty, King Stephan of Dečani and his son Dushan, King and later Emperor of the Serbians and Greeks, the monastery took only eight years to complete (1327-1335). What might be an inspirational example of father-son cooperation, however, is actually more of a gruesome tragedy: King Stephan was killed in 1331 during fighting between his supporters and his son's supporters in their struggle for the crown, and his remains were the first to be laid to rest in the monastery that his son then completed (he's in the coffin in front of the altar). It may be somewhat of a consolation to Stephan that he is celebrated as a saint by the Serbian Orthodox Church; his day is November 24.

Inside the monastery, there are frescoes galore—around 1000 beautiful renditions of different Biblical scenes, crafted by artists belonging to the Greek School. These frescoes were intended to portray the entire text of the Bible to the many illiterate of the 14th century; today, they remain astonishingly well-preserved, particularly in light of the two fires that devastated Dečani in the 17th and 18th centuries. After the second of these fires, in fact, the monastery was so ravaged that its new administrator, Daniel Pastrovič-Kazanegra, earned the title of the second Dečani founder for his success in restoring and reawakening the complex. Especially noteworthy is the iconostasis in the church, rebuilt thanks to Brother Daniel's efforts.

Today, Dečani is a functional and thriving monastery; the 22 monks inhabiting it continue the traditional monastic activities of translating and publishing books and Web pages (http://www.prishtina.com/Religion/Decani/decani.htm), wood carving, and icon painting, as well as providing spiritual guidance to Christians in the predominantly Muslim Kosovo area. To visit the monastery, take the bus from Peć (15 per day, 15min., 5din) and get off in Dečani. From the stop, continue on foot 100m and turn right at the major intersection. Farther on, the local school should appear on your right; the monastery is about 2km down the road.

GATEWAY CITIES

Berlin, Germany

US$1	= DM1.82 (Deutschmarks)	DM1 =	US$0.55
CDN$1=	DM1.32	DM1 =	CDN$0.76
UK£1	= DM2.90	DM1 =	UK£0.35
IR£1	= DM2.67	DM1 =	IR£ 0.37
AUS$1	= DM1.32	DM1 =	AUS$0.75
NZ$1	= DM1.16	DM1 =	NZ$0.86
SAR1	= DM0.39	DM1 =	SAR2.58
Country Phone Code: 49		**International Dialing Prefix: 00**	

Berlin's population is united by a common notion that a city isn't just where people live and conduct business, but a place where things happen, citizens congregate, and politics are played out *en masse*. This mentality is a result of Berlin's extraordinary role in world history during the last half-century, from the 1950s and 60s, when the city embodied the Cold War, to the late 1980s and early 1990s, when the fall of Communism found Berlin straddling two distinct but no longer separate worlds. Even as money is finally allocated to rebuild the eastern sectors, the disparity between East and West is troubling to residents of both. Raised in the shadow of global conflict, Berliners respond with a glorious storm of cultural activity and the nightlife you might expect from a population that has its back against the wall. A kaleidoscope of GDR apartment blocks and designer boutiques, decaying buildings and gleaming modern office complexes, Berlin's gritty melancholy is balanced by the exhilaration of being on the cutting edge.

ORIENTATION AND PRACTICAL INFORMATION

Berlin surveys the Prussian plain in the northeast corner of reunited Germany, about four hours southeast of Hamburg by rail and eight hours north of Munich. Berlin is also well-connected to other European cities: Prague is five hours away by rail, Warsaw six hours. For now, Western Berlin's **Bahnhof Zoologischer Gerten (Bahnhof Zoo)** remains the city's principal train station and a major focus of the its subway and surface rail systems. The situation is changing, though, as the eastern **Berlin Hauptbahnhof** surpasses the space-constricted Zoo Station. **Friedrichstraße, Alexanderplatz**, and **Lichtenberg** are other important eastern subway and rail stations.

Berlin's historic east and commercial west halves are connected by the grand tree-lined boulevard **Straße des 17 Juni**, which runs through the massive **Tiergarten** park. The commercial district of West Berlin centers on Zoo Station and **Breitscheidplatz.** The district is marked by the bombed-out Kaiser-Wilhelm-Gedächtniskirche. A star of streets radiates from Breitscheidpl. Toward the west run **Hardenbergstraße, Kantstraße,** and the commercial boulevard **Kurfürstendamm,** known as **Ku'damm.** Down Hardenbergstr. lies Steinpl. and the enormous Berlin Technical University. Down Kantstr., **Savignyplatz** is lined with cafes, restaurants, and hotels.

The newly asphalted **Ebert Straße** runs along the path of the deconstructed Berlin Wall from the Reichstag to **Potsdamer Platz.** The landmark **Brandenburger Tor** and surrounding Pariser Pl., reconstructed with the aid of EU funds, open onto **Unter den Linden,** which leads to the historic heart of Berlin. Farther east is the ugly but active **Alexanderplatz,** the East's growing business district. The alternative **Kreuzberg** and **Mitte,** for 45 years the fringe neighborhoods of the West and East, are once again at the city's heart. If you're planning to stay more than a few hours in Berlin, the blue and yellow **Falk Plan** (DM11), available at most kiosks, is an immensely useful **map.**

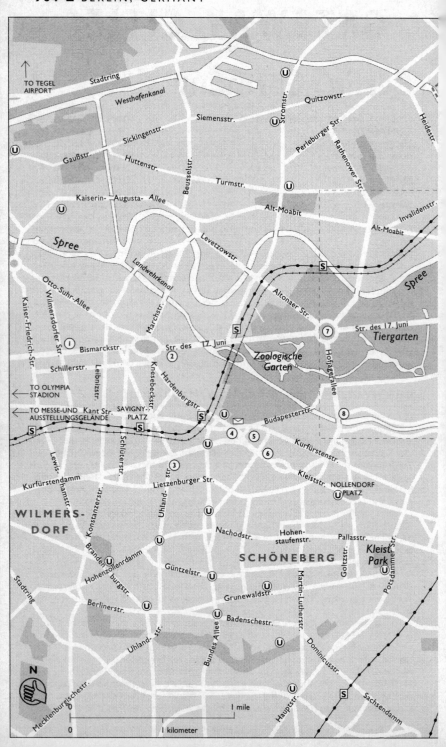

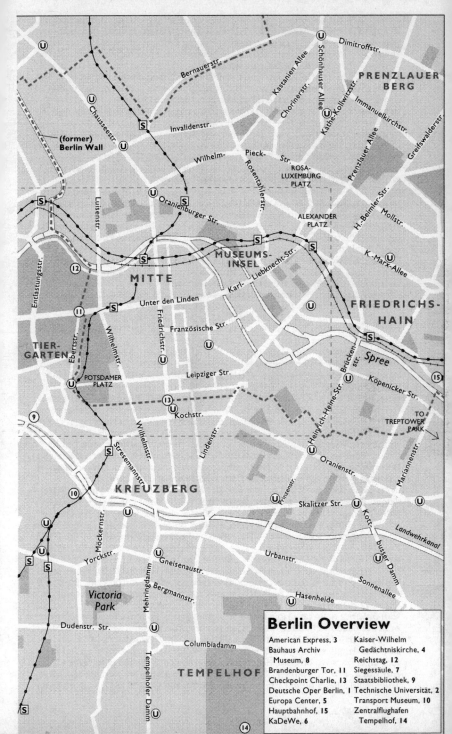

Berlin Overview

American Express, 3
Bauhaus Archiv
   Museum, 8
Brandenburger Tor, 11
Checkpoint Charlie, 13
Deutsche Oper Berlin, 1
Europa Center, 5
Hauptbahnhof, 15
KaDeWe, 6

Kaiser-Wilhelm
   Gedächtniskirche, 4
Reichstag, 12
Siegessäule, 7
Staatsbibliothek, 9
Technische Universität, 2
Transport Museum, 10
Zentralflughafen
   Tempelhof, 14

Tourist Offices: For tourist info, call 25 00 25. **Berlin-Touristen-Information, Europa Center,** Budapesterstr. 45. From Bahnhof Zoo, walk along Budapesterstr. past the Kaiser-Wilhelm-Gedächtniskirche about 5min. Free copies of city magazines *030* and *Serge* (for gays and lesbians), which have entertainment listings. The German-language *Tip* and *Zitty* are better (DM4). Open Mon.-Sat. 8am-10pm, Sun. 9am-9pm. Also in the main hall of **Tegel Airport** (open daily 5:15am-10pm) and inside the **Brandenburger Tor,** south wing (open daily 9:30am-6pm). All offices provide a simple city **map** (DM1) and book rooms for a DM5 fee.

Tours: Berlin Walks (tel. 301 91 94) offers a range of English-language walking tours, including the famous Discover Berlin tour. Tours last about 2½hr. and meet at 9:15am, 10am, and 2:30pm in front of the Zoo station. DM14, under 26 DM10. The **Insider Tour** of Berlin also hits all the major sights. Tours last 3hr. and leave from the McDonald's by the Zoo station May-Nov. at 10am and 2:30pm. DM10.

Embassies and Consulates: Australia (consulate), Uhlandstr. 181-183 (tel. 880 08 80). Open Mon.-Fri. 9am-noon. **Canadian (embassy),** Friedrichstr. 95 (tel. 261 11 61; fax 262 92 06). Open Mon.-Fri. 8:30am-12:30pm and 1:30-5pm. **Ireland (consulate),** Ernst-Reuter-Pl. 10 (tel. 34 80 08 22; fax 34 80 08 63). Open Mon.-Fri. 10am-1pm. **New Zealand** citizens should contact their embassy in Bonn (Bundeskanzlerpl. 2-10; tel. (0228) 22 80 70). **South Africa (consulate),** Douglasstr. 9 (tel. 82 50 11; fax 826 65 43). Open Mon.-Fri. 9am-noon. **U.K. (embassy),** Unter den Linden 32 (tel. 20 18 40; fax 20 18 41 58). Open Mon.-Fri. 9am-noon and 2-4pm. **U.S. Citizens Service:** 170 Clayallee (tel. 832 92 33; fax 831 49 26). U1: Oskar Helene Heim. Open Mon.-Fri. 9am-noon. Telephone advice available Mon.-Fri. 9am-5pm; after hours, call for recorded emergency instructions.

Currency Exchange: Deutsche Verkehrs-Kredit Bank (tel. 881 71 17), Bahnhof Zoo on Hardenbergstr. 1% commission on traveler's checks (min. DM7.50). Open daily 7:30am-10pm. The **Reisebank** at *Hauptbahnhof* (tel. 296 43 93) changes traveler's checks for DM7.50. Open Mon.-Fri. 7am-10pm, Sat.-Sun. 7am-4pm. **Berliner Bank** in Tegel Airport is open daily 8am-10pm.

American Express: Uhlandstr. 173, 10719 (tel. 884 58 80). Mail held; all banking services. Long lines on weekends. Open Mon.-Fri. 9am-5:30pm, Sat. 9am-noon. **Branch office** at Bayreutherstr. 37 (tel. 21 49 83 63). Open Mon.-Fri. 9am-6pm.

Flights: Flughafen Tegel (tel. 41 01 23 06). Berlin's main airport. From UX: Bahnhof Zoo or UX: Jakob-Kaiser-Pl., take bus 109 to "Tegel." **Flughafen Tempelhof** (tel. 69 51 22 88). Take bus 119 to "Pl. der Luftbrücke." **Flughafen Schönefeld** (tel. 60 91 51 66), in East Berlin, is connected by S3 to the city center.

Trains: Bahnhof Zoo generally sends trains west, while **Hauptbahnhof** serves lines to the south and east; many exceptions exist. The stations are connected by S-Bahn. Trains from the east also arrive at **Berlin-Lichtenberg.** To reach **Deutsche Bahn Information,** dial 194 19; be prepared for a long wait. Similarly long lines at offices in Bahnhof Zoo (open daily 5:30am-10:30pm) and Hauptbahnhof.

Buses: ZOB, the central bus station (tel. 301 80 28), is by the *Funkturm.* U2: Kaiserdamm. *Zitty* and *Tip* list deals on long-distance buses, often cheaper than trains.

Public Transportation: Construction will affect S- and U-Bahn service for the next few years. **Max,** a bespectacled mole, appears on posters and signs announcing minor disruptions to service. Information and tickets are available at the **BVG Pavillon,** Bahnhof Zoo (tel. 25 62 25 62). Open daily 8am-8pm. An *Einzelfahrschein Normaltarif* (single ticket) costs DM3.90 and is good for 2hr. after validation. An *Einzelfahrschein Kurzstreckentarif* (short-trip fare, DM2.50) allows travel through up to 6 bus stations (with no transfers; not valid on airport bus lines) or 3 U- or S-Bahn stops (with unlimited transfers). A 4-trip *Sammelkarte* (multiple ticket) costs DM13; each "click" is good for 2hr. A short-trip 4-ride *Kurzstreckensammelkarte* is also available for DM8.50. Buy tickets from machines, bus drivers, or ticket windows in the U- and S-Bahn stations. The **Berlin Tagesticket** (DM13) is a 24hr. pass for the bus and U- and S-Bahn. A **7-Day Ticket** (DM40) is good for moderate-length stays. A calendar-month **Umweltkarte** costs DM93, a good value for longer stays. To be valid, tickets must be canceled in the red box marked *"hier entwerten"* before boarding. Tickets bought on board a bus are automatically valid. The U- and S-Bahn do not run 1-4am, except for the **U9** and **U12,** which run all night Fri.-Sat. **Night buses,** centered on Bahnhof Zoo, run every 15min. Pick up the free *Nachtliniennetz* map. All night bus numbers are preceded by **N.**

Luggage Storage: In Bahnhof Zoo. Lockers DM2 per day, larger ones DM4; 3-day max. At **Hauptbahnhof,** lockers run DM2, larger ones DM4. At Bahnhof **Lichtenberg** and S-Bahnhof **Alexanderplatz,** lockers cost DM2; 24hr. max.

Bookstores: Marga Schoeler Bücherstube, Knesebeckstr. 34 (tel. 881 11 12). Many books in English. Open Mon.-Wed. 9:30am-7pm, Thurs.-Fri. 9:30am-8pm, Sat. 9am-4pm. **British Bookshop,** Mauerstr. 83-83 (tel. 238 46 80). English newspapers and magazines. Open Mon.-Fri. 9am-6pm, Sat. 10am-4pm.

Laundromat: Wasch Centers are at Leibnizstr. 72 in Charlottenburg; Wexstr. 34 in Schöneberg; Bergmannstr. 61 in Kreuzberg; Behmstr. 12 in Mitte; and Jablonskistr. 21 in Prenzlauer Berg. Wash DM6 per 6kg. Dry DM2 for 30min. Soap included. All open daily 6am-10pm.

Crisis Lines: Sexual Assault Hotline, tel. 251 28 28. Open Tues. and Thurs. 6-9pm, Sun. noon-2pm. **Schwüles Überfall** hotline and legal help for gays, tel. 216 33 36. Open daily 6-9pm. **Drug Crisis,** tel. 192 37. **Frauenkrisentelefon,** a women's crisis line, tel. 615 42 43. Open Mon. and Thurs. 10am-noon, Tues., Wed., and Fri. 7-9pm, Sat.-Sun. 5-7pm. English-speakers staff all lines.

Pharmacies: Europa-Apotheke, Tauentzienstr. 9-12 (tel. 261 42 44), by Europa Center (close to Bahnhof Zoo). Open daily 9am-9pm. Closed *Apotheken* post signs directing you to the nearest one open, or call 011 41.

Emergency: The U.S. and U.K. embassies have a list of English-speaking doctors. **Emergency Doctor:** tel. 31 00 31. **Emergency Dentist:** tel. 841 91 00. English speaking dentists available.

Police: Pl. der Luftbrücke 6 (tel. 110 or 69 90).

Internet Access: Cyberb@r Zoo, Joachimtalerstr. 5-6 (tel. 88 02 40; email cyberbar-zoo@hotmail.com), in the Karstadt Sport Megastore. DM5 for 30min. Open Mon.-Fri. 10am-8pm, Sat. 9am-4pm. Also in **Cybermind's Virtuality Cafe,** Lewishamstr. 1 (tel. 327 51 43). DM7 for 15min. Open daily from 2pm.

Post Offices: In **Bahnhof Zoo** (tel. 313 97 99). Open Mon.-Fri. 6am-midnight, Sat.-Sun. 8am-midnight. *Poste Restante,* held at window 7, should be addressed: Poste Restante/Hauptpostlagernd, Postamt Bahnhof Zoo, 10612 Berlin. The branch office at **Tegel Airport** (tel. 430 85 23) is open daily 6:30am-9pm. In East Berlin, in the **Hauptbahnhof,** Postamt Berlin 17, Str. der Pariser Kommune 8-10, 10243 Berlin. Open Mon.-Fri. 7am-9pm, Sat. 8am-8pm.

Telephones: At any post office or around Bahnhof Zoo. **Phone code:** 030.

ACCOMMODATIONS AND CAMPING

Although tourists mob Berlin during the summer, same-day accommodations aren't impossible to find. As always, it's best to call ahead, particularly during the Love Parade, a huge technofest the second weekend of July. For a DM5 fee, **tourist offices** will find you a room: be prepared to pay DM70 for singles and DM100 for doubles.

The Backpacker, Köthenerstr. 44, 10963 Berlin (tel. 262 51 40; email ante@aol.com). U2: Potsdamerpl. From the Stresemannstr. exit, turn right on Stresemannstr., then right again. Close to Mitte's action. Kitchen and hip staff that updates you on nightlife. Reception open 7am-11pm. No curfew. First night DM30, DM25 thereafter. Sheets DM3. Laundry facilities DM5. On January 15, 1998, a **second location** will open in Mitte at Chausseestr. 102 (tel. 251 52 02). U6: Zinnowitzer Str., or S1 and S2: Nordbahnhof. Discounted public transportation tickets and **Internet access.** DM25-30. Sheets DM4. Breakfast DM5-10.

Die Fabrik, Schlesischestr. 18, 10997 Berlin (tel. 611 71 16; fax 618 29 74). U1: Schlesisches Tor. *Pension qua* hostel in a beautifully converted factory within walking distance of Kreuzberg's mad nightlife. Reception open 24hr. No curfew. Singles DM66; doubles DM94 (honeymoon suite DM110); triples DM120; quads 144. 16-bed dorm DM30 per person. Breakfast DM10. Call ahead.

Circus, Am Zirkus 2-3, 10117 Berlin (tel. 28 39 14 33; email circus@mind.de), near Alexanderpl. Brand new and trying hard to achieve hostel hipness, offering **Inter-**

net access, laundry machines, and a disco ball in the lobby. No curfew. Singles DM38; doubles DM60; triples DM84; dorms DM25 per person. Sheets DM3.

Jugendgästehaus (HI), Kluckstr. 3, 10785 Berlin (tel. 261 10 97; fax 265 03 83), in the Schöneberg/Wilmersdorf area. From Ku'damm, take bus 129 (dir. "Hermannpl.") to "Gedenkstätte," or U1: Kurfürstenstr., then walk up Potsdamerstr., go left on Pohlstr., then right. Clean and modern. Reception open 1pm-midnight with 30min. breaks; ring the bell. Curfew midnight; door opened at 12:30 and 1am. Lockout 9am-1pm. DM32, over 26 DM41. Sheets and breakfast included. Key deposit DM10. Lockers and laundry facilities available. Call at least 2 weeks ahead.

Hotelpension Cortina, Kantstr. 140, 10623 Berlin (tel. 313 90 59; fax 31 73 96). S3, S5, S7, S9, or bus 149: Savignypl. Convenient and hospitable. Reception open 24hr. Singles DM70; doubles DM120, with shower DM130. Breakfast included.

Pension Knesebeck, Knesebeckstr. 86, 10623 Berlin (tel. 312 72 55; fax 313 34 86). S3, S5, S7, or S9: Savignypl. Just north of the park. Large *Alt-Berliner* rooms, many with couches and sinks. Hearty buffet breakfast. Reception open 24hr. Singles with showers DM85; doubles DM120-140. Big *Mehrbettzimmer* DM50-60 per person. Laundry DM2.50. Phone reservations must be confirmed by fax or letter.

Hotel-Pension München, Güntzelstr. 62 (tel. 857 91 20; fax 85 79 12 22). U9: Güntzelstr. *Pension cum* gallery with art by contemporary Berlin artists and sculptures by the owner. Superclean rooms with TVs. Singles DM60-110; doubles DM80-125. Breakfast DM9. Written reservations are best, or call before 2pm.

Hotel Sachsenhof, Motzstr. 7, 10777 Berlin (tel. 216 20 74; fax 215 82 20). Small, plain rooms, but clean and well-furnished. Reception open 24hr. Singles DM57-65; doubles DM99-156. Extra beds DM30. Breakfast DM10.

Pension Kreuzberg, Grossbeerenstr. 64, 10963 Berlin (tel. 251 13 62; fax 251 06 38). U6, 7: Mehringdamm. Small but well-decorated rooms in an old, grand building near the Kreuzberg scene. Reception open 8am-10pm. Singles DM70; doubles DM95. *Mehrbettzimmer* DM42 per person. Breakfast DM5.

Hotel Transit, Hagelbergerstr. 53-54, 10965 Berlin (tel. 785 50 51; fax 785 96 19). U6, 7: Mehringdamm, or bus 119 or night bus N19. Party hard and crash gently. Singles DM90; doubles DM152; triples DM140; quads DM180. *Mehrbettzimmer* DM34. Breakfast included.

FOOD

Berlin's restaurant scene is as international as its population; German food and drink should be a second priority here. One exception is the smooth, sweet *Berliner Weiße mit Schuß,* a concoction of local beer with a shot of fruit syrup. Much Berlin food is Turkish: almost every street has its own Turkish *Imbiß* (snack bar; often open 24hr.). The *Döner Kepab,* a sandwich of lamb and salad, has cornered the fast food market, but falafel runs a close second. For DM3-5, either makes a small meal. A second wave of immigration has brought quality Indian restaurants to Berlin, and Italian is always a safe choice. A gloriously civilized tradition in Berlin's cafes is *Frühstück,* breakfast served well into the afternoon, sometimes 24 hours.

Aldi, Bolle, and **Penny Markt** are the cheapest supermarket chains, along with the many **Plus** stores in Wilmersdorf, Schönberg, and Kreuzberg. Supermarkets are usually open Monday through Friday 9am to 6pm and Saturday 9am to 1pm. There's a kaleidescopic **Turkish market** in Kreuzberg on the banks of the Landwehrkanal (near U1: Kottbusser Tor) every Friday.

Mensa TU, Hardenbergstr. 34. Bus 145 to "Steinpl.," or walk 10min. from Bahnhof Zoo. The mightiest of Berlin's mensae, serving rather good vegetarian (*Bio Essen*) dishes. Meals DM4-6. *Mensa* open Mon.-Fri. 11:15am-2:30pm.

Schwarzes Cafe, Kantstr. 148, near Savignypl. Dark walls, big-band music, and dapper waiters. A bit pricey, but breakfast served at all hours (DM7-13). Open 24hr., except for Tues., when closed early morning-6pm.

Baharat Falafel, Winterfeldtstr. 37. U1, 2: Nollendorfpl. Perhaps the best falafel in Berlin (DM6). Open Mon.-Sat. 10am-3am, Sun. 11am-3am.

Rani, Goltzstr. 32, behind the church on Winterfeldtpl. U1, 2: Nollendorfpl. Very casual and cheap Indian restaurant popular with students. Most dishes DM6-10. Generous portions. Open daily 11am-2am.

Kurdistan, Uhlandstr. 161. U15: Uhlandstr. One of Berlin's most exotic and most appetizing offerings. Fabulous *Yekawe* (meat with rice, raisins, and cinnamon) DM15. Most entrees DM15-20. Open Mon.-Sat. 5pm-late.

Morena, Wiener Str. 60. U1, 12: Görlitzer Bahnhof. A gracious, roomy cafe with some of Kreuzberg's best *Frühstück* (DM5-8.50, served 9am-5pm). Open Sun.-Thurs. 9am-4am, Fri.-Sat. 9am-5am.

Die Rote Harfe, Oranienstr. 13, in Heinrichpl., the center of Kreuzberg. U8: Moritzpl. or U1: Kottbusser Tor. Leftists and grizzled types eating solid German food are bound to spark the radical in you. Daily 3-course lunch menu DM15. Open Sun.-Thurs. 10am-2am, Fri.-Sat. 10am-3am.

SIGHTS

Between Eastern and Western Berlin

For decades a barricaded gateway to nowhere, the **Brandenburger Tor** (Brandenburg Gate) is the structure that commonly symbolizes the reunited Berlin. The central point of the city, it opens east onto Unter den Linden (S-Bahn: Unter den Linden or bus 100). Built during the reign of Friedrich Wilhelm II as an emblem of peace, the gate served as a locked door embedded in the Berlin Wall and wasn't opened until December 22, 1989, over a month after the Wall came down. The **Berlin Wall** itself is a dinosaur with only fossil remains. Fenced in overnight on August 13, 1961, the 160km long wall separated families and friends, sometimes running through homes. Portions of it are preserved near the *Hauptbahnhof* and the Reichstag. The longest remaining bit is the brightly painted **East Side Gallery** (S-Bahn: Hauptbahnhof). The demolished Wall has left an incompletely healed scar across the city center. From the west side, trees have been planted extending the Tiergarten park a few meters more. But on the east side, a grassy no-man's-land strewn with cinder blocks awaits construction. **Potsdamer Platz,** cut off by the Wall, was once a major transportation hub of Berlin designed under Frederick Wilhelm I to approximate Parisian boulevards. Daimler-Benz now plans to convert the land surrounding the *Platz* into a sprawling office complex. South of Potsdamer Platz stands the **Martin-Gropius-Bau,** Stresemanstr. 110. The decorous edifice was designed by Martin Gropius, a pupil of Schinkel and uncle of *Bauhausmeister* Walter Gropius. The **Haus am Checkpoint Charlie,** Friedrichstr. 44 (U-bahn: "Kochstr." or bus 129), narrates the history of the Wall through film and photos. Upstairs are exhibits on human rights, as well as artistic renderings of the Wall (open daily 9am-10pm; DM7.50, students DM4.50).

Western Berlin

Just north of the Brandenburger Tor sits the imposing, stone-gray **Reichstag,** former seat of the parliaments of the German Empire and the Weimar Republic, and future home of Germany's governing body, the *Bundestag*. In 1918 Philipp Scheidemann proclaimed a German republic from one of its balconies. His move turned out to be wise, since two hours later Karl Liebknecht, in the Imperial Palace a few kilometers away on Unter den Linden, announced a German Socialist Republic, ironically on the site that later supported the parliament of the GDR. As the Republic declined, Nazi members showed up to sessions in uniform, and on February 28, 1933, a month after Hitler became Chancellor, fire mysteriously broke out in the building. The fire provided a pretext for Hitler to declare a state of emergency, giving the Nazis broad powers to arrest and intimidate opponents before the upcoming elections. The infamous end result was the Enabling Act, which established Hitler as legal dictator and abolished democracy. In the summer of 1995, the Reichstag metamorphosed into an artsy parcel, when husband-and-wife team **Christo** and **Jeanne-Claude** wrapped the dignified building in 120,000 yards of shimmery metallic fabric. The government held a massive design competition for the building's new dome; the current plans call for a huge glass dome, but will likely change, since a scale model of the design fried the miniature model ministers inside. The lush **Tiergarten** in the northwest corner of western Berlin is a relief from the neon lights of the Ku'damm to the west and the din and dust of construction work to the east.

A sobering reminder of the devastation caused by WWII, the shattered **Kaiser-Wilhelm-Gedächtniskirche** now houses an exhibit dedicated to peace (open Tues.-Sat. 10am-4pm). The exhibit, however, has lost some of its didactic force amid the giddy neon of the **Ku'damm** and the Europa Center shopping mall. The renowned **Zoo,** with entrances across from the train station and at Budapesterstr. 34 (the famous Elephant Gate), houses an excellent collection of fauna. (Open May-Sept. daily 9am-6:30pm; Oct.-Feb. 9am-5pm; March-April 9am-5:30pm. DM11, students DM9.) Next door at Budapesterstr. 32 stands the spectacular **Aquarium.** (Open daily 9am-6pm. DM8, students DM5. Zoo and aquarium DM17, students DM14.)

Schloß Charlottenburg (U-Bahn: Sophie-Charlotte-Pl. or bus 145 from Bahnhof Zoo), the vast Baroque palace built by Friedrich I for his second wife, presides over a carefully landscaped Baroque park. The *Schloß*'s many buildings include **Neringbau,** the palace proper, which contains rooms filled with historical furnishings. (Castle open Tues.-Fri. 9am-5pm, Sat.-Sun. 10am-5pm. Entire palace complex *Tageskarte* DM15, students DM10.) Seek out the **Palace Gardens,** with their carefully planted rows of trees, footbridges, and fountains which surround the **Royal Mausoleum, Belvedere,** an 18th-century residence housing a porcelain exhibit and the **Schinkel Pavilion,** with furniture designed by Schinkel (open Tues.-Sun. 6am-9pm; free).

Indispensable for a sense of Berlin's famous *alternative Szene* is a visit to **Kreuzberg.** Much of the area was occupied by *Hausbesetzer* (squatters) during the 60s and 70s; they were forcibly evicted in the early 1980s, provoking riots and throwing the city into upheaval. For a look at the district's more respectable face, take U6 or U7 to Mehringdamm and wander. At night, many bohemian cafes and punk clubs spill onto **Gneisenaustraße,** which heads west from the intersection with Mehringdamm. The cafes and bars on Oranienstr. boast a more radical element; the May Day parades always start on Oranienpl. (U1, 8: Kottbusser Tor).

Eastern Berlin

The Brandenburger Tor opens eastward onto **Unter den Linden,** once one of Europe's best-known boulevards and the spine of old Berlin. All but the most famous buildings have been destroyed, but farther down, many 18th-century structures have been restored to their original Prussian splendor. Past Friedrichstr., the first massive building on your left is the **Deutsche Staatsbibliothek** (library), with a pleasant café inside. Beyond the library is **Humboldt Universität,** once one of the finest in the world. Next door, the former **Neue Wache** (New Guard House), designed by the Prussian architect Friedrich Schinkel, is today the somber **Monument to the Victims of Fascism and Militarism.** Buried inside are urns filled with earth from the Nazi concentration camps Buchenwald and Mauthausen and from the battlefields of Stalingrad, El Alamein, and Normandy. Across the way is **Bebelplatz,** the site of Nazi book-burning. The square houses a monument to the book-burning that consists of a hallowed-out chamber lined with illuminated, empty white bookshelves. The impressive building with the curved facade is the **Alte Bibliothek.** The most striking of the monumental buildings is the **Zeughaus,** now the **Museum of German History.** From the museum you can enter the courtyard and see the tormented faces of Andreas Schlüter's *Dying Warriors.*

Berlin's most striking ensemble of 18th-century buildings is a few blocks south of Unter den Linden at **Gendarmenmarkt,** graced by the twin cathedrals of **Deutscher Dom** and **Französischer Dom,** built for the French Huguenot community. Enclosing the far end of the square, the classical **Schauspielhaus** is Berlin's most elegant concert space and hosts many international orchestras and classical performers.

As it crosses the bridge, Unter den Linden opens out onto **Museuminsel** (Museum Island). To the left is the **Altes Museum,** with a big polished granite bowl in front, and the poly-domed **Berliner Dom** (Berlin Cathedral). Severely damaged by an air raid in 1944, the cathedral emerged from 20 years of restoration in 1993; the interior is ornately gaudy (open Mon.-Sat. 9am-8pm, Sun. noon-8pm; DM5, students DM3). Behind the Altes Museum lie three other enormous museums and the reconstructed **Neues Museum.** The cobblestone square in front of the Altes Museum is known as the **Lustgarten.** Once a small park, it became a military parade ground under the Nazis. Across the street, the Lustgarten turns into Marx-Engels-Pl. under the amber-colored **Palast der Republik,** where the GDR parliament once met.

Across the Liebknecht Brücke, in the park, stands the "conceptual memorial" consisting of steel tablets engraved with images of worker struggle and protest surrounding a twin statue of Marx and Engels. The park and the street behind it used to be known as the **Marx-Engels Forum;** the street is now called **Rathausstraße.**

On the other side of the Museumsinsel, Unter den Linden leads to teeming, concrete **Alexanderplatz,** the landmark of which is the **Fernsehturm** (television tower), the tallest structure in Berlin. The cross that marks it in sunlight was seen by some as a cosmic joke on the Communists (open March-Oct. daily 9am-1am; Nov.-Feb. 10am-midnight; DM8). The graceful 15th-century **Marienkirche** stands on the open plaza behind the *Fernsehturm.* Nearby is the gabled **Rotes Rathaus,** Old Berlin's famous red-brick town hall. Behind the *Rathaus,* the twin spires of the **Nikolaikirche** mark Berlin's oldest building. Inside the 13th-century structure, a small museum documents the early history of the city (open Tues.-Sun. 10am-6pm; DM3, students DM1). The church gives the surrounding **Nikolaiviertel,** a reconstructed *Altstadt,* its name.

Northwest of Alexanderpl. lies the **Scheunenviertel,** once the center of Berlin's Orthodox Jewish community (U- or S-Bahn: Alexanderpl., or S1, 2: Oranienburgerstr.). Prior to WWII, wealthier and more assimilated Jews tended to live in Western Berlin, while more Orthodox Jews from Eastern Europe settled in the *Scheunenviertel.* The shell of the **Neues Synagoge** stands at Oranienburgerstr. 30. This huge "oriental-style" building was designed by the famous Berlin architect Knoblauch. The temple's beautiful gold-laced domes and some of the sumptuous interior have been reconstructed. **The New Synagogue 1866-1995,** chronicling the synagogue's history, and **Jewish History in Berlin,** documenting the history of Jews in Berlin since the 1660s are housed here (open Sun.-Thurs. 10am-6pm, Fri. 10am-2pm; DM5, students DM3). **Oranienburgerstraße** has become a center of the squatter and artist communities, with a correspondingly rich cultural and cafe life.

East of Oranienburgerstr. is **Prenzlauer Berg,** a former working-class district largely neglected by East Germany's reconstruction efforts. Many of its old buildings are falling apart; others still have shell holes and embedded bullets from WWII. Home to cafes, restaurants, and a few museums, restored **Husemannstraße** is especially worthy of a stroll. The area's population belies the aging architecture; there are heaps of students, artists, clubs, and communes, but the city government's anti-commune policy is in danger of destroying this counter-cultural renaissance. The scene around **Kollwitzplatz** is especially vibrant.

Museums

Four major complexes—Charlottenburg, Dahlem, Museumsinsel, and Tiergarten—form the hub of the city's museum culture. Their prices and hours are standardized: Tues.-Fri. 9am-5pm, Sat.-Sun. 10am-5pm; DM4, students DM2. A *Tageskarte* (good for all of the national museums) is DM8, students DM4. All national museums and most private ones close on Monday; on the first Sunday of each month, admission to the national museums is free.

Pergamonmuseum, Kupfergraben, in Museumsinsel. One of the world's great ancient history museums. The scale is mind-boggling: the Babylonian Ishtar Gate (575 BC), the Roman Market Gate of Miletus, and the majestic Pergamon Altar of Zeus (180 BC). Extensive collection of Greek, Islamic, and Far Eastern art. Last admission 30min. before closing.

Dahlem Museum, Arnimallee 23-27 and Lansstr. 8. U-Bahn: Dahlem-Dorf. Huge complex of 7 museums, each worth a half-day. Particularly superb are the **Gemäldegalerie** (Painting Gallery), a collection of Italian, German, Dutch, and

Flemish Old Masters (including 26 Rembrandts), and the **Museum für Indische und Islamische Kunst,** extensive collections of Indian and Islam culture.

Schloß Charlottenburg, Spandauer Damm. U2: Sophie-Charlotte-Pl., or bus 145. The **Ägyptisches Museum,** across Spandauer Damm from the castle's main entrance, houses a fascinating collection of ancient Egyptian art, including the 3300-year-old bust of Queen Nefertiti. Also check out the **Sammlung Berggruen** and the **Galerie der Romantik.** *Tageskarte* for the non-SMPK parts of the *Schloß* costs DM15, students DM10.

Neue Nationalgalerie, Potsdamerstr. 50. S1, 2 or U2: Potsdamer Pl. Part of the Tiergarten complex. This sleek building, gives quantity its own quality in a collection devoted to large art displays. Permanent collection includes works by Kokoschka, Barlach, Kirchner, and Beckmann.

Martin-Gropius Bau, Stresemannstr. 110 (tel. 25 48 60). S-Bahn or U-Bahn: "Anhalter Bahnhof." The **Berlinische Galerie,** on the second floor, is devoted to rotating exhibits of contemporary art, much of it very famous. On the top floor, the **Jüdisches Museum** hosts extremely varied exhibits of painting, sculpture, and design related to Jews in Germany. Most exhibits in both are open Tues.-Sun. 10am-8pm. DM12, students DM6. Adjacent to the museums, built on top of the ruins of a Gestapo kitchen, the **Topographie des Terrors** details the development of Nazism in Germany. Open Tues.-Sun. 10am-6pm. Free. The adjacent **Prinz-Albrecht-Gelände** contains the ruins of many Gestapo buildings. Signs describe what once took place. Open during daylight hours. Free.

ENTERTAINMENT

Berlin is *wild,* all night, every night. The best guides to theater, nightlife, and the extremely active music scene are the bi-weekly magazines *Tip* and *Zitty* (both DM4). The monthly *Berlin Program* lists more events. The free magazine *Siegessäule* details gay events for the month and is available in gay bars and bookstores.

Nightlife

In western Berlin, the **Savignypl., Schöneberg, Wilmersdorf,** and **Kreuzberg** districts rock the house, but the focus of the *Szene* is shifting inexorably eastward. The east, in a word, is hot: low rents and a rising "alternative" population give its cafes and bars a grittier edge that the slicker west side can't touch.

Quasimodo, Kantstr. 12a (tel. 312 80 86). S3, 5, 7, or 9: Savignypl. This unassuming basement pub with attached *Biergarten* is one of Berlin's most crucial jazz venues, drawing in big names and lively crowds. Cover depends on performance, ranging from free to DM30. Concert tickets available from 5pm or at Kant Kasse ticket service (tel. 313 45 54; fax 312 64 40). Open daily from 8pm.

M, Goltzstr. 33. U7: Eisenacherstr. One of the more interesting Schöneberg bars, stark and neon-lit, and slightly wild late at night. Black is eternally in. "Karlheinz, you are beautiful and angular." Open daily 8am-whenever.

Yaam, Eichenstr. 4. U1: Schlesisches Tor. Neither club nor bar, but rather *the place* to chill on weekend afternoons. African and Caribbean food market Sun. and Berlin's largest pick-up basketball league. Open Fri.-Sun. 2pm-10pm. Cover DM5.

SO 36, Oranienstr. 190 (http://www.SO36.de). U1: Görlitzer Bahnhof. A mish-mash of wild oeuvres: Sun. is ballroom dancing, Wed. means gay and lesbian disco night, Thurs. keeps heads banging with ska, metal, punk, and hardcore. Fri.-Sat., the crowd gets younger for the slightly raucous parties. Open Sun. after 7pm, Mon. after 11pm, Wed.-Thurs. after 10pm, Fri.-Sat. 11pm-late.

Tresor, Leipzigerstr. 8. U2: Mohrenstr. or Potsdamer Platz. One of the most rocking techno venues in Berlin, packed from wall to wall with enthusiastic ravers. Open Wed. and Fri.-Sun. after 11pm. Cover DM5 on Wed., DM12 on weekends. The garden stays open all day Sat., with free entry after 7am.

Tacheles, Oranienburgerstr. 53-56 (tel. 282 61 85). U6: Oranienburger Tor. Perhaps the greatest source of artistic pretense in all of Berlin. The art commune has decorated the interior with graffiti, collages, and exhibits. Bands, films, raves, and three bars serve up nightly entertainment. Open 24hr.

Insel der Jugend, Alt Treptow 6. S8,9. or 10: Treptower Park, then bus 265 or N65 to "Alt-Treptow." Located on an island in the middle of the park. Top 2 floors spin reggae, hip-hop, ska, and house; basement has a frantic techno scene. Hipsters chill in the cafe. Cafe open daily 2-9pm. Club open after 9pm on Thurs., after 10pm on Fri., after 11pm on Sat. Cover for club DM5-15.

Rose's, Oranienstr. 182, U1, 8: Kottbusser Tor. Popular and energetic gay and lesbian bar. Open daily 10pm-6am.

90°, Dennewitzstr. 37. U1: Kurfürstenstr. Exceptionally popular gay and lesbian techno dance scene for the sartorially splendiferous (dress sleekly!) on Thurs. and Sun. Open Thurs.-Sun. after 11pm

Concerts and Opera

Berliner Philharmonisches Orchester, Matthäikirchstr. 1 (tel. 25 48 81 32; fax 25 48 81 35). Bus 129 from Ku'damm to "Potsdamerstr." and walk 3 blocks north; or S-Bahn 2: "Potsdamerpl." The Berliner Philharmoniker, led for decades by the late Herbert von Karajan, is perhaps the finest orchestra in the world. Check an hour before concert time for seats or write at least eight weeks in advance. Often closed during the summer months. Box office open Mon.-Fri. 3:30-6pm, Sat.-Sun. and holidays 11am-2pm. Fax or write to: Kartenbüro, Berliner Philharmonisches Orchester, Matthäikirchstr.1, 10785 Berlin.

Deutsche Oper Berlin, Bismarckstr. 34-37 (tel. 341 02 49 or 343 84 01 for tickets). U-Bahn 2 or 12: "Deutsche Oper." Berlin's best opera. Main box office open Mon.-Sat. 11am-1hr. before performance, Sun. 10am-2pm. Tickets DM15-125.

Helsinki, Finland

US$1	= 5.48mk (markka, FIM)	1mk =	US$0.18
CDN$1	= 3.96mk	1mk =	CDN$0.25
UK£1	= 8.72mk	1mk =	UK£0.11
IR£1	= 8.00mk	1mk =	IR£0.12
AUS$1	= 4.00mk	1mk =	AUS$0.25
NZ$1	= 3.48mk	1mk =	NZ$0.28
SAR1	= 1.16mk	1mk =	SAR0.85
Country Phone Code: 358		**International Dialing Prefix: 990**	

A meeting point of East and West, Helsinki combines the relaxed feeling of Finland with a metropolitan elegance. Lutheran and Russian Orthodox cathedrals stand almost face to face, Red Army uniforms and medals are sold on the street, and St. Petersburg and Tallinn are but a short cruise across the Gulf of Finland. Cobblestone streets, well-tended parks, and a boat-thronged coastline make Helsinki an ideal city for strolling; Mannerheimintie and the Esplanadi offer great people-watching. The southeast corner of the city is a nest of diplomats, elegant mansions, and aggressive traffic, while the area around the train station offers cafes, shops, and street vendors.

ORIENTATION AND PRACTICAL INFORMATION

Helsinki dangles off Finland's southern edge. The central city's layout resembles a "V" with a large, bulbous point and several smaller peninsulas. The train station lies just north of the vertex, from which the **Mannerheimintie** and **Unioninkatu** thoroughfares radiate. The harbor and most sights are southeast of the train station. All street signs have both Finnish and Swedish names. For candid and practical info on what's hot, the free paper *City* is unbeatable, while *Helsinki This Week* provides local information and a list of lodgings, restaurants, and current happenings.

Tourist Offices: City Tourist Office, Pohjoisesplanadi 19 (tel. 169 37 57). From the train station, walk 2 blocks south on Keskuskatu and turn left on Pohjoisesplanadi. Open late May-early Sept. Mon.-Fri. 9am-7pm, Sat.-Sun. 9am-3pm; mid-Sept. to mid-May Mon.-Fri. 9am-5pm, Sat.-Sun. 9am-3pm. **Hotellikeskus** (Hotel Booking Center; tel. 17 11 33), in the train station, specializes in finding rooms (12mk booking fee), but also has **maps** and youth hostel lists. Open late May-Aug. Mon.-Sat. 9am-7pm, Sun. 10am-6pm; Sept. to mid-May Mon.-Fri. 9am-5pm. Both offices sell the **Helsinki Card,** offering unlimited local transportation and museum discounts (1-day 105mk, 2-day 135mk, 3-day 165mk). The **Finnish Tourist Board,** Eteläesplanadi 4 (tel. 41 76 93 00; fax 41 76 93 01), can tell you all about transportation and campgrounds. Open June-Aug. Mon.-Fri. 8:30am-5pm, Sat. 10am-2pm; Sept.-May Mon.-Fri. 8:30am-4pm. **Finnish Youth Hostel Association,** Yrjönkatu 38B (tel. 694 03 77), on the south side of the bus station, lists hostels and arranges Lapland lodgings. Open Mon.-Fri. 9am-4pm.

Budget Travel: Kilroy Travels, Kaivokatu 100 (tel. 680 78 11). Sells Transalpino tickets, ISIC, and YIEE cards. Open Mon.-Fri. 10am-6pm, Sat. 10am-2pm.

Embassies: Canada, Pohjoisesplanadi 25B (tel. 17 11 41). Open Mon.-Thurs. 8:30am-4:30pm, Fri. 8:30am-1:30pm. **Estonia,** Itäinen Puistotie 10 (tel. 62 20 260). **Ireland,** Evottajankatu 7A (tel. 64 60 06). **Latvia,** Armfeltintie 10 (tel. 47 64 72 44). **Lithuania,** Rauhankatu 13A (tel. 60 82 10). **Poland,** Armas Lindgrenin tie 21 (tel. 684 80 77). **Russia,** Tehtaankatu 1B (tel. 66 18 76). **South Africa,** Rahapajankatu 1A (tel. 658 288). **U.K.,** Itäinen Puistotie 17 (tel. 22 86 51 00). **U.S.,** Itäinen Puistotie 14A (tel. 17 19 31). Open Mon.-Fri. 9am-noon.

Currency Exchange: Rates are generally the same throughout the city, with a minimum 10mk commission on traveler's checks. **Forex,** in the train station, charges a 10mk fee for cash and 10mk per traveler's check, but no fee to exchange markka into foreign currency. Open daily 8am-9pm. Same rates in the main post office. Open Mon.-Fri. 7am-9pm, Sat. 9am-6pm, Sun. 11am-9pm. The airport terminal has money exchange (cash only); open daily 6:30am-11pm. **Merita** banks at ferry terminals are open Mon.-Fri. 9am-6pm, Sat. 9-11:30am and 3:45-7:30pm, Sun. 9-11:30am and 3:45-6pm. Visa cash advances available 24hr. from most ATMs.

American Express: Area Travel, Mikonkatu 2D, 2nd floor, 00100 (tel. 62 87 88). No commission on traveler's checks. Open Mon.-Fri. 9am-1pm and 2:15-4:30pm.

Flights: Info tel. 818 81. Bus #615 runs between the **Helsinki-Vantaa** airport and the station square (Mon.-Fri. 2-3 times per hr. 5:20am-10:20pm, 15mk). The Finnair bus shuttles between the airport and the Finnair building at Asema-aukio 3, next to the train station (every 20min. 5am-midnight, 35min., 25mk).

Trains: Info tel. 101 01 15. Trains chug regularly to Turku (2hr., 90mk), Tampere (2hr., 90mk), and Rovaniemi (10hr., 2304mk). Call 010 01 24 for info on trains to Moscow (16hr., sleeper 506mk) and St. Petersburg (7½hr., 265mk, Eurail and Scanrail 148mk). The station has **lockers** and **luggage service** (10mk each; service open daily 6:35am-10pm).

Buses: Info tel. 96 00 40 00. The station with routes throughout Finland and to St. Petersburg (3 per day, 8hr., 190-250mk) sits west of the post office, between Salomonkatu and Simonkatu. Buy tickets at the station or on the bus.

Ferries: Silja Line, Mannerheimintie 2 (tel. 180 41). Open Mon.-Fri. 8:30am-6pm, Sat. 9am-2pm. **Viking Line,** Mannerheimintie 14 (tel. 123 51). Open Mon.-Fri. 8:30am-6pm, Sat. 9am-3pm. **Viking Line** and **Finnjet** (contact Silja Line) ferries leave from Katajanokka island east of Kauppatori (take tram 2 or 4). The departure point for **Silja Line, Polferries** (tel. 980 07 45 52), **Estonian Line** (tel. 66 99 44), and **Tallink** (tel. 22 82 12 77) is south of Kauppatori (take tram 3T). For more information about touring the Baltics, call the Baltic tourist info line at 63 05 22.

Public Transportation: The metro and most trams and buses run approximately 6am-11pm (certain bus and tram lines, including tram 3T, run until 1:30am). On the weekend, trams run until 2:30am. Within Helsinki, rides cost 9mk; 10-trip ticket 75mk. Travel between Helsinki, Espoo, and Vantaa costs 15mk; 10-trip ticket 125mk. All tickets are valid 1hr. (free transfers) and are available at R-Kiosks and City Transport offices at Simonkatu 1, the Rautatientori metro station, and the Hakaniemi train station. Punch your ticket on board. Ask on trams or at the City Transport office for maps; some routes are more direct than others. The **Tourist Ticket** provides limitless travel in Helsinki, Espoo, and Vantaa (1-day 90mk, 3-day 45mk); purchase it at City Transport or tourist offices.

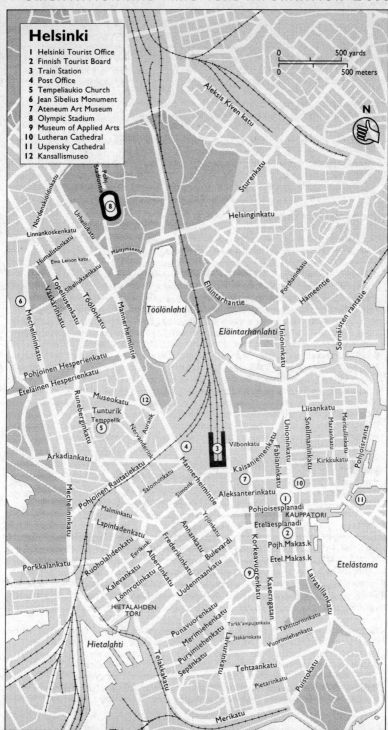

Helsinki

1 Helsinki Tourist Office
2 Finnish Tourist Board
3 Train Station
4 Post Office
5 Tempeliaukio Church
6 Jean Sibelius Monument
7 Ateneum Art Museum
8 Olympic Stadium
9 Museum of Applied Arts
10 Lutheran Cathedral
11 Uspensky Cathedral
12 Kansallismuseo

GATEWAY CITIES

Bookstore: The Academic Bookstore, Pohjoisesplanadi 39 (tel. 121 41). Dazzling selection of books in English (including travel guides) and classic novels for 15mk. Popular hang-out spot, with cafe. Open Mon.-Fri. 9am-8pm, Sat. 9am-5pm.

Pharmacy: Yliopiston Apteekki, Mannerheimintie 5 (tel. 17 90 92). Open daily 7am-midnight. Another branch at Mannerheimintie 96 (tel. 41 57 78). Open 24hr.

Medical Assistance: Aleksin lääkäriasema, Mannerheimintie 8 (tel. 601 911). Receives and refers foreigners.

Emergencies: tel. 112.

Police: tel. 100 22. Stations at Olavinkatu 1A, Kasarmikatu 25B, 2 Pikku Roobertinkatu 1-3, and the train station near platform 11.

Post Office: Mannerheimintie 11 (tel. 195 51 17). Open Mon.-Fri. 9:30am-5pm. *Poste Restante* office in the same building sells stamps and exchanges money. Open Mon.-Fri. 7am-9pm, Sat. 9am-6pm, Sun. 11am-9pm. **Postal code:** 00100.

Telephones: In the same building as the post office. Open Mon.-Fri. 9am-10pm, Sat.-Sun. 10am-4pm. Get the best rates by using a Tele or Nonstop phone card, which work in green Nonstop card phones. **Telephone Code:** 09.

ACCOMMODATIONS

Hosting the 1952 Olympics compelled Helsinki to provide abundant lodgings. During the summer, it's wise to make reservations, but just showing up is not extraordinarily risky. Most hostels offer laundry facilities, breakfast, and saunas.

Hotel Satakuntatalo (HI), Lapinrinne 1 (tel. 69 58 51; fax 694 22 26), 500m south-west of the train station—turn right on Mannerheimintie, then left up Salomonkatu past the bus station; go down Lapinrinne. A dorm-*cum*-summer hotel; clean and well-run, with some great rooms. Kitchen and baggage storage. Reception open 24hr. Dorms 55mk. Singles 195mk; doubles 230mk. Nonmembers add 15mk. Breakfast included. Sauna 20mk. Laundry 15mk. Open June-Aug.

Stadion Hostel (HI), Pohj. Stadiontie 3B (tel. 49 60 71; fax 49 64 66), in the Olympic Stadium complex. Take tram 3T or 7A from the train station. 200-bed hostel with high ceilings, huge windows, a kitchen, and TV. Reception open June-early Sept. daily 8am-2am; mid-Sept. to May 8-10am and 4pm-2am. Dorms 55mk, non-members 70mk. Doubles 160mk. Locked room for luggage. Sheets 20mk.

Academica (HI), Hietaniemenkatu 14 (tel. 13 11 43 34; fax 44 12 01). Just 700m from the train station; walk up Mannerheimintie and turn right, then left onto Ark-adiankatu, left on Mechelininkatu, and right onto Hietaniemenkatu. Kitchen. Reception open 24hr. Singles 215mk. Doubles 220mk. Triples 255mk per person. Quads 300mk per person. Nonmembers add 15mk per person. Open June-Aug.

Kallio Youth Hostel, Porthaninkatu 2 (tel. 70 99 25 90; fax 70 99 25 98). From the train station, walk 15min. north on Unioninkatu, or take the metro to Hakaniemi. Cozy 35-bed hostel. TV room and kitchen. Reception open daily 8am-11pm. 70mk, disposable sheets 10mk. Free lockers and storage room. Open July-Aug.

FOOD

In Finland, even groceries are expensive; find relief at the **Alepa** chain (the branch under the train station is open Mon.-Sat. 10am-10pm, Sun. noon-10pm). Energetic epicureans can find a variety of wares, including fresh fruit, veggies and fish, at the **Kauppatori** (Market Square) by the port (open June-Aug. Mon.-Sat. 7am-2pm and 4-8pm; Sept.-May Mon.-Fri. 7am-2pm), and the nearby **Kauppahalli** (Market Hall; open Mon.-Sat. 8am-5pm, Sun. 8am-2pm).

Zetor, Kaivokatu 10. Finnish specialties, a lively crowd, and a real tractor inside make this the essence of Finland: food, drinks, music, dancing, and of course, a sauna. Opens Sun.-Fri. 3pm, Sat. 1pm; closes when the last customer leaves.

Suola Ja Pippuri, Snellmaninkatu 17. On a quiet side street. Lunch 38-44mk. Mainly seafood dinners. Open Mon.-Fri. 11am-midnight, Sat. 1pm-midnight.

Ravintola Pikku Satama, Pikku Satamakatu 3, by the harbor. Charming outdoor terrace and good prices. Lunch 33mk. Pizza 40mk. Pasta 40mk. Moussaka 39mk. Open Sun.-Fri. 10:30am-midnight, Sat 2pm-midnight.

Kasvis, Korkeavuorenkatu 3. Serves organically grown vegetable dishes (25-45mk) and amazing homemade bread that they've been perfecting for 20 years. Enjoy your meal outside or inside. Open Mon.-Fri. 11am-10pm, Sat.-Sun. noon-10pm.

Cafe Engel, Aleksanterinkatu 26. Sip coffee for hours (8.50mk) or try the delicious lingonberry pie (17mk). Open Mon.-Sat. 9am-midnight, Sun. 11am-midnight.

Kappeli, Eteläesplanadi 1. Victorian Parisian fantasy that has catered to trendies since 1837 (Sibelius had a favorite table here). Warm pies 15mk per slice. Mouth-watering entrees 38-55mk. Lunch 25-37mk. Beer 25mk. Open daily 9am-4am.

University Cafeterias: Fabianinkatu 33; outdoor-terraced Porthania, Hallituskatu 6. Entrees 20mk. Students only. Both open June-Aug. Mon.-Fri. 10am-4pm; Sept.-May Mon.-Fri. 8am-6pm, Sat. 10:30am-2:30pm.

SIGHTS

Tram 3T offers the city's cheapest tour (pick up a free itinerary on board). Better yet, just walk—most sights are packed within 2km of the train station and the city has few hills. The tourist office stocks the booklet *See Helsinki on Foot.*

The famed architect Alvar Aalto once said of Finland, "Architecture is our form of expression because our language is so impossible," and the bold 20th-century creations amid slick Neoclassical works that suffuse the region prove him right. Much of the layout and architecture of the old center, however, is the brainchild of a German, Carl Engel. After Helsinki became the capital of the Grand Duchy of Finland in 1812, Engel was chosen to design an appropriate city. In **Senaatintori** (Senate Sq.), on the corner of Unioninkatu and Aleksanterinkatu, his work is well represented by the **Tuomiokirkko** (Dome Church). After marveling at the Neoclassical exterior, though, you may be disappointed by the austere interior of the Lutheran cathedral, completed in 1852. (Open June-Aug. 9am-6pm, Sun. noon-4pm; Sept.-May Sun.-Fri. 10am-4pm, Sat. 10am-6pm.) A few blocks to the east, on Katajanokka island, the spectacular Byzantine-Slavonic **Uspensky Katedraali** (Orthodox Cathedral) guards the island with its red spikes. (Ornate interior open May-Sept. 30 Mon. and Wed.-Fri. 9:30am-4pm, Tues. 9:30am-6pm, Sat. 9am-4pm, Sun. noon-3pm. Oct.-April irregular hours.) The cosmopolitan **Esplanadi,** behind the cathedral, offers a wonderful, crowded melange of cafes and street entertainment.

Across from the train station sprawls Finland's largest art museum, the **Art Museum of the Ateneum,** Kaivokatu 2, with Finnish and foreign art from the 1700s to the 1960s. (Open Tues. and Fri. 9am-6pm, Wed.-Thurs. 9am-8pm, Sat.-Sun. 11am-5pm. 10mk, students 5mk; special exhibits 25mk.) The **Kansallismuseo** (National Museum), 500m northwest of the train station at Mannerheimintie 34, displays intriguing bits of Finnish culture, from Gypsy and Sami costumes to *ryijyt* (rugs), along with a splendid history exhibit. (Open June-Aug. Tues. 11am-8pm, Wed.-Sun. 11am-5pm; Sept.-May Tues. 11am-8pm, Wed.-Sun. 11am-4pm. 15mk, students 5mk.) The intriguing **Temppeliaukion Kirkko** (Church In the Rock), designed in the late 60s by Tuomo and Timo Suomalainen, is built into a hill, with only the roof visible from the outside. From the train station, head west on Arkadiankatu and then right on Fredrikinkatu to the square where the church is buried (open Mon.-Fri. 10am-8pm, Sat. 10am-6pm, Sun. between services). The striking **Jean Sibelius Monument,** 750m north of the church in Sibelius Park, on Mechelininkatu, was dedicated to one of the 20th century's greatest composers by sculptor Eila Hiltunen. The monument looks like a cloud of organ pipes blasting into outer space. About one mile north of the city center looms the **Olympiastadion,** the main arena for the 1952 Helsinki Olympics. The stadium was ready to welcome athletes in 1940, but had to wait after World War II canceled the games that year. The stadium tower offers a great view of the city (open Mon.-Fri. 9am-8pm, Sat.-Sun 9am-6pm; 10mk). Outside, check out the nude statue of athlete Paavo Nurmi, "The Flying Finn." Although the Finns have no qualms about baring all in the sauna, the statue stirred considerable controversy when it was unveiled. Check out the cacti and palms at the **City Wintergarten,** Hammarskjöldin-tie 1 (open Mon.-Sat. noon-3pm, Sun noon-4pm, free), or follow the sea gulls to **Mar-**

ket Square and **Old Market Hall** at the north end of Esplanadi, where fresh fish and souvenirs are sold daily.

Surrounding islands provide a welcome relief from the fast pace of Helsinki's center. Ferries leave hourly from Market Square (round-trip 20mk) for the now-demilitarized fortress island of **Suomenlinna,** built by the Swedes in the 18th century on five interconnected islands to repel attacks on Helsinki. If museumed-out, relax on the rocky **beach** or head to **Seurasaari,** linked to the mainland by a walkway, for a picnic, swim, or saunter. To reach Seurasaari, take bus 24 from Erottaja, outside the Swedish Theater, to the last stop. There's also summer boat service from Market Square.

ENTERTAINMENT

Much of Helsinki nods off early, but only because the days are so packed. Sway to afternoon street music in the leafy **Esplanadi** or party on warm nights at **Hietaniemi beach.** Consult *Helsinki This Week* for current happenings and *City,* printed in English in summer, for popular cafes, bars, and nightclubs; both are free. Starting in the last week in August, the two-week **Helsinki Festival** brings together a melange of arts events, from ballet to theater to rock concerts.

Manala (Hell), Dagmarinkatu 2, just behind the Parliament building. Live bands, celebrity acts, and a maze-like, mysterious environment draw an international crowd. Rock, disco, and tango. Cover varies. Open daily until 4am.
Old Students' House, Mannerheimintie 3. 19th-century establishment with pubs, dancing, restaurant, and sociable students. Beer 15-20mk. Cover 20-50mk for live bands. Open Mon.-Thurs. 11am-1am, Fri.-Sat. 11am-2am.
Nylon, Kaivokatu 10. Trendy club with women in platform shoes and men up to date on the fashion mags. Open Tues.-Thurs. 11pm-4am, Fri.-Sat. 10pm-4am.
Storyville, Museokatu 8, near the National Museum. Helsinki's choice jazz club. Live music nightly. Cover varies. Open Mon.-Sat. 8pm-4am, Sun. 8pm-2am.
Don't Tell Mama, Annankatu 32. Hopping gay dance club with disco, techno, and rock. Open Tues.-Sun 11pm-4am.

Vienna (Wien), Austria

US$1 = 13.14AS (schilling, or ATS)	10AS = US$0.76
CDN$1= 9.58AS	10AS = CDN$1.04
UK£1 = 21.38AS	10AS = UK£0.47
IR£ = 19.13AS	10AS = IR£0.52
AUS$1 = 9.79AS	10AS = AUS$1.02
NZ$1 = 8.53AS	10AS = NZ$1.17
SAR1 = 2.86AS	10AS = SAR3.50
Country Phone Code: 43	**International Dialing Prefix: 900**

Smoke lingering in brooding coffeehouses, bronze palace roofs faded gentle green, the hush that awaits the conductor's baton—serene and softly aged Vienna is grand in a way that cradles rather than confronts. The center of the Habsburg empire and a prime mover in annals of European history, Vienna treats dreamers to a collector's bin of imperial tastes and proportions. Yet as buildings rose and coffeehouse klatchers scribbled, Vienna's *fin de siècle* veneer provided a fine gloss for the slow boil of Zionism, Nazism, and the Viennese schizophrenia that kept Freud's waiting room full. The memory of WWII's atrocities still lurks in the collective conscience of Vienna, yet the shades of Haydn and Mozart seem still to keep watch over the city's busy streets.

ORIENTATION AND PRACTICAL INFORMATION

Vienna is in eastern Austria, 40km from the Hungarian, Czech, and Slovak borders. The city is divided into 23 **districts** (*Bezirke*), with the old **Innere Stadt** (inner city) occupying the first district. From this center, the city spreads out in a series of concentric rings. The first ring, which surrounds the Innere Stadt, is the **Ringstraße,** known simply as the Ring. Many of Vienna's attractions are located in this area, including several museums and the **Rathaus.** Along the southern section of the Ring, the intersection of **Opernring, Kärntner Ring,** and **Kärntner Straße** forms the epicenter of the city; the Opera House, tourist office, and the **Karlsplatz** U-Bahn stop are nearby. Roman numerals have been added to most of the addresses listed below to indicate the district in which particular establishments are located.

Vienna is a metropolis with **crime** like any other; use common sense, especially after dark. Be extra careful in the beautiful Karlsplatz, home to many pushers and junkies, and avoid areas in the 5th, 10th, and 14th districts, as well as Landstr.-Hauptstr. Beware of pickpockets in the parks and on **Kärntner Straße,** where the hordes of tourists make tempting targets. Vienna's skin trade operates in some sections of the Gürtel; **Prater Park** is also questionable at night.

> The Austrian telephone network is becoming digitized, and phone numbers may change without notice after this book goes to press.

Tourist Offices: I, Kärntnerstr. 38 (tel. 58 86 60), behind the Opera House. Free **maps** and brochures; *Youth Scene* provides vital info for travelers of all ages. The office also books rooms (300-400AS) for a 40AS fee and the first night's deposit. Open daily 8am-5pm. **Branch offices** at Westbahnhof (open daily 6:15am-11pm), Südbahnhof (open May-Oct. daily 6:30am-9pm), and the airport (open June-Sept. 8:30am-9pm). **Jugend-Info Wien** (Vienna Youth Information Service), Bellaria-Passage (tel. 17 99; email jugendinfo.vie@blackbox.ping.at), in the underground passage at the Bellaria intersection. Enter at the "Dr.-Karl-Renner-Ring/Bellaria" tram stop (lines 1, 2, 46, 49, D, and J) or the Volkstheater U-Bahn. The hip and knowledgeable staff has an accommodations list, cheap tickets, and *Jugend in Wien.* Open Mon.-Fri. noon-7pm, Sat. 10am-7pm.

Budget Travel: Österreichisches Verkehrsbüro (Austrian National Travel Office), I, Operngasse 3-5 (tel. 588 62 38), opposite the Opera House. Sells BIJ tickets and the *Thomas Cook Timetable* (270AS). Open Mon.-Fri. 9am-6pm, Sat. 9am-noon.

Embassies and Consulates: Australia, IV, Mattiellistr. 2-4 (tel. 512 85 80), behind the Karlskirche. Open Mon.-Thurs. 8:30am-1pm and 2-5:30pm, Fri. 8:30am-1:15pm. **Canada,** I, Laurenzerburg 2, 3rd fl. (tel. 531 38, ext. 3000). Open Mon.-Fri. 8:30am-12:30pm and 1:30-3:30pm. **Ireland,** III, Hilton Center, 16th fl., Landstraßer Hauptstr. 2 (tel. 715 42 47; fax 713 60 04). **New Zealand,** XIX, Springsiedlegasse 28 (tel. 318 85 05; fax 37 76 60). **South Africa,** XIX, Sandgasse 33 (tel. 32 46 93). **U.K.,** III, Jauresgasse 10 (tel. 716 13 53 38). Open Mon.-Fri. 9:15am-noon and 2-4pm. **U.S.,** IX, Boltzmangasse 16 (tel. 313 39), off Währingerstr. Open Mon.-Fri. 8:30am-5pm.

Currency Exchange: Most **banks** are open Mon.-Wed. and Fri. 8am-3pm, Thurs. 8am-5:30pm, with a break from 12:30-1:30pm. Bank and airport exchanges have the same official exchange rates; expect a min. 50AS commission for traveler's checks, 10AS for cash. Longer hours and smaller commissions are available at the **train stations.** The 24hr. exchange at the **main post office** has excellent rates.

American Express: I, Kärntnerstr. 21-23, P.O. Box 28, A-1015 (tel. 515 40), down from Stephansplatz. Cashes AmEx (commission free) and Thomas Cook (3% commission) checks. Holds mail for 4 weeks for members only. Open Mon.-Fri. 9am-5:30pm, Sat. 9am-noon.

Trains: 24hr. info tel. 17 17 (http://www.bahn.at). 3 main stations in the city. The **Westbahnhof,** XV, Mariahilferstr. 132, serves Salzburg (3hr., 396AS); Innsbruck (6hr., 690AS); Budapest (3-4hr., 348AS); and major Western cities, including Amsterdam, Paris, and Munich. To reach the city center, take U-3 (dir. "Erdberg") to "Volkstheater" or "Stephansplatz." The **Südbahnhof,** X, Wiedner Gürtel 1a,

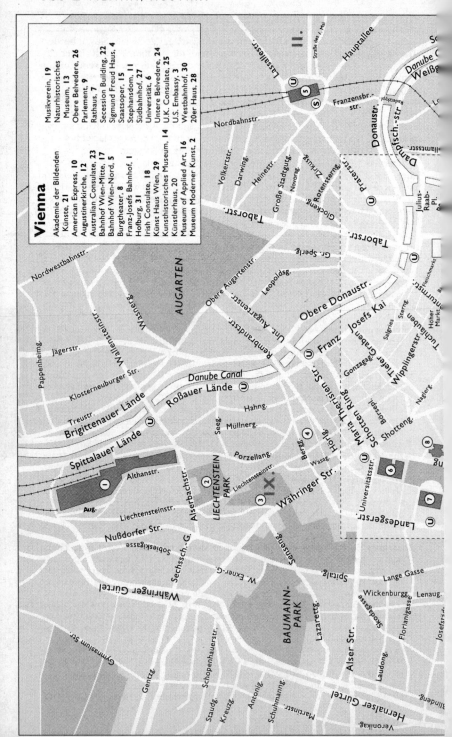

Vienna

Akademie der Bildenden
  Künste, 21
American Express, 10
Augustinerkirche, 12
Australian Consulate, 23
Bahnhof Wien-Mitte, 17
Bahnhof Wien-Nord, 5
Burgtheater, 8
Franz-Josefs Bahnhof, 1
Hofburg, 31
Irish Consulate, 18
Kunst Haus Wien, 29
Kunsthistorisches Museum, 14
Künstlerhaus, 20
Museum of Applied Art, 16
Museum Moderner Kunst, 2

Musikverein, 19
Naturhistorisches
  Museum, 13
Obere Belvedere, 26
Parlement, 9
Rathaus, 7
Secession Building, 22
Sigmund Freud Haus, 4
Staatsoper, 15
Stephansdom, 11
Südbahnhof, 27
Universität, 6
Untere Belvedere, 24
U.K. Consulate, 25
U.S. Embassy, 3
Westbahnhof, 30
20er Haus, 28

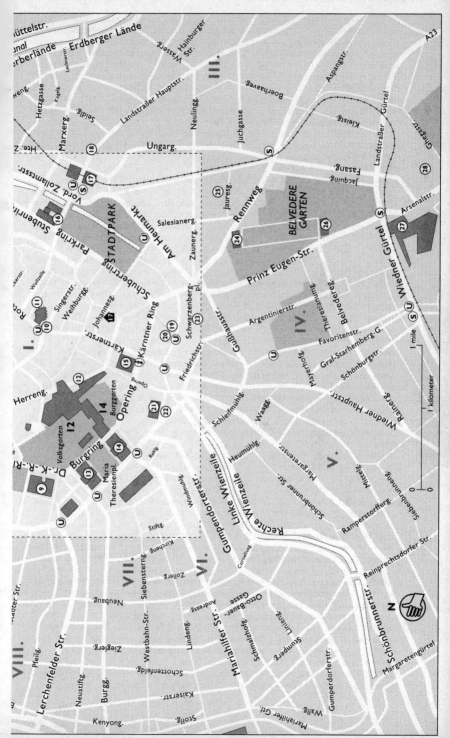

sends trains to Prague (5½hr., 468AS); Rome (14hr., 987AS); and Venice (7½hr., 660AS). If you arrive at this station, take tram D (dir. "Nußdorf") from the right side of the station or S-Bahn 1, 2, 3, or 15 to "Südtirolerplatz," where you can switch to U-Bahn. The **Franz-Josefs Bahnhof,** IX, Althamstr. 10, handles commuter trains but also serves Berlin (12hr., 1002AS). There are 2 smaller stations: **Bahnhof Wien Mitte,** in the center of town, serves commuter trains and the shuttle to the airport; **Bahnhof Wien-Nord,** by the Prater on the north side of the Danube Canal, is one of the main S-Bahn and U-Bahn links for trains heading north.

Buses: Info tel. 711 01; open daily 7am-7pm. Catch buses at the **City Bus Terminals** at Wien-Mitte/Landstraße, Hüttelsdorf, Heiligenstadt, Floridsdorf, Kagran, Erdberg, or Reumannplatz. Domestic **BundesBuses** run from these stations to local and international destinations. Ticket counters open Mon.-Fri. 6am-5:50pm, Sat.-Sun. 6am-3:50pm. International private lines have travel agencies in the stations as well. Bus travel is seldom cheaper than train travel.

Public Transportation: Excellent **U-Bahn** (subway), **bus,** and **S-bahn** (tram) systems cover the city. Single fare is 20AS (17AS if purchased in advance at a ticket office or tobacco shop); a 24hr. pass costs 50AS, a 72hr. pass 130AS. All passes allow unlimited travel, except on night buses. To validate a ticket, punch it immediately upon entering the bus, tram, etc. in the orange machine, or risk a 500AS fine. Tickets can be purchased from *Tabak* kiosks or *Automaten* in major U-Bahn stations. Trams and subways close from 12:30-5:30am, but **night buses** run on reduced routes (25AS, passes not valid). Night bus stops are designated by "N" signs. Streetcar lines and U-Bahn stops are listed on a free city map, available at the tourist office; ticket counters sell comprehensive maps for 15AS. The public transportation **information** number (tel. 587 31 86) will give you directions to any point in the city. Open Mon.-Fri. 6:30am-6:30pm, Sat.-Sun. 8:30am-4pm.

Ferries: Cruise with **DDSG Donaureisen** (tel. 523 80) to Budapest for 750AS, round-trip 1100AS (daily April 8-Oct. 29). Buy tickets at tourist offices. Boats dock at the *Reichsbrücke* on the New Danube; take U-1 to "Vorgartenstr."

Taxis: tel. 313 00, 401 00, 601 60, 814 00, or 910 11. Stands at Westbahnhof, Südbahnhof, and Karlspl. in the city center. Accredited taxis have yellow and black signs on the roof. Basic rate generally 27AS, plus a charge per km. 16AS surcharge for taxis called by radiophone; 10AS surcharge nights (11pm-6am), Sun., and holidays. 12AS surcharge for luggage over 20kg, 24AS for over 50kg.

Luggage Storage: Lockers (40AS per 24hr.) at all train stations. Adequate for sizable backpacks. **Luggage watch** 30AS. Open daily 4am-1:15am.

Bookstores: Shakespeare & Company, I, Sterngasse 2 (tel. 535 50 53; fax 535 50 53 16; email bookseller@shakespeare.co.at). Eclectic and intelligent. Great English magazine selection. Open Mon.-Fri. 9am-7pm, Sat. 9am-5pm.

Bisexual, Gay, and Lesbian Organizations: Rosa Lila Villa, VI, Linke Wienzeile 102 (tel. 586 81 50), is a favored resource. Friendly staff provides counseling, information, a lending library, and nightclub listings. Open Mon.-Fri. 5-8pm.

Laundromat: Schnell und Sauber, VII, Westbahnhofstr. 60; U-6 to "Burggasse Stadthalle." Wash 60AS for 6kg. Detergent included. Spin-dry 10AS. Open 24hr. Many hostels offer laundry facilities (50-70AS).

Crisis Hotlines: Rape Crisis, tel. 523 22 22. Open Mon. 10am-6pm, Tues. 2-6pm, Wed. 10am-2pm, Thurs. 5-11pm. 24hr. immediate help: tel. 717 19. **English-language "Befrienders" Suicide Hotline,** tel. 713 33 74. Open Mon.-Fri. 9:30am-1pm and 6:30-10pm, Sat.-Sun. 6:30-10pm.

Medical Assistance: Allgemeines Krankenhaus, IX, Währinger Gürtel 18-20 (tel. 404 00). Your embassy can provide a list of English-speaking physicians.

Emergencies: Police, tel. 133. **Ambulance,** tel. 144. **Fire,** tel. 122. Alert your consulate of any emergencies or legal problems.

Internet Access: Libro, Donauzentrum (tel. 202 52 55). Free access at its 6 terminals. **Public Netbase, VII,** Museumsquartier, Museumpl. I (tel. 522 18 34). Free surfing 2-7pm. **Jugend-Info des Bundesministeriums,** Franz-Josefs-kai 51 (tel. 533 70 30). Free access at 1 PC. Mon.-Fri. 11am-6pm.

Post Offices: Hauptpostamt, I, Fleischmarkt 19. Exchange windows, telephones, faxes, and mail services. Open 24hr. Address *Poste Restante* to "Postlagernde

Briefe, Hauptpostamt, Fleischmarkt 19, A-1010 Wien." **Postal codes:** In the 1st district A-1010, in the 2nd A-1020, in the 3rd A-1030, and so on, to the 23rd A-1230. **Phone code:** 0222 from within Austria, 1 from outside the country.

ACCOMMODATIONS

One of Vienna's few unpleasant aspects is the hunt for cheap rooms during the summer season. Write or call for reservations at least five days ahead, and pick up lists of hostels and hotels from the tourist office. University dorms (actually singles and doubles) alleviate the problem slightly in July when they metamorphose into hostels.

Hostels

Myrthengasse (HI), VII, Myrthengasse 7, and **Neustiftgasse (HI),** VII, Neustiftgasse 85 (both tel. 523 63 16 or 523 94 29; fax 523 58 49). From the Westbahnhof, take U-6 (dir. "Heiligenstadt") to "Burggasse-Stadthalle," then bus 48A ("Ring") to "Neubaugasse." Walk back on Burggasse one block, and take the 1st right (15min.). From the Südbahnhof, take bus #13A (dir. "Skodagasse/Alerstr.") to "Kellermanngasse," then walk 2 blocks to your left on Neustiftgasse and turn left on Myrthengasse. The hostels, under the same management, are around the corner from each other. Comfortable, modern rooms with pine furniture and lockers. Curfew 1am. Lockout 9am-3:45pm. 160-190AS. Laundry 50AS. Reserve ahead.

Believe-It-Or-Not, VIII, Myrthengasse 10, #14 (ring bell; tel. 526 46 58), across the street from the Myrthengasse (see above). Funky and social. Kitchen, living room, and 2 bedrooms with high ceilings. Eccentric caretaker's personal crash-course on Vienna is a must. Reception open 8am until early afternoon. 160AS. Reserve ahead.

Jugendgästehaus Wien Brigittenau (HI), XX, Friedrich-Engels-Pl. 24 (tel. 332 82 940 or 330 05 98; fax 330 83 79). U-1 or U-4: "Schwedenplatz," then tram N to "Floridsdorferbrücke/Friedrich-Engels-Pl.," and follow the signs. Spacious hostel with exceptional facilities for the disabled. Reception open 24hr. Dorms 190AS with shower. Singles 160AS. Lockers and breakfast included.

Kolpingfamilie Wien-Meidling (HI), XIII, Bendlgasse 10-12 (tel. 813 54 87; fax 812 21 30). U-4 or U-6: "Niederhofstr." Head right on Niederhofstr., and take the 4th right. Well-lit and modern. Reception open daily 6am-midnight. Dorms 100-155AS. Doubles 430AS. Nonmembers add 20AS. Breakfast 45AS. Sheets 65AS.

Hostel Zöhrer, VIII, Skodagasse 26 (tel. 406 07 30; fax 408 04 09). From Westbahnhof, take U-6 (dir. "Heiligenstadt") to "Alserstr." then streetcar #43 (dir. "Schottentor") to "Skodagasse." From Südbahnhof, take bus #13A to "Alserstr./Skodag." Crowded but comfy. Kitchen. Reception open 7:30am-10pm. Check-out 9am. No curfew. Dorms with showers 170AS. 2-bed dorms 230AS. Breakfast and sheets included. Laundry 60AS. Front door/locker key deposit 100AS, with ID 50AS.

University Dormitories

The following dorms usually become summer hostels from July to September.

Porzellaneum der Wiener Universität, IX, Porzellangasse 30 (tel. 31 77 28 20). From Südbahnhof, take tram D (dir. "Nußdorf") to "Fürstengasse." From Westbahnhof, take tram #5 to "Franz-Josefs Bahnhof," then tram D: "Südbahnhof." Reception open 24hr. Singles 175AS; doubles 350AS. Sheets included. Reserve ahead.

Ruddfinum, IV, Mayerhofgasse 3 (tel. 505 53 84). U-1: "Taubstummengasse." Reception open 24hr. Singles 270AS; doubles 480AS; triples 600AS. Sheets, showers, and breakfast included.

Hotels and Pensions

F. Kaled and Tina, VII, Lindengasse 42 (tel. 523 90 13). U-3: "Ziedergasse." Follow Ziedergasse 2 blocks to Lindengasse; the hotel is on the right. Lovely private rooms. Singles 400AS, with bath 450AS; doubles 550-650AS; triples 800AS.

Hotel Quisisana, VI, Windmühlgasse 6 (tel. 587 71 55; fax 587 71 56). U-2: "Babenbergerstr." Turn right on Mariahilferstr., go 3 blocks, and bear left on Windmühlg. An old-fashioned hotel run by a charming older couple. Singles 320AS, with shower 370AS; doubles 500-600AS; triples 750AS; quads 1000AS.

Pension Hargita, VII, Andreasgasse (tel. 526 19 28). U-3: "Zieglergasse" then head down Mariahilferstr. Singles 400AS, with shower 450AS; doubles 550-800AS.

Pension Falstaff, IX, Müllnergasse 5 (tel. 317 91 27; fax 317 91 864). U-4: "Roßauer Lände." Cross Roßauer Lände and head down Grünentorgasse, taking the 3rd left onto Müllnergasse. Singles 360AS, with shower 470AS; doubles 600-820AS. Extra bed 200AS. Breakfast included.

FOOD

In an uncertain world, the Viennese take it as a given that the least you can do is face it all with a full stomach. Culinary offerings in the city reflect the patchwork empire of the Habsburgs. *Serbische Bohnensuppe* (Serbian bean soup) and *Ungärische Gulaschsuppe* (Hungarian goulash) exemplify the Eastern European influence. *Knödel,* bread dumplings found in most side dishes, originated in the former Czechoslovakia. Even the famed *Wiener Schnitzel* (fried and breaded veal cutlets) was first cooked in Milan. Vienna is perhaps most renowned for its sublime desserts and chocolates, such as *Sacher Torte, Imperial Torte,* and *Apfel Strudel;* they're unbelievably rich, but most are priced for patrons who are likewise blessed—though most residents maintain that they are worth every *Groschen.* The cafe is a centerpiece of Vienna's unhurried charm. *Konditoreien* are no less traditional, but here the focus shifts from coffee to delectable pastries.

Restaurants in the touristy **Kärntnerstraße** area are generally overpriced. A better bet is the neighborhood just north of the university where **Universitätsstraße** and **Währingerstraße** meet. The **Rathausplatz** hosts inexpensive food stands most of the year. The aromatic delicacies at the open-air **Naschmarkt** (U-4: "Kettenbrückegasse") are an especially filling option for vegetarians who travel to this carnivorous city (open Mon.-Fri. 7am-6pm, Sat. 7am-1pm). For discount **supermarket** fare, try the ubiquitous **Billa, Konsum, Hoffer,** or **Sparmarkt.** To conquer the summer heat, pick up some ice cream at **Gelateria Hoher Markt,** I, Hoher Markt, just off Rotenturmstr. (open March-Oct. daily 9am-11pm). Be aware that grocery stores and most restaurants close from Saturday afternoon to Monday morning.

Trześniewski, I, Dorotheergasse 1, 3 blocks down the Graben from the Stephansdom. A famous stand-up restaurant that has been serving petite open-faced sandwiches for over 80 years. The preferred haunt of Franz Kafka. Lots of veggie options. Open Mon.-Fri. 8:30am-7:30pm, Sat. 9am-1pm; 1st Sat. of the month 9am-6pm. **Branch** at VII, Mariahilferstr. 26-30 in the Hermansky store. Same hours.

Blue Box, VII, Richtergasse 8. U-3: "Neubaugasse." You absolutely can't come to Vienna and miss this place. Dishes are fresh, flamboyant, and above all, original. Choose from Viennese, French, English, vegetarian, you name it. Open Tues.-Thurs. 10am-2am, Fri.-Sat. 10am-4am, Sun. 10am-2am, Mon. 6pm-2am.

Levante, I, Wallnerstr. 2. Greek-Turkish restaurant features heaps of affordable dishes, including vegetarian delights. Meals 78-130AS. **Branches** at I, Wollzeile 19; Mariahilferstr. 88a; and VIII, Josefstädterstr. 14. All open daily 11am-11:30pm.

Brezelgwölb, I, Lederhof 9 (tel./fax 533 88 11). Excellent hearty cuisine even the Viennese call *"Altwiener"* (old Viennese). Rare standing pieces of the medieval city wall reside in the courtyard—the rest was torn down to build the Ringstraße. Reserve in the evening. Open daily 11:30am-1am.

Tunnel, VIII, Florianigasse 39. U-2: "Rathaus." Dark and smoky, prized for its dilapidated hipness, live music, and really affordable food. Open daily 9am-2am.

Cafe Central, I, at the corner of Herrengasse and Strauchgasse, inside Palais Ferstel. Sigmund Freud was a patron; Lenin and Trotsky played chess here, fingering imperialist miniatures with cool anticipation. Oh, the cafe serves coffee, too. Open Mon.-Sat. 9am-8pm. Live piano music 4-7pm.

Demel, I, Kohlmarkt 14. Walk 5min. from the Stephansdom down Graben. The premier Viennese *Konditorei.* The atmosphere is divine in this legendary *fin-de-siècle* cathedral of sweets. Waitresses in convent-black serve the tasty confections (35-50AS). Don't miss the *crème-du-jour.* Open daily 10am-6pm.

Hotel Sacher, I, Philharmonikerstr. 4, around the corner from the main tourist information office. This historic sight has been serving the world-famous *Sacher Torte* (50AS) in red velvet opulence for years. Open daily 7am-11:30pm.

SIGHTS

Vienna from A to Z (60AS from the tourist office, more in bookstores) gives all you need for a self-tour. The free *Museums* brochure from the tourist office lists all opening hours and admission prices. Museum tickets usually cost 20-80AS.

The Innere Stadt

If you begin your tour from the main tourist office, the first prominent building in view will be the **Staatsoper** (State Opera House). Apart from the Stephansdom, no other building is as close to the hearts of the Viennese as the Opera. The cheapest way to see the glittering gold, crystal, and red-velvet interior may be to see an opera; standing-room tickets with excellent views are only 20AS. If you can't find tickets, tours of the house cost 40AS, students 25AS (July-Aug. daily 11am-3pm on the hour; Sept.-June upon request). Alfred Hrdlicka's poignant 1988 sculpture **Monument Gegen Krieg und Faschismus** (Memorial Against War and Fascism), behind the opera on Albertinapl., commemorates the suffering of Austria's people—especially its Jews—during WWI. From Albertinapl., Tegetthoffstr. leads to the spectacular **Neuer Markt,** where a graceful fountain and 17th-century church greet visitors. Continue north from here to reach Vienna's most revered landmark, the Gothic **Stephansdom;** the cathedral's smoothly tapering **Sudturm** has become Vienna's emblem. Take a lap around the building before checking out the view from the **Nordturm** (North Tower). In the catacombs, the **vault** stores Hapsburgs' innards. (Tours of the cathedral in English Mon.-Sat. 10:30am and 3pm, Sun. 3pm. 30AS. Spectacular July-Sept. evening tour Sat. 7pm; 100AS. North Tower open April-Sept. daily 9am-6pm; Oct.-March 8am-5pm. Elevator ride 50AS. Tours of the vault Mon.-Sat. 10am-noon and 2-4:30pm, Sun. 2-5pm. 50AS.)

The **Hofburg** (Imperial Palace), rising from the southeast side of Michaelerpl., was inhabited by the Habsburg emperors until 1918; it now houses the President's office. The enormous complex also includes the **Burggarten** (Gardens of the Imperial Palace), the **Burgkapelle** (where the Vienna Boys' Choir sings Mass on Sun. and religious holidays), and the **Schauräume** (State rooms), the former private rooms of Emperor Franz Josef and Empress Elisabeth. Perhaps the grandest part of the complex is the **Neue Hofburg** (New Palace); the double-headed golden eagle crowning the roof symbolizes the double empire of Austria-Hungary. Also check out the **Nationalbibliothek** (National Library), which has outstanding papyrus scrolls and musical manuscripts. Keep walking around the Hofburg, away from the Michaeler-kirche, to wander through the Baroque **Josefsplatz,** which features an equestrian monument to Emperor Josef II and the stunning 14th-century **Augustinerkirche.** Between Josefsplatz and Michaelerplatz, the Palace Stables (*Stallburg*) are home to the famous Royal Lipizzaner stallions of the **Spanische Reitschule** (Spanish Riding School). Performances (April-June and Sept. Sun. at 10:45am and Wed. at 7pm; March and Nov. to mid-Dec. Sun. at 10:45am) are always sold out; for reservations six months in advance (do not send money), write to: Spanische Reitschule, Hofburg, A-1010 Wien (tickets 250-900AS, standing-room 200AS). Watching the horses train is much cheaper.

The Hofburg's Heldenplatz gate presides over the Burgring segment of the **Ringstraße.** In 1857, Emperor Franz Josef commissioned this 187ft. wide and 2½mi. long boulevard to replace the medieval city walls that separated Vienna's center from the suburban districts. Follow Burgring west through the **Volksgarten's** hundreds of varieties of roses to reach the Neoclassical, sculpture-adorned **Parliament** building. Just up Dr.-Karl-Renner-Ring is the **Rathaus,** an intriguing remnant of late 19th-century neo-Gothic with Victorian mansard roofs and red geraniums in the windows. There are numerous art exhibits inside, and the city holds outdoor festivals in the square outside. Opposite the Rathaus, the **Burgtheater** contains frescoes by Klimt. Immediately to the north on Dr.-Karl-Lueger-Ring is the **Universität,** and the surrounding sidestreets overflow with cafes, bookstores, and bars.

Outside the Ring

Music lovers trek out to the **Zentralfriedhof** (Central Cemetery), XI, Simmeringer Hauptstr. 234; the second gate leads to the graves of Beethoven, Strauss, and Schönberg, and an honorary monument to Mozart (open May-Aug. daily 7am-7pm; March-April and Sept.-Oct. 7am-6pm; Nov.-Feb. 8am-5pm). To reach the Zentralfriedhof, take streetcar #71 from Schwarzenbergplatz (35min.). If you need some cheering up after this experience, visit the **Hundertwasser Haus,** at the corner of Löwenstraße and Kegelgasse in the third district. A wild fantasia of pastel colors, ceramic mosaics, and oblique tile columns contributes to the eccentricity of this blunt rejection of architectural orthodoxy. Hundertwasser fans shouldn't miss **Kunst Haus Wien,** III, Untere Weißgerberstr. 13, built specifically for the artist's works. This crazily pastiched building also hosts international contemporary exhibits (open daily 10am-7pm; 90AS, students 50AS).

Another must-see is the **Schloß Schönbrunn** (U-4: "Schönbrunn") and its surrounding gardens, which comprise one of the greatest palace complexes in Europe. Tours of some of the palace's 1500 rooms reveal the elaborate taste of Maria Theresa's era. The six-year-old Mozart played in the **Hall of Mirrors** at the whim of the Empress. The **Great Gallery's** frescoes are a highlight, but the **Million Gulden Room** wins the prize for excessiveness; Indian miniatures cover the chamber's walls. In summer, many concerts and festivals take place in the palace. (Palace apartments open April-Oct. daily 8:30am-5pm; Nov.-March 8:30am-4:30pm. 100AS, tours in English 40AS.)

The **Prater,** extending southeast from the Wien-Nord Bahnhof, is a notoriously touristed amusement park that functioned as a private game reserve for the Imperial family until 1766. The park is dotted with various arcades, restaurants, and casinos. Rides range from garish thrill machines to the stately 65m **Riesenrad** (Giant Ferris Wheel), which offers one of the best views of Vienna. (Open Feb.-Oct. daily 10am-10pm, sometimes until midnight; Nov. 10am-8pm. Entrance to the complex is free, but each attraction charges admission.) Beloved by children during the day, the Prater becomes less wholesome and more dangerous after sunset.

Museums

On the Burgring in what used to be the *Neue Hofburg* is the famous **Kunsthistorisches Museum.** The building is home to one of the world's best art collections, including a number of Brueghels, Vermeer's *Allegory of Painting,* and numerous works by Rembrandt, Rubens, Titian, Dürer, and Velázquez. Cellini's famous golden salt cellar is here, along with a superb collection of ancient art and a transplanted Egyptian burial chamber. Gustav Klimt decorated the lobby (open Tues.-Wed. and Fri.-Sun. 10am-6pm, Thurs. 10am-9pm; 100AS, students 50AS). Across the way sits the **Naturhistorisches Museum,** identical in appearance but less interesting in content. Fans of Klimt and fellow radicals Schiele and Kokoschka should visit the **Austrian Gallery** in the **Belvedere Palace,** entrance at Prinz-Eugenstr. 27. The Lower Belvedere houses the Baroque Museum and the Museum of Medieval Austrian Art (both museums open Tues.-Sun. 10am-5pm; 60AS, students 30AS).

The greatest monument of *fin-de-siècle* Vienna is the **Secession Building,** I, Friedrichstr. 12, built by Wagner's pupil Josef Maria Olbrich to accommodate the artists—led by Klimt—who scorned traditional styles and broke with the uptight Viennese art establishment. Olbrich designed this extraordinary ivory-and-gold edifice as a reaction against the overblown Neoclassicism of the Ring museums (open Tues.-Fri. 10am-6pm, Sat.-Sun. 10am-4pm; 30AS, students 15AS). The **Künstlerhaus,** from which the Secession seceded, is to the east at Karlspl. 5 (open Mon.-Wed. and Fri.-Sun. 10am-6pm, Thurs. 10am-9pm; 90AS, students 40AS).

ENTERTAINMENT

Music and Theater

You can enjoy Viennese opera in the imperial splendor of the **Staatsoper** for a mere 20-50AS. Get in line on the west side about three hours before curtain for standing room (*Stehplätze*) tickets, sold only on the day of performance. Get tickets for the center to enjoy the best views, and bring a scarf to tie on the rail to save your place during the show. Costlier advance tickets (100-850AS) are on sale at the **Bundestheaterkasse**, I, Hanuschgasse 3 (tel. 514 44 22 60), next to the opera along the Burggarten (open Mon.-Fri. 8am-6pm, Sun. 9am-noon). Get there between 6 and 7am opening day for a good seat.

Vienna, the most musical of cities, quiets somewhat in summer; the Staatsoper, the Philharmonic, and the **Wiener Sängerknaben** (Vienna Boys' Choir) vacation during July and August. During the rest of the year, the pre-pubescent prodigies sing mass each Sunday at the **Burgkapelle** (Royal Chapel) of the Hofburg. The **Wiener Philharmoniker** (Vienna Philharmonic Orchestra) is also world-renowned, performing in the **Musikverein**, I, Dumbastr. 3 (tel. 505 81 90), on the northeast side of Karlspl.

Vienna is almost as famous for its *Heurigen* (wine gardens with outside seating at picnic tables) as for its art and music. The worn picnic benches and old shade trees provide an ideal spot to contemplate, converse, or listen to *Schrammelmusik* (sentimental folk songs played by aged musicians). **Grinzing** is the largest *Heurigen* area, but atmosphere and prices are better in **Sievering, Neustift am Wald, Stammersdorf,** and **Neuwaldegg.** Hidden from tourists and therefore beloved by locals, **Buschenschank Heinrich Niersche,** XIX, Strehlgasse 21, overlooks the field of Grinzing. To reach it, take U-Bahn 1 to "Währingerstraße/Volksoper," then bus 41A to "Pötzleindorfer Höhe." Walk uphill one block, and make a right on Strehlgasse (open Wed.-Mon. 3pm-midnight).

The city parties until dawn, though public transportation stops around midnight. Pick up a copy of *Falter* (28AS) for the best entertainment listings. Revelers tend to lose themselves in the infamous **Bermuda Dreieck** (Triangle), a collection of a dozen or so bars down Rotenturmstr., away from the Stephansdom. Other locals congregate in the cool, ancient grottos of the **Bäckerstraße** area behind the Stephansdom, or in the eighth district behind the university.

Benjamin, I, Salzgries 11-13, just outside the Triangle. Go down the steps from Ruprecht's church, left onto Josefs Kai, and left on Salzgries. Persian rugs, velvet lounge, soul grooves, and airplane seats. *Budvar* 37AS, *Kapsreiter* 43AS. Open Sun.-Thurs. 7pm-2am, Fri.-Sat. 7pm-4am.

Krah Krah, I, Rabensteig 8. From Stephanspl., head down Rotenturmstr., and continue slightly to your left on Rabensteig. 50 kinds of beer on tap. Outdoor seating until 10pm. Open Sun.-Wed. 11am-2am, Thurs.-Sat. 11am-3am.

Zwölf Apostellenkeller, I, Sonnenfelsgasse 3, behind the Stephansdom. To reach this underground tavern, walk into the archway, take a right, go down the long staircase, and discover grottoes that date back to 1561. Beer 37AS. *Viertel* of wine from 25AS. Open Aug.-June daily 4:30pm-midnight.

Esterházykeller, I, Haarhof 1, off Naglergasse. Vienna's least expensive *Weinkeller*. Try the Burgenlander *Grüner Veltliner* wine (26AS). Open in summer Mon.-Fri. 11am-11pm; off-season Mon.-Fri. 11am-11pm and Sat.-Sun. 4-11pm.

Kaktus, I, Seitenstettengasse 5, in the heart of the triangle. Packed with the bombed and the beautiful. Open Sun.-Thurs. 6pm-2am, Fri.-Sat. 6pm-4am.

U-4, XII, Schönbrunnerstr. 222 (tel. 85 83 18). U-4: "Meidling Hauptstr." 5 floors and theme nights please a varied clientele. Thurs. is "Gay Heavens Night." Cover 50-100AS. Open daily 11pm-5am.

Why Not, I, Tiefer Graben 22 (tel. 535 11 58). A gay bar/disco for women and men. Open Fri.-Sat. 11pm-6am, Sun. 9pm-2am. Women-only one Thurs. per month.

Istanbul, Turkey

US$1 = 173,000TL (Turkish Lira)	100,000TL = US$0.58
CDN$1 = 124,993TL	100,000TL = CDN$0.80
UK£1 = 279,984TL	100,000TL = UK£0.36
IR£1 = 253,949TL	100,000TL = IR£0.39
AUS$1 = 125,418TL	100,000TL = AUS$0.79
NZ$1 = 111,025TL	100,000TL = NZ$0.90
SAR1 = 36,885TL	100,000TL = SAR2.71

The only city in the world that straddles two continents, Istanbul has always been a meeting place of diverse cultures and peoples. Constantine consolidated Roman power here in the 4th century, and the following centuries brought Christian and Greek influences under the Byzantine Empire. Eventually, internal crises and unruly Crusaders weakened the western stronghold, and in 1453 Mehmet II conquered the city and established the reign of the Ottoman Empire. The magnificent legacies of these three great empires coexist today with a new set of cultures and customs. Sophisticated Euro-chic tourists cross paths with conservative, veiled Muslims on their way to prayer, and thousands of solemn mosques and ancient ruins share street space with boisterous markets and teahouses throughout the city.

ORIENTATION AND PRACTICAL INFORMATION

Waterways divide Istanbul into three sections. The **Bosphorus Strait** (Boğaziçi) splits the European (west) and Asian (east) sections. The Turks call the western, European side "Arupa" and the eastern, Asian side "Asya." The area south of the **Golden Horn,** where most of the sites of interest are located, is known as **Haliç.** Most directions in Istanbul are further specified by city precinct or district. Budget travelers converge in **Sultanahmet** and **Laleli** (Askaray), the area around the Aya Sophia mosque, south of and up the hill from Sirkeci. The main boulevard—leading west from Sultanahmet towards the university, the Grand Bazaar, and Askaray—changes names from **Divan Yolu** to **Ordu Caddesi** as it nears Aksaray. Shoppers crowd the district between the **Grand Bazaar,** east of the university, and the less touristy **Egyptian Bazaar,** southeast of Eminönü. The **Kumkapı** district is south of the university and Yeniçeriler Caddesi. Stay near landmarks and use the tourist office's free map and you won't get lost.

Tourist Offices: Free country and city maps in various offices. **Sultanahmet,** 3 Divan Yolu (tel./fax 518 18 02), at the north end of the Hippodrome, across from the Sultan Pub. Open daily 9am-5pm. **Taksim,** in the Hilton Hotel Arcade (tel. 233 05 92) and near the French Consulate (tel. 245 68 76). Both open Mon.-Sat. 9am-5pm. Also in the **Karaköy Maritime Station** (tel. 249 57 76; open daily 8:30am-5pm), the **Sirkeci Train Station** (tel. 511 58 88; open daily 8:30am-5:30pm), and the **Atatürk Airport** (tel. 663 07 93; open 24hr.).
Budget Travel Offices: Gençtur, Prof. K. Ismail Gürkan Cad. Cağaloğlu, Hamamı, Sok. Kardeşler Iştlan, 4th fl. (tel. 520 52 74; fax 519 08 64), in central Sultanahmet. Sells ISICs and GO25 cards. Open Mon.-Fri. 9:30am-noon and 1-5pm, Sat. 9:30am-1pm. **Seventur Travel Shop,** 2-C Alemdar Cad. (tel. 512 41 83; fax 512 36 41). Follow the Sirkeci tram tracks past Aya Sophia. Sells ISICs and youth IDs, offers airport shuttle service, and sells reliable plane and bus tickets. Open Mon.-Fri. 9am-1pm, Sat. 9am-6pm. **Indigo Tourism and Travel Agency,** 24 Akbıyık Cad. (tel. 517 72 66; fax 518 53 33), in the heart of the cluster of hotels in Sultanahmet. Sells ISICs, GO25 cards, bus, plane, and ferry tickets. Open in summer daily 8:30am-7:30pm; off-season Mon.-Sat. 9:30am-6pm.
Consulates: All are open Mon.-Fri. **Australia,** 58 Tepecik Yolu, Etiler (tel. 257 70 50). **Canada,** 107/3 Büyükdere Cad., Gayrettepe (tel. 272 51 74; fax 272 34 27). **Ireland** (Honorary), 26-a Cumhuriyet Cad., Mobil Altı, Elmadağ (tel. 246 60 25). **New Zealand** nationals should get in touch with the embassy in Ankara, at 24/1

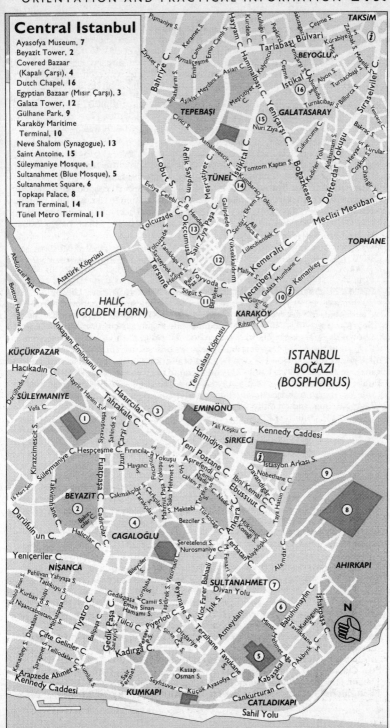

Central Istanbul

Ayasofya Museum, 7
Beyazit Tower, 2
Covered Bazaar
(Kapalı Çarşı), 4
Dutch Chapel, 16
Egyptian Bazaar (Mısır Çarşı), 3
Galata Tower, 12
Gülhane Park, 9
Karaköy Maritime
Terminal, 10
Neve Shalom (Synagogue), 13
Saint Antoine, 15
Süleymaniye Mosque, 1
Sultanahmet (Blue Mosque), 5
Sultanahmet Square, 6
Topkapı Palace, 8
Tram Terminal, 14
Tünel Metro Terminal, 11

GATEWAY CITIES

Kız Kulesi Sok. (tel. (312) 445 05 56). **South Africa,** 106 Büyükdere Cad., Esentepe (tel. 275 47 93; fax 288 25 04). **U.K.,** 34 Meşrutiyet Cad., Beyoğlu/Tepebaşı (tel. 293 75 45). **U.S.,** 104-108 Meşrutiyet Cad., Tepebaşı (tel. 251 36 02).

Currency Exchange: Banks' exchange counters are open Mon.-Fri. 8:30am-noon and 1:30-5pm. Most don't charge commission. **ATMs** are scattered across the city. **Garanti Bankası** branches are open on Sat. and during noon breaks.

American Express: Türk Express, 91 Cumhuriyet Cad., 2nd fl. (tel. 230 15 15), up the hill from Taksim Sq., handles lost checks and cards. Open Mon.-Fri. 9am-6pm. The office in the **Hilton Hotel lobby,** Cumhuriyet Cad. (tel. 241 02 48), deals with lost cards only when Türk Express is closed. Open daily 8:30am-8pm.

Flights: Atatürk Airport, 30km from the city, has a domestic and an international terminal connected by bus (every 20min. 6am-10pm). Take a Havaş bus from either terminal to the city (5:50am-10:50pm, 30min., US$2.50). The bus stops at Aksaray, where you can catch the tram to Sultanahmet, and at Şişhane.

Trains: Haydarpaşa Station (tel. (216) 336 04 75 or 336 20 63), on the Asian side. Ferries (US$0.50) run daily 6am-midnight from the station to Karaköy pier 7, on the European side. This station serves destinations in Turkey. Europe-bound trains leave from **Sirkeci Station** (tel. 527 00 50), in Eminönü. To: Sofia (US$31), Athens (US$62.50), and Munich (US$212).

Buses: Intercity buses leave from the **Esenler Otobüs Terminalı** (*otogar*). To get there from Sultanahmet, take the tram 6 stops to **Yusufpaşa,** then walk to the **Aksaray Metro station** on Adnan Menderes Blvd. Take the Metro to *otogar* (15min., US$0.35), where dozens of bus companies have offices. **Varan Tours** (tel. 658 02 77; fax 658 02 80) operates throughout Western Europe; **Ulusoy** (tel. 658 30 00; fax 658 30 10) serves Greece as well as domestic destinations; **Kamil Koç** (tel. 658 20 00; fax 658 20 08), **Pamukkale** (tel./fax 658 22 22), and **Çanakkale Seyahat** (tel. 658 36 40) are also recommended. Unlicensed companies have been known to offer discounts to Western countries and then abandon passengers in Eastern Europe—be very cautious. Frequent buses leave for Ankara (6hr., US$12-15); Izmir (9hr., US$14-17); and Bodrum (13hr., US$21.25). European destinations include Athens (16hr., US$24-27) and Vienna (1 per week, 36hr., US$95).

Public Transportation: AKBİL, or the Akıllı Bilet, are new electronic tickets for metros, trams, seabuses, public buses, and double-decker buses. Deposit an initial US$3.50, then add credit to your AKBİL from any of the IETT bus booths with the sign "AKBİL satılır." AKBİL ticket prices are usually 30-50% cheaper than cash fares.

Ferries: Turkish Maritime Lines, the blue-awninged "*Denizcilik İşletmeleri*" building, is near Pier 7 at Karaköy, just west of Haydarpaşa ferry terminal. Combination ticket to Izmir (US$10-25): sails to Bandırma, then takes the train (3 per week). For **local ferries,** head to the Sirkeci area, around the Galata Bridge. Pier 1 serves Üsküdar (6:30am-11pm), Pier 2 serves Kadıköy (7:30am-9pm, US$0.50), and Pier 3 sends cruises along the Bosphorus (round-trip US$4) and to the Princes Isles. Pier 4 serves Kadıköy (8am-7:25pm, US$0.60); Pier 5 Adalar; Pier 6 Bağlat (past the Galata Bridge). Pier 7, in Kadıköy across the Galata Bridge, serves the Haydarpaşa railway station (6am-midnight, US$0.50). Timetables are posted at each terminal.

Taxis: Make sure the meter is on, and don't pay more than it says. One light on the meter indicates the day rate; two lights the night rate (50% higher; midnight-8am). Steer away from taxis at the airport or from drivers who approach you in Sultanahmet. If you don't speak Turkish, have your destination written down.

English Bookstores: Aypa Bookstore, 19 Mimar Mehmet Ağa Cad., Sultanahmet (tel. 517 44 92), behind the Blue Mosque. Open daily 6:30am-8pm. **International Press Büffe,** 91 İstiklâl Cad., has international magazines and newspapers.

Laundromats: Star Laundry, 18 Akbıyık Cad. (tel. 638 23 02), below Star Pension. Wash and dry US$1.25 per kg, minimum 2kg. Open daily 8am-10pm.

Emergencies: Tourist Police (tel. 527 45 03 or 528 53 69; fax 512 76 76), in Sultanahmet at the beginning of Yerebatan Cad., behind the obelisk in the park across from the tourist office. Open 24hr. In **emergencies** call 155.

Post Office (PTT): Main branch at 25 Büyük Postane Sok. Better for those in Sultanahmet is the booth opposite the Aya Sophia entrance. Open daily 8:30am-7pm.

Phone Code: 212 (European side) or 216 (Asian side).

ACCOMMODATIONS AND CAMPING

Istanbul's budget rooms (and all *Let's Go* listings) concentrate in the safe, central **Sultanahmet** district. Hotels around **Sirkeci** railway station are in the US$5-10 range. **Aksaray** offers hotels in every price range. Hotels in **Laleli,** the city's center of prostitution, should be avoided. Rates rise about 20% in July and August.

Yücelt Hostel (HI), 6/1 Caferiye Cad. (tel. 513 61 50; fax 512 76 28). From the Sultanahmet tram stop, follow the tracks downhill toward Sirkeci; Aya Sophia is the red-tinted mosque on your right, and the hostel is in the alley to the left as you face the mosque's gate. Free storage and showers. Doubles US$8-11 per person. Dorms US$4-9. 10% *Let's Go* discount. Laundry US$1.25 per kg. Reserve 2 weeks ahead.

Orient Youth Hostel, 13 Akbıyık Cad. (tel. 517 94 93; fax 518 38 94), near Topkapı Palace. A/C, cable TV. Bring own toilet paper and towel. Luggage room, safe, and a travel agency. Doubles US$5.50 per person; quads US$5. Dorms US$4.50.

Sultan Turist Otel, 3 Terbıyık Sok. (tel. 516 92 60; fax 517 16 26). Around the corner from the Orient Hostel. Immaculate and professional. Roof restaurant/bar. Safe-deposit and laundry services. In-house travel office and international phone services. Singles US$16.50; doubles US$20; triples US$25. Dorms US$6.90.

Hotel Anadolu, Yerebatan Cad. 3 Salkım Söğüt Sok. (tel. 512 10 35; fax 527 76 95). From the Sultanahmet tram, walk 50m down to Sirkeci along the tram tracks; take a left at the major intersection (Yerebatan Cad.), then the first right. Rudimentary, well-kept rooms. US$12 per person. Roof beds US$7.

Bahaus Guesthouse, Akbıyık Cad. Bayram Fırını Sok. #11 (tel./fax 517 66 97). Comfortable. View of the Bosphorus. Singles US$15; doubles US$25-30; triples US$35-40. Basement US$5. 10% *Let's Go* discount.

Hotel Pamphylia, Yerebatan Cad. 47 (tel. 526 89 35 or 513 95 48; fax 513 95 49). Immaculate rooms, some with balcony and TV. Terrace with a great view. Safe deposit. Singles US$25; doubles US$35; triples US$50. Rates US$5 less off season.

Hanedan Hotel, Akbıyık Cad., 3 Adliye Sok. (tel. 516 48 69; fax 517 45 24). Pleasant view from terrace. Beautiful cafeteria. Currency exchange. 24hr. airport transport. 24hr. hot water. Doubles US$20-$26. Breakfast included.

FOOD

If you like to eat, you'll love Istanbul. The **Kumkapı** district, south of the Grand Bazaar, is famous for its seafood, and **Beyoğlu** boasts a wide variety of establishments around İstiklâl Cad. To get to İstiklâl Cad. from Sultanahmet, follow the tram lines to Sirkeci, take a left, and follow the water, crossing the Galata Bridge and taking a left onto the first major street; the Tünel, which goes to İstiklâl Cad., will be on the right. **Cengelköy** is known for its fish restaurants; **Kanlıca** is reputed to have the most delicious yogurt in Istanbul. Two **open-air markets** are centrally located: one next to Çiçek Pasajı, in Beyoğlu, and a fruit market next to the **Mısır Çarşısı** (Egyptian Spice Bazaar). **Mısır Çarşısı** itself sells an astonishing and mouth-watering collection of oriental sweets. Stop at a *büfe* (snack shop) for *tost* and a soft drink, both less than US$1.

Türkistan Aşevi, 36 Tavukhane Sok. A feast for the eyes and taste buds. 7-course lunch US$14. 8-course dinner US$17. No alcohol served.

Dârüzziyâfe, 6 Şifahane Cad., in the Süleymaniye Mosque. Main courses US$4.50-6. Mellow atmosphere. *Sülemaniye Çorbası* is a must (meat and veggie soup, US$1.75). Live Ottoman music Sat. nights. No alcohol. Open noon-11pm.

Pudding Shop, 6 Divan Yolu. A major pitstop on the Hippie Trail to the Far and Middle East in the 1970s. Self-serve. Meat dishes US$2-2.50. Veggie dishes US$1.50. Super dessert stop. The cappuccino rocks at only US$0.65.

Cennet, 90 Divan Yolu, on the right as you walk along Divan Yolu from Sultanahmet towards Aksaray, 3min. from the Sultanahmet tram. A full meal is US$3-6. Specializes in Anatolian pancakes (*gözeme*). Open daily 10am-midnight.

House of Medusa Restaurant, Yerebatan Cad. 19 Muhteremefendi Sok., on a cross street off Divan Yolu. This internationally renowned eatery is a must-see. Excellent Turkish cuisine in the 1st floor garden (open in summer), 3rd floor divan area, and

4th floor bar. Delicious *piliç* (chicken stuffed with vegetables) US$3.75. Veggie specialties US$2.75-4.25. Tasty pudding US$1.75. All are best capped with the delicious Turkish coffee. Open daily 8am-midnight.

Şampiyon, Balık Pazarı. Famous all around Turkey; believed to prepare the best *kokoreç* in the country. Lamb innards are grilled, then cooked with spices and tomatoes. Try the smallest portion, *çeyrek ekmek kokoreç* (US$1.50).

Cumhuriyet Meyhanesi, at the far end of the fruit market. Turkey's top poets, artists, and journalists gather here in the evenings. Serves delectable items such as eggplant salad (US$2.25). Open daily 10am-1am, possibly later.

Ağa Lokanta Restaurant, 7 Sakızağacı Cad., Beyoğlu. A traditional Turkish restaurant. Okra and spinach US$1.75. *Sebze graten* US$2. *Karışık komposto* dessert US$1. Great for vegetarians.

SIGHTS

Istanbul's incomparable array of attractions could keep an ardent sightseer busy for weeks; try to allow at least a few days to hit the highlights listed here. A FIYTO card grants free entry to many museums. An ISIC is generally good for half price.

Built in 537 by Emperor Justinian, **Aya Sophia** (Haghia Sophia) has served both as a cathedral and a mosque, but now functions as a museum featuring wall mosaics of Christ and the Virgin Mary. (Museum open Tues.-Sun. 9:30am-4:30pm. Mosaic gallery open Tues.-Sun. 9:30am-11:30 and 1-4pm. US$3.30, students US$1.30.) Sultan Ahmet I built the **Blue Mosque** (*Sultanahmet Camii*), opposite Aya Sophia, in an attempt to one-up Justinian. The mosque's formidable silhouette is unforgettable, and the interior, with its blue Iznik tiles, is stunning. You may visit the mosque outside of the five daily prayer times; modest dress is required. Across the street to the right from Aya Sophia is the **Yerebatan Cistern,** a vast underground cavern whose shallow water eerily reflects the 336 columns that support the structure (open daily 9am-5pm; US$1.65). To the northwest is the **Hippodrome,** where Byzantine emperors presided over chariot races and put down uprisings. Across from the Hippodrome, the 16th-century **İbrahim Paşa Palace** houses a museum of Turkish and Islamic art (open Tues.-Sun. 10am-5pm).

From the mid-15th century until the mid-19th century, the **Topkapı Sarayı** (Topkapı Palace) was the nerve center of the Ottoman Empire. This magnificent maze of buildings was originally the site of the Ottoman government and the home of the Sultan. Don't miss the **Second Court** and its huge East Asian porcelain collection, or the **Treasury,** with an inestimable wealth of diamonds, emeralds, gold, and jade. Nearby, the **Pavilion of Holy Relics** contains remnants of the prophet Muhammad: his footprint, a lock of hair, a tooth, his original seal, and a letter written in his hand. You can also take a tour of the **Harem** (every 30min., US$2.50) and view beautiful blue-green tiles in the ominous-sounding **Circumcision Chamber** (palace grounds open daily 9:30am-5pm; US$3.30, students US$1.30).

A museum complex is located through a gate marked "Archaeological Museum," downhill from the Topkapı Palace. The **Çinili Köşk** (Tiled Pavilion), once a petite pleasure retreat attached to the palace, now houses the **Tile Museum.** Replete with yellows, blues, and greens, the building's own tiles constitute one of Turkey's best examples of the Tabrizi Persian style (open May-Sept. Tues.-Thurs. and Sat.-Sun. 9am-4pm; US$1.35). The **Museum of the Ancient Orient** has Hittite, Babylonian, Sumerian, Assyrian, and Egyptian artifacts including tablets of the Hammurabi Code and a peace treaty signed by Egyptian Pharoh Ramses II (open daily May-Sept. 9am-4pm; US$1.35). The **Archaeological Museum** displays a prize-winning collection of early Greek, Hellenistic, and Roman marbles and bronzes, including a famous sarcophagus with carvings of Alexander the Great (open May-Sept. daily 9am-4pm; US$1.35).

To get to the vast, ornate, and chaotic **Kapalı Çarşı** (Grand Bazaar) from Sultanahmet, follow the tram tracks toward Askaray until you see the mosque on your right. Enter the mosque's side gate, and walk, with the park to your left, to the bazaar entrance. You'll get lost, but just enjoy it. Beware, though, that hawkers prey on tourists and that prices skyrocket in the summer. Few Turks are naïve enough to buy anything here—follow their example and just enjoy the spectacle (open Mon.-Sat. 9am-7pm). At the opposite entrance to the bazaar is the **Sahaflar Çarşısı** (used book market) which sells a wide selection of books along with Kur'anic inscriptions, artwork, and university texts. The market opens onto a bustling square. Opposite stands the huge gate of **İstanbul University,** where peaceful respites are interrupted only by the frequent appearance of riot police, often on Fridays after prayer. The campus contains **Beyazıt Camii,** the oldest mosque in Istanbul. Just north of the university is the **Süleymaniye** mosque complex. Together with the **Şehzade Mehmet** (a few blocks southwest) and the **Selimiye** (in the city of Edirne), the Süleymaniye (completed 1557) is one of the three masterpieces of Sinan, who almost single-handedly codified Ottoman Classical architecture. The complex includes a mosque, seven religious schools, a charitable soup kitchen, and the tomb of Süleyman the Magnificent.

In the northwest corner of the city, the impeccably preserved **Kariye Camii,** with its superb 14th-century frescoes is a mandatory stop for Byzantine art connoisseurs. The museum is a long way up Fevzipaşa Cad. near the Edirne Gate and is accessible by *dolmuş,* bus #58 from Eminönü, or any bus in the direction Edirnekapı (open Wed.-Mon. 9:30am-4:30pm).

Across the Galata Bridge, the 62m high **Galata Tower,** built by Justinian in 528 and rebuilt for spying purposes in 1348 by the Genoese, offers spectacular views of the Golden Horn. Along the Bosphorus, **Dolmabahçe Palace** was the home of sultans from 1856 until the demise of the Ottoman Empire after WWI, and soldiers still guard the collection of imperial treasures (open Tues.-Sun. 9:30am-4pm; US$5). To reach the palace from Eminönü, take the ferry (US$0.50) or bus 58 to Beşiktaş. The number of visitors per day is limited, so go early. For a closer look at the waters around Istanbul, take a **Bosphorus cruise;** boats leave from Pier 3, beside the Galata Bridge in Eminönü (US$3.35). When the ferry makes its final stop on the Asian side, disembark and treat yourself to the fish *kebap* and mussels of street vendors. Double-decker bus #210 also runs hourly from behind the tourist office to points along the European side of the Bosphorus (2 bus tickets each way).

ENTERTAINMENT

For an authentic **Turkish bath** (*hamam*), it's best to go to the nearby cities of Edirne and Bursa. Istanbul baths, however, can provide a reprieve for the down and dirty. The much-publicized **Cağaloğlu Hamamı** (tel. 522 24 24), in Sultanahmet on Yerebatan Cad., is fancy, but avoid it if you are at all claustrophobic (open daily 8am-10pm; US$10-20). Istanbul's other famous *hamam,* the historical **Çemberlitaş Bath,** 8 Vezirhan Cad. (tel. 522 79 74; fax 511 25 35), is the 1584 product of master architect Mimar Sinan (open daily 6am-midnight; US$10). Nightlife rages from midnight to dawn in the Taksim district. Do not club-hop here in a haphazard manner: some clubs are reputable, but some are run by hustlers who have ties to the nearby red-light district. Stick to places that have been specifically recommended by *Let's Go* or by trustworthy locals.

Kemançı, Sıraselviler Cad., on an alley off İstiklâl Cad. Wild and loud rock bar that frequently hosts live bands. US$5 cover on weekends includes a drink.

Bilsak, Sıraselviler Cad., Soğana Sk. 7. The place for a more mellow and artsy scene.

Carnival Pub, in the fruit market beside the Flower Passage. Heavy metal and punk bands nightly. Beers US$2.

Hayal Kahvesi, Büyükparmakkapı Sok., an alley off İstiklâl Cad. Popular haven for artists. Live music starts at 11pm. House special Hayal cocktail US$4.25.

North Shield, Çalıkuşu Sok. in Levent. Authentic British pub with an incredible variety of European beers. Foreigners tend to hang here.

2019, Atatürk 100, Tıl Oto Sanayi Sitesi. Hard rock with car wreck decor. Gays, Istanbul's jet-set, and assorted funky types frequent this bar.

VAT 69, İman Adnan Sok. Popular with gay men. Open until early morning.

APPENDIX

CLIMATE

Temp. (in °C) Rain (in cm)	January		April		July		October	
	Temp.	Rain	Temp.	Rain	Temp.	Rain	Temp.	Rain
Albania:								
Tirana	12/2	13.5	18/8	11.7	31/17	3.2	23/10	10.5
Belarus:								
Minsk	-4/-8	4.2	10/7	4.9	19/17	5.5	12/8	5.1
Bosnia:								
Sarajevo	03/-3	4.7	18/7	5.4	28/17	6.1	18/8	5.5
Bulgaria:								
Sofia	02/-3	3.6	16/5	6.1	27/16	6.8	17/8	6.5
Croatia:								
Zagreb	02/-4	8.8	15/4	9.8	27/14	11.3	15/6	15.1
Czech Rep.:								
Prague	0/-5	1.8	12/3	2.7	23/13	6.8	12/5	3.3
Estonia:								
Tallinn	-4/-10	3.1	10/1	3.3	22/11	5.3	11/4	6.2
Hungary:								
Budapest	01/-4	3.7	17/7	4.5	28/16	5.6	16/7	5.7
Latvia:								
Riga	-4/-10	3.1	10/1	3.3	22/11	5.3	11/4	6.2
Lithuania:								
Vilnius	-4/-10	3.1	10/1	3.3	22/11	5.3	11/4	6.2
Macedonia:								
Skopje	05/-3	3.9	19/5	3.8	31/15	2.9	19/6	6.1
Romania:								
Bucharest	01/-7	4.6	18/05	5.9	30/16	5.3	18/6	2.9
Poland:								
Warsaw	0/-6	2.7	12/03	3.7	24/15	9.6	13/5	3.8
Russia:								
Moscow	-9/-16	3.9	10/1	3.9	23/13	8.8	09/3	4.5
Slovakia:								
Bratislava	01/-4	3.9	15/6	4.5	25/15	8.4	14/7	1.3
Slovenia:								
Ljubljana	02/-4	8.8	15/4	9.8	27/14	11.3	15/6	15.1
Ukraine:								
Kiev	-4/-10	5.8	14/5	4.5	25/15	9.1	13/6	3.3
Yugoslavia:								
Belgrade	4/-2	4.1	17/6	5.7	27/16	6.3	28/8	5
Gateways:								
Berlin	02/-3	4.6	13/04	4.2	24/14	7.3	13/06	4.9
Helsinki	-3/-9	5.6	6/-1	4.4	22/13	6.8	8/3	7.3
Istanbul	8/3	9.1	15/8	4.2	26/19	2.4	19/13	6.5
Vienna	01/-4	3.9	15/06	4.5	25/15	8.4	14/07	5.6

TRAIN TRAVEL TIME (IN HOURS)

	Budapest	Kiev	Prague	Moscow	Bucharest	Warsaw
Budapest		22	9	39	13	10
Kiev	22		30	13-17	17	20
Prague	9	30		39	22	12-14
Moscow	39	13-17	39		34	27-30
Bucharest	13	17	22	34		23
Warsaw	10	20	12-14	27-30	23	

COUNTRY CODES

Albania	355	**Latvia**	371	**Slovenia**	386
Belarus	375	**Lithuania**	370	**Ukraine**	380
Bosnia	387	**Macedonia**	389	**Yugoslavia**	381
Bulgaria	359	**Moldova**	373	**Berlin, GER**	49
Croatia	385	**Poland**	48	**Helsinki, FIN**	358
Czech Republic	420	**Romania**	40	**Vienna, AUS**	43
Estonia	372	**Russia**	7	**Istanbul, TUR (Europe)**	212
Hungary	36	**Slovakia**	421	**(Asia)**	216

MEASUREMENTS

Like most of the world, Eastern Europe uses the metric system. The following are fairly precise metric equivalents of common English measurements.

1 millimeter (mm) = 0.04 inch   1 inch = 25mm
1 meter (m) = 1.09 yards   1 yard = 0.92m
1 kilometer (km) = 0.62 mile   1 mile = 1.61km
1 gram (g) = 0.04 ounce   1 ounce = 25g
1 kilogram (kg) = 2.2 pounds   1 pound = 0.55kg
1 liter = 1.06 quarts   1 quart = 0.94 liter

To convert from Fahrenheit degrees into Celsius, subtract 32 and multiply by 5/9. To from Celsius to Fahrenheit, multiply by 9/5 and add 32.

°C	-5	0	5	10	15	20	25	30	35	40
°F	23	32	41	50	59	68	77	86	95	104

APPENDIX

Glossaries

The Cyrillic Alphabet

The Cyrillic alphabet is a script used in Bulgaria, Macedonia, Serbia, Russia, and many parts of the former Soviet Union. On mission in Great Moravia (part of modern-day Czech Republic and Slovakia), two 9th-century monks developed the alphabet's first form in order to translate the Bible into Slavic. The monks, Cyril and Methodius, were Greek (which is why many Cyrillic letters look Greek) and Orthodox, so when Catholic powers gained control of the region that the monks were proselytizing, their disciples fled to the shores of Lake Ohrid (Macedonia) which, at the time, belonged to Bulgaria. There they founded the first Slavic university, and the script spread swiftly to other Slavic lands.

For many centuries, Cyrillic was a source of unity to the Slavic nations who wrote in it, and its use (or non-use) still makes a political statement in some parts of the world. One of the major differences between the otherwise very similar Serb and Croat languages is that Croatian is written in the Latin alphabet, while Serbian is written in Cyrillic. Furthermore, as republics of the former Soviet Union are discovering their roots, they are learning their own scripts instead of Cyrillic, which for decades Moscow had made the empire's *scripta franca*.

The transliteration index given below is that of Russian Cyrillic. Other languages include some additional letters and pronounce certain letters differently. Each country's language section outlines these disparities.

Cyrillic	English	Pronunciation	Cyrillic	English	Pronunciation
А, а	a	*G*a*rden*	Р, р	r	*R*andom
Б, б	b	Mr. *B*urns	С, с	s	*S*aucy
В, в	v	The *V*illage People	Т, т	t	*T*antalize
Г, г	g	*G*alina	У, у	u	D*oo*dle
Д, д	d	*D*avid	Ф, ф	f	Absolutely *F*ab
Е, е	ye or e	*Y*ellow	Х, х	kh	*Ch*utzpah (*hkh*)
Ё, ё	yo	*Yaw*n	Ц, ц	ts	Let'*s* Go
Ж, ж	zh	*Zh*irinovsky	Ч, ч	ch	*Ch*inese diplomacy
З, з	z	*Z*any	Ш, ш	sh	*Ch*ampagne
И, и	i	*Kathleen*	Щ, щ	shch	Khru*shch*ev
Й, й	y	*Y*ak	Ъ, ъ	(hard)	(no sound)
К, к	k	*K*illjoy	Ы, ы	y	l*i*t
Л, л	l	*L*ouis	Ь, ь	(soft)	(no sound)
М, м	m	*M*eteor	Э, э	eh	Al*e*xander
Н, н	n	*N*utty	Ю, ю	yoo	*You*
О, о	o	*L*a*w*	Я, я	yah	*Ya*hoo!
П, п	p	*P*eter the Great			

ALBANIAN (SHQIP)

English	Albanian	Pronunciation
Yes/no	Po/jo	poh/voh
Please	Ju lutem	yoo LOO-tehm
Thank you	Faleminderit	FAH-leh-meen-DEH-reet
Hello	Mirëdita	meer-DEE-tah
Good-bye	Mirupafshim	mee-roo-PAHFS-hihm

English	Albanian	Pronunciation
Good morning	Mirëmëngjes	meer-mhen-JEHS
Good evening	Mirëmbrëma	meer-mbreh-MAH
Excuse me	Më fal	muh-FAHL
When?	kur?	KOOR
Where is...?	Ku është..?	KOO uhsht
Help!	Ndihmë!	n-DEE-mih
How much does this cost?	Sa kushton/sa bën?	sah koosh-TOHN/sah bihn
Do you have...?	A keni ...?	ah KEH-nee
Do you speak English?	A flisni anglisht?	ah FLEES-nee ahn-GLEESHT
I don't understand	Unë nuk kuptoj.	oon nook KOOP-toy
Please write it down.	Të lutem m'a shkruaj.	ter LOO-tehm mah shkrooay
I'd like to order...	Dua...	doo-ah
Check, please.	Faturën ju lutem.	fah-TUR-en yoo LUH-tem
I'd like a room.	Dua një dhomë.	doo-ah njer DHOH-mer
With shower	me dush?	meh doosh

English	Albanian	Pronunc.	English	Albanian	Pronunc.
open	hapet	HAH-peht	meat	mish	mish
closed	mbyllet	MBU-leht	vegetables	perime	PEH-ri-meh
arrival	arritje	ARIT-yer	water	ujë	ooy
departure	ndarjë	NDAR-yer	coffee	kafe	kah-FEH
station	stacion	STATS-ion	wine	verë	VEH-rer
round-trip	vajtje-ardhje	VAY-te ARD-ye	juice	lëng	lerng
one-way	vajtje	VAY-tye	milk	qumësht	CHOO-mersht
bread	bukë	BOO-ker	beer	birrë	BEE-rer
one	një	nyer	six	gjashtë	jy-asht
two	dy	duy	seven	shtatë	shtaht
three	tre	treh	eight	tetë	teht
four	katër	KAH-ter	nine	nëntë	nernt
five	pesë	PEH-ser	ten	dhjetë	dhyet
one hundred	njëqind	ner-CHEEND	one thousand	njëmijë	NER-meey

BULGARIAN (БЪГАРСКИ)

English	Bulgarian	Pronunciation
Yes/no	Да/Не	dah/neh
Please	Моля	MO-lya
Thank you	Благодаря	blahg-oh-dahr-YAH
Hello	Добър ден	DOH-bur den
Good-bye	Добиждане	doh-VIZZ-dan-eh
Good morning	Добро утро	doh-BRAW U-troh
Good night	Добър вечер	doh-BER VEH-cher
Excuse me	Извиниете	iz-VI-ne-te

English	Bulgarian	Pronunc.
When?	Кога?	ko-GA
Where is...?	Къде?	kuh-DEH
Help	Помощ	PO-mosht
How much does this cost?	Колко струва?	KOHL-ko STROO-va
Do you have...?	Имате ли...?	IH-mah-teh lee...?
Do you speak English?	Говорите ли английски?	go-VO-rih-te li an-GLIS-kih
I don't understand	Не разбирам.	neh rahz-BIH-rahm
Please write it down.	Моля, напишете.	MO-lyah, nay-pee-SHESH-teh
I'd like to order...	Искам...	ISS-kahm
Check, please.	Искам да платя, моля.	ISS-kahm dah plah-TYAH, MO-lya
I'd like a room.	Искам стая	EES-kahm STAH-yah
With shower	с душ	s dush

English	Bulgarian	Pronunc.	English	Bulgarian	Pronunc.
open	отварят	ot-VAR-yaht	meat	месо	MEH-so
closed	затварят	zaht-VAR-yaht	vegetables	зеленчуци	zelenchuyee
arrival	пристигащи	pristigashti	water	вода	vo-DAH
departure	заминаваши	zaminavashti	coffee	кафе	kah-FEH
station	гара	gara	wine	вино	VEE-no
round-trip	отиване и Връщане	o-TEE-van-e ee VRI-shtah-neh	juice	сок	sok
one-way	отиване	o-TEE-vahn-eh	milk	мляко	MLYAH-ko
grocery	бакалия	bah-kah-LIH-ya	beer	бира	BEE-rah
bread	хляб	hlyab	tea	чай	tchai
one	едно	ehd-NO	six	шест	shesht
two	две	dveh	seven	седем	SEH-dehm
three	три	tree	eight	осем	O-sehm
four	четири	CHEH-tee-ree	nine	девет	DEH-veht
five	пет	peht	ten	десет	DEH-seht
one hundred	сто	stoh	one thousand	хиляда	hi-LYA-da

CROATIAN

English	Croatian	Pronunciation
Yes/no	Da/Ne	Da/Neh
Please/You're welcome	Molim	MO-leem
Thank you	Hvala	FA-la
Hello/Hi	Zdravo/Bok	ZDRAH-vo/bock
Good-bye	Dovidjenja	DO vidg-en-ya
Good morning	Dobro jutro	DO-bro YOO-tro
Good night	Laku noć	LA-koo noch
Excuse me	Molim vas	MO-leem vas
When?	Kada?	KA-da
Where is...?	Gdje je?	GDYE je

English	Croatian	Pronunciation
Help	U pomoć	OO pomoch
Leave me alone	Pusti me na miru.	PU-sti me na MI-ru
How much does this cost?	Koliko to košta?	KO-li-KOH toh KOH-shta
Do you have...?	Imate li…?	EEM-a-teh lee
Do you speak English?	Govorite li engleski?	go-VOR-i-teh lee eng-LEH-ski
I don't understand.	Ne razumijem.	neh ra-ZOO-mi-yem
Please write it down?	Možete li napisati?	MOZH-e-te lee na-PIH-sa-tee
I'd like to order...	Želio bih naručiti…	Jelim na-ROO-chiti
Check, please.	Račun, molim.	RACH-un, mo-leem
I'd like a room.	Želio bih imati sobu.	ZNEL-i-o bih EE-ma-tee so-bu

English	Croatian	Pronunc.	English	Croatian	Pronunc.
open	otvoren	OT-vo-ren	meat	meso	MEH-so
closed	zatvoreno	zat-VOR-eno	vegetables	povrče	POH-ver-chay
arrival	dolazak	DOL-a-zak	water	voda	VO-dah
departure	odlazak	OD-la-zak	coffee	kava	KAH-vah
station	kolodvor	KOL-o-dvor	wine	vino	VEE-no
round-trip	kružno putovanje	KRUH-zhno put-OH-van-ye	juice	sok	sok
one-way	jenosmjerna	JE-no SMI-er-na	milk	mlijeko	mil-YEH-koh
grocery	trgovina	terg-OH-vee-na	beer	pivo	PEE-voh
bread	kruh	krooh	tea	čaj	chi
one	jedan	ehd-NO	six	šest	shesht
two	dva	dveh	seven	sedam	SEH-dahm
three	tri	tree	eight	osam	O-sehm
four	četiri	CHEH-tee-ree	nine	devet	DEH-veht
five	pet	peht	ten	deset	DEH-seht
one hundred	sto	sto	one thousand	tisuća	TEE-soo-chah

CZECH (ČESKY)

English	Czech	Pronunciation
Yes/no	Ano/ne	AH-no/neh
Please/You're welcome	Prosím	PROH-seem
Thank you	Dékuji	DYEH-koo-yih
Hello	Dobrý den	DO-bree den
Good-bye	Na shledanou	nah SLEH-dah-noh-oo
Good morning	Dobré ráno	DO-breh RAH-no
Good night	Dobrou noc	DO-broh NOTS
Excuse me	S dovolením	z-DOH-voh-leh-neem
Sorry	Promiňte	PROH-mihn-teh
My name is...	Jmenuji se	Y-mehn-oo-yee se
What is your name?	Jak se jmenujete?	yak se Y-mehn-oo-ye-teh
Help!	Pomoc!	poh-MOTS

English	Czech	Pronunciation
When?	Kdy?	k-DEE
Where is...?	Kde?	k-DEH
How do I get to...?	Jak se dostanu do...?	YAK seh dohs-TAH-noo doh
How much does this cost?	Kolik?	KOH-lihk
Do you have...?	Máte..?	MAH-teh
Do you speak English?	Mluvité anglicky?	MLOO-vit-eh ahng-GLIT-ski
I don't understand.	Nerozumím.	neh-rohz-oo-MEEM
Please write it down?	Prosím napište.	PRO-seem nah-PEESH-tye
A little slower, please.	Prosím pomalu.	PRO-seem poh-MAH-loo
I'd like to order...	Chtel bych...	khtyel bikh
I'd like to pay.	Zaplatím.	ZA-pla-teem
Have you a vacancy?	Máte volný pokoj?	MAH-te VOL-nee PO-koy
With shower	se sprchou	SE sprkh-oh

English	Czech	Pron.	English	Czech	Pron.
bank	banka	BAN-ka	post office	pošta	POSH-ta
exchange	směnárna	smyeh-NAR-na	stamps	známka	ZNAHM-ka
arrival	prijezd	PREE-yezd	departure	odjezd	OD-yezd
one-way	jedním směrem	YED-nyeem SMNYE-rem	round-trip	zpáteční	SPAH-tech-nyee
ticket	listek	LIS-tek	reservation	místenka	mis-TEN-kah
station	nádraží	NA-drah-zhee	train	vlak	vlahk
bus	autobus	OUT-oh-boos	airport	letiště	LEH-tish-tyeh
bakery	pekařství	PE-karzh-stvee	grocery	potraviny	PO-tra-vee-nee
breakfast	snídaně	SNEE-dan-ye	lunch	oběd	OB-yed
dinner	večeře	VE-cher-zhe	menu	listek	LIS-tek
water	voda	VO-dah	bread	chléb	khleb
pork	vepřové	VE-przhov-eh	vegetables	zelenina	ZE-le-nee-na
fish	ryba	REE-ba	beef	hovězí	HO-vye-zee
cheese	sýr	seer	chicken	kuře	KOO-rzheh
tea	čaj	tchai	coffee	káva	KAH-va
juice	sok	sok	milk	mléko	MLEH-koh
wine	víno	VEE-no	beer	pivo	PEE-voh
Monday	pondělí	PON-dye-lee	Sunday	neděle	NEH-dyeh-leh
Tuesday	úterý	OO-teh-ree	holiday	prazdniny	PRAHZ-dni-nee
Wednesday	středa	stshreh-dah	today	dnes	dness
Thursday	čtvrtek	CHTV'R-tek	tomorrow	zítra	ZEE-tra
Friday	pátek	PAH-tek	open	otevřen	O-te-zhen

English	Czech	Pron.	English	Czech	Pron.
Saturday	sobota	SO-boh-ta	closed	zatveřen	ZA-tev-zhen
one	jeden	YEH-den	twenty	dvacet	dvah-TSEHT
two	dvě	dv-YEH	thirty	třicet	tr-zhih-TSEHT
three	tři	tr-ZHIH	forty	čtyřicet	chteer-zhee-TSEHT
four	čtyři	SHTEER-zhee	fifty	padesát	pah-des-AHT
five	pět	p-YEHT	sixty	šedesát	sheh-des-AHT
six	šest	shest	seventy	sedmdesát	SE-dum-des-AT
seven	sedm	SEH-duhm	eighty	osmdesát	os-um-des-AHT
eight	osm	OSS-uhm	ninety	devadesát	deh-vah-des-AT
nine	devět	dehv-YEHT	one hundred	sto	stoh
ten	deset	des-SEHT	one thousand	tisíc	TI-seets

ESTONIAN (ESTI KEEL)

English	Estonian	Pronunciation
Yes/no	Jaa/Ei	yah/rhymes with "hay"
Please	Palun	PAH-luhn
Thank you	Tänan	TÆ-nan
Hello	Tere	TEH-re
Good-bye	Head aega	hehaht EYE-kah
Good morning	Tere hommikust	TEH-re ho-mih-KUHST
Good night	Head ööd	hehaht euht
Excuse me	Vabandage	vah-pan-TAGE-euh
When?	Millal?	mih-LAL?
Where is...?	Kus on...?	Kuhs on...
Help!	Appi!	APP-pi
How do I get to...?	Mina soovisin minna...?	MIH-nah soo-VIK-sin MIH-na
How much does this cost?	Kui palju?	Kwee PAL-you?
Do you have...?	Kas teil on ...?	kass tayl on ...?
Do you speak English?	Kas te räägite inglise keelt?	kass teh rah-KIHT-eh ihn-KLIS-eh keelt
I don't understand.	Ma ei saa aru.	mah ay saw AH-rooh
I'd like to order...	Ma sooviksin...	mah SOO-vik-sin
Check, please.	Arve, palun.	AR-vet, PAH-lun.
I'd like a room.	Ma sooviksin tuba.	mah SOO-vik-sin TUH-bah
With shower	duššiga?	DUSH-shi-ga

English	Estonian	Pronunc.	English	Estonian	Pronunc.
arrival	saabub	SAA-boob	vegetables	juurvili	YUR-vi-li
departure	väljub	VAL-yoob	water	vesi	VEH-si
round-trip	edasi-tagasi piletit	E-dasi-TA-gasi PI-let-it	coffee	kohvi	KOH-fee
one-way	üheotsa piletit	EW-he-OHT-sah PI-le-tiht	wine	vein	VAY-een

English	Estonian	Pronunc.	English	Estonian	Pronunc.
station	jaam	yaam	juice	jamahl	ya-MAXL
grocery	toidupood	TOY-du-POOD	milk	piim	peem
bread	leib	LAY-eeb	beer	ôlu	elu
meat	liha	LI-ha	tea	tee	teee
one	üks	ewks	six	kuus	koose
two	kaks	kaks	seven	seitse	SEIT-se
three	kolm	kohlm	eight	kaheksa	KAH-eks-ah
four	neli	NEH-lih	nine	üheksa	EUW-eks-ah
five	viis	veese	ten	kümme	KEUW-meh
one hundred	sada	SA-da	one thousand	tuhat	TU-hat

HUNGARIAN (MAGYAR)

English	Hungarian	Pronunciation
Yes/no	Igen/nem	EE-ghen/nem
Please	Kérem	KAY-rem
Thank you	Köszönöm	KUH-suh-num
Hello	Szervusz	SAIR-voose
Good-bye	Viszontlátásra	Vi-sont-lah-tah-shraw
Good morning	Jó reggelt	YOH reh-gehlt
Good night	Jó éjszakát	YOH ay-sokat
Excuse me	Sajnálom	shoy-nah-lawm
My name is...	...vagyok	vah-djawk
What is your name?	Hogy hívják	hawdj HEE-vyahk
When?	Mikor?	MI-kor
Where is...?	Hol van...?	hawl von
May I?	Kaphatok?	kop-huh-tok
How do you get to...?	Hogy jutok...?	hawdj YOO-tawk
How much does this cost?	Mennyibe kerül?	MEN-yee-beh KEH-rewl
Do you have...?	Van...?	von
Do you speak English?	Beszél angolul?	BESS-ayl ON-goal-ool
I don't understand	Nem értem	nem AYR-tem
Please write it down?	Kérem, írja fel.	KAY-rem, EER-yuh fell.
Speak a little slower, please.	Kérem, beszéljen lassan	KAY-rem, BESS-ayl-yen LUSH-shun
I'd like to order...	...kérek.	KAY-rek
Check, please.	A számlát, kérem.	uh SAHM-lot KAY-rem
Have you a vacancy?	Van szabad szobájuk?	von sub-od soh-bah-yook
Private bath	privát fürdő?	pree-VAHT FIR-duh

English	Hungarian	Pronunc.	English	Hungarian	Pronunc.
bank	bank	bonk	post office	posta	pawsh-tuh
exchange	valutabeválto	VO-loo-tob-be-vaal-taw	stamps	bélyeg	BAY-yeg

English	Hungarian	Pronunc.	English	Hungarian	Pronunc.
arrival	érkezés	ayr-keh-aysh	departure	indulás	IN-dool-ahsh
one-way	csak oda	chok AW-do	round-trip	oda-vissza	AW-do-VEES-so
ticket	jegyet	YED-et	train	vonat	VAW-not
station	pályaudvar	pa-yo-OOT-var	airport	repülőtér	rep-ewlu-TAYR

English	Hungarian	Pronunc.	English	Hungarian	Pronunc.
bakery	pékség	PAYK-shayg	grocery	élelmiszerbolt	Ay-lel-meser-balt
breakfast	reggeli	REG-gell-ee	lunch	ebéd	EB-ehd
dinner	vacsora	VOTCH-oh-rah	menu	étlap	ATE-lop
water	víz	veez	bread	kenyér	KEN-yair
cheese	sajt	shoyt	vegetables	zöldségek	ZULD-segek
fish	hal	hull	beef	marhahús	MOR-ho-hoosh
juice	gyümölcslé	DYEW-murl-chlay	pork	sertéshúst	SHER-taysh-hoos
coffee	kávé	KAA-vay	milk	tej	tay
wine	bor	bawr	beer	sör	shurr

English	Hungarian	Pronunc.	English	Hungarian	Pronunc.
Monday	hétfő	hayte-phuuh	Saturday	szombat	SAWM-baht
Tuesday	kedd	ked	Sunday	vasárnap	VO-shahr-nahp
Wednesday	szerda	sayr-dah	holiday	ünnepnap	ewn-nap-nop
Thursday	csütörtök	chew-ter-tek	today	ma	mo
Friday	péntek	paine-tek	tomorrow	holnap	HAWL-nahp

English	Hungarian	Pronunc.	English	Hungarian	Pronunc.
one	egy	edge	twenty	húsz	hoose
two	kettő	ket-tuuh	thirty	harminc	har-mintz
three	három	hah-rom	forty	negyven	nedj-ven
four	négy	naydj	fifty	ötven	ut-ven
five	öt	uh-t	sixty	hatvan	hut-von
six	hat	hut	seventy	hetven	het-ven
seven	hét	hayte	eighty	nyolcvan	nyoltz-van
eight	nyolc	nyoltz	ninety	kilencven	kih-lentz-ven
nine	kilenc	kih-lentz	one hundred	száz	sah-z
ten	tíz	tease	one thousand	ezer	eh-zayr

LATVIAN (LATVISKA)

English	Latvian	Pronunciation
Yes/no	Jā/nē	yah/ney
Please	Lūdzu	LOOD-zuh

English	Latvian	Pronunciation
Thank you	Paldies	PAHL-dee-yes
Hello	Labdien	LAHB-dyen
Good-bye	Sveiki	SVEY-kee
Good morning	Labrīt	LAHB-reet
Good night	Labvakar	LAHB-vah-kahr
Excuse me	Atvainojiet	AHT-vye-no-yet
When?	Kad?	KAHD
Where is...?	Kur ir...?	kuhr ihr
Help!	Palīgā!	PAH-lee-gah
How do I get to...?	Es gribu iet uz...?	ehs GREE-boo EE-yet ooze
How much does this cost?	Cik maksā?	sikh MAHK-sah
Do you have...?	Vai jums ir...?	vai yoomss ir
Do you speak English?	Vai jūs runājiet angliski?	vye yoos RUH-nah-yee-eht AHN-glee-ski
I don't understand.	Es nesaprotu.	ehs NEH-sah-proh-too
I'd like to order...	Es vēlos...	ess VE-lwass
Check, please.	Rēķins, lūdzu.	RAY-kins, LOOD-zu
Do you have any vacancies?	Vai jums ir brīvas istabas?	vai yums ir BREE-vas IS-tab-as

English	Latvian	Pronunc.	English	Latvian	Pronunc.
arrival	pienāk	PEE-en-ak	vegetables	dārzeņi	DAR-ze-nyih
departure	atiet	AH-tee-it	water	ūdens	OH-dens
station	stacija	STAH-tsee-uh	coffee	kafija	KAH-fee-yah
round-trip	turp un atpakaļ	toorp oon AT-pakal	wine	vins	veens
one-way	vienā virzienā	VEEA-nah VIR-zee-an-ah	juice	sula	SOO-la
grocery	pārtikas veikals	PAHR-tih-kas VEY-kalss	milk	piens	PEE-ins
bread	maize	MAY-zuh	beer	alus	AH-lus
meat	mēsa	MAY-sah	tea	tēja	TAY-yah
one	viens	vee-YENZ	six	seši	SEH-shih
two	divi	DIH-vih	seven	septini	SEHP-tih-nyih
three	tris	TREESE	eight	astoni	AHS-toh-nyih
four	četri	CHEH-trih	nine	devini	DEH-vih-nyih
five	pieci	PYET-sih	ten	desmit	DEZ-miht

LITHUANIAN (LIETUVIŠKAI)

English	Lithuanian	Pronunciation
Yes/no	Taip/ne	TAYE-p/NEH
Please/You're welcome	Prašau	prah-SHAU
Thank you	Ačiu	AH-chyoo
Hello	Labądien	Lah-bah-DEE-yen

APPENDIX

English	Lithuanian	Pronunciation
Good-bye	Viso gero	VEE-soh GEh-roh
Good morning	Labas rytas	LAH-bass REE-tass
Good night	Labanakt	lah-bah-NAKT
Excuse me	Atsiprašau	aHT-sih-prh-SHAU
When?	Kada?	KAH-da
Where is…?	Kur yra…?	Koor EE-rah..
Help!	Gelbėkite!	GYEL-behk-ite
How do I get to…?	Norėčiau nueiti h…?	nor-RAY-chee-yow new-ih-tih ee
How much does this cost?	Kiek kainuoja?	KEE-yek KYE-new-oh-yah
Do you have…?	Ar turite..?	ahr TU-ryite
Do you speak English?	Ar kalbate angliškai?	AHR AHN-gleesh-kye
I don't understand.	Aš nesuprantu	AHSH neh-soo-PRAHN-too
I'd like to order…	Norėčiau…	nor-RAY-cee-yow
Check, please.	Sąskaitą, prašau	SAHS-kai-ta, prah-SHAU
Do you have any vacancies?	Ar turite laisvų kambarių?	ahr TU-ryite lai-SVOO KAHM-bah-rio

English	Lithuanian	Pronunc.	English	Lithuanian	Pronunc.
arrival	atvyksta	at-VEEK-stah	vegetables	daržovė	dar-ZHO-ve
departure	išvyksta	ish-VEEK-stah	water	vanduo	van-DAW
station	stotis	sto-TEES	coffee	kava	KAH-vah
round-trip	grįžtamasio bilieto	GREEZH-tah-mah-sio BI-lieto	wine	vynas	VEE-nas
one-way	į vieną galą	ee VIE-naa GAH-laa	juice	sultys	SUL-tyees
grocery	bakalejos krautuvė	bah-kah-LYEH-yos KRA-tu-veh	milk	pienas	PEE-nas
bread	duona	DAW-na	beer	alus	AH-lus
one	vienas	vee-AYN-ahss	six	šeši	SHEH-shih
two	du	doo	seven	septyni	sehp-TEE-nih
three	trys	treese	eight	aštuoni	ahsh-too-OH-ni
four	keturi	keh-TUH-ree	nine	devyni	deh-VEE-nih
five	penki	PEHN-kee	ten	dešimt	deh-SHIMT
one hundred	šimtas	SHIM-tahs	one thousand	tukstantis	TOOK-stan-tis

MACEDONIAN

English	Macedonian	Pronunciation
Yes/no	Да/не	dah/neh
Please	Повелете	poh-VEL-et-ey
Thank you	Фала	FAH-lah
Hello	Добар ден	DAW-bahr-den
Good-bye	Довидување	DAW-ve-DOO-va-ne

English	Macedonian	Pronunciation
Good morning	Добро утро	DAW-broh OOT-raw
Good night	Добро вечер	DAW-broh VYEH-cher
Excuse me	Дозволете	dohz-VOH-leh-teh
When?	Кога?	koh-GAG
Where is...?	Каде?	kah-DEY
Help!	Помош!	pah-MASH
Leave me alone.	Оставете ме на мира.	Ohs-TA-ve-te mey na MEE-ra
How much does this cost?	Колку чини?	KOL-koo CHEE-nee
Do you speak English?	Зборивате ли англиски?	ZVOR-oo-va-te li an-GLEE-ski
I don't understand.	Не разбирам.	neh rahz-BEE-rahm

English	Macedon.	Pronunc.	English	Macedon.	Pronunc.
arrival	пристигнување	pristignuvanye	vegetables	зеленчуии	zelenchuyee
departure	тругвање	trugvanye	water	вода	vo-DAH
station	станица	stanitsa	coffee	кафе	kah-FEH
round-trip	отивањеи вращање	o-TEE-vahn-e ee VRI-shta-ne	wine	вино	VEE-no
one-way	отивање	o-TEE-vahn-eh	juice	сок	sok
grocery	бакалија	bah-kah-LEE-ya	milk	мляко	MLYAH-ko
bread	хляб	khlyab	beer	бира	BEE-rah
meat	месо	MEH-so	tea	чай	chahy
one	едно	ehd-NO	six	шест	shesht
two	две	dveh	seven	седем	SEH-dem
three	три	tree	eight	осем	O-sehm
four	четири	CHEH-tee-ree	nine	девет	DEH-veht
five	пет	peht	ten	десет	DEH-seht
one hundred	сто	stoh	one thousand	илјада	il-YAH-da

POLISH (POLSKI)

English	Polish	Pronunciation
Yes/no	Tak/nie	tahk/nyeh
Please/You're welcome	Proszę	PROH-sheh
Thank you	Dziękuję	jen-KOO-yeh
Hello	Cześć	cheshch
Good-bye	Do widzenia	doh vee-DZAY-nyah
Good morning	Dzień dobry	jeen DOH-brih
Good night	Dobranoc	doh-BRAH-nots
Excuse me/I'm sorry	Przepraszam	psheh-PRAH-shahm
Help!	Na pomoc!	nah POH-mots
My name is...	Nazywam się	nah-ZIH-vahm sheh
What is your name?	Jak się pan(i) nazywa?	yak sheh PAN(ee) nah-ZIH-vah

English	Polish	Pronunciation
When?	Kiedy?	KYEH-dih
Where is...?	Gdzie jest?	g-JAY yehst
How do I get to...?	Ktorędy do...?	ktoo-REN-dih doh
How much does this cost?	Ile to kosztuje?	EE-leh toh kohsh-TOO-yeh
Do you have...?	Czy są...?	chih sawn
Do you speak English?	Czy pan(i) mówi po angiel-sku?	chih PAH(-nee) MOO-vee poh ahn-GYEL-skoo
I don't understand.	Nie rozumiem.	nyeh roh-ZOO-myem
Please write it down.	Proszę napisać.	PROH-sheh nah-PEE-sahtch
A little slower, please.	Proszę mówić wolniej.	PROH-sheh MOO-veetch VOHL-nee–eh
Have you a vacancy?	Czy są jakieś wolne pokoje?	chih sawn YAH-kyesh VOHL-neh poh-KOY-eh
Private shower?	z prysznicem	zeh prish-NEE-tsem

English	Polish	Pronunc.	English	Polish	Pronunc.
bank	bank	bahnk	**post office**	poczta	POTCH-tah
exchange	wymiany walut	vih-MYAH-nih VAH-loot	**stamps**	znaczki	ZNATCH-kee
arrivals	przyjazdy	pshi-YAHZ-dih	**departures**	odjazdy	ohd-YAHZ-dih
ticket	bilet	BEE-leht	**reservation**	miejscówka	mye-SOOV-ka
station	dworzec	DVOH-zhets	**train**	pociąg	POH-chawnk
bus	autobus	OW-toh-boos	**airport**	lotnisko	laht-NEE-skoh
bakery	piekarnia	pyeh-KAHR-nee-ah	**beef**	wołowina	vo-wo-VEE-na
grocery store	sklep spożywczy	sklehp spoh-ZHIV-chih	**pork**	wieprzowina	vye-psho-VEE-nah
breakfast	śniadanie	shnee-ah-DAHN-yeh	**chicken**	kurczę	KOOR-cheh
lunch	obiad	OH-byaht	**fish**	ryba	RIH-bah
dinner	kolacja	koh-LAH-tsyah	**cheese**	ser	sehr
menu	menu	meh-NOO	**coffee**	kawa	KAH-vah
salt	sól	sool	**tea**	herbata	hehr-BAH-tah
bread	chleb	khlehp	**milk**	mleko	MLEH-koh
water	woda	VOH-dah	**wine**	wina	VEE-nah
vegetables	jarzyny	yahr-ZHIH-nih	**beer**	piwo	PEE-voh
vegetarian	wegetariań	ve-ge-tahr-YAN	**juice**	sok	sohk
Monday	poniedziałek	poh-nyeh-JAH-wehk	**Saturday**	sobota	soh-BOH-tah
Tuesday	wtorek	FTOH-rehk	**Sunday**	niedziela	nyah-JEH-lah
Wednesday	środa	SHROH-dah	**holiday**	święto	shvee-EN-toh
Thursday	czwartek	CHVAHR-tehk	**today**	dzisiaj	JEESH-eye
Friday	piątek	PYAWN-tehk	**tomorrow**	jutro	YOO-troh

English	Polish	Pronunc.	English	Polish	Pronunc.
one	jeden	YEH-den	twenty	dwadzieścia	dva-JEESH-cha
two	dwa	dvah	thirty	trzydzieści	tshi-JEESH-chi
three	trzy	tshih	forty	czterdzieści	chter-jes-chih
four	cztery	ch-TEH-rih	fifty	pięćdziesiąt	pyench-JEE-shawnt
five	pięć	pyench	sixty	sześćdziesiąt	sheshch-JEE-shawnt
six	sześć	sheshch	seventy	siedemdziesiąt	shedem-JEE-shawnt
seven	siedem	SHEH-dem	eighty	osiemdziesiąt	ohshem-JEE-shawnt
eight	osiem	OH-shem	ninety	dziewięć dziesiąt	JYEH-vyen-JEE-shawnt
nine	dziewięć	JYEH-vyench	one hundred	sto	stoh
ten	dziesięć	JYEH-shench	one thousand	tysiąc	TIH-shawns

ROMANIAN (ROMAN)

English	Romanian	Pronunciation
Yes/no	Da/nu	dah/noo
Please	Vă rog	vuh rohg
Thank you	Mulţumesc	mool-tsoo-MESK
You're welcome	Cu placere	coo pla-CHEH-reh
Hello	Bună ziua	BOO-nuh zee wah
Good-bye	La revedere	lah reh-veh-DEH-reh
Good morning	Bună dimineaţa	BOO-nuh dee-mee-NYAH-tsa
Good night	Noapte bună	NWAP-teh BOO-ner
Excuse me	Scuzaţi-mă	skoo-ZAH-tz muh
Sorry	Pare rău	PA-reh rau
My name is...	Mă cheamă...	muh-KYAH-muh
What is your name?	Cum vă numiţi?	koom vuh noo-MEETS
Help!	Ajutor!	AH-zhoot-or
When?	Cind?	kihnd
Where is...?	Unde?	OON-deh
How do I get to...?	Cum se ajunge la...?	koom seh-ZHOON-jeh-la
How much does this cost?	Cît costă?	kiht KOH-stuh
Do you have...?	Aveţi...?	a-VETS
Do you speak English?	Vorbiţi englezeşte?	vor-BEETS ehng-leh-ZESH-te
I don't understand	Nu înţeleg	noo-ihn-TZEH-lehg
Please write it down?	Vă rog scrieţi aceasta.	vuh rog SCREE-ets a-CHAS-ta
A little slower, please.	Vorbiţi mai vă rog.	vor-BEETS my vuh rohg
I'd like to order...	Aş vrea nişte...	ash vreh-A NEESH-teh

English	Romanian	Pronunciation
Check, please.	Plata, vă rog.	PLAH-tah, VUH rohg
Do you have a vacancy?	Aveţi camere libere?	a-VETS CA-mer-eh LEE-ber-e
With private shower?	cu duş?	koo doosh

English	Romanian	Pronunc.	English	Romanian	Pronunc.
bank	bancă	BAN-cuh	post office	poşta	POH-shta
exchange	un birou de de schimb	oon bee-RO deh skeemb	stamps	timbru	TEEM-broo
	schimb valutar	deh skeemb valutar			
arrivals	sosiri	so-SEER	departures	plecări	play-CUHR
one-way	dus	doos	round-trip	dus-întors	doos-in-TORS
ticket	bilet	bee-LET	reservation	rezervarea	re-zer-VAR-eh-a
station	gară	GAH-ruh	train	trenul	TRAY-null
bus	autobuz	AHU-toh-booz	airport	aeroportul	air-oh-POR-tull
bakery	o brutărie	o bru-ter-REE-e	grocery	o alimentară	a-lee-men-TA-ra
breakfast	micul dejun	MIK-ul DAY-zhun	dinner	cină	CHEE-nuh
lunch	prînz	preunz	menu	meniu	menyoo
salt	sare	SAH-ray	bread	pîine	PUH-yih-nay
water	apă	AH-puh	vegetables	legume	LEH-goom-eh
pork	carne de porc	CAR-neh deh pork	beef	carne de vacă	CAR-ne de VA-cer
		pork			cuh
coffee	cafea	CAH-fay-ah	milk	lapte	LAHP-tay
wine	vin	VAY-een	beer	bere	BE-reh
juice	suc	sooc	tea	ceai	CHAH-ee
Monday	luni	loon	Sunday	duminică	duh-MIH-ni-ku
Tuesday	marţi	marts	today	azi	az
Wednesday	miercuri	MEER-kur	tomorrow	mîine	MUH-yih-neh
Thursday	joi	zhoy	open	deschis	DESS-kees
Friday	vineri	VEE-ner	closed	închis	un-KEES
Saturday	sîmbătă	SIM-buh-tuh			
one	unu	OO-noo	twenty	douăzeci	doh-wah-ZECH
two	doi	doy	thirty	treizeci	tray-ZECH
three	trei	tray	forty	paizeci	pa-ee-ZECH
four	patru	PAH-tru	fifty	cincizeci	chin-ZECH
five	cinci	CHEEN-ch	sixty	şaizeci	shay-ZECH
six	şase	SHAH-seh	seventy	şaptezeci	shap-teh-ZECH
seven	şase	SHAHP-teh	eighty	optzeci	ohpt-ZECH
eight	opt	ohpt	ninety	nouăzeci	noah-ZECH
nine	nouă	NO-uh	one hundred	o sută	o SOO-tuh
ten	zece	ZEH-cheh	one thousand	o mie	oh MIH-ay

RUSSIAN (РУССКИЙ)

English	Russian	Pronunciation
Yes/no	Да/Нет	Dah/N-yet
Please/You're Welcome	Пожалуйста	pa-ZHOW-a-sta
Thank you	Спасибо	spa-SEE-bah
Hello	Добрый день	DOH-breh DEN
Good-bye	До свидания	dus-vee-DAHN-ya
Good Morning	Доброе утра	DOH-breh OO-tra
Excuse me	Извините	eez-vee-NEET-yeh
My name is...	Меня зовут...	men-YA-za-VOOT...
What is your name?	Как вас зовут?	kak vac zah-VOOT
Help!	Поможите!	pah-mah-ZHEE-te
When?	Когда?	kahg-DAH
Where is...?	Где?	g-dyeh
How much does this cost?	Сколько стоит?	SKOHL-ka STOW-eet
Do you have...?	У вас есть...?	oo vas YEST
Do you speak English?	Вы говорите по-английски?	vee go-vo-REE-te po an-GLEE-skee
I don't understand	Я не понимаю.	ya nee pa-nee-MAH-yoo
Please write it down?	Напишите, пожалуйста?	nah-pee-SHIT-yeh, pah-ZHAHL-stah
A little slower, please.	Медленее, пожалуйста.	MYED-lee-nyay-eh
I'd like to order...	Я хотел(а) бы...	ya khah-TYEL(ah) bi
Check, please.	Чч ёт, пожалуйста.	shchyot, pah-ZHAHL-stah
Do you have a vacancy?	У вас есть свободный номер?	oo vahss yehst svah-BOD-niy NO-mmeer
Private shower?	с душом?	s dushom

English	Russian	Pronunc.	English	Russian	Pronunc.
bank	банка	BANK-a	post office	почта	POSH-tah
exchange	обмен валут	ob-MEN va-lut	stamps	марка	MAHR-doo
arrival	приезд	pree-JEZD	departure	отъезд	ot-JEZD
one-way	бодин конец	v ah-DEEN kah-NYEHTS	round-trip	туда и обратно	too-DAH ee ah0BRAHT-nah
ticket	билет	beel-YET	reservation	заповедник	za-po-VED-nik
station	вокзал	vok-ZAL	train	поезд	POY-ezd
bus	автобус	av-toh-BOOS	airport	аэропорт	ayro-PORT
bakery	булочная	BOO-lahch-nah-yah	grocery	продукты	prah-DOOK-ti
breakfast	завтрак	zav-TRAK	lunch	обед	ob-YED

English	Russian	Pronunc.	English	Russian	Pronunc.
dinner	ужин	OO-zhin	menu	меню	menu
water	вода	vod-DAH	bread	хлеб	khlyeb
vegetarian	вегетариан	vegh-e-tah-rian	vegetables	обоши	ob-ah-shchee
pork	свиниу	svee-NEE-noo	beef	говядину	ga-VA-dee-noo
fish	рыба	REE-ba	chicken	курицу	KOO-ree-tsoo
coffee	кофе	KO-fee	cheese	шыру	SEE-roo
juice	сок	sok	milk	молоко	mah-lah-KOH
wine	вино	vee-NO	beer	пиво	PEE-vah
Monday	понедельник	pa-nee-DEH-lek	Sunday	воскрешенье	va-skree-SE-ne
Tuesday	вторник	FTOR-neek	holiday	день отдыха	dyen OT-di-kha
Wednesday	среда	sree-DAH	today	севодня	se-VOHD-nya
Thursday	четверг	cheet-VERK	tomorrow	завтра	ZAHV-trah
Friday	пятница	PAHT-neet-sah	closed	закрыте	za-KRI-te
Saturday	суббота	soo-BOT-tah	open	открыте	ot-KRI-te
one	один	ah-DEEN	twenty	двадцать	d-VAHD-tset
two	два	d-VAH	thirty	тридцать	TREE-dtset
three	три	tree	forty	сорок	SOR-ok
four	четыре	che-TIH-rih	fifty	пятьдесят	pya-de-SAHT
five	пять	p-YAHT	sixty	шестьдесят	shays-de-SAHT
six	шесть	SHAY-st	seventy	семьдесят	SIM-de-set
seven	семь	s-YIM	eighty	восемьдесят	VO-sim-de-set
eight	восемь	VOH-sem	ninety	девяносто	de-vya-NO-sta
nine	девять	DEV-yat	one hundred	сто	stoh
ten	десять	DES-yat	one thousand	тысяча	TIS-see-cha

SLOVAK (SLOVENSKY)

English	Slovak	Pronunciation
Yes/no	áno/nie	ah-NOH/NEH
Please	prosím	PROH-seem
Thank you	Ďakujem	DAK-oo-yem
Hello	Dobrý deň	doh-BREE den
Good-bye	Na shledanou	nah SLEH-dah-noh-oo
Good morning	Dobré ráno	doh-BREH RAH-no
Good night	Dobrú noc	doh-BROO NOTS
Excuse me	Prepáčte mi	PREH-pach-te mee
Sorry	Prepáčte	PREH-pach-te
Help!	Pomoc!	pah-MOTS
When?	Kedy?	keh-DEE
Where is...?	Kde existovat?	k-DEH ex-ih-STOH-vat
How do I get to...?	Jak se dostanu do...?	YAK seh dohs-TAH-noo doh

English	Slovak	Pronunciation
How much does this cost?	Coto stojí?	KOH-to STOH-yee
Do you have...?	Máte..?	MAH-teh
Do you speak English?	Hovoríte anglicky?	ho-vo-REE-te ahng-GLIT-ski
I don't understand.	Nerozumiem	neh-rohz-OOM-ee-em
Please write it down?	Prosím napište.	PRO-seem nah-PEESH-tye
A little slower, please.	Prosím pomalu.	PRO-seem poh-MAH-lo
I'd like to order...	Chtel bych...	khtyel bikh
Check, please.	Prosím, ucet.	PRO-seem, OO-chet
Do you have a vacancy?	Máte volnú izbu?	MAH-te VOL-noo iz-BOO
Private shower?	se sprchou?	SE-sprkh-oh

English	Slovak	Pron.	English	Slovak	Pron.
arrival	príchod	PREE-khod	vegetables	zelenína	ze-LEH-nee-na
departure	odchod	OD-khod	water	voda	VO-da
station	stanica	STAH-nee-tsa	coffee	káva	KAH-va
round-trip	zpátečni	SPAH-tech-nee	wine	víno	VEE-no
one-way	jedním směrem	YED-nyeem SMNYE-rem	juice	štava	SHTA-va
ticket	lístok	LEE-stok	milk	mlieko	m-LYE-ko
bread	chlieb	kh-LYEB	beer	pivo	PEE-vo
meat	mäso	MEH-so	tea	čaj	chay
one	jeden	YED-en	six	šest	shest
two	dva	dvah	seven	sedem	SE-dem
three	tri	tree	eight	osem	O-sem
four	štyri	sh-TEE-ree	nine	devät	DEH-veht
five	pät	peht	ten	desat	DEH-saht
one hundred	sto	stoh	one thousand	tisíc	tih-SEETS

SLOVENIAN (SLOVENSKO)

English	Slovenian	Pronunciation
Yes/no	Ja/Ne	yah/neh
Please	Prosim	PROH-seem
Thank you	Hvala	HVAA-lah
Hello	Zdravo	ze-drah-voh
Good-bye	Na svidenje	nah SVEE-den-yeh
Excuse me	Oprostite	oh-proh-stee-teh
Where is...?	Kje?	k-yeh
Help!	Na pomoč!	nah poh-MOHCH
How much does this cost?	Koliko to stane?	koh-lee-koh toh stah-neh
Do you have...?	Ali imate...?	AA-li i-MAA-te
Do you speak English?	Govorite angleško?	go-vo-REE-teh ang-LEH-shko

English	Slovenian	Pronunciation
I don't understand	Ne razumem	neh rah-ZOO-mehm
open	odprto	od-prto
closed	zaprto	za-prto
one	ena	ena
two	dva	dva
three	tri	tree

UKRAINIAN

English	Ukrainian	Pronunciation
Yes/no	Так/Ні	tak/nee
Please	Прошу	PRO-shoo
Thank you	Дякую	DYA-kou-yoo
Hello	Добрий день	doh-bree-DEN
Good-bye	До побачення	doh poh-BAH-chen-nya
Excuse me	Вибачте	VIH-bach-te
Where is...?	Де?	deh?
Help!	Поможіт!	pah-mah-ZHEET
How much does this cost?	Скільки коштує?	SKEL-kih kahsh-TOO-ye
Do you have...?	чи є у вас...?	chih yeh oo vahs...
Do you speak English?	Ви говорите по-англиськи?	Vih-ho-VOR-ihte poh-anh-lih-skih
I don't understand	Я не позумю	Ya ne roh-zoo-meee-yu
open	отчинено	ot-chi-ne-no
closed	зачинено	zah-chi-ne-no
one	один	ah-DEEN
two	два	dvah
three	три	tREE

Index

Key

Numerics

A

B

★Let's Go 1998 Reader Questionnaire★

> Please fill this out and return it to **Let's Go, St. Martin's Press,** 175 Fifth Ave., New York, NY 10010-7848. All respondents will receive a free subscription to **The Yellowjacket, the Let's Go Newsletter.**

Name: _____

Address: _____

City: _____ **State:** _____ **Zip/Postal Code:** _____

Email: _____ **Which book(s) did you use?** _____

How old are you? under 19   19-24   25-34   35-44   45-54   55 or over

Are you (circle one)   in high school   in college   in graduate school   employed   retired   between jobs

Have you used Let's Go before? yes no **Would you use it again?** yes no

How did you first hear about Let's Go? friend   store clerk   television   bookstore display   advertisement/promotion   review   other

Why did you choose Let's Go (circle up to two)? reputation budget focus   price   writing style   annual updating   other: _____

Which other guides have you used, if any?   Frommer's $-a-day   Fodor's   Rough Guides   Lonely Planet   Berkeley   Rick Steves   other: _____

Is Let's Go the best guidebook?   yes no

If not, which do you prefer? _____

Please rank each of the following parts of Let's Go 1 to 5 (1=needs improvement, 5=perfect). packaging/cover   practical information   accommodations   food   cultural introduction   sights   practical introduction ("Essentials")   directions   entertainment   gay/lesbian information   maps   other: _____

How would you like to see the books improved? (continue on separate page, if necessary) _____

_____

How long was your trip?   one week   two weeks   three weeks   one month   two months or more

Which countries did you visit? _____

What was your average daily budget, not including flights? _____

Have you traveled extensively before? yes no

Do you buy a separate map when you visit a foreign city? yes no

Have you seen the Let's Go Map Guides? yes no

Have you used a Let's Go Map Guide? yes no

If you have, would you recommend them to others? yes no

Did you use the Internet to plan your trip? yes no

Would you use a Let's Go: recreational (e.g. skiing) guide gay/lesbian guide   adventure/trekking guide   phrasebook   general travel information guide

Which of the following destinations do you hope to visit in the next three to five years (circle one)? South Africa   China   South America   Russia   Caribbean   Scandinavia   other: _____

Where did you buy your guidebook?   Internet   chain bookstore   independent bookstore   college bookstore   travel store   other: _____

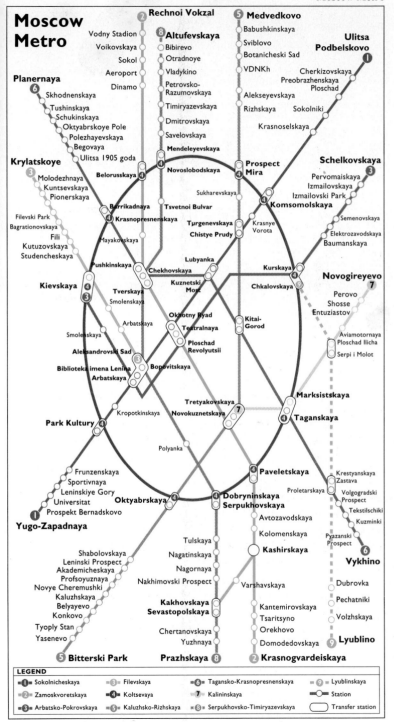

Moscow Metro

Moscow Metro

LEGEND

- ① Sokolnicheskaya
- ② Zamoskvoretskaya
- ③ Arbatsko-Pokrovskaya
- ③ Filevskaya
- ④ Koltsevaya
- ⑤ Kaluzhsko-Rizhskaya
- ⑥ Tagansko-Krasnopresnenskaya
- ⑦ Kalininskaya
- ⑧ Serpukhovsko-Timiryazevskaya
- ⑨ Lyublinskaya
- ○━━○ Station
- ◯ Transfer station

Moscow

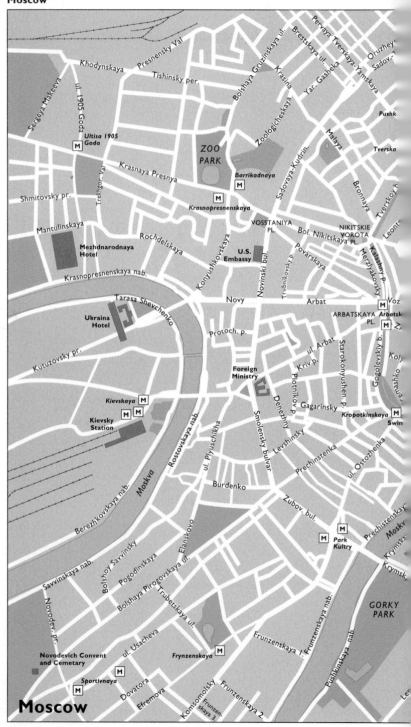

Moscow

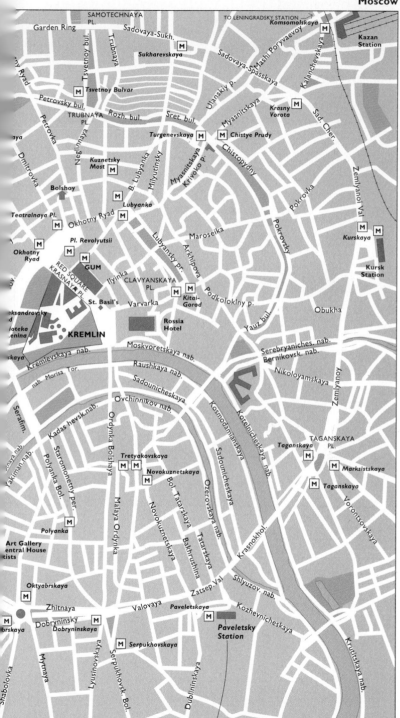

SAMOTECHNAYA
PL.
Garden Ring
Sadovaya-Sukh.
TO LENINGRADSKY STATION
Komsomolskaya
Kazan
Station
Trubnaya
Sukharevskaya
Sadovaya-Spasskaya
Sadovaya-Spasskaya
Mashi Poryvaevoy
Kalanchevskaya
ny Ryad
Tsvetnoy bul.
Tsvetnoy Bulvar
Ulanskiy p.
Petrovsky bul.
Rozh. bul.
Sret. bul.
Krasny
Vorota
Sad. Cher.
Petrovka
TRUBNAYA
PL.
Neglinnaya
Myasnitskaya
Zemlyanoi Val
Dmitrovka
Turgenevskaya
Chistye Prudy
Krivoko p.
Chistopydny
Kuznetsky
Most
B. Lubianka
Milyutinsky
Myasnitskaya
Pokrovka
Kurskaya
Bolshoy
Lubianka
Maroseika
Pokrovsky
Teatralnaya Pl.
Okhotny Ryad
Lubyansky pr.
Arkhipova
Kursk
Station
Pl. Revolyutsii
Okhotny
Ryad
RED SQUARE
KRASNAYA PL.
GUM
Ilyinka
CLAVYANSKAYA
PL.
Podkolokiny p.
Obukha
St. Basil's
Varvarka
Kitai-
Gorod
eksandrovsky
d
ioteka
enina
KREMLIN
Rossia
Hotel
Yauz bul.
Kremlevskaya nab.
Moskvoretskaya nab.
Serebryaniches. nab.
Bernikovsk. nab.
skaya
nab. Morisa Tor.
Raushkaya nab.
Nikoloyamskaya
Sadounicheskaya
Kosmodamianskaya
Zemlyanoy
Ovchinnikov nab.
Kadas hevsk nab.
Kotelnicheskaya nab.
Serafim.
Staromonetny per.
Ordynka Bolshaya
Pohanka Bol.
TAGANSKAYA
PL.
akiman. nab.
zkaya nab.
Tretyakovskaya
Taganskaya
Marksistskaya
Novokuznetskaya
Ozerovskaya nab.
Taganskaya
Malaya Ordynka
Bol. Tatarskaya
Sadounicheskaya
Voronrsovskaya
Polyanka
Novokuznetskaya
Bakhrushina
Tatarskaya
Krasnokhol.
Art Gallery
entral House
tists
Krasnokhol.
Oktyabrskaya
Zatsep Val
Shlyuzov. nab.
Zhitnaya
Valovaya
Paveletskaya
Kozhevnicheskaya
brskaya
Dobryninsky
Dobryninskaya
Paveletsky
Station
Mytnaya
Serpukhovskaya
Lyusinovskaya
Serpukhovsk. Bol.
Dublininskaya
Krutitskaya nab.
Shabolovka

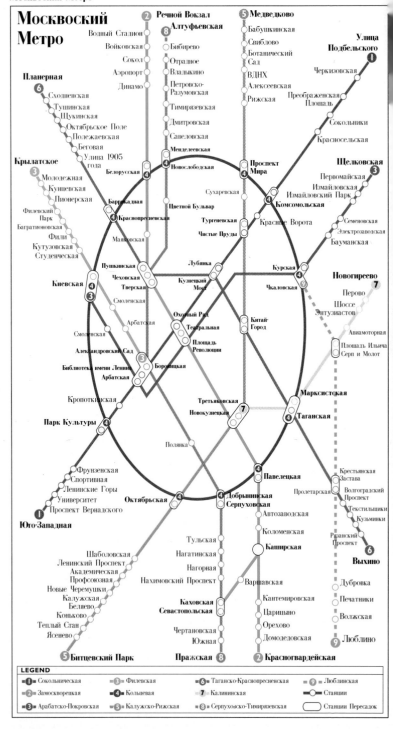

Москвоский Метро

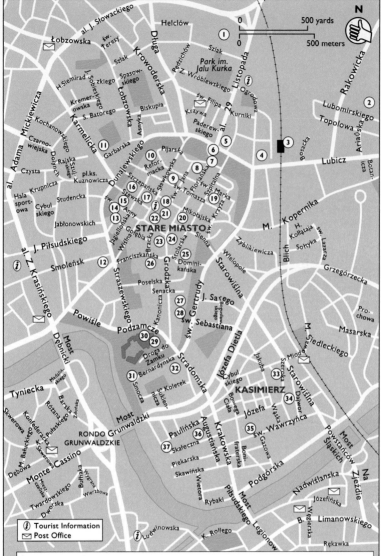

Central Kraków

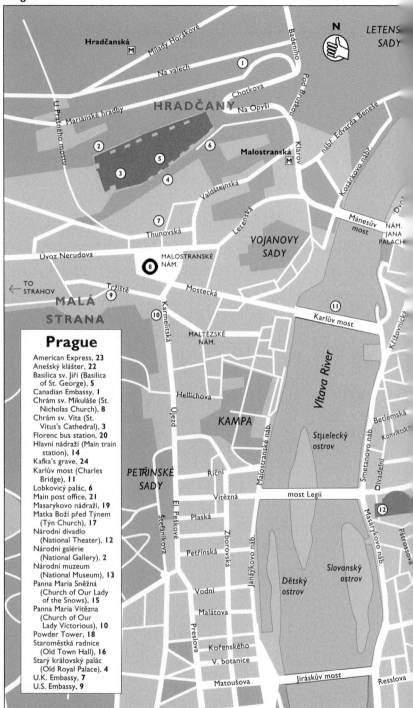

Hradčanská Ⓜ Milady Horákové Na valech ① Chotkova Badeniho Pod Bruskou nábř. Edvarda Beneše Kosarkovo nábř. LETENS SADY N

U Prašného mostu Mariánské hradby HRADČANY Na Opyši Klárov Malostranská Ⓜ

② National Gallery ③ ⑤ ④ ⑥ Lobkovicý palác Valdštejnská Letenská

⑦ Thunovská Úvoz Nerudova Mánesův most NÁM. JANA PALACH

MALOSTRANSKÉ NÁM. ⑧ VOJANOVY SADY

TO STRAHOV → Tržiště ⑨ MALÁ STRANA ⑩ Mostecká Karmelitská ⑪ Karlův most Křižovnická

MALTÉZSKÉ NÁM.

Hellichova Vltava River Betlémská Konviktsk.

Újezd KAMPA Stŗelecký ostrov Smetanovo nábř. Divadelní

PETŘINSKÉ SADY Říční Malostranské náb.

Vítězná most Legií ⑫ Masarykovo nábř. Pštrossova

El. Peškové Plaská Zborovská Janáčkovo náb. Slovanský ostrov

Štefánikova Petřínská Dětský ostrov

Vodní Malátova

Preslova Kořenského V. botanice Jiráskův most Resslova

Matoušova

Prague

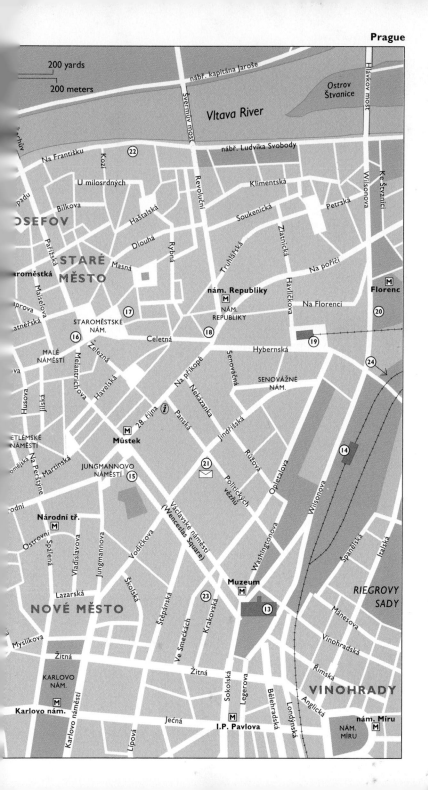

Central Budapest

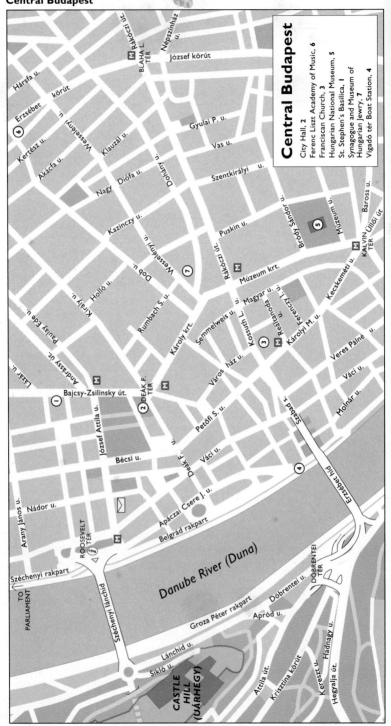

Central Budapest

City Hall, **2**
Ferenc Liszt Academy of Music, **6**
Franciscan Church, **3**
Hungarian National Museum, **5**
St. Stephen's Basilica, **1**
Synagogue and Museum of Hungarian Jewry, **7**
Vigadó tér Boat Station, **4**